Behavioral Economics of Preferences, Choices, and Happiness

Shinsuke Ikeda • Hideaki Kiyoshi Kato
Fumio Ohtake • Yoshiro Tsutsui
Editors

Behavioral Economics of Preferences, Choices, and Happiness

Springer

Editors
Shinsuke Ikeda
Institute of Social and Economic Research
Osaka University
Ibaraki, Osaka, Japan

Hideaki Kiyoshi Kato
Graduate School of Economics
Nagoya University
Nagoya, Aichi, Japan

Fumio Ohtake
Institute of Social and Economic Research
Osaka University
Ibaraki, Osaka, Japan

Yoshiro Tsutsui
Faculty of Economics
Konan University
Kobe, Hyogo, Japan

ISBN 978-4-431-55401-1 ISBN 978-4-431-55402-8 (eBook)
DOI 10.1007/978-4-431-55402-8

Library of Congress Control Number: 2015942514

Springer Tokyo Heidelberg New York Dordrecht London

Printed on acid-free paper

Springer Japan KK is part of Springer Science+Business Media (www.springer.com)

Preface

This book aims to provide new and broader directions for the future development of behavioral economics and finance. To do so, we collect important contributions in behavioral economics/finance and related topics from journal publications of Japanese researchers to date.

All four editors of this book have been interested in extending the reach of standard theories in their own fields using behavioral economics. A project to edit some sort of readings or handbooks on behavioral economics for the promotion of economic research came about naturally as a result of our frequent interactions while running academic meetings on behavioral economics, especially those of the Association of Behavioral Economics and Finance (ABEF), the Japanese Economic Association (JEA), and the Nippon Finance Association (NFA). In addition, these meetings gave us access to important works that were motivated by behavioral economics. We therefore have compiled and edited a couple of independent volumes in an attempt to capture the many worthy articles that lie within this topic. The first, titled *Behavioral Economics of Preferences, Choices, and Happiness*, focuses on works on behavioral economics; and the second, *Behavioral Interactions, Markets, and Economic Dynamics: Topics in Behavioral Economics*, on economics-oriented studies on topics in behavioral economics. This book is the former.

The present book can be characterized by three specific features. First, it focuses on single-agent behavioral issues such as decision making, preference formation, and subjective well-being. These topics comprise the core of behavioral economics, at least at present. In contrast, the other book focuses on economic studies that examine interactions of multiple agents or market phenomena through the use of behavioral economics models. The two books thus are complementary.

Second, the chapter authors have added newly written addenda to the original articles, in which they discuss their own subsequent works and provide supplementary analyses, detailed information on the underlying data, and/or recent literature surveys. The addendum of each chapter is based on discussion at the Development of Behavioral Economics and Finance Conference held in February 2014. During this conference, participants, including the authors of the book chapters, discussed the original studies to be included in these volumes in light of contributions, limitations, and implications for future research developments. We accordingly believe that this work creates a bridge between the original studies and future research development.

Third, reflecting the diverse fields of the editors, this book, as well as its companion volume, captures the broad influence of behavioral economics and finance on various topics. The topics of this book cover time preference and risk attitudes, addiction, health, social preferences, happiness, various types of decisions, biological foundations, and investor behavior.

Part I collects six studies concerning attitudes toward risk and time, which is one of the main topics of behavioral economics. It starts with an article that appeared in the *American Economic Review* and was authored by Professors Tomomi Tanaka, Colin F. Camerer, and Quang Nguyen. This chapter is unique in that it measures risk and time preferences by conducting experiments in Vietnamese villages. It investigates how wealth, political history, and economic circumstances are correlated with risk and time discounting. Their main finding is that people are less loss-averse and more patient in villages with higher mean income. Chapter 2, authored by Professors Takanori Ida and Rei Goto, has two characteristics. First, it develops a new method to simultaneously measure the rate of time preference and the coefficient of risk aversion. Since time preference is usually measured by assuming a linear utility function, resulting in estimates that are biased, this is an important contribution. Second, it investigates relationships between preference parameters and cigarette smoking. The authors find that current smokers are more impatient and risk-prone than nonsmokers. Chapter 3, written by Professors Yusuke Kinari, Fumio Ohtake, and Yoshiro Tsutsui, measures present bias, paying special attention to the separation of delay and interval effects. This constitutes an important contribution because most of the previous studies did not separate them. They find that present bias transpires when delay is less than 8 weeks. They also find that the interval and magnitude effects are a result of intertemporal choice being partially based on the differential in reward amount. Chapter 4, by Professor Kan Takeuchi, analyzes not only the present bias, but also future bias using laboratory experiments. Future bias means that subjects tend to undervalue the immediate reward, which is the opposite of present bias. Although present bias has been frequently reported, this chapter is unique in reporting that many subjects exhibit future bias, and in proposing an inverse S-curve time discount function to capture this bias. It also presents a new non-parametric model of time preference that assumes neither separability between delay and reward nor any specific form of the utility function. Chapter 5, by Professor Taiki Takahashi, proposes that hyperbolic discounting, which is often observed in biology, psychopharmacology, behavioral neuroscience, and neuroeconomics in humans and non-human animals, can be explained by Weber's law. Weber's law states that the external stimulus (e.g., loudness) is scaled into a logarithmic internal representation of sensation. This chapter demonstrates that even if subjects discount delayed rewards exponentially, their actual discounting of delayed rewards may follow the hyperbolic function. This chapter is unique in querying the reason why people exhibit hyperbolic discounting. Chapter 6, by Professors Shunichiro Sasaki, Shiyu Xie, Fumio Ohtake, Jie Qin, and Yoshiro

Tsutsui, investigates risk attitudes of Chinese students by conducting a laboratory economic experiment of selling and buying lotteries in Fudan University, Shanghai. They find that subjects in the selling experiment were risk loving when there was a low win probability and risk averse under a high win probability, whereas they were risk averse with any win probability in the buying experiment. They investigate how risk attitude relates to the attributes of the subject. They also find that subjects' risk attitudes revealed in the experiments can account for their risky asset holding.

Part II collects five studies that relate to smoking (or addiction). As four of these studies investigate the effect of smoking on time discounting, Part II has a deep connection to Part I. Chapter 7 was written by Professors Takanori Ida and Rei Goto. This chapter presents the results of a survey conducted in 2006 of four addictive behaviors: smoking, drinking, pachinko (a popular Japanese form of pin-ball gambling), and horse-race betting. This chapter provides a unique perspective on the interdependencies among the four addictive behaviors and finds that highly significant interdependencies exist between smoking and drinking and between pachinko and horse-race betting. This finding suggests that quitting one addictive behavior is not sufficient for completely escaping from addiction. One more merit of this study is that it estimates time discounting and risk aversion simultaneously, as is done in Chap. 2. Chapter 8 was written by Professors Yu Ohmura, Taiki Takahashi, and Nozomi Kitamura and investigates the effect of smoking on delay effect. In an experiment using 27 smokers and 23 never smokers, the subjects are required to choose between immediate and delayed monetary rewards. The authors find that the degree to which delayed monetary gains were discounted was significantly and positively correlated with both the number of cigarettes smoked, indicating that the frequency of nicotine self-administration is positively associated with greater delay discounting of gain. Chapter 9 was written by Professors Myong-Il Kang and Shinsuke Ikeda and investigates the effect of smoking on delay and sign effect using a nationwide panel survey of Japanese adults, the Japan Household Panel Survey on Consumer Preferences and Satisfaction. They divide the respondents into naïve and sophisticated people and categorize them by smoking participation and cigarette consumption. They find that (1) discount rates are positively associated with both the probability of smoking participation and the number of cigarettes consumed, (2) the sign effect restrains both types of smoking behavior, and (3) the degree of hyperbolic discounting positively relates to both decisions. Chapter 10 was authored by Professors Shoko Yamane, Hiroyasu Yoneda, Taiki Takahashi, Yoshio Kamijo, Yasuhiro Komori, Fumihiko Hiruma, and Yoshiro Tsutsui. This study is unique in that the authors compare time discount rates not only between smokers and non-smokers but also between smokers and deprived smokers. Additionally, subjects receive not only monetary rewards but also actual tobacco in order to elicit smokers' true preferences. They find that smokers are more impatient than non-smokers and that nicotine deprivation makes smokers even more impatient, suggesting that nicotine concentration has different effects on short-run and long-run time preferences. Chapter 11 was written by Professor Eiji Yamamura. This chapter differs from the others in that it does not examine the relationship between smoking and time discounting, but instead examines the effect of social norms on cigarette consumption. Using prefecture-level panel data, the author finds that a tightly knit society results in a reduction in smoking. He also finds that smoking and drinking have a complementary relationship. That is, a greater initial consumption of alcohol results in a larger consumption of cigarettes. This finding is consistent with that in Chap. 7.

Part III is composed of two chapters that address health-related behaviors. In Chap. 12, Professors Shinsuke Ikeda, Myong-Il Kang, and Fumio Ohtake use nationwide survey data to examine how the Japanese people's body weights are related to their personal traits captured by time discounting. Their unique contribution is that an association between time discounting and body weight is detected not only via impatience, but also via preference time-inconsistency, captured by hyperbolic discounting, and the again-loss asymmetry of time discounting, captured by the sign effect. Body weight is found to be positively associated with survey responses indicative of impatience and hyperbolic discounting, whereas negatively associated with those indicative of the sign effect. The finding implies that obesity and underweight at least partially come from temporal decision biases. In Chap. 13, Professors Yoshiro Tsutsui, Uri Benzion, and Shosh Shahrabani address economic and behavioral determinants of Japanese people's decisions to receive influenza vaccinations. Based on a large-scale questionnaire, decisions are shown to depend not only on factors that are predictable from rational decision models, such as the cost and benefits of the vaccination, infection risk, severity of the disease, side effects, and the attitudes toward time and risks, but also on behavioral tendencies due to status-quo bias, overconfidence, and altruism. Policy implications are also discussed, especially regarding the effectiveness of disseminating related medical information.

The two chapters of Part IV address social aspects of consumer preferences. In Chap. 14, Professors Katsunori Yamada and Masayuki Sato estimate income comparison effects using the decision utility approach instead of the standard experienced utility approach, in which subjects state preferences over combinations of hypothetical income amounts for themselves and certain reference persons. The authors conduct hypothetical discrete choice experiments in an original, large-scale, Internet-based survey of Japanese subjects to estimate the utility function parameters for the intensity and sign of the income comparisons. They find that the income comparison effects depend on the characteristics of the subjects themselves and their reference persons. In the addendum, Yamada and Sato show that their estimates of the preference parameters were quite stable after the Great East Japan Earthquake. Social aspects of consumer preferences may well depend on how frequently people interact in society. In Chap. 15, Professor Eiji Yamamura measures the amounts of social capital in prefectures by the average rates of participation in local community activities to estimate the relationship between social capital and preferences for income redistribution. People in areas with greater social capital are found to be more likely to prefer income redistribution. The addendum summarizes further developments with respect to the effect of trust in the government on redistribution preferences and perception of tax burden.

Part V collects three articles concerning happiness and well-being. In Chap. 16, Professors Yoshiro Tsutsui, Miles Kimball, and Fumio Ohtake analyze how election results make some voters happy and others unhappy. Using monthly survey data, they examine the general election conducted on September 11, 2005, in which Prime Minister Koizumi won a landslide victory. Although there are consistent tendencies that supporters of ruling parties are happier and supporters of opposition parties are less happy, the effect is not significant. From this result they conclude that the Japanese people are indifferent to politics compared with people in the United States. Chapter 17 was written by Professors Yoshiro Tsutsui and Fumio Ohtake, who ask why the level of happiness is constant over time, which is known as the Easterlin paradox. Their hypothesis is that the manner in which the question is asked may be one of the causes of the paradox. Thus, they ask about changes in happiness in their daily survey and investigate whether the level of happiness and the integrated process of changes in happiness are the same. They find that the level of happiness is stationary, whereas the integrated process of changes is non-stationary with a rising trend, implying that they are different series. This result is interesting because if we use the integrated process of change in happiness rather than the level of happiness, the Easterlin paradox would probably not be observed. Chapter 18, written by Professors Hiroshi Ono and Kristen Schultz Lee, proposes an innovative concept of happiness redistribution. Using data on 42,000 individuals from 29 countries, they find that aggregate happiness is not greater in social democratic welfare states, but that happiness closely reflects the redistribution of resources in these countries. For example, they find that the happiness gap between high- and low-income earners is considerably smaller in social democratic welfare states, suggesting that happiness is redistributed from the privileged to the less privileged. Their idea is unique and has seldom been analyzed in the happiness literature.

Part VI collects theoretical contributions on choices and decisions. In Chap. 19, Professors Yusufcan Masatlioglu, Daisuke Nakajima, and Erkut Y. Ozbay develop a new theory of revealed attention to show how to deduce a decision maker's preferences and the alternatives he pays attention to given his observed choices. The study, originally published in the *American Economic Review*, is a unique, important contribution that fundamentally revises the standard revealed preference theory so as to make it applicable to more general and plausible cases in which decision makers pay only limited attention to their potentially feasible choice set. The critical importance of distinguishing a preference and (in)attention in understanding a decision maker's observed behavior is clarified, thereby revealing policy and welfare implications. The limited attention theory is also shown to be capable of explaining the often observed "anomalous" behaviors, such as attraction effect and cyclical choice. In Chap. 20, Professors Youichiro Higashi, Kazuya Hyogo, and Norio Takeoka contribute to the literature of intertemporal decision making. Their study provides an axiomatic foundation for the random discounting model, where the decision maker believes her discount factor fluctuates randomly over time. The degree of uncertainty about future discount factors, measured by second-order stochastic dominance, is characterized in terms of behavioral preference for flexibility. A consumption-savings problem under random discounting is also discussed. The effects of time-discounting uncertainty on consumption-saving choices are discussed as well. Professor Koji Abe in Chap. 21 develops a unique geometric way to prove correctly Gul and Pensendofer's utility representation theorem (*Econometrica* 69, 2001, 1403–1435). He applies an extended version of the standard utility representation theorem to the case of tempted consumers without self-control. He also shows testable implications.

Part VII consists of two studies on the biological foundation of decision making. Chapter 22 is a pioneering work written by Professors Saori C. Tanaka, Kenji Doya, Go Okada, Kazutaka Ueda, Yasumasa Okamoto, and Shigeto Yamawaki, and published in *Nature Neuroscience*; they provide a neuroscientific foundation for intertemporal decision making. Using functional magnetic resonance imaging (fMRI), the authors examine brain function for reward prediction in the short and long run when subjects engage in a Markov decision making task, where they have to learn actions from past rewards/losses with different time scales. Based on the theoretical framework of temporal difference learning, the future reward prediction and associated prediction errors are estimated from each subject's performance data. The analysis shows that there is a gradient of activation within the insula and the striatum, depending on the timing of the reward, from short run to long run. That is, their ventroanterior parts relate to immediate reward predictions, whereas dorsoposterior parts relate to future reward predictions. Thus, to maintain its importance in intertemporal decision making, the brain functions differently in predicting immediate reward and future rewards. In Chap. 23, Professors Sun Youn Lee and Fumio Ohtake and Rie Tamiya investigate the correlation between the relative length of the second and fourth digits (2D:4D) and physical competition using sports ability as a proxy. 2D:4D has been suggested as a marker for prenatal exposure to testosterone and testosterone-driven attributes are known to be associated with physical performance in a wide range of sports. The unique contribution of their research is that they collected data from retired professional sumo wrestlers, measuring 2D:4D from handprints collected from 1970 to present. The results indicate that sumo wrestlers with lower 2D:4D tend to have a higher winning percentage and higher rank performance. The addendum reviews how 2D:4D differs between ethnic groups and sexes and how 2D:4D possibly affects individual performance other than sports ability, such as personality, behavioral and psychological traits, and success in school and the labor market.

Part VIII consists of three articles related to how investors' behavior affects stock returns. In Chap. 24, Professors Yoshio Iihara, Hideaki Kiyoshi Kato, and Toshifumi Tokunaga examine the tendency of individual, institutional, and foreign investors in Japan to that of herds using an ownership change as a proxy for investor herding. The annual data covers the period from 1975 to 1996. Both local institutional investors and foreign investors followed intra-year positive feedback trading. The significantly positive excess returns of foreign investors in the post-herding period imply that their trade is related to information. On the other hand, domestic investors' trade/herding is not related to information since the excess returns of the post-herding period are negative. These findings are surprising because during the period of study, the Japanese market was so regulated that the major players in the market were local, not foreign, investors. Chapter 25 identifies the characteristics of online traders using survey data. Professor Konari Uchida documents several interesting findings. Young men are more likely to invest online. Employed investors are more likely to trade online than unemployed ones. In contrast to investment behavior in the U.S., a good performance in the past does not seem to lead investors to online trading in Japan. Thus, self-attribution bias is not observed for Japanese online traders. Online traders tend to tilt their portfolios to highly volatile stocks relying on historical price data analysis. In other words, they are overly confident in their ability to select stocks using this chart. In Chap. 26, Professors Takehide Hirose, Hideaki Kiyoshi Kato, and Marc Bremer find a significant cross-sectional relationship between margin buying and stock returns. Both market- and firm-level analyses indicate that margin buying traders show herding behavior. The information on outstanding margin buying shares predicts future stock returns, especially for small-firm stocks. The predictive power does not diminish even when controlling for liquidity. These findings imply that individual investor trades move the stock price away from the fundamental value.

Ibaraki, Japan — Shinsuke Ikeda
Nagoya, Japan — Hideaki Kiyoshi Kato
Ibaraki, Japan — Fumio Ohtake
Kobe, Japan — Yoshiro Tsutsui

Acknowledgements

We thank Emi Kurimune and Azusa Ohishi of the Research Center of Behavioral Economics, Osaka University, for all the hard work, and Springer Japan for their support for this project. We appreciate the financial support from the Joint Usage/Research Center Project of the Institute of Social and Economic Research, Osaka University (project title: Overview and Future Issues of Behavioral Economics in Japan, 2014 and 2015), which was granted from the Ministry of Education, Culture, Sports, Science and Technology.

Contents

Contributors

Shinsuke Ikeda is a professor at the Institute of Social and Economic Research (ISER), Osaka University, and serves as the director of the Research Centre of Behavioral Economics in ISER. He got a B.Com. of Kobe University in 1980 and a Ph.D. (Doctor) of Osaka University (economics) in 1997. He was the former president of the Association of Behavioral Economics and Finance. He published articles on behavioral economics, macroeconomic dynamics, and asset pricing in Journal of Finance, Journal of Health Economics, Journal of International Economics, Journal of Monetary Economics, International Economic Review, etc. His work on behavioral economics is incorporated into the book The Economics of Self-Destructive Choices, Springer, to appear in 2015.

Hideaki Kiyoshi Kato is a professor of finance at Graduate School of Economics, Nagoya University, Nagoya, Japan. Before joining Nagoya University, he taught at Kobe University. He received his Ph.D. degree from the University of Utah in 1985. He has published several books and more than 30 articles in the leading finance journals such as Review of Financial Studies, Management Science, Journal of Financial Economics, Journal of Financial and Quantitative Analysis, International Review of Finance, Japan and the World Economy, Pacific Basin Finance Journal, Journal of Portfolio Management, Journal of Financial Research, Journal of Banking and Finance, and Journal of Futures Markets on subjects including the market efficiency and anomalies, stock options, investor behavior, dividend policy, equity offerings, and stock index futures. He is currently an associate editor of Pacific Basin Finance Journal and International Review of Finance.

Fumio Ohtake is Osaka University distinguished professor and a professor in the Institute of Social and Economic Research at Osaka University and an executive vice president of Osaka University. He earned his M.A. and a Ph.D. from Osaka University in 1985 and 1996, respectively, and a B.A. from Kyoto University in 1983. He is the president of the Association of Behavioral Economics and Finance, and an executive director of the Japanese Economic Association. His research topics are behavioral economics, labor economics, income distribution, and household behavior. He is also a recipient of the 2005 Nikkei Prize for Excellent Books in Economic Science; the 2005 Suntory Prize for Social Science and Humanities; the 2005 Economist Prize; the 2006 Ishikawa Prize of the Japanese Economic Association; and the 2008 Japan Academy Prize.

Yoshiro Tsutsui is a professor of economics at Konan University. He had previously taught at Nagoya City University and Osaka University. He was awarded a Ph.D. (economics) from Osaka University. He was the first president of the Association of Behavioral Economics and Finance, and the president of Japan Society of Monetary Economics. His primary areas of teaching and research are behavioral economics and banking and finance. Currently, his research includes happiness study, time discounting, international linkage of stock prices, and regional banking and finance. His publications appeared in journals including Review of Economics and Statistics, Journal of Financial and Quantitative Analysis, Journal of Banking and Finance, Journal of Risk and Uncertainty, Regional Science and Urban Economics, and Journal of Research in Personality. In 1988, his book, The Financial Markets and Banking Industry: Economic Analysis of Industrial Organization (Toyokeizai-Shinpo Sha, in Japanese) was awarded the Nikkei Prize for Excellent Books in Economic Science.

Part I
Attitude Toward Risk and Time

Chapter 1
Risk and Time Preferences: Linking Experimental and Household Survey Data from Vietnam

Tomomi Tanaka, Colin F. Camerer, and Quang Nguyen

Abstract We conducted experiments in Vietnamese villages to determine the predictors of risk and time preferences. In villages with higher mean income, people are less loss-averse and more patient. Household income is correlated with patience but not with risk. We expand measurements of risk and time preferences beyond expected utility and exponential discounting, replacing those models with prospect theory and a three-parameter hyperbolic discounting model. Comparable risk parameter estimates have been found for Chinese farmers, using our method.

Keywords Prospect theory • Hyperbolic discounting • Wealth

1 Introduction

A fundamental question in development economics is the extent to which economic success is linked to basic features of human preferences. If people are extremely averse to financial risk, they may be reluctant to create businesses that may have inherently risky cash flows. If people are impatient, they may be reluctant to invest and educate their children. Taken together, risk-aversion and impatience may explain, in part, why some people remain poor.

The original article first appeared in the American Economic Review 100(1):557–571, 2010. A newly written addendum has been added to this book chapter.

T. Tanaka (✉)
World Bank, Washington, DC, USA
e-mail: ttanaka@worldbank.org

C.F. Camerer
Division of the Humanities and Social Sciences, California Institute of Technology, Pasadena, CA, USA
e-mail: camerer@hss.caltech.edu

Q. Nguyen
Department of International Management and Innovation, Middlesex University, London, UK
e-mail: Q.Nguyen@mdx.ac.uk

S. Ikeda et al. (eds.), *Behavioral Economics of Preferences, Choices, and Happiness*, DOI 10.1007/978-4-431-55402-8_1

We conducted experiments in Vietnamese villages to directly measure risk and time preferences of individuals, and investigated how these preferences correlate with economic circumstances. Vietnam has several advantages as a field site:

1. Access to a 2002 living standard survey enabled us to link detailed survey responses from individuals directly to experimental responses by the same individuals.
2. Most Vietnamese villagers are poor but literate. As a result, it is both easy to motivate them with modest financial stakes, and to ensure they comprehend instructions.
3. The rise of household businesses in the market economy has created substantial variation in income. This income variation can be correlated with preference measures.

In any cross-sectional study like this, it is difficult to infer the direction of causality from correlation: Do preferences cause economic circumstances (e.g., through business formation, for example), or do circumstances create preferences (as described by Samuel Bowles (1998))? An ideal study would use randomized assignment of individuals to economic circumstances. As an alternative, we employ an instrumental variable approach, using rainfall and household head's ability to work at the time of survey, which are unlikely to be correlated with preferences, as instrumental variables for income.

Besides contributing new data, this chapter makes a methodological contribution to experimental development economics. Most previous experiments conducted in the field tested models of risk and time preferences that can be characterized by one parameter. (See Jeffrey Carpenter and Juan-Camilo Cardenas (2008) for a review). These models often fit experimental data in Western educated populations (Frederick et al. 2002; Starmer 2000) and field data (Camerer 2000) less well than models with multiple components of risk and time preferences. For example, in expected utility theory (EU), risk preferences are characterized solely by the concavity of a utility function for money. But if risky choices express prospect theory preferences (Daniel Kahneman and Amos Tversky 1979), then utility concavity is not the only parameter influencing risk preferences—nonlinear weighting of probabilities, and aversion to loss compared to gain, also influence risk preferences. Our instruments are designed to measure these three parameters of prospect theory, rather than just one in EU.

Similarly, we measure three parameters in a general time discounting model (Benhabib et al. 2007), rather than measuring a single exponential discount rate as in most other studies. If the exponential model is an adequate approximation, then our richer instruments will deliver parameter values of the extra variables which affirm the virtue of the simpler exponential.

Before proceeding to design details and results, it is useful to discuss how our approach compares to other field experiments. Field experiments in development are powerful tools for policy evaluation because they can randomize treatments in naturally-occurring decision making to see how well a specific policy works in a specific setting with a proper control group (see Esther Duflo (2005) for a review).

For example, Ashraf et al. (2006) found that women who displayed lower discount rates in a hypothetical-question survey were more likely to open a commitment savings account offered by a bank in the Philippines.

Our approach is different. Our study is designed to collect preference measures experimentally and correlate those measures with demographic and economic variables (income, in particular) from the previous household survey. The goal is to contribute basic tools for field experimentation and to generate tentative observations about the correlation between preferences and economic circumstances. No single result will be as conclusive as more targeted studies which explore the effect of a specific policy. Nevertheless, the policy-specific approach and our broad approach are complementary. Targeted studies like Ashraf et al.'s tell broader studies like ours what to look for. Broader studies like ours give a rich set of tentative results for more targeted studies like Ashraf et al.'s to explore more carefully. Accumulation of regularity will come fastest from doing both types of studies.

2 Selection of Research Sites and Research Methods

In July–August 2005, risk and time discounting experiments were conducted with members of households who were previously interviewed during a 2002 living standard measurement survey.[1] In the 2002 survey, 25 households were interviewed in each of 142 and 137 rural villages in the Mekong Delta (in the South) and the Red River Delta (in the North).[2] From these, we chose nine villages, five villages in the south and four villages in the north, with substantial differences in mean village income and market access. Some descriptive statistics about the nine experimental village sites are given in Table 1.1. The southern villages are indexed by S1–S5 (where S1 indexes the highest village wealth and S5 indexes the lowest), and northern villages are indexed by N1–N4.[3]

A week before the experiments, research coordinators contacted local government officials in each research site, and asked them to invite one person from each of the 25 previously surveyed households to the experiments. Experiments started at approximately 9 A.M. in the morning, and lasted about 4 h. Subjects were given instructions and separate record sheets for each game. Illiterate subjects (8 %) were given verbal instruction by research assistants. Subjects who had difficulty

[1]Discrete trust game was conducted before the risk and time discounting experiments. Trust outcomes were not revealed until the end of the session and are reported elsewhere.

[2]The 2002 living standard survey covers total 354,360 households in Vietnam. According to the local government officials in our research sites, lists of all households in selected villages were submitted to district offices, and households were randomly selected from the lists for the survey.

[3]Villages S1 and S3 are in Can Tho City, Village S2 is in Ca Mau Province, Villages S4 and S5 are in Tra Vinh Province, Villages N1 and N2 are in Vinh Phuc Province, and Villages N3 and N4 are in Thai Binh Province.

Table 1.1 Descriptive statistics

	S1	S2	S3	S4	S5	N1	N2	N3	N4
Number of subjects	22	16	18	21	21	17	22	24	20
Of which ethnic Chinese	9	1	0	0	0	0	0	0	0
Mean household income in 2002 (in 1 million dong)	36.6	35.8	20.3	18.5	15.0	28.0	17.5	9.1	7.2
Age (mean)	47.7	44.6	48.8	42.8	47.9	55.1	42.5	49.9	48.6
Gender (1 = male) (mean)	0.59	0.88	0.83	0.71	0.81	0.47	0.36	0.50	0.50
Education (years) (mean)	7.2	7.1	8.4	6.0	5.0	7.5	8.0	4.8	7.6
Literacy rate (mean)	0.95	0.94	0.95	0.95	0.91	0.89	0.95	0.83	0.90
Distance to nearest market	0.0	5.0	0.0	4.2	0.0	0.0	1.0	3.0	0.3
Rainfall (mm)	1,442	2,328	1,442	1,202	1,202	1,399	1,399	1,442	1,442
Number of household heads who were not able to work at the time of survey	1	0	0	1	1	0	1	1	2
Daily wage for male labor for harvesting (1,000 dong)	–	–	30	30	30	18	18	20	20

completing record sheets by themselves were also helped by research assistants who carefully avoided giving specific instructions about how to answer. The average experimental earning for three games was 174,141 dong (about 11 dollars[4]), roughly 6–9 days' wages for casual unskilled labor.

3 Risk

3.1 Previous Findings

Ravi Kanbur and Lyn Squire (2001) describe the risk attitude of the poor as "a feeling of vulnerability". Market fluctuations and natural disasters could put these

[4]The exchange rate between Vietnamese Dong and US Dollar does not fluctuate very much. On July 23 2005, the exchange rate was 15,880 Dong for one US Dollar, while it was 15,947 Dong for one Dollar on July 23, 2002.

villagers in a state of having little or losing what little they have. Empirical evidence suggests wealthier households invest in more risky productive activities, and earn higher returns (Rosenzweig and Binswanger 1993). These premises are consistent with decreasing absolute risk aversion in expected utility theory (EU); wealthier people are willing to take more risk than poorer people.

However, previous experimental studies conducted in developing countries give mixed results on wealth and risk preferences. Binswanger (1980, 1981) and Paul Mosley and Arjan Verschoor (2005) find no significant association between risk aversion and wealth. Uffe Nielsen (2001) finds positive relations between wealth and risk aversion, while Matte Wik et al. (2004) and Mahmud Yesuf (2004) find negative correlations. However, they used EU and mix gain-only and gain-loss gambles in their analysis, making it difficult to tell whether risk aversion comes solely from the concavity of utility function.

3.2 Measurement of Prospect Theory Parameters

We consider prospect theory as an alternative theoretical framework to EU, and conduct experiments with lotteries involving both gains and losses. We use cumulative prospect theory and the one-parameter form of Drazen Prelec (1998)'s axiomatically-derived weighting function. The values of prospects are $v(y) + \pi(p)(v(x) - v(y))$ (for $xy > 0$ and $|x| > |y|$) or $v(y) + \pi(p)v(x) + \pi(q)v(y)$ where p and q are the probabilities of outcomes x and y. We assume a piecewise power function for value, $v(x) = x^{\sigma}$ for gains $x > 0$ and $v(x) = -\lambda(-x)^{\sigma}$ for losses $x < 0$. The probability weighting function is $\pi(p) = 1/\exp[\ln(1/p)]^{\alpha}$.

Parameters σ and λ represent concavity of the value function, and the degree of loss aversion. The probability weighting function is linear if $\alpha = 1$, as it is in EU. If $\alpha < 1$, the weighting function is inverted S-shaped, i.e., individuals overweight small probabilities and underweight large probabilities, as shown by Tversky and Kahneman (1992). If $\alpha > 1$, then the weighting function is S-shaped, i.e., individuals underweight small probabilities and overweight large probabilities. The above model reduces to EU (with a reflected utility function at zero) if $\alpha = 1$ and $\lambda = 1$.

To elicit the three prospect theory parameters, we designed three series of paired lotteries as shown in Table 1.2. Each row is a choice between two binary lotteries, A or B. We enforced monotonic switching by asking subjects at which question they would "switch" from Option A to Option B in each Series. They can switch to Option B starting with the first question, and they do not have to switch to Option B at all.[5] After they completed three series of questions with the total of 35 choices,

[5]The instructions gave three examples. In one example a subject switches at the sixth question, in one example the subject chooses option A for all questions, and in one example the subject chooses Option B for all questions. The three examples were given to help ensure that subjects do not feel that they are forced to switch.

Table 1.2 Three series of pairwise lottery choices (in 1,000 dong)

Option A		Option B		Expected payoff difference (A−B)
Series 1				
Balls 1–3	Balls 4–10	Ball 1	Balls 2–10	
40	10	68	5	7.7
40	10	75	5	7.0
40	10	83	5	6.0
40	10	93	5	5.2
40	10	106	5	3.9
40	10	125	5	2.0
40	10	150	5	−0.5
40	10	185	5	−4.0
40	10	220	5	−7.5
40	10	300	5	−15.5
40	10	400	5	−25.5
40	10	600	5	−45.5
40	10	1,000	5	−85.5
40	10	1,700	5	−155.5
Series 2				
Balls 1–9	Ball 10	Balls 1–7	Balls 8–10	
40	30	54	5	−0.3
40	30	56	5	−1.7
40	30	58	5	−3.1
40	30	60	5	−4.5
40	30	62	5	−5.9
40	30	65	5	−8.0
40	30	68	5	−10.1
40	30	72	5	−12.9
40	30	77	5	−16.4
40	30	83	5	−20.6
40	30	90	5	−25.5
40	30	100	5	−32.5
40	30	110	5	−39.5
40	30	130	5	−53.5
Series 3				
Balls 1–5	Balls 6–10	Ball 1–5	Ball 6–10	
25	−4	30	−21	6.0
4	−4	30	−21	−4.5
1	−4	30	−21	−6.0
1	−4	30	−16	−8.5
1	−8	30	−16	−10.5
1	−8	30	−14	−11.5
1	−8	30	−11	−13.0

Note: The amounts displayed to subjects are in thousands of dong

we draw a numbered ball from a bingo cage with 35 numbered balls, to determine which row of choice will be played for real money. We then put back 10 numbered balls in the bingo cage and played the selected lottery.

The difference in expected value between the lotteries (A relative to B) is shown in the right column. As one moves down the rows, the higher payoff in Option B increases and everything else is fixed. The choices are carefully designed so any combination of choices in the three series determines a particular interval of prospect theory parameter values. Table 1.3 illustrates the combinations of approximate values of σ, α and λ for each switching point. "Never" indicates the cases in which a subject does not switch to Option B (i.e., always choose A). The switching points in Series 1 and 2 jointly determine σ and α. For example, suppose a subject switched from Option A to B at the seventh question in Series 1. The combinations of (σ, α) which can rationalize this switch are (0.4, 0.4), (0.5, 0.5), (0.6, 0.6), (0.7, 0.7), (0.8, 0.8), (0.9, 0.9) or (1, 1). Now suppose the same subjects also switched from Option A to B at the seventh question in Series 2. Then the combinations of (σ, α) which rationalize that switch are (0.8, 0.6), (0.7, 0.7), (0.6, 0.8), (0.5, 0.9), or (0.4, 1). By intersecting these parameter ranges from Series 1 and 2, we obtain the approximate values of (σ, α) = (0.7, 0.7). Predictions of (σ, α) for all possible combinations of choices are given in Table 1.9 in the Appendix.

The loss aversion parameter λ is determined by the switching point in Series 3. Notice that λ cannot be uniquely inferred from switching in Series 3. Questions in Series 3 were constructed to make sure that λ takes similar values across different levels of σ. Table 1.3 shows the range of λ for each switching point for three values $\sigma = 0.2$, 0.6 and 1.

3.3 *Empirical Results*

Figure 1.1 shows the distributions of choices made by subjects in Series 1 and 2. The numbers in the axes correspond to the switching points in Series 1 and 2.[6] The height of a cone represents the number of subjects who switched at that particular combination of switching points in Series 1 and 2. Black cones represent the choices which are consistent with EU. There are not many subjects whose choices are consistent with EU. The mean estimated values of (σ, α) are (0.59, 0.74) and (0.63, 0.74) in the south and north, respectively. Elaine M. Liu (2013) replicated this risk experiment with Chinese farmers and estimated average values (0.48, 0.69), which are reasonably close. The average derived value of α is significantly different from 1 at the 1 % significance level by t-test, rejecting EU in favor of inverted-S shaped

[6]Switching point 15 implies the subject never switched in that series.

Table 1.3 Switching point (question at which preference switches from option A to option B) and approximations of σ, α and λ

Series 1 (Question 1–14)							
σ	α						
	0.4	0.5	0.6	0.7	0.8	0.9	**1.0**
0.2	9	10	11	12	13	14	**Never**
0.3	8	9	10	11	12	13	**14**
0.4	7	8	9	10	11	12	**13**
0.5	6	7	8	9	10	11	**12**
0.6	5	6	7	8	9	10	**11**
0.7	4	5	6	7	8	9	**10**
0.8	3	4	5	6	7	8	**9**
0.9	2	3	4	5	6	7	**8**
1.0	1	2	3	4	5	6	**7**
Series 2 (Question 15–28)							
σ	α						
	0.4	0.5	0.6	0.7	0.8	0.9	**1.0**
0.2	Never	14	13	12	11	10	**9**
0.3	14	13	12	11	10	9	**8**
0.4	13	12	11	10	9	8	**7**
0.5	12	11	10	9	8	7	**6**
0.6	11	10	9	8	7	6	**5**
0.7	10	9	8	7	6	5	**4**
0.8	9	8	7	6	5	4	**3**
0.9	8	7	6	5	4	3	**2**
1.0	7	6	5	4	3	2	**1**

Series 3 (Question 29–35)			
Switching question	σ = 0.2	σ = 0.6	σ = 1
1	λ > 0.14	λ > 0.20	λ > 0.29
2	0.14 < λ < 1.26	.20 < λ < 1.38	0.29 < λ < 1.53
3	1.26 < λ < 1.88	1.38 < λ < 1.71	1.53 < λ < 1.71
4	1.88 < λ < 2.31	1.71 < λ < 2.25	1.71 < λ < 2.42
5	2.31 < λ < 4.32	2.25 < λ < 3.73	2.42 < λ < 3.63
6	4.32 < λ < 5.43	3.73 < λ < 4.82	3.63 < λ < 4.83
7	5.43 < λ < 9.78	4.82 < λ < 9.13	4.83 < λ < 9.67

Bold indicates choices compatible with EU (α=1) and risk-aversion

probability weighting (see (Hsu et al. 2009) for a review and neural measures). We regressed the curvature of the utility function (σ) using OLS regressions, and loss-aversion (λ) by interval regressions using maximum likelihood techniques against

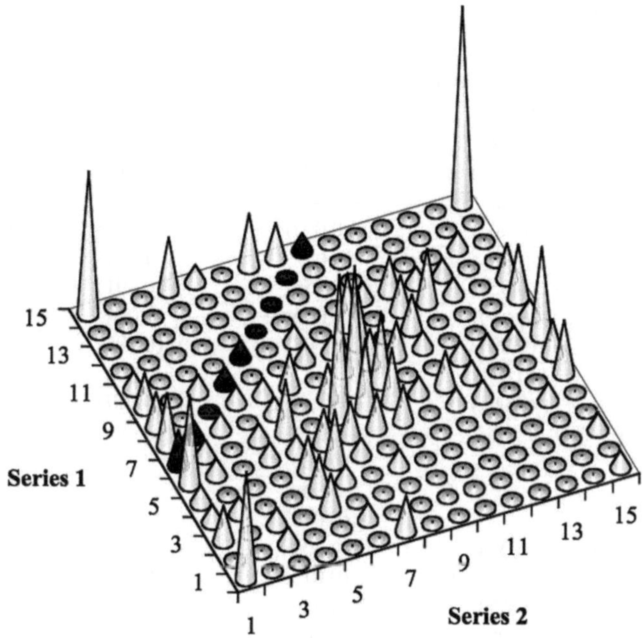

Fig. 1.1 Distribution of switching points in Series 1 & 2 (experimental data). *Black* denotes switching point pairs consistent with EU

individual-specific variables.[7] We first ran regressions using household income as an independent variable.

The regression results are shown in columns (1) and (3) in Table 1.4. Looking first at σ (curvature of the utility function), the strongest effects suggest subjects who are more educated and older are more risk-averse. The estimation result for loss aversion (λ) shows ethnic Chinese are less loss averse and people living in the South are more loss averse. Household income is not significantly correlated with either σ or λ.

Having learned that household income does not correlate with either risk aversion (in terms of concavity of utility function) or loss aversion, we decomposed household income into two variables, mean village income and relative income within the village (subtracting the mean and dividing by the within-village standard deviation).

Columns (2) and (4) in Table 1.4 contain the regression results of the estimations. Neither relative income nor mean income of the village correlates with concavity of utility function. However, mean village income is strongly correlated with loss

[7]The average estimated value of λ is 2.63, close to the 2.25 estimated by Tversky and Kahneman (1992), and is significantly different from one by t-test ($p < .001$). Liu's (2013) estimate is 3.47.

Table 1.4 Correlations with dimensions of risk aversion (OLS)

	Dependent variable			
	σ (Value function curvature)		λ (Loss aversion)	
	(1)	(2)	(3)	(4)
Chinese	0.039 (0.115)	0.027 (0.121)	−3.273* (1.711)	−2.341 (1.769)
Age	−0.005** (0.002)	−0.005** (0.002)	0.042 (0.030)	0.049 (0.030)
Gender	−0.035 (0.056)	−0.028 (0.056)	−0.524 (0.791)	−0.557 (0.781)
Education	−0.019** (0.007)	−0.020*** (0.008)	0.098 (0.105)	0.141 (0.106)
Income	−0.001 (0.001)		−0.028 (0.017)	
Relative income		−0.011 (0.026)		−0.600 (0.371)
Mean income		0.000 (0.003)		−0.086** (0.043)
Distance to market	−0.008 (0.014)	−0.008 (0.015)	−0.178 (0.206)	−0.151 (0.205)
South	−0.033 (0.057)	−0.052 (0.064)	1.479* (0.810)	1.994** (0.888)
Constant	1.054*** (0.141)	1.038*** (0.144)	0.514 (1.997)	0.722 (2.000)
Observations	181	181	181	181
R^2	0.07	0.06		
Log likelihood			−436	−434
Hausman test	$\chi^2 = 5.23$ (p = 0.022)	$\chi^2 = 5.52$ (p = 0.063)	$\chi^2 = 0.27$ (p = 0.999)	$\chi^2 = 3.33$ (p = 0.853)
Davidson & MacKinnon test	F-statistic =5.36 (p = 0.021)	F-statistic =2.82 (p = 0.063)	$\chi^2 = 0.06$ (p = 0.814)	$\chi^2 = 0.87$ (p = 0.814)

Note: ***Significant at the 1 % level; **Significant at the 5 % level; *Significant at the 10 % level. Standard errors are in parentheses

aversion. Nevertheless, income variables may be endogenous, and it is difficult to know whether income variables explain risk preferences or vice versa. We used rainfall and household head's ability to work at the time of survey as exogenous instruments for income variables[8] and conducted the Hausman and Davidson-MacKinnon tests to investigate whether OLS is an inconsistent estimator for curvature of the utility function (σ) and loss aversion (λ). The results of both tests suggest OLS is an inconsistent estimator for σ (see Table 1.4). Therefore, we

[8]We tested several instrumental variables e.g., funeral costs, natural disaster relief, crop failure due to natural disaster and pests, and selected rainfall and household head's ability to work as instruments, since these variables yield the highest F-statistic in the regression.

Table 1.5 IV-2SLS regressions for risk aversion (σ)

First stage						
	Dependent variable					
	Income		Relative income		Mean income	
Rainfall	0.018	(0.006)***	−0.000	(0.000)	0.019	(0.002)***
Head can't work (dummy)	−11.846	(7.786)	−0.930	(0.380)**	−2.869	(2.584)
Chinese	6.741	(6.824)	0.196	(0.333)	10.942	(2.265)***
Age	0.035	(0.128)	0.003	(0.006)	0.054	(0.042)
Gender	−5.129	(3.282)	−0.012	(0.160)	−2.063	(1.089)*
Education	0.706	(0.440)	0.036	(0.021)*	0.281	(0.146)*
Distance to market	−1.0673	(0.974)	0.021	(0.048)	−1.137	(0.323)***
South	10.483	(3.277)***	−0.040	(0.160)	9.340	(1.088)***
Constant	−13.122	(10.671)	−0.179	(0.521)	−14.209	(3.541)***
Observations	181		181		181	
R^2	0.15		0.05		0.58	
F-statistic	3.89		1.17		30.22	

Second stage				
	Dependent variable			
	σ (Value function curvature)			
Chinese	−0.035	(0.143)	−0.096	(0.138)
Age	−0.006	(0.003)**	−0.006	(0.002)***
Gender	0.022	(0.073)	−0.006	(0.059)
Education	−0.029	(0.010)***	−0.028	(0.010)***
Income (IV)	0.010	(0.006)		
Relative income (IV)			0.049	(0.148)
Mean income (IV)			0.010	(0.005)*
Distance to market	−0.012	(0.017)	−0.013	(0.010)
South	−0.155	(0.094)	−0.148	(0.080)*
Constant	0.980	(0.174)***	0.992	(0.160)***
Observations	181		181	
R^2	0.08		0.08	

Note: ***Significant at the 1 % level; **Significant at the 5 % level; *Significant at the 10 % level. Standard errors are in parentheses

conducted instrumental variable two-stage least squares (IV-2SLS) regressions for the curvature of the utility function (σ). The IV regression results are shown in Table 1.5. The variable "head can't work " is a dummy variable, taking the value 1 if the household head was not able to work at the time of the survey. The effect of mean income is now significant at the 10 % level, i.e., individuals living in wealthier villages are less loss averse and also less risk averse. There are no significant effects of gender, which is interesting because many studies find that men are less averse to financial risk than women (e.g., Eckel and Grossman 2008). Our findings suggest that these previous effects of gender may be due to confounds with variables that often correlate with gender, such as income and education, which can be controlled for using our household survey.

4 Time Discounting

4.1 Previous Findings

Time discounting is another fundamental preference which may affect wealth accumulation. Most studies linking discount rates to wealth in both developed and developing societies use the exponential discounting model and show richer people are more patient (lower r).[9] However, exponential discounting model is often rejected by experimental and field data (Frederick et al. 2002). For example, measured discount rates tend to decline over time[10] (Ainslie 1992) and exhibit a "present bias" or preference for immediate reward.[11] David Laibson (1997) proposed "quasi-hyperbolic" discounting model.[12]

4.2 Measurement of Time Discounting Parameters

We use a general model proposed by Benhabib et al. (2007) which allows us to test exponential, hyperbolic, quasi-hyperbolic discounting, and a more general form. The model assigns a value to reward y at time of $y\beta(1-(1-\theta)rt)^{1/(1-\theta)}$ for $t > 0$ (or simply y for immediate reward at $t = 0$).

The three factors r, β and θ separate conventional time discounting (r), present-bias (β) and hyperbolicity (θ) of the discount function. When $\beta = 1$, as θ approaches 1 the discounted value reduces to exponential discounting (e^{-rt}) in the limit. When $\theta = 2$ and $\beta = 1$, it reduces to true hyperbolic discounting ($1/(1 + rt)$). When $\theta = 1$

[9]Jerry Hausman (1979), Emily C. Lawrance (1991) and Harrison et al. (2002) report this relation in the United States and Denmark. John L. Pender (1996), Nielsen (2001) and Yesuf (2004) also report it in India, Madagascar, and Ethiopia, respectively. Kris N. Kirby et al. (2002) and C. Leigh Anderson et al. (2004) did not find a wealth-patience relation in Bolivia and Vietnam, but their villages did not have as much income variation as we were able to design in by handpicking villages.

[10]See Richard Thaler (1981), Uri Benzion et al. (1989), Loewenstein and Prelec (1992), and John L. Pender (1996).

[11]See Laibson (1997), Laibson et al. (1998), O'Donoghue and Rabin (1999), and Angeletos et al. (2001).

[12]This formulation has been used to study retirement planning, gym membership, procrastination, deadlines, and addiction (Bernheim et al. 2001; DellaVigna and Malmendier 2006; Diamond and Koszegi 2003; Laibson et al. 1998; O'Donoghue and Rabin 1999, 2001).

(in the limit) and β is free, it reduces to quasi-hyperbolic discounting (βe^{-rt}). The three-parameter form enables a way to compare three familiar models at once.

In our experiments, subjects make 75 choices between smaller rewards delivered today, and larger rewards delivered at specified times in the future as follows: Option A: Receive x dong today; or Option B: Receive y dong in t days.

The reward x varies between 30,000 and 300,000 and the time delay t varies between 3 days and 3 months (see Table 1.10 in the Appendix).[13]

Before conducting the experiment, we chose and announced a trusted agent who would keep the money until delayed delivery date to ensure subjects believed the money would be delivered. The selected trusted persons were usually village heads or presidents of women's associations. In five villages, the trusted agents were also experimental subjects. Agreement letters of money delivery were signed between the trusted agents and the first author. Agents were instructed to deliver the money to the houses of experimental subjects, which tries to equalize the pure transaction costs of receiving money immediately (i.e., at the end of the experiment) or in the future.[14]

After subjects completed all 75 questions, we put 75 numbered balls in the bingo cage and drew one ball to determine a pairwise choice. The option chosen for that pair (i.e., A or B) determined how much money was to be delivered, and when.

We denote the probability of choosing immediate reward of x over the delayed reward of y in t days by P(x > (y, t)), and use a logistic function to describe this relation as follows:

$$P(x > (y,t)) = \frac{1}{1 + \exp\left(-\mu\left(x - y\beta(1 - (1-\theta)\,rt)^{\frac{1}{1-\theta}}\right)\right)} \tag{1.1}$$

We estimate the parameters μ, β, θ and r in the above logistic equation. The variable μ is a response sensitivity or noise parameter.

4.3 Empirical Results

Estimation results comparing specific functions are given in Table 1.6. We fitted the logistic function (1) by using a nonlinear least-squares regression procedure.[15] The

---

[13]The largest amount of y, 300,000 dong (about 19 dollars), is 15 days' wages in the rural north.

[14]A referee suggested appropriately cautious wording: "There are many risks involved with leaving the money with the village head; one is that the village head will give out the money early, another is that the village head will keep the money for himself, another is that the village head will encourage those players who will be receiving a lot of money in the future to redistribute it within the village as earnings are no longer anonymous. These issues may affect the values of r, β, and θ in different ways. Given the difficulties in experimental design we did the best we can, and these are interesting issues for future research."

[15]We excluded data from 3 subjects who made alternating responses across consecutive rows.

Table 1.6 Comparison of exponential, hyperbolic and quasi-hyperbolic discounting models

	Exponential	Hyperbolic	Quasi-hyperbolic	Equation (1)
μ ($\times 10^{-6}$)	6.26*** (0.319)	7.60*** (0.408)	8.58*** (0.544)	8.70*** (0.553)
r	0.021*** (0.001)	0.046*** (0.004)	0.008*** (0.001)	0.078 (0.074)
β			0.644*** (0.019)	0.820*** (0.070)
θ				5.070*** (0.659)
Observations	5,340	5,340	5,340	5,340
Adjusted R^2	0.515	0.519	0.522	0.523

Note: ***Significant at the 1 % level. Robust standard errors are in parentheses. Standard errors are adjusted for within subject correlations

estimated values of (r, β, θ) are (0.078, 0.82, 5.07).[16] This implies subjects should trade 6,151 dong today for 10,000 dong in a week, and 4,971 dong today for 10,000 dong in 3 weeks.

In addition to the general model (1) (shown in the far right column), we estimated exponential, hyperbolic, and quasi-hyperbolic discounting models. Estimating the full model (1) with unrestricted θ does not improve R^2 much compared with the estimation of the quasi-hyperbolic model, so we focus attention only on the quasi-hyperbolic discounting.

Next, we estimate the following logistic function (2) to see whether demographic variables correlate with individual difference in present bias (β) and discount rates (r).

$$P(x > (y,t)) = \frac{1}{1 + \exp(-\mu(x - y\beta \exp[-rt]))} \tag{1.2}$$

where $\beta = \beta_0 + \sum \beta_i X_i$, $r = r_0 + \sum r_i X_i$ and demographic variables and associated coefficients are represented by X_i and β_i or r_i.

Table 1.7 shows the results from regressing estimates of the quasi-hyperbolic discounting model, allowing ß and r to depend on demographic variables. We conducted non-linear estimations of the logistic function (2), using household income as an independent variable for the first regression (reported in column (1)), and relative and mean village income as independent variables for the second regression (reported in column (2)).[17] The variable "trusted agent" is a dummy variable, taking the value 1 if the subject is a trusted agent for money delivery. The variable "risk payment" corresponds to the amount of money the subject received in the risk experiment.

[16] t-tests of θ = 1 (quasi-hyperbolic discounting) and each of the restrictions ß = θ = 1 (exponential discounting) and ß = 1 and θ = 2 (hyperbolic discounting) reject all restrictions at p > 0.0001.

[17] The coefficients of explanatory variables for r (discount rates) are multiplied by 100.

Table 1.7 Correlations with present bias and discount rates (OLS)

	β (Present bias)		r (Discount rate)	
	(1)	(2)	(1)	(2)
μ ($\times 10^{-6}$)	8.93*** (0.59)	9.14*** (0.61)		
Constant (β_0, r_0)	0.673*** (0.096)	0.676*** (0.098)	0.021*** (0.004)	0.023*** (0.004)
Chinese	−0.037 (0.086)	−0.046 (0.089)	−0.199 (0.337)	−0.019 (0.316)
Trusted agent	−0.043 (0.080)	−0.032 (0.080)	−0.189 (0.265)	0.085 (0.293)
Age	0.001 (0.002)	0.001 (0.002)	−0.013** (0.005)	−0.012** (0.005)
Gender	0.013 (0.039)	0.015 (0.039)	−0.122 (0.141)	−0.121 (0.130)
Education	−0.009 (0.005)	−0.009 (0.006)	−0.037** (0.017)	−0.023 (0.015)
Income	0.510 (0.658)		−4.530** (1.782)	
Relative income		0.000 (0.019)		0.016 (0.065)
Mean village income		1.196 (2.381)		−29.838*** (7.512)
Distance to market	0.013 (0.012)	0.013 (0.012)	−0.010 (0.037)	0.000 (0.034)
South	−0.053 (0.046)	−0.059 (0.050)	−0.153 (0.152)	0.080 (0.163)
Risk payment	−0.819 (1.011)	−0.928 (1.015)	−7.144** (3.593)	−4.115 (3.602)
Observations	5,340	5,340		
Adjusted R^2	0.52	0.52		
Davidson and MacKinnon test	F-statistic =4.58 (p = 0.011)	F-statistic =3.18 (p = 0.014)		

Note: ***Significant at the 1 % level; **Significant at the 5 % level; *Significant at the 10 % level. Standard errors are in parentheses. Standard errors are adjusted for within subject correlations. The estimated coefficients of explanatory variables for r (discount rates) are multiplied by 100

The largest effects are on discount rates r. Household income and mean village income are positively related with patience (lower r). None of the income variables explain individual difference in present bias (β) while the estimated coefficient of β in Table 1.6 (0.644) indicates subjects are present biased. This implies people are present biased regardless of their wealth, and the degree of present bias is comparable to estimates from a variety of other studies.[18]

[18]See Brown et al. (2009) for a review of quasi-hyperbolic model estimates.

Table 1.8 Correlations with present bias and discount rates (IV-2SLS)

	β (Present bias)		r (Discount rate)	
	(3)	(4)	(3)	(4)
μ (×10^{-6})	9.09*** (0.61)	9.09*** (0.18)		
Constant (β_0, r_0)	0.664*** (0.098)	0.643*** (0.113)	0.024*** (0.004)	0.023*** (0.004)
Chinese	−0.055 (0.078)	−0.086 (0.106)	−0.023 (0.337)	0.161 (0.358)
Trusted agent	−0.039 (0.078)	−0.065 (0.075)	−0.334 (0.223)	−0.147 (0.239)
Age	0.000 (0.001)	0.000 (0.001)	−0.015** (0.006)	−0.013** (0.006)
Gender	0.037 (0.045)	0.032 (0.040)	−0.162 (0.140)	−0.051 (0.140)
Education	−0.012 (0.007)	−0.010 (0.008)	−0.002 (0.020)	−0.019 (0.022)
Income (IV)	3.801 (4.497)		−38.985*** (13.313)	
Relative income (IV)		−0.044 (0.144)		−0.128 (0.437)
Mean village income (IV)		5.994 (4.878)		−36.264** (14.907)
Distance to market	0.012 (0.012)	0.010 (0.012)	0.034 (0.039)	0.034 (0.040)
South	−0.081 (0.060)	−0.091 (0.055)	0.239 (0.213)	0.176 (0.212)
Risk payment	−1.078 (1.104)	−1.605 (1.417)	−5.404 (3.993)	−5.022 (4.4507)
Observations	5,340	5,340		
Adjusted R^2	0.52	0.52		

Note: ***Significant at the 1 % level; **Significant at the 5 % level; *Significant at the 10 % level. Standard errors are in parentheses. We adjusted standard errors for correlations within individuals. The estimated coefficients of explanatory variables for r (discount rates) are multiplied by 100

The amount of money made in the risk game earlier in the experimental session is weakly correlated with patience: individuals who received higher payments in the risk game exhibit lower discount rates r. The choices made by the individuals who were assigned the role of money delivery were not significantly different from other subjects.[19] We also conducted regressions using instrumental variables (IV) for income variables, because the results of the Davidson-MacKinnon test suggest OLS is an inconsistent estimator. Table 1.8 shows the regression results from the

[19]We also conducted regressions without the data of five subjects who were assigned the role of money delivery. There were few changes in regression results (see Table 1.11 in Appendix).

IVthe regression results from the IV estimations. It indicates household income as well as mean village income correlate with lower discount rates.

5 Conclusion

We conducted experiments in Vietnamese villages to investigate how income and other demographic variables are correlated with risk and time preference.

Our results suggest mean village income is related to risk and time preferences. People living in poor villages are not necessarily afraid of uncertainty, in the sense of income variation; instead, they are averse to loss. When we introduce instrumental variables for income variables, mean village income is also significantly correlated with risk aversion (concavity of the utility function). From the time discounting experiment, we found that mean village income is correlated with lower discount rates, that is, people living in wealthy villages are not only less risk averse but also more patient.

Household income is correlated with patience (lower interest rate) but not with risk preference, which is consistent with the classic result of Binswanger (1980, 1981). Our results also demonstrate that people are present biased regardless of their income levels and economic environments.

These results are exploratory and the experimental measures are not perfect. Furthermore, in a cross-sectional study like this, it is difficult to conclude much about the direction of causality between preferences and economic circumstances because the study was not designed to do so. We used instrumental variables to deal with the income endogeneity problem. However, preferences and circumstances may be causal in both directions.

Finally, one contribution of our study is to show how to expand measurements of risk and time preferences beyond one-parameter expected utility and exponential discounting, replacing those models with prospect theory and the Benhabib et al. three-parameter discounting model. The parameters we measure are comparable to those in other studies (particularly the first direct replication using our risk preference measurement method, by Liu (2013) studying Chinese farmers) and correlate in interesting ways with household measures.

Acknowledgments This research was supported by a Behavioral Economics Small Grant from the Russell Sage Foundation, Foundation for Advanced Studies on International Development, and internal Caltech funds to author Camerer. Comments from participants at the ESA meeting (October 2005), SEA meeting (November 2005), SJDM (November 2005), ASSA meeting (January 2007), audiences at Columbia, NYU, Bocconi, Emory, Hawaii, Caltech, UCSC, Claremont McKenna, Guelph, Carleton, Arizona State, a conference at UT-Dallas, and five thoughtful anonymous referees were helpful. Thanks to our research coordinators, Phan Dinh Khoi, Huynh Truong Huy, Nguyen Anh Quan, Nguyen Mau Dung, and research assistants, Bui Thanh Sang, Nguyen The Du, Ngo Nguyen Thanh Tam, Pham Thanh Xuan, Nguyen Minh Duc, Tran Quang Trung, and Tran Tat Nhat. We also thank Nguyen The Quan of the General Statistical Office, for allowing us to access the 2002 household survey data.

Appendix

Table 1.9 Switching point (question) in Series 1 and 2, and approximations of σ (parameter for the curvature of power value function) and α (probability sensitivity parameter in Prelec's weighting function)

σ	Switching question in Series 1														
Series 2	1	2	3	4	5	6	7	8	9	10	11	12	13	14	Never
1	1.50	1.40	1.35	1.25	1.15	1.10	1.00	0.95	0.90	0.85	0.80	0.75	0.65	0.55	0.50
2	1.40	1.30	1.25	1.15	1.10	1.00	0.95	0.90	0.85	0.80	0.75	0.70	0.60	0.55	0.50
3	1.30	1.20	1.15	1.10	1.00	0.95	0.90	0.85	0.80	0.75	0.70	0.65	0.55	0.50	0.45
4	1.20	1.15	1.05	1.00	0.95	0.90	0.85	0.80	0.75	0.70	0.65	0.60	0.50	0.45	0.40
5	1.15	1.05	1.00	0.95	0.90	0.85	0.80	0.75	0.70	0.65	0.60	0.55	0.50	0.40	0.35
6	1.05	1.00	0.95	0.90	0.85	0.80	0.75	0.70	0.65	0.60	0.55	0.50	0.45	0.40	0.35
7	1.00	0.95	0.90	0.85	0.80	0.75	0.70	0.65	0.60	0.55	0.50	0.45	0.40	0.35	0.30
8	0.95	0.90	0.85	0.80	0.75	0.70	0.65	0.60	0.55	0.50	0.45	0.40	0.35	0.30	0.25
9	0.90	0.85	0.80	0.75	0.70	0.65	0.60	0.55	0.50	0.45	0.40	0.35	0.30	0.25	0.20
10	0.85	0.80	0.75	0.70	0.65	0.60	0.55	0.50	0.45	0.40	0.35	0.30	0.25	0.20	0.20
11	0.80	0.70	0.65	0.65	0.60	0.55	0.50	0.45	0.40	0.35	0.30	0.25	0.20	0.15	0.15
12	0.75	0.65	0.60	0.55	0.50	0.50	0.45	0.40	0.35	0.30	0.25	0.20	0.20	0.15	0.10
13	0.65	0.60	0.55	0.50	0.45	0.45	0.40	0.35	0.30	0.25	0.20	0.15	0.15	0.10	0.10
14	0.60	0.55	0.50	0.45	0.40	0.35	0.35	0.30	0.25	0.20	0.15	0.10	0.10	0.10	0.05
Never	0.50	0.45	0.40	0.40	0.35	0.30	0.30	0.25	0.20	0.15	0.10	0.10	0.05	0.05	0.05
α	Switching question in Series 1														
Series 2	1	2	3	4	5	6	7	8	9	10	11	12	13	14	Never
1	0.60	0.75	0.75	0.85	0.90	0.95	1.00	1.05	1.10	1.15	1.20	1.25	1.30	1.40	1.45
2	0.60	0.70	0.75	0.80	0.85	0.90	0.95	1.00	1.05	1.10	1.15	1.20	1.25	1.35	1.40
3	0.55	0.60	0.70	0.75	0.80	0.85	0.90	0.95	1.00	1.05	1.10	1.15	1.20	1.25	1.30
4	0.50	0.60	0.65	0.70	0.75	0.80	0.85	0.90	0.95	1.00	1.05	1.10	1.15	1.20	1.25
5	0.45	0.55	0.60	0.65	0.70	0.75	0.80	0.85	0.90	0.95	1.00	1.05	1.10	1.15	1.20
6	0.45	0.50	0.55	0.60	0.65	0.70	0.75	0.80	0.85	0.90	0.95	1.00	1.05	1.10	1.15
7	0.40	0.45	0.50	0.55	0.60	0.65	0.70	0.75	0.80	0.85	0.90	0.95	1.00	1.05	1.10
8	0.35	0.40	0.45	0.50	0.55	0.60	0.65	0.70	0.75	0.80	0.85	0.90	0.95	1.00	1.05
9	0.30	0.35	0.40	0.45	0.50	0.55	0.60	0.65	0.70	0.75	0.80	0.85	0.90	0.95	1.00
10	0.25	0.30	0.35	0.40	0.45	0.50	0.55	0.60	0.65	0.70	0.75	0.80	0.85	0.90	0.95
11	0.20	0.25	0.30	0.35	0.40	0.45	0.50	0.55	0.60	0.65	0.70	0.75	0.80	0.85	0.90
12	0.15	0.20	0.25	0.30	0.35	0.40	0.45	0.50	0.55	0.60	0.65	0.70	0.75	0.80	0.85
13	0.10	0.15	0.20	0.25	0.30	0.35	0.40	0.45	0.50	0.55	0.60	0.65	0.70	0.75	0.80
14	0.05	0.10	0.15	0.20	0.25	0.30	0.35	0.40	0.45	0.50	0.55	0.60	0.65	0.70	0.75
Never	0.05	0.05	0.10	0.15	0.20	0.25	0.30	0.35	0.40	0.45	0.45	0.55	0.55	0.65	0.60

Note: σ and α are approximated to the nearest 0.05 increments. When subjects do not switch, the approximate values at the boundaries were used

Table 1.10 Pairwise time discounting choices

	Option A	Option B
1–1	Receive 120,000 dong in 1 week	Receive 20,000 dong today
1–2	Receive 120,000 dong in 1 week	Receive 40,000 dong today
1–3	Receive 120,000 dong in 1 week	Receive 60,000 dong today
1–4	Receive 120,000 dong in 1 week	Receive 80,000 dong today
1–5	Receive 120,000 dong in 1 week	Receive 100,000 dong today
2–1	Receive 120,000 dong in 1 month	Receive 20,000 dong today
2–2	Receive 120,000 dong in 1 month	Receive 40,000 dong today
2–3	Receive 120,000 dong in 1 month	Receive 60,000 dong today
2–4	Receive 120,000 dong in 1 month	Receive 80,000 dong today
2–5	Receive 120,000 dong in 1 month	Receive 100,000 dong today
3–1	Receive 120,000 dong in 3 months	Receive 20,000 dong today
3–2	Receive 120,000 dong in 3 months	Receive 40,000 dong today
3–3	Receive 120,000 dong in 3 months	Receive 60,000 dong today
3–4	Receive 120,000 dong in 3 months	Receive 80,000 dong today
3–5	Receive 120,000 dong in 3 months	Receive 100,000 dong today
4–1	Receive 300,000 dong in 1 week	Receive 50,000 dong today
4–2	Receive 300,000 dong in 1 week	Receive 100,000 dong today
4–3	Receive 300,000 dong in 1 week	Receive 150,000 dong today
4–4	Receive 300,000 dong in 1 week	Receive 200,000 dong today
4–5	Receive 300,000 dong in 1 week	Receive 250,000 dong today
5–1	Receive 300,000 dong in 1 month	Receive 50,000 dong today
5–2	Receive 300,000 dong in 1 month	Receive 100,000 dong today
5–3	Receive 300,000 dong in 1 month	Receive 150,000 dong today
5–4	Receive 300,000 dong in 1 month	Receive 200,000 dong today
5–5	Receive 300,000 dong in 1 month	Receive 250,000 dong today
6–1	Receive 300,000 dong in 3 months	Receive 50,000 dong today
6–2	Receive 300,000 dong in 3 months	Receive 100,000 dong today
6–3	Receive 300,000 dong in 3 months	Receive 150,000 dong today
6–4	Receive 300,000 dong in 3 months	Receive 200,000 dong today
6–5	Receive 300,000 dong in 3 months	Receive 250,000 dong today
7–1	Receive 30,000 dong in 1 week	Receive 5,000 dong today
7–2	Receive 30,000 dong in 1 week	Receive 10,000 dong today
7–3	Receive 30,000 dong in 1 week	Receive 15,000 dong today
7–4	Receive 30,000 dong in 1 week	Receive 20,000 dong today
7–5	Receive 30,000 dong in 1 week	Receive 25,000 dong today
8–1	Receive 30,000 dong in 1 month	Receive 5,000 dong today
8–2	Receive 30,000 dong in 1 month	Receive 10,000 dong today
8–3	Receive 30,000 dong in 1 month	Receive 15,000 dong today
8–4	Receive 30,000 dong in 1 month	Receive 20,000 dong today
8–5	Receive 30,000 dong in 1 month	Receive 25,000 dong today
9–1	Receive 30,000 dong in 3 months	Receive 5,000 dong today
9–2	Receive 30,000 dong in 3 months	Receive 10,000 dong today
9–3	Receive 30,000 dong in 3 months	Receive 15,000 dong today

(continued)

Table 1.10 (continued)

	Option A	Option B
9–4	Receive 30,000 dong in 3 months	Receive 20,000 dong today
9–5	Receive 30,000 dong in 3 months	Receive 25,000 dong today
10–1	Receive 240,000 dong in 3 days	Receive 40,000 dong today
10–2	Receive 240,000 dong in 3 days	Receive 80,000 dong today
10–3	Receive 240,000 dong in 3 days	Receive 120,000 dong today
10–4	Receive 240,000 dong in 3 days	Receive 160,000 dong today
10–5	Receive 240,000 dong in 3 days	Receive 200,000 dong today
11–1	Receive 240,000 dong in 2 weeks	Receive 40,000 dong today
11–2	Receive 240,000 dong in 2 weeks	Receive 80,000 dong today
11–3	Receive 240,000 dong in 2 weeks	Receive 120,000 dong today
11–4	Receive 240,000 dong in 2 weeks	Receive 160,000 dong today
11–5	Receive 240,000 dong in 2 weeks	Receive 200,000 dong today
12–1	Receive 240,000 dong in 2 months	Receive 40,000 dong today
12–2	Receive 240,000 dong in 2 months	Receive 80,000 dong today
12–3	Receive 240,000 dong in 2 months	Receive 120,000 dong today
12–4	Receive 240,000 dong in 2 months	Receive 160,000 dong today
12–5	Receive 240,000 dong in 2 months	Receive 200,000 dong today
13–1	Receive 60,000 dong in 3 days	Receive 10,000 dong today
13–2	Receive 60,000 dong in 3 days	Receive 20,000 dong today
13–3	Receive 60,000 dong in 3 days	Receive 30,000 dong today
13–4	Receive 60,000 dong in 3 days	Receive 40,000 dong today
13–5	Receive 60,000 dong in 3 days	Receive 50,000 dong today
14–1	Receive 60,000 dong in 2 weeks	Receive 10,000 dong today
14–2	Receive 60,000 dong in 2 weeks	Receive 20,000 dong today
14–3	Receive 60,000 dong in 2 weeks	Receive 30,000 dong today
14–4	Receive 60,000 dong in 2 weeks	Receive 40,000 dong today
14–5	Receive 60,000 dong in 2 weeks	Receive 50,000 dong today
15–1	Receive 60,000 dong in 2 months	Receive 10,000 dong today
15–2	Receive 60,000 dong in 2 months	Receive 20,000 dong today
15–3	Receive 60,000 dong in 2 months	Receive 30,000 dong today
15–4	Receive 60,000 dong in 2 months	Receive 40,000 dong today
15–5	Receive 60,000 dong in 2 months	Receive 50,000 dong today

Addendum: The Impacts of Risk Preferences on Technology Adoption in Agriculture[20]

In the chapter entitled "Risk and time preferences: Linking experimental and household survey data from Vietnam", we examined how basic preferences, namely risk and time preferences, are linked to wealth. We hypothesized that (1) risk

[20]This addendum has been newly written by Tomomi Tanaka for this book chapter.

Table 1.11 Correlations with present bias and discount rates (OLS) without trusted agents

	β (Present bias)		r (Discount rate)	
	(1)	(2)	(1)	(2)
μ (×10^{-6})	8.78*** (0.81)	8.99*** (0.61)		
Constant (β_0, r_0)	0.680*** (0.098)	0.681*** (0.099)	0.022*** (0.004)	0.023*** (0.004)
Chinese	−0.043 (0.087)	−0.049 (0.089)	−0.193 (0.328)	0.029 (0.309)
Age	0.001 (0.002)	0.001 (0.002)	−0.014** (0.005)	−0.013** (0.005)
Gender	0.007 (0.040)	0.008 (0.040)	−0.124 (0.143)	−0.146 (0.130)
Education	−0.009 (0.005)	−0.009 (0.006)	−0.035** (0.017)	−0.021 (0.015)
Income	0.469 (0.669)		−4.350** (1.829)	
Relative income		0.001 (0.019)		0.021 (0.065)
Mean village income		1.034 (2.458)		−30.132*** (7.468)
Distance to market	0.013 (0.012)	0.013 (0.012)	−0.008 (0.036)	0.004 (0.034)
South	−0.047 (0.047)	−0.050 (0.050)	−0.187 (0.153)	0.067 (0.165)
Risk payment	−0.751 (1.026)	−0.820 (1.113)	−8.035** (3.669)	−4.828 (3.665)
Observations	5190	5190		
Adjusted R^2	0.52	0.53		

Note: ***Significant at the 1 % level; **Significant at the 5 % level; *Significant at the 10 % level. Standard errors are in parentheses. Standard errors are adjusted for within subject correlations. The estimated coefficients of explanatory variables for r (discount rates) are multiplied by 100

averse people are reluctant to enter into risky but profitable economic activities, and (2) impatient people do not engage in long-term projects such as educating their children, so thus remain poor. We conducted risk and time discounting experiments in nine villages in Vietnam and investigated whether risk and time preferences correlate with income, relative income within village, and mean income of village. We found mean village income is correlated with risk and time preferences. People living in poor villages are not necessarily risk averse but they are loss averse. They also have higher discount rates, suggesting they are less patient. These results imply economic circumstances are important in shaping people's preferences. On the other hand, household income is not strongly related to preferences. Lower income is linked to impatience (higher discount rates) but is not correlated with risk preferences. By conducting experiments in multiple villages with various mean income levels, we were able to investigate whether mean village income (economic environments) or absolute income levels are related with wealth. Our contribution was to show how to expand measurement of risk and time preference beyond expected utility and exponential discounting models, by replacing them with prospect theory and quasi-hyperbolic discounting models with present bias. However, we could not link these preferences with economic activities and decision making in productive activities.

Using our experimental design, Elaine M. Liu (2013) examine whether risk preferences can explain the difference in adoption of agricultural technology among Chinese farmers. Liu shows the adoption of genetically modified Bt cotton is slower among risk averse and loss averse farmers. Also, the farmers who overweight small probabilities adopt genetically modified Bt cotton earlier. Elaine M. Liu and JiKun Huang (2013) further examine whether risk preferences explain overuse of pesticides among these farmers. They show risk averse farmers overuse pesticides, but loss averse farmers use less amounts of pesticides. They hypothesize loss averse farmers are more concerned about the impact of pesticides use on health. The two studies extended our study by using the experimental design we developed in our study and linking risk preferences with actual economic activities, i.e., agricultural technology adoption.

References

Ainslie G (1992) Picoeconomics: the strategic interaction of successive motivational states within the person. Cambridge University Press, New York

Anderson CL, Dietz M, Gordon A, Klawitter M (2004) Discount rates in Vietnam. Econ Dev Cult Chang 52(4):873–888

Angeletos GM, Laibson D, Repetto A, Tobacman J, Weinberg S (2001) The hyperbolic consumption model: calibration, simulation, and empirical evaluation. J Econ Perspect 15(3):47–68

Ashraf N, Karlan DS, Yin W (2006) Tying odysseus to the mast: evidence from a commitment savings product in the Philippines. Q J Econ 121(2):635–672

Benhabib J, Bisin A, Schotter A (2007) Hyperbolic discounting: an experimental analysis. http://homepages.nyu.edu/~as7/pshype1205withfigures.pdf. Accessed 12 Jan 2015

Benzion U, Rapoport A, Yagil J (1989) Discount rates inferred from decisions – an experimental-study. Manag Sci 35(3):270–284

Bernheim BD, Skinner J, Weinberg S (2001) What accounts for the variation in retirement wealth among U.S. households? Am Econ Rev 91(4):832–857

Binswanger HP (1980) Attitudes toward risk: experimental measurement in rural India. Am J Agric Econ 62:395–407

Binswanger HP (1981) Attitudes toward risk: theoretical implications of an experiment in rural India. Econ J 91(364):867–890

Bowles S (1998) Endogenous preferences: the cultural consequences of markets and other economic institutions. J Econ Lit 36(1):75–111

Brown AL, Camerer CF, Chua ZE (2009) Learning and visceral temptation in dynamic savings experiments. Q J Econ 124(1):197–231

Camerer CF (2000) Prospect theory in the wild: evidence from the field. In: Kahneman D, Tversky A (eds) Choices, values, and frames. Cambridge University Press, Cambridge, pp 288–300

Carpenter J, Cardenas JC (2008) Behavioral development economics: lessons from field labs in the developing world. J Dev Stud 44(3):337–364

DellaVigna S, Malmendier U (2006) Paying not to go to the gym. Am Econ Rev 96(3):694–719

Diamond P, Koszegi B (2003) Quasi-hyperbolic discounting and retirement. J Public Econ 87:1839–1872

Eckel CC, Grossman P (2008) Differences in the economic decisions of men and women: experimental evidence. In: Plott C, Smith V (eds) Handbook of experimental economics results. Elsevier, New York, pp 509–519

Esther D (2005) Field experiments in development economics. Paper presented at the world congress of the econometric society, London

Frederick S, Loewenstein G, O'Donoghue T (2002) Time discounting and time preference: a critical review. J Econ Lit 40(2):351–401

Harrison GW, Lau MI, Williams MB (2002) Estimating individual discount rates in Denmark: a field experiment. Am Econ Rev 92(5):1606–1617

Hausman J (1979) Individual discount rates and the purchase and utilization of energy-using durables. Bell J Econ 10(1):33–54

Hsu M, Krajbich I, Zao C, Camerer CF (2009) Neural response to reward anticipation under risk is nonlinear in probabilities. J Neurosci 29(7):2231–2237

Kahneman D, Tversky A (1979) Prospect theory: an analysis of decision under risk. Econometrica 47(2):263–291

Kanbur R, Squire L (2001) The evolution of thinking about poverty. In: Meier GM, Stiglitz JE (eds) Frontiers of development economics. Oxford University Press, Oxford

Kirby KN, Godoy R, Reyes-Garcia V, Byron E, Apaza L, Leonard W, Perez E, Vadez V, Wilkie D (2002) Correlates of delay-discount dates: evidence from Tsimane' Amerindians of the Bolivian Rain Forest. J Econ Psychol 23:291–316

Laibson DI (1997) Golden eggs and hyperbolic discounting. Q J Econ 112(2):443–477

Laibson D, Repetto A, Tobacman J (1998) Self-control and saving for retirement. Brook Pap Econ Act 1:91–196

Lawrance EC (1991) Poverty and the rate of time preference: evidence from panel data. J Polit Econ 99(1):54–77

Liu EM (2013) Time to change what to sow: risk preferences and technology adoption decisions of cotton farmers in China. Rev Econ Stat 95(4):1386–1403

Liu EM, Huang JK (2013) Risk preferences and pesticide use by cotton farmers in China. J Dev Econ 103:202–215

Loewenstein G, Prelec D (1992) Anomalies in intertemporal choice: evidence and an interpretation. Q J Econ 107(2):573–597

Mosley P, Verschoor A (2005) Risk attitudes and the 'Vicious Circle of Poverty'. Euro J Dev Res 17(1):59–88

Nielsen U (2001) Poverty and attitudes towards time and risk – experimental evidence from Madagasca. Working paper, Royal Veterinary and Agricultural University of Denmark

O'Donoghue T, Rabin M (1999) Doing it now or later. Am Econ Rev 89(1):103–124

O'Donoghue T, Rabin M (2001) Choice and procrastination. Q J Econ 116(1):121–160

Pender JL (1996) Discount rates and credit markets: theory and evidence from rural India. J Dev Econ 50:257–296

Prelec D (1998) The probability weighting function. Econometrica 66(3):497–527

Rosenzweig MR, Binswanger HP (1993) Wealth, weather risk and the composition and profitability of agricultural investments. Econ J 103(416):56–78

Starmer C (2000) Developments in non-expected utility theory: the hunt for a descriptive theory of choice under risk. J Econ Lit 38(2):332–382

Tanaka T, Camerer CF, Nguyen Q (2010) Risk and time preferences: linking experimental and household survey data from Vietnam. Am Econ Rev 100(1):557–571

Thaler R (1981) Some empirical-evidence on dynamic inconsistency. Econ Lett 8(3):201–207

Tversky A, Kahneman D (1992) Advances in prospect-theory - cumulative representation of uncertainty. J Risk Uncertain 5(4):297–323

Wik M, Kebede TA, Bergland O, Holden S (2004) On the measurement of risk aversion from experimental data. Appl Econ 36(21):2443–2451

Yesuf M (2004) Risk, time and land management under market imperfections: applications to Ethiopia. Dissertation, Göteborg University

Chapter 2
Simultaneous Measurement of Time and Risk Preferences: Stated Preference Discrete Choice Modeling Analysis Depending on Smoking Behavior

Takanori Ida and Rei Goto

Abstract Measuring time and risk preferences and relating them to economic behaviors are important topics in behavioral economics. We developed a new method to simultaneously measure the rate of time preference and the coefficient of risk aversion. Analyzing the individual-level relationships between preference parameters and cigarette smoking, we conclude that current smokers are more impatient and risk-prone than non-smokers. Heavy smokers are the most impatient and risk-prone, while ex-smokers are the most patient and risk-averse. Among non-smokers, neither age-related nor gender-related differences were found. On the other hand, risk and time preferences are significantly different according to age and gender for smokers.

Keywords Time preference • Risk aversion • Conjoint analysis • Mixed logit model

1 Introduction

In behavioral economics, measuring preference parameters regarding time and risk and analyzing relationships between preference parameters and economic behaviors, including smoking, are becoming increasingly important. Currently, economic psychology is expected to provide significant insights for such fields as consumer choice theory and public policy. This chapter develops a new method to

---

The original article first appeared in International Economic Review 50(4):1169–1182, 2009. A newly written addendum has been added to this book chapter.

T. Ida (✉) • R. Goto
Graduate School of Economics, Kyoto University, Yoshida, Sakyoku, Kyoto 606-8501, Japan
e-mail: ida@econ.kyoto-u.ac.jp; goto.rei.7w@kyoto-u.ac.jp

S. Ikeda et al. (eds.), *Behavioral Economics of Preferences, Choices, and Happiness*, DOI 10.1007/978-4-431-55402-8_2

simultaneously measure time and risk preferences and investigates the relationship between preference parameters and smoking behavior.

Many studies including Mitchell (1999) have examined the economic-psychological effects of smoking behavior. Time preference is generally measured by time discounting tasks, while risk preference is derived from probability discounting tasks. For the former, respondents choose between two kinds of rewards: small but immediate and large but delayed. Impatient respondents prefer the small but immediate alternative. For the latter, respondents choose between small but certain and large but risky rewards.

Because smoking remains a serious public health issue, it is important to clarify how time and risk preferences are linked to addictive behaviors at the individual level. Previous experimental research analyzed this problem by separately measuring time and risk preferences. Research on time preference reported that smokers were more impatient than non-smokers; smokers more frequently chose the earlier-smaller reward over the later-larger reward. Examples include Mitchell (1999), Bickel et al. (1999), Odum et al. (2002), Baker et al. (2003), Reynolds et al. (2004), positive correlation between the number of cigarettes smoked per day and a delay discounting rate. Ohmura et al. (2005) suggested that the frequency of nicotine self-administration as well as the dosage were positively associated with greater delay discounting. Risk preference research has been unable to determine whether smoking and risk-prone preference is related. Mitchell (1999), Reynolds et al. (2003), and Ohmura et al. (2005) reported negligible correlations.[1] Further research on the relationship between time and risk preferences and smoking behaviors is required.[2] In this chapter, we classified smokers into three categories based on the Fagerström Test for Nicotine Dependence (FTND) (Heatherton et al. 1991) and then measured the rate of time preference and the coefficient of risk aversion by dependence category.

Time and risk preferences are the two main focuses in behavioral economics. There have been many attempts to measure the rate of time preference and the coefficient of risk aversion. Interestingly, Prelec and Loewenstein (1991) argued that the discounted utility model (time preference) and the expected utility model (risk preference) have similar structures regarding their known anomalies. Nevertheless, as Rachlin and Siegel (1994) suggest, the nature of the interaction between time and risk preferences remains controversial. Barsky et al. (1997) measured preference parameters related to risk tolerance and intertemporal substitution and analyzed interaction with "risky" behaviors, including smoking, drinking, noninsurance, and stock speculation. Most previous studies measured time and risk preferences

---

[1]Reynolds et al. (2004) indicated that although smokers were more impatient and risk-prone than non-smokers, delay discounting was a stronger predictor of smoking than probability discounting.

[2]Other delay-discounting research has shown that children are more impatient than adults (Green et al. 1994, 1996); males are more impatient than females (Kirby and Markovic 1996); pathological gamblers and drug-dependent populations are more impatient than the general population (Alessi and Petry 2003; Petry 2001; Bickel and Marsch 2001).

separately, which is analytically unsatisfactory. Preference parameters regarding delay and probability discounting must be simultaneously measured.

A few studies have integrated the measurements of time and risk preferences, including Rachlin et al. (1991), Keren and Roelofsma (1995), Anderhub et al. (2001), and Yi et al. (2006). However, there is still room to improve both the methodology and results.[3] Our chapter simultaneously measures the rate of time preference and the coefficient of risk aversion at the individual level using Stated Preference Discrete Choice Model (SPDCM) analysis.

Our two main conclusions can be summarized as follows. First, we analyzed the relationship between smoking and time and risk preferences and found that smokers are more impatient and risk-prone than non-smokers. Heavy smokers tend to be more impatient and risk-prone, while ex-smokers are more patient and risk-averse than never-before smokers. Second, we investigated whether smoking or gender is more closely related to differences in preference parameters. Our results show that gender differences are not linked to differences in time and risk preferences for non-smokers. On the other hand, they are significantly related to differences in time and risk preferences for smokers. Similar results are observed for age differences.

This chapter is organized as follows. Section 2 explains the data sampling method and discusses the data characteristics. Section 3 introduces this chapter's conjoint analysis. Section 4 proposes discounted and expected utility models for estimating parameters, and Sect. 5 presents a mixed logit model analysis. After displaying the basic statistics and estimation results in Sect. 6, the relationship between smoking and time/risk preferences is investigated in Sect. 7. In Sect. 8, the influences of individual characteristics on smoking are examined. Finally, Sect. 9 gives some concluding remarks.

2 Data Sampling Method

In this section, we explain the data sampling method and the data characteristics. We surveyed Japanese adults registered with a consumer monitor investigative company (with about 220,000 monitors). Data sampling was performed in the following three stages. First, we randomly drew 10,000 respondents from the monitors and classified them as current or non-smokers.[4] Non-smokers were divided into never-before and ex-smokers. Based on FTND, current smokers were classified as heavy (H), moderate (M), and light (L). FTND is composed of the following six questions (Heatherton et al. 1991).

---

[3]Furthermore, it is important to investigate which is psychologically more fundamental, time or risk preference. At this point, opinions are divided into two camps. Some think that probabilistic discounting is a result of delay discounting (Rachlin et al. 1986, 1991), while others argue that delay discounting reflects the inherent uncertainty in the delay to a reward (Green and Myerson 1996; Stevenson 1986).

[4]A current smoker is defined as somebody who has been smoking for 1 month or more and has smoked at least 100 cigarettes so far.

1. How soon after you wake up do you smoke your first cigarette? (1) Within 5 min (3 points), (2) 6–30 min (2 points), (3) 31–60 min (1 point), (4) After 60 min (0 points)
2. Do you find it difficult to refrain from smoking in places where it is forbidden e.g. in church, at the library, in cinema, etc.? (1) Yes (1 point), (2) No (0 points)
3. Which cigarette would you hate most to give up? (1) The first one in the morning (1 point), (2) All others (0 points)
4. How many cigarettes/day do you smoke? (1) 10 or less (0 points), (2) 11–20 (1 point), (3) 21–30 (2 points), (4) 31 or more (3 points)
5. Do you smoke more frequently during the first hours after waking than during the rest of the day? (1) Yes (1 point), (2) No (0 points)
6. Do you smoke if you are so ill that you are in bed most of the day? (1) Yes (1 point), (2) No (0 points)

By aggregating the responses, we defined respondents with 0–3 points as low nicotine dependence (L-smokers), 4–6 points as moderate nicotine dependence (M-smokers), and 7 and over as high nicotine dependence (H-smokers). Consequently, the rates were 37 % for L-smokers, 42 % for M-smokers, and 21 % for H-smokers.

At the second stage, we surveyed a random sample of 200 respondents from the five categories (H-, M-, L-, never-, and ex-smokers) and asked them about smoking. The ratio of female smokers at the first stage was 40 %, which is higher than the national ratio for adult Japanese female smokers (23 %), based on a 2004 survey of the Ministry of Health, Labor, and Welfare. Therefore, we set the ratio of female smokers at the second stage to correspond to the national figure (23 %): 30 % for L-smokers, 23 % for M-smokers, and 15 % for H-smokers. At the third stage, we collected replies from the conjoint analysis regarding time and risk preferences from around 70 % of the respondents and measured the time preference rate and the risk aversion coefficient based on replies to the conjoint analysis. The respondents received a slight remuneration after completing the questionnaire. Table 2.1 summarizes the demographics of the sample data.

3 Conjoint Analysis

In this section, we explain conjoint analysis, a stated preference method that we carried out on 692 respondents sampled at the third stage to simultaneously measure time and risk preferences. The conjoint analysis assumes that a service is a profile composed of attributes. If we include too many attributes and levels, respondents have difficulty answering the questions. On the other hand, if we include too few, the description of the alternatives becomes inadequate. After conducting several pretests, we determined the alternatives, attributes, and levels as follows:

Alternative 1:

Reward, probability, and delay are fixed across profiles.
Reward: JPY100,000 (US$909)
Winning probability: 100 %
Time delay: None.

Table 2.1 Sample data

1st-stage sampling	No. of samples	Sample ratio	Sub-sample ratio	Female ratio	Average age
Sample	10,816	–	–	51 %	40.0
Non-smokers	7,632	71 %	–	56 %	39.7
(1) Never-before smokers	6,089	56 %	80 %	60 %	38.4
(2) Ex-smokers	1,546	14 %	20 %	38 %	45.1
Smokers	3,184	29 %	–	40 %	40.6
(1) H-smokers	671	6 %	21 %	38 %	43.4
(2) M-smokers	1,340	12 %	42 %	38 %	40.8
(3) L-smokers	1,173	11 %	37 %	43 %	38.8

2nd-stage sampling	No. of samples	Sample ratio	Sub-sample ratio	Female ratio	Average age
Sample	1,022	–	–	34 %	41.1
Non-smokers	406	40 %	–	50 %	40.7
(1) Never-before smokers	203	20 %	50 %	66 %	40.2
(2) Ex-smokers	203	20 %	50 %	35 %	41.3
Smokers	616	60 %	–	23 %	41.3
(1) H-smokers	205	20 %	33 %	15 %	44.2
(2) M-smokers	206	20 %	33 %	23 %	40.4
(3) L-smokers	205	20 %	33 %	30 %	39.3

3rd-stage sampling	No. of samples	Sample ratio	Sub-sample ratio	Female ratio	Average age
Sample	692	–	–	35 %	40.2
Non-smokers	288	42 %	–	50 %	39.6
(1) Never-before smokers	139	20 %	48 %	65 %	36.1
(2) Ex-smokers	149	22 %	52 %	37 %	42.8
Smokers	404	58 %	–	25 %	40.7
(1) H-smokers	125	18 %	31 %	18 %	43.8
(2) M-smokers	127	18 %	31 %	21 %	39.9
(3) L-smokers	152	22 %	38 %	34 %	38.8

Alternative 2:

Reward, probability, and delay vary across profiles.
Reward is either JPY150,000 (US$1,364), JPY200,000 (US$1,818), JPY250,000 (US$2,273), or JPY300,000 (US$2,727).
Winning probability is 40, 60, 80, or 90 %.
Time delay is 1 month, 6 months, 1 year, or 5 years.

Since the number of profiles becomes unwieldy if we consider all possible combinations, we adopted an orthogonal planning method to avoid this problem (see Louviere et al. 2000 Ch. 4 for details). Figure 2.1 depicts a representative questionnaire covering profiles and attributes. We asked eight questions per respondent and

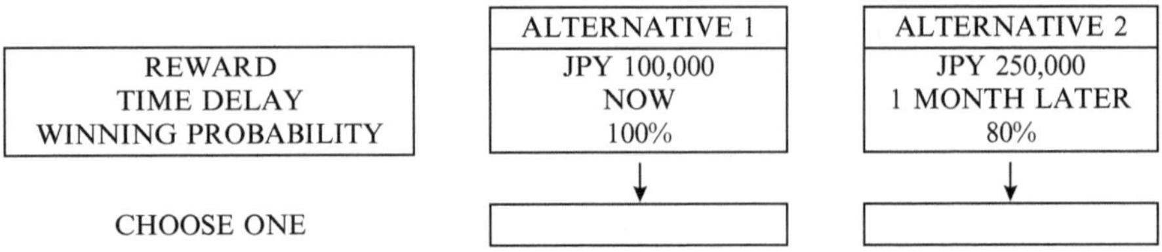

Fig. 2.1 Representative questionnaire

used a stratified random sampling method (explained in Sect. 2) that totaled 1,112 samples for never-before smokers, 1,192 for ex-smokers, 1,000 for H-smokers, 1,016 for M-smokers, and 1,216 for L-smokers.

4 Discounted and Expected Utility Models

In this section, we explain the discounted and expected utility models that form the basis for estimating the time preference rate and the risk aversion coefficient. Let a utility of alternative i be V_i (reward$_\mathrm{i}$, probability$_\mathrm{i}$, timedelay$_\mathrm{i}$). The exponential discounted utility model and the (linear in probability) expected utility model are used for the functional form of V_i[5]:

Discounted utility: $\exp\left(-TIME * \mathrm{timedelay}_\mathrm{i}\right) * \mathrm{utility}\left(\mathrm{reward}_\mathrm{i}\right)$,

where parameter *TIME* denotes the rate of time preference.

Expected utility[6]: $\mathrm{probability}_\mathrm{i} * \mathrm{utility}(\mathrm{reward}_\mathrm{i})$.

Accordingly, rewriting V_i, we obtain

$$V_i\left(\mathrm{reward}_\mathrm{i},\ \mathrm{probability}_\mathrm{i},\ \mathrm{timedelay}_\mathrm{i}\right)$$
$$= \exp\left(-TIME * \mathrm{timedelay}_\mathrm{i}\right) * \mathrm{probability}_\mathrm{i} * \mathrm{utility}\left(\mathrm{reward}_\mathrm{i}\right).$$

At this point, we simply specify the functional form of utility as the *RISK*-th power of reward. Such a utility function is called the constant relatively risk-averse form, where the coefficient of the relative risk aversion is denoted by 1-*RISK*. Taking logarithms of both sides, we obtain:

[5]As is commonly known, the exponential discounted utility model was advocated by Samuelson (1937) and axiomatically defined by Koopmans (1960) and Fishburn and Rubinstein (1982). The expected utility model is attributed to Von Neumann and Morgenstern (1953).

[6]If we consider index s the state of nature, $s = 1, \ldots, S$, expected utility is written as $\sum_{s=1,\ldots,S}$ probability$_\mathrm{s}$*utility(reward$_\mathrm{s}$). Note that we simply assume here that one alternative has only one state of nature other than the state of zero reward.

$$\ln V_i(\text{reward}_i,\ \text{probability}_i,\ \text{timedelay}_i) = -TIME * \text{timedelay}_i + \ln\ \text{probability}_i + RISK * \ln\ \text{reward}_i.$$

Two points should be noted here: first, a greater level of impatience implies a larger *TIME*; second, since a risk-averse attitude means $1\text{-}RISK \in [0,1]$, a greater level of risk-aversion implies a larger $1\text{-}RISK$.

One main objective of behavioral economics is discovering and elucidating anomalies. The most famous anomaly in time preference is hyperbolic discounting, where the rate of time preference decreases with time delay (Frederick et al. 2002). Two well-known anomalies in risk preference are certainty effect and loss aversion (Kahneman and Tversky 1979) for which many models have struggled to account. Nonetheless, this chapter will measure the rate of time preference and the coefficient of relative risk aversion based on the standard discounted and expected utility models for two reasons. First, both the constant rate of time preference and the coefficient of the relative risk aversion still provide good benchmarks, and therefore comparing preference parameters based on other general models with the preceding observations is difficult.[7] Second, some models explaining anomalies may be compatible with the standard model by a simple transformation of variables. For example, if psychological time is set as a logarithm of physical time, an exponential discounted model with respect to physical time can be transformed into a hyperbolic discounted model for psychological time (Takahashi 2005).

5 Mixed Logit Model

Conditional logit (CL) models, which assume independent and identical distribution (IID) of random terms, have been widely used in past studies. However, independence from the irrelevant alternatives (IIA) property derived from the IID assumption of the CL model is too strict to allow flexible substitution patterns. A nested logit (NL) model partitions the choice set and allows alternatives to have common unobserved components compared with non-nested alternatives by partially relaxing strong IID assumptions. However, even the NL model is not suited for our analysis because it cannot deal with the distribution of parameters at the individual level (Ben-Akiva et al. 2001). Consequently, the most prominent model is a mixed logit (ML) model that accommodates differences in the variance of random components (or unobserved heterogeneity). These models are flexible enough to overcome the limitations of CL models by allowing random taste variation, unrestricted substitution patterns, and the correlation of random terms over time (McFadden and Train 2000).

[7] Rubinstein (2003) interestingly argued that the same type of evidence, which rejected the exponential discounted utility model, could just as easily reject hyperbolic discounted utility models as well.

Assuming that parameter β_n is distributed with density function $f(\beta_n)$ (Train 2003; Louviere et al. 2000), the ML specification allows for repeated choices by each sampled decision maker in such a way that the coefficients vary over people but are constant over choice situations for each person. The logit probability of decision maker n choosing alternative i in choice situation t is expressed as

$$L_{nit}(\beta_n) = \prod_{t=1}^{T} \left[\exp(V_{nit}(\beta_n)) / \sum_{j=1}^{J} \exp\left(V_{njt}(\beta_n)\right) \right] \tag{2.1}$$

which is the product of normal logit formulas, given parameter β_n, the observable portion of utility function V_{nit}, and alternatives $j = 1, \ldots, J$ in choice situations $t = 1, \ldots, T$. Therefore, ML choice probability is a weighted average of logit probability $L_{nit}(\beta_n)$ evaluated at parameter β_n with density function $f(\beta_n)$, which can be written as

$$P_{nit} = \int L_{nit}(\beta_n) f(\beta_n)\, d\beta_n \tag{2.2}$$

In the linear-in-parameter form, the utility function can be written as

$$U_{nit} = \gamma' x_{nit} + \beta_n' z_{nit} + \varepsilon_{nit} \tag{2.3}$$

where x_{nit} and z_{nit} denote observable variables, γ denotes a fixed parameter vector, β_n denotes a random parameter vector, and ε_{nit} denotes an independently and identically distributed extreme value (IIDEV) term.

Because the ML choice probability is not expressed in closed-form, simulations need to be performed for the ML model estimation. Let θ denote the mean and (co-)variance of parameter density function $f(\beta_n|\theta)$. ML choice probability is approximated through the simulation method (see Train 2003, p. 148 for details). We can also calculate the estimator of the conditional mean of the random parameters, conditioned on individual specific choice profile y_n (see Revelt and Train 1998 for details), given as

$$h\left(\beta \middle| y_n\right) = \left[P\left(y_n \middle| \beta\right) f(\beta)\right] \Big/ \int P\left(y_n \middle| \beta\right) f(\beta)\, d\beta \tag{2.4}$$

In what follows, we assume that preference parameters regarding time and risk follow normal distribution:

TIME (rate of time preference)
RISK (coefficient of relative risk aversion represented by 1-*RISK*).

The random utility that person n obtains from choosing alternative i in choice situation t can be written as follows:

$$U_{nit} = -\alpha * TIME * timedelay_{nit} + \alpha * \ln probability_{nit} + \alpha * RISK * \ln reward_{nit} + \varepsilon_{nit} \quad (2.5)$$

where α is a scale parameter that is not separately identified from free parameters and is normalized to one (Hensher et al. 2005, p. 536).[8]

Accordingly, we can demonstrate variety in the parameters at the individual level with the maximum simulated likelihood (MSL) method for estimation by setting 100 Halton draws.[9] Furthermore, since a respondent repeatedly completes eight questionnaires in the conjoint analysis, the data form a panel, and we can also apply a standard random effect estimation.

6 Basic Statistics and Estimation Results

Table 2.2 presents the proportion where Alternative 1 (default) is chosen, and the average values of the attributes of Alternative 2 where this is chosen. Smokers are classified as heavy (H), moderate (M), and light (L), and non-smokers are divided into never-before and ex-smokers.

Table 2.3 gives the estimation results. Having assumed that random parameters are distributed normally, each parameter has mean and standard-deviation (SD)

Table 2.2 Basic statistics

	Smokers	H-smokers	M-smokers	L-smokers	Non-smokers	Never-smokers	Ex-smokers
Ratio of Alt 1 chosen	64.1 %	63.9 %	63.6 %	64.9 %	64.1 %	63.6 %	64.5 %
	Averages	Averages	Averages	Averages	Averages	Averages	Averages
Time delay (per month)	10.232	9.972	10.311	10.384	11.011	10.941	11.078
ln probability	−0.232	−0.243	−0.235	−0.221	−0.228	−0.228	−0.227
ln reward	12.370	12.371	12.373	12.366	12.355	12.350	12.361

Note: Averages are of Alt 2 chosen

[8]Louviere et al. (2000, pp. 142–143) showed that variance is an inverse function of the scale as $\sigma^2 = \pi^2/6\alpha^2$. Therefore, associated variance σ^2 becomes 1.645.

[9]Louviere et al. (2000, p. 201) suggested that 100 replications are normally sufficient for a typical problem involving five alternatives, 1,000 observations, and up to 10 attributes (also see Revelt and Train 1998). The adoption of Halton sequence draw is an important problem to be examined (Halton 1960). Bhat (2001) found that 100 Halton sequence draws are more efficient than 1,000 random draws for simulating an ML model.

Table 2.3 Estimation results

	Smokers	H-smokers	M-smokers	L-smokers	Non-smokers	Never-smokers	Ex-smokers
No. of samples	3,232	1,000	1,016	1,216	2,304	1,112	1,192
LL Max	−1664.532	−512.547	−525.702	−624.071	−1220.735	−587.972	−630.015
LL(0)	−2240.2517	−693.1472	−704.238	−842.867	−1597.011	−770.780	−826.231
Pseudo R2	0.257	0.261	0.254	0.260	0.236	0.237	0.237
	Coeff./S.E.						
TIME (MEAN)	0.0664 ***	0.0693 ***	0.0611 ***	0.0669 ***	0.0447 ***	0.0516 ***	0.0390 ***
	0.0068	0.0133	0.0115	0.0105	0.0054	0.0084	0.0064
RISK (MEAN)	0.9104 ***	0.9557 ***	0.9230 ***	0.8496 ***	0.6999 ***	0.7619 ***	0.6461 ***
	0.0714	0.1408	0.1295	0.1102	0.0785	0.1076	0.1152
TIME (S.D.)	0.0398 ***	0.0388 ***	0.0347 ***	0.0423 ***	0.0222 ***	0.0321 ***	0.0126
	0.0061	0.0121	0.0110	0.0091	0.0062	0.0082	0.0103
RISK (S.D.)	0.3030 *	0.5526 ***	0.4028 *	0.0442	0.4203***	0.0288	0.6368 ***
	0.1622	0.2003	0.2405	0.2793	0.1476	0.3312	0.1533

Note: Coefficients in the upper row, standard errors (S.E.) in the lower row, ***at the 1 % significance level; *at the 10 % significance level

estimates. Furthermore, estimation results are separately reported for smokers (H-, M-, and L-smokers) and non-smokers (never-before and ex-smokers). For time preference parameter *TIME*, all mean estimates are statistically significant based on t values, and standard deviation estimates are statistically significant, except for ex-smokers at the 1 % significance level. For risk preference parameter *RISK*, all mean estimates are statistically significant based on t values at the 1 % significance level, and standard deviation estimates are at least statistically significant at the 10 % significance level, except for L- and never-before smokers.

7 Time Preference, Risk Aversion, and Smoking Behaviors

In this section, the rate of time preference and the coefficient of relative risk aversion are simultaneously measured based on estimation results. The results are presented in Table 2.4.

A higher rate of time preference, defined as *TIME*, implies greater impatience. The main findings can be summarized as follows:

- Smokers are more impatient than non-smokers; the rate of time preference of the former (0.0664) is higher than the latter (0.0447).
- Heavy smokers are the most impatient among smokers; they have the highest rate of time preference (0.0693).[10]
- Ex-smokers are more patient than never-before smokers; the rate of time preference of the former (0.0390) is lower than the latter (0.0516).

Our finding that smokers are more impatient than non-smokers is consistent with preceding observations (Mitchell 1999; Bickel et al. 1999; Odum et al. 2002; Baker et al. 2003; Reynolds et al. 2004; Ohmura et al. 2005). As expected, heavy smokers

Table 2.4 Time preference and risk aversion

		Smokers	H-smokers	M-smokers	L-smokers	Non-smokers	Never-smokers	Ex-smokers
Time preference (TIME)	Estimates	0.0664	0.0693	0.0611	0.0669	0.0447	0.0516	0.0390
	S.E.	0.0068	0.0133	0.0115	0.0105	0.0054	0.0084	0.0064
Relative risk aversion (1-RISK)	Estimates	0.0896	0.0443	0.0770	0.1504	0.3001	0.2381	0.3539
	S.E.	0.0714	0.1408	0.1295	0.1102	0.0785	0.1076	0.1152

[10]Note here that the estimated rate of time preference is the lowest for those moderately dependent on nicotine. Therefore, we will verify whether preferences truly differ depending on nicotine dependence using the likelihood ratio (LR) test below.

are the most impatient.[11] Note that ex-smokers are more patient than never-before smokers, implying that successful smoking cessation may be related to patience.[12]

Defined as 1-*RISK*, the higher the coefficient of relative risk aversion, the more risk-averse is the result. The main findings can be summarized as follows:

- Smokers are more risk-prone than non-smokers; the coefficient of the relative risk aversion of the former (0.0896) is lower than the latter (0.3001).[13]
- Heavy smokers are the most risk-prone among smokers; they have the lowest coefficient of relative risk aversion (0.0443).
- Ex-smokers are more risk-averse than never-before smokers; the coefficient of the relative risk aversion of the former (0.3539) is higher than the latter (0.2381).

Although many studies have investigated the relationship between smoking and attitudes toward risk, the issue remains inconclusive (Mitchell 1999; Reynolds et al. 2003; Ohmura et al. 2005). It follows from our simultaneous measurement of the rate of time preference and the coefficient of risk aversion that smokers are more risk-prone than non-smokers; furthermore, heavy smokers are the most risk-prone, while ex-smokers are the most risk-averse. This reflects our intuition that a strongly nicotine-dependent person is insensitive to risk, while one who has successfully stopped smoking is sensitive to risk, since smoking is a large risk factor causing serious diseases including lung cancer (Chaloupka and Warner 2000).

However, at this point, two reservations must be mentioned. First, although Table 2.4 compares how the rates of time preference and the coefficients of relative risk aversion depend on smoking, we need to verify whether preferences truly differ among groups. We statistically investigated whether preferences, expressed as parameters, are equal between different groups using the likelihood ratio (LR) test. Table 2.5 summarizes the results as follows:

- A statistically significant difference in time and risk preferences exists between smokers and non-smokers.
- No statistically significant difference in time and risk preferences exists that depends on nicotine dependence among smokers.
- No statistically significant difference in time and risk preferences exists between never-before and ex-smokers.

---

[11]We followed convention in health economics by classifying smokers into three groups depending on FTND scores (see Haberstick et al. 2007; Guillon et al. 2007, for example). However, since the number of classifications and the selection of cut-points may be arbitrary, we need to verify how sensitive our results are to small changes in cut-points (De Leon et al. 2003; Storr et al. 2005). After slightly changing the cut-points to the left and to the right, we verified that higher dependent smokers are more impatient and risk-prone than lower dependent smokers.

[12]The success rate of smoking cessation is around 50 %, and, furthermore, the heavier the nicotine-dependency, the lower the success rate is (Akkaya et al. 2006).

[13]Since the coefficients of relative risk aversion for smokers and non-smokers lie in the interval [0,1], both smokers and non-smokers are still classified as risk-averse types.

Table 2.5 LR test of joint preference equality

	Test statistics	*p* values
Smokers vs. Non-smokers	15.851	0.003
Smokers: H-smokers vs. M-smokers vs. L-smokers	4.424	0.352
Non-smokers: Never-smokers vs. Ex-smokers	5.496	0.240

Note: χ^2(d.f. = 4) are 13.276 for p = 0.01, 9.488 for p = 0.05, and 7.779 for p = 0.1

Current smoking or non-smoking is significantly associated with time and risk preferences.

Second, since this research only investigated the relationship between smoking and time/risk preferences, we reserve judgment about causality because we cannot determine here whether an impulsive person tends to smoke or a smoker tends to become impulsive. A detailed study of causality lies outside the scope of this chapter. We consider this the most crucial area for future research.[14]

8 Individual Characteristics and Smoking

In an ML model, we can indicate varieties of individual preferences by standard deviations of random parameters. As explained in Sect. 5, we can also calculate the estimator of the conditional mean of random parameters based on the Bayes theorem (see Revelt and Train 1998). Figure 2.2 displays the conditional distributions of the time preference rate and the risk aversion coefficient for smokers and non-smokers. Preferences vary at individual levels.[15]

We concluded above that smokers were more impatient and risk-prone than non-smokers. However, according to a 2004 survey conducted by the Ministry of Health, Labor, and Welfare, the percentages of adult male and female Japanese smokers are 43.3 % and 12.0 %, respectively. When discussing differences in preferences between smokers and non-smokers, differences in smoking rates by individual characteristics including gender must be considered (Kirby and Markovic

[14]Rimm et al. (1995) discussed that the prevalence of smoking is higher in heavy drinkers than in moderate or non-drinkers, and alcohol consumption is higher in smokers than in non-smokers. Madden et al. (2000) pointed out a positive genetic correlation between smoking and drinking. Furthermore, Rose et al. (2004) investigated subjective and behavioral interactions among nicotine, ethanol, and nicotinic antagonist mecamylamine. There may be some commonality in the neural pathways mediating the effects of nicotine and ethanol.

[15]The presence of multiple observations on stated choice responses for each sampled individual means that the potential for correlated responses across observations violates the independence of observation assumptions in classical choice model estimation (Hensher and Greene 2003). However, since ML models address unobserved heterogeneity by a random parameters specification, the correlation is automatically accommodated through the explicit modeling of preference heterogeneity across choice situations (Daniels and Hensher 2000).

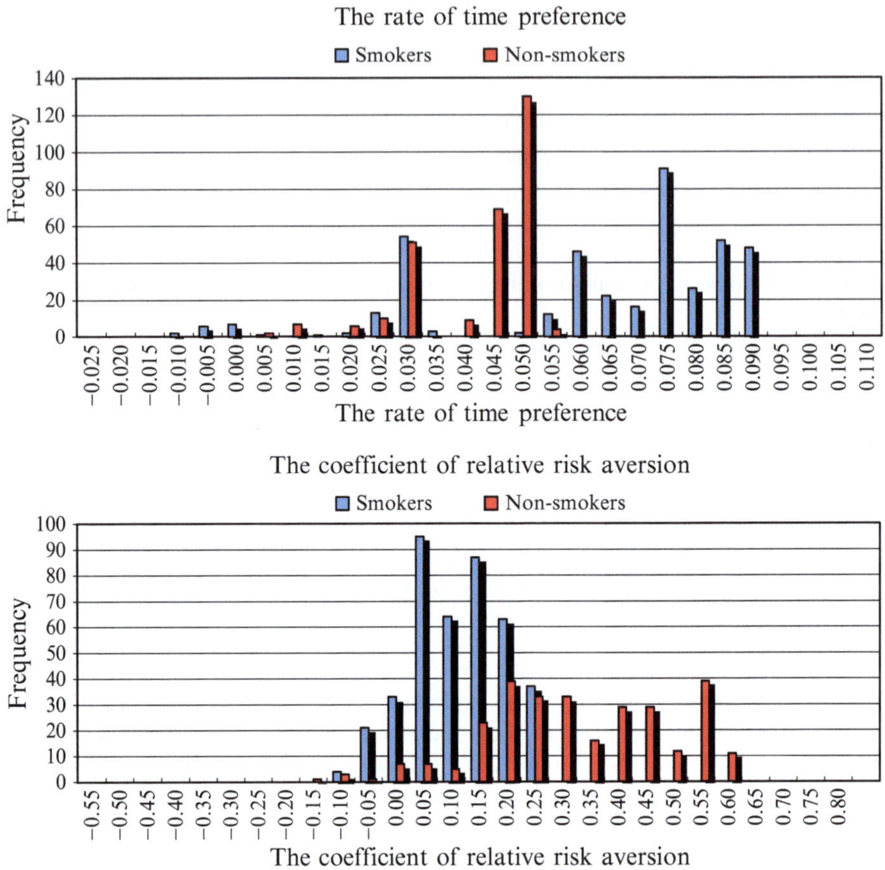

Fig. 2.2 Conditional distributions of random parameters

1996). Thus, we further investigated the differences in time/risk preferences using a likelihood ratio (LR) test between male and female smokers, between male and female non-smokers, between older (over 50) and younger (less than 50) smokers, and between older and younger non-smokers.

The estimation results, given in Table 2.6, are separately reported for male and female smokers, male and female non-smokers, older and younger smokers, and older and younger non-smokers. For time preference parameter *TIME*, all mean estimates are statistically significant based on t values, and standard deviation estimates are statistically significant except for female non-smokers. For risk preference parameter *RISK*, all mean estimates are statistically significant based on t values, but standard deviation estimates are not statistically significant for some cases.

Next the rate of time preference and the coefficient of relative risk aversion were simultaneously measured based on estimation results (Table 2.7). We compared

Table 2.6 Estimation results (gender and age)

	Male smokers	Female smokers	Male non-smokers	Female non-smokers	Older (50≤) smokers	Younger (<50) smokers	Older (50≤) Non-smokers	Younger (<50) Non-smokers
No. of Samples	2,432	800	1,144	1,160	896	2,336	656	1,648
LL Max	−1238.821	−421.102	−615.110	−603.665	−453.1487	−1206.547	−351.471	−867.609
LL(0)	−1685.734	−554.518	−792.960	−804.051	−621.0599	−1619.192	−454.705	−1142.307
Pseudo R2	0.265	0.241	0.224	0.249	0.270	0.255	0.227	0.240
	Coeff./S.E.	Coeff./S.E.	Coeff./S.E.	Coeff./S.E.	Coeff./S.E.	Coeff./S.E.	Coeff./S.E.	Coeff./S.E.
TIME (MEAN)	0.0736 ***	0.0468 ***	0.0456 ***	0.0432 ***	0.0753 ***	0.0644 ***	0.0472 ***	0.0448 ***
	0.0082	0.0102	0.0078	0.0076	0.0131	0.0077	0.0114	0.0063
RISK (MEAN)	1.0284 ***	0.5951 ***	0.7289 ***	0.6651***	1.1631 ***	0.8350 ***	0.6536 ***	0.7130***
	0.0856	0.1269	0.1081	0.1146	0.1540	0.0799	0.1616	0.0898
TIME (S.D.)	0.0434 ***	0.0275 ***	0.0293 ***	0.0147	0.0390 ***	0.0411 ***	0.0298 **	0.0209 ***
	0.0071	0.0102	0.0085	0.0108	0.0106	0.0069	0.0124	0.0072
RISK (S.D.)	0.4139 ***	0.0009	0.2719	0.5210 ***	0.7134 ***	0.0041	0.6377 ***	0.2872
	0.1531	0.3999	0.2954	0.1783	0.1901	0.2978	0.2274	0.2319

Note: Coefficients in the upper row, standard errors (S.E.) in the lower row, ***at the 1 % significance level; **at the 5 % significance level; *at the 10 % significance level

Table 2.7 Time preference and risk aversion (gender and age)

		Male smokers	Female smokers	Male non-smokers	Female non-smokers
Time preference (TIME)	Estimates	0.0736	0.0468	0.0456	0.0432
	S.E.	0.0082	0.0102	0.0078	0.0076
Relative risk aversion (1-RISK)	Estimates	−0.0284	0.4049	0.2711	0.3349
	S.E.	0.0856	0.1269	0.1081	0.1146
		Older (50≤) smokers	Younger (<50) smokers	Older (50≤) non-smokers	Younger (<50) non-smokers
Time preference (TIME)	Estimates	0.0753	0.0644	0.0472	0.0448
	S.E.	0.0131	0.0077	0.0114	0.0063
Relative risk aversion (1-RISK)	Estimates	−0.1631	0.1650	0.3464	0.2870
	S.E.	0.1540	0.0799	0.1616	0.0898

Table 2.8 LR test of joint preference equality (gender and age)

	Test statistics	*p* values
Male smokers vs. Female smokers	9.218	0.056
Male non-smokers vs. Female non-smokers	3.920	0.417
Older smokers vs. Younger smokers	9.673	0.046
Older non-smokers vs. Younger non-smokers	3.311	0.507

Note: χ^2(d.f. = 4) are 13.276 for p = 0.01, 9.488 for p = 0.05, and 7.779 for p = 0.1

male/female smokers/non-smokers and then older/younger smokers/non-smokers. The main findings can be summarized as follows:

- Male smokers are more impatient and risk-prone than female smokers.
- Male non-smokers are only slightly more impatient and risk-prone than female non-smokers.
- Older smokers are more impatient and risk-prone than younger smokers.
- Older non-smokers are only slightly more impatient than younger non-smokers. On the other hand, older non-smokers are only slightly less risk-prone than younger non-smokers.

Last, we carried out an LR test whose results are shown in Table 2.8. If a test statistic is larger than the critical value, the time and risk preferences statistically differ between the two groups. The main findings can be summarized as follows:

- Male smokers are significantly more impatient and risk-prone than female smokers as a result of the LR test (*p* value is 0.056).
- On the other hand, male and female non-smokers do not differ significantly in delay and probability discounting (*p* value is 0.417).

A possible explanation for these results is that the nicotine dependence of male smokers is generally higher than female smokers; males comprise 82 % of

H-smokers and 66 % of L-smokers. Since H-smokers are more impatient and risk-prone than L-smokers, it seems reasonable that male smokers are more impatient and risk-prone than female smokers. On the other hand, note that we did not observe gender differences among non-smokers. These conclusions suggest that gender is irrelevant, but smoking behavior itself matters in time/risk preferences.

- Older smokers are significantly more impatient and risk-prone than younger smokers as a result of the LR test (p value is 0.046).
- On the other hand, older and younger non-smokers do not differ significantly in time and risk discounting (p value is 0.507).

A possible explanation for these results is that the nicotine dependence of older smokers is generally higher than younger smokers; the average ages of H- and L-Smokers are 43.8 and 38.8, respectively. Since H-smokers are more impatient and risk-prone than L-smokers, it seems reasonable that older smokers are more impatient and risk-prone than younger smokers. Differences in life expectancy might also influence time/risk preference. Note, however, that we did not observe distinctions resulting from age among non-smokers. It follows that age is irrelevant, but smoking behavior itself matters in time/risk preferences.

9 Concluding Remarks

Measuring preference parameters regarding time and risk and applying them to analyze economic behavior are important topics in behavioral economics. This chapter contributes to these fields in two ways. First, we simultaneously measured the rate of time preference and the coefficient of risk aversion that have so far only been addressed separately in the literature. They were measured by a mixed logit model that can display individual-level variety in preferences. Second, we studied the relationship between time/risk preferences and smoking.

We reached two major conclusions. First, smokers are more impatient and risk-prone than non-smokers. Furthermore, heavy smokers tend to be more impatient and risk-prone, while ex-smokers are more patient and risk-averse than never-before smokers. Second, female non-smokers (older non-smokers) were not observed to be significantly different from male non-smokers (younger non-smokers) in time and risk preferences, while male smokers (older smokers) were significantly different from female smokers (younger smokers) in time and risk preferences.

Finally,the following problems remain unsolved. First, we did not consider how the decision to smoke is affected by preferences. Second, we only dealt with smoking, but in the future analyzing such addictive behaviors as drinking, gambling, and substance abuse might also be interesting. Third, we must conduct international comparisons to determine whether our conclusions hold across cultures and countries. These potential topics are future research.

Addendum: Recent Developments[16]

Measuring time and risk preferences and relating them to economic behaviors are important topics in behavioral economics. Ida and Goto (2009a) have developed a new method to simultaneously measure the rate of time preference and the coefficient of risk aversion. Analyzing the individual-level relationships between preference parameters and cigarette smoking, we conclude that current smokers are more impatient and risk-prone than non-smokers. Heavy smokers are the most impatient and risk-prone, while ex-smokers are the most patient and risk-averse. Among non-smokers, neither age-related nor gender-related differences were found. On the other hand, risk and time preferences are significantly different according to age and gender for smokers.

Furthermore, Ida and Goto (2009b) have simultaneously measured the rate of time preference and the coefficient of risk aversion, as well as investigates the interdependencies of four addictive behaviors: smoking, drinking, pachinko (a popular Japanese form of pinball gambling), and horse betting among a sample of the Japanese population. We reach two main conclusions. First, there are significant interdependencies among the four addictive behaviors, in particular between smoking and drinking and between gambling on pachinko and the horses. Second, we conclude that the higher the time preference rate and the lower the risk aversion coefficient becomes, the more likely individuals smoke, drink frequently, and gamble on pachinko and the horses.

In health-care situations, it is important to find risk factors to help clinicians to forecast the outcomes of various interventions. Goto et al. (2009) have also investigated whether time and risk preference predicts relapse among smokers trying to quit. A total of 689 smokers who began quitting smoking within the previous month is followed for 6 months. At the baseline, we estimate time discount rate and coefficient of risk-aversion individually using the method developed in Ida and Goto (2009a) and collected known risk factors of relapse of smoking. During the follow-up course, data such as duration of smoking cessation, methods of cessation supports and mood variation is surveyed. Cox's proportional hazard model with a time-dependent covariate is used. See also Ida et al. (2011) for a developed research.

In the unadjusted model, Cox's proportional hazard regression shows that those with a high time discount rate are more likely to relapse [hazard ratio: 1.18, 95 % confidence interval (CI): 1.11–1.25]. A high coefficient of risk-aversion reduces the hazard of relapse (0.96, 0.96–0.97). When adjusted for other predictors of relapse (age, gender, self-efficacy of quitting, health status, mood variation, past quitting experience, the use of nicotine replacement therapy, nicotine dependence), the hazard ratios of time discount rate and the coefficient of risk-aversion is 1.17 (95 % CI: 1.10–1.24) and 0.98 (95 % CI: 0.97–0.99), respectively. Those who emphasize future rewards (time–patient preference) and those who give more importance

[16] This addendum has been newly written for this book chapter.

to rewards that are certain (higher risk-aversion) are significantly more likely to continue to abstain from smoking. This research shows that time preference and risk preference are independent predictors of failure or success of a quit attempt.

We have lastly investigated smoking status, including cigarette dependence (the most common form of addiction), using the quasi-hyperbolic discounting approach proposed by Laibson (1997). When one compares the current utility of smoking (i.e., temporary stress relief) with the future utility of non-smoking (long-term good health), individuals that have a higher time preference rate tend to attach larger importance to the former compared with the latter and are thus more likely to smoke (and moreover be heavily addicted). Further, if an individual has a present bias, namely his or her current utility is especially high compared with future utility, he or she is more likely to start smoking and to fail to quit smoking many times despite acknowledging the health benefits of not smoking.

Ida (2014) have first tested the likelihood that the stationarity axioms, which are required according to discounted utility theory, are violated and then investigated whether these parameters can successfully predict smoking status, including cigarette dependence, based on a quasi-hyperbolic discount function. By analyzing whether quasi-hyperbolic discounting parameters are associated with smoking, we see that both the present bias and the constant time preference parameters account for smoking behavior very well. Elasticity, which measures how changing one economic variable affects others, also helps quantify this relationship. The analysis shows that a 1 % increase in the present bias parameter significantly increases smoking probability by 0.42 %, while a 1 % increase in the constant time preference parameter increases smoking probability by 0.68 %.

Second, we have investigated how these parameters elucidate cigarette dependence and find that both the present bias and the constant time preference parameters also account for cigarette dependence very well. The analysis shows that a 1 % increase in the present bias parameter decreases the proportion of low nicotine-dependent smokers by 0.43 % but increases that of highly nicotine-dependent smokers by 0.27 %. Furthermore, a 1 % increase in the constant time preference parameter decreases the proportion of low nicotine-dependent smokers by 1.21 % but increases that of highly nicotine-dependent smokers by 0.84 %. Thus, I can conclude that quasi-hyperbolic discounting parameters function as good predictors of smoking status. See also Ida (2010) for a related research.

References

Akkaya A, Ozturk O, Cobanoglu H, Bircan HA, Simsek S, Sahin U (2006) Evaluation of patients followed up in a cigarette cessation clinic. Respirology 11:311–316

Alessi SM, Petry NM (2003) Pathological gambling severity is associated with impulsivity in a delay discounting procedure. Behav Process 64:345–354

Anderhub V, Guth W, Gneezy U, Sonsino D (2001) On the interaction of risk and time preferences: an experimental study. Ger Econ Rev 2:239–253

Baker F, Johnson MW, Bickel WK (2003) Delay discounting in current and never-before cigarette smokers: similarities and differences across commodity, sign, and magnitude. J Abnorm Psychol 112:382–392

Barsky RB, Juster FT, Kimball MS, Shapiro MT (1997) Preference parameters and behavioral heterogeneity: an experimental approach in the health and retirement study. Q J Econ 112:537–579

Ben-Akiva M, Bolduc D, Walker J (2001) Specification, estimation and identification of the logit kernel (or continuous mixed logit) model. Working paper, Department of Civil Engineering, MIT

Bhat C (2001) Quasi-random maximum simulated likelihood estimation of the mixed multinomial logit model. Transp Res B 35:677–693

Bickel WK, Marsch LA (2001) Toward a behavioral economic understanding of drug dependence: delay discounting processes. Addiction 96:73–86

Bickel WK, Odum AL, Madden GJ (1999) Impulsivity and cigarette smoking: delay discounting in current never, and ex-smokers. Psychopharmacology (Berl) 146:447–454

Chaloupka FJ, Warner KE (2000) The economics of smoking. In: Culyer AJ, Newhouse JP (eds) Handbook of health economics, vol 1. Elsevier Science B.V., Amsterdam

Daniels R, Hensher DA (2000) Valuation of environmental impacts of transportation projects: the challenge of self-interest proximity. J Transp Econ Policy 34:189–214

De Leon J, Diaz FJ, Becona E, Gurpegui M, Jurado D, Gonzalez-Pinto A (2003) Exploring brief measures of nicotine dependence for epidemiological surveys. Addict Behav 28:1481–1486

Fishburn PC, Rubinstein A (1982) Time preference. Int Econ Rev 23:677–694

Frederick S, Lowenstein G, O'Donoghue T (2002) Time discounting and time preference: a critical review. J Econ Lit 40:351–401

Goto R, Takahashi Y, Nishimura S, Ida T (2009) A cohort study to examine whether time and risk preference is related to smoking cessation success. Addiction 104:1018–1024

Green L, Myerson J (1996) Exponential versus hyperbolic discounting of delayed outcomes: risk and waiting time. Am Zool 36:496–505

Green L, Fry A, Myerson J (1994) Discounting of delayed rewards: a life-span comparison. Psychol Sci 5:33–36

Green L, Myerson J, Lichtman D, Rosen S, Fry A (1996) Temporal discounting in choice between delayed rewards: the role of age and income. Psychol Aging 11:79–84

Guillon MS, Crocq MA, Bailey PE (2007) Nicotine dependence and self-esteem in adolescents with mental disorders. Addict Behav 32:758–764

Haberstick BC, Timberlake D, Ehringer MA, Lessem JM, Hopfer CJ, Smolen A, Hewitt JK (2007) Genes, time to first cigarette and nicotine dependence in a general population sample of young adults. Addiction 102:655–665

Halton J (1960) On the efficiency of evaluating certain quasi-random sequences of points in evaluating multi-dimensional integrals. Numer Math 2:84–90

Heatherton TF, Kozlowski LT, Frecker RC, Fagerström KO (1991) The Fagerström test for nicotine dependence: a revision of the Fagerström tolerance questionnaire. Br J Addict 86:1119–1127

Hensher DA, Greene WH (2003) The mixed logit model: the state of practice. Transportation 30:133–176

Hensher DA, Rose JM, Greene WH (2005) Applied choice analysis. Cambridge University Press, Cambridge

Ida T (2010) Anomaly, impulsivity, and addiction. J Socio-Econ 39:194–203

Ida T (2014) A Quasi-hyperbolic discounting approach to smoking behavior. Heal Econ Rev 4:1–11

Ida T, Goto R (2009a) Simultaneous measurement of time and risk preferences: stated preference discrete choice modeling analysis depending on smoking behavior. Int Econ Rev 50:1169–1182

Ida T, Goto R (2009b) Interdependency among addictive behaviors and time/risk preferences: discrete choice model analysis of smoking, drinking, and gambling. J Econ Psychol 30:608–621

Ida T, Goto R, Takahashi Y, Nishimura S (2011) Can economic-psychological parameters predict successful smoking cessation? J Socio-Econ 40:285–295

Kahneman D, Tversky A (1979) Prospect theory: an analysis of decision under risk. Econometrica 47:263–291

Keren G, Roelofsma P (1995) Immediacy and certainty in intertemporal choice. Organ Behav Hum Decis Process 63:287–297

Kirby KN, Markovic N (1996) Delayed-discounting probabilistic rewards: rates decrease as amounts increase. Psychon Bull Rev 3:100–104

Koopmans TC (1960) Stationary ordinal utility and impatience. Econometrica 28:287–309

Laibson D (1997) Golden eggs and hyperbolic discounting. Q J Econ 62:443–477

Louviere JJ, Hensher DA, Swait JD (2000) Stated choice methods. Cambridge University Press, Cambridge

Madden PA, Bucholz KK, Martin NG, Heath AC (2000) Smoking and the genetic contribution to alcohol-dependence risk. Alcohol Res Health 24:209–214

McFadden D, Train KE (2000) Mixed MNL models of discrete choice models of discrete response. J Appl Econ 15:447–470

Ministry of Health, Labour and Welfare of Japan (2004) National health and nutrition survey 2002 (in Japanese "Kokumin Kenko Eiyo Tysa"). Daiichi-Shuppan, Tokyo

Mitchell SH (1999) Measures of impulsivity in cigarette smokers and non-smokers. Psychopharmacology (Berl) 146:455–464

Odum AL, Madden GJ, Bickel WK (2002) Discounting of delayed health gains and losses by current, never- and ex-smokers of cigarettes. Nicotine Tob Res 4:295–303

Ohmura Y, Takahashi T, Kitamura N (2005) Discounting delayed and probabilistic monetary gains and losses by smokers of cigarettes. Psychopharmacology (Berl) 182:508–515

Petry NM (2001) Pathological gamblers, with and without substance use disorders, discount delayed rewards at high rates. J Abnorm Psychol 110:482–487

Prelec D, Loewenstein G (1991) Decision making over time and under uncertainty: a common approach. Manag Sci 37:770–786

Rachlin H, Siegel E (1994) Temporal pattering in probabilistic choice. Organ Behav Hum Decis Process 59:161–176

Rachlin H, Logue AW, Gibbon J, Frankel M (1986) Cognition and behavior in studies of choice. Psychol Rev 93:33–45

Rachlin H, Raineri A, Cross D (1991) Subjective probability and delay. J Exp Anal Behav 55:233–244

Revelt D, Train K (1998) Mixed logit with repeated choices: households' choices of appliance efficiency level. Rev Econ Stat 80:647–657

Reynolds B, Karraker K, Horn K, Richards JB (2003) Delay and probability discounting as related to different stages of adolescent smoking and non-smoking. Behav Process 64:333–344

Reynolds B, Richards JB, Horn K, Karraker K (2004) Delay discounting and probability discounting as related to cigarette smoking status in adults. Behav Process 65:35–42

Rimm EB, Can J, Stampfer MJ, Colditz GA, Willett WC (1995) Prospective study of cigarette smoking, alcohol use, and the risk of diabetes in men. Br Med J 310:555–559

Rose JE, Brauer LH, Behm FM, Cramblett M, Calkins K, Lawhon D (2004) Psychopharmacological interactions between nicotine and ethanol. Nicotine Tob Res 6:133–144

Rubinstein A (2003) Economics and psychology? The case of hyperbolic discounting. Int Econ Rev 44:1207–1216

Samuelson P (1937) A note on measurement of utility. Rev Econ Stud 4:155–161

Stevenson MK (1986) A discounting model for decisions with delayed positive and negative outcomes. J Exp Psychol 115:131–154

Storr CL, Reboussin BA, Anthony JC (2005) The Fagerstrom test for nicotine dependence: a comparison of standard scoring and latent class analysis approaches. Drug Alcohol Depend 80:241–250

Takahashi T (2005) Loss of self-control in intertemporal choice may be attributable to logarithmic time-perception. Med Hypotheses 65:691–693

Train KE (2003) Discrete choice methods with simulation. Cambridge University Press, Cambridge

Von Neumann J, Morgenstern O (1953) Theory of games and economic behavior. Princeton University Press, Princeton

Yi R, de la Piedad X, Bickel WK (2006) The combined effects of delay and probability in discounting. Behav Process 73:149–155

Chapter 3
Time Discounting: Declining Impatience and Interval Effect

Yusuke Kinari, Fumio Ohtake, and Yoshiro Tsutsui

Abstract Most studies have not distinguished delay from intervals, so that whether the declining impatience really holds has been an open question. We conducted an experiment that explicitly distinguishes them, and confirmed it at short delay such as less than 8-week delay. This implies that people make dynamically inconsistent plans. We also found the interval effect that the time discount rate decreases with prolonged intervals. We show that the interval and the magnitude effects are caused because intertemporal choice is made partially based on the differential in reward amount, while Weber's law explains neither the delay nor the interval effects sufficiently.

Keywords Time discount rate • Declining impatience • Interval effect • Subadditivity • Weber's law

JEL Classification D81, D9

The original article first appeared in Journal of Risk and Uncertainty 39:87–112, 2009. A newly written addendum has been added to this book chapter.

Y. Kinari
School of Economics, Nagoya University of Commerce and Business, 4-4 Sagamine Komenoki-cho, Nisshin-shi, Aichi 470-0193, Japan
e-mail: kinari-yusuke@nucba.ac.jp

F. Ohtake
Institute of Social and Economic Research, Osaka University, 6-1 Mihogaoka, Ibaraki, Osaka 567-0047, Japan
e-mail: ohtake@iser.osaka-u.ac.jp

Y. Tsutsui (✉)
Faculty of Economics, Konan University, 8-9-1 Okamoto, Higashinada-ku, Kobe 658-8501, Japan
e-mail: tsutsui@center.konan-u.ac.jp

S. Ikeda et al. (eds.), *Behavioral Economics of Preferences, Choices, and Happiness*, DOI 10.1007/978-4-431-55402-8_3

Decision-making is time consistent if the per-period time discount rate is constant over time.[1] Many experiments in economics and psychology, however, have found declining impatience in that the per-period time discount rate of the immediate future is higher than that of the distant future. Declining impatience implies a reversal of preference, and people regret plans they have made in the past (Laibson 1997). Declining impatience has been formalized as a (quasi) hyperbolic time discounting function and has become a standard decision-making model in behavioral sciences.

However, in many economic experiments on declining impatience so far, two elements—delay and interval—are mixed. To measure the time discount rate in experiments, three timings should be distinguished—now, an earlier option, and a later option. Because "now" is fixed, two quantities define the situation fully: delay represents the time difference between now and an earlier option, and interval represents the time difference between earlier and later options. Although the time discount rates may depend on these two factors, most experiments have not distinguished them. Nevertheless, researchers have interpreted their results indicating that the time discount rates depend solely on the delay, and have reported that the per-period time discount rate decreases as the delay increases. However, people's discounting may depend heavily on the interval, not on the delay, so that decision-making may be time consistent.

Read (2001) was innovative in conducting experiments that explicitly distinguish the delay from the interval and in demonstrating the importance of the interval.[2] He divided the total interval (18 months) into three subintervals (6 months each) and compared the discount rates elicited by the choice method, which requires subjects to choose one of two options: one according to which they get a smaller reward sooner and another according to which they get a larger reward, but later. He found with "subadditive time discounting" that the product of three discount rates (plus unity) for subintervals is higher than the discount rate (plus unity) for the total interval. However, he denied the phenomenon of declining impatience because of a lack of evidence when intervals are controlled.

According to Read (2001), who investigated declining impatience by distinguishing delay from interval, decision-making by human beings is time consistent. Declining impatience or hyperbolic discounting, which is a standard model in psychology and physiological neuroscience as well as in behavioral economics, has not indeed had a firm empirical foundation. However, as will be shown in the next section, there are pros and cons with regard to declining impatience, even in the experimental studies that explicitly distinguish the delay from the interval.

[1]This chapter does not consider the case of endogenous time discount rate (Uzawa 1968). If time discount rate of an individual changes over time, which he or she does not know ex ante, his or her decision-making may be time inconsistent. However, these cases are not objects of this chapter.

[2]In the field of psychology, several studies had distinguished the delay from the interval (e.g., Baron 2000; Van der Pol and Cairns 2001; Bleichrodt and Johannesson 2001). However, most of them aimed to measure time discounting for non-pecuniary goods.

Given these lines of study, this chapter has two aims. The first is to elucidate whether declining impatience is really a behavioral characteristic of human beings. Since declining impatience is confirmed when a matching method in which subjects are asked the amount at a specified date—which makes them indifferent to a specified option—is used, we examine it using the choice method. We request subjects to choose one of two options: an earlier option according to which they get a smaller reward sooner and a later option according to which they get a larger reward, but later. Specifying these options, we control the amount of the reward, the interval, and the delay. As we rigorously distinguish the delay from the interval in our experiments, our investigation of the delay effect leads to an examination of the interval effect as a by-product.

To solve the puzzle of whether the delay effect is really the important characteristic of human beings, this chapter distinguishes the delay from the interval, as Read (2001) appropriately has done. However, we are different from him with respect to two points: first we set the delay at less than 12 weeks, and secondly, we adopt a "random order choice method" in which we ask subjects to choose between earlier and later options whose conditions are randomly specified to avoid the biases that sequential and logical order methods may contain. The first point is especially important because we indeed find the delay effect between 2 week and 8 week delays. Read (2001) did not observe the delay effect because he set the delay at over 6 months where people would not explicitly show the delay effect. We also believe that the random order choice method is a powerful method for eliciting subjects' true time discounting. Thus, this chapter finds that people show the delay effect under the choice method, in which subjects choose between earlier and later options. Since the delay effect has been confirmed using other methods, which will be explained in Sect. 1.2, we believe that this corroborates declining impatience, which is especially important because it brings about time inconsistency. Our point is that declining impatience is observed in the case of rather short delays, which Read (2001) overlooked.

A by-product of this analysis is the discovery of the interval effect, according to which the per-period time discount rate decreases as the interval lengthens. The interval effect, which turns out to be a very significant anomaly and should be focused on more in future work, is a sufficient condition for the subadditive time discounting found by Read (2001), and thus the finding is consistent with his results.

The second aim of this chapter is to investigate possible causes of time discounting anomalies. Recent studies show that the anomalies depend heavily on various experimental conditions, which in turn suggests that these anomalies reflect subjects' psychological characteristics. Thus, we investigate the causes along these lines. In particular, we investigate the possibility that the anomalies turn up because human beings make intertemporal choices in a heuristic way to save on the cost of difficult thinking, proposing "the differential effect hypothesis" whereby the differential in the amount of the reward plays an important role in intertemporal choice. Empirical results reveal that the interval and magnitude effects are caused, at least partially, because subjects make choices based on the differential in the reward amount.

We also examine whether or not Weber's law that asserts logarithmic time perception is the source of the anomalies. We first show theoretically that the assumption of subjective logarithmic time perception may explain the anomalies of the delay and interval effects. Our estimation results indicate, however, that Weber's law does not actually explain these anomalies. Nonetheless, logarithmic time perception has some explanatory power for the choice between the earlier and later options, suggesting that Weber's law still remains as a promising tool to investigate intertemporal choice.

The rest of this chapter is organized as follows: In Sect. 1, we point out problems in previous studies. Section 2 explains our experimental procedure. Section 3 reports our experimental results. In Sect. 4, we check the robustness of our results using a questionnaire survey conducted at the end of the experiment. In Sect. 5, we inquire as to the cause of the anomalies on time discounting and examine the differential amount hypothesis and Weber's law. Section 6 concludes this chapter.

1 Distinguishing Delay from Interval

1.1 *Problems Faced in Previous Studies*

Many studies, including those by Richards et al. (1999), Pender (1996), Kirby and Marakovic (1995), Myerson and Green (1995), Benzion et al. (1989), and Thaler (1981)typically asked subjects how much they will demand if, instead of receiving X dollars now, they receive it at time t (in the future). Varying t and X in their experiments, they drew the conclusion that per-period time discount rates diminish with delay, since the per-period time discount rate from now to t, $R(0, t)$, is smaller than that from now to s, $R(0, s)$, $s < t$, that is,

$$R(0, s) \geq R(0, t), s < t. \tag{3.1}$$

In their deduction, however, they ignore the fact that at the same time, the interval changes from s to t. One can interpret inequality (3.1) as the per-period time discount rate decreases with an increase in the interval. In order to test declining impatience rigorously, we need to compare discount rates for various delays by controlling the intervals.

1.2 *Declining Impatience*

Read (2001) conducts experiments, distinguishing explicitly the delay from the interval. By doing this, he elicited a pure effect of change in delay by fixing the intervals at 6 months, but found no evidence of declining impatience.

Several studies that explicitly distinguish the delay and the interval have appeared. For example, Read and Roelofsma (2003) focus on the method that elicits time discounting from questions. They found that declining impatience is observed with the matching method that asks subjects of the amount at specified date, which makes them indifferent to a specified option, but not with the choice method that asks subjects to choose the better one from specified two options. On the other hand, Read et al. (2005) focus on how the timing of two options is described. They found that declining impatience is observed when the timing is specified with calendar dates, but not when it is specified by the length of the delay. Thus, there are pros and cons on declining impatience even in experimental studies that explicitly distinguish the delay from the interval.

Given these arguments, we examine whether declining impatience is really the case, setting the delay at an adequately short period. With regard to the results of Read (2001), we point out that his analysis has a problem, because even the shortest delay in his experiments is 6 months, which is too long to analyze the effect of a change in the delay. Frederick et al. (2002) reported that there is no evidence of declining impatience when the delay is over 1 year. In fact, using the matching method and a shorter delay than that of Read (2001), Read and Roelofsma (2003) found evidence of declining impatience. Ikeda et al. (2005) also found that a change in the delay longer than 1 month does not affect time discount rates. These researches suggest that declining impatience is a phenomenon of short delays. In our experiment, we test much shorter delays, such as 1 day or 1 week, to find declining impatience within 8 weeks of delay, with the intervals being controlled.

Another feature of our study is to employ a random order method in which options were presented to subjects randomly, irrespective of their past choice. Experimental conditions such as the length of the delay, the length of the interval, and the amount of the reward are chosen randomly for each question. In contrast, many studies used a sequential order method in which the options that are shown to subjects are arranged according to some experimental condition like discount rate. This method may suffer a bias originating from the sequential order. Read (2001) and Read and Roelofsma (2003) employ a logical order method according to which the future options available for subjects depend on the current options chosen by them. Although this method has an advantage that it is immune from a possible sequential order bias, it contains the risk that a series of subjects' choices may be affected by the first presented options. In other words, a solution by logical order method may not achieve global maximum, but rather local maximum near the initial value.[3] The random order method has merits that make it immune from a possible sequential order bias, and so the global maximum is more warranted. A stressful burden is imposed upon subjects because the timing of acceptance and the amount of reward change randomly with every question, which may help to elicit subjects' true preference.

[3]The situation is similar to the Newton–Raphson method of numerical optimization, which sometimes depends on initial value that researchers set.

1.3 Interval Effect

While Read (2001) found a negative answer to declining impatience, he found an affirmative answer to "subadditive time discounting" represented by the following inequality (3.2).

$$1+\beta\,(0m,18m)\le(1+\beta\,(0m,6m))\times(1+\beta\,(6m,12m))\times(1+\beta\,(12m,18m)) \tag{3.2}$$

where m stands for month(s), and $\beta(a, b)$ indicates time discount rate for the period from time a to time b, that is, if receiving X dollars at time a is indifferent to receiving Y dollars at time b, $\beta(a, b)$ is $(Y-X)/X$. Using the per-period time discount rate $R(a, b)$, defining 6 months as a unit period, inequality (3.2) is rewritten as

$$(1+R\,(0m,18m))^3\le(1+R\,(0m,6m))\times(1+R\,(6m,12m))\times(1+R\,(12m,18m)). \tag{3.3}$$

In short, "declining impatience", falsely argued by studies so far that mixed the delay and the interval, is actually subadditivity and not true declining impatience: this is what Read (2001) found.

In this chapter, we define the interval effect such that the longer the interval, the lower the per-period time discount rate with the delay and magnitude effects being adjusted. That is,

$$R\,(a,b)\le R(a',b'),\ \mathit{if}\ b\text{–}a\ge b'\text{–}a',\ \forall a,b,a',b', \tag{3.4}$$

and we investigate whether the interval effect is confirmed with our subjects. It is easy to prove that inequality (3.3) is satisfied if inequality (3.4) is satisfied. Therefore, the interval effect is a sufficient condition for subadditive time discounting. In this sense, the interval effect is a more general concept than subadditive time discounting.

2 Experiment

2.1 Subjects

Our experiment was conducted in the morning and afternoon for 4 days from February 14 to 17, 2006. The experiment consists of eight sessions in total, using different subjects. Subjects were 219 students in total who were affiliated with

Table 3.1 Attributes of subjects

	Number of subjects					
Departments	Total	Male	Female	Undergraduates	Graduates	Average age
Letters	25	7	18	22	3	21.08
Law	15	9	5	14	1	20.73
Economics	24	16	8	19	5	21.67
Human science	16	4	12	15	1	21.13
Engineering	68	63	5	59	9	20.65
Engineering science	34	32	2	26	8	21.62
Science	22	19	3	17	5	22.32
Medicine	12	8	4	7	5	23.58
Pharmaceutical science	3	3	0	3	0	19.67
Total	219	161	57	182	37	21.32

Osaka University. Most of the experiments on time discounting employ 30 or 40 subjects; however, our experiment was large-scale.[4]

Table 3.1 provides some information about our subjects. As for age, subjects are 18–37 years of age, but most of them are around 20 years old. Among 219 subjects, 26 % are female and 17 % are graduate students. Subjects are well-diversified over nine departments of Osaka University.[5]

2.2 *Procedure*

Each subject is required to choose one of the two options displayed on a computer screen in front.[6] One is option A wherein subjects get a smaller reward earlier, and the other is option B in which subjects get a larger rewards later.

As noted in the previous sections, we control three factors: the amount of reward, interval, and delay. We define the delay as the difference between the present (time 0) and the time of receipt stated in the option A, and specify eight different delays. We define the interval as the difference between the time of receipt stated in the options A and B, and specify four intervals. Pairing these delays and intervals, we specify 15 combinations of receipt timing shown in Table 3.2.

We define the amount of reward as the amount stated in the option A; 180 different amounts are generated randomly from the truncated normal distribution with the mean of 2,000; standard deviation of 1,000; upper bound of 4,000; and lower bound of 500. These 180 amounts are randomly assigned to each question.

[4]Benzion et al. (1989) experimented with 282 students, but they did not reward the subjects.

[5]No subjects are from the department of dentistry.

[6]The experiment was programmed and conducted with the software z-Tree (Fischbacher 1999).

Table 3.2 Fifteen combinations of receipt timing in earlier and later options

Delay (timing of receipt in option A)	Interval	Delay + Interval (timing of receipt in option B)
0 day	2 weeks	2 weeks
0 day	4 weeks	4 weeks
0 day	6 weeks	6 weeks
0 day	8 weeks	8 weeks
1 day	2 weeks	15 days
1 week	2 weeks	3 weeks
2 weeks	2 weeks	4 weeks
2 weeks	4 weeks	6 weeks
2 weeks	6 weeks	8 weeks
4 weeks	2 weeks	6 weeks
4 weeks	4 weeks	8 weeks
6 weeks	2 weeks	8 weeks
8 weeks	2 weeks	10 weeks
10 weeks	2 weeks	12 weeks
12 weeks	2 weeks	14 weeks

Twelve rates of return (1 %, 2 %, 3 %, 4 %, 5 %, 7.5 %, 10 %, 12.5 %, 15 %, 25 %, 35 %, and 50 %) are also randomly assigned to 12 questions of each combination. The amount of reward stated in the option B is calculated by adding the amount of reward tantamount to the above rates of return to the amount in the option A.

Thus, there are 15 combinations of receipt timing in the options A and B as shown in Table 3.2, and we ask 12 questions for each combination, each of which is specified with different rates of return ranging from 1 to 50 %. Consequently, subjects are requested to answer 180 questions. These 180 questions are determined in advance, and all subjects answer the same questions. However, the order that the questions are presented to subjects is randomly determined for each subject.

Subjects are paid 2,000 yen in cash for participation in the experiment. At the end of the experiment, we randomly select one question out of the 180 questions, for which we will actually pay the reward. Subjects will receive a reward, a gift voucher from amazon.co.jp, on the date stated in the option they have chosen in this selected question.

2.3 *Estimation of Time Discount Rates*

We estimate 15 per-period time discount rates per subject, each of which corresponding to each combination of time of receipt. The procedure of the estimation is as follows. As noted in the previous subsection, 12 questions are asked for each combination of receipt timing, changing the rate of return. The answers for these 12 questions, A or B, were sorted in ascending order as per the rates of return implied by the options. If a subject chooses the option A when the rate of return is low and option B when it is high, so that they switch from the option A to B only once, then we determine the time discount rate of the subject as an average of the two rates of return immediately before and after the switch.

However, some subjects made two or more switches between the two options during answering of the 12 questions with the same combination of the receipt timing.[7] This is probable because the questions were asked randomly. In such a multi-switching case, we estimate the time discount rates using a logit model. Specifically, the dependent variable is a dummy variable that takes unity when a subject chooses B (later option) and zero otherwise, and is regressed over the 12 rates of return. Then, using the estimates of the coefficient, we calculate back a rate of return where a probability of choosing B becomes just 0.5, and regard it as the time discount rate of the subject for this combination of receipt timing. We exclude the data from our analyses if the estimated time discount rates using the logit model are out of the 1–50 % range. Moreover, if a subject consistently chooses A (or B) for 12 questions of the same combination of receipt timings, we exclude those observations from our analyses.[8]

In this chapter, we denote the subjects' time discount rates between time a and b calculated by the above procedure as $\beta(a, b)$, and the corresponding per-period time discount rate $R(a, b)$, where the unit period is set at 2 weeks.[9] In Table 3.3, we show the number of observations, the mean and the standard deviation of per-period time discount rates, and the mean of the amount of reward for each combination of receipt timing.

3 Results

3.1 Declining Impatience

To confirm that the per-period time discount rates are declining with the delay, we choose the combinations in which the delays are different but the intervals are the same, and compare their discount rates.[10] In other words, we select the observations

[7]1,352 out of 3,285 time discount rates (219 subjects × 15 combinations of receipt timings) fall into this multi-switching case.

[8]957 out of 3,285 observations are excluded; 625 (43 respectively) observations are excluded because subjects chose B (A) for all questions; 289 observations are excluded because the time discount rates estimated by the logit model are not in the range from 1 to 50 %.

[9]For example, the value of $1 + R(0\,day, 4\,weeks)$ is calculated as the square root of $1 + \beta(0\,day, 4\,weeks)$, and the value of $1 + R(0\,day, 6\,weeks)$ is calculated as the cube root of $1 + \beta(0\,day, 6\,weeks)$.

[10]We cannot control the amount of reward because it is randomly chosen for each question. As shown in the far-right column of Table 3.3, however, the average amounts do not differ substantially

Table 3.3 Per-period time discount rates

Delay (timing of receipt in option A)	Delay + Interval (timing of receipt in option B)	Number of observations	Per-period time discount rate		Average amount of reward in option A
			Mean	Standard error	
0 day	2 weeks	167	0.090	0.091	2,263
0 day	4 weeks	170	0.060	0.047	1,803
0 day	6 weeks	161	0.066	0.046	1,789
0 day	8 weeks	164	0.039	0.027	2,238
1 day	15 days	173	0.094	0.074	2,181
1 week	3 weeks	165	0.091	0.082	2,198
2 weeks	4 weeks	157	0.095	0.095	1,776
2 weeks	6 weeks	158	0.052	0.044	1,814
2 weeks	8 weeks	171	0.044	0.030	1,961
4 weeks	6 weeks	149	0.077	0.064	2,135
4 weeks	8 weeks	164	0.051	0.044	1,903
6 weeks	8 weeks	132	0.081	0.069	2,131
8 weeks	10 weeks	135	0.063	0.068	2,279
10 weeks	12 weeks	128	0.069	0.079	2,155
12 weeks	14 weeks	134	0.070	0.065	2,304

Notes: Table shows the number of observations, mean and standard deviation of per-period time discount rates, and the average of the amount of reward for each combination of receipt timing. The number of observations is less than the number of subjects, 219, because we exclude the observations if a subject consistently chooses A (or B) for 12 questions of the same combination, and that the estimated time discount rates using a logit model are out of the 1–50 % range

of the same interval and examine whether there exists a negative correlation between the delay and the time discount rate within these observations.

Let us first analyze the case where the interval is set at 2 weeks. Figure 3.1, which depicts the relation of the per-period time discount rates (vertical axis) and the delay (horizontal axis), reveals that the per-period time discount rate tends to decline as the delay increases, keeping the interval at 2 weeks. While the discount rates are in a range from 0.090 to 0.095 when the delay is within 2 weeks, they are less than 0.085 on and over a 4-week delay, suggesting that the per-period time discount rates shift downward during the 2-week to 4-week delay.

To examine its significance, we pick up observations whose intervals are the same and conduct a mean-difference test among groups with different delays. The test results are shown in Table 3.4, which reveals that the discount rates within a 2-week delay are significantly different from those over a 4-week delay. In addition, the discount rates within a 2-week delay are not significantly different from each

among 15 combinations of receipt timing. Therefore, possible biases due to the uncontrolled amount may be trivial.

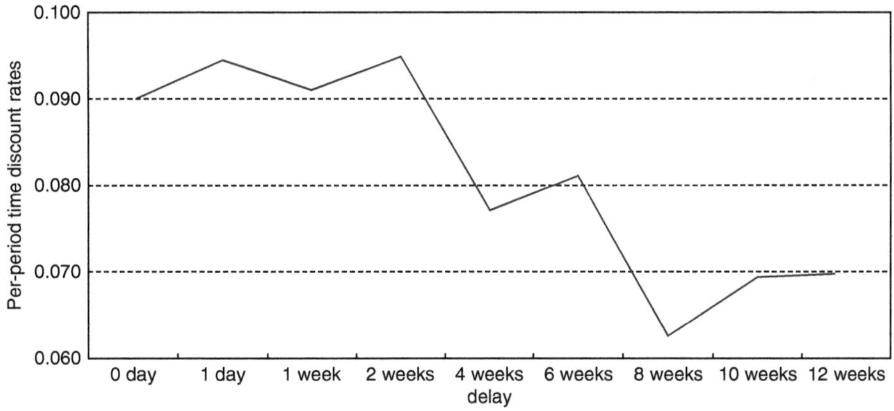

Fig. 3.1 Declining impatience in the case where the interval is kept at 2 weeks. Note: The average of the per-period time discount rates for each delay designated at the horizontal axis is plotted. The interval is kept at 2 weeks

Table 3.4 Test results for the declining impatience for the case that the interval is held at 2 weeks

	1 day	1 week	2 weeks	4 weeks	6 weeks	8 weeks	10 weeks	12 weeks
0 day	−0.491	−0.110	−0.464	1.451	0.961	2.976***	2.079**	2.208**
1 day	–	0.397	−0.040	2.235**	1.620*	3.899***	2.794***	3.060***
1 week	–	–	−0.380	1.670*	1.135	3.268***	2.291**	2.464**
2 weeks	–	–	–	1.907*	1.419	3.352***	2.470**	2.622***
4 weeks	–	–	–	–	−0.482	1.862*	0.908	0.938
6 weeks	–	–	–	–	–	2.197**	1.276	1.341
8 weeks	–	–	–	–	–	–	−0.736	−0.917
10 weeks	–	–	–	–	–	–	–	−0.082

Notes: Observations whose interval is 2 weeks are picked up and a mean-difference test among groups with different delays is applied. The figures in each cell are t-values for the mean-difference test between per-period time discount rates of two groups with different delays shown in the first column and the first row; ***, **, and * indicate that the values are statistically significant at the 1 %, 5 %, and 10 % levels, respectively

other, and the discount rates over a 4-week delay seldom differ significantly from each other. These results suggest that the per-period time discount rates with a 2-week interval substantially decrease during a 2-week to 4-week delay.

Figure 3.2 depicts the relationship between the per-period time discount rates and the delay, with the interval being kept at 4 weeks. Table 3.5 presents the result of the mean-difference tests for the case of a 4-week interval. Although there is no significant difference between the per-period time discount rate with a 2-week delay and that with a 4-week delay, the per-period time discount rate with 0-day delay is significantly different from the per-period time discount rates with 2-week and 4-week delays. These results confirm the declining impatience between the 0-day and 2-week delays, for the case of a 4-week interval.

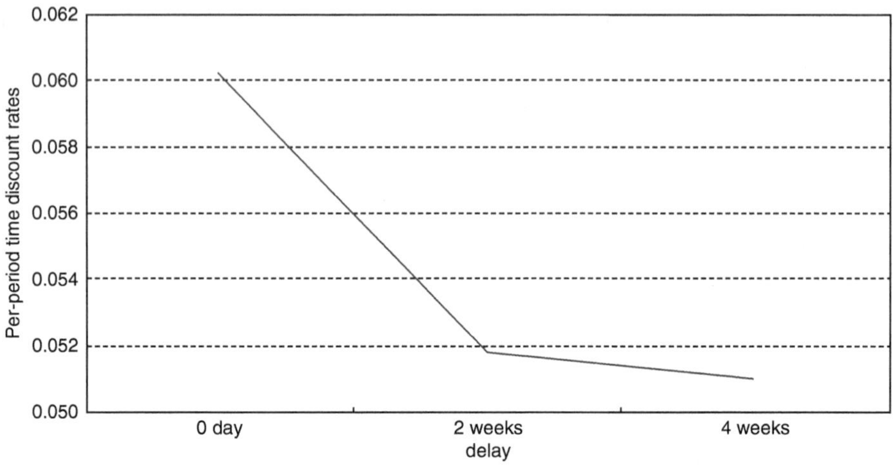

Fig. 3.2 Declining impatience in the case where the interval is kept at 4 weeks. Note: The average of the per-period time discount rates for each delay designated at the horizontal axis is plotted. The interval is kept at 4 weeks

Table 3.5 Test results for the declining impatience for the case that the interval is held at 4 weeks

	2 weeks	4 weeks
0 day	1.663*	1.857*
2 weeks		0.167

Notes: Observations whose interval is 4 weeks are picked up and a mean-difference test among groups with different delays is applied. The figures in each cell are t-values for the mean-difference test between per-period time discount rates of two groups with different delays shown in the first column and the first row; * indicates that the values are statistically significant at the 10 % level

When the interval is fixed at 6 weeks, the average time discount rate of the 0-day delay R (0 day, 6 weeks) is 0.066, while that of the 2-week delay R (2 weeks, 8 weeks) is 0.044; the latter is significantly lower than the former (t-value is 4.948). This indicates that the per-period time discount rates also diminish with the delay in the case of the 6-week interval. In sum, declining impatience is recognized during the shorter delays irrespective of the interval.

3.2 *Regression Analysis with Panel Data*

In the previous subsection, we conducted mean-difference tests keeping the intervals fixed and found declining impatience. In this subsection, we run a regression to confirm declining impatience controlling the magnitude effect and subjects' attributes in addition to the interval effect. The analysis will elucidate how time discount rates depend on the delay, interval, amount of reward, and attributes of the subjects.

Specifically, we regress the panel data of the per-period time discount rates of 3,285 observations (i.e., 219 subjects × 15 combinations of receipt timing) on experimental conditions (the delay, interval, and amount of reward) and subjects' attributes (gender, age, and their affiliated department).[11] This analysis has an advantage of comprehensive use of the experimental results. The following variables of experimental conditions and attributes of subjects are employed in the estimation: eight dummy variables for delay, taking the 0-day delay as a benchmark; three dummy variables for the interval, taking the 2-week interval as a benchmark; and the average amount of reward that is defined as the average of the amount of reward of 12 questions in the same combination of receipt timing.[12] As for subjects' attributes, we employ a male dummy variable for gender, age, a dummy variable standing for graduates, and eight dummy variables standing for each department, taking the department of engineering as the reference group.

The regression results are presented in Table 3.6. Model 1 is a regression which considers only experimental conditions, while Model 2 stands for a regression which incorporates subjects' attributes into Model 1. The results of Model 1 reveal that although 1-day and 1-week delays do not affect significantly, the longer delay dummies have significant negative effects. In addition, the coefficients of the dummies keep decreasing until the 8-week delay. These results imply that the declining impatience is observed even when the effect of the amount of reward as well as the interval is controlled.

All the intervals have significant negative coefficients, supporting the interval effect that the per-period time discount rate is declining with the interval. Closer inspection reveals that it may decrease monotonically if we evaluate the coefficients of 4-week and 6-week intervals as similar. The logarithmic average amount of reward has a significantly negative coefficient, indicating the magnitude effect wherein the larger the amount of reward, the lower the per-period time discount rate.

When the attribute variables are added (see Model 2), the coefficients of the delay and interval dummies and the logarithmic average amount of reward are almost unchanged, implying that the above results are fairly robust. The male dummy has a significant positive coefficient, indicating male is more impatient than female, as Ikeda et al. (2005) report. As for the age, Ikeda et al. (2005) report that the older subjects tend to have lower per-period time discount rates; however, this age effect is not confirmed in our experiment. This may be because most of our subjects are around 20 years old, while the age of their subjects spreads over a wide range. All the department dummies, taking the department of engineering as the benchmark, did not have significant coefficients, although departments of medicine and science are relatively low and departments of economics and pharmaceutical science are

---

[11] Subjects' attributes are based on the questionnaire survey conducted at the end of the experiment.

[12] We use the average of 12 amounts of reward because it is hard to identify the amount of reward corresponding to the dependent variable, especially in the case where the time discount rate is estimated by a logit model.

Table 3.6 Regression results of per-period time discount rates on experimental conditions and attributes of subjects

Independent variables		Model 1 Coefficients	Model 1 Standard errors	Model 2 Coefficients	Model 2 Standard errors
Constant		0.709***	0.147	0.661***	0.152
Delay dummies	1 day	0.003	0.004	0.004	0.004
	1 week	−0.001	0.004	−0.001	0.004
	2 weeks	−0.014***	0.003	−0.014***	0.003
	4 weeks	−0.014***	0.003	−0.014***	0.003
	6 weeks	−0.022***	0.005	−0.022***	0.005
	8 weeks	−0.032***	0.005	−0.032***	0.005
	10 weeks	−0.029***	0.005	−0.029***	0.005
	12 weeks	−0.022***	0.005	−0.022***	0.005
Interval dummies	4 weeks	−0.036***	0.003	−0.036***	0.003
	6 weeks	−0.034***	0.003	−0.034***	0.003
	8 weeks	−0.041***	0.004	−0.041***	0.004
Logarithmic average amount of reward		−0.080***	0.019	−0.081***	0.019
Male dummy				0.028***	0.010
Age of subjects				0.002	0.002
Graduates dummy				−0.005	0.014
Department dummies	Letters			0.004	0.014
	Law			−0.005	0.014
	Economics			0.018	0.012
	Human science			0.007	0.016
	Engineering			−0.002	0.008
	Science			−0.013	0.013
	Medicine			−0.018	0.016
	Pharmaceutical science			0.052	0.034
Number of observations		2,328		2,316	
R-squared	Within	0.132		0.133	
	Between	0.140		0.110	
	Overall	0.067		0.089	

Notes: Only the regression results from random effect model are shown because it was not rejected against fixed effect model by Hausman specification test. Dependent variable is the per-period time discount rates; *** indicates that the values are significant at the 1 % level. The number of observations is less than the total observations (219 subjects 15 combinations of receipt timing) because we exclude the observations that a subject consistently chooses A (or B) for 12 questions of the same combination, and that the estimated time discount rates using a logit model are out of the 1–50 % range high. When we set the department of economics as the reference group, however, a dummy representing the department of medicine has a significantly negative coefficient, indicating that students of the department of medicine are more patient than those of the department of economics.

3.3 Subadditive Time Discounting

As noted in Sect. 1, time discounting is subadditive if the interval effect exists. Therefore, the results of the interval effect presented in the previous subsection imply that the time discounting should be subadditive. In this subsection, we directly confirm that the time discounting of our subjects is actually subadditive.

We denote the time discount rate (plus unity) between time a and time b, for the case where the period is not divided, as $U\ (a, b)$. This corresponds to the left-hand side of inequality (3.2). Meanwhile, we denote the same time discount rate (plus one), for the case where the period is divided into n subintervals, as $D\ (n, a, b)$. Specifically, $D\ (n, a, b)$ is defined as the product of the time discount rates of the subintervals, which corresponds to the right-hand side of inequality (3.2). In this subsection, we use the time discount rates for various periods instead of the per-period one for the sake of simplicity of notation.

While Read (2001) divides the total intervals of 18 months and 24 months into three equal-length subintervals for the test of the subadditivity, we employ various shorter total intervals of 4 weeks, 6 weeks, and 8 weeks, and divide them into shorter subintervals such as 2 weeks.

Table 3.7, which presents the results on the subadditivity, reveals that the time discount rates in the divided cases are significantly higher than those of the undivided cases irrespective of the number of divisions. As expected, the subadditive time discounting is observed in our experiment as in Read (2001). Furthermore, since *U (0 day, 8 weeks)* < *D (2, 0 days, 8 weeks)* < *D (4, 0 days, 8 weeks)*, we conclude that the subadditivity is stronger as the number of divisions is larger. This is consistent with the result of Read and Roelofsma (2003).

Division is a kind of shortening of an interval, and the interval effect is a sufficient condition for the subadditivity as explained in Sect. 1. Thus, it is no surprise that we observe the subadditive time discounting, because we have already found the interval effect. In addition, since the larger number of divisions implies shorter intervals, the result in which the subadditivity for a larger number of divisions is stronger is also consistent with the interval effect.[13]

[13]Of course, this chapter does not dismiss the possibility that the subadditivity is caused by some additional factors to the interval effect. For instance, when the divided and undivided cases are compared, delay is also different between the cases: while only one delay is involved in the undivided case, a couple of delays are involved in the divided case. In addition, it might be the case that division itself affects the time discount rate. However, this chapter does not pursue how

Table 3.7 Test results on the subadditive time discounting

	Number of observations	Time discount rates				Difference in mean
		Mean	Standard error	Minimum	Maximum	
$n = 4$						
U(0 day, 8 weeks)	164	1.169	0.127	1.016	1.457	0.320***
D(4, 0 day, 8 weeks)	107	1.490	0.396	1.057	3.280	
$n = 3$						
U(0 day, 6 weeks)	161	1.218	0.159	1.012	1.482	0.103***
D(3, 0 day, 6 weeks)	130	1.320	0.277	1.040	2.521	
U(2 weeks, 8 weeks)	171	1.142	0.100	1.016	1.465	0.188***
D(3, 2 weeks, 8 weeks)	113	1.330	0.258	1.045	2.415	
$n = 2$						
U(0 day, 4 weeks)	170	1.126	0.102	1.017	1.473	0.071***
D(2, 0 day, 4 weeks)	148	1.198	0.180	1.028	1.939	
U(2 weeks, 6 weeks)	158	1.108	0.097	1.015	1.473	0.084***
D(2, 2 weeks, 6 weeks)	137	1.193	0.168	1.027	1.856	
U(4 weeks, 8 weeks)	164	1.106	0.095	1.011	1.464	0.075***
D(2,4 weeks, 8 weeks)	120	1.181	0.129	1.028	1.692	
U(0 day, 8 weeks)	164	1.169	0.127	1.016	1.457	0.076***
D(2, 0 day, 8 weeks)	152	1.246	0.189	1.028	1.901	

Notes: U (a, b) denotes the time discount rate (plus one) of the undivided case between time a to b. D (n, a, b) denotes the time discount rate (plus one) of the divided case between time a to b; n represents the number of subintervals of equal length; *** indicates that the difference in mean is significant at the 1 % level

the subadditivity is different from the interval effect. To elucidate this point, it is necessary to devise specific experiments, which will be a future task.

4 Robustness Check with Survey Data

In this section, we check the robustness of the declining impatience observed in our experiment by analyzing the results of a questionnaire survey conducted at the end of the experiment. In our experiment, subjects are requested to answer 180 questions presented in random order. This randomness of presentation might cause bias. On the other hand, in the questionnaire survey, subjects are asked two questions. Which one do they prefer: (A) 10,000 yen in 2 days or (B) X yen in 9 days; and the other is between (A) 10,000 yen in 90 days or (B) Y yen in 97 days. Eight values are assigned for Xs and Ys in these questions.[14] Because both questions differ only in the delay and their interval and amount of reward are the same, we can test the declining impatience by just comparing the responses to both the questions. The largest difference from the questions asked in the experiment is that these questions are aligned in ascending order of X and Y, and subjects can read all eight questions before they answer. Therefore, subjects' choice may depend on these eight questions. In addition, the questionnaire survey is also different from the experiment in that subjects are not paid a reward based on their choices.

As in the case of the experiment, we determine time discount rates of the subjects at the average of the two rates of return immediately before and after a switch.[15] The result of the mean-difference test is shown in Table 3.8, which reveals that the mean of subjects' per-period time discount rates in the questionnaire is substantially lower than the corresponding figure in the experiment shown in Table 3.3. For example, *R (2 days, 9 days)* is 0.013 in Table 3.8, while *R (1 day, 15 days)* is 0.094 in Table 3.3. This discrepancy arises probably because the amount of reward in the questionnaire is about five times larger than that in the experiment.[16]

Table 3.8 reveals that the discount rate of a 2-day delay is significantly higher than that of a 90-day delay, implying that the declining impatience is also observed in the answers to survey questions. In sum, the results of the declining impatience is robust depending on whether the questions are presented one by one in random order or simultaneously in ascending order, and whether or not a reward is paid depending on their choice.

[14]Pender (1996) adopts this method in their economic experiment.

[15]In this analysis, we regard multi-switching cases as irrational choices and exclude them from the analysis. There are only a few such cases in the questionnaire survey.

[16]The estimated coefficient of the logarithmic average amount of reward in Table 3.6 indicates that the time discount rate decreases by about 0.1 when the average amount of the reward changes from 2,000 to 10,000 yen ($0.080 \times (\ln(10000) - \ln(2000))$). The time discount rates in the experiment come close to the questionnaire survey when the magnitude effect is considered.

Table 3.8 Test results on the declining impatience using the questionnaire survey

	Number of observations	Time discount rates		Difference in mean
		Mean	Standard error	
R(2 days, 9 days)	193	0.013	0.013	0.005***
R(90 days, 97 days)	203	0.008	0.010	

Notes: *R (2 days, 9 days)* stands for per-period time discount rate with 2-day delay and 7-day interval. *R (90 days, 97 days)* stands for per-period time discount rate with 90-day delay and 7-day interval. The number of observations is less than the number of subjects, 219, because we exclude the observations that a subject consistently chose all A or all B and those with multi-switching; *** indicates that the difference in mean is statistically significant at the 1 % level

5 What Causes the Anomalies?

5.1 Traditional Assumptions and Time Discounting Anomalies

In the previous sections, we confirmed three anomalies: declining impatience and interval and magnitude effects. This section pursues the reason why these anomalies occur.

When subjects consider which is preferable, (A) receiving X yen at time s or (B) receiving Y yen at time t ($t > s$), information on the amount of reward in the two options X and Y and on the timing of receipt of the two options s and t is at hand. Traditional economics, however, assumes that people are rational, so that they have their own per-period time discount rate, $\tilde{R}$, a priori, and compare $\tilde{R}$ with the rate of return, R, calculated from the four pieces of information as

$$R = \left(\frac{Y}{X}\right)^{1/(t-s)} - 1 \tag{3.5}$$

to determine their choices. The four pieces of information are condensed into the rate of return, R, and only R is compared with $\tilde{R}$ to determine the subjects' decision on the earlier or later options; no other information has any additional effect on their decision. As we observed in the previous sections, such an assumption does not evidently match with the reality. The time discount rate, $\tilde{R}$, of the people is not a constant, but is dependent on the experimental conditions of each question, X, Y, t, and s. These facts imply that the traditional assumption of a rational human being does not apply and. The subjects' time discount rates, $\tilde{R}$, may depend on the delay, interval, and amount of reward; and the choice of people is not determined only by the rate of return, R, implied in the two options, or subjects may not compare R with $\tilde{R}$ to make a choice between earlier and later options, but use a handier heuristic way. In this section, we examine two hypotheses that may explain these anomalies.

5.2 Differential Effect Hypothesis

In this subsection, we examine the reason why the length of the interval and the amount of reward affected subjects' decision-making in addition to the rate of return, R. In particular, we propose a hypothesis that subjects focus on a differential in the amount of earlier and later options (hereafter, the differential effect hypothesis) when they choose between two options.

One possible reason why there exist anomalies like delay, interval and magnitude effects is that people make decisions in a heuristic way to save calculation costs. Two options are completely specified with four conditions on timing of receipts and the amount of rewards of each option, i. e., s, t, X, and Y. The rate of return defined by the two options is not easily known: it is calculated with these four items of information. It is known that human beings usually use a heuristic method for decision-making (Tversky and Kahneman 1974); therefore, it is natural to suppose that our subjects also made their intertemporal decisions in a heuristic way. In this chapter, we examine the hypothesis that the difference in amounts plays an important role in intertemporal choice. Of course, there should be many ways to save calculation costs, and a comprehensive analysis of the heuristic method in intertemporal choice should be an important task of future research.

Subjects may choose the earlier (later) option when the differential in amount of rewards, $Y-X$, is substantially small (large).[17] We call it the "differential effect hypothesis". Of course, it is not reasonable to assume that subjects will always reason in this way.[18] For example, even if subjects have some threshold for the difference in amounts and choose an option based on whether the interval and the amount of reward fall in a certain small range, it is not reasonable to think that they will apply the same threshold when the interval becomes very long and/or the amount of reward becomes very large. However, in our case, the interval is from 2 weeks to 8 weeks and the amount of rewards is from 500 to 4,000 yen, so that the experimental conditions are not very diversified. Thus, subjects may follow this heuristic way in the experiments.

If the subjects follow the differential amount hypothesis, the interval and magnitude effects will be observed. Since the differential in amount is described as

$$Y - X = X\left[(R+1)^{(t-s)} - 1\right], \tag{3.6}$$

it increases as the length of the interval and the amount of reward increase. If our subjects make a decision based on the differential in amount, subjects choose the later option when the interval becomes longer or the amount of reward gets larger, even though the rate of return does not change. Consequently, when the differential in the amount of reward is large, subjects report a lower discount rate, so that we will find negative coefficients on the intervals and on the amount of reward

[17] Read and Scholten (2006) examine a similar idea.

[18] We are grateful to an anonymous referee for explaining this with a concrete example.

when discount rates are regressed over these variables. This is actually what we observed in Table 3.6. If this differential effect hypothesis is true, we can expect that coefficients on the interval and the amount become larger when the variable of the differential is added to this regression.

However, this regression is problematic because, as noted in footnote 12, it is difficult to identify the amount (and, therefore, also the differential) corresponding to the time discount rate estimated by a logit model. To solve this problem, we regress subjects' binary choices on the earlier or later option over the four experimental conditions, instead of the two-step method in which we estimate the discount rate at the first step, and then explain it with the experimental conditions in the second step. The method in this section has an advantage of making efficient use of all the information from the 180 choices per subject. More importantly, while the two-step method requires a premise that subjects make a decision based only on their specific per-period time discount rate, $\tilde{R}$, the current method does not require such a premise, which was already found to be incorrect.

We regress the dependent variable, a dummy variable that takes unity in case a subject chooses the later option and zero otherwise, over dummy variables standing for each delay, dummy variables for each interval, the amount of reward, and the logarithm of the per-period rate of return, $\ln(1+R)$. The estimation results of this specification (Model 3), as well as the specification (Model 4) that incorporates the differential in amount as an independent variable, are presented in Table 3.9.[19] The estimation method is a panel logit cum random effect model.

First, let us examine the results of Model 3. The rate of return has a significantly positive coefficient, implying that the rate of return is an important factor in decision-making, as traditional economics assumes. However, the rate of return is not the only factor that determines the intertemporal choice. In addition to the rate of return, the delay has an additional explanatory power. The dummy variables for the delays, except for those representing a 1-day and 1-week-delay, have significant positive coefficients and become larger for longer delays. In short, subjects tend to choose later options as the delay becomes larger, even when the rate of return is controlled. This fact is a counterpart to the declining impatience reported in Table 3.6, because the result that subjects choose the later option as the delay is extended, indicates that the switch from the earlier option to the later option occurs at a lower discount rate, as the delay is larger. This in turn implies that lower per-period time discount rates are found as the delay is extended.

The interval dummies are also significantly positive, implying that subjects increasingly choose the later options, as the interval extends. This fact corresponds to the interval effect observed in Table 3.6. The coefficient of the amount of reward is also significantly positive, implying that subjects tend to increasingly choose the later option as the amount of the reward increases. This result corresponds to the magnitude effect observed in Table 3.6.

[19]Four variables out of these five explanatory variables determine the remaining one variable. However, as the relation is nonlinear, the collinear problem does not arise.

Table 3.9 Test result of the differential effect hypothesis

Independent variables		Model 3 Coefficients	Model 3 Marginal effects	Model 4 Coefficients	Model 4 Marginal effects
Constant		−4.140***		−2.967***	
Rate of return, ln (1 + R)		39.511***	5.812***	17.750***	2.476***
Amount of reward × 10^{-4}		6.437***	0.947***	2.389***	0.333***
Differential in amount × 10^{-3}				7.565***	1.055***
Delay dummies	1 day	−0.165*	−0.254*	−0.302***	−0.046***
	1 week	0.104	0.149	0.105	0.014
	2 weeks	0.532***	0.071***	0.495***	0.063***
	4 weeks	0.661***	0.083***	0.659***	0.078***
	6 weeks	1.043***	0.113***	0.961***	0.100***
	8 weeks	1.284***	0.129***	1.239***	0.119***
	10 weeks	1.347***	0.133***	1.248***	0.119***
	12 weeks	0.981***	0.108***	0.867***	0.093***
Interval dummies	4 weeks	0.418***	0.057***	−0.393***	−0.059***
	6 weeks	0.436***	0.058***	−0.626***	−0.101***
	8 weeks	0.576***	0.072***	−0.950***	−0.169***
Number of observations		29,748		29,748	
Log likelihood		−10669.556		−10182.963	

Notes: Only the regression results of random effect model are shown because it is not rejected against fixed effect model by Hausman specification test. Dependent variable is the response to the binary questions; *** and * indicate that the values are statistically significant at the 1 % and 10 % levels, respectively. The number of observations is less than the total observations (219 subjects × 15 combinations of receipt timing) because we exclude the observations when a subject consistently chooses A (or B) for 12 questions of the same combination, and that the estimated time discount rates using a logit model are out of the 1–50 % range

Now, let us turn to Model 4, which incorporates the differential in amount as an explanatory variable. Compared with Model 3, the marginal effects of the interval dummies change their signs from significantly positive to significantly negative, while those of the delay dummies are unchanged. The marginal effect of the amount of reward also becomes smaller by about one-third in the case of Model 3. These results support our hypothesis that the interval and the amount of reward affect the subjects' choices through a change in the differential in amount. In other words, the interval and the magnitude effects are caused at least partially by the differential effect.

How strong is the differential effect? The coefficient of the differential in amount is significantly positive, which means that subjects increasingly choose the later option as the differential increases. Its marginal effect is 1.055×10^{-3}. On the other hand, when the differential is added to the regression, the marginal effect of the rate of return decreases to 2.476, about two-fifth of Model 3. These values of the marginal effects imply that a 1 % increase in the logarithm of the rate of return and a 20-yen increase in the differential in amount will cause nearly the same increase in the probability of choosing the later option.[20] Thus, a change in the differential in amount has an effect on the subjects' choice comparable to a change in the rate of return.

As possible causes of subadditivity, Read (2001) pointed out a psychological effect of focusing stronger attention on smaller intervals when they are divided (support theory), and a bias toward the midpoint in subjective estimates leading to overestimates of small quantities (regression effect). This chapter argues that the differential effect may be an additional cause of the interval effect. Table 3.9 suggests that once the differential effect is adjusted, the remaining interval effect is that subjects increasingly choose the earlier option as the interval gets longer, which is the opposite of the total interval effect.[21]

5.3 *Weber's Law*

Many psychophysicists have traditionally considered that people perceive an external stimulus (e.g., loudness) after transforming it by a nonlinear function. This is called Weber's law. Recent studies further suggest that time perception also follows Weber's law, implying that the relationship between objective and subjective time is nonlinear (Takahashi 2005, 2006; Dehaene 2003; Okamoto and Fukai 2001).

Weber's law gives us another hypothesis that may explain anomalies in intertemporal choice. Takahashi (2005) argues that the hyperbolic time discounting function is derived from exponential discounting and Weber's law. In other words, if time perception follows Weber's law, people show declining impatience even if they discount future rewards exponentially. In addition, Takahashi (2006) shows that the interval effect may be explained by exponential discounting and Weber's law. In this section, we empirically investigate whether or not both anomalies are actually dissolved by Weber's law.

Following Takahashi (2005), we define subjective time as a logarithm of objective time (logarithmic time perception).

$$\tau \equiv \alpha \ln(1 + t), \tag{3.7}$$

where τ stands for subjective time, t is objective time, and α is a parameter. Let us describe how the rate of return is perceived by a subject with logarithmic time perception. The rate of return of a reward, R, in the experiments is defined as (3.5), where t and s are objective time. However, if the subject perceives time as

[20]The results that use the rate of return R instead of $\ln(1 + R)$ may appeal more to our intuition. The estimation results are almost the same as those of Model 3 in Table 3.9, which imply that a 1 % increase in the rate of return and a 16-yen increase in the differential amount will cause nearly the same increase in the probability of choosing the later option.

[21]This is a phenomenon that Scholten and Read (2006) call superadditivity.

transformed by (3.7), he evaluates the rate of return of a reward not by objective but by subjective time. This rate of return of a reward evaluated by subjective time τ, $\widehat{R}$, is obtained by substituting subjective time for objective time in Eq. (3.5).

$$\widehat{R} = \left(\frac{Y}{X}\right)^{\frac{1}{\alpha\{\ln(1+t)-\ln(1+s)\}}} - 1 \tag{3.8}$$

Also, we obtain following relationship from Eq. (3.5).

$$\left(\frac{Y}{X}\right) = (1+R)^{t-s} \tag{3.9}$$

Substituting Eq. (3.9) into (3.8), we obtain Eq. (3.10), which shows the relationship between the rate of return of a reward evaluated by subjective time and that by objective time.

$$\begin{aligned} \ln\left(1+\widehat{R}\right) &= \frac{t-s}{\ln(1+t)-\ln(1+s)} \ln(1+R) + \frac{1}{\alpha} \ln(1+R) \\ &\equiv A(t,s,R) + \frac{1}{\alpha} \ln(1+R)\,. \end{aligned} \tag{3.10}$$

To examine the validity of Weber's law, we will conduct the following two tests. First, if Weber's law has relevancy, $\ln\left(1+\widehat{R}\right)$ should be able to explain the choice between earlier and later options. The results of this test are shown in the left-hand columns of Table 3.10. In Model 5, the binary choice is regressed over $A(t, s, R)$ and the amount of reward; in Model 6, $\ln(1+R)$ is added to Model 5. In both cases, all the independent variables are highly significant, supporting Weber's law.[22]

The second test is to examine whether or not the delay and the interval terms become insignificant when the rate of return R is replaced with the perceived rate of return $\widehat{R}$. If Weber's law is the only source of the delay and interval effects, as Takahashi (2005, 2006) argues, delay dummies and/or interval dummies should be insignificant when $A(t, s, R)$ and $\ln(1+R)$ are included in the regression.

The estimation results of this regression (Models 7–9) are presented in the right columns of Table 3.10. The results reveal that $A(t, s, R)$ is insignificant when the delay dummies are included in regressions such as Model 7 and Model 9, but significant when only interval dummies and the amount of reward are considered as explanatory variables. However, even in the latter case, interval dummies have significant positive coefficients, suggesting that the interval effect does not disappear when considering Weber's law. In sum, while the first test reveals that Weber's law has some power in the intertemporal choice, the second test elucidates that the delay

[22]In these models we added the amount of reward, because Weber's law as defined in this chapter does not explain the magnitude effect theoretically. However, when we delete the amount of reward, the results are essentially unchanged.

Table 3.10 Test result of the Weber's law

Independent variables		Model 5 Coefficients	Model 5 Marginal effects	Model 6 Coefficients	Model 6 Marginal effects	Model 7 Coefficients	Model 7 Marginal effects	Model 8 Coefficients	Model 8 Marginal effects	Model 9 Coefficients	Model 9 Marginal effects	Model 10 Coefficients	Model 10 Marginal effects
Constant		−1.673***		−3.388***		−3.685***		−3.528***		−4.147***		−2.956***	
Logarithmic time perception effect, $A(t, s, R)$		4.596***	0.970***	2.147***	0.312***	0.290	0.043	2.182***	0.314***	−0.083	−0.012	0.176	0.025
Rate of return, ln (1 + R)				32.389***	4.707***	37.809***	5.609***	32.758***	4.718***	39.747***	5.858***	17.219***	2.401***
Amount of reward × 10^{-4}		5.562***	1.173***	6.181***	0.898***	6.368***	0.945***	6.328***	0.911***	6.437***	0.949***	2.386***	0.333***
Differential in amount × 10^{-3}												7.573***	1.056***
Delay dummies	1 day					−0.470***	−0.079***			−0.181*	−0.028*	−0.267***	−0.040***
	1 week					−0.265***	−0.042***			0.106	0.015	0.101	0.014
	2 weeks					0.447***	0.061***			0.536***	0.071***	0.487***	0.062***
	4 weeks					0.491***	0.065***			0.670***	0.084***	0.642***	0.076***
	6 weeks					0.624***	0.077***			1.057***	0.114***	0.932***	0.098***
	8 weeks					0.852***	0.098***			1.301***	0.130***	1.201***	0.116***
	10 weeks					0.900***	0.102***			1.369***	0.134***	1.202***	0.116***
	12 weeks					0.518***	0.066***			1.007***	0.110***	0.810***	0.088***
Interval dummies	4 weeks							0.258***	0.035***	0.420***	0.057***	−0.398***	−0.060***
	6 weeks							0.154***	0.021***	0.440***	0.058***	−0.635***	−1.023***
	8 weeks							0.050	0.071	0.582***	0.073***	−0.963***	−1.715***
Number of observations		29,748		29,748		29,748		29,748		29,748		29,748	
Log likelihood		−14411.936		−10828.383		−10711.218		−10809.562		−10669.571		−10182.627	

Notes: Only the regression results of random effect model are shown because it is not rejected against fixed effect model by Hausman specification test. Dependent variable is the response to the binary questions; *** and * indicate that the values are statistically significant at the 1 % and 10 % levels, respectively. The number of observations is less than the total observations (219 subjects × 15 combinations of receipt timing) because we exclude the observations when a subject consistently chooses A (or B) for 12 questions of the same combination, and that the estimated time discount rates using a logit model are out of the 1–50 % range and the interval effects still remain as anomalies, which are not solved by Weber's law.[23]

Finally, let us confirm whether the differential effect hypothesis is supported even though Weber's law is considered. In the far-right column, the estimation results that both $A(t, s, R)$ and the differential in amount are included in the regression are shown (Model 10). The results are almost the same as those of Model 4, so that the conclusion of the previous subsection is retained.[24]

6 Conclusion

This chapter examined the effects of delay and interval on the subjects' time discount rates, as well as the effect of differential in the amount of reward on the subjects' choice, using the result of an experiment on time discount rates and a questionnaire survey conducted together with the experiment. Most previous researches did not distinguish the delay from the interval. Although Read and his collaborators conducted various experiments that distinguish them, the results on declining impatience are ambiguous. Thus, whether the phenomenon of declining impatience really holds has been an open question.

Our hypothesis is that declining impatience should be a phenomenon that occurs at short delay. We conducted an experiment that explicitly distinguished the delay from the interval and set the delay less than 12 weeks, and found that per-period time discount rates keep decreasing up to an 8-week delay when the interval is controlled. This implies that people make dynamic inconsistent plans and show a preference reversal.

This chapter also focused on whether time discount rates depend on the interval between the two options. Although this problem has seldom been investigated, we found the interval effect according to which the per-period time discount rate decreases as the interval lengthens. This interval effect is a sufficient condition for the subadditive time discounting proposed by Read (2001).

Finally, we investigated the possible cause of three time discounting anomalies confirmed in this chapter: declining impatience, the interval effect, and the magnitude effect. We speculated that the anomalies are caused because human beings use heuristic thinking when they make intertemporal choices, and proposed the differential in amount hypothesis. Empirical results reveal that the interval and the magnitude effects are caused, at least partially, because subjects' choices are influenced by the differential in reward amount.

---

[23]Of course, we do not deny the possibility that Weber's law will solve the anomalies using a different approach from ours. For example, Read and Scholten (2006) apply Weber's law not only to scaling time but also to scaling the amount of money and examine the validity of the law.

[24]When we delete the delay and interval dummies, $A(t, s, R)$ becomes significant, while the differential in amount remains significant.

We also examine the hypothesis that Weber's law applied to time perception actually solves the delay and the interval effects, as the theory predicts. Our estimation results indicate that Weber's law has some relevancy to intertemporal decision, but it does not explain either effect.

Acknowledgments An earlier version of this chapter was presented at the Behavioral Economics Conference and Annual Meeting of Japanese Economic Association. The authors are grateful to comments by Takanori Ida, Fumihiko Hiruma, Shinsuke Ikeda, Yuichi Fukuta, Kazumasa Umeda, and the participants of the conferences. Especially, we would like to thank an anonymous referee of this journal for comments, which resulted in a substantial revision and improvement.

Addendum: Examination of Elicitation Designs[25]

In the text of this chapter, we report that declining impatience is recognized at short delays of less than 8 weeks. As was noted in Sect. 1.2, this is a new finding, because it involves (1) selection of one of two options randomly shown on computer display, (2) asking subjects to choose from specified two options, and (3) specifying the timing by the length of the day instead of by calendar date. Using methods (2) and (3) and a multiple price list (MPL) format that presents whole choices simultaneously instead of (1), Read (2001) found no evidence of declining impatience. However, declining impatience has been observed with a matching method that asks subjects regarding an amount at a specified date, making them indifferent between the specified options (Read and Roelofsma 2003). It is also observed when the timing is specified with calendar dates (Read et al. 2005). These results motivate us to investigate under which method declining impatience is more easily observed. One of the authors of the text (Fumio Ohtake) studied this topic, and wrote about it in Hanaoka et al. (2014). In this addendum we briefly introduce that paper.

Hanaoka et al. (2014) mainly focuses on two designs for elicitation of time discounting.[26] The first of these is (1) the elicitation format, in which options are presented as a multiple price list (MPL) or a titration. In a titration, a subject is presented with each intertemporal choice, based on a decision tree; according to each chosen outcome, the options presented in the subsequent choice are adjusted to present the remaining options as the range of remaining discount rates becomes narrower. The second is (2) the framing, which concerns whether subjects are asked amounts or delays.

[25]This addendum has been newly written for this book chapter.

[26]The paper also investigate time horizon, concerning two different points starting either at different points in time or at the same point in time. However, since we criticized the latter method, arguing that declining impatience cannot be separated from the interval effect, we do not report the results that were obtained with this method.

An original nationwide web survey on time and preferences was conducted in 2011, with 4,970 subjects surveyed. Analysis of the responses indicates that using the net comparison approach, declining discounting is observed only for the titration elicitation format within the framing of "ask amount," whereas the other procedures show no bias. As per the framing, increasing discounting is more likely to be observed when using the framing of "ask delay" than when using "ask amount."

The paper further investigates whether the elicited discount rates can accurately predict behavior such as debt, credit card borrowing, obesity, smoking, and gambling. A subject is classified as having dynamically inconsistent time preferences if the subject exhibits either declining discounting (present-biased preferences) or increasing discounting (future-biased preferences); a subject is classified as having dynamically consistent time preferences (no-biased preferences) if he/she exhibits constant discounting. Each behavior is regressed over the two dummy variables according to the classification (present-bias and future-bias) and the discount factor.

The estimation reveals a weak correlation between behavior and the values elicited by the MPL; none of the coefficients on present bias and future bias are statistically significant. In sharp contrast, most of the coefficients elicited by the titration are significantly correlated with behavior and show the expected signs. Thus, the discount rate is more correlated with behavior such as debt, credit card borrowing, obesity, smoking, and gambling when elicited with the titration method than with the MPL, when amount is asked. On the other hand, the parameters of present- or future-biased preferences elicited under the framing of "ask delay" fail to capture behavior in both the MPL and the titration, whereas asking amount often produces reasonable outcomes in the titration method.

The results are summarized as follows. (1) Whether subjects exhibit dynamically consistent or inconsistent time preferences depends on which elicitation designs are adopted. (2) Whether the elicited discount rates accurately predict behavior varies across elicitation designs. Specifically, the results suggest that an elicitation design using a titration format and/or asking subjects on amount would provide more relevant measures for predicting behavior than other designs.

References

Baron J (2000) Can we use human judgments to determine the discount rate? Risk Anal 20:861–868

Benzion U, Rapoport A, Yagil J (1989) Discount rates inferred from decisions: an experimental study. Manag Sci 35:270–284

Bleichrodt H, Johannesson M (2001) Time preference for health: a test of stationary versus decreasing timing aversion. J Math Psychol 45:265–282

Dehaene S (2003) The neural basis of the Weber–Fechner law: a logarithmic mental number line. Trends Cogn Sci 7:145–147

Fischbacher U (1999) Z-Tree: Zurich toolbox for readymade economic experiment – experimenter's manual, IEW working paper 21. University of Zurich, Zurich

Frederick S, Loewenstein G, O'Donoghue T (2002) Time discounting and time preference: a critical review. J Econ Lit 40:351–401

Hanaoka C, Ikeda S, Ohtake F (2014) Elicitation designs and time discounting: comparisons of predictive power on behavior, mimeo

Ikeda S, Ohtake F, Tsutsui Y (2005) Time discount rates: an analysis based on economic experiments and questionnaire surveys. Institute of Social and Economic Research discussion paper, 638, pp 1–36. (in Japanese)

Kirby KN, Marakovic NN (1995) Modeling myopic decisions: evidence for hyperbolic delay-discounting within subjects and amounts. Organ Behav Hum Decis Process 64:22–30

Laibson D (1997) Golden eggs and hyperbolic discounting. Q J Econ 112:443–477

Myerson J, Green L (1995) Discounting of delayed rewards: models of individual choice. J Exp Anal Behav 64:263–276

Okamoto H, Fukai T (2001) Neural mechanism for a cognitive timer. Phys Rev Lett 86:3919–3922

Pender JL (1996) Discount rates and credit markets: theory and evidence from rural India. J Dev Econ 50:257–296

Read D (2001) Is time-discounting hyperbolic or subadditive? J Risk Uncertain 23:5–32

Read D, Roelofsma PHMP (2003) Subadditive versus hyperbolic discounting: a comparison of choice and matching. Organ Behav Hum Decis Process 91:140–153

Read D, Scholten M (2006) Beyond discounting: the tradeoff model of intertemporal choice, Working paper LSEOR 06.88. London School of Economics and Political Science, London, pp 1–63

Read D, Frederick S, Orsel B, Rahman J (2005) Four score and seven years from now: the date/delay effect in temporal discounting. Manage Sci 51:1326–1335

Richards JB, Zhang L, Mitchell SH, De Wit H (1999) Delay or probability discounting in a model of impulsive behavior: effect of alcohol. J Exp Anal Behav 71:121–143

Scholten M, Read D (2006) Discounting by intervals: a generalized model of intertemporal choice. Manag Sci 52:1424–1436

Takahashi T (2005) Loss of self-control in intertemporal choice may be attributable to logarithmic time-perception. Med Hypotheses 65:691–693

Takahashi T (2006) Time-estimation error following Weber-Fechner law may explain subadditive time-discounting. Med Hypotheses 67:1372–1374

Thaler R (1981) Some empirical evidence on dynamic inconsistency. Econ Lett 8:201–207

Tversky A, Kahneman D (1974) Judgment under uncertainty: heuristics and biases. Science 85:1124–1131

Uzawa H (1968) Time preference, the consumption function and optimum asset holdings. In: Wolfe JN (ed) Value capital and growth: papers in honour of Sir John Hicks. Aldine, Chicago

Van der Pol M, Cairns J (2001) A comparison of the discounted utility model and hyperbolic discounting models in the case of social and private intertemporal preferences for health. J Econ Behav Organ 49:79–96

Chapter 4
Non-parametric Test of Time Consistency: Present Bias and Future Bias

Kan Takeuchi

Abstract This chapter reports the elicited time preference of human subjects in a laboratory setting. The model allows for non-linear utility functions, non-separability between delay and reward, and time inconsistency including future bias in addition to present bias. In particular, the experiment (1) runs a non-parametric test of time consistency and (2) estimates the form of time discount function independently of instantaneous utility functions, and then (3) the result suggests that many subjects exhibiting *future bias*, indicating an inverse S-curve time discount function.

Keywords Time preference • Experiment • Future bias

1 Introduction

People are typically averse to a delayed reward and prefer an option that pays a smaller reward immediately. This positive *time preference* has been observed in experiments on pigeons, rats, and humans.[1] It has been shown that when a reward is delayed into the future, its present value decreases. More interestingly, the time inconsistent preference referred to as *present bias* has been frequently reported:

The original article first appeared in Games and Economic Behavior 71:456–478, 2011. A newly written addendum has been added to this book chapter.

[1]For humans, Frederick et al. (2002) provide a comprehensive review of time preference from an economic perspective, while Green and Myerson (2004) provide an overview of studies in psychology. In the experiments on pigeons and rats, the reward is food/water or the access to it. Time preference is referred to as impulsive behavior in the literature. See Monterosso and Ainslie (1999) for a survey.

K. Takeuchi (✉)
Hitotsubashi University, Tokyo, Japan
e-mail: kan@econ.hit-u.ac.jp

S. Ikeda et al. (eds.), *Behavioral Economics of Preferences, Choices, and Happiness*, DOI 10.1007/978-4-431-55402-8_4

subjects put more weight on the value of a present reward than a future one. This phenomenon is also called *decreasing impatience*, as the subject's impatience decreases into the future (Prelec 2004).[2]

There are many experimental studies on time preference, most of which commonly rely on several assumptions. Those assume, for instance, that the time discounting function is separable from the reward amount, the subjects believe that delayed rewards will be delivered for sure, the monetary rewards are non-fungible, and that the utility function is linear and time invariant. These often become the common confounding factors in experimental studies on time preferences.

Among these, this chapter particularly addresses the separability assumption between discounting and utility and the linearity assumption on the utility function, presenting an experiment that elicits the time preference of subjects in a laboratory setting. Suppose that $V(x, t) = D(t, x)u(x)$ denotes the present discounted value of a reward x that will be paid at time t. The separability assumption forces us to ignore the second element of $D(t, x)$, which necessarily biases the result. As seen in this formula, any parametric assumption on the utility function u also naturally entails a bias in the estimation of time discount D. To incorporate these estimation biases, the present study develops a non-parametric test of time preference.

Specifically, this experiment runs a non-parametric test based on *equivalent delay function*. It also estimates the form of time discount function independently of that of the instantaneous utility function by converting delay into risk. Then I find the result suggesting that many subjects exhibit future bias.

First, I define the equivalent delay function on two reward options ($T : X \times Y \to \mathbb{R}_+$) and show that the modularity of the function T characterizes time inconsistent behavior. For a present reward x and a larger but delayed reward y, the equivalent delay $T(x, y)$ specifies the delay of y with which the two reward options are equally valuable. Then I show the sub(super)modularity of the function corresponds to the decreasing (increasing) impatience. Eliciting T for several pairs of (x, y) provides non-parametric characterization of time inconsistency. To the best of my knowledge, this method is new to the literature.

Second, the experiment converts delay into risk and attempts to estimate the form of the time discount function independently of the utility function. The advantage of this approach is to separate the time discount factor from the non-linearity of the utility function, both of which are often confounded in the literature. Section 4 illustrates the potential biases in the estimation that might be caused if the utility function is assumed to be linear.

Finally, the result indicates that many subjects exhibit future bias and increasing impatience for few weeks from the present moment. The previous experimental studies assumed that subjects exhibited present bias and hyperbolic time discounting, but they seemingly overlooked the other time inconsistency, which I call *future bias*. While the present bias means that subjects tend to overvalue the immediate reward and result in a myopic preference reversal, the future bias is the

[2]Halevy (2008) calls this diminishing impatience.

opposite. Although there have been few studies of future bias, Loewenstein (1987) has already found the same type of anomaly as *reverse time inconsistency*. With reverse time inconsistency, subjects tend to postpone taking a reward until the near future. Rubinstein (2006) also introduces future bias as a possible (hypothetical) time inconsistent behavior. Very recently Sayman and Öncüler (2009) observed subjects actually exhibiting reverse time inconsistent behavior in their longitudinal experiment. My concurrent study finds similar evidence for future bias.

Notice that future bias and present bias are not conflicting, but they may coexist within a subject. Future bias, however, has not been frequently observed, since it can be elicited under certain conditions. Specifically, the interval between two future options has to be sufficiently short and the options have to be close to $t = 0$. In addition, to capture such a time preference, an inverse S-curve time discount function must be employed. Thus, I use the generalized Weibull function and show that some subjects have such time discount functions, i.e., they are concave for the first part and convex for the rest.

The rest of the chapter is organized as follows. The next section explains the motivation and the model. Section 3 presents the experimental design. Section 4 presents the analysis and main results. In Sect. 5 I discuss the results, and Sect. 6 concludes the chapter.

2 The Model

This section describes a new experimental design. Unlike existing studies, this experiment estimates time preference without making any parametric assumption on the utility function. Before introducing the design, I highlight the importance of the approach.

Let $(x, t) \in \mathbb{R}^2_+$ represent an option that pays x at time t. The present value V of the option is

$$V(x, t) = D(t, x)u(x),$$

where D is a discount function and u is the instantaneous utility of the reward x. By observing preferences of subjects over several options, the experiments estimate the functional form of D. Although there is extensive research on this matter, the utility function $u(x)$ is, in most experimental studies, assumed to be linear (see Table 4.1).[3]

[3]There are a few exceptions. Kirby and Santiesteban (2003) compare $u(x) = x$ with $u(x) = \sqrt{x}$ and find no significant difference in goodness-of-fit. Andersen et al. (2008) , Fernández-Villaverde and Mukherji (2006) and Ida and Goto (2009) assume a constant relative risk-aversion (CRRA) utility function. Rubinstein (2003) does not impose any assumptions. The novel experimental design of Attema et al. (2010) does not require the functional form (utility-free). Tanaka et al. (2010) estimate parameters for CRRA utility functions incorporating with loss aversion and probability weighting function.

Table 4.1 Methodologies of empirical estimations of time preference

Study	Utility function	Adjustment procedure	Elicitation method
Thaler (1981)	Linear	Amount	Matching
Benzion et al. (1989)	Linear	Amount	Matching
Rachlin et al. (1991)	Linear	Amount/delay	Choice
Holcomb and Nelson (1992)	n.a.	Amount/delay	Choice
Bohm (1994)	Linear	Amount	Choice/matching
Keren and Roelofsma (1995)	Linear	Amount/delay	Choice
Kirby and Maraković (1995)	Linear	Amount	Matching
Wahlund and Gunarsson (1996)	Linear	Amount	Matching
Ahlbrecht and Weber (1997)	Linear	Amount	Choice/matching
Cairns and van der Pol (1997)	Linear	Amount	Matching
Green et al. (1997)	Linear	Amount	Choice
Kirby (1997)	Linear	Amount	Matching
Chapman and Winquist (1998)	Linear	Amount	Matching
Holden et al. (1998)	Non-linear	Amount	Matching
Chapman et al. (1999)	Linear	Amount	Matching
Coller and Williams (1999)	Linear	Amount	Choice
Kirby et al. (1999)	Linear	Amount/delay	Choice
Chesson and Viscusi (2000)	n.a.	Delay	Matching
Hesketh (2000)	Linear	Amount/delay	Choice
Anderhub et al. (2001)	Linear	Amount	Matching
Read (2001)	Linear	Amount	Matching
van der Pol and Cairns (2001)	Linear	Amount/delay	Choice
Warner and Pleeter (2001)	Linear	Amount	Choice
Harrison et al. (2002)	Linear	Amount	Choice
Kirby and Santiesteban (2003)	Linear and $x^{0.5}$	Amount	Matching
Rubinstein (2003)	Non-linear	Amount/delay	Choice
Harrison et al. (2005)	Linear	Amount	Choice
Fernández-Villaverde and Mukherji (2006)	CRRA	—	Choice
Andersen et al. (2008)	CRRA	Amount	Choice
Kinari et al. (2009)	Linear	Amount/delay	Choice
Sayman and Öncüler (2009)	Linear	Amount	Matching
Ida and Goto (2009)	CRRA	Amount/delay	Choice
Tanaka et al. (2010)	CRRA	Amount	Choice
Benhabib et al. (2010)	Linear	Amount	Matching
Attema et al. (2010)	n.a.	Delay	Matching
Coller et al. (2012)	CRRA	Amount	Choice
This concurrent study	n.a.	Delay	Matching

The instantaneous utility of reward x is usually assumed to be *linear*, i.e., $u(x) = x$. The adjustment procedure is either *amount* or *delay* or both. In the amount-adjustment procedure, subjects are asked to choose what amount of a present (future) reward x makes itself equally valuable to the other future (present) reward, and the delay of the future option is fixed. In the delay-adjustment procedure, subjects are asked to choose the delay of a future reward that makes it equally worth to a given present reward. Elicitation Method: In order to elicit those amounts or delays, subjects are given (a list of) two fixed options in the *choice method* or asked to specify the amount or delay in the *matching method*

The linear utility assumption may become problematic, in particular, when we are interested in the functional form of D, e.g., whether it is exponential or hyperbolic discounting. Suppose that, for example, a subject is indifferent to any pair of options from $\{x_i, t_i\}_{i \in I}$, that is $V(x_i, t_i) = V(x_j, t_j)$ for any $i, j \in I$. Next suppose that one researcher assumes $u(x) = x$ and that she finds $D(t) = e^{-rt}$ fits the data perfectly. Given the same data, however, another researcher assumes that $u(x) = \log(x)$ and finds that $D(t) = 1/kt$ explains the behavior of the subject well. Thus, the former concludes that D is exponential, while the latter concludes D is hyperbolic. Notice that these two different conclusions do not necessarily contradict each other: they simply reflect the difference in the assumptions on the utility function.[4]

Furthermore, a parametric assumption on u can produce a *magnitude effect*, one of the anomalies commonly reported in the literature.[5] Thaler (1981) reports that subjects answered, on average, that they were indifferent between the two options in each of the following pairs respectively: ($15, now) vs. ($60, 1 year later) and ($3,000, now) vs. ($4,000, 1 year later). As long as the utility function is assumed to be linear, there is no discount factor that is consistent with these two choices ($15/60 \neq 3{,}000/4{,}000$). This anomaly is called the magnitude effect because the discount factor depends on the amount of the reward. It becomes easy, however, to find a constant discount factor once we allow general utility functions.[6] This observation does not necessarily contradict the discounted utility framework; it just reflects the restrictive assumption made on the utility function.

A new experimental design, therefore, should elicit time preference without invoking the linearity assumption on the utility function. The following subsections present two methods that estimate time preference independently of u. The first one elicits time preference or time inconsistent behavior without considering the utility function, and the second one estimates the time discount function without the linearity assumption on u.

I have to stress that the second method still relies on the separability between x and t. Almost all experimental research on time preference make the separability assumption and do not capture possible interactions.[7]

---

[4]A trivial example of such a data set is $\{(x_i, t_i) \big| x_i = e^{rt_i}.\}$.

[5]Frederick et al. (2002) refer to the magnitude effect as one of the six commonly observed anomalies. It is referred to as *amount-dependent discounting* in the psychology literature. See the extensive survey by Green and Myerson (2004).

[6]For example, $u(x) = x^{0.42} + 45.9$ can accommodate the anomaly above. That is, $u(15)/u(60) = u(3{,}000)/u(4{,}000) = 0.95$. Masatlioglu and Ok presented this numerical example in an earlier version of their paper.

[7]There is an exception, which is, the research by Benhabib et al. (2010) that allows for a fixed cost of present bias.

2.1 Modularity of Equivalent Delay Function

The first part of this experiment elicits time preference for a set of rewards, $x_0 < x_1 < x_2$. I define the equivalent delay that makes the present value of a future large reward equal to the value of a present small reward. Then, I show that the modularity of that equivalent delay function characterizes time inconsistency.

Suppose that a subject is indifferent between two options (x, t) and (x', t'). I set $t = 0$ for the following argument. For a given $(x, 0)$ and x', this experiment elicits the equivalent delay $T(x, x')$ that makes the two options the same to a subject.[8] Let T be such a function on $\{(x, x') \in \mathbb{R}^2_+ | x \leq x'.\}$. defn $T(x, x')$ is an *equivalent delay* such that $(x, 0) \sim (x', T(x, x'))$. defn Present and future biases, if any, are detected in the properties of this function T. Notice that, by transitivity, $D(T(x_0, x_1), x_1) \times D(T(x_1, x_2), x_2) \equiv D(T(x_0, x_2), x_2)$ holds regardless of the form of D and T. First, the following definition is straightforward.

Definition A subject is *time consistent* if T is modular.

If T is modular, a subject will not exhibit time inconsistent preference reversal. For example, the standard exponential discount function, $D(t, x) = e^{-rt}$, implies that

$$T(x_0, x_1) + T(x_1, x_2) = T(x_0, x_2).$$

Figure 4.1 illustrates this concept. Suppose that a subject responds as follows: (\$5 today)$\sim$(\$10 in 10 days), (\$5 today)$\sim$(\$15 in 16 days) and (\$10 today)$\sim$(\$15 in Z days). This means $T(5, 10) = 10$, $T(5, 15) = 16$ and $T(10, 15) = Z$. Assume that the subject is given the (\$15 in 16 days) option. Then, suppose the first 10 days have passed and there are still 6 days to go. Imagine that she is offered another option of (\$10 today) at that moment. She compares the two options (\$10 today) and (\$15 in 6 days). If she is time consistent, she is still indifferent and she is willing to wait 6 days to get \$15. Recall she has already answered (\$10 today)$\sim$(\$15 in Z days). Thus, $Z = 6$ corresponds to time consistency, implying $T(5, 10) + T(10, 15) = T(5, 15)$.

In the example above, the subject compares (\$10 today) and (\$15 in 6 days) at day $T(5, 10)$. But she would be willing to wait only Z days to get \$15. If she has present bias, then the immediate \$10 becomes more attractive than the future option of (\$15 in 6 days). Thus, $Z < 6$ or $T(5, 15) - T(5, 10) > T(10, 15)$. Formally, I define this present bias as follows.

[8]Noor (2010) similarly defines more general *time compensation function*, $\Psi_{s,l}(t)$. $T(x, x')$ is equivalent to $\Psi_{x,x'}(0)$.

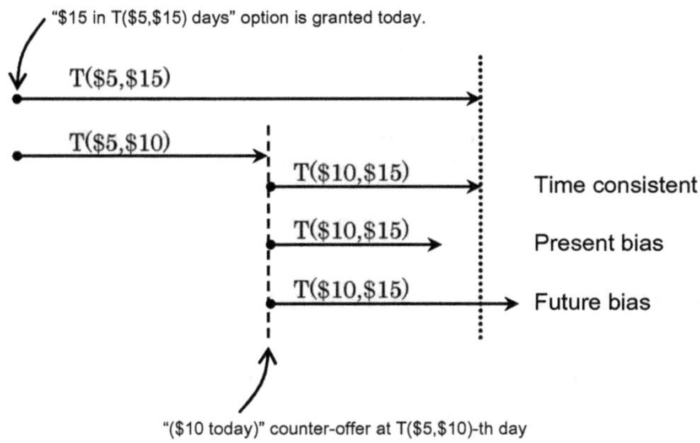

Fig. 4.1 Present and future bias. ($5 today), ($10 in 10 days) and ($15 in 16 days) are equally valuable to a subject by transitivity. Assume that the subject is given the ($15 in 16 days) option and then 10 days have passed. Note that she stands on the broken line in the middle of the figure and there are still 6 days to go for $15. Then, imagine she is offered another option of ($10 today) at that moment. She compares the two options ($10 today) and ($15 in 6 days). If she is time consistent, she is still indifferent and she is willing to wait 6 days to get $15. Thus, $Z = 6$ or $T(5, 10) + T(10, 15) = T(5, 15)$. If her preference is present biased, then she is not willing to wait 6 days. Instead, she chooses ($10 today) option. It implies $Z < 6$ or $T(5, 10) + T(10, 15) < T(5, 15)$. The future bias is defined for the opposite reversal

Definition A subject exhibits *present bias* if T is strictly submodular.

Observe, for example, that hyperbolic discount functions imply $T(x_0, x_1) + T(x_1, x_2) < T(x_0, x_2)$. In fact, when u is continuous, this present bias is consistent with the *decreasing impatience* of Prelec (2004). See the appendix for proof.

Definition (Prelec (2004)) A subject is said to exhibit *decreasing impatience* if for any $\delta > 0$, $x_2 > x_1 > 0$, $(x_1, t_1) \sim (x_2, t_2)$ implies $(x_1, t_1 + \delta) \prec (x_2, t_2 + \delta)$.

Proposition 1 *Decreasing impatience is equivalent to present bias.*

As this nonparametric test does not depend on the separability between x and t, it is compatible with the fixed cost representation of present bias proposed by Benhabib et al. (2010). Following their approach, let us suppose that any future option incurs a fixed cost of b and that the discount function is exponential (e.g., $V(x, t) = e^{-rt}u(x) - b$ or $V(x, t) = e^{-rt}u(x - b)$). These representations also imply that $T(x_0, x_1) + T(x_1, x_2) < T(x_0, x_2)$. See the appendix for the derivation.

Remark 1 The present bias due to the fixed cost of future reward is also characterized by the submodularity of T.

Accordingly, the opposite time inconsistent preference, future bias, implies that subjects become more impatient with delay as time goes into the future. *Future bias* or *increasing impatience*, can be defined in the following way.

Definition A subject exhibits *future bias* if T is strictly supermodular. Equivalently, a subject exhibits *increasing impatience* if for any $\delta > 0$, $x_2 > x_1 > 0$, $(x_1, t_1) \sim (x_2, t_2)$ implies $(x_2, t_2 + \delta) \prec (x_1, t_1 + \delta)$.

This experiment runs a longitudinal analysis for $x_0 < x_1 < x_2$ and finds that most subjects exhibit future bias (see Result 1 in Sect. 4).

2.2 Converting Delay into Uncertainty

The second part of the experiment is to estimate the time discount function D independently of u. That is, the experiment does not estimate the form of the utility function. Note however this estimation still relies on the separability assumption. The discounted present value of (x, t) is denoted by $D(t)u(x)$ hereafter.

This method observes data points for the time discount function without using any parametric assumption on the utility function. To do so, it elicits both of the equivalent delay and the equivalent probability in within-subject design.[9] Thus, in this part, we need to estimate the ratio of the instantaneous utilities of two rewards.

Let $(x, p) \in \mathbb{R}^2_+$ represent a lottery that pays x with probability p and 0 otherwise. Suppose a subject is indifferent between a pair of lotteries, (x, p) and (x', p'). The separability assumption yields the following:

$$pu(x) = p'u(x'), \text{if}(x, p) \sim (x', p'). \tag{4.1}$$

For a given (x, p) and x', I elicit the probability p' that makes the subject indifferent between the two lotteries.[10] In this experiment, I set $p = 1$, so one option definitely pays the reward, and it follows that

$$p' = \frac{u(x)}{u(x')}. \tag{4.2}$$

Recall that the same subject has reported the equivalent delay t' that makes herself indifferent between the immediate option that pays x and the delayed option that pays x' in t'. By the separability assumption, It follows that

$$D(t') = \frac{u(x)}{u(x')}. \tag{4.3}$$

[9]Notice there are two underlying assumptions. One is that subjects are expected utility maximizers and the other is that u is time invariant.

[10]I use only this probability equivalence (PE) method, not a certainty equivalence (CE) method, which elicits the certainty equivalent x for a given lottery (x', p'). Since this experiment intends to examine the correspondence between the time delay and the risk for a pair of fixed rewards, the CE method cannot be applicable. However, note that the systematic bias and the discrepancy between the PE and CE method are reported in Hershey and Schoemaker (1985).

The two Eqs. (4.2) and (4.3) yield one point for D in time-probability space; this point satisfies the following identity:

$$D(t') = p', \tag{4.4}$$

which holds without any parametric assumption on u.[11]

In the first part, $t = 0$ means that one option pays x immediately without any delay, while in the second part, the lottery with $p = 1$ pays x for sure. Thus, subjects compare the delayed reward with the immediate one, and they assess an uncertain option by comparing it with the certain reward.[12] By transitivity, $(x, t) \sim (x, p)$, so subjects use such comparisons to indirectly convert p into t (or vice versa).

2.3 *Discount Function and Hazard Function*

This subsection introduces the basic concept of survival analysis into the time preference framework. Because the experiment lets subjects convert delay into risk, the survival analysis framework is appropriate. To understand the underlying concept better, let us consider why humans, even animals, discount future rewards. There can be several explanations: they are mortal, there is a future uncertainty, (opportunity) cost of waiting, and so forth (Yaari 1965). Alternatively, one can simply say that they have *pure* time preference, aside from risk. Yet, I compound all of those plausible explanations into one function of time, $D(t)$; this is consistent with assuming that time discounting is caused by the uncertain nature of the future (Green and Myerson 1996; Stevenson 1986). I similarly suppose there is an underlying

[11]Recall that subjects are assumed to be EU maximizer. If the prospect theory applies here, that is, subjects transform p into subjective weighting $\pi(p)$, then the identity above should be $D(t') = \pi(p')$. Note that, however, the estimated time discount function represents the corresponding risk p' to the given delay t'. Thus, this experimental design still integrates the risk and time preferences.

[12]The front end delay (FED) design is used to control the transaction cost of the rewards and the immediacy effect in the recent experimental studies (Andersen et al. 2008; Benhabib et al. 2010; Coller and Williams 1999). With the FED, the earlier option will not be paid immediately; instead, it will be paid with a little delay (see Harrison and Lau (2005) for a discussion). Although I was aware of the advantage, I did not adopt it for the following reason. Suppose two delayed options are offered, (x, t) and (x', t') where $0 < t < t'$. Note that, in theory, the time discount function depends on both timings (see Masatlioglu and Ok 2007). That is, $D(t, t')$ is not necessarily equal to $D(0, t'-t)$ or $D(0, t')/D(0, t)$. Thus, we cannot use that observation to elicit $D(0, t')$. In addition, It is important to keep the symmetric structure between the time and risk preference tasks. As Keren and Roelofsma (1995) and Halevy (2008) argue, the immediacy effect and the certainty effect have several common properties. If that is the case, the immediate reward ($t = 0$) corresponds to the certain reward ($p = 1$). It is not certain, however, what p would correspond to a seven-day FED ($t = 7$).

single process of discounting any uncertainty or risk, including the future.[13] For further discussion and justification, see Bommier (2006), Dasgupta and Maskin (2005) and Rachlin et al. (1991).

Suppose a subject makes an intertemporal decision, at time 0, as if she presumes that the future reward is uncertain for some reason. I assume that she has consciously or subconsciously determined her subjective probability that the reward is no longer available to her at time t. Denote this by $F(t)$, which is called the *failure function* in this context. The *survival function* is defined as $D(t) = 1 - F(t)$. Note that it corresponds to the time discount function. Then, the *hazard function* is defined as follows:

$$h(t) = F'(t)/D(t),$$

which is the conditional probability that the reward becomes unavailable at time t given that it has been available up to time t. The hazard rate is also referred to as the instantaneous discount rate (e.g., Laibson 1997), and it represents her impatience at a given moment t.

Prelec (2004) shows that $\ln D(t)$ is convex in t if and only if the time preference exhibits decreasing impatience. Then, a corollary immediately follows, since $-h(t) = d \ln D(t)/dt$:

Corollary 1 *The hazard function $h(t)$ is decreasing (increasing) in t if and only if the time preference exhibits decreasing (increasing) impatience.*

That is, when I characterize the time inconsistent behavior of subjects, it is sufficient to examine the hazard function. Compared to the hazard function, the time discount function is more familiar and intuitive. Therefore, I estimate both.

As for the functional form of D, I assume the following:

$$D(t, \theta, r, q) = \frac{1}{[1 + \theta(rt)^q]^{\frac{1}{\theta}}}, \tag{4.5}$$

where $\theta \in (0, 1], r \in [0, \infty)andq \in [0, \infty)$. This D, called the generalized Weibull model, is a further-generalized version of the *generalized hyperbolic* of Loewenstein and Prelec (1992). They propose $D(t) = (1 + \alpha t)^{-\beta/\alpha}$ in their original notation, which is a special case of the above $D(t)$ when $q = 1$, $\alpha = \theta r$, and $\beta = r$. Note that, while the generalized hyperbolic form represents only decreasing impatience (present bias), the generalized Weibull function (4.5) can represent increasing

[13]Prelec and Loewenstein (1991) review and contrast the anomalies in both expected utility theory and discount utility theory. For example, the decreasing impatience ("common difference effect") corresponds to the "common ratio effect (anomaly)" in expected utility theory, and the present bias is equivalent to the certainty effect anomaly. The similar structures of those anomalies support my view.

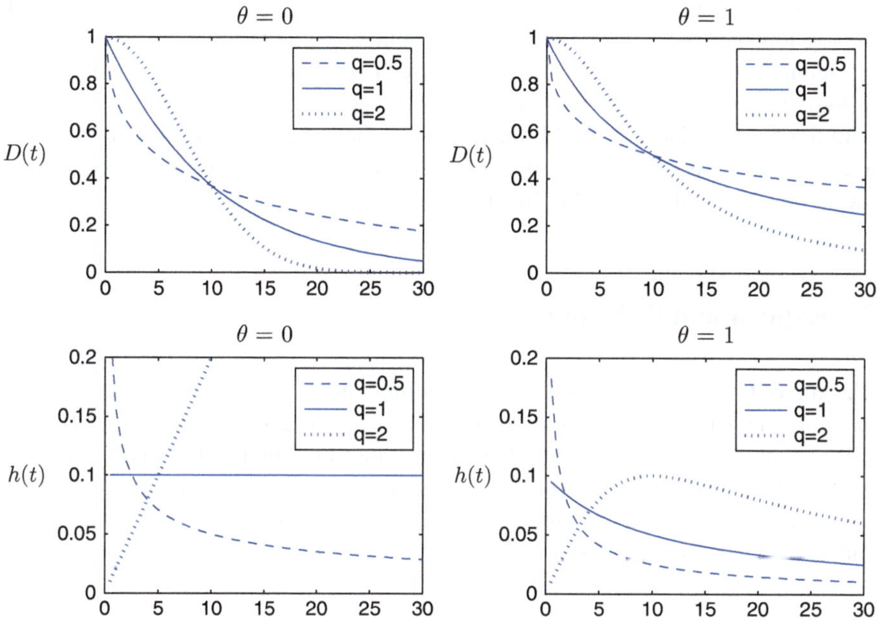

Fig. 4.2 Example plots of $D(t)$ and hazard functions

impatience (future bias) as well.[14] This is the advantage of the generalized Weibull function.

Remark 2 (slope of hazard functions)

1. If $q \leq 1$, then $h'(t) \leq 0$ (with strict inequality if $\theta > 0$), implying present bias and decreasing impatience.
2. If $q = 1$ and $\theta = 0$, then $h'(t) = 0$, implying time consistency and constant impatience.
3. If $q > 1$, then $h'(t) \geq 0$ for $t < \bar{t}$ and $h'(t) \leq 0$ for $t > \bar{t}$ where $\bar{t} = \left[(q-1)/r^q\theta\right]^{1/q}$, implying future bias and increasing impatience.

Remark 3 (inverse S-curve $D(t)$) If $q > 1$, then $D(t)$ is an inverse S-curve function. That is, $D(t)$ is concave for $0 \leq t \leq \hat{t}$ and convex for $\hat{t} \leq t$, where $\hat{t} = \left[(q-1)/r^q(\theta+q)\right]^{1/q}$.

Figure 4.2 illustrates the functional form of D for several parameter values. When $\theta = 1$, D is called the Weibull model, and its hazard rate depends on q: constant for

[14] θ is introduced to capture any unobservable heterogeneity, or *frailty*. Assume that the frailty a is a multiplicative effect on the hazard function, $h(t|a) = ah(t)$ and that the unobserved a follows a Gamma distribution, $G(1/\theta, \theta)$. This results in the D given above Mudholkar et al. (1996).

$q = 1$ and increasing (decreasing) when $q > 1$ (when $q < 1$). If $\theta = 0$, D is called the log-logistic model, which nests a hyperbolic discount function ($q = 1$).

Benhabib et al. (2010) use a novel approach to determine whether an exponential or hyperbolic discount function fits better. They parameterize time preferences by θ with fixed $q = 1$. Here, I would like to expand their approach by estimating both θ and q together. As Corollary 1 shows, it is sometimes more informative to estimate the slope of $h(t)$ rather than the functional form of D.

3 Experimental Design

The aim of this experiment is (i) to find any time inconsistent behavior (present bias or future bias), (ii) to specify the functional form of the discount function, $D(t)$, and (iii) to evaluate biases that would have been caused by the linearity assumption on $u(x)$. The experiment consists of four components: a delayed-payment task to elicit time preferences, a lottery choice task to elicit risk preferences, a psychological survey, and a demographic survey.

3.1 Assessing Time and Risk Preferences

In the time preference part, subjects are asked a set of ten questions in the following format:

> To me, 'receiving \$x today' is equally as good as 'receiving \$y in __ days',

where $x < y$. Subjects are told that they must wait longer to get the larger amount of money, \$y, and they are asked to identify the *longest acceptable delay* that makes the two options the same. In every case, subjects receive their earnings as money orders. The actual amounts of x and y are one of \$5, \$10, \$15, \$20 and \$25; thus, the combinations of two different rewards make 10 questions in total.

Similarly, in the risk preference part, subjects answer questions having the following format:

> To me, 'receiving \$x for sure' is equally as good as 'receiving \$y with __ % chance'.

I ask subjects to report the *lowest acceptable odds of winning* the lottery for \$y. Again, subjects are told that they must play the lottery to get the larger amount, \$y. The actual values of x and y are identical to those in the time preference part. Earnings were paid in cash for this part.

To induce subjects to report their true *delay* and *odds*, I employ the Becker-DeGroot-Marschak (BDM) mechanism.[15] In the time preference part, a computer

[15] Becker et al. (1964).

program randomly chooses a proposed delay. If it is shorter than the longest acceptable delay that a subject reports, then the subject gets \$y right after the proposed delay; otherwise, the subject gets \$x at the end of the experiment. In the risk preference part, a number between 0 to 100 is randomly selected. If it is less than the lowest acceptable odds of winning, then the subject does not play the lottery and receives \$x for sure; otherwise, she plays the lottery. Her chance of winning the lottery is the probability (%) that the computer generates. She gets \$y if she wins the lottery and nothing if she loses.

Regarding the BDM mechanism, there are two possible issues: (i) it may be too complicated for subjects to understand and (ii) subjects may form decisions based on the underlying distribution of the possible valuation.[16] The instructions, therefore, explain the incentive compatibility property through the use of examples and the instructions go on to explain why any false report may make them worse off. Then the instructions explicitly tell subjects that their "best response is always to answer the questions truthfully."[17] As for the range of the potential valuation, in the risk preference part, subjects are told that $p \sim U[0, 100]$. This range is the most neutral to behavior because it suggests nothing particular about the odds of winning. In the time preference part, I set $t \sim U[1, 120]$. Since any range of t can be an anchor in the decision-making process, subjects are not told anything about the range of the possible proposed delay.[18]

The multiple choice list of Holt and Laury (2002) may be ideal for eliciting risk attitude; however, its grid size is too coarse to fit into Eq. (4.4). Alternatively, I could adopt the iterative multiple price list or the newly developed adaptive instrument (see Harrison et al. (2005) and Eckel et al. (2005), respectively), which would provide a finer grid and increment unit. However, both mechanisms require subjects to answer many questions to elicit a single t.[19] Thus, I run BDM.[20] After subjects complete the tasks, they fill out a survey.

---

[16]See Bohm et al. (1997) that find the sensitivity of BDM to the underlying distribution of valuation.

[17]Since the purpose of the BDM mechanism in this experiment is not to test the mechanism but to make subjects reveal their valuation, I believe that it is appropriate to teach the subjects about the incentive property. After they read the instructions for the time preference part, subjects answer two review questions on the mechanism. Out of 55 subjects, 35 answered both questions correctly and 12 answered one of the questions correctly.

[18]There were two subjects who asked about the possible range of the delay. I answered them by saying that there was a range of a proposed delay, from which the computer program would choose a number and I did not tell the range. Then, I repeated their best response was still to answer questions truthfully regardless of the range.

[19]In addition, it seemed that these two methods were not always incentive compatible. However, I leave this issue for future research on the methodology, as it calls for a rigorous investigation.

[20]Attema et al. (2010) independently develop another experimental design with the same spirit. For a given pair of rewards $x < x'$, they elicit the length of interval between the two rewards that makes the two options equally good. Suppose $(x, 0) \sim (x', t_1)$. In the next question, let subjects compare (x, t_1) and (x', t_2) and elicit t_2 that makes $(x, t_1) \sim (x', t_2)$. This sequence of adaptive questions yields the shape of the time discount function. See their paper for more detail. Note that, due to its adaptive nature, this method would not be incentive compatible if the reward were real money.

3.2 Procedure

Each session involves 10–15 subjects; 5 sessions yield 56 subjects in total. In three of these sessions, subjects firstly complete the time preference part and then the risk preference part. The order of the two parts is reversed in the other two sessions.[21]

At the beginning of each session, subjects are given printed instructions. After the instructions for the first part are read aloud, subjects are encouraged to ask questions. Then, they answer the ten questions for the first part. The same procedure is repeated for the second part. The ten questions are separated into four groups depending on the amount of the smaller reward in the question.[22] The computer screen displays each group of questions individually and subjects report their *delay* (or *odds*) by answering questions. When the submit button is clicked, the computer proceeds to another screen. After she goes through those four screens, the computer shows her ten answers in a table format and offers a chance to revise the answers. On average, it takes 2 min and 25 s to complete ten questions.[23] To prevent any wealth effect and/or feedback, subjects are informed of the result at the end of the experiment session, not at the end of each part.

In the time preference part, the reward is paid with a US Postal Money Order.[24] If a subject earns the "$x today" option, she will get the money order when she leaves the session. Those who get the future option are asked to write their mailing address on a stamped envelope and the money order, and seal it into the envelope. Then I collect the envelopes and mail them after the proposed delay. All of these procedures are written in the instructions.

The 56 student subjects were recruited at the University of Michigan. No subject was used in more than one session. All sessions were conducted in the RCGD lab at the University of Michigan, and each session lasted approximately 70 min.

[21]I do not observe a significant order effect in the reported *delays*. However, the subjects in the last two sessions who completed the risk preference part first significantly reported the lower *lowest acceptable odds* than those in the first three sessions. The mean difference is 8.48 % points and the p-value of t-test is 0.051.

[22]The first group consists of four questions, whose reward pairs are ($5, $10), ($5, $15), ($5, $20) and ($5, $25). The next group includes ($10, $15), ($10, $20) and ($10, $25).

[23]It took 145.1 s on average for a subject to complete the time preference task and 144.7 s for the risk preference task. Of 56 subjects, 21 revised their answers in the time preference part and 18 revised their answers in the risk preference part.

[24]There are several implementations of delayed payments. Harrison et al. (2005) have the Danish Ministry of Economic and Business Affairs transfer the delayed payment into the subjects' bank account. Anderhub et al. (2001) and Coller and Williams (1999) give a post-dated check to subjects. Benhabib et al. (2010) send a check to the subject's mailing address. Tanaka et al. (2010) assign to a village leader to deliver future rewards to participants in the village.

Table 4.2 Session summary

Session	Number of subjects	Task 1	Task 2	Survey
1	10	Time	Risk	Yes
2	10	Time	Risk	Yes
3	10	Risk	Time	Yes
4	11	Risk	Time	Yes
5	15	Risk	Time	Yes

The average earning (including money orders) was \$22.77 plus \$5 for a participation fee. I used a z-Tree program to run this experiment (Fischbacher 2007). Table 4.2 summarizes the tasks and number of subjects for each of the five sessions I conducted.

4 Results

In this section, I present three main results. First, I characterize time inconsistent behavior and observe the future bias. Second, I estimate the time discount function using the inverse S-curve function. Finally, I illustrate the biases caused by the linearity assumption on $u(x)$.

Figure 4.3 gives an overview of the distribution of responses.[25] On average, subjects are willing to wait longer and take higher risk as the distance between the small and large rewards becomes larger. In what follows, I examine individual subject behavior in more detail.

4.1 Future Bias

To run the longitudinal analysis, I select three different rewards from $\{5, 10, 15, 20, 25\}$ to classify subject responses according to the criteria above. For each subject, there are 10 combinations, generating 550 observations in total.[26] Figure 4.4 summarizes the distribution of the difference, $T(x_0, x_1) + T(x_1, x_2) - T(x_0, x_2)$ for $x_0 < x_1 < x_2$. As seen, it is skewed to the right and the number and

[25]There was a subject who answered 366 (days) to all 10 delay questions. The value 366 was the longest delay that subjects could input. I refer this subject as ID56.

[26]In this analysis, I excluded the data of ID56, since his response always implies future bias no matter what his true time preference is.

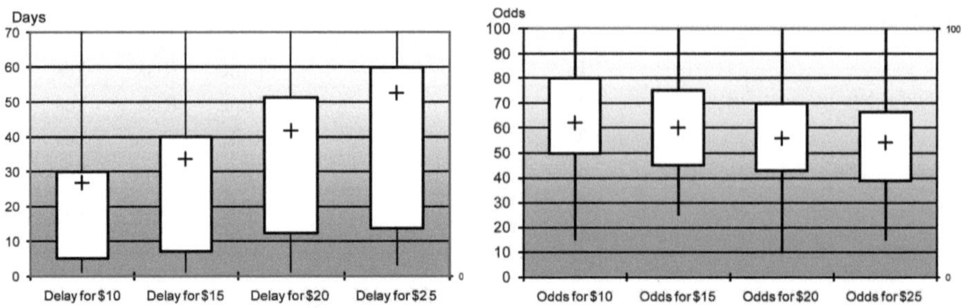

Fig. 4.3 Reported delay and odds for the larger reward against \$5 today (for sure) option. These boxplots summarize the responses of 56 subjects to the first four questions in the time and risk preference parts. In the questions for the time (risk) preference part, they are asked to report how many days of delay (what odds) make the larger reward option and the \$5 today (for sure) option equal. The box covers the half of those responses in the middle and the cross symbol indicates the mean. As the amount of the larger reward increases, they are willing to wait longer and take higher risks, on average

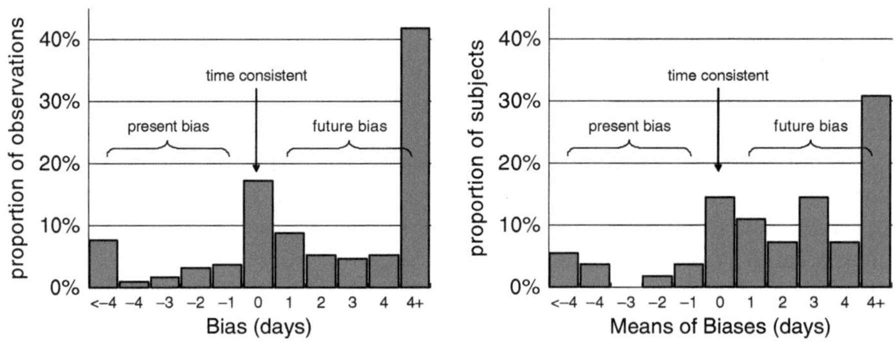

Fig. 4.4 Distributions of time preference. This figure summarizes the distributions of time consistent behavior, the present and future biases. $T(x_i, x_j)$ denotes the delay that makes two options, (x_i today) and (x_j in $T(x_i, x_j)$ days), the same to a subject. The bias (days) is defined $T(x_0, x_1) + T(x_1, x_2) - T(x_0, x_2)$ for any three rewards, $x_0 < x_1 < x_2$. Thus, positive (negative) bias corresponds to future (present) bias. There are ten combinations of three rewards for each of 55 subjects. The left panel shows the distribution of the biases for all 550 combinations and the right panel shows the distribution of the mean value of bias of each subject. In the right panel, the range of k days includes any mean value in $[k - \frac{1}{2}, k + \frac{1}{2})$. As seen in both panels, the distributions are skewed to the right

magnitudes of future biases are greater than those of present biases. The first main finding in this chapter is that subjects exhibit significantly more future bias than present bias.

Result 1 (Future Bias) Of the 550 observations, 362 are future biased preference reversals and 93 are present biased preference reversals. The number of future biases is significantly greater than that of present biases.

Support *The null hypothesis is that the median is zero for the difference between* $T(x_0,x_1)+T(x_1,x_2)$ *and* $T(x_0,x_2)$. *The sign test, assuming a binomial distribution of* $B(n=550,p=0.5)$, *indicates that the null hypothesis can be rejected at any level above 0.00 %. Furthermore, for each subject, I take the mean of the ten observations of the difference between* $T(x_0,x_1)+T(x_1,x_2)$ *and* $T(x_0,x_2)$ *and run the sign test. Assuming* $B(n=55,p=0.5)$, *the p-value is 0.01 %.*

This future bias result is surprising, since most analyses in the literature assume present bias. Only recently have Read (2001) and Attema et al. (2010) found increasing impatience in subject behaviors that indicates future bias preference. Sayman and Öncüler (2009) conducted experiments with longitudinal design and found *reverse* time-inconsistent choice behavior, which is also consistent with the future bias found in this experiment. Most of experiments in the literature, however, support present bias. I suppose there are two reasons for that: the time range and the estimation methods of those experiments.

First, in many of the prior experiments, subjects reveal their time preferences over a long time range which is usually longer than 1 month. Thus, those experiments do not capture future bias that seemingly occurs in the immediate future. According to Table 1 of Frederick et al. (2002) which summarizes the time range of 42 experiments, there are eight studies in which the time range is shorter than 1 month. The other 34 experiments elicit the time preference over future options that would pay a reward after 1 month.

As seen in Table 4.3 of the next subsection, however, the subjects exhibit future bias within a short period, which is on average 22.4 days from the current moment and then exhibit present bias thereafter. Sayman and Öncüler (2009) also report that the reverse time inconsistency is more likely to be observed when the delay is shorter than 4 weeks. Therefore, it is indicated that future bias has been overlooked due to the long time range of the experiments in prior research.

Secondly, although the previous studies found present bias behavior, they did not necessarily mean that the subjects did not have a future bias preference. The present bias and the future bias can coexist within a subject; while she exhibits future bias in the short period, the same person may also exhibit present bias over a long time range. Although she seems to have two inconsistent biases simultaneously, an inverse S-curve time discount function can consistently account for them together. Figure 4.5 illustrates the concept. The left panel shows that a subject who has the inverse S-curve time discounting exhibits both of the present and future bias. Notice, however, that the future bias can be elicited only when the interval between the two delayed options is sufficiently short. The right panel of the figure shows the case where the subject exhibits only present bias since the interval is too long to elicit the future bias.

To my knowledge, all previous studies that estimate time discount function focus on whether subjects have a present bias or not. Therefore, they did not need to employ an inverse S-curve function to estimate the subjects' time preference and they did not detect future bias. This is another reason why future bias has been rarely reported before.

Table 4.3 Estimates of time preference

ID	θ	r	q	R^2	D(1 year)	$\hat{t}$
7	0.00	0.013	3.30	0.683	0.000	67.3
10	0.00	0.029	2.15	0.679	0.000	26.0
30	0.37	0.043	1.97	0.587	0.000	15.0
18	0.03	0.056	1.78	0.604	0.000	11.1
22	0.00	0.010	1.71	0.891	0.000	61.5
23	0.00	0.083	1.70	0.602	0.000	7.1
8	0.00	0.008	1.70	0.641	0.001	70.9
1	0.13	0.054	1.69	0.416	0.000	10.5
25	0.00	0.056	1.66	0.382	0.000	10.3
15	0.85	0.020	1.59	0.829	0.027	20.2
48	0.00	0.041	1.41	0.624	0.000	10.2
40	0.82	0.223	1.37	0.839	0.001	1.2
27	0.00	0.007	1.28	0.893	0.034	43.2
43	0.00	0.010	1.18	0.615	0.009	19.7
2	0.03	0.005	1.15	0.999	0.170	36.8
11	0.57	0.011	1.15	0.735	0.098	10.9
5	0.01	0.014	1.12	0.492	0.003	9.8
28	0.00	0.007	1.10	0.655	0.053	14.8
36	0.92	0.037	1.02	0.665	0.057	0.3
6	0.00	0.020	1.02	0.205	0.001	0.8
44	1.00	0.002	0.93	0.367	0.546	–
4	0.00	0.116	0.85	0.554	0.000	–
9	0.04	0.136	0.83	0.575	0.000	–
29	0.01	0.055	0.79	0.312	0.000	–
45	1.00	0.002	0.70	0.338	0.533	–
34	0.12	0.007	0.58	0.856	0.196	–
17	0.00	0.052	0.56	0.379	0.006	–
42	0.18	0.017	0.54	0.863	0.112	–
49	0.27	0.007	0.53	0.846	0.263	–
35	0.87	0.004	0.46	0.063	0.428	–
21	0.41	0.001	0.40	0.421	0.566	–
26	0.05	0.020	0.36	0.135	0.143	–
24	0.83	0.000	0.21	0.335	0.733	–
mean	0.26	0.04	1.18	0.578	0.121	22.4

This table presents the estimates for 33 subjects for whom the model predicts well ($R^2 > 5\,\%$). See Table 4.4 for the other 23 subjects. The extrapolation of the function with the estimated parameters to $t = 365$ provides D(1 year). The last column shows $\hat{t} = \left[(q-1)/r^q(\theta+q)\right]^{1/q}$ at which the form of the inverse S-curve D changes from concave to convex

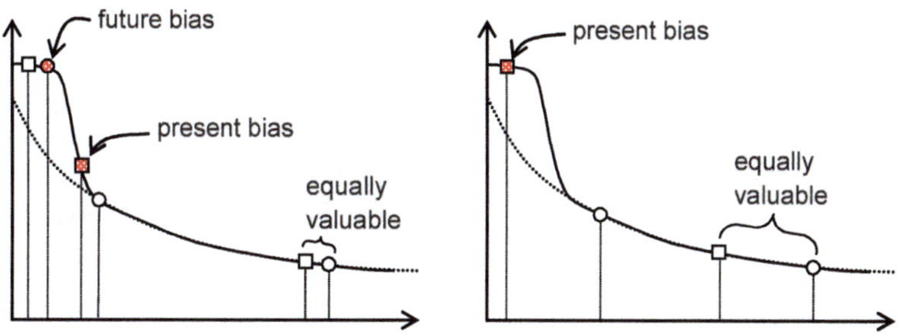

Fig. 4.5 The interval between options and elicitation of future bias. The square and circle represent two delayed reward options. The dotted curve is a quasi-hyperbolic discount function and the solid curve is an inverse S-curve time discount function. Suppose that as long as the two options are on the dotted curve, they are equally valuable to a subject. Left panel: In the middle, the subject strictly prefers the square option and exhibits present bias, since the square is above the exponential discounting curve while the circle is still on the curve. However, when both are close to $t = 0$ and belong to the extended present in the subject's perception, the circle is further above the exponential curve than the square. Thus, she strictly prefers the circle option and exhibits future bias. Right panel: it shows the case where the interval between the two options is too long to elicit her future bias time preference

I discuss other psychological reasoning for future bias and its implication in Sect. 5.

There is a remark on the result; decreasing discounting is not so prevalent in this experiment. I suppose that most of the subjects do not exhibit a present bias since the immediate reward is paid in a money order, which incurs some cost to cash out. If we paid the subjects the immediate reward in cash and the future reward in a money order, they would probably have shown a present bias more frequently due to the transaction cost associated with the future option. There are other experiments that observe little decreasing discounting for the same reason. For example, Anderhub et al. (2001), who use a (post-dated) check for both immediate and future payments, observe little hyperbolic discounting (only 14 of their 61 subjects). The front-end delay (FED) also serves to equalize the transaction cost between immediate and future payments (see Harrison and Lau (2005) for discussion). In fact, Harrison et al. (2002) use a 1-month FED and observe little hyperbolic discounting. This evidence implies that the hyperbolic discounting and decreasing discounting observed in other experiments might be attributed to, in part, the transaction cost of the future payment.

4.2 The Inverse S-Curve Discounting

To characterize the future bias observations, I estimate parameters q_i, θ_i and r_i by a non-linear least-squares fit for each subject. Recall each subject generates ten paired-observations. Let (t_{ij}, p_{ij}) denote a data point obtained from subject i's

Fig. 4.6 Estimated discount functions

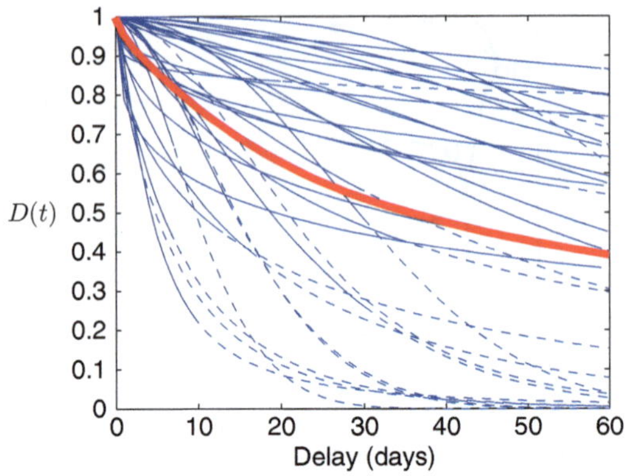

response to question j, where t_{ij} is the reported delay and p_{ij} is the reported odds. For each subject, I solve a non-linear least-squares problem of the following form:

$$\min_{\theta,r,q} \sum_j \left[p_{ij} - D(t_{ij}, \theta, r, q)\right]^2, \tag{4.6}$$

where D is the generalized Weibull function defined in Eq. (4.5).

Table 4.3 summarizes the estimated parameters for 33 subjects.[27] Figure 4.6 shows the estimated $D(t)$ for those 33 subjects. The solid portions of each curve depict $D_i(t)$ for $0 \leq t \leq \max_j \{t_{ij}\}$. The bold line in the middle represents the average discount factor for given t, that is $\bar{D}(t) = \sum D_i(t)/33$. Note that $\bar{D}(35.9) = 0.50$ means that a 36-day delay is equivalent to 50 % of the risk, on average.

Result 2 (Inverse S-curve discounting) Some subjects have an inverse S-curve $D_i(t)$. Overall, however, the average discount function $\bar{D}$ is hyperbolic.

Support *For 20 out of the 33 subjects in Table 4.3, the estimated q is greater than 1. This hump-shaped hazard function implies increasing impatience (future bias) at the beginning and decreasing impatience (present bias) later on. Non-linear least-squares for $t \in \{1, \ldots, 60\}$ finds $(\theta, r, q) = (0.915, 0.028, 0.890)$ fitting $\bar{D}$ with $R^2 = 0.9995$. Though not all $D_i(t)$ are hyperbolic, the average discount function $\bar{D}$ appears to be hyperbolic.*

Remark 4 (Extended present) Result 2 suggests a concept of *extended present* (or extended immediacy). This means that the subjects recognize that the first few days following today all belong to the extended present and they discount rewards paid in those days moderately. Observe also that extended present is corresponding to future bias.

[27]Note, however, that for the other 22 subjects the model has little explanatory power ($R^2 < 0.05$). I treat them separately and discuss this later.

This concept is consistent with the experimental results of Coller et al. (2012) and Holcomb and Nelson (1992). Coller et al. (2012) show that a short (front end) delay attached to a small-soon reward eliminates the immediate effect or the present premium.[28] Their result shows that a 7-day front end delay eliminates the premium. On the other hand, Holcomb and Nelson (1992) do not find any effect of a 1-day front end delay. Thus, the period between 2 and 7 days from today constitutes the present in a sense that the present premium is still attached to those days. Similarly, in this experiment, the "present" seems to continue as the hazard rate remains low for the first few days of the future.

There are two caveats to the results. Observe that the discounting is unreasonably steep and that converting delay into risk does not work for some subjects.

First, as shown in Table 4.3, the annual discount factors estimated by extrapolation are very low, i.e., the discount function is very steep. The average time discount function also has a very short "half-life", which is only 36 days (i.e., $D(35.9\text{ days}) = 0.50$). This result seems to be unreasonable, since the imputed annual discount rate from the average estimated $D(1\text{ year}) = 0.121$ is 726 %. Notice, however, that this incredibly high discount rate is not unique in the literature. For example, Table 1 of Frederick et al. (2002) summarizes 42 studies on time preference and includes ten experiments that similarly observe unreasonably high discount rates. One may think that subjects were not certain whether they would really receive their future payment. If that was the case, the discount rates would be overestimated reflecting not only their time preference but also their suspicion about the plausibility of the future payment. However, half of those ten experiments whose elicited discount rates are very high do not involve real future reward. Even though subjects do not need to, or simply cannot, be suspicious about the plausibility for the hypothetical rewards in the experiments, they still exhibit a very steep discounting function. Thus, the high discount rate itself does not indicate that the result is unacceptable.

The second caveat is that, for two-fifths of our subjects, the conversion of delay into risk does not work. The experimental method could not identify time preference by their risk-taking behavior or risk preference. While they are not willing to take higher risk for larger reward, they are still willing to wait longer for a larger reward.

Table 4.4 presents the estimated parameters with and without assuming $u(x) = x$ for those 23 subjects. The R^2 is almost zero, implying that the acceptable longest delay $T(x, y)$ for the larger reward y is not corresponding to the acceptable odds $p = u(x)/u(y)$ in our framework. The method intends to convert delay into risk (or vise versa) using BDM, but the result shows its limitation. In particular, the R^2 becomes much higher if $u(x) = x$ is assumed. It indicates that the elicited probability equivalence through BDM is not consistent with the subjects' risk preferences.

[28] The experiment has two treatments. In the first treatment, subjects are asked to choose one of two future rewards. In the second treatment, they are asked to choose from one immediate reward and another future reward. If there is an immediate effect (present bias) and a premium to accept any delayed reward instead of an immediate one, then the premium is present only in the second treatment.

Table 4.4 Estimates of time preference

	No assumption on $u(x)$				Assumed $u(x) = x$				
ID	θ	r	q	R^2	θ	r	q	R^2	D(1 year)
3	0.78	0.000	0.00	0.000	0.00	0.027	1.11	0.819	0.000
50	0.74	0.000	0.00	0.000	0.00	0.024	1.63	0.787	0.000
31	0.70	0.000	0.02	0.000	0.00	0.076	1.00	0.736	0.000
41	0.63	0.000	0.01	0.000	0.00	0.076	1.00	0.736	0.000
13	1.00	0.000	0.12	0.000	0.62	0.091	1.33	0.726	0.001
39	0.11	0.055	0.00	0.000	0.00	0.049	0.92	0.717	0.000
55	1.00	0.000	0.18	0.000	0.03	0.083	0.51	0.581	0.006
33	0.56	0.030	0.08	0.038	0.86	0.087	1.35	0.517	0.005
54	0.63	0.000	0.03	0.000	0.00	0.149	1.32	0.511	0.000
38	0.31	0.223	0.22	0.040	0.00	0.209	0.78	0.480	0.000
19	0.39	0.419	0.00	0.000	0.00	0.111	1.13	0.453	0.000
12	0.57	0.000	0.10	0.000	0.65	0.051	0.59	0.384	0.094
51	0.88	0.000	0.02	0.000	0.00	0.115	0.70	0.382	0.000
46	0.68	0.000	0.01	0.000	0.07	0.050	0.62	0.279	0.007
16	0.13	0.017	0.48	0.050	0.01	0.021	1.05	0.201	0.000
47	0.90	0.000	0.01	0.000	0.00	0.011	0.42	0.084	0.171
52	0.85	0.000	0.06	0.001	0.55	0.008	0.24	0.021	0.381
20	0.98	0.000	0.03	0.000	0.38	0.081	0.26	0.017	0.177
14	0.39	0.000	0.03	0.000	0.35	0.065	0.18	0.005	0.256
32	1.00	0.002	8.51	0.000	0.57	0.005	1.58	0.000	0.203
53	0.14	0.010	2.23	0.000	0.14	0.010	2.25	0.000	0.000
37	0.67	0.000	0.06	0.000	1.00	99.997	0.00	0.000	0.500
56	n.a.	n.a.	n.a.	n.a.	n.a.	n.a.	n.a.	n.a.	>0.800
Mean	0.64	0.034	0.56	0.006	0.24	4.61	0.91	0.383	0.082

The model, that converts delay into the equivalent risk, does not fit to responses for 23 subjects. As seen in this table, R^2 is almost zero for these subjects. The right half part shows the parameter estimation, imposing $u(x) = x$. In terms of R^2, the linearity assumption on $u(x)$ improves the fitting. The last row is corresponding to the subject, all of whose equivalent delays are binding at 366 days

Remark 5 (Discrepancy between PE and delay) For two-fifths of the subjects, there is a significant discrepancy between the probability equivalence (PE) and the acceptable delay elicited by BDM. It can be mostly attributed to the inconsistency between PE and $u(x)/u(y)$.

4.3 The Effect of the Linear Utility Assumption

In this subsection, I examine the effect and biases caused by the linear utility assumption. Thus, I explicitly assume $u(x) = x$, replacing p_{ij} by the ratio of rewards.

For example, suppose that a subject is indifferent between ($15 today) and ($20 in 7 days), and between ($15 for sure) and ($20 with 90 % chance). A paired observation should be (7 days, 90 %) and infer $D(7) = 0.9$. In this subsection, assuming $u(x) = x$, I ignore the second part of the responses and thus I observe (7 days, 75 %) where 75 % = $15/$20. This infers $D(7) = 0.75$ instead.

4.3.1 Downward Bias

In general, the ratio of two rewards is lower than the acceptable odds; $15/$20 < 90 % in the example above. Subjects are not willing to take the high risk (25 %) of losing $15 for an additional $5. Thus, the linearity assumption causes downward bias on $D(t)$.

Result 3 (downward bias) The linearity assumption biases estimates of $D(t)$ downward.

Support *The acceptable risks that subjects report is 66.26 % on average, while the ratio of rewards is 0.50 overall. The difference is statistically significant ($p <$ 0.001). Figure 4.7 compares the average discount factors, with and without the $u(x) = x$ assumption. As seen in Fig. 4.7, the $u(x) = x$ assumption causes an overestimation of the discount factor. Fitting $D(t) = e^{-rt}$ to those $\bar{D}(t)$, I find that $\hat{r} = 0.0282$ for $\bar{D}(t)$ without the linearity assumption and $\hat{r} = 0.0560$ for the other. That is, the linearity assumption increases the discount rate (hazard rate) from 2.82 to 5.60 %.*

Figure 4.8 illustrates such a downward bias for two subjects. For subject ID = 34, the assumption shifts $D(t)$ so low that the discount rate becomes almost double. By comparing the equivalent delay and the equivalent uncertainty, the experiment estimates $D(t)$ independently of the functional form of $u(x)$. For example, for subject

Fig. 4.7 Overall downward bias

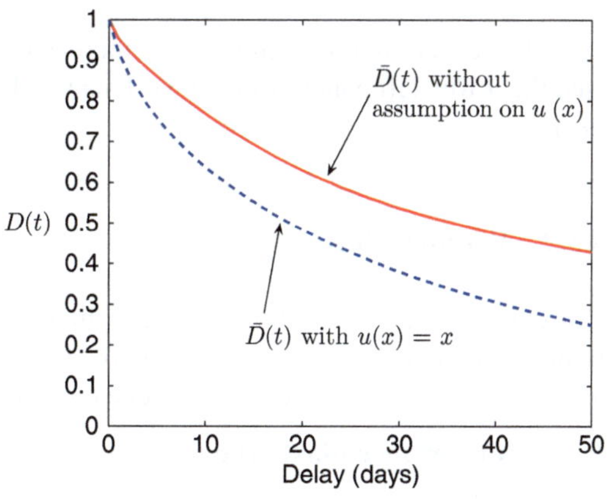

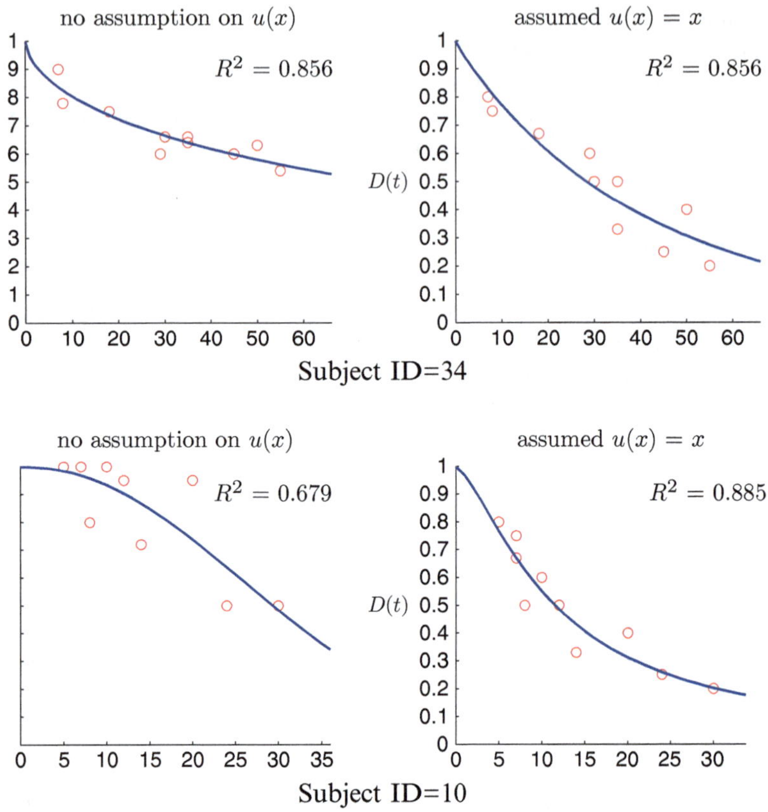

Fig. 4.8 Downward bias. These figures compare two estimations of $D(t)$: one without an assumption on $u(x)$ and the other with a $u(x) = x$ assumption. The linearity assumption causes downward bias. For ID=10, the experiment successfully elicits the concavity of $D(t)$ (the left panel). This would not be observed if I had assumed the linearity assumption

ID $= 10$, it successfully estimates the increasing impatience or the concavity of $D(t)$ (see the lower-left panel of Fig. 4.8). This would not be observable if I had assumed $u(x) = x$.

4.3.2 Variance Bias

Our experimental method also reduces the variance in the data. For some subjects, it may be that $\mathrm{var}(x_k/x_j) > \mathrm{var}(u(x_k)/u(x_j))$, since u can be concave. Then, eliciting $u(x_k)/u(x_j)$, this experiment can reduce the variance of the data.

Result 4 (Variance bias) The linearity assumption increases variance.

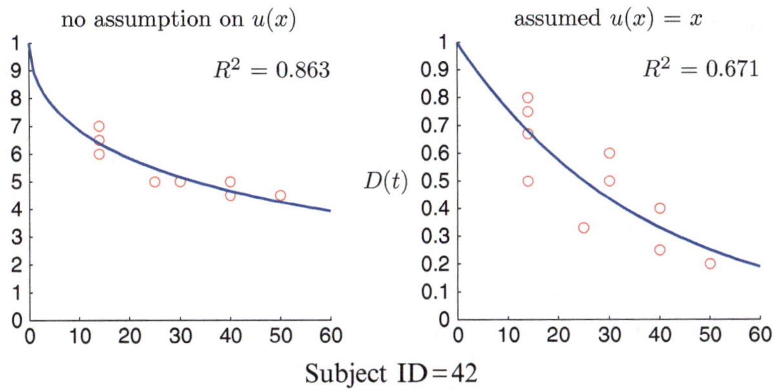

Fig. 4.9 Variance bias

Support *The variance of the reported odds* $\sigma_i^2 = \mathrm{var}(p_{ij})$ *is significantly less than the variance of the ratios of the rewards, 383.5. For 50 subjects,* $\sigma_i^2 < 383.5$.

Figure 4.9 illustrates that the linearity assumption increases the variance of the data for subject ID = 42. For this subject, 14 days of delay discount the value of rewards down to 65 % on average (see the left panel). In fact, in this subject's responses, there are four paired observations: (14 days, 60 %), (14 days, 65 %), (14 days, 65 %) and (14 days, 70 %). However, the linearity assumption biases the reported odds into 0.5, 0.67, 0.75 and 0.8, respectively. As a result, R^2 also decreases from 0.863 to 0.671.

5 Discussion

This section discusses the following: the existence of pure time preference, the issues in the experimental method including plausibility of delay and fungibility of rewards, and psychological accounts for future bias, including the extended notion of present.

First, although this experimental design has some advantages, the interpretation needs to be done carefully. In this study, some subjects seem to have a pure time preference that cannot be attributed to a risk preference. For those 19 subjects, the R^2 of the non-linear least-squares of (4.6) is less than 0.01, meaning that $D(t)$ has no explanatory power. However, if I impose $u(x) = x$, then R^2 will be 0.38 on average, indicating that their time preferences are not identified by their elicited probability equivalences. It also suggests that there may be some other factor than risk causing time discounting. Detecting those factors is left for future research.

5.1 Confounds in the Experimental Method

The potential confounds in the experimental method should be addressed.[29] In particular, the plausibility of future rewards and the fungibility of monetary rewards are the confounding factors that many experimental studies, including this chapter, do not control.

When estimating the time preference of a subject, it is assumed that she is not skeptical about the plausibility of a future reward. However, the subject may avoid a future reward just because she does not think she will actually receive it. For example, the subject feels that an experimenter is unreliable, or she anticipates she may be moving far in the near future.[30] Then, her revealed time preference does not correctly reflect her true time preference. This type of subjective uncertainty cannot be easily separated from time preference and might result in an overestimation of time discounting.

The other issue is that a money order is a fungible reward in principle. Thus, most of the experiments including this chapter do not necessarily elicit the psychological time preference for consumption of subjects. Note, however, that Reuben et al. (2010) recently showed that the time discounting for non-fungible chocolate and fungible money correlates with each other within a subject, indicating that monetary rewards are still useful for time preference experiments.

5.2 Psychological Accounts of Future Bias

As for future bias, I consider other interpretations and psychological accounts, which include the unreliability of own future memory and the notion of extended present.[31]

First, a subject may anticipate that she is going to forget about a delayed reward. Suppose that she thinks her short-term memory is most likely to fade after several weeks, i.e., the hazard rate of the memory loss is increasing in time during those weeks and decreasing thereafter. Assume she is a little skeptical about the

---

[29]I thank an anonymous referee for his/her detailed comments pointing out these issues.

[30]In our study, to minimize the skepticism, subjects were given a postal money order and wrote their addresses and names on the money order and an envelope, in which they sealed their money order.

[31]I am aware that the future bias can be explained by the same psychological process that causes a subadditive discounting (Read 2001; Scholten and Read 2006). The subadditive discount function means $D(0,t) > D(0,s) \times D(s,t)$ and implies present biased behavior. Read explains that "when an object or event is subdivided, each part is paid more attention than if it is part of a larger whole (p. 10)." Notice that a similar subadditivity of attention can lead to the opposite future bias in this framework: namely, if a subject interprets the difference between x_0 and x_1 as an object, then the acceptable delay is a function of the difference, i.e. $\tilde{T}(x_1 - x_0) = T(x_0, x_1)$. When there is subadditivity in $\tilde{T}$, it results in future bias observations.

plausibility of the future payment but she still thinks the future payment will be delivered as long as she remembers it, by reclaiming it for example. Then, the revealed time preference results in the inverse S-shaped time discount function. It is left for further research to control this psychological factor.

Secondly, but most importantly, future bias observations suggest that the present is not a single point on the time line but, rather, that it extends into the immediate future. Observe also that the inverse S-shaped time discount function fits to this concept of the extended present. Then, a question arises: When does the *future* really start?

One can ask when does the future really start and how many seconds, minutes, hours, days, or weeks separate the present from the future. If the next 10 min do not belong to the future, then one would not discount any reward paid within those 10 min. This suggests the notion that the present extends into the future and that, immediately after the current moment, a time discount function will not necessarily decrease. This concept of the extended present is also important for the application of quasi-hyperbolic discounting models.

Suppose that a subject perceives the period $[0, \bar{t}]$ as the "present" and discounts any reward arriving thereafter. Her time discount function can be simply characterized as follows:

$$D(t) = \begin{cases} 1 & \text{if } t \in [0, \bar{t}] \\ e^{-rt} & \text{if } t > \bar{t}. \end{cases}$$

This still captures the nature of quasi-hyperbolic discounting. But, notice also that it is consistent with both present bias and future bias. The concept of the extended present naturally adds another dimension to the quasi-hyperbolic discount function, and it will deepen our understanding of the time preference.

6 Concluding Remarks

Time preference is one of the fundamental factors in any decision-making process. Understanding the nature of this time preference provides us with deep insight into human behaviors and economic decisions in both microeconomics and macroeconomics. In fact, there are many applications of this line of research: savings and investments, credit card markets, retirement, clinical decisions,[32] procrastination, and addiction.[33]

[32]Time-related aspects and delay discounting play important roles in clinical decisions. See Bos et al. (2005) and Ortendahl and Fries (2006) for reviews and discussions.

[33]For example, nicotine-dependent (Reynolds et al. 2004) and alcoholic (Petry 2001) individuals have more myopic time preferences than individuals without any addiction.

In this chapter, I elicit the time preference of subjects using a new experiment design. This experimental design is unique in the sense that it runs a non-parametric test of time consistency and it does not impose any parametric assumption on the utility function. The non-parametric test can be done by introducing equivalent delay function, and it is shown that the modularity of the function is corresponding to the standard definition of time inconsistency. This test is also independent of the separability assumption between x and t, which is the very first one of this kind in the literature.

In the parametric estimation of time discount function, I employ the generalized Weibull model to accommodate an inverse S-curve time discount function.

The experimental results suggest that some subjects exhibit both of increasing and decreasing impatience (i.e., future bias and present bias). These behavior patterns, future bias in particular, were rarely observed in previous experimental studies, as the standard experimental designs could estimate only present bias. The finding of future bias implies that the immediate future constitutes an extended present for subjects. That is, the future does not really start right away, but it starts after some delay. This time preference is characterized by an inverse S-curve discount function that is concave for the first 22 days, on average, and convex thereafter. My method also corrects biases caused by the linearity assumption on utility functions, i.e., $u(x) = x$. The result shows that the estimated discount rate with the linearity assumption could be roughly twice as high as that without the assumption.[34]

This study considers delay as a risk factor and integrates risk and time preference. Although there is no definitive answer about how delay relates to risk, there are some clues. Many studies in psychopharmacology, for example, show that substance dependent (addicted) individuals tend to make impulsive intertemporal choices.[35] If drug abuse is high-risk behavior, there must be a common impulsive nature in both myopic time preference and risk-taking behavior. It is also known that the perception of a short time interval is influenced by dopamine.[36] More recently, McClure et al. (2007) find, by observing the fMRI images of subjects' brain, a brain region that seems to be responsible for the present bias.[37] These clues from various fields will reveal the relationship between risk and time preferences in a more systematic manner. At present, this chapter serves to show the need for a systematic approach to the integration of time and risk, as well as the boundary between the present and the future.

---

[34]This result supports one of the main findings of Andersen et al. (2008).

[35]In psychopharmacology, there is extensive research on the relationship between addictive behavior and discounting. Reynolds (2006) and Bickel et al. (2007) provide comprehensive reviews of the literature.

[36]See the extensive survey by Cardinal (2006) for other examples.

[37]See also Kable and Glimcher (2007) for other arguments.

Acknowledgements I thank Yan Chen, Fuhito Kojima, Yusufcan Masatlioglu, Daisuke Nakajima, Emre Ozdenoren, Scott Page, Matthew Rabin, Shunichiro Sasaki, Andrew Schotter, Lones Smith, Nathaniel Wilcox and seminar participants at Michigan, Caltech, Hitotsubashi, Amsterdam, and French Economic Association meetings (Lyon), Japan Economic Association meetings (Tokyo) and the ESA meetings (Osaka, Shanghai and Tucson) for helpful comments and discussions. I thank Benjamin Taylor and Xiao Liu for their excellent research assistance. I specially thank Yan Chen, two anonymous referees and an advisory editor for valuable feedbacks. All errors are mine. The research support provided by NSF grant SES0339587 to Chen is gratefully acknowledged. This work was also supported by JSPS KAKENHI Grant Number 22730156.

Appendix

Proof

Proof (Proof of Proposition 1) Assume a subject exhibits decreasing impatience. Choose arbitrary $w < z \leq x_1 < x_2$. Let $t_1 = T(z, x_1)$, $t_2 = T(z, x_2)$ and $t_1 + \delta = T(w, x_1)$. By transitivity, it follows that $(z, 0) \sim (x_1, t_1) \sim (x_2, t_2)$. Decreasing impatience implies $(x_1, t_1 + \delta) \prec (x_2, t_2 + \delta)$, that is, $(x_1, T(w, x_1)) \prec (x_2, T(z, x_2) + T(w, x_1) - T(z, x_1))$. Substituting $(x_1, T(w, x_1)) \sim (x_2, T(w, x_2))$, it yields

$$(x_2, T(w, x_2)) \prec (x_2, T(z, x_2) + T(w, x_1) - T(z, x_1)).$$

Comparing these two options with the same reward x_2, observe $T(w, x_2) > T(z, x_2) + T(w, x_1) - T(z, x_1)$, which means submodularity.

Assume the present bias and T is submodular. Choose arbitrary $t_1 \geq 0$, $\delta \geq 0$ and $x_2 > x_1 > 0$. Suppose $(x_1, t_1) \sim (x_2, t_2)$. We want to show $(x_1, t_1 + \delta) \prec (x_2, t_2 + \delta)$. Find $y < z \leq x_1$ such that $t_1 = T(z, x_1)$ and $\delta = T(y, z)$. By submodularity there exists $w < y$ such as $t_1 + \delta = T(w, x_1)$. Notice that $T(w, x_2) > T(w, y) + T(y, z) + T(z, x_2) > T(y, z) + T(z, x_2) = \delta + t_2$. Therefore,
$(x_1, t_1 + \delta) \sim (x_1, T(w, x_1)) \sim (x_2, T(w, x_2)) \prec (x_2, t_2 + \delta)$. □

Proof (Derivation of Remark 1) Let b denote the fixed cost of future rewards. b is zero if the reward is paid immediately.

First, it is straightforward that the representation of $V(x, t) = e^{-rt}u(x) - b$ result in $T(x_0, x_1) + T(x_1, x_2) < T(x_0, x_2)$ for any three rewards $x_0 < x_1 < x_2$. Notice that $u(x) = e^{-rT(x,y)}u(y) - b$ for a pair of rewards $x < y$ and apply this equation for the three combinations of x_0, x_1 and x_2. Eliminate $u(x_0)$ and $u(x_1)$ from those equations and observe $u(x_2)\left[e^{-r[T(x_0,x_1)+T(x_1,x_2)]} - e^{-rT(x_0,x_2)}\right] = b$. For any positive fixed cost $(b > 0)$, this means $T(x_0, x_1) + T(x_1, x_2) < T(x_0, x_2)$ and present bias.

Next, let us show that another representation of the fixed cost, $V(x, t) = e^{-rt}u(x - b)$, may also lead the present bias result. Consider $u(x_0) = V(x_1, T(x_0, x_1)) = V(x_2, T(x_0, x_2))$ and $u(x_1 - b) = V(x_2, T(x_1 - b, x_2))$. Altogether, they yield $T(x_0, x_1) + T(x_1 - b, x_2) = T(x_0, x_2)$. Notice that this equation implies $T(x_0, x_1) + T(x_1, x_2) < T(x_0, x_2)$, since $T(x_1 - b, x_2) > T(x_1, x_2)$ for $b > 0$. □

Instruction

Experimental Instruction — T/R

Instruction
You are about to participate in an economics experiment in which you will earn dollars as well as money orders based on the decisions you make. All earnings you make in the experiment are yours to keep. Please do not talk to each other during the experiment. If you have a question, please raise your hand and the experimenter will come and help you.

Overview

1. This experiment consists of two different parts and two parts of follow-up survey.
2. In the first part, you will be asked several questions about your timing preferences and will earn a money order. The amount of the money order depends on your answers.
3. In the second part, you will be offered several lotteries to choose from.
   If you win any, the cash reward will be paid to you at the end of this experiment.
4. Note that the two parts are completely independent of one another. That is, your choices and the earnings in one part do not affect those in the other part.
5. We will read the instruction for each part separately. First, we will read the instruction for the first part and you will complete the first task. Then, we will read the instruction for the second part and you will complete the second task. Finally, we will ask you to fill out some survey questions.
6. At the end of the experiment, each of you will be informed individually of your earnings for both parts, and you will then get paid.

Part 1: Delayed Payment Decision
In this part, we will pay you with a money order. The money order is issued by the US Postal Service and redeemable for the face value cash at any postal office. It may be also deposited to your bank account.

Task
You will answer a set of ten questions assuming the following situation:

> A money order of $A will be given to you at the end of experiment.
> Alternatively, if you are willing to wait, then instead of $A, we will mail you a money order for $B which is greater than $A, i.e., $B > $A. Consider the acceptable longest delay for which you would be willing to wait to receive the larger amount.

Then, the question asks you to fill out the blank below:

Q: To me, "receiving $A today" is equally as good as "receiving $B in ____ days."

You must wait to get the larger amount. Decide what length of delay makes the two options the same to you, and fill in that amount.

Note that “Receiving $B in **T** days”, it means you expect to receive the money order of $B by mail in **T** days. The actual amounts of $A and $B vary from question to question.

If you get $B money order, you will write your mailing address on a stamped envelope, sign the money order and seal it into the envelope. We will then mail the envelope later.

After each one of you answers all ten questions, the computer will randomly select one of the questions. Your actual payment will be based on your answer to the selected question.

Procedure

To determine which of $A or $B you get, the computer will randomly choose a number. It will be generated independently of your answers to the questions. This number will become the actual delay for $B, if you get $B. Call that the *proposed delay*.

If the proposed delay is longer than your longest acceptable delay, you will not get $B. Instead, you will get $A at the end of the experiment.

If the proposed delay is shorter than or equal to your longest acceptable delay, you will get $B. The proposed delay will be the actual delay. Thus, the $B money order will arrive at your mailing address right after the proposed delay.

Example: (For purposes of illustration, we replace days with weeks.)

Suppose that you were asked the following question.

Q: To me, “receiving $70 today” is equally as good as “receiving $100 in __ weeks.”

If your answer was 10 weeks, i.e.,

To me, “receiving $70 today” is equally as good as “receiving $100 in <u>10</u> weeks,” then, the computer randomly generates a number. If the number is greater than 10, e.g., if it is 14, then you do not get $100. Instead, you will get $70 today.

If the number is less than or equal to 10, then you will get $100. For example, suppose that the number generated is 8. In this case, you will get $100 in 8 weeks.

Any question?

Strategy:

Note that this procedure is such that your best response is to write down the longest delay for which you are willing to wait to get the larger amount, $B.

We now show that truthful reporting is your best strategy. We will illustrate why you will never be better off sending a false report. Let us work through one example. Say that we offer you two amounts $70 and $100 and ask you to choose a time, **T** that is such that you would be indifferent to waiting **T** weeks and receiving $100 as opposed to receiving $70 today. Let us just assume, for the sake of argument, that you would be indifferent between receiving $70 today and receiving $100 in <u>10</u> weeks. The question is should you tell us **T** = 10 when we ask you?

To see why the answer is yes, let us say that you are thinking of not telling us the truth. There are two possible cases, under-reporting or over-reporting. We will show that in either case you might be worse off compared to telling the truth.

1. Under-reporting can make you worse off.

By reporting any shorter delay than your actual acceptable delay, **T**, you can never be better off, and sometimes be worse off.

Suppose that you falsely answered by saying that your acceptable delay was only 6 weeks, even though your true acceptable delay was 10 weeks, i.e.,

To me, "receiving $70 today" is equally as good as "receiving $100 in _6_ weeks." The computer randomly chooses a number to propose a delay. Suppose that the number generated is between 6 and 10, say, it is 9. Since this proposed delay is longer than that you reported, i.e., $9 > 6$, you receive $70 today. But, the proposed delay is still shorter than your acceptable delay, and thus you would be willing to wait 9 weeks for $100. Receiving $70 today is worse than receiving $100 in 9 weeks. You lose the opportunity to get the better outcome by falsely reporting shorter delay.

Thus, under-reporting will never make you better off.

What about stating **T** greater than 10 weeks?

2. Over-reporting can make you worse off as well.

By reporting any longer delay than your actual acceptable delay, **T**, you may end up waiting too long.

Suppose that you falsely answered by saying that your acceptable delay was 14 weeks, even though your true acceptable delay was 10 weeks. That is,

To me, "receiving $70 today" is equally as good as "receiving $100 in _14_ weeks."

The computer randomly chooses a number to propose a delay. Suppose that the number generated is between 10 and 14, say, it is 13. Since the proposed delay is shorter than that you reported, i.e., $13 < 14$, you will get $100. But, the actual delay, 13 weeks, is longer than your acceptable delay. You end up waiting too long. Thus, you lose the opportunity to get the better outcome by falsely reporting a longer delay.

Thus, over-reporting will never make you better off.

In sum, your best strategy is always to answer the questions truthfully.

Any question?

[the next part starts in a new page in the original format]

Part 2: Lottery Choice

Your earnings in this part will be paid in cash at the end of this experiment.

Task You will answer a set of ten questions assuming the following situation:

You are given two options:

1. Receive \$Y for sure; or
2. Play a lottery for \$Z, where \$Z > \$Y, and your odds of winning the lottery are P%.

Consider the lowest acceptable odds of winning with which you would be willing to play the lottery.

In a series of questions, you will be asked to fill out the blank below:

Q: To me, "receiving \$Y for sure" is equally as good as "receiving \$Z with __ % chance."

You need to play a lottery to get the larger amount. Decide what odds of winning make the two options the same to you, and fill in that amount.

The actual amounts of \$Y and \$Z vary from question to question.

After each one of you answers all ten questions, the computer will select one of the questions at random. Your actual payment will be based on your answer to the selected question.

Payment
To determine your chance of winning the lottery, the computer will randomly choose a number between 0 and 100 %. Each of those numbers will be equally likely to be drawn, and the selected number will be the chance of winning.

If the chance of winning the lottery is less than your lowest acceptable odds of winning, you will not play the lottery. Instead, you will receive \$Y for sure.

If the chance of winning the lottery is greater than or equal to your lowest acceptable odds of winning, you will play the lottery. If you win the lottery, you will get \$Z; and if you lose, you will get nothing.

Example: (For purposes of illustration, we use different amounts than those actually given to you in the experiment.)
Suppose that you were asked the following question.

Q: To me, "receiving \$70 for sure" is equally as good as "receiving \$120 with __ % chance." '

Suppose your answer is 58 %, i.e.,

To me, "receiving \$70 for sure" is equally as good as "receiving \$120 with 58 % chance."
Then, the computer randomly generates a number between 0 and 100.

If the number is less than 58, e.g., if it is 23, then you do not get to play the lottery. Thus, you get \$70 for sure.

If the number is greater than or equal to 58, then you will play the lottery. For example, suppose that the number generated is 84. In this case, you will play a lottery for \$120 and your chance of winning is 84 %. If you win the lottery, you will get \$120; and if you lose the lottery you will get nothing.

Any question?

Strategy:
Note that this procedure is such that your best response is to write down the minimum odds with which you are willing to play a lottery for $Z.

We now show that truthful reporting is your best strategy. We will illustrate why you will never be better off sending a false report. Let us work through one example. Say that we offer you two amounts $70 and $120 and ask you to choose odds of a lottery, **P%**. Let us just assume, for the sake of argument, that you would be indifferent between receiving $70 for sure and receiving $120 with 58 % chance. The question is should you tell us **P** = 58 when we ask you?

To see why the answer is yes, let us say that you are thinking of not telling us the truth. There are two possible cases, under-reporting or over-reporting. We will show that in either case you might be worse off compared to telling the truth.

1. Under-reporting can make you worse off. By reporting any lower odds than your actual acceptable odds, you can never be better off, and sometimes be worse off.

Suppose that you falsely answered by saying that your acceptable odds were 43 %, even though your true acceptable odds were 58 %, i.e.,

To me, "receiving $70 for sure" is equally as good as "receiving $120 with _43_ % chance."

The computer randomly chooses a number between 0 and 100 % to determine the chance of winning the lottery. Suppose that the number generated is between 43 and 58, say, it is 51. Since the number generated is greater than that you reported, i.e., 51 > 43, you play the lottery and your odds of winning the lottery are 51 %. But, it is lower than your acceptable odds, and thus playing the lottery is worse than receiving $70 for sure. You end up playing a lottery with unacceptably low odds by falsely reporting lower odds.

Thus, under-reporting will never make you better off.

What about stating **P** greater than 58 %?

2. Over-reporting can make you worse off as well. By reporting any higher odds than your acceptable odds, you may lose the opportunity to play a lottery even if it is preferred to receiving $70 for sure.

Suppose that you falsely answered by saying that your acceptable odds were 77 %, even though your true acceptable odds were 58 %.

'To me, "receiving $70 for sure" is equally as good as "receiving $120 with _77_ % chance." '

The computer randomly chooses a number between 0 and 100 % to determine the chance of winning the lottery. Suppose that the number generated is between 58 and 77, say, it is 66. Since the number generated is smaller than that you reported, i.e., 66 < 77, you do not play the lottery and you receive $70 for sure. But, the chance of winning the lottery, 66 %, is greater than your acceptable odds. It means you still prefer playing the lottery to receiving $70 for sure. Thus, you lost the opportunity to get the better outcome by falsely reporting higher odds.

Thus, over-reporting will never make you better off.

In sum, your best strategy is always to answer the questions truthfully.

Any question?

Addendum: Further Analysis[38]

Summary

Takeuchi (2011) separates time preference and risk preference by characterizing the consistency of time preference independently of utility function. Many experiments have done in the literature to elicit time discount function D in the following equation.

$$u(y) = D(x, t) \cdot u(x),$$

where y is the present value of a future option that pays x at time t, D is the discount function, and u is the instantaneous utility function. Notice that almost all of the experiments adjust the level of x and y to find the present value of a future option and then accumulate observations so that those observations will reveal the property of D.

There is, however, a confounding factor. As far as we try to observe the property of D by alternating the level of payments, we cannot separate the variance of D from the variance of u.

Takeuchi (2011), therefore, invents a new elicitation method that adjusts timing t instead of the level of reward x. My idea successfully results in the theoretical characterization of time consistency solely based on timing (See the definitions and Proposition 1 in Sect. 2). Then, I test my theory in the experiment and observe not only present biases but also future biases.

Readers should notice that the test usually has to involve four different reward levels and the corresponding four equivalent delays in accordance with Proposition 1, while Fig. 4.1 of the paper compares only three reward levels and three equivalent delays for illustration purpose. If there is any sort of fixed cost to the equivalent delay, a test that consists of only three equivalent delays will have a bias toward future biases.

[38]This addendum has been newly written for this book chapter.

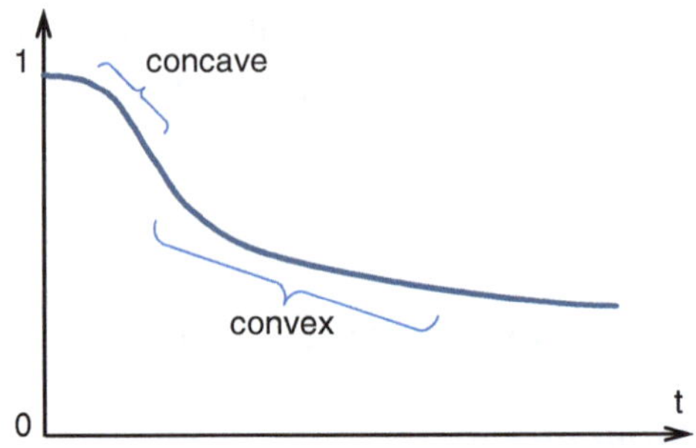

Fig. 4.10 The inverse S-shape time discount function. Future bias implies that the time discount function is concave

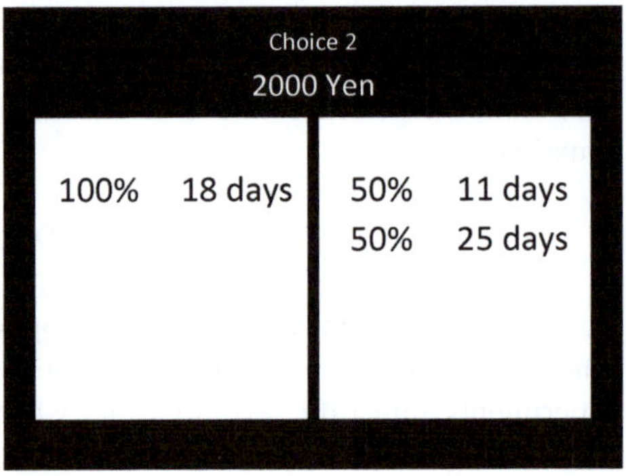

Fig. 4.11 Questionnaire sample screen shot (Translated from Japanese). If a decision maker chooses the left option (100 % 18 days), then it implies that his/her time discount function is concave around $t = 18$ and inverse S-shaped

The Follow-Up Experiment on S-Shape Discount Function

The result indicates that time discount function may be concave or inverse S-shape as shown in Fig. 4.10. Thus, I conduct another experiment to test the concavity of time discount function.

I invent another non-parametric test to check the convexity of time discount function in Takeuchi (2012). Figure 4.11 shows one of the simplest choice tasks in the experiment. The reward is fixed at 2,000 Japanese Yen (JPY), though the delay of the payment is uncertain. The decision-maker (DM) is given two options. When she or he chooses the left option, the DM receives 2,000 JPY in 18 days for sure. If the DM chooses the right option, then the delay will be determined whether it is 11 or 25 days on the given probability that is 50 %:50 % in this example. Notice that the expected length of the delay is identical to each other option, namely $18\text{days} = \frac{1}{2}(11 \text{ days} + 25 \text{ days})$.

When the DM chooses the left option over the right one, it implies that

$$D(x, 18)u(x) > 0.5D(x, 11)u(x) + 0.5D(x, 25)u(x)$$

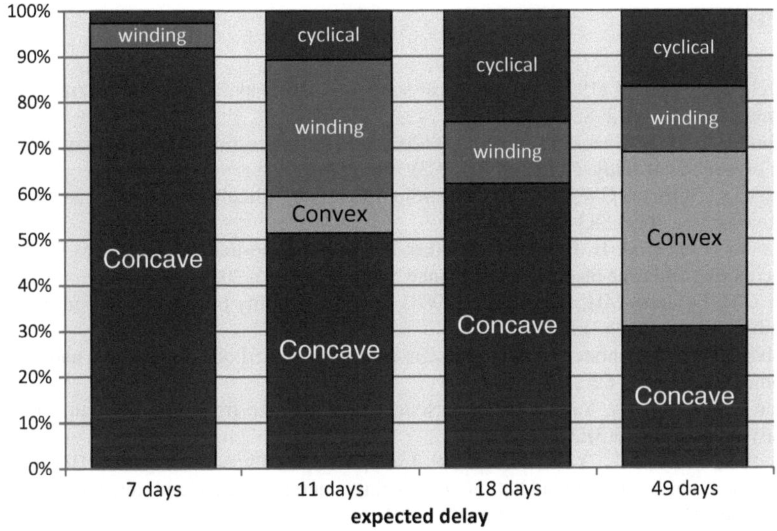

Fig. 4.12 The composition of responses for each group. The proportion of choices indicating concavity is decreasing in the expected delay. This pattern is consistent with the inverse S-shape time discount function

where $x = 2{,}000$ JPY. This inequality immediately implies the time discount function is concave around 18 regardless of the shape of u.[39]

If time discount function is inverse S-shape, the fraction of subjects who indicate concavity of their time preference is decreasing in the expected delay. The experiment result supports this hypothesis as shown in Fig. 4.12.

The inverse S-shaped time discount function fits this observation better than the standard convex time discount function. Most of the subjects reveal their concavity of time discounting around $t = 7$ days, which is consistent with the previous result that observed many of the subjects exhibited future bias around $t = 2$ weeks. Few of the subjects are Convex at questions where the expected delays are 7, 11 and 18 days, although one third of them are Convex when the expected delay is 49 days.

The result tells us that our time perception is not necessarily monotone. Time pasts slow around $t = 0$ probably because we feel that the very near future is part of the present. Then it runs fast and the discount function changes its shape from concave into convex. Again, it seems that time runs slow in far future since it is too far to feel the disutility of any additional delay. The concept of time flow is not solid but more elastic and flexible in our cognition.

[39]This simple example includes the for-sure option of (100 % 18 days) for illustration. For some other choice tasks, the assigned delay is uncertain for both of the left and the right options. For example, in another task, the DM is asked to choose either of the following options, (Left; 50 % 11 days; 50 % 25 days) and (Right; 75 % 11 days; 25 % 39 days). Note that the expected delay of these future options is 18 days.

References

Ahlbrecht M, Weber M (1997) An empirical study on intertemporal decision making under risk. Manag Sci 43(6):813–826

Anderhub V, Güth W, Gneezy U, Sonsino D (2001) On the interaction of risk and time preferences: An experimental study. Ger Econ Rev 2(3):239–253

Andersen S, Harrison GW, Lau MI, Rutström EE (2008) Eliciting risk and time preferences. Econometrica 76(3):583–618

Attema AE, Bleichrodt H, Rohde KI, Wakker PP (2010) Time-tradeoff sequences for analyzing discounting and time inconsistency. Manag Sci 56(11):2015–2030

Becker GM, DeGroot MH, Marschak J (1964) Measuring utility by a single-response sequential method. Behav Sci 9(3):226–232

Benhabib J, Bisin A, Schotter A (2010) Present-bias, quasi-hyperbolic discounting, and fixed costs. Games Econ Behav 69(2):205–223

Benzion U, Rapoport A, Yagil J (1989) Discount rates inferred from decisions: an experimental study. Manag Sci 35(3):270–284

Bickel WK, Miller ML, Yi R, Kowal BP, Lindquist DM, Pitcock JA (2007) Behavioral and neuroeconomics of drug addiction: competing neural systems and temporal discounting processes. Drug Alcohol Depend 90:S85–S91

Bohm P (1994) Time preference and preference reversal among experienced subjects: the effects of real payments. Econ J 104(427):1370–1378

Bohm P, Lindén J, Sonnegård J (1997) Eliciting reservation prices: becker-DeGroot-Marschak mechanisms vs. markets. Econ J 107:1079–1089

Bommier A (2006) Uncertain lifetime and intertemporal choice: risk aversion as a rationale for time discounting. Int Econ Rev 47:1223–1246

Bos JM, Postma MJ, Annemans L (2005) Discounting health effects in pharmacoeconomic evaluations: current controversies. Pharmacoecon 23:639–649

Cairns JA, van der Pol MM (1997) Constant and decreasing timing aversion for saving lives. Soc Sci Med 45(11):1653–1659

Cardinal RN (2006) Neural systems implicated in delayed and probabilistic reinforcement. Neural Netw 19:1277–1301

Chapman GB, Winquist JR (1998) The magnitude effect: temporal discount rates and restaurant tips. Psychon Bull Rev 5(1):119–123

Chapman GB, Nelson R, Hier DB (1999) Familiarity and time preferences: decision making about treatments for migraine headaches and Crhon's disease. J Exp Psychol Appl 5:17–34

Chesson H, Viscusi WK (2000) The heterogeneity of time-risk tradeoffs. J Behav Decis Mak 13(2):251–258

Coller M, Williams MB (1999) Eliciting individual discount rates. Exp Econ 2:107–127

Coller M, Harrison GW, Rutström EE (2012) Latent process heterogeneity in discounting behavior. Oxf Econ Pap 64(2):375–391

Dasgupta P, Maskin E (2005) Uncertainty and hyperbolic discounting. Am Econ Rev 94(4):1290–1299

Eckel C, Engle-Warnick J, Johnson C (2005) Adaptive elicitation of risk preference. Working paper

Fernández-Villaverde J, Mukherji A (2006) Can we really observe hyperbolic discouting? Working paper

Fischbacher U (2007) z-Tree: Zurich toolbox for ready-made economic experiments. Exp Econ 10(2):171–178

Frederick S, Loewenstein G, O'Donoghue T (2002) Time discounting and time preference: a critical review. J Econ Lit 40(2):351–401

Green L, Myerson J (1996) Exponential versus hyperbolic discounting of delayed outcomes: risk and wating time. Am Zool 36(4):496–505

Green L, Myerson J (2004) A discounting framework for choice with delayed and probabilistic rewards. Psychol Bull 130(5):769–792

Green L, Myerson J, McFadden E (1997) Rate of temporal discounting decreases with amount of reward. Mem Cogn 25(5):715–723
Halevy Y (2008) Strotz meets Allais: diminishing impatience and the certainty effect. Am Econ Rev 98(3):1145–1162
Harrison G, Lau MI, Williams MB (2002) Estimating individual discount rates in Denmark: a field experiment. Am Econ Rev 92:1606–1617
Harrison GW, Lau MI (2005) Is the evidence for hyperbolic discounting in humans just an experimental artefact? Behav Brain Sci 28:657
Harrison GW, Lau MI, Rutström EE, Sullivan MB (2005) Eliciting risk and time preferences using field experiments: some methodological issues. In: Carpenter J, Harrison GW, List JA (eds) Field experiments in economics. Research in experimental economics, vol 10. JAI Press, Greenwich, pp 125–218
Hershey JC, Schoemaker PJ (1985) Probability versus certainty equivalence methods in utility measurement: are they equivalent? Manag Sci 31(10):1213–1231
Hesketh B (2000) Time perspective in career-related choices: applications of time discounting principles. J Vocat Behav 57:62–84
Holcomb JH, Nelson PS (1992) Another experimental look at individual time preference. Ration Soc 4:199–220
Holden ST, Shiferaw B, Wik M (1998) Poverty, market imperfections and time preferences of relevance for environmental policy? Env Devel Econ 3:105–130
Holt CA, Laury SK (2002) Risk aversion and incentive effects. Am Econ Rev 92(5):1644–1655
Ida T, Goto R (2009) Simultaneous measurement of time and risk preferences: stated preference discrete choice modeling analysis depending on smoking behavior. Int Econ Rev 50(4):1169–1182
Kable JW, Glimcher PW (2007) The neural correlates of subjective value during intertemporal choice. Nat Neurosci 10:1625–1633
Keren G, Roelofsma P (1995) Immediacy and certainty in intertemporal choice. Org Behav Hum Decis Process 63(3):287–297
Kinari Y, Ohtake F, Tsutsui Y (2009) Time discounting: declining impatience and interval effect. J Risk Uncertain 39(1):87–112
Kirby KN (1997) Bidding on the future: evidence against normative discounting of delayed rewards. J Exp Psychol Gen 126(1):54–70
Kirby KN, Maraković NN (1995) Modeling myopic decisions: evidence for hyperbolic delay-discounting within subjects and amounts. Org Behav Hum Decis Process 64(1):22–30
Kirby KN, Santiesteban M (2003) Concave utility, transaction costs, and risk in measuring discounting of delayed rewards. J Exp Psychol Learn Mem Cogn 29(1):66–79
Kirby KN, Petry NM, Bickel W (1999) Heroin addicts have higher discount rates for delayed rewards than non-drug-using controls. J Exp Psychol Gen 128(1):78–87
Laibson D (1997) Golden eggs and hyperbolic discounting. Quart J Econ 112(2):443–477
Loewenstein G (1987) Anticipation and the valuation of delayed consumption. Econ J 97(387):666–684
Loewenstein G, Prelec D (1992) Anomalies in intertemporal choice: evidence and an interpretation. Q J Econ 107(2):573–597
Masatlioglu Y, Ok EA (2007) A theory of (relative) discounting. J Econ Theory 137(1):214–245
McClure SM, Ericson KM, Laibson DI, Loewenstein G, Cohen JD (2007) Time discounting for primary rewards. J Neurosci 27:5796–5804
Monterosso J, Ainslie G (1999) Beyond discounting: possible experimental models of impulse control. Psychopharmacology 146:339–347
Mudholkar GS, Srivastava DK, Kollia GD (1996) A generalization of the Weibull distribution and application to the analysis of survival data. J Am Stat Assoc 91:1575–1583
Noor J (2010) Time preference data and functional equations. Boston University, working paper
Ortendahl M, Fries JF (2006) Discounting and risk characteristics in clinical decision-making. Med Sci Monit 12:RA41–45
Petry NM (2001) Delay discounting of money and alcohol in activity using alcoholics, currently abstinent alcoholics, and controls. Psychopharmacology 154:243–250

Prelec D (2004) Decreasing impatience: a criterion for non-stationary time preference and "hyperbolic" discounting. Scand J Econ 106(3):511–532
Prelec D, Loewenstein G (1991) Decision making over time and under uncertainty: a common approach. Manag Sci 37(7):770–786
Rachlin H, Raineri A, Cross D (1991) Subjective probability and delay. J Exp Anal Behav 55(2):233–244
Read D (2001) Is time-discounting hyperbolic or subadditive? J Risk Uncertain 23(1):5–32
Reuben E, Sapienza P, Zingales L (2010) Time discounting for primary and monetary rewards. Econ Lett 106(2):125–127
Reynolds B (2006) A review of delay-discounting research with humans: relations to drug use and gambling. Behav Pharmacol 17:651–667
Reynolds B, Richards JB, Hornc K, Karraker K (2004) Delay discounting and probability discounting as related to cigarette smoking status in adults. Behav Process 65:35–42
Rubinstein A (2003) "Economics and psychology"? the case of hyperbolic discounting. Int Econ Rev 44(4):1207–1216
Rubinstein A (2006) Discussion of "behavioral economics". In: Blundell R, Newey WK, Persson T (eds) Advances in economics and econometrics. Econometric Society monographs, vol 42. Cambridge University Press, Cambridge, pp 246–257
Sayman S, Öncüler A (2009) An investigation of time-inconsistency. Manag Sci 55(3):470–482
Scholten M, Read D (2006) Discounting by intervals: a generalized model of intertemporal choice. Manag Sci 52(9):1424–1436
Stevenson MK (1986) A discounting model for decisions with delayed positive and negative outcomes. J Exp Psych 115:131–154
Takeuchi K (2011) Non-parametric test of time consistency: present bias and future bias. Games Econ Behav 71(2):456–478
Takeuchi K (2012) Time discounting: the concavity of time discount function: an experimental study. J Behav Econ Financ 5:2–9
Tanaka T, Camerer CF, Nguyen Q (2010) Risk and time preferences: linking experimental and household survey data from Vietnam. Am Econ Rev 100(1):557–571
Thaler R (1981) Some empirical evidence on dynamic inconsistency. Econ Lett 8:201–207
van der Pol M, Cairns J (2001) Estimating time preferences for health using discrete choice. Soc Sci Med 52:1459–1470
Wahlund R, Gunarsson J (1996) Mental discounting and financial strategies. J Econ Perspect 17(6):709–730
Warner JT, Pleeter S (2001) The personal discount rate: evidence from military downsizing programs. Am Econ Rev 91(1):33–53
Yaari ME (1965) Uncertain lifetime, life insurance, and the theory of the consumer. Rev Econ Stud 32:137–150

Chapter 5
Loss of Self-Control in Intertemporal Choice May Be Attributable to Logarithmic Time-Perception

Taiki Takahashi

Abstract Impulsivity and loss of self-control in drug-dependent patients have been associated with the manner in which they discount delayed rewards. Although drugs of abuse have been shown to modify perceived time duration, little is known regarding the relationship between impulsive decision-making in intertemporal choice and estimation of time-duration. In classical economic theory, it has been hypothesized that people discount future reward value exponentially. In exponential discounting, a temporal discounting rate is constant over time, which has been referred to as dynamic consistency. However, accumulating empirical evidence in biology, psychopharmacology, behavioral neuroscience, and neuroeconomics does not support the hypothesis. Rather, dynamically inconsistent manners of discounting delayed rewards, e.g., hyperbolic discounting, have been repeatedly observed in humans and non-human animals. In spite of recent advances in neuroimaging and neuropsychopharmacological study, the reason why humans and animals discount delayed rewards hyperbolically is unknown. In this study, we hypothesized that empirically-observed dynamical inconsistency in intertemporal choice may result from errors in the perception of time duration. It is proposed that perception of temporal duration following Weber's law might explain the dynamical inconsistency. Possible future study directions for elucidating neural mechanisms underlying inconsistent intertemporal choice are discussed.

Keywords Intertemporal choice • Time perception • Neuroeconomics • Dopamine • Psychophysics

---

The original article first appeared in Medical Hypotheses 65(4):691–693, 2005. A newly written addendum has been added to this book chapter.

T. Takahashi (✉)
Department of Behavioral Science, Hokkaido University, N10 W7, Kita-ku, Sapporo 060-0810, Japan
e-mail: ttakahashi@lynx.let.hokudai.ac.jp

S. Ikeda et al. (eds.), *Behavioral Economics of Preferences, Choices, and Happiness*, DOI 10.1007/978-4-431-55402-8_5

1 Background

Discounting of delayed rewards refers to the observation that the value of a delayed reward is discounted (reduced in value or considered to be worth less) compared to the value of an immediate reward (Bickel and Marsch 2001; Frederick et al. 2002). Studies in psychopharmacology, psychiatry, behavioral neuroscience, and economics have been focused on how subjects discount delayed rewards. Notably, it has repeatedly been demonstrated that substance abusers more steeply discount delayed rewards than non-drug dependent subjects (Bickel and Marsch 2001).

According to classical economic theory, including a rational addiction theory, it has been assumed that individuals discount delayed reward in a rational manner (Frederick et al. 2002). This type of discounting (exponential discounting) follows the exponential equation:

$$V(D) = A \exp(-kD), \tag{5.1}$$

where V is the subjective value of a reward, A is the (objective) amount of the reward, and D is the length of delay until the delivery of reward. The free parameter k is an index of the degree of discounting, i.e., larger k values correspond to steeper delay discounting. However, subsequent empirical studies have revealed that the following (general) hyperbolic equation fits the behavioral data better than Eq. 5.1 (Bickel and Marsch 2001; Frederick et al. 2002):

$$V(D) = A/(1 + jD)^s, \tag{5.2}$$

where j and s are free parameters. Note that when $s = 1$, the function is referred to as a simple hyperbolic equation. Discounting delayed rewards following this hyperbolic equation is called "hyperbolic discounting". Larger j and s values again correspond to steeper delay discounting. A remarkable distinction between the exponential and hyperbolic discounting exists in the time-course of a discounting rate, defined as $(\mathrm{d}V/\mathrm{d}D)/V$ (Frederick et al. 2002). Specifically, in hyperbolic discounting, the discounting rate is a decreasing function of delay, resulting in "preference reversal", which is an example of dynamically inconsistent behavior and loss of self-control (commonly observed in drug addicts) (Bickel and Marsch 2001); while in exponential discounting, the discounting rate is independent of delay and keeps constant, which is called dynamical consistency (Bickel and Marsch 2001; Frederick et al. 2002).

Recently, in the emerging field of neuroeconomics (Glimcher and Rustichini 2004), how neural substrates mediate discounting of delayed rewards attracts much attention. For instance, dopaminergic reward-processing brain regions, orbitofrontal and limbic regions play pivotal roles in delay discounting (Fellows 2004; Winstanley et al. 2004).

We have also examined a neuroendocrine correlate of delay discounting (Takahashi 2004). However, in spite of extensive neuropsychopharmacological and neuroimaging studies, it is still unknown why individuals discount delayed rewards hyperbolically, rather than exponentially (Fellows 2004). In this chapter, we propose that the empirically-observed inconsistency in discounting may result from errors in the estimation of time-duration.

2 Hypothesis

The psychophysicists Weber and Fechner proposed that the external stimulus (e.g., loudness) is scaled into a logarithmic internal representation of sensation (Weber's law), rather than a linear internal representation (Dehaene 2003). Some recent studies further suggest that the mental timer also seems to be logarithmic, rather than linear, following Weber's law (Okamoto and Fukai 2001; Grondin 2001), although it is still controversial whether time estimation is processed in distributed neural networks or in central time-keeping neural circuitry (Grondin 2001). Therefore, it is reasonable to suppose that discounting of delayed rewards with logarithmic time-perception differs from that with linear time-perception. Let τ be logarithmically perceived (subjective) time-duration which can be represented as:

$$\tau(D) = \alpha \ln(1 + \beta D), \tag{5.3}$$

where α and β denote constants independent of D and τ. Note that $\tau(0) = 0$ and τ is no less than 0. Suppose that individuals *try* to discount delayed rewards exponentially, with this type of logarithmic time-perception. In this case, D in Eq. 5.1 is replaced with τ. Then, exponential discounting with Weber-type time-perception follows the exponential function with τ:

$$V = A \exp(-k\tau). \tag{5.1'}$$

If this equation is expressed in terms of D,

$$\begin{aligned} V(D) &= A \exp\{-k\alpha \ln(1 + \beta D)\} \quad \text{(from Eq. 5.3)} \\ &= A \exp\left\{-\ln(1 + \beta D)^{k\alpha}\right\} \\ &= \frac{A}{(1 + \beta D)^{k\alpha}}. \end{aligned} \tag{5.4}$$

Here, if we denote $j = \beta$ and $s = k\alpha$, Eq. 5.4 (exponential discounting with logarithmic time-perception) is the same as Eq. 5.2 (the general hyperbolic function). As can be seen from the derivation of this equation, even if subjects with logarithmic time-perception try to discount delayed rewards exponentially (i.e., in a dynamically consistent manner), rather than hyperbolically, their actual discounting of delayed rewards may follow the hyperbolic function, possibly due to an error in time-perception which follows Weber's law.

3 Several Neuropsychopharmacological Findings Supporting Our Hypothesis

Neuropsychopharmacological studies have revealed that both acute and chronic administration of dopaminergic drugs (e.g., alcohol, heroin, and nicotine) dramatically affect individual's degree of discounting delayed rewards (Bickel and Marsch 2001). For instance, parameters of hyperbolic discounting (e.g., β in Eq. 5.4) have been shown to be increased in drug addicts, which is supposed to associate with their impulsive decision-making in intertemporal choice and loss of self-control (Bickel and Marsch 2001; Petry 2001; Mitchell 1999; Kirby et al. 1999; Reynolds et al. 2004). Interestingly, it has been reported that dopaminergic drugs also markedly affect subject's time-perception (Rammsayer 1993, 1997; Odum and Ward 2004). Together, it is possible that dopaminergic drugs modulate neural processing underlying time-perception and increase non-linearity of time-perception, resulting in exaggerated inconsistency in discounting and loss of self-control.

4 Conclusions

Relations between non-linearity of time-perception and subject's parameters in discounting equations should be empirically investigated in future studies, in order to test our hypothesis. Studies employing substance abusers and administrations of dopaminergic drugs would be especially important.

Acknowledgements The research reported in this chapter was supported by a grant from the Grant-in-Aid for Scientific Research ("21st century center of excellence" grant and grant #17650074) from the Ministry of Education, Culture, Sports, Science and Technology of Japan and Yamaguchi endocrinological disorder grant.

Addendum: Recent Developments[1]

Recent progress in studies on intertemporal choice witnessed a dramatic shift of research focus from the role of valuation (i.e., utility functions) to temporal cognition. Since Takahashi (2005) proposed that "hyperbolic" discounting (one of

[1]This addendum has been newly written for this book chapter.

the most widely-known anomalies in intertemporal choice) may be attributable to nonlinear time perception during intertemporal decision making, much evidence which confirms the idea of the nonlinear time perception theory of hyperbolic discounting has accumulated (Takahashi et al. 2008; Zauberman et al. 2009; Han and Takahashi 2012). Notably, Han and Takahashi (2012) demonstrated that hyperbolicity (i.e., decreasing impatience) is better explained by nonlinearity of psychological time than concavity of utility functions, rejecting the well-known Loewenstein-Prelec theory (1992) of hyperbolic discounting.

In addition to hyperbolic discounting, other prominent anomalies in intertemporal choice may be explained by the psychophysical characteristics of psychological time (Takahashi and Han 2012), which is proposed as "tempospect" theory of intertemporal choice. For instance, the sign effect (i.e., gain is more rapidly time-discounted than loss) is due to gain-loss asymmetry in psychological time (i.e., psychological time in waiting delayed gain is longer than that in waiting delayed loss) (Takahashi and Han 2012). Other anomalies in intertemporal choice (e.g., delay-speed up asymmetry, magnitude effect, and domain effect) can also be accounted for by the characteristics of psychological time (the subjective time-interval during intertemporal decision making) (see Takahashi and Han 2012, for details).

Neurobiologically, dopamine D2 receptors, known to be associated with temporal cognition, strongly modulates temporal discounting (Kawamura et al. 2013a). This finding is consistent with our tempospect theory of intertemporal choice. Furthermore, FKBP5 gene (a "suicide gene", related to glucocorticoid stress hormone receptor functioning) polymorphism was shown to modulate temporal discounting (Kawamura et al. 2013b). This is the first neurogenetic evidence of our neuroeconomic theory of suicide (Takahashi 2011).

In addition to anomalies in intertemporal choice, those in decision under risk may also be explained by the nonlinearity of psychological time in repeated gambles (Takahashi 2011; Takahashi et al. 2012). This theory was also confirmed by our recent experiment (Takahashi and Han 2013). Taken together, various anomalies in economic decision can be accounted for by psychophysical characteristics of psychological time.

References

Bickel WK, Marsch LA (2001) Toward a behavioral economic understanding of drug dependence: delay discounting processes. Addiction 96(1):73–86

Dehaene S (2003) The neural basis of the Weber-Fechner law: a logarithmic mental number line. Trends Cogn Sci 7(4):145–147

Fellows LK (2004) The cognitive neuroscience of human decision making: a review and conceptual framework. Behav Cogn Neurosci Rev 3(3):159–172

Frederick S, Loewenstein G, O'Donoghue T (2002) Time discounting and timepreference: a critical review. J Econ Lit 40(2):351–401

Glimcher PW, Rustichini A (2004) Neuroeconomics: the consilience of brain and decision. Science 306(5695):447–452

Grondin S (2001) From physical time to the first and second moments of psychological time. Psychol Bull 127(1):22–44

Han R, Takahashi T (2012) Psychophysics of time perception and valuation in temporal discounting of gain and loss. Phys A Stat Mech Appl 391(24):6568–6576

Kawamura Y, Takahashi T, Liu X, Nishida N, Noda Y, Yoshikawa A et al (2013a) Variation in the DRD2 gene affects impulsivity in intertemporal choice. Open J Psychiatry 3(1):26–31

Kawamura Y, Takahashi T, Liu X, Nishida N, Tokunaga K, Umekage T et al (2013b) DNA polymorphism in the FKBP5 gene affects impulsivity in intertemporal choice. Asia Pac Psychiatry 5(1):31–38

Kirby KN, Petry NM, Bickel WK (1999) Heroin addicts have higher discount rates for delayed rewards then non-drug-using controls. J Exp Psychol Gen 128(1):78–87

Mitchell SH (1999) Measures of impulsivity in cigarette smokers and non-smokers. Psychopharmacology 146(4):455–464

Odum AL, Ward RD (2004) The effects of morphine on the production and discrimination of interresponse times. J Exp Anal Behav 82(2):197–212

Okamoto H, Fukai T (2001) Neural mechanism for a cognitive timer. Phys Rev Lett 86(17):3919–3922

Petry NM (2001) Delay discounting of money and alcohol in actively using alcoholics, currently abstinent alcoholics, and controls. Psychopharmacology 154(3):243–250

Rammsayer TH (1993) On dopaminergic modulation of temporal information processing. Biol Psychol 36(3):209–222

Rammsayer TH (1997) Are there dissociable roles of the mesostriatal and mesolimbocortical dopamine systems on temporal information processing in humans? Neuropsychobiology 35(1):36–45

Reynolds B, Richards JB, Horn K, Karraker K (2004) Delay discounting and probability discounting as related to cigarette smoking status in adults. Behav Process 65(1):35–42

Takahashi T (2004) Cortisol levels and time-discounting of monetary gain in humans. Neuroreport 15(13):2145–2147

Takahashi T (2005) Loss of self-control in intertemporal choice may be attributable to logarithmic time-perception. Med Hypotheses 65(4):691–693

Takahashi T (2011) Psychophysics of the probability weighting function. Phys A Stat Mech Appl 390(5):902–905

Takahashi T, Han R (2012) Tempospect theory of intertemporal choice. Psychology 3(8):2152–7180

Takahashi T, Han R (2013) Psychophysical neuroeconomics of decision making: nonlinear time perception commonly explains anomalies in temporal and probability discounting. Appl Math 4(11):1520–1525

Takahashi T, Oono H, Radford MHB (2008) Psychophysics of time perception and intertemporal choice models. Phys A Stat Mech Appl 387(8):2066–2074

Takahashi T, Han R, Nakamura F (2012) Time discounting: psychophysics of intertemporal and probabilistic choices. J Behav Econ Financ 5:10–14

Winstanley CA, Theobald DEH, Cardinal RN, Robbins TW (2004) Contrasting roles of basolateral amygdala and orbitofrontal cortex in impulsive choice. J Neurosci 24(20):4718–4722

Zauberman G, Kim BK, Malkoc SA, Bettman JR (2009) Discounting time and time discounting: Subjective time perception and intertemporal preferences. J Mark Res 46(4):543–556

Chapter 6
Experiments on Risk Attitude: The Case of Chinese Students

Shunichiro Sasaki, Shiyu Xie, Fumio Ohtake, Jie Qin, and Yoshiro Tsutsui

Abstract This chapter examines Chinese students' risk attitudes using selling and buying experiments with lotteries. We found that subjects were more risk averse during the buying experiment than during the selling experiment, suggesting an endowment effect. In the selling experiment, subjects were risk loving when there was a low win probability and risk averse with a high win probability, whereas they were risk averse in the buying experiment. Using the prize money won during the experiment as a measure of wealth, we found decreasing absolute risk aversion. Subjects' risk attitudes as revealed in the experiments explain their risky asset holding behavior.

The original article first appeared in China Economic Review 19:245–259, 2008. A newly written addendum has been added to this book chapter.

S. Sasaki
Faculty of Economics, Kindai University, 3-4-1 Kowakae, Higashiosaka, Osaka 577-8502, Japan
e-mail: ssasaki@kindai.ac.jp

S. Xie
Department of World Economics, Fudan University, 220 Handan Road, Shanghai 200433, P. R. China
e-mail: syxie@fudan.edu.cn

F. Ohtake
Institute of Social and Economic Research, Osaka University, 6-1 Mihogaoka, Ibaraki, Osaka 567-0047, Japan
e-mail: ohtake@iser.osaka-u.ac.jp

J. Qin
Faculty of Economics, Ritsumeikan University, 1-1-1 Noji-higashi, Kusatsu, Shiga 525-8577, Japan
e-mail: jieqinjp@yahoo.co.jp

Y. Tsutsui (✉)
Faculty of Economics, Konan University, 8-9-1 Okamoto, Higashinada-ku, Kobe 658-8501, Japan
e-mail: tsutsui@center.konan-u.ac.jp

S. Ikeda et al. (eds.), *Behavioral Economics of Preferences, Choices, and Happiness*, DOI 10.1007/978-4-431-55402-8_6

Keywords Risk aversion • Economic experiment • China

JEL Classification C91, D81

1 Introduction

This chapter examines Chinese students' risk attitudes by using selling and buying experiments with lotteries, based on the BDM method (Becker et al. 1964). Experiments in China are especially interesting, in that prizes won by subjects are relatively large compared to those in developed countries because of the high purchasing power of the Chinese yuan. It is often argued that economic experiments are not reliable because prizes are too small to give subjects an adequate incentive. Experiments in China might be immune to such criticism.[1] Indeed, the cost of living in 2005 was 6.5 times lower for our Chinese subjects than for Japanese subjects, after the exchange rate conversion.[2] Nevertheless, to our knowledge, there have been few such experiments carried out in China.[3]

Our experiment is unique, in that we conducted both the selling and buying experiments with the same subjects. Previous studies conducted the selling experiments (Eichberger et al. 2003; Kachelmeier and Shehata 1992) and the buying experiments (Cramer et al. 2002; Hartog et al. 2002; Shavit et al. 2001) separately. However, to our knowledge, no studies have examined both the selling and the buying experiments, comprehensively.[4] Comparing the results of previous studies based on the selling and buying experiments, one could argue that subjects participating in the buying experiment were more risk averse than those in the selling experiment. However, it is not convincing to draw the conclusion that people are more risk averse when they buy lottery tickets than when they sell them, as the difference may be due to a difference in subject characteristics. Thus, it is important to conduct an experiment where the same subjects participate in both the selling and the buying experiments.

Our study was also unique, in that we asked the subjects to answer a detailed questionnaire that included scenario questions on risk attitude. We analyzed how risk attitudes were related to their demographic and economic attributes, such

[1]Another response to this criticism is to use the results of TV shows that pay huge prizes. Fullenkamp et al. (2003) and Beetsma and Schotman (2001) reported that people are risk averse, while Metrick (1995) does not reject the proposition that they are risk neutral.

[2]This figure is based on responses to our questionnaire from subjects of the experiment done in Shanghai and Tokyo. We asked about the cost of living per month.

[3]Kachelmeier and Shehata (1992) is a notable exception. They paid Chinese students monetary rewards three times their monthly revenue.

[4]Knetsch and Sinden (1984) is a notable exception. Their TEST3 consisted of selling and buying experiments which ask similar questions to ours. However, they are different from ours, in that different subjects are used for the selling and buying experiments.

as knowledge of financial economics and wealth. Although Barsky et al. (1997), Donkers et al. (2001), and Hartog et al. (2002) examined these relationships using questionnaire surveys, our method has merit in that we measured risk attitude in a controlled experiment where subjects had monetary incentives. We examined whether subjects' risk attitudes can explain their risky asset holdings. We also investigated whether subjects' risk attitudes, as revealed in the experiments, were consistent with those in the questionnaire. Finally, we examined how subjects' risk aversion correlated with their time discount rates, which was measured in our experiment.

The rest of the chapter is organized as follows. In the next section, we explain our experimental method. In Sect. 3, we show the risk attitude according to the probability of winning a lottery and compare the results with those of Kachelmeier and Shehata (1992). In Sect. 4, we investigate how risk attitude relates to the attributes of the subjects. In Sect. 5, we analyze whether subjects' risk attitudes can account for their actual behaviors. In Sect. 6, we compare the risk attitude revealed in the experiment and in the questionnaire. In Sect. 7, we examine the relationship between time discount rate and risk aversion. Section 8 concludes our findings.

2 Experimental Method

The experiment was conducted on March 11, 2005, at Fudan University in Shanghai. Subjects were 30 undergraduate students of the Department of World Economics at Fudan University.[5] Their attributes are summarized in Table 6.1. Out of 30 subjects, 26 (86 %) were female. The subjects were 20 or 21 years old. Their income and wealth was widely dispersed; household incomes ranged from less than 20,000 yuan (US$2,400) to over 220,000 yuan (US$26,400) and the mode was 20,000 (US$2,400) to 40,000 yuan (US$4,800).

The experiment on risk attitude started at 6 pm and ended around 8 pm. An experiment on time discounting was conducted until 9 pm. The subjects were then requested to complete a test on financial economics and fill in a questionnaire. The session finished around 10 pm.[6]

The experiment was based on the BDM method as follows.

[5]One subject felt unwell and left after the selling experiment was completed, so the number of the subjects for the buying experiment was 29.

[6]According to teachers and students at Fudan University, the students there study until around 10 pm every day, so the evening experiment was not a burden to them. We conducted the experiment in the evening, because it was difficult to recruit students during the daytime, as they were expected to attend classes.

Table 6.1 Attributes of the subjects

		Frequency	Ratio			Frequency	Ratio
Gender	Male	4	0.13	Age	20	14	0.47
	Female	26	0.86		21	13	0.43
	None	2	0.07		NA	3	0.1
Own annual income	<1,000	1	0.03	Household's real estate	<100,000	3	0.1
	1,000-2,000	3	0.1		100,000–200,000	4	0.13
	2,000–4,000	1	0.03		200,000–400,000	3	0.1
	4,000–6,000	3	0.1		400,000–600,000	5	0.17
	6,000–8,000	3	0.1		600,000–800,000	2	0.07
	8,000–10,000	2	0.07		800,000–1,000,000	2	0.07
	10,000–12,000	2	0.07		1,000,000–1,200,000	3	0.1
	12,000–14,000	3	0.1		1,200,000–1,400,000	1	0.03
	14,000–16,000	3	0.1		1,400,000–1,600,000	0	0
	>16,000	1	0.03		>1,600,000	1	0.03
	NA	6	0.2		NA	6	0.2

Household's annual income	<20,000	2	0.07	Household's financial assets	<20,000	4	0.13
	20,000–40,000	8	0.27		20,000–40,000	2	0.07
	40,000–60,000	3	0.1		40,000–60,000	2	0.07
	60,000–80,000	3	0.1		60,000–80,000	0	0
	80,000–100,000	2	0.07		80,000–100,000	0	0
	100,000–120,000	0	0		100,000–120,000	8	0.27
	120,000–140,000	0	0		120,000–140,000	0	0
	140,000–160,000	1	0.03		140,000–160,000	1	0.03
	160,000–180,000	0	0		160,000–180,000	0	0
	180,000–200,000	0	0		180,000–200,000	0	0
	200,000–220,000	1	0.03		200,000–220,000	2	0.07
	>220,000	3	0.1		>220,000	0	0
	NA	7	0.23		NA	11	0.37

Note: Income and assets are in yuan. Own annual income includes spouse's income and support by parents. Household income/assets include own income/assets and those of parents

2.1 The Selling Experiment

In each round of the selling experiment, subjects were given a lottery ticket, by which they receive 1,000 points if they win and nothing otherwise. The computer randomly chose the win probability of the lottery ticket from 0 to 100 % and showed it to the subjects. After confirming the win probability, subjects put their selling price into the computer. Then the computer drew the buying price randomly from a uniform distribution in a range from 0 to 1,000 points. If the buying price exceeded the selling price, the lottery ticket was traded at the buying price. Otherwise, subjects retained their tickets and they proceeded to the lottery stage. In the lottery stage, the computer determined win or lose status on the basis of the win probability. Subjects who won got 1,000 points. Subjects who lost received nothing. After each round, points obtained by the trade or the lottery appeared on the display and subjects wrote it down on the record sheet in order to check the results and to have time to consider their strategies. The entire procedure of the experiment above was explained using a written instruction, and whether or not the subjects fully understood the procedure was confirmed with a couple of questions. Then, five rounds were tried by the subjects for practice. Six staff served to answer questions raised by the subjects. Finally, 20 rounds were conducted. At the end of the real session, the cumulative total points obtained were converted to yuan, with 1,000 points being equal to 20 yuan (US$2.4); that amount was paid at the end of all experiments on that day as the prize for the selling experiment.

2.2 The Buying Experiment

The buying experiment was the same as the selling experiment, with the following exception. Subjects were given 10,000 points at the outset.[7] They input their buying price (the highest value that they could offer) for a lottery ticket for which the win probability was shown on their own display. If this buying price exceeded the selling price offered by the computer, the ticket was traded to the subject at the selling price. In this case, if they won, the payoff was 1,000 points minus the selling price; if they lost, they suffered a loss equal to the selling price.

Points won by subjects and their converted payoffs in yuan are presented in Table 6.2. The average payoff was 261 yuan (US$31, 13,033points) for the selling experiment and 260 yuan (US$31, 12,977 points) for the buying experiment.[8]

[7]This is necessary because in the selling experiment, subjects were given 20 lottery tickets with the expected payoff of 10,000 points. Furthermore, subjects would have been too embarrassed to buy a lottery ticket if they had no points at the outset.

[8]In addition to payoffs, subjects received a 120 yuan (US$14) participation fee.

Table 6.2 Points and payoffs won by the subjects

		Number of subjects	Average	Standard deviation	Minimum	Maximum
Selling experiment	Points	30	13,033	1,564	10,183	16,699
	Payoffs in yuan	30	261	31	204	334
Buying experiment	Points	29	12,997	1,148	10,804	15,786
	Payoffs in yuan	29	260	23	217	316
Total	Points	30	25,597	2,983	12,812	29,282
	Payoffs in yuan	30	512	60	257	586

Note: Points won in the buying experiment include 10,000 points given to the subjects at the outset of the buying experiment. In addition to the payoffs above, each subject was given 120 yuan as the participation fee

3 Risk Attitudes in the Selling and Buying Experiment

We adopted the following measure of absolute risk aversion (*ARA*), developed by Cramer et al. (2002):

$$ARA = \frac{aZ - p}{1/2 \times (aZ^2 - 2apZ + p^2)},$$

where Z is the lottery prize, p is the price evaluated by a subject, and a is the win probability. We also present the result of the "transformed risk averse price (*TP*)," defined as:

$$TP = 1 - \frac{p}{aZ}.$$

To compare our results with those in Kachelmeier and Shehata (1992), we calculated the average *ARA* and *TP* for each category of win probability, 0–10 %, 10–20 %, and so on. The results are presented in Figs. 6.1, 6.2, 6.3, and 6.4, where the horizontal axis represents the win probability. Note also that the bold line represents the mean of *ARA* or *TP* and the thin lines represent its upper and lower limits of the 95 % confidence interval for each win probability.

Figure 6.1 shows the *TP* for the selling experiment, which corresponds to Figs. 6.1 and 6.2 in Kachelmeier and Shehata (1992).[9] These figures appear superficially similar. The subjects were risk loving in lotteries with win probabilities of less than 20 %, and almost risk neutral in the others. Close examination, however, reveals a difference. As Fig. 6.1 in our chapter shows, subjects were risk averse in the lotteries with win probabilities over 30 %, at the 5 % significance level, whereas Kachelmeier and Shehata (1992) reported that the subjects were, at most, risk

[9]Note that Kachelmeier and Shehata (1992) show the certainty-equivalent ratio, which is equivalent to 1-*TP*.

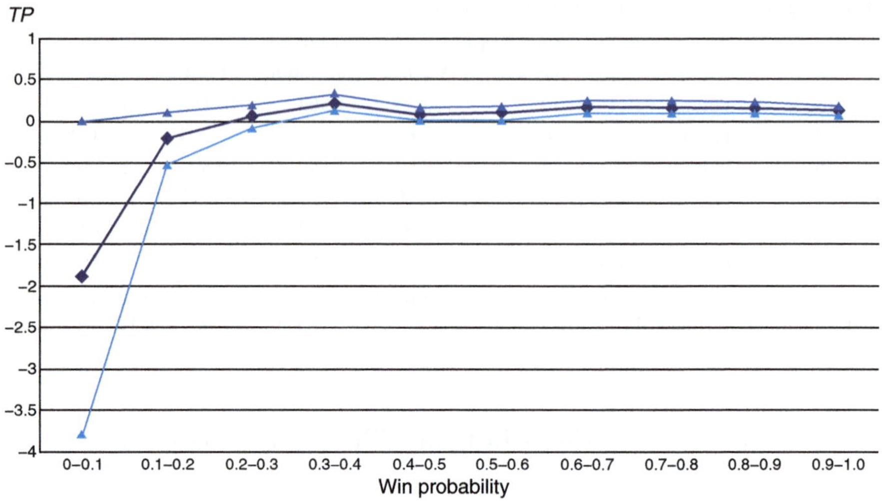

Fig. 6.1 *TP* by win probability: selling experiment. Note: —▲— indicates 95 % confidence interval

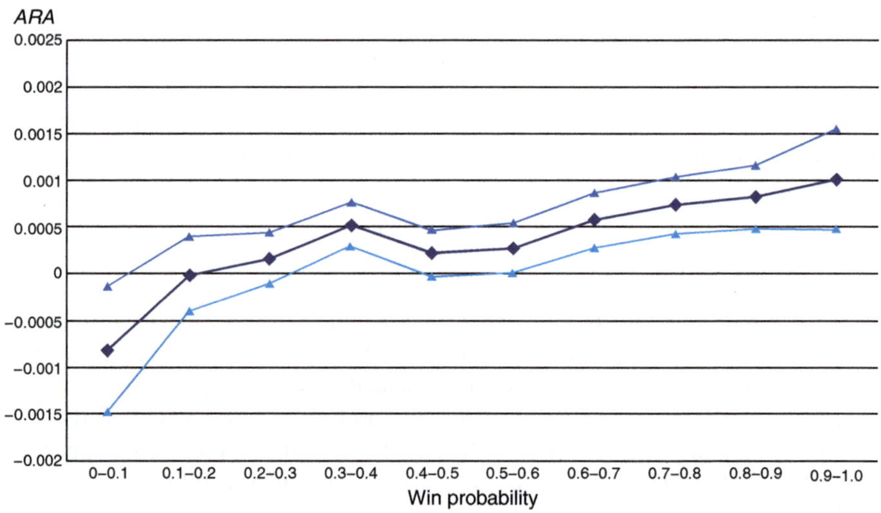

Fig. 6.2 *ARA* by win probability: selling experiment. Note: —▲— indicates 95 % confidence interval

neutral.[10] Kachelmeier and Shehata's result was important because subjects facing very high rewards in the experiment were risk loving or neutral, implying that these characteristics did not appear just because they were gambling for smaller amounts of money. Indeed, they show that the subjects were risk loving in lotteries with

[10]They do not show the confidence interval, so we cannot evaluate the significance of their results.

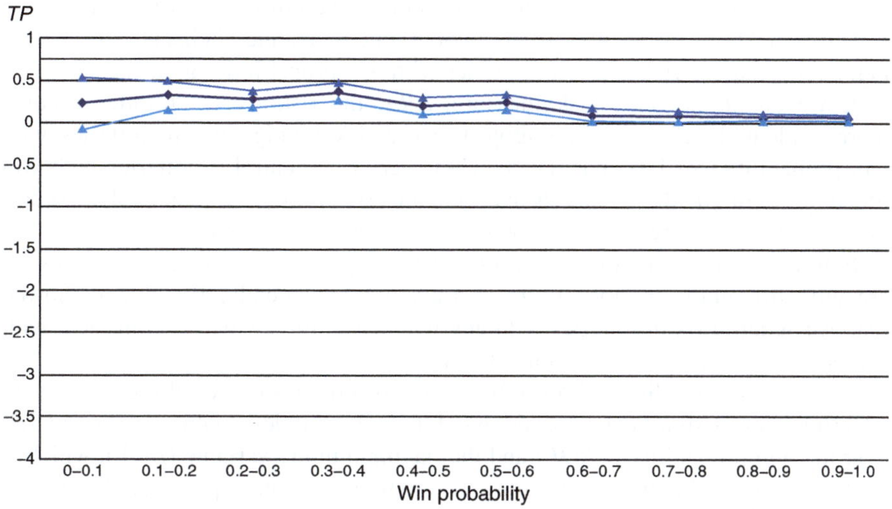

Fig. 6.3 *TP* by win probability: buying experiment. Note: —▲— indicates 95 % confidence interval

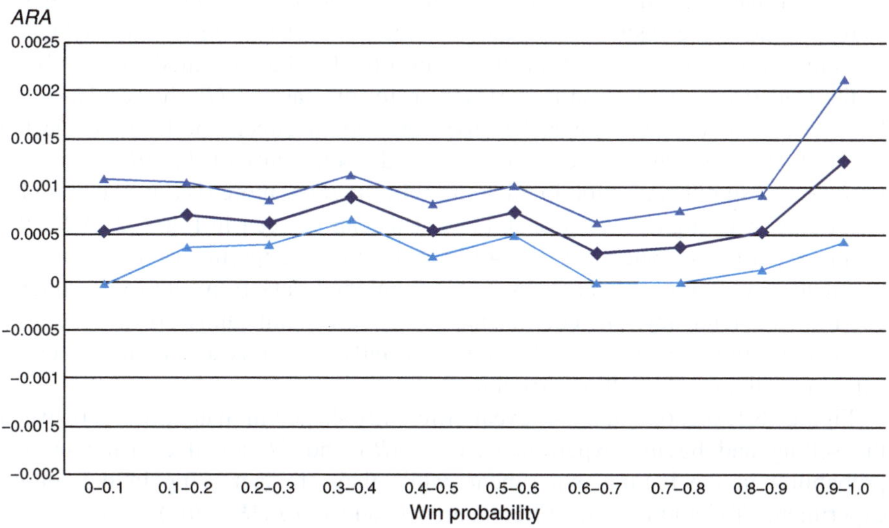

Fig. 6.4 *ARA* by probability: buying experiment. Note: —▲— indicates 95 % confidence interval

small prizes, but risk neutral in lotteries with large prizes, implying that the subjects became more risk averse as prizes became larger. If subjects' risk attitudes vary depending on the amount of prizes, as they observed, it would be possible to interpret our results as meaning that our subjects show a risk-averse attitude because the prize was very large. The average prize won by the subjects was 632 yuan (US$76), while they reported that their average monthly living expenses were 2,048 yuan

(US\$246); subjects therefore earned, on average, one third of their monthly living expenses in 2 h.[11] Our results cast doubt on Kachelmeier and Shehata (1992)'s finding: people may be risk averse in lotteries with win probabilities greater than 30 %.

If we adopt the other risk measure, *ARA*, the risk-averse attitudes become more evident. In Fig. 6.2, the subjects were risk loving only in lotteries with win probabilities of less than 10 %. They were risk neutral in lotteries with win probabilities of 10–50 %, and risk averse in those over 60 %.[12] Specifically, it seems that they became more risk averse with higher win probabilities.

Figures 6.3 and 6.4 show the results of the buying experiment.[13] These results are quite different from those in Figs. 6.1 and 6.2. Specifically, the subjects showed risk-averse attitudes in lotteries with any win probability, which is consistent with the usual assumptions of economic theory.

To check whether the difference between risk attitudes in the selling and buying experiments was significant, we regressed the risk attitude variables (*ARA* and *TP*) over the win probability (*PROB*) and the buying dummy variable (*BUY*), which is set at unity for the buying experiment and zero for the selling experiment. We pooled all the data, 20 rounds for each of the selling and buying experiments multiplied by the number of subjects, and estimated fixed effects and random effects models.

The estimation results are presented in the first and second columns of Table 6.3. Here, we show the results of a random effects model for the case of *ARA*; the random effects model was not rejected against the fixed effects model on the basis of the Hausman specification test. However, for the case of *TP*, the results of the fixed effects model are shown, because the random effects model was rejected at the 1 % significance level. The estimated coefficients of *PROB* are always positive and significant, implying that the subjects show more risk-averse attitudes to lotteries with higher win probabilities. This can be seen in Fig. 6.2 (*ARA*; the selling experiment), whereas Fig. 6.4 (*ARA*; the buying experiment) does not show this tendency. Regression analysis of the combined data from both experiments confirms this tendency. The coefficients of *BUY* are significantly positive for both cases, indicating that the subjects are significantly more risk averse in the buying experiment than in the selling experiment.

Figures 6.1, 6.2, 6.3, and 6.4 reveal differently shaped in many aspects between the selling and buying experiments; e.g., *ARA* and *TP* are decreasing in win probability in the buying experiment, while they are increasing in the selling experiment. To confirm the differences, we added $PROB^2$, $BUY \times PROB$, and $BUY \times PROB^2$ into the regression equation. The estimation results are shown in the third and fourth columns of Table 6.3. *ARA* and TP are increasing in *PROB*

[11]According to a teacher at Fudan University, most Chinese students' living expenses per month should be under or around 1,000 yuan (US\$120). If this is true, our prize is tantamount to more than half their monthly living expenses.

[12]These results are the same as those from Japanese experiments. See Tsutsui et al. (2005).

[13]In the calculation of *ARA* data, we excluded one sample because the subject assigned 999 points to a lottery with a win probability of 100 %, leading to an extreme value of 2.

Table 6.3 Risk attitude, win probability, and endowment effect

Experiment	Sell and buy		Sell and buy		Sell		Buy	
Dependent variable	*ARA × 1,000*	*TP*	*ARA × 1,000*	*TP*	*ARA × 1,000*	*TP*	*ARA × 1,000*	*TP*
Model of estimation	RE	FE	RE	RE	FE	FE	RE	FE
BUY	0.292 (0.000)	0.295 (0.002)	1.4352 (0.000)	1.7671 (0.000)				
PROB	0.845 (0.000)		2.8677 (0.000)	6.2530 (0.000)	1.7953 (0.010)	5.4547 (0.000)	−1.3995 (0.094)	0.0945 (0.705)
BUY × PROB			−4.3646 (0.000)	−6.1079 (0.000)				
$PROB^2$			−1.4341 (0.068)	−5.0875 (0.000)	−0.5133 (0.440)	−4.5084 (0.000)	1.5289 (0.054)	−0.3976 (0.094)
$BUY \times PROB^2$			3.1312 (0.005)	4.6847 (0.000)				
Constant	−0.051 (0.729)	−0.305 (0.003)	−0.5795 (0.006)	−1.4981 (0.000)	−0.3538 (0.018)	−1.2940 (0.000)	0.8513 (0.000)	0.2807 (0.000)
Number of observations	1,179		1,179		600		579	
Number of subjects	30		30		30		29	
R^2	0.0356	0.0143	0.0544	0.0601	0.0854	0.0536	0.0060	0.0393

Note: *P*-values are in parentheses. RE represents random effects model, FE represents fixed effects model

in the selling experiment, while *ARA* is decreasing in the buying experiment. The tendency is not clear in the case of TP in the buying experiment. *ARA* and TP are concave in the selling experiment, while *ARA* is convex and TP is concave in the buying experiment. These results are also confirmed by the estimation, splitting the samples between the selling and buying experiments (see columns 5–8 in Table 6.3).

The finding that subjects are risk averse in the buying experiment has been reported in Shavit et al. (2001), Hartog et al. (2002), and Cramer et al. (2002). In addition, the finding that subjects are risk loving or risk neutral in the selling experiment has been reported in Kachelmeier and Shehata (1992) and Eichberger et al. (2003). Our experimental results confirm that subjects exhibit different risk attitudes in selling and buying lotteries, even when the same subjects participated in both experiments.

Why does risk attitude differ between selling and buying experiments? One argument is that the subjects learned the structure of the experiment and the optimal strategy during the selling experiment (which was conducted before the buying experiment), so they revealed their true attitude in the buying experiment. However, this interpretation is not very convincing, because the amount of money won by the subjects did not differ between both experiments, leading us to reject the notion of a learning effect. Another possible interpretation for higher risk aversion in the buying experiment is the endowment effect (Kahneman et al. 1990). Among other studies, Knetsch and Sinden (1984) observed that subjects' willingness to accept (*WTA*) in a lottery was higher than their willingness to pay (*WTP*), which implies that they were more risk averse when they bought a lottery ticket than when they sold one. Our finding is consistent with this endowment effect.

Needless to say, our results are dependent on various experimental conditions, so they may not be ubiquitous. Among others, the results of higher risk aversion in the buying experiment may depend on the order of the selling and buying experiments.[14] The order may affect the results in two ways. One is the learning effect, which is already mentioned. The second possibility is that subjects, on average, earn a positive reward in the selling experiment, which may affect their risk aversion in the buying experiment.

As will be demonstrated in the next section, the subjects showed decreasing risk aversion, implying that risk aversion in the buying experiment is lowered with the reward obtained in the selling experiment. Thus, risk aversion in the buying experiment is expected to become larger if we adjust the wealth effect. This is indeed shown by a regression incorporating the reward obtained in the selling experiment (*POINTS*) as an explanatory variable: the coefficient of *BUY* is still positive and becomes even larger as expected, implying higher risk aversion in the buying experiment.

Nevertheless, it is necessary to do the experiments in reverse order to confirm whether our conclusion is robust, because there may be unpredictable reasons for the order to affect risk aversion.

[14]We would appreciate a comment by a referee on this point.

4 How Does the Risk Attitude Relate to Attributes of the Subjects?

In this section, we examine how the risk attitude revealed in the experiments relates to the socioeconomic attributes of the subjects. Specifically, we focus on wealth, knowledge of financial economics, and gender.

How risk attitude depends on wealth has been an important topic. Arrow (1970) argues decreasing absolute risk aversion and increasing relative risk aversion with respect to wealth. As for absolute risk aversion, using the results of a questionnaire survey, Hartog et al. (2002) found decreasing absolute risk aversion with respect to respondents' annual income. Based on survey results, Donkers et al. (2001) also report that risk aversion decreases as income increases, although they do not use absolute risk aversion as the risk measure. In an experiment in which subjects invest money into risky projects, Levy (1994) found decreasing absolute risk aversion and decreasing (or constant, at most) relative risk aversion with respect to wealth, which varied during the experiment. As for relative risk aversion, most studies measure relative risk aversion using the risky asset holding ratio, and decreasing relative risk aversion has been reported instead (Cohn et al. 1975; Guiso et al. 1996, and Kessler and Wolf 1991).

The effect of education on risk attitude has also been studied. Donkers et al. (2001) and Hartog et al. (2002) report that subjects with higher education levels tend to be more risk loving. In this chapter, the subjects are all university students, and our aim was to investigate the effect of knowledge of financial economics on their risk attitude. As standard finance theory is based on the assumption that economic agents are risk averse, students who study finance theory may believe that they must behave as if they are risk averse. To test this hypothesis, after the experiments, we requested the subjects to complete a test that consisted of seven economics problems including three on risk aversion. We analyzed the relationship between the test score and risk attitude.

As in the previous section, we pooled all the data, 40 rounds multiplied by the number of subjects, and estimated fixed and random effects models with them. Because some of the subjects did not answer questions about their income and assets, their observations were dropped from the estimation. Win probability (*PROB*) and the dummy variable representing the buying experiment (*BUY*) are considered in the regression analysis, since risk attitude is systematically influenced by these, as shown in the previous section.

For the gender variable, we adopted a dummy variable *MALE*, which takes the value of unity if the subject is a male, and zero otherwise. For the variable representing knowledge on financial economics, we adopted TEST, which is the score of the subjects on the test conducted immediately after the experiment. For the wealth data, we considered three different variables, *INCOME*, *ASSETS*, and *POINTS*, whose definitions will be explained below.

The results of the random effects model are shown in Table 6.4 for the cases of *ARA* and *TP*, because the Hausman specification test does not reject random

Table 6.4 Risk attitude and subjects' attributes

Dependent variable	*ARA* × *1,000*	*TP*	*ARA* × *1,000*	*TP*	*ARA* × *1,000*	*TP*	*ARA* × *1,000*	*TP*	*RRA* (*ARA* × *POINTS* × 1,000)
Model of the estimation	RE	RE	RE	RE	RE	RE	REIV	REIV	REIV
PROB	0.747 (0.000)	0.592 (0.002)	1.015 (0.000)	0.687 (0.001)	0.910 (0.000)	0.458 (0.004)	0.907 (0.001)	0.448 (0.005)	0.542 (0.000)
BUY	0.397 (0.000)	0.377 (0.001)	0.380 (0.000)	0.357 (0.004)	0.543 (0.000)	0.511 (0.000)	0.615 (0.000)	0.403 (0.004)	0.648 (0.000)
MALE	−0.388 (0.329)	−0.681 (0.014)	−0.412 (0.298)	−0.629 (0.016)	−0.545 (0.116)	−0.704 (0.003)	−0.539 (0.184)	−0.714 (0.107)	−0.625 (0.126)
ASSETS	0.102 (0.458)	0.046 (0.633)							
INCOME			−0.158 (0.405)	−0.114 (0.363)					
POINTS/10,000					−0.481 (0.001)	−0.419 (0.010)	−0.620 (0.001)	−0.210 (0.297)	−0.191 (0.272)
TEST	0.085 (0.532)	0.050 (0.600)	0.289 (0.077)	0.168 (0.118)	0.148 (0.207)	0.073 (0.356)	0.150 (0.274)	0.070 (0.639)	0.112 (0.418)
Constant	−1.730 (0.337)	−1.134 (0.368)	0.066 (0.964)	−0.084 (0.930)	−0.268 (0.556)	−0.245 (0.448)	−0.188 (0.723)	−0.359 (0.536)	−0.317 (0.552)
Number of observations	959		879		1,159		1,159		1,159
Number of subjects	24		22		29		29		29
R^2	0.0537	0.0424	0.0876	0.0472	0.0710	0.0440	0.0712	0.0424	0.0678

Note: *P*-values are in parentheses. RE represents random effect model, REIV represents random effect instrumental variable model. We used each subject's cumulative total of win probability as the instrumental variable. Number of observations varies due to the lack of data for *ASSETS* and/or *INCOME*

effects models against fixed effects models. In the first and second columns, the results when *ASSETS* is adopted as the wealth variable are shown, where *ASSETS* is the logarithm of the amount of financial and real assets owned by a subject's household. *PROB* and *BUY* are significantly positive, confirming the results in Table 6.3. *TEST* is positive, but insignificant. *MALE* is negative, but only significant in the TP case. *ASSETS* is positive, but insignificant. This unexpected result might be because *ASSETS* includes assets owned by the subjects' parents. *ASSETS* probably does not represent most subjects' personal wealth.

Considering the above problem, we adopted *INCOME*, which is defined as the logarithm of subjects' annual income including support from their parents. The results are presented in the third and fourth columns. *PROB*, *BUY*, and *MALE* produce similar results to the case of *ASSETS*. *TEST* is positive and significant at around the 10 % level. *INCOME* is negative as expected, but insignificant.

A problem with *INCOME* may be that it is constant for all the rounds of the experiments, whereas risk attitude measured as *ARA* or *TP* differed between rounds. Meanwhile, actual wealth of the subjects was also changed by the prizes they won in each round. We should not neglect this change in wealth during the experiment, which the subjects confirmed on their PC monitors in each round; they also wrote the value on their record sheets. According to the prospect theory (Kahneman and Tversky 1979), subjects may recognize the outset of the experiment as the "reference point" and focus on the change in wealth resulting from wins and losses in each lottery.

In the fifth and sixth columns, we present the results, with *POINTS* adopted as the wealth variable, where *POINTS* is the cumulative total of points that subjects had won before each round of the experiment. The effect of *INCOME*, which varies only among subjects, if at all, may be captured in individual constant terms. *POINTS* is significantly negative as expected. The coefficients of the other variables are similar to the results obtained when *INCOME* or *ASSETS* are used.

However, *POINTS* may be an endogenous variable because points subjects won in the experiment should be affected by their risk attitudes. For example, points won by risk averse subjects or risk loving subjects would be less than those by risk neutral subjects, on average. Thus, if most of subjects are risk averse, the estimated coefficient of *POINTS* would be negatively biased. In fact, average *ARA* and TP for all subjects were 0.000513, which was significantly positive at the 1 % level and 0.0503, which was not significantly positive at the 10 % level, respectively, implying that *POINTS* may be biased for the case of *ARA*.

In order to correct this bias, we need to introduce an instrumental variable, which correlates with *POINTS* but is uncorrelated with the error term. In our experiment, subjects' cumulative total of win probabilities that they faced before each round of the experiment (*CUMPROB*) can work as an instrumental variable, because it correlates with *POINTS* but is independent of subjects' fixed effects. The regression results using *CUMPROB* as an instrumental variable of *POINTS* is presented in the columns designated as REIV of Table 6.4. *POINTS* is still significantly negative for the *ARA* case, indicating that decreasing absolute risk aversion is confirmed when the endogeneity of *POINTS* is corrected.

From the regression results using *POINTS* as a wealth variable, *POINTS* always negatively correlates with risk aversion and almost all of them are statistically significant, even when we assume that *POINTS* is negatively biased. This observation is consistent with decreasing absolute risk aversion.

Arrow (1970) argued that relative risk aversion (*RRA*) may be increasing with wealth. However, the empirical evidence is not decisive. Although most of the studies on relative risk aversion adopted a risky asset holding ratio as the measure of relative risk aversion, our study is unique in that we used a more direct measure of relative risk aversion derived from the pricing of lotteries. We constructed *RRA* by multiplying *ARA* by *POINTS*, and regressed it against *POINTS* (representing wealth), *PROB*, and *BUY* by using the instrumental variable *CUMPROB*. The results are presented in the far-right column of Table 6.4. *POINTS* is not significant, implying constant relative risk aversion. We repeated the analysis using *RRA* defined as $ARA \times \exp(ASSETS)$ and $ARA \times \exp(INCOME)$ and obtained similar results. These results suggest that relative risk aversion is constant with respect to wealth, supporting the conventional use of the constant relative risk averse (CRRA) utility function in macrofinance.

Let us summarize the results of the other variables. The coefficient of *PROB* is always significantly positive, implying that the subjects are more risk averse in lotteries with higher win probabilities. The coefficient of *BUY* is always significantly positive, confirming the estimation results in the preceding section. The coefficient of *MALE* is always negative, but significant at the 5 % level only when the dependent variable is TP. The observation that males are more risk loving than females is consistent with the findings of Barsky et al. (1997), Donkers et al. (2001), and Hartog et al. (2002), all of which were based on questionnaire surveys.

The coefficient of *TEST* is always positive but significant at the 10 % level only when the dependent variable is *ARA* and when *INCOME* was utilized as the wealth variable. Although this result is not strong, it suggests that students who have more knowledge of financial economics are likely to be more risk averse. Levy and Levy (2001, 2002) measured risk attitudes of business school students and practitioners (fund managers and financial analysts) to find that practitioners were more risk averse than students. As practitioners would have more knowledge about financial economics than students, these results are consistent with ours. Meanwhile, Donkers et al. (2001) and Hartog et al. (2002) reported that subjects with higher education levels tend to be more risk loving. Thus, a consistent interpretation is that higher general education levels make people more risk loving, but specific knowledge of financial economics makes people more risk averse.

5 Subjects' Risky Asset Holdings and Their Risk Attitudes

Can risk attitude revealed in the experiment explain subjects' actual behavior? In this section, we investigate the relationship between subjects' risk attitudes and their risky asset holdings. We postulate that more risk-averse subjects have smaller proportions of risky assets, and we test this hypothesis with our data.

Table 6.5 Risky asset holdings and risk attitudes

Dependent variable	*RISK*	*RISK*	*RISK*	*RISK*	*RISK*	*RISK*
AVARA × *1,000*	−11.8035 (0.061)	−22.0727 (0.004)			−10.9523 (0.088)	
AVTP			−5.3120 (0.519)	−8.5712 (0.349)		−8.4272 (0.221)
ASSETS	8.1034 (0.030)		7.2039 (0.066)			
FINASSETS					5.7523 (0.151)	3.4924 (0.359)
INCOME		1.4512 (0.718)		3.3515 (0.508)		
MALE	13.4902 (0.164)	8.6895 (0.346)	14.2525 (0.216)	8.5020 (0.501)		
Constant	−81.2837 (0.081)	12.2248 (0.727)	−74.7764 (0.133)	−12.1098 (0.780)	−39.7429 (0.348)	−19.9415 (0.631)
Number of observations	21	17	21	17	18	18
Pseudo R^2	0.0518	0.0815	0.0329	0.0247	0.0267	0.0159

Note: *P*-values are in parentheses. Estimation method is Tobit

As for the risky asset holdings, we asked the following question in the questionnaire completed at the end of the experiment.

What percentage of the financial assets of your entire household are in Investment Trusts, Stocks, Futures/Options, Corporate Bonds, Foreign Currency Deposits, Government Bonds of Foreign Countries?

Let us define the variable *RISK* as the percentage that subjects reported in response to this question. As the variable for risk attitude for each subject, we define *AVARA* and *AVTP* as the average *ARA* and average *TP* over the 40 rounds in the selling and buying experiments.

We regressed *RISK* against *AVARA* (or *AVTP*), *ASSETS* (or *INCOME*), and *MALE*.[15] The estimation results are shown in Table 6.5. Tobit was used for the estimation because one subject answered that she had no risky assets.[16] The estimated coefficients of *AVARA* were significantly negative, supporting our hypothesis, while those of *AVTP* were negative but insignificant.

This is somewhat surprising, considering that *AVARA* represents the subjects' risk attitude, while the risky asset holding ratio is usually determined by their parents. Thus, to understand this result, we need to assume that risk attitudes of parents

[15]We do not use *POINTS* as the wealth variable here because risky asset holding has nothing to do with the change in wealth during the experiments.

[16]The results by OLS are almost the same as those in Table 6.5.

and children correlate. Is this assumption reasonable? The answer is "yes." Indeed, Hirata et al. (2006) conducted a questionnaire survey of parents and their children and found that the correlation coefficient between the risk aversion of parents and their children was 0.18 when lottery questions were used.[17] Thus, the finding of a negative correlation between parents' risky asset holding ratio and children's absolute risk aversion may be reasonable.

ASSETS is significantly positive, whereas *INCOME* is positive but insignificant. This result is reasonable because *ASSETS* comprises assets owned by the household, whereas *INCOME* is the income of the subjects (i.e., the children). The risky asset holding ratio of a household may relate more strongly to the former than to the latter.[18]

However, the positive correlation between *RISK* and *ASSETS* is not consistent with the theoretical model of Friend and Blume (1975). They developed a model based on the Capital Asset Pricing Model (CAPM), in which the proportion of risky assets to total assets (*RISK*) is equal to the ratio of expected excess return $\left(r_m - r_f\right)$ and variance of return on the market portfolio (${\sigma_m}^2$) divided by relative risk aversion (*RRA*). That is:

$$RISK = \frac{\left(r_m - r_f\right)}{{\sigma_m}^2 RRA}$$

Most previous researchers, including Friend and Blume (1975) themselves, relied on this relation to use risky asset share (*RISK*) as a proxy for risk tolerance $\left(\frac{1}{RRA}\right)$ and examined how *RRA* relates to wealth. Thus, in their analyses, if relative risk aversion is increasing with respect to wealth, risky asset share should negatively

[17]The sample size was 260, so the correlation coefficients were significant (5 % critical value is 0.12). Hirata et al. (2006) report that the correlation coefficient between time discount rates of parents and their children is around 0.2, while the correlation coefficient between random pairs who have no relationship is zero.

[18]It cannot be denied that the questions on the subjects' parents, *RISK*, *ASSETS*, and *FINASSETS* may not be answered correctly, so they may suffer from a measurement error. Nonetheless, the coefficient of *AVARA* is immune from such a measurement error, so its coefficient is not biased. As for the coefficients of *ASSETS* and *FINASSETS*, they may be biased if the measurement errors of *RISK* and *ASSETS* (*FINASSETS*) are correlated. However, because *RISK* is defined as the ratio of risky asset to *FINASSETS*, and because measurement errors of risky asset and *FINASSETS* are thought to be correlated, the measurement error of *RISK* is probably independent of that of *FINASSETS*. In addition, if we look at correlations between subjects' own wealth (income, food consumption, expenditure per month, etc.) and their households' wealth (annual income, real estate, financial assets, etc.) in the responses to some questions of the questionnaire, nine correlations out of 21 are significantly positive. This fact suggests that subjects may have adequate information about their parents' wealth and those variables are somewhat reliable.

relate to wealth. However, in many cases, the opposite is detected, indicating that the relation does not describe reality (e.g. McCarthy 2004).[19]

Our chapter is unique, in that we can test the relation between risky asset share and *RRA* because we have data on absolute risk aversion as well as the wealth. As relative risk aversion is absolute risk aversion multiplied by wealth, Friend and Blume's (1975) model predicts that the share of risky assets negatively correlates with *ARA* and *ASSETS*, when both of them are included in the regression equation to explain *RISK*. This is indeed what we report in Table 6.5. Although our result is consistent with the model in that *ARA* negatively correlates to the share, it does not support the model because the coefficient of *ASSETS* is significantly positive. Our results suggest that use of risky asset share as a proxy for *RRA* may be problematic. Moreover, we found that *RRA* is constant with respect to wealth in the preceding section, implying that *RISK* would have been constant with respect to wealth, if Friend and Blume's (1975) model is true. The fact that *RISK* positively correlates to wealth suggests the rejection of their model.

A problem of this estimation is that *ASSETS* consists of real asset and financial asset, while *RISK* is defined as the ratio of financial asset only. Thus, it may be appropriate to estimate the equation adopting financial asset (*FINASSETS*) instead of *ASSETS*. The results are shown in the far right columns of Table 6.5. The results generally confirm the above conclusion: that *AVARA* is significantly negative at the 10 % level and *FINASSETS* is positive, even if it is not significant at the 10 % level.

The risky asset holding of male subjects is higher than that of female subjects (32.6 % vs. 22.2 %), and males are less risk-averse than females (*AVARA* is 0.09 vs. 0.58). However, *MALE* is positive but insignificant in Table 6.5, implying that the higher risky asset holding of males is due to their lower risk aversion and nothing else.

6 Subjects' Risk Attitude in Experiments and in the Questionnaire

In the questionnaire completed at the end of the experiment, we asked several questions to elicit subjects' attitudes toward various types of risk. Specifically, we asked:

When you go out, how high does the probability of rain usually have to be before you take an umbrella?

We define the variable RAIN as 100–*x*, where *x*(%) is the answer to this question. We also asked:

[19]Friend and Blume (1975) themselves reported that risky asset share positively correlates to financial assets. However, when wealth is defined as the total of financial and real assets, they found a negative correlation.

One proverb, "Nothing ventured, nothing gained," reveals a belief that it is necessary to take risks if you expect excellent results. On the other hand, another proverb, "A wise man never courts danger," reveals a belief that you should avoid risks as much as possible. Which way of thinking is closest to yours? On a scale of 0–10 with "10" being completely in agreement with the former statement, and "0" being completely in agreement with the latter statement, please rate your behavioral pattern.

We define *VENTURE* as 10–*x*, where *x* is the answer to this question.

Another question was:

When you go out, are you usually careful about locking doors/windows and turning off appliances to prevent a fire? On a scale of 0–10 with "10" being the "least careful", and "0" being the "most careful", please rate your level of caution.

We define *FIRE* as 10–*x*, where *x* is the answer to this question.

Questions 13–16 asked the subjects their subjective price in various lotteries, which are similar to the trials in the experiment. Specifically, in Q13 subjects were asked what their buying price would be in a lottery with a prize of 160 yuan (US$19) with a win probability of 50 %. Question 14 asked their buying price in a lottery with the prize of 8,000 yuan (US$960) with a win probability of 1 %. Question 15 asked the selling price of the lottery in Q13. Question 16 asked about insurance against losses instead of a lottery. Specifically, we asked:

Assume that you know there is a 1 % chance of being robbed of 8,000 yuan (US$960). However, you can take out an insurance policy that covers losses from a robbery. How much would you pay for this insurance?

For Q13–Q16, we calculated the *ARA* and *TP* for each subject. The correlation coefficient between *AVARA* in the experiment and risk attitude in the questionnaire is shown in the first column in the top panel of Table 6.6.

AVARA revealed in the experiment significantly correlated with *RAIN* and *VENTURE*, but it did not significantly correlate with *FIRE*. *AVARA* has a relatively high correlation with *Q13ARA* and *Q15ARA*, which are the questions with the highest similarity in the experiment. These results imply that the risk attitudes revealed in the experiments and in the questionnaire are generally consistent.[20]

At the same time, however, the results in Table 6.6 suggest that risk attitude varies substantially depending on the types of risk asked about. The correlation between *AVARA* and *Q14ARA* is almost zero. These two questions ask about risk attitudes in quite different situations: the prize in *Q14ARA* was very large (8,000 yuan (US$960)), while the prize in the experiment was only 20 yuan (US$2.4). The correlation between *Q16ARA* and *AVARA* is also close to zero. These two questions are also quite different. In *Q16ARA*, subjects were asked their subjective

[20]Therefore, the low correlation mentioned below is not due to the difference in methods (experiment and questionnaire).

Table 6.6 Correlation coefficient between risk attitude in the experiment and risk attitude in the questionnaire

ARA

	AVARA	*RAIN*	*VENTURE*	*FIRE*	*Q13ARA*	*Q14ARA*	*Q15ARA*	*Q16ARA*
AVARA	1.0000							
RAIN	0.3880**	1.0000						
VENTURE	0.5469***	0.2389	1.0000					
FIRE	−0.0563	0.0643	−0.0024	1.0000				
Q13ARA	0.1899	−0.2246	0.2424	0.1007	1.0000			
Q14ARA	−0.0171	0.1437	0.1058	0.3080	0.0982	1.0000		
Q15ARA	0.1660	0.0197	0.1323	0.1054	0.5387***	0.0114	1.0000	
Q16ARA	0.0409	0.0797	−0.1360	0.1073	−0.2953	−0.4129**	0.1680	1.0000

Note: *Q13ARA–Q16ARA* are *ARA* of each subject derived from Q13–Q16 in the questionnaire. ***stands for significance at 1 %; and **stands for significance at 5 % level

TP

	AVTP	*RAIN*	*VENTURE*	*FIRE*	*Q13TP*	*Q14TP*	*Q15TP*	*Q16TP*
AVTP	1.0000							
RAIN	0.1882	1.0000						
VENTURE	0.1324	0.2389	1.0000					
FIRE	0.2077	0.0643	−0.0024	1.0000				
Q13TP	0.1948	−0.3590*	0.2117	0.1085	1.0000			
Q14TP	0.1905	0.1427	0.1056	0.3076	0.1949	1.0000		
Q15TP	0.2374	−0.0293	0.1925	0.0746	0.4586**	−0.0433	1.0000	
Q16TP	0.2247	0.0861	−0.0285	0.0697	−0.2809	−0.4087**	0.2531	1.0000

Note: *Q13ARA–Q16TP* are TP of each subject derived from Q13–Q16 in the questionnaire. **stands for significance at 5 % level; and * stands for significance at 10 % level

price of insurance in instances where the possible loss was very large (8,000 yuan (US$960)), while attitude towards an uncertain small gain (20 yuan (US$960)) is asked in the experiment.

In sum, although one may expect all the variables in Table 6.6 to be highly correlated because they all represent risk attitude, this is not the case at all. The risk attitude is quite different depending on the type of risk.

This finding is confirmed if we look at the correlations between items in the questionnaire instead of looking at the correlations between those in the experiment and in the questionnaire. In the top panel of Table 6.6, a positive correlation is significant at the 5 % level in only three cases out of 28.[21] This result may be due to the following reasons. One is that the measures based on psychological questions, *RAIN*, *VENTURE*, and *FIRE*, ask about attitudes toward different types of risks. Rain risk is a small risk, while fire risk is a large risk, and people may show different attitudes depending on the risk size. The second possible reason, already argued above, is that Q13 and Q14 have different win probabilities and different prizes, which results in the different risk attitudes demonstrated in Sect. 3. Question 16 is concerned with insurance against an expected loss, while Q13–Q15 are concerned with the evaluation of an expected gain. Thus, "loss aversion" proposed by Kahneman and Tversky (1979) produces a different risk attitude. If the difference is not identical among the subjects, correlation will be weak or even negative.

In the bottom panel of Table 6.6, we show the correlation between *AVTP* of the experiment and several variables from the questionnaire. Here, *AVTP* in the experiment has a positive correlation with all the measures in the questionnaire, although it is insignificant. Most of the correlation coefficients are positive, but they are not significant, confirming the results of *AVARA*.

7 Risk Aversion Negatively Correlates with Time Discount Rate

In this section, we examine the relationship between time discounting and risk aversion. The time discount rate is calculated from the results of an experiment conducted after the experiment on risk attitude. Let us briefly explain the experiment on time discount rate.

Subjects were asked to choose whether they would prefer to (A) receive u yuan after x months (or x' days) or (B) receive v yuan after y ($>x$) months (or y' ($>x'$) days). We fix u, x, and y, and change v from a small amount to a large amount for 32 pairs to find the point at which the subjects switch from A to B. Specifically, on a record sheet distributed to subjects in each round, subjects were asked to circle

[21] Only one case is significantly positive out of 21 cases between items in the questionnaire, which is the correlation between the most similar questions (Q13 and Q15).

one of the two options which they prefer to for all 32 pairs of options. Let us call the interest rate corresponding to this switching R (%). Higher R indicates a higher discount rate. We conducted the experiments for 12 combinations of (u, x, y), including experiments with and without prizes, so that there are 12 items of data on R for each subject.[22] We took the logarithm of these Rs and averaged them (*TD*).

The correlation between the time discount rate *TD* and *AVARA* is −0.274, and between *TD* and *AVTP* is −0.114. Although insignificant, they are negative, suggesting that less patient people may tend to be less risk averse. The negative correlation between the time discount rate and risk aversion is also reported in Hiruma and Tsutsui (2005) and Tsutsui et al. (2005), who based their findings on experiments with Japanese subjects. Thus, the observation may be a robust fact, even if the correlation is not strong. The reason for this observation is an interesting question for future investigation.

8 Conclusion

In this chapter, we present the results of an experiment on risk attitudes conducted at Fudan University in Shanghai. First, we investigated how risk attitude depends on win probabilities of lotteries. The results of the selling experiment were similar to those of Kachelmeier and Shehata (1992) in that risk-loving attitudes with a win probability of less than 20 % were confirmed. However, subjects held risk-averse attitudes when the win probability exceeded 30 %. Thus, Kachelmeier and Shehata's results need to be reconsidered.

In buying experiments, subjects showed risk-averse attitudes for all win probabilities. We found that subjects were more risk averse in the buying experiment than in the selling experiment, which is generally consistent with previous literature. Our results are unique in that this tendency was confirmed even when the same subjects participated in both the selling and the buying experiments. The higher risk aversion in the buying experiment can be interpreted as an endowment effect, as proposed by Knetsch and Sinden (1984) and Kahneman et al. (1990).

Using the data from the questionnaire completed after the experiment, we observed that (1) males may be more risk loving than females, (2) those who have more knowledge of financial economics are more risk averse, and (3) absolute risk aversion is decreasing and relative risk aversion is constant with respect to changes in wealth.

Subjects' risk attitudes revealed in the experiments, can account for their risky asset holding. The risk attitudes revealed in the experiment are generally consistent with those revealed in the questionnaire, but risk attitudes are different depending

[22] Whether the prizes would be really paid or not for each round was written in the instruction and was announced carefully. The prizes were announced to pay for eight out of 12 rounds.

on the various types of risks. Finally, we found a negative correlation between risk aversion and time discount rate.

Conducting an experiment in China is interesting for the following two reasons. One is that we could offer large monetary rewards to Chinese students – as much as one third of their monthly living expenses – in a 2-h experiment. Such a large reward scheme enhances the reliability of the experimental results in that it provides subjects with adequate incentives in decision making. The other one is that we can consider the relationship between subjects' risk attitudes and their cultural backgrounds. Because China has developed an undoubtedly different culture and history from western countries, and it has been growing rapidly in these two decades, Chinese people may show different risk attitudes. There have been many studies that measured risk attitudes in various countries: Eichberger et al. (2003) for Germany, Cramer et al. (2002) for The Netherlands, Shavit et al. (2001) for Israel, and so on. However, it is difficult to compare these experimental results directly because experimental design and procedure vary between studies. In this sense, Kachelmeier and Shehata (1992) is a notable exception because it compared subjects' risk attitudes among China, U.S., and Canada, utilizing the same experimental design, and found no difference in subjects' risk attitudes among these countries. Of course, we need further studies to examine the robustness of their result in a comprehensive way.

Acknowledgments This research was supported by the 21st Century COE (Center of Excellence) Program at Osaka University and Grant-in-Aid for Scientific Research 17203025 of the Ministry of Education, Culture, Sports, Science and Technology in Japan.

Addendum: Comparison of Risk Attitudes Between Chinese and Japanese, and Between Students and Non-students[23]

Similar selling and buying experiments reported in the text had been conducted by some of the same authors at Osaka University and Waseda University in Japan. In this addendum, we compare subjects' risk attitudes in those experiments with the experimental result described in the text.

The experiments at Osaka University were conducted on March 2004 with 63 subjects (32 working people and 31 elderly retirees).[24] The experiments at Waseda University were conducted on March 2005 using 32 subjects (all undergraduate students)[25]. Table 6.7 summarizes the subjects' characteristics (gender and age) and the monetary payoffs obtained in each experiment.

[23]This addendum has been newly written for this book chapter.

[24]For the details of the experimental results, see Ohtake and Tsutsui (2012).

[25]The similar experiments conducted in Waseda University are reported in Hiruma and Tsutsui (2005).

Table 6.7 Subjects' characteristics and monetary payoffs

Experiment		Osaka		Waseda
Date		3/2/2004	3/6/2004	**3/5/2005**
Subject's backgrounds		Elderly people	Working people	**Undergraduate students**
Number of subjects		31	32	**32**
Gender	Male	22	17	**19**
	Female	8	15	**13**
Mean age		67.50	43.13	**23.13**
Mean monetary payoff (yen)		**5,981**	**6,264**	**7,560**

Table 6.8 Overall mean *ARA* and *TP* in each experiment

		Selling experiment		Buying experiment	
		Overall mean *ARA*	Overall mean *TP*	Overall mean *ARA*	Overall mean *TP*
Experiment	Osaka	0.000078	−0.103203	0.000403	−0.568130
	Fudan	0.000373	−0.087086	0.000660	0.192737
	Waseda	0.000284	0.032012	0.000617	0.164187

Subjects in each experiment played the selling experiment for 20 rounds and the buying experiment for 20 rounds, with exactly the same procedure as described in the text. Using selling and buying prices that each subject assigned to a lottery ticket, *ARA* and *TP* were estimated for each subject.

Table 6.8 shows the overall mean *ARA* and *TP* in each experiment. For the comparison of the overall mean *ARA* and *TP* in the buying and selling experiment, we confirm that the overall mean *ARA* and *TP* in the buying experiment are larger than those in the selling experiment for all experiments, except for the overall mean *TP* of Osaka University. The fact that subjects are more risk averse in the selling experiment than in the buying experiment is consistent with the conclusion in the text, implying that the endowment effect for the lottery ticket is robustly observed.

Comparison of the overall mean *ARA* and *TP* between the three experiments reveals that the overall mean *ARA* and *TP* in the Osaka University experiment are always smaller than those in the Fudan University and Waseda University experiments. The result that subjects in the Osaka University experiment are more risk loving than subjects in the other two experiments might be attributed to their different backgrounds: subjects in the Osaka University experiment are working/elderly people, while subjects in Fudan University and Waseda University experiments are students. However, more investigation is called for in order to verify that non-students are generally more risk loving than students.

Figures 6.5 and 6.6 show the mean *ARA* and *TP* for each win probability in the selling experiment. From these figures, we can see that subjects tend to be risk loving or risk neutral for low win probabilities and risk neutral or risk averse for high win probabilities.

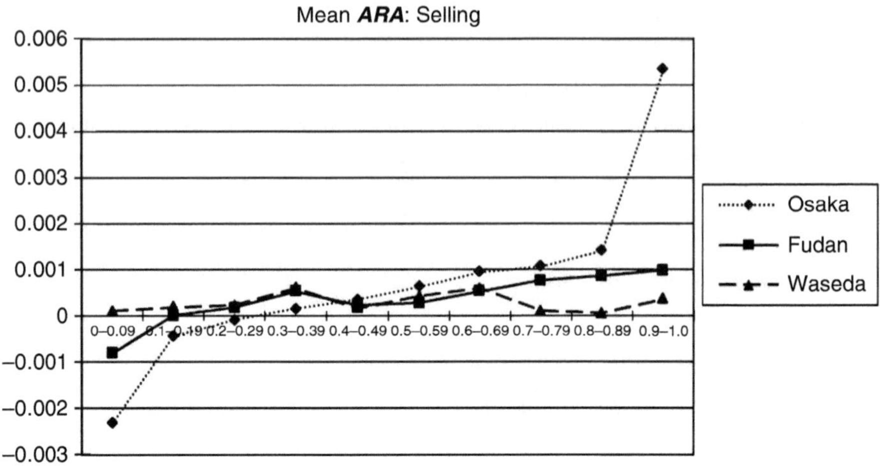

Fig. 6.5 Mean *ARA* for each win probability: sell experiment

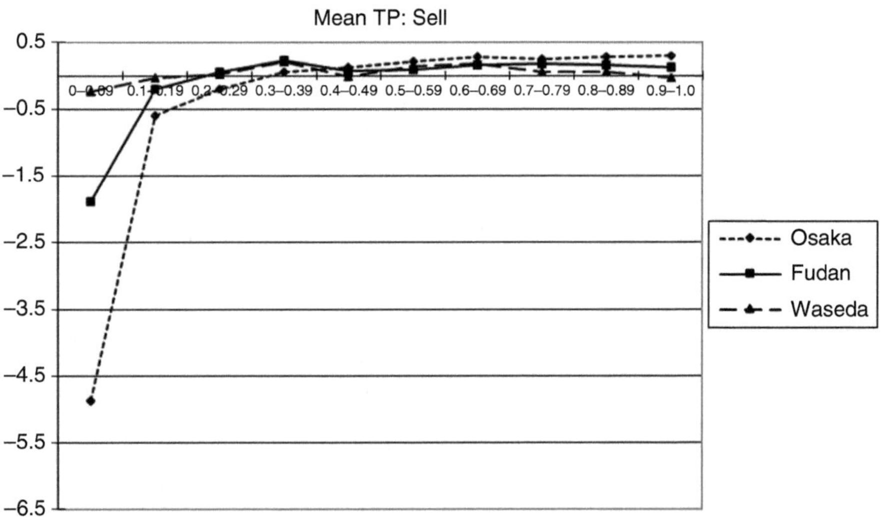

Fig. 6.6 Mean *TP* for each win probability: sell experiment

Figures 6.7 and 6.8 show the mean *ARA* and *TP* for each win probability in the buying experiment. From these figures, we confirm that the mean *ARA* and *TP* in the buying experiment are greater than those in the selling experiment, except for the *TP* in the Osaka University experiment. This result probably reflects the endowment effect of the lottery ticket as discussed above.

From these figures, we can see that the mean *ARA* and *TP* for the smallest win probability (less than 10 %) in the Osaka University experiment are much smaller than those in the Fudan University and the Waseda University experiment in both the

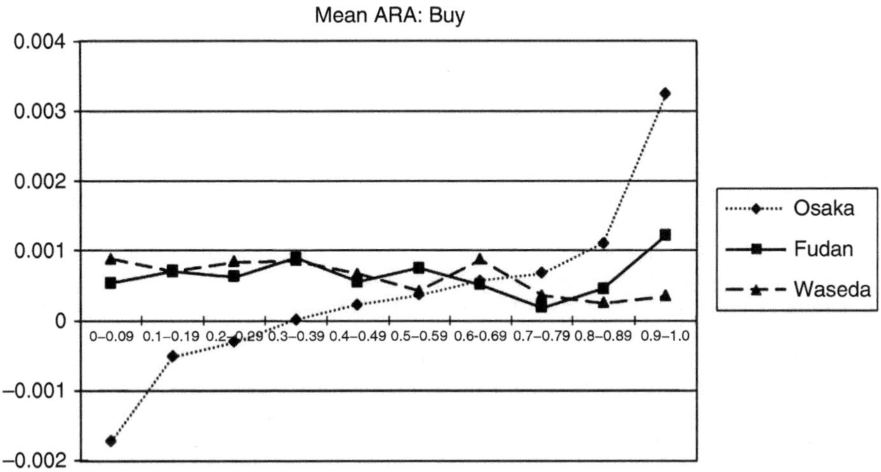

Fig. 6.7 Mean *ARA* for each win probability: buy experiment

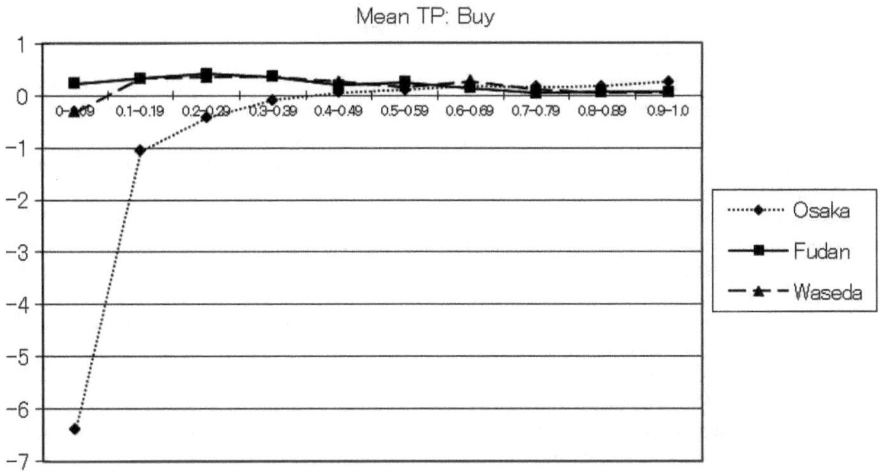

Fig. 6.8 Mean *TP* for each win probability: buy experiment

selling and the buying experiments. On the other hand, looking at the highest win probability, Osaka University shows an extremely high value compared with the other two universities. Basically the shapes of the graphs in these four figures are relatively similar between Fudan and Waseda Universities, whereas that of Osaka University is quite different. This suggests that risk attitude is not different between China and Japan, but is different between students and non-students. Of course, more research should be done to confirm this conjecture.

References

Arrow KJ (1970) Essays in the theory of risk-bearing. North-Holland, Amsterdam

Barsky RB, Juster FT, Kimball MS, Shapiro MD (1997) Preference parameters and behavioral heterogeneity: an experimental approach in the health and retirement study. Q J Econ 112(2):537–579

Becker GM, Degroot J, Marschak J (1964) Measuring utility by a single response sequential method. Behav Sci 9:226–232

Beetsma RMW-J, Schotman PC (2001) Measuring risk attitudes in a natural experiment: data from the television game show Lingo. Econ J 111:821–848

Cohn RA, Lewellen WG, Lease RC, Schlarbaum GG (1975) Individual investor risk aversion and investment portfolio composition. J Finance 30:605–620

Cramer JS, Hartog J, Jonker N, Van Praag CM (2002) Low risk aversion encourages the choice for entrepreneurship: an empirical test of a truism. J Econ Behav Organ 48:29–36

Donkers B, Melenberg B, Van Soest A (2001) Estimating risk attitudes using lotteries: a large sample approach. J Risk Uncertain 22(2):165–195

Eichberger J, Guth W, Muller W (2003) Attitudes towards risk: an experiment. Metroeconomica 54(1):89–124

Friend I, Blume ME (1975) The demand for risky assets. Am Econ Rev 65(5):900–922

Fullenkamp C, Tenorio R, Battalio R (2003) Assessing individual risk attitudes using field data from lottery games. Rev Econ Stat 85(1):218–226

Guiso L, Jappelli T, Terlizzese D (1996) Income risk, borrowing constraints, and portfolio choice. Am Econ Rev 86:158–172

Hartog J, Carbonell FI, Jonker N (2002) Linking measured risk aversion to individual characteristics. Kyklos 55(1):3–26

Hirata K, Ohtake F, Tsutsui Y (2006) Is time preference inherited? mimeo

Hiruma F, Tsutsui Y (2005) Are people really risk-averse? An experimental study. Osaka Econ Pap 55(2):43–68. (in Japanese)

Kachelmeier SJ, Shehata M (1992) Examining risk preference under high monetary incentives: experimental evidence from the People's Republic of China. Am Econ Rev 82(5):1120–1141

Kahneman D, Tversky A (1979) Prospect theory: an analysis of decision under risk. Econometrica 47:263–291

Kahneman D, Knetsch JL, Thaler R (1990) Experimental tests of the endowment effects and the Coase theorem. J Polit Econ 98:1325–1348

Kessler D, Wolf EN (1991) A comparative analysis of household wealth patterns in France and the United States. Rev Income Wealth 37:249–266

Knetsch JL, Sinden JA (1984) Willingness to pay and compensation demanded: experimental evidence of an unexpected disparity in measures of value. Q J Econ 99:507–521

Levy H (1994) Absolute and relative risk aversion: an experimental study. J Risk Uncertain 8(3):289–307

Levy M, Levy H (2001) Testing for risk aversion: a stochastic dominance approach. Econ Lett 71:233–240

Levy M, Levy H (2002) Experimental test of the prospect theory value function: a stochastic dominance approach. Organ Behav Hum Decis Process 89:1058–1081

McCarthy D (2004) Household portfolio allocation: a review of the literature. mimeo

Metrick A (1995) A natural experiment in "Jeopardy!". Am Econ Rev 85:240–253

Ohtake F, Tsutsui Y (2012) Investigation of risk attitude with an economic experiment. Behav Econ Finance 5:26–44 (in Japanese)

Sasaki S, Xie S, Ohtake F, Qin J, Tsutsui Y (2008) Experiments on risk attitude: the case of Chinese students. China Econ Rev 19:245–259

Shavit S, Sonsino D, Benzion U (2001) A comparative study of lotteries-evaluation in class and on the web. J Econ Psychol 22:483–491

Tsutsui Y, Ohtake F, Ikeda S (2005) Estimation of degree of risk aversion: an experiment at Osaka University. mimeo. (in Japanese)

Part II
Addiction

Chapter 7
Interdependency Among Addictive Behaviours and Time/Risk Preferences: Discrete Choice Model Analysis of Smoking, Drinking, and Gambling

Takanori Ida and Rei Goto

Abstract This chapter simultaneously measures the rate of time preference and the coefficient of risk aversion, as well as investigates the interdependencies of four addictive behaviours: smoking, drinking, *pachinko* (a popular Japanese form of pinball gambling), and horse betting among a sample of the Japanese population. We reach two main conclusions. First, there are significant interdependencies among the four addictive behaviours, in particular between smoking and drinking and between gambling on *pachinko* and the horses. Second, we conclude that the higher the time preference rate and the lower the risk aversion coefficient becomes, the more likely individuals smoke, drink frequently, and gamble on *pachinko* and the horses.

Keywords Time preference • Risk aversion • Smoking • Addiction

1 Introduction

In currently developing economic psychology, or behavioural economics, one crucial topic is investigating addictive behaviours including smoking, drinking, and gambling.[1] Referring to the related literature, there are two models of research regarding addictive behaviours: rational addiction and bounded rational addiction (Messinis 1999). The rational addiction model argues that utility maximizing consumers consider the future consequences of their past and current consumption

---

The original article first appeared in Journal of Economic Psychology 30(4):608–621, 2009. A newly written addendum has been added to this book chapter.

[1]See DiClemente and Hantula (2003) as to a review of the applied behavioural literature in consumer choice.

T. Ida (✉) • R. Goto
Graduate School of Economics, Kyoto University, Yoshida, Sakyoku, Kyoto 606-8501, Japan
e-mail: ida@econ.kyoto-u.ac.jp; goto.rei.7w@kyoto-u.ac.jp

S. Ikeda et al. (eds.), *Behavioral Economics of Preferences, Choices, and Happiness*, DOI 10.1007/978-4-431-55402-8_7

of addictive substances (Stigler and Becker 1977; Becker and Murphy 1988). On the other hand, the bounded rational addiction model assumes that many drug, tobacco, and alcohol addicts regret their reliance on these substances (Winston 1980; Akerlof 1991) and argues that addiction results from mistaken beliefs about the likelihood of being addicted (Orphanides and Zervos 1995, 1998). From this point of view, we investigate the following issue. Although recently many studies have investigated addiction based on bounded rational addiction models (Bernheim and Rangel 2005; Kan 2007), discussion has concentrated on the transition of addictive behaviour over time (*vertical addiction*). In this chapter, we emphasize the interdependencies among addictive behaviours (*horizontal addiction*).

Following rational addiction models, vertical addiction is defined as habit forming behaviour; utility function is given by U(c, S), where c denotes current consumption, S denotes its consumption stock, and vertical addiction is indicated by $d[\partial U/\partial c]/dS > 0$. Turning to horizontal addiction, the utility function is given by $U(c_1, c_2, \ldots, c_i, \ldots, c_n)$, where c_i represents some addictive behaviour, and horizontal addiction is indicated by $d[\partial U/\partial c_i]/dc_j > 0$ for $i \neq j$.[2]

When investigating addictive behaviours, economic-psychological parameters including the rate of time preference and the coefficient of risk aversion play key roles. For example, research on time preference has reported that smokers are more impatient than non-smokers; furthermore, a significant positive correlation between the amount smoked per day and a higher discounting rate has been observed (Mitchell 1999; Bickel et al. 1999; Odum et al. 2002; Baker et al. 2003; Reynolds et al. 2004; Ohmura et al. 2005).[3] The research on risk preference remains unable to determine whether smoking and impulsive probability discounting are related (Mitchell 1999; Reynolds et al. 2003; Ohmura et al. 2005). We also introduce studies on addictive behaviours other than smoking: heavy drinkers highly discount delayed monetary rewards more than social or non-drinkers (Madden et al. 1997, 1999); pathological gamblers more readily discount monetary rewards than non-gambler (Petry and Casarella 1999; Petry 2001; Alessi and Petry 2003); furthermore, the severity of gambling problems is associated with discounting rates, and pathological gamblers with substance abuse disorders (alcohol, cocaine, or marijuana) more impulsively discount delayed rewards than those without such problems (Petry and Casarella 1999; Petry 2001; Alessi and Petry 2003). Based on these viewpoints, we will explore the following: expanding upon the previous studies concerning

[2]It would be interesting to extend the analysis to 'beneficial addiction' ($d[\partial U/\partial c_i]/dS > 0$) including jogging and swimming. There is some controversy as to whether jogging and swimming can be also considered addictions (Holden 2001); excessive exercise can cause unhealthy outcomes (McKenzie 1999) and can also be a harmful addiction in this case.

[3]Some research found the opposite: smokers exhibited lower discount rates (Chesson and Viscusi 2000).

the relationship between addictive behaviours and the rate of time preference, this chapter investigates the relationship between addictive behaviours and risk aversion coefficients that has not yet been fully addressed.

At this point, we explain the two approaches adopted in this chapter. First, we develop a simple method to simultaneously measure the rate of time preference and the coefficient of risk aversion. As Rachlin and Siegel (1994) suggest, the nature of the interaction between the rate of time preference and the coefficient of risk aversion has remained controversial because most previous studies measured them separately, which is analytically unsatisfactory.[4] Accordingly, this chapter simultaneously measures the rate of time preference and the coefficient of risk aversion at the individual level based on discrete choice experiment (DCE) and mixed logit (ML) model analysis.[5]

Second, we examine the interdependencies of plural addictive behaviours and time/risk preferences. Barsky et al. (1997) measured preference parameters related to risk tolerance and intertemporal substitution and analyzed their interaction with "risky" behaviours, including smoking, drinking, noninsurance, and stock speculation. Kapteyn and Teppa (2003) exploited hypothetical choices among different consumption streams to infer the rates of time preference and considered some interesting behavioural extensions, including habit formation.[6] Donkers and van Soet (1999) also showed that household behaviour depended on the rate of time preference, the rate of risk aversion, and the information set. This chapter deals with such addictive behaviours as smoking, drinking, playing *pachinko* (a form of Japanese gambling involving the use of a Pinball machine), and betting on the horses and analyzes the influence of time/risk preferences on those addictive behaviours.[7] Also, considering the problem of endogeneity, this chapter investigates interdependencies among addictive behaviours by a two-step probit estimation method.

Finally, the main conclusions of this chapter can be summarized in two points. First, we conclude that one who smokes, plays *pachinko*, and gambles on horses has a higher rate of time preference and a lower coefficient of risk aversion. On the other hand, drinkers have a lower rate of time preference and a higher coefficient of risk aversion. However, if we narrow the definition of drinker (i.e., drinking every day), we discover that regular drinkers conversely become more

[4]A few studies have tried to integrate the measurements of time and risk preferences. Examples include Rachlin et al. (1991), Keren and Roelofsma (1995), Anderhub et al. (2001), and Yi et al. (2006).

[5]In health economics, obtaining reveal preference (RP) data is sometimes difficult, since the market is incomplete; it is advantageous to utilize stated preference (SP) data using experiments and questionnaire surveys. As such, this hypothetical technique has been applied in healthcare settings, and previous results have revealed that SP results have internal validity and consistency (Viney et al. 2002).

[6]They interestingly discovered that the rate of time preference was robust with respect to the different assumptions regarding habit formation, while the coefficient of relative risk aversion changed substantially across specifications.

[7]In pachinko, the object is to increase the number of pachinko balls to exchange for cash or prizes.

impatient and risk-seeking. Second, we find strong interdependencies between smoking and drinking and between *pachinko* and gambling on horses. Furthermore, weak interdependencies are found between smoking and *pachinko* and between drinking and gambling on horses.

The chapter is organized as follows. Section 2 explains the method of sampling data and discusses their characteristics. Section 3 proposes discounted and expected utility models for estimating preference parameters and portrays a mixed logit model analysis. Section 4 discusses the interdependencies among addictive behaviours based on a two-step probit estimation method. Section 5 draws concluding remarks.

2 Sample Data

In this section, we explain our data sampling method and the data characteristics. We surveyed Japanese adults registered with a consumer monitoring investigative company (whose total number of monitors is about 220,000). Data sampling was performed in July 2006 based on the following two stages. First, we randomly drew 1,022 respondents from the monitors and asked them about their habits and paid them JPY150 (US$1.40, given JPY110 = US$1). Second, we collected 692 replies from around 70 % of the respondents and paid JPY500 (US$4.50) to those who answered the DCE questionnaire. The average age of the respondents was 40.2, and 35 % of the final respondents were female. Table 7.1 summarizes the demographics of the sample data.

At this point, we scrutinize the detailed features of the sample data. Table 7.2 depicts the pattern of the relations of such addictive behaviours as smoking, drinking, playing *pachinko,* and gambling on horses. For each behaviour, we assign discrete choice variable 1 for respondents (*treatment* group) who replied YES, and 0 for those (*comparison* group) who responded NO. Thus, figures represent the conditional ratios of addictive behaviours. For example, *FROM smoking X TO drinking = 76.2 %* means that 76.2 % of smokers also drink. Since these conditional ratios are all higher than the figures in Table 7.1 (for example, 74.1 % for drinking), we assume positive correlations among addictive behaviours. Especially, strong relations are observed from *pachinko* to smoking and horse races and from horse races to drinking and *pachinko*.

Table 7.1 Demographics of sample data

No. of samples	Age	Male	Married	No. of children	Household income (JPY1,000)	Employed	University graduate	Smoking	Drinking	Pachinko	Horse race
692	40.64	64.6 %	67.8 %	1.07	6,813	84.5 %	52.6 %	58.4 %	74.1 %	18.4 %	12.1 %

Note: Figures are sample averages or their % ratios

Table 7.2 Pattern of relations of addictive behaviours

		TO			
		Smoking	Drinking	Pachinko	Horse race
FROM	Smoking	**100.0** %	76.2 %	24.5 %	13.1 %
	Drinking	60.0 %	**100.0** %	18.7 %	14.0 %
	Pachinko	78.0 %	75.6 %	**100.0** %	31.5 %
	Horse race	63.1 %	85.7 %	47.6 %	**100.0** %

Note: FROM smoking X TO drinking = 76.2 % means that 76.2 % of smokers drink

3 Simultaneous Measurement of Time/Risk Preferences

This section explains a method that simultaneously measures the rate of time preference and the coefficient of risk aversion.

3.1 Discrete Choice Experiment

First, we conducted the following discrete choice experiment (DCE) for the 692 respondents to simultaneously measure time/risk preferences.[8] DCE analysis assumes that a service is a profile composed of attributes. If we include too many attributes and levels, respondents have difficulty answering the questions. On the other hand, if we include too few, the description of alternatives becomes inadequate. After conducting several pretests, we finally determined the attributes and their levels.

The following are the alternatives, attributes, and levels set in this research[9]:

Alternative 1:

Reward, probability, and delay are fixed across profiles.
Reward: JPY100,000 (US$909), Winning probability: 100 %, Time delay: None.

Alternative 2:

Reward, probability, and delay vary across profiles.
Reward is one of the following: JPY150,000 (US$1,364), JPY200,000 (US$1,818), JPY250,000 (US$2,273), or JPY300,000 (US$2,727).
Winning probability is 40 %, 60 %, 80 %, or 90 %.
Time delay is 1 month, 6 months, 1 year, or 5 years.

Since the number of profiles becomes unwieldy if we consider all possible combinations, we adopt an orthogonal planning method to avoid this problem

[8]Tsuge et al. (2005) is interesting because it applies the DCE analysis of risk preference.

[9]In our survey, a respondent was told that when choosing Alternative 2, which included delay and risk, she first drew lots; when a winning number was drawn, she would get a prize after a given period of time.

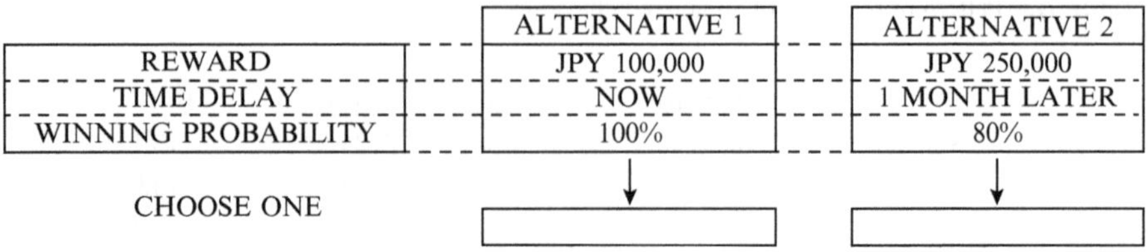

Fig. 7.1 Representative questionnaire

(Louviere et al. 2000 Ch. 4). Figure 7.1 depicts a representative questionnaire covering profiles and attributes. We asked eight questions per respondent. We assumed that Alternative 1 was always both *sure* and *immediate* while Alternative 2 was always both *risky* and *delayed*. This setting may lead to a predetermined relationship between time preference rates and risk aversion coefficients. In addition, in the pretest, we tried another questionnaire in which Alternatives 1 and 2 were both *risky* and *delayed*. At that moment, we observed that the goodness of fit always decreased when regressing the response data by the ML model. This was probably because the respondents required immense information processing abilities since all attributes in both alternatives varied randomly. In this respect, Carson et al. (1994) argued that if the attribute levels were so complex that extra cognitive effort had to be expended to comprehend them, the number of profiles to which individuals were asked to respond should be reduced.

3.2 *Discounted and Expected Utility Models*

Next, we explain discounted and expected utility models that form the basis for estimating the rate of time preference and the coefficient of risk aversion. Let the utility of alternative i be V_i (reward_i, $\text{probability}_\text{i}$, time delay_i). The exponential discounted utility model and the (linear in probability) expected utility model are used for the functional form of $V_{i.}$[10] Specifically, we write

Discounted utility: $\exp(-TIME * \text{timedelay}_\text{i}) * \text{utility}(\text{reward}_\text{i})$,

where parameter *TIME* denotes the rate of time preference

Expected utility[11]: $\text{probability}_\text{i} * \text{utility}(\text{reward}_\text{i})$.

[10] As is commonly known, the exponential discounted utility model was advocated by Samuelson (1937) and axiomatically defined by Koopmans (1960) and Fishburn and Rubinstein (1982). The expected utility model is attributed to von Neumann and Morgenstern (1953).

[11] If we consider index s the state of nature, s = 1, …, S, expected utility is written as $\Sigma_{\text{s}=1,\ldots,\text{S}}$ $\text{probability}_\text{s}*\text{utility}(\text{reward}_\text{s})$. Note that we simply assume here that one alternative has only one state of nature other than the state of zero reward.

Accordingly, rewriting V_i, we obtain

$$\begin{aligned} &V_i\left(\mathrm{reward_i},\ \mathrm{probability_i},\ \mathrm{time\ delay_i}\right) \\ &\quad = \exp\left(-\mathit{TIME} * \mathrm{time\ delay_i}\right) * \mathrm{probability_i} * \mathrm{utility}\left(\mathrm{reward_i}\right). \end{aligned}$$

At this point, we simply specify the functional form of utility as the *RISK*-th power of reward. Such a utility function is called the constant relative risk-averse form, where the coefficient of relative risk aversion is denoted by 1-*RISK*. Taking logarithms of both sides, we obtain

$$\begin{aligned} &\ln\ V_i\left(\mathrm{reward_i},\ \mathrm{probability_i},\ \mathrm{time\ delay_i}\right) \\ &\quad = -\mathit{TIME} * \mathrm{time\ delay_i} + \ln\ \mathrm{probability_i} + \mathit{RISK} * \ln\ \mathrm{reward_i}. \end{aligned}$$

Note two points here: first, the higher the time-impatient (myopic) value, the larger *TIME* is; second, since a risk averse attitude means 1-*RISK*∈(0,1), the more risk-averse, the larger 1-*RISK* is.

One of the main objectives of behavioural economics is discovering and elucidating anomalies. The most famous anomaly in time preference is hyperbolic discounting, where the rate of time preference decreases with time delay (Frederick et al. 2002). Two well-known anomalies in risk preference are certainty effect and loss aversion (Kahneman and Tversky 1979). Many models have been suggested to explain these anomalies. Nevertheless, our chapter measures the rate of time preference and the coefficient of relative risk aversion based on the standard discounted and expected utility models.[12] Note, however, some models that explain anomalies may be compatible with the standard model by a simple transformation of variables. For example, if setting psychological time as a logarithm of physical time, the exponential discounted model with respect to physical time can be transformed into a hyperbolic discounted model for psychological time (Takahashi 2005).

3.3 *Mixed Logit Model*

This subsection describes our econometric model. Conditional logit (CL) models, which assume independent and identical distribution (IID) of random terms, have been widely used in past studies. However, independence from the irrelevant alternatives (IIA) property derived from the IID assumption of the CL model is too strict to allow flexible substitution patterns. The most prominent model is a mixed logit (ML) scheme that accommodates differences in the variance of random

[12]This is partly because both the constant rate of time preference and the coefficient of relative risk aversion still provide good benchmarks.

components (unobserved heterogeneity).[13] They are flexible enough to overcome the limitations of CL models by allowing random taste variation, unrestricted substitution patterns, and the correlation of random terms over time (McFadden and Train 2000).

Here we explain the ML model assuming that parameter β_n is distributed with density function $f(\beta_n)$ (Train 2003; Louviere et al. 2000). The ML specification allows for repeated choices by each sampled decision maker in a way that the coefficients vary over people but are constant over choice situations for each person. The logit probability of decision maker n choosing alternative i in choice situation t is expressed as

$$L_{nit}(\beta_n) = \prod_{t=1}^{T} \left[\exp\left(V_{nit}(\beta_n)\right) / \sum_{j=1}^{J} \exp\left(V_{njt}(\beta_n)\right) \right], \tag{7.1}$$

which is the product of normal logit formulas, given parameter β_n, the observable portion of utility function V_{nit}, and alternatives $j = 1, \ldots, J$ in choice situations $t = 1, \ldots, T$. Therefore, the ML choice probability is a weighted average of logit probability $L_{nit}(\beta_n)$ evaluated at parameter β_n with density function $f(\beta_n)$, which can be written as

$$P_{nit} = \int L_{nit}(\beta_n) f(\beta_n)\, d\beta_n. \tag{7.2}$$

In the linear-in-parameter form, the utility function can be written as

$$U_{nit} = \gamma' x_{nit} + \beta' z_{nit} + \varepsilon_{nit}, \tag{7.3}$$

where x_{nit} and z_{nit} denote observable variables, respectively, γ denotes a fixed parameters vector, β denotes a random parameter vector, and ε_{nit} denotes an independently and identically distributed extreme value (IID-EV) term.

Because the ML choice probability is not expressed in closed-form, simulations need to be performed for the ML model estimation. Let θ denote the mean and (co-)variance of parameter density function $f\left(\beta_n \middle| \theta\right)$. ML choice probability is approximated through the simulation method (see Train 2003, p. 148 for details).

We can also calculate the estimators of the conditional means of the random parameters, conditioned on individual specific choice profile y_n (Revelt and Train 2000), which are given as

$$h\left(\beta \middle| y_n\right) = P\left(y_n \middle| \beta\right) f(\beta) / \int P\left(y_n \middle| \beta\right) f(\beta)\, d\beta. \tag{7.4}$$

[13] ML models are also called random parameter models if focusing on the distribution of parameters, or error component models if focusing on flexible substitution patterns (Revelt and Train 1998; Brownstone and Train 1999).

In what follows, we assume that preference parameters regarding time and risk follow normal distribution. Accordingly, we can demonstrate variety in parameters at the individual level. Here we use the MSL method for estimation by setting 100 Halton draws.[14] Furthermore, since a respondent repeatedly completes eight questionnaires in the DCE analysis, we consider the data to be panel data. Thus, we apply a standard random effects method in which random draws are repeatedly reused for the same respondent.

The following are the explanatory variables used in the ML model:

TIME (therefore, the rate of time preference is represented by *TIME*)
RISK (therefore, the coefficient of relative risk aversion is represented by 1-*RISK*).

At this point, we can write the random utility that person n obtains from choosing alternative i in choice situation t as follows:

$$U_{nit} = -\alpha * TIME * timedelay_{nit} + \alpha * \ln probability_{nit} + \alpha * RISK * \ln reward_{nit} + \varepsilon_{nit}, \tag{7.5}$$

where α is a scale parameter that is not separately identified from free parameters and is here normalized to one (Hensher et al. 2005, p. 536).[15]

If we divide respondents based on the discrete choices of four addictive behaviours as much as possible, we obtain $2^4 = 16$ categories. Dividing respondents into 16 categories leads to a small number of samples per category and thus results in less efficient estimation results. Therefore, we divide the respondents into YES or No category for each addictive behaviour and then separately measure the rate of time preference and the coefficient of relative risk aversion.

3.4 Estimation Results

Table 7.3 shows the estimation results. Having assumed that the random parameters are distributed normally, each parameter has mean and standard-deviation (S.D.) estimates. The estimation results are reported for smoking, drinking, *pachinko*, and horse races, respectively. For time-preference parameter TIME, all mean estimates are statistically significant based on t values, and all standard deviation estimates

[14]Louviere et al. (2000, p. 201) suggest that 100 replications are normally sufficient for a typical problem involving five alternatives, 1,000 observations, and up to 10 attributes (Revelt and Train 1998). The adoption of the Halton sequence draw is an important problem to be examined (Halton 1960). Bhat (2001) found that 100 Halton sequence draws are more efficient than 1,000 random draws for simulating ML models.

[15]Louviere et al. (2000, pp. 142–143) showed that the variance is an inverse function of the scale as $\sigma^2 = \pi^2/6\alpha^2$. Therefore, the associated variance σ^2 becomes 1.645.

Table 7.3 Estimation results of ML model

(a) Smoking				(b) Drinking			
No. of samples	3232 (404*8)			No. of samples	4104 (513*8)		
Maximum LL	−1665.2			Maximum LL	−2148.9		
Initial LL	−2240.3			Initial LL	−2844.7		
McFadden R^2	0.2567			McFadden R^2	0.2446		
Variables		Estimates	S.E.	Variables		Estimates	S.E.
TIME	Mean	0.0663	0.0068***	TIME	Mean	0.0505	0.0046***
	S.D.	0.0397	0.0061***		S.D.	0.0263	0.0049***
RISK	Mean	0.9139	0.0714***	RISK	Mean	0.7779	0.0607***
	S.D.	0.3242	0.1605**		S.D.	0.4068	0.1136***
(c) Pachinko				(d) Horse race			
No. of samples	1776 (222*8)			No. of samples	800 (100*8)		
Maximum LL	−518.8			Maximum LL	−2889.4		
Initial LL	−704.2			Initial LL	−3837.3		
McFadden R^2	0.2633			McFadden R^2	0.2470		
Variables		Estimates	S.E.	Variables		Estimates	S.E.
TIME	Mean	0.0647	0.0116***	TIME	Mean	0.0790	0.0178***
	S.D.	0.0370	0.0102***		S.D.	0.0465	0.0142***
RISK	Mean	0.8484	0.1245***	RISK	Mean	0.8695	0.1608***
	S.D.	0.2770	0.2965		S.D.	0.0477	0.8089

Note 1: ***significant at the 1 % level, **significant at the 5 % level, *significant at the 10 % level
Note 2: As space is limited, the estimation results for NO groups are omitted

are statistically significant. For risk preference parameter RISK, all mean estimates are statistically significant based on *t* values, and standard deviation estimates are statistically significant except *pachinko* and horse races.

3.5 Time Preference, Risk Aversion, and Addictive Behaviours

In this subsection, the time preference rates and the relative risk aversion coefficients are simultaneously measured for addictive behaviours. The results are presented in Table 7.4. Table 7.4a indicates the rates of time preference and the coefficients of relative risk aversion for those who smoke, drink, play *pachinko,* or gamble on horses (YES group). Table 7.4b displays the rates of time preference and the coefficients of relative risk aversion for those who do not smoke, drink, play *pachinko,* or gamble on horses (NO group). Table 7.4c shows the results of Welch's *t* test regarding the difference in mean estimates between the YES and NO groups. Also, if readers are interested, they can see how preferences differ among addictions: the time preference rates are 0.066 for smokers and 0.051 for drinkers, while the risk aversion coefficients are 0.086 for smokers and 0.222 for drinkers, which are indicated in Table 7.4a.

The main findings can be summarized as follows:

- For smoking, playing *pachinko,* and gambling on horses, the YES groups are *more impatient* and *risk-seeking* than the NO groups; the rates of the time

Table 7.4 Time preference and relative risk aversion

(a) The rates of time preference and the coefficients of relative risk aversion for YES groups					
		Smoking	Drinking	Pachinko	Horse race
Time preference (TIME)	Estimates	0.066	0.051	0.065	0.079
	S.E.	0.007	0.005	0.012	0.018
Risk aversion (1-RISK)	Estimates	0.086	0.222	0.152	0.131
	S.E.	0.071	0.061	0.124	0.161
(b) The rates of time preference and the coefficients of relative risk aversion for NO groups					
		Smoking	Drinking	Pachinko	Horse race
Time preference (TIME)	Estimates	0.045	0.074	0.054	0.053
	S.E.	0.005	0.011	0.005	0.004
Risk aversion (1-RISK)	Estimates	0.300	0.074	0.196	0.192
	S.E.	0.079	0.105	0.058	0.056
(c) Welch *t* test between YES and NO groups					
		Smoking vs. Non-smoking	Drinking vs. Non-drinking	Pachinko vs. Non-pachinko	Horse race vs. Non-horse race
Welch t values	Time preference	47.1 ***	27.7 ***	10.4 ***	13.1 ***
	Risk aversion	36.6 ***	17.8 ***	3.9 ***	3.5***

Note: ***significant at the 1 % level, **significant at the 5 % level, *significant at the 10 % level

preference of the former are statistically significantly higher than the latter, while the coefficients of the relative risk aversion of the former are statistically significantly lower than the latter.

- Only for drinking, the YES groups are *less impatient* and *risk-seeking* than the NO groups; the rates of time preference of the former are statistically significantly lower than the latter, while the coefficients of relative risk aversion of the former are statistically significantly higher than the latter.

Our finding that smokers are more impatient in delay discounting than non-smokers is consistent with preceding observations (Mitchell 1999; Bickel et al. 1999; Odum et al. 2002; Baker et al. 2003; Reynolds et al. 2004; Ohmura et al. 2005).[16] On the other hand, although many studies have investigated the relationship between smoking and attitudes toward risk, the issue remains inconclusive (Mitchell 1999; Reynolds et al. 2003; Ohmura et al. 2005). From our simultaneous measurements of the rate of time preference and the coefficient of relative risk aversion, it follows that smokers are more risk-prone and more time-impatient than non-smokers.

Yi et al. (2007) compared smokers and non-smokers using a probability discounting procedure; when these data were fit to a hyperbolic discounting model, nonstatistically significant group differences between them were observed; indifference points obtained from high probabilities were lower for heavy cigarette smokers relative to non-smokers. One reason that explains the difference between Yi et al. (2007) and our chapter lies in a difference in the method we adopted; we estimated time preference rates and risk aversion coefficients simultaneously by asking respondents to choose between certain-immediate and risky-later rewards, which leads to the different result by Yi et al. (2007).

In the ML model, we can indicate varieties of individual preferences by standard deviations of random parameters. As explained above, we can also calculate the estimator of the conditional mean of random parameters based on the Bayes theorem (Revelt and Train 2000). Figure 7.2 displays conditional distributions of the rate of time preference and the coefficient of risk aversion for smokers and non-smokers. Preferences vary at the individual level.

The above results mark a breakthrough in the research of the interaction between addictive behaviours including smoking and time/risk preferences. However, one reservation should be mentioned. Since this research only investigated the relationship between addictive behaviours including smoking and time/risk preferences, we reserve judgment about causality. For example, we cannot determine here whether an impulsive person tends to smoke or a smoker tends to become impulsive. A detailed study of causality lies outside the scope of this chapter. This is a crucial area for future research. Furthermore, we assumed that delay and risk were distinguished by our questionnaires. However, the literature including Rachlin et al. (1991)

[16]It is not necessarily a long-established hypothesis that smoking is positively correlated with impulsive delay discounting. Famous research by Fuchs (1982) reported weak relations between them, for example.

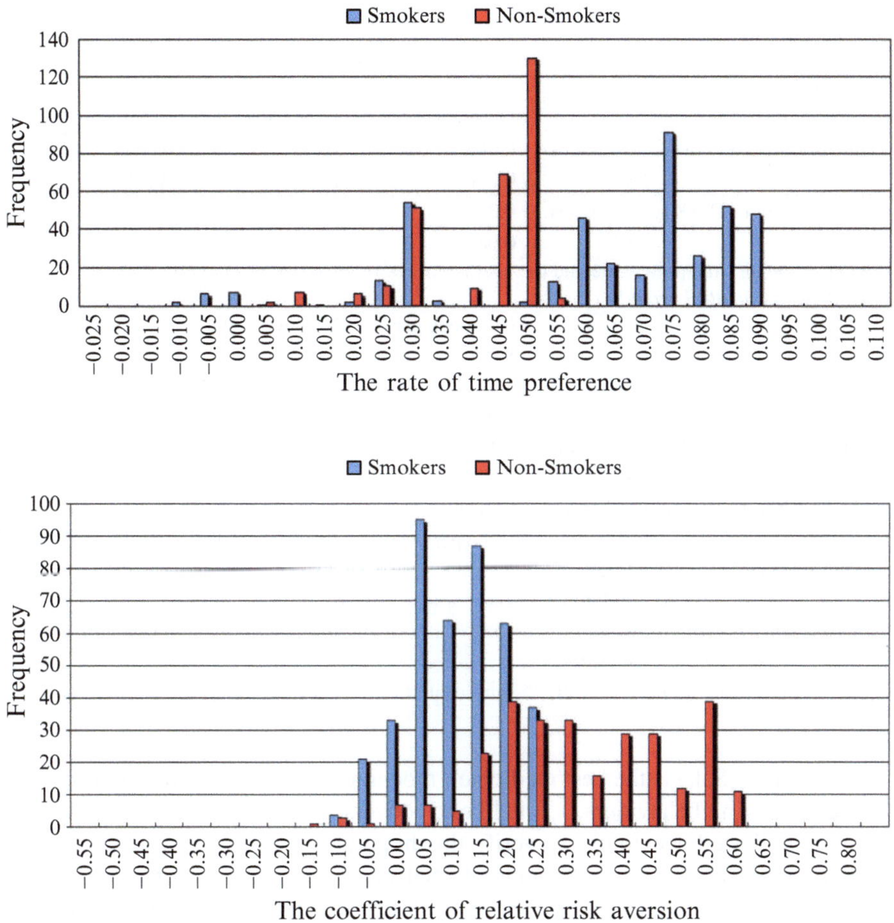

Fig. 7.2 Conditional distributions of random parameters

and Sozou (1998) demonstrated that both risk and delay of reward elicited the same underlying form of intolerance, because a future reward's value should be discounted such that there is a risk that the reward will not realize. On the other hand, other studies including Green and Myerson (2004) have shown that both time and probability discounting are different and dissociable processes. There is still much room to be studied here.

3.6 Detailed Analysis of Time Preference, Risk Aversion, and Drinking

The result that drinkers are less impatient in time discounting and less risk-seeking in probability discounting than non-drinkers may be counterintuitive. As a Japanese

Table 7.5 Time preference and relative risk aversion for various drinking definitions

(a) The rates of time preference and the coefficients of relative risk aversion for *drinkers (treatment group)*

		Once per week	Every other day	Every day
Time preference (TIME)	Estimates	0.048	0.052	0.059
	S.E.	0.006	0.008	0.013
Risk aversion (1-RISK)	Estimates	0.212	0.185	0.057
	S.E.	0.081	0.116	0.013

(b) The rates of time preference and the coefficients of relative risk aversion for *non-drinkers (control group)*

		Non once per week	Non every other day	Non every day
Time preference (TIME)	Estimates	0.061	0.056	0.055
	S.E.	0.006	0.005	0.005
Risk aversion (1-RISK)	Estimates	0.179	0.192	0.208
	S.E.	0.070	0.058	0.055

(c) Welch t test between drinkers and non-drinkers

		Once per week	Every other day	Every day
Welch t values	Time preference	27.2***	5.8***	3.1***
	Risk aversion	5.8***	0.7	57.4***

Note: ***significant at the 1 % level, **significant at the 5 % level, *significant at the 10 % level

proverb says, 'Sake is the best medicine', moderate drinking may control impatient and risk-seeking behaviours.[17] It is likely, conversely, that excessive drinking may encourage these behaviours. To verify this hypothesis, we re-estimate the rates of time preference and the coefficients of relative risk aversion for drinking at least once per week, drinking at least every other day, and drinking every day respectively. At this point, drinkers represent the *treatment* group who drink *every day*, while non-drinkers represent the *control* group who do not drink *every day*, for example.

The estimation results indicated in Table 7.5 are interesting. Table 7.5a indicates the rates of time preference and the coefficients of relative risk aversion for various types of drinkers. Table 7.5b displays the rates of time preference and the coefficients of relative risk aversion for various types of the control groups. Table 7.5c shows the results of Welch's t test regarding the differences in mean estimates between them.

The main findings can be summarized as follows:

- In cases where a drinker is defined as drinking at least *once per week*, drinkers are *less impatient* and *risk-seeking* than the control group; the rates of time

[17] Our finding that social drinking exhibited more self-control than no drinking was predicted by Ainslie (2001) and Rachlin (2004).

preference of the former are statistically significantly lower than the latter, while the coefficients of relative risk aversion of the former are statistically significantly higher than the latter.

- In cases where a drinker is defined as drinking *every day*, drinkers are *more impatient* and *risk-seeking* than the control group; the rates of time preference of the former are statistically significantly higher than the latter, while the coefficients of relative risk aversion of the former are statistically significantly lower than the latter.

In summary, the more narrowly "drinker" is defined, the higher the rate of time preference and the lower the coefficient of relative risk aversion. It must be noted that all drinkers represent shallower delay discount functions than non-drinkers while light drinkers must have shallower delay discounting than heavy-drinkers. As a result, there is indeed a "golden mean" between teetotalling and drunkenness. As for time preference rates, the values are 0.074 for non-drinkers, 0.045 for *light* (once per week or every other day) drinkers, and 0.059 for *heavy* (every day) drinkers. Thus we observed the U-shaped curve among non-, light, and heavy drinkers, which indicates that teetotalling (i.e., an overreaction to impulsiveness) is a kind of impulsivity itself. The same thing can be said of risk aversion coefficients, since the inverse U-shaped curve among non-, light, and heavy drinkers is observed. The coefficients are 0.074 for non-drinkers, 0.265 for *light* (once per week or every other day) drinkers, and 0.057 for *heavy* (every day) drinkers.

4 Interdependencies Among Addictive Behaviours

This section explains the method for investigating the interdependencies among addictive behaviours.

4.1 Two-Stage Probit Estimation Method

In this section, we explain a method to measure the directions and impacts of interdependencies among four addictive behaviours (smoking, drinking, playing *pachinko,* and gambling on horses). For our purpose, we consider the four simultaneous equations model and address the problem of endogeneity across these equations.

We adopt a two-stage probit estimation method that consists of the following two-stage analysis. In the first stage, we separately estimate the induced form equations of addictive behaviours by the probit model. We use such exogenous variables as age, gender (female dummy variable), married dummy variable, number of children, household annual income (unit: JPY 1,000), employed dummy variable, university graduate dummy variable, the rate of time preference, and the coefficient of relative risk aversion. In the second stage, we estimate the structural form equations by the probit model, letting the expected choice probabilities be instrumental variables. We use such explanatory variables as expected choice probabilities of addictive behaviours, the rate of time preference, the coefficient of relative risk aversion, and other statistically significant exogenous variables (including age and female dummy variables).

For details, a simultaneous probit system is specified as follows:

$$Y_{ki}^{*} = \sum_{\substack{k=1 \\ j \neq k}}^{K} \alpha_{kj} Y_{ji}^{*} + \beta_k' X_i + \varepsilon_{ki}, \quad k = 1, \ldots, K \tag{7.6}$$

$$Y_{ki}^{*} = \pi_k' X_i + v_{ki}, \quad k = 1, \ldots, K \tag{7.7}$$

$$Y_{ki} = \begin{bmatrix} 1 \text{ if } Y_{ki}^{*} > 0 \\ 0 \text{ if } Y_{ki}^{*} \leq 0 \end{bmatrix}, \tag{7.8}$$

where Y_{ki}^{*} denotes a latent dependent variable indicating the utility of individual i to choose addictive behaviour k, Y_{ki} denotes an observed dependent variable equalling 1 for an YES choice and 0 for a NO choice, X_i denotes a vector of observed exogenous variables, α_{kj} denotes a scalar unknown parameter, β_k and π_k denote vectors of unknown parameters, and $\varepsilon_i = (\varepsilon_{1i}, \ldots, \varepsilon_{Ki})$ and $v_i = (v_{1i}, \ldots, v_{Ki})$ denote random terms from a K-dimensional multivariate $N(0, \Omega)$ distribution. The simultaneous equations system (7.6) is a structural form since it includes latent independent variables, while the simultaneous equations system (7.7) is a reduced form since it does not.

The two-stage probit estimation method is as follows (Nelson and Olson 1978):

1. Estimate π_k', $k = 1, \ldots, K$ in the reduced form equations (7.7) by probit maximum likelihood separately applied to each K equation and form instruments $\widehat{Y}_{ki}^{*} = \widehat{\pi}_k' X_i$.
2. Replace the Y_{ji}^{*}s on the right hand sides of the structural form equations (7.6) by the corresponding $\hat{Y}_{ki}^{*}$s, and treating these instruments as fixed regressors and the resulting equations as single equation models, estimate the structural form equations (7.6) by the probit maximum likelihood again. Estimates of the structural parameters are consistent and asymptotically normal with asymptotic covariance matrix.[18]

Important applications of the two-stage probit (or tobit) estimation method include Evans et al. (1992), Evans and Schwab (1995), and Brooks et al. (1998).

[18]The correction of the asymptotic covariance matrix at the second step requires some additional computation (Murphy and Topel 1985).

4.2 Estimation Results

Table 7.6 displays the estimation results, in which the figures are the probit model estimations at the second stage. Explanatory variables are expected choice probabilities of addictive behaviours, the rate of time preference, the coefficient of relative risk aversion, and other statistically significant exogenous variables.

First, note the parameters of the choice probabilities of addictive behaviours. When the sign of a parameter estimate is positive, there is a positive interdependency from one behaviour (explanatory variable) to the other behaviour (explained variable). The main findings can be summarized as follows:

- *Drinking* and *playing pachinko* are positively associated with *smoking*.
- *Smoking* and *horse races* are positively associated with *drinking*.
- *Smoking* and *horse races* are positively associated with *playing pachinko*.
- *Drinking* and *playing pachinko* are positively associated with *horse races*. Note that *smoking* has statistically significant negative interdependency.

Next, we scrutinize the parameters representing the rate of time preference and the coefficient of relative risk aversion. If we consider that addictive behaviours are associated with impatient and risk-seeking preferences, the expected effects of the rate of time preference on the choice probabilities of addictive behaviours are *positive*, while the expected effects of the coefficient of relative risk aversion on the choice probabilities of addictive behaviours are *negative*. The main findings can be summarized as follows:

- Expected results are observed for *smoking*, *pachinko,* and *horse races*. On the other hand, the results were opposed to our hypothesis regarding drinking.
- In addition, some exogenous variables including the female dummy variable and age have statistically significant effects on addictive behaviours.

4.3 Interdependencies Among Addictive Behaviours

Next we investigate interdependencies among addictive behaviours based on the estimation results. Figure 7.3 depicts statistically significant interdependencies by arrows. The figures are the elasticities of choice probability. For example, a 1 % increase in the choice probability of smoking increases the choice probability of drinking by 0.154 %; similarly, a 1 % increase in the rate of time preference increases the choice probability of smoking by 1.021 %.

The main findings can be summarized as follows:

- *Smoking* and *drinking* are highly associated with each other.
- *Pachinko* and *horse races* are highly associated with each other.
- *Smoking* and *pachinko* are weakly associated with each other.
- *Drinking* and *horse races* are associated with each other.

Table 7.6 Estimation results of two-step probit models

(a) Smoking

No. of samples	692		
Maximum LL	−633.4		
Initial LL	−959.3		
McFadden R^2	0.3398		
Variables	Estimates	S.E.	Elasticities
Constant	−0.7049	0.2272***	
Drinking	0.8416	0.1361***	0.328
Pachinko	0.5794	0.2967*	0.226
Horse race	−0.2301	0.2741	−0.09
Time preference	45.9375	3.6435***	1.021
Risk aversion	−10.0123	0.8206***	−0.696
Age	−0.015	0.0057***	−0.238
University	0.0166	0.0077**	0.022

(b) Drinking

No. of samples	692		
Maximum LL	−606.8		
Initial LL	−959.3		
McFadden R^2	0.3674		
Variables	Estimates	S.E.	Elasticities
Constant	−1.312	0.2602***	
Smoking	0.4732	0.1129***	0.154
Pachinko	−0.2249	0.3202	−0.073
Horse race	0.7569	0.323**	0.247
Time preference	−30.8143	3.62***	−0.57
Risk aversion	9.1743	0.6854***	0.544
Female dummy	0.3774	0.1569**	0.167
Age	0.0284	0.0061***	0.3765
Employed	0.7467	0.1491***	0.157

(c) Pachinko

No. of samples	692		
Maximum LL	−609.2		
Initial LL	−959.3		
McFadden R^2	0.365		
Variables	Estimates	S.E.	Elasticities
Constant	−0.4088	0.1768**	
Smoking	0.2568	0.1045**	0.107
Drinking	0.1279	0.1446	0.053
Horse race	1.3355	0.1944***	0.558
Time preference	15.3153	4.336***	0.357
Risk aversion	−3.8184	0.6703***	−0.296
Age	−0.0168	0.0072**	−0.286
Married	−0.2853	0.1416**	−0.2

(d) Horse race

No. of samples	692		
Maximum LL	−424.9		
Initial LL	−959.3		
McFadden R^2	0.5571		
Variables	Estimates	S.E.	Elasticities
Constant	−0.235	0.249	
Smoking	−0.5705	0.1284***	−0.268
Drinking	0.563	0.1929***	0.265
Pachinko	1.8336	0.3002***	0.862
Time preference	22.207	4.3187***	0.588
Risk aversion	−4.855	0.5756***	−0.418
Female dummy	−1.2039	0.2351***	−0.766
Income	−0.1634	0.0558***	−0.243

Note: ***significant at the 1 % level, **significant at the 5 % level, *significant at the 10 % level

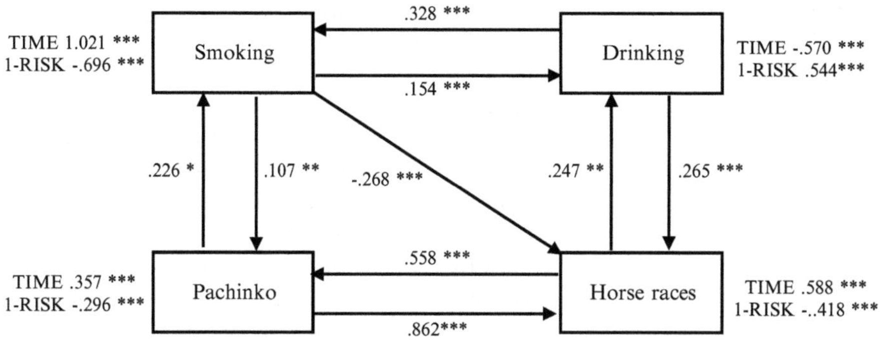

Fig. 7.3 Interdependencies among addictive behaviours. Note 1: ***significant at the 1 % level, **significant at the 5 % level, *significant at the 10 % level. Note 2: Figures are elasticities

- *Smoking* and *horse races,* as well as *drinking* and *pachinko*, are not associated with each other.
- The rates of time preference and the coefficients of relative risk aversion have the expected effects on *smoking*, *pachinko,* and *horse races*.

We can intuitively understand the above results. Since smoking and drinking are frequently conducted simultaneously at home, restaurants (if permitted), or resorts, a high degree of interdependence probably exists between them. Also, since both *pachinko* and horse races involve gambling, people who like one tend to like the other. On the other hand, since many race tracks have recently regulated smoking and most *pachinko* parlors ban drinking, it is difficult to simultaneously gamble on horse races and smoke, or play *pachinko* and drink. Therefore, it is not strange that no interdependency exists between horse races and smoking and between *pachinko* and drinking.

Horizontal (cross) addiction means that a person has plural addictive habits including smoking, drinking, taking drugs, and gambling. It has been reported that the more they are addicted, the more impatient they are (Alessi and Petry 2003; Petry 2001; Bickel and Marsch 2001). Rimm et al. (1995) discussed that the prevalence of smoking was higher in heavy drinkers than in moderate or non-drinkers, and alcohol consumption was higher in smokers than in non-smokers. Madden et al. (2000) pointed out a positive genetic correlation between smoking and drinking. Furthermore, Rose et al. (2004) investigated subjective and behavioural interactions among nicotine, ethanol, and nicotinic antagonist mecamylamine. There may be some commonality in the neural pathways mediating the effects of nicotine and ethanol.

Based on previous literature, it is accepted that the higher the rate of time preference and the lower the coefficient of relative risk aversion, the higher the choice probabilities of smoking, *pachinko,* and horse races. However, drinking is the only exception because a decrease in the rate of time preference or an increase in the coefficients of relative risk aversion leads to an increase in the choice probability of drinking.

Table 7.7 Estimation results for drinking every day

No. of samples	692		
Maximum LL	−779.4		
Initial LL	−959.3		
McFadden R^2	0.1875		
Variables	Estimates	S.E.	Elasticities
Constant	−0.2098	0.2071	
Smoking	0.2839	0.0985***	0.112
Pachinko	−1.1261	0.2754***	−0.446
Horse race	0.4394	0.2612*	0.174
Time preference	5.5386	2.6309**	0.122
Risk aversion	−0.5200	0.2293**	−0.038
Female dummy	−0.0423	0.1213	−0.123
Age	0.0096	0.0044**	0.154
Occupation	0.4372	0.1202***	0.117

Note: ***significant at the 1 % level, **significant at the 5 % level, *significant at the 10 % level

4.4 Detailed Analysis of Interdependencies and Drinking

We re-estimate the interdependencies by using the two-step probit estimation method for drinking every day. Table 7.7 indicates the new estimation results.

Consequently, the rate of time preference and the coefficient of relative risk aversion have the expected effects on the choice probability of drinking. Thus, by narrowing the definition of drinking, the expected interdependencies exist between drinking and time/risk preferences.

5 Concluding Remarks

The following are two important themes in behavioural economics: measuring preference parameters regarding time and risk and investigating interdependencies among addictive behaviours. The increase in health risks caused by smoking and drinking leads to increases in national medical expenditures, and gambling frequently leads to financial difficulties and bankrupts. If we have detailed knowledge about such addictive behaviours as smoking, drinking, and gambling, we can consider accurate countermeasures.

The following are our conclusions. First, there are interesting interdependencies among addictive behaviours including smoking, drinking, playing *pachinko,* and gambling on horses. Especially highly significant interdependencies exist between smoking and drinking and between *pachinko* and horse races. Therefore, quitting one addictive behaviour is not sufficient to totally escape from addiction. It is necessary to go *cold turkey* on all addictions. Second, these addictive behaviours are closely associated with a higher rate of time preference and a lower coefficient of risk aversion. Therefore, there are variations among individuals regarding addictive tendencies, and preventive measures must consider individual differences in time/risk preferences.

The positive relationship between time preference and addiction and the inverse relationship between risk preference and addiction may indicate that rational addiction models are not rejected in the present study. Blondel et al. (2007) showed that addicts were not less consistent with standard theories of behaviour over time and under risk. Becker and Murphy (1988) proposed a rational addiction model in which people who heavily discounted future utilities were more likely to become addicted.[19] As for smoking, much research on time preference has reported that smokers are more impatient than non-smokers and more frequently choose earlier-smaller rewards over later-larger rewards. On the other hand, sufficient research on risk preference has not been accumulated to determine whether smoking and risk-prone preferences are associated.[20] Thus, further research on the relationship between risk preference and additive behaviour is required.

Although our findings show that addicts are impatient and less risk-averse, this does not necessarily imply that they are irrational. When one whose preference is impatient but rational is addicted, direct government intervention is not strongly justified to stop addiction. However, an interesting study reported that individual time preference rates were associated with education and income levels (Warner and Pleeter 2001). Therefore, if one receives more education, one's time preference rate might decrease, lowering the likelihood of addiction; governments might consider education as an effective countermeasure for stopping addictions.

Finally, unsolved problems remain. First, we have not covered any detailed analysis of vertical addiction. Integrating studies of horizontal and vertical addictions is desirable. Second, a detailed study of causality lies outside the scope of this chapter. Third, we should carry out international comparisons to analyze whether the conclusions obtained in this chapter hold in different cultures and countries. We consider these issues potential topics for future research.

[19]Whether addiction is intertemporally rational or irrational depends on whether choice is time-consistent or time-inconsistent. Several studies have regarded addiction as time-inconsistent behaviour. For example, Gruber and Koszegi (2001) demonstrated that preferences with respect to smoking were time inconsistent; individuals both failed to recognize the true difficulty of quitting and sought self-control devices to help them quit. Kan (2007) empirically studied time-inconsistent preferences in the context of cigarette smoking behaviour and concluded that a smoker who wanted to quit had a demand for control devices, e.g., a smoking ban in public areas or a hike in cigarette taxes.

[20]Mitchell (1999) and Reynolds et al. (2003) reported negligible correlations between them.

Addendum: Recent Developments[21]

Smoking is still the most common cause of morbidity and mortality in Japan, with about 130,000 people estimated to die annually from smoking-related diseases (Ikeda et al. 2012). Decreased tobacco use has been shown to reduce the development of smoking-related diseases and death in smokers (Glantz and Gonzalez 2012). Therefore, anti-tobacco policies have been a global issue. In Japan, the enforcement of the Health Promotion Law (2002) promote various tobacco-controlling approaches such as restricting smoking in public places and raising the tax on tobacco. However, in Japan, these measures have proven inadequate compared with other industrialized nations (WHO 2013).

In order to explore factors drive smokers' attempts to quit as well as the investigations about different features of preferences according to smoking history, Goto et al. (2007) have analyzed the willingness of smokers to quit their habit in given hypothetical conditions using discrete choice experiments (DCEs). See also Goto et al. (2011) for a developed research.

In the DCE, any goods or services are described by bundling their attributes or characteristics. The extent to which an individual values goods or services can be evaluated by the selection of hypothetical choices that mimic the daily decision-making process. This technique has often been applied in health-care settings. In this study, the following five attributes were identified as the most important factors: the price of a pack of cigarettes, fines for smoking in public places, long-term health risks (mortality risk), short-term health risks (risk of upper respiratory infection), and health risks to others.

Table 7.8 shows summary of results of the DCE which collects the data from 616 smokers, stratified with Fagerstrom test for nicotine dependence (FTND). The impacts of attributes other than the cigarette price differ remarkably among smokers with different levels of nicotine dependence. The price of cigarettes has the shortest term and certain effect on smokers relative to other variables such as health risks

Table 7.8 Impacts of attributes on smoking on quit attempts

	FTND high	FTND middle	FTND low
Price	+***	+***	+***
Fine	NS	+*	NS
Long-tern health risk (Mortality risk)	NS	NS	+***
Snort-tern health risk (Risk of upper respiratory infection)	NS	+***	+**
Health risk by passive smoking	NS	+***	+***

Notes: *, **, *** 10, 5, 1 % significant level, respectively. + means that the attribute elevate the probability of quit attempts. NS means that the attribute has no impact on quit attempts

[21] This addendum has been newly written for this book chapter.

and penalties—that is, our DCE results indicated that the shortest term and certain effects are significant or all types of smokers, while the longer and risky term effects such as health risks are found only in smokers with lower nicotine dependence. These results imply the importance of time/risk preference parameters also from tobacco-controlling policy perspective.

References

Ainslie G (2001) Breakdown of will. Cambridge University Press, New York

Akerlof G (1991) Procrastination and obedience. Am Econ Rev 81:1–19

Alessi SM, Petry NM (2003) Pathological gambling severity is associated with impulsivity in a delay discounting procedure. Behav Process 64:345–354

Anderhub V, Guth W, Gneezy U, Sonsino D (2001) On the interaction of risk and time preferences: an experimental study. Ger Econ Rev 2:239–253

Baker F, Johnson MW, Bickel WK (2003) Delay discounting in current and never-before cigarette smokers: similarities and differences across commodity, sign, and magnitude. J Abnorm Psychol 112:382–392

Barsky RB, Juster FT, Kimball MS, Shapiro MT (1997) Preference parameters and behavioral heterogeneity: an experimental approach in the health and retirement study. Q J Econ 112:537–579

Becker GS, Murphy KM (1988) A theory of rational addiction. J Polit Econ 96:675–700

Bernheim BD, Rangel A (2005) Behavioral public economics: welfare and policy analysis with non-standard decision makers, NBER working paper, #11518. National Bureau of Economic Research, Cambridge, MA

Bhat C (2001) Quasi-random maximum simulated likelihood estimation of the mixed multinomial logit model. Transp Res B 35:677–693

Bickel WK, Marsch LA (2001) Toward a behavioral economic understanding of drug dependence: delay discounting processes. Addiction 96:73–86

Bickel WK, Odum AL, Madden GJ (1999) Impulsivity and cigarette smoking: delay discounting in current never, and ex-smokers. Psychopharmacology 146:447–454

Blondel S, Lohéac Y, Rinaudo S (2007) Rationality and drug use: an experimental approach. J Health Econ 26:643–658

Brooks J, Cameron AC, Carter CA (1998) Political action committee contributions and U.S. congressional voting on sugar legislation. Am J Agric Econ 80:441–454

Brownstone D, Train KE (1999) Forecasting new product penetration with flexible substitution patterns. J Econ 89:109–129

Carson RT, Louviere JJ, Anderson DA, Arabie P, Bunch DS, Hensher DA, Johnson RM, Kuhfeld WF, Steinberg D, Swait J, Timmermans H, Wiley JB (1994) Experimental analysis of choice. Mark Lett 5:351–367

Chesson H, Viscusi WK (2000) The heterogeneity of time-risk tradeoffs. J Behav Decis Mak 13:251–258

DiClemente DF, Hantula DA (2003) Applied behavior economics and consumer choice. J Econ Psychol 24:589–602

Donkers B, van Soet A (1999) Subjective measures of household preferences and financial decisions. J Econ Psychol 20:613–642

Evans WN, Schwab RM (1995) Finishing high school and starting college: Do catholic make a difference? Q J Econ 110:941–974

Evans WN, Oates WE, Schwab RM (1992) Measuring peer effects: a study of teenage behavior. J Polit Econ 100:966–991

Fishburn PC, Rubinstein A (1982) Time preference. Int Econ Rev 23:677–694

Frederick S, Lowenstein G, O'Donoghue T (2002) Time discounting and time preference; a critical review. J Econ Lit 40:351–401
Fuchs V (1982) Time preferences and health: an exploratory study. In: Fuchs V (ed) Economics aspects of health. University of Chicago Press, Chicago
Glantz S, Gonzalez M (2012) Effective tobacco control is key to rapid progress in reduction of non-communicable diseases. Lancet 379:1269–1271
Goto R, Nishimura S, Ida T (2007) Discrete choice experiment of smoking cessation behaviour in Japan. Tob Control 6:336–343
Goto R, Takahashi Y, Ida T (2011) Changes of smokers' attitudes to intended cessation attempts in Japan. Value Health 14:785–791
Green L, Myerson J (2004) A discounting framework for choice with delayed and probabilistic rewards. Psychol Bull 130:769–792
Gruber J, Koszegi B (2001) Is addiction "rational"? Theory and evidence. Q J Econ 116:1261–1303
Halton J (1960) On the efficiency of evaluating certain quasi-random sequences of points in evaluating multi-dimensional integrals. Numer Math 2:84–90
Hensher DA, Rose JM, Greene WH (2005) Applied choice analysis. Cambridge University Press, Cambridge
Holden C (2001) 'Behavioral' addictions: do they exist? Science 294:980–982
Ikeda N, Inoue M, Iso H, Ikeda S, Satoh T, Noda M et al (2012) Adult mortality attributable to preventable risk factors for non-communicable diseases and injuries in Japan: a comparative risk assessment. PLoS Med 9(1):e1001160
Kahneman D, Tversky A (1979) Prospect theory: an analysis of decision under risk. Econometrica 47:263–291
Kan K (2007) Cigarette smoking and self-control. J Health Econ 26:61–81
Kapteyn A, Teppa F (2003) Hypothetical intertemporal consumption choices. Econ J 113:140–152
Keren G, Roelofsma P (1995) Immediacy and certainty in intertemporal choice. Organ Behav Hum Decis Process 63:287–297
Koopmans TC (1960) Stationary ordinal utility and impatience. Econometrica 28:287–309
Louviere JJ, Hensher DA, Swait JD (2000) Stated choice methods. Cambridge University Press, Cambridge
Madden GJ, Petry NM, Bodger GJ, Bickel WK (1997) Impulsive and self-control choices in opioid-dependendent patients and non-drug-using control participants: drug and monetary rewards. Exp Clin Psychopharmacol 5:256–262
Madden GJ, Bickel WK, Jacobs EA (1999) Discounting of delayed rewards in opioid-dependent outpatients: exponential or hyperbolic discounting function? Exp Clin Psychopharmacol 7:284–293
Madden PA, Bucholz KK, Martin NG, Heath AC (2000) Smoking and the genetic contribution to alcohol-dependence risk. Alcohol Res Health 24:209–214
McFadden D, Train KE (2000) Mixed MNL models of discrete choice models of discrete response. J Appl Econ 15:447–470
McKenzie DC (1999) Markers of excessive exercise. Can J Appl Physiol 24:66–73
Messinis G (1999) Habit formation and the theory of addiction. J Econ Surv 13:417–442
Mitchell SH (1999) Measures of impulsivity in cigarette smokers and non-smokers. Psychopharmacology 146:455–464
Murphy KM, Topel RH (1985) Estimation and inference in two-step econometric models. J Bus Econ Stat 3:370–379
Nelson F, Olson L (1978) Specification and estimation of a simultaneous-equation model with limited dependent variables. Int Econ Rev 19:695–709
Odum AL, Madden GJ, Bickel WK (2002) Discounting of delayed health gains and losses by current, never- and ex-smokers of cigarettes. Nicotine Tob Res 4:295–303
Ohmura Y, Takahashi T, Kitamura N (2005) Discounting delayed and probabilistic monetary gains and losses by smokers of cigarettes. Psychopharmacology 182:508–515
Orphanides A, Zervos D (1995) Rational addiction with learning and regret. J Polit Econ 103:739–758

Orphanides A, Zervos D (1998) Myopia and addictive behaviour. Econ J 108:75–91
Petry NM (2001) Pathological gamblers, with and without substance use disorders, discount delayed rewards at high rates. J Abnorm Psychol 110:482–487
Petry NM, Casarella T (1999) Excessive discounting of delayed rewards in substance abusers with gambling problems. Drug Alcohol Depend 56:25–32
Rachlin H (2004) The science of self-control. Harvard University Press, Cambridge, MA
Rachlin H, Siegel E (1994) Temporal pattering in probabilistic choice. Organ Behav Hum Decis Process 59:161–176
Rachlin H, Raineri A, Cross D (1991) Subjective probability and delay. J Exp Anal Behav 55:233–244
Revelt D, Train K (1998) Mixed logit with repeated choices: households' choices of appliance efficiency level. Rev Econ Stat 80:647–657
Revelt D, Train K (2000) Specific taste parameters and mixed logit, Working paper no. E00-274. Department of Economics, University of California, Berkeley
Reynolds B, Karraker K, Horn K, Richards JB (2003) Delay and probability discounting as related to different stages of adolescent smoking and non-smoking. Behav Process 64:333–344
Reynolds B, Richards JB, Horn K, Karraker K (2004) Delay discounting and probability discounting as related to cigarette smoking status in adults. Behav Process 65:35–42
Rimm EB, Can J, Stampfer MJ, Colditz GA, Willett WC (1995) Prospective study of cigarette smoking, alcohol use, and the risk of diabetes in men. Br Med J 310:555–559
Rose JE, Brauer LH, Behm FM, Cramblett M, Calkins K, Lawhon D (2004) Psychopharmacological interactions between nicotine and ethanol. Nicotine Tob Res 6:133–144
Samuelson P (1937) A note on measurement of utility. Rev Econ Stud 4:155–161
Sozou PD (1998) On hyperbolic discounting and uncertain hazard rates. Proc R Soc B Biol Sci 265:2015–2020
Stigler GJ, Becker GS (1977) De Gustibus Non Est Dispuandum. Am Econ Rev 67:76–90
Takahashi T (2005) Loss of self-control in intertemporal choice may be attributable to logarithmic time-perception. Med Hypotheses 65:691–693
Train KE (2003) Discrete choice methods with simulation. Cambridge University Press, New York
Tsuge T, Kishimoto A, Takeuchi K (2005) A choice experiment approach to the valuation of mortality. J Risk Uncertain 31:73–95
Viney R, Lanscar E, Louviere J (2002) Discrete choice experiments to measure preference for health and health care: expert review. Pharmacoecon Outcomes Res 2:319–326
von Neumann J, Morgenstern O (1953) Theory of games and economic behaviour. Princeton University Press, Princeton
Warner JT, Pleeter S (2001) The personal discount rate: evidence from military downsizing programs. Am Econ Rev 91:33–53
Winston GC (1980) Addiction and backsliding: a theory of compulsive consumption. J Econ Behav Organ 1:295–324
World Health Organization (2013) WHO report on the global tobacco epidemic, 2013: enforcing bans on tobacco advertising, promotion and sponsorship. World Health Organization, Geneva
Yi R, de la Piedad X, Bickel WK (2006) The combined effects of delay and probability in discounting. Behav Process 73:149–155
Yi R, Chase WD, Bickel WK (2007) Probability discounting among cigarette smokers and nonsmokers: molecular analysis discerns group differences. Behav Pharmacol 18:633–639

Chapter 8
Discounting Delayed and Probabilistic Monetary Gains and Losses by Smokers of Cigarettes

Yu Ohmura, Taiki Takahashi, and Nozomi Kitamura

Abstract *Rationale:* Nicotine dependence has been associated with impulsivity and discounting delayed/uncertain outcomes. *Objectives:* This study had two main objectives: (1) to examine the relationship between the number of cigarettes consumed per day and the degree to which delayed and uncertain monetary gains and losses are discounted by smokers, and (2) to determine the relationship between the estimated dose of nicotine intake per day and the degree to which four types of discounting occur. *Methods:* Twenty seven habitual smokers and 23 never smokers participated in this experiment. They were required to choose between immediate and delayed monetary rewards (or losses), or between guaranteed and probabilistic rewards (or losses). *Results:* The degree to which delayed monetary gains were discounted was significantly and positively correlated with both the number of cigarettes smoked and the estimated dose of nicotine intake per day. Conversely, there was no relationship between smoking and the remaining three types of discounting. Also, mild smokers in our sample did not differ from never smokers in discounting monetary gains or losses. *Conclusions*: In general, our results suggest that both the frequency of nicotine self-administration, as well as the dosage, are positively associated with greater delay discounting of gains. One

The original article first appeared in Psychopharmacology (Berlin) 182(4):508–515, 2005. A newly written addendum has been added to this book chapter.

Y. Ohmura
Department of Neuropharmacology, Graduate School of Medicine, Hokkaido University, N15 W7, Kita-ku, Sapporo, 060-8638 Japan
e-mail: yohmura@med.hokudai.ac.jp

T. Takahashi (✉)
Department of Behavioral Science, Hokkaido University, N10 W7, Kita-ku, Sapporo 060-0810, Japan
e-mail: ttakahashi@lynx.let.hokudai.ac.jp

N. Kitamura
Hokkaido University, Sapporo, Japan

S. Ikeda et al. (eds.), *Behavioral Economics of Preferences, Choices, and Happiness*, DOI 10.1007/978-4-431-55402-8_8

neuropsychopharmacological explanation for this effect is that chronic nicotine intake may induce neuroadaptation of the neural circuitry involved in reward processing.

Keywords Addiction • Delay discounting • Probability discounting • Cigarette smoking • Nicotine • Impulsivity • Neuroeconomics • Intertemporal choice

1 Introduction

Impulsive behavior, broadly defined as "actions that are poorly conceived, prematurely expressed, unduly risky, or inappropriate to the situation and that often result in undesirable outcomes" (Daruna and Barnes 1993), are frequently observed in drug-dependent subjects (see Bickel and Marsch 2001 for a review). In most psychopharmacological studies of intertemporal choice, impulsivity is often operationalized in terms of delay discounting—the tendency to choose smaller, relatively immediate rewards over larger but more delayed rewards (e.g., Kirby et al. 1999; Richards et al. 1999b; Petry 2001; Pietras et al. 2003).

Dependence on drugs such as cocaine, heroin, nicotine, or alcohol has been associated with greater discounting of delayed rewards in a number of psychopharmacological studies (e.g., Kirby and Petry 2004; Kirby et al. 1999; Bickel et al. 1999; Petry 2001). However, to date, little is known regarding the relationship between the frequency of drug administration, or the drug dosage, and delay discounting. One notable exception is a recent study by Reynolds (2004) reporting that the number of cigarettes consumed per day was positively correlated with impulsive choice in delay discounting. Understanding the dose-dependent relationship between a drug and delay discounting is critical to (a) better estimate a drug's effect on impulsive behavior in general, and intertemporal decision-making specifically, which can often result in problematic outcomes for the drug user (see Bickel and Marsch 2001 for a review) and (b) predict vulnerability to drug dependence as a function of discounting behavior, as suggested by a previous study (Perry et al. 2005).

Recently, in the emerging field of neuroeconomics (see Glimcher and Rustichini 2004; Schultz 2004 for a review), several neuroscientists and economists have collaborated to reveal some of the neural substrates involved in economic decision making, including those governing delay discounting. For instance, we have reported that low cortisol levels were associated with impulsive choice in delay discounting (Takahashi 2004) partly via modulation of the reward-processing, dopaminergic circuitry in the brain. In one neuroimaging study, Loewenstein and Cohen's group demonstrated that choosing a smaller, immediate monetary reward was associated with activation of the reward-processing dopaminergic circuitry located in the midbrain (McClure et al. 2004). Montague and Berns (2002) have proposed that estimating future reward values is mediated by dopaminergic circuitry (e.g., the ventral tegmental area). Taken together, dopaminergic systems may play a pivotal role in impulsive choice in delay discounting.

Concerning the relationship between chronic self-administration of nicotine and dopaminergic response to monetary gains, Schultz and his colleagues have reported a lower dopaminergic response to monetary rewards in habitual cigarette smokers when compared to nonsmokers, which may indicate an exaggerated devaluation of delayed monetary rewards (i.e., greater delay discounting) in smokers (Martin-Solch et al. 2001, 2003). Nevertheless, the relationship between self-administration of a dopaminergic drug such as nicotine and discounting behavior can be better defined. Therefore, it is of neuropsychopharmacological interest to investigate delay discounting as a function of both the frequency of nicotine self-administration and the strength of the dosage.

Moreover, although most studies have focused on discounting delayed monetary gain, we feel it is important to expand the current research design to include additional forms of discounting. Neuroeconomic research has revealed that distinct brain regions are activated in response to monetary gains and losses (Knutson et al. 2000, 2003; Breiter et al. 2001). Therefore, in examining the relationship between cigarette smoking and impulsive discounting delayed outcomes, it is important to include the tendency to discount delayed monetary losses in addition to the discounting of delayed monetary gains. Furthermore, the relationship between drug intake and the discounting of uncertain rewards (probability discounting) has been attracting more attention recently, but with mixed results. For instance, Mitchell, a psychopharmacologist, failed to observe a difference between smokers and never smokers in discounting of uncertain rewards (Mitchell 1999). On the other hand, although there was no significant correlation between probability discounting and breath CO levels taken at the time of participation, smokers in the Reynolds study discounted an uncertain monetary reward more dramatically when compared to never smokers (Reynolds et al. 2004). One possible reason for the discrepant findings may have to do with the degree to which the samples engaged in smoking: smokers in the Mitchell study consumed as few as 15 cigarettes per day, whereas those in the Reynolds study smoked more than 20 per day. Thus, an elevation in probability discounting may only be observed in relatively heavy smokers. Nevertheless, the inconsistency of these findings suggests that the link between smoking and probability discounting requires further investigation. It should also be noted that whether impulsive behavior can be defined as strong probability discounting is still controversial (cf. Myerson et al. 2003). Again, considering that the neural responses involved in economic gains and losses are distinct, it is important to examine discounting of both uncertain monetary gains and losses with regard to smoking frequency and nicotine dosage.

As far as we know, this study is the first to investigate the relationship between the frequency and dosage of nicotine self-administration and the tendency toward four types of decision making (i.e., discounting of delayed and uncertain monetary gains and losses) within the same subjects. It should also be noted that, as far as we know, this study is the first to examine discounting of uncertain monetary losses in smokers of cigarettes. Furthermore, we examined differences in four types of discounting between never smokers and smokers. Additionally, to further elucidate their distinct psychological processes (and possibly the distinct neural mechanisms underlying these processes as well), we compared discounting of gains and losses. Finally, we examined whether a positive correlation is observed between delay and probability discounting as expected from the hypothesis that an increase in delay is equivalent to a decrease in probability (Rachlin et al. 1991).

2 Materials and Methods

2.1 Participants

A total of 50 subjects participated in the present study, including 27 young-adult habitual smokers (20 males and 7 females) between 21 and 33 years of age ($M = 24.15$; $SD = 3.68$), and 23 never smokers (16 males and 7 females) between 21 and 28 years of age ($M = 23.26$; $SD = 1.96$). It should be noted that the present smoker population was relatively mild in comparison to other studies (e.g., Bickel et al. 1999; Reynolds et al. 2004; in their studies, only heavy smokers who consumed a minimum of 20 cigarettes per day were employed); only eight smokers consumed a minimum of 20 cigarettes per day, and the mean number of cigarettes consumed per day was 14.38 (Table 8.1). Graduate and undergraduate students were recruited to participate through advertisements posted on bulletin boards at Hokkaido University in Sapporo, Japan. The participants were informed that the experiment involved a decision-making task involving monetary gains and losses. They signed an informed consent form before participating and received 1,000 yen (about US $10) following completion of the experiment.

Table 8.1 Mean and standard deviations for demographic variables, smoking behavior, and AUCs for current and never smokers

	Currentsmokers		Neversmokers	
	Mean	SD	Mean	SD
Sex (% men)	69.57		74.07	
Age (years)	24.15	3.68	23.26	1.96
Education (% graduate)	32.00		47.83	
Cigarette number (per day)	14.38	6.66		
Smoking history (months)	69.04	48.89		
DD of gain	0.54	0.27	0.58	0.33
PD of gain	0.23	0.15	0.18	0.08
DD of loss	0.69	0.25	0.74	0.29
PD of loss	0.36	0.16	0.39	0.17

In calculating the AUC, the horizontal axis is delay (in delay discounting) or odds-against (=1/probability − 1, in probability discounting), and the vertical axis is the indifference point. Note that smaller AUC values correspond to greater discounting. Regarding education and cigarette number, two data points are missing due to the participants' omission in answering these questions
DD Delay discounting, *PD* probability discounting

2.2 Materials and Procedure

Because Johnson and Bickel (2002) showed a strong correlation between discounting rates for hypothetical and real monetary gains, and Baker et al. (2003) demonstrated that discounting rates for hypothetical and real money were not significantly different, a computerized procedure consisting of hypothetical monetary outcomes was used to assess discounting in the laboratory. The procedure was composed of four different types of discounting (i.e., delay of gain, delay of loss, uncertain gain, and uncertain loss). Participants were seated individually in a semisoundproof room and received the following instruction on the computer screen in Japanese:

> [From now, you are required to perform tasks of decision-making on monetary reward/loss. The task is to choose between two options. The monetary reward/ loss in this experiment is hypothetical, but we want you to think as though it is real money].

Next, they received instructions describing the four discounting tasks with corresponding examples. At the beginning of each trial, the participant was asked to select one of two cards displayed on their computer monitor. The left card indicated the sum of money that could be received (or lost) immediately (or certainly, in the probability-discounting tasks), whereas the right card always indicated 100,000 yen (about US $1,000) that could be received (or lost) after a certain delay (or with a certain probability).

The sum of money indicated on the left card ranged from 100,000 to 5,000 yen (or from −100,000 to −5,000 yen, in loss-frame tasks) in 5,000-yen intervals. In the delay-discounting task, the delay indicated on the right card changed between five time frames (1 week, 1 month, 6 months, 1 year, and 5 years). For the probability-discounting task, the right card indicated one of five probability values (90, 70, 50, 30, and 10 %). These changes were computerized according to the algorithm used by Richards et al. (1999b). This algorithm is designed to determine the point at which the participant switches his or her preference from the left card (immediate/guaranteed reward or loss) to the right card (delayed/probabilistic reward or loss) by changing the type of task and the sum of money in accordance with previous decisions. The switching point is regarded as the indifference point and was used to calculate the dependant variable. In the present study, 20 indifference points were determined (five for each type of discounting). This algorithm masks the true nature of the procedure, and in the present study, distractor trials were inserted after ten indifference points were established (for more details, see Richards et al. 1999b).

Following the computer task, all participants were required to answer four questions regarding their smoking behavior, including the number of months they had smoked, the average number of cigarettes they smoked per day, the variation (i.e., the minimum and maximum number of cigarettes they smoked in a day), and their usual brand of cigarettes. The entire experimental procedure took between 30 and 60 min to complete. For no subject did the variation in the number of cigarettes they smoked per day exceed five cigarettes. It should also be noted that the results remained essentially unchanged when the number of cigarettes smoked per day was

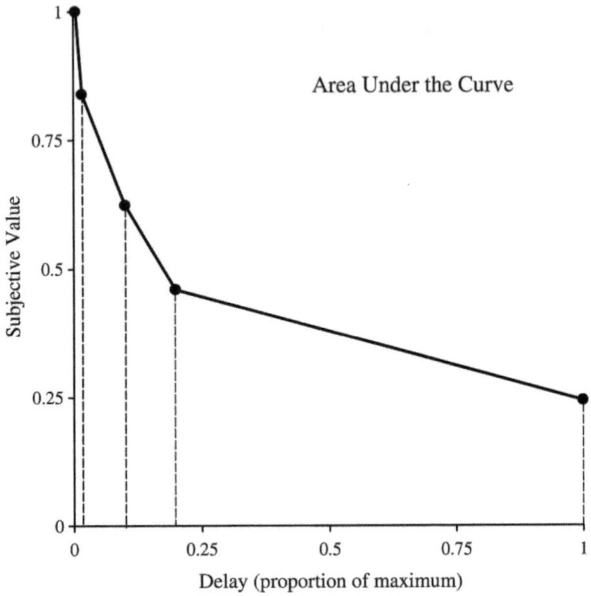

Fig. 8.1 Calculation of the area under the indifference curve in delay discounting of monetary gain, a linkage of subjective values of delayed monetary gain, for representative example (Subject 12). Note that in probability discounting, the horizontal axis is odds-against (=1/probability − 1)

recoded into categories of low (1–10 cigarettes), medium (11–20 cigarettes), and high (21 cigarettes or more) frequencies.

2.3 *Data Analysis*

To parametrize the degree to which each subject discounted delayed and uncertain monetary gains and losses, we computed an area under the curve (AUC) for each of the four discounting tasks (cf. Fig. 8.1). The procedure for calculating an AUC was as follows (for more details, see Myerson et al. 2001). First, indifference points were plotted in two dimensions, with either delay or odds-against [=(1/probability) − 1] (cf. Rachlin et al. 1991) plotted along the horizontal axis and gain (or the absolute value of loss) plotted along the vertical axis. Connecting the individual indifference points defined the indifference curve. Note that the steepness of the indifference curve indicates the degree to which the monetary outcomes were discounted by the subject. Second, both the horizontal and vertical scales were divided by the largest value on their respective axes to produce a range of values between 0 and 1. Third, the AUC was defined as the total area under this normalized indifference curve. The smaller this area, the more dramatic the subject's discounting tendency. We adopted the use of AUCs primarily to avoid equation-dependent systematic errors that can result from specific fitting functions, something the AUC parameter does not depend on.

Additionally, although it is well established that delayed and probabilistic gains are discounted hyperbolically rather than exponentially (e.g., Mazur 1987; Rachlin et al. 1991; Richards et al. 1999b; Simpson and Vuchinich 2000), we compared the four types of discounting (delayed and uncertain, gains and losses), to determine whether losses are also discounted hyperbolically. Specifically, we performed a nonlinear regression (SAS, PROC NLIN) to fit hyperbolic and exponential discounting functions to the indifference points at each level of delay and probability. The exponential function was defined as

$$V = Ae^{-kD},$$

where *V* is the subjective value of a reward, *A* is the (objective) amount of the reward (the monetary gain or loss), *k* is a free parameter and an index of the steepness of the discounting function (i.e., larger *k* values correspond to steeper delay discounting), and *D* is the length of the delay (delay discounting) or the odds-against (probability discounting). The hyperbolic function was defined as

$$V = A/(1 + kD),$$

with the same notations. To determine which equation fits the data better, we compared the respective R^2 values of the hyperbolic and exponential equations.

The estimated amount of daily nicotine intake was calculated by multiplying the average number of cigarettes smoked per day by the amount of nicotine per cigarette that was printed on the cigarette pack of the brand consumed by the subject. It is noteworthy that the number of cigarettes smoked per day indicates the frequency of nicotine self-administration, whereas the estimated amount of nicotine intake per day indicates the level of chronic nicotine exposure. To test statistical significance of correlations and mean differences, Pearson's product-moment correlation coefficients and *t* tests were utilized, respectively. Alpha level was set at 5 % throughout.

3 Results

3.1 Relationships Involving Demographics and Discounting Behavior

Means and standard deviations for demographic variables, smoking behavior, and AUCs for discounting are summarized in Table 8.1. Smoking and nonsmoking samples did not differ in age, sex, or level of education, but there was a significant difference in the average number of cigarettes smoked per day between men and women (16.36 vs 9.29, $t(23) = 2.67$, $P < 0.05$). The correlation between the average number of cigarettes smoked per day and age was not significant.

The present AUC values were similar to values reported in previous studies (Myerson et al. 2001). A participant's age did not correlate with any of the AUCs for discounting, and there were no significant differences between the AUCs of men and women or between the AUCs of graduate and undergraduate students. Thus, neither age, sex, nor education seemed to have any effect on discounting behavior in our sample.

3.2 Fitness of Discounting Equations

Hyperbolic and exponential R^2 values were calculated using both group medians and individual scores. For the group data, each R^2 value associated with the hyperbolic function (delay discounting of gain, 0.99; probability discounting of gain, 0.98; delay discounting of loss, 0.97; and probability discounting of loss, 0.98) was larger than its corresponding exponential function (delay discounting of gain, 0.91; probability discounting of gain, 0.81; delay discounting of loss, 0.96; and probability discounting of loss, 0.84). Moreover, except when discounting delayed gains, each individual R^2 value associated with the hyperbolic function was significantly larger than its corresponding exponential function [dependent sample t tests: delay discounting of gain $t(39) = 1.77$, $P = 0.08$; probability discounting of gain $t(39) = 2.80$, $P < 0.01$; delay discounting of loss $t(33) = 4.93$, $P < 0.01$; and probability discounting of loss $t(38) = 4.82$, $P < 0.01$]. These results suggest that the subjects discounted most types of monetary outcomes hyperbolically, rather than exponentially, as a number of previous studies have reported (e.g., Rachlin et al. 1991; Vuchinich and Simpson 1998; Richards et al. 1999b; Bickel et al. 1999; Simpson and Vuchinich 2000).

3.3 Relationships Involving Smoking Status and Discounting Behavior

First, we investigated the relationship between the frequency of nicotine intake and discounting behavior in smokers by calculating the Pearson product-moment correlation between the number of cigarettes smoked per day and each of the four types of discounting. The correlational analysis revealed that the AUC for discounting delayed gains in smokers decreased significantly with the number of cigarettes they smoked per day [$r(25) = -0.66$, $P < 0.01$, see Fig. 8.2], suggesting that more frequent smokers are more impulsive when discounting delayed monetary gains. It should be noted that this finding is consistent with the recent study by Reynolds (2004), which reported a positive correlation between the number of cigarettes smoked per day and a delay discounting rate (logged hyperbolic k) of monetary rewards. Regarding the number of cigarettes smoked per day and

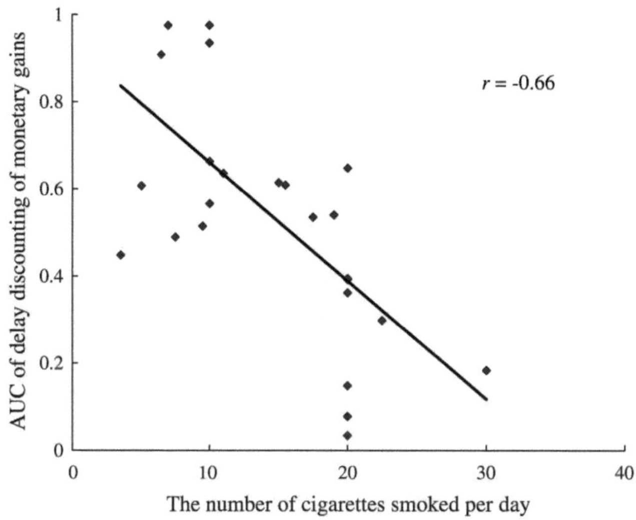

Fig. 8.2 Scatterplot of the number of cigarettes smoked per day and the AUC for delay discounting of monetary gains in smokers. A significant negative correlation was observed ($n = 25$, $P < 0.01$). Note that a smaller AUC indicates a higher degree of discounting. Two data points are missing due to the participants' omission in answering questions about their smoking behavior

the remaining three types of discounting, no other significant correlations were observed in the present study [probability discounting of gain $r(25) = -0.00059$, $P = 0.9978$; delay discounting of loss $r(25) = -0.12$, $P = 0.58$; and probability discounting of loss $r(25) = 0.10$, $P = 0.63$]. In addition, because (a) the number of male and female smokers (20 males and 7 females) was different and, (b) as stated earlier, there was a significant difference in the average number of cigarettes smoked per day between the sexes, we omitted the female participants and repeated the correlational analysis. Again, the AUC for delay discounting of gains in male smokers was significantly correlated with the number of cigarettes smoked per day [$r(18) = -0.69$, $P < 0.01$], and no other significant correlations were observed.

Second, correlations between the level of chronic nicotine exposure and the degree of discounting similarly revealed a significant relationship between the AUC for discounting delayed gains by smokers and the estimated amount of nicotine intake per day [$r(25) = -0.57$, $P < 0.01$, see Fig. 8.3]. This indicates that subjects with higher levels of chronic nicotine exposure were more impulsive in discounting delayed monetary gains. Regarding the relationships between the estimated amount of nicotine intake per day and the remaining three types of discounting, no other significant relationships were observed [probability discounting of gain $r(25) = 0.22$, $P = 0.29$; delay discounting of loss $r(25) = -0.05$, $P = 0.82$; and probability discounting of loss $r(25) = -0.12$, $P = 0.56$]. When the analysis was restricted to male participants, the results were the same; the only significant correlation between nicotine intake per day and discounting was that involving delay discounting of gains by male smokers [$r(18) = -0.56$, $P < 0.05$].

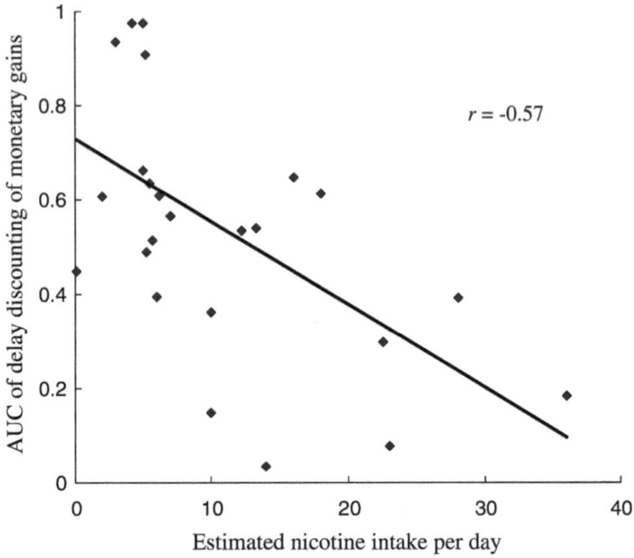

Fig. 8.3 Scatterplot of the estimated amount of nicotine intake per day and the AUC for delay discounting of monetary gains in smokers. A significant negative correlation was observed ($n = 25$, $P < 0.01$). Note that a smaller AUC indicates a higher degree of discounting. Two data points are missing due to the participants' omission in answering questions about their smoking behavior

Additionally, the number of months the subject had smoked was unrelated to his or her discounting behavior [delay discounting of gain $r(25) = -0.18$, $P = 0.38$; probability discounting of gain $r(25) = -0.10$, $P = 0.63$; delay discounting of loss $r(25) = 0.34$, $P = 0.08$; and probability discounting of loss $r(25) = 0.21$, $P = 0.30$] but was significantly correlated with both the estimated nicotine intake per day and the number of cigarettes smoked per day ($r(25) = 0.46$, $P < 0.05$ and $r(25) = 0.42$, $P < 0.05$, respectively). These findings are consistent with those reported in the report of Reynolds (2004). Also, the number of cigarettes smoked per day was correlated with the amount of nicotine per cigarette [$r(25) = 0.55$, $P < 0.01$]. This indicates that habitual smokers who consume more cigarettes regularly tend to smoke stronger cigarettes. Consequently, the number of cigarettes smoked per day was correlated with the estimated amount of nicotine intake per day [$r(25) = 0.87$, $P < 0.01$].

3.4 Group Differences in the Degree of Discounting Between Never Smokers and Smokers

To examine whether a previously reported group difference between never smokers and heavy smokers was replicated in the present study, we compared delay discounting of monetary gains in smokers and never smokers and found no significant difference [$t(48) = 0.48$, $P = 0.63$]. Moreover, there was no difference between smokers and never smokers in any of the other three types of discounting [probability discounting of gain $t(40.5) = -1.78$, $P = 0.08$; delay discounting of loss $t(48) = 0.57$, $P = 0.57$; and probability discounting of loss $t(48) = 0.78$, $P = 0.44$]. It has already been noted that the smokers in our sample were relatively mild nicotine users compared to those who have participated in previous studies (e.g., Bickel et al. 1999; Mitchell 1999; Reynolds et al. 2004), which may have resulted in a nonsignificant group difference.

3.5 Relationship Between Discounting Gains and Discounting Losses

In addition, we examined the relationship between discounting a gain and discounting a loss across all 50 participants for delay and probability discounting and confirmed positive and negative relationships, respectively [delay discounting $r(50) = 0.60$, $P < 0.01$; probability discounting $r(50) = -0.49$, $P < 0.01$]. Moreover, mean AUCs for discounting gains were significantly smaller than those for losses [dependent sample t tests: delay discounting $t(49) = 4.34$, $P < 0.01$; probability discounting $t(49) = 4.66$, $P < 0.01$]. This implies that people more steeply discount future/uncertain gains than losses.

3.6 Relationship Between Delay Discounting and Probability Discounting

Finally, we analyzed the relationship between delay discounting and probability discounting independently for gains and losses across all 50 participants. For gains, Pearson product–moment correlations revealed a positive, but nonsignificant, relationship between the AUCs of delay and probability discounting [$r(50) = 0.17$, $P = 0.23$]. This observation is consistent with the study of Myerson et al. (2003) reporting a relatively weak to modest positive relationship between discounting of delayed and uncertain gains. The correlation between discounting delayed and uncertain losses was likewise nonsignificant [$r(50) = 0.16$, $P = 0.28$]. Together, these results suggest that the cognitive processes involved in evaluating delayed rewards (or losses) may differ from those involved with uncertain rewards (or losses).

4 Discussion

Our study is the first to examine the relationships between the number of cigarettes smoked per day, the estimated amount of nicotine intake per day, and four types of discounting (i.e., delay and probability discounting of monetary gains and losses) within the same subjects. Our data suggest five general conclusions: (1) the frequency of nicotine self-administration is positively associated with impulsive behavior in discounting delayed monetary rewards, (2) the level of chronic nicotine exposure is similarly associated with impulsive behavior in discounting delayed monetary gains, (3) relatively mild smokers do not discount delayed or uncertain gains or losses more than never smokers, (4) discounting monetary losses is not strongly associated with smoking, and (5) the relationship between smoking and probability discounting is not as strong as that observed between smoking and delay discounting of gains.

The correlations observed between smoking behavior and delay discounting of monetary rewards are consistent with previous studies. For example, Reynolds (2004) recently reported a significant positive correlation between the number of cigarettes smoked per day and a delay discounting rate (logged hyperbolic k). In addition to the positive relationship observed between discounting of delayed rewards and smoking frequency (Fig. 8.1), we also reported a positive association involving nicotine dosage (Fig. 8.2), whereby higher doses of nicotine were associated with a greater tendency to discount delayed rewards. Neuropsychopharmacologically, because chronic nicotine exposure is known to associate with strong neuroadaptation, predominantly in reward-processing brain regions (Liu and Jin 2004; Rahman et al. 2004), it is possible that chronic exposure to nicotine may reduce dopaminergic activity in the neural circuitry, resulting in augmented devaluation of delayed monetary gains. However, whether drug-intake-induced neuroadaptation actually causes strong delay discounting of gain should be more extensively studied. Moreover, it was observed that habitual smokers who consume more cigarettes regularly tend to smoke stronger cigarettes. Therefore, smoking frequency (i.e., the number of cigarettes consumed per day) can alternatively be adopted to estimate nicotine exposure when more biologically significant measures are unavailable (e.g., the amount of daily nicotine intake or cotinine level).

Although smokers and never smokers did not differ in their discounting behavior overall, this likely resulted from the number of relatively mild nicotine users in our sample. Most studies have focused on heavy smokers who consume no less than 20 cigarettes per day (e.g., Bickel et al. 1999; Reynolds et al. 2004); in contrast, only eight of the nicotine users in our study met this criterion. As such, our investigation is the first to demonstrate that relatively mild smokers do not more rapidly discount delayed monetary rewards than never smokers. One possible interpretation of this result is that the level of chronic nicotine exposure in mild smokers might not be strong enough to affect impulsivity.

Although there was a relationship with delay discounting of gains, we did not detect a relationship between smoking behavior and delay discounting of monetary losses. This observation may reflect the unique neural activation patterns observed in response to gains and losses during decision making; dopaminergic neural responses are evoked in response to monetary gains, whereas other brain regions (e.g., the right anterior cingulate, thalamus, and left amygdala) are more strongly activated in response to monetary losses (Knutson et al. 2000, 2003; Breiter et al. 2001). It should be noted that several studies have shown that heavy smokers tend to discount delayed losses more steeply than never smokers (Odum et al. 2002; Baker et al. 2003). Again, this discrepancy might be explained by the relatively mild nicotine use exhibited by our sample of smokers. This point should be further investigated in future studies to draw more definitive conclusions.

Whereas delay discounting of gain was associated with smoking behavior, we did not observe a significant correlation between probability discounting of gain and smoking behavior. Likewise, we did not find a significant difference in probability discounting of gain between smokers and never smokers. The smokers employed in both our present study and Mitchell's (1999) study were relatively light smokers, which may have resulted in a nonsignificant difference in probability discounting of gain between smokers and never smokers. On the other hand, the study of Reynolds and his colleagues reported that heavy smokers discounted an uncertain monetary reward more dramatically when compared to never smokers, possibly because they employed heavier smokers (Reynolds et al. 2004). Considering these results, it is possible that probability discounting is related to smoking only in heavy smokers.

We further examined the relationships between the four types of discounting regardless of smoking status. It was revealed that the participants discounted both delayed and uncertain gains more steeply than delayed and uncertain losses, respectively, which is in line with previous reports of an asymmetry in the decisions made regarding gains and losses in discounting tasks (Tversky and Kahneman 1981; Thaler 1981; Baker et al. 2003). It was also demonstrated that the association between the tendency to discount rewards and the tendency to discount losses was positive in direction for delay discounting, but negative for probability discounting. The latter finding can explain paradoxical behavior observed in antisocial psychiatric patients with comorbid drug dependence (Kausch 2003) who exhibit both low discounting of probabilistic rewards (e.g., a preference for gambling) and high discounting of probabilistic losses (e.g., low aversion to possible HIV infection caused by needle sharing or high-risk sexual behavior). Finally, although the direction of the correlation observed between delay and probability discounting of gains was positive, the coefficient did not reach statistical significance. This is consistent with the conclusion of Myerson et al. (2003) that the tendencies to discount delayed and uncertain gains is only weakly to modestly related at best. However, because several studies have shown a strong positive correlation between them (e.g., Richards et al. 1999b; Reynolds et al. 2003), further studies are required to elucidate this relationship.

Although promising, there are limitations to our present study. First, we did not restrict the participant's access to nicotine prior to the experiment. In our opinion, it is improbable that the time of the last cigarette prior to participating in the experiment significantly affected our results, since (1) the time to complete our study was typically less than 1 h, and (2) one previous study (Mitchell 2004) has shown that even a 24-h nicotine deprivation did not change the discounting behavior of monetary outcomes (although discounting cigarettes was significantly increased). Nevertheless, future studies should examine how the time of last cigarette affects the subject's discounting behavior. Second, we did not assess breath CO levels or urine cotinine levels. It is, however, noteworthy that a number of studies (Ueda et al. 2002; Benowitz et al. 2003; Binnie et al. 2004) have shown that there is a significant correlation between self-reported smoking status and urinary cotinine levels, especially in mild smokers, suggesting that self-reported smoking status is a good estimate of actual nicotine intake. It should also be noted that our results are consistent with the study of Reynolds et al. (2004) reporting that CO levels were positively associated with delay discounting of gains, but not with probability discounting of gains. Nevertheless, it would be preferable for future studies to assess biological markers of nicotine exposure such as plasma cotinine levels and CSF (cerebrospinal fluid) nicotine levels.

Finally, we suggest future directions: (1) the effects of acute and chronic nicotine administration on discounting should be compared since psychopharmacological studies have revealed that an acute administration of a dopaminergic drug may actually reduce impulsive behavior in delay discounting of gains, whereas chronic exposure may induce neuroadaptation and thereby increase impulsive behavior in delay discounting of gains (Richards et al. 1999a; Cardinal et al. 2000; Wade et al. 2000; de Wit et al. 2002; Pietras et al. 2003), and (2) future investigations should combine a genetic analysis with a psychopharmacological methodology to further elucidate the neuropsychopharmacological correlates of delay and probability discounting of gains and losses because considerable evidence indicates that nicotine use is influenced by our genotype, such as DRD2 polymorphism (see Munafo et al. 2004 for a review).

Acknowledgements The research reported in this chapter was supported by grants from the Grant-in-Aid for Scientific Research ("21st century center of excellence" grant and grant #17650074) and Grant-in-Aid for Scientific Research on Innovative Areas (23118001 & 23118002; Adolescent Mind & Self-Regulation) from the Ministry of Education, Culture, Sports, Science and Technology of Japan, and a Yamaguchi endocrinological disorder grant. We are grateful to Dr. Paul Wehr, Dr. Yoshiro Tsutsui and anonymous reviewers for critical reading of our manuscript.

Addendum: Recent Developments[1]

A number of studies on the relationships between temporal (social and probability) discounting and impulsivity associated with smoking behavior (nicotine addiction) have recently been conducted. In behavioral economics, Kang and Ikeda (2013) utilized questionnaires which may be related to impulsivity and hyperbolicity in temporal discounting and observed that both psychological tendencies are positively associated with smoking behavior. Although Ohmura et al. (2005) did not examine a causal direction from nicotine intake to greater impulsivity in temporal discounting, recent studies demonstrated the causality. For instance, Kelsey and Niraula (2013) studied the effect of acute and sub-chronic administration of nicotine on temporal discounting by rats. They reported that nicotine administration increased impulsivity

[1] This addendum has been newly written by Taiki Takahashi for this book chapter.

in temporal discounting. Secades-Villa et al. (2014) reported that prolonged (1 year) decreased impulsivity in temporal discounting by human ex-smokers. These reports indicate that nicotine intake increases impulsivity in temporal discounting. Other recent studies suggest the opposite causal direction may also exists. Harris et al. (2014) studied the roles of impulsivity in temporal discounting by humans in response to smoking cessation treatments and observed that temporal discounting predicts the treatment outcomes. Consistent with this finding, Kayir et al. (2014) demonstrated that trait impulsivity predicts the effects of nicotine withdrawal on impulsive choice by rats. It is therefore probable that there are two causal directions in the relationship between nicotine intake and impulsive temporal discounting: from nicotine intake to impulsivity in temporal discounting and vice versa. Our previous study on the relationship between alcoholism and temporal discounting also supports this interpretation (Takahashi et al. 2007).

In Neuroeconomics, several advances have been made on the neurobiological foundations of the relationship between smoking (and other dopaminergic drugs) and temporal discounting (Takahashi 2009; MacKillop et al. 2012). Kobiella et al. (2013) observed that the activation of smokers' ventral striatum is weaker than that of non-smokers' during intertemporal choice for delayed gains. Sheffer et al. (2013) studied the effect of high-frequency transcranial magnetic stimulation of the left dorsolateral prefrontal cortex on temporal discounting by smokers and reported that the stimulation decreased temporal discounting of gains, but increased temporal discounting of loss. Theoretically, Takahashi (2011) proposed that addicts' time-inconsistency in temporal discounting may be related to nonlinearity in time perception (Takahashi 2005) via alteration of dopaminergic systems (e.g., D2 receptors and electrical coupling between dopaminergic neurons, Takahashi 2007; Kawamura et al. 2013), which should be examined in future studies in psychophysical neuroeconomics (Han and Takahashi 2012; Takahashi and Han 2013).

References

Baker F, Johnson MW, Bickel WK (2003) Delay discounting in current and never-before cigarette smokers: similarities and differences across commodity sign and magnitude. J Abnorm Psychol 112:382–392

Benowitz NL, Pomerleau OF, Pomerleau CS, Jacob P III (2003) Nicotine metabolite ratio as a predictor of cigarette consumption. Nicotine Tob Res 5:621–624

Bickel WK, Marsch LA (2001) Toward a behavioral economic understanding of drug dependence: delay discounting processes. Addiction 96:73–86

Bickel WK, Odum AL, Madden GJ (1999) Impulsivity and cigarette smoking: delay discounting in current never and ex-smokers. Psychopharmacology (Berl) 146:447–454

Binnie V, McHugh S, Macpherson L, Borland B, Moir K, Malik K (2004) The validation of self-reported smoking status by analyzing cotinine levels in stimulated and unstimulated saliva, serum and urine. Oral Dis 10:287–293

Breiter HC, Aharon I, Kahneman D, Dale A, Shizgal P (2001) Functional imaging of neural responses to expectancy and experience of monetary gains and losses. Neuron 30:619–639

Cardinal RN, Robbins TW, Everitt BJ (2000) The effects of D-amphetamine chlordiazepoxide alpha-flupenthixol and behavioural manipulations on choice of signalled and unsignalled delayed reinforcement in rats. Psychopharmacology (Berl) 152:362–375
Daruna JH, Barnes PA (1993) A neurodevelopmental view of impulsivity. In: McCown WG, Johnson JL, Shure MB (eds) The impulsive client: theory research and treatment. American Psychological Association, Washington, DC, pp 23–37
de Wit H, Enggasser JL, Richards JB (2002) Acute administration of D-amphetamine decreases impulsivity in healthy volunteers. Neuropsychopharmacology 27:813–825
Glimcher PW, Rustichini A (2004) Neuroeconomics: the consilience of brain and decision. Science 306:447–452
Han R, Takahashi T (2012) Psychophysics of valuation and time perception in temporal discounting of gain and loss. Phys A Stat Mech Appl 391(24):6568–6576
Harris M, Penfold RB, Hawkins A, Maccombs J, Wallace B, Reynolds B (2014) Dimensions of impulsive behavior and treatment outcomes for adolescent smokers. Exp Clin Psychopharmacol 22(1):57–64
Johnson MW, Bickel WK (2002) Within-subject comparison of real and hypothetical money rewards in delay discounting. J Exp Anal Behav 77:129–146
Kang M-I, Ikeda S (2013) Time discounting and smoking behavior: evidence from a panel survey. Health Econ. 18 October 2013. doi:10.1002/hec.2998. [Epub ahead of print]
Kausch O (2003) Patterns of substance abuse among treatmentseeking pathological gamblers. J Subst Abuse Treat 25:263–270
Kawamura Y, Takahashi T, Liu X, Nishida N, Noda Y, Yoshikawa A, Sasaki T (2013) Variation in the DRD2 gene affects impulsivity in intertemporal choice. Open J Psychiatry 3(1):26–31
Kayir H, Semenova S, Markou A (2014) Baseline impulsive choice predicts the effects of nicotine and nicotine withdrawal on impulsivity in rats. Prog Neuropsychopharmacol Biol Psychiatry 48:6–13
Kelsey JE, Niraula A (2013) Effects of acute and sub-chronic nicotine on impulsive choice in rats in a probabilistic delay-discounting task. Psychopharmacology (Berl) 227(3):385–392
Kirby KN, Petry NM (2004) Heroin and cocaine abusers have higher discount rates for delayed rewards than alcoholics or non-drug-using controls. Addiction 99:461–471
Kirby KN, Petry NM, Bickel WK (1999) Heroin addicts have higher discount rates for delayed rewards than non-drug-using controls. J Exp Psychol Gen 128:78–87
Knutson B, Westdorp A, Kaiser E, Hommer D (2000) FMRI visualization of brain activity during a monetary incentive delay task. Neuroimage 12:20–27
Knutson B, Fong GW, Bennett SM, Adams CM, Hommer D (2003) A region of mesial prefrontal cortex tracks monetarily rewarding outcomes: characterization with rapid event-related fMRI. Neuroimage 18:263–272
Kobiella A, Ripke S, Kroemer NB, Vollmert C, Vollstädt-Klein S, Ulshöfer DE, Smolka MN (2013) Acute and chronic nicotine effects on behaviour and brain activation during intertemporal decision making. Addict Biol. 16 May 2013. doi:10.1111/adb.12057. [Epub ahead of print]
Liu ZH, Jin WQ (2004) Decrease of ventral tegmental area dopamine neuronal activity in nicotine withdrawal rats. Neuroreport 15:1479–1481
MacKillop J, Amlung MT, Wier LM, David SP, Ray LA, Bickel WK, Sweet LH (2012) The neuroeconomics of nicotine dependence: a preliminary functional magnetic resonance imaging study of delay discounting of monetary and cigarette rewards in smokers. Psychiatry Res 202(1):20–29
Martin-Solch C, Magyar S, Kunig G, Missimer J, Schultz W, Leenders KL (2001) Changes in brain activation associated with reward processing in smokers and nonsmokers. A positron emission tomography study. Exp Brain Res 139:278–286
Martin-Solch C, Missimer J, Leenders KL, Schultz W (2003) Neural activity related to the processing of increasing monetary reward in smokers and nonsmokers. Eur J Neurosci 18:680–688

Mazur JE (1987) An adjusting procedure for studying delayed reinforcement. In: Commons ML, Mazur JE, Nevin JA, Rachlin H (eds) Quantitative analysis of behavior, vol 5, The effects of delay and of intervening events on reinforcement value. Erlbaum, Hillsdale, pp 55–73

McClure SM, Laibson DI, Loewenstein G, Cohen JD (2004) Separate neural systems value immediate and delayed monetary rewards. Science 306:503–507

Mitchell SH (1999) Measures of impulsivity in cigarette smokers and non-smokers. Psychopharmacology (Berl) 146:455–464

Mitchell SH (2004) Effects of short-term nicotine deprivation on decision-making: delay, uncertainty and effort discounting. Nicotine Tob Res 6:819–828

Montague PR, Berns GS (2002) Neural economics and the biological substrates of valuation. Neuron 36:265–284

Munafo M, Clark T, Johnstone E, Murphy M, Walton R (2004) The genetic basis for smoking behavior: a systematic review and meta-analysis. Nicotine Tob Res 6:583–597

Myerson J, Green L, Warusawitharana M (2001) Area under the curve as a measure of discounting. J Exp Anal Behav 76:235–243

Myerson J, Green L, Hanson JS, Holt DD, Estle SJ (2003) Discounting delayed and probabilistic rewards: processes and traits. J Econ Psychol 24:619–635

Odum AL, Madden GJ, Bickel WK (2002) Discounting of delayed health gains and losses by current never- and ex-smokers of cigarettes. Nicotine Tob Res 4:295–303

Ohmura Y, Takahashi T, Kitamura N (2005) Discounting delayed and probabilistic monetary gains and losses by smokers of cigarettes. Psychopharmacology (Berl) 182(4):508–515

Perry JL, Larson EB, German JP, Madden GJ, Carroll ME (2005) Impulsivity (delay discounting) as a predictor of acquisition of IV cocaine self-administration in female rats. Psychopharmacology (Berl) 178:193–201

Petry NM (2001) Delay discounting of money and alcohol in actively using alcoholics currently abstinent alcoholics and controls. Psychopharmacology (Berl) 154:243–250

Pietras CJ, Cherek DR, Lane SD, Tcheremissine OV, Steinberg JL (2003) Effects of methylphenidate on impulsive choice in adult humans. Psychopharmacology (Berl) 170:390–398

Rachlin H, Raineri A, Cross D (1991) Subjective probability and delay. J Exp Anal Behav 55:233–244

Rahman S, Zhang J, Engleman EA, Corrigall WA (2004) Neuroadaptive changes in the mesoaccumbens dopamine system after chronic self-administration: a microdialysis study. Neuroscience 129:415–424

Reynolds B (2004) Do high rates of cigarette consumption increase delay discounting? A cross-sectional comparison of adolescent smokers and young-adult smokers and nonsmokers. Behav Processes 67:545–549

Reynolds B, Karraker K, Horn K, Richards JB (2003) Delay and probability discounting as related to different stages of adolescent smoking and non-smoking. Behav Processes 64:333–344

Reynolds B, Richards JB, Horn K, Karraker K (2004) Delay discounting and probability discounting as related to cigarette smoking status in adults. Behav Processes 65:35–42

Richards JB, Sabol KE, de Wit H (1999a) Effects of methamphetamine on the adjusting amount procedure, a model of impulsive behavior in rats. Psychopharmacology (Berl) 146:432–439

Richards JB, Zhang L, Mitchell SH, de Wit H (1999b) Delay or probability discounting in a model of impulsive behavior: effect of alcohol. J Exp Anal Behav 71:121–143

Schultz W (2004) Neural coding of basic reward terms of animal learning theory game theory microeconomics and behavioural ecology. Curr Opin Neurobiol 14:139–147

Secades-Villa R, Weidberg S, García-Rodríguez O, Fernández-Hermida JR, Yoon JH (2014) Decreased delay discounting in former cigarette smokers at one year after treatment. Addict Behav 39(6):1087–1093

Sheffer CE, Mennemeier M, Landes RD, Bickel WK, Brackman S, Dornhoffer J, Kimbrell T, Brown G (2013) Neuromodulation of delay discounting, the reflection effect, and cigarette consumption. J Subst Abuse Treat 45(2):206–214

Simpson CA, Vuchinich RE (2000) Reliability of a measure of temporal discounting. Psychol Rec 50:3–16

Takahashi T (2004) Cortisol levels and time-discounting of monetary gain in humans. Neuroreport 15:2145–2147

Takahashi T (2005) Loss of self-control in intertemporal choice may be attributable to logarithmic time-perception. Med Hypotheses 65(4):691–693

Takahashi T (2007) Hyperbolic discounting may be reduced to electrical coupling in dopaminergic neural circuits. Med Hypotheses 69(1):195–198

Takahashi T (2009) Theoretical frameworks for neuroeconomics of intertemporal choice. J Neurosci Psychol Econ 2(2):75–90

Takahashi T (2011) A neuroeconomic theory of rational addiction and nonlinear time-perception. Neuro Endocrinol Lett 32(3):221–225

Takahashi T, Han R (2013) Psychophysical neuroeconomics of decision making: nonlinear time perception commonly explains anomalies in temporal and probability discounting. Appl Math 4:1520–1525

Takahashi T, Furukawa A, Miyakawa T, Maesato H, Higuchi S (2007) Two-month stability of hyperbolic discount rates for delayed monetary gains in abstinent inpatient alcoholics. Neuro Endocrinol Lett 28(2):131–136

Thaler R (1981) Some empirical evidence on dynamic inconsistency. Econ Lett 8:201–207

Tversky A, Kahneman D (1981) The framing of decisions and the psychology of choice. Science 211:453–458

Ueda K, Kawachi I, Nakamura M, Nogami H, Shirokawa N, Masui S, Okayama A, Oshima A (2002) Cigarettes nicotine yields and nicotine intake among Japanese male workers. Tob Control 11:55–60

Vuchinich RE, Simpson CA (1998) Hyperbolic temporal discounting in social drinkers and problem drinkers. Exp Clin Psychopharmacol 6:292–305

Wade TR, de Wit H, Richards JB (2000) Effects of dopaminergic drugs on delayed reward as a measure of impulsive behavior in rats. Psychopharmacology (Berl) 150:90–101

Chapter 9
Time Discounting and Smoking Behavior: Evidence from a Panel Survey

Myong-Il Kang and Shinsuke Ikeda

Abstract By using a panel survey of Japanese adults, we show that smoking behavior is associated with personal time discounting and its biases, such as hyperbolic discounting and the sign effect, in the way that theory predicts: smoking depends positively on the discount rate and the degree of hyperbolic discounting and negatively on the presence of the sign effect. Positive effects of hyperbolic discounting on smoking are salient for naïve people, who are not aware of their self-control problem. By estimating smoking participation and smokers' cigarette consumption in Cragg's two-part model, we find that the two smoking decisions depend on different sets of time-discounting variables. Particularly, smoking participation is affected by being a naïve hyperbolic discounter, whereas the discount rate, the presence of the sign effect, and a hyperbolic discounting proxy constructed from sign effect behavior vis-à-vis doing homework assignments affect both types of decision making. The panel data enable us to analyze the over-time instability of elicited discount rates. The instability is shown to come from measurement errors, rather than preference shocks on time preference. Several evidences indicate that the detected associations between time preferences and smoking behavior are interpersonal one, rather than within-personal one.

Keywords Smoking • Discount rate • Hyperbolic discounting • The sign effect • Panel

---

The original article first appeared in the Health Economics 23(12):1443–1464, 2014. A newly written addendum has been added to this book chapter.

M.-I. Kang (✉)
Department of Business Administration, Korea University, 1-700 Ogawa-cho, Kodaira, Tokyo 187-8560, Japan
e-mail: mkang@korea-u.ac.jp

S. Ikeda
Institute of Social and Economic Research, Osaka University, 6-1 Mihogaoka, Ibaraki, Osaka 560-0047, Japan
e-mail: ikeda@iser.osaka-u.ac.jp

S. Ikeda et al. (eds.), *Behavioral Economics of Preferences, Choices, and Happiness*, DOI 10.1007/978-4-431-55402-8_9

1 Introduction

We examine empirically how personal time discounting relates to smoking behavior, such as smoking participation and the quantity of cigarettes consumed. Our focus is on the association of smoking with three aspects of personal time discounting: (i) *impatience*, measured by the discount rate; (ii) *hyperbolic discounting*, where a person is less patient in immediate future choices than in distant future choices (e.g., Thaler 1981; Benzion et al. 1989; Ainslie 1992); and (iii) *the sign effect*, where a person discounts positive payoffs more intensely than negative payoffs (e.g., Khwaja et al. 2007; Ikeda et al. 2010). To determine the impact of hyperbolic discounting on smoking, we place hyperbolic discounters into two types in terms of their self-awareness of the time-inconsistent property inherent in their behavior: *sophisticated* hyperbolic discounters, who recognize themselves as being time-inconsistent, and *naïve* hyperbolic discounters, who misconceive themselves as being time-consistent.

The economic theory of smoking predicts that people with a higher discount rate tend to put less weight on future disutility of addiction relative to present satisfaction from smoking, and hence smoke more (see, e.g., Becker and Murphy 1988; Chaloupka 1991). In the more recently developed behavioral economics framework, with hyperbolic discounting and the resulting self-control problem, people are predicted to smoke more than with exponential discounting. This tendency is especially strong for naïve hyperbolic discounters: they do not take their self-control problem into account in the smoking decision and hence, are likely to smoke excessively in a time-inconsistent way (see, e.g., Gruber and Kőszegi 2001, 2004). In addition, behavioral economics predicts that gain-loss asymmetry in time discounting, captured by the sign effect, makes consumers averse to future losses (Wakai 2008, 2011), which would lead to moderation in smoking. Although these predictions are logical and testable, there have been few attempts at direct and systematic empirical confirmation.

Motivated by these predictions, this chapter tests four hypotheses: (1) persons with higher discount rates smoke more than others, (2) hyperbolic discounters smoke more than exponential discounters, (3) naïve hyperbolic discounters smoke more than sophisticated ones, and (4) people who display the sign effect smoke less than others. In testing these hypotheses, the effects of time discounting on both the probability of being a smoker and the quantity of cigarettes consumed are estimated by adopting a two-part model developed by Cragg (1971) as an alternative to the Tobit specification to a sample comprising both smokers and nonsmokers.

The analysis is conducted based on a unique nationwide panel survey of Japanese adults, the Japan Household Panel Survey on Consumer Preferences and Satisfaction (hereafter, JHPS), during the 2005–2008 period. In the survey, roughly 3,000–5,000 Japanese adults each year replied to questionnaires regarding their various choices and background attributes, including smoking status. Time-discounting data, including those of hyperbolic discounting and the sign effect, are constructed from the respondents' replies to hypothetical questions on intertemporal monetary tradeoffs with different choice conditions. The survey also asked respondents two questions regarding their tendency toward procrastination vis-à-vis doing homework assignments. One is how likely they were, in fact, to procrastinate in doing onerous homework assignments during school vacations in their childhood. The other is how late they planned to do the particular homework assignments. From the responses to the first question, we construct a proxy variable of hyperbolic discounting. Moreover, by using the response data for the two questions, hyperbolic respondents who self-reported unplanned procrastination are identified as naïve, and the other hyperbolic respondents as sophisticated.[1]

We find that in total, respondents' smoking status depends on time discounting in the predicted ways. In particular, smoking depends positively on the discount rate and negatively on the presence of the sign effect. In addition, survey responses indicating inclination toward procrastination, a proxy of hyperbolic discounting, have a significantly positive association with smoking and, as expected, the tendency is more significant for naïve hyperbolic discounters than for sophisticated ones. However, hyperbolic discounting estimated from monetary choice questions exhibits neither a predicted nor a stable correlation with smoking.

One noticeable finding is that the two behavioral decisions of smoking, i.e., smoking participation and the quantities of cigarettes consumed, depend on different sets of time-discounting variables. In particular, whether a hyperbolic respondent is a smoker or not depends crucially on whether he is naïve or sophisticated. The discount rate, the sign effect, and a hyperbolic discounting proxy commonly affect both types of smoking decision.

The contribution of this chapter is threefold. First, this is the first attempt to measure direct and systematic associations between smoking and the three aspects of time discounting: impatience, hyperbolic discounting, and the sign effect. In the previous studies that determine associations between time discounting and smoking,[2] impatience and hyperbolic discounting have been regarded as mutually exclusive aspects of discounting. Grignon (2009) is a typical example: it compares smoking decisions among impatient, patient, and present-biased agents, identified by virtue of their answers to two questions regarding monetary intertemporal choices. However, impatience and hyperbolic discounting (and the sign effect) are different aspects of time discounting: people can be patient and hyperbolic, or

[1]Ikeda et al. (2010) construct a similar proxy of hyperbolic discounting and detect a positive association between it and the degree of obesity. In Ikeda and Kang (2015), we adopt the same idea to identify whether a respondent is naïve or sophisticated, and thereby show that a naïve, hyperbolic discounter is more likely to be a debtor than an exponential discounter, whereas a sophisticated hyperbolic respondent is as likely to be a debtor as an exponential respondent.

[2]With regard to the assertion that there are higher discount rates among addicts, see, for the issue of smoking, Mitchell (1999), Odum et al. (2002), Bickel et al. (1999), Baker et al. (2003), Ohmura et al. (2005), Reynolds et al. (2004) and Ida and Goto (2009); for the issue of drug abuse, Madden et al. (1997) and Kilby et al. (1999). With regard to the prevalence of hyperbolic discounting among addicts, see Madden et al. (1999) for heroin users and Bickel et al. (1999), Odum et al. (2002), and Ida (2010) for smokers. See also Blondel et al. (2007), a study whose findings show that there is no difference between the discount rates of drug users and drug nonusers if risk attitudes are controlled for.

impatient and exponential. In view of this, we incorporate the three time-discounting variables into smoking equations as regressors, and thereby determine the partial association between smoking and each of the three. Furthermore, to our best knowledge, no previous study on smoking incorporates the sign effect.[3]

Second, our study is the first to verify the excessive smoking of naïve hyperbolic discounters. Economic theory has shown that in many cases, time-inconsistent over-consumption behavior due to hyperbolic discounting is more salient for the naïve, who misperceive their self-control problem, than for the sophisticated, who incorporate the effect of the self-control problem into their decision making.[4] In the context of the smoking decision, theory shows that naïve hyperbolic discounters have a higher smoking propensity than sophisticated hyperbolic discounters and the exponential discounters, whereas the difference in the smoking propensity between sophisticated hyperbolic discounters and exponential discounters is not that large (see Gruber and Kőszegi 2004). Irrespective of the predictions, there has been no attempt to test their empirical validity. By sorting hyperbolic respondents into naïfs and sophisticates, we fill the void.

Third, the present research is the first study using panel data to detect the association between time discounting and smoking. The use of panel data enables us to confirm the existence of time variations in time-preference measures coming from preference shocks and measurement errors. The examination of the within-person variation is necessary to check the validity of the presumption in the literature that personal time preferences are constant over time (e.g., Grignon 2009; Sato and Ohkusa 2003). Further, the use of panel data enables us to examine how large the measurement errors of time-preference measures are, compared with the effect of preference shocks on smoking behavior. We do that by comparing estimation results using time-variant preference variables and those using the variables to eliminate within-person variations.

The remainder of this chapter is constructed as follows. In Sect. 2, we discuss the motivation for our hypotheses regarding the relationships between time discounting and smoking. Section 3 presents a description of the data and assessments of the within-person stability of constructed time-preference variables, and Sect. 4 reports the basic estimation results and checks their robustness. Section 5 examines the relative impacts of preference shocks and measurement errors on our estimation results. Finally, Sect. 6 concludes the chapter.

---

[3]Baker et al. (2003) and Khwaja et al. (2007) detect the presence of the sign effect using a sample comprising both smokers and nonsmokers. However, they did not examine the impact of the presence of the sign effect on smoking decisions.

[4]Behavioral differences between naïfs and sophisticates are discussed in terms of procrastinating behavior by O'Donoghue and Rabin (1999), and in terms of borrowing behavior by Heidhues and Kőszegi (2010).

2 Time Discounting and Smoking

After Becker and Murphy (1988) proposed a rational addiction model, empirical evidence has widely supported the forward-looking property of decision making with regard to addictive consumption (e.g., Chaloupka 1990, 1991; Keeler et al. 1993; Becker et al. 1994; Bardsley and Olekalns 1999; Luo et al. 2003; Wan 2006). This implies that the degree of impatience, measured by the discount rate, plays a critical role in smoking behavior: a higher discount rate—and hence, a higher degree of impatience—would lead to more cigarette consumption. As in many of the previous studies (see footnote 2), we hypothesize that persons with higher discount rates tend to smoke more than others.

Hyperbolic discounting, in which the discount rate for immediate future choices is higher than that for distant future choices, causes the self-control problem: people at each point in time always prefer immediate gratification to a larger future benefit. This makes intertemporal choices present-biased and thus would lead hyperbolic individuals to smoke more than exponential ones. Note, however, that the behavior of hyperbolic persons differs between sophisticates, who are well aware of their tendency to be less patient in the future because of hyperbolic discounting, and naïfs, who are unaware of the future incidence of the preference reversal. Sophisticates smoke time-consistently by incorporating the effect of the preference reversal in time discounting, whereas naïve hyperbolic discounters do not take their self-control problem into account in the smoking decision and hence, are likely to smoke excessively in a time-inconsistent way. We hypothesize that hyperbolic discounters are likely to smoke more than exponential discounters, and that the tendency is stronger for naïve hyperbolic discounters than for sophisticated hyperbolic discounters.[5]

Many empirical studies have reported that discount rates for future losses are lower than those for future gains. This sign effect makes people dislike suffering future losses, and they have a strong desire to avoid future losses by bearing costs at present. Indeed, many subjects in experiments are reported to prefer to incur a loss immediately rather than delay it (e.g., Benzion et al. 1989; Chapman 1996). For example, Ikeda et al. (2010) report that people who are subject to the sign effect are likely to control their weight to avoid the future costs of obesity. In Ikeda and Kang (2015), we show that questionnaire respondents who exhibit the sign effect have an aversion to money borrowing to avoid the future burden of repayments.

---

[5]Theoretically, it is difficult to show analytically the precise effect of hyperbolic discounting on smoking behavior by obtaining a closed-form solution in a dynamic optimization framework. However, Gruber and Kőszegi (2004) verify, using a quadratic utility model, that naïve hyperbolic discounters have a higher marginal propensity to smoke than sophisticated hyperbolic discounters, and that sophisticated hyperbolic discounters in turn display a higher smoking propensity than exponential discounters. Laibson (1997, 1998) shows that under certain conditions, the effective discount rate obtained by transforming the hyperbolic discounting function into the exponential one is greater than the pure exponential discount rate. This implies that persons with hyperbolic discounting tend to smoke more than those with exponential discounting.

Similarly, the sign effect would lead people to consider seriously the future psychological and monetary losses of smoking, such as the detrimental effects on future health and the hardship of quitting smoking under addiction. This would cause people to keep their smoking down or not to initiate smoking. We thus hypothesize that a person who exhibits the sign effect is likely to smoke less than others.[6]

3 The Data

Our empirical research is based on the annual panel data of the JHPS from the 2005–2008 period.[7] The JHPS is a household survey conducted by a drop-off/pick-up method. It was initiated in 2004 with randomly selected respondents: 4,224 Japanese adults between the ages of 20 and 65. In 2005, respondents dropped by 1,237 to 2,987. In 2006, 620 individuals were dropped, and 1,396 new random-sampled individuals were added to the survey; in total, 3,763 individuals responded in 2006. In 2007, the respondents dropped by 651 to 3,763. As of 2008, the number of respondents had increased to 4,018, with 2,731 respondents continuing from the previous year and 1,287 being newly added through a mail-in data-capture method. All surveys were conducted in February except in 2006, when the survey was conducted in February and March. In total, the four-wave data from 2005 to 2008 contain 13,880 observations composed of 5,670 survey participants, of which 2,233 have participated in JHPS once, 488 twice, 1,125 three times, and 1,824 four times.[8] On average, the participants took part in our survey 2.45 times during the 2005–2008 period.

[6]In the economics literature, there have been two attempts to incorporate the sign effect into economic models. First, Wakai (2008, 2011) provide a utility-smoothing model in which future felicity is discounted at a lower rate when it is smaller than the current utility level (i.e., when felicity is going to decrease in the future) than when it is larger than the current utility level (i.e., when felicity is going to increase in the future). Second, Loewenstein and Prelec (1992) propose a property of loss amplification, by which the rate of change in the values of gains is perceived as smaller than that in the values of equivalent losses.

[7]The JHPS was initiated in 2004 as a project of the Osaka University COE program and continues as a project of the Osaka University Global COE program, both of which are supported by the Ministry of Education, Culture, Sports, Science and Technology.

[8]We exclude from our sample the data from 2004, for two reasons. Unlike in 2005–2008, the queries to elicit discount rates in the 2004 survey were asked in a matching form in which respondents were asked to write down equivalent amounts of present-day money to a given amount of future money. The resulting discount rate data are considered to contain large measurement errors. The descriptive statistics of elicited discount rates in the 2004 survey indeed differ from those in other years. In addition to the choice conditions of the discounting, the queries also differ from those in other years.

3.1 Cigarette Consumption

In the JHPS, respondents' smoking habits are surveyed by asking them, 'How many cigarettes do you smoke regularly? Select a proximal option from the following: (i) Never smoke, (ii) Hardly smoke, (iii) Smoke sometimes, (iv) About 10 cigarettes per day, (v) About a pack per day, (vi) More than two packs per day.' For 2007 and 2008, the option '(vii) I used to smoke but have quit' was added.

To quantify cigarette consumption, we take the respondents who selected options (i), (ii), or (vii) as nonsmokers, those who selected (iii) as smokers consuming not over five cigarettes per day, (iv) as smokers consuming over five and not over 15, (v) as smokers consuming over 15 and not over 40, and (vi) as smokers consuming over 40.

By using the category data, we apply the method developed by Kimball et al. (2008) to estimate a log normal distribution for the distribution of the respondents' cigarette consumption each year, where each respondent's cigarette consumption is estimated as an expected value conditional on his or her categorical level of smoking.

The summary statistics of cigarette consumption and smoking rates are shown in Table 9.1. For the male sample, both the number of cigarettes consumed and the smoking rates decreased during the full sample period. For the female sample, on the other hand, the number of cigarettes consumed increased from 2005 to 2007, although the smoking rates decreased throughout the full sample period.[9]

3.2 Eliciting Discount Rates and Their Behavioral Biases

In the JHPS, the respondents' discount rates were measured by asking five questions about intertemporal choice under alternative conditions. The respondents were asked to choose a preferable option from two options, 'A' and 'B': in 'A', the respondent receives JPY 10,000 (around USD 93.32) in 2 days, and in 'B', receives JPY 10,000 plus a certain amount of JPY α—say, JPY 10,038 (around USD 93.67), in 9 days; here, choosing the delayed receipt 'B' instead of 'A' implies receiving 20 % of the annual interest rate. In each question, eight such problems were posed in the form of a payoff table with alternative α values, from small to large, and hence, with alternative imputed interest rates, from low to high. Table 9.2 shows QUESTION 1, which is one of the five questions asked; there, the amount of receipt

[9] These trends are consistent with the reported data of the National Survey of Health and Nutrition (NSHN) conducted by the Ministry of Health, Labour and Welfare of Japan. According to NSHN data from 2004 to 2005, the number of cigarettes consumed by male smokers decreased from 21.5 to 21.0 per day, and the rates of regular smoking declined from 43.3 to 39.3 %. For females, the number of cigarettes consumed increased from 14.6 to 15.6 per day, while their rates of regular smoking decreased from 12.0 to 11.3 %.

Table 9.1 Summary statistics of smoking behavior

			2005	2006	2007	2008
(Panel A) Cigarette consumption	All	Mean	6.502	6.226	5.873	5.238
		S.D.	11.971	11.679	11.294	10.724
		# of Obs.	2,972	3,746	3,084	4,001
	Male	Mean	11.373	10.937	10.218	9.172
		S.D.	14.728	14.378	13.703	13.394
		# of Obs.	1,395	1,763	1,437	1,870
	Female	Mean	2.193	2.038	2.081	1.785
		S.D.	6.223	6.054	6.649	5.748
		# of Obs.	1,577	1,983	1,647	2,131
(Panel B) Cigarette consumption (smokers)	All	Mean	21.517	21.879	21.82	20.873
		S.D.	12.296	11.697	11.222	11.488
		# of Obs.	898	1,066	830	1,004
	Male	Mean	24.483	24.253	23.76	23.368
		S.D.	12.077	11.635	10.712	11.193
		# of Obs.	648	795	618	734
	Female	Mean	13.832	14.916	16.166	14.092
		S.D.	9.136	8.734	10.777	9.355
		# of Obs.	250	271	212	270
(Panel C) Smoking rates	All	Mean	0.264	0.258	0.245	0.224
		S.D.	0.441	0.437	0.43	0.417
		# of Obs.	2,972	3,746	3,084	4,001
	Male	Mean	0.424	0.419	0.404	0.367
		S.D.	0.494	0.494	0.491	0.482
		# of Obs.	1,395	1,763	1,437	1,870
	Female	Mean	0.122	0.114	0.106	0.099
		S.D.	0.327	0.318	0.308	0.299
		# of Obs.	1,577	1,983	1,647	2,131

The data are from the Japan Household Panel Survey on Consumer Preferences and Satisfaction from the 2005–2008 period. Summary statistics of Panel A include nonsmokers in the sample. Panel B shows the summary statistics of regular smokers. Panel C shows rates of regular smokers

for option 'A' is specified as JPY 10,000, and the imputed interest rate for option 'B' varies, ranging from −10 to 300 %. Respondents are expected to choose option 'A' at low interest rates, but as the imputed interest rate increases, they are expected to switch to 'B' at some critical high threshold rate. The individual respondents' discount rates can be inferred by estimating the interest rate at which the delayed receipt of 'B' is irrelevant compared to the more immediate receipt of 'A'. The elicited discount rates are associated with particular choice conditions, e.g., 2 days vs. 9 days, and JPY 10,000 for option 'B' in QUESTION 1.[10]

[10]In contrast to some experimental studies (e.g., Harrison et al. 2002), the current study is based on the non-incentivized hypothetical question survey. We have a great deal of evidence that there is no

Table 9.2 Question to elicit discount rates: an example (QUESTION 1 for DR_1)

Question 1.
Suppose you have two options to receive some money. You may choose Option 'A', to receive 10,000 JPY in two days; or Option 'B', to receive a different amount in 9 days. Compare the amounts and timing in Option 'A' with Option 'B' and indicate which amount you would prefer to receive for each of all 8 choices.

Option A (Receipt in 2 days)	Option B (Receipt in 9 days)	Interest rate (Annual) (%)	Circle A or B	
JPY 10,000 (USD93.32)	JPY 9,981 (USD93.14)	−10	A	B
JPY 10,000 (USD93.32)	JPY 10,000 (USD93.32)	0	A	B
JPY 10,000 (USD93.32)	JPY 10,019 (USD93.50)	10	A	B
JPY 10,000 (USD93.32)	JPY 10,038 (USD93.67)	20	A	B
JPY 10,000 (USD93.32)	JPY 10,096 (USD94.21)	50	A	B
JPY 10,000 (USD93.32)	JPY 10,191 (USD95.10)	100	A	B
JPY 10,000 (USD93.32)	JPY 10,383 (USD96.89)	200	A	B
JPY 10,000 (USD93.32)	JPY 10,574 (USD98.67)	300	A	B

This is a question to elicit the discount rate in the Japan Household Panel Survey on Consumer Preferences and Satisfaction from the 2005–2008 period. The US dollar amounts are computed by using the average JPY/USD exchange rate, 107.16, in February, 2008

As summarized in Table 9.3, we developed five such questions to elicit discount rates by controlling the choice conditions, such as (i) *timings of payoff realization* (2 days vs. 9 days, etc.), (ii) *money amounts* for option 'A' (JPY 10,000 or JPY 1 million), and (iii) *the signs of payoffs* (receipt or payment). In 'payment' question 5, the respondents were asked to choose between 'A', which pays JPY 1 million in 1 month, and 'B', which pays JPY 1 million plus some amount in 13 months and from which acceptable interest-rate payments to delay a JPY 1 million payment for 12 months were measured.

From each question, we obtain response data in the form of category numbers, which tell us between which two interest rates a respondent's choice switched from option 'A' to 'B', if any switch takes place; some subjects did not switch from 'A' to 'B' at all for any of the offered interest rates.[11]

To estimate the individual respondents' discount rates from the category data, and hence, to identify whether a time-discounting bias, e.g., hyperbolic discounting, takes place even when a respondent's choice switched at the same category in the relating two questions (e.g., the immediate future and distant future questions), we

systematic difference between discount rates estimated from real and hypothetical monetary reward choices (e.g., Baker et al. 2003; Johnson and Bickel 2002; Simpson and Vuchinich 2000). See also Khwaja et al. (2007), Grignon (2009), and Ikeda et al. (2010) for studies that use hypothetical choice surveys to elicit discount rates. However, we could be still skeptical of the usefulness of responses to our limited hypothetical questions in explaining smoking behavior. We shall discuss on within-person variations in our response data in Sect. 3.3, and on measurement errors in Sect. 5.

[11]As in the literature (e.g., Harrison et al. 2002), respondents who displayed multi-switching points are omitted from the sample. Respondents who left an option unselected are also omitted.

Table 9.3 Elicited discount rates under alternative choice conditions

Choice conditions	DR_1			DR_2			DR_3			DR_4			DR_5		
Timings ((A) or (B))	2 days or 9 days			90 days or 97 days			1 month or 13 months			1 month or 13 months			1 month or 13 months		
Amounts for (A)	JPN 10,000 (USD93.32)			JPN 10,000 (USD93.32)			JPN 10,000 (USD93.32)			JPY 1 m (USD9331.84)			JPY 1 m (USD9,331.84)		
Receipt or payment	Receipt			Receipt			Receipt			Receipt			Payment		
	Mean	S.D.	Obs.	Mean	S.D.	Obs.	Mean	S.D.	Obs.	Mean	S.D.	Obs.	Mean	S.D.	Obs.
2005	1.904	2.390	2,737	1.892	2.421	2,768	0.153	0.193	2,790	0.023	0.042	2,771	−0.008	0.044	2,331
2006	1.798	2.274	3,444	1.843	2.387	3,464	0.147	0.183	3,475	0.024	0.042	3,475	−0.008	0.040	2,912
2007	1.591	1.968	2,905	1.623	2.059	2,872	0.137	0.166	2,902	0.022	0.036	2,891	−0.001	0.028	2,292
2008	1.561	1.952	3,761	1.515	1.941	3,765	0.136	0.166	3,765	0.022	0.036	3,756	−0.002	0.027	3,103
Pooled	1.704	2.148	12,847	1.708	2.206	12,869	0.143	0.177	12,932	0.023	0.039	12,893	−0.005	0.036	10,638
Time discounting biases	Hyperbolic discounting: $DR_1 > DR_2$									Sign effect: $DR_4 > DR_5$					

This table shows the questions to elicit discount rates under alternative choice conditions and the summary statistics in the Japan Household Panel Survey on Consumer Preferences and Satisfaction from the 2005–2008 period. The US dollar amounts are computed by using the average JPY/USD exchange rate, 107.16, in February, 2008

apply the method developed by Kimball et al. (2008). We first estimate a log-normal distribution for the cross-respondent distribution of gross discount rates; next, from the distribution, each respondent's gross discount rate for a certain question—i.e., from a certain payoff table—is estimated as an expected value conditional on his or her switch taking place at a certain observed category. By using the imputed discount rates, the incidence of the two time-discounting biases are identified. Table 9.3 summarizes the descriptive statistics of the elicited discount rates, where DR_i ($i = 1, \cdots, 5$) represents the discount rate estimated from question i.[12,13]

To quantify the degree of impatience, we construct DISCRATE, which represents the simple average of the standardized values of the elicited discount rates $DR_{i,t}$ ($i = 1, \cdots, 5, t = 2005, \cdots, 2008$):

$$DISCRATE_t = (1/5) \sum_{i=1}^{5} \left[\left(DR_{i,t} - E\left(DR_i\right) \right) / \sigma \left(DR_i\right) \right], \qquad (9.1)$$

where $E(DR_i)$ and $\sigma(DR_i)$ represent the sample means and standard deviations of $DR_{i,t}$ over the entire sample period, respectively.

Note that specification (9.1) of the impatience index has two merits. First, since five discount rates are incorporated into one impatience index, possible measurement errors in individual discount-rate estimates are averaged out. Second, since the standardization is conducted by using over-period sample means and standard deviations, DISCRATE can capture time variations in the degree of impatience. We hypothesize that with all other things being equal, a respondent's cigarette consumption depends positively on the value of his or her impatience index DISCRATE. Table 9.4 summarizes the definitions and summary statistics of the variables.[14]

---

[12]It is well known that the discount rates differ wildly depending on various choice conditions. See, e.g., Frederick et al. (2002), which summarizes the elicited discount rates reported in the vast literature. It is also known that discount rates elicited from experiments and questionnaire surveys are much higher than market interest rates. See Frederick et al. (2002).

[13]It is not unusual for the discount rate for future payments (or losses) to be negative. Indeed, many subjects in experiments are reported to prefer to incur a loss immediately rather than delay it (e.g., Benzion et al. 1989; Chapman 1996). Average discount rates for losses are sometimes reported as negative (Loewenstein 1987; Chapman 1996; Ganiats et al. 2000). Wakai (2011) shows theoretically that a negative discount rate for deteriorating future felicity causes people to strongly dislike future volatility, so that intertemporal preferences become non-monotonic. Our result that average respondents prefer earlier repayment with a negative interest rate is consistent with this kind of non-monotonicity of intertemporal preferences.

[14]Although the standardized average DISCRATE of the elicited discount rates should theoretically satisfy E (DISCRATE) = 0 and σ (DISCRATE) = 1, neither equality is actually met, as seen in Table 9.4. This comes from the fact that the numbers of effective responses differ among the five discount rate questions.

Table 9.4 Definitions and summary statistics of variables

Variables		Definition	Mean	S.D.	Obs.
Cigarette consumption	The number of cigarette consumption	The number of cigarettes consumed per day	5.920	11.398	13,803
Time preference factors	DISCRATE	The simple mean, defined by equation (1), of the standardized values of the elicited discount rates $DR_{i,t}$ $(i = 1, \ldots, 5)$ as a measure of the degree of impatience	−0.058	0.325	10,125
	HYPERBOL	A binary indicator for hyperbolic discounting which equals one if $DR_1 > DR_2$, and zero otherwise	0.673	0.469	12,639
	HYPERBOLPROXY	A binary indicator of a proxy measure of hyperbolic discounting or the degree of procrastination, which takes one if a respondent's responses to the question A (QA), are always equal or greater than four in all the waves in which he participated, and takes zero otherwise	0.461	0.499	13,827
	NAÏVE	A binary indicator of time-inconsistent behavior which equals one if respondents display differences between responses to QA and QB, excluding the response to option (6) in QB, being equal to or greater than two in both the 2007 and 2008 waves, and zero otherwise.	0.287	0.452	11,638
	HYPERBOL*NAÏVE	A binary indicator of naïve hyperbolic discounters constructed by the interaction of HYPERBOL with NAÏVE	0.202	0.401	10,662
	HYPERBOLPROXY*NAÏVE	A binary indicator of naïve hyperbolic discounters constructed by the interaction of HYPERBOLPROXY with NAÏVE	0.249	0.433	11,638
	SIGN	A binary indicator for the sign effect which equals one if $DR_4 > DR_5$, and zero otherwise	0.903	0.296	10,450
Control variables	Degree of risk aversion	A variable which measures the degree of risk aversion, constructed by subtracting from 100 the respondents' responses to the question: 'When you go out, how high probability of rainfall makes you bring an umbrella with you?'	50.160	20.203	13,654
	Gender	A binary indicator for gender which equals one for male respondents and, zero otherwise	0.469	0.499	13,880
	Education	A binary indicator for university graduates which equals one for university graduates, and zero otherwise	0.218	0.413	13,454
	Income	Per capita household income in JPY 10,000	223.615	174.910	11,608
	Age	Ages of respondents	49.686	13.058	13,880

3.2.1 Time-Discounting Biases

By comparing the mean values of the elicited discount rates, we examine whether our average respondent displays the two aforementioned time-discounting biases. First, in no year is hyperbolic discounting observed, on average, since the mean of the discount rate DR_1, imputed from the immediate future choice (i.e., 2 days or 9 days), is not significantly higher than that of DR_2, imputed from a distant future choice (i.e., 90 days or 97 days). Second, in all years, the discount rate for future receipts DR_4 is significantly higher than that for future payments DR_5. This implies that our average respondent displays the sign effect.[15]

To examine the effects of the time-discounting biases on respondents' cigarette consumption, we construct the binary indicators HYPERBOL and SIGN for hyperbolic discounting and the sign effect, respectively, where, for example, HYPERBOL = 1 if $DR_1 > DR_2$, and HYPERBOL = 0 otherwise. From the mean values of HYPERBOL and SIGN, shown in Table 9.4, the percentages of the respondents who display the anomalies are 67.3 % for hyperbolic discounting and 90.3 % for the sign effect. Our hypothesis is that with all other things being equal, respondents' cigarette consumption relates positively to HYPERBOL and negatively to SIGN.

3.2.2 A Proxy for Hyperbolic Discounting

To strengthen our analysis regarding the correlation between hyperbolic discounting and smoking, we also construct a proxy variable for hyperbolic discounting from self-reported behavioral data. This would be necessary because, as we will show later, HYPERBOL might contain serious measurement errors.

In the JHPS, to measure the respondents' degrees of hyperbolic discounting or present bias from their behavioral tendency to procrastinate, we asked them about their likelihood to procrastinate in doing homework assignments during vacations in their childhood:

QA: Thinking about when you were a child and were given an assignment in school, when did you usually do the assignment?[16]

(1) Got it done right away
(2) Tended to get it done early, before the due date
(3) Worked on it daily, up until the due date

[15] In addition, although we have not included the results of the *t*-test in the table, DR_3, the discount rate for JPY 10,000 (around USD 93.32) is significantly higher than DR_4, which applies for JPY 1 million (around USD 9,331.84). This implies that people are more patient for larger amounts than for smaller amounts. This tendency, called the *magnitude effect*, is also commonly observed in the literature (e.g., Benzion et al. 1989; Frederick et al. 2002).

[16] In Japanese elementary and high schools, students are usually assigned a great deal of homework during summer vacation.

(4) Tended to get it done toward the end
(5) Got it done at the last minute

The higher the number a respondent chose in this question, the more strongly he procrastinated, and hence, the more likely he would be hyperbolic. Question QA was asked every year, and in the absence of measurement errors, a respondent's response to it should be the same every year. In fact, owing to measurement errors, there are some within-respondent variations in the data. To reduce the effect of those measurement errors, we construct a proxy indicator for hyperbolic discounters based on longitudinally consistent responses: By using the response data to QA, we identify a respondent as hyperbolic if he self-reports that he did unplanned procrastination consistently in all the waves that he participated in. Specifically, we define a proxy variable for hyperbolic discounting, HYPERBOLPROXY, as one if a respondent's responses to QA are always equal to or greater than 4 in all the waves that he participated in, and zero otherwise. With the indicator HYPERBOLPROXY, 46.1 % of the responses are identified as hyperbolic. Although HYPERBOLPROXY does not capture the respondents' current behavioral inclination, but rather that of their childhood, it has been empirically reported in psychological research that a person's self-control ability toward present rewards in preschool days accurately predicts his or her cognitive power and self-control ability in later years (e.g., Shoda et al. 1990). Similarly, Ikeda et al. (2010) and Ikeda and Kang (2015) empirically show that people's degrees of obesity and their inclination toward over-borrowing, respectively, have expected positive associations with their degrees of procrastination in childhood, which are measured using the same question as QA.

3.2.3 Naïve or Sophisticated

To determine whether each of the hyperbolic respondents is naïve or sophisticated, the JHPS also asked respondents in 2007 and 2008 how they had planned to do homework assignments during their childhood vacations:

QB: Thinking about when you were a child and were given an assignment in school, when did you plan to do your assignment?

(1) I planned to get it done right away
(2) I planned to get it done rather early, before the due date
(3) I planned to work on it daily, up until the due date
(4) I planned to get it done toward the end
(5) I planned to get it done at the last minute
(6) I didn't make any plans

The planned timing of doing homework assignments in options (1)–(5) in QB correspond to the execution timing in options (1)–(5) in QA, respectively. After excluding respondents who chose (6) in QB (i.e., who did not make any plan), we can identify naïve respondents by comparing the responses to QA with those to

QB: respondents who chose a larger number in QA than in QB could be considered naïve, as they tended to procrastinate on jobs in a time-inconsistent manner.

An indicator variable for time-inconsistent behavior, NAÏVE, is constructed which equals one if respondents display differences between responses to QA and QB that are equal to or greater than two in both the 2007 and 2008 waves, and zero otherwise. The naïve hyperbolic discounters are identified by an interaction of the hyperbolic indicator HYPERBOL (respectively, HYPERBOLPROXY) with NAÏVE, denoted by HYPERBOL*NAÏVE (respectively, HYPERBOLPROXY*NAÏVE).[17] The interaction indicator HYPERBOL*NAÏVE indicates that 20.2 % of the respondents are naïve hyperbolic discounters; HYPERBOLPROXY*NAÏVE implies that this number is 24.9 %. These proportions of naïve hyperbolic discounters are consistent with those in the Japanese Internet survey of Ikeda and Kang (2015), in which naïve hyperbolic discounters are reported to comprise 25.3 % of respondents.

3.3 *Longitudinal Within-Person Stability of Time-Preference Data*

Before proceeding to the main analysis, we check the within-person stability of our time-preference data by examining the longitudinal within-person variation in time-discounting characteristics.[18] This is important because, in the literature, it has been sometimes assumed that people's preference data at a point in time can explain, to some extent, their choices and behavior in other years (e.g., Grignon 2009). The validity of this presumption crucially depends on how stable people's preferences actually are. This should be checked using panel data.

We check the stability of our time-discounting data by estimating autocorrelation in the limited sample of respondents for whom we have all the time-preference data—i.e., DISCRATE, HYPERBOL, and SIGN—throughout the entire period. In

[17]Options for QA and QB do not have any categories to capture behavior to do homework late or not to do it at all. As another problem, responses may capture other respondent attributes than an inclination toward procrastination (e.g., their upbringing by parents, availability of other options, or any social connections). To partially take this possibility into account, we conducted another main regression analysis by controlling for the education levels of parents, and we found our main results to be robust, even against this consideration. Furthermore, in spite of the above-mentioned limitations, HYPERBOLPROXY and the interaction with NAÏVE (HYPERBOLPROXY*NAÏVE) obtained from QA and QB have strong correlations with respondents' degrees of obesity, inclination toward over-borrowing, and addictive behavior other than smoking (e.g., drinking and gambling), all of which are predicted by economic theory to be affected by peoples' present-biased tendency. See Appendix, which shows the correlations of HYPERBOLPROXY and HYPERBOLPROXY*NAÏVE with the actual current behavior.

[18]Note that throughout the sample period, JHPS asked the same set of questions regarding time discounting.

Table 9.5 Autocorrelations of time-preference variables.

	DISCRATE	HYPERBOL	SIGN
L1	0.6161*** (0.000) [2346]	0.1769*** (0.000) [4293]	0.1769*** (0.000) [2508]
L2	0.5774*** (0.000) [1564]	0.1266*** (0.000) [2862]	0.1261*** (0.000) [1672]
L3	0.5362*** (0.000) [782]	0.0037 (0.889) [1431]	0.1549*** (0.000) [836]

This table shows the autocorrelations of time preference variables. 'L1', 'L2', and 'L3' indicate the first-order, second-order, and third-order lagged variables, respectively. The p-values are in parentheses, and the number of observations are in square brackets.
*** denotes statistical significance at 1 % level

this limited sample, the numbers of respondents are 782 for DISCRATE, 1,431 for HYPERBOL, and 836 for SIGN.

Table 9.5 summarizes the first- to third-order autocorrelations of each time-preference variable. All the time-preference variables display positive autocorrelations. In particular, note that DISCRATE, which is constructed by averaging out measurement errors that would be contained in the individual discount-rate data, has strong positive autocorrelations and could be taken as fairly stable and hence reliable.

In contrast, the autocorrelations of HYPERBOL and SIGN are not so strong. The third-order autocorrelation of HYPERBOL is insignificant. In fact, it can be shown that the binary indicator HYPERBOL takes different values in the first and last waves with probability 39.8 %. The autocorrelations of SIGN are not so large although they are all significant. The evidences show that there are non-negligible time-variations in our measures of time-discounting biases, HYPERBOL and SIGN. These results also indicate that the presumption that time preference is invariant over time is empirically invalid.

Note that there are two possibilities for the existence of time-variations in the time-preference measures. Firstly, they can be caused by preference shocks. In this case, the within-person variations in the time-preference variables lead to time-varying smoking behavior that cannot be explained by control variables. Secondly, the variations could reflect measurement errors which would arise for various reasons (e.g., non-incentivized, demanding nature of questions etc.) when eliciting discount rates.

Table 9.6 shows the autocorrelations of self-reported behavior from which the proxy of hyperbolic discounting (HYPERBOLPROXY) and the time-inconsistent indicator (NAÏVE) are constructed. The variable QA, which indicates how late the respondents did homework, and QB, which indicates how late they planned to do homework, show strong and positive autocorrelations with those lags, e.g., QA has

Table 9.6 Autocorrelations of responses to the homework questions

	QA	QB	QA-QB
L1	0.7406*** (0.000) [5121]	0.4891*** (0.000) [2329]	0.6053*** (0.000) [2322]
L2	0.7047*** (0.000) [3414]		
L3	0.6863*** (0.000) [1707]		

This table shows the autocorrelations of responses to homework questions. 'QA' indicates the response to the question regarding doing homework assignments explained in Sect. 3.2.2. 'QB' indicates the responses to the question regarding planning homework assignments explained in Sect. 3.2.3, where respondents who choose option (6) are excluded. 'QA-QB' indicates the differences between QA and QB. 'L1', 'L2', and 'L3' indicate the first-order, second-order, and third-order lagged variables, respectively. The *p*-values are in parentheses and the number of observations are in square brackets
*** denotes statistical significance at the 1 % level

a 68.6 % correlation with the third-order lagged variable and QB displays a 48.9 % correlation with the first-order one. The difference between QA and QB, which indicates the degree of naïveté, also has a strong autocorrelation, 60.5 %. It could be concluded that the self-reported data are reasonably stable during our sample period.

However, without measurement errors, the response data to retrospective questions QA and QB must be completely time-invariant. The detected time variations in variables QA and QB thus reflect measurement errors. When constructing HYPERBOLPROXY and NAÏVE as explained in Sect. 3.2, we reduce the effect of the measurement errors by using the longitudinally consistent responses.[19]

In view of all the above points, we adopt the following estimation strategy. First, we conduct regression of smoking behavior by using the time-varying preference variables DISCRATE, HYPERBOL, and SIGN as regressors. Second, the same regression is conducted using HYPERBOLPROXY, instead of HYPERBOL, which may contain serious measurement errors. Third, we check the relative impacts of preference shocks and measurement errors on our estimation results. To do so, in addition to those two basic analyses, we re-conduct regression by applying alternative time-invariant indicators for hyperbolic discounting and the sign effect,

[19]We also construct the variables that are time-averaged responses to QA instead of HYPERBOLPROXY, and that which are constructed by taking time-averaged differences between responses to QA and QB instead of NAÏVE. With these alternative specifications, the main results in the present study do not change substantially. The estimation results are available upon request.

whose preference shocks and measurement errors are averaged out by taking across-wave means, and compare the results in the case of the time-variant indicators and the time-invariant ones.

4 Regression Results: Cragg's Two-Part Model

In this section, we examine the impacts of time discounting on smoking behavior by using econometric models. Since our cigarette consumption data including the nonsmoker sample are left-censored, we estimate smoking behavior by using Cragg's (1971) two-part model. In Cragg's model, a probit model is adopted to estimate smoking participation, whereas a least squares model is used to estimate smokers' cigarette consumption. The model allows for estimating two different sets of parameters: smoking participation and the number of cigarettes consumed.[20]

We first estimate a basic model (model (1)) that includes DISCRATE, HYPERBOL, and SIGN as regressors. We then estimate revised models by using HYPERBOLPROXY in place of HYPERBOL (model (3)) and adding the product term of a naïve dummy and hyperbolic discounting (models (2) and (4)). Each estimation is conducted for the full, male, and female samples.

Throughout the estimation, we incorporate year dummies and control variables for various personal attributes, including the degree of risk aversion, gender, education, age, and per-capita household income. Detailed explanations and summary statistics for the controls are given in Table 9.4.

Table 9.7 shows the marginal effects of time-preference variables on cigarette consumption in the two-part model.

Consistent with our hypothesis, the coefficients of discount rate, DISCRATE, display positive signs in all models. In many cases, the positive associations are significant. Particularly in the full sample, all of them are significant for both smoking participation and cigarette consumption. Quantitatively, an increase in DISCRATE by one unit of standard deviation, *ceteris paribus*, leads to a 4.1–4.7 percentage point higher probability of being a smoker, whereas it increases smokers' cigarette consumption by 1.22–1.67 per day.

As for the impact of the sign effect, it restrains cigarette consumption but not smoking participation. Smokers with the sign effect smoke less than do the other smokers, by 1.47–1.99 cigarettes per day in the full samples and by 1.91–2.51 in the male samples. Although a smoking rate of the full sample in model (4) displays a significant association with the sign effect, it is not robust in the other models. Other estimated coefficients of the sign effect are negative, as we hypothesize, but are insignificant.

Hyperbolic discounting, HYPERBOL, shows unstable association with cigarette consumption, except that, opposite to our prediction, significantly negative associ-

[20]This model is also called the 'double-hurdle model' or 'two-tier model.'

Table 9.7 Marginal effects via the estimation made through Cragg's two-part models

	Model (1)						Model (2)					
	All		Male		Female		All		Male		Female	
	Smoking participation	Cigarette consumption by smokers	Smoking participation	Cigarette consumption by smokers	Smoking participation	Cigarette consumption by smokers	Smoking participation	Cigarette consumption by smokers	Smoking participation	Cigarette consump-tion by smokers	Smoking participation	Cigarette consumption by smokers
DISCRATE	0.045***	1.525**	0.064***	1.152	0.029	3.360***	0.041***	1.677**	0.055*	1.277	0.032*	3.143*
	(0.015)	(0.771)	(0.023)	(0.755)	(0.020)	(1.249)	(0.016)	(0.680)	(0.029)	(0.999)	(0.017)	(1.650)
HYPERBOL	−0.004	0.288	−0.018	0.289	0.011	0.409	−0.019*	−0.151	−0.036*	−0.215	0.000	−0.017
	(0.011)	(0.485)	(0.018)	(0.612)	(0.013)	(0.856)	(0.010)	(0.629)	(0.021)	(0.737)	(0.014)	(1.126)
HYPERBOL*NAÏVE							0.052***	0.285	0.050**	0.427	0.048***	−0.195
							(0.011)	(0.598)	(0.023)	(0.694)	(0.014)	(0.935)
SIGN	−0.023	−1.474**	−0.028	−1.905**	−0.018	−0.484	−0.021	−1.985***	−0.016	−2.509***	−0.024	−0.858
	(0.016)	(0.659)	(0.023)	(0.797)	(0.016)	(1.116)	(0.016)	(0.757)	(0.026)	(0.886)	(0.017)	(1.321)
# of Obs.	8,446		4,118		4,328		7,223		3,395		3,828	
Log pseudolikelihood	−13088.344		−9323.606		−3739.909		−10707.521		−7475.578		−3204.426	
	Model (3)						Model (4)					
DISCRATE	0.047***	1.224**	0.073***	0.745	0.022	3.105**	0.042***	1.628**	0.063**	1.141	0.024	3.313**
	(0.014)	(0.594)	(0.023)	(0.666)	(0.016)	(1.361)	(0.014)	(0.661)	(0.027)	(0.882)	(0.020)	(1.371)
HYPERBOLPROXY	0.035***	1.704***	0.044***	2.544***	0.026***	−0.148	0.017	1.712***	0.044**	2.589***	−0.013	−0.853
	(0.010)	(0.429)	(0.015)	(0.543)	(0.010)	(0.805)	(0.011)	(0.567)	(0.019)	(0.762)	(0.017)	(1.400)
HYPERBOLPROXY *NAÏVE							0.035***	−0.269	0.008	−0.491	0.060***	0.992
							(0.013)	(0.602)	(0.024)	(0.748)	(0.018)	(1.478)
SIGN	−0.024*	−1.556**	−0.028	−1.961**	−0.019	−0.508	−0.021	−1.963***	−0.014	−2.387***	−0.023	−0.865
	(0.014)	(0.610)	(0.026)	(0.825)	(0.016)	(1.326)	(0.017)	(0.628)	(0.029)	(0.925)	(0.017)	(1.305)
# of Obs.	8,422		4,106		4,316		7,223		3,395		3,828	
Log pseudolikelihood	−13022.774		−9260.521		−3735.949		−10700.131		−7467.136		−3202.178	

This table shows the results of the Cragg's two-part model. Estimated coefficients are transformed into the marginal effects. The results are controlled by incorporating following variables as regressors: year dummies, the degree of risk aversion, gender, education, age, squared age, per capita household income, and squared per capita household income. Standard errors adjusted for clustering are in parentheses
* denotes statistical significance at the 10 % level. ** denotes statistical significance at the 5 % level. *** denotes statistical significance at the 1 % level

ations are detected for the full and male samples in model (2), where the estimated coefficients are insignificant with mixed signs. The unstable results might be due to large measurement errors of HYPERBOL, which are mentioned in the previous section.

In contrast, consistent with our hypothesis, HYPERBOLPROXY displays significantly positive impacts on smoking participation and cigarette consumption, particularly in the basic model (model (4)). Quantitatively, procrastinators show higher probabilities of smoking than do non-procrastinators, by 3.5 percentage points in the full sample, by 4.4 percentage points in the male sample, and by 2.6 percentage points in the female sample. Similarly, procrastinators consume more cigarettes than non-procrastinators, by 1.70–1.71 per day in the full sample and by 2.54–2.59 per day in the male sample.

A noticeable result is that most of the coefficients to the product terms of hyperbolic discounting and naïveté, which capture the smoking of naïve hyperbolic discounters in excess of that of the sophisticated hyperbolic, have significant and positive association with smoking participation in models (2) and (4). For example, in model (2), naïve hyperbolic discounters display a higher probability of smoking participation than the sophisticated, by 5.2, 5.0, and 4.8 percentage points in the full, male, and female samples, respectively.[21]

5 Measurement Errors, Preference Shocks, and Interpersonal Variations in Smoking

As pointed out in Sect. 3.3, within-respondent variations of HYPERBOL and SIGN could be attributed to the meaningful effect of preference shocks and the meaningless effect of measurement errors. We shall discuss on this issue by making use of the merits of multiple-wave data.

The use of multi-wave data is expected to have several advantages, compared to the case of a one-wave analysis. First, the resulting increase in the sample size makes estimations more efficient. Second, the data enable us to improve the predictive power of discount measures because multi-wave data could capture the effect of preference shocks on within-person changes of smoking behavior. Third, the use of multi-waves could reduce harmful influences of measurement errors on estimation, whereas the one-wave estimation is likely to directly suffer the influences. In fact, we can confirm that one-wave regressions show weaker and less stable associations between time discounting measures and smoking behavior than

[21]For robustness checks, we estimate five alternative specifications by using both the pooled regression and random-effects models: (i) the binary probit model, (ii) the linear regression model, (iii) the Tobit model, (iv) the ordered probit model, and (v) the interval data regression model. The results are fairly consistent with those in Table 9.7: the estimated impacts of time-preference variables on smoking behavior are confirmed in all specifications in the same manner as in the Cragg model. These results are available upon request.

multi-wave regressions in Table 9.7.[22] The use of multi-wave data actually improves the predictive power of time-discounting measures.

To examine which is larger, the effect of preference shocks or that of measurement errors, we construct binary indicator HYPERBOLM (respectively, SIGNM) by identifying a respondent as a hyperbolic discounter (respectively, as exhibiting the sign effect) if his across-wave average value of the HYPERBOL (respectively, SIGN) is greater than a certain critical value, say 0.5.[23] In these time-invariant binary indicators, within-person preference shocks and possible measurement errors are averaged out. Note also that associations between time discounting and smoking that are detected for by using the time-invariant indicators are not within-personal associations, but interpersonal associations between them. We re-conduct regressions by using HYPERBOLM and SIGNM for regressors.

Table 9.8 summarizes the results. By comparing it with Table 9.7, we see that the estimation result is improved by using HYPERBOLM and SIGNM in two points. First, the significance levels of the sign effects become higher. In particular, by estimating exclusively interpersonal associations using the averaging-out procedure, we detect significant associations of the sign effect not only with cigarette consumption but also with the probability of being a smoker. Second, the values of the log pseudolikelihood are improved. The improvements of the results imply that considerable measurement errors that might be contained in the time-varying indicator of the sign effect (SIGN) dominate the impacts of preference shocks on smoking in Table 9.7. It also implies that the detected significant associations between smoking and the sign effect represent interpersonal associations between them, rather than their within-personal associations.

To focus simply on the interpersonal associations, we re-estimate the same models by using only the 'consistent' sample in which both HYPERBOL and SIGN consistently take the same values of 1 or 0 over all the waves that the respondent participates in. As shown by Table 9.9, the marginal effects on DISCRATE, HYPERBOLPROXY, and the interaction terms of the naïf become larger in size, with the levels of statistical significance being almost unchanged. This implies that interpersonal differences of the time-discounting properties actually induce the differences of cigarette consumption levels between individuals.[24]

6 Concluding Remarks

By using a unique panel survey of Japanese adults, we have detected associations between smoking behavior and time discounting including its behavioral biases. Discount rates have positive associations with both the probability of smoking

[22] The results of one-wave estimations are available upon request.

[23] The cases of taking 0.75 and 1 as the threshold values are also estimated, wherein our results are robust against the modifications. The results are available upon request.

[24] However, in the consistent sample, the negative impacts of SIGN become weaker, possibly due to the sample reduction.

Table 9.8 Marginal effects via the estimation made through Cragg's two-part models by averaging out time-variations in HYPERBOL and SIGN

	Model (1)						Model (2)					
	All		Male		Female		All		Male		Female	
	Smoking participation	Cigarette consumption by smokers	Smoking participation	Cigarette consumption by smokers	Smoking participation	Cigarette consumption by smokers	Smoking participation	Cigarette consumption by smokers	Smoking participation	Cigarette consumption by smokers	Smoking participation	Cigarette consumption by smokers
DISCRATE	0.047***	1.589***	0.077***	1.322*	0.019	3.279**	0.045***	1.887***	0.072***	1.607	0.022	3.247**
	(0.014)	(0.577)	(0.024)	(0.722)	(0.021)	(1.406)	(0.016)	(0.716)	(0.025)	(1.007)	(0.018)	(1.281)
HYPERBOLM	−0.001	0.584	0.004	0.808	−0.006	0.306	−0.012	0.193	−0.007	0.408	−0.016	−0.063
	(0.012)	(0.550)	(0.021)	(0.708)	(0.013)	(1.115)	(0.014)	(0.671)	(0.020)	(0.743)	(0.015)	(1.022)
HYPERBOLM* NAÏVE							0.051***	1.037*	0.056**	1.323*	0.044***	0.370
							(0.012)	(0.582)	(0.023)	(0.776)	(0.013)	(0.892)
SIGNM	−0.051**	−1.448*	−0.066**	−2.482**	−0.035	0.942	−0.050**	−1.913**	−0.048	−3.215**	−0.047*	0.500
	(0.022)	(0.839)	(0.031)	(1.213)	(0.024)	(1.334)	(0.022)	(0.903)	(0.035)	(1.320)	(0.024)	(1.569)
# of Obs.	8,446		4,118		4,328		7,223		3,395		3,828	
Log pseudolikelihood	−13086.953		−9321.963		−3739.599		−10704.361		−7472.367		−3204.545	
	Model (3)						Model (4)					
DISCRATE	0.047***	1.152*	0.073***	0.664	0.022	3.106**	0.042***	1.531**	0.064***	1.035	0.025	3.263**
	(0.013)	(0.594)	(0.022)	(0.721)	(0.016)	(1.314)	(0.013)	(0.773)	(0.021)	(0.989)	(0.020)	(1.331)
HYPERBOLPROXY	0.035***	1.692***	0.044***	2.517***	0.025**	−0.202	0.017	1.725***	0.044**	2.591***	−0.013	−0.914
	(0.010)	(0.453)	(0.015)	(0.562)	(0.011)	(0.819)	(0.012)	(0.613)	(0.019)	(0.727)	(0.017)	(1.369)
HYPERBOLPROXY* NAÏVE							0.034***	−0.309	0.008	−0.536	0.060***	0.982
							(0.013)	(0.612)	(0.021)	(0.679)	(0.017)	(1.344)
SIGNM	−0.051**	−1.540**	−0.068**	−2.475**	−0.035*	0.916	−0.048**	−1.838**	−0.046	−3.000**	−0.045**	0.586
	(0.022)	(0.771)	(0.033)	(1.095)	(0.018)	(1.341)	(0.021)	(0.886)	(0.041)	(1.455)	(0.022)	(1.658)
# of Obs.	8,422		4,106		4,316		7,223		3,395		3,828	
Log pseudolikelihood	−13021.980		−9259.266		−3735.31		−10700.543		−7466.994		−3201.572	

This table shows the results of the Cragg's two-part model by averaging out within-person variations by identifying a respondent as a hyperbol discounter (respectively as exhibiting the sign effect) if his across-wave average value of HYPERBOL (respectively, SIGN) is greater than 0.5. Estimated coefficients are transformed into the marginal effects. The results are controlled by incorporating following variables as regressors: year dummies, degree of risk aversion, gender, education, age, squared age, per capita household income, and squared per capita household income. Standard errors adjusted for clustering are in parentheses

* denotes statistical significance at the 10 % level. ** denotes statistical significance at the 5 % level. *** denotes statistical significance at the 1 % level

Table 9.9 Marginal effects via the estimation made through Cragg's two-part models with consistent sample

	Model (1)						Model (2)					
	All		Male		Female		All		Male		Female	
	Smoking participation	Cigarette consumption by smokers	Smoking participation	Cigarette consumption by smokers	Smoking participation	Cigarette consumption by smokers	Smoking participation	Cigarette consumption by smokers	Smoking participation	Cigarette consumption by smokers	Smoking participation	Cigarette consumption by smokers
DISCRATE	0.063***	2.692***	0.072*	2.898*	0.054*	3.638*	0.052*	2.424**	0.043	2.657	0.061*	3.282
	(0.024)	(1.021)	(0.041)	(1.496)	(0.031)	(1.927)	(0.03)	(1.216)	(0.043)	(1.883)	(0.036)	(2.53)
HYPERBOL	−0.018	0.117	−0.023	0.428	−0.01	−0.364	−0.022	−1.699	−0.012	−1.738	−0.024	−1.276
	(0.019)	(0.925)	(0.03)	(1.203)	(0.023)	(1.53)	(0.024)	(1.306)	(0.044)	(1.732)	(0.031)	(2.576)
HYPERBOL* NAÏVE							0.069***	2.159**	0.05	3.94***	0.079***	−0.512
							(0.016)	(0.883)	(0.031)	(1.38)	(0.019)	(1.203)
SIGN	−0.023	−0.909	−0.016	−2.044	−0.027	1.588	−0.026	−2.503	0.008	−5.142**	−0.05	1.557
	(0.028)	(1.178)	(0.045)	(1.655)	(0.031)	(2.27)	(0.04)	(1.54)	(0.06)	(2.131)	(0.042)	(3.857)
# of Obs.	3,569		1,666		1,903		2,697		1,175		1,522	
Log pseudolikelihood	−5238.098		−3532.529		−1694.156		−3571.122		−2280.592		−1272.489	
	Model (3)						Model (4)					
DISCRATE	0.066***	1.55**	0.091***	1.491*	0.041*	2.168	0.066***	1.9**	0.088***	1.92*	0.05***	2.08
	(0.014)	(0.704)	(0.023)	(0.803)	(0.021)	(1.353)	(0.017)	(0.752)	(0.024)	(1.095)	(0.019)	(1.35)
HYPERBOLPROXY	0.041***	1.776***	0.05***	2.65***	0.031**	−0.205	0.016	1.821***	0.045*	2.756***	−0.014	−0.864
	(0.01)	(0.44)	(0.015)	(0.723)	(0.013)	(0.924)	(0.013)	(0.64)	(0.027)	(0.863)	(0.017)	(1.522)
HYPERBOLPROXY* NAÏVE							0.048***	−0.42	0.018	−0.692	0.075***	0.792
							(0.016)	(0.71)	(0.028)	(0.909)	(0.018)	(1.757)
SIGN	−0.037	−1.505	−0.024	−2.733*	−0.039	1.454	−0.029	−1.435	0.018	−2.823	−0.054	0.843
	(0.024)	(1.146)	(0.037)	(1.581)	(0.029)	(1.877)	(0.033)	(1.306)	(0.055)	(2.071)	(0.034)	(2.248)
# of Obs.	6,985		3,444		3,541		5,904		2,802		3,102	
Log pseudolikelihood	−10722.045		−7691.848		−3005.682		−8648.622		−6099.28		−2518.831	

This table shows the results of the Cragg's two-part model by using only the sample in which both of HYPERBOL and SIGN take consistently the same values of one or zero over all the waves that the respondent participates in. Estimated coefficients are transformed into the marginal effects. The results are controlled by incorporating following variables as regressors: year dummies, degree of risk aversion, gender, education, age, squared age, per capita household income, and squared per capita household income. Standard errors adjusted for clustering are in parentheses

* denotes statistical significance at the 10 % level. ** denotes statistical significance at the 5 % level. *** denotes statistical significance at the 1 % level

participation and, among smokers, the number of cigarettes consumed. The incidence of the sign effect restrains both types of smoking behavior. The degree of hyperbolic discounting which is elicited from each respondent's procrastination behavior positively relates to the both decisions. Particularly, naïve hyperbolic discounters are more likely to initiate smoking than sophisticated hyperbolic discounters. This implies that paternalistic intervention such as cigarette tax hikes would be desirable to enhance the welfare of smokers, as Gruber and Kőszegi (2001) and Gruber and Mullainathan (2005) commonly suggest.

By making use of the merit of the panel data, we have contributed to the empirical literature on time preference and smoking in several points. First, we have shown that elicited time preferences and their behavioral biases display large within-person variations. To our best knowledge, there is no study which investigates the within-person stability of time preference, either based on incentivized experiments or on non-incentivized survey. A straightforward implication of the large within-person variations is that the usual simplifying presumption that elicited time preference is stable over time may be empirically invalid. Second, by smoothing out the variations by taking within-person averages, and by conducting estimation in the subsample of stable responses, we have shown that the within-person variations in the elicited time-preference biases seem to reflect considerable measurement errors, rather than preference shocks.[25] Third, faced with the measurement errors, associations between smoking and time preferences are shown to be clearly detected as inter-personal associations by averaging out the within-person variations or by using the consistent sample. The analyses indicate that using panel data with multiple observations per person helps to show evidence of a link between preferences and behaviors.

Further research is needed to overcome problems in this study. First, our analysis owes much to the Kimball method in imputing discount rates. Although the method has the merit of using entire information of the cross-respondent distribution of responses, the estimated proportions of hyperbolic discounters and those of respondents who indicate the sign effect seem to be higher than reported in the

[25]There could be several reasons for the measurement errors. First, our data are not based on incentivized experiments. For this point, see footnote 10. Second, our questions to elicit discount rates might be somewhat demanding for respondents. However, we do not think that this possibility is so serious for the following reasons. First, our average respondents replied to the same time-discounting questions in 2.5 waves. It would not be so difficult for them to reply to the questions. Second, in the 2011 wave, more than 80 % of respondents made consistent choices even though options in payoff tables (e.g., Table 9.2) were arranged in more complex manners, i.e., in random orders without listing imputed interest rates, instead of the order in accordance with the listed value of imputed interest rates as in Table 9.2. Third, our time discounting data display associations with various behavioral attributes, such as the degree of obesity, debt holdings, and habits of gamble and drinking, in theoretically predicted ways. For the same reasons, we do not guess that the measurement errors in our data are larger than in computer-based studies in the literature where series of simple binary choices are posed stepwise.

previous literature.[26] This could be partly attributable to the nature of the Kimball method.[27]

Second, we could not identify association between preference shocks in time-discounting biases and smoking behavior. It would be an important issue to develop a method to identify preference shocks to time preferences by removing measurement errors from within-personal variations in time preferences.

Another direction of the future research will be to examine how tax hikes affect different types of discounters. In particular, we should discern smoking moderation behavior in response to cigarette tax hikes from the recent decreasing trend of cigarette consumption. It is also interesting to identify respondents' degree of naïveté by conducting experiments in an incentivized manner.

Acknowledgment Our special thanks go to Y. Fukuta, K. Hirata, M. Nakagawa, F. Ohtake, J. Wan, and participants at the International Workshop on the Economics of Obesity and Health 2009 for helpful comments. We acknowledge financial supports from: the COE and Global COE Programs of Osaka University; a Grant-in-Aid for Scientific Research (B 21330046) from the Japan Society for the Promotion of Science; and the Joint Usage/ Research Center Projects of ISER from the Ministry of Education, Culture, Sports, Science and Technology.

Appendix

Table 9.10 shows the correlation coefficients of HYPERBOLPROXY and HYPERBOLPROXY*NAÏVE with actual behavioral traits.

Addendum: Validation Using Recent Wave Data in JHPS[28]

This addendum checks robustness of the results in the Kang and Ikeda (2014) text article. To do so, we use the most recent waves of JHPS in 2009 and 2010. These waves of data enable us to reconsider whether time-variations of preference data are attributed to individual preference shocks or possible measurement errors, and whether detected relationships between time preferences and smoking capture

[26]For example, the proportion of hyperbolic discounters in our dataset is 67.3 % (see Sect. 3.2.1), whereas hyperbolic discounters occupy 25 % of 3,200 Italians and 1,400 Dutch respondents (see Eisenhauer and Ventura 2006), 36 % of 606 Americans (see Meier and Sprenger 2010), and 44.9 % of 2,236 Japanese (see Ikeda and Kang 2015).

[27]Instead of using Kimball's procedure, we could impute discount rates by simply assigning median interest rates of categories to their estimates. In that case, however, we cannot elicit discount rates when respondents do not switch at any given choices. Partly due to the resulting reduction of the sample size, estimation results become weaker when using the median interest rates. The Kimball method enables us to estimate discount rates even when responses do not switch.

[28]This addendum has been newly written for this book chapter.

Table 9.10 The correlations of HYPERBOLPROXY and HYPERBOLPROXY*NAÏVE with actual behavioral traits

	Debt holdings	Body Mass Index	Alcohol	Gambling
HYPERBOLPROXY	0.0687*** (0.000)	0.0779*** (0.000)	0.0832*** (0.000)	0.0948*** (0.000)
HYPERBOLPROXY * NAÏVE	0.0631*** (0.000)	0.0343*** (0.000)	0.0546*** (0.000)	0.0665*** (0.000)

This table shows the correlation coefficients of HYPERBOLPROXY and HYPERBOLPROXY*NAÏVE with following actual behavioral traits: (i)'Debt holdings', which takes one if a respondent is in debt other than mortgages and zero otherwise; (ii)'Body Mass Index', which is defined as weight in kilograms divided by height in meters squared (kg/m2); (iii)'Alcohol', which indicates the strength of drinking habits on 6-point scale from one (don't drink at all) to six (5 cans of beer (12 oz.*5) or its equivalent a day, everyday); and (iv)'Gambling', which indicates frequency of gambling behavior on 6-point scale from one (don't gamble at all) to six (almost everyday). The p-values are in parentheses and the number of observations are in square brackets
*** denotes statistical significance at the 1 % level

behavioral differences due to within-personal preference shocks or interpersonal differences of time preferences.[29]

Table 9.11 shows that associations between time-discounting and smoking in the 2009 and 2010 data are consistent with those in the text article. All of the individual discount rates (DR1 to DR4), with the exception of the discount rate for paying money (DR5), and the impatience measure (DISCRATE) show significant and positive associations with smoking.

In the 2009 and 2010 waves, associations regarding behavioral biases of time discounting also show consistency with our previous findings, in that heavier smokers are less likely to exhibit the sign effect (SIGN), and more likely to exhibit tendencies toward procrastination (HYPERBOLPROXY) and time-inconsistency (NAÏVE).[30] In contrast, we find association between smoking and hyperbolic discounting regarding monetary choices (HYPERBOL) to be different from our hypothesis again.

As discussed in the text, time-varying indicators regarding monetary discounting biases, such as HYPERBOL and SIGN, might contain non-negligible measurement errors. Table 9.12 shows autocorrelations of DISCRATE, HYPERBOL, and SIGN in the 2009 and 2010 waves. In spite of the significant autocorrelations observed in case of the three variables, the reported magnitudes for HYPERBOL and SIGN are not large enough. The time-variations in the indicators are attributable to measurement errors. Indeed, associations between time-discounting biases and smoking become stronger when we use time-invariant indicators that take one only

[29]Since the 2010 JHPS wave does not make inquiries regarding behavioral inclinations for the homework assignment, we assume here that variables HYPERBOLPROXY and NAÏVE take the same values as in the 2009 wave.

[30]The relationships are robust even if the cut-off points of HYPERBOLPROXY and NAÏVE are arbitrarily changed.

Table 9.11 Comparisons of time-discounting properties among smoking statuses using 2009 and 2010 waves

	DR_1	DR_2	DR_3	DR_4	DR_5	DISCRATE	HYPERBOL	SIGN	HYPERBOLPROXY	NAÏVE
Smoker	3.551	4.315	0.228	0.052	−0.005	0.092	0.679	0.879	0.675	0.418
	[2,316]	[2,346]	[2,364]	[2,356]	[1,960]	[1,859]	[2,290]	[1,921]	[2,504]	[2,111]
Heavy smoker	4.900	5.692	0.269	0.074	−0.014	0.224	0.663	0.845	0.741	0.445
	[189]	[197]	[200]	[200]	[153]	[143]	[187]	[148]	[216]	[173]
Light smoker	3.431	4.189	0.224	0.050	−0.005	0.081	0.680	0.882	0.669	0.416
	[2,127]	[2,149]	[2,164]	[2,156]	[1,807]	[1,716]	[2,103]	[1,773]	[2,288]	[1,938]
Non-smoker	2.830	3.231	0.177	0.040	−0.004	−0.013	0.717	0.901	0.545	0.360
	[8,407]	[8,434]	[8,473]	[8,464]	[7,074]	[6,740]	[8,277]	[6,954]	[8,895]	[8,017]
Differences:										
Heavy vs light (t-value)	(2.154)	(1.805)	(1.758)	(2.202)	(−1.378)	(2.129)	(−0.474)	(−1.323)	(2.149)	(0.746)
	**	**	**	**	*	**		*	**	
Smoker vs non-smoker (t-values)	(3.553)	(4.529)	(6.929)	(3.759)	(−0.725)	(5.774)	(−3.620)	(−2.806)	(11.685)	(4.947)
	***	***	***	***		***	***	***	***	***

The data are from 2009 and 2010 waves in the Japan Household Panel Survey on Consumer Preferences and Satisfaction (JHPS). 'Heavy smoker' indicates smokers who smoke more than two packs, i.e., 40 cigarettes, per day, and 'light smokers' indicates smokers who smoke more than 10 cigarettes and less than two packs per day

*, **, and *** denote statistical significances of mean differences of time-discounting variables between groups at the 10 %, 5 %, and 1 % levels, respectively

Table 9.12 Autocorrelations of time-preference variables using 2009 and 2010 waves

	DISCRATE	HYPERBOL	SIGN
L1	0.369*** (0.000) [5121]	0.090*** (0.000) [2329]	0.121*** (0.000) [2322]

This table shows the autocorrelations of time preference variables. 'L1' indicates the first-order lagged variable. The p-values are in parentheses, and the number of observations are in square brackets

*** denotes statistical significance at the 1 % level

if a respondent reports the incident of the corresponding time-discounting biases in both waves.[31] This fact implies that, in time-variations of time preferences in JHPS, measurement errors dominate preference shocks, and therefore, in accordance with our assertion in the text article, the results in Table 9.11 reflect interpersonal associations between time discounting and smoking, rather than within-personal ones.

By using a titration-type questionnaire, which asks sequentially three queries of binary choices on immediate future and distant future trade-offs, we successfully detect expected associations between monetary hyperbolic discounting and several actual behaviors, such as health-related behavior including smoking in Kang and Ikeda (2013) and borrowing behavior in Ikeda and Kang (2015). Therefore, we now believe that unstable associations of monetary hyperbolic discounting in the text article might not reflect any true relations between hyperbolic discounting and smoking, but would rather reflect some shortcomings of the methodology in detecting hyperbolic discounting.

References

Ainslie G (1992) Picoeconomics. Cambridge University Press, Cambridge

Baker F, Johnson MW, Bickel WK (2003) Delay discounting in current and never-before cigarette smokers: similarities and differences across commodity, sign, and magnitude. J Abnorm Psychol 112(3):382–392

Bardsley P, Olekalns N (1999) Cigarette and tobacco consumption: have anti-smoking policies made a difference? Econ Rec 75(3):225–240

Becker GS, Murphy KM (1988) A theory of rational addiction. J Polit Econ 96(4):675–700

Becker GS, Grossman M, Murphy KM (1994) An empirical analysis of cigarette addiction. Am Econ Rev 84(3):396–418

[31]Time-invariant indicators make associations in Table 9.11 stronger: in the case of hyperbolic discounting, the t-values are changed to -5.480 for the mean difference between smokers and nonsmokers, and to -1.210 for the difference between heavy smokers and light smokers; and in the case of the sign effect, the former is changed to -3.627, and the latter to -1.843.

Benzion U, Rapoport A, Yagil J (1989) Discount rates inferred from decisions: an experimental study. Manag Sci 35(3):270–284
Bickel WK, Odum AL, Madden GJ (1999) Impulsivity and cigarette smoking: delay discounting in current never, and ex-smokers. Psychopharmacology 146(4):447–454
Blondel S, Lohéac Y, Rinaudo S (2007) Rationality and drug use: an experimental approach. J Health Econ 26(3):643–658
Chaloupka F (1990) Men, women, and addiction: the case of cigarette smoking, NBER working paper 3267. National Bureau of Economic Research, Cambridge, MA
Chaloupka F (1991) Rational addictive behavior and cigarette smoking. J Polit Econ 99(4): 675–700
Chapman G (1996) Temporal discounting and utility for health and money. J Exp Psychol Learn Mem Cogn 22(3):771–791
Cragg JG (1971) Some statistical models for limited dependent variables with application to the demand for durable goods. Econometrica 39(5):829–844
Eisenhauer J, Ventura L (2006) The prevalence of present bias: some european evidence. Appl Econ 38(11):1223–1234
Frederick S, Loewenstein G, O'Donoghue T (2002) Time discounting and time preference: a critical review. J Econ Lit 40(2):351–401
Ganiats G, Teodore RT, Carson RM, Hamm SB, Cantor W, Summer S, Spann J, Hagen M, Miller C (2000) Health status and preferences: population-based time preferences for future health outcome. Med Decis Mak 20(3):263–270
Grignon M (2009) An empirical investigation of heterogeneity in time preferences and smoking behaviors. J Socio-Econ 38(5):739–751
Gruber J, Kőszegi B (2001) Is addiction "rational"? Theory and evidence. Q J Econ 116(4): 1261–1303
Gruber J, Kőszegi B (2004) Tax incidence when individuals are time-inconsistent: the case of cigarette excise taxes. J Public Econ 88(9–10):1959–1987
Gruber J, Mullainathan S (2005) Do cigarette taxes make smokers happier. Adv Econ Anal Policy 5(1):1–43
Harrison GW, Lau MI, Williams MB (2002) Estimating individual discount rates in Denmark: a field experiment. Am Econ Rev 92(5):1606–1617
Heidhues P, Kőszegi B (2010) Exploiting naïvete about self-control in the credit market. Am Econ Rev 100(5):2279–2303
Ida T (2010) Anomaly, impulsivity, and addiction. J Socio-Econ 39(2):194–203
Ida T, Goto R (2009) Simultaneous measurement of time and risk preferences: stated preference discrete choice modeling analysis depending on smoking behavior. Int Econ Rev 50(4): 1169–1182
Ikeda S, Kang M-I (2015) Hyperbolic discounting, borrowing aversion, and debt holding. Japanese Economic Review. doi:10.1111/jere.12072
Ikeda S, Kang M-I, Ohtake F (2010) Hyperbolic discounting, the sign effect, and the body mass index. J Health Econ 29(2):268–284
Johnson MW, Bickel WK (2002) Within-subject comparison of real and hypothetical money rewards in delay discounting. J Exp Anal Behav 77(2):129–146
Kang M-I, Ikeda S (2013) Time discounting, present biases, and health-related behavior, ISER discussion paper 885. ISER, Osaka
Kang M-I, Ikeda S (2014) Time discounting and smoking behavior: evidence from a panel survey. Health Econ 23(12):1443–1464
Keeler TE, Hu T-W, Barnett BG, Manning WG (1993) Taxation, regulation, and addiction: a demand function for cigarettes based on time-series evidence. J Health Econ 12(1):1–18
Khwaja A, Silverman D, Sloan F (2007) Time preference, time discounting, and smoking decisions. J Health Econ 26(5):927–979
Kilby KN, Petry NM, Warren WK (1999) Heroin addicts have higher discount rates for delayed rewards than non-drug-using controls. J Exp Psychol 128(1):78–87

Kimball MS, Sahm CR, Shapiro MD (2008) Imputing risk tolerance from survey responses. J Am Stat Assoc 103(483):1028–1038

Laibson D (1997) Golden eggs and hyperbolic discounting. Q J Econ 112(2):443–477

Laibson D (1998) Life-cycle consumption and hyperbolic discount functions. Eur Econ Rev 42(3–5):861–871

Loewenstein G (1987) Anticipation and the valuation of delayed consumption. Econ J 97(387):666–684

Loewenstein G, Prelec D (1992) Anomalies in intertemporal choice: evidence and an interpretation. Q J Econ 107(2):573–597

Luo F, Abdel-Ghany M, Ogawa I (2003) Cigarette smoking in Japan: examination of myopic and rational models of addictive behavior. J Fam Econ Iss 24(3):308–317

Madden GJ, Petry NM, Barger GJ, Bickel WK (1997) Impulsive and self-control choices in opioid-dependent patients and non-drug-using control patients: drug and monetary rewards. Exp Clin Psychopharmacol 5(3):256–262

Madden GJ, Bickel WK, Eric EA (1999) Discounting of delayed rewards in opioid-dependent outpatients: exponential or hyperbolic discounting functions? Exp Clin Psychopharmacol 7(3):284–293

Meier S, Sprenger C (2010) Present-biased preferences and credit card borrowing. Am Econ J Appl Econ 2(1):193–210

Mitchell SH (1999) Measures of impulsivity in cigarette smokers and non-smokers. Psychopharmacology 146(4):455–464

O'Donoghue T, Rabin M (1999) Doing it now or later. Am Econ Rev 89(1):103–124

Odum AL, Madden GJ, Bickel WK (2002) Discounting of delayed health gains and losses by current, never- and ex-smokers of cigarettes. Nicotin Tob Res 4(3):295–303

Ohmura Y, Takahashi T, Kitamura N (2005) Discounting delayed and probabilistic monetary gains and losses by smokers of cigarettes. Psychopharmacology 182(4):508–515

Reynolds B, Karraker K, Horn K, Richards JB (2004) Delay and probability discounting as related to different stages of adolescent smoking and non-smoking. Behav Process 64(3):333–344

Sato M, Ohkusa Y (2003) The relationship between smoking initiation and time discounting factor, risk aversion and information. Appl Econ Lett 10(5):287–289

Shoda Y, Mischel W, Peake PK (1990) Predicting adolescent cognitive and self-regulatory competencies from preschool delay of gratification: identifying diagnostic conditions. Dev Psychol 26(6):978–986

Simpson CA, Vuchinich RE (2000) Reliability of a measure of temporal discounting. Psychol Rec 50(1):3–16

Thaler R (1981) Some empirical evidence on dynamic inconsistency. Econ Lett 8(3):201–207

Wakai K (2008) A model of utility smoothing. Econometrica 76(1):137–153

Wakai K (2011) Modeling nonmonotone preferences: the case of utility smoothing. J Math Econ 47(2):213–226

Wan J (2006) Cigarette tax revenues and tobacco control in Japan. Appl Econ 38(14):1663–1675

Chapter 10
Smokers, Smoking Deprivation, and Time Discounting

Shoko Yamane, Hiroyasu Yoneda, Taiki Takahashi, Yoshio Kamijo, Yasuhiro Komori, Fumihiko Hiruma, and Yoshiro Tsutsui

Abstract This chapter investigates whether smokers exhibit greater time discounting than non-smokers, and how short-term nicotine deprivation affects time discounting. A unique feature of our experiment is that our subjects receive rewards not only of money, but also of actual tobacco. This is done in order to elicit smokers' true preferences. Smokers are more impatient than non-smokers, consistent with

---

The original article first appeared in the Journal of Socio-Economics 45:47–56, 2013. A newly written addendum has been added to this book chapter.

S. Yamane
Faculty of Economics, Kindai University, 3-4-1 Kowakae, Higashi-Osaka, Osaka 577-8502, Japan
e-mail: syamane@kindai.ac.jp

H. Yoneda
Graduate School and Faculty of Pharmaceutical Sciences, Kyoto University, 46-29 Yoshida-Shimo-Adachi-cho, Sakyo-ku, Kyoto 606-8501, Japan
e-mail: yoneda@pharm.kyoto-u.ac.jp

T. Takahashi
Center for Experimental Research in Social Sciences, Department of Behavioral Science, Hokkaido University, N.10, W.7, Kita-ku, Sapporo 060-0810, Japan
e-mail: ttakahashi@lynx.let.hokudai.ac.jp

Y. Kamijo
School of Management, Kochi University of Technology, 185 Miyanokuchi, Tosayamada-cho, Kami-Shi, Kochi 782-8502, Japan
e-mail: yoshio.kamijo@gmail.com

Y. Komori
5-43-4 Minamisenju, Arakawaku, Tokyo 116-0003, Japan
e-mail: yasuhiro.komori@gmail.com

F. Hiruma
School of Commerce, Waseda University, 1-6-1 Nishiwaseda, Shinjuku-ku, Tokyo 169-8050, Japan
e-mail: hiruma@waseda.jp

Y. Tsutsui (✉)
Faculty of Economics, Konan University, 8-9-1 Okamoto, Higashinada-ku, Kobe 658-8501, Japan
e-mail: tsutsui@center.konan-u.ac.jp

S. Ikeda et al. (eds.), *Behavioral Economics of Preferences, Choices, and Happiness*, DOI 10.1007/978-4-431-55402-8_10

previous studies. Additionally, nicotine deprivation makes smokers even more impatient. These results suggest that nicotine concentration has different effects on time preferences in the short and long runs.

Keywords Time discounting • Nicotine concentration • Smoking deprivation • Panel logit analysis • Economic experiment

JEL Classification D03, D90, I10, Q57

1 Introduction

It is well-established that smokers are more impatient than non-smokers (Brick et al. 1999; Mitchell 1999; Baker et al. 2003; Ohmura et al. 2005; Reynolds 2004; Reynolds and Schiffbauer 2004, 2007).[1] Experiments using animals suggest that this is due to a chronic (but not acute) increase in nicotine concentration (Dallery and Locey 2005; Tsutsui-Kimura et al. 2010).[2]

The purpose of this study is twofold. We first seek to confirm the result that smokers display greater time discounting than non-smokers. We then investigate the short-term effects of nicotine deprivation on time discounting.

If time discounting simply corresponds to the concentration of nicotine in a person's body, a short-term deprivation of nicotine should reduce a person's time discount rate, by reducing this concentration. Indeed, Dallery and Locey (2005) report that an increase in impulsiveness induced by chronic nicotine administration is reversible in rats. However, casual observation suggests that smokers become more irritated and impatient when they abstain from smoking for a while. Several studies support this intuition. An experiment by Sayette et al. (2005) finds that the urge to smoke may affect time perception, and that smokers who crave nicotine overpredict the duration and intensity of their own future smoking urges. Using opioids rather than tobacco, Badger et al. (2007) find that heroin addicts value an extra dose of the heroin substitute Buprenorphine more highly when they are currently craving than when they are currently satiated. Similarly, Giordano et al. (2002) find that the degree of discounting was significantly higher when subjects are opioid-deprived, and conclude that opioid deprivation increases the degree to which dependent individuals discount delayed heroin and money. These studies suggest a negative rather than a positive relationship between time discounting and the concentration of a drug in an addict's body.

---

[1]However, Khwaja et al. (2007), based on survey results, report that there are no significant differences in revealed rates of time discounting between smokers and non-smokers.

[2]Note that there exists reverse causality, in that the time discount rate significantly affects an individual's decision to start smoking (Sato and Ohkusa 2003).

Examining the relation between nicotine deprivation and impatience, Mitchell (2004), Field et al. (2006), and Yi and Landes (2012) report that deprivation makes subjects more impulsive. However, comparing 1-day and 14-day abstinence groups, Yoon et al. (2009) find no significant difference in time discounting tasks. Using a 3-h deprivation period, Dallery and Raiff (2007) report no significant differences in time discounting between active nicotine patch and placebo patch groups. Although these results are not conclusive, they suggest that the long-term and short-term effects of nicotine deprivation on impatience may differ. To resolve this puzzle, we propose that when a non-smoker starts smoking, the long-term increase in nicotine concentration makes her more impatient in general, but a decrease in nicotine concentration due to a brief cessation of smoking makes her even more impatient for the duration of deprivation.[3]

To explore both the long- and short-term effects of nicotine addiction, we conduct an experiment comparing time discounting between smokers and non-smokers, as well as between deprived smokers and non-deprived smokers. The salient difference of our experiments from previous studies such as Mitchell (2004), Field et al. (2006), and Yi and Landes (2012) is that our subjects are asked to choose between receiving nicotine earlier and receiving nicotine later. In contrast, Mitchell (2004) asks her subjects to choose between receiving a number of cigarettes (up to 60) and US$10 immediately, or receiving a larger amount of money in the future (up to 365 days). This task does not give subjects the opportunity to choose the time at which they will be allowed to smoke. In addition, the 60 cigarettes are not all smoked at the time they are received, leaving some ambiguity in the timing of the nicotine receipt. Thus, subjects facing this cigarette-money tradeoff should show the same rate of time preference as if both alternatives were purely monetary (since they presumably assign a fixed monetary value to the immediate receipt of 60 cigarettes). Surprisingly, however, Mitchell finds that nicotine-deprived subjects become more impulsive in a cigarette-money session, but not in a money-money session, suggesting that the framing of the choice has some impact on the intertemporal decisions of her subjects.

Field et al. (2006) ask subjects in their money-money task to choose between fixed amounts of money (£ 500) received later vs. some amount of money received immediately. The delay is set at either 1 week, 2 weeks, 1 month, 6 months, 1 year,

[3]Several studies investigate what kinds of people more easily abstain from smoking. For example, Krishnan-Sarin et al. (2007) study 30 adolescent smokers, who participated in a high school based smoking cessation program; 16 participants (53 %) were abstinent from smoking at the completion of the 4-week study. Compared to abstinent adolescents, those not achieving abstinence discounted monetary rewards more. Thus, it may be the case that more impulsive adolescents were unable to achieve abstinence. Dallery and Raiff (2007) report that those who had higher time discounting tended to choose smoking more often than money, suggesting that they had more difficulty abstaining. Conducting a 5-month follow-up survey of 608 Japanese adults who had just begun smoking cessation, Ida et al. (2011) found that cessation successes are more risk averse than cessation failures, and that time preference rates decrease for cessation successes and increase for cessation failures.

5 years, or 25 years. The subjects in their cigarette-cigarette task are asked to choose between amounts of cigarettes that correspond to the monetary rewards in the money-money task.[4] They find that nicotine-deprived participants show more pronounced delay discounting in both tasks. However, our critique of Mitchell (2004) applies to Field et al. (2006) as well; we doubt that either the "cigarette-money task" in Mitchell (2004) or the "cigarette-cigarette task" in Field et al. (2006) and Yi and Landes (2012) is the best way to elicit preferences on smoking. In our experiment, in contrast, subjects choose both the amount and the timing of their smoking reward. Our experiment is unique in that we pay actual rewards not only in the "money session," but also in the "tobacco session"; at the end of the experiment, subjects actually smoke according to their choices earlier in the session.[5] We do this because we believe that precision in the specification of incentives is crucial to the accurate elicitation of preferences, especially in the case of smoking.

It is known that people have different discount rates for different consumed goods; these differences are called "domain effects" (Frederick et al. 2002; Odum and Baumann 2007). In our case, deprived smokers may be highly impatient with regards to tobacco, but more patient with regards to other goods such as money.

The rest of the chapter proceeds as follows. In the next section, we explain our experimental design. In Sect. 3, we present the preliminary results of the experiments. In Sect. 4, we explain the main results of our panel logit estimation and give two robustness checks. Section 5 concludes.

2 Experimental Design

2.1 Basic Setup

Our subjects consist of three groups: non-smokers, smokers who smoked as usual on the day of the experiment, and smokers who were deprived of smoking for 12 h before the beginning of the experiment. Subjects who comprised the "usual smoker group" on the first day became members of the "deprived smoker group" on the second day, and vice versa. Using the same subjects in the two sessions enabled within-subject comparisons between deprived and non-deprived conditions. If we had used different subjects for deprived and non-deprived groups, selection bias may have arisen e.g. because those who can easily abstain from smoking would join the deprived group. Our method guarantees internal validity.

---

[4]£500 corresponds to 100 packs, where one pack contains 20 cigarettes. The rewards are hypothetical in Field et al. (2006), and are not actually paid to the subjects.

[5]Yoon et al. (2009) conduct a choice task involving real money and cigarettes; however, subjects are requested to choose between one puff now and $0.25 now, so that their task is not an intertemporal choice.

Subjects were requested to choose one of two options, A or B, displayed on a computer in front of each subject.[6] Those who chose option A received a smaller reward earlier, and those who chose option B received a larger reward later.

We varied four variables over our treatment groups: (1) the size of the reward in option A, (2) the "delay," (3) the "interval," and (4) the "rate of return." The "delay" is defined as the difference between the time at which the option is chosen ($t = 0$) and the time at which option A is received. The "interval" is defined as the difference between the times at which options A and B are received. The "rate of return" is defined as the amount of reward in option B minus the amount in option A, divided by the interval.

2.2 *Hypothetical Tobacco, Money, and Real Tobacco Sessions*

The experiment consisted of three sessions: the "hypothetical tobacco," "money," and "real tobacco" sessions.

2.2.1 Real Tobacco Session

We begin with the explanation of the real tobacco session, as this is, to our knowledge, the first time such a choice has been offered to experimental subjects. The rationale behind using real tobacco is that the desire to smoke is an instinctive rather than a rational motivation, so that the belief that rewards will actually be paid (i.e. that subjects will be able to smoke) is necessary to elicit true preferences. Thus, we set up the experiment so that each subject would smoke a specified amount at the exact time specified in the option she selected.

80 questions are asked in the real tobacco session, one of which is randomly selected to determine actual rewards, meaning that a subject actually smokes the specified amount of tobacco at the time specified in the chosen option of the selected question. In order to avoid complications, we constructed the session in such a way that those who selected the earlier option smoked immediately after the experiment regardless of which question was selected to give the reward, and those who chose the later option smoked 30 min later. To do this, we divided the 80 questions into five blocks, each of which consisted of 16 questions (see Fig. 10.1). The same time delay is displayed in each block, and the 16 questions differ only in the amount of tobacco (in the figure we present an example of 1 puff vs. 2 puffs, but different combinations are displayed in the other questions). In the first block, the delay associated with the earlier option is 32 min, and the delay associated with the later option is 62 min (30 min later than the earlier option). These values are the same in all of the 16 questions. As subjects had 3 min to answer all 16 questions in each block, 15 min is

[6]The experiment was carried out using the software Hot Soup Play.

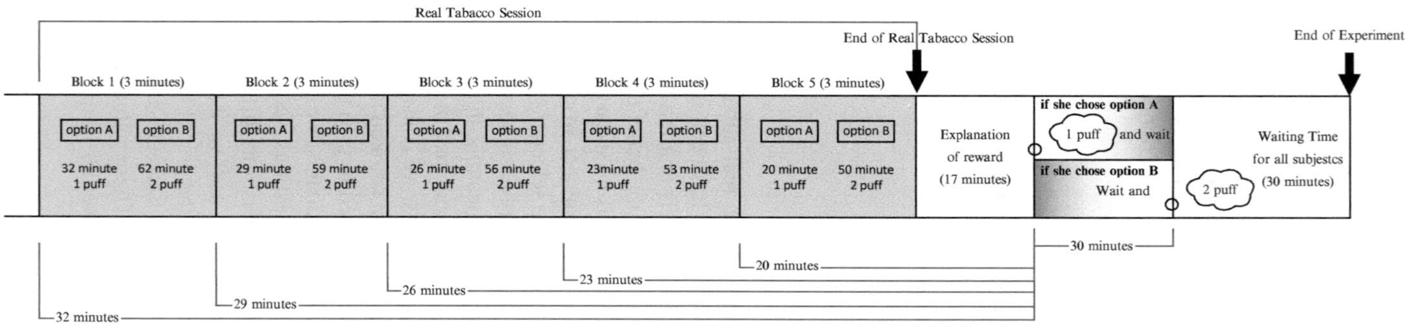

Fig. 10.1 Procedure of real tobacco session

necessary to answer all the questions in the five blocks; 17 min is then spent giving monetary rewards and guiding subjects to the smoking area. Therefore, in the case that a question in the first block is selected as the actual reward, those who chose the earlier option smoke 32 min later, and those who chose the later option smoke an additional 30 min later.[7]

Let us explain what happens in the second block. The time delay associated with the "earlier" option in any question is 29 min, and the time delay associated with the "later" option is 59 min (the interval between the two options is fixed at 30 min). Because 3 min passed since the beginning of the first question block, in the case that a question in the second block is selected to give the rewards, those who chose the "earlier" option smoke 29 min after they make their choice, and those who chose the "later" option smoke 59 min after they make their choice. These represent the same timing as the case in which a question in the first block is selected to give the actual reward.

This mechanism also applies to the third to fifth blocks. In other words, the time delay associated with the "earlier" option in the third, the fourth, and the fifth block, respectively, gets shorter by 3 min each, so that these become 26, 23, and 20 min, respectively (the interval between the two options, as always is fixed at 30 min). Consequently, all subjects smoke at exactly the chosen time delay, measured from the time that they actually selected that delay.

The tobacco reward took one of six possible values: one puff, two puffs, a half cigarette, one cigarette, one and a half cigarettes, and two cigarettes. After some preliminary trials, it was decided that eight puffs was equivalent to smoking one cigarette

Ten rates of return were used; 0, 33.3, 50, 100, 200, 300, 500, 700, 1,100, and 1,500 (%) for a 30-min interval. Using these parameter values, 16 questions were asked for each delay, so that 80 questions were asked in total in the real tobacco session (Table 10.1).[8]

2.2.2 Hypothetical Tobacco Session

Although our real tobacco session was able to elicit the subjects' preferences over the given time horizon of 50 min, longer time periods could not be explored. To ask questions concerning longer delays and intervals, we added a "hypothetical tobacco session," in which subjects did not actually smoke at the end of the experiment.

In this session, the hypothetical smoking rewards were the same as those in the real tobacco session. The five delays were zero, 1 h, 3 h, 12 h, and 24 h. The interval was fixed at 12 h. The ratios of the rates of return were the same asthose of the

[7]However, the time delays displayed in each block are the same, implying that we ignored the gap between the displayed time and the real time. This gap was less than 3 min.

[8]Note that we did not ask all the possible combinations.

Table 10.1 The amounts of the rewards corresponding to option B in 16 questions asked in real tobacco and hypothetical tobacco sessions

	Rate of return									
Amount(A)	0 %	33.3 %	50 %	100 %	200 %	300 %	500 %	700 %	1,100 %	1,500 %
1 puff	1 puff			2 puffs		0.5		1	1.5	2
2 puffs				0.5		1	1.5	2		
0.5				1	1.5		2			
1			1.5	2						
1.5		2								

Note: The amounts of the rewards corresponding to option B are shown in each cell. Each number represents a number of cigarettes, unless otherwise mentioned. The length of the period used to determine rates of return is 30 min in the real tobacco session and 12 h in the hypothetical tobacco session

Table 10.2 The amount of rewards in option B of the 16 questions asked for each delay in money session

	Rate of return (annual)					
Amount(A)	0 %	50 %	100 %	150 %	200 %	300 %
1,000	1,000	1,019	1,039	1,058	1,077	1,116
2,000		2,039	2,077	2,116	2,154	2,231
3,000		3,058	3,116	3,174	3,231	3,347

Note: The amount of rewards (yen) in option B is shown in each cell

real tobacco session, relative to the interval. Based on these conditions, 16 questions were asked for each delay, so that 80 questions were asked in total in the hypothetical tobacco session (Table 10.1).

2.2.3 Money Session

The money session had three possible rewards; 1,000, 2,000, and 3,000 yen.[9] Five delays were considered: today, 1 week, 2 weeks, 3 weeks, and 4 weeks. The interval was fixed at 2 weeks. Six different annualized rates of returns were chosen: 0, 50, 100, 150, 200, and 300 (%). Based on these conditions, 16 questions were asked for each delay, so that a total of 80 questions were asked in the money session (Table 10.2).

At the end of the experiment, one question was randomly selected out of 80 questions for the money and real tobacco sessions respectively, and subjects received a reward (both money and smoking), based on their choice in the selected question, at the time stated in the chosen option. Smokers in both the "usual" and "deprived" smoking groups earned an average of ¥4,450 ($49) for 2 days, and non-smokers, who attended only the money session on 1 day, earned ¥1,923 ($21). In addition,

[9]At this time the exchange rate was about $1 = ¥90.

smokers and non-smokers were paid ¥6,666 ($74; for 2 days) and ¥2,222 ($25), respectively, in cash as compensation for participation, so that total per-capita rewards were ¥11,116 ($124) for smokers and ¥4,145 ($46) for non-smokers.

2.3 *Flow of the Experiment*

After the instructions were read, the hypothetical tobacco session, money session, and real tobacco sessions were conducted in that order. Only the usual smoker group was allowed to smoke during the breaks between the sessions. The real tobacco session was divided into five blocks, each of which involved 16 questions in 3 min. After each real tobacco session finished, one of the 80 questions was randomly selected, and each subject smoked the amount of tobacco at the time designated in her chosen option in the selected question. During this 50-min smoking time, subjects answered a questionnaire and were paid the show-up fee.[10] After all the subjects smoked, they waited for 30 min in the laboratory, during which time they were allowed to do anything other than smoke (if applicable). This 30-min prohibition of smoking was announced in the instructions at the beginning of the experiment, before subjects made their choices. This was done to assure that subjects did not smoke on their own immediately after leaving the experiment, since this opportunity would distort their intertemporal choice.[11]

2.4 *Implementation of the Experiment*

The experiment was conducted on January 12–14 (first wave) and February 20–21 (second wave), 2010 at Osaka University, Japan. The subjects consisted of 50 smokers (male = 49, female = 1) and 17 non-smokers (male = 13, female = 4).[12] All of the non-smokers were in the first wave. Of the smokers, 14 subjects (all male) were in the first wave and the rest of the subjects, 36 (male = 35, female = 1) were in the second wave of the experiment.

[10]Most of the rewards in the money session, except for the ones received immediately, were paid later at the specified times by bank transfer.

[11]In the hypothetical tobacco session, we asked the subjects to "suppose you were unable to smoke for 24 h after the experiment" when they made their choices.

[12]Mitchell (2004) uses only 11 smokers. Field et al. (2006) use 30 smokers.

3 Preliminary Results

3.1 Compliance with the No-Smoking Requirement

We asked the subjects of the deprived smoker group to stop smoking 12 h prior to the beginning of the experiment.[13] In order to verify that this was done, we gave these subjects a breath test and checked the CO concentration of their exhalations, using a "smokerlyzer" tool produced by Bedfont Scientific Ltd. The tool provides two measures of the likelihood of recent smoking; ppm (parts per million) of CO in the lungs, and %COHb (percent of carboxyhemoglobin) in the blood.

The mean of ppm among the deprived smokers was 3.24, while that of the usual smokers was 8.20, so that the deprived smokers showed significantly lower ppm ($t(98) = 4.74$, $p < 0.0001$). The deprived smokers had 1.04%COHb on average, while the usual smokers had 1.86, so that again the deprived smokers showed significantly lower smoking activity by this measure ($t(98) = 4.53$, $p < 0.0001$). These results indicate that the 12-h injunction against smoking was generally obeyed. Inspection of the individual records revealed that all the subjects who showed high nicotine concentrations under the usual smoking condition show a large decline in concentration levels when deprived.

3.2 Effectiveness of the 12-h Nicotine Deprivation Period

It is important that the 12-h nicotine deprivation period be long enough to strengthen the subjects' desire to smoke.[14] In order to verify this, we asked the following question four times during the experiment ((1) just after the start of the experiment, (2) just after the hypothetical tobacco session, (3) just after the money session, and (4) just after the real tobacco session):

Question: How strongly do you want to smoke now? Please rate your desire from 1 (I do not want to smoke now) to 10 (I do want very much to smoke now).

The result is shown in Fig. 10.2. The deprived group reported significantly higher desire to smoke than the usual smoker group ((1): $t(98) = -6.16$, $p < 0.0001$, (2): $t(98) = -4.97$, $p = <0.0001$, (3): $t(98) = -7.17$, $p < 0.0001$, (4): $t(98) = -7.10$, $p < 0.0001$). Also, while the smoking desire reported by the usual smoker group does not show an upward trend over the course of the experiment, that of the deprived group does. This is to be expected, because the usual smoker group is allowed to smoke during the breaks between the sessions, while the deprived group is not.

[13]The experiments began at either 10 am or 1 pm.

[14]Mitchell (2004) asked her subjects to stop smoking for 24 h; Field et al. (2006) 13 h; and Dallery and Raiff (2007) 3 h.

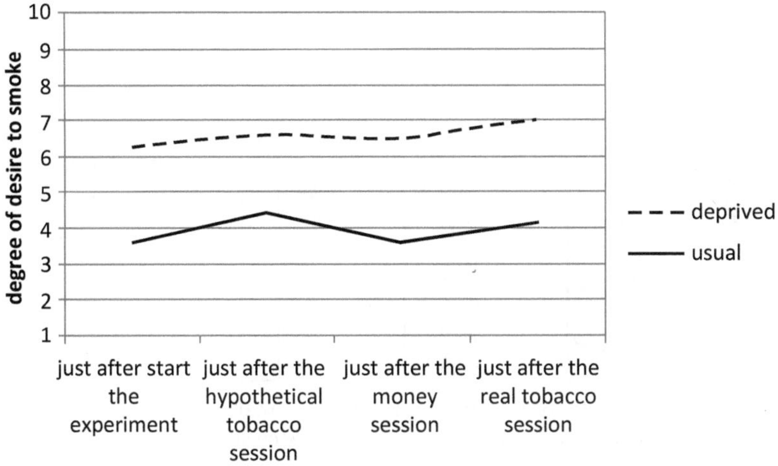

Fig. 10.2 How strongly do you want to smoke now? Note: 49 subjects are asked to choose from 1 ("I do not want to smoke now") to 10 ("I want very much to smoke now." They were asked the question twice, so that the number of responses is 98

We also asked the subjects the following question at the end of the experiment.

Question: Suppose that you were not allowed to smoke at all for 24 h, starting now. How much would you pay in order to smoke one cigarette now?

The average answer of usual smokers was ¥116.4, while that of deprived smokers was ¥210.8. Again these two groups' smoking appetites differed during the experiment, although the difference is not statistically significant at the 5 % level ($t(70) = -1.67, p = 0.100$).

3.3 *Average Choices of the Subject Groups*

First, we report the number of rounds in which non-smokers, usual smokers, and deprived smokers, respectively, chose the later option. We code the choice as a dummy variable that equals 1 if option B (the later option) is chosen, and 0 otherwise. The results are shown in Fig. 10.3. The vertical axis in the figure gives the mean of this variable for each group.

From this figure it is apparent that non-smokers tend to choose the later option. The difference in the mean between all smokers and non-smokers is significant ($t(9358) = 8.792, p = 0.000$).

Although the difference between deprived smokers and usual smokers is small in size, it is significant at the 5 % level in the real tobacco session ($t(7998) = 2.142$, $p = 0.032$). However, it is not significant in the hypothetical tobacco session ($t(7998) = -0.631$, $p = 0.528$) and money session ($t(7998) = -0.761$, $p = 0.447$).

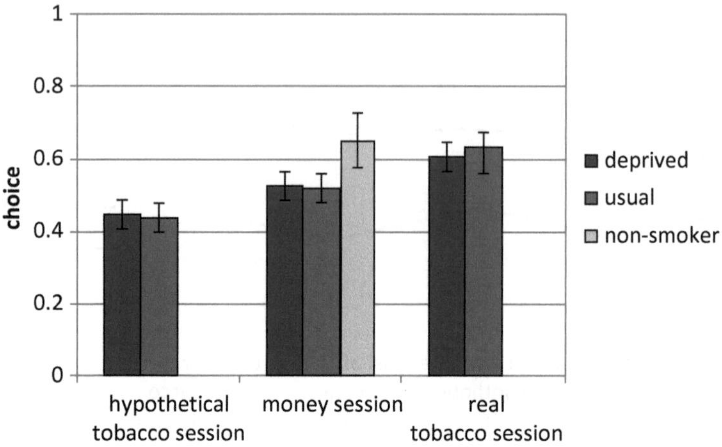

Fig. 10.3 Fraction who chose the later option (B). Note: *Vertical bars* represent ± SEM (standard error of means)

This simple analysis suggests that deprived smokers are more impatient than usual smokers when it comes to choices involving actual tobacco.

4 Panel Logit Analysis

4.1 Estimation Method

To quantify time discounting for the three groups, we estimate a panel logit model, where the dependent variable is a choice dummy that takes a value of unity if a subject chooses a later option and zero if she chooses an earlier option. An alternative method would have been to first estimate separately the time discount rates for each treatment group specified by the delay, the interval, and the amount of rewards, and then to compare these. However, the method we use has the advantage of efficient use of all the information contained in the 240 total choices made by the subjects. More importantly, the two-step method assumes that each subject makes all decisions based only on her personal constant per-period time discount rate, an assumption that has been found questionable by a number of studies (Frederick et al. 2002; Kirby and Marakovic 1995; Benzion et al. 1989; Loewenstein and Prelec 1992); our method requires no such assumption.

Other studies have adopted approaches that differ than ours. Previous studies such as Bickel et al. (1999), Reynolds (2004), Dallery and Raiff (2007), and Ohmura et al. (2005) estimate hyperbolic discounting functions. Field et al. (2006) use area under the curve (AUC), first proposed by Myerson et al. (2001), to measure time discounting. However, we have reasons for not using either of these approaches.

Evaluation of the degree of hyperbolic discounting by estimation of the hyperbolic function is limited in that it assumes a specific functional form. AUC does not; however, calculating AUC for each subject at the first stage, and then comparing AUCs between smokers and non-smokers, sacrifices efficiency compared to the full-information method that we use.

It is believed that intertemporal choice is affected by the delay, the interval, and the magnitude of the reward (Kinari et al. 2009). Therefore, our explanatory variables are the rate of return (*RETURN*), the delay (*DELAY*), and the amount of reward (*AMOUNT*).[15] We also include a dummy variable for whether a subject is a smoker (*D_SMOKER*) for the analysis of smokers vs. non-smokers, i.e. the estimation using the data of the money session. If the coefficient on this dummy is negative, it implies that smokers tend to choose later options, and are therefore less patient.

On the other hand, in the analysis of deprivation, the key variable measuring the effect of short-term nicotine deprivation is a dummy variable for deprived smokers (*D_DEPRIVATION*). All the data obtained in the three sessions are used for the analysis of deprivation.[16] Explanations of all variables used in the regression analysis are given in the Appendix.

4.2 Smokers vs. Non-smokers

The results of the estimation for smokers vs. non-smokers are presented in Table 10.3. The total number of observations is 5,360. Only in the "money session" do we compare smokers with non-smokers. The left-most columns of the table show the coefficients on *DELAY* and *AMOUNT*. The coefficient on the smoker dummy is significantly negative, implying that smokers are more impatient than non-smokers. Although the coefficient on *AMOUNT* is significantly positive, implying that subjects become more patient for large rewards (the magnitude effect), the coefficient on the *DELAY* variable is not significant. Thus, we see no delay effect in this regression specification.

In the middle columns, the results for the delay and amount dummies are shown. The dummy variables representing whether the reward was given today (*D_DELAY_M1*, where "*M1*" represents the money session) and whether the amount was ¥1,000 (*D_AMOUNT_M1*) are omitted for the benchmark specification. Again, the coefficient on *D_SMOKER* is significantly negative, confirming that smokers are more impatient. The amount dummies are significantly positive, and the coefficient on the dummy representing ¥3,000 (*D_AMOUNT_M3*) is larger than that for ¥2,000 (*D_AMOUNT_M2*), confirming the existence of magnitude effects

---

[15]The interval is fixed in each session, so that its effect is included in the constant term.

[16]Although smokers are also compared with non-smokers in the money session, only the results for deprived vs. non-deprived smokers are used in the analysis of deprivation.

Table 10.3 Estimation results of panel logit regression: smokers vs. non-smokers

	Coef.	p value	Coef.	p value	Coef.	p value
Constant	−2.205	[0.000]**	−1.691	[0.000]**	−1.434	[0.000]**
D_SMOKER	−0.658	[0.000]**	−0.662	[0.000]**	−0.663	[0.000]**
DELAY	0.03	[0.170]				
AMOUNT	0.001	[0.000]**				
RETURN	0.01	[0.000]**	0.01	[0.000]**		
D_DELAY_M2			0.3	[0.003]**	0.3	[0.003]**
D_DELAY_M3			0.285	[0.004]**	0.285	[0.004]**
D_DELAY_M4			0.201	[0.043]*	0.201	[0.043]*
D_DELAY_M5			0.201	[0.043]*	0.201	[0.043]*
D_AMOUNT_M2			0.987	[0.000]**	1.017	[0.000]**
D_AMOUNT_M3			1.434	[0.000]**	1.471	[0.000]**
D_RETURN_M4					0.84	[0.000]**
D_RETURN_M5					1.459	[0.000]**
D_RETURN_M6					1.692	[0.000]**
D_RETURN_M7					2.594	[0.000]**
Pseudo R^2		0.184		0.184		0.185
Observation		5,360		5,360		5,360

Note: ** indicates significance at the 1 % level and * at the 5 % level

over the entire range of rewards. The delay dummies representing 1 and 2 weeks later (*D_DELAY_M2 and D_DELAY_M3*) are significantly positive at the 1 % level, while those for 3 and 4 weeks later (*D_DELAY_M4* and *D_DELAY_M5*) are only significant at the 5 % level, with smaller point estimates, so that delay effect can only be unambiguously observed over periods of 1 or 2 weeks.[17] This last result is consistent with Kinari et al. (2009) and Sasaki et al. (2012).

The right-hand columns of Table 10.3 show the results when dummies for the different rates of return are used as regressors instead of the return variable itself. The coefficients on the return dummies are significantly positive, and are larger for larger returns, confirming that subjects' choices were rational with respect to returns. The coefficients on the delay and amount dummies are similar in size to the corresponding coefficients in the previous regression.

4.3 Effects of Smoking Deprivation

In the upper panel of Table 10.4, we present the results for the effect of nicotine deprivation for all three sessions, using *DELAY*, *AMOUNT*, and *RETURN* as

[17]This may be the reason why no delay effect is found when the delay variable itself is used as a regressor instead of these dummies.

Table 10.4 Estimation results of panel logit regression: effect of deprivation

	Real tobacco session		Hypothetical tobacco session		Money session	
	Coef.	p value	Coef.	p value	Coef.	p value
D_DEPRIVATION	−0.161	[0.006]**	0.048	[0.411]	0.089	[0.219]
DELAY	−0.031	[0.000]**	−0.0002	[0.951]	0.087	[0.001]**
AMOUNT	−1.750	[0.000]**	−1.321	[0.000]**	0.002	[0.000]**
RETURN	0.002	[0.000]**	0.002	[0.000]**	0.021	[0.000]**
Pseudo R^2		0.208		0.201		0.432
Observation	49 persons	7,840	47 persons	7,520	50 persons	8,000

	Real tobacco session		Hypothetical tobacco session			Money session	
	Coef.	p value	Coef.	p value		Coef.	p value
D_DEPRIVATION	−0.166	[0.005]**	0.051	[0.400]	*D_DEPRIVATION*	0.090	[0.215]
RETURN	0.002	[0.000]**	0.003	[0.000]**	*RETURN*	0.022	[0.000]**
D_DELAY_T2	−0.113	[0.234]	−0.118	[0.216]	*D_DELAY_M2*	0.637	[0.000]**
D_DELAY_T3	−0.185	[0.052]	−0.195	[0.041]*	*D_DELAY_M3*	0.624	[0.000]**
D_DELAY_T4	−0.158	[0.096]	0.127	[0.183]	*D_DELAY_M4*	0.524	[0.000]**
D_DELAY_T5	−0.462	[0.000]**	−0.149	[0.117]	*D_DELAY_M5*	0.498	[0.000]**
D_AMOUNT_T2	0.552	[0.000]**	0.753	[0.000]**	*D_AMOUNT_M2*	2.084	[0.000]**
D_AMOUNT_T3	0.060	[0.472]	0.535	[0.000]**	*D_AMOUNT_M3*	3.120	[0.000]**
D_AMOUNT_T4	−1.684	[0.000]**	−1.280	[0.000]**			
D_AMOUNT_T5	−1.854	[0.000]**	−1.368	[0.000]**			
Pseudo R^2		0.228		0.234	Pseudo R^2		0.442
Observation	49 persons	7,840	47 persons	7,520	Observation	50 persons	8,000

Note: The numbers of observations differ because those who only chose A or only chose B are excluded; * p value<0.05. ** p value<0.01

explanatory variables in addition to a dummy for the deprived smoker group. The smoking deprivation dummy is significant only for the real tobacco session. The coefficient on the dummy variable is negative, implying that smoking deprivation makes subjects more impatient. In the hypothetical tobacco and money sessions, the dummy variable is not significant. These results suggest that subjects reveal their true smoking preferences only when incentives are appropriate; i.e., when the smoking reward is real.[18]

The coefficient on the delay differs over the three sessions. It is significantly negative in the real tobacco session, implying that the subjects become more impatient with respect to smoking as the delay becomes longer. This is the opposite of the typical delay effect. In the money session, the coefficient on the delay is significantly positive, showing the usual delay effect. In the hypothetical tobacco session, the coefficient is not significant.

The coefficient on the amount of reward is significantly positive in the money session, implying the usual magnitude effect; subjects become more patient when the amount of reward is large. However, in the real and hypothetical tobacco sessions, the effect is reversed; when the reward is larger, subjects are *less* patient.

The coefficient on the rate of return is positive in all sessions, indicating that subjects are rational with respect to rates of return.

When dummies for the delay and amount are used as regressors instead of the raw variables, the results are essentially unchanged (Table 10.4, lower panel). The smoking deprivation dummy is significant only in the real tobacco session. For the return variable, we do not use dummies; this is in order to avoid the dummy variable trap, as the return dummies are linearly dependent with the delay and amount dummies in the real and hypothetical tobacco sessions. The return variable is positive and significant in all sessions, as shown in the upper panel of the table.[19]

The usual delay effect is only observed in the money session, as shown in the upper panel. However, we find that the delay effect only operates over 1 week. In the real and hypothetical tobacco sessions, the coefficients on the delay dummies are negative, implying that the opposite of the usual delay effect is found for some delays (shown in the upper panel)

For the magnitude effect, the coefficients of the amount dummies in the money session are positive and increasing in the amount, again confirming the usual magnitude effect. In the real and hypothetical tobacco sessions, the coefficients of the dummies on two puffs and half a cigarette are significantly positive, while those for larger amounts are significantly negative, suggesting that the amount of smoking has a nonlinear and complex effect on the choice.

---

[18]The real tobacco session dealt with an immediate delay, while the hypothetical tobacco and money sessions assumed longer delays. Therefore, it might be the case that the difference in the magnitude of the delays in the different sessions is responsible for this result.

[19]For the money session, we also estimate an equation including all return dummies (the results are omitted to save space). All the coefficients on the dummies are significantly positive and increasing in the amount. Thus, rationality of subjects' choices with respect to returns is again confirmed. The delay and magnitude effects are unchanged from those in the upper panel.

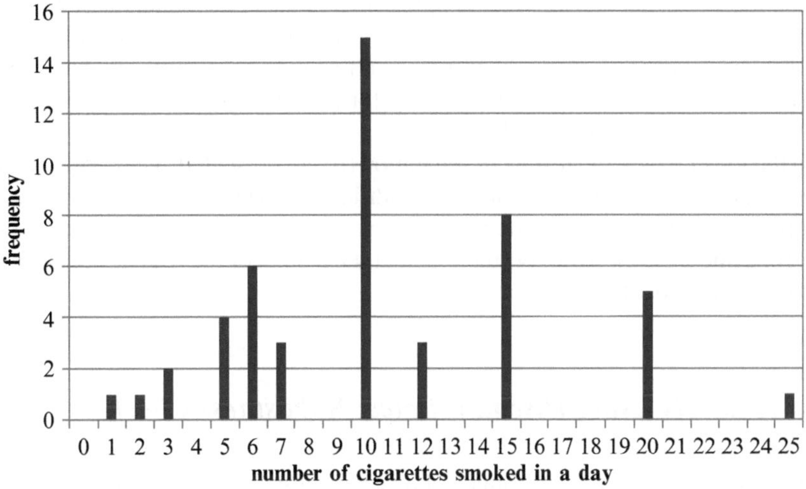

Fig. 10.4 Histogram of the number of cigarettes that subjects typically smoke per day

In sum, nicotine deprivation makes subjects more impatient with regards to smoking, but not to money. The delays and amount of rewards matter for intertemporal choices, but differ depending on whether the choice is over tobacco or money. Thus, we find a domain effect for time discounting.

4.4 Light and Heavy Smokers: Robustness Check 1

Our subjects consist of both light and heavy smokers. Figure 10.4 presents a histogram of the number of cigarettes that the subjects smoke per day, which ranges from 1.5 to 25 cigarettes with a mode of ten cigarettes. In the previous subsection, we found that short-term deprivation makes subjects impatient in the real tobacco session. This tendency should be stronger for heavy smokers and weaker for light smokers. Thus, as a robustness check, we separate our 50 smokers into "heavy smoker" and "light smoker" groups, and measure the difference between the two.

It seems natural to separate the groups at the mode of ten cigarettes. In one specification (specification (a)), the light smoker group consists of those who smoke less than or equal to ten cigarettes (31 subjects) and the heavy smoker group consists of the other 17 subjects; in specification (b), the light smoker group consists of those who smoke less than ten cigarettes (17 subjects) and the heavy smoker group consists of the remaining 31 subjects.[20]

[20]The number of observations is smaller than 50 because those who chose only A or only B are excluded.

The results for specification (a) are presented in the upper panel of Table 10.5. In the real tobacco session, although the deprivation dummy is significantly negative for the heavy smoker group, it is not significant for the light smoker group.[21] The coefficient on the deprivation dummy for the heavy smoker group is larger in absolute value than for the whole sample.

In the lower panel, the results of separation (b) are presented. They are essentially the same, confirming our hypothesis. In addition, the heavy smoker group becomes significantly impatient when deprived, even in the hypothetical tobacco session. This robustness check strongly suggests that the results of the previous section have captured a real effect.

4.5 Analysis Using Discount Rates: Robustness Check 2

Thus far, we have analyzed the binary choice data directly using our logit estimation. This method has the advantage of more efficient use of data, as well as avoidance of the questionable assumptions necessary for the estimation of discount rates. However, a two-step method using estimated discount rates should produce results that are not dramatically different from those presented in the previous sections. In this sub-section, we check the robustness of our results by estimating discount rates corresponding to our choice data, and using this as the dependent variable in our regression equation.

To this end, we first must estimate discount rates. The answers for each combination of delay and amount, A or B, were sorted in ascending order as per the rates of return implied by the options. If a subject chooses the "earlier" option when the rate of return is low and the "later" option when it is high, so that they switch from the "earlier" option to the "later" option only once, then we measure the time discount rate of the subject as the average of the two rates of return immediately before and after the switch. If they choose all "earlier" options or all "later" options, the tail end values are treated as the time discount rate. We discard the cases in which subjects made multiple switches between the two options. By this method, we estimate 1,724 (deprived = 864, usual = 860) discount rates for the hypothetical tobacco session, 1,610 (deprived = 687, usual = 678, non-smoker = 245) for the money session, and 1,809 (deprived = 916, usual = 893) for the real tobacco session.

In the second stage, we examine the effect of smoking and deprivation from smoking. In Fig. 10.5, the averages of the discount rates are presented. Discount rates are measured per 12 h in the hypothetical tobacco session, per 1 year in the money session, and per 30 min in the real tobacco session. Non-smokers

[21]When amount dummies and delay dummies are used as regressors instead of the corresponding variables, similar results are obtained. The results for the money session are not presented, since the estimation routine did not converge.

Table 10.5 Estimation results of panel logit regression: light vs. heavy smokers

Separation (a)								
	Real tobacco session				**Hypothetical tobacco session**			
	Light smokers		Heavy smokers		Light smokers		Heavy smokers	
	Coef.	p value	Coef.	p value	Coef.	p value	Coef.	p value
D_DEPRIVATION	0.014	[0.886]	−0.391	[0.000]**	−0.161	[0.098]	0.129	[0.089]
RETURN	0.002	[0.000]**	0.003	[0.000]**	0.002	[0.000]**	0.003	[0.000]**
DELAY	−0.017	[0.121]	−0.042	[0.000]**	−0.005	[0.401]	0.002	[0.707]
AMOUNT	−2.311	[0.000]**	−1.46	[0.000]**	−1.634	[0.000]**	−1.075	[0.000]**
Pseudo R^2		0.210		0.232		0.202		0.214
Observations	17 persons	2,720	31 persons	4,960	17 persons	2,720	29 persons	4,640
Separation (b)								
	Real tobacco session				**Hypothetical tobacco session**			
	Light smokers		Heavy smokers		Light smokers		Heavy smokers	
	Coef.	p value	Coef.	p value	Coef.	p value	Coef.	p value
D_DEPRIVATION	0.058	[0.424]	−0.876	[0.000]**	0.185	[0.010]*	−0.363	[0.001]**
RETURN	0.002	[0.000]**	0.004	[0.000]**	0.002	[0.000]**	0.003	[0.000]**
DELAY	−0.024	[0.005]**	−0.05	[0.000]**	0.003	[0.524]	−0.008	[0.172]
AMOUNT	−2.114	[0.000]**	−1.169	[0.000]**	−1.557	[0.000]**	−0.736	[0.000]**
Pseudo R^2		0.218		0.249		0.211		0.215
Observation	31 persons	4,960	17 persons	2,720	30 persons	4,800	16 persons	2,560

Note: The numbers of observations differ because those who only chose A or only chose B are excluded; * p value<0.05. ** p value<0.01

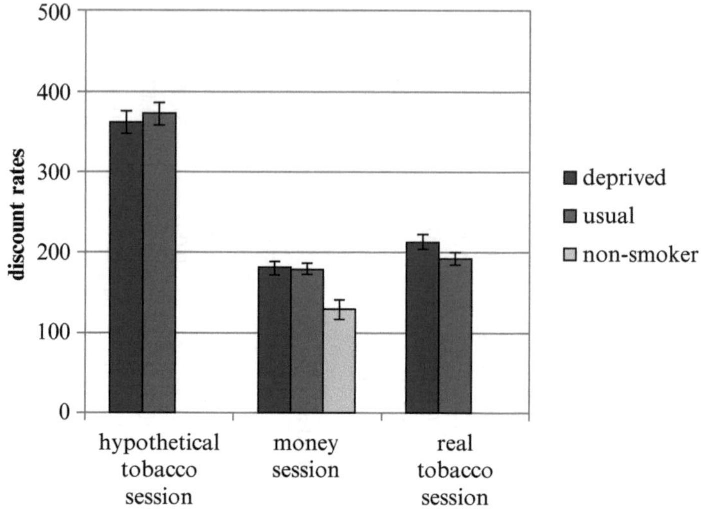

Fig. 10.5 Comparison of discount rates. Note: Vertical axis shows discount rates (%). Discount rates are measured per 12 h in the hypothetical tobacco session, per 1 year in the money session, and per 30 min in the real tobacco session. *Vertical bars* represent ± SEM (standard error of means)

clearly show lower discount rates, and the difference is significant ($t(921) = -3.53$, $p = 0.0004$). Also, deprived smokers show significantly higher discount rates in the real tobacco session ($t(1807) = -1.684$, $p = 0.092$), while the difference is not significant in the hypothetical tobacco ($t(1722) = 0.470$, $p = 0.638$) and money ($t(1363) = -0.117$, $p = 0.907$) sessions.

We regressed the estimated discount rates over the two conditions, the delay and the amount, and the dummy variables of smokers and deprived smokers. The results are shown in Table 10.6. The coefficient on the dummy variable for smokers (*D_SMOKER*) is significantly positive, implying that smokers show higher discount rates. Coefficients on the delay and the amount are significantly negative, revealing the usual delay and amount effects. These results confirm those of the panel logit regression (Table 10.3). The coefficient on the dummy variable for deprived smokers (*D_DEPRIVATION*) is significantly positive in the real tobacco session, but insignificant in the hypothetical tobacco and money sessions. These results indicate that deprivation makes subjects impatient only in the real tobacco session, reiterating the results of the panel logit regression (Table 10.4). The usual delay and amount effects are found in the hypothetical tobacco and money sessions, while the opposite effect is seen in the real tobacco session, which are similar to the results found in the panel logit regression (Table 10.4), except for the hypothetical tobacco session. Table 10.6 gives us an idea of the economic significance of smoking and deprivation. Smokers' annual discount rates are 51 percentage points higher than those of non-smokers, and deprivation raises 30-min. discount rates by 20 percentage points; these effects are of considerable magnitude!

Table 10.6 Estimation results of discount rates regression

	Smoker vs. Non-smoker		Deprived vs. Usual smoker					
			Real tobacco session		Hypothetical tobacco session		Money session	
	Coef.	p value	Coef.	p value	Coef.	p value	Coef.	p value
DELAY	−1.217	[0.772]	2.277	[0.045]*	−1.393	[0.091]	−3.07	[0.163]
AMOUNT	−0.074	[0.000]**	92.898	[0.000]**	−223.929	[0.000]**	−0.076	[0.000]**
D_SMOKER	51.408	[0.000]**						
D_DEPRIVATION			20.173	[0.036]*	−5.365	[0.718]	−3.624	[0.562]
Constant	278.921	[0.000]**	89.135	[0.004]**	491.37	[0.000]**	341.182	[0.000]**
Observation	50 smokers and 17 non-smokers	923	50 persons	1,809	50 persons	1,724	50 persons	1,365

Note: The dependent variable is a discount rate. A fixed-effects model is estimated, in which STATA does not report R^2; * p value<0.05. ** p value<0.01

In sum, the analysis using discount rates produces essentially the same results found in the previous section.

5 Conclusions

In this chapter, we investigated whether smokers show higher time discounting than non-smokers, and how short-term nicotine deprivation affects time discounting. A unique feature of our experiment is to offer subjects a choice between two smoking options, and to give rewards to subjects according to their choices not only in the money session, but also in the tobacco session, in order to measure domain effects on preferences by eliciting their true preference on nicotine.

We unequivocally confirmed that smokers are more impatient than non-smokers in the money, hypothetical tobacco, and real tobacco sessions, which is consistent with previous studies. On the other hand, short-term nicotine deprivation makes smokers even more impatient. This latter result is obtained only in the real tobacco session, where subjects actually consume their tobacco rewards at the specified time. This suggests that giving appropriate incentives is crucial for the elicitation of true preferences when smoking is involved. When the sample is restricted to heavy smokers, the effect is even stronger.

Overall, these results suggest that nicotine concentration has different effects in the short-run than in the long-run; although long-term intake of nicotine, which implies higher nicotine concentrations over time, makes people more impatient, short-term nicotine deprivation, which causes a *lower* nicotine concentration, makes smokers even more impatient. In other words, nicotine intake has different effects on the time preferences of addicted and non-addicted subjects.[22] Investigation of the neurological basis for these effects remains as a target for future research.

However, a second interpretation is also possible. We focus here on the result that deprivation does not have any effect in the hypothetical tobacco and money sessions. These results may suggest that nicotine per se has *no* causal effect on time discounting.[23] If that is the case, the result that smokers are more impatient than non-smokers should not be inferred as the result of nicotine concentration at all, rather, the causality would run in the opposite direction. If this is the case, smoking does not make people impatient, but impatient people start smoking. Which interpretation is correct is an interesting topic for future work.

---

[22]However, an alternative hypothesis exists. Long-term smokers may simply experience the repeated frequent occurrence of short-term deprivation, and thus become impatient. In this case, the long-term and short-term effects of nicotine would be due to the same phenomenon.

[23]In this interpretation, the results obtained in the real tobacco session would have to be due to a different phenomenon from time discounting; e.g. impulsiveness.

Appendix

A1. Definition of Variables Used in Regressions

Variable name	Explanation
D_SMOKER	Smoker dummy variable: 1 when subjects is smoker, 0 otherwise
D_DEPRIVATION	Deprivation dummy variable: 1 when subjects is nicotine deprived, 0 otherwise
DELAY	Time of earlier reward
D_DELAY_M2	Delay dummy variable in money session: 1 when delay is 1 week, 0 otherwise
D_DELAY_M3	Delay dummy variable in money session: 1 when delay is 2 weeks, 0 otherwise
D_DELAY_M4	Delay dummy variable in money session: 1 when delay is 3 weeks, 0 otherwise
D_DELAY_M5	Delay dummy variable in money session: 1 when delay is 4 weeks, 0 otherwise
D_DELAY_T2	Delay dummy variable in tobacco sessions: 1 when delay is 10 min, 0 otherwise in real tobacco session, 1 when delay is 1 h, 0 otherwise in hypothetical tobacco session
D_DELAY_T3	Delay dummy variable in tobacco sessions: 1 when delay is 20 min, 0 otherwise in real tobacco session, 1 when delay is 3 h, 0 otherwise in hypothetical tobacco session
D_DELAY_T4	Delay dummy variable in tobacco sessions: 1 when delay is 30 min, 0 otherwise in real tobacco session, 1 when delay is 12 h, 0 otherwise in hypothetical tobacco session
D_DELAY_T5	Delay dummy variable in tobacco sessions: 1 when delay is 40 min, 0 otherwise in real tobacco session, 1 when delay is 24 h, 0 otherwise in hypothetical tobacco session
AMOUNT	Amount of earlier rewards
D_AMOUNT_M2	Delay amount variable in money session: 1 when amount is 2,000 yen, 0 otherwise
D_AMOUNT_M3	Delay amount variable in money session: 1 when amount is 3,000 yen, 0 otherwise
D_AMOUNT_T2	Delay amount variable in tobacco sessions: 1 when amount is 2 puffs, 0 otherwise
D_AMOUNT_T3	Delay amount variable in tobacco sessions: 1 when amount is 0.5 cigarettes, 0 otherwise
D_AMOUNT_T4	Delay amount variable in tobacco sessions: 1 when amount is 1 cigarettes, 0 otherwise
D_AMOUNT_T5	Delay amount variable in tobacco sessions: 1 when amount is 1.5 cigarettes, 0 otherwise
RETURN	Return of later reward
D_RETURN_M4	Delay return variable in money session: 1 when return is 100 %, 0 otherwise

(continued)

Variable name	Explanation
D_RETURN_M5	Delay return variable in money session: 1 when return is 150 %, 0 otherwise
D_RETURN_M6	Delay return variable in money session: 1 when return is 200 %, 0 otherwise
D_RETURN_M7	Delay return variable in money session: 1 when return is 300 %, 0 otherwise

A2. Supplementary Data

Supplementary data associated with this chapter can be found, in the online version, at http://dx.doi.org/10.1016/j.socec.2013.4.005.

Addendum: Two Experiments Related to the Experiment in the Text[24]

In this addendum, we introduce two experiments related to the experiment described in the text of this chapter. One is our future work, and the other is a past experiment that served as a foundation for this study.

B1. Neuroeconomics Experiment

It will be interesting to apply the present study to a neuroeconomics experiment. To define the brain areas and networks correlated with intertemporal choice is an important topic of neuroeconomics. For example, McClure et al. (2004), using fMRI neuroimaging, found that two separate systems are involved in intertemporal decisions. One of these systems is comprised of the "beta areas," which include the limbic and paralimbic cortical structures. McClure et al. demonstrated that this structure is activated when people make intertemporal decisions, including decisions with immediate rewards. The other system is comprised of the "delta areas", including the lateral prefrontal and parietal areas. This system is activated in response to choices that do or do not include immediate rewards. Kable and Glimcher (2007) also showed that the activities in the ventral striatum, medial prefrontal cortex and posterior cingulate cortex are positively correlated with the amount of rewards and negatively correlated with the delay. Both of the studies focused on general human behavior and did not focus on specific subject groups such as smokers. On the other hand, Peters et al. (2011) and Luo et al. (2010) found that the neural activity in the ventral striatum of smokers is significantly lower than that of non-smokers when faced with intertemporal choices that involve delay.

[24]This addendum has been newly written for this book chapter.

There are also some fMRI studies related to nicotine addiction, but these do not involve intertemporal choice. For example, Beaver et al. (2011) separated subjects into two conditions after deprivation of smoking for 8 h. Their subjects were told to do a cognitive task after being administered either nicotine or placebo tablets. Beaver found that the activity of dopamine circuits such as the ventromedial prefrontal cortex and posterior cingulate cortex were significantly increased in the control group with the placebo tablet.

McClernon et al. (2009) examined brain activity when smoking cues were showed to subjects who were under 24 h smoking deprivation. They found that the activities of brain areas related to visual sensory processing, attention, and action planning, such as the left occipital gyrus and the bilateral precuneus, were increased by smoking deprivation. In addition, they reported that the degree of pre-scan craving and the activation of the right dorsomedial prefrontal cortex were positively correlated.

To reveal the neurological basis of the influence of nicotine on intertemporal choice will be worthwhile work. Just like our present laboratory experiment, the neuroimaging work will be able to find the correlates of the effects of nicotine concentration in the long-run (by comparing smokers and non-smokers), and also in the short-run (by comparing deprived and non-deprived smokers). Furthermore, it may be possible to find different correlates in the different domains: money and tobacco. In our future neural experiment, we predict that the same areas as in the previous studies noted above will be activated by smoking deprivation, and we expect to find a neural foundation for the domain effects observed in our present behavioral experiment.

B2. Preliminary Experiment in Waseda University

We conducted an experiment in Waseda University prior to the present Osaka University experiment. In the Waseda experiment, we also had three sessions: real tobacco, hypothetical tobacco, and money. The basic setup in the Waseda experiment was quite similar to the one we used at Osaka University. However, an important difference was that we did not allow subjects to smoke during the resting time between the sessions. Since the experiment lasted about 3 h, we inadvertently imposed 3 h of smoking deprivation on the subjects in the non-deprived condition. Therefore, in the Waseda experiment, the "deprived" condition was a long-period deprivation condition, and the "non-deprived" condition was actually a short-period deprivation condition. Since this is not what we wanted to do, we reconstructed our experiment to solve this and other weaknesses (not reported here).

The details of experimental design are of paramount importance. Experimenters should examine them, considering all relevant possibilities. However, some problems are often not recognized until an experiment is actually conducted. Thus, preparatory experiments are usually extremely helpful to the eventual success of a study.

References

Badger GJ, Bickel WK, Giordano LA, Jacobs EA, Loewenstein G, Marsch L (2007) Altered states: the impact of immediate craving on the valuation of current and future opioids. J Health Econ 26:865–876

Baker F, Johnson MW, Bickel WK (2003) Delay discounting in current and never-before cigarette smokers: similarities and differences across commodity, sign, and magnitude. J Abnorm Psychol 112:382–392

Beaver JD, Long CJ, Cole DM, Durcan MJ, Bannon LC, Mishra RG, Matthews PM (2011) The effects of nicotine replacement on cognitive brain activity during smoking withdrawal studied with simultaneous fMRI/EEG. Neuropsychopharmacology 36:1792–1800

Benzion U, Rapoport A, Yagil J (1989) Discount rates inferred from decisions: an experimental study. Manag Sci 35(3):270–284

Bickel WK, Odum AL, Madden GJ (1999) Impulsivity and cigarette smoking: delay discounting in current, never, and exsmokers. Psychopharmacology 146:447–454

Dallery J, Locey ML (2005) Effects of acute and chronic nicotine on impulsive choice in rats. Behav Pharmacol 16(1):15–23

Dallery J, Raiff BR (2007) Delay discounting predicts cigarette smoking in a laboratory model of abstinence reinforcement. Psychopharmacology 190:485–496

Field M, Santarcangelo M, Sumnall H, Goudie A, Cole J (2006) Delay discounting and the behavioural economics of cigarette purchases in smokers: the effects of nicotine deprivation. Psychopharmacology 186:255–263

Frederick S, Loewenstein G, O'donoghue T (2002) Time discounting and time preference: a critical review. J Econ Lit 40(2):351–401

Giordano LA, Bickel WK, Loewenstein G, Jacobs EA, Marsch LA, Badger GJ (2002) Mild opioid deprivation increases the degree that opioid-dependent outpatients discount delayed heroin and money. Psychopharmacology 163(2):174–182

Ida T, Goto R, Takahashi Y, Nishimura S (2011) Can economic-psychological parameters predict successful smoking cessation? J Socio-Econ 40(3):285–295

Kable JW, Glimcher PW (2007) The neural correlates of subjective value during intertemporal choice. Nat Neurosci 10:1625–1633

Khwaja A, Silverman D, Sloan F (2007) Time preference, time discounting, and smoking decisions. J Health Econ 26:927–949

Kinari Y, Ohtake F, Tsutsui Y (2009) Time discounting: declining impatience and interval effect. J Risk Uncertain 39:87–112

Kirby KN, Marakovic NN (1995) Modeling myopic decisions: evidence for hyperbolic delay-discounting within subjects and amounts. Organ Behav Hum Decis Process 64:22–30

Krishnan-Sarin S, Reynolds B, Duhig AM, Smith A, Liss T, McFetridge A, Cavallo DA, Carroll KM, Potenza MN (2007) Behavioral impulsivity predicts treatment outcome in a smoking cessation program for adolescent smokers. Drug Alcohol Depend 88:79–82

Loewenstein G, Prelec D (1992) Anomalies in intertemporal choice: evidence and an interpretation. Q J Econ 107:573–597

Luo S, Ainslie G, Giragosian L, Monterosso JR (2010) Striatal hyposensitivity to delayed rewards among cigarette smokers. Drug Alcohol Depend 116:18–23

McClernon FJ, Kozink RV, Lutz AM, Rose JE (2009) 24-h smoking abstinence potentiates fMRI-BOLD activation to smoking cues in cerebral cortex and dorsal striatum. Psychopharmacology 204:25–35

McClure SM, Laibson DI, Loewenstein G, Cohen JD (2004) Separate neural systems value immediate and delayed monetary rewards. Science 306:503–507

Mitchell SH (1999) Measures of impulsivity in cigarette smokers and non-smokers. Psychopharmacology 146(4):455–464

Mitchell SH (2004) Effects of short-term nicotine deprivation on decision-making: delay, uncertainty, and effort discounting. Nicotine Tob Res 6:819–828

Myerson J, Green L, Warusawitharana M (2001) Area under the curve as a measure of discounting. J Exp Anal Behav 76:235–243

Odum AL, Baumann AAL (2007) Cigarette smokers show steeper discounting of both food and cigarettes than money. Drug Alcohol Depend 91:293–296

Ohmura Y, Takahashi T, Kitamura N (2005) Discounting delayed and probabilistic monetary gains and losses by smokers of cigarettes. Psychopharmacology (Berl) 182(4):508–515

Peters J, Bromberg U, Schneider S, Brassen S, Menz M, Banaschewski T, Conrod PJ, Flor H, Gallinat J, Garavan H, Heinz A, Itterman B, Lathrop M, Martinot J, Paus T, Poline J, Robbins TW, Rietschel M, Smolka M, Ströhle A, Struve M, Loth E, Schumann G, Büchel C (2011) Lower ventral striatal activation during reward anticipation in adolescent smokers. Am J Psychiatry 168(5):540–549

Reynolds B (2004) Do high rates of cigarette consumption increase delay discounting? A cross-sectional comparison of adolescent smokers and young-adult smokers and nonsmokers. Behav Process 67:545–549

Reynolds B, Schiffbauer R (2004) Measuring state changes in human delay discounting: an experiential discounting task. Behav Process 67(3):343–356

Reynolds B, Patak M, Shroff P, Penfold RB, Melanko S, Duhig AM (2007) Laboratory and self-report assessments of impulsive behavior in adolescent daily smokers and nonsmokers. Exp Clin Psychopharmacol 15:264–271

Sasaki S, Xie S, Ikeda S, Qin J, Tsutsui Y (2012) Time discounting: delay effect and procrastinating behavior. J Behav Econ Finance 5:15–25

Sato M, Ohkusa Y (2003) The relationship between smoking initiation and time discount factor, risk aversion and information. Appl Econ Lett 10:287–289

Sayette MA, Loewenstein G, Kirchner TR, Travis T (2005) Effects of smoking urge on temporal cognition. Psychol Addict Behav 19(1):88–93

Tsutsui-Kimura I, Ohmura Y, Izumi T, Yamaguchi T, Yoshida T, Yoshioka M (2010) Nicotine provokes impulsive-like action by stimulating alpha4beta2 nicotinic acetylcholine receptors in the infralimbic, but not in the prelimbic cortex. Psychopharmacology (Berl) 209(4):351–9

Yi R, Landes RD (2012) Temporal and probability discounting by cigarette smokers following acute smoking abstinence. Nicotin Tob Res, published online

Yoon JH, Higgins ST, Bradstreet MP, Badger GJ, Thomas CS (2009) Changes in the relative reinforcing effects of cigarette smoking as a function of initial abstinence. Psychopharmacology 205:305–318

[illegible]

Chapter 11
The Effects of the Social Norm on Cigarette Consumption: Evidence from Japan Using Panel Data

Eiji Yamamura

Abstract Using Japan's prefecture-level panel data from 1989 to 2001, this chapter examines the influence of the social norm on a person's smoking behavior when the complementary relationship between smoking and drinking is taken into account. The key findings through a dynamic panel model controlling for unobserved prefecture-specific fixed effects are as follows: (1) Influence from others is stronger when people live more closely and cohesively. A tightly knit society results in a reduction of smoking through smoking-related interaction. (2) Smoking and drinking have a complementary relationship: greater initial consumption of alcohol results in larger consumption of cigarettes. (3) The complementary relationship between smoking and drinking is attenuated if the cost of committing the annoying conduct (i.e., smoking) is high.

Overall, this empirical study provides evidence that the psychological effect of the presence of surrounding people has a direct significant effect upon smoking behavior and, furthermore, that it attenuates the complementary relationship between smoking and drinking, thereby reducing cigarette consumption. These results indicate that not only formal rules but also tacitly formed informal norms are effective deterrents to smoking.

Keywords Smoking behavior • Social norm • Panel data

JEL Classification I10, I12, Z10

The original article first appeared in the Japan and the World Economy 23:6–12, 2011. A newly written addendum has been added to this book chapter

E. Yamamura (✉)
Department of Economics, Seinan Gakuin University, 6-2-92 Nishijin, Sawara-ku, Fukuoka 814-8511, Japan
e-mail: yamaei@seinan-gu.ac.jp

S. Ikeda et al. (eds.), *Behavioral Economics of Preferences, Choices, and Happiness*, DOI 10.1007/978-4-431-55402-8_11

1 Introduction

It is generally acknowledged that Japan's per capita cigarette consumption and smoking rate has been remarkably high among major industrialized nations (World Bank 1999). However, in Japan, some literature has pointed out that compared with other industrialized nations, the government did not sufficiently make an effort to raise public awareness about the health hazards of smoking (Yorozu and Zhou 2002; Luo et al. 2003).[1] For instance, Yorozu and Zhou (2002) refer to the absence of antismoking ordinances and regulations and the lack of dissemination of information about the health hazards of smoking. Nonetheless, the consumption of cigarettes has declined gradually in Japan. Thus, given that the formal rules and laws enacted by the government were not sufficiently effective in reducing cigarette consumption, there should be other mechanisms involved in the control of smoking which has lead to a reduction of cigarette consumption.

A person innately does not pay much attention to which side of the road they drive on, and thus they would normally choose to simply drive on the same side as everyone else. This phenomenon shows an aspect of human nature that relates to social existence. The influence of the attitude and conduct of others on a person's behavior seems apparent among neighbors and colleagues in schools and workplaces (Becker and Murphy 2000; Brock and Durlauf 2001; Crane 1991; Evans et al. 1992; Gaviria and Rapahel 2001; Glaeser et al. 1996; Manski 1993). The interactive mechanism above also applies to a person's choice of demand behavior. What others consume stimulates a person's demand for it as well. That is to say, the more popular goods are, the more people want them. Consequently, interactions among people through conversations and daily life may affect aggregated demand behavior toward goods such as cigarettes (Powell et al. 2005). When this interactive mechanism is considered, as Coleman (1990) pointed out, actors harmed by an action that benefits the actor in control of the action experience negative externalities, as exemplified by nonsmokers sitting near a smoker. The problem for nonsmokers, therefore, is how to limit such actions taken by smokers.

Compared with Europe or North America, in general the smoking prevalence of females is remarkably lower than that of males in the Asian nations of Japan, Korea, Thailand, and Singapore. For example, the smoking prevalences of males and females in the United States are 27.7 % and 22.5 %, respectively. On the other hand, those of Japan are 59.0 % and 14.8 %, respectively (World Bank 1999). These data imply that as a whole the smoking prevalence of Japan is higher than that of the United States, although that of females is distinctly lower in Japan than in the United States. Japan ratified its "Convention on the Elimination of all Forms of Discrimination Against Women" in 1979 at the United Nations General Assembly.[2]

[1]The situation in Korea is similar (Kim and Seldon 2004). Other existing work examining smoking behavior in Asia includes Japan (Haden 1990) and China (Yuanliang and Zongyi 2005).

[2]See http://www.un.org/womenwatch/daw/cedaw/

Consequently, females have risen in social standing and therefore have a larger influence on the social lives of the Japanese. With regard to smoking, most females in Japan are non-smokers who dislike smoking behavior. As the social status of females has risen, the anti-smoking atmosphere has become more prevalent.[3] Such an atmosphere also seems to shape the general anti-smoking social norm in Japan.

If one smokes in a public place and the surrounding people indicate their annoyance against him, then the person may feel embarrassed and thereby generate the psychological cost of committing the impolite behavior of smoking. The psychological cost of smoking depends on anti-smoking social norms, which are shaped by local interactions (Funk 2005). Furthermore, the apprehension of bad behavior such as crime or smoking depends on the watchfulness of citizens (Huck and Kosfeld 2007). Neighborhood watch efforts are likely to be more effective if the community members have closer relationships. Accordingly, assuming that neighborhood watch and psychological cost are complementary and that the majority of a community's members consist of nonsmokers, then the social norm that bans community members from smoking will be stronger in a more cohesive community. In the long run, the entire community will come to ostracize those who break such informal rules, such as smokers (Posner and Rasmusen 1999). I believe that informal rules such as social norms are the key determinants of the attitudes of smokers in Japan. This is why, in this study, I pay particular attention to the role of social norms in the regulation of smoker attitudes and thus include the proxy variables of social disorganization.[4]

The empirical studies of Dee (1999) and Gruber et al. (2003) provide evidence of a robust complementarity between cigarettes and alcohol.[5] To put it differently, reductions in drinking are associated with a lower prevalence of smoking. Such a complementarity seems to be affected by the informal social norm created through the watchfulness of the neighborhood or colleagues at work. The anti-smoking social norm appears to attenuate the complementarity between smoking and drinking. Nevertheless, the empirical links between social norms and complementary goods has yet to be considered in the literature. Therefore, the object of this chapter is to explore such links using the panel data of Japan from 47 Japanese prefectures for the years 1989–2001 and controlling for unobservable fixed effects. The contribution of this chapter is a combined analysis of the importance of the social norm and complementary goods on smoking behavior.

This chapter also contributes to the cigarette demand literature by examining the determinants of smoking incorporating both the direct and indirect effects of

---

[3]Due to limitations of data, the effect of females on cigarette consumption is not directly estimated in this research.

[4]The cohesiveness of society has another aspect as well. According to Putnam (2000), social networks built in a cohesive society may reinforce healthy norms, and socially isolated people are more likely to smoke or engage in various health damaging behaviors.

[5]Recently, Arcidacono et al. (2007) also investigated the relationship between smoking and drinking.

the social norm (via reduction of the complementarity of alcohol consumption) on smoking behavior. The organization of this chapter is as follows: Sect. 2 surveys cigarette consumption in Japan and advances a testable hypothesis. Section 3 presents the simple econometric framework. Section 4 discusses the results of the estimations. The final section offers concluding observations.

2 Review of Cigarette Consumption in Japan

2.1 Review

I begin this section by studying the figures that outline the current state of smoking in Japan. A cursory examination of Fig. 11.1, which demonstrates the transition of per capita consumption of cigarettes in Japan, suggests that consumption declined gradually over time until 1996.[6] Subsequently, Fig. 11.2 illustrates the average per capita consumption of cigarettes by prefecture for both high alcohol consumption and low consumption groups, which are equally divided by the initial year's alcohol consumption.[7] Figure 11.2 reveals that the consumption of cigarettes by the high alcohol consumption group is obviously higher than that of the low alcohol consumption group. Monthly expenditures of cigarettes declined from 1,500 yen (in 1988) to 1,100 yen (after 1996) in the high alcohol consumption group, whereas it declined from 1,100 yen (in 1988) to 950 yen (after 1996) in the low alcohol consumption group. Thus the reduction in cigarette expenditures was approximately 400 yen for the high alcohol consumption group but only 150 yen for the low alcohol consumption group, indicating a difference in cigarette consumption between these two groups. Furthermore, the consumption of alcohol was positively associated with that of cigarettes, and the decrease in cigarette consumption was more evident in the high alcohol consumption group than in the low consumption group.

The relationship between cigarette and alcohol consumption is shown in Fig. 11.3, in which alcohol and cigarette consumption are represented in the horizontal and the vertical axis, respectively. Alcohol and cigarette consumption per year are measured in millions of yen. I used their log forms to create the figures. Furthermore, Fig. 11.3a, b show the high and low alcohol consumption groups, respectively, which are divided in the same manner used in Fig. 11.2. As I explain later, the data comprises panel data, consisting of 47 prefectures and spanning 13 years. There were a total of 611 observations, which were then divided into the high alcohol consumption group (312 observations) and the low alcohol consumption group (299 observations). From these figures it can be seen that the sample regression line in Fig. 11.3a is steeper than that in Fig. 11.3b. That is,

[6]The evolution of cigarette consumption is unchanged even when expenditures on cigarettes are divided by the unit price of cigarettes. That is, consumption had been in decline until 1996, even when the unit price change is taken into account.

[7]The initial year is defined as 1989.

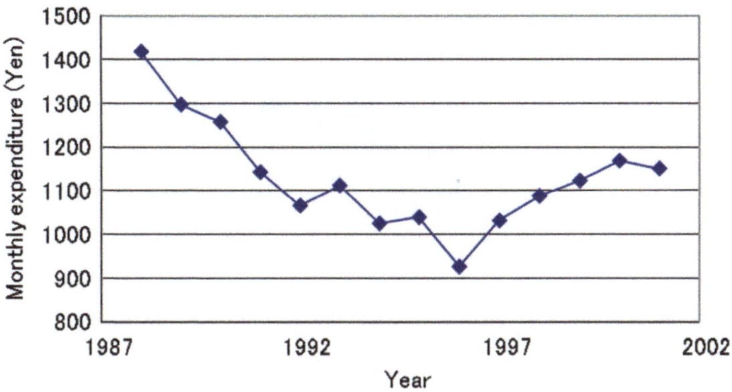

Fig. 11.1 Monthly household expenditures on cigarettes (Note: Data source: *Minryoku*, edited by Asahi Shimbun (2004))

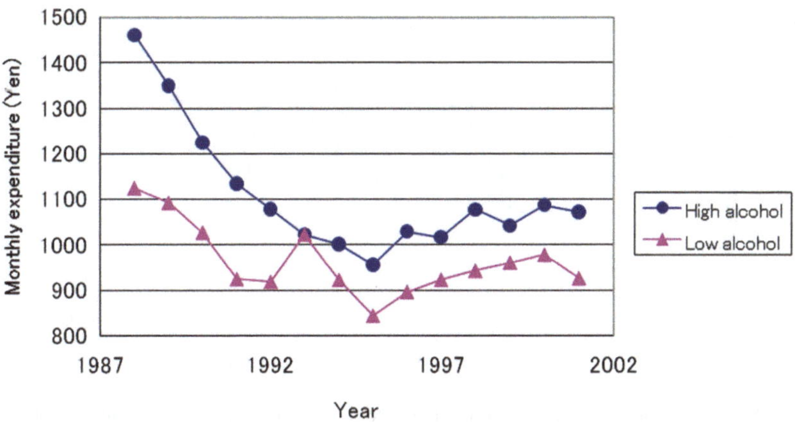

Fig. 11.2 Monthly household expenditures on cigarettes for high alcohol consumption and low alcohol consumption areas (*Note:* Data source: *Minryoku*, edited by Asahi Shimbun (2004))

a positive relationship is observed more clearly in Fig. 11.3a than in Fig. 11.3b, indicating that the complementarity between drinking and smoking is more obvious if the consumption of alcohol is higher.

To sum up the evidence presented above, smoking is associated more positively with drinking despite the fact that their complementarity declines more rapidly in the areas where the consumption of alcohol is higher.

2.2 *Hypothesis*

As suggested earlier, the per capita cigarette consumption in Japan has dominated industrialized nations in recent years. However, there is a remarkable difference in the smoking prevalences of males and females, which are about 60 % and

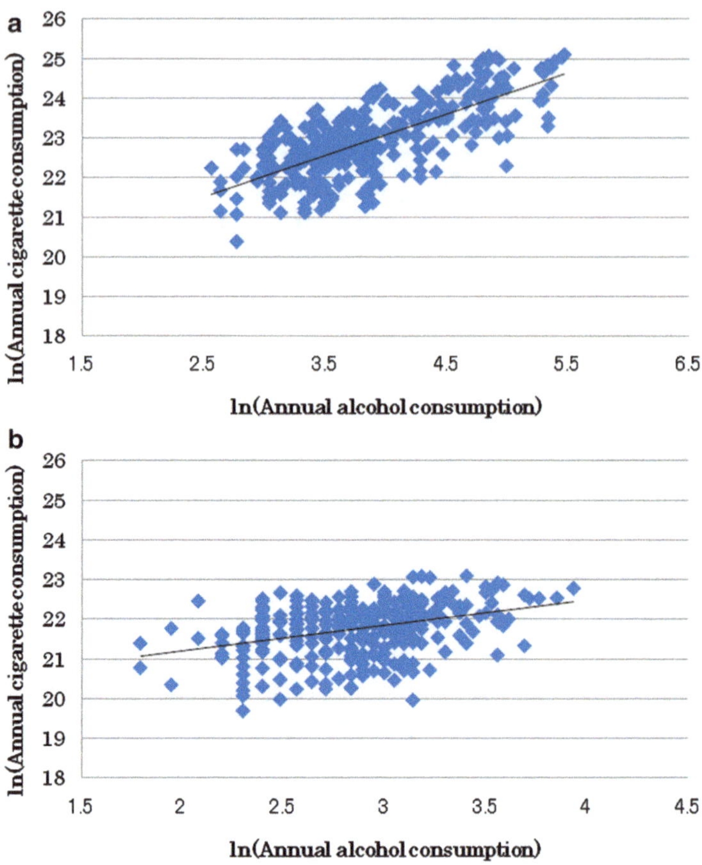

Fig. 11.3 Relationship between monthly household cigarette expenditures and alcohol consumption for high alcohol consumption and low alcohol consumption areas. (**a**) High alcohol consumption region. (**b**) Low alcohol consumption region. Note: The log form of annual alcohol and cigarettes consumption (millions of yen) was applied (Source: Data collected from *Minryoku*, edited by Asahi Shimbun (2004))

15 %, respectively (World Bank 1999). A growing body of literature suggests that social interaction mechanisms may be crucial determinants of behavior. It has been asserted that an increase in the prevalence of a given behavior at the peer level may lead to an increased probability of such behavior at the individual level (Manski 1993; Becker 1996; Becker and Murphy 2000; Glaeser et al. 1996). Assuming that society consists mainly of males in Japan, there may be a social interaction mechanism that enhances the prevalence of smoking since the majority of people in the society are smokers. Indeed, it is widely acknowledged that females have a relatively low social position in Japan. Under such circumstances, it is generally believed to be merely a matter of etiquette in Japan to ask another person sitting beside one for permission to smoke (Yorozu and Zhou 2002).

However, in recent years, the social position of females has improved and females have become influential in the modern society of Japan. This change reflects the Equal Employment Opportunities Law for Men and Women, which was enacted in 1985 in order to improve the employment opportunities of females. In the process of their rise in social position, females tend to increase their influence on modern social behaviors such as smoking at workplaces and accelerate the social norm of "not smoking for the sake of nonsmokers" through smoking-related interaction.[8] The higher the psychological cost, the stronger the nonsmoking norm becomes. The strength of nonsmoking norms plays a critical role in deterring members of a society from smoking. In short, as the social standing of females improves, the nonsmoking social norm emerges and leads to decreases in cigarette consumption. Informal norm enforcement among interacting male and female members of society tends to be stronger and more effective if the members communicate more cohesively and closely (Putnam 2000). Accordingly, I raise the following Hypothesis 1 concerning the effect of social norms on smoking.

Hypothesis 1: *A tightly knit society can achieve a reduction in smoking through smoking-related interaction.*

Dee (1999) presents evidence of the complementarity of drinking and smoking in line with the findings shown in the figures presented in the previous subsection. In addition to their complementarity, both cigarettes and alcohol are considered addictive goods. Hence, the initial consumption of alcohol is positively associated with the subsequent consumption of cigarettes.[9] Accordingly, I advance the following empirical Hypothesis 2.

Hypothesis 2: Greater consumption of alcohol in the past results in greater current consumption of alcohol, eventually leading to greater current consumption of cigarettes.

The psychological cost of committing an impolite behavior comes from the watchfulness of the neighborhood or colleagues at a workplace. On the condition that the cost rises, smokers drink but are less likely to smoke at a party where nonsmokers are present, even if smokers would like to jointly consume cigarettes and alcohol. This psychological cost is expected to have an influence not only directly on smoking but also indirectly on its complementarity. As a consequence, I postulate Hypothesis 3 with respect to the effects of the informal social norm upon smoking.

[8] Smoking related interactions are supposed as follows: Females tend to ask smokers at work not to smoke. When females are employed equal numbers to males, then smokers are more likely to be informed that their smoke bothers someone at work.

[9] From a medical and health science point of view, if people can become addicted to both types of products, then a cure should be sought for both. Hence, addictiveness should be regarded as a kind of disease rather than simply a habit.

Hypothesis 3: *The complementarity between smoking and drinking is attenuated if the cost of committing the annoying conduct of smoking is high.*

3 Model

3.1 Data

Except for cigarette price, data used in the regression estimation as independent variables are collected from Asahi Shimbun (2004). The price data are obtained from the Japan Statistical Yearbook (various years) published by the Statistics Bureau of the Ministry of Internal Affairs and Communication. The structure of the data is panel, consisting of 47 prefectures and spanning 13 years (1989–2001). The raw data set includes various prefecture-level data on various variables. Table 11.1 depicts the descriptive statistics for all of the variables used in the regression estimation.

3.2 Econometric Framework

To test the hypotheses raised in the previous section, first I examine whether the social norm reduced the current cigarette consumption directly. Second, I examine how the social norm attenuates the complementarity of alcohol and cigarette consumption.

Table 11.1 Variable definitions, means, and standard deviations

Variable	Definition	Mean	Standard deviation
CIGA	Cigarette expenditure[a]	9,370	12,909
PRIC	Cigarette price (Yen)	227.2	13.9
DENS	Population density of (number of population per km^2)	623	1,060
SN1	Number of public baths	547	525
SN2	Number of community centers	377	277
DSN1	Population turnover within prefecture (number of people)[b]	72.1	86.1
DSN2	Number of immigrants from other prefectures[b]	64.0	79.9
INCOM	Regional real income[a]	8,228	9,297
ALCOL	Alcohol consumption[a]	41.9	41.9
SERVI	Number employed in service sector[b]	834.0	867.3
CAR	Number of cars[b]	142.8	122.2
POP	Total population[b]	2,645	2,387

Notes: [a]In Millions of Yen
[b]In 1000s
Values are the simple averages of the yearly values over the period 1988–2001. Data source is *Minryoku* edited by Asahi Shimbun (2004)

Following Becker and Murphy (2000), the estimated function takes the following myopic addiction form[10]:

$$\begin{aligned} CIGA_{it} = {} & \alpha_1 CIGA_{it-1} + \alpha_2 PRIC_{it} + \alpha_3 DENS_{it} + \alpha_4 SN1_{it} + \alpha_5 SN2_{it} \\ & + \alpha_6 DSN1_{it} + \alpha_7 DSN2_{it} + \alpha_8 ALCOL_{it} + \alpha_9 INCOM_{it} + \alpha_{10} SERVIC_{it} \\ & + \alpha_{11} CAR_{it} + \alpha_{12} POP_{it} + \delta_t + \nu_i + u_{it}, \end{aligned}$$

where $CIGA_{it}$ represents the dependent variable in prefecture i and year t. α's represents the regression parameters. In this estimation, as the main stress does not fall on the rational addictive behavior, I hypothesized that current cigarette consumption depends on past consumption but not future consumption. If the myopic addictive behavior holds, then the expected signs of the lagged *CIGA* and *PRIC* become positive and negative, respectively.[11]

δ_t, ν_i, u_{it} represent the unobservable specific effects in the t th year (a fixed effect time vector), the individual effects of i's prefecture (a fixed effects prefecture vector) and an error term, respectively. δ_t represents the year specific effects and ν_i holds the time invariant feature, while u is an error term. The structure of the data set used in this study is panel, and the independent variables include a lagged dependent variable. To address potential endogenous problems with the lagged independent variable, I carry out dynamic panel estimation developed by Arellano-bond (Arellano and Bond 1991), because dynamic panel models allow past realizations of the dependent variable to affect its current level. In this model, the set of valid instruments is $CIGA_{i1}, CIGA_{i2}, \ldots, CIGA_{i,t-2}$. In addition, special attention must be paid to the omitted variable bias stemming from unobservable individual specific effects. This can be also controlled for by means of dynamic panel estimation. Year dummies were also incorporated to subdue δ_t, which represents the conditional and structural changes at the macro level that could affect cigarette consumption.

The problem of simultaneous consumption between alcohol and cigarettes seems to remain, however, resulting in estimation bias. To control for this bias, I conducted fixed effect model estimation, in which past alcohol consumption was used as the instrument. Then, the predicted value of alcohol consumption was used for the estimation of cigarette consumption.

[10]The focus of this chapter is not on rational addictive behavior. I thus used the myopic function form. Nonetheless, when the rational addiction model is employed, the results of estimation are unchanged.

[11]Although the price measure is a single nationwide uniform cigarette price in Japan, the deflator is different among prefectures. The cigarette price can be deflated by the consumer price index, and therefore the relative cigarette price varies across prefectures.

3.3 Proxies for Social Norms

Nonsmokers would suffer seriously from the smoking of surrounding people if they lived in a densely populated area since the externality of smoking is strong and directly affects others. Nonsmokers have a tendency to request that smokers not smoke or to express their annoyance with the smoking behavior. This is why the expected signs of *DENS* representing the density of the population measured by the population per km^2 are negative.

I now proceed to characterize the social norm that captures the informal social pressure on smokers from nonsmokers.[12] The cost of annoying others depends on the social norms, which are shaped by local interactions (Funk 2005). As pointed out by Jacobs (1969), in urban areas, face-to-face communication is easier, resulting in economic benefits. This suggests that interpersonal interactions are more frequent in denser areas because the distances among people are shorter, allowing social norms to form. Individuals are more apt to smoke due to the decrease in the expected cost of annoying surrounding people such as community members or workplace colleagues if the community is disorganized and social norms are weak. According to the view of Putnam (2000), social disorganization can be regarded as the engine of impolite behavior. Such disorganization undermines the social norms and marks urban areas where population turnover is high, one's neighbors are anonymous, and local organization is rare. The degree to which one is integrated into one's community depends upon the community's condition. To borrow an argument of Putnam (2000), frequent movers have weaker ties within the community, and so mobile communities seem to have less interactivity among neighbors than more stable communities. To put it differently, the more mobile a community is, the weaker the connectedness within it becomes. Hence, *DSN*1 and *DSN*2, denoting the number of population turnovers within a prefecture and the number of immigrants from other prefectures, respectively, can be considered as proxies for the decay of social norms.[13] Accordingly, these coefficients are predicted to take a positive sign.

The following independent variables are used as proxies of the social norm. In traditional Japanese daily life, public baths were used by community members who, apart from the wealthy, ordinarily lived in houses without a private bath. Through the use of such baths, people could get acquainted with neighbors and generate social networks. In modern Japan, most residences have their own baths, and people

[12]The proxies of social norms are constructed based on the prefecture-level aggregated data. It should be noted that prefecture may not be adequate as the unit of analysis because social norms are formed through interpersonal interaction in neighborhoods and workplaces. Thus, attention should be paid to the possible limitations of the data. Future studies will need to incorporate micro data to examine the effects of social norms.

[13]In previous studies (e.g., Yamamura 2008a, b, 2011a), the number of population turnovers within a prefecture and the number of immigrants from other prefectures are also used as proxies of social norms in prefectural-level data. These studies provide evidence that these social norm proxies have significant influences on the demands for lawyers, driving mannerisms, and voting behavior.

are therefore more likely to take a bath at home. However, a new type of public bath featuring more deluxe baths and saunas has recently developed, and these are used by all sectors of society, thus providing a place to meet neighbors and form social networks. The community center can be also considered as a place where people interact closely and enhance the cohesiveness among community members. Closely-knit networks formed through interpersonal interactions are thought to ostracize their members if they are considered to be against the informal rules that exist within the network (Hayami 2001). The higher the cost of suffering from ostracism, the more tightly the network is knitted (Greif 1993, 1994). The degree of the cost of suffering from ostracism can therefore be considered a measure of the strength of social norms. Therefore, the number of public baths and community centers, represented as *SN*1 as *SN*2, respectively, where people can contact neighbors and deter them from annoying the others surrounding them, can thus also serve as a proxy for social norms.[14] Therefore, I expect the signs of *SN*1 and *SN*2 to be negative.

3.4 Control Variables

In addition to social norms, I also focus on the effects of drinking[15] following the argument of Dee (1999) that the consumption of alcohol and cigarettes might constitute an important case as these products are complementary. Thus, the *ALCOL*standing for alcohol consumption is expected to take a positive sign.[16]

The cost of smoking is not only psychological but also economic. In the workplace, if ones customers, business partners, or counterparts dislike smoking, then a smoker cannot build good relationships with them, and as a result, team performance in the workplace is lowered. In particular, the cost of smoking appears to be high in the service sector, as employees tend to work within a locked room and can suffer more health damage from smoking. Following the enactment of a restrictive smoking policy (Gottlieb et al. 1990), informal rules of preventing smoking should also form naturally and necessarily become effective. Hence, *SERVI*, denoting the number of people employed in the service sector, would take a negative sign. Similarly, because the space inside vehicles is closed, people riding inside vehicles should be more sensitive to smoking and the likelihood of more serious damage to their health from its effects. The sign of *CAR*, which represents the number of vehicles, is expected to be negative.

[14]Yamamura (2009) considered the number of public baths and the number of community centers as proxies of social norms by using prefectural level data, and found that these variables were negatively associated with the number of crimes committed.

[15]The case Dee (1999) presents is of teenage smoking and drinking. I conjecture that this relationship holds in not only teens but also in other generations.

[16]It should be noted that the price of alcohol must be used as the explanatory variable in order to more precisely examine the complementarity. However, I found difficulty in measuring the price of alcohol since there are a number of kinds of alcohol, such as beer, whiskey and wine.

3.5 Interaction Terms with Alcohol

In the subsequent estimation, I incorporate the additional cross-products of $ALCOL_{it}$ and some dependent variables as follows: $DENS_{it} * ALCOL_{it}$, $SN1_{it} * ALCOL_{it}$, $SN2_{it} * ALCOL_{it}$, $DSN1_{it} * ALCOL_{it}$, and $DSN2_{it} * ALCOL_{it}$. As stated previously in Hypothesis 3, the complementarity between smoking and drinking becomes weaker when the cohesiveness of a tightly knit community leads to raising the psychological cost of smoking. If this holds, then the expected signs of $DENS_{it} * ALCOL_{it}$, $SN1_{it} * ALCOL_{it}$, and $SN2_{it} * ALCOL_{it}$ become negative. On the other hand, $DSN1_{it} * ALCOL_{it}$ and $DSN2_{it} * ALCOL_{it}$ are expected to take a positive sign.

As explained in Sect. 3.2, to control for the problem of simultaneous consumption of alcohol and cigarettes, I conduct the Fixed Effects 2SLS estimation. In this estimation, I use a data set consisting of past alcohol consumption and the cross-products of $ALCOL_{it-1}$ and proxies for the norm ($DENS_{it}$, $SN1_{it}$, $SN2_{it}$, $DSN1_{it}$, and $DSN2_{it}$) as instruments.

4 Results

4.1 Basic Results

Table 11.2 presents the results of the dynamic panel estimations. Results that do not control for the endogenous bias are shown in columns (1)–(3). Results that control for the endogenous bias are shown in columns (4)–(6). Furthermore, estimations were conducted using not only the entire sample shown in (1) and (4), but also the high alcohol consumption prefectures shown in columns (2) and (5) and the low alcohol consumption prefectures shown in (3) and (6). Information derived from the estimations of splitting samples can be of great use for comparing the differences of social norm effects on smoking behavior between the two groups. Looking at the second row from the bottom of Tables 11.2 and 11.3 reveals that there is no second-order serial correlation for disturbances of the first-differenced equation for any of the dynamic panel (GMM) estimations. Therefore, Arellano-Bond type GMM estimators are consistent.

From the results of columns (1) and (4), it can be seen that *CIGA* and *PRIC* take positive and negative signs, respectively, which is in line with the myopic addiction model. Turning to the key variables of this research, most of the proxies for the social norm or the decay of the social norm such as *DENS*, *SN*1, *SN*2, *DSN*1, and *DSN*2, take the predicted signs. In particular, *DSN*1, and *DSN*2 are statistically significant, which is consistent with Hypothesis 1. *ALCOL*, *SERVI*, and *CAR* also take the expected signs and are statistically significant. *INCOM* takes a negative sign, implying that cigarettes are inferior goods. This finding is contrary to that of the existing literature (Haden 1990; Yorozu and Zhou 2002). The reason why cigarettes become inferior goods is likely due to the emergence of substitute

Table 11.2 Comparison of regression results for cigarette smoking between high and low alcohol consumption areas

Variable	Endogeneity of current alcohol consumption not controlled			Endogeneity of current alcohol consumption controlled		
	(1) All areas	(2) High alcohol consumption areas	(3) Low alcohol consumption areas	(4) All areas	(5) High alcohol consumption areas	(6) Low alcohol consumption areas
CIGA$_{-1}$	0.12** (2.98)	0.15** (2.76)	0.002 (0.04)	0.11** (2.63)	0.15** (2.53)	−0.005 (−0.08)
PRIC	−30.0 (−0.14)	−135.3 (−0.38)	74.1 (0.98)	−32.8 (−0.15)	−149.5 (−0.40)	15.0 (0.19)
DENS	−63.3 (−1.24)	−62.1 (−0.90)	−129.6 (−1.39)	−79.9 (−1.51)	−80.5 (−1.09)	−73.9 (−0.78)
SN1	−1.86 (−0.25)	6.08 (0.63)	−2.67 (−0.44)	−8.08 (−1.08)	−3.64 (−0.37)	−1.66 (−0.27)
SN2	−7.58 (−0.65)	−63.3* (−2.16)	0.24 (0.09)	−7.92 (−0.66)	−59.8* (−1.95)	−0.93 (−0.36)
DSN1	190.1** (4.01)	173.9** (2.61)	−138.2 (−1.44)	164.9** (3.33)	121.6* (1.73)	−189.1* (−1.93)
DSN2	230.7** (3.85)	224.9** (2.91)	−98.7 (−1.14)	205.2** (3.33)	187.0* (2.33)	−74.1 (−0.85)
ALCOL	224.9** (6.14)	251.2** (4.79)	−30.9 (−1.32)	201.6** (4.06)	166.6** (2.39)	63.1 (1.56)
INCOM	−2.13** (−3.75)	−1.44* (−1.93)	−1.00 (−1.02)	−2.05** (−3.48)	−1.43* (−1.82)	−1.16 (−1.19)
SERVIC	−141.4** (−12.9)	−129.2** (−8.51)	−43.0** (−3.08)	−147.0** (−13.1)	−136.4** (−8.64)	−39.4** (−2.80)
CAR	−128.5** (−6.19)	−140.6** (−4.71)	−67.8* (−2.27)	−118.0** (−5.54)	−122.2** (−3.99)	−48.0 (−1.60)
POP	96.6** (4.67)	86.3** (3.06)	47.1* (1.68)	106.8** (4.83)	102.5** (3.35)	28.6 (0.99)
Second-order autocorrelation	Z = 0.55 p-value = 0.58	Z = 0.15 p-value = 0.88	Z = 1.61 p-value = 0.10	Z = 0.47 p-value = 0.63	Z = 0.27 p-value = 0.78	Z = 0.71 p-value = 0.47
Sample groups	564 47	288 24	276 23	564 47	288 24	276 23

Table 11.3 Regression results of cigarette smoking considering the interaction between alcohol consumption and social norm proxies

Variables	(1) Endogeneity of current alcohol consumption not controlled Dynamic panel	(2) Endogeneity of current alcohol consumption controlled Fixed effects 2SLS
$CIGA_{-1}$	0.05 (0.44)	0.14 (1.49)
PRIC	15.0 (0.07)	123.1 (1.18)
ALCOL	55.0 (0.43)	−233.0** (−2.81)
DENS ALCOL*	−0.15** (−2.80)	−0.14* (−1.95)
SN1 ALCOL*	0.21 (1.41)	0.23 (1.59)
SN2 ALCOL*	−0.52 (−1.63)	−0.14 (−1.00)
DSN1 ALCOL*	2.14** (3.72)	1.81** (2.39)
DSN2 ALCOL*	−0.48 (−0.57)	0.01 (0.02)
INCOM	−2.47* (−1.78)	−1.48* (−1.66)
SERVIC	−134.3** (−5.50)	−112.9** (−5.35)
CAR	−132.5** (−2.72)	−155.1** (−4.51)
POP	78.0** (2.95)	38.0 (1.56)
Second-order autocorrelation	Z = 0.23 p-value = 0.81	
Wald Chi^2	4,134	
R-square		0.65
Sample groups	564 47	564 47

Notes: Numbers in parentheses are z-statistics in column (1) and t-statistics in column (2), which are obtained by robust standard error. * and ** indicate significance at the 5 and 1 % levels, respectively (one-sided tests). Year dummies *DENS*, *SN*1, *SN*2, *DSN*1, and *DSN*2 are included in all estimations but not reported here to save space

goods in the process of the economic development in Japan. These results strongly support my prediction that the social norm plays an important role in the decrease of cigarette consumption.

Next, let us compare the results of the high and low alcohol consumption groups. In columns (2) and (5), whereas the coefficients of *DENS* and *SN*2 take negative signs, those of *DSN*1and *DSN*2 take positive signs, and they are all statistically significant with the exception of *DENS*. The fact that the coefficient of *ALCOL* takes the expected positive sign implies that the complementarity of drinking and smoking is valid. On the other hand, it is interesting to observe that in columns (3) and (6) most of the proxies for the social norm or the decay of the social norm do not take the predicted signs, and none of them are statistically significant. Furthermore, contrary to the expected result, the coefficient sign of *ALCOL* is negative. Considering Fig. 11.2 and Table 11.2 together, the social norm effects on smoking depend upon the initial consumption of alcohol, which is positively associated with the initial consumption of cigarettes. The effects of antismoking norms declined as the initial consumption of smoking and drinking fell, presumably because the smaller the externality from smoking, the less aggressive nonsmoker attitudes toward smokers became, which is in line with previously published results finding that the proportion of nonsmokers that suggested to smokers that they quit smoking decreased after the implementation of restrictive smoking policies in the United States (Gottlieb et al. 1990). Another likely reason for the decrease in the effectiveness of antismoking norms is that when the number of places where people are allowed to smoke decreases, there are fewer opportunities for nonsmokers to express their opinions of annoyance to smokers. In short, these results can be interpreted to mean the following. (1) Social norms have a tremendous effect on smoking when the consumption of alcohol is high, but not when it is low. (2) The degree of current consumption of cigarettes depends upon the initial consumption of alcohol, thus confirming Hypothesis 2.

4.2 The Impact of Norms on Complementarity

Switching now to the interaction terms of $ALCOL_{t-1}$ and the proxy variables for the social norm or its decay, the results are shown in Table 11.3. Column (1) presents the result when the endogeneity bias of alcohol is not controlled for. Column (2) shows the result when the endogeneity bias of alcohol is controlled for. Because the focus of this study is on the impact of the social norm on the complementarity of smoking and drinking, it can be seen from Table 11.3 that in all estimations, as expected, the signs of $DENS_{it} * ALCOL_{it}$ are negative while those of $DSN1_{it} * ALCOL_{it}$ are positive and statistically significant. With respect to $SN2_{it} * ALCOL_{it}$, its coefficients take the predicted negative signs and but are not statistically significant. As shown in Table 11.2, *SERVI* and *CAR* take significant negative signs, conforming to the expectations. My interpretation of the results drawn from Table 11.3 is consistent with the prediction described earlier and supports Hypothesis 3.

Up to this point I have presented the various estimated results of this study. Summing them up, I arrive at the conclusion that the estimation results examined in this section are consistent and reasonably support Hypotheses 1 to 3 raised in the preceding section.

5 Conclusion

The consumption of cigarettes is considered to be influenced by the informal social norm and social interaction. Therefore, the mechanisms related to the social norm and social interaction seem to be more influential among industrialized countries, and especially in Japan since it is a relatively homogeneous society. However, researchers have heretofore not paid attention to this relationship, and therefore little is known about the effect of the social norm on smoking behavior.

The key findings through a dynamic panel model controlling for unobserved fixed effects are as follows:

(1) Influence from others is stronger when people live more closely and cohesively together. Thus, a tightly knit society can help to create a reduction of smoking through smoking-related interaction.
(2) Smoking and drinking have a complementary relationship; greater initial consumption of alcohol results in greater consumption of cigarettes.
(3) Complementarity between smoking and drinking is attenuated if the cost of committing the annoying conduct (i.e., smoking) is high.

Summing up the evidence presented here, overall this empirical study provides evidence that the high psychological cost caused by those surrounding smokers has a direct significant effect upon smoking behavior and, furthermore, that it attenuate the complementarity between smoking and drinking, thereby reducing cigarette consumption. I found that this research helps to explain one aspect of human nature related to social existence. The influence of the attitude of others on a person's behavior seems apparent. The findings derived from the current investigation using regression analysis can further bridge the complementary relationship between social norms and smoking behavior, and as such they are of value to researchers.

Social norms are thought to be formed through the interpersonal interactions among people in close proximity. This chapter used prefecture-level aggregated data, but due to limitations inherent in such data, the effects of social norms could not be investigated as accurately as this inquiry requires. Therefore, for more precise estimation, it is necessary to use micro-level data to better analyze the effects of social norms; we intend to incorporate such date in our future work. Moreover, my chief argument in this chapter is in part based on the critical assumption that as the social position of females improved, it more strongly affected smoking behavior. Nevertheless, it is not clear whether this assumption is valid. A future direction for this study will be to examine how the improvement of the social position of females has an influence on smoking behavior and thereby helps reduce the consumption of cigarettes in Japan.

Addendum: Related Literature[17]

As suggested in Yamamura (2011b), social norms shared by a community influence cigarette consumption. However, there is also the possibility that smokers influence norms and social relationships. It has been recently acknowledged that smokers, when compared with non-smokers, are more impatient and prefer immediate benefits. In other words, smokers are more present-oriented (e.g., Khwaja et al. 2006a, b; Ida and Goto 2009a, b). If this holds true, then various questions concerning the behavior of smokers naturally arise. For instance, can such impatient people maintain long-term personal relationships? This question is important because relationships with people are thought to influence economic outcomes. Maintaining trust with one's business partner creates a large benefit in the future, and this deters people from deviating from such relationships (despite possible short-term benefits of cheating on one's partner). However, presented-oriented people are thought to betray their partners at the expense of any long-term benefit.

Family stability can be considered similarly because the family group is regarded as the most basic unit of all social groups. Stable family relations lead to peace of mind, which seems to increase happiness. Furthermore, family stability seems to positively influence performance in the workplace, all other things being equal. That is, the maintenance of intimate spousal relationships is considered to result in various benefits in the long run, even if it requires patience and compromise. However, it is difficult for smokers to be patient and to compromise because of their characteristics. Thus, it would be worthwhile to examine the marital life of smokers to better understand the behavior of smokers. Some recent research has attempted to compare the behavior of smokers and non-smokers by focusing on interpersonal relationships.

Yamamura (2014) compared the martial lives of smokers with non-smokers. He considered that the frequency of sexual contact between spouses to be an investment in the maintenance of marital life. However, the role of having sex differs with the situation. If people follow their primitive instincts, they will engage in sexual behavior. Impatient people are thus likely to have sex. For the purpose of exploring such an inference, Yamamura investigated how sexual behavior differs between smokers and non-smokers using individual-level data from Japan. In addition, determinants of life satisfaction were also investigated. The key findings are: (1) frequency of sex is positively associated with family satisfaction; (2) unmarried smokers are more likely to have sex than unmarried non-smokers; and (3) married smokers are less likely to have sex than married non-smokers. However, the causality is ambiguous because survey data was used in that paper. That is, estimation bias is thought to exist and a more refined method based on experiments is necessary to further scrutinize the findings.

[17] This addendum has been newly written for this book chapter.

References

Arcidiacono P, Sieg H, Sloan F (2007) Living rationally under the volcano? An empirical analysis of heavy drinking and smoking. Int Econ Rev 48:37–65

Arellano M, Bond S (1991) Some tests of specification for panel data: Monte Carlo evidence and an application to employment equations. Rev Econ Stud 58:277–297

Asahi Shimbun (2004) Minryoku: Todofuken-Betsu Minryoku Sokutei Shiryoshu (CD-ROM edition). Asahi-Shimbunsha, Tokyo

Becker G (1996) Account for tastes. Harvard University Press, Cambridge

Becker G, Murphy K (2000) Social economics: market behavior in a social environment. The Belknap Press of Harvard University Press, Cambridge

Brock WA, Durlauf SN (2001) Discrete choice with social interactions. Rev Econ Stud 68:235–260

Coleman JS (1990) Foundation of social theory. Harvard University Press, Cambridge

Crane J (1991) The epidemic theory of ghettos and neighborhood effects on dropping out and teenage childbearing. Am J Sociol 96(5):1226–1259

Dee TS (1999) The complementarity of teen smoking behavior and drinking. J Health Econ 18:769–793

Evans WN, Oates WE, Schwab RM (1992) Measuring peer group effects: a study of teenage behavior. J Polit Econ 100(5):966–991

Funk P (2005) Government action, social norms, and criminal behavior. J Inst Theor Econ 161:522–35

Gaviria A, Rapahel S (2001) School-based peer effects and juvenile behavior. Rev Econ Stat 83(2):257–268

Glaeser EL, Sacerdote B, Scheinkman JA (1996) Crime and social interaction. Q J Econ 111(2):507–548

Gottlieb NH, Eriksen MP, Lovato CY, Weinstein RP, Green LW (1990) Impact of a restrictive work site smoking policy on smoking behavior, attitudes, and norms. J Occup Med 32(1):16–23

Greif A (1993) Contract enforceability and economic institutions in early trade: The Maghribi Traders' Coalition. Am Econ Rev 83:525–548

Greif A (1994) Cultural beliefs and the organization of society: a historical and theoretical reflection on collectivist and individualist societies. J Polit Econ 102:912–950

Gruber J, Sen A, Stabile M (2003) Estimating price elasticities when there is smuggling: the sensitivity of smoking to price in Canada. J Health Econ 22:821–841

Haden K (1990) The demand for cigarettes in Japan. Am J Agric Econ 72(2):446–450

Hayami Y (2001) Development economics: from the poverty to the wealth of nations. Oxford University Press, New York

Huck S, Kosfeld M (2007) The dynamics of neighbourhood watch and norm enforcement. Econ J 117:270–286

Ida T, Goto R (2009a) Simultaneous measurement of time and risk preferences: stated preference discrete choice modeling analysis depending on smoking behavior. Int Econ Rev 50:1169–1182

Ida T, Goto R (2009b) Interdependency among addictive behaviours and time/risk preferences: discrete choice model analysis of smoking, drinking and gambling. J Econ Psychol 30:608–621

Jacobs J (1969) The economy of cities. Vintage, New York

Khwaja A, Sloan F, Salm M (2006a) Evidence on preferences and subjective beliefs of risk takers: the case of smokers. Int J Ind Organ 24:667–682

Khwaja A, Sloan F, Chung S (2006b) Learning about individual risk and decision to smoke. Int J Ind Organ 24:683–699

Kim S, Seldon BJ (2004) The demand for cigarettes in the Republic of Korea and implication for government policy to lower cigarette consumption. Contemp Econ Policy 22(2):299–308

Luo F, Abdel-Ghany M, Ogawa I (2003) Cigarette smoking in Japan: examination of myoptic and rational models of addictive behavior. J Fam Econ Iss 24(3):305–317

Manski CF (1993) Identification of endogenous social effects: the reflection problem. Rev Econ Stud 60:531–542

Posner RA, Rasmusen E (1999) Creating and enforcing norms, with special reference to sanction. Int Rev Law Econ 19:369–82

Powell LM, Tauras JA, Ross H (2005) The importance of peer effects, cigarette prices and tobacco control policies for youth smoking behavior. J Health Econ 24:950–968

Putnam R (2000) Bowling alone: the collapse and revival of American community. A Touchstone Book, New York

World Bank (1999) Economics of tobacco control, Country data online document available at www.worldbank.Org/tobacco/brieflist_db_print.asp

Yamamura E (2008a) The market for lawyers and social capital: are informal rules a substitute for formal ones? Rev Law Econ 4(1):23. doi: 10.2202/1555-5879.1295

Yamamura E (2008b) Impact of formal and informal deterrents on driving behavior. J Socio-Econ 37(6):2505–2512

Yamamura E (2009) Impact of formal and informal deterrents on crime. J Socio-Econ 38(4):611–621

Yamamura E (2011a) Effects of social norms and fractionalization on voting behavior in Japan. Appl Econ 43(11):1385–1398

Yamamura E (2011b) The effects of the social norm on cigarette consumption: evidence from Japan using panel data. Jpn World Econ 23(1):6–12

Yamamura E (2014) Smokers' sexual behavior and their satisfaction with family life. Soc Indic Res 118:1229–1247

Yorozu I, Zhou Y (2002) The demand of cigarettes in Japan: impact of information dissemination on cigarette consumption. Contemp Econ Policy 20(1):72–82

Yuanliang B, Zongyi Z (2005) Aggregate cigarette demand and regional differences in China. Appl Econ 37:2523–2528

Part III
Health

Chapter 12
Hyperbolic Discounting, the Sign Effect, and the Body Mass Index

Shinsuke Ikeda, Myong-Il Kang, and Fumio Ohtake

Abstract Analysis of a broad survey of Japanese adults confirms that time discounting relates to body weight, not only via impatience, but also via hyperbolic discounting, proxied by inclination toward procrastination, and the sign effect, where future negative payoffs are discounted at a lower rate than future positive payoffs. Body mass index is positively associated with survey responses indicative of impatience and hyperbolic discounting, and negatively associated with those indicative of the sign effect. A one-unit increase in the degree of procrastination is associated with a 2.81 percentage-point increase in the probability of being obese. Subjects exhibiting the sign effect show a 3.69 percentage-point lower probability of being obese and a 4.02 percentage-point higher probability of being underweight than those without the sign effect. These effects are substantial compared with the prevalence rates of the corresponding body mass status. Obesity and underweight thus result in part from the temporal decision biases.

Keywords Obesity • Hyperbolic discounting • Sign effect • BMI • Underweight • Discount rate

---

The original article first appeared in Journal of Health Economics 29:268–284, 2010. A newly written addendum has been added to this book chapter.

S. Ikeda (✉) • F. Ohtake
Institute of Social and Economic Research, Osaka University, 6-1 Mihogaoka, Ibaraki, Osaka 567-0047, Japan
e-mail: ikeda@iser.osaka-u.ac.jp; ohtake@iser.osaka-u.ac.jp

M.-I. Kang
Department of Business Administration, Korea University, 1-700 Ogawa-cho, Kodaira, Tokyo 187-8560, Japan
e-mail: mkang@korea-u.ac.jp

S. Ikeda et al. (eds.), *Behavioral Economics of Preferences, Choices, and Happiness*, DOI 10.1007/978-4-431-55402-8_12

1 Introduction

This chapter examines how interpersonal differences in the body mass index (hereafter, BMI), defined as weight in kilograms divided by height in meters squared (kg/m^2), are related to differences in time discounting, using data from a broad survey of Japanese adults. The focus is on the association of body mass not only with impatience, measured by the level of discount rates, but also with two behavioral properties of time discounting: hyperbolic discounting or the immediacy effect, where a person discounts his immediate future more intensely than his distant future, and the sign effect, where a person discounts positive payoffs more intensely than negative payoffs (e.g., Thaler 1981 and Benzion et al. 1989). To do so, we included questions in the survey that enabled us to measure the respondents' behavioral inclinations in time discounting.

We find that respondents' BMI is associated positively with the degree of impatience and negatively with the sign effect, where the significance levels are higher for the female sample than for the male sample. For example, an increase in impatience by one unit of the standard deviation is associated with an increase in BMI by 1.09 % of the BMI mean, a 2.28 percentage-point increase in the probability of being obese, and a 0.83 percentage-point decrease in the probability of being underweight. Subjects exhibiting the sign effect show a 3.69 percentage-point lower probability of being obese and a 4.02 percentage-point higher probability of being underweight than those without the sign effect. These marginal effects are substantial compared with the prevalence rates, i.e., the unconditional probabilities, of the corresponding body mass status (e.g., 18.92 % for obesity and 6.97 % for underweight).

We also show that survey responses indicating predilection toward procrastination, a proxy for hyperbolic discounting, have a significantly positive correlation with body mass. For example, a one-unit increase in the degree of procrastination is associated with a 2.81 percentage-point increase in the probability of being obese and a 0.92 percentage-point decrease in the probability of being underweight. The marginal impacts of procrastination on the probabilities of being obese, severely obese, and underweight are all more than 13 % of the corresponding unconditional probabilities. However, hyperbolic discounting estimated from monetary choice questions displays neither significant nor robust correlation with body mass.

When we consider the relation between body weight and time discounting, one interesting question is how underweight might be related to time discounting. Underweight has equally long-run harmful effects on health as overweight. We could thus expect that underweight people, as well as obese people, tend to be less patient than those with normal weight, and hence that the discount rate might be non-monotonically associated with body weight. The monotonic relation between time discounting and body mass that we detect implies that the theoretical prediction is not valid for our respondents.

Although many studies have reported empirically positive association between people's body mass and their time preference or discount rates (e.g., Komlos et al. 2004; Smith et al. 2005; Borghans and Golsteyn 2006), obesity might not be really problematic insofar as body mass is an optimal outcome of rational decision makings.[1] When body mass is determined by some distorted decision makings, obesity should be taken as a serious problem and be resolved by hard dieting and/or governments' policy intervention.

The novelty of this chapter is to incorporate relations between body mass and the behavioral biases in time discounting, caused by hyperbolic discounting and the sign effect. As Cutler et al. (2003) discuss, hyperbolic discounting leads people to procrastinate time-inconsistently in controlling their immediate appetite and to instead eat excessively cheap, fatty foods. The sign effect leads people to control caloric intake in order to avoid bearing the future psychological and monetary costs of obesity, such as the hardships of dieting, costs of having to buy new larger sized clothes, and medical services. This may actually induce underweight due to excessive dieting. Although the importance of the influence of the temporal decision biases has been recognized in the literature of health-related behaviors (e.g., Ainslie 2001; Cutler et al. 2003; and Khwaja et al. 2007), there is no previous study, to our knowledge, that examines directly how body mass is associated with the behavioral inclinations in time discounting. [2]

Komlos et al. (2004), examining international cross-sectional macro data, find that the prevalence rate of obesity in Western countries is negatively correlated with the national savings rate, a reverse proxy for national discount rates. Similarly, Smith et al. (2005), using cross-sectional data from a National Longitudinal Survey of Youth (NLSY) conducted in the U.S., report a significant negative correlation between BMI and savings, again, a reverse proxy for the discount rate. From Dutch survey data, Borghans and Golsteyn (2006) construct a variety of proxies for time discounting to show that the respondents' BMI is positively correlated with the discount rate proxies. However, the proxies used in those studies are somewhat unrefined. For example, savings may well depend on variables other than the discount rate, such as income, age, and especially hyperbolic discounting and the sign effect.

---

[1]Note, however, that associations between discount rates and body mass status do not necessarily imply "rational" obesity. People's time preferences may be controlled by external pressures from corporations. For example, fast food companies do not want people to wait until tomorrow to consume and will coerce them into having a high discount rate by using various advertisements.

[2]Shapiro (2005) shows that participants in low-income families who were provided food stamps by the U.S. government displayed less smoothed time profiles of caloric intake that are consistent with hyperbolic discounting. There are studies reporting that participations in the food stamp program is related to obesity (e.g., Chen et al. 2005). Combining these results implies that hyperbolic discounting may relate to the incidence of obesity. By showing empirically that obese people likely fail to use information and commitment devices to protect long-term heath, Scharff (2009) provides indirect evidences to the association between hyperbolic discounting and body mass formation.

To eliminate this problem, we construct two kinds of time preference data. First, by administering questionnaires on various intertemporal monetary choices, we obtain individuals' discount rates under alternative choice conditions. This enables us (i) to construct time preference data as a measure of impatience by computing the normalized mean of the elicited discount rates, and (ii) to construct indicator variables for hyperbolic discounting and the sign effect. Second, we construct a time preference proxy from the debt-holding data. This proxy is estimated as the residual after regressing debt holdings on hyperbolic discounting, the sign effect, and the determinants other than time preference. We also construct a proxy variable for hyperbolic discounting by measuring respondents' tendencies toward procrastination.

The remainder of the chapter is structured as follows. In Sect. 2, the relation between time discounting and caloric intake is discussed from the viewpoint of intertemporal decision making. In Sect. 3, after providing the definitions of body mass status including obesity and underweight, we explain our Japanese survey data and construct variables regarding body mass and time discounting that are used for empirical analysis. Section 4 shows the regression results. Finally, Sect. 5 concludes the chapter.

2 Time Discounting and Caloric Intake Behavior

When we make intertemporal decisions including those on caloric intake, the subjective discount rate plays a key role in determining how much of our resources we consume for present gratification and how much we save for future gratification. We hypothesize that interpersonal differences in BMI are, in part, related to differences in time discounting. To investigate the effects of time discounting on BMI and hence on the incidence of obesity, we consider three aspects of time discounting: (i) impatience, (ii) hyperbolic discounting, and (iii) the sign effect.

2.1 Impatience

A higher subjective discount rate, i.e., a higher degree of impatience, implies a stronger preference for present consumption relative to future consumption. In advanced countries, where the costs of caloric intake in terms of both money and time are so low that nutrition and calories required for subsistence are easily obtainable, those with less patience would tend to have higher BMI values and a higher probability of being obese. As in Komlos et al. (2004) and Smith et al. (2005), we hypothesize that persons with higher discount rates tend to have greater body mass.

2.2 *Hyperbolic Discounting*

As a stylized fact, it has often been reported that people have high discount rates for very short horizons but have considerably lower discount rates for longer horizons (e.g., Thaler 1981; Benzion et al. 1989). This implies that people are less patient in immediate future choices than in distant future choices. Since the resulting discount factor is better described by a hyperbolic function of time than by an exponential one, the phenomenon is referred to as hyperbolic discounting.

Hyperbolic discounters make time-inconsistent choices with regard to dieting and health care. They overeat, which harms their long-term health and body shape (e.g., Ainslie 2001). Cutler et al. (2003) argue that reductions in the cost of food due to recent technological advance have accelerated this time-inconsistent overeating, which may account for the increased prevalence of obesity. Chapman (1995) also points out that hyperbolic discounting gives rise to underinvestment in health capital. We hypothesize that persons with a stronger tendency toward hyperbolic discounting will tend to have a greater body mass.

2.3 *The Sign Effect*

Many studies have reported that losses are discounted at a lower rate than gains. For example, Thaler (1981) finds that the discount rates for gains were 3–10 times higher than those for losses. The evaluations of Loewenstein's (1987) subjects reveal that they are indifferent as regards either receiving $100 immediately or receiving $157 in a year; they are also indifferent as regards either losing $100 immediately or losing $133 in a year. This gain-loss asymmetry is referred to as the sign effect.

The sign effect makes people reluctant to borrow because persons who operate under this effect require a more favorable (i.e., lower) interest rate to borrow than they would to save (e.g., Loewenstein and Prelec 1992). Similarly, the sign effect induces people to control food consumption and avoid the future costs of obesity, such as the hardships associated with dieting and the costs of obesity-related medical care. We hypothesize that persons whose time preferences exhibit the sign effect are likely to have smaller body mass.

In sum, we hypothesize that body weight is associated positively with impatience and hyperbolic discounting, and negatively with the sign effect. However, since being underweight has a commonly detrimental effect on long-run health as being overweight, these hypotheses might be inconsistent with traditional theory. Underweight respondents who care more about being thin now than being ill in the future would be less patient than those with normal body weight. Respondents with a high discount rate could thus be either underweight or overweight, so that the discount rate might be related to BMI in a U-shaped manner. Similarly, hyperbolic discounting and the sign effect could have non-monotonic associations with BMI. In Appendix A.1, by conducting a multinomial regression analysis, we show that such a non-monotonic association is not actually observed between body mass and time discounting. We thus conduct the main analysis below based on the assumption that associations between body mass and time discounting, if present, are monotonic.

3 The Data

Our empirical research is based on the Japan Household Survey on Consumer Preferences and Satisfaction 2005 (hereinafter, JHS05), a survey that the authors conducted in February 2005. We carried out this survey as part of the Osaka University COE program, supported by the Ministry of Education, Culture, Sports, and Science and Technology. This is a household survey, in which we randomly selected 6,000 Japanese respondents older than 20 years of age and asked them to fill out questionnaires. Out of the 6,000, 2,987 responded. The proportion of male respondents was 47.0 %, with the average age of the respondents being 49.080. We included in the survey various questions to elicit information about the respondents' attitudes toward time discounting and risk; their demographic, social, and economic attributes; and their health status including height and weight.

3.1 Definitions of Obesity, Severe Obesity, and Underweight

In Japan, as in other advanced countries, the number of obese individuals has been increasing, resulting in increased social costs including those of health care. However, one distinctive feature in Japan is that in addition to obese individuals, underweight individuals, too, are widely observed. According to the National Survey of Health and Nutrition 2004 (hereinafter, NSHN04), conducted by Japan's Ministry of Health, Labour and Welfare, the prevalence rate of obesity in Japanese adults amounts to nearly 30 % for males and 20 % for females. On the other hand, nearly 5 % of adult males and 10 % of adult females are underweight. In particular, the prevalence rate of underweight individuals among females in their 20s exceeds 20 %.

While the international criterion for obesity provided by the World Health Organization (WHO) is that a person has a BMI ≥ 30, the Examination Committee of Criteria for "Obesity Disease in Japan", affiliated with the Japan Society for the Study of Obesity (JSSO), provided in 2000 a new criterion specific to Japan,[3] according to which a person is regarded as obese if he or she has a BMI ≥ 25 (see Table 12.1). The JSSO criterion is based on the scientific findings that (i) the average number of obesity-related disorders exceeds 1.0 at a BMI of 25, with a progressive

[3]For the English-language version of the report, see Examination Committee (2002).

Table 12.1 Definitions of obesity and underweight

<table>
<tr><th>BMI</th><th>WHO criteria</th><th>JSSO criteria</th><th colspan="2">This paper</th></tr>
<tr><td>BMI <18.5</td><td>Underweight</td><td>Underweight</td><td colspan="2">Underweight</td></tr>
<tr><td>18.5 ≤ BMI < 25</td><td>Normal range</td><td>Normal range</td><td colspan="2">Normal range</td></tr>
<tr><td>BMI = 22</td><td>Standard (ideal)</td><td>Standard (ideal)</td><td colspan="2">Standard (ideal)</td></tr>
<tr><td>25 ≤ BMI < 30</td><td>Preobese</td><td>Obese (degree1)</td><td rowspan="4">Obese</td><td></td></tr>
<tr><td>30 ≤ BMI < 35</td><td>Obese (class I)</td><td>Obese (degree2)</td><td rowspan="3">Severe-obese</td></tr>
<tr><td>35 ≤ BMI < 40</td><td>Obese (class II)</td><td>Obese (degree3)</td></tr>
<tr><td>40 ≤ BMI</td><td>Obese (class III)</td><td>Obese (degree3)</td></tr>
</table>

Note: The JSSO criteria are based on The Examination Committee of Criteria for Obesity Disease in Japan (2002)

increase in such disorders for a BMI ≥ 25, and (ii) in screening tests, the sensitivity and specificity for detecting subjects with multiple disorder-risk factors display the best trade-off at a cut-off BMI of 25.[4,5] Since then, research on the health of Japanese people as well as on the medical care policy of the Japanese government has been conducted based on the JSSO criterion.

We define obesity, therefore, as a condition where a person has a BMI ≥ 25 and severe obesity as a condition where a person has a BMI ≥ 30. Similarly, individuals with a BMI < 18.5 are classified as being underweight. A BMI of 22, at which the probability of diseases becomes minimal, is regarded as standard or ideal.[6]

3.2 BMI

From the JHS05 data on height and weight, we computed each respondent's BMI. Table 12.2 provides the by-gender summary statistics of the respondents' body mass indices. Note that the JHS05 data are self-reported, and hence the BMI data may contain underreporting bias (see, e.g., Cawley 2004; Chou et al. 2004). The

[4]The use of the WHO criterion for Asian populations has been criticized since Asian populations have a high body fat deposit at a lower BMI than Caucasians, and type 2 diabetes mellitus and cardiovascular diseases are prevalent even with a BMI lower than 25 in Asian countries. For detailed discussions, see Low et al. (2009).

[5]The same obesity criterion as that of JSSO was provided for Asian populations by the International Association for the Study of Obesity and the International Obesity Task Force (2000). See also WHO Expert Consultation (2004), which advised further study on appropriate ethnic-specific BMI cut-off points.

[6]The JSSO criteria for underweight (BMI < 18.5) and ideal weight (BMI = 22), which are the same as the corresponding WHO criteria, are based on the research by Tokunaga et al. (1991). By using the sample of the Japanese adults, they estimated quadratic regression curves relating BMI to morbidity, thereby showing that (i) the BMI value associated with the lowest morbidity was 22.2 for males and 21.9 for females, and (ii) the morbidity rates at a BMI of 18.5 are as high as those at a BMI of 25.

Table 12.2 Summary statistics of the respondents' body mass in JHS05

		Male	Female
BMI	Means	23.347	21.938
	S.D.	3.119	2.962
Prevalence rates	Underweight	0.042	0.095
	Obesity	0.240	0.143
	Severe obesity	0.029	0.015
Obs.		1,369	1,501

BMI means in the JHS05 sample are smaller than those in the NSHN04 data, which were actually measured in 2004. For example, the females' mean BMI in the JHS05 equals 21.94, which is significantly smaller than the corresponding mean BMI of 22.37 in NSHN04.[7] Notwithstanding the concerns about self-reporting bias, we shall conduct the main analysis below by using the original self-reported JHS05 data.[8] In Appendix A.2, we show that our main results are robust even when adjusting for self-reporting bias by using the by-age distribution of actually measured BMI in NSHN04.

3.3 *Time Discounting*

3.3.1 Eliciting Discount Rates

In JHS05, we measured the respondents' discount rates by asking five questions on intertemporal choice under alternative conditions. As in previous surveys (e.g., Harrison et al. 2002; Borghans and Golsteyn 2006), we told the respondents to choose between two options, "A" and "B." For example, we asked them to choose between "A" – receiving in 2 days JPY 10,000 (around USD 95.35 using the conversion rate [104.88] in February 2005), and "B" – receiving in 9 days JPY 10,000 plus a certain amount of JPY α, say JPY 10,038 (around USD 95.71). Here, choosing the delayed receipt "B" instead of "A" implies receiving 20 % of the

[7]For detailed comparison between the body mass distributions of JHS05 and NSHN04, see Tables 12.15 through 12.18 in Appendix A.2.

[8]Following Cawley (2004), Chou et al. (2004) corrected for the underreporting biases in the original self-reported data by (1) estimating the quadratic relations between actual and self-reported values of weight and height using the Third National Health and Nutrition Examination Survey (NHANES III), U.S.A., and (2) applying the estimated relations to their American self-reported data (the BRFSS) pertaining to weight and height to obtain bias-corrected data and to compute bias-corrected BMI. Michaud et al. (2007) applied the quadratic correction function estimated by Burkhauser and Cawley (2008) to their European self-reported data. In Japan, we have no data set that, like NHANES III, is composed of self-reported as well as actually measured data of the same subjects. Furthermore, it might be questionable to directly apply Burkhauser and Cawley's (2008) estimated correction function to the Japanese data because the BMI distribution in Japan and the definition of obesity therein both differ from those in Western countries.

Table 12.3 Question to elicit discount rates: an example (QUESTION 1 for DR1) QUESTION 1. Suppose you have two options to receive some money. You may choose Option "A", to receive 10,000 JPY in two days; or Option "B", to receive a different amount in nine days. Compare the amounts and timing in Option "A" with Option "B" and indicate which amount you would prefer to receive for each of all 8 choices

Option A – Receipt in 2 days	Option B – Receipt in 9 days	Interest rate (Annual) (%)	Circle A or B	
JPY 10,000 (USD 95.35)	JPY 9,981 (USD 95.17)	−10	A	B
JPY 10,000 (USD 95.35)	JPY 10,000 (USD 95.35)	0	A	B
JPY 10,000 (USD 95.35)	JPY 10,019 (USD 95.53)	10	A	B
JPY 10,000 (USD 95.35)	JPY 10,038 (USD 95.71)	20	A	B
JPY 10,000 (USD 95.35)	JPY 10,096 (USD 96.26)	50	A	B
JPY 10,000 (USD 95.35)	JPY 10,191 (USD 97.17)	100	A	B
JPY 10,000 (USD 95.35)	JPY 10,383 (USD 99.00)	200	A	B
JPY 10,000 (USD 95.35)	JPY 10,574 (USD 100.82)	300	A	B

Note: This is a question in the Japan Household Survey on Consumer Preferences and Satisfaction, 2005. The US dollar amounts are computed by using the average JPY/USD exchange rate, 104.88, in February, 2005

annual interest rate. In each question, we posed eight such queries with alternative α values (from small to large) and hence with alternative imputed interest rates (from low to high).

Table 12.3 represents the query QUESTION 1, where the amount received under option "A" is specified as JPY 10,000 and the imputed interest rate for option "B" changes from −10 to 300 %. We expected the respondents to choose option "A" at low interest rates, but as the imputed interest rate rises, expected they would ultimately switch to option "B" at a certain critical high rate. The individual respondents' discount rates can be inferred by estimating the interest rate at which respondents are indifferent as to the delayed receipt of option "B" or the more immediate receipt of option "A" Note, however, that the elicited discount rates are associated with the particular choice conditions, for example, 2 days versus 9 days, and the amount of JPY 10,000 for option "A" in QUESTION 1.

To detect various tendencies in time discounting, we developed five questions by controlling for (i) money amounts for option "A" – JPY 10,000 (around USD 95.35) or JPY 1 million (around USD 95,347); (ii) time horizons for "A" – 2 days, 1 month, or 90 days; (iii) time delays – 7 days or 12 months; and (iv) receipt or payment. In the "payment" question, QUESTION 5, we asked the respondents to choose either "A" – paying JPY 1 million in 1 month or "B" – paying JPY 1 million + some amount in 13 months, from which we elicited acceptable interest rate payments to ask for postponing a 1 million payment for 12 months.

From each question, we obtain raw response data, which indicate the interest rates between which each respondent switched his or her choice from option "A" to "B." Some subjects, however, stuck to option "A" regardless of the interest rates that were offered. To elicit the respondents' discount rates from these data,[9] we follow Kimball et al. (2005) in estimating a log-normal distribution for the cross-respondent distribution of gross discount rates. From the estimated distribution, we estimated each respondent's gross discount rate for a certain question table as an expected value, conditional on the respondent's changing his/her choice between certain interest rates. The descriptive statistics of the elicited discount rates, together with the choice conditions under which they are elicited, are summarized in Table 12.4, where DR_i $(i = 1, \ldots, 5)$ represent the discount rates that we estimated from responses to QUESTION *i*.

To investigate the associations of body mass with impatience, we construct DISCRATE, which represents the simple average of the standardized values of the elicited discount rates DR_i $(i = 1, \ldots, 5)$:

$$\mathrm{DISCRATE} = \frac{1}{5}\sum_{i=1}^{5} \frac{(\mathrm{DR}_i - E(\mathrm{DR}_i))}{\sigma(\mathrm{DR}_i)}, \tag{12.1}$$

where E (•) and σ (•) represent sample means and standard deviations. For $E(\mathrm{DR}_i)$ and $\sigma(\mathrm{DR}_i)$, see Table 12.4. Table 12.5 summarizes the definitions of variables that we use in the analysis below as well as their basic statistics.[10] We hypothesize that the respondents' body mass is associated positively with the impatience index DISCRATE.[11]

3.3.2 Hyperbolic Discounting and the Sign Effect

By comparing the mean values of the elicited discount rates, we can examine whether our average respondent displays either hyperbolic discounting or the sign effect. First, hyperbolic discounting or the immediacy effect is not observed on average since the mean of the discount rate DR_1, imputed from the immediate future choice (i.e., 2 days or 9 days), is not significantly higher than DR_2, which is applied to a more distant future choice (i.e., 90 days or 97 days). Second, the

[9]Some respondents switched their choices between "A" and "B" more than once. As in the literature (e.g., Harrison et al. 2002), we removed those data from the sample.

[10]Although the standardized average DISCRATE of the elicited discount rates should theoretically satisfy $E(\mathrm{DISCRATE}) = 0$ and $\sigma(\mathrm{DISCRATE}) = 1$, neither of the equalities is fulfilled, as seen in Table 12.5. This is due to the fact that the number of effective responses differs in the five discount rate questions.

[11]Instead of DISCRATE, we also tried for an alternative impatience index factor scores to the first factor that was extracted by factor analysis from the discount rate data. Although our main results did not change qualitatively, the significance levels were slightly weakened compared with the case in which DISCRATE is used for the impatience variable.

Table 12.4 Elicited discount rates under alternative choice conditions

		DR_1	DR_2	DR_3	DR_4	DR_5
Choice conditions	Timings ((A) or (B))	2 days or 9 days	90 days or 97 days	1 month or 13 months	1 month or 13 months	1 month or 13 months
	Amounts for (A)	JPY 10,000 (USD 95.374)	JPY 10,000 (USD 95.374)	JPY 10,000 (USD 95.374)	JPY 1million (USD 9534.70)	JPY 1million (USD 9534.70)
	Receipt or payment	Receipt	Receipt	Receipt	Receipt	Payment
Descriptive statistics	Mean	1.904	1.892	0.153	0.023	−0.008
	Median	0.741	0.741	0.080	0.008	0.001
	S.D.	2.390	2.421	0.193	0.042	0.044
	Obs.	2,737	2,768	2,790	2,771	2,331
Time discounting properties (*P*-value)		Hyperbolic discounting: DR1 > DR2 (0.426)			Sign effect: DR4 > DR5 (0.00)	

Note: The data are from the Japan Household Survey on Consumer Preferences and Satisfaction, 2005. The USD amounts are computed by using the average JPY/USD exchange rate, 104.88, in February, 2005

Table 12.5 Definitions of variables and basic statistics

Variables	Definition	Mean	S.D.	Obs.
BMI	Body mass index, defined as weight in kilograms divided by height in meters squared (kg/m^2)	22.610	3.128	2,870
OBESITY	A binary indicator for obesity which equals 1 if BMI $\geq$ 25 and 0 otherwise	0.189	0.392	2,870
SEVERE OBESITY	A binary indicator for severe obesity which equals 1 if BMI $\geq$ 30 and 0 otherwise	0.022	0.147	2,870
UNDERWEIGHT	A binary indicator for underweight which equals 1 if BMI $<$ 18.5 and 0 otherwise	0.070	0.255	2,870
DISCRATE	Simple mean, defined by Eq. (12.1), of the standardized values of the elicited discount rates DR_i ($i = 1,\ldots,5$) as a measure of the degree of impatience	0.042	0.688	2,202
DEBTIMP	A proxy of the degree of impatience, measured by standardized residuals of debt holding DEBT after regressing it on explanatory variables other than the degree of impatience (see the first regression in Table 12.6)	0.000	1.000	1,704
HYPERBOL	A binary indicator for hyperbolic discounting which equals 1 if $DR_1 > DR_2$, and 0 otherwise.	0.621	0.485	2,694
PROCR	Response to the question 'When did you do homework assignments in the summer vacation in your high school days?' on a 5-point scale, from 1 (homework was finished at 'the beginning of the vacation') to 5 (it was not done until 'the very end of the vacation'), which is a proxy measure of the degree of procrastination.	3.282	1.300	2,910
SIGN	A binary indicator for the sign effect which equals 1 if $DR_4 > DR_5$, and 0 otherwise	0.885	0.319	2,289
RISKAV	A variable which measures the degree of risk aversion, constructed by subtracting from 100 the respondents' responses to the question: "When you go out, how high probability of rainfall makes you bring an umbrella with you?"	0.505	0.205	2,941
MALE	A binary indicator for males which equals 1 for male respondents and 0 otherwise	0.470	0.499	2,987
UNIV	A binary indicator for university graduates which equals 1 for university graduates and 0 otherwise	0.204	0.403	2,893
AGE	Ages of respondents	49.080	12.968	2,983
DEBT	A binary indicator for debt holding other than morgages which equals 1 for debt holders and 0 otherwise.	0.251	0.434	2,806
INCOME	Per capita household income in million yen (USD values)	2.213 (21,100)	1.583 (15,093)	2,361
ΔINCOME	The expected percentage change of income in a forthcoming year, estimated from responses to the question: 'What is the expected percentage of change in your whole household income this year?'	−0.948	3.914	2,707
WORKHOUR	Work hours for a week	27.191	22.922	2,879
SMOKING	A ordered variable indicating the strength of smoking habits on a 6-point scale, from 1 (smoking no cigarette a day) to 6 (smoking more than two packages of cigarettes a day)	2.125	1.713	2,972

discount rate DR_4 applied to future receipts is significantly higher than DR_5, the discount rate used for discounting future payments. This implies that our average respondent displays the sign effect.[12]

To examine the associations of body mass with the two behavioral properties in time discounting, we construct the binary indicator HYPERBOL for hyperbolic discounting, and the binary indicator SIGN for the sign effect, where, for example, HYPERBOL = 1 if $DR_1 > DR_2$, and HYPERBOL = 0 otherwise. From the mean values of HYPERBOL and SIGN, shown in Table 12.5, the proportions of respondents who display hyperbolic discounting and the sign effect are, respectively, 61.1 and 88.5 %.[13]

Our hypothesis is that, *ceteris paribus*, the respondents' body mass is positively related to HYPERBOL and negatively related to SIGN.

3.3.3 Alternative Proxies for Impatience and Procrastination

Besides DISCRATE and HYPERBOL, we construct alternative proxy variables for impatience (DEBTIMP) and hyperbolic discounting (PROCR). To measure respondents' degrees of hyperbolic discounting or procrastination, we asked them to indicate, on a 5-point scale ranging from 1 to 5, what used to be the extent of their tendency to procrastinate over homework assignments during school vacations.[14] Variable PROCR represents the response data to this question, wherein a larger value implies a stronger inclination toward procrastination or hyperbolic discounting.

As an alternative proxy for the degree of impatience, we estimate DEBTIMP from the respondents' debt holding behavior. In the JHS05, we asked the respondents to indicate whether they have debts other than mortgages. Let DEBT denotes a binary indicator for the debt holding. Intertemporal consumption theory predicts that the debt holding variable DEBT to be associated with time discounting in three ways: via (i) impatience, where high impatience implies a high probability of debt holdings, (ii) hyperbolic discounting, which causes people to save less, leading to

---

[12] In addition, although we have not included the results of the *t* test in Table 12.4, DR_3, the discount rate for JPY 10,000 is significantly higher than DR_4, applied for JPY 1 million, implying that people are more patient in the case of larger amounts than in the case of smaller amounts. This tendency is called the magnitude effect (e.g., Benzion et al. 1989; Frederick et al. 2002).

[13] Although the means of DR_1 and DR_2 do not differ greatly, the mean of HYPERBOL is high (61.1 %). This is because, even when in the corresponding two choice tables like Table 12.3, a respondent's choice switches from "A" to "B" at the same step, say, when the implied interest rate moves from 20 to 50 %, the estimate of DR_1, obtained by the method of Kimball et al. (2005), is larger than that of DR_2, reflecting the fact that the average respondents switch from "A" to "B" at a higher interest rate.

[14] In Japanese elementary and high schools, students are usually given many homework assignments during vacations.

Table 12.6 Time discounting and debt holdings

Dependent variable: DEBT	Marginal effects (t-value)	Marginal effects (t-value)
DISCRATE		0.085 (5.434)***
PROCR	0.015 (1.819)*	0.013 (1.617)
SIGN	−0.057 (−1.724)*	−0.066 (−1.892)*
RISKAV	−0.174 (−3.342)***	−0.174 (−3.228)***
UNIV	−0.054 (−2.141)**	−0.062 (−2.429)**
AGE	0.021 (3.315)***	0.021 (3.227)***
AGE^2	0.000 (−4.000)***	0.000 (−3.935)***
INCOME	−0.036 (−2.168)**	−0.043 (−2.441)**
INCOME^2	0.004 (2.337)**	0.006 (2.708)***
ΔINCOME	−0.006 (−2.099)**	−0.007 (−2.440)**
Log likelihood	−928.902	−875.692
#obs	1,704	1,640

Note: The probability of debt holding is estimated by using binary probit models
*, **, *** Statistical significance at the 10 %, 5 %, and 1 % levels, respectively

excessive debt holding (see Laibson 1997, 1998), and (iii) the sign effect, which makes people reluctant to pay interest in the future, thereby inducing "borrowing aversion" behavior (see Loewenstein and Prelec 1992).

Impatience proxy DEBTIMP is the standardized residual of Prob (DEBT = 1) after regressing it using a probit model on the following: PROCR, as a proxy for (ii); SIGN, the binary indicator for (iii); and other control variables capturing the degree of risk aversion (RISKAV), per-capita household income (INCOME and INCOME squared), the expected percentage change of income in a forthcoming year (ΔINCOME), and ages (AGE and AGE squared). We construct the risk aversion index RISKAV by subtracting from 100 % the respondents' responses to the question "When you go out, how high a probability of rainfall makes you carry an umbrella?"

Table 12.6 shows the results of the first stage probit regression for Prob (DEBT = 1) and those of the regression in which impatience variable DISCRATE is introduced to the set of explanatory variables. As shown in the second column, which reports the result of the first probit model without DISCRATE as a regressor, the marginal effects for all the explanatory variables are statistically significant. In particular, as predicted by theory, debt holding is positively related to the tendency to procrastinate PROCR, and negatively related to the sign effect SIGN, and both coefficients are significant at the 10 % level. As seen in the third column of the table, the result is robust, except that the P-value for PROCR becomes a little lower than 10 % when we introduce, as an impatience measure, the standardized mean of the elicited discount rates DISCRATE to the set of explanatory variables.[15]

[15]This is probably because of multicollinearity between DISCRATE and PROCR.

Table 12.7 Correlations between impatience proxy (DEBTIMP) and elicited discount rates

	DISCRATE	DR_1	DR_2	DR_3	DR_4	DR_5
DEBTIMP	0.137	0.091	0.071	0.115	0.110	0.080
(*t*-values)	(5.583)***	(3.711)***	(2.919)***	(4.762)***	(4.555)***	(3.325)***

Note: Impatience proxy DEBTIMP is constructed from standardized residuals of the binary probit estimation of the probability of debt holding (see the first result in Table 12.6)
*** Statistical significance at the 1 % level

The proxy DEBTIMP for impatience is constructed by standardizing the residuals of the first regression model, that is, the model that does not include the impatience variable as a regressor. To check the relevancy of using DEBTIMP as an impatience proxy, Table 12.7 examines correlations of DEBTIMP with the elicited individual discount rates and DISCRATE. In fact, the impatience proxy shows highly significant positive correlation with each of the respondent's discount rates and DISCRATE. This is consistent with the impatience measure DISCRATE having a positive and highly significant correlation with debt holdings.[16]

4 Results

We estimate two regression models (1) and (2). In model (1), we use time discounting variables elicited from hypothetical intertemporal monetary choices, namely, DISCRATE, HYPERBOL, and SIGN. Due to a domain effect, however, the time discounting variables constructed from hypothetical monetary choices might not succeed in capturing the correlation between time discounting and BMI.[17] Thus, instead, model (2) regresses body mass variables including BMI on the proxies for time discounting, namely, DEBTIMP for impatience and PROCR for hyperbolic discounting (procrastination). The indicator SIGN is common to the two models.

The two regression models are estimated first in a basic specification, where only the three time discounting variables are included as explanatory variables, and then, in a second specification, where control variables for other personal attributes are also included. In the second specification, the controls include (i) the degree of risk aversion RISKAV; (ii) demographic factors, including gender (MALE),

[16]We also conducted the same analysis by using the money amount data of debt, instead of the debt holding dummy DEBT. The results including those of body mass regressions below were very similar to the case of DEBT, except that the negative correlation between debt and the sign effect was insignificant, unlike in Table 12.6, when the debt amount was used.

[17]For example, Chapman (1995) reports that monetary discount rates do not have a strong explanatory power for intertemporal choices regarding health investments. In fact, in Borghans and Golsteyn (2006), monetary discount rates elicited from hypothetical pecuniary choices do not display as strong correlations with BMI as do other impatience proxies that are constructed from responses to behavioral and/or psychological questions.

education (UNIV), and age (AGE), where MALE and UNIV are binary indicators for males and university graduates, respectively; (iii) economic factors such as per-capita household income (INCOME) and working hours (WORKHOUR), where, to control for possible non-monotonic correlations, AGE squared, INCOME squared, and the square root of WORKHOUR are also added; and (iv) smoking habits SMOKING, which indicates the strength of the respondents' smoking habit on a 6-point scale.[18]

The regressions are conducted in the full, male, and female samples. The OLS method is used for the BMI regressions and the binary probit method is used to estimate the probabilities of being obese, severely obese, and underweight.[19]

4.1 BMI

Panels (a) and (b) of Table 12.8 summarize the results of the OLS regressions for BMI. In model (1) (see panel (a)), BMI displays, in either specification, with or without control variables, significantly positive correlation with impatience (DISCRATE) for the full sample and significantly negative correlation with the sign effect (SIGN) for the female sample. In the full sample, for example, a discount rate that exceeds the average by one unit of standard deviation (SD), with all other personal attributes being equal, leads to a BMI that is around 0.273 higher than the average. In this sample, the BMI of the average respondent who displays the sign effect is around 0.550 smaller than that of respondents who do not display the sign effect. However, correlation with HYPERBOL is either wrong in sign or insignificant. Although HYPERBOL has a significant, negative coefficient in the female sample under the attribute-uncontrolled specification, it turns positive and insignificant when other personal attributes are controlled for. As a whole, in model (1), expected correlations with impatience and the sign effect are present in the full and female samples, respectively, but expected correlations with hyperbolic discounting are not evident.[20]

---

[18]Smoking suppresses appetite and reduces BMI (e.g., Michaud et al. 2007). As is often stressed in the literature (e.g., Becker and Murphy 1988; Khwaja et al. 2007), less patient people are likely to smoke more since the future loss caused by smoking is likely to be discounted more intensely. Unless the smoking habit is controlled for, true positive correlation between BMI and impatience, if present, might be underestimated due to the confounding negative correlation via smoking. The same logic is also true for the correlations of BMI with hyperbolic discounting and the sign effect. By reporting the regression results for BMI when smoking is not controlled for, Appendix A.3 shows that these predictions hold fairly valid.

[19]Even when the effects of the regional and occupational differences are controlled for by adding the prefecture and occupation dummies to the set of the explanatory variables, the main results do not change substantially. See Ikeda et al. (2009).

[20]Our data of time discounting variables contain measurement errors due to decision errors (see, e.g., the special issue of Experimental Economics, introduced by Starmer and Bardsley 2005). Especially the measurement errors of HYPERBOL and SIGN might be magnified as they are

In model (2) (see panel (b) of Table 12.8), in contrast, BMI displays fairly significant correlations with all three time discounting variables in both specifications, with and without controls. In particular, for the full and female samples, the coefficients of all the time discounting variables, namely, impatience (DEBTIMP), procrastination or hyperbolic discounting (PROCR), and the sign effect (SIGN),

Table 12.8 OLS regressions of BMI

(a) Model (1)						
	Uncontrolled			Controlled		
	All	Male	Female	All	Male	Female
DISCRATE	0.383*** (3.07)	0.300* (1.68)	0.152 (0.90)	0.273** (2.03)	0.276 (1.42)	0.256 (1.36)
HYPERBOL	−0.084 (−0.48)	0.142 (0.55)	−0.398* (−1.74)	0.105 (0.57)	0.177 (0.65)	0.014 (0.06)
SIGN	−0.229 (−1.08)	0.066 (0.21)	−0.500* (−1.83)	−0.550** (−2.40)	−0.300 (−0.86)	−0.723** (−2.40)
RISKAV				−0.659* (−1.81)	−0.972* (−1.87)	−0.465 (−0.90)
MALE				1.301*** (7.19)		
UNIV				−0.118 (−0.65)	−0.256 (−1.08)	0.059 (0.20)
AGE				0.238*** (5.47)	0.230*** (3.51)	0.235*** (3.87)
AGE^2				−0.002*** (−4.64)	−0.002*** (−3.24)	−0.002*** (−2.92)
INCOME				−0.257** (−2.30)	−0.130 (−0.88)	−0.518*** (−2.60)
INCOME^2				0.038*** (3.00)	0.026* (1.73)	0.067** (2.53)
WORKHOUR				0.030** (2.22)	0.008 (0.43)	0.037* (1.73)
WORKHOUR ^(1/2)				−0.202** (−2.04)	−0.032 (−0.21)	−0.264* (−1.85)
SMOKING				−0.055 (−1.20)	−0.046 (−0.82)	−0.097 (−1.16)
Constant	22.828*** (97.68)	23.165*** (66.5)	22.582*** (75.79)	17.019*** (17.01)	18.705*** (12.97)	17.103*** (12.15)
Adj. R^2	0.008	0.000	0.008	0.094	0.021	0.079
#obs	2,118	1,026	1,092	1,658	818	840

(continued)

constructed based on the differences of two discount rates. The weakness of the results regarding HYPERBOL may be partially attributable to underestimation bias due to measurement errors.

Table 12.8 (continued)

(b) Model (2)

	Uncontrolled			Controlled		
	All	Male	Female	All	Male	Female
DEBTIMP	0.232*** (3.12)	0.136 (1.31)	0.306*** (3.02)	0.246*** (3.40)	0.167 (1.57)	0.314*** (3.20)
PROCR	0.280*** (4.89)	0.179** (2.12)	0.187** (2.42)	0.217*** (3.80)	0.179** (2.08)	0.240*** (3.18)
SIGN	−0.366 (−1.58)	−0.202 (−0.61)	−0.532* (−1.70)	−0.490** (−2.16)	−0.165 (−0.49)	−0.743** (−2.45)
RISKAV				−0.815** (−2.24)	−0.992* (−1.93)	−0.725 (−1.41)
MALE				1.212*** (6.62)		
UNIV				−0.137 (−0.75)	−0.247 (−1.05)	−0.046 (−0.16)
AGE				0.238*** (5.44)	0.226*** (3.47)	0.242*** (3.97)
AGE^2				−0.002*** (−4.54)	−0.002*** (−3.18)	−0.002*** (−2.97)
INCOME				−0.271** (−2.35)	−0.105 (−0.68)	−0.604*** (−3.03)
INCOME^2				0.037*** (2.80)	0.021 (1.34)	0.076*** (2.86)
WORKHOUR				0.027* (1.95)	0.004 (−0.21)	0.048 (2.20)
WORKHOUR^(1/2)				−0.184* (−1.85)	0.056 (0.36)	−0.337** (−2.31)
SMOKING				−0.068 (−1.48)	−0.041 (−0.74)	−0.149* (−1.76)
Constant	22.036*** (77.01)	22.861*** (53.79)	21.851*** (58.10)	16.458*** (16.18)	18.063*** (12.34)	16.537*** (11.65)
Adj. R^2	0.019	0.004	0.018	0.102	0.023	0.110
#obs	1,670	840	830	1,629	812	817

Notes: *, **, *** Statistical significance at the 10 %, 5 %, and 1 % levels, respectively

have the expected signs and are highly significant in the attribute-controlled specification. The coefficients of procrastination are significantly positive in all the regressions of model (2), including the male sample.

Those correlations of BMI with the time discounting variables are illustrated by Figs. 12.1 and 12.2. Figure 12.1 depicts the means of attribute-nonadjusted and -adjusted BMI in the quintiles stratified by the values of impatience proxy DEBTIMP. In either case, the BMI means are shown to be positively associated with impatience. Figure 12.2 computes the BMI means stratified by whether the sign effect is present or not, and whether PROCR =5 (strong HD: strong hyperbolic discounting) or PROCR $\leq$4 (weak HD), where other personal attributes are nonadjusted for in

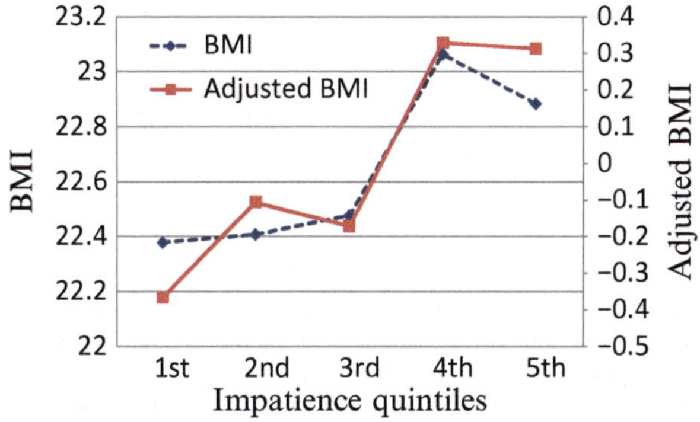

Fig. 12.1 BMI means in impatience quintiles. Note: In the full sample, BMI means are compared in quintiles stratified by the degree of impatience DEBTIMP. "1st" represents the most patient quintile whereas "the 5th" the least patient. "Adjusted BMI" represents BMI which is adjusted for personal attributes, other than impatience, which are incorporated in model 2

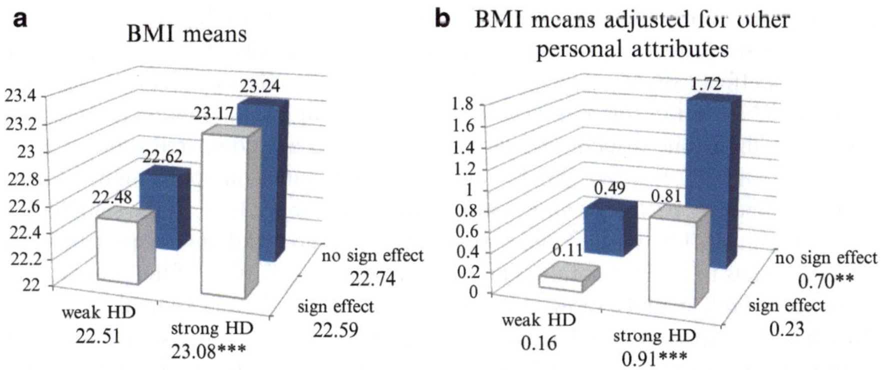

Fig. 12.2 BMI with/without hyperbolic discounting (procrastination) and the sign effect. Note: In the full sample, BMI means are compared among subsamples stratified by the degree of hyperbolic discounting and the incidence of the sign effect. "Strong HD" represents strong hyperbolic discounting with PROCR = 5; and "weak HD" weak hyperbolic discounting with PROCR < 5. In panel (**b**), BMI values are adjusted for personal attributes including impatience (DEBTIMP). *, **, *** Statistical significance at the 10 %, 5 %, and 1 % levels, respectively, in the t-tests of mean differences between respective pairs of subsamples

panel (a) and adjusted for in panel (b). These figures both show clearly positive associations between BMI and hyperbolic discounting and negative associations between BMI and the sign effect.

To quantitatively evaluate the associations of BMI with the time discounting variables as reported in Table 12.8 and Figs. 12.1 and 12.2, Table 12.9 computes normalized associations by dividing the marginal effects in the controlled regression of model (2) by the sample mean or the SD of BMI. The row "Δ impatience" reports relative increases in BMI associated with an increase in the impatience proxy DEBTIMP by one unit of the SD; the row "Δ procrastination" shows

Table 12.9 Impacts of time discounting variables on BMI: The case of Model (2)

	All		Male		Female	
	/average BMI	/BMI S.D.	/average BMI	/BMI S.D.	/average BMI	/BMI S.D.
Δimpatience	1.09 %	7.86 %	0.72 %	5.32 %	1.43 %	10.61 %
Δprocrastination (hyperbolic discounting)	0.96 %	6.93 %	0.77 %	5.70 %	1.09 %	8.11 %
Δsign effect	−2.17 %	−15.65 %	−0.71 %	−5.25 %	−3.39 %	−25.10 %

Note: The row of "Δimpatience" shows the impacts of an increase in the average of the discount rates DR's by one unit of the sample S.D. of the average discount rate. The row of "Δprocrastination" shows the impacts of a one-point increase in the degree of procrastination (PROCR). The row of "Δsign effect" summarizes the effect of the presence of the sign effect (SIGN = 1), compared with the case without the effect (SIGN = 0). The columns of "/average BMI" report the marginal effects relative to the average BMI, whereas in the "/BMI S.D." columns the marginal impacts are measured in terms of relative magnitudes to sample S.D. in the corresponding samples. The impacts are evaluated by the estimation results of model (2)

relative increases in BMI associated with a one-point increase in the propensity to procrastinate over homework (PROCR), the proxy of hyperbolic discounting; and the row "Δ sign effect" represents relative differences between BMI in the presence of the sign effect (SIGN = 1) and BMI without the sign effect (SIGN = 0). As seen from the table, in the full and, especially female samples, the marginal effects on BMI of the three time-discounting variables are substantial, compared with the mean and the SD of BMI. For example, female respondents with a one-point higher degree of procrastination, *ceteris paribus*, have a BMI greater by 8.11 % of the sample SD. Difference in BMI between female respondents who do and do not display the sign effect amounts to −3.39 % of the sample mean and to −25.10 % of the sample SD.

In sum, both models show that, especially for the full and female samples, BMI has the expected correlations with impatience and with the sign effect.[21] A significant positive correlation between BMI and hyperbolic discounting is also consistently observed in all the samples when the tendency toward procrastination is used as a proxy for the degree of hyperbolic discounting.[22]

[21]The accuracy of BMI in diagnosing obesity is known to be limited especially for males because muscular persons can have large BMI even when they are not really fat (see, e.g., Burkhauser and Cawley 2008; and Romero-Corral et al. 2008). The poor performance for the male sample may be partially attributable to this property of BMI. If exercise habits need patience, patient men are likely to be muscular and hence have a high BMI, which makes true positive correlations between obesity and impatience underestimated unless the exercise habits are controlled for.

[22]As for associations of BMI with the control variables, Table 12.8 shows that (i) males have significantly greater BMI than females, and (ii) BMI depends non-monotonically on age, per capita household income, and work hours. Finding (i) contrasts to the tendency in Western countries (e.g., Komlos et al. 2004; Borghans and Golsteyn 2006). The U-shaped relation between BMI and income in finding (ii) is in contrast with monotonic, negative correlations between the two which are observed in Western countries (e.g., Chou et al. 2004; Zagorsky 2005). For detailed discussions, see Ikeda et al. (2009).

Table 12.10 Binary probit regression of obesity

	Uncontrolled			Controlled		
	All	Male	Female	All	Male	Female
(a) Model (1)						
DISCRATE	0.043*** (2.74)	0.037 (1.53)	0.027 (1.40)	0.037** (2.09)	0.036 (1.34)	0.032 (1.51)
HYPERBOL	−0.001 (−0.00)	0.020 (0.55)	−0.247 (−0.91)	0.013 (0.54)	0.027 (0.69)	0.001 (0.04)
SIGN	−0.020* (−0.75)	0.085 (0.20)	−0.458 (−1.38)	−0.046 (−1.49)	−0.018 (−0.36)	−0.063* (−1.67)
Log likelihood	−1015.51	−566.08	−430.77	−762.03	−439.38	−316.05
#obs	2,118	1,026	1,092	1,658	818	840
(b) Model (2)						
DEBTIMP	0.024** (2.56)	0.021 (1.51)	0.024** (2.09)	0.023** (2.47)	0.021 (1.42)	0.023** (2.03)
PROCR	0.030*** (4.01)	0.028** (2.30)	0.021** (2.23)	0.028*** (3.67)	0.029** (2.33)	0.024*** (2.61)
SIGN	−0.030 (−1.00)	−0.007 (−0.16)	−0.053 (1.38)	−0.037 (−1.21)	0.004 (0.08)	−0.065* (−1.68)
Log likelihood	−793.83	−450.22	−335.35	−748.95	−428.96	−310.27
#obs	1,670	840	830	1,629	812	817

Notes: *, **, *** Statistical significance at the 10 %, 5 %, and 1 % levels, respectively

4.2 Probabilities of Being Obese and Severely Obese

Let OBESITY and SEVERE OBESITY be binary indicators for obesity and severe obesity, respectively. By using binary probit models, we estimate the marginal effects on the probabilities Prob (OBESITY = 1) and Prob (SEVERE OBESITY = 1) in models (1) and (2) under the two specifications, uncontrolled and controlled for personal attributes. Tables 12.10 and 12.11 show the results for obesity and severe obesity, respectively.

As for obesity, the estimated marginal effects of the impatience variables DISCRATE and DEBTIMP are both positive and reasonably significant in both models. In the full sample, with all other personal attributes being equal, the respondents who are impatient by one unit of a SD more than the average are obese with a 3.7 percentage-point higher probability in model (1), and with a 2.3 percentage-point higher probability in model (2).

With regard to the other discounting variables, the result of model (1) is not that strong, whereas in model (2), the association of the obesity probability with procrastination (PROCR) is positive at the 1 % significance level for the full and female samples in either specification, adjusted or non-adjusted for personal attributes. In model (2), a one-unit higher degree of procrastination, ceteris paribus, implies a 2.8 percentage-point higher probability of being obese in the full sample

Table 12.11 Binary probit regression of severe obesity

	Uncontrolled			Controlled		
	All	Male	Female	All	Male	Female
(a) Model (1)						
DISCRATE	0.001 (0.12)	0.004 (0.46)	−0.005 (−0.88)	−0.003 (−0.56)	−0.005 (−0.64)	0.000 (−0.13)
HYPERBOL	−0.006 (−0.75)	0.013 (0.09)	−0.012 (−1.41)	−0.004 (−0.62)	−0.006 (−0.52)	0.000 (0.04)
SIGN	−0.011 (−1.12)	0.001 (0.06)	−0.021* (−1.83)	−0.017* (−1.75)	0.000 (0.02)	−0.025** (−2.45)
Log likelihood	−209.09	−131.86	−72.41	−143.28	−91.65	−47.11
#obs	2,118	1,026	1,092	1,658	818	840
(b) Model (2)						
DEBTIMP	0.002 (0.63)	0.002 (0.50)	0.001 (0.34)	0.002 (0.75)	0.002 (0.62)	0.001 (0.38)
PROCR	0.010*** (3.74)	0.015*** (2.80)	0.005** (2.08)	0.007*** (3.18)	0.011** (2.45)	0.003* (1.71)
SIGN	−0.013 (−1.36)	0.002 (0.14)	−0.027** (−2.25)	−0.011* (−1.67)	−0.000 (−0.00)	−0.020** (−2.31)
Log likelihood	−152.21	−96.33	−53.65	−139.33	−87.16	−47.89
#obs	1,670	840	830	1,629	812	817

Notes: *, **, *** Statistical significance at the 10 %, 5 %, and 1 % levels, respectively

and a 2.4 percentage-point higher probability in the female sample. The associations are quantitatively noteworthy, compared with the unconditional probabilities of being obese, i.e., the corresponding obesity prevalence rates (18.9 % and 14.3 % for the full and female samples, respectively). Associations between obesity and the sign effect, however, are not strong.

The probability of being severely obese has a significant negative correlation with the sign effect in the full and female samples, implying that respondents who do not display the sign effect are more likely to be severely obese. For example, in model (1), the probability of respondents who do not display the sign effect being severely obese is, for the full sample, 1.7 percentage-point higher than the corresponding probability for those who do display the sign effect and, for the female sample, 2.5 percentage-point higher than that for those who display the sign effect. The increases in the probability associated with the absence of the sign effect are as large as, or even larger than the unconditional probabilities of being severely obese (2.2 % and 1.5 % for the full and female samples, respectively).

Although the associations with hyperbolic discounting in model (1) are insignificant, those with inclination toward procrastination PROCR in model (2) are significantly positive in all three samples. In particular, compared with the males' unconditional probability of being severely obese (2.9 %), the marginal effect of PROCR (1.1 %) on the males' probability of being severely obese is substantial.

Table 12.12 Binary probit regression of underweight

	Uncontrolled			Controlled		
	All	Male	Female	All	Male	Female
(a) Model (1)						
DISCRATE	0.003 (0.30)	0.005 (0.40)	0.011 (0.67)	0.009 (0.86)	0.004 (0.39)	0.011 (0.64)
HYPERBOL	0.024 (1.63)	0.000 (0.01)	0.048** (2.11)	0.010 (0.70)	−0.006 (−0.39)	0.030 (1.31)
SIGN	0.023 (1.37)	0.000 (0.02)	0.042 (1.62)	0.040** (2.46)	0.023 (1.19)	0.053** (2.12)
Log likelihood	−531.33	−190.69	−330.37	−382.24	−140.44	−228.67
#obs	2,118	1,026	1,092	1,658	818	840
(b) Model (2)						
DEBTIMP	−0.009 (−1.41)	−0.006 (−0.87)	−0.010 (−1.02)	−0.008 (−1.43)	−0.005 (−0.93)	−0.009 (−0.99)
PROCR	−0.011** (−2.44)	−0.006 (−1.11)	−0.010 (−1.37)	−0.009** (−2.20)	−0.005 (−1.42)	−0.013* (−1.86)
SIGN	0.040** (2.22)	0.026 (1.23)	0.055* (1.86)	0.040** (2.54)	0.018 (1.47)	0.055** (2.14)
Log likelihood	−401.49	−149.96	−245.99	−369.86	−133.42	−223.86
#obs	1,670	840	830	1,629	812	817

Notes: *, **, *** Statistical significance at the 10 %, 5 %, and 1 % levels, respectively

4.3 Probability of Being Underweight

In the full and female samples, consistent with our hypothesis, models (1) and (2) show that the probability of being underweight has a significantly positive correlation with the sign effect when other personal attributes are controlled for (see Table 12.12). For either model, respondents displaying the sign effect belong to the underweight group with a 4.0 percentage-point higher probability in the full sample, and with around a 5.5 percentage-point higher probability in the female sample, than those who did not display the effect. Again, the effects are not that small, compared to the corresponding unconditional probabilities of being underweight (i.e., 7.0 % and 9.5 % in the full and female samples, respectively). In model (2), procrastination has a significant negative association with the probability of being underweight in the full and female samples.

To summarize, by using the above results in the full sample for model (2), Table 12.13 lists the marginal effects of differences in the time discounting variables on the probabilities of being obese, severely obese, and underweight, relative to the corresponding unconditional probabilities, where "Δimpatience," "Δprocrastination," and "Δsign effect" are the same as in Table 12.9. All the marginal effects have the expected signs, and many of them (i.e., 6 out of 9) are significant. Compared with the corresponding unconditional probabilities,

Table 12.13 Relative marginal effects of time discounting variables on the prob. of being obese, severely obese, and underweight: the case of model (2) in the full sample

	Obesity		Severe obesity		Underweight	
Unconditional probabilities (shares)	18.92 %		2.20 %		6.97 %	
	Marginal effects (percentage points)	/Uncond. prob.	Marginal effects (percentage points)	/Uncond. prob.	Marginal effects (percentage points)	/Uncond. prob.
Δimpatience	2.28**	12.04 %	0.16	7.09 %	−0.83	−11.85 %
Δprocrastination (hyperbolic discounting)	2.81***	14.87 %	0.73***	33.28 %	−0.92**	−13.24 %
Δsign effect	−3.69	−19.48 %	−1.06*	−48.22 %	4.02**	57.71 %

Note: The row of "Δimpatience" shows the impacts of an increase in the average of the discount rates DR's by one unit of sample S.D. of the average discount rate. The row of "Δprocrastination" shows the impacts of a one-point increase in the degree of procrastination (PROCR). The row of "Δsign effect" summarizes the effect of the presence of the sign effect (SIGN = 1), compared with the case without the effect (SIGN = 0). The marginal effects are evaluated by the estimation results of model (2)
*, **, ***Statistical significance at the 10 %, 5 %, and 1 % levels, respectively. The columns of "/Uncond. prob." represent the ratios of the marginal effects to the unconditional probabilities of the corresponding body mass status

the magnitudes of the marginal effects of these time discounting variables are substantial.[23] In particular, the marginal effects of the presence of the sign effect on the probabilities of being underweight and severely obese are around half of the corresponding unconditional probabilities. The marginal impacts of procrastination on the probabilities of being obese, severely-obese, and underweight are all greater than 13 % of the corresponding unconditional probabilities.

5 Concluding Remarks

Based on analysis of a survey of Japanese adults, we have found that the body mass status of respondents are expectedly related to their time discounting via impatience, hyperbolic discounting, and the sign effect. The marginal impacts of these preferences on the probabilities of being obese and underweight are not that small, especially compared with the corresponding prevalence rates. Caloric intake and the resulting body mass formation could thus be taken as determined by intertemporal decision-making with behavioral decision bias toward immediacy and/or toward aversion of future losses.

[23]These results remain unchanged even when the probabilities of being obese, severely obese, and underweight are jointly estimated by estimating multivariate probit models with correlated error terms. For the results of the multivariate probit regression, see Ikeda et al. (2009).

Three policy implications arise from this. First, policies that raise the immediate costs of choices which lead to obesity are likely to be effective at reducing the prevalence of obesity. For example, greasy food tax would directly raise the present costs of being obese in the future, and thereby suppress the obesity rate.[24,25]

Second, policies that ease self-control problems are also likely to be effective. As suggested by Bernheim et al. (2001), school education can contribute to correcting children's distorted decision making by instructing them the merits of various commitment devices. Counteracting advertisements that stimulate consumers' impulsiveness and/or weaken patience may be effective.[26]

Third, to prevent hyperbolic people from overeating, "nudging" policies that change the defaults of choices would also be effective. For example, by conducting field experiments in fast food restaurants, Downs et al. (2009) report that consumers' calorie intake is reduced by arranging the menu so that the front page contains only low-calorie food.

Future research needs to extend the analysis to a panel set to explain recent BMI dynamics in Japan. As reported by Borghans and Golsteyn (2006), it may be difficult to explain time-series changes in BMI solely by changes in time preference. It would be interesting to examine how the behavioral properties of time discounting influence the effect that dynamic changes in exogenous economic factors – such as food prices and medical care costs – have on body mass. It would also be interesting to examine why people, especially women, who are less hyperbolic and display the sign effect are more likely to be underweight, contrary to economic intuition.

Acknowledgements This is a revised version of Ikeda, Kang, and Ohtake (2009), which has been circulated under the title: "Fat debtors: Time discounting, its anomalies, and body mass index." Our special thanks go to I. Shimomura and T. Hunahashi (Graduate School of Medicine, Osaka University) for helpful discussions from the viewpoint of medical science, and D.J. Flath, C.Y. Horioka, and two anonymous referees for helpful comments. We are also grateful to Y. Fukuta, R. Goto, D. Kawaguchi, K. Hirata, and participants at the 2008 meeting of the Association of Behavioral Economics and Finance, the International Workshop on the Economics of Obesity and Health 2009, and the faculty seminars of Hitotsubashi University, Osaka University, University of New South Wales, and Bond University for beneficial discussions. We acknowledge financial support from the COE and Global COE Programs of Osaka University. Ikeda and Ohtake

[24]Taiwan's Bureau of Health Promotion is drafting a bill to levy the special tax on unhealthy food leading to obesity.

[25]As another example, Japan's Ministry of Health, Labour and Welfare started in 2008 the Specific Health Check-Up System, which aimed at an early detection of metabolic syndrome and obesity. In the system, the insurers of health insurances are required to check up every year the body mass status of the people insured, and give practical advice for healthier life to the insured who are diagnosed with metabolic syndrome, or in danger of developing metabolic syndrome. Because receiving compulsory consultation takes time and psychological costs, the system raises the present costs of being obese for incipiently obese people.

[26]As for the information-oriented policy, the Nutrition Labeling and Education Act, which took effect in 1994 in U.S., made labeling mandatory for most processed food. Varyam and Cawley (2006) report a negative association between implementation of the new labels and body weight among non-Hispanic white women.

acknowledge financial support from a Grant-in-Aid for Scientific Research (B 21330046 and B [2]1214207, respectively) from the Japan Society for the Promotion of Science. A part of this study is the result of "Development of biomarker candidates for social behavior" carried out under the Strategic Research Program for Brain Sciences by the Ministry of Education, Culture, Sports, Science and Technology of Japan.

Appendices

A.1 Multinomial Probit Estimation of the Body Mass Status Function

Theoretically, time discounting variables may be non-monotonically correlated with body mass because being underweight, with a BMI much lower than the optimal level, 22, might have equally detrimental effects on health in the long run as being obese. If body mass were non-monotonically correlated to the time discounting variables, linear relations between BMI and time discounting as assumed in the regressions in the text would not be appropriate. Further, in the probit regressions for obesity, the reference category of dependent variable OBESITY would be inappropriate, too, since it includes the underweight status which may be positively correlated with discount rates, etc., as is the obese status.

To show that such non-monotonic associations are not observed between body mass and each of the time discounting variables, we put the results of multinomial probit regressions in panels (a) and (b) of Table 12.14, wherein, with the constraint that the sum of the probabilities of being underweight ($BMI < 18.5$), normal ($18.5 \leq BMI < 25$), degree-1 obese ($25 \leq BMI < 30$),[27] and severely obese ($BMI \geq 30$) should equal one, marginal correlations between each of the probabilities and time discounting variables are estimated simultaneously by using the full sample and controlling for other personal attributes.

Panel (b) shows that, in the case of model (2), correlations between body mass and DEBTIMP, PROCR, and SIGN are all monotonic[28]: DEBTIMP and PROCR are both negatively correlated with underweight and normal body weight, whereas positively correlated with degree-1 obesity and severe obesity; SIGN is positively associated with underweight, whereas negatively associated with degree-1 obesity and severe obesity. For model (1), likewise, SIGN is monotonically correlated with body mass. However, as for DISCRATE and HYPERBOL, we can find no stable patterns of correlations.[29]

---

[27]For the degrees of obesity in the JSSO criterion, see Table 12.1.

[28]The significance levels in the multinomial probit regressions are much lower than in the binary probit regressions in the text because the number of parameters to be estimated is much larger than in the binary probit regressions.

[29]To check the possibilities that underweight respondents are more likely to manifest high discount rates, hyperbolic discounting, and/or to be without the sign effect than those of normal body mass,

Table 12.14 Multinomial probit regressions for body mass status

	Controlled			
	Underweight	Normal	Obesity	Severe obesity
(a) Model (1)				
DISCRATE	0.009 (0.85)	−0.047** (−2.42)	0.040** (2.38)	−0.003 (−0.53)
HYPERBOL	0.011 (0.72)	−0.026 (−0.96)	0.019 (0.83)	−0.004 (−0.59)
SIGN	0.042*** (3.55)	0.002 (0.05)	−0.027 (−0.86)	−0.017 (−1.35)
Log likelihood	−1216.341			
#obs	1,658			
(b) Model (2)				
DEBTIMP	−0.009 (−1.48)	−0.014 (−1.34)	0.021** (2.32)	0.002 (0.81)
PROCR	−0.010** (−2.27)	−0.017** (−2.04)	0.019*** (2.58)	0.008*** (3.41)
SIGN	0.042*** (3.65)	−0.008 (−0.24)	−0.021 (−0.68)	−0.014 (−1.26)
Log likelihood	−1190.650			
#obs	1,629			

Note: The regressions are conducted using the full sample by incorporating all the control variables. *, **, ***Statistical significance at the 10 %, 5 %, and 1 % levels, respectively

In sum, as far as our data are concerned, associations between body mass and each of the time discounting variables seem to be monotonic, and the regression models in the text could be considered as appropriate.

A.2 Estimating with Corrected BMI Data

A.2.1 Correcting for Self-reporting Biases

As discussed in the text, the self-reported BMI data in the JHS05 may well contain underreporting biases. To check the robustness of the main results, we re-conduct the analysis by correcting for self-reporting bias.

We roughly examine whether or not the JHS05 data contain self-reporting biases by comparing the by-age BMI distributions of our JHS05 data with those

we also conducted BMI regressions by using (1) the sample of non-obese respondents of BMI < 25 and (2) the sample of those with BMI ≤ 22. For either sample, however, we could find no significant correlations that are opposite in signs to those obtained in the text.

of the NSHN04 data (sample size: 7689) that are actually measured.[30] Tables A2(a) through A2(d) describe statistically the by-age body mass distributions in the NSHN04 and JHS05 data. Results of the comparison suggest that the BMI means, the obesity rates, and the severe obesity rates in the original JHS05 data may contain underreporting biases. Particularly in the case of females, the BMI means and the obesity rate in JHS05 are significantly lower than those in NSHN04. Consistent with this tendency, the sample SDs of the females' BMI in JHS05 are significantly smaller than those in NSHN04. As for the male sample, although the bias is not as large as in the female sample, the obesity rates are smaller in JHS05. There is no significant difference between the rates of severe obesity among males in the two data sets. Although the prevalence rate of underweight in JHS05 is slightly lower than that in NSHN04, the difference does not seem to be large.

Based on these findings, we correct for the underreporting bias in the female sample by specifying, from the JHS05 BMI data in generations i ($i = 20$, 30, 40, 50, 60), quadratic functions $f_i(x) = a_i x^2 + b_i x + c_i$, which transform self-reported BMI values $x \geq 22$ to corrected BMI values $f_i(x)$.[31] The coefficients a_i, b_i, and c_i are determined such that the function satisfies: (1) $f_i\left(x_i^*\right) = 25$; (2) $f_i\left(x_i^{**}\right) = 30$; and (3) $f_i(22) = 22$, where x_i^* and x_i^{**} represent the critical BMI values by which to define obesity and severe obesity for generation i, respectively, that equilibrate the prevalence rates of obesity and severe obesity across JHS05 and NSHN04. Conditions (1) and (2) ensure that the corrected BMI distribution generates the same obesity and severe obesity rates as those in the NSHN04. Condition (3) is the assumption that since a BMI of 22 is known to be the healthiest,[32] people with BMI ≤ 22 could be regarded as having no incentive to underreport their weights or overreport their height, and hence, would have no tendency to underreport their BMI values. The corrected values of the female BMI for $x \geq 22$ are computed by using the quadratic functions obtained for the corresponding generations, whereas for $x < 22$, no adjustment is made as there seems to be no serious reporting bias. As for the male BMI data, similar adjustment is made except that we do not correct data for $x > 30$ since the prevalence rate of severe obesity in the JHS05 does not differ significantly from that in the NSHN04 (see Table 12.17). Tables 12.15, 12.16, 12.17, and 12.18 show that the correction eliminates, to a great extent, the underreporting bias in the mean and the SD of each body mass status in each generation.[33]

---

[30]Because the NSHN04 survey was conducted in November 2004, and the JHS05 survey was conducted in February 2005, possible differences in the two BMI data sets due to time difference can be regarded as negligible.

[31]Our procedure is a modified version of what is proposed in the literature (e.g., Cawley 2004; Chou et al. 2004; Burkhauser and Cawley 2008; and Michaud et al. 2007). See also footnote 9.

[32]See Table 12.1 and the related discussions in Sect. 3.1.

[33]However, the corrections of the downward bias in the SDs remain insufficient for males in their 20s and 30s and for females in their 30s and 40s.

Table 12.15 By-age BMI distributions: NSHN04, JHS05, and corrected data

Age		Male			Female		
		NSHN04	JHS05	Corrected data	NSHN04	JHS05	Corrected data
20s	Means	22.52	22.46 (0.448)	22.66 (0.623)	20.28	20.23 (0.428)	20.29 (0.572)
	S.D.	3.62	3.98 (0.107)	4.09 (0.054)*	2.54	2.55 (0.474)	2.64 (0.281)
30s	Means	23.42	23.25 (0.284)	23.38 (0.451)	20.95	20.84 (0.302)	20.85 (0.699)
	S.D.	3.36	3.61 (0.111)	3.69 (0.060)*	2.99	2.62 (0.008)***	2.62 (0.008)***
40s	Means	24.07	23.63 (0.045)*	23.85 (0.202)	22.64	22.03 (0.004)***	22.19 (0.027)**
	S.D.	3.37	3.30 (0.353)	3.40 (0.432)	3.57	2.98 (0.000)***	3.12 (0.004)***
50s	Means	23.69	23.57 (0.262)	23.76 (0.640)	22.97	22.36 (0.001)***	22.71 (0.999)
	S.D.	2.89	2.92 (0.399)	3.02 (0.169)	3.21	2.80 (0.001)***	3.21 (0.492)
60-71	Means	23.75	23.24 (0.002)***	23.61 (0.237)	23.35	22.87 (0.010)**	23.29 (0.396)
	S.D.	3.00	2.60 (0.001)***	2.99 (0.478)	3.47	3.01 (0.001)***	3.57 (0.273)
All	Means	23.65	23.35 (0.003)***	23.59 (0.298)	22.37	21.94 (0.000)***	22.17 (0.027)**
	S.D.	3.15	3.14 (0.457)	3.31 (0.022)**	3.25	2.96 (0.000)***	3.29 (0.291)
	Obs.	2,286	1,368	1,368	2,789	1,499	1,499

Note: Values in parentheses represent P-values for the null hypotheses that corresponding statistics equal those of the NSHN04 data
*, **, ***Statistical significance at the 10 %, 5 %, and 1 % levels, respectively

A.2.2 Results with Corrected Data

Tables 12.19, 12.20, and 12.21 provide the estimation results with the corrected data. As a whole, the association reported in the text between body mass and each of the three time discounting variables is robust even when corrected for self-reporting bias. For example, across the original and corrected data sets, there are few differences in the signs and significance levels of the estimated coefficients in the BMI regressions (see Tables 12.8 and 12.19).

As a result of the correction, however, there are marginal changes in the results of the obesity regressions. In particular, as seen from the comparison of Tables 12.10 and 12.20, the magnitudes of the coefficients of impatience variables, especially those of DISCRATE, and their associated *t*-values become greater, whereas the opposite is true for the coefficients of the sign effect. Provided that our procedure successfully corrects for the actual underreporting biases, these marginal changes

Table 12.16 By-age obesity distributions: NSHN04, JHS05, and corrected data

	Male			Female		
Age	NSHN04	JHS05	Corrected data	NSHN04	JHS05	Corrected data
20s	0.199	0.133 (0.025)**	0.195 (0.876)	0.054	0.035 (0.261)	0.049 (0.915)
30s	0.289	0.252 (0.167)	0.292 (0.922)	0.083	0.079 (0.745)	0.086 (0.782)
40s	0.327	0.267 (0.012)**	0.324 (0.885)	0.179	0.139 (0.016)**	0.179 (0.976)
50s	0.308	0.248 (0.003)***	0.305 (0.918)	0.241	0.161 (0.000)***	0.240 (0.955)
60–71	0.299	0.237 (0.002)***	0.298 (0.984)	0.298	0.218 (0.000)***	0.297 (0.964)
All	0.297	0.240 (0.000)***	0.296 (0.893)	0.195	0.143 (0.000)***	0.195 (0.956)
Obs.	2,286	1,368	1,368	2,789	1,499	1,499

Note: Values in parentheses represent P-values for the null hypotheses that corresponding statistics equal those of the NSHN04 data

*, **, ***Statistical significance at the 10 %, 5 %, and 1 % levels, respectively

Table 12.17 By-age severe obesity distributions: NSHN04, JHS05, and corrected data

	Male			Female		
Age	NSHN04	JHS05	Corrected data	NSHN04	JHS05	Corrected data
20s	0.021	0.035 (0.290)	0.035 (0.290)	0.008	0.007 (0.655)	0.007 (0.655)
30s	0.030	0.050 (0.052)*	0.050 (0.052)**	0.012	0.008 (0.523)	0.008 (0.523)
40s	0.034	0.036 (0.960)	0.036 (0.960)	0.027	0.015 (0.106)	0.024 (0.848)
50s	0.032	0.034 (0.779)	0.034 (0.780)	0.036	0.015 (0.001)***	0.032 (0.541)
60–71	0.031	0.008 (0.000)***	0.031 (0.956)	0.045	0.025 (0.013)**	0.048 (0.724)
All	0.031	0.029 (0.586)	0.036 (0.159)	0.029	0.015 (0.000)***	0.027 (0.516)
Obs.	2,286	1,368	1,368	2,789	1,499	1,499

Note: Values in parentheses represent P-values for the null hypotheses that corresponding statistics equal those of the NSHN04 data

*, **, ***Statistical significance at the 10 %, 5 %, and 1 % levels, respectively

could be considered as the results of association between underreporting behavior and the two time discounting variables. For example, if obese respondents with high discount rates are more likely to underreport their weight, true positive correlations between the probability of being obese and the discount rate will be underestimated in the uncorrected sample. Similarly, if obese people with the sign effect tend to underreport BMI, true negative correlation between obesity and the sign effect

Table 12.18 By-age underweight distributions: NSHN04 and JHS05

	Male			Female		
Age	NSHN04	JHS05		NSHN04	JHS05	
20s	0.084	0.115	(0.114)	0.214	0.211	(0.913)
30s	0.038	0.074	(0.000)***	0.156	0.143	(0.431)
40s	0.021	0.032	(0.112)	0.066	0.103	(0.000)***
50s	0.020	0.016	(0.523)	0.054	0.057	(0.680)
60-71	0.036	0.036	(0.994)	0.066	0.050	(0.105)
All	0.033	0.042	(0.010)**	0.093	0.095	(0.625)
Obs.	2,286		1,368	2,789		1,499

Note: Values in parentheses represent P-values for the null hypotheses that statistics of the JHS05 data equal those of the NSHN04 data
*, **, ***Statistical significance at the 10 %, 5 %, and 1 % levels, respectively

Table 12.19 BMI regressions with corrected data

	Uncontrolled			Controlled		
	All	Male	Female	All	Male	Female
(a) Model (1)						
DISCRATE	0.401*** (2.99)	0.300 (1.60)	0.186 (1.01)	0.300** (2.06)	0.277 1.35	0.302 1.47
HYPERBOL	−0.098 (−0.52)	0.138 (0.51)	−0.423* (−1.67)	0.123 (0.62)	0.192 (0.66)	0.041 (0.15)
SIGN	−0.238 (−1.04)	0.067 (0.20)	−0.517* (−1.71)	−0.582** (−2.36)	−0.322 (−0.87)	−0.761** (−2.30)
Adj. R^2	0.008	0.000	0.008	0.092	0.018	0.088
#obs	2,117	1,026	1,091	1,658	818	840
(b) Model (2)						
DEBTIMP	0.246*** (3.07)	0.137 (1.24)	0.334*** (2.98)	0.261*** (3.35)	0.167 (1.49)	0.340*** (3.15)
PROCR	0.284*** (4.59)	0.176** (1.96)	0.194** (2.27)	0.228*** (3.69)	0.182** (1.99)	0.256*** (3.09)
SIGN	−0.384 (−1.53)	−0.225 (−0.64)	−0.542 (−1.57)	−0.520** (−2.12)	−0.177 (−0.50)	−0.784** (−2.35)
Adj. R^2	0.017	0.003	0.017	0.099	0.020	0.117
#obs	1,670	840	830	1,629	812	817

Notes: *, **, *** Statistical significance at the 10 %, 5 %, and 1 % levels, respectively

will be overestimated in the uncorrected sample.[34] These findings suggest the importance of further study on behavioral aspects of underreporting behavior to detect unbiased correlations between time discounting and body mass.

[34]In fact, for the subsample of the respondents who self-reported not to be obese, i.e., those with an uncorrected BMI < 25, the implied magnitude of underreporting, computed as corrected BMI minus uncorrected BMI, displays significant positive correlations with DISCRATE and SIGN after individual attributes including self-reported BMI are adjusted for.

Table 12.20 Obesity regressions with corrected data

	Uncontrolled			Controlled		
	All	Male	Female	All	Male	Female
(a) Model (1)						
DISCRATE	0.065*** (3.76)	0.056** (2.15)	0.509** (2.30)	0.058*** (2.96)	0.045 (1.51)	0.065*** (2.59)
HYPERBOL	0.019 (0.79)	0.055 (1.46)	−0.022 (−0.70)	0.040 (1.49)	0.060 (1.45)	0.020 (0.59)
SIGN	0.008 (0.27)	0.018 (0.38)	0.001 (0.02)	−0.007 (−0.19)	0.006 (0.12)	−0.005 (−0.13)
Log likelihood	−1160.73	−624.53	−517.76	−875.78	−488.20	−373.46
#obs	2,117	1,026	1,091	1,658	818	840
(b) Model (2)						
DEBTIMP	0.026*** (2.56)	0.287* (1.86)	0.023* (1.67)	0.028*** (2.64)	0.031** (1.97)	0.022* (1.66)
PROCR	0.030*** (3.65)	0.201 (1.57)	0.026** (2.44)	0.027*** (3.17)	0.020 (1.53)	0.030*** (2.82)
SIGN	0.001 (0.04)	−0.003 (0.948)	0.005 (0.11)	−0.003 (−0.09)	0.014 (0.27)	−0.008 (−0.18)
Log likelihood	−921.92	−508.57	−403.81	−863.59	−481.21	−366.51
#obs	1,670	840	830	1,629	812	817

Notes: *, **, *** Statistical significance at the 10 %, 5 %, and 1 % levels, respectively

Table 12.21 Severe obesity regressions with corrected data

	Uncontrolled			Controlled		
	All	Male	Female	All	Male	Female
(a) Model (1)						
DISCRATE	0.001 (0.10)	0.009 (0.86)	−0.114 (−1.36)	−0.005 (−0.73)	−0.003 (−0.30)	−0.008 (−1.01)
HYPERBOL	−0.009 (−0.98)	−0.005 (−0.33)	−0.013 (−1.14)	−0.007 (−0.70)	−0.012 (−0.76)	0.001 (0.09)
SIGN	−0.161 (−1.33)	−0.028 (−0.15)	−0.027* (−1.83)	−0.026* (−1.95)	−0.005 (−0.26)	−0.041** (−2.51)
Log likelihood	−278.45	−158.25	−116.52	−204.53	−115.74	−83.24
#obs	2,117	1,026	1,091	1,658	818	840
(b) Model (2)						
DEBTIMP	0.005 (1.45)	0.003 (0.46)	0.007 (1.59)	0.006* (1.83)	0.004 (0.80)	0.005* (1.87)
PROCR	0.009*** (2.87)	0.012** (2.09)	0.006* (1.69)	0.009*** (2.80)	0.011** (2.05)	0.005* (1.69)
SIGN	−0.020 (−1.57)	0.002 (0.09)	−0.039** (−2.32)	−0.023* (−1.90)	−0.001 (−0.05)	−0.034** (−2.50)
Log likelihood	−214.62	−123.56	−89.10	−199.34	−116.40	−76.71
#obs	1,670	840	830	1,629	812	817

Notes: *, **, *** Statistical significance at the 10 %, 5 %, and 1 % levels, respectively

Table 12.22 OLS regressions of BMI without controlling for smoking

	(a) Model (1)			(b) Model (2)		
	All	Male	Female	All	Male	Female
DISCRATE	0.277**	0.285	0.255	0.242***	0.169	0.299***
	(2.05)	(1.47)	(1.36)	(3.36)	(1.61)	(3.05)
HYPERBOL	0.121	0.205	0.021	0.216***	0.182**	0.235***
	(0.65)	(0.75)	(0.08)	(3.78)	(2.11)	(3.11)
SIGN	−0.546**	−0.310	−0.704**	−0.481**	−0.174	−0.724**
	(−2.39)	(−0.90)	(−2.34)	(−2.13)	(−0.52)	(−2.39)
RISKAV	−0.645	−0.943*	−0.480	−0.786**	−0.959*	−0.741
	(−1.77)	(−1.83)	(−0.93)	(−2.17)	(−1.88)	(−1.44)
MALE	1.23***			1.123***		
	(7.25)			(6.53)		
UNIV	−0.093	−0.229	0.079	−0.104	−0.224	0.003
	(−0.52)	(−0.98)	(0.27)	(−0.57)	(−0.96)	(0.01)
AGE	0.236***	0.225***	0.235***	0.235***	0.222	0.244***
	(5.43)	(3.45)	(3.87)	(5.38)	(3.42)	(4.00)
AGE^2	−0.002***	−0.002***	−0.002***	−0.002***	−0.002	−0.002***
	(−4.58)	(−3.17)	(−2.91)	(−4.47)	(−3.12)	(−2.96)
INCOME	−0.253**	−0.133	−0.504***	−0.265**	−0.108	−0.584***
	(−2.27)	(−0.90)	(−2.53)	(−2.30)	(−0.70)	(−2.93)
INCOME^2	0.037***	0.026*	0.066**	0.036***	0.021	0.074***
	(2.95)	(1.71)	(2.49)	(2.73)	(1.33)	(2.80)
WORKHOUR	0.030**	0.008	0.037*	0.027*	−0.004	0.048
	(2.24)	(0.43)	(1.75)	(1.97)	(−0.22)	(2.19)
WORKHOUR^(1/2)	−0.205**	−0.032	−0.270*	−0.189*	0.056	−0.342**
	(−2.08)	(−0.21)	(−1.89)	(−1.90)	(0.36)	(−2.35)
Constant	16.939***	18.639***	16.888***	16.367***	18.009	16.205***
	(16.98)	(12.97)	(12.10)	(16.12)	(12.34)	(11.50)
Adj. R^2	0.094	0.022	0.079	0.102	0.024	0.108
#obs	1,659	813	840	1,630	813	817

Notes: *, **, *** Statistical significance at the 10 %, 5 %, and 1 % levels, respectively

A.3 BMI Regressions Without Controlling for Smoking

Table 12.22 reports the results of the BMI regressions without controlling for smoking. By comparing the results with those with controlling for smoking in Table 12.8, we first see that our results do not change substantially even without controlling for smoking. Secondly, however, the magnitudes of coefficients and the associated *t*-values for significant time discounting variables are smaller in the smoking-uncontrolled regressions (Table 12.22) than in the smoking-controlled regressions (Table 12.8), with the coefficient of DISCRATE in model (1) being the only exception. As discussed in footnote 19, this implies that correlations between BMI and time discounting are underestimated when smoking is not controlled for.

Addendum: Robustness and Related Research[35]

In this addendum, we review recent evidence that demonstrates the robustness of the results in the previous article (Ikeda et al. 2010) regarding the association between time discounting and body weight found using the 2005 JHS data.

Our results remain valid for the post-2005 waves of the JHS. Based on the 2010 wave data, i.e., those of the most recent survey in which all the data required for the present purpose are available, time discounting and other related attributes continue to differ between obese and non-obese individuals, as summarized in Table 12.23. Consistent with our previous results based on the 2005 wave data, the average obese respondent exhibited higher personal discount rates (DR1 though DR5), higher inclination toward debt holding and procrastination (PROC), and a lower tendency of the sign effect. Additionally, as in the previous study, hyperbolic discounting, estimated from intertemporal monetary choice questions, does not have the expected (positive) association with obesity.[36]

Conducting an original Internet survey in 2010 (N = 2,351) in which discount rates are estimated from Newton-type sequential binary choice questions, rather than from the reward lists like Table 12.3 in the text, Kang and Ikeda (2013) show that the respondents' health-related attributes, including body weight, are associated with time discounting as predicted by our previous research. In particular, they successfully show that obesity was positively related to hyperbolic discounting: hyperbolic discounters have a 3.6 percentage-point higher probability of being obese.

However, the above studies are based on non-incentivized responses to hypothetical questions. Several experimental studies have successfully detected the associations between time discounting and body status. In Chabris et al. (2008) and Richards and Hamilton (2012), individual laboratory-measured discount rates are shown to predict inter-personal variations in BMI and other behavioral indices. In both studies, the subjects' discount factors are estimated to be the hyperbolic type. Unlike our results reported in the preceding article, however, the effects of the degree of impatience and steepness (or hyperbolic discounting) on body weight are not disentangled.

The original title of our article was "Fat debtors" (Ikeda et al. 2009). The empirical observation that obese people tend to have debts was the motivation behind the article. Similarly, Guthrie and Sokolowsky (2012) explore obesity as credit risk and show that the loan delinquency rate among obese people is 20 percent higher than that for the non-obese.

Regarding the relationship between underweight and time discounting, Steinglass and colleagues find that individuals with anorexia nervosa show *less* temporal

[35]This addendum has been newly written for this book chapter.

[36]The robustness of these tendencies is confirmed for the JHS data of each annual wave from 2005 to 2010.

Table 12.23 Time discounting and debt holding of obese and non-obese respondents in the 2010 wave data

	DR_1	DR_2	DR_3	DR_4	DR_5	PROCR	The proportions of respondents with:		
							Debts	Hyperbolic discounting	Sign effects
Obese	5.731	7.018	0.288	0.080	−0.0003	3.477	0.299	0.492	0.861
[N]	[961]	[982]	[983]	[981]	[825]	[1,027]	[987]	[950]	[805]
Non-obese	4.377	5.488	0.242	0.064	−0.0073	3.240	0.231	0.531	0.888
[N]	[3,814]	[3,862]	[3,892]	[3,894]	[3,316]	[4,078]	[3,892]	[3,773]	[3,269]
(t-values)	3.068	2.922	3.065	2.288	1.623	5.158	4.440	−2.168	−2.120
Significance (one-sided test)	***	***	***	**	*	***	***	**	**

Notes: The data are from the Japan Household Survey on Consumer Preferences and Satisfaction, 2010. The definitions of the variables are the same in the text article

*, **, *** Statistical significance at the 10 %, 5 %, and 1 % levels, respectively

discounting than individuals at a healthy weight (Steinglass et al. 2012). Together with our findings, this suggests that being underweight is associated with excessive self-control, rather than a lack of self-control. This relationship is in contrast to other unhealthy behavior and psychiatric disorders, such as smoking and substance abuse, and consistent with the Guthrie and Sokolowsky (2012) finding that underweight people have the lowest delinquency rate in their sample.

References

Ainslie G (2001) Breakdown of will. Cambridge University Press, Cambridge
Becker GS, Murphy KM (1988) A theory of rational addiction. J Polit Econ 96:675–700
Benzion U, Rapoport A, Yagil J (1989) Discount rates inferred from decisions: an experimental study. Manag Sci 35:270–284
Bernheim BD, Garrett DM, Maki DM (2001) Education and saving: the long-term effects of high school financial curriculum mandates. J Public Econ 80:435–465
Borghans L, Golsteyn HH (2006) Time discounting and the body mass index: evidence from the Netherlands. Econ Hum Biol 4:39–61
Burkhauser RV, Cawley J (2008) Beyond BMI: the value of more accurate measures of fatness and obesity in social science research. J Health Econ 27:519–529
Cawley J (2004) The impact of obesity on wages. J Hum Resour 39:452–474
Chabris CF, Laibson D, Morris CL, Schuldt JP, Taubinsly D (2008) Individual laboratory-measured discount rates predict field behavior. J Risk Uncertain 37:237–269
Chapman GE (1995) Valuing the future, temporal discounting of health and money. Med Decis Mak 15:373–386
Chen Z, Yen ST, Eastwood DB (2005) Effects of food stamp participation on body weight and obesity. Am J Agric Econ 87:1167–1173
Chou S, Grossman M, Saffer H (2004) An economic analysis of adult obesity: results from the Behavioral Risk Factor Surveillance System. J Health Econ 23:565–587
Cutler DM, Glaeser EL, Shapiro JM (2003) Why have Americans become more obese? J Econ Perspect 17:93–118
Downs J, Loewenstein G, Wisdom J (2009) Strategies for promoting healthier food choices. Am Econ Rev 99:1–10
Frederick SG, Loewenstein G, Donoghue TO (2002) Time discounting and time preference: a critical review. J Econ Lit 40:351–401
Guthrie K, Sokolowsky J (2012) Obesity and credit risk, SSRN No. 1786536
Harrison GW, Lau MI, Williams MB (2002) Estimating individual discount rates in Denmark: a field experiment. Am Econ Rev 92:1606–1617
Ikeda S, Kang M-I, Ohtake F (2009) Fat debtors: time discounting, its anomalies, and body mass index, ISER Discussion Paper 732, Osaka University
Ikeda S, Kang M-I, Ohtake F (2010) Hyperbolic discounting, the sign effect, and the body mass index. J Health Econ 29:268–284
Kang M-I, Ikeda S (2013) Time discounting, present biases, and health-related behavior, Osaka University ISER Discussion Paper No. 885, Osaka University
Khwaja A, Silverman D, Sloan F (2007) Time preference, time discounting, and smoking decisions. J Health Econ 26:927–949
Kimball MS, Sahm CR, Shapiro MD (2005) Using survey-based risk tolerance, mimeo.
Komlos J, Smith PK, Bogin B (2004) Obesity and the rate of time preference: is there a connection? J Biosoc Sci 36:209–219
Laibson D (1997) Golden eggs and hyperbolic discounting. Q J Econ 112:443–477

Laibson D (1998) Life-cycle consumption and hyperbolic discount functions. Eur Econ Rev 42:861–871

Loewenstein G (1987) Anticipation and the valuation of delayed consumption. Econ J XLVII:666–687

Loewenstein G, Prelec D (1992) Anomalies intertemporal choice: evidence and an interpretation. Q J Econ 107:573–597

Low S, Chin MC, Ma S, Heng D, Deurenberg-Yap M (2009) Rationale for redefining obesity in Asians. Ann Acad Med Singap 38:66–74

Michaud P-C, van Soest AHO, Andreyeva T (2007) Cross-country variation in obesity patters among older Americans and Europeans. Forum Health Econ Policy 10:1–30, Article 8

Richards TJ, Hamilton SF (2012) Obesity and hyperbolic discounting: an experimental analysis. J Agric Resour Econ 37:181–198

Romero-Corral A, Somers VK, Sierra-Johnson J, Thomas RJ, Collazo-Clavell ML, Korinek J, Allison TG, Batsis JA, Sert-Kuniyoshi FH, Lopez-Jimenez F (2008) Accuracy of body mass index in diagnosing obesity in the adult general population. Int J Obes 32:959–966

Scharff RL (2009) Obesity and hyperbolic discounting: evidence and implications. J Consum Policy 32:3–21

Shapiro JM (2005) Is there a daily discount rate? Evidence from the food stamp nutrition cycle. J Public Econ 89:303–325

Smith PK, Bogin B, Bishai D (2005) Are time preference and body mass index associated? Econ Hum Biol 3:259–270

Starmer C, Bardsley N (2005) Introduction to the special issue: Exploring the error in experimental economics. Exp Econ 8:295–299

Steinglass JE, Figner B, Berkowitz S, Simpson HB, Weber EU, Walsh BT (2012) Increased capacity to delay reward in anorexia nervosa. J Int Neuropsychol Soc 18:1–8

Thaler R (1981) Some empirical evidence on dynamic inconsistency. Econ Lett 8:201–207

The Examination Committee of Criteria for 'Obesity Disease' in Japan, chaired by Y. Matsuzawa, Japan Society for the Study of Obesity (2002) New criteria for 'obesity disease' in Japan. Circulation J 66:987–992

The International Association for the Study of Obesity and the International Obesity Task Force (2000) The Asia-Pacific perspective: redefining obesity and its treatment, Australia. http://www.diabetes.com.au/pdf/obesity_report.pdf

Tokunaga K, Matsuzawa Y, Kotani K, Keno Y, Kobatake T, Fujioka S, Tarui S (1991) Ideal body weight estimated from the body mass index with the lowest morbidity. Int J Obes 15:1–5

Varyam JN, Cawley J (2006) Nutrition labels and obesity, NBER Discussion Papers 11956, NBER, Cambridge

WHO Expert Consultation (2004) Appropriate body-mass index for Asian populations and its implications for policy and intervention strategies. Lancet 363:157–163

Zagorsky JL (2005) Health and wealth The late-20th century obesity epidemic in the U.S. Econ Hum Biol 3:269–313

[illegible]

Chapter 13
Economic and Behavioral Factors in an Individual's Decision to Take the Influenza Vaccination in Japan

Yoshiro Tsutsui, Uri Benzion, and Shosh Shahrabani

Abstract In this chapter, we investigate what people in Japan consider when deciding to take the influenza vaccination. We develop an economic model to explain the mechanism by which people decide to take the influenza vaccination. Using our model and the data obtained from a large-scale survey we conducted in Japan, we demonstrated that people make rational decisions about vaccinations after considering its cost and benefits. People consider the probability of infection, severity of the disease, and the vaccination's effectiveness and side effects. The time discount rate is another consideration because the timing of costs and benefits of the vaccination differ. Risk aversion (fearing the contraction of the flu and vaccination's side effects) also affects the decision. People also deviate from rationality—altruism and status quo bias play important roles in the decision-making. Overconfidence indirectly affects the decision via perception variables such as the subjective probability of infection and assessment of influenza's severity. The decision also depends on attributes such as gender, age, and marital status. If the general perception of flu and vaccination is inaccurate, supplying accurate information regarding those may increase or decrease the vaccination rate, depending on whether this perception is, respectively, higher or lower than the objective rates. Thus, we examine whether the

---

The original article first appeared in the Journal of Socio-Economics 41:594–602, 2012. A newly written addendum has been added to this book chapter.

Y. Tsutsui (✉)
Faculty of Economics, Konan University, 8-9-1 Okamoto, Higashinada-ku, Kobe 658-8501, Japan
e-mail: tsutsui@center.konan-u.ac.jp

U. Benzion
Department of Economics, Ben Gurion University, Beer Sheva 84105, Israel
e-mail: uriusa@gmail.com

S. Shahrabani
Economics and Management Department, Max Stern Academic College of Emek Yezreel, Emek Yezreel 19300, Israel
e-mail: shoshs@yvc.ac.il

S. Ikeda et al. (eds.), *Behavioral Economics of Preferences, Choices, and Happiness*, DOI 10.1007/978-4-431-55402-8_13

general perception is biased. Our survey suggests that disseminating information on the vaccination's effectiveness may increase the rate of vaccination, whereas that on the probability of infection may have the opposite effect.

Keywords Influenza • Vaccination • Survey • Time preference • Japan

JEL Classification I19

1 Introduction

Influenza can be a serious disease in modern societies. As a serious pandemic, it can cause morbidity and mortality, as in 2009 with the swine flu. Since vaccination against flu can potentially prevent it, a study of the factors that are considered when making the decision to take or not to take the influenza vaccine can help prevent outbreaks of the disease. The objective of the current study is to examine how willingness to take the influenza vaccination depends on economic aspects such as costs and benefits as well as behavioral aspects including perceptions of influenza and the vaccination against it, preference parameters, and personal attributes. To achieve this aim, we use the behavioral economic model and results of a large data survey in Japan.

The Health Belief Model (HBM) developed by Rosenstock et al. (1988) is a traditional psychological approach to explaining and predicting preventive health behavior. HBM has been used to explore a variety of health behaviors, including vaccination (Blue and Valley 2002; Chen et al. 2007; Lau et al. 2008; Shahrabani et al. 2009; Tsutsui et al. 2010). According to the HBM, the acceptance of an influenza vaccine depends on the following predictors: perception of susceptibility to influenza, beliefs about the severity of influenza, perceived benefits of the vaccine in preventing influenza, and perceived barriers to accepting a vaccine (Blue and Valley 2002; Chapman and Coups 1999).

The economic approach also has been used to examine individual decisions regarding whether or not to take the vaccine (see for example: Brito et al. 1991; Mullahy 1999; Shahrabani et al. 2008). The theoretical framework of Shahrabani et al. (2008) show that the decision to take the vaccine based on objective factors can differ from that based on subjective or psychological factors. Their results show that values of objective factors predict a very high vaccination rate, implying that an individual's perceptions and beliefs do not accurately reflect actual values; further, it predicts that behavioral factors may be important in the decision. For example, perceived risks of infection may affect an individual's propensity to be immunized (Mullahy 1999). Thus, psychological factors, in addition to economic variables, should be considered to fully understand the reasons for the vaccination rate.

This chapter takes an economic approach and determines the relationship between vaccine taking and the costs/benefits of vaccination from utility-maximizing behavior. Based on the classic expected utility framework, we assume that people compare the benefits and costs of taking the vaccine, and choose to be vaccinated if the benefits exceed the costs. Our model predicts that the decision to be vaccinated depends on the perceived probability of infection, severity of the disease, side effects of vaccination, and inoculation costs. Thus, the factors that explain vaccination behavior according to utility-maximizing behavior are very similar to those of the HBM. However, it is an innovation of our theory to predict that an individual's time discount and risk aversion also play important roles in the decision to take a vaccination or not.

We hypothesize that people rationally choose to take a flu vaccination, but introduce an extended model that takes into account behavioral aspects which may affect the decision to be vaccinated. In particular, we examine whether psychological factors such as altruism, overconfidence, and the status quo effect play an important role in the decision.

We designed questions concerned with a respondent's beliefs and preferences with regard to influenza and vaccination, and conducted a large-scale survey in Japan to test our theoretical hypothesis. Thus, although we rely on the economic approach, we actually use perception or belief variables, as does the HBM. The use of perception or belief variables is, we believe, more appropriate than using actual data to explain decision making, considering the critique of Shahrabani et al. (2008).

Furthermore, the current study applies the survey results to derive policy implications with regard to dissemination of information on influenza and the vaccination against it.

The chapter is organized as follows. In Sect. 2, we explain the analytical framework including the basic model and extended model. In Sects. 2.1 and 2.2, we develop a model based on rationality, while in Sect. 2.3, we introduce behavioral variables to the basic model. Section 3 explains the methods and describes the survey in Japan. Section 4 is devoted to the results. Section 5 summarizes the study and concludes by showing how the inoculation rate can be increased.

2 Analytical Framework

2.1 Model

Benefits: The benefits of vaccination are (a) improving current and future health and (b) reducing the degree of inconvenience to one's family and friends when one is infected with flu. The magnitude of the benefits depends on how one perceives (1) the seriousness of the disease, (2) how the vaccination relieves the condition, and (3) the probability of infection, as well as his/her time discount rate, and risk aversion. Time discounting matters because the benefits of vaccination are received in the future, while the costs are paid earlier. Risk aversion involves assessing the risk of contracting flu and the side effects of the vaccination.

We denote the probability of contracting flu by *PROB*, the effectiveness of the vaccination by *EFFECT*, and the damage of contracting flu by *DAMAGE*. Thus, the damage of contracting flu is reduced to (1–*EFFECT*) × *DANAGE*, where *EFFECT* is assumed to take on a value between zero and one.

Costs: The cost of vaccination (*COST*) consists of the fee for inoculation (*FEE*), opportunity, and psychological costs of taking the vaccination, and perceived side effects of vaccination (*SIDEEFFECT*). We assume that people suffer these costs at the time of vaccination.

Decision to be vaccinated: The utility of the individual in our model is defined over consumption in two periods, x_1 and x_2. In period 1, the individual decides whether he/she wants to take the vaccine, and in period 2, the individual may be infected by influenza. Thus, the expected utility in the case of taking vaccination is:

$$u(x_1 - COST) + \theta\,[(1 - PROB) \times u(x_2) + PROB \times u(x_2 - (1 - EFFECT) \times DAMAGE)] \tag{13.1}$$

while the expected utility of not taking vaccination is:

$$u(x_1) + \theta\,[(1 - PROB) \times u(x_2) + PROB \times u(x_2 - DAMAGE)] \tag{13.2}$$

where θ is the discount factor. A person will take the vaccination if the value of Eq. (13.1) is larger than the value of Eq. (13.2).

Assuming that $x_1 \approx x_2 \gg COST$ and *DAMAGE*, and expanding the utility function to the second order, we find that people take the vaccination, if:

$$-COST + \theta PROB \times EFFECT \times DAMAGE - \frac{1}{2}\alpha\left[COST^2 - \theta \times PROB \times EFFECT \times (2 - EFFECT) \times DAMAGE^2\right] > 0 \tag{13.3}$$

where α stands for the absolute risk aversion, $-u''/u'$ (see Appendix A). This inequality implies that people are more likely to take the vaccination when (a) *PROB*, (b) *EFFECT*, or (c) *DAMAGE* is greater, (d) *COST* or (e) time discount rate $(1/\theta - 1)$ is smaller, or (f) risk aversion (α) is higher (lower, respectively), in the case where the fear of getting the flu is greater (smaller) than the fear of side effects (see Appendix A). Conditions (a) – (d) conform to the results of the HBM.

Assuming a linear function, (a) – (f) are described in Eq. (13.4), which is the basic equation for estimating willingness to take the vaccination (*WTVACCIN*).

$$WTVACCIN_i = a_0 + a_1 PROB_i + a_2 EFFECT_i + a_3 DAMAGE_i + a_5 COST_i + a_6 \theta_i + a_7 \alpha_i + u_i \tag{13.4}$$

where the subscript *i* stands for the individual *i*, $a_1, a_2 > 0$, $a_3, a_5, a_6 < 0$, and a_7 will be positive when *DAMAGE* dominates *SIDEEFFECT*.

To identify the channels through which risk aversion affects *WTVACCIN*, we adopt cross terms of risk aversion and *COST*, and risk aversion and *DAMAGE* resulting in the following equation.

$$WTVACCIN_i = a_0 + a_1 PROB_i + a_2 EFFECT_i + a_3 DAMAGE_i + a_5 COST_i + a_6 \theta_i + a_8 \alpha_i DAMAGE_i + a_9 \alpha_i COST_i + u_i \quad (13.5)$$

where it is demonstrated that $a_8 > 0$ and $a_9 < 0$.

2.2 Variables in the Basic Equation

Willingness to get the vaccination: *WTVACCIN* is the respondent's intention to take the vaccination within 12 months.

Probability of infection: *PROB* is the respondent's assessment of the probability of being infected with flu within 12 months, expressed as a percentage.

Damage of flu: *DAMAGE* is the respondent's assessment of the damage suffered if he/she contracts flu. It consists of two elements: SEVERITY, the respondent's assessment of the potential severity of the disease; and BOTHER, the respondent's assessment of the degree to which his/her family and friends would be inconvenienced if the respondent were infected.

Effectiveness of vaccination: Effectiveness of vaccination is denoted as *EFFECT*.

Cost of vaccination: We examine *COST* using the following: (a) the respondent's assessment of the seriousness of the side effects of a flu shot, *SIDEEFFECT*, (b) the monetary cost of the shot, and (c) the psychological costs. Variables relating to the monetary cost include respondents' assessment of the inoculation fee, *FEE*, and per capita income, *INCOME*. *INCOME* is included because the same *FEE* should be felt cheaper for people with higher income. Variables associated with the opportunity costs of taking the injection include wage and regional dummies, which are proxies for factors such as the cost of transportation to the administering hospital.

Preferences: Preferences include time discount rate, *TDR*, and absolute risk aversion, *ARA*. To determine *TDR*, we ask respondents which option they prefer: an earlier receipt with a smaller reward or a later receipt with a larger reward. To determine *ARA*, we ask respondents which option they prefer: lower wage with lower risk or higher wage with higher risk, following the method of Barsky et al. (1997). Definitions of all the variables we used are presented in Appendix B.

Using these notations of the variables, our basic Eq. (13.4) is now described as

$$WTVACCIN_i = b_0 + b_1 PROB_i + b_2 EFFECT_i + b_3 SEVERITY_i + b_4 BOTHER_i + b_5 FEE_i + b_6 SIDEEFFECT_i + b_7 INCOME_i + b_8 TDR_i + b_9 ARA_i + u_i \quad (13.6)$$

2.3 Extension of the Model Considering Behavioral Variables

Our basic model assumes that rational individuals decide whether they want to take the vaccination based only on the costs and benefits of vaccination. However, other variables representing behavioral preferences and attributes may also affect the decision. In this subsection, we present an extended model that incorporates behavioral preferences and socio-economic variables into the basic Eq. (13.6).

Our extended model takes into consideration an individual's altruism, overconfidence, anxiety regarding his/her health, and experiences of vaccination and flu, i.e., behavioral preferences that are often disregarded in traditional economics.

Altruism: Those who are more altruistic and caring may be more likely to take a vaccine because they want to avoid troubling other people. If so, the degree of altruism, *ALTRUISM*, has a positive effect on taking a vaccination. To examine this, we insert $(b_4 + b_{22}ALTRUISM)BOTHER$ or $b_{10}ALTRUISM + b_4BOTHER$ instead of $b_4BOTHER$ in the regression, where b_4 and b_{22} represent concern for family and friends, and b_{10} for the public. We expect b_4 and $b_{22} > 0$. In addition, $b_{10} > 0$ if a respondent believes that vaccination will mitigate flu epidemics and improve social welfare.

Overconfidence: Overconfidence may lower a respondent's assessment of the potential level of *PROB*, *SEVERITY*, *SIDEEFFECT*, or *BOTHER*. However, these variables are already included in the regression. To examine whether or not overconfidence affects vaccination behavior through some other channel not already specified in the regression, we add a variable for overconfidence, *OVERCON*.

Anxiety over health condition: Those who are concerned about their health will tend to take the vaccination. Thus, we take into account three variables: the degree of their health anxiety, *UNHEALTH*, and whether they undergo blood tests periodically, *TESTP*, or when disease is suspected, *TESTS*.

Psychological costs: Status quo bias means that people are reluctant to try new things (Knetsch and Sinden 1984). Accordingly, people who have never been vaccinated may resist taking the vaccination while those who are accustomed to being vaccinated every year may be reluctant to stop being vaccinated. We measure this psychological cost of taking the vaccination by the respondent's experience with flu vaccination, *EXVACCIN*. Those vaccinated in recent years are more likely to be vaccinated again.

Past experience of catching flu: Past experience of being ill with the flu, *EXFLU*, is also expected to influence *WTVACCIN*. Those seriously affected in the past will tend to take the vaccination, while those who experienced a mild infection may think that inoculation is unnecessary. Those seriously affected would have clearer memories of their illness and *EXFLU* is expected to be positive.

Attributes: We include gender, age, marital status, whether or not the respondent has children, and level of education in our extended regression Eq. (13.7):

$$
\begin{aligned}
WTVACCIN_i = {} & b_0 + b_1 PROB_i + b_2 EFFECT_i + b_3 SEVERITY_i \\
& + b_4 BOTHER_i + b_5 FEE_i + b_6 SIDEEFFECT_i + b_7 INCOME_i \\
& + b_8 TDR_i\,(HOMEWORK_i) + b_9 ARA_i\,(UMBRELLA_i) \\
& + b_{10} ALTRUISM_i + b_{11} OVERCON_i + b_{12} HEALTH_i + b_{13} TESTP_i \\
& + b_{14} TESTS_i + b_{15} EXVACCIN_i + b_{16} EXFLU_i + b_{17} MALE_i \\
& + b_{18} AGE_i + b_{19} UNMARRY_i + b_{20} NOCHILD_i + b_{21} SCHOOL_i \\
& + b_{22} ALTRUISM_i \times BOTHER_i + u_i
\end{aligned} \tag{13.7}
$$

3 Data

Data used in this chapter were obtained from a survey conducted by the COE (Center of Excellence) project of Osaka University in February 2005 with 4,300 people from throughout Japan, randomly selected by the double stratified random sampling method.[1] The selected participants were visited in their homes and given a questionnaire. Several days later, the filled-out questionnaires were picked up from their homes; 2,987 questionnaires (70 %) were returned. The range, means, and standard deviations of the main variables used for the analysis are presented in Table 13.1.

A possible critique of the use of survey data is that statements of intent may differ from actual actions. In our case, however, we were able to examine the relationship between respondents' declared intentions with their actual actions, since we re-contacted to the same survey respondents 2 years later and ask them whether they had received a flu shot in the past years. Two thousand and thirty five people responded. The results reveal that our respondents acted in close accordance with their stated intentions in the initial survey.[2]

[1]The questionnaire (in Japanese) is found at http://www2.econ.osaka-u.ac.jp/coe/project/survey-0502.pdf

[2]Out of 237 people who chose 1 ("Yes, certainly"), 223 (94.1 %) actually received vaccinations. Out of 327 people who chose 2 ("Yes, probably"), 227 (69.4 %) actually received vaccinations. Out of 480 people who chose 3 ("I have not decided yet"), 122 (25.4 %) actually received vaccinations. Out of 687 people who chose 4 ("No, probably not") 107 (15.6 %) actually received vaccinations. Out of 304 people who chose 5 ("No, certainly not"), 27 (8.9 %) actually received vaccinations.

Table 13.1 Definitions and mean values of variables in the study

Variable	Definition	Range		Mean	Standard error
		Min	Max		
WTVACCIN	Willingness to be vaccinated	1	5	2.712	0.029
PROB	Subject assessment of probability of getting flu (%)	0	100	23.868	0.469
SEVERITY	Self-assessment of seriousness of flu	1	6	3.260	0.026
BOTHER	Degree of bothering one's family and friends if infected	1	4	2.874	0.018
EFFECT	Effectiveness of vaccination	1	5	2.950	0.016
SIDEEFFECT	Seriousness of side effects of vaccination	1	7	3.055	0.039
FEE	Fee for inoculation	1	6	4.539	0.021
INCOME	Annual income per family member (ten thousand yen)	8.333	1,500	222.807	3.632
TDR	Time discount rate	−0.562	26.890	7.904	0.272
ARA	Absolute risk aversion	0.000	0.444	0.036	0.001
OVERCON	Degree of overconfidence	1	5	2.784	0.022
UNHEALTH	Anxiety regarding health	1	5	3.223	0.025
ALTRUISM	Degree of altruism	0	1	0.551	0.012
EXVACCIN	Experience of flu vaccination	0	1	0.521	0.012
EXFLU	Experience of contracting flu	0	1	0.113	0.008
TESTP	Had a periodic blood test in the last 12 months	0	1	0.652	0.011
TESTS	Had a blood test because of suspected disease in the last 12 months	0	1	0.096	0.007
DMAN	A dummy variable where male = 1, female = 0	0	1	0.492	0.012
AGE	Age of respondent	22	72	49.215	0.302
UNMARRY	A dummy variable where unmarried = 1, otherwise = 0	0	1	0.128	0.008
NOCHILD	A dummy variable where no children = 1, otherwise = 0	0	1	0.192	0.009
SCHOOL	Level of education where 1 = lowest and 11 = highest	1	11	4.081	0.048

4 Results

4.1 Results of Basic Eq. (13.6)

Estimates of basic Eq. (13.6) are presented in Table 13.2. Because the dependent variable, *WTVACCIN* (Willingness to be vaccinated), is denoted in integers from 1 to 5, and larger values indicate stronger willingness, we estimate the equation

Table 13.2 Results of basic Eq. (13.6) for estimating vaccination behavior, *WTVACCIN*

Variable		Estimate	*p*-value	ME	SE
PROB		0.007	0.000	0.008	0.001
DAMAGE	*SEVERITY*	0.129	0.000	0.145	0.027
	BOTHER	0.241	0.000	0.270	0.038
EFFECT		0.247	0.000	0.277	0.043
COST	*SIDEEFFECT*	−0.046	0.004	−0.051	0.018
	FEE	0.014	0.611	0.016	0.031
	INCOME	0.0004	0.038	0.0004	0.0002
TDR		−0.005	0.020	−0.006	0.002
ARA		1.154	0.012	1.293	0.517
			S.E.		
Boundary value	cut1	0.951	0.201		
	cut2	2.020	0.203		
	cut3	2.695	0.206		
	cut4	3.300	0.208		
Pseudo R^2		0.037			
Number of observations		1,861			

Note: The first column contains the variables that determine *WTVACCIN*. When the variable in the first column consists of multiple variables, those are shown in the second column. The estimation method is ordered probit. Cut1 to cut4 indicate boundary values of categories for which standard errors (S.E.) are given instead of *p* values. ME is weighted average of marginal effects. SE is the standard error of ME

with Ordered Probit. Most of the estimates are significant and show the expected sign, suggesting that basic Eq. (13.6), assuming rational choice, explains vaccination behavior well. In the table, average Marginal Effect (ME) and its Standard Error (SE) are shown. These values are similar to the estimates of Ordered Probit equation.

PROB, *EFFECT*, *SEVERITY*, *BOTHER*, and *SIDEEFFECT* are highly significant, showing a positive sign as expected. *FEE* is not significant, implying that monetary cost is not important in Japan. However, per capita household income has a positive sign and is significant at the 5 % level, suggesting that higher income promotes *WTVACCIN*. This may be because the fee is of less importance to households with a higher income.

To save space, we do not show the results associated with opportunity costs in this regression in Table 13.2. Therefore, the following is a brief report on the effect of opportunity costs. Important opportunity costs include those for transportation and lost revenue. Direct data are not available for transportation costs, so we make do with dummy variables dependent on the size of the respondent's city and region. Lost revenue is defined as the time required to take the vaccination multiplied by the wage rate. In the questionnaire, we ask respondents how many hours they work per week, how many days per year, and how much income they receive for their labor. Thus, *WAGE* is calculated as labor income/(work hours × work days/7). We add *WAGE* and regional and city-size dummies (proxies for lost time) to Eq. (13.6). Although *WAGE* was expected to negatively affect *WTVACCIN*, the estimate is not significant. Likewise, none of the regional and city-size dummies were significant at the 5 % level. However, while we found no evidence that opportunity costs significantly affect vaccination behavior, this may not necessarily imply that opportunity costs are unimportant since our data regarding opportunity costs are far from perfect.

TDR, the time discount rate for the immediate future, has a significant negative sign, as predicted in our model, implying that those who heavily discount the expected benefits of vaccination are less likely to take the vaccination. Discount rates over a long time horizon, such as 1 year, however, are not significant, implying that time discounting for the immediate future is crucial for *WTVACCIN* (results not shown to save space). These results are reasonable, since the time difference between inoculation and prevalence of flu is usually a couple of months.

ARA has a significant positive sign, suggesting that fear of contracting flu dominates any fear of side effects from the vaccination. Thus, risk aversion promotes taking the vaccination.

One might suspect that there are reverse causalities from *WTVACCIN* to perception variables, such as *PROB*, *SEVERITY*, and *BOTHER*. It is true that those who decide to take the vaccination usually assess *PROB* to be lower than those who choose not to be vaccinated. Thus, a reverse causality between *WTVACCIN* and *PROB* probably exists, making *PROB* an endogenous variable.[3] However, this reverse causality would imply that those with higher *WTVACCIN* show lower *PROB*, giving rise to a negative correlation between them. Thus, the positive correlation found in our estimates strongly suggests that there is causality from *PROB* to *WTVACCIN*, which is strong enough to overcome the reverse causality. By the same token, those who decide to take the vaccination usually assess *SEVERITY* and *BOTHER* to be lower than those who choose not to be vaccinated. Thus, the same logic can apply to these variables, and the results of the effects of the perception variables on willingness to take vaccination hold, despite the existence of the reverse causality.

4.2 Results of Extended Eq. (13.7)

Results of the extended model Eq. (13.7), including *ALTRUISM* in the regression, are presented in the right columns of Table 13.3. The fit of this specification is good. The adjusted R^2 is much improved, compared to the basic Eq. (13.6).[4] The estimates of the variables included in basic Eq. (13.6) are almost the same.

The coefficient of *ALTRUISM*, b_{10}, is significant at the 0.1 % level, suggesting that those who are altruistic tend to take vaccinations in order to avoid flu epidemics

[3]We tried to estimate the magnitude of the effect of *PROB* on *WTVACCIN* by correcting the endogeneity. However, an appropriate instrumental variable was difficult to find.

[4]This is partly due to the inclusion of experience of vaccination, *EXVACCIN*.

Table 13.3 Results of extended regression Eq. (13.7) for estimating vaccination behavior, *WTVACCIN*

		using ALTRUISM				*using ALTRUISM*BOTHER*			
Variable		Estimate	*p*-value	ME	SE	Estimate	*p*-value	ME	SE
PROB		0.009	0.000	0.009	0.001	0.009	0.000	0.009	0.001
DAMAGE	*SEVERITY*	0.105	0.000	0.108	0.026	0.106	0.000	0.109	0.026
	BOTHER	0.266	0.000	0.273	0.037	0.225	0.000	0.231	0.038
EFFECT		0.226	0.000	0.232	0.041	0.225	0.000	0.231	0.041
COST	*SIDEEFFECT*	−0.053	0.001	−0.055	0.017	−0.054	0.001	−0.055	0.017
	FEE	0.039	0.187	0.040	0.030	0.039	0.188	0.040	0.030
	INCOME	0.0004	0.053	0.0004	0.0002	0.0004	0.047	0.0004	0.0002
TDR		−0.004	0.054	−0.004	0.002	−0.004	0.050	−0.004	0.002
ARA		1.032	0.037	1.059	0.508	1.034	0.037	1.060	0.508
Behavioral variables	*OVERCON*	0.010	0.731	0.010	0.028	0.011	0.687	0.011	0.028
	UNHEALTH	0.058	0.021	0.059	0.026	0.058	0.022	0.059	0.026
	ALTRUISM	0.227	0.000	0.233	0.053	–	–	–	–
	*ALTRUISM*BOTHER*	–	–	–	–	0.078	0.000	0.080	0.018
	EXVACCIN	0.884	0.000	0.896	0.052	0.885	0.000	0.896	0.052
	EXFLU	0.108	0.187	0.112	0.085	0.110	0.178	0.114	0.085
	TESTP	0.118	0.054	0.121	0.062	0.119	0.052	0.122	0.062
	TESTS	0.113	0.252	0.117	0.103	0.112	0.257	0.116	0.103
	MALE	−0.171	0.001	−0.175	0.054	−0.172	0.001	−0.176	0.054
	AGE	0.018	0.000	0.019	0.003	0.018	0.000	0.019	0.003
	UNMARRY	0.249	0.045	0.259	0.131	0.252	0.042	0.262	0.131
	NOCHILD	−0.295	0.005	−0.298	0.103	−0.296	0.005	−0.299	0.103
	SCHOOL	−0.013	0.360	−0.013	0.014	−0.012	0.370	−0.013	0.014

(continued)

Table 13.3 (continued)

Variable		*using ALTRUISM*				*using ALTRUISM*BOTHER*			
		Estimate	*p*-value	ME	SE	Estimate	*p*-value	ME	SE
			S.E.				S.E.		
	cut1	2.509	0.292			2.402	0.292		
	cut2	3.681	0.296			3.574	0.296		
	cut3	4.465	0.300			4.359	0.300		
	cut4	5.201	0.304			5.096	0.304		
Pseudo R^2		0.108				0.109			
Number of observations		1,798				1,798			

Note: Refer to note of Table 13.2

in the society. *UNHEALTH* has a significant positive sign, as expected. However, *TESTP* and *TESTS* are insignificant at the 5 % significant level, even though they have positive signs. *OVERCON* is insignificant, suggesting that it does not affect vaccination behavior through channels other than those specified in the regression, such as *PROB*.

EXVACCIN is highly significant, indicating that having been vaccinated in the past reduces the psychological costs of taking a vaccination. The large coefficient suggests that psychological costs carry great weight in the decision to be vaccinated, supporting the "status quo bias" hypothesis that human beings are reluctant to change. *EXFLU* is positive but insignificant, suggesting that painful memories of previous experiences with flu dominate relatively pleasant memories, but only slightly.

Among attributes, females, the elderly, the unmarried, and those who have children are more likely to take a vaccination. Schooling does not affect vaccination behavior.

When *ALTRUISM*BOTHER* replaces *ALTRUISM* in the equation (right-hand columns of Table 13.3), the cross term is highly significant with a positive sign, implying that those who are altruistic tend to take the vaccination to avoid troubling their families and not only in consideration of avoiding flu epidemics in the society.[5]

4.3 Examination of Time Discount Rate (TDR) and Risk Aversion (ARA)

While the total number of responses to the survey was 2,987, only 1,861 of these observations were available for estimating Eq. (13.6). This was because many respondents failed to answer either the question regarding income and/or the questions on *TDR* and *ARA* (quantitative style questions). Thus, to check the robustness of our results, we did two things:

In Table 13.4, we present the results using *qualitative* data associated with *TDR* and *ARA*. *HOMEWORK* represents a respondent's homework habits in childhood (those who made it a rule to do homework, i.e. get an unpleasant obligation out of the way, at the beginning of a school holiday are regarded as more patient or more future-oriented). *UMBRELLA* is determined by asking how high the probability of rain has to be to motivate the respondent to carry an umbrella (those who report that a low probability is sufficient are regarded as more risk-averse). Using these alternative variables, the sample size is 2,184. *UMBRELLA* is positive and significant at the 0.1 % level, and *HOMEWORK* is negative and significant at the 5 % level, confirming the results for *TDR* and *ARA*. Estimates of other variables are almost unchanged from those presented in Table 13.2, indicating that our results are robust for the sample size.

[5]However, neither is significant when both terms are included at the same time.

Table 13.4 Robustness check of the basic results using *HOMEWORK* and *UMBRELLA* as the variables for time discounting and risk aversion

Variable		Estimate	*p*-value	ME	SE
PROB		0.007	0.000	0.008	0.001
DAMAGE	*SEVERITY*	0.125	0.000	0.142	0.025
	BOTHER	0.235	0.000	0.267	0.035
EFFECT		0.247	0.000	0.280	0.039
COST	*SIDEEFFECT*	−0.047	0.002	−0.053	0.017
	FEE	−0.001	0.968	−0.001	0.029
	INCOME	0.0002	0.279	0.0002	0.0002
TDR	*HOMEWORK*	−0.037	0.036	−0.042	0.020
ARA	*UMBRELLA*	0.004	0.0000	0.005	0.001
			S.E.		
Boundary value	cut1	0.836	0.197		
	cut2	1.901	0.199		
	cut3	2.582	0.202		
	cut4	3.168	0.204		
Pseudo R^2		0.036			
Number of observations		2,184			

Note: Refer to note of Table 13.2

In order to further check the robustness, we delete the variable of income in addition to the use of qualitative data for time discounting and risk aversion. The number of observations increased to 2,694 (90 % of the total observations). The estimates are almost identical to those shown in Table 13.3 (results not shown here).

In Table 13.5, we show the estimation results of Eq. (13.5), which examines two channels through which risk aversion impacts *WTVACCIN*. When cross terms for risk aversion and severity (representing *DAMAGE*; *ARA*SEVERITY*) and risk aversion and side effects (representing *COST*; *ARA*SIDEEFFECT*) are used, the coefficient of the former, i.e. a_8 in Eq. (13.5), is positive and significant at the 1 % level, and that of the latter, i.e. a_9 in Eq. (13.5), is negative and significant at the 5 % level (left columns). This result supports our hypothesis that risk aversion operates through the fear of getting the flu, which is stronger than the fear of side effects of the vaccination. When a cross term for risk aversion, severity, and effect (*ARA*SEVERITY*EFFECT*) is used instead of *ARA*SEVERITY*, the results are unchanged (right-hand columns). This result is consistent with the result that risk aversion, in general, negatively affects *WTVACCIN*.

5 Discussion and Conclusion

This chapter develops an economic model to explain the mechanism by which people in Japan decide whether or not to take the influenza vaccination. Using our model and data obtained from a large-scale survey we conducted in Japan,

Table 13.5 Examination of two channels through which risk aversion impacts as shown in Eq. (13.5)

Variable		Equation (13.5) using *ARA*SEVERITY*				Equation (13.5) using *ARA*EFFECT*SEVERITY*			
		Estimate	*p*-value	ME	SE	Estimate	*p*-value	ME	SE
PROB		0.007	0.000	0.008	0.001	0.007	0.000	0.008	0.001
DAMAGE	*SEVERITY*	0.102	0.000	0.114	0.029	0.106	0.000	0.118	0.029
	BOTHER	0.240	0.000	0.268	0.038	0.239	0.000	0.268	0.038
EFFECT		0.245	0.000	0.274	0.043	0.218	0.000	0.244	0.044
COST	*SIDEEFFECT*	−0.026	0.175	−0.029	0.021	−0.030	0.098	−0.034	0.020
	FEE	0.014	0.626	0.015	0.031	0.014	0.606	0.016	0.031
	INCOME	0.0003	0.074	0.0003	0.0002	0.0003	0.074	0.0003	0.0002
Time discount	*TDR*	−0.005	0.017	−0.006	0.002	−0.005	0.017	−0.006	0.002
Risk aversion	*ARA*SEVERITY*	0.754	0.004	0.844	0.290	–	–	–	–
	*ARA*EFFECT*SEVERITY*	–	–	–	–	0.215	0.004	0.241	0.083
	*ARA*SIDEEFFFECT*	−0.587	0.037	−0.657	0.315	−0.444	0.064	−0.497	0.268
			S.E.				S.E.		
Boundary value	cut1	0.878	0.197			0.801	0.198		
	cut2	1.947	0.199			1.870	0.200		
	cut3	2.623	0.202			2.546	0.202		
	cut4	3.229	0.204			3.152	0.205		
Pseudo R^2		0.037				0.037			
Number of observations		1,861				1,861			

Note: Refer to note of Table 13.2

we demonstrate that people rationally make the decision considering the costs and benefits of vaccination. People take into account the probability of infection, severity of the disease, and effectiveness and side effects of the vaccination. Time discount rate matters because the timing of costs and benefits of vaccination differs. Risk aversion also affects the decision through the fear of contracting the flu and the fear of side effects of the vaccination. However, we found no evidence that subjective assessment of monetary cost is important in making the decision.[6] The results of this Japanese sample are compatible with the findings of Tsutsui et al. (2010) with respect to their USA sample.

Yet, people also deviate from rationality. Altruism, a behavioral variable, plays an important role in making the decision. To the best of our knowledge, the effect of altruism on the willingness to be vaccinated has not yet been examined. The status quo bias is clearly recognized, in that people who have never been vaccinated tend to avoid taking the vaccination. Overconfidence does not affect the decision directly. However, it does indirectly via perception variables such as the subjective probability of infection and assessment of the severity of influenza, similar to findings in the USA sample of Tsutsui et al. (2010) (the results are not shown to save space). The decision also depends on attributes such as gender, age, and marital status.

The results of this chapter have interesting implications. First, raising the inoculation rate is often thought to be socially desirable because taking a vaccination has strong externality. However, we found that the degree of altruism affects the willingness to take vaccination not only through the channel of concern for one's family and friends (the coefficient of *ALTRUISM*, b_{22}, in Table 13.2), but also through a channel of caring about a wider range of people (the coefficient of *ALTRUISM*BOTHER*, b_{10}, in Table 13.2). Therefore, if most Japanese people are altruistic, the spontaneous vaccination rate will not differ substantially from the social optimum. However, our survey indicates that 44 % of Japanese respondents show no altruism, suggesting that it is desirable for the society to raise the vaccination rate to a level higher than the rate that people choose spontaneously.[7] This conclusion is consistent with casual observation that the flu shot is given for free in many systems and in several systems the rate of elderly (60+) taking the flu shot is considered a measure of the quality of care, meaning that the social optimum might be quite high.

Second, if the general perception of flu and vaccination is inaccurate, supplying accurate information on the illness, its possible complications, and the effectiveness of the vaccination will probably raise or lower the vaccination rate, depending on whether this perception is higher or lower than the objective rates. Thus, we examine whether the general perception is biased, although our

[6]However, since previous studies, such as Steiner et al. (2002), found that monetary cost has an impact on the decision to take a vaccination, our results should be examined further from various aspects.

[7]In the USA, only 24 % are not altruistic based on our survey results.

caveat is that the following assessment is crude. *WTVACCIN* depends on six perceptions: *PROB*, *SEVERITY*, *BOTHER*, *EFFECT*, *SIDEEFFECT*, and *FEE*. The mean *PROB* is 24 %, which is very high considering the fact that according to the website of "global security" (http://ww.globalsecurity.org/security/ops/hsc-scen-3_flu-pandemic-deaths.htm), theinfluenza infection rate is 5–15 % (except during pandemic periods). Although there are no statistics on the total number of flu cases in Japan, based on the 1.56 million infections reported in 2005 from 4,700 hospitals, the probability of infection is only 1.5 % (A website of National Infectious Disease Surveillance Center: http://dsc.nih.go.jp/idwr/ydata/report-Jb.html). This number, of course, underestimates the true rate because it is based on reports from the limited number of hospitals. More reliable information can be derived from our survey. Some 10.5 % of our respondents indicated that they were infected with flu during the previous 2 years, reflecting a yearly probability of infection of about 5 %.[8] Since this rate is still substantially lower than the subjective probability of being infected (24 %), providing information on the probability of contracting flu would probably reduce the average vaccination rate.[9]

However, the infection rates differ between different age groups and between those who took the vaccine and those who did not take it. Therefore, we examined the subjective infection rates and the infection rates in the following sub-samples: male vs. female, over-60s vs. under-60s, those who took the flu shot during the past 2 years vs. those who did not take it.

Our results (not shown in the chapter) indicate that the subjective probability differs between the sub-groups: female-25.5 % vs. male-22.5 %; people under 60 years-25.6 % vs. people over 60 years-20.0 %; those who took the vaccine during the last 2 years-26.4 % vs. those who did not take the vaccine during this period-23.3 %. Nonetheless, in all sub-groups we found that the subjective probability was substantially higher than the experienced flu rate during the last 2 years.

Most of the other perception variables are qualitative and not easy to compare with actual figures. For *FEE*, 55 % chose "the fee is 2,000–5,000 yen," and for *SEVERITY*, 60 % chose "a disease from which it takes about a week to recover," both of which do not seem to radically contradict the facts. However, with regard to the effectiveness of the vaccination, while 60 % of the respondents correctly answered "the shot can prevent certain types of flu," 20 % selected "despite the flu shot, a high possibility of getting the flu remains," which contradicts the truth and underestimates the effectiveness of vaccination. With reference to the side effects

[8] Yet, it could be that this number reflects also "flu-like" symptoms which are sometimes wrongly attributed to the influenza illness, suggesting that the true rate is lower than 5 %.

[9] One may argue that the flu rate varies substantially from year to year, so that we should not compare the subjective probability of 2005 with experienced probability for the past 2 years. According to the statistics reported by the National Infectious Disease Surveillance Center, the number of influenza infections reported by the hospitals designated to report the infection in 2005 was almost double the number reported in 2004, and 1.3 times the number reported in 2003. Thus, the actual rate of infection is probably larger than 5 %. Yet, there is no reason to believe that this rate exceeds 10 %.

of vaccination, although 50 % accurately answered that "side effects have little influence," about 10 % selected "very serious side effects that could cause after-effects" and 5 % selected "extremely serious side effects that could cause death," which overestimate potential side effects of flu vaccination.

In sum, although the comparisons are crude, they seem to suggest that Japanese people evaluate the effectiveness of vaccination as too low and the side effects as too high in number and level of severity. In this case, dissemination of information on the effectiveness of vaccination may help raise the vaccination rate. On the other hand, they seem to perceive too high a probability of getting the flu. If this is true, provision of correct information on the probability of infection may mitigate their willingness to be vaccinated. Nevertheless, it is difficult to evaluate theses speculations without knowing the social optimal vaccination rate, which could be quite high, as we mentioned before.

It is interesting to note that the current chapter and Tsutsui et al. (2010) used the same questionnaire in Japan and the U.S., respectively, and found in general similar results. For example, basic statistics, such as the willingness to receive vaccination and subjects' assessment of the probability of getting flu, are extremely similar between the two countries. Yet there are some discrepancies; for example, Japanese people tend to consider influenza to be a less serious disease in comparison to the U.S. people. Nonetheless, Japanese people tend to worry more than Americans about the burden they will place on their family and colleagues if they get sick. This discrepancy may reflect cultural differences between the two countries, which is a topic for future research.

Appendix A. Derivation of Eq. (13.3) and the Expected Sign of the Coefficients

For simplicity, let us assume that x_1 and x_2 are independent of the decision on vaccination and they are much larger than the costs and benefits due to vaccination. Then, expanding the utility (13.1) and (13.2) around x_1 and x_2 respectively, we obtain,

$$\begin{aligned}&-u'(x_1)\,COST + \tfrac{1}{2}u''(x_1)\,COST^2 + \theta PROB \times EFFECT \times DAMAGE\\&\times\left[u'(x_2) + \tfrac{1}{2}u''(x_2) \times DAMAGE \times (EFFECT - 2)\right] > 0\end{aligned} \tag{13.8}$$

Assuming that $x_1 = x_2$, and denoting $-u''/u'$, the absolute risk aversion, as α, Eq. (13.3) is derived.

Denoting the left side of (13.8) as Ω, a larger Ω implies more willingness to take the vaccination. Therefore, the derivative of Ω to these elements implies the effect of each element of the equation on the willingness to be vaccinated against flu. Differentiating Ω from each term, we obtain

$$\begin{aligned}
\frac{d\Omega}{dCOST} &= -\alpha \times COST - 1 < 0 \\
\frac{d\Omega}{dDAMAGE} &= \theta \times PROB \times EFFECT \times [1 + \alpha \times DAMAGE \\
&\qquad \times (2 - EFFECT)] > 0 \\
\frac{d\Omega}{dPROB} &= \theta \times EFFECT \times DAMAGE \times [1 + \alpha \times DAMAGE \\
&\qquad \times (2 - EFFECT)] > 0 \\
\frac{d\Omega}{dEFFECT} &= \theta \times PROB \times DAMAGE \times [1 + \alpha \times DAMAGE \\
&\qquad \times (1 - EFFECT)] > 0 \\
\frac{d\Omega}{d\theta} &= PROB \times EFFECT \times DAMAGE \times \left[1 + \tfrac{1}{2}\alpha \times DAMAGE \right. \\
&\qquad \left. \times (2 - EFFECT)\right] > 0 \\
\frac{d\Omega}{d\alpha} &= -\tfrac{1}{2}\left[COST^2 - \theta \times PROB \times EFFECT \times (2 - EFFECT) \right. \\
&\qquad \left. \times DAMAGE^2\right], \\
\frac{d\Omega}{d\alpha} &> 0 \quad \text{if } DAMAGE \text{ is sufficiently larger than } COST,
\end{aligned} \tag{13.9}$$

which prove (a)–(f) in the text.

Appendix B. Definition of the Data

In this appendix, we explain the variables used in the analysis.

WTVACCIN: Willingness to take the vaccination, which is defined as 6 minus the answer to the question "Do you intend to receive the flu shot in the next 12 months?" The answer is given on a five-point scale from "1 Yes, certainly" to "5 No, certainly not." A larger *WTVACCIN* implies greater willingness to take vaccination.

PROB: Subject probability of infection (*PROB*) is defined as the answer (%) to the question "Estimate your chances of being infected with the flu during the next 12 months."

EFFECT: With reference to the effectiveness of a flu shot, we asked, "How effective do you think the flu shot is?" and define a variable *EFFECT* as 6 minus the answer to this question, which is any one of five options on a scale from "1 The shot can completely prevent the flu" to "5 The shot is never effective."

SEVERITY: For seriousness of the disease, we define *SEVERITY* as 7 minus the answer to the question "How serious a disease do you think the flu is?" which is one of six options on a scale from "1 An extremely serious disease which could cause death" to "6 A disease which has little influence."

BOTHER: With regard to the degree of bother for one's family and friends when one is infected, we defined *BOTHER* as 5 minus the answer to the question "When you are infected with the flu, to what extent do you bother your family and friends?" which is one of four options on a scale from "1 I bother them tremendously" to "4 I hardly bother them."

SIDEEFECT: With regard to the seriousness of the side effects of a flu shot, we defined *SIDEEFFECT* as 8 minus the answer to the question "How serious do you think the side effects caused by a flu shot are?" This is one of the seven options on a scale from "1 Extremely serious side effects which could cause death" to "7 There are no side effects."

FEE: For the injection fee, we defined *FEE* as the answer to the question "How much do you think a flu shot costs?" which is any of six options on a scale from "1 free" to "6 more than $50.00."

TDR: Discount rates are estimated from the following questions: "Which would you choose, receiving $100 in 2 days or in 9 days?" Eight different pairs of options that correspond to different interest rates ranging from −10 to 300 % are presented. Respondents are requested to choose earlier or later receipt in these eight cases. Most respondents rationally chose earlier options during low interest rates, switched to a later option at some interest rate, and kept choosing it for higher interest rates. We define a variable *TDR* as the interest rate at which they switch.

ARA: Risk aversion is measured using a question that asks what payment pattern is preferred. The options are: 1 Your monthly income has a 50 % chance of increasing by 30 %, but also has a 50 % chance of decreasing by 10 % or 2 Your monthly income is guaranteed to increase by 5 %. Those who choose 1 are asked the question in which the increasing rate is altered from 30 to 20 %. Those who choose 2 are asked the question in which the increasing rate is altered from 30 to 50 %. From these answers, we classify all the respondents into four groups, and assuming constant relative risk aversion utility function, we calculate relative risk aversion for each group, which is named *RRA* following Barsky et al. (1997). Dividing *RRA* by their household income, we calculate the absolute risk aversion, *ARA*.

ALTRUISM: Altruism is measured using the question "Suppose that you found a well-known charity that gave financial help to people who typically had about one-fifth of your family income per person. Up to how much of your own family income per month would you be willing to give the charity if you knew the money would go directly to benefit these people?" We define a dummy variable where "No help at all" =1 and 0 otherwise.

OVERCON: A variable measuring overconfidence of respondents is defined by the responses to the statement "I will never be robbed." *OVERCON* is defined as 6 when the answers are five options on a scale from "1 It is particularly true for you" to "5 It doesn't hold true for you at all."[10]

UNHEALTH: We define a variable *UNHEALTH* from the response to the statement "I am anxious about my health," which is any of five options on a scale from "1 It is particularly true for you" to "5 It doesn't hold true for you at all." Larger *UNHEALH* implies greater anxiety for health.

[10]The confidence of "never be robbed" may exist for good reasons for some people. They might be too poor to be robbed. Or they might have taken the most foolproof measures for security. Or they live in safer places. In order to adjust these elements, we regress *OVERCON* over financial wealth of respondents and variables representing size of city where respondents live and 10 regions of Japan and define *OVERCON2* as the constant term plus estimated residuals. However, no explanatory variables of the regression were significant and the regression as a whole was insignificant by F-test (p-value was 0.8). Thus, we report only the results with *OVERCON*.

TESTP and *TESTS*: *TESTP* takes on unity if respondents took a periodic blood test in the previous 12 months and zero otherwise. *TESTS* takes on unity if respondents took a blood test because of suspicion of disease in the last 12 months and zero otherwise.

EXVACCIN: We define *EXVACCIN* that takes unity if the answer to the question "Have you ever received a flu shot?" is yes and zero otherwise.

EXFLU: We define *EXFLU* that takes unity if the answer to the question "Have you been infected by the flu during the last two years?" is yes and zero otherwise.

MALE: A dummy variable with male = 1 and female = 0.

AGE: Age of the respondent.

UNMRRY: A dummy variable with unmarried = 1 and 0 otherwise.

NOCHILD: A dummy variable with those who have no children = 1 and 0 otherwise.

SCHOOL: School career, which is defined by "the highest level of education completed" from "1 Grade school" to "11 Doctorial degree."

WAGE: Wage is defined based on the following three questions as $Q62/(Q35 \times (Q36/7))$

*Q*35. About how many hours per week do you work for pay in a typical week?
*Q*36. About how many days do you work for pay per year?
*Q*62. How much was your annual income earned for 2004?

Sixty-nine percent answered "yes" to the question "Are you currently employed?" so that we got only 1,147 observations for the equation including *WAGE*.

HOMEWORK: This is a proxy for time discounting, since those who finish unpleasant tasks earlier are considered to be more patient, or more future-oriented. *HOMEWORK* is defined using the answers to the following question: When you were a child, if you were given an assignment in school, when did you usually do the assignment? 1 Got it done right away 2 Tended to get it done early, before the due date 3 Worked on it daily up until the due date 4 Tended to get it done toward the end 5 Got it done at the last minute

UMBRELLA: This is a proxy for risk aversion and is defined as an answer to the following question: When you usually go out, how high does the probability of rain have to be before you take an umbrella? (Percentages between 0 and 100).

Addendum: Flu Vaccination in the US[11]

We conducted a parallel survey in the U.S. using the same questions, in order to examine uptake of flu vaccination among Americans.[12]

[11]This addendum has been newly written for this book chapter.

[12]The following findings are based on the paper titled "A Policy to Promote Influenza Vaccination: A Behavioral Economic Approach" by Tsutsui et al. 2010.

In January 2005, 12,338 questionnaires were distributed in the U.S., and 4,979 (40 %) received responses. Using these, we estimated an equation similar to Eq. (13.7) in the text. The main differences between Eq. (13.7) and the specification for the U.S. analysis were as follows: (1) time discount rates and risk aversion were specified using the simple questions shown below; (2) the variable of income was not included; (3) variable *ALTRUISM* was not included; and (4) some control variables were different.

Surprisingly, the estimation results were almost the same, at least for the sign conditions. Specifically, the coefficients of the key variables – *PROB*, *SEVERITY*, *BOTHER*, and *EFFECT* – were significant and positive, the coefficient of *SIDEEFFECT* was significant and negative, and the coefficient of *FEE* was not significant. The variable of the discount rate (*TDR*) was defined using a different question than in the text, namely: "I want to save joys for later" (1 = do not agree at all; 5 = certainly agree), and its coefficient was negative and significant at 10 %. The risk aversion (*RA*) variable was also defined using a different question from the text, namely: "When you usually go out, how high does the probability of rain have to be before you take an umbrella?" In this case the coefficient was positive at the 1 % significance level. In sum, both in Japan and in the U.S., people rationally decided whether or not to take flu vaccinations based on cost-benefit considerations.

The effects of behavioral variables were also similar in both countries.[13] Overconfidence (*OVERCON*) was not significant in the regression. While the coefficients of *UNHEALTH* and *EXVACCIN* were significant and positive, that of *EXFLU* was insignificant. In addition, the *TESTP* and *TESTS* coefficients were significant. These results are the same as those described in the text. Thus, behavioral rules are also similar in Japan and in the U.S.

The effects of demographic variables on willingness to take the flu vaccination are also similar. For example, elderly people tended to get vaccinated in both countries. Neither school career (*SCHOOL*) nor marital status (*UNMARRY*) were significant in either of the countries. However, the results for the gender variable are different. While in Japan women were significantly more likely to get vaccinated than men, in the US there was no significant difference between women and men with respect to the decision to get vaccinated.

Willingness to be vaccinated was measured by the following question: "Do you intend to obtain a flu shot in the next 12 months?" (1 = certainly no, 5 = certainly yes). The average answer was almost the same: 2.7 in Japan and 2.8 in the U.S. Subjective assessment of the probability of coming down with the flu (%) did not radically differ between the two countries: 23.9 % in Japan and 26.0 % in the U.S. People's assessments of the effectiveness of the vaccination and the severity of side effects were also similar in both countries. However, some items were different. First, Americans think the flu is more serious than do the Japanese (Japan: U.S. = 3.3: 4.2). The Japanese are more concerned about being a burden on family

[13] *ALTRUISM* is not included as a regressor in the case of the U.S.

members and friends after they have been infected (Japan: U.S. = 2.9: 1.7). Finally, the Japanese think that the flu shot is more costly (Japan: U.S. = 4.5: 3.4).

In the text, we concluded that overconfidence does not affect vaccination. In our analysis of the US case, we considered this point in greater depth. As noted above, overconfidence does not directly affect people's willingness to be vaccinated (*WTV*) in the U.S. or in Japan. However, it does have an indirect effect via subjective variables, such as *PROB*, *SEVERITY*, *FEE*, *EFFECT*, and *SIDEEFFECT*. Similarly, as in Japan, the education level does not affect *WTV* directly in the U.S. However it does have an indirect impact via subjective variables.

References

Barsky RB, Juster FT, Kimball MS, Shapiro MD (1997) Preference parameters and behavioral heterogeneity: an experimental approach in the health and retirement study. Q J Econ 112:537–579

Blue CL, Valley JM (2002) Predictors of influenza vaccine: acceptance among healthy adult workers. AAOHN J 50:227–235

Brito DL, Sheshinski E, Intriligator MD (1991) Externalities and compulsory vaccinations. J Public Econ 45:69–90

Chapman GB, Coups EJ (1999) Predictors of influenza vaccine acceptance among healthy adults. Prev Med 29:249–262

Chen JY, Fox SA, Cantrell CH, Stockdale SE, Kagawa-Singer M (2007) Health disparities and prevention: racial/ethnic barriers to flu vaccinations. J Community Health 32:5–20

Knetsch JL, Sinden JA (1984) Willingness to pay and compensation demanded: experimental evidence of an unexpected disparity in measures of value. Q J Econ 99:507–521

Lau J, Kim J, Yang X, Tsui HY (2008) Cross-sectional and longitudinal factors predicting influenza vaccination in Hong Kong Chinese elderly aged 65 and above. J Infect 56:460–468

Mullahy J (1999) It'll only hurt a second? Microeconomic determinants of who gets flu shots. Health Econ 8:9–24

Rosenstock LM, Strecher VJ, Becker MH (1988) Social learning theory and the Health Belief Model. Health Educ Q 15:175–183

Shahrabani S, Gafni A, Benzion U (2008) Low flu shot rates puzzle – some plausible behavioral explanations. Am Econ 52:66–72

Shahrabani S, Benzion U, Yom DG (2009) Factors affecting nurses' decision to get the flu vaccine. Eur J Health Econ 10:227–231

Steiner M, Vermeulen LC, Mullahy J, Hayney MS (2002) Factors influencing decisions regarding influenza vaccination and treatment: a survey of healthcare workers. Infect Control Hosp Epidemiol 23:625–627

Tsutsui Y, Benzion U, Shahrabani S, Yom DG (2010) A policy to promote influenza vaccination: a behavioral economic approach. Health Policy 97:238–249

Tsutsui Y, Benzion U, Shahrabani S (2012) Economic and behavioral factors in an individual's decision to take the influenza vaccination in Japan. J Socio-Econ 41:594–602

Part IV
Social Preferences

Chapter 14
Another Avenue for Anatomy of Income Comparisons: Evidence from Hypothetical Choice Experiments

Katsunori Yamada and Masayuki Sato

Abstract We propose a new avenue for studying income comparisons effects, namely hypothetical discrete choice experiments in which respondents are presented with alternative combinations of hypothetical monthly income amounts, both for themselves and certain reference persons. With this experimental method we can avoid the problems associated with researcher-imposed reference persons' incomes that are found in most of the happiness studies testing comparison effects. This approach allows investigation of the differences in comparison effects across types of reference groups as well as respondents' individual characteristics, including specific comparison benchmarks, which are the main open questions in the literature. Some results from our original, large-scale, Internet-based survey are provided.

Keywords Relative utility • Hypothetical choice experiment • Reference group • Comparison benchmark

JEL classification Number: C9; D1; D3

The original article first appeared in the Journal of Economic Behavior & Organization 89:35–57, 2013. A newly written addendum has been added to this book chapter.

K. Yamada (✉)
Faculty of Economics, Kindai University, Higashiosaka, Osaka, Japan
e-mail: kyamada@kindai.ac.jp

M. Sato
Graduate School of Human Development and Environment, Kobe University, Kobe, Hyogo, Japan
e-mail: msat@port.kobe-u.ac.jp

S. Ikeda et al. (eds.), *Behavioral Economics of Preferences, Choices, and Happiness*, DOI 10.1007/978-4-431-55402-8_14

1 Introduction

Traditional economic theories focus on the role of absolute income or consumption, whereas behavioral evidence suggests that social comparisons influence well-being and decisions (Fliessbach et al. 2007, p. 1305). Whether social comparisons do in fact affect individual utility is critically important in understanding human behavior in any social context, and in evaluating the outcomes of economic behavior.

This study provides a new way to measure income comparison effects using hypothetical discrete choice experiments. A critical component in empirical studies of income comparison and relative utility is defining the appropriate reference person or group for each subject. Our approach estimates the income comparison parameters in the utility function through the *decision utility approach*, which was originally put forth by Kahneman et al. (1997) in the field of environmental valuation. Hence, this method is different from the standard *experienced utility approach* used in happiness studies, where respondents' subjective reports of well-being and proxies for reference income are used to estimate the relative utility effects. By using the decision utility approach, we are able to avoid the use of researcher-imposed reference persons' incomes, which must be constructed by econometricians without knowledge of the subjects who provided data on happiness but who were not asked with whom they made a comparison or how much they think their rivals earn.[1] In our experimental approach, we impose alternative combinations of hypothetical monthly income amounts on subjects, both for themselves and certain reference persons. Using data on respondents' choices of preferred income scenario, we can estimate the utility function parameters that capture the intensity and sign of income comparisons with certain reference persons. As such, the methodological merits of our study include that (i) the subjects can see the characteristics of reference persons and how much these persons earn compared with themselves in clear situation choice tasks, and (ii) the subjects can choose discrete choices with a lower cognitive burden than when evaluating their lives with more general happiness scores.

Exploiting the features of the choice experiment, we can investigate differences in comparison effects by reference person type through changing the characteristics of reference persons in hypothetical income scenarios. Another important issue that can be addressed with our method is determining how individual characteristics such as age, gender, educational attainments, and respondents' specific comparison benchmarks affect attitudes in income comparisons. Among these variables, the comparison benchmarks are of particular interest for researchers in the field, because these were recently studied by Clark and Senik (2010) via the experienced utility approach. We provide empirical results on these issues by using our original, large-scale, Internet-based survey of Japanese subjects. Our data set is socially representative in terms of age and gender distribution, which is an important virtue

[1]Critiques of using researcher-imposed reference persons' incomes to estimate income comparison effects in happiness regressions were detailed in Manski (1993) and Sloane and Williams (2000).

of our sample, as many studies often rely on potentially biased student samples. Problems of sample bias also affect experimental studies that provide incentives for a small number of subjects such as Fehr and Schmidt (1999, 2006).[2] Our Internet-based survey overcomes this issue by accessing an enormous number and wide variety of registered subjects through a reliable subcontracted research company.

While the Internet offers immediate access to a large and diverse subject pool and research opportunities at cheaper costs, there are also caveats and potential pitfalls that pertain to Internet-based experiments. Typical critiques include the inability to monitor the motivations and understanding of participants and uncertainty about the precise identity of the experimental subjects, among others. On these issues, Horton et al. (2011) provided clear evidence that online experiments on social preferences through Amazon Mechanical Turk (MTurk) replicate previous experimental results from physical laboratories, encouraging the use of Internet-based surveys.[3] The fact that our experiment was hypothetical may be another source of concern, but neuroscience studies such as Bickel et al. (2009) and Kang et al. (2011) show that incentivized and hypothetical experiments do not generate significant differences in human neural activity. In addition, Amir et al. (2012) found that experimental participants in MTurk showed no differences in responses between incentivized experiments and non-incentivized experiments in the public goods game and in the trust game.

The remainder of the chapter is organized as follows. Section 2 reviews the empirical literature on income comparisons and relative utility and places this study in historical context. In Sect. 3 we explain the experimental design of hypothetical discrete choices for income comparisons and the methods employed in our original Internet-based survey. The questionnaire and data construction for empirical analyses are also explained in the section. Section 4 outlines the estimation method following Train (2009). Section 5 presents the results for our benchmark task, in which the reference person is defined as "the social average" as in the series of studies by Richard Easterlin. Section 6 provides some additional results when different types of reference persons are presented in hypothetical income scenarios. Section 7 discusses potential biases related to experimental studies and concludes the chapter.

[2]Recent experimental studies on social preferences by Falk et al. (2013) and Exadaktylos et al. (2012) report that only slight student bias can be observed, if any, and argue that experimental results from student samples are useful even in designing policy for the whole population.

[3]See also Paolacci et al. (2010), Suri and Watts (2011), Rand (2011), and Amir et al. (2012) for the potential pitfalls of Internet-based experiments and surveys and rebuttals to those critiques in the literature of social preferences.

2 Related Studies on Income Comparisons

In the literature of happiness studies on income comparisons, reference persons are defined according to the researchers' choices, and the list of reference groups examined in previous studies is almost endless: an average (representative) person in society (Easterlin 1974, 1995, 2001; Stevenson and Wolfers 2008), someone like you (Clark and Oswald 1996; Ferrer-i Carbonell 2005), colleagues (Brown et al. 2008; Cappelli and Sherer 1988; Clark et al. 2009b), friends (Senik 2009), family (Senik 2009), neighbors (Clark et al. 2009a; Knight et al. 2009; Luttmer 2005; Senik 2009), and so forth. The accumulated evidence on the various cases is plentiful, and a prominent area of progress in the happiness literature recently is reported by Clark and Senik (2010), who investigated the effects of individual-specific comparison benchmarks on comparison attitudes using data on *who compares to whom*. They found that the intensity of social comparison changes in combination with specific groups that people ascribe to their comparison benchmarks. For example, those who think that their reference group is *friends* tend to make more comparisons than those whose think the comparison benchmark group is *work colleagues*.[4]

Despite all these evidence from field data on happiness scores, an alternative experimental approach for testing the relative utility hypothesis is necessary (Falk and Heckman 2009). One reason is that the reference income proxies used in empirical tests in previous happiness studies were imposed on subjects by an econometrician because information on both the *direct* and *cardinal* measures of reference income typically was missing. To our knowledge, the only exception in the literature that has information on both the *direct and cardinal* measures of reference income is de la Garza et al. (2010). Knight et al. (2009) and Senik (2009) used information on the perceptions of relative position in the respondents' villages or among friends and family members. However, their proxies of relative comparisons were ordinal, so interpretations of the magnitudes of coefficients for comparison effects were not straightforward. Another reason is that the use of information on subjective well-being is sometimes a cause for criticism by economists in other fields, even though the view that subjective well-being information is valid has been well established (Ferrer-i Carbonell and Frijters 2004; Hollander 2001; Kahneman and Krueger 2006; Oswald and Wu 2010).

Aiming to overcome these issues, we present an alternative approach to hypothetical discrete choice experiments. In our experiments, similar to Clark and Senik (2010), we investigate how people change their comparison behavior (intensity and sign of social comparison) on the basis of their demographics, including comparison benchmarks. Moreover, similar to Senik (2009), heterogeneity of comparison effects driven by differences in reference groups can be examined by changing the definition of reference persons in hypothetical situation choice tasks. This method provides a much easier way of clarifying such heterogeneity compared with

[4] See also Mayraz et al. (2009).

researchers who collect information in surveys on direct and cardinal measure of reference income for each reference group, together with happiness scores.

Solnick and Hemenway (1998), Johansson-Stenman et al. (2002), Alpizar et al. (2005), Carlsson et al. (2007), and Andersson (2008) investigated the intensity of social comparisons by addressing the methodologies of hypothetical choice experiments. One issue in Johansson-Stenman et al. (2002), Alpizar et al. (2005), and Andersson (2008) is that the choice format was designed in such a way that respondents made iterative choices to arrive at the point of indifference. This strategy is known to result in starting point bias (Carson 1991). Solnick and Hemenway (1998) and Carlsson et al. (2007) did not use iterative choices. Instead, each respondent only made a single choice between two alternatives related to relative income. With these strategies, we cannot apply a mixed logit framework to estimate the distribution of a parameter of relative utility. Also, the *degree of positionality* inferred by these previous studies, except for Solnick and Hemenway (1998), contained measurement error because the assigned value for the degree of positionality was given arbitrarily. To our knowledge, Carlsson et al. (2009) is the only study that conducted hypothetical and discrete choice experiment on income comparisons with repeated choice questions. They considered changes in the intensity of relative utility across different caste classes in India, but they did not provide results from factorial design analyses with different reference persons being tested in the same experiment. In Carlsson et al. (2009), sample representativeness is also an issue, as they conducted in-person surveys of 498 college students.[5]

Finally, studies on social preferences that differ from income comparison studies are mentioned. Using game theoretical frameworks such as the dictator game, the ultimatum game, and the public goods provision game, researchers had subjects interact in their experiments and examined the implications on reciprocity, trust and fairness. These studies include, for example, Andreoni and Bernheim (2009), Paolacci et al. (2010), Andreoni and Rao (2011), Suri and Watts (2011), Rand (2011), Horton et al. (2011), and Amir et al. (2012). Unlike these studies, studies on income comparisons, including happiness studies and our study of discrete choice experiments, there are no strategic interactions among subjects. This feature is actually important when we would like to estimate parameters of utility functions that can be used for macroeconomics analyses, e.g., Abel (1990), Gali (1994), Futagami and Shibata (1998), Liu and Turnovsky (2005), and Garcia-Penalosa and Turnovsky (2008), as in macroeconomics the number of agents is infinite, which is different from game theoretical situations.

[5]In terms of the representativeness of the sample, the respondents in Solnick and Hemenway (1998), Johansson-Stenman et al. (2002), and Alpizar et al. (2005) included only students and the respondents in Andersson (2008) were only people in academia. In contrast, the respondents in Carlsson et al. (2007) were from a socially representative survey.

3 Experimental Design, Questionnaire, and Data Collection

3.1 Hypothetical Discrete Choice Question: Social Average Task

First we explain the experimental paradigm in the survey, using the example of a benchmark experiment called the social average task. The methods described for the social average task are representative of the methods for all the tasks we conducted in our study. We discuss the results of the other two tasks in Sect. 6 and provide detailed explanations of their experimental settings and empirical results in the Appendix because of space constraints.

The Easterlin paradox, which suggests that "increasing the income of society as a whole will not increase the well-being of anyone," has been discussed in the literature on *experienced utility* that considers how national average income acts as a driving force of relative utility effects. The social average task provides a useful alternative method for investigating the validity of the paradox and relative utility effects in general. The merits of our method are that subjects recognize that they are competing with the Japanese social average when making choices and that the economic situations are explicitly shown to them.

Before the subjects began responding to repeated choice questions, they were shown an instruction screen displaying the following:

> The following figures show your hypothetical monthly income (before tax). Also displayed in the same figure is Japan's overall average monthly income (before tax). Suppose that these are current situations of your monthly income (before tax) and Japan's overall average monthly income (before tax).

In the subsequent screens, we asked respondents hypothetical discrete choice questions while showing them various figures for different alternatives after the question as shown below.[6]

> Comparing situation 1 and situation 2 shown in the figures, which is more preferable to you? Suppose that the price levels in the two situations are the same. Please choose from the following options.

As it is seen in Fig. 14.1, each situation is defined by two *attributes*, one's own monthly pre-tax income and the monthly pre-tax income of the reference group. The choice scenario also provided the option "Don't know/Cannot answer."[7] Section 4

[6] In the survey information in the figures was presented in Japanese. The images for monthly income differ in terms of number of banknotes shown according to the attribute levels. Subjects repeated five questions and they were not allowed to go back to a previous question once they had made a choice. This survey format was also used in the other two tasks: the Leyden task and the "who-compares-to-whom task.

[7] We provided this no-choice option because of the suggestion by Arrow et al. (1993) and Haaijer et al. (2001), who pointed out the importance of including a no-choice option in hypothetical choice experiments. We then removed observations in which the no-choice option was selected

Fig. 14.1 An example of choice question (social average task)

explains how we estimate parameters for a utility function using observations of discrete choices on preferred income scenarios. Next, we explain how we constructed our choice questions.

Considering the monthly income distribution in Japan, the levels of the attributes are set using the following distribution: 180,000 JPY, 240,000 JPY, 400,000 JPY, 640,000 JPY, and 900,000 JPY. The 2 attributes (own income and reference income) and 5 possible income levels for each attribute provide 25 potential variations in the income situation scenario. In the literature, these scenarios are called *alternatives*.

Researchers have to make their own choices about which alternatives to use in survey questions and which ones to discard. Following Louviere et al. (2000), we conducted *orthogonal planning* in choosing the alternatives to be used in choice questions. This method effectively pairs multi-dimensional and multiple-level attributes in alternatives, and provides an experimental plan with the greatest amount of information using the least number of observations. Further, employing orthogonal planning, we can avoid multicollinearity problems in the regressions of the random utility model explained in Sect. 4, because the independent variables

from our regressions. An alternative way of coping with these observations is to interpret them as showing indifference between the two situations, rather than a failure to understand the survey question. Unfortunately, we have no information about the true reason why the no-choice option was chosen. Hence, following the literature, we use the results of the first choice out of the five questions for a robustness check and found that the results presented are robust (not shown here due to space constraints, but available upon request).

in the regressions become orthogonal. We used SPSS Conjoint (ver. 15.0) for orthogonal design of alternatives in this study.

Next, we constructed *choice sets* consisting of pairs of alternatives and the no-choice option. By the requirement of orthogonal design, we generated two different alternative vectors, each of which consists of 25 pairs of own income levels and reference income levels.[8] Finally, choice sets, with a no-choice option, are created by pairing two alternatives, one of which is taken from an alternative vector and the other of which is chosen from the other alternative vector. The pairing strategy is at the discretion of the researchers, but all the variations must be exploited and same alternative cannot be used twice. Because the orthogonality in the alternative matrix is maintained for each row permutation, we can arbitrarily pair alternatives to meet the requirement.

As documented in Huber and Zwerina (1996) and Viscusi et al. (2008), it is ideal if the choice design can be paired so as to balance the utility of each alternative. One difficulty in choice experiments of relative utility, however, is that an increase (decrease) in a reference group's income does not necessarily mean that there is a decrease (increase) in one's own utility level; as such, we did not exclude the possibility of altruistic preference. Given these constraints, our best strategy for pairing alternatives is as follows.

Suppose we have the scenario $S = (x, y)$, where x denotes the level of one's own income and y is others income. Then, qualitatively, candidates of paired scenarios consist of the following 8 variations: $(x, y+)$, $(x, y-)$, $(x+, y)$, $(x+, y+)$, $(x+, y-)$, $(x-, y+)$, $(x-, y)$, and $(x-, y-)$, where $x+$ means some value greater than x and $x-$ means some value smaller than x. Since we do not exclude the possibility of altruism a priori, there are no a priori dominant choices for S from these eight alternatives. We then made pairs such that these eight situations appear as evenly as possible. Using the procedures discussed here, we were able to efficiently obtain parameter estimates. Table 14.1 of income levels (in 10,000 JPY) shows the set of questions we used in the survey. Each respondent answered five randomly assigned questions out of the 25 total questions.

3.2 Logistics of the Survey and Questionnaire

Our data set was created using an original, Internet-based survey.[9] A Japanese consumer monitoring company, Nikkei Research Inc., conducted the survey under

[8]As such, in the social average task, 25 alternatives out of 25 potential variations *had to be used* to meet the requirement of orthogonal design. In the case of the Leyden task, 25 out of 1,000 potential alternatives were chosen to make an alternative vector, while in the "who-compares-to-whom task, 25 out of 125 potential variations were selected via orthogonal design. These alternative vectors were generated from different random seeds.

[9]We conducted three preliminary tests before the main test. We then took differences in reference groups into account in designing the questions used in the choice questions.

Table 14.1 Parameter sets in social average task

	Alternative 1		Alternative 2			Alternative 1		Alternative 2	
Q	Own income	Ref. income	Own income	Ref. income	Q	Own income	Ref. income	Own income	Ref. income
1	64	40	40	18	14	64	90	90	90
2	90	90	40	90	15	18	64	24	40
3	90	64	64	90	16	24	90	18	64
4	90	18	90	40	17	24	18	64	24
5	90	40	90	64	18	18	90	40	40
6	90	24	90	18	19	24	24	64	18
7	24	40	64	64	20	18	24	24	90
8	64	64	90	24	21	18	40	18	24
9	40	40	64	40	22	40	64	24	64
10	64	24	18	18	23	40	18	18	90
11	40	24	24	4	24	18	18	18	40
12	64	18	40	24	25	24	64	24	18
13	40	90	40	64					

the direction of the authors. As clearly documented in Horton et al. (2011), "[t]he validity of economics experiments depends heavily upon trust, particularly subjects' trust that the promulgated rules will be followed and that all stated facts about payment, ⋯, are true." In Japanese society, the Nihon Keizai Shimbun (NIKKEI) Group is widely viewed as a trustworthy and neutral media outlet. Nikkei Research, Inc., as a part of NIKKEI group, has established a high reputation among researchers and consumers. For example, in order to provide highly reliable research data, its registered subjects are subject to monthly screenings. The company keeps information up to date and excludes double registrations. Incentives for respondents are provided by cash voucher, rather than by points; point incentives can lead to bias, as particular respondents with points tend to answer.

Nikkei Research, Inc., and the authors reached an agreement that the number of subjects should be over 10,000, given the volume of the research fund. Then, in consideration of the unweighted average of response rates for seven similar academic choice experiment surveys conducted by the same company in 2008 and 2009, the company sent an invitation email for the survey to 60,482 subjects (out of more than 160,000 total registered subjects in the Nikkei Database). Subjects between the ages of 20 and 65 were selected using stratified random sampling so that the cohort profile of our sample mirrored the Japanese census statistics of age and gender distribution. Because subjects are not required to declare their educational attainments during the registration process, we did not use such information in our stratified sampling. In the email, we specified that the survey is being conducted for research purposes and followed the disclosure requirements for research involving human beings provided with incentives as set forth by the ethics committee. We specified our payment rules in the invitation email and stated that the incentive would be on a lottery basis. We informed subjects that 800 winners among those who completed the survey would be paid 500 JPY per person. The anonymity of subjects was completely secured. If subjects wished to participate in the survey, they were instructed to follow the link in the email that directed them to our stand-alone survey website, written in html, that was launched in February 2010. The survey was open for 1 week (Feb. 18 to 25, 2010), and 14,370 subjects completed the survey.[10] This approach is in contrast to 1-day research, which many other research companies typically adopt for cost reasons. With 1-day research, subjects are chosen on a first-come first-served basis, causing potential bias as the resulting sample may well not be representative. Sampling over a 1-week period likely reduces this bias. The structure of the questionnaire is as follows.

3.2.1 Part 1: Introductory Questions

At the beginning of the survey, respondents were asked to choose one of five possible categories on their level of satisfaction about *income*. Category 1 corresponds to "Not at all satisfied," while category 5 denotes "Extremely satisfied". The second question related to social comparison and was phrased as "How much are you concerned, anxious, or jealous about the amounts of income received by other people?" The respondents were asked to choose from five response options, where category 1 corresponded to "Not at all" and category 5 denoted "Very concerned." The third question concerned the respondents' definition of their reference group. They were asked to choose one category, from those applicable to them, as their reference group, with the choices being: (i) family, (ii) neighbors, (iii) friends, (iv) colleagues, (v) do not care, and (vi) others. From these last two questions, we can observe "who compares to whom?" and "how much?," which were investigated as the framework of the happiness study of European countries by Clark and Senik (2010). Table 14.2 shows the distribution of the reference groups chosen by the respondents. We can see that the most often cited reference group is *friends*, followed by *work colleagues*. These rankings are the opposite of those in European countries, as documented in Clark and Senik (2010), but it is interesting that in both Europe and Japan these two groups are the two most important reference groups.

Table 14.2 Distribution of comparison benchmark

	Family	Neighbors	Friends	Colleagues	Do not compare	Others
Observations	483	578	4,279	2,024	2,592	247
%	4.73	5.67	41.94	19.84	25.40	2.42

[10] This response rate of 23.8 % (14,370/60,482) is smaller than might have been desired. The decision of subjects to participate in the survey was driven by unobservable characteristics that likely differ between participants and non-participants. If the unobservable characteristics are independent of the income comparison effects, then sample selection will not bias the results.

Family and *neighbors* play minor roles as reference groups. These findings were used in setting up our hypothetical choice experiment in the "who-compares-to-whom" task. In our data set, one-fourth of subjects answered they do not have comparison groups.

3.2.2 Part 2: Hypothetical Discrete Choice Questions

1. Social average task (randomly assigned 5 questions)
2. Leyden task (randomly assigned 5 questions)
3. Who-compares-to-whom task (randomly assigned 5 questions)

3.2.3 Part 3: Demographic Questions

The last part of the survey consisted of questions about individual characteristics, including age, gender, educational background, employment, marital status, type of residence, residence area, and annual pre-tax personal income in 2009.

3.3 *Survey Strategy and Data Construction*

One clear deficiency of such web-based surveys is that researchers cannot actively monitor and encourage subjects to participate in the survey. In particular, when subjects do not have a clear understanding of questions, they will try to complete questions as quickly as possible by making up answers without contemplation. Hence, there is a trade-off between (1) better understanding of the questionnaire by subjects, which reduces the cognitive experimenter demand effect (EDE), and (2) the benefits of conducting the survey "behind the veil of ignorance," which reduces the social EDE (Zizzo 2010). In our case, given that the survey was on the Internet and that specificity was required to meet the study's academic purpose and the requirements of the ethics committee, we leaned toward the former (better understanding by subjects) and explicitly stated that the survey was a "Survey on socio-economic attitudes by Osaka University" in both the invitation email and the top page of the survey website.[11]

[11]In our survey, the questionnaire started with questions about income satisfaction and comparison attitudes. Because these introductory questions are followed by the hypothetical choice tasks, the question order might make individuals conscious of making pecuniary comparisons. If this is the case, this bias will also be related to social EDE. That said, the fact that the subjects were reminded about social comparisons does not necessarily lead to over- or under-estimates of the true effect. On the one hand, after the instructions subjects may be motivated to "beat" the reference persons in the hypothetical choices, which will over-estimate the true effects of social comparison. On the other hand, one can just as easily think of mechanisms shifting the results in the other direction. Namely, many people dislike thinking of themselves as status-seeking and they therefore underestimate the degree to which they state that they care about social comparisons. This resembles the purchase

A good way to monitor subjects' willingness to participate in the survey is to look at the elapsed time for completing the survey.[12] If the elapsed time is extremely short for a subject, it is obvious that he completed the survey without contemplation, and it is plausible that he just wanted to join the lottery for the research reward. The average elapsed time to finish the survey was 9 min 9 s for our survey, with the median value of 6 min 5 s.[13] For subjects, the easiest way to finish the survey is to provide the same answers for conjoint questions documented above. We eliminated those who provided the same number for all five questions in any tasks (2,218) after we confirmed that those who provided the same answers on five consecutive questions in a task tended to finish the survey very quickly, most likely without contemplation.[14] We also discarded the information of subjects whose elapsed time is shorter than 4 min (968) on the basis of feedback from an internal company pilot test by NIKKEI. So far, we are left with 10,988 respondents.

Next, observations were dropped if they were either missing information for some of the variables used in the empirical analysis below (219), or contained an inconsistency in the data, such as retirement before the age of 55 (1). Finally, we excluded observations of respondents who report their personal annual pre-tax income in 2009 to be higher than 12 million JPY (565).[15] To ensure that this cut-off for the income variable was not a result of sample selection, we compared the observations in the two groups along different dimensions including age, education, marital status, and residence area. We are happy to report that the number of observations excluded from our working sample does not seem to be a result of any sample selection problems, and that the main results documented below remain qualitatively unchanged when we use the whole sample as our study sample. At the final stage, we were left with 10,203 respondents.

---

of moral satisfaction in Kahneman and Knetsch (1992). See the concluding section for more discussion on potential biases in experimental studies.

[12]Rubinstein (2007) conducted an Internet-based survey experiment and recorded response time for some questions. He found significant differences in response time across types of questions, and suggested that choices made on the basis of an emotional response require less response time than choices that require the use of cognitive reasoning. In our case, we have information on total response time to complete the entire survey, while response times for individual questions are not available.

[13]Observations with no time records (90) and elapsed time longer than 60 min (106) are excluded from our study sample.

[14]Rand (2011) reported that at least 80 % of experiment participants in MTurk were not merely making random selections on survey questions, which resembles the figure in our case.

[15]The cut-off point, 12 million JPY, is higher than the sum of the average of personal pre-tax annual income and three standard deviations of the income distribution. There are two major reasons for the high frequency of high-income level subjects. One reason is that survey participation is biased toward persons with higher education, Internet access, and urban residence. It is natural that these individuals have higher income than others without these characteristics. The other reason is that they tried to cheat by inflating their income levels. According to the exchange rate in March 2009, 12 million JPY is around 130,000 USD.

The descriptive statistics of our data are shown in Table 14.3. Because the stratified random sample was designed to mirror the population cohort profile of Japanese census statistics, the age and gender structures of our sample appear quite similar to national statistics. There is however considerable under-representation of women who are divorced, separated or widowed. This difference from national statistics comes about because the latter include everyone aged over 15. As the average length of life for Japanese women is around 87 (with that of men being around 78), women tend to be widowed towards the end of their lives, which is reflected in the rate of female divorce/separation/widowhood in national statistics. However, as our sample only includes those who are aged up to 65, the rates of divorce/separation/widowhood for both men and women are lower than those in national statistics.

With respect to educational attainment, in our samples of males, just 1 % of the sample completed middle school only, 18 % completed high school only, 10 % completed some of college, and the remaining 70 % held college or post-graduate degrees. This bias toward higher education also holds for the female samples. This is an over-sampling of more highly educated participants. Related to this issue, the average income levels from our sample are greater than that in the national statistics. The survey requests that subjects indicate their own income level from a list of 11 categories, where category 1 denotes annual wages of less than 2 million JPY and category 11 corresponds to an annual income level of more than 50 million JPY. When we measure individual income levels as the mid-point in each of the 9 intermediate categories, and use ad hoc values of 1.5 and 55 million JPY for the two extreme categories, respectively, we obtained that the average annual income of our whole sample was 5.69 million JPY for males and 2.93 million JPY for females.

The differences from the national statistics for students and the unemployed do not look severe. Information on residence location is compared. There is an over-sampling from the Kanto region, which includes Tokyo. Also, people from the Kansai region, which contains Osaka, are slightly over-sampled. Overall, we find that our data set captures significant features of Japanese society, except for the distribution of educational attainment. It is difficult to obtain a representative sample with small face-to-face surveys.

4 Random Utility Model and Empirical Method

In this section we introduce the econometric foundation on how subjects' choice data can be used to estimate their utility functions. We start by describing a discrete choice model with a general utility function. To analyze decisions in hypothetical choice experiments, we use a random utility model framework. The model deals with data on repeated choices over available alternatives. It is assumed that subjects choose an alternative since they obtain higher utility out of the alternative than from the other available alternatives. When there are two alternatives available (A and B, for example), and if they chose A rather than B, then the choice data

Table 14.3 Descriptive statistics

	(1) Our survey (whole sample)		(2) Our survey (study sample)		(3)	(4) National data[b]	
	Male	Female	Male	Female	NIKKEI	Male	Female
Age category							
20s	18.20	22.18	18.06	21.51	13.73	19.48	18.75
30s	24.53	22.90	25.37	23.18	36.42	24.48	24.06
40s	20.53	24.47	19.2	24.8	30.07	21.78	21.73
50s	23.07	18.61	22.54	18.85	13.88	22.11	22.64
60s	13.68	11.83	14.83	11.66	5.89	12.15	12.82
Education[a]							
Middle school	1.00	0.97	0.94	0.89	N.A.	18.18	20.80
High school	19.62	26.19	21.20	25.89		41.60	43.39
Some college	10.47	31.89	11.14	32.12		11.36	24.54
College	68.91	40.95	66.73	41.10		28.33	10.67
Marital status							
Single	32.69	26.50	33.23	25.75	29.99	32.00	23.40
Married	63.95	67.24	63.27	67.92	60.66	61.80	57.60
Divorced/widowed	3.36	6.26	3.50	6.34	9.35	6.20	19.00
Region							
Hokkaido	4.31		4.65		3.97	4.30	
Tohoku	4.21		4.36		4.06	7.40	
Kanto	45.32		44.23		46.94	32.90	
Koshinetsu	3.95		4.19		3.67	6.70	
Chubu	10.09		9.96		9.45	11.90	
Kansai	20.23		20.55		19.73	16.30	
Chugoku	3.92		3.92		3.82	6.00	
Shikoku	1.84		1.88		1.90	3.10	
Kyushu	6.14		6.28		6.45	11.40	
Female [0.1]	52.57		55.59		56.64	51.27	
Student [0,1]	3.60		3.41		N.A.	7.60	
Annual income[b]	5.69	2.93	4.90	2.71	N.A.	4.87	1.85
Unemployment	4.05		4.01		N.A.	4.90	

All figures except for annual income (in million JPY) are percentages for each category

[a]Those who are currently students are excluded from the figure

[b]Demographic characteristics are from the Population Estimates by the Statistics Bureau (Sep. 2009); education attainment data are from the Employment Status Survey (Table 3; 2007) by the Statistics Bureau; marital status data are from the Population Statistics of Japan (Table 6.21; 2008) by the National Institute of Population and Social Security Research; region data are from the Population Statistics of Japan (Table 9.5; 2008); income information is from the Employment Status Survey (2008); and unemployment data are from the Labour Force Survey (Feb. 2010) by the Statistics Bureau

is recorded as 1 for alternative A and 0 for alternative B, along with the levels of the explanatory variables (attributes) in alternatives A and B, respectively. These pieces of information comprise the observation for regression analyses.

Now more specifically, there are N subjects and they answer $T(\geq 1)$ repeated choice questions. The utility of subject n when s/he chooses alternative i at question $t \in T$, U_{itn}, consists of observable components in experiments V_{itn} and unobservable components ϵ_{itn} so that utility can be viewed as $U_{itn} = V_{itn} + \epsilon_{itn}$. Utility from observable components are assumed to be linear combinations of each attribute as $V_{itn} = \sum_{k=1}^{K} \beta_k X_{ik}$, where $k = 1, \cdots, K(K \geq 2)$ represents the variety of attributes, X_k denotes the levels of kth attributes, and β_k measures marginal utility of each attribute. In the following analysis, the vector of $\beta \equiv (\beta_1, \cdots, \beta_K)$ that maximizes the log likelihood function of observed choice patterns by subject is the estimator of conditional or mixed logit model regressions. Following McFadden (1974), ϵ_{itn} is distributed following independent and identical distribution of extreme value type 1 (IIDEV1) with variance σ^2.

The logit formula of choice probability P_{itn} that subject n chooses alternative i from the set of alternatives S_t (choice set) in question $t \in T$ can be written as

$$P_{itn} = prob(U_{itn} > U_{jtn}, \forall j \neq i \in S_t) = prob(\epsilon_{jtn} - \epsilon_{itn} < V_{itn} - V_{jtn}, \forall j \neq i \in S_t).$$

McFadden (1974) showed that $P_{itn} = \exp(\lambda V_{itn}) / \sum_{j \in S} \exp(\lambda V_{jtn})$, where $\lambda = \pi / \sqrt{6}\sigma$ is the scale parameter.

Finally, a dummy variable d_{itn} is defined, taking a value of 1 if subject n choose alternative i for question $t \in T$, and 0 otherwise. Together with the logit formula of choice probability P_{itn}, the log likelihood function of repeated choices observed in experiments can be written as

$$LL(\beta) = \sum_n \sum_t \sum_{i \in S_t} d_{itn} \ln P_{itn}.$$

In the conditional logit model, the parameters of utility function, β, can be obtained with the first-order condition of $\partial LL(\beta)/\partial\beta = 0$ (McFadden 1974). To be more specific, when we estimate the model assuming that the independence of irrelevant alternatives (IIA) holds, we obtain a conditional logit model where all of N subjects share the same set of parameter in β. Alternatively, when we allow for distributions of some parameters in β across subjects, we obtain the mixed logit model. In the latter case, while we assume that the error term is independently and identically distributed as in the conditional logit model, non-IIA situations are allowed. In the case of the mixed logit model, we can obtain the distribution of parameters $f(\beta)$ as follows. Following Train (2009), we specify that $f(\beta)$ is either a normal or a log normal distribution function with parameters set as θ. The choice probability function P_{itn}^{ML} for the mixed logit model can be written as

$$P_{itn}^{ML} = \int P_{itn}(\beta) f(\beta|\theta) d\beta,$$

where P_{itn} is the logit choice probability in the conditional logit model given β. θ can be obtained via simulation which maximizes the simulated log likelihood function[16]

$$SLL(\theta) = \sum_n \sum_t \sum_{i \in S_t} d_{itn} \ln P_{itn}^{ML}.$$

Next, we specify the shape of the utility function for our own purposes. Here we present the specific theoretical framework for the social average task only because of space constraints. Individuals derive utility not only from their own income $X_1 = y$ but also from the social average income $X_2 = \bar{y}$. From textbook assumptions, we suppose that subjects value attribute y positively. On the other hand, the social average income $\bar{y}$ can be valued positively (altruism) or negatively (jealousy). Following Johansson-Stenman et al. (2002), Dupor and Liu (2003), Liu and Turnovsky (2005), we consider the constant relative risk aversion-type utility function as

$$V = \frac{(y\bar{y}^{\gamma})^{1-\rho}}{(1-\rho)}, \tag{14.1}$$

where $\rho > 0$. If $\rho = 1$, it reduces to the log felicity function. The parameter γ regulates the intensity and sign of relative utility and is the central topic of this study. If $\gamma < 0$, the individual has jealousy. If $\gamma > 0$, the individual has an altruistic preference, whereas if $\gamma = 0$, there is no relative utility.

Again, let i denote the alternative and n denote the subject. We take the logarithms of both sides in Eq. 14.1 to obtain

$$\ln V_{ni} = (1-\rho) \ln y_{ni} + (1-\rho)\gamma \ln \bar{y}_{ni} - \ln(1-\rho). \tag{14.2}$$

With an error term ϵ_n, the probability P_{in} that respondent n prefers alternative i to alternative j is given by

$$\begin{aligned} P_{in} = Prob\big(&(1-\rho)\ln y_{in} + (1-\rho)\gamma \ln \bar{y}_{in} - \ln(1-\rho) + \epsilon_{in} \\ &> (1-\rho)\ln y_{jn} + (1-\rho)\gamma \ln \bar{y}_{jn} - \ln(1-\rho) + \epsilon_{jn}\big), \quad \text{forall} \quad j \neq i. \end{aligned}$$

Using maximum-likelihood estimation we obtain coefficients for $\ln y$ as $\beta_1 = 1 - \rho$ and $\ln \bar{y}$ as $\beta_2 = (1-\rho)\gamma$. β_1 and β_2 are regarded as marginal utility in the random utility model framework. It is noteworthy here that estimated β_1 and β_2 are divided by the scale parameter λ, which is unknown to researchers (Train 2009, p. 41).

[16]See Section 6 of Train (2009) for details.

This means that we cannot obtain true magnitudes of all the parameters in Eq. 14.2. However, we can obtain true estimates of our interested variable γ by dividing β_2 with β_1, thus canceling λ out.[17]

5 Benchmark Results from the Social Average Task

Our benchmark results from social average task are shown here. Results in this section will be informative to theoretical macroeconomists because previous theoretical studies on relative utility effects such as Abel (1990), Gali (1994), Liu and Turnovsky (2005), and Garcia-Penalosa and Turnovsky (2008) were conducted without estimating important parameters in the utility function. As such, they put forward various propositions in accordance with the parameters assumed and do not necessarily reflect "reality."

Table 14.4 provides results for the whole sample. The first column shows the results from the conditional logit model. We see that a person's own income affects utility positively and significantly, as is expected. Next, from the coefficient of the reference income term, it is shown that relative utility exists among Japanese respondents, and that, on average, the effect appears in the form of *jealousy*. These

Table 14.4 Conditional logit and mixed logit estimates (social average task)

	(1)	(2)	(3)	
Model	Conditional logit		Mixed logit	
Dep. Var: Utility			Mean	SD
Own income	0.048***	0.039***	0.097***	0.077***
	(0.001)	(0.002)	(0.002)	(0.002)
Reference income	−0.022***	−0.021***	−0.044***	0.081***
	(0.001)	(0.001)	(0.001)	(0.002)
Estimated γ	−0.458	−0.546		
Observations	48,172	48,172	48,172	
Pseudo R-squared	0.249			

Robust standard errors clustered by subject in parentheses
$^{*}p < 0.1$; $^{**}p < 0.05$; $^{***}p < 0.01$

[17] Ida and Goto (2009) compared estimated parameters in a logit model framework by assuming that $\sigma = 1$ through all regressions of subsamples. However, researchers cannot compare estimates from different subsamples without taking differences in σ into consideration. As stated in the body, the coefficients that are estimated indicate the effect of each *observed* variable relative to the variance of the *unobserved* factors. It is useful to recognize that the likelihood ratio test designed for confirming statistically significant difference of parameters among subgroups is not suitable here. For example, a larger σ in a subsample leads to smaller coefficients in its regression, even when the observed factors in two subsamples have the *same* effect on utility. A heteroscedastic logit model can be used in investigating the difference of σ between the subgroups.

two coefficients provide the true magnitude for the parameter of relative utility γ, by dividing the second by the first. From the estimates in column (1) of Table 14.4, we obtain that $\gamma = -0.458$. From a decision utility framework, this result stands in the middle of two extremes in experienced utility frameworks: the fully relative utility function of Easterlin (1995) and the solely absolute utility function of Stevenson and Wolfers (2008).[18] It is noteworthy that a recent finding in the happiness studies literature by de la Garza et al. (2010) reached the same conclusion that money buys happiness *to some extent* in Japan, through the use of direct and cardinal measures of reference income. Also note that our result is perfectly in line with the other studies based on hypothetical choices in different societies such as Solnick and Hemenway (1998), Johansson-Stenman et al. (2002), Alpizar et al. (2005), and Carlsson et al. (2007).

5.1 Representativeness of the Result

As was documented in Sect. 3.3, our data set under-sampled those who completed middle school only. A simple estimation of Mincer equation with our data showed that educational attainment was positively correlated with income levels. As was shown by Ravallion and Lokshin (2010), it is well known in the literature that people with lower income tend to become less jealous, and we found the same result in our data set, as is documented below in Sect. 5.2. Hence, the representativeness of our results is an issue, and it is likely that we *over-estimated* the relative utility effects because of the oversampling of persons with higher educational attainment. In column (2) of Table 14.4, we show the result when we adjust the sampling weights using a post-stratification method.[19] The estimated γ after the post-stratification adjustment suggests, against our expectation, that the original γ in Column (1) was a slight *under-estimation* of the negative relative utility effect compared with the adjusted, representative data set in terms of gender, age, and educational attainment.

The reason for this result is as follows. First, the coefficient of the own income term in Column (2) is smaller in comparison with that in Column (1). Comparing coefficients of own income term from columns (1) and (2), we see that subjects with higher educational attainment and higher income levels enjoy higher marginal utility from own income.[20] Second, after the adjustment, the coefficient of the

[18]According to Figure 3 in Easterlin (1995), the Easterlin paradox evidently held for Japan in the period from 1958 to 1987. One reason why the comparison intensity we estimated falls short of the level validating the paradox reason is that the social comparison effect is just one of many explanations of the Easterlin paradox. Habit formation, for example, explains the paradox as well (van de Stadt et al. 1985).

[19]We computed post-stratification adjustments to survey sampling weights. The sampling weights in gender and educational attainments were adjusted such that the sum of the weights equals the control total for each stratum.

[20]Because marginal utility from consumption becomes smaller as your consumption levels increases in neoclassical economics theory, at first sight this seems odd. This observation, however,

reference income term in Column (2) is smaller in absolute value than the one in Column (1). The direction of the change is hence in line with the presumption that people with higher educational attainment and higher income levels tend to become more jealous. In our data set, the first effect dominates the second effect to provide γ of stronger jealousy after adjusting for the over-sampling of persons with higher educational attainment.

Given the results, an accurate depiction of the representative relative utility effects in Japanese may not be necessary since, as described above, samples with lower educational attainment are under-sampled. Nonetheless, because of the large size of our sample, the breadth of coverage across Japan's 47 prefectures, and the wide variety of job types from public servants to students and the unemployed, we believe that our data set does capture significant features of the relative utility effects in Japan. Hereafter, we show results using the unweighted sample for brevity.

5.2 *Heterogeneity of Preference Parameters*

In the last columns of Table 14.4, we show the result from the mixed logit model in which normal distributions of parameters across subjects are allowed.[21] We find that own income affects utility positively, whereas the reference income has a negative impact on utility on average. We also find a similar ratio in the values estimated for the own income term to that of reference income term in both the conditional logit model and the mixed logit model, which validates the robustness of previous findings from the conditional logit model.

It is interesting to note that the standard deviation terms estimated in the mixed logit model are both significant at the 1 % level. Behavioral economics has provided evidence that demographic differences lead to substantial differences in preference parameters, such as the time discount rate and the level of risk aversion.[22]

---

can be justified when we allow for heterogeneity of a parameter in the utility function between the poor and the rich. When a shift parameter of the utility function is greater for the rich than the poor, the marginal utility of consumption at a certain level of consumption becomes higher for the rich. The heterogeneity of the utility function, reversely, could explain why some become rich while the other stay poor, even when the other demographic conditions are the same for all the subjects.

[21] The STATA module for mixed logit model estimation is provided by Hole (2007).

[22] Small et al. (2005) applied the framework of a mixed logit model to investigate the distribution of commuters' preferences for speedy and reliable highway travel, finding that there was substantial heterogeneity in motorists' values of travel time and reliability. Hole (2008) investigated the preferences of patients about general practitioner appointments using standard logit, mixed logit, and latent class logit models. He showed that there was significant preference heterogeneity for all the attributes in the experiment. Viscusi et al. (2008) showed that eco-conscious individuals have a lower rate of time discounting than those who are not eco-friendly. Ida and Goto (2009) showed that smokers have with a higher value of time discounting and a lower value of risk aversion than nonsmokers.

Following Viscusi et al. (2008), we identify the effects of individual characteristics on preference parameters by controlling for interaction terms of attributes in the surveys and demographic variables in conditional logit models.[23] In doing so, we consider two organic factors, six acquired individual characteristics, and three subjective variables as potential sources of parameter heterogeneity. The two organic variables are age and gender. We consider annual income level, educational attainment, urban residence, marital status, unemployment status, and student dummies for the six individual characteristics. The three subjective dummy variables include a "do not compare" dummy, a "very happy" dummy, and a "very comparison conscious" dummy.

We report the results without a detailed table to save space (the full results are available upon request). We find that people tend to become more jealous if they are rich, female, highly educated, or married. Interestingly, urban residents do not have stronger comparison attitudes when compared to those who do not live in major cities. It is also interesting that age does not affect comparison intensity. In terms of the marginal utility of own income, as previously introduced, those with higher income and higher educational attainment tend to obtain higher utility from a certain amount of income. Regarding the subjective variables, we find that those who report that they do not compare have weaker comparison attitudes, which we discuss in more depth in the following section, and that the more they care about comparisons, the stronger their jealousy becomes. These findings are as expected. Feelings of being happier do not affect comparison intensity. Our findings are robust against changes in the threshold level for the comparison conscious group, the happy group, high income group, and elder group.

Thus, we can confirm that heterogeneity plays a role in determining the intensity of social comparison, just as previous behavioral economics studies have found in other fields.

5.3 Analysis with Comparison Benchmark Information

A recent caveat from the happiness study of Clark and Senik (2010) is that comparison attitudes can differ depending on the reference group that people ascribe as their comparison benchmark. In our data set, similar to Clark and Senik (2010), information on specific and relevant reference groups for each subject is available. It is interesting to see how people change the intensity of comparison on the basis of their comparison benchmarks.

[23]The introduction of interaction terms into conditional logit frameworks is acceptable as long as we confine our attention to the sign and significance of the interaction terms, as is clearly explained on page 22 in Train (2009). See Ai and Norton (2003) for interpretations of the *marginal effects* of dummy interaction terms in logit models. As long as one can interpret the coefficients as marginal utilities, as we do in a random utility model framework, Ai and Norton's point is not relevant.

Since the target reference group is based on a general concept, the differences in relative utility intensity derived in this task reflect basic differences in the intensity of relative utility across subgroups. We divide our study sample into subgroups of individually relevant reference groups and compare the obtained *true* magnitudes of γ across the subgroups.

The variances of the estimated γ by subgroup for the comparison benchmarks are obtained by using the Delta method to examine the statistical significance of the differences. Since γ takes the form $\gamma = r/s$, where r and s are stochastic variables, the variance of γ is obtained as follows:

$$\begin{aligned} Var(\gamma) &= \begin{pmatrix} \frac{\partial\gamma}{\partial r} & \frac{\partial\gamma}{\partial s} \end{pmatrix} \begin{pmatrix} Var(r) & Cov(r,s) \\ Cov(r,s) & Var(s) \end{pmatrix} \begin{pmatrix} \frac{\partial\gamma}{\partial r} \\ \frac{\partial\gamma}{\partial s} \end{pmatrix} \\ &= \frac{1}{\beta_s^2} Var(r) + \frac{\beta_r^2}{\beta_s^4} Var(\beta_s) - \frac{2\beta_r}{\beta_s^3} Cov(r,s), \end{aligned}$$

where for r and s, β_r and β_s are the averages and $Var(r)$ and $Var(s)$ are the variances, respectively. $Cov(r,s)$ is the covariance of r and s.

Columns (1) through (5) of Table 14.5 show the coefficients and estimated γ across subgroups for the comparison benchmarks. We exclude the subgroup of "others." An interesting estimate of γ appears in column (2), where the comparison benchmark is neighbors. People who tend to compare themselves with neighbors are the most jealous in Japan. The value of γ for the "neighbors" subgroup is significantly different from the other subgroups ($p < 0.01$).

Table 14.5 Conditional logit estimates across comparison benchmark subgroups (social average task)

	(1)	(2)	(3)	(4)	(5)
Comparison benchmark	Family	Neighbor	Friend	Colleague	Do not compare
Model	Conditional logit				
Dep. Var: Utility					
Own income	0.045***	0.056***	0.052***	0.050***	0.041***
	(0.003)	(0.003)	(0.001)	(0.002)	(0.001)
Reference income	−0.021***	−0.031***	−0.025***	−0.022***	−0.017***
	(0.002)	(0.002)	(0.001)	(0.001)	(0.001)
Estimated γ	−0.467	−0.554	−0.481	−0.440	−0.415
Estimated variance of γ	0.049	0.018	0.064	0.073	0.026
γ same as?	Colleague	Friend	Family	Do not compare	
T statistics	68.2	16.8	21.5	52.4	
Observations	2,255	2,739	20,442	9,581	11,982
Pseudo R-squared	0.228	0.320	0.279	0.253	0.190

Robust standard errors clustered by subject in parentheses. For estimates of γ, we report variances constructed via the Delta method

$^{*}p < 0.1$; $^{**}p < 0.05$; $^{***}p < 0.01$

The finding that those who compare themselves with neighbors have the strongest intensity of relative utility requires further attention. The reference group of neighbors is characterized by close contact. Hence, the result seems natural if we accept that people endogenously choose their reference groups from groups of close contacts, as Clark et al. (2008) argued. However, it is interesting to see a weaker intensity of relative utility for those whose comparison benchmark is work colleagues, another type of close contact, shown in column (4). The difference of estimated γ between the two subgroups of comparison benchmark is significant ($p < 0.01$). Regarding this finding, it may make sense when considering the tunnel effect proposed by Hirschman and Rothschild (1973). He argued that an increase in work colleagues' income could be interpreted as a positive signal regarding likely future outcomes. However, the effect seems not so strong as to provide *positive* relative utility, as was found by Senik (2004) using a Russian data set.[24]

It is important to note that the "Do not compare" group in column (5) has a significantly smaller estimated γ than the other groups ($p < 0.01$).[25] However, the fact that social comparison effects are observed among those who explicitly state that they do not compare, and that differences in the estimated gamma from other subgroups appears marginal, despite being significant, draws our attentions.

The benefits of our experimental approach are that we showed subjects clearly illustrated income comparison scenarios with information on their own income levels and reference income levels, and that we elicited information on comparison benchmarks. This procedure resolves uncertainty in existing happiness studies that do not elicit comparison benchmarks as to whether the negative coefficients for the relative income proxies in happiness regressions are in fact capturing social comparisons. Hence, a natural expectation for the results from our experimental approach is that we find no social comparisons effects among those who say they do not compare. It is also noteworthy that we did not get the result because of a biased construction of the experiment: from the construction of choice sets as explained in Sect. 3.1, we can obtain positive, negative, or no relative utility effects depending on patterns of subjects' choices.

Table 14.6 shows the results when we divide the observations of the "Do not compare group" into subgroups of survey-elicited intensity of jealousy (from 1 to 5). The number of subjects who declared the maximum intensity of jealousy (5) was too few to provide a relevant result, as shown in Column (5) of Table 14.6. As it can be seen, the estimated values of γ across subgroups of survey elicited intensity of jealousy make some sense. In subjects who declared weaker jealousy in the questionnaire, their choice patterns in the choice experiment provided weaker intensity of income comparisons of γ. For those who declared the minimum

[24]Card et al. (2012) compared the positive effects of the tunnel effects and negative effects of relative utility in a social experiment setting, and showed that the negative effects are dominant in the United States.

[25]In the previous section we picked up the same effect when we interacted a "Do not compare" dummy variable with reference income terms.

Table 14.6 Conditional logit estimates in the "Do Not Compare" subgroup by intensity of jealousy (social average task)

	(1)	(2)	(3)	(4)	(5)
Intensity of Jealousy	1	2	3	4	5
Model	Conditional logit				
Dep. Var: Utility					
Own income	0.038***	0.041***	0.044***	0.034***	−0.003
	(0.003)	(0.002)	(0.002)	(0.011)	(0.018)
Reference income	−0.013***	−0.015***	−0.022***	−0.038***	−0.035
	(0.002)	(0.001)	(0.002)	(0.010)	(0.040)
Estimated γ	−0.342	−0.366	−0.500	−1.118	N.A.
Estimated variance of γ	0.004	0.001	0.002	0.147	
γ same as?	jealous = 2	jealous = 3	jealous = 4		
T statistics	17.5	145.8	22.1		
Observations	2,181	5,935	3,662	188	16
Pseudo R-squared	0.162	0.183	0.224	0.229	0.127

Robust standard errors clustered by subject in parentheses. For estimates of γ, we report variances constructed via the Delta method
$^{*}p < 0.1$; $^{**}p < 0.05$; $^{***}p < 0.01$

intensity of jealousy (1), the estimated γ was −0.342. This figure is a 25 % reduction from the comparison effect for the whole sample, but again, is significantly different from zero. Our interpretation of the result, considering that the result is not found because of a biased construction of the experiment favoring negative comparisons, is that ultimately humans make comparisons, even though they themselves declare that they do not. In support of this argument, Fliessbach et al. (2007), Takahashi et al. (2009), and Tricomi et al. (2010) revealed a neurological basis for making comparisons in human brains. These studies imply that we inherently cannot escape from making comparisons. We even suggest that our study has provided stronger support for the existence of negative relative utility effects than research that relies on evaluation and rating data can provide: it is easy for subjects to "cheat" in questionnaires to say that they do not make comparisons, or to rate their intensity of jealousy very low, even when they indeed are very jealous. It is not, however, very easy for them to expect what their choices in choice experiments will indicate about their jealousy without knowing the technical aspects of discrete choice experiments.

6 Discussion of Results from Extended Tasks

A salient feature of the hypothetical discrete choice experiment on income comparisons is that we can investigate differences in such effects across various types of reference persons in well-controlled experimental conditions. Here we introduce the main results from other such applications. The detailed construction of the experiments and empirical results are given in the Appendix.

6.1 Leyden Task

In the Leyden task, reference persons are characterized by specific demographic variables of age, gender, and educational attainment, which we adapted from the Leyden School definition of reference group (van Praag and Frijters 1999). We then would like to see how the intensity and sign of relative utility change in accordance with the characteristics of reference persons.

We found that reference groups with higher educational attainment tend to be the target of stronger jealousy. We also find that if the reference person is older than the subject, feelings of pecuniary emulation are mitigated. The altruistic attitudes toward elderly persons, or admiration of them, are interesting since both higher age and higher education are associated with higher income on average. As we confirmed in the social average task, reference persons with higher income levels draw stronger jealousy. These intriguing relative utility effects for the elderly may be a good reflection of Japanese culture. Regarding the effect of gender, it was found that males are the target of stronger jealousy from both males and females. To sum up, from the Leyden task, we can say that comparison attitudes change on the basis of the features of reference persons. These findings suggest that consideration of social averages as the salient reference group is not sufficient when examining the relative utility effects in the whole society. Instead, researchers should pay attention to the features of the true reference groups of subjects, since they greatly affect the outcome of empirical investigations of relative utility.

6.2 Who-Compares-to-Whom Task

In this task, we simultaneously consider two types of reference groups, friends and work colleagues, in choice questions. The selection of these reference groups comes from the result of our preliminary tests, which showed that these two groups were the most cited by respondents.

In addition to the simultaneous treatment of two external reference groups, in this study we also have information on subjects' specific comparison benchmark, and we examine the following issues: (i) if friends and colleagues are recognized as different type of reference groups, and if so, (ii) how different they are; and (iii) if comparison attitudes toward these two groups vary by specific comparison benchmarks. The answers are as follows.

(i) The result suggests that friends and colleagues are recognized as different types of reference groups and subjects frequently change their comparison benchmarks from one to the other, rather than stick to one, in accordance with situations they face. This result hints at the fact that reference groups are chosen endogenously.[26]

(ii) The average comparison effects toward the friend group and the work colleague group are very different in magnitude. The intensity of jealousy toward work colleague group is more than 10 times stronger than that toward the friend group.

(iii) A noteworthy finding is the large standard deviation of the income comparisons effect toward "friends," compared with the small mean effect. We found that a mean estimate of comparison effects toward friends reflected differing attitudes in the subjects toward their friends. In fact, around 30 % of subjects feel altruism toward friends. Another intriguing pattern is found when we compare the estimates of standard deviations for the relative utility effects toward work colleagues by two subgroups of subjects with friends and those with work colleagues as the comparison benchmark. On one hand, the standard deviation is found to be significant (though it is not particularly large) in the subgroup with a comparison benchmark of friends. On the other hand, for the subgroup with a comparison benchmark as work colleagues, the standard deviation is found to be *insignificant*, implying that the negative relative utility effect against work colleagues spikes near the group average. These outcomes suggest that reference groups of friends and work colleagues are different, not only in terms of the average intensities of the relative utility effects, but also in the sense that their distributions differ by subsample groups of specific comparison benchmarks. We argue that this outcome reflects that *friends* encompasses many aspects of life, such as benevolent rivals, persons of understanding, and so forth, and that work colleagues tend to be regarded as rivals.

7 Concluding Remarks

In this concluding section, we discuss biases that are normally associated with *stated preference methods*.

As Hausman (1993) and Carson et al. (2001) pointed out, there are some potential biases in stated choice methods. Bateman et al. (2002) categorized these biases into three broad categories: (i) incentives to misrepresent responses, (ii) implied value cues, and (iii) scenario misspecification. The first category relates to false answers to the survey questions. This bias arises when the questions and scenario settings are not well designed. The second and the third biases result from respondents' misunderstandings of the survey questions, namely cognitive EDE as coined by Zizzo (2010). To avoid these potential biases, researcher should carefully design

[26]See Train et al. (1987) and Herriges and Kling (1996) for technical discussion on the nested logit model that derived this implication.

choice tasks through pilot surveys, repeated preliminary tests and close investigation of the preliminary results. In the present study, we conducted pilot surveys and three preliminary tests to fine tune our questionnaire. The most substantial change in our main test from the preliminary test was the introduction of visual images in the choice situation tasks. By introducing visual images, the cognitive burden on subjects was decreased, with the average elapsed time for finishing the survey reduced by half from the initial preliminary test without images. We also see that standard errors in the logit model estimations were also reduced compared to the estimations obtained from preliminary test data. By comparing our results with those from the preliminary tests, we also find that the order of questions and selection of questions, other than the choice questions in the present study, do not seem to seriously affect the main results of our study.

Dolan and Kahneman (2008) critically summarized biases associated with stated preference methods including hypothetical discrete choice experiments. They then advocated happiness (or experienced utility) research for situations where researchers would like to infer the market values of non-market goods. Note, however, that footnote 4 in Dolan and Kahneman (2008) holds that "[their] critique is focused on the use of measures of decision utility to elicit values of this kind, rather than their usefulness in other contexts, such as predicting behavior." The purpose of this chapter is to elicit the sign and the intensity of comparison effects which affect human behavior.[27]

In stated choice method studies of Johansson-Stenman et al. (2002), Alpizar et al. (2005), Carlsson et al. (2007), and Andersson (2008), respondents were asked to consider the well-being of their offspring, rather than their own well-being. This framing was used in order to help the respondents liberate themselves from their current circumstances, disentangling their actual consumption from the hypothetical consumption choices in the survey. In the present study, we instead asked about the respondents' own interests. This design choice was made because we would like to know the current situation within Japanese society. The biases associated with ignoring the previous strategy are not expected to be especially severe because we can control for individual fixed effects, as we asked respondents to make five repeated choices in each task, unlike in the previous studies. Our strategy here was also motivated by Dolan and Kahneman (2008), who took a critical view on having subjects make hypothetical choices on the basis of future expectations and past memory.

We suggest a future research agenda as follows. The merit of the hypothetical choice experiment framework under a random utility model is that we do not rely on information of subjective well-being to obtain the true parameters of

[27]The other drawback inherent in stated choice methods that is often mentioned is the artificial nature of the questions and incentive incompatibility for subjects in making choices. Regarding the issue, Lusk and Schroeder (2004) showed that stated choice methods provided similar results for marginal effects compared with the results in non-hypothetical settings. They held that careful design of the survey is the key issue in avoiding this bias, a requirement that we argue that we have satisfied through the use of multiple preliminary tests. See also Falk and Heckman (2009).

the (decision) utility function for the relative utility. Because subjective well-being information is usually strongly influenced by country fixed effects and by social norms, hypothetical choice experiment frameworks will be useful alternative avenues in conducting international comparisons of the relative utility effects.

Appendices

Leyden Task

Construction of Choice Tasks

The general method of constructing the choice scenarios in the Leyden task is the same as in social average task, including orthogonal planning. However, in this task, the reference group is not simply the social average, but instead is characterized by the gender, age, and educational attainment of the reference person.

Hence, a total of five alternatives were defined in this task. After the preliminary tests, we determined the levels of these attributes as follows. First, as before, the income variables contain the following variations: 180,000 JPY, 240,000 JPY, 400,000 JPY, 640,000 JPY, and 900,000 JPY. For age, we included four level 2, 32, 45, and 58 years old with the goal of reflecting different stages of workers' careers. Gender was male and female. For the levels of educational attainment, we included five variations: middle school, high school, technical school, undergraduate, and graduate.

One thousand potential variations in the combinations of these attributes exist. The computer algorithm for orthogonal planning in SPSS Conjoint provided 25 sets of alternatives out of 1,000 potential variations. We replicated this procedure to obtain two sets of alternative vectors. To pair the alternatives for this task, we used the same strategy as in the social average task, with the exception that information on the three attributes of socioeconomic characteristics were not taken into account. We also added the no-choice options as in the previous task. Table 14.7 shows the set of questions we used in the survey.

Instructions in the Survey

Before the subjects started the repeated choice questions, they were shown an instruction screen saying that:

> The next figure shows your hypothetical monthly income (before tax). It also shows the monthly income (before tax) of a certain other person. As in the previous question [social average task], suppose that the current situation of your monthly income (before tax) and the other person's monthly income (before tax) are both as shown.

Table 14.7 Parameter sets in Leyden task

	Alternative 1					Alternative 2				
			Reference person's characteristics					Reference person's characteristics		
Q	Own income	Ref. income	Gender	Education	Age	Own income	Ref. income	Gender	Education	Age
1	18	90	Female	Under graduate	32	40	40	Male	Junior high	32
2	40	18	Male	Graduate	32	64	40	Male	Tech school	45
3	24	24	Male	Graduate	45	40	24	Male	Tech school	22
4	90	24	Female	Junior high	32	64	64	Female	Junior high	22
5	18	40	Female	Graduate	58	24	40	Male	Under graduate	22
6	40	40	Male	Under graduate	22	64	24	Male	Graduate	22
7	40	24	Female	High school	22	90	24	Male	High school	32
8	40	64	Male	Junior high	58	24	64	Male	High school	45
9	64	40	Female	Junior high	45	24	24	Female	Junior high	58
10	90	90	Male	High school	58	64	90	Female	Under graduate	32
11	24	64	Female	Under graduate	22	18	64	Male	Graduate	32
12	90	40	Male	Tech school	22	90	90	Male	Junior high	45
13	64	90	Male	Graduate	22	24	18	Female	Tech school	32
14	64	24	Male	Under graduate	58	24	90	Male	Graduate	22
15	18	24	Male	Tech school	22	40	64	Male	Under graduate	58
16	64	18	Female	High school	22	90	18	Male	Under graduate	22
17	18	64	Male	High school	45	18	40	Female	High school	22
18	40	90	Female	Tech school	45	18	18	Male	Junior high	22
19	90	64	Female	Graduate	22	40	18	Female	Graduate	45
20	90	18	Male	Under graduate	45	40	90	Female	High school	22
21	24	40	Male	High school	32	18	90	Male	Tech school	58
22	64	64	Male	Tech school	32	64	18	Male	High school	58
23	18	18	Male	Junior high	22	18	24	Female	Under graduate	45
24	24	90	Male	Junior high	22	90	40	Female	Graduate	58
25	24	18	Female	Tech school	58	90	64	Female	Tech school	22

This certain other person might, for example, be a 28-year-old woman with a university degree, or a 58-year-old man with a high school diploma. The characteristics of this other person vary in each question.

In the subsequent screens, we asked respondents to answer the following question while showing them various figures for different alternatives after the question, as shown below (Fig. 14.2).[28]

[28] In the survey information in the figures was presented in Japanese. The images for monthly income differ in terms of number of banknotes shown according to the attribute levels. Also, images for reference person differ, depending on his or her characteristics. Subjects repeated five questions and they were not allowed to go back to previous questions once they had made their choices.

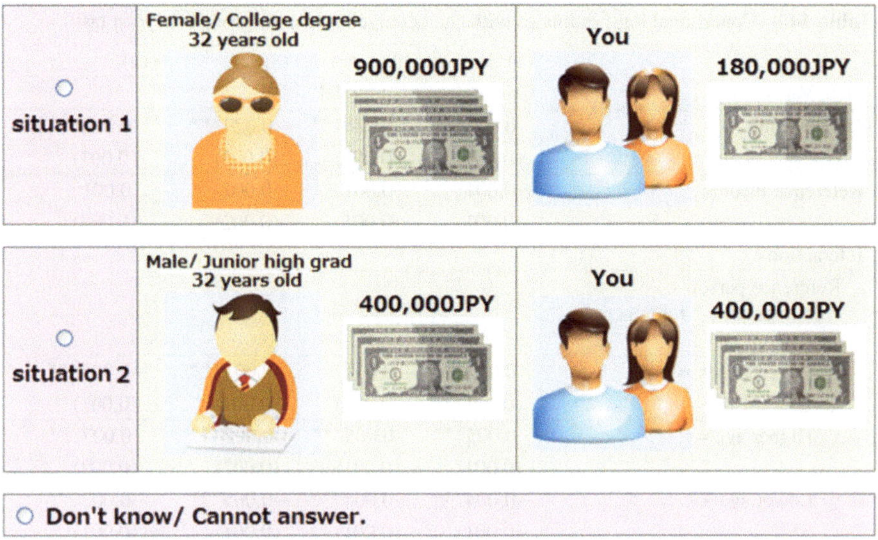

Fig. 14.2 An example of choice question (Leyden task)

> Comparing situation 1 and situation 2 shown in the figures, which is more preferable to you? Suppose that the price levels in the two situations are the same.

As we documented above, we prepared in a total of 25 choice sets consisting of specific hypothetical amounts for a person's own pre-tax monthly income and for the reference person. Each respondent answered five randomly assigned questions out of the 25 total questions.

Empirical Results

We identify the effects of the reference person's characteristics on marginal utility by adding interaction terms for reference income levels and reference person characteristic dummy variables. We created these dummy variables as follows. Regarding gender, we made a *different gender* dummy variable, with information of the subjects' own gender and that of the reference group in the choice scenario (0 = "same gender"). With respect to age, we created dummy variables for *higher age* and *younger age* (0 = "same age") using information on the subjects' own age and that of the reference group in the choice scenarios. Finally, using information on the subjects' own level of educational attainment and that of the reference group in the choice scenarios, we created dummy variables for *higher education* and *lower education* (0 = "same education"). These interaction terms are added into the conditional logit model estimation, thereby examining how this additional information on reference groups affects social comparison. Table 14.8 presents the results.

Table 14.8 Conditional logit estimates with characterized reference groups (Leyden task)

	(1)	(2)	(3)	(4)
Dep. Var: Utility	Conditional logit model			
Own income	0.028***	0.028***	0.029***	0.020***
	(0.001)	(0.001)	(0.002)	(0.001)
Reference income	−0.001	−0.001	−0.002	0.001
	(0.001)	(0.001)	(0.002)	(0.002)
Interactions:				
Reference person's demographic * reference income				
Different sex $*\bar{y}$	0.001	0.001	0.003***	−0.007***
	(0.001)	(0.001)	(0.001)	(0.001)
Higher age $*\bar{y}$	0.005***	0.005***	0.007***	0.007***
	(0.001)	(0.001)	(0.002)	(0.002)
Lower age $*\bar{y}$	−0.004***	−0.004***	−0.005***	−0.003***
	(0.001)	(0.001)	(0.001)	(0.001)
Higher education $*\bar{y}$	−0.004***	−0.004***	−0.004***	−0.001
	(0.001)	(0.001)	(0.001)	(0.001)
Lower education $*\bar{y}$	−0.000	−0.000	−0.000	−0.000
	(0.001)	(0.001)	(0.001)	(0.001)
Interactions of own individual characteristics and income levels[a]	No	Yes	Yes	Yes
Observations	45,554	45,554	20,328 (male)	25,226 (female)
Pseudo R-squared	0.194	0.213	0.253	0.186

Standard errors clustered by subject in parentheses. Omitted categories are "Same age $*\bar{y}$" and "Same education $*\bar{y}$"

[a]If Yes, individual characteristics are controlled with interaction terms for the own income term, and for reference income. The same set of individual characteristic variables controlled in the social average task regressions are taken into account

$^{*}p < 0.1$; $^{**}p < 0.05$; $^{***}p < 0.01$

In column (1) of Table 14.8, we show the results of a conditional logit model estimation when we do not control for the effects of subjects' own individual characteristics on their own income, reference income, and reference group type dummy interactions. Column (2) of Table 14.8 shows the results when controlling for these effects.[29] The columns show that one's own income effect is positive and significant, as is the case in the previous task. The main effect of reference income identified is negative and significant.

[29]Our findings are robust against changes in the threshold level for the comparison-conscious group, the happy group, the high-income group, and the elder group. These results are available upon requests.

As columns (1) and (2) show, reference groups with higher educational attainment tend to be the target of stronger jealousy. We also find that if the reference person is older than you are, feelings of pecuniary emulation are mitigated. The altruistic attitudes toward elderly persons, or admiration of them, are interesting since both higher age and higher education are associated with higher income on average. As it was confirmed in the social average task, reference persons with higher income levels draw stronger jealousy. These intriguing relative utility effects for the elderly may be a good reflection of Japanese culture.

While columns (1) and (2) do not provide strong evidence showing effects of reference persons' gender on comparisons, we actually have significant effects when we divide our sample into subgroups of male and females. Column (3) (male) and column (4) (female) suggest that males have stronger jealousy toward people of the same gender than they do toward females, whereas females have weaker jealousy toward people of the same gender than they do toward males. Hence, we conclude that males are the target of stronger jealousy in Japanese society. Columns (3) and (4) also suggest that the previous results on the effects of age and educational backgrounds of reference groups remain unchanged.

To sum up, from the Leyden task we can say that comparison attitudes change on the basis of the features of reference persons. These findings suggest that consideration of social averages as the salient reference group is not sufficient when examining relative utility effects. Instead, researchers should pay attention to the features of the true reference groups of subjects, since they can greatly affect the outcome of empirical investigations on relative utility.

Who-Compares-to-Whom Task

Construction of Choice Tasks

In the descriptive statistics from the pre-test, we could see that the most often cited reference group is *friends*, followed by *work colleagues*. Now these two groups are treated as reference persons.[30] We thus use three attributes, one's own income, reference income of friends, and reference income of colleagues. While we can elicit the intensity and signs of relative utility for friends and colleagues using a two-situation-choice framework as in the previous tasks, the framework of this choice task has five options: (i) situation 1, (ii) situation 2, (iii) situation 3, (iv) situation 4, and (v) do not know/cannot answer.

We created this expanded framework so as to use a *tree structure* for the choice options. Our purpose is to investigate whether people perceive two different

[30]In the Japanese social context, the two reference groups (friends/classmates and work-related) may not be mutually exclusive. The nested-logit regressions, however, show that respondents distinguished these two reference groups clearly. We thank Charles Yuji Horioka for pointing out this potential flaw in the structure of the choice experiment.

reference groups as actually different. More specifically, we would like to exclude the possibility that people define their comparison benchmark to simply be others and that the exact characterizations of others are not important.

As before, the levels of the three attributes have five variations: 180,000 JPY, 240,000 JPY, 400,000 JPY, 640,000 JPY, and 900,000 JPY. Given that we have three attributes in this task, there are 125 potential variations of alternatives. Again, orthogonal design was used to pick up 25 out of the 125 variations to make a vector of alternatives. We repeated this procedure four times to form the four-situation choice task used in the survey. We paired these four situations to form a choice set such that we can make use of a tree structure in the hypothetical choice experiments. Two attributes for situation 1 and situation 2 are characterized by the same level of income for *colleagues*, while one's own income and income levels of *friends* are randomly chosen. Regarding the attributes of situation 3 and situation 4, the income level of *friends* is fixed, while one's own income and income levels of *colleagues* are randomly chosen. We call the nest of situation 1 and situation 2 *C-fixed*, while the second nest of situation 3 and situation 4 is called *F-fixed*. For respondents who consider that *only* the reference income of friends matters, the F-fixed nest exhibits the similarity of the choice options in the nest. Also, for respondents who consider that only reference income of work colleagues matters, the C-fixed nest shows the equivalence of the choice options in the nest. With this tree structure, if subjects think that there is no difference between the reference group of friends and that of work colleagues– in other words, if they think of both reference groups of friends and work colleagues as being simply "others"–the tree structure of the choice options becomes irrelevant. If this is the case, from the nested logit model estimation, we would obtain that *Inclusive Value (IV)* parameters related to respective nests are estimated to be significantly different from one. Table 14.9 shows the set of questions we used in the survey.

Instructions in the Survey

Before the subjects started the repeated choice questions, they were shown an instruction screen saying that:

> The next figure shows your hypothetical monthly income (before tax). And in the same way as before, it pairs that amount with the monthly income (before tax) of certain other persons. Suppose that the current situations for these sets are as shown.
> This time for the question, imagine that the certain other persons as (1) a co-worker, (2) a friend.

In the subsequent screens, we asked respondents to answer the following question while showing the various figures for different alternatives, as shown below (Fig. 14.3).[31]

[31] In the survey everything in the figures was presented in Japanese. Subjects repeated five questions and they were not allowed to go back to previous questions once they had made their choices.

Table 14.9 Parameter sets in who compares to whom task

	Alternative 1			Alternative 2			Alternative 3			Alternative 4		
		Ref. income			Ref. income			Ref. income			Ref. income	
Q	Self	Colleague	Friend	Self	Colleague	Friend	Self	Colleague	Friend	Self	Colleague	Friend
1	90	40	64	18	40	90	90	64	40	64	18	40
2	90	64	24	64	64	40	64	24	90	18	90	90
3	64	64	64	18	64	24	90	40	18	24	24	18
4	40	90	64	40	90	40	40	64	90	64	40	90
5	18	24	64	24	24	90	24	64	18	18	18	18
6	64	18	90	90	18	64	64	90	18	40	40	18
7	64	40	18	40	40	64	90	18	24	40	64	24
8	40	40	40	64	40	18	40	90	24	24	44	24
9	24	64	40	90	64	94	18	40	90	24	18	90
10	18	40	24	90	40	40	24	44	64	64	24	64
11	24	18	64	64	18	24	40	24	18	64	64	18
12	64	24	40	90	24	18	90	28	64	24	90	64
13	64	90	24	18	90	64	64	40	24	18	24	24
14	90	90	90	24	90	18	64	64	64	40	18	64
15	24	90	18	90	90	24	64	18	40	90	24	40
16	40	64	18	24	64	64	24	18	90	90	68	90
17	40	24	90	64	24	64	18	18	18	90	90	18
18	24	40	90	24	40	24	18	24	40	40	90	40
19	18	64	90	40	64	18	40	40	40	24	68	40
20	18	18	18	40	18	90	24	24	24	64	90	24
21	90	18	40	18	18	18	90	90	90	40	24	90
22	40	18	24	24	18	40	24	90	40	18	40	40
23	24	24	24	18	24	40	18	90	64	18	64	64
24	18	90	40	64	90	90	18	64	24	90	18	24
25	90	24	18	40	24	24	40	18	64	90	40	64

Comparing situations 1 through 4 as shown in the figures, which would be the most preferable to you? Suppose that the price levels in the four situations are all the same.

Each respondent answered five randomly assigned questions out of the 25 total questions.

Empirical Results

In the questionnaire for this task, we provided four choice options and a "Don't know/Cannot answer" option, since we aim to use a tree structure for the choice options. The first two options are the *F-fixed* nest, while the third and the fourth options are the *W-fixed* nest in this task. Our purpose in making these nests is to test if people perceive the friend and colleague groups as independent from each other. If people define their rivals as being merely "others", then the characterization of reference persons is not important, nullifying the nested structure of the four options.

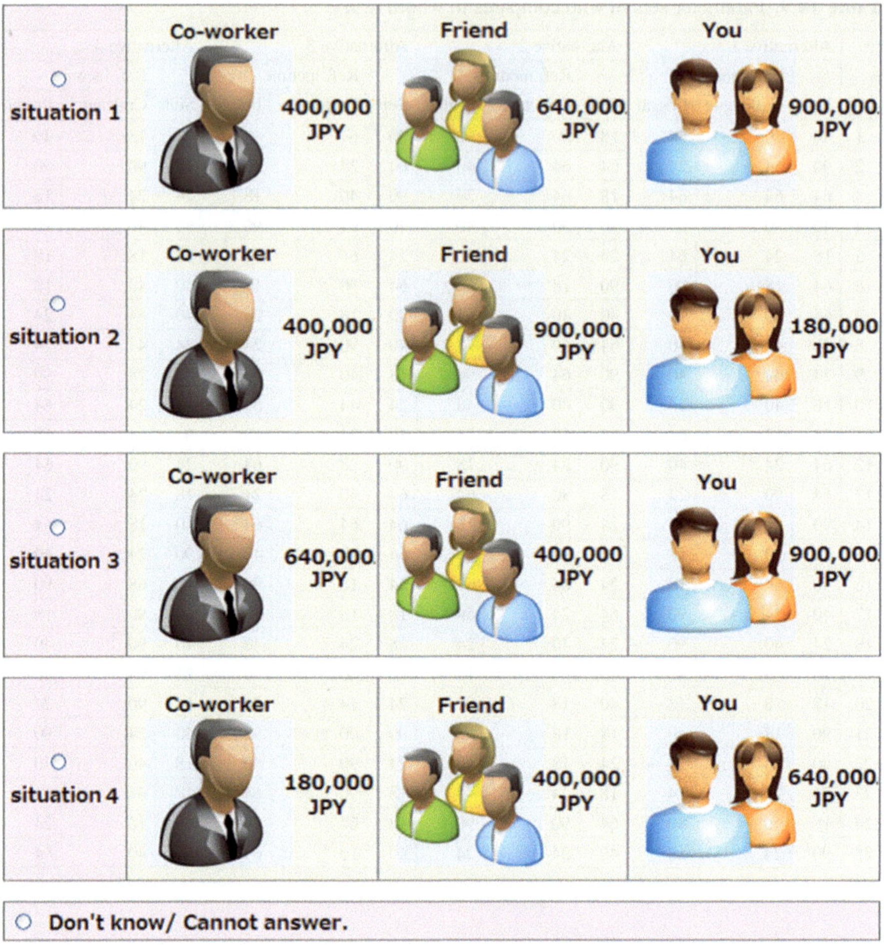

Fig. 14.3 An example of choice question (who compares to whom task)

The results from the nested logit model are as follows (not shown in tabular form). First, the IV parameter for the *F-fixed* nest becomes 1.556, while that for the *W-fixed* nest becomes 1.627. Both of these results are significantly different from 1 at the 1 % confidence level. These figures indicate that respondents perceive the two reference groups as different from each other. Secondly, an interesting finding here is that the estimated IV parameters exceed 1. According to Train et al. (1987), from a purely statistical perspective, the values of IV parameters indicate the relative substitutability within and among nests, and if they are greater than 1, it means that choice substitutability among nests are more frequent.[32] In our choice setting, the outcome suggests that subjects frequently change their comparison benchmarks from one to the other, rather than stick to a single benchmark group, in accordance with situations they face. This result hints at the fact that reference groups are chosen endogenously.

To investigate the difference in relative utility effects toward friends and colleagues, we first employ a conditional logit model framework as is shown in Table 14.10. In this task, the true parameters of relative utility, γ_f and γ_w, are calculated by dividing the estimates of the reference income terms for friends and for work colleagues by the estimates of the own income term.

The first column of Table 14.10 shows the result of conditional logit estimation for the whole study sample. Firstly, it shows that the own income effect is found to be positive and significant, which validates the framework of the choice task in this study. Secondly, the relative utility effects toward the friend group and colleague group are both estimated to be significantly negative, as is the case when the reference group is the social average.

The difference in magnitudes for the terms of these two reference groups, however, warrants attention. Looking at the true estimates of relative utility parameters, the intensity of jealousy toward work colleague group is more than 10 times stronger than that of the friend group. Another interesting finding is that from columns (2) to (6), where estimation results of subgroups of individual-specific comparison benchmark are provided, the relative utility effect toward certain types of friends disappears in some cases.

Especially, in column (4), for those who state that their reference group is friends, the relative utility effect toward friends is not significantly different from zero; whereas in column (5), for those whose reference group is work colleagues, the relative utility effect toward friends is significantly negative.[33] At first glance, this outcome is puzzling.

A mixed logit model framework helps to understand the issue of the weak intensity of comparison attitude toward friends. Column (7) of Table 14.10 shows that we obtain very similar magnitudes for the mean effects of one's own income, the reference income of friends, and that of work colleagues, as is the case in the conditional logit model in column (1). The column, on the other hand, shows that the relative magnitudes of the standard deviation terms compared to their mean estimates are very different from each other.

A noteworthy finding is the large standard deviation for the reference income level for friends compared to the mean. With this finding, we conclude that a

[32]See Herriges and Kling (1996) for the relationship between the magnitude of IV parameters and the global necessary and sufficient condition of utility maximization behavior in a random utility model framework.

[33]We point out that the intensity of jealousy toward the reference group of work colleagues by those who answered that they do not compare is the weakest among subgroups (column 6). Together with the same finding in the social average task, this result validates our data set.

Table 14.10 Conditional logit and mixed logit estimates (who-compares-to-whom task)

	(1)	(2)	(3)	(4)	(5)	(6)	(7)	
Comparison benchmarks		Family	Neighbor	Friend	Colleague	Do not compare		
	Conditional logit						Mixed logit	
Dep. Var: Utility							Mean	SD
Own income	0.028*** (0.000)	0.028*** (0.001)	0.031*** (0.001)	0.028*** (0.000)	0.030*** (0.001)	0.025*** (0.001)	0.035*** (0.000)	0.029*** (0.001)
Reference income (Friend)	−0.001*** (0.000)	−0.001 (0.001)	0.000 (0.001)	0.000 (0.000)	−0.003*** (0.001)	−0.002*** (0.000)	−0.002*** (0.000)	−0.011*** (0.000)
Reference income (Colleague)	−0.011*** (0.000)	−0.012*** (0.001)	−0.012*** (0.001)	−0.012*** (0.000)	−0.011*** (0.001)	−0.007*** (0.000)	−0.011*** (0.000)	0.006*** (0.001)
Estimated γ_f	−0.036	0	0	0	−0.100	−0.080		
Estimated variance of γ_f		0.039	0.030	0.013	0.017	0.017		
Estimated γ_w	−0.393	−0.429	−0.387	−0.429	−0.367	−0.280		
Estimated variance of γ_w		0.047	0.036	0.015	0.019	0.019		
Observations	47,180	2,226	2,664	20,131	9,387	11,639	47,180	
Pseudo R-squared	0.140	0.143	0.168	0.147	0.158	0.111		

Robust standard errors clustered by subject in parentheses. For estimates of γ, we report variances constructed via the Delta method
Result omitted for the case of "other comparison benchmarks"
$^{*}p < 0.1$; $^{**}p < 0.05$; $^{***}p < 0.01$

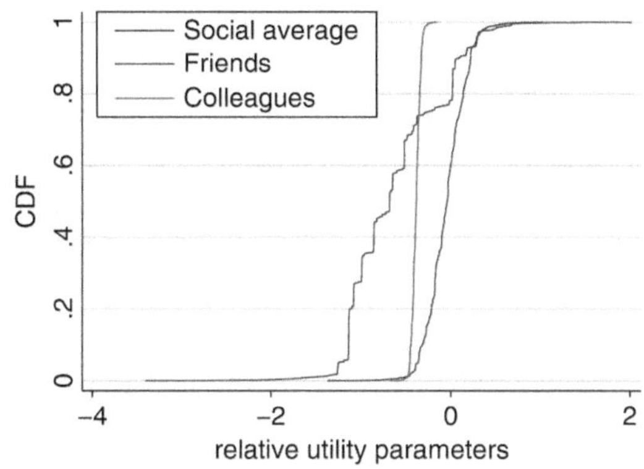

Fig. 14.4 Distributions of relative utility parameters (social average, friends, and colleagues)

mean estimate of reference income for friends that is close to zero reflects differing attitudes in the subjects toward their friends. In order to visualize the intuition of this point, we provide Fig. 14.4 in which the cumulative distribution functions (CDFs) of the true parameters of relative utility for the social average (γ_a), for the friend group (γ_f), and for the work colleague group (γ_w) are illustrated.[34] Figure 14.4 clearly shows that the distributions of these true magnitudes of relative utility effects exhibit different patterns from each other. The CDF of γ_w shows that all the subjects in our study sample have negative relative utility toward work colleagues, whereas the CDF of γ_f shows that around 30 % of subjects feel altruism toward friends. We also see from the CDF of γ_a that the distribution of γ_a has the largest variance.

It is also interesting to note the differences in the distribution of relative utility effects, in addition to those in the intensity of comparisons, by separately regressing subsamples of specific comparison benchmarks using the mixed logit model framework. Results are shown in Table 14.11.

The first noteworthy finding is that in each subgroup of specific comparison benchmarks, the means of the effect of one's own income provides quite similar magnitudes to each other. The means of relative utility effects for friends are found to be significantly negative, except for subgroups with neighbors as the comparison benchmark. For the subgroups with family as the comparison benchmark, the mean relative utility effect of friend's income is estimated to be significant, but it is only at the 10 % confidence level. In all subgroups, the absolute values of the mean estimates of relative utility effects for friends are close to zero. Another noteworthy observation is that the estimated standard deviation terms of the reference income terms for friends are large compared to the means. Notice that those terms are significant for all subgroups, including the subgroup with work colleagues as the comparison benchmark.

[34] γ_a is obtained in the social average task. We obtained individual parameters of relative utility using the inverse Bayesian formula after the mixed logit model estimation (Train 2009).

Table 14.11 Mixed logit estimates for subgroups of comparison benchmarks (who-compares-to-whom task)

	(1)		(2)		(3)		(4)		(5)	
Comparison benchmark	family		neighbor		friend		colleague		Do not compare	
	Mixed logit									
Dep. Var: Utility	Mean	SD	Mean	SD	Mean	SD	Mean	SD	Mean	SD
Own income	0.036*** (0.002)	0.031*** (0.003)	0.036*** (0.002)	0.024*** (0.002)	0.035*** (0.001)	0.028*** (0.001)	0.038*** (0.001)	0.028*** (0.001)	0.032*** (0.001)	0.030*** (0.001)
Reference income (Friend)	−0.002* (0.001)	0.013*** (0.002)	−0.000 (0.001)	0.006* (0.003)	−0.001** (0.000)	0.012*** (0.001)	−0.004*** (0.001)	0.011*** (0.001)	−0.003*** (0.000)	0.008*** (0.001)
Reference income (Colleague)	−0.013*** (0.001)	0.010*** (0.003)	−0.012*** (0.001)	0.006** (0.003)	−0.013*** (0.000)	0.007*** (0.001)	−0.011*** (0.001)	0.003 (0.005)	−0.007*** (0.000)	0.003 (0.002)
Observations	2,226		2,664		20,131		9,387		11,639	

Robust standard errors in parentheses
Result omitted for the case of "other comparison benchmarks"
$^{*}p < 0.1$; $^{**}p < 0.05$; $^{***}p < 0.01$

The mean relative utility effects of work colleagues' income are found to be significantly negative for all subsample regressions. The magnitudes of the mean estimates compared to the own income terms are larger than they were in the case of using friends as the reference group.

An intriguing pattern is found when we compare the estimates of standard deviations for the relative utility effects toward work colleagues for the two subgroups of subjects with friends (column 3) and with work colleagues (column 4) as the comparison benchmark. On one hand, the standard deviation is found to be significant (though it is not particularly large) in the friend subgroup. On the other hand, for the work colleague subgroup, the standard deviation is found to be *insignificant*, implying that the negative relative utility effect against work colleagues spikes near the average point among those subsamples. This outcome suggests that reference groups of friends and work colleagues are different, not only in terms of the average intensities of the relative utility effects, but also in the sense that their distributions differ by subsample group for specific comparison benchmarks. We argue that this outcome reflects that *friends* encompass many aspects of life, such as benevolent rivals, persons of understanding, and so forth, and that work colleagues tend to be regarded as rivals.

Addendum: Additional Survey[35]

The stability of experimentally measured deep parameters over time in response to exogenous shocks such as macroeconomic events and natural disasters is a new research topic. If the utility parameters are vulnerable to such shocks, economists may no longer want to treat utility parameters as "deep." Since this research area is rather new, only a few papers are available, including Volk et al. (2011), Krupka and Stephens (2013), and Kuziemko et al. (2013).

We investigate whether the experience of a huge natural disaster in Japan, the Great East Japan Earthquake, affected a deep parameter of utility function. After we conducted the first survey in March 2010 on income comparisons following Yamada and Sato (2013), the earthquake occurred in March 2011. Our new data set for the second experiment, which was socially representative just as the first survey, was created using an original Internet-based survey in March 2013. We maintained the structure of our questionnaire as almost identical between the surveys, which made it relevant to compare elicited parameters of income comparisons from the two waves of experiments: Framing effects should not be a concern.

For the new survey, we again worked with Nikkei Research Inc. Nikkei Research and the authors reached an agreement that the number of subjects should be greater than 2,500 given the volume of research funding. Then, considering the unweighted average response rate for seven similar academic experimental surveys conducted by

[35]This addendum has been newly written for this book chapter.

the same company in 2008 and 2009, the company sent invitation emails to potential survey subjects. Registered subjects who answered our 2010 survey were not invited to participate in the second experiment. Subjects between the ages of 20 and 65 were selected using stratified random sampling so that the cohort profile of our sample mirrored the Japanese census statistics of age and gender distribution. In the invitation email, we specified that the survey would be conducted for research purposes. We followed the disclosure requirements for research involving human beings provided with incentives, as set forth by the ethics committee. We specified our payment rules in the invitation email and stated that the incentive would be provided on a lottery basis. We informed subjects that lottery winners among those who completed the survey would be paid 500 JPY per person. The anonymity of subjects was completely secured. If subjects wished to participate in the survey, they were instructed to follow the link in the email that directed them to our stand-alone survey website, written in html, which was launched in March 2013. The survey was open from March 25 through March 27, 2013, and 2,950 subjects completed the survey. Our main results are discussed below.

First, Table 14.12 shows the distribution of the reference groups chosen by the respondents, namely, the direction of income comparisons. The first row of Table 14.12 is for 2010 and the second is for 2013.

Table 14.13 shows the distribution of happiness levels and the intensity of jealousy, with their means in the last column.

Finally, elicited utility parameters of income comparisons from the conditional logit model are shown in Table 14.14. The first column replicates the results from the 2010 survey, while the second column shows the results from the 2013 survey.

As reflected in Tables 14.12–14.14, what we found was rather surprising to Japanese eyes. Even after the precedent disaster of the Great East Japan Earthquake, distributions of important subjective variables such as happiness and the intensity and direction of income comparisons were unchanged. Moreover, elicited parameters of income comparisons are remarkably similar between the surveys. Our findings favor the presumption about deep parameters: They are indeed deep.

Table 14.12 Change in the distribution of comparison benchmark

	Family	Neighbors	Friends	Colleagues	Do not compare	Others
% (2010)	4.73	5.67	41.94	19.84	25.40	2.42
% (2013)	5.39	5.05	37.05	18.41	32.20	1.90

Table 14.13 Change in survey elicited subjective scores

	1	2	3	4	5	Mean
Happiness (2010)	21.03	40.09	31.09	6.04	0.94	2.25
Happiness (2013)	20.85	37.69	33.22	6.88	1.36	2.30
Jealousy (2010)	6.22	24.16	29.42	35.65	4.73	3.09
Jealousy (2013)	7.19	25.97	32.68	29.76	4.41	2.98

Table 14.14 Change in parameter of income comparisons

	2010	2013
Model	Conditional logit	
Dep. Var: Utility		
Own income	0.048*** (0.001)	0.038*** (0.001)
Reference income	−0.022*** (0.001)	−0.021*** (0.000)
Estimated γ	−0.458	−0.563
Observations	48,172	26,040
Pseudo R-squared	0.249	0.189

References

Abel AB (1990) Asset prices under habit formation and catching up with the Joneses. Am Econ Rev 80:38–42

Ai C, Norton EC (2003) Interaction terms in logit and probit models. Econ Lett 80:123–129

Alpizar F, Carlsson F, Johansson-Stenman O (2005) How much do we care about absolute versus relative income and consumption? J Econ Behav Organ 56:405–421

Amir O, Rand G, Gal Y (2012) Economic games on the internet: the effect of $1 stakes. PLoS One 7:e31461

Andersson FW (2008) Is concern for relative consumption a function of relative consumption. J Socio-Econ 37:353–364

Andreoni J, Bernheim BD (2009) Social image and the 50–50 norm: a theoretical and experimental analysis of audience effects. Econometrica 77:1607–1636

Andreoni J, Rao JM (2011) The power of asking: how communication affects selfishness, empathy, and altruism. J Public Econ 95:513–520

Arrow K, Solow R, Portney PR, Leamer EE, Radner R, Schuman H (1993) Report of the NOAA panel on contingent valuation. Technical report, National Oceanic and Atmospheric Administration

Bateman I, Carson R, Day B, Hanemann M, Hanley N, Hett T, Jones-Lee M, Loomes G, Mourato S, Ozdemiroglu E, Pearce D, Sugden R, Swanson J (2002) Economic valuation with stated preference techniques. Edward Elgar, Cheltenham

Bickel WK, Pitcock JA, Yi R, Angtuaco EJC (2009) Congruence of BOLD response across intertemporal choice conditions: fictive and real money gains and losses. J Neurosci 29:8839–8846

Brown GDA, Gardner J, Oswald AJ, Qian J (2008) Does wage rank affect employees' well-being? Ind Relat 47:355–389

Cappelli P, Sherer PD (Winter 1988) Satisfaction, market wages, & labor relations: an airline study. Ind Relat 27:56–73

Card D, Mas A, Moretti E, Saez E (2012) Inequality at work: the effect of peer salaries on job satisfaction. Am Econ Rev 102:2981–3003

Carlsson F, Johansson-Stenman O, Martinsson P (2007) Do you enjoy having more than others? Survey evidence of positional goods. Economica 74:586–598

Carlsson F, Gupta G, Johansson-Stenman O (2009) Keeping up with the Vaishyas? Caste and relative standing in India. Oxf Econ Pap 61:52–73

Carson R (1991) Constructed arkets. In: Braden JB, Kolstad CD (eds) Measuring the demand for environmental quality, vol 198. Elsevier, North Holland, pp 122–162

Carson R, Flores N, Meade N (2001) Contingent valuation: controversies and evidence. Environ Resour Econ 19:173–210

Clark AE, Oswald AJ (1996) Satisfaction and comparison income. J Public Econ 61:359–381
Clark AE, Senik C (2010) Who compares to whom? The anatomy of income comparisons in Europe. Econ J 120:573–594
Clark AE, Frijters P, Shields MA (2008) Relative income, happiness, and utility: an explanation for the easterlin paradox and other puzzles. J Econ Lit 46:95–144
Clark AE, Kristensen N, Westergard-Nielsen N (2009a) Economic satisfaction and income rank in small neighbourhoods. J Eur Econ Assoc 7:519–527
Clark AE, Kristensen N, Westergard-Nielsen N (2009b) Job satisfaction and co-worker wages: status or signal? Econ J 119:430–447
de la Garza A, Mastrobuoni G, Sannabe A, Yamada K (2010) The relative utility hypothesis with and without self-reported reference wages. Iser discussion paper, Institute of Social and Economic Research, Osaka University
Dolan P, Kahneman D (2008) Interpretations of utility and their implications for the valuation of health. Econ J 118:215–234
Dupor B, Liu W-F (2003) Jealousy and equilibrium overconsumption. Am Econ Rev 93:423–428
Easterlin RA (1974) Does economic growth improve the human lot? Some empirical evidence. In: David PA, Reder MW (eds) Nations and households in economic growth: essays in honour of Moses Abramowitz. Academic, New York
Easterlin RA (1995) Will raising the incomes of all increase the happiness of all? J Econ Behav Organ 27:35–47
Easterlin RA (2001) Income and happiness: towards an unified theory. Econ J 111:465–484
Exadaktylos F, Espin AM, Branas-Garza P (2012) Experimental subjects are not different. Technical report. Scientific Reports 3, Article number: 1213. doi: 10.1038/srep01213
Falk A, Heckman JJ (2009) Lab experiments are a major source of knowledge in the social sciences. Science 326:535–538
Falk A, Meier S, Zehnder C (2013) Do lab experiments misrepresent social preferences? The case of self-selected student samples. J Eur Econ Assoc 11(4):839–852
Fehr E, Schmidt KM (1999) A theory of fairness, competition, and cooperation. Q J Econ 114:817–868
Fehr E, Schmidt KM (2006) The economics of fairness, reciprocity and altruism – experimental evidence and new theories. In: Kolm S-C, Ythier JM (eds) Handbook on the economics of giving, reciprocity and altruism, vol 1. Elsevier, Amsterdam, pp 615–691
Ferrer-i Carbonell A (2005) Income and well-being: an empirical analysis of the comparison income effect. J Public Econ 89:997–1019
Ferrer-i Carbonell A, Frijters P (2004) How important is methodology for the estimates of the determinants of happiness? Econ J 114:641–659
Fliessbach K, Weber B, Trautner P, Dohmen T, Sunde U, Elger CE, Falk A (2007) Social comparison affects reward-related brain activity in the human ventral striatum. Science 318:11305–11308
Futagami K, Shibata A (1998) Keeping one step ahead of the Joneses: status, the distribution of wealth, and long run growth. J Econ Behav Organ 36:109–126
Gali J (1994) Keeping up with the Joneses: consumption externalities, portfolio choice, and asset prices. J Money Credit Bank 26:1–8
Garcia-Penalosa C, Turnovsky S (2008) Consumption externalities: a representative consumer model when agents are heterogeneous. Econ Theory 37:439–467
Haaijer R, Kamakura W, Wedel M (2001) Mixed logit with repeated choices: households' choices of appliance efficiency level. Int J Mark Res 43:93–106
Hausman J (1993) Contingent valuation: a critical assessment. North-Holland, Amsterdam/New York
Herriges JA, Kling CL (1996) Testing the consistency of nested logit models with utility maximization. Econ Lett 50:33–39
Hirschman AO, Rothschild M (1973) The changing tolerance for income inequality in the course of economic development; with a mathematical appendix. Q J Econ 87:544–566

Hole AR (2007) Fitting mixed logit models by using maximum simulated likelihood. Stata J 7:388–401
Hole AR (2008) Modelling heterogeneity in patients' preferences for the attributes of a general practitioner appointment. J Health Econ 27:1078–1094
Hollander H (2001) On the validity of utility statements: standard theory versus Duesenberry's. J Econ Behav Organ 45:227–249
Horton J, Rand D, Zeckhauser R (2011) The online laboratory: conducting experiments in a real labor market. Exp Econ 14:399–425
Huber J, Zwerina K (1996) The importance of utility balance in efficient choice designs. J Mark Res 33:307–317
Ida T, Goto R (2009) Simultaneous measurement of time and risk preferences: stated preference discrete choice modeling analysis depending on smoking behavior. Int Econ Rev 50:1169–1182
Johansson-Stenman O, Carlsson F, Daruvala D (2002) Measuring future grandparents' preferences for equality and relative standing. Econ J 112:362–383
Kahneman D, Knetsch JL (1992) Valuing public goods: the purchase of moral satisfaction. J Environ Econ Manage 22:57–70
Kahneman D, Krueger AB (Winter 2006) Developments in the measurement of subjective well-being. J Econ Perspect 20:3–24
Kahneman D, Wakker PP, Sarin R (1997) Back to Bentham? Explorations of experienced utility. Q J Econ 112:375–405
Kang MJ, Rangel A, Camus M, Camerer CF (2011) Hypothetical and real choice differentially activate common valuation areas. J Neurosci 31:461–468
Knight J, Song L, Gunatilaka R (2009) Subjective well-being and its determinants in rural China. China Econ Rev 20:635–649
Krupka EL, Stephens M (2013) The stability of measured time preferences. J Econ Behav Organ 85:11–19
Kuziemko I, Norton MI, Saez E, Stantcheva S (2013) How elastic are preferences for redistribution? Evidence from randomized survey experiments. CEPR Discussion Papers 9438, C.E.P.R. Discussion Papers
Liu W-F, Turnovsky S (2005) Consumption externalities, production externalities, and long-run macroeconomic efficiency. J Public Econ 89:1097–1129
Louviere JJ, Hensher DA, Swait JD (2000) Stated choice methods: analysis and applications. Cambridge University Press, Cambridge
Lusk JL, Schroeder TC (2004) Are choice experiments incentive compatible? A test with quality differentiated beef steaks. Am J Agric Econ 86:467–482
Luttmer EFP (2005) Neighbors as negatives: relative earnings and well-being. Q J Econ 120:963–1002
Manski CF (1993) Identification of endogenous social effects: the reflection problem. Rev Econ Stud 60:531–542
Mayraz G, Schupp J, Wagner GG (2009) Life satisfaction and relative income: perceptions and evidence. CEP Discussion Papers dp0938, Centre for Economic Performance, LSE
McFadden D (1974) Conditional logit analysis of qualitative choice behavior. In: Zarembka P (ed) Frontiers in econometrics. Academic, New York
Oswald A, Wu S (2010) Objective confirmation of subjective measures of human well-being: evidence from the USA. Science 327:576–579
Paolacci G, Chandler J, Ipeirotis PG (2010) Running experiments on Amazon mechanical turk. Judgm Decis Making 5:411–419
Rand DG (2011) The promise of mechanical turk: how online labor markets can help theorists run behavioral experiments. J Theor Biol 299:172–179
Ravallion M, Lokshin M (2010) Who cares about relative deprivation? J Econ Behav Organ 73:171–185
Rubinstein A (2007) Instinctive and cognitive reasoning: a study of response times. Econ J 117:1243–1259

Senik C (2004) When information dominates comparison: learning from Russian subjective panel data. J Public Econ 88:2099–2123

Senik C (2009) Direct evidence on income comparisons and their welfare effects. J Econ Behav Organ 72:408–424

Sloane PJ, Williams H (2000) Job satisfaction, comparison earnings, and gender. LABOUR 14:473–502

Small KA, Winston C, Yan J (2005) Uncovering the distribution of motorists' preferences for travel time and reliability. Econometrica 73:1367–1382

Solnick SJ, Hemenway D (1998) Is more always better? A survey on positional concerns. J Econ Behav Organ 37:373–383

Stevenson B, Wolfers J (Spring 2008) Economic growth and subjective well-being: reassessing the easterlin paradox. Brookings Papers on Economic Activity 39:1–87

Suri S, Watts DJ (2011) A study of cooperation and contagion in web-based, networked public goods experiments. Plos One 6:e16836

Takahashi H, Kato M, Matsuura M, Mobbs D, Suhara T, Okubo Y (2009) When your gain is my pain and your pain is my gain: neural correlates of envy and schadenfreude. Science 323:937–939

Train K (2009) Discrete choice methods with simulation, 2nd edn. Cambridge University Press, Cambridge

Train KE, McFadden DL, Ben-Akiva M (Spring 1987) The demand for local telephone service: a fully discrete model of residential calling patterns and service choices. RAND J Econ 18:109–123

Tricomi E, Rangel A, Camerer CF, O'Doherty JP (2010) Neural evidence for inequality-averse social preferences. Nature 463:1089–1091

van de Stadt H, Kapteyn A, van de Geer S (1985) The relativity of utility: evidence from panel data. Rev Econ Stat 67:179–187

van Praag BM, Frijters P (1999) The measurement of welfare and well-being; the Leyden approach. Paul frijters discussion papers, School of Economics and Finance, Queensland University of Technology

Viscusi WK, Huber J, Bell J (2008) Estimating discount rates for environmental quality from utility-based choice experiments. J Risk Uncertain 37:199–220

Volk S, Thoeni C, Ruigrok W (2011) Temporal stability and psychological foundations of cooperation preferences. Economics working paper series 1101, School of Economics and Political Science, University of St. Gallen

Yamada K, Sato M (2013) Another avenue for anatomy of income comparisons: evidence from hypothetical choice experiments. J Econ Behav Organ 89:35–57

Zizzo D (2010) Experimenter demand effects in economic experiments. Exp Econ 13:75–98

Chapter 15
Social Capital, Household Income, and Preferences for Income Redistribution

Eiji Yamamura

Abstract This chapter explores how social capital influences individual preferences for income redistribution. Social capital is measured by participation in community activities. After controlling for individual characteristics, I find that people are more likely to express preferences for income redistribution in areas with higher rates of community participation. This is more clearly so in high-income groups than in low-income groups. I infer that individuals' preferences for income redistribution are influenced by psychological externalities. Because the data is from surveys, I also consider the role of expressive behavior. I also consider the hypothesis that behavior is influenced by social distance.

Keywords Redistribution • Social capital • Inequality

JEL Classification D30, D63, H20, Z13

1 Introduction

A major activity of governments is to redistribute income. In principle, although income redistribution is more complex and subject to political calculations (Tullock 2005), in western democracies, redistribution increases the welfare of the poor, while decreasing that of the wealthy (Milanovic 2000). Income inequality also has several indirect effects—it can lead to a decrease in trust among people (Alesina and La Ferrara 2002) and impede levels of community involvement (Alesina and La Ferrara 2000; La Ferrara 2002). Social capital, which is defined as trust or participation within a community, is considered to play a critical role in increasing

The original article first appeared in the European Journal of Political Economy 28:498–511, 2012. A newly written addendum has been added to this book chapter.

E. Yamamura (✉)
Department of Economics, Seinan Gakuin University, 6-2-92 Nishijin, Sawara-ku, Fukuoka 814-8511, Japan
e-mail: yamaei@seinan-gu.ac.jp

S. Ikeda et al. (eds.), *Behavioral Economics of Preferences, Choices, and Happiness*, DOI 10.1007/978-4-431-55402-8_15

social welfare (Putnam 1993, 2000). Hence, income redistribution is thought to increase social welfare, in part through social capital formation. However, the reverse causality that social capital influences political redistribution has not been investigated to date, with the exception of Bergh and Bjørnskov (2011).[1]

Since 2000, a growing number of studies have attempted to explore how and why people prefer income redistribution (e.g., Ravallion and Lokshin 2000; Corneo and Grüner 2002; Alesina and La Ferrara 2005; Rainer and Siedler 2008; Alesina and Giuliano 2009; Klor and Shayo 2010). Theoretical models suggest that expectations of upward and downward mobility play an important role in determining individual attitudes toward redistribution (Piketty 1995). The "prospect of upward mobility" hypothesis supposes that people who expect to move up the income scale will not favor a distributive policy even if they are currently poor (Bénabou and Ok 2001). This hypothesis is empirically supported by prior works (Alesina and La Ferrara 2005; Rainer and Siedler 2008). In contrast, it has also been found that people with current wealth tend to support redistribution if they expect their welfare to fall (Ravallion and Lokshin 2000).

The existing literature that explores the determinants of preference for redistribution does not sufficiently consider the effect of interaction among people. However, an individual's perception and behavior are thought to be influenced by the people around them and the neighboring community structure (e.g., Alesina and La Ferrara 2000, 2002; La Ferrara 2002; Jensen and Harris 2008; Shields et al. 2009). There are empirical works that support the hypothesis that it is "relative" income rather than "absolute income" that has an effect on the degree of happiness (e.g., Clark and Oswald 1996; Neumark and Postlewaite 1998; McBride 2001; Stutzer 2004; Luttmer 2005). Veblen (1899) argued that "conspicuous consumption" by rich people serves to impress other people. However, it seems plausible that poor people envy rich people, and therefore hope that the rich will become poor. Owing to such externalities, rich people are likely to be unhappy. In this case, rich people tend to support income redistribution, thereby reducing the externality, and achieving increased levels of happiness.[2] This possibility seems to be more likely when the rich and poor meet and interact more frequently. In other words, rich people are more likely to support income redistribution when people are more inclined to participate in social activities. However, little is known regarding the interaction mechanism for redistribution. Thus, it is worthwhile to examine how and the extent to which the preference for redistribution is affected by interactions among people. Furthermore, preference appears to be significantly affected by structure and traditional societal values (Alesina et al. 2004; Chang 2010). However, existing literature on redistribution preferences has focused largely on Western countries, with the exception of Ohtake and Tomioka (2004) and Chang (2010).

[1]Using cross-country data, Bergh and Bjørnskov (2011) found that trust aids the creation of welfare states, reducing inequality. Algan and Cahuc (2010) also addressed a similar question.

[2]Social capital possibly influences the fairness of people, leading to change the equilibrium level of redistribution (Galasso 2003).

Asian countries are characterized by the fact that their cultures and societies are different from those of Western countries, and as such it would be a valuable and necessary exercise to consider the preference for income redistribution in Asian countries. To this end, this chapter attempts to compare the effect of social capital on preferences for redistribution between poor and rich groups using Japanese General Social Surveys (JGSS), which include more than 10,000 observations. I found that people are more inclined to prefer income redistribution in areas where residents are more actively involved in community activities. This tendency was more clearly observed for people from high-income groups than with people in low-income groups. This chapter is in line with Alesina et al. (2004), which marks the crossroad for the determinants of happiness and preferences for redistribution.

The remainder of this chapter is organized as follows. In Sect. 2, the testable hypotheses are discussed. Section 3 provides an explanation regarding data and the empirical method used. Section 4 presents the estimation results and their interpretation. The final section offers some conclusions.

2 Hypotheses

The seminal work of Becker (1974) stated that social interaction is defined in terms of a consumption externality or as the utility function of a person to include the reactions of others in his/her actions. Along similar lines, there is an argument that relative income is related to happiness (e.g., Clark and Oswald 1996; Neumark and Postlewaite 1998; McBride 2001; Luttmer 2005). Luttmer concluded "that the negative effect of a neighbor's earnings on well-being is real and that it is most likely caused by a psychological externality" (Luttmer 2005, 990). It follows from this that an individual's preference depends, in part, on those that surround them (Luttmer 2001). Furthermore, frequency of contact with neighboring people reinforces this effect (Stutzer 2004). Luttmer provided the evidence that "increased neighbors' earnings have the strongest negative effect on happiness for those who socialize more in their neighborhood" (Luttmer 2005, 989–990).

If one's household income is higher than the average household income within a residential area, they are considered as relatively wealthy. The remainder of the people are regarded as relatively poor. Rich people are more likely to meet people with lower household income than to meet higher-income people within their residential area. In contrast, poorer people are more likely to meet people with higher household incomes than people with lower incomes within their residential area. As suggested in previous works, people tend to consider the extent to which their income is higher (or lower) than the income of others. That is, people are believed to care about their relative position. Because of interpersonal preferences, higher earnings of neighbors are related with lower levels of happiness (e.g., Frank 1985; Luttmer 2005; Layard 1980). "An envious or malicious person presumably would feel better off if some other persons become worse off in certain respects. He could "harm" himself (i.e., spend his own resources) in order to harm others"

(Becker 1996, 190). Further, envy possibly causes poorer people to engage in criminal behaviors such as theft or vandalism, not only to increase their "wealth" but also to reduce rich people's wealth (Skaperdas 1992; Mitsopoulos 2009). Thus, such criminal behavior caused by envy is considered to result in "illegal" income redistribution.

When there is greater societal interaction among residents (i.e., more frequent contact between rich and poor), there is also an increase in the degree of envy felt by poorer residents toward the richer ones, leading to an increase in negative effects (crimes committed against them by the poor) on the wealthy. Hence, I advance Hypothesis 1[3]:

Hypothesis 1: *Poor people are more inclined to prefer income redistribution when they live in areas where residents are more likely to interact with each other.*

This effect gives poorer people an incentive to support a "legal" redistribution policy. In contrast, richer people are more averse to redistribution simply because redistribution policies transfer their income to the poor. For example, a rich person's welfare depends not only on his/her own income and consumption levels but also on how the neighboring poorer people view his/her income and consumption. If a rich person enjoys the goodwill of those neighboring him/her or fears their envy, that rich person may transfer some of his/her own income to them up to the point where his/her marginal utility loss from the income transfer equals the marginal utility gain owing to an improvement in the evaluation from the neighboring people. As a consequence, a rich person's utility is maximized. To put it more concisely, when the effect of negative externality caused by the envy of poorer people outweighs the negative effect of a reduction of income caused by a redistribution policy, rich people will support a redistribution policy. Whether rich people prefer income redistribution depends on the frequency of interaction among residents because the negative externality is considered to be an increasing function of contact with neighboring poor people.[4] This leads me to propose Hypothesis 2:

Hypothesis 2: *Rich people are more inclined to prefer income redistribution when they live in an area where residents are more likely to interact with each other.*

[3]It should be noted that Hypothesis 1 will only hold if comparison effects actually exist. This is because comparison effects are difficult to separate from purely individual aspiration effects at the individual level (Stutzer 2004).

[4]There are possibly other mechanisms with which to arrive at Hypothesis 2. For instance, richer people support redistribution from purely moral or altruistic motives. In addition, it can be argued that richer people tend to display their charitable natures to the poor only in surveys, and in reality they are not.

3 Data and Methods

3.1 Data

This chapter used JGSS data, which are individual-level data.[5] JGSS surveys use a two-stage stratified sampling method and were conducted throughout Japan from 2000. This chapter used a dataset covering 2000, 2001, 2002, 2003, 2005, 2006, and 2008.[6] JGSS was designed as a Japanese counterpart to the General Social Survey (GSS) from the United States. JGSS asks standard questions concerning an individual's characteristics via face-to-face interviews. The data cover information related to preferences regarding income redistribution policies, marital and demographic (age and gender) status, annual household income,[7] years of schooling, age, prefecture of residence, and prefecture of residence at 15 years old. A Japanese prefecture is the equivalent to a state in the United States or a province in Canada. There are 47 prefectures in Japan, and the average values for the variables included in the JGSS can be calculated for each prefecture. The construction of the research sample is presented in Table 15.1. Data were collected from 22,796 adults, between 20 and 89 years old. Respondents did not answer all of the survey questions; therefore, data regarding some variables are not available, and the number of samples used in the regression estimations is reduced, ranging between 11,048 and 11,808. The use of JGSS data in this chapter has certain advantages. First, compared with international data (e.g., Corneo and Grüner 2002; Alesina and Angeletos 2005; Aristei and Perugini 2010), "within country analysis is much less likely to be subject to measurement error due to changes in institutional structures of redistributive policies" (Alesina and Giuliano 2009, 22). Second, previous works related to preferences for income redistribution used the United States GSS (e.g., Alesina and La Ferrara 2005; Alesina and Giuliano 2009; Derin-Güre and Uler 2010). JGSS was designed as the Japanese counterpart to the United States GSS, and therefore analysis using JGSS enables researchers to compare findings between Japan and United States. Recent studies have highlighted the significant effect that cultural and social backgrounds have on "happiness" (Alesina et al. 2004), as well as their influence on individual preferences for income redistribution (Luttmer 2011). Hence, the findings of this chapter will help researchers to examine how social,

---

[5]Data for this secondary analysis, "Japanese General Social Surveys (JGSS), Ichiro Tanioka," was provided by the Social Science Japan Data Archive, Information Center for Social Science Research on Japan, Institute of Social Science, The University of Tokyo.

[6]Surveys were not conducted in 2004 and 2007. Surveys were conducted in 2009 and 2010 but the data is not available.

[7]In the original dataset, annual earnings were grouped into 19 categories, and we assumed that everyone in each category earned the midpoint value. For the top category of "23 million yen and above," I assumed that everybody earned 23 million yen. Of the 11,808 observations used in the regression estimations, there were only 116 observations in this category. Therefore, the problem of top-coding should not be an issue here.

Table 15.1 Construction of research sample

Year	Observations from original sample	Observations used in analysis
2000	2,893	1,920
2001	2,790	1,786
2002	2,953	1,915
2003	3,663	1,287
2005	2,023	1,056
2006	4,254	1,248
2008	4,220	2,596
Total	27,790	11,808

Note: Observations were used in the analysis when they were available to be used for all variables in the estimations

historical, and cultural differences influence redistribution preferences. Finally, previous works have not fully investigated how and why Japanese people prefer redistribution, with the exception of Ohtake and Tomioka (2004). Ohtake and Tomioka (2004) used a smaller sample (approximately 1,000 observations) than that used in this chapter. The JGSS data used in this chapter contain approximately 11,000 observations, and as such these results are more accurate and reliable than previous works.

Following the discussion in Putnam (2000), the degree of participation in community activities is considered to be social capital in this research. The aim of this chapter is to examine the externality from neighboring people on preferences for income redistribution policies. The influence of neighboring people is thought to be greater when people are more likely to participate in community activities. That is, people are influenced by neighboring people to a greater extent when they live in areas with higher levels of community involvement. In 1996, the Japan Broadcasting Corporation conducted a survey on the consciousness and behaviors of prefecture residents, capturing community activity involvement rates in prefectures (Japan Broadcasting Corporation 1997). One of the survey questions asked "Do you actively participate in community activities?" Respondents could choose one of three responses: "yes", "unsure", or "no". I calculated the rates for those who answered "yes" within a prefecture, and used this value as a measure of social capital (however, it should be noted that care should be taken with regard to the definition of social capital). Furthermore, I assumed that the rate of participation in community activities was stable over time. As mentioned earlier, there are 47 prefectures, and I obtained a proxy for each prefecture.[8]

[8]Trust is regarded as a kind of social capital (Putnam 2000). Generalized trust is predicted to be related with preferences or the acceptance of policies that actively redistribute strangers (Uslaner 2008). JGSS data contains variables that will capture the degree of generalized trust. However, the proxy variable for generalized trust is considered as an endogenous variable because the causality between redistribution preferences and generalized trust is ambiguous. Therefore, estimation results are thought to suffer from endogeneity bias if the proxy for generalized trust is

Gini data coefficients for prefecture level household income were calculated using data from the "National Survey of Family Income and Expenditure", conducted by the Ministry of Internal Affairs and Communications (1999, 2004). These surveys are conducted every 5 years, e.g., 1999, 2004, and 2009. However, the data for 2009 are not available. The data used in this chapter cover the period 2000–2008. Therefore, as explained in the following section, I used Gini coefficients for 1999 as an initial value. In addition, I also used Gini coefficients for 2004 as independent variables. I matched the information regarding individual characteristics sourced from the JGSS data with prefecture characteristics such as community participation rates and Gini coefficients. Thus, I was able to investigate how income inequality within a community affects an individual's preference for income redistribution.

The variables used in the regression estimations are shown in Table 15.2, which provides definitions and mean comparisons of the high- and low-income groups. High-income earners are defined as those with a household income that is higher than the average household income within a prefecture. The remainder of the residents are defined as low-income earners. The average household income within a prefecture (*AVINCOM*) is calculated using JGSS data. The utility of people is thought to be affected not only by one's own income but also by the income level of neighboring people (e.g., Clark and Oswald 1996; Neumark and Postlewaite 1998; McBride 2001; Stutzer 2004). In other words, not only absolute income but also relative income is considered to be related to an individual's utility and, therefore, perceptions. This chapter controls for both individual-level household income and average household income within residential prefectures to capture the relative income effect. The regional characteristics used in this chapter are *SC* (rate of those who participate in community events), *GINI*99 and *GINI*04 (Gini coefficients for 1999 and 2004, respectively), and *AVINCOM* (average household income within a prefecture).

Turning to individual characteristics, OEQUAL and *EQUAL* are proxies for preferences for income redistribution. The question regarding income redistribution asked: What is your opinion of the following statement? "It is the responsibility of the government to reduce the differences in income between families with high incomes and those with low incomes." There were five response options, ranging from "1 (strongly disagree)" to "5 (strongly agree)". OEQUAL is the values that the respondents chose. Figure 15.1 shows the distribution of views regarding political redistribution, and reveals that the number of respondents who chose "1" or "2" is smaller than those who chose "4" or "5". Thus, the shape of histogram is skewed towards the right. Respondents most frequently chose the median number "3". However, there is a problem with this proxy for redistribution preferences. Of the five possible responses, "3 (depends)" requires the greatest care in interpretation. It is unclear whether "depends" can be considered as an intermediate category, or whether it includes a number of respondents who might have answered in

---

included as an independent variable. It is for this reason that the proxy for generalized trust is not included as an individual-level control variable.

Table 15.2 Mean values for high-income household group and low-income household group

	Definitions	High-income	Low-income	t-statistics
Regional characteristics				
SC	Rate of those who actively participate in community events	0.48	0.47	4.18***
AVINCOM	Average household income within a prefecture (million yen)	6.14	6.09	4.31***
GINI99	Gini coefficients for 1999	0.295	0.295	1.26
GINI04	Gini coefficients for 2004	0.302	0.303	3.02***
Individual characteristics				
OEQUAL	Degree of agreement with the argument that the government should reduce income inequality: 1 (strongly disagree) – 5 (strongly agree)	3.62	3.82	14.1***
EQUAL	Response to the question regarding income redistribution, those whose response was 4 (agree) or 5 (strongly agree) take 1, otherwise 0.	0.52	0.60	11.6***
INCOME	Individual household income (million yens)	9.79	3.43	140***
AGE	Ages	50.0	55.3	22.4***
MARRY	It takes 1 if respondents are currently married, otherwise 0.	0.81	0.75	10.1***
SCHOOL	Years of schooling	12.4	11.6	22.8***
UNEMP	It takes 1 if respondents are currently unemployed, otherwise 0.	0.01	0.02	2.58***
MALE	It takes 1 if respondents are male, otherwise 0.	0.44	0.47	4.38***
PROG_1	Concerning political views, it takes 1 if respondents choose 1, otherwise 0. 1 (conservative) – 5 (progressive)	0.07	0.07	1.25
PROG_2	Concerning political views, it takes 1 if respondents choose 2, otherwise 0. 1 (conservative) – 5 (progressive)	0.20	0.20	0.25
PROG_3	Concerning political views, it takes 1 if respondents choose 3, otherwise 0 1 (conservative) – 5 (progressive)	0.52	0.51	1.49
PROG_4	Concerning political views, it takes 1 if respondents choose 4, otherwise 0. 1 (conservative) – 5 (progressive)	0.16	0.16	1.02

(continued)

Table 15.2 (continued)

	Definitions	High-income	Low-income	t-statistics
PROG_5	Concerning political views, it takes 1 if respondents choose 5, otherwise 0. 1 (conservative) – 5 (progressive)	0.03	0.04	3.59***
BLIFE_1	Concerning "opportunity for better life", it takes 1 if respondents choose 1, otherwise 0. 1 (not sufficient at all) – 5 (sufficient)	0.08	0.11	8.03***
BLIFE_2	Concerning "opportunity for better life", it takes 1 if respondents choose 2, otherwise 0. 1 (not sufficient at all) – 5 (sufficient)	0.37	0.39	2.58***
BLIFE_3	Concerning "opportunity for better life", it takes 1 if respondents choose 3, otherwise 0. 1 (not sufficient at all) – 5 (sufficient)	0.37	0.34	4.24***
BLIFE_4	Concerning "opportunity for better life", it takes 1 if respondents choose 4, otherwise 0. 1 (not sufficient at all) – 5 (sufficient)	0.13	0.11	4.13***
BLIFE_5	Concerning "opportunity for better life", it takes 1 if respondents choose 5, otherwise 0. 1 (not sufficient at all) – 5 (sufficient)	0.24	0.21	1.39

Note: All observations used. Absolute values of t-statistics are the results of a mean difference test between high- and low-income household groups. *, **, and *** indicate significance at the 10 %, 5 %, and 1 % levels, respectively

other categories if other possible responses were included in the questionnaire. To alleviate any bias arising from this, in addition to OEQUAL, I also used an alternative dummy variable "*EQUAL*" as a proxy for preferences for redistribution. *EQUAL* takes the value of 1 if the response is "4 (agree)" or "5 (strongly agree)", and is otherwise 0. As explained later in the chapter, an ordered probit model is used for the estimations when OEQUAL is the dependent variable. In the alternative specification, a probit model is used when *EQUAL* is the dependent variable. It can be seen from Table 15.2 that OEQUAL and *EQUAL* are larger for the low-income group than for the high-income group and are statistically significant at the 1 % level, which is consistent with the inference that poorer people are more likely to prefer income redistribution to increase their welfare.

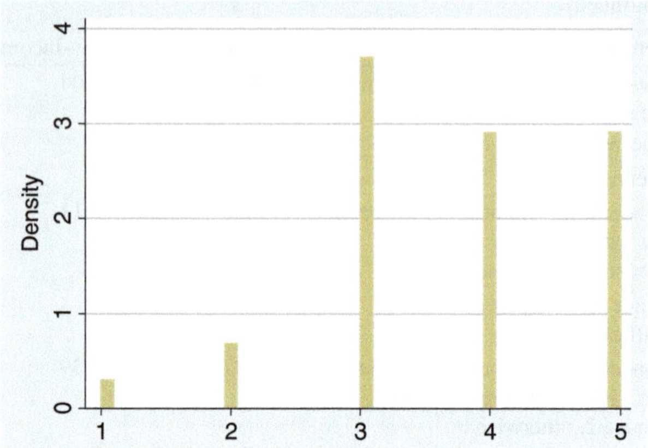

Fig. 15.1 Distribution of views regarding income redistribution. Note: The question asked of respondents was: What is your opinion of the following statement? "It is the responsibility of the government to reduce the differences in income between families with high incomes and those with low incomes." There were five response options: "1 (strongly disagree)" to "5 (strongly agree)". The number indicated in the figure is equivalent to the number of responses

Years of schooling, *SCHOOL*, is significantly greater for the high-income group than the low-income group, suggesting that human capital contributes to an increase in income levels.

Political ideology plausibly influences preferences for redistribution and so should be controlled for when preferences for income redistribution are estimated (Bernasconi 2006; Alesina and Giuliano 2009). I constructed a proxy for capturing this effect based on responses to the question: "Where would you place your political views on a five-point scale?" There are five response options: "1 (conservative)" to "5 (progressive)". The placement of political views is captured by dummies: $PROG\_5$ takes the value of 1 when the response is "5", otherwise 0. $PROG\_1$, $PROG\_2$, $PROG\_3$, and $PROG\_4$ are defined in a similar manner. It is of interest that political views did not differ between the high- and low-income groups, with the exception of $PROG\_5$. This tells us that political views are unrelated to individual income levels in Japan.

An expectation of future income is a key determinant in preferences for income redistribution (e.g., Alesina and La Ferrara 2005; Rainer and Siedler 2008). A JGSS question asks "In your opinion, how much opportunity would you say there is in Japanese society to improve the standard of living for you and/or your family?" There are five response options: "1 (not sufficient at all)" to "5 (sufficient)". Dummies capture the degree of improvements in standards of living: $BLIFE\_5$ takes the value of 1 when the response is "5", otherwise 0. $BLIFE\_1$, $BLIFE\_2$, $BLIFE\_3$, and $BLIFE\_4$ are defined in a similar manner. As shown in Table 15.2, there are significantly larger values for $BLIFE\_1$ and $BLIFE\_2$ in the low-income group than for the high-income group. These results indicate that people in the low-income group are less likely to believe that there is an opportunity for improvements in standards of living than high-income people. The significantly larger value of *BLIFE_4* for the high-income group shows that they are more likely to believe that there is sufficient opportunity for improvement compared with the low-income group. This appears to imply that income mobility is less likely to occur in Japan. However, interestingly, there is no significant difference in the values for *BLIFE_5* between the high- and low-income group, which suggests that both poor and rich people have a similar expectation regarding upward mobility. As a whole, Japanese people appear to hold a mixed perception regarding income mobility.

3.2 Social Capital and Its Definition

According to Putnam (2000), social capital is defined as the features of a social organization such as networks and norms, and that social trust facilitates coordination and cooperation. Hence, social capital can be interpreted in various ways, thereby causing ambiguity and criticism regarding its measurement and definition (e.g., Paldam 2000; Sobel 2002; Durlauf 2002; Bjørnskov 2006). The effects of social capital are considered to differ according to its definition and choice of proxy. Therefore, for an in-depth study, it is important to focus on just one aspect of social capital. In recent works, researchers have tended to indicate exactly what type of social capital was used as a proxy when analyzing the effect of social capital. As stated earlier, this study uses community involvement as social capital to examine its externality on preferences for redistribution. Frequency of participation in community events can be theoretically interpreted as an investment in social capital (Glaeser et al. 2002). With regard to Japan, prior works have reported that community involvement increases the benefit for community members by decreasing crime rates (Yamamura 2009) and the number of deaths in natural disasters (Yamamura 2010). These studies show that involvement in one's community has an important role in Japanese society. In contrast, frequent interaction among community members is also thought to increase negative externalities such as envy toward richer members. Japan has a different cultural and historical background from Western countries. Thus, an examination into the effect of social capital in Japan is considered useful to compare the role of social capital in Eastern countries with that in Western countries.

3.3 Econometric Framework and Estimation Strategy

In Figs. 15.2a and 15.3a, the vertical axis shows the average *OEQUAL* within a prefecture. In Figs. 15.2b and 15.3b, the vertical axis shows *EQUAL* (rate of those who prefer redistribution within a prefecture). A cursory examination of Fig. 15.2a, b reveals a positive association between social capital and a preference for redistribution, which is congruent with the hypotheses raised previously. However, this relationship is observed when individual characteristics are not controlled

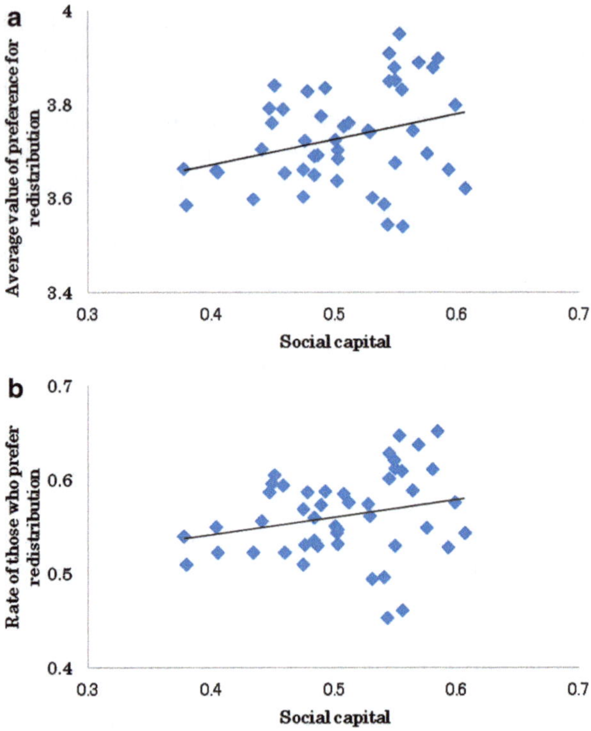

Fig. 15.2 (**a**) Relationship between social capital and preference for income distribution. (**b**) Relationship between social capital and preference for income distribution

for. A more precise examination calls for a regression analysis using individual-level data matched with characteristics from residential areas.

Turning now to the relationship between income inequality and preferences for redistribution, Fig. 15.3a, b show that the Gini coefficients for 1999 are not associated with a preference for income redistribution. Derin-Güre and Uler (2010) found that income inequality had a differing effect on the private charitable contributions of high-income earners and those of low-income earners. Preference for redistribution within a prefecture is calculated using observations from both high- and low-income groups. Therefore, the effect of income inequality is thought to be neutralized, and as such it is worth comparing the effects of income inequality on preferences for redistribution between high- and low-income groups using regression estimations.

For the purpose of examining the hypotheses proposed previously, the estimated function of the baseline model takes the following form:

$$\begin{aligned} &OEQUAL_{im} \text{ (or } EQUAL_{im}\text{)} \\ &\quad = \alpha_0 + \alpha_1 SC_m + \alpha_2 AVINCOM_m + \alpha_3 GINI99_m \\ &\qquad + \alpha_4 INCOM_{im} + \alpha_5 AGE_{im} + \alpha_6 MARRRY_{im} \\ &\qquad + \alpha_7 SCHOOL_{im} + \alpha_8 UNEMP_{im} + \alpha_9 MALE_m \\ &\qquad + \alpha_{10} PROG2_{im} + \alpha_{11} PROG3_{im} + \alpha_{12} PROG4_{im} + \alpha_{13} PROG5_{im} + u_{im} \end{aligned}$$

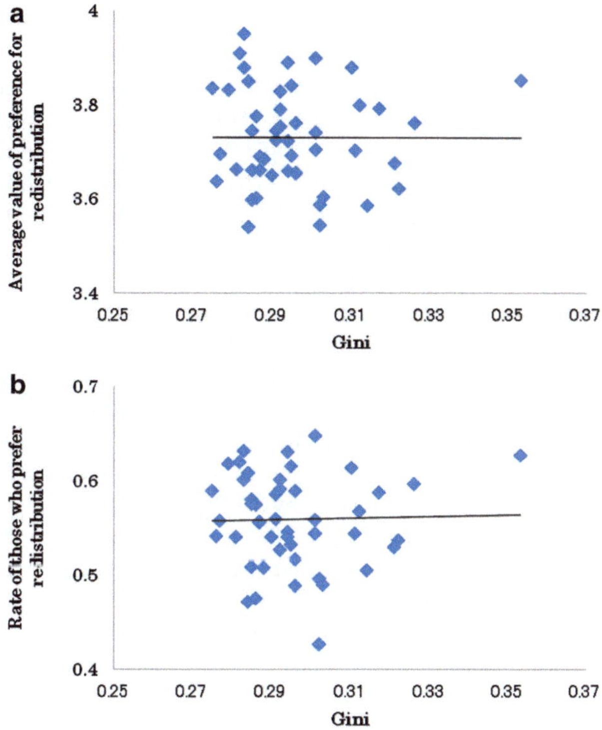

Fig. 15.3 (**a**) Relationship between Gini coefficients for 1999 and preference for income distribution. (**b**) Relationship between Gini coefficients for 1999 and preference for income distribution

where $OEQUAL_{im}$ (or $EQUAL_{im}$) represents the dependent variable in individual *i*, and prefecture *m*. Regression parameters are represented by α. As explained earlier, values for OEQUAL range from 1 to 5 and so the ordered probit model is used to conduct the estimations. In the alternative specification, *EQUAL* is the dummy variable and so takes either 1 or 0. Hence, the probit model is used when *EQUAL* is the dependent variable. The error term *is* represented by u_{im}. It is reasonable to assume that the observations may be spatially correlated within a prefecture, as the preference of one agent may well relate to the preference of another in the same prefecture. To consider such spatial correlation in line with this assumption, I used the Stata cluster command and calculated z-statistics using robust standard errors. The advantage of this approach is that the magnitude of spatial correlation can be unique to each prefecture.

In previous works, individual characteristics have been used to measure levels of socialization in a neighborhood (Stutzer 2004; Luttmer 2005). It seems plausible that people who feel happier are more likely to have contact with their neighbors. If so, those who are satisfied and do not prefer redistribution are less likely to have contact with neighbors. Therefore, the causality between socialization and preference for redistribution is ambiguous. To alleviate this bias, this chapter examined the effect of social capital formed in residential areas rather than an individual's socialization. Hence, *SC* is incorporated as an independent variable and is anticipated to take the positive sign. *AVINCOM* and *GINI99* are included to control for relative income and income inequality within a prefecture. As suggested by Luttmer (2005), increases in average income within a locality lead to reductions in the residents' welfare. People are thought to support redistribution to improve their welfare. In this chapter, *AVINCOM* is expected to take the positive sign. However, an increase in *AVINCOM* appears to lead people to expect that they can earn more. If so, the sign for *AVINCOM* becomes negative. If people wish to address inequality, the sign for *GINI*99 should be positive. Furthermore, income inequality increases the psychological externality of poor against rich, leading rich people to support income redistribution. Therefore, *GINI*99 is more likely to take the positive sign for rich people than for poor people. In the alternative specification, *GINI*04 is also included in addition to *GINI*99.

Following existing literature (e.g., Ravallion and Lokshin 2000; Corneo and Grüner 2002; Ohtake and Tomioka 2004; Alesina and La Ferrara 2005; Rainer and Siedler 2008; Alesina and Giuliano 2009), *INCOME*, *AGE*, *MARRY*, *SCHOOL*, and *MALE* are included as independent variables to control for individual characteristics. Political views are captured by $PROG\_2 - PROG\_5$, with $PROG\_1$ (conservative view) as the reference group. Progressive views generally support left-wing policies such as political income redistribution. Hence, the coefficients of $PROG\_2 - PROG\_5$, are predicted to take the positive sign, with the absolute value of the coefficient $PROG\_5$ to be largest among them.

4 Estimation Results

The estimation results of the ordered probit model are presented in Tables 15.3a, 15.4, and 15.5. The probit model results that correspond to Table 15.3a are shown in Table 15.3b. The results of the baseline model are reported in Table 15.3. Table 15.4 shows the results for when both *GINI*99 are *GINI*04 are included. As presented in the theoretical model (Piketty 1995; Bénabou and Ok 2001), expectations regarding upward and downward mobility determine an individual's attitude or preference for redistribution. Prior empirical works estimating preference for redistribution are in line with the theoretical model and stress the role of expectation regarding future income or social position (e.g., Alesina and La Ferrara 2005; Rainer and Siedler 2008).

Aside from the inclusion of the baseline model to capture this effect, I also incorporated $BLIFE\_2$, $BLIFE\_3$, $BLIFE\_4$, and $BLIFE\_5$ as independent variables in an alternative model. These results are exhibited in Table 15.5.

In each table, the estimation results, based on a sample of rich and poor respondents, are shown in columns (1) and (4). The results for the rich respondents are presented in columns (2) and (5), while the results for the poor respondents are presented in columns (3) and (6). As argued by Luttmer (2005), there is "the possibility that cross-section results are driven by selection of people who are happier by nature into areas that are relatively poor ... One might worry that movers

Table 15.3 Baseline model

a Dependent variable is OEQUAL (ordered probit model). Values are coefficients

	All			People live in the same prefecture they lived in at 15 years of age		
	(1) All	(2) High-income	(3) Low-income	(4) All	(5) High-income	(6) Low-income
Regional characteristics						
SC	0.50*** (2.78)	0.69*** (2.77)	0.39 (1.40)	0.55** (2.31)	0.62* (1.67)	0.58* (1.90)
AVINCOM	−0.02* (−1.80)	−0.01 (−0.61)	−0.04** (−2.13)	−0.02* (−1.86)	−0.001 (−0.06)	−0.05*** (−2.81)
GINI99	−0.22 (−0.30)	2.41*** (3.30)	−2.16* (−1.70)	0.13 (0.17)	3.28** (2.53)	−2.16 (−1.58)
Individual characteristics						
INCOME	−0.03*** (−9.99)	−0.03*** (−5.83)	−0.01 (−0.91)	−0.03*** (−8.24)	−0.03*** (−5.22)	−0.01 (−0.81)
AGE	0.004*** (6.81)	0.006*** (4.79)	0.003*** (4.45)	0.003*** (4.04)	0.006*** (3.76)	0.002** (2.49)
MARRY	0.04* (1.91)	0.01 (0.32)	0.002 (0.93)	0.03 (1.22)	−0.001 (−0.03)	0.01 (0.53)
SCHOOL	−0.03*** (−6.46)	−0.03*** (−5.50)	−0.02*** (−4.21)	−0.03*** (−5.11)	−0.04*** (−5.00)	−0.02*** (−2.82)
UNEMP	0.16* (1.74)	0.35** (2.25)	0.09 (0.81)	0.08 (0.74)	0.26 (1.38)	0.02 (0.22)
MALE	0.07*** (3.14)	0.04 (1.44)	0.08*** (2.70)	0.08*** (3.82)	0.05 (1.33)	0.11*** (3.28)
PROG_1	<Reference group>			<Reference group>		
PROG_2	−0.005 (−0.12)	−0.02 (−0.43)	0.007 (0.11)	0.03 (0.60)	0.01 (1.33)	0.03 (0.45)
PROG_3	0.07 (1.56)	0.04 (0.59)	0.09 (1.33)	0.09 (1.57)	0.05 (0.24)	0.11 (1.41)
PROG_4	0.15*** (3.51)	0.09 (1.32)	0.21*** (2.99)	0.17*** (3.55)	0.13 (0.67)	0.21*** (2.88)
PROG_5	0.25*** (3.27)	0.21* (1.71)	0.27** (2.44)	0.27*** (2.80)	0.28* (1.99)	0.25** (2.05)
Wald Statistics	1,065	630	348	775	412	240
Observations	11,808	5,152	6,656	8,479	3,680	4,799

(continued)

Table 15.3 (continued)

b Dependent variable is EQUAL (probit model). Numbers indicate marginal effect

	All			People live in the same prefecture they lived in at 15 years of age		
	(1) All	(2) High-income	(3) Low-income	(4) All	(5) High-income	(6) Low-income
Regional characteristics						
SC	0.19** (2.09)	0.21* (1.74)	0.18 (1.52)	0.22* (1.86)	0.28* (1.69)	0.20 (1.46)
AVINCOM	−0.006 (−1.14)	−0.006 (−0.97)	−0.01 (−1.50)	−0.006 (−1.06)	−0.003 (−0.36)	−0.01* (−1.86)
GINI99	−0.009 (−0.03)	0.93*** (2.91)	−0.70 (−1.36)	0.04 (0.13)	1.30** (2.34)	−0.84 (−1.63)
Individual characteristics						
INCOME	−0.01*** (−7.73)	−0.01*** (−4.40)	−0.0007 (−0.18)	−0.01*** (−6.27)	−0.01*** (−3.49)	−0.001 (−0.36)
AGE	0.001*** (6.52)	0.002*** (4.37)	0.001*** (4.89)	0.001*** (3.64)	0.002*** (3.46)	0.001*** (2.93)
MARRY	0.01 (1.25)	−0.005 (−0.22)	−0.008** (−2.58)	0.01 (0.85)	−0.01 (−0.56)	0.01 (0.61)
SCHOOL	−0.01*** (−3.85)	−0.01*** (−3.70)	0.04 (1.07)	−0.01*** (−3.12)	−0.01*** (−3.27)	−0.006* (−1.71)
UNEMP	0.06* (1.80)	0.11 (1.46)	0.04 (1.07)	0.04 (1.06)	0.08 (0.96)	0.03 (0.72)
MALE	0.05*** (5.30)	0.05*** (3.62)	0.05*** (3.67)	0.05*** (4.85)	0.05*** (2.82)	0.05*** (3.39)
PROG_1	<Reference group>			<Reference group>		
PROG_2	0.02 (1.37)	0.01 (0.54)	0.03 (1.18)	0.04* (2.03)	0.04 (1.17)	0.04 (1.55)
PROG_3	0.02 (1.57)	0.23 (0.81)	0.03 (1.25)	0.03 (1.28)	0.03 (0.99)	0.02 (0.90)
PROG_4	0.09*** (5.38)	0.06** (2.32)	0.12*** (4.48)	0.10*** (5.34)	0.10*** (2.72)	0.11*** (3.96)
PROG_5	0.10*** (3.74)	0.12*** (2.69)	0.08** (2.52)	0.10*** (2.64)	0.15*** (2.69)	0.06 (1.54)
Wald statistics	585	417	292	545	408	180
Observations	11,808	5,152	6,656	8,479	3,680	4,799

Note: Numbers in parentheses are z-statistics calculated using robust standard errors clustered in the prefecture. *, **, and *** indicate significance at the 10 %, 5 %, and 1 % levels, respectively. In all estimations, constant and year dummies are included as independent variables but are not reported because of space limitations

Table 15.4 Dependent variable is OEQUAL (ordered probit model including GINI04)

	All			People live in the same prefecture they lived in at 15 years of age		
	(1) All	(2) High-income	(3) Low-income	(4) All	(5) High-income	(6) Low-income
Regional characteristics						
SC	0.50*** (2.75)	0.69*** (2.95)	0.38 (1.34)	0.53** (2.35)	0.66* (1.81)	0.53* (1.70)
AVINCOM	−0.02* (−1.80)	−0.01 (−0.60)	−0.04** (−2.13)	−0.02* (−1.84)	−0.001 (−0.06)	−0.05*** (−2.72)
GINI99	−0.16 (−0.15)	2.41** (2.31)	−2.09 (−1.20)	0.42 (0.39)	2.73* (1.80)	−1.36 (−0.75)
GINI04	−0.13 (−0.12)	−0.0002 (−0.00)	−0.14 (−0.09)	−0.62 (−0.44)	1.08 (0.54)	−1.57 (−0.90)
Wald statistics	1,067	632	392	803	445	242
Observations	11,808	5,152	6,656	8,479	3,680	4,799

Note: Values are coefficients. Numbers in parentheses are z-statistics calculated using robust standard errors clustered in the prefecture. *, **, and *** indicate significance at the 10 %, 5 %, and 1 % levels, respectively. In all estimations, constant, year dummies and other independent variables used in Table 3(a) are included as independent variables but are not reported because of space limitations

may have had something unobserved happen to them" (Luttmer 2005, 977). This unobserved factor is a possible reason for estimation bias. The JGSS provided data regarding not only current residential prefectures but also the residential prefectures of the respondents at 15 years of age. If the current residential prefecture is not the same prefecture at 15 years old, respondents are defined as "movers". For the purpose of alleviating this bias, following Luttmer (2005), I also conducted the estimations by excluding all respondents who had moved to a different prefecture. These results are exhibited in columns (4)–(6) of Tables 15.3a,b 15.4, and 15.5.

In Table 15.3a, the signs for *SC* take the expected positive signs and are statistically significant, with the exception of column (3). *AVINCOM* takes the negative sign and is statistically significant in columns (1), (3), (4), and (6). This suggests that an increase in the average income leads low-income earners to be less inclined to support a redistribution policy. Hence, concerning redistribution policies, average income is not related to poorer people's negative feelings (e.g., envy) but to positive feelings such as expectations of higher earnings. Interestingly, *GINI*99 takes a significantly positive sign only for the high-income group. It follows then that income inequality represents a psychological externality for rich people, and hence they support income redistribution. As for individual characteristics, the sign for INCOME is negative in all estimations, and is not statistically significant for the low-income group. This indicates that a reduction in income via a policy of income redistribution leads rich people to oppose such a policy. Significant negative values for *SCHOOL* are observed in all estimations. I interpret this result as suggesting that people with higher education are more likely to expect higher

Table 15.5 Dependent variable is OEQUAL (ordered probit model including "expected better life" dummies and GINI04)

	All			People live in the same they lived in at 15 years of age		
	(1) All	(2) High-income	(3) Low-income	(4) All	(5) High-income	(6) Low-income
Regional characteristics						
SC	0.40** (2.29)	0.52** (2.01)	0.38 (1.36)	0.40* (1.80)	0.44 (1.14)	0.49 (1.54)
AVINCOM	−0.02 (−1.54)	−0.007 (−0.41)	−0.04* (−1.87)	−0.02* (−1.79)	0.0003 (0.01)	−0.05*** (−2.67)
GINI99	0.07 (0.07)	2.88** (2.54)	−2.09 (−1.25)	0.79 (0.68)	3.45** (2.16)	−1.32 (−0.72)
GINI04	−0.36 (−0.30)	−0.57 (−0.33)	−0.04 (−0.03)	−0.99 (−0.66)	0.28 (0.13)	−1.57 (−0.85)
Individual characteristics						
BLIFE_1	<Reference group>			<Reference group>		
BLIFE_2	−0.06 (−1.53)	−0.04 (−0.59)	−0.06 (−1.30)	−0.05 (−1.48)	−0.02 (−0.33)	−0.07 (−1.64)
BLIFE_3	−0.16*** (−4.15)	−0.10 (−1.26)	−0.19*** (−4.29)	−0.15*** (−3.64)	−0.09 (−1.04)	−0.18*** (−4.02)
BLIFE_4	−0.16*** (−3.91)	−0.13 (−1.54)	−0.17*** (−3.17)	−0.14*** (−3.07)	−0.12 (−1.31)	−0.15** (−2.40)
BLIFE_5	−0.41*** (−6.48)	−0.31** (−2.22)	−0.51*** (−5.22)	−0.47*** (−4.65)	−0.38** (−2.20)	−0.54*** (−4.28)
Wald statistics	1,218	593	526	998	431	228
Observations	11,048	4,814	6,234	7,932	3,440	4,492

Note: Values are coefficients. Numbers in parentheses are z-statistics calculated using robust standard errors clustered in the prefecture. *, **, and *** indicate significance at the 10 %, 5 %, and 1 % levels, respectively. In all estimations, constant, year dummies, and other independent variables used in Table 3(a) are included as independent variables but are not reported because of space limitations

future earnings. UNEMP takes the positive signs in all estimations, but is only statistically significant in columns (1) and (2), implying that the effect of job status on preference for redistribution is ambiguous. Consistent with expectations, *PROG*_5 takes a significant positive sign in all estimations. This implies that political views influence preferences for redistribution.

Results reported in Table 15.3b are similar to those in Table 15.3a. The coefficients exhibited in Table 15.3a cannot be interpreted as marginal effects and it is difficult to interpret them in the ordered probit model. Therefore, I will focus largely on the reported marginal effects of the probit model. In Table 15.3b, the positive sign for *SC* continues to be statistically significant in columns (1), (2), (4) and (5), but not in columns (3) and (6). Therefore, *SC* influences rich people but not poor people. The focus is further narrowed to the results that are obtained after "movers" were excluded from the sample. Its marginal effects are 0.28 in column

(5), meaning that a 1 % increase in the rate of participation in community events leads to a 0.28 % increase in support for redistribution policies. The negative sign of *AVINCOM* is only statistically significant in column (6). *GINI99* takes a significant positive sign only in columns (2) and (5), implying that income inequality results in richer people supporting redistribution policies but not poorer people. The marginal effect shown in column (5) can be interpreted as suggesting that a 0.1-point increase in Gini coefficients leads to a 0.13-point increase in support from rich people for income redistribution.

As demonstrated in Fig. 15.2b, there are outliers with a rate of redistribution preferences that are clearly below 0.50.[9] These outliers possibly drive the results of Tables 15.2 and 15.3. Thus, it is necessary to show that the main results of Tables 15.3 are indeed robust. For this purpose, a prefecture-level jackknife exercise was performed with the outliers excluded from the sample. Tables 15.6 and 15.7 appear in the Appendix. The results corresponding to Table 15.3a and b are presented in Tables 15.6 and 15.7, respectively. Results of Tables 15.6 and 15.7 are nearly identical to those in Table 15.3. It follows then that the results of Table 15.3 are not driven by the outliers.

Turning now to Table 15.4, results for *SC*, *AVINCOM*, and *GINI99* are similar to those presented in Table 15.3a. The sign for *GINI04* is negative with the exception of column (5). Furthermore, *GINI04* is not statistically significant in all estimations. This indicates that *GINI99* has a significant effect on preferences of rich people, whereas *GINI04* has no influence at all. This shows that the effects of income inequality are not stable and so care should be taken when interpreting these results. Concerning Table 15.5, results for *SC*, *AVINCOM*, *GINI99*, and *GINI04* in columns (1)–(3) are similar to those in Table 15.4. However, the sign for *SC* is positive but not statistically significant in columns (5) and (6). This result is partly because of the reduction in observations used for the estimations. In line with the prediction, the signs for *BLIFE_2* – *BLIFE_5* are negative in all estimations. Furthermore, *BLIFE_3* – *BLIFE_5* are statistically significant at the 1 % level in columns (1), (3), (4), and (6). In contrast, only *BLIFE_5* is statistically significant in columns (2) and (5). Thus, expectations for a "better life" have a greater influence on preferences for income redistribution for poor people than rich people.

To sum the various estimated results presented thus far, I conclude, as a whole, that the estimation results examined in this section are consistent with Hypothesis 2, and support it reasonably well, but not Hypothesis 1. I interpret these results as suggesting the following: Hypothesis 1 will only hold when we assume that the higher earnings of others will reduce levels of happiness (e.g., Frank 1985; Luttmer 2005; Layard 1980). However, as indicated by previous empirical works (Snowdon 2012), income inequality is not negatively associated with happiness levels. This is not consistent with the assumption. Further, the fact that Hypothesis 1 was not supported by the estimations in this chapter implies that the assumption does not

[9]The rates of redistribution preferences for Gunma and Saga prefectures are 0.45 and 0.46, respectively.

apply here. The above findings imply that rich people are more likely to support a redistribution policy when they live in an area where residents have frequent contact with each other. This is in line with findings from the United States, where rich people are more likely to increase charitable contributions for inequality reduction than poor people (Derin-Güre and Uler 2010). These results imply that, for rich people, the effect of negative externalities caused by the envy of poor people is greater in areas supporting a tightly knit community. In contrast, poor people's attitudes regarding redistribution policies are unlikely to depend on the degree of residential contact within a community.

The results of this chapter can be interpreted in the context of expressive behavior (Hillman 2010). Applied to voting, the hypothesis is that individuals vote in order to participate in expressing their opinions regarding particular issues, and not because they expect to affect the outcomes of the election (e.g., Tullock 1971; Copeland and Laband 2002; Sobel and Wagner 2004). This chapter has used survey data. Survey responses can be considered as expressive because the cost of giving a response is low. There is expressive utility from signaling conformity with group-defined norms of niceness or generosity but there is no material loss from expressing a preference for income redistribution (Tullock 1971). In this chapter, expressing a preference for redistribution can be interpreted as increasing expressive utility. Actually implementing the policy would reduce material utility. Another interpretation of the results is therefore that social capital makes people more expressive and I have shown how income affects expressiveness. Baron (2010) proposes that socio-economic distance influences the degree of enforcement of altruistic moral preferences, which provides the motivation for redistribution. The greater the socio-economic distance between individuals, the weaker moral preferences are. Socio-economic distance is positively related to the degree of community participation. The findings of this chapter are also consistent with the social-distance hypothesis (Baron 2010).

5 Conclusions

Individuals feel worse off when others around them earn more, and so residents are concerned not only about their income but also the average local income. The influence of relative income is greater for those who socialize more in their neighborhood (Stutzer 2004; Luttmer 2005). Preference for income redistribution are inevitably influenced by relative income and also by social capital captured by frequency of contact with neighbors. However, little is known about the effect of social capital on preferences for income redistribution. Further, there is the possibility that people who feel happier are more likely to socialize with neighbors. Accordingly, the causality between socialization and happiness is ambiguous. To alleviate this bias, this chapter focused on the degree of social capital present in the neighborhoods of individuals, rather than by looking at socialization. In this chapter, social capital was measured by the rate of participation in community activities in

1996. Matching this data with micro data from JGSS for 2000–2008, I estimated the effect of social capital in residential areas on preferences for income redistribution.

The major findings are that after controlling for various individual characteristics, people are more likely to prefer income redistribution in areas where there are higher rates of community participation. This is in line with Luttmer (2005), implying that the consumption externality suggested by Becker (1974) depends on the degree of frequency of personal interaction within a community. The effect of social capital on preference for income redistribution was more clearly observed in the high-income group than the low-income group. From this, I derive the argument that for rich people, frequency of interaction increases the effect of the negative externality caused by the envy of poorer people. Further, the effect of the negative externality outweighs the negative effect of reducing the income of the wealthy via income redistribution policies. Because the data is from surveys, the findings of this chapter are also consistent with expressive behavior. The results also support the social distance hypothesis.

In rural Asian villages, it has been observed that an individual with a higher socioeconomic status will use his/her own influence and resources to provide protection and/or benefits to someone with a lower status (Hayami 2001). Such relationships are called patron–client relationships by anthropologists and sociologists (Scott 1972). Rural Asian villages are characterized by long-term and intensive personal interactions between village members. Even in modern Japanese society, when community members frequently attend community events and interact with each other, the relationships between members mirror the relationships in rural villages. If such relationships exist to a certain extent in modern Japanese society, then the wealthy are expected to play the role of patron and offer patronage to the poor (client). The finding that social capital leads the rich to prefer income redistribution possibly reflects the cultural and anthropological characteristics of parts of Asia.

However, the effect of the residential area characteristics appeared to vary according to individual characteristics. That is, even when individuals live in tightly-knit communities with significant social capital, their preferences are not necessarily influenced by neighboring people if they do not socialize in the neighborhood. Owing to a lack of data, however, this chapter cannot explore this issue further. Furthermore, Japan is generally characterized as a racially homogenous society. Aside from such homogeneity, Japan's historical and cultural backgrounds also distinguish it from Western countries. Effect of social capital varies according to institutional strength (Ahlerup et al. 2009). Hence, to test the generality of these findings, it is necessary to examine the hypotheses proposed in this chapter using other countries with different characteristics. In addition, the generalized trust appears to be related to income inequality (Uslaner 2008). Inevitably, generalized trust is thought to influence redistribution preferences. Thus, it would be worthwhile to investigate how generalized trust affects preferences by controlling for endogeneity bias. These remaining issues require attention in future studies.

Appendix

Table 15.6 Excluding outliers: dependent variable is OEQUAL (ordered probit model)

	All			People live in the same prefecture they lived in at 15 years of age		
	(1) All	(2) High-income	(3) Low-income	(4) All	(5) High-income	(6) Low-income
Regional characteristics						
SC	0.58*** (3.03)	0.82*** (3.16)	0.43 (1.33)	0.65** (2.57)	0.81* (1.96)	0.63* (1.77)
AVINCOM	−0.02 (−1.52)	−0.01 (−0.34)	−0.04* (−1.88)	−0.02 (−1.57)	0.0003 (0.15)	−0.05** (−2.52)
GINI99	−0.19 (−0.23)	2.49*** (3.14)	−2.15 (−1.44)	0.20 (0.23)	3.44** (2.18)	−2.08 (−1.38)
Individual characteristics						
INCOME	−0.03*** (−9.61)	−0.03*** (−5.57)	−0.01 (−0.74)	−0.03*** (−7.96)	−0.03*** (−5.07)	−0.01 (−0.74)
AGE	0.004*** (6.62)	0.006*** (4.71)	0.003*** (4.40)	0.003*** (3.82)	0.005*** (3.71)	0.002** (2.38)
MARRY	0.03 (1.58)	0.01 (0.29)	0.002 (0.60)	0.02 (0.91)	−0.001 (−0.00)	0.004 (0.13)
SCHOOL	−0.03*** (−6.33)	−0.03*** (−5.66)	−0.02*** (−4.00)	−0.03*** (−5.19)	−0.04*** (−5.31)	−0.02*** (−2.73)
UNEMP	0.16* (1.73)	0.35** (2.08)	0.10 (0.86)	0.09 (0.75)	0.25 (1.24)	0.04 (0.29)
MALE	0.07*** (3.02)	0.04 (1.46)	0.08** (2.50)	0.08*** (3.71)	0.05 (1.32)	0.11*** (3.12)
PROG_1	<Reference group>			<Reference group>		
PROG_2	−0.01 (−0.24)	−0.04 (−0.63)	0.005 (0.08)	0.02 (0.44)	−0.002 (−0.04)	0.03 (0.44)
PROG_3	0.06 (1.46)	0.02 (0.41)	0.09 (1.32)	0.08 (1.45)	0.03 (0.42)	0.12 (1.41)
PROG_4	0.15*** (3.32)	0.08 (1.14)	0.21*** (2.86)	0.17*** (3.36)	0.12 (1.33)	0.21*** (2.82)
PROG_5	0.25*** (3.22)	0.19 (1.53)	0.28** (2.50)	0.28*** (2.70)	0.25* (1.78)	0.27** (2.11)
Wald Statistics	1,013	753	370	818	446	251
Observations	11,581	5,050	6,531	8,284	3,591	4,693

Note: Values are coefficients. Numbers in parentheses are z-statistics calculated using standard errors obtained by prefecture-level jackknife method. *, **, and *** indicate significance at the 10 %, 5 %, and 1 % levels, respectively. In all estimations, constant and year dummies are included as independent variables but are not reported because of space limitations. The two prefectures where redistribution preferences were below 0.50 are considered as outliers and are excluded from the sample

Table 15.7 Excluding outliers: Dependent variable is EQUAL (probit model)

	All			People live in the same prefecture they lived in at 15 years of age		
	(1) All	(2) High-income	(3) Low-income	(4) All	(5) High-income	(6) Low-income
Regional characteristics						
SC	0.24** (2.56)	0.29** (2.29)	0.21 (1.55)	0.29** (2.28)	0.39** (2.14)	0.23 (1.50)
AVINCOM	−0.004 (−0.84)	−0.004 (−0.59)	−0.01 (−1.09)	−0.005 (−0.75)	0.008 (0.00)	−0.01* (−1.55)
GINI99	0.02 (0.06)	0.98*** (2.77)	−0.67 (−1.27)	0.09 (0.26)	1.37** (2.05)	−0.79 (−1.35)
Individual characteristics						
INCOME	−0.01*** (−7.23)	−0.01*** (−4.14)	−0.0006 (−0.06)	−0.01*** (−5.92)	−0.01*** (−3.39)	−0.001 (−0.28)
AGE	0.001*** (6.27)	0.002*** (4.10)	0.001*** (4.92)	0.001*** (3.35)	0.002*** (3.16)	0.001*** (2.81)
MARRY	0.01 (1.04)	−0.006 (−0.24)	0.005 (0.41)	0.01 (0.74)	−0.01 (−0.50)	0.007 (0.45)
SCHOOL	−0.01*** (−3.95)	−0.01*** (−4.05)	−0.008** (−2.53)	−0.01*** (−3.33)	−0.01*** (−3.73)	−0.006* (−1.69)
UNEMP	0.06* (1.83)	0.11 (1.34)	0.05 (1.16)	0.05 (1.10)	0.08 (0.85)	0.04 (0.83)
MALE	0.05*** (5.04)	0.05*** (3.57)	0.05*** (3.39)	0.05*** (4.61)	0.05*** (2.69)	0.05*** (3.18)
PROG_1	<Reference group>			<Reference group>		
PROG_2	0.02 (1.22)	0.01 (0.39)	0.03 (1.06)	0.04* (1.85)	0.03 (0.98)	0.04 (1.45)
PROG_3	0.02 (1.50)	0.02 (0.79)	0.03 (1.22)	0.03 (1.22)	0.03 (0.86)	0.02 (0.91)
PROG_4	0.09*** (5.14)	0.06** (2.17)	0.11*** (4.25)	0.10*** (5.09)	0.09** (2.55)	0.11*** (3.82)
PROG_5	0.10*** (3.75)	0.12*** (2.48)	0.09** (2.77)	0.10*** (2.64)	0.14** (2.46)	0.07* (1.79)
Wald statistics	594	452	308	539	393	198
Observations	11,581	5,050	6,531	8,284	3,591	4,693

Note: Values are coefficients. Numbers in parentheses are z-statistics calculated using standard errors obtained by prefecture-level jackknife method. *, **, and *** indicate significance at the 10 %, 5 %, and 1 % levels, respectively. In all estimations, constant and year dummies are included as independent variables but are not reported because of space limitations. The two prefectures where redistribution preferences were below 0.50 are considered as outliers and are excluded from the sample

Addendum: Recent developments[10]

It is widely acknowledged that the morals and virtues shared by members of society influence the effectiveness of economic policy (Aghion et al. 2010; Algan and Cahuc 2009). To identify the policy implications of preferences for redistribution, it is important to first systematically investigate subjective perceptions concerning policy. Algan et al. (2011) claimed that trust in society plays a critical role in ensuring an efficient welfare state. Furthermore, recent research has shown that the degree of support for economic policy depends on the level of trust in government.

Yamamura (2014a) used a similar analytical framework to that in Yamamura (2012) to explore the effect of trust in government on perceived tax burden and preference for redistribution. As is demonstrated in Fig. 15.4, there is a positive relationship between trust in members of parliament and support for redistribution policy in the high-income group. However, this relationship is not observed for the low-income group. In contrast, Fig. 15.5 exhibits a negative relationship between trust in members of parliament and perceived tax burden for the high-income

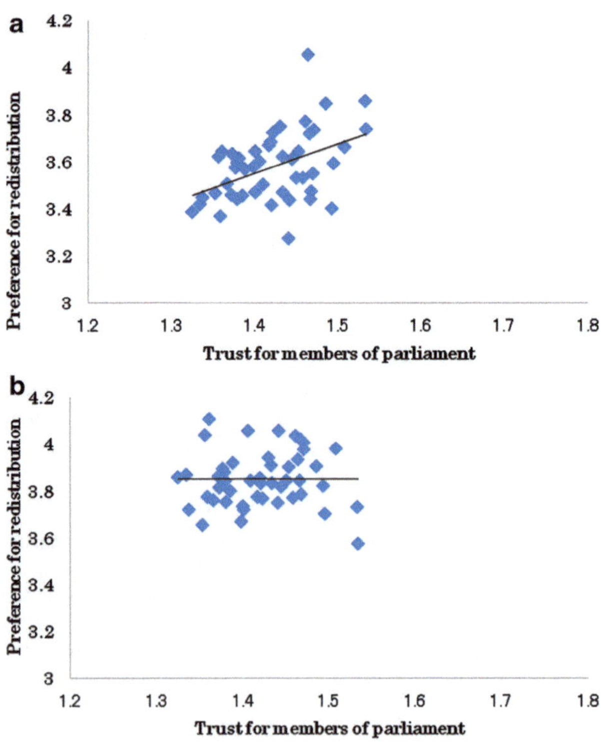

Fig. 15.4 Relationship between preference for income distribution and trust for diet members. (**a**) high-income group. (**b**) low-income group

[10]This addendum has been newly written for this book chapter.

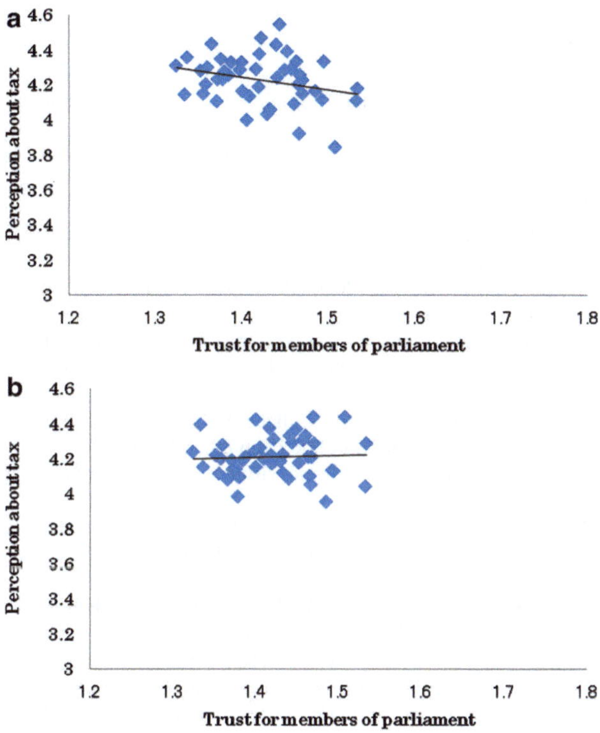

Fig. 15.5 Relationship between perceptions regarding tax and trust for diet members. (**a**) high-income group. (**b**) low-income group

group. Again, this relationship is not observed for the low-income group. Although not reported here, after controlling for various factors the results of a regression analysis are consistent with Figs. 15.4 and 15.5. Hence, perceptions about the cost of redistribution policies are considered to influence the support for redistribution policies. This implies that trust in government affects calculations regarding the cost and benefit of redistribution policies.

In addition to Japan, preferences for redistribution have been examined using data from Western countries and cross-country data. In Italy, differences in social capital and civic morals were found to produce different levels of regional economic efficiency (Putnam 1993). Sabatini et al. (2014) found that people are more likely to prefer redistribution in those areas where people are less likely to become free riders. In contrast, those who are more likely to become free riders are inclined to prefer income redistribution for their own benefit, at the expense of society as a whole. Based on individual-level data covering countries in Asia, Europe and other areas, Yamamura (2014b) examined how the conflict between high- and low-income groups affects the preference for redistribution and perceived inequality. They found that the conflict caused high-income people to prefer redistribution policies and perceive a high degree of inequality. However, such a tendency was not observed for low-income earners. All in all, the influence of surrounding conditions on subjective perceptions concerning redistribution is observed for high-income earners but not for low-income earners.

References

Aghion P, Algan Y, Chahuc P, Shleifer A (2010) Regulation and distrust. Q J Econ 125(3):1015–1049

Ahlerup P, Olsson O, Yanagizawa D (2009) Social capital vs institutions in the growth process. Eur J Polit Econ 25:1–14

Alesina A, Angeletos GM (2005) Fairness and redistribution. Am Econ Rev 95:960–980

Alesina A, Giuliano P (2009) Preferences for redistribution, NBER working paper 14825. National Bureau of Economic Research, Cambridge MA

Alesina A, La Ferrara E (2000) Participation in heterogeneous communities. Q J Econ 115:847–904

Alesina A, La Ferrara E (2002) Who trusts others? J Public Econ 85:207–234

Alesina A, La Ferrara E (2005) Preferences for redistribution in the land of opportunities. J Public Econ 89:897–931

Alesina A, De Tella R, MacCulloch R (2004) Inequality and happiness: are Europeans and Americans different? J Public Econ 88:2009–2042

Algan Y, Cahuc P (2009) Civic virtue and labor market institutions. Am Econ J Macroecon 1(1):111–145

Algan Y, Cahuc P (2010) Inherited trust and growth. Am Econ Rev 100:2060–2092

Algan Y, Cahuc P, Sangnier M (2011) Efficient and inefficient welfare states, IZA discussion paper 5445. IZA institute, Bonn

Aristei D, Perugini C (2010) Preferences for redistribution and inequality in well-being across Europe. J Policy Model 32:176–195

Baron DP (2010) Morally motivated self-regulation. Am Econ Rev 100:1299–2329

Becker G (1974) Theory of social interaction. J Polit Econ 82:1063–1093

Becker G (1996) Accounting for tastes. Harvard University Press, Cambridge, MA

Bénabou R, Ok EA (2001) Social mobility and the demand for redistribution: the PAUM hypothesis. Q J Econ 116:447–487

Bergh A, Bjørnskov C (2011) Trust, welfare states and income equality: what causes what? Unpublished paper, University of Aarhus

Bernasconi M (2006) Redistributive taxation in democracies: evidence on people's satisfaction. Eur J Polit Econ 22:809–837

Bjørnskov C (2006) The multiple facets of social capital. Eur J Polit Econ 22:22–40

Chang WC (2010) Religion and preferences for redistributive policies in an East Asian country. Poverty Public Policy 2:81–109

Clark A, Oswald A (1996) Satisfaction and comparison income. J Public Econ 61:359–381

Copeland C, Laband DN (2002) Expressiveness and voting. Public Choice 110:351–363

Corneo G, Grüner HP (2002) Individual preferences for political distribution. J Public Econ 83:83–107

Derin-Güre P, Uler N (2010) Charitable giving under inequality aversion. Econ Lett 107:208–210

Durlauf SN (2002) On the empirics of social capital. Econ J 122:F459–F479

Frank RH (1985) Choosing the right pond. Oxford University Press, Oxford

Galasso V (2003) Redistribution and fairness: a note. Eur J Polit Econ 19:885–892

Glaeser E, Laibson D, Sacerdote B (2002) An economic approach to social capital. Econ J 122:F437–F458

Hayami Y (2001) Development economics: from poverty to the wealth of nations, 3rd edn. Oxford University Press, New York

Hillman AL (2010) Expressive behavior in economics and politics. Eur J Polit Econ 26:403–418

Japan Broadcasting Corporation (1997) Data book: survey on consciousness of prefecture residents (Zenkoku Kenmin Ishiki Chosa, 1996). Japan Broadcasting Corporation Press, Tokyo

Jensen B, Harris MN (2008) Neighbourhood measures: quantifying the effects of neighbourhood externalities. Econ Rec 84:68–81

Klor EF, Shayo M (2010) Social identity and preferences over redistribution. J Public Econ 94:269–278

La Ferrara E (2002) Inequality and group participation: theory and evidence from rural Tanzania. J Public Econ 85:235–273
Layard R (1980) Human satisfactions and public policy. Econ J 90:737–750
Luttmer E (2001) Group loyalty and the taste for redistribution. J Polit Econ 109:500–528
Luttmer E (2005) Neighbors as negatives: relative earnings and well-being. Q J Econ 120:963–1002
Luttmer E (2011) Culture, context, and the taste for redistribution. Am Econ J Econ Policy 3:157–179
McBride M (2001) Relative-income effects on subjective well-being in the cross-section. J Econ Behav Organ 45:251–278
Milanovic B (2000) The median voter hypothesis, income inequality and income redistribution: an empirical test with the required data. Eur J Polit Econ 16:367–410
Mitsopoulos M (2009) Envy, institutions and growth. Bull Econ Res 61:201–222
Neumark D, Postlewaite A (1998) Relative income concerns and the rise in married women's employment. J Public Econ 70:157–183
Ohtake F, Tomioka J (2004) Who supports redistribution? Jpn Econ Rev 55:333–354
Paldam M (2000) Social capital: one or many? Definition and measurement. J Econ Surv 14:629–653
Piketty T (1995) Social mobility and redistributive politics. Q J Econ 110:551–584
Putnam R (1993) Making democracy work: civic traditions in modern Italy. Princeton University Press, Princeton
Putnam R (2000) Bowling alone: the collapse and revival of American community. A Touchstone Book, New York
Rainer H, Siedler T (2008) Subjective income and employment expectations and preferences for redistribution. Econ Lett 99:449–453
Ravallion M, Lokshin M (2000) Who wants to redistribute? The tunnel effect in 1990 Russia. J Public Econ 76:87–104
Sabatini F, Sarracino F, Yamamura E (2014) Social norms on rent seeking and preferences for redistribution, EconStor Preprints 98662. ZBW – German National Library of Economics, Berlin
Scott J (1972) The erosion of patron-client bonds and social change in Rural Southeast Asia. J Asian Stud 33:5–37
Shields MA, Wheatley PS, Wooden M (2009) Life satisfaction and economic and social characteristics of neighborhoods. J Popul Econ 22:421–443
Skaperdas S (1992) Cooperation, conflict and power in the absence of property rights. Am Econ Rev 82:720–739
Snowdon C (2012) Are more equal countries happier? In: Booth P (ed) ...and the pursuit of happiness. Institute of Economic Affairs, London, pp 98–127
Sobel J (2002) Can we trust social capital? J Econ Lit 40:139–154
Sobel RS, Wagner GA (2004) Expressive voting and government redistribution: testing Tullock's charity of the uncharitable. Public Choice 119:143–159
Statistics Bureau of the Ministry of Internal Affairs and Communications (1999, 2004) National Survey of Family Income and Expenditure (Zenkoku shohi zhittai chosa). Statistics Bureau of the Ministry of Internal Affairs and Communications, Tokyo
Stutzer A (2004) The role of income aspirations in individual happiness. J Econ Behav Organ 54:89–109
Tullock G (1971) The charity of the uncharitable. West Econ J 9:379–392
Tullock G (2005) The economics and politics of wealth redistribution. The selected works of Gordon Tullock. Edited by and with an introduction by Charles K. Rowley. Liberty Fund, Indianapolis
Uslaner E (2008) Corruption, inequality, and the rule of law: the bulging pocket makes the easy life. Cambridge University Press, Cambridge
Veblen T (1899) The theory of leisure class. Modern Library, New York
Yamamura E (2009) Impact of formal and informal deterrents on crime. J Socio-Econ 38:611–621

Yamamura E (2010) Effects of interactions among social capital, income and learning from experiences of natural disasters: a case study from Japan. Reg Stud 44:1019–1032

Yamamura E (2012) Social capital, household income, and preferences for income redistribution. Eur J Polit Econ 28(4):498–511

Yamamura E (2014a) Trust in government and its effect on preferences for income redistribution and perceived tax burden. Econ Gov 15(1):71–100

Yamamura E (2014b) Comparing the influence of conflict on the perceptions of rich and poor: testing the hypothesis of Acemoglu and Robinson. ISER Discussion Paper 0911, Institute of Social and Economic Research, Osaka University, Osaka

Part V
Happiness and Well-Being

Chapter 16
Koizumi Carried the Day: Did the Japanese Election Results Make People Happy and Unhappy?

Yoshiro Tsutsui, Miles Kimball, and Fumio Ohtake

Abstract This chapter investigates whether Japanese people were happy and unhappy with the general election conducted on September 11, 2005, in which the Prime Minister, Koizumi, won a landslide victory. We conducted a large survey just after the election to ask people how happy they were and which party they had supported. Although there are consistent tendencies that supporters of ruling parties were happier and supporters of opposition parties were unhappier, the effect was not significant. Considering the results of previous studies that showed that Americans demonstrated significant responses to the result of a presidential election, this study suggests that Japanese people are indifferent to politics.

Keywords Election • Happiness • Koizumi Cabinet • Survey • Japan

JEL Classification I31, D72, C42

The original article first appeared in European Journal of Political Economy 26: 12–24, 2010. A newly written addendum has been added to this book chapter.

Y. Tsutsui (✉)
Faculty of Economics, Konan University, 8-9-1 Okamoto, Higashinada-ku, Kobe 658-8501, Japan
e-mail: tsutsui@center.konan-u.ac.jp

M. Kimball
Department of Economics, University of Michigan, 312 Lorch Hall, 611 Tappan St., Ann Arbor, MI 48109-1220, USA
e-mail: mkimball@umich.edu

F. Ohtake
Institute of Social and Economic Research, Osaka University, 6-1 Mihogaoka, Ibaraki, Osaka 567-0047, Japan
e-mail: ohtake@iser.osaka-u.ac.jp

S. Ikeda et al. (eds.), *Behavioral Economics of Preferences, Choices, and Happiness*, DOI 10.1007/978-4-431-55402-8_16

1 Introduction

Standard economic theory assumes that people's utility depends on their own consumption, and so the importance of political institutions is often disregarded, although the latter essentially determine overall economic outcomes. Of course, people admit that the political system is an infrastructure necessary to achieve high economic performance and is very important from the view point of improving the level of happiness of people (Frey and Stutzer 2002a, b). Nevertheless, many people do not participate in political activities because the political system is seen as a public good that can be free-ridden. On the other hand, the political process can be regarded as a battle between two competing opinions rather than the provision of public goods. However, even in this case, people tend to think that they are too small and helpless to influence the outcome, and so they do not participate in political activities. This is also a kind of a free-rider problem within a political group. In fact, the voting rate has been declining in many countries, including Japan and the U.S., and indifference to politics is an important social problem in democratic countries.

This chapter investigates whether Japanese people were happy and unhappy with the election outcomes. Although democratic countries worry about their nations' indifference to politics, there are no good ways to measure the degree of interest in an election amongst a nation's population. Asking people about their happiness after an election and comparing the levels of happiness of winners and losers may be a good method to measure their interest in an election; people who are interested in victory or defeat in an election should become happy or unhappy with the results. Nevertheless, there have been only a few studies (Wilson et al. 2003 and Gilbert et al. 1998), to our knowledge, that have investigated the degree of happiness amongst voters.[1] These previous studies asked only 52 and 57 voters respectively; therefore, these results cannot be seen as a convincingly robust representation of any tendency in the United States. We conducted a large survey in which we obtained about 1,400 responses every month, randomly sampled from all over Japan. Thus, this is the first comprehensive study to investigate how much people are interested in an election.

Our study is unusual in focusing on the *dynamics* of happiness in response to news, rather than the level of happiness. The focus on the dynamics of happiness in response to news is motivated by the theory in Kimball and Willis (2006). In order to explain hedonic adaptation—the tendency of happiness to return to a baseline—they model happiness as spiking up temporarily in response to good news ("elation") and dipping temporarily in response to bad news ("dismay"). In this study, in order to

[1]Of course there is a great deal of literature studying happiness data, including studies on the effect of the degree of democracy on people's happiness. For a survey on economics of happiness, see Frey and Stutzer (2002a, b), Bruni and Porta (2005), Di Tella and MacCulloch (2006) and Clark et al. (2008). Elections have also been studied in numerous literatures such as Vergne (2009), Hindriks and Lockwood (2009), and Taniguchi (2005). However, there have been quite limited number of studies that relate these two topics.

investigate how happiness depends on news and personal events, we conducted a survey on happiness every month with respondents in Japan and asked them about their current feeling.[2]

In this chapter, we analyze the effect of the Japanese general election conducted on September 11, 2005. This election was a rather heated one. The Koizumi Cabinet won an overwhelming victory that exceeded predictions by the media. Surprisingly, our study does not find any significant change in happiness amongst winners or losers, suggesting that Japanese people are relatively indifferent to politics, though comparable results on the effect of election results on politics are not yet available for other countries.[3]

This chapter is organized as follows. In Sect. 2, we first explain how the election was conducted and provide an outline of our survey. Then, we show that there is a tendency for supporters of ruling parties to become happier and for those of opposition parties to become unhappier, but that this tendency is insignificant. In Sect. 3, by looking at the level of happiness over the 6 days following the election, we examine how the elation and dismay at the result of the election faded away. In Sect. 4, we show how to adjust for the fact that the percentage of respondents who said they supported the cabinet changed from month on to the next. Such an adjustment is important, because those who supported Koizumi well before the election tended to be happier than those who only decided to support Koizumi later on. In Sect. 5, we examine whether the happiness of voters was affected by the win or loss of their party's candidates in their own prefectures. Section 6 is devoted to discussion of our findings and conclusions that can be drawn from them.

2 Did Japanese Become Happy and Unhappy According to Their Political Allegiance?

2.1 *The General Election on September 11, 2005*

The general election was conducted on Sunday, September 11, 2005, and the Prime Minister, Koizumi, won a landslide victory. The Liberal Democratic Party (hereafter LDP) carried 296 seats of the 480 seats in the House of Representatives. Combining these with the seats carried by New Komeito (Komei), with which the LDP has concluded an alliance, the ruling parties carried over 2/3 (327/480) of the seats in the House of Representatives. The Japanese Diet consists of the House of Representatives and the House of Councilors, and to be approved, bills should clear both. However, even if they are rejected in the House of Councilors after approval

[2]We conducted a similar survey in the U.S., from which we found that Hurricane Katrina made Americans significantly unhappy. See Kimball et al. (2006).

[3]We discuss what evidence has been published for the effects of election results on happiness in the U.S. in Sect. 6.

by the House of Representatives, they are approved if they win over 2/3 of the votes in the House of Representatives on a second vote. Therefore, the victory of over 2/3 of the seats in the House of Representatives meant that Prime Minister Koizumi could pass any bills even if they were opposed by the House of Councilors.

To understand why this election result was important, we need to explain the situation under which Koizumi dissolved the House of Representatives on August 8. The alliance of the LDP and Komei commanded a majority in both Houses; therefore, in principle, they could have passed any bill. However, the privatization of the Japan Postal Service Public Corporation, which was the most important public promise made by Koizumi, met strong opposition from many Diet members of his own LDP. In consequence, the bill passed the House of Representatives by a close margin, but was rejected in the House of Councilors on August 8. Prime Minister Koizumi dissolved the House of Representatives at once, saying that he wanted to ask the nation's opinion on the privatization. Thus, the general election became a kind of national referendum on the policy of reforming the Postal Service. How this election attracted the nation's attention was reflected in the high turnout rate of voters: 68 % this time around, as against 60 % at the last general election.

2.2 *Our Survey*

We conducted monthly surveys from August 2005 to February 2006, and focused on the impact of the general election conducted on September 11, 2005.

Let us explain the outline of our survey, taking the September survey as an example. The surveys in the other months have similar features. In each case, 2,000 people over 20 years old were randomly selected from all over Japan and interviewed.[4] In the September survey, the number of effective responses was 1,399; the response rate was 70.0 %. The survey was conducted from September 13 to 20, and the number of respondents on each date is shown in Table 16.1.[5] 749 respondents (53.5 %) supported the Koizumi Cabinet, 416 (29.7 %) were opposed to it, and 234 (16.7 %) answered "do not know." The parties supported by respondents are shown in Table 16.2. 32 % supported the LDP and 15 % supported the Democratic Party of Japan (DP), while 42 % did not support any party. Thus, how to attract those who did not support a specific party was the key, and according to exit polls, about a half of them voted for the LDP, leading to the victory of Koizumi.

As for happiness, the following question was asked:

[4] The survey is not a panel. Different people are randomly chosen every time.

[5] Although one answer and four answers were obtained on September 13 and 20, respectively, we disregard them when analyzing the effect on each day because they are very few in number.

Table 16.1 Number of responses on each day in September survey

	Total	13-Sep	14-Sep	15-Sep	16-Sep	17-Sep	18-Sep	19-Sep	20-Sep
Count	1,399	1	149	192	183	327	353	190	4
Proportion (%)	100	0.1	10.7	13.7	13.1	23.4	25.2	13.6	0.3

Table 16.2 Number of supporters for each party

	Total	LDP	DP	Komei	Communist	SDP	PNP	NPN	Other parties	No party	Do not know
Count	1,399	446	207	61	32	23	3	1	3	589	34
Proportion (%)	100	31.9	14.8	4.4	2.3	1.6	0.2	0.1	0.2	42.1	2.4

Note: Communist stands for Japanese Communist Party
SDP Social Democratic Party, *PNP* The People's New Party, *NPN* New Party Nippon

Please remember how you felt in this one week. To what degree were you feeling happy in the last week? On a scale of 0–10, where "10" is "very happy" and "0" is "very unhappy," how do you rate your level of happiness in the last week?

We define a variable, *Happiness,* for this value. According to the survey conducted in September, out of 1,399, those who chose 5 formed the largest group (397 = 28.4 %), and those who chose 6, 7, or 8 numbered over 200 each (about 15 %). The average happiness value was 6.3. We also have data on gender, age, academic background, household income, occupation, residence location, and the size of cities, as well as attitude towards the Koizumi Cabinet, which party a respondent supports, and his or her view on the state of business.[6]

2.3 *Level of Happiness of Supporters of Ruling Parties*

We want to investigate whether the level of happiness of supporters of the ruling parties rose from August to September, and whether the degree of happiness of supporters of opposition parties fell during the same period. In this subsection, we calculate the averages of happiness for these groups for each month in order to compare them. Since happiness changes from month to month due to various reasons, we must be careful to adjust the figures to allow for variation caused by events other than the election.

As can be seen from Fig. 16.1, the average happiness of all respondents substantially varied over the period. In particular, we are interested in the change in happiness from August to September and the figures show that the average level of happiness of all respondents in August is higher than in September. Thus, if we

[6]Household income has not been asked in the surveys for several months.

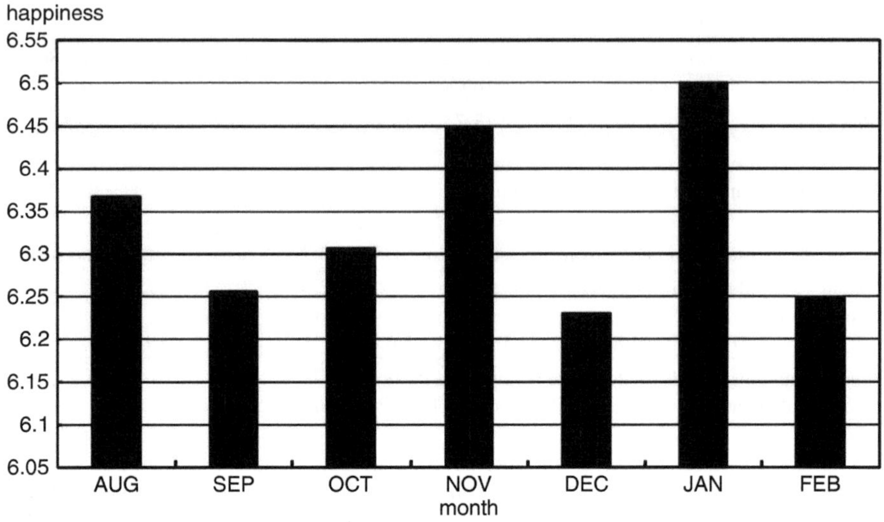

Fig. 16.1 Average happiness of all respondents

find a decrease in happiness amongst supporters of the ruling parties in September, it does not necessarily imply that the election results affected the supporters in a negative way. In order to identify the effect of the election results on the level of happiness amongst supporters of the ruling and opposition parties, it is necessary to adjust the change in average happiness between months. To do so, we divide the happiness of supporters of ruling and opposition parties by the average happiness of all respondents for each month.

Indeed, happiness amongst supporters of the ruling parties in September was lower than that in August. However, when we adjust the change in average happiness of all respondents, the outcome is reversed. The dark color columns in Fig. 16.2, which represent the level of normalized happiness, reveal that supporters of the ruling parties rose in September, declined until December, and rose again in January and February. The rise in September may be due to the victory in the election. The grey color columns in Fig. 16.2 represent the normalized happiness of supporters of opposition parties. The normalized happiness fell in September, fell even more in October before going up until January.[7] The result that the level of happiness fell in September is consistent with the notion that it was caused by the defeat in the election. However, one may argue that the result fell more in October than in September makes this an unreasonable explanation.

Our survey also asks whether or not people support the Koizumi Cabinet. According to the results, a large proportion of supporters of opposition parties also supported the Koizumi Cabinet in September. This is not strange because the Prime

[7]Original happiness of supporters of opposition parties before normalization fell in September.

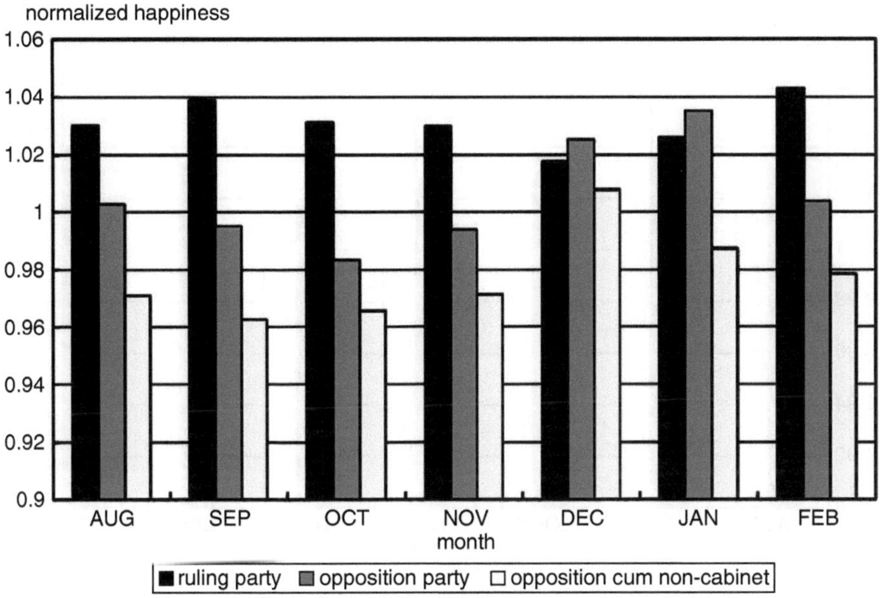

Fig. 16.2 Normalized happiness of supporters of ruling parties, opposition parties, and those who support opposition but not the Koizumi Cabinet. Note: Normalized happiness is (average happiness of a group)/(average happiness of the whole sample)

Minister, Koizumi, claimed that he was the real reformer of the LDP, and so people who are against the LDP may, nonetheless, support Koizumi. They may have felt happy to hear that Koizumi won.

Considering this fact, it may be appropriate to focus on the happiness of those who supported the opposition and did not support the Koizumi Cabinet. The light color columns in Fig. 16.2 represent the results, which reveal that the happiness of those people fell in September and rose in October, and then continued to go up until December. This result is consistent with the supposition that people who were against both Koizumi and the LDP became unhappy with the defeat in the general election in September, 2005.

The ruling party consists of the LDP and Komei, while the opposition consists of the Democratic Party of Japan (DP), the Japanese Communist Party (Communist), the Social Democratic Party (SDP), the People's New Party (PNP), and New Party Nippon (NPN). Let us examine whether the results on ruling and opposition parties mentioned above apply for each party. The supporters of Communist, SDP, PNP, and NPN are too few to get reliable statistics for each party; therefore, we aggregated the supporters of these small parties into one group (SMALL) and considered the LDP, Komei, DP, and SMALL.

The dark color columns in Fig. 16.3 show the results for the LDP. The level of happiness rose in September. However, the difference from August to September was only 0.004 and the happiness rose more in October. Thus, the rise in happiness

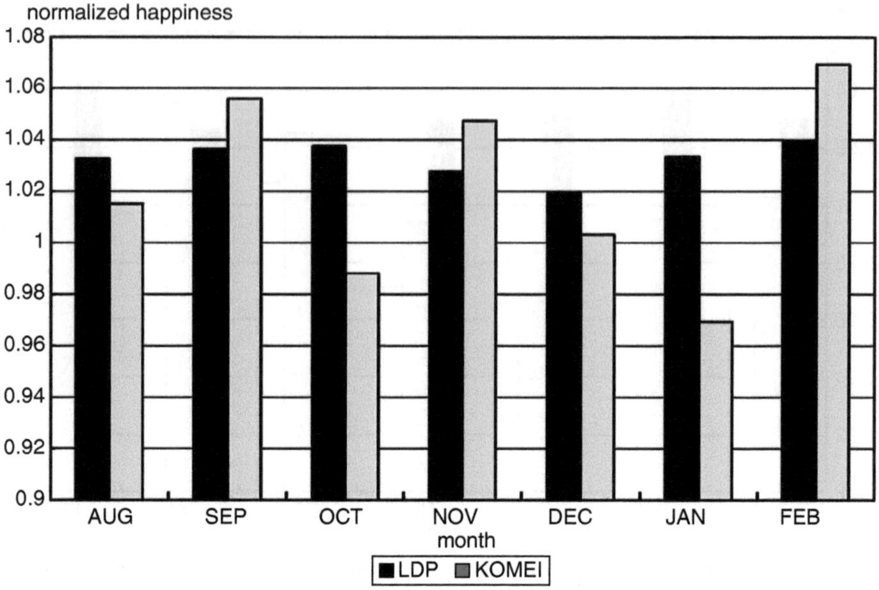

Fig. 16.3 Normalized happiness of supporters of LDP and KOMEI

of LDP supporters was small in September. The light color columns in Fig. 16.3 show the results for Komei. The level of happiness rose in September and fell in October. The difference from August to September is 0.04, which is ten times larger than that of supporters of the LDP. Thus, the rise in happiness of Komei (the smaller ruling party) supporters is more pronounced than that of LDP (the larger ruling party) supporters.

The dark color columns in Fig. 16.4 show the results for the DP. The level of happiness fell in September and rose in October. However, the difference from August to September was only 0.001. The grey color columns in Fig. 16.4 show the results for SMALL, i.e., Communist, SDP, NPN, and PNP taken together. The level of happiness fell in September. The difference from August was 0.04, which is 40 times larger than that for the DP. Thus, the fall in happiness of SMALL's supporters was more pronounced than that of DP's supporters. Considering the results for the LDP and Komei together, these results suggest that the supporters of smaller parties were more strongly affected by the results of the election.

However, the result that the level of happiness dropped much more in October than in September is strange. This may be due to the fact that a considerable proportion of the supporters of opposition parties also supported the Koizumi Cabinet. For example, among the 32 supporters of Communist in September, 19 did not support the Cabinet and ten did support the Cabinet.[8] The average happiness

[8]Three answered 'do not know'.

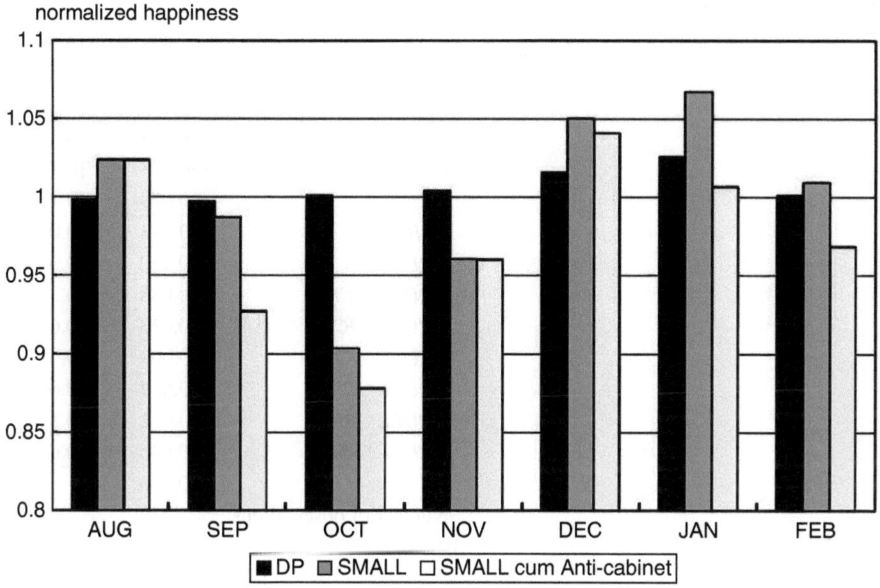

Fig. 16.4 Normalized happiness of supporters of DP, SMALL, and SMALL cum anti-cabinet

of the former group was 5.2, while that of the latter was 8.0. Thus, in September, the anti-cabinet Communist supporters were much unhappier than pro-cabinet Communist supporters.

To get rid of the bias from pro-cabinet supporters of opposition parties, we show the happiness of supporters of SMALL who were anti-cabinet as the light color columns in Fig. 16.4. Their level of happiness fell in September by almost 0.10. While the happiness was lower in October than in September, the change between September and October was only half that between August and September.

The results in Figs. 16.2, 16.3, and 16.4 suggest that the supporters of ruling parties felt relatively happier in September than in August, while those of opposition parties felt less happy in September than in August. Considering that the survey was conducted a few days after the election, the landslide victory of Koizumi may be the cause of this rise and fall in happiness. The effect was larger for the supporters of smaller parties; for ruling parties, the effect on Komei was larger than that on the LDP, and for the opposition parties, the effect on SMALL was larger than that on the DP.

2.4 Is the Change Significant?

In this subsection, we examine whether the rise and fall in the level of happiness in September is significant. To test the significance of the change in happiness of supporters of the ruling parties, we estimate the following equation.

Table 16.3 Estimates of Eq. (16.1)

Variable	Coefficient	p-value
Constant	2.421	[0.000]
SEP	−0.100	[0.045]
OCT	−0.045	[0.370]
NOV	0.028	[0.573]
DEC	−0.073	[0.148]
JAN	0.079	[0.112]
FEB	−0.098	[0.043]
DRULE	0.130	[0.044]
*DRULE*SEP*	0.088	[0.315]
*DRULE*OCT*	0.038	[0.670]
*DRULE*NOV*	−0.009	[0.919]
*DRULE*DEC*	−0.039	[0.664]
*DRULE*JAN*	−0.022	[0.802]
*DRULE*FEB*	0.046	[0.614]
R^2	0.008	
Number of observations	8,592	

$$\begin{aligned} Happiness_i = {} & \alpha_1 + \alpha_2 SEP_i \times DRULE_i + \alpha_3 OCT_i \times DRULE_i + \alpha_4 NOV_i \times DRULE_i \\ & + \alpha_5 DEC_i \times DRULE_i + \alpha_6 JAN_i \times DRULE_i + \alpha_7 FEB_i \times DRULE_i \\ & + \beta_1 DRULE_i + \beta_2 SEP_i + \beta_3 OCT_i + \beta_4 NOV_i + \beta_5 DEC_i + \beta_6 JAN_i + \beta_7 FEB_i \end{aligned} \tag{16.1}$$

where '$Happiness_i$' stands for original (not normalized) happiness of respondent *i*, *AUG*, *SEP*, *OCT*, *NOV*, *DEC*, *JAN*, and *FEB* are dummy variables standing for each month. *DRULE* is a dummy variable, which is 1 if the respondent is a supporter of ruling parties and 0 otherwise. Subscript *i* stands for the respondents from August to February ($i = 1, \ldots, 8{,}592$). The change in happiness of supporters of ruling parties from August to September is measured by the coefficient of $SEP \times DRULE$, α_2.

The estimates of Eq. (16.1) are shown in Table 16.3, which reveal that average happiness in September is significantly lower (at the 5 % level) than that in August (see *SEP*).[9] Supporters of the ruling parties are significantly happier (at the 5 % level) than others (see *DRULE*). The supporters of the ruling parties were happier in September than in August, but this is not significant (*p*-value is 0.315, see *DRULE SEP*). However, the coefficient is larger and more significant than those of other months, suggesting that this coefficient may reflect the impact of the election.

We estimate equations similar to Eq. (16.1) for the supporters of opposition parties, SMALL (Communist, SDP, NPN, and PNP), LDP, and Komei.[10] In order to save space, only the estimates of α_2 are presented in Table 16.4. The indicators are

[9]The average happiness is also significantly lower in February.

[10]*DRULE* in Eq. (16.1) is replaced with corresponding dummy variables.

Table 16.4 Estimates of: change in happiness from August to September for each party

	Regression analysis		*t*-test of mean difference			
			Mean of September	# of September	*t*-value	*p*-value
Party	Coefficient	*p*-value	Mean of August	# of August	*df*	
Ruling party	0.088	[0.315]	1.039	498	0.434	[0.332]
			1.030	384	880	
LDP	0.058	[0.526]	1.037	437	0.175	[0.431]
			1.033	328	763	
Komei	0.153	[0.448]	1.056	61	0.751	[0.227]
			1.015	56	115	
Opposition party	−0.026	[0.814]	0.995	257	−0.263	[0.396]
			1.003	174	429	
DP	−0.012	[0.924]	0.998	203	0.001	[0.499]
			0.998	140	341	
SMALL	−0.068	[0.769]	0.986	53	−0.512	[0.305]
			1.021	34	85	
SMALL cum non-cabinet supporter	−0.25	[0.341]	0.919	36	−1.344	[0.092]
			1.024	27	61	

Note: *df* stands for degree of freedom. # stands for number of observations

consistent with our expectation in all cases: those belonging to ruling parties, LDP, and Komei, are positive, while those belonging to opposition parties, SMALL, and SMALL cum anti-cabinet, are negative. This suggests that the results may not be accidental. However, the estimates are all insignificant, suggesting that the effect of political events on the happiness of the Japanese was quite limited, if it existed at all. The coefficient is larger for Komei and SMALL (cum non-cabinet supporter) compared with the LDP and the opposition parties in total, suggesting that the supporters of smaller parties like Komei, Communist, and SDP have stronger loyalty than supporters of larger parties like the LDP and DP.[11]

Alternatively, we can test the difference of the means of the normalized happiness between August and September. Since the normalization is done by taking ratio to the mean happiness of each month, while monthly dummies are added in the regression Eq. (16.1) to adjust the month-specific variation, the adjustment is not completely same. They might produce different outcomes, so that it is worth checking the results of the mean difference tests. The results are presented in the right columns of Table 16.4. Looking at the *p*-values in the rightmost column, it reveals that there are no cases that the difference between August and September is significant at the 5 % level.[12] Thus the conclusion based on the regression analysis is confirmed by the mean difference tests.

[11]These estimates are not significant, probably because the number of supporters is small.

[12]Those who support small opposition parties and anti-cabinet became unhappier at the 10 % level.

3 Daily Change in Happiness in September

Happiness of supporters of political parties varies over a period of months, as shown in Figs. 16.2, 16.3, and 16.4. However, it is not likely that the effect of the election results on the happiness of average Japanese people lasts over months. The effect, if it exists, should fade away in a shorter period. Kimball et al. (2006) showed that Hurricane Katrina made American people unhappier, but the effect faded away within a week or two. In this section, we investigate, by looking at the daily data to see how long the effect of the election lasted. Given that the main effect of the election is not significant, we do not expect to find a statistically significant interaction with the day, but it seems worthwhile to see the pattern.

The survey was conducted from September 13 to 20. The number of respondents on each date, shown in Table 16.1, varies from 150 to 350, with the exception of September 13 and 20.[13]

We calculate average happiness of supporters of ruling parties each day. Since happiness possibly fluctuated in line with macro news every day, we divide the average by the mean of happiness of all respondents for each day. No specific trend is observed (figure is not shown in order to save space).

The results of the supporters of Komei are represented by the dark color columns in Fig. 16.5. The average happiness declined from September 14 to 16, while the trend thereafter is unclear. The light color columns in Fig. 16.5 represent the results of opposition parties.[14] The level of happiness rose from September 14 to 17 and thereafter declined. These two results in Fig. 16.5 may suggest that the effect of the election results lasted until September 16 or 17.

To examine if this change in happiness by day is significant, we estimate the following equation:

$$\begin{aligned} Happiness_i &= a_0 + a_1 DAY15_i + a_2 DAY16_i + a_3 DAY17_i + a_4 DAY18_i + a_5 DAY19_i \\ &\quad + b_0 DRULE_i + b_1 DRULE_i \times DAY15_i + b_2 DRULE_i \times DAY16_i \\ &\quad + b_3 DRULE_i \times DAY17_i + b_4 DRULE_i \times DAY18_i + b_5 DRULE_i \times DAY19_i \end{aligned} \tag{16.2}$$

where *DAY*15 stands for a dummy variable for September 15 and so on. i stands for respondents of the September survey ($i = 1, \ldots, 1{,}361$). b_1 represents the discrepancy in happiness of supporters of ruling parties between September 15 and 14. The coefficients b_1-b_5 are not significant (results are not shown). The coefficients for supporters of Komei and opposition parties are not significant either. Therefore, like the overall effect of the election, the day-effect in Fig. 16.5 is weak, if it exists.

[13]Although one answer and four answers were obtained on September 13 and 20, respectively, we disregard them when we analyze the effect for each day because they are very few in number.

[14]We expected that the happiness of supporters of SMALL would show a clearer pattern. Unfortunately, the analysis of "smaller opposition parties" is impossible because the observations are too few in number.

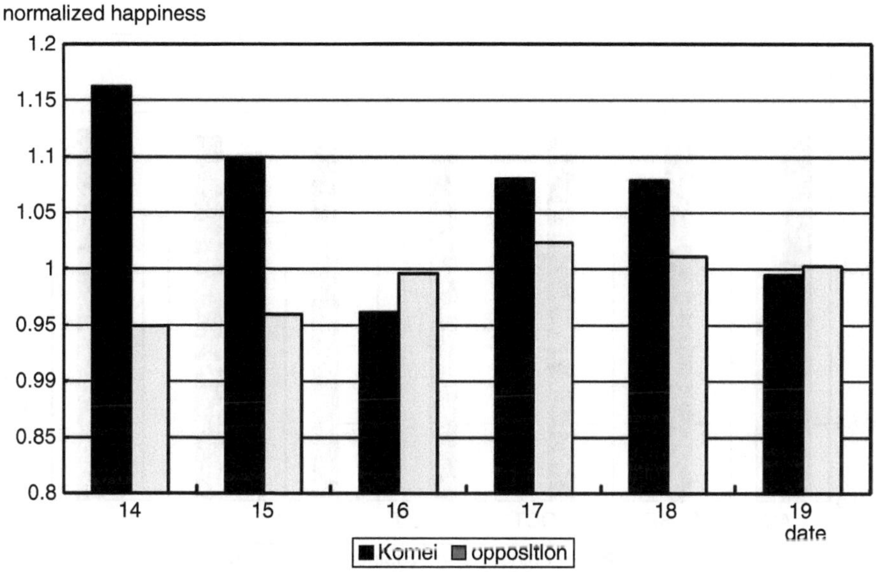

Fig. 16.5 Normalized happiness of supporters of Komei and opposition parties for each day

4 Happiness of Cabinet Supporters

Who carried the day; the LDP or Koizumi? This is the question asked by the media after the election. The answer was Koizumi. It may be interesting to see if the cabinet supporters were happier than supporters of each party in September.

The dark color columns in Fig. 16.6 represent the average happiness of cabinet supporters in each month divided by the average happiness of all respondents for each month.[15] Unexpectedly, the normalized happiness of cabinet supporters declined in September. The grey color columns in Fig. 16.6 represent the happiness of anti-cabinet supporters. Their happiness also declined in September. These results mean that only those who answered "do not know" were happier in September, as shown by the light color columns in Fig. 16.6.

Why did this happen? There are two key facts to consider. The first is that the number of cabinet supporters increased from 549 in August to 733 in September (see Table 16.5). The other is that cabinet supporters are always happier than anti-cabinet supporters; 6.62 as against 6.20 in August. Given these facts, a possible explanation for the fall of happiness of pro-cabinet supporters is as follows. The increase in the number of pro-cabinet supporters means that many people who would not have been pro-cabinet in September, if the exogenous factors such as occurrence of the general election had been the same as in August, actually changed their opinion

[15]Cabinet supporters are consistently happier than anti-cabinet supporters.

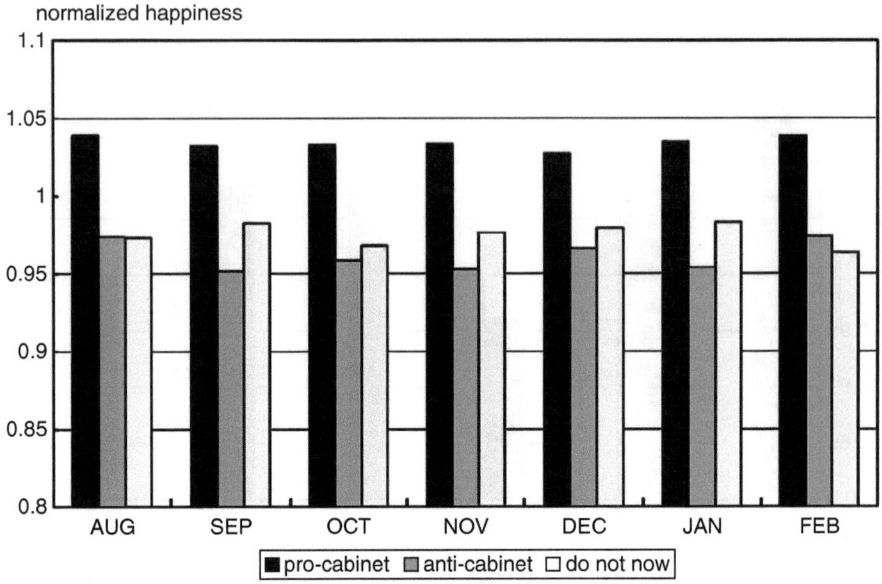

Fig. 16.6 Normalized happiness of pro-cabinet supporters, anti-cabinet supporters, and those who answered "do not know"

Table 16.5 The number of cabinet supporters in August and September

	August		September	
	Number of respondents	Happiness	Number of respondents	Happiness
Pro-cabinet	549	6.62	733	6.46
Anti-cabinet	493	6.2	410	5.95
Others	315	6.2	218	6.14

to pro-cabinet. Since non-pro-cabinet are generally unhappier than pro-cabinet, this shift produces a downward bias of happiness of cabinet supporters in September. In short, the number of people who support the cabinet is endogenously determined and an increase in their number implies the inclusion of unhappier people into this category.

Thus, to measure the effect of the victory in the election on the level of happiness amongst pro-cabinet supporters, we need to identify imaginary cabinet supporters in September who were also pro-cabinet in August. Since the survey chooses different random samples every month and our sample is not panel data, we need to estimate hypothesized pro-cabinet supporters.

To solve this problem, we first estimate a model that explains what type of people tend to support the Koizumi Cabinet. Adopting all the information available in our survey, we estimate the following equation:

$$
\begin{aligned}
DCAB_i = {} & a_0 + a_1 GOODNEWS_i + a_2 DMAN_i + a_3 AGE_i + a_4 SCHOOL_i \\
& + a_5 LARGE15CITY_i + a_6 OTHERCITY_i + a_7 AGRICULTURE_i \\
& + a_8 FIELD_i + a_9 FREE\_MANAGE_i + a_{10} HOUSEWIFE_i \\
& + a_{11} STUDENT_i + a_{12} OTHERJOB_i + a_{13} HOKKAIDO_i \\
& + a_{14} TOHOKU_i + a_{15} KANTO_i + a_{16} KEIHIN_i \\
& + a_{17} KOSHINETSU_i + a_{18} HOKURIKU_i + a_{19} TOKAI_i \\
& + a_{20} KINKI_i + a_{21} HANSHIN_i + a_{22} TYUGOKU_i \\
& + a_{23} SHIKOKU_i + a_{24} GOODBC_i + a_{25} LDP_i + a_{25} DP_i \\
& + a_{26} KOMEI_i + a_{27} COMMUNIST_i + a_{28} SDP_i \qquad (16.3)
\end{aligned}
$$

where *DCAB* is a dummy variable, which is 1 when a respondent supports the Koizumi Cabinet and 0 otherwise. *GOODNEWS* is a variable that takes a value from 1 to 12 corresponding to the range between "they had very good personal news or event in the last week" and "they had very bad personal news or event in the last week." *DMAN* is a dummy variable, which is 1 when a respondent is a man and 0 otherwise. *AGE* is the age of each respondent, *SCHOOL* is a variable which takes 1 if the respondent's academic education is grade school, 2 if high school, and 3 if university. *LARGE15CITY* is a dummy variable that takes 1 if a respondent lives in one of the 15 largest cities in Japan and 0 otherwise. *OTHERCITY* is a dummy variable that takes 1 if the respondent lives in the other cities. Variables from *AGRICULTURE* to *OTHERJOB* are dummy variables that take 1 if a respondent engages in a certain occupation. Variables from *HOKKAIDO* to *SIKOKU* stand for a dummy variable representing regions in Japan. *GOODBC* is a variable that takes a value from 1 to 5 corresponding to "business conditions will definitely become better" to "business conditions will definitely become worse." Variables from *SLDP* to *SSDP* are dummy variables for supporters of each party. Subscript i stands for all respondents of the whole period ($i = 1, \ldots, 8{,}592$).

Using all the data from August to February, we estimate Eq. (16.3) with a probit. The estimation results are not shown to save space. Those who have higher education, who think that business conditions will become better, and who received good personal news in the last week tend to be cabinet supporters. Some regions are significant: HOKKAIDO and KOSINETSU have negative indicators, while KEIHIN and KINKI have positive indicators. Naturally, the LDP and Komei supporters also tended to support the cabinet, whilst DP, Communist, and SDP supporters tended to be anti-cabinet. Then, using these estimates, we construct the fitted value for each respondent, and transform it into a probability with F (fitted value), where $F(\cdot)$ stands for the cumulative normal distribution function. The number of cabinet supporters was 521 and at its lowest in August; therefore, we select the top 521 respondents based on the probability from those who answered "pro-cabinet" in the survey for each month.[16]

[16]Alternatively, we could have selected the top 521 respondents disregarding the information on their answer of the pro-cabinet question. We believe, however, that the information is important, since the R-squared of Eq. (16.3) is only 0.29.

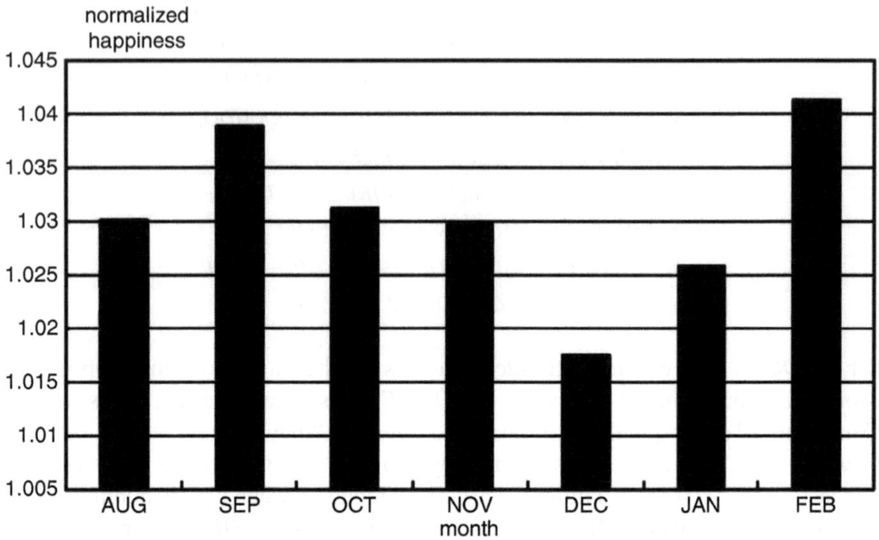

Fig. 16.7 Normalized happiness of hypothetical pro-cabinet supporters. Note: Hypothetical pro-cabinet supporters are the top 521 respondents selected from those who answered 'pro-cabinet' in the survey of each month. The rank of 'pro-cabinet' was determined based on the estimates of pro-cabinet characteristic function Eq. (16.3)

The average happiness of these 521 hypothetical pro-cabinet supporters for each month, normalized by the average happiness of all respondents for each month, is presented in Fig. 16.7. The normalized average happiness of cabinet supporters rose in September, then declined until December, and went up thereafter. In contrast to Fig. 16.6, happiness in September is higher than that in August. This outcome confirms that the reason why the happiness of pro-cabinet supporters declined in September is the sharp increase in pro-cabinet supporters in September who are unhappier than cabinet supporters. Once the endogeneity of cabinet supporters is adjusted by picking up the same number of cabinet supporters, we found that their happiness rose relatively in September, suggesting that the victory in the general election was good news to pro-cabinet supporters.

Is this rise in happiness significant? To investigate this, we use Eq. (16.1), in which *DRULE* is substituted by *ADDCAB* standing for a dummy variable that is 1 for 521 hypothetical cabinet supporters and 0 otherwise. The results are shown in Table 16.6. *SEP* is negative, even though insignificant at the 10 % level, suggesting that happiness declined in September. *ADDCAB* is significantly positive, suggesting that the hypothetical pro-cabinet supporters were happier than others. *ADDCAB*SEP* is positive, which suggests that the hypothetical pro-cabinet supporters were happier in September than in August; however, this value is not significant.

The insignificant results raise the doubt that the rise in September is perhaps only accidental. However, considering that all the results on the rise and fall of happiness

Table 16.6 Significance of the rise in happiness of hypothetical pro-cabinet supporters

Variable	Coefficient	*p*-value
C	6.226	[0.000]
SEP	−0.120	[0.234]
OCT	−0.092	[0.375]
NOV	0.105	[0.307]
DEC	−0.027	[0.793]
JAN	0.199	[0.050]
FEB	−0.152	[0.130]
ADDCAB	0.415	[0.000]
*ADDCAB**SEP*	0.049	[0.753]
*ADDCAB**OCT*	0.084	[0.598]
*ADDCAB**NOV*	−0.104	[0.515]
*ADDCAB**DEC*	−0.278	[0.080]
*ADDCAB**JAN*	−0.113	[0.475]
*ADDCAB**FEB*	−0.008	[0.961]
R^2	0.011	
Number of observations	8,592	

amongst supporters of the ruling parties, the opposition parties, and the cabinet are consistent with our hypothesis, it may be the case that the election results really affected the happiness of the Japanese, albeit only weakly.

5 Number of Elected Representatives and Happiness of the Inhabitants

The prefecture where each respondent lives was documented, so that it is possible to estimate the effect of the number of winners of the LDP by prefecture in the general election on the level of happiness of the LDP supporters.[17] We construct a variable, *WLDP*, defined as (number of winners of LDP in a prefecture where a respondent lives)/(total number of winners (i.e., seats) of the prefecture). To examine whether LDP supporters became happier with the victory of the LDP in their home prefecture, we estimate the following equation.

$$Happiness_i = a_0 + a_1 SLDP_i + a_2 SLDP_i * WLDP_i \qquad (16.4)$$

[17] We also estimate the effect of the number of winners of parties other than the LDP, leading to insignificant results. There are small electoral districts and proportional electoral districts in the current Japanese electoral system. In this chapter, we consider only the winners of the former districts because we suspect that people are most interested in the results for the small electoral districts they are in.

Table 16.7 Estimation results of Eq. (16.4)

Variable	Coeff.	*p*-value	Coeff.	*p*-value	Coeff.	*p*-value	Coeff.	*p*-value
Constant	6.148	[0.000]	6.158	[0.000]	6.148	[0.000]	5.982	[0.000]
SLDP	0.289	[0.414]			0.337	[0.003]		
*SLDP*WLDP*	0.064	[0.887]	0.411	[0.004]				
WLDP							0.378	[0.114]
R^2	0.005		0.005		0.006		0.007	
Number of observations	1,361		1,361		1,361		1,361	

where *SLDP* is a dummy variable, which takes 1 if a respondent supports the LDP and 0 otherwise. Subscript i stands for respondents in September ($i = 1, \ldots, 1{,}361$).

The estimation results are presented in the first column of Table 16.7. Both coefficients, a_1 and a_2, have a positive indicator, but they are not significant.

Incidentally, *SLDP* and the cross term are significant when *Happiness* is regressed on them separately, implying that LDP supporters are happier than others (see the second and third columns of Table 16.7). *WLDP* is also positive when *Happiness* is regressed on only this variable, suggesting that the LDP won in the prefectures where a larger proportion of the inhabitants support the LDP, and they tend to be happier (see the extreme right column of Table 16.7).

6 Discussion and Conclusions

This chapter examines whether the landslide victory of the Koizumi Cabinet in the general election on September 11, 2005 made Japanese people happy and unhappy. Relative changes in the happiness of supporters and non-supporters of the ruling parties from August to September were not significant. However, we found that the indicators representing the effects are consistent with our expectation in most cases, which suggests that the Japanese people were only slightly happy and unhappy with the election results.

This result seems to imply that Japanese are relatively indifferent to politics. However, we need to examine a few elements before drawing this conclusion. Our results could possibly have been obtained, even if the Japanese were deeply committed to politics. One might argue that in the election the ruling parties won implying that nothing had changed, so that it is natural that people did not feel either elation or dismay in response to the news. However, even in the case that 'nothing had changed', people should feel elation and dismay, if they had expected the contrary, that is that the ruling party would lose in the election. Thus, this argument can be specified in a more general manner and examined as follows: There was a possibility that the election results were anticipated beforehand, and so the historic victory of Koizumi was not really a surprise. However, according to the articles based on polls before the election, this supposition is not correct.

All predictions made by newspapers underestimated the number of seats gained by the ruling parties. For example, the Asahi Shinbun, based on their poll (118,616 responses), reported on September 4 that the ruling parties would win 254–310 seats (their best estimate was 283). The Mainichi Shinbun also announced their prediction on September 4, based on their poll (90,043 respondents), that the ruling parties would win 275–327 (the average is 301) seats. In fact, the ruling parties won 327. Thus, the prediction in the media that the ruling parties would win the majority was proved correct, and so winning the majority itself was not a surprise. However, winning two thirds of the seats should have been a surprise.

In addition, one important point is that this overwhelming victory may not be good news even to the supporters of the ruling parties. The majority of people thought that Koizumi (or the ruling parties) won too many seats. Interestingly, according to polls after the election, about one third of those who had voted for the LDP answered that fewer seats for the ruling parties would have been better (the Nikkei and the Yomiuri, September 14). This suggests that one third of those who voted for the LDP might have been unhappy because they thought that the LDP won too many seats. They may have regretted that they had voted for the LDP, suggesting that many people supported the LDP only relatively, and not absolutely. Considering this fact, it is not surprising that supporters of ruling parties did not become significantly happier, even if they were deeply interested in politics. However, the fact does not explain why supporters of opposition parties did not become significantly unhappier, if they cared a great deal about politics. This provides some evidence that the Japanese are relatively indifferent to politics.

Hedonic adaptation is the final point which makes us hesitate to conclude that Japanese people are indifferent to politics. Since our survey started 3 days after the election, the results might merely indicate that people returned to their baseline feelings quickly, although they were very excited with the news on the election day. Thus, our results might imply that Japanese people adapted to the election results very quickly.

The next question is whether the Japanese are more indifferent to politics than people in other countries. A good measure of people's interest in politics may be the voting rate. The voting rate in the general elections in Japan has been declining over the years since the first general election in 1890, reaching about 60 % in recent years. On the other hand, the voting rate in the presidential election in the U.S. was 51 % in 2000. Thus, the voting rate is not low in Japan, at least for general elections. We should note, however, that people need to register beforehand to vote in the U.S., while registration is not necessary in Japan.[18] Thus, it is easier for Japanese to vote; therefore, a simple comparison may not be appropriate.[19] The voting rate has been declining over the years in many countries, and so the governments of

[18]The US registration rate was 75 % in 2000.

[19]In France, where people need to register to vote, the voting rate for presidential elections has been over 70 % over the last 30 years. As for the parliamentary elections in France, the voting rate

these countries warn of the crisis of democracy and try to increase the voting rate. Although they lament people's indifference to elections in their home countries, it is difficult to know which nation is more indifferent to elections because voting rates depend heavily on the electoral system.

Another barometer for interest in politics may be the number of members of political parties. The number of registered Republicans in the United States is approximately 60 million, while the number of the members of the LDP in Japan is 1.2 million.[20] The number is much smaller in Japan than in the U.S., which suggests that politics is more popular in the U.S. than in Japan. However, a simple comparison may lead to a fallacy, since the definition of a party member is different in the two countries.[21]

The two measures, voting rate and the number of members, are vulnerable to differences between the systems and do not offer reliable evidence for comparison of people's indifference to politics. Rather, a survey on happiness of supporters of political parties like the one in this chapter is expected to elucidate the degree of interest in elections.

There have been two studies that examined the effect of election results on happiness of supporters of candidates. One is Gilbert et al. (1998), which analyzed happiness amongst 57 voters at a gubernatorial election in Texas in 1994. Losers were happier than winners both before and after the election; however, on the basis of evaluations 1 month after the election, there was no evidence that winners became happier than losers. Losers' happiness was 5.00 just before the election and 5.33 one month after the election, while winners' happiness was 4.10 and 4.40 before and after the election. The other study is Wilson et al. (2003), which investigated a U.S. presidential election in 2000. They asked 52 college students about their happiness one day after Gore conceded. Bush supporters were significantly (at the 1 % level) happier than Gore supporters.[22] However, since they chose only students who were especially interested in politics, their significant results are not easily compared with our insignificant results.

Thus, whether an effect of the election results on happiness was established depended on when respondents were asked: in the U.S. the effect remained on the next day of the event, but didn't remain after a month. We interviewed respondents 3 days after the election, which is closer to Wilson et al. (2003), suggesting that Japanese are more indifferent than Americans. Of course, we should be careful because of the fact that there is discrepancy of 2 days. Kimball et al. (2006) found

---

has been around 60 % since 1988, which implies a higher incentive for voting than applies in the Japanese case, considering the trouble of registration.

[20] According to information provided by the Republican National Committee and from administration office of the LDP, respectively.

[21] Members of the LDP are required to pay 4,000 yen as an annual fee, while nothing special is required for registration in the U.S.

[22] They subtracted people's initial happiness from the happiness after the election to evaluate the change.

that dismay caused by Hurricane Katrina faded away in a week; therefore, the difference of 2 days might have resulted in different outcomes.[23]

Acknowledgments An earlier version of this chapter was presented at the conference of behavioral economics held in Kyoto, Annual meetings of Japanese Economic Association and The Japan Society of Household Economics. The authors are grateful to two anonymous referees of this journal, Daiji Kawaguchi, Fumihiko Hiruma, and the participants for their comments. The study is financially supported by the 21st Century COE (Center of Excellence) Program funded by the Ministry of Education, Culture, Sports, Science and Technology.

Addendum: Investigation of the Effect of Election Results on Happiness Using Daily Data[24]

In the text, we found that the effect of election results on happiness is weak, and concluded that Japanese people are largely indifferent to politics. However, as we remarked in the text, since our survey started 3 days after the election, the results might merely indicate that people returned to their baseline feelings quickly, and in fact may have been very excited about the news on election day itself. To overcome this problem, we need to collect data on happiness over several days before and after the election day, including the day itself.

We thus conducted a daily survey that covers the period before, after, and including an election day. The sample included about 70 students of Osaka University, and examined the change in happiness for 7 days before and after the election for the House of Councillors held on July 29, 2007. This election was epochal, since the Democratic Party of Japan (DPJ) won a landslide victory, resulting that opposition parties became the majority in the House of Councillors. Nonetheless, we did not find a clear change in the happiness of respondents due to this event. Does this mean that Japanese people are indifferent to politics? The result might merely reflect the following possibilities: (1) the small sample might result in insignificant estimates; (2) the younger generation is more indifferent to politics and elections than older generations; (3) the House of Councillors receives much less popular attention than the House of Representatives.

To exclude these possibilities, we conducted a survey covering an election for member of the House of Representatives, conducted on August 30, 2009, and obtained 1,068 responses from people of various generations. The election was a historical event in that the Liberal Democratic Party (LDP) and Komei Party, then in power, lost the election in a landslide, and the DPJ took power.

---

[23]Whether the election attracted people's attention may be another point. Both the general election in Japan and the Bush vs. Gore struggle attracted much attention: it is not easy to say which one is more focused on by the nations.

[24]This addendum has been newly written for this book chapter.

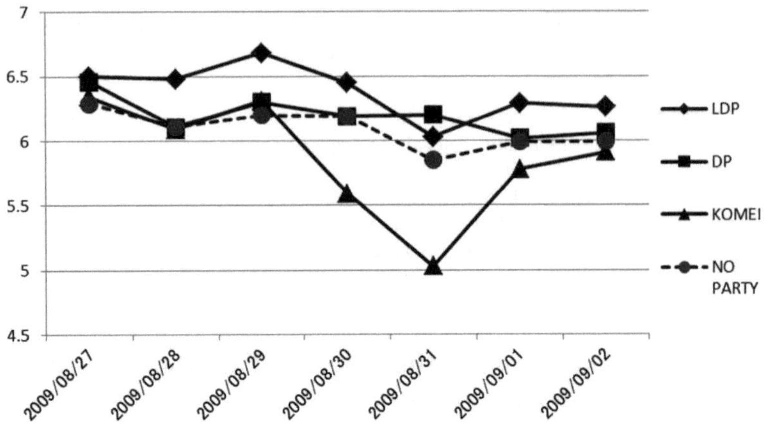

Fig. 16.8 Happiness of supporter of each party

Here we report preliminary results based on this survey. Figure 16.8 shows the average happiness level of supporters of each party. The figure reveals that the happiness of the supporters of the LDP and Komei (which lost power in this election) substantially declined on August 31, the first day respondents reported their happiness after knowing the election results. However, their happiness substantially recovered on the next day. This result suggests that the analysis of the Koizumi election in the text, which was based on the data 3 days after the election, failed to catch a large change in happiness on the election day.

However, the decline of happiness of LDP and Komei supporters on the election day turned out to be statistically insignificant. Why? There are two possibilities. The one is that "supporters" includes "weak supporters" who are largely indifferent to election results. The other is that the media reported their expectations for the election results far ahead of time, allowing many people to anticipate a landslide victory for the DPJ, so that their happiness stayed unchanged when the anticipated result actually happened. In order to examine the first possibility, when we asked respondents about their party affiliation, we also asked them whether that support was strong. Respondents were requested to choose from "strong," "somewhat strong," "somewhat weak," and "weak." In addition, we asked on the next day of the election (August 31) whether the respondents went to vote or not, and for which party they voted.

To investigate the second possibility, we asked the respondents about their expectations about election results 2 days before the election (August 28). We also asked them on the next day of the election "Are the election results about the same as you expected?" Furthermore, on the same day, we asked how many seats they wished the DPJ to gain, requesting them to choose one from "I hope they gain more seats," "I'm satisfied with this gain," and "I hope they gain fewer seats."

Using this data, we find:

1. The happiness of "strong" and "somewhat strong" supporters of LDP significantly declined on August 31 (the day following the election).

2. The happiness of LDP voters significantly declined on August 31.
3. The happiness of those who *expected* a smaller DPJ gain than actually occurred significantly declined on August 31.
4. The happiness of those who *wished* for a smaller DPJ gain than actually occurred significantly declined on August 31.

These results suggest that both the strength of party affiliation and expectations are crucial elements in deciding whether election results significantly affect happiness in Japan.

Figure 16.8 reveals that the happiness of DPJ supporters was barely moved by the election. Although we have not fully found the reason for this lack of movement, we confirmed the following:

5. The happiness of "strong" DPJ supporters did not change much during the sample period.
6. Even when we select for party affiliation, expectations, and desired outcome, we find no significant rise in happiness among DPJ supporters on the day following the election (August 31).[25]

We see two possible explanations for these results. The first is that many supporters of the DPJ became supporters relatively recently, and did not really love the party. The second is that a substantial number of DPJ supporters might think after the election that the DPJ's victory was too large. In our dataset, 52 % of all respondents wished the DPJ had won less seats, while only 10 % wished they had won more seats. Among the supporters of the DPJ, these 27 % and 19 %, respectively; even many DPJ supporters wished their party's victory had been smaller.

References

Bruni L, Porta PL (2005) Economics and happiness: framing the analysis. Oxford University Press, New York

Clark AE, Frijters P, Shields MA (2008) Relative income, happiness, and utility: an explanation for the Easterlin paradox and other puzzles. J Econ Lit 46:95–144

Di Tella R, MacCulloch R (2006) Some uses of happiness data in economics. J Econ Perspect 20:25–46

Frey BS, Stutzer A (2002a) Happiness and economics. Princeton University Press, Princeton

Frey BS, Stutzer A (2002b) What can economists learn from happiness research? J Econ Lit 40:402–435

Gilbert DT, Pinel EC, Wilson TD, Blumberg SJ (1998) Immune neglect: a source of durability bias in affective forecasting. J Pers Soc Psychol 75:617–638

Hindriks J, Lockwood B (2009) Decentralization and electoral accountability: incentives, separation and voter welfare. Eur J Polit Econ 25:385–397

Kimball M, Willis R (2006) Utility and happiness. Mimeo

[25] However, happiness significantly rose on some other days.

Kimball M, Levy H, Ohtake F, Tsutsui Y (2006) Unhappiness after Hurricane Katrina, NBER working paper no. 12062. National Bureau of Economic Research, Cambridge, MA

Taniguchi N (2005) Electoral behavior in contemporary Japan. Keio Gijuku University Press, Tokyo (in Japanese)

Tsutsui Y, Kimball M, Ohtake F (2010) Koizumi carried the day: did the Japanese election results make people happy and unhappy? Eur J Polit Econ 26:12–24

Vergne C (2009) Democracy, elections and allocation of public expenditures in developing countries. Eur J Polit Econ 25:63–77

Wilson TD, Meyers J, Gilbert DT (2003) How happy was I, anyway?: a retrospective impact bias. Soc Cogn 21:421–446

Chapter 17
Asking About Changes in Happiness in a Daily Web Survey and Its Implication for the Easterlin Paradox

Yoshiro Tsutsui and Fumio Ohtake

Abstract This chapter investigates whether the level of happiness and integrated process of changes in happiness are the same. Using the daily data of two waves of 4 and 6 months each, we found that the level of happiness is stationary, whereas the integrated process of changes is non-stationary with a rising trend, implying that they are different series. An examination of the causes of the difference indicated that although adaptation completely influences the level of happiness, it only partially influences the change in happiness. This may be because the latter is based on a comparison between today and yesterday,

Keywords Change in happiness • Easterlin paradox • Daily web survey • Adaptation

JEL Classification I31

1 Introduction

The aim of this chapter is to shed some light on the Eastern paradox, which is the phenomenon that average happiness in a country is stable at a constant level for a long period, whereas the country's GDP grows substantially (Easterlin 1974;

The original article first appeared in the Japanese Economic Review 63(1): 38–56, 2012. A newly written addendum has been added to this book chapter.

Y. Tsutsui (✉)
Faculty of Economics, Konan University, 8-9-1 Okamoto, Higashinada-ku, Kobe 658-8501, Japan
e-mail: tsutsui@center.konan-u.ac.jp

F. Ohtake
Institute of Social and Economic Research, Osaka University, 6-1 Mihogaoka, Ibaraki, Osaka 567-0047, Japan
e-mail: ohtake@iser.osaka-u.ac.jp

S. Ikeda et al. (eds.), *Behavioral Economics of Preferences, Choices, and Happiness*, DOI 10.1007/978-4-431-55402-8_17

Clark et al. 2008).[1] The literal policy implication of the paradox is that economic growth is meaningless, as long as greater happiness is the goal (Frank 2005). This interpretation radically contradicts ordinary intuition and common sense. On the other hand, based on traditional economics, the paradox appears to be evidence that subjective happiness is not reliable for economic analysis. Indeed, many economists do not believe that subjective happiness is comparable between individuals, so that averaging the stated happiness over individuals is not justified. Thus, although the economics of happiness, which is defined as the research area that uses data on subjective happiness, has experienced significant development in recent years (Frey and Stutzer 2002a, b; Bruni and Porta 2005; Dolan et al. 2008), it is still at the stage where the validity of the analyses that use subjective happiness is being examined.

In this chapter, we propose a new interpretation of the Easterlin paradox; we argue that the Easterlin paradox may disappear once we measure subjective happiness in a different way from that measured in the conventional manner. It is known that one of the reasons why the average of happiness is flat over time is that people adapt to new standards of living quickly (adaptation hypothesis). This implies that people become happier with an increase in income in the short run; however, in the long run, a part of the increase in happiness is cancelled by adaptation (Easterlin 2005; Di Tella et al. 2007; Clark et al. 2008).[2] However, we speculate that if we ask about "change in happiness" and derive the level of happiness by summing up the answered change in happiness, then the calculated level of happiness will not be significantly affected by adaptation and it will correlate with the standard of living over time, thereby contradicting the Easterlin paradox.

However, this chapter only offers indirect evidence to resolve the Easterlin paradox. This chapter actually reports the results of a daily web survey, wherein we asked respondents the level of and change in happiness every day over 660 days. Although the sum of the changes ought to coincide with the level by definition, we will show that these two series diverge dramatically. Subsequently, we will investigate the cause of the divergence. We examine two possible causes: one is that the degree of adaptation is different between the two series. In the survey, we asked how good or bad the news that respondents received every day was.[3] Using these data, we investigate how the level of and change in happiness respond to the news on that day and adapt to it thereafter. If change in happiness is less adaptable to the news, then this suggests that the Easterlin paradox may not occur when we use the sum of changes in happiness as the data of the level of happiness. In short,

[1] Stevenson and Wolfers (2008) questioned the existence of the paradox in Japan and the EU.

[2] Another cause of the Easterlin paradox is that people evaluate their happiness in comparison with others' situations. This is called the relative income hypothesis (Duesenberry 1949; Clark and Oswald 1996; Clark et al. 2008); however, this chapter does not focus on this hypothesis.

[3] We asked six questions on various elements, including personal and macro news, that may affect happiness in the survey, which are explained in Sect. 2.

we attempt to disentangle controversy on the Easterlin paradox by proposing a new type of question for tracking subjective happiness.[4]

The remainder of the chapter is organized as follows. Section 2 explains our daily survey, which includes questions on the level of happiness and on the daily change in happiness. Section 3 analyzes whether the integrated process of the changes in happiness differs from the level of happiness. Given the result that the series differ, Sect. 4 investigates three possible reasons for the difference. Section 5 discusses the implications of the obtained results to the Easterlin paradox and concludes the chapter.

2 The Daily Survey

2.1 Two Waves

We solicited undergraduate and graduate students at Osaka University and requested them to report their happiness every day for several months.[5] They responded using their personal computers and mobile phones.[6] To the best of our knowledge, administering a daily survey like this for a long period of time is unique to this study. The survey enables us to estimate a happiness function with panel data, which has the merit of excluding the difference in happiness between people with a fixed (or random) effect model. In other words, it enables us to estimate a within-subjects happiness function, which is immune to a direct comparison of subjective happiness between people.

Our daily survey consisted of two waves. The first (2008-survey) was from December 1, 2007 to March 31, 2008, and the number of respondents decreased slightly during this period from 68 to 64.[7] The second wave (2009-survey) was from January 1 to June 30, 2009. During this period, the number of respondents decreased from 52 to 41.[8]

[4]Regarding developments in the measurement of subjective happiness, refer to Kahneman and Krueger (2006).

[5]We also asked questions including valuations of personal and macro news (how good or bad they were) arriving on that day, as explained below.

[6]Most younger residents of Japan carry mobile phones that have the capability of connecting to the Internet and sending emails.

[7]The first wave started in 1 November 2006. However, the survey did not include a question on changes in happiness until December 2007.

[8]The second phase was initially planned to conclude at the end of March; however, it was extended until the end of June. This is the reason why the number of respondents decreased substantially. In fact, the number of respondents decreased from 47 in March to 41 in April.

2.2 Questions and Definition of Variables

In the survey, we asked 13 questions; here, we explain those questions that were used in the analysis in this chapter.[9]

Q1. How happy are you now?
Choose a number between 0 and 10. 0 is "very unhappy," 10 is "very happy."

10 9 8 7 6 5 4 3 2 1 0

LEVEL is defined as the answer, which represents the level of happiness on a scale from 0 to 10.

Q5. Recall the most important personal news or event that occurred since you answered this questionnaire yesterday. How did you evaluate the news?
Choose a number between −5 and 5. 5 is "very good," −5 is "very bad."

−5 −4 −3 −2 −1 0 1 2 3 4 5

P_NEWS is defined as the answer, which represents the rating of the importance of the personal news that the respondent received that day.

Q7. Recall the most important news that was in the newspaper or on TV since you answered this questionnaire yesterday. How did you evaluate the news?
Choose a number between −5 and 5. 5 is "very good," −5 is "very bad."

−5 −4 −3 −2 −1 0 1 2 3 4 5

M_NEWS is defined as the answer, which represents the rating of the macro news that appeared on TV and/or in newspapers that day.

Q9. Did you sleep well last night?

1. poor sleep, 2. slightly poor sleep, 3. slept well, 4. slept very well

SLEEP is defined as the answer, which represents the quality of sleep. A larger number means better sleep.

Q10. How is your health now?

1. good, 2. generally good, 3. generally not good, 4. bad

HEALTH is defined as four minus the answer to Q10, which represents the quality of health. A larger number means better health.

---

[9]Questions 2, 3, 4, 6, and 8 are not used in this chapter; therefore, we have omitted their explanation.

Q11. Do you feel any anxiety and stress now?

1. a lot, 2. a little, 3. not much, 4. none

NOANXIETY is defined as the answer, which represents the level of anxiety and stress. A larger number means less stress.

Q12: Have you already attended a class today or are you going to attend a class today?

1. I have attended a class, 2. I will be attending a class, 3. I am attending a class now, 4. No class today

We define *NOCLASS* as 1 if the respondent has no class today, and 0 otherwise

Q13: Your happiness today compared with your happiness yesterday (before) is

1. much happier, 2. reasonably happier, 3. slightly happier, 4. same as yesterday (before), 5. slightly unhappier, 6. reasonably unhappier, 7. much unhappier

We define *CHANGE* as four minus the answer to Q13, which represents change in happiness from yesterday (or the time when they answered the last survey) and ranges from −3 (much unhappier) to 3 (much happier).

We present descriptive statistics of these variables for both waves in Table 17.1. In 2008-survey, the mean of *LEVEL* is 5.8, which is relatively lower than the level of happiness, 6.4, reported in "Kokumin Seikatsu Senkodo Chosa" (Survey on preferences in life of nations; webpage of the Cabinet Office). The mean of *CHANGE* is positive, implying that the respondents were becoming happier during the observed period. The mean of *P_NEWS* is slightly positive, implying that overall, they received good news, which is consistent with the fact that the mean of *CHANGE* is positive. In contrast, *M_NEWS* is slightly negative, which implies that overall, the macro news was bad. *SLEEP* and *HEALTH* are larger than 2.5, that is, the average on the scale of 1 to 4, suggesting that overall, respondents were in good health and slept well. However, the mean of *NOANXIETY* is smaller than the average on the scale of 1 to 4, suggesting that the average respondent was bothered by stress and anxiety. The mean of *NOCLASS* is 0.68.[10]

The values of the variables of 2009-survey are not radically different from those of 2008-survey. However, the values of *LEVEL*, *CHANGE*, and *P_NEWS* in the 2009-survey were larger than those of the corresponding variables in the 2008-survey, thereby suggesting that the respondents of 2009-survey were happier than those of 2008-survey.

[10]Since Osaka University has 26 school days from 1 January to 31 March (there is a spring vacation in February and March), this number implies that respondents attended most of the school days and responded to the questionnaire. In 2009-survey, the mean of *NOCLASS* is 0.58, implying that they attended classes for approximately 76 days out of the 81 school days from January to June. However, "Class" in the question includes experiments at laboratories in natural science and technology departments, which are conducted on days when school is not in session. Therefore, the above assessment is crude.

Table 17.1 Descriptive statistics

	Mean	Standard deviation	Standard error	95 % lower band	95 % upper band	Min.	Max.
2008-survey							
LEVEL	5.875	2.036	0.024	5.829	5.922	0	10
CHANGE	0.115	1.223	0.014	0.088	0.143	−3	3
INTEG	10.585	40.639	0.473	9.659	11.512	−151	347
DIFFERENCE	0.003	1.656	0.019	−0.035	0.041	−10	10
P_NEWS	0.544	2.297	0.027	0.492	0.597	−5	5
M_NEWS	−0.4	1.981	0.023	−0.445	−0.354	−5	5
SLEEP	2.645	0.984	0.011	2.622	2.667	1	4
HEALTH	2.737	0.813	0.009	2.718	2.756	1	4
NOANXIETY	2.021	0.952	0.011	1.999	2.043	1	4
NOCLASS	0.684	0.465	0.005	0.673	0.695	0	1
Number of observations	7,389						
2009-survey							
LEVEL	6.216	2.036	0.024	6.170	6.263	0	10
CHANGE	0.199	1.141	0.013	0.173	0.225	−3	3
INTEG	23.836	56.939	0.666	22.531	25.140	−167	476
DIFFERENCE	−0.003	1.573	0.018	−0.039	0.033	−9	10
P_NEWS	0.794	2.577	0.030	0.735	0.853	−5	5
M_NEWS	−0.064	2.068	0.024	−0.112	−0.017	−5	5
SLEEP	2.652	0.988	0.012	2.629	2.674	1	4
HEALTH	2.817	0.872	0.010	2.797	2.837	1	4
NOANXIETY	2.271	1.061	0.012	2.247	2.295	1	4
NOCLASS	0.580	0.494	0.006	0.569	0.591	0	1
Number of observations	7,319						

2.3 *Rewards*

Respondents were requested to connect to the webpage and to answer the questions every day. They were paid 160 yen per answer for the daily survey. Those who responded to the daily survey for over 22 days and those who answered the hourly survey more than once a month were paid 1,300 yen as a bonus for the month, and those who responded to the daily survey for over 27 days and answered the hourly survey received 2,600 yen as a monthly bonus.[11]

[11]In the web survey, respondents were also requested to report their hourly happiness on one day of their choice each month. We call this the hourly survey. The hourly survey essentially follows an experience sampling method (Csikszentmihalyi and Hunter 2003; Scollon et al. 2003), which is better than the day reconstruction method by Kahneman et al. (2004a, b), wherein respondents

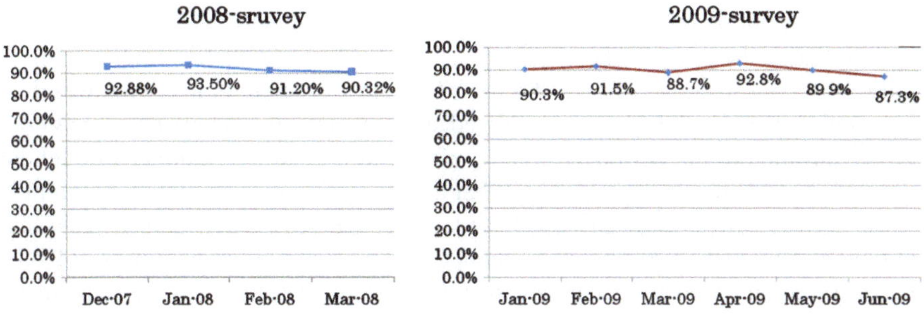

Fig. 17.1 Response rate

2.4 *Response Rate*

Figure 17.1 shows the response rate of the daily survey for each month. In both 2008- and 2009- surveys, the response rate is approximately 90 %.

3 Comparison Between the Level of Happiness and the Integrated Process of the Change in Happiness

3.1 *Comparison of the Averaged Data*

In this section, we check if the two series of happiness, *LEVEL* (Q1; level of happiness) and *CHANGE* (Q13; change in happiness) are consistent with each other. To this aim, we define the following two variables associated with *LEVEL* and *CHANGE*.

DIFFERENCE: the difference in LEVEL from the day before; and
INTEG: the sum of the *LEVEL* on the first day and *CHANGE* of the consecutive days until the current day

Table 17.1 presents the descriptive statistics of *INTEG* and *DIFFERENCE*. *INTEG* widely ranged from −151 to 347 in the 2008-survey and from −167 to 476 in the 2009-survey. *DIFFERENCE* was very small in both the surveys and was not statistically different from zero.

Aside from the scaling of *CHANGE* in its definition, by mathematical definition, *DIFFERENCE* and *CHANGE* (and therefore, *LEVEL* and *INTEG*) should follow the same series. In order to check if they are in fact the same, we calculate the average of

answer questions in real time, so that the responses are immune to memory biases. We do not explain the hourly survey in detail because we do not use the results in this chapter.

these four variables over respondents for each day. Specifically, we calculate *INTEG* by calculating the integrated process of each respondent, and then averaging them.[12] In Fig. 17.2, the averages of *LEVEL* and *INTEG* are presented for the two waves. It is apparent that although *LEVEL* is stabilized at a constant level in both phases, *INTEG* grows throughout the periods.[13] *INTEG* also shows growing volatility throughout the periods.[14] Thus, the figure reveals that the two series are completely different.

In Fig. 17.3, we show *CHANGE* and *DIFFERENCE*. The figure reveals that although *DIFFERENCE* is positive and negative with similar probability, *CHANGE* is more frequently positive than negative. In fact, the hypothesis of the same mean for *CHANGE* and *DIFFERENCE* is rejected at the 1 % level in both the waves. Although the mean of *CHANGE* is significantly positive, that of *DIFFERENCE* is not significantly different from zero (see Table 17.1).

3.2 Panel Unit Root Tests

Figure 17.2 gives us the impression that *LEVEL* is a stationary series, whereas *INTEG* is non-stationary. If this is the case, the two series are certainly different. In order to check this, we conduct panel unit root tests for the four series *LEVEL*, *INTEG*, *CHANGE*, and *DIFFERENCE* for the two waves.

Specifically, we employ pooled tests based on Fisher's type statistic, as defined in Choi (2001). Choi's (2001) test combines *P*-values from a unit root test applied to each individual under the null hypothesis that all cross-section units have a unit root, against the alternative that some of the panel units are stationary. Choi's (2001) test statistic, termed P_{N} statistic in this chapter, is as follows:

$$P_{\mathrm{N}} = \frac{1}{2\sqrt{N}}\sum_{i=1}^{N}\left(-2\ln p_{\mathrm{i}} - 2\right) \rightarrow \mathrm{N}\left(0,\ 1\right),\ \ as\ T \rightarrow \infty, N \rightarrow \infty, \qquad (17.1)$$

where p_{i} is the *P*-value associated with the unit root test statistic for individual *i*. We use two types of unit root tests: the Augmented Dickey-Fuller (ADF) test where the

[12]Alternatively, we can first average *CHANGE* over respondents each day and then construct an integrated process of these averages. *INTEG* constructed in this way is smoother than that in Fig. 17.2, and it does not show an increase in volatility. This is because averaging *CHANGE* over respondents makes the variance much smaller (i.e., the variance is denominated by the number of respondents). However, it increases with time as in Fig. 17.2, so that the essential conclusions are unaltered. See footnote 14.

[13]Comparing *INTEG* of the two phases, we found that the one in the 2009-survey grows more rapidly: in the 2008-survey, it reaches 20 in 4 months, whereas in the 2009-survey it reaches 40 in 6 months.

[14]This is because the disturbance term of the integrated process of an individual increases in proportion with time; therefore, its variance increases in the quadratic function of time.

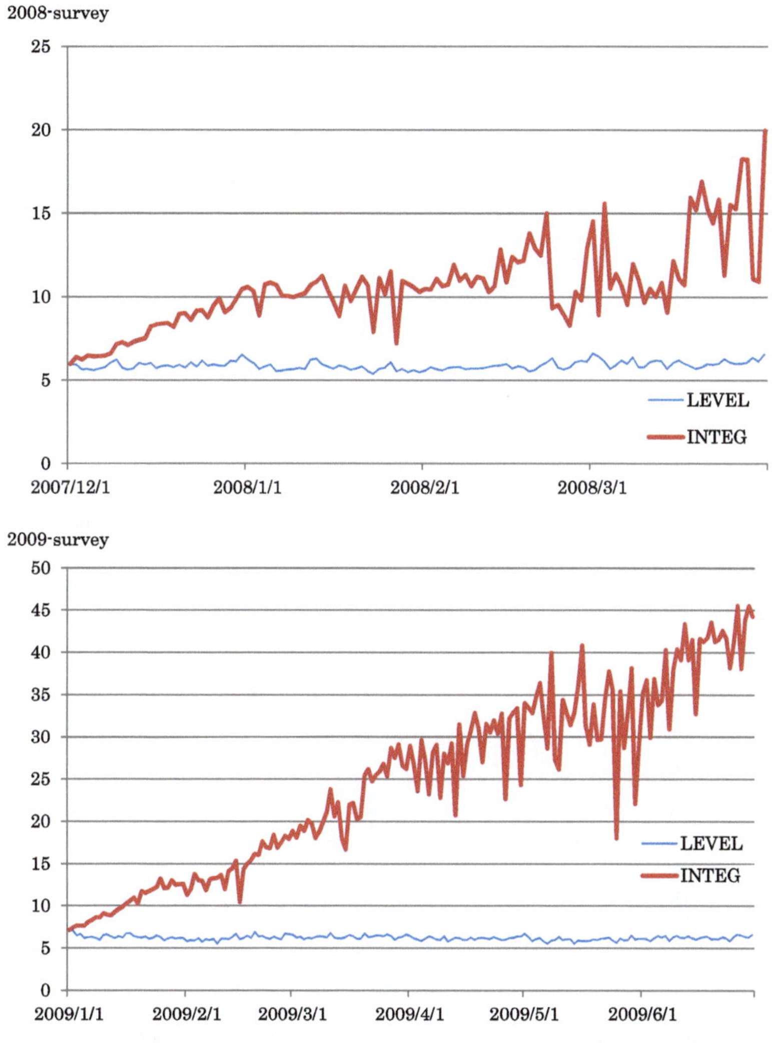

Fig. 17.2 *LEVEL* and *INTEG*

null hypothesis is a unit root (Dickey and Fuller 1979) and the Kwiatkowsk-Phillips-Schmidt-Shin (KPSS) test where the null hypothesis is stationarity (Kwiatkowski et al. 1992). Because the power of the tests of the unit root null is low in small samples, testing the stationarity null is indispensable. We examine two specifications: "with constant" and "with constant and time trend (*TREND*)."

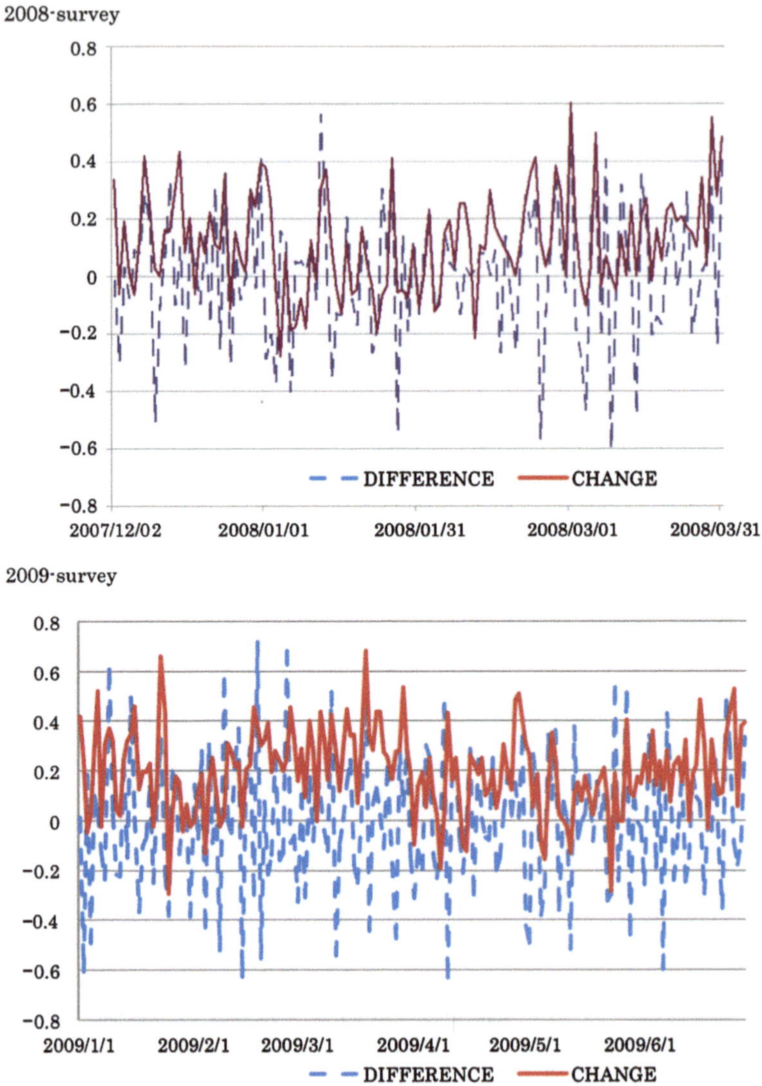

Fig. 17.3 *CHANGE* and *DIFFERENCE*

Table 17.2 presents the test results.[15] The upper panel shows the results of 2008-survey. In the two specifications, with or without TREND, the results are almost identical. As for *LEVEL*, *DIFFERENCE*, and *CHANGE*, the ADF test rejects the

[15]The number of lags of the lagged difference terms of the ADF test is selected according to Akaike information criterion (AIC) for each regression. The number of lags truncation in the KPSS tests is set at 12.

Table 17.2 Results of panel unit root tests

	without *TREND*				with *TREND*			
	ADF		KPSS		ADF		KPSS	
	P_N	*p* value	P_N	*p* value	P_N	*p* value	P_N	*p* value
2008-survey								
LEVEL	4.745	0.000	0.096	0.924	4.473	0.000	−0.867	0.386
INTEG	−0.675	0.500	10.513	0.000	0.545	0.586	10.513	0.000
CHANGE	4.745	0.000	−0.196	0.845	2.713	0.007	−0.617	0.537
DIFFERENCE	8.210	0.000	−0.928	0.354	8.210	0.000	−0.972	0.331
2009-survey								
LEVEL	8.210	0.000	−0.605	0.545	8.210	0.000	−0.299	0.765
INTEG	−0.249	0.804	10.513	0.000	0.310	0.757	10.513	0.000
CHANGE	8.210	0.000	−0.697	0.486	5.725	0.000	−0.876	0.381
DIFFERENCE	8.210	0.000	−1.000	0.317	8.210	0.000	−1.000	0.317

Note: P_N is a Fisher's statistic as defined in Choi (2001) based on a *P*-value of the individual augmented Dickey and Fuller (1979) of the null of a unit root and the individual Kwiatkowski et al. (1992) test of the null of no unit root. The lag length of the lagged difference terms to be added to the individual ADF test was selected according to Akaike information criterion (AIC) for each regression, and truncation lags in the KPSS test was set at 12. A Fisher's statistic P_N as defined in Choi (2001) has a N(0, 1) distribution under the null hypothesis

ADF Augmented Dickey–Fuller, *KPSS* Kwiatkowsk–Phillips–Schmidt–Shin

null of non-stationarity, and the KPSS test accepts the null of stationarity, suggesting that these series follow a stationary process. On the other hand, as for *INTEG*, the ADF test accepts the null of non-stationarity, and the KPSS test rejects the null of stationarity, suggesting that the series is non-stationary. The same results are obtained for the 2009-survey, and they are shown in the lower panel. Thus, the results unequivocally indicate that *INTEG* is non-stationary, whereas the other variables are stationary, implying that *LEVEL* and *INTEG* cannot be the same series.

As for *CHANGE* and *DIFFERENCE*, although both series are stationary, the mean of *CHANGE* is significantly positive, whereas that of *DIFFERENCE* is not significantly different from zero. In addition, their correlation coefficient is only 0.456 in 2008 and 0.417 in 2009. These results suggest that they are not the same series, even if they have some relationship.

In summary, the results of the unit root tests indicate that *LEVEL* and *INTEG* cannot be the same series. This also applies to *CHANGE* and *DIFFERENCE*.

4 Why Are the Two Series Different?

Mathematically, the results of the integrated process of *CHANGE* must be identical to the level itself. Thus, we need to question why the two series differ. We suggest and examine two possible reasons for this.

4.1 Asking About Happiness Within a Certain Range

The first possibility arises from the style of the question that investigates the level of happiness on a range from 0 (very unhappy) to 10 (very happy). Assume that the level of happiness is linearly increasing with time similarly to *INTEG*. In this case, respondents cannot report their actual level of happiness because the answer is limited by an upper bound of 10. Therefore, they may report their level of happiness by transforming the linear function to a function that is asymptotic to 10 and 0 as the level of original happiness goes to infinity and minus infinity, respectively. An example of such a function is the logistic function:

$$H = L + \frac{U - L}{1 + \exp\left(-r\tilde{H}\right)}, \tag{17.2}$$

where H is the reported level of happiness, $\tilde{H}$ is the original level of happiness, U and L are the upper and lower limits, respectively, and r is a parameter determining the slope of the function. By a simple calculation, we can recover $\tilde{H}$ from H with the inverse function of Eq. (17.2), which is called the logit function:

$$\tilde{H} = \frac{1}{r}\left(\ln\left(H - L\right) - \ln\left(U - H\right)\right). \tag{17.3}$$

Let us examine whether the recovered series $\tilde{H}$ using Eq. (17.3) resembles *INTEG*. Specifically, we set $U = 10$, $L = 0$, and $r = 0.1$, and first calculate $\tilde{H}$ for each respondent using Eq. (17.3) and then average them.[16] The recovered $\tilde{H}$ using the actual values of H is depicted in Fig. 17.4.[17] As shown in the figure, $\tilde{H}$ is a kind of enlarged figure of *LEVEL* in both waves, and does not increase with time as *INTEG* does.[18]

Thus, the supposition that asking about happiness in a certain range is the cause of the gap between *LEVEL* and *INTEG* is invalid. This result is consistent with our intuition, because *LEVEL* in Fig. 17.2 fluctuates around a constant level and does not show an increasing trend. A transformation using Eq. (17.3) simply extends the form; therefore, it cannot be expected that a constant series will be transformed into an increasing function.

However, one may argue that the transformation using Eq. (17.3) is biased because the extension of H is symmetrical around $H = 5$ in spite of the fact that the average of H is approximately 6. Therefore the region below $H = 6$ should be

[16]Here, r is chosen arbitrarily.

[17]Alternatively, we can use average H over respondents to calculate $\tilde{H}$ with Eq. (17.3). The results are similar to the graph in Fig. 17.4; thus, the calculated $\tilde{H}$ is not increasing and does not resemble *LEVEL* either.

[18]We also depict the case of $U = 7.5$, $L = 5.5$, and $r = 0.02$. The graph is extended more; however, it does not show an increasing trend.

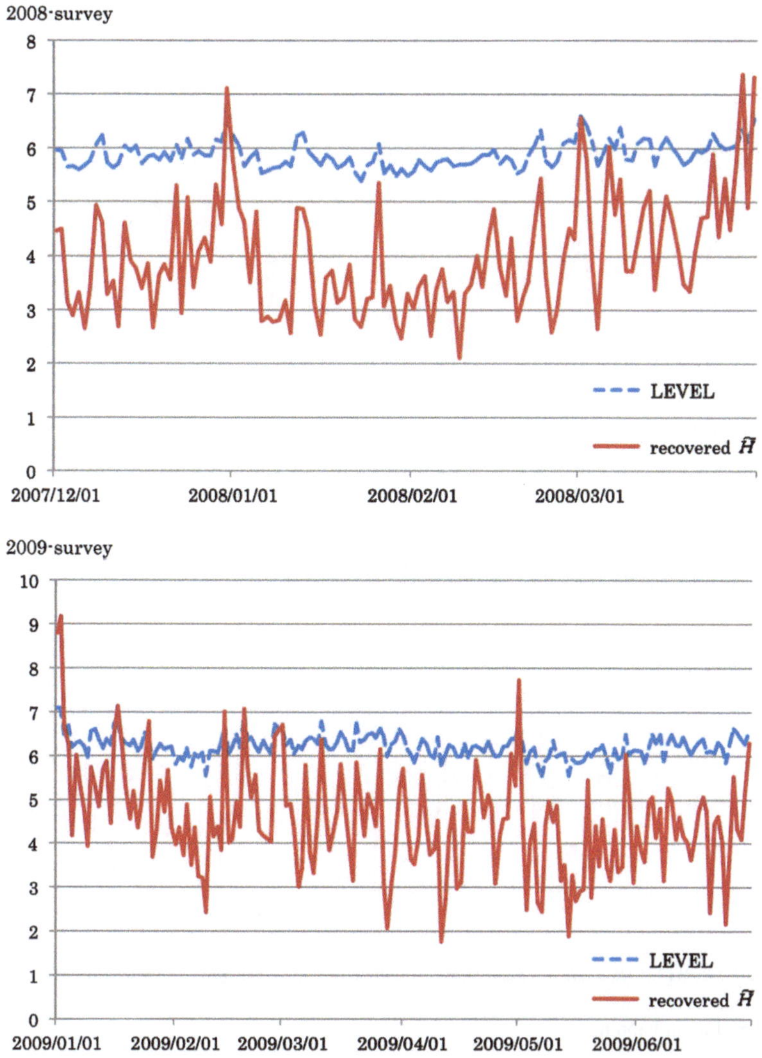

Fig. 17.4 Recovered $\tilde{H}$ using Eq. (17.3)

extended more intensively compared with the region above $H = 6$. If this is done, then the result may change. In order to address this concern, we estimate an ordered probit model of H in order to obtain the estimates of the cutoff values of 0 to 10. Then, we calculate the expected value of each class by fitting a standardized normal distribution to the actual frequencies falling in these classes. These estimates represent "standardized latent happiness," which corresponds to $\tilde{H}$ in Eq. (17.3).

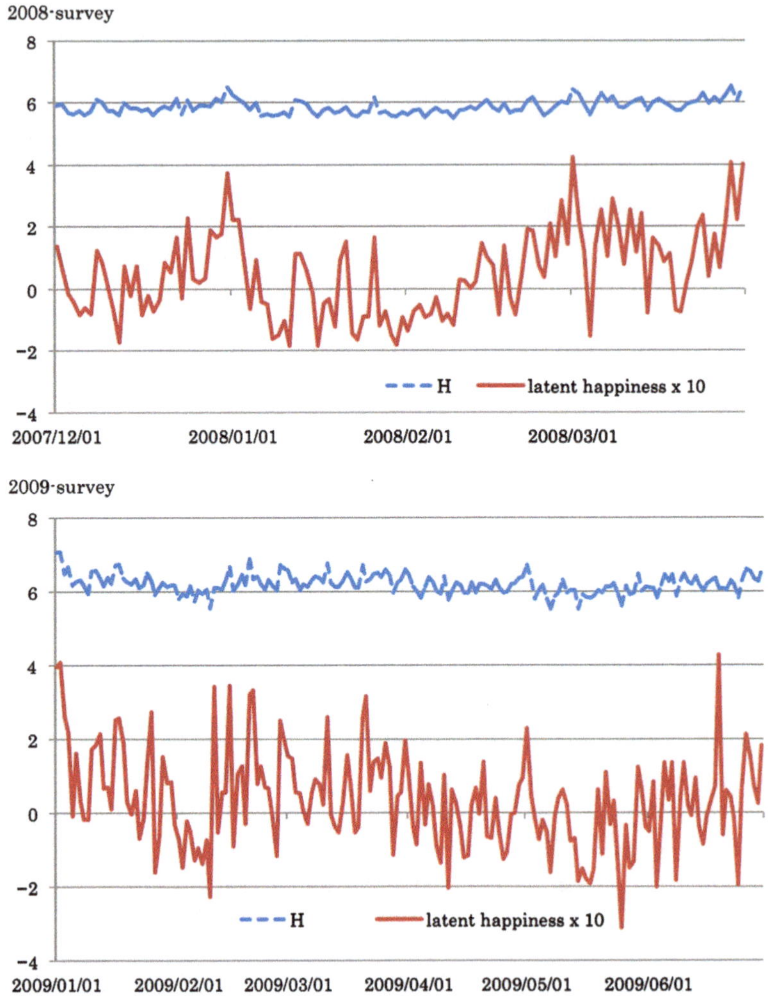

Fig. 17.5 Latent happiness

The latent happiness thus calculated is depicted in Fig. 17.5.[19] It is apparent from the figure that these estimates do not show an upward trend. Thus, the conclusion that asking about happiness in a certain range is not the cause of the difference is confirmed.

[19]In the figure, latent happiness is multiplied by 10 because the variation is too small to be observed otherwise.

4.2 Adaptation

The second possibility examined in this chapter is that although *LEVEL* (and therefore, *DIFFERENCE*) is affected by adaptation, *CHANGE* (and therefore *INTEG*) is not.

Although our respondents tend to become happier every day because of, for example, the receipt of good personal news, they may adapt themselves to the happier situation brought about by the good news and return to their original level of happiness in a few days. We speculate that *CHANGE* is less affected by adaptation than *DIFFERENCE*. In this subsection, we compare *CHANGE* and *DIFFERENCE*, rather than *INTEG* and *LEVEL*, because we conduct a regression analysis, which requires that the variables be stationary.

In our questionnaire, variables that may affect the respondents' happiness are *P_NEWS*, *M_NEWS*, *SLEEP*, *HEALTH*, *NOANXIETY*, and *NOCLASS*. We regress *CHANGE* and *DIFFERENCE* over these variables and their lagged variables and check whether the lagged variables have opposite effects on happiness to those of the current variables. If the lagged variables have opposite effects to those of the current ones, the effect of the current variables is cancelled, at least partially, in the consecutive periods (Clark et al. 2008). For the exposition, assume that happiness, *H*, depends on *P_NEWS* for four periods such that

$$H_t = \text{constant} + \alpha P_{NEWS_t} - \sum_{i=1}^{3} \beta_i P_{NEWS_{t-1}} + u_t, \quad \alpha, \beta_1 > 0. \tag{17.4}$$

Then, a one-unit increase in *P_NEWS* raises happiness by α units in the short-run (the current day); however, it raises happiness by only $\alpha - \sum_{i=1}^{3} \beta_i$ units in the long-run (3 days later). If our respondents adapt to the news, such a result will be obtained by the regression of Eq. (17.4).

Table 17.3 presents the results for 2008- and 2009-surveys estimated by random or fixed effect models.[20] Since the two results are essentially similar, we only explain the results for the 2009-survey (lower panel) in order to save space. The results are summarized in the following four points.

First, the coefficients of the current variables show the expected positive signs for most cases. In particular, *P_NEWS*, *HEALTH*, and *NOANXIETY* have large effects on happiness.

Second, regarding the current variables, the magnitudes of the estimates are similar for *CHANGE* and *DIFFERENCE* for all the variables except *SLEEP* and *NOCLASS*.

[20] We selected the model based on the Hausman test.

Table 17.3 Estimation results on adaptation hypothesis

	2008				2009			
	CHANGE		*DIFFERENCE*		*CHANGE*		*DIFFERENCE*	
	Fixed effect		Random effect		Random effect		Random effect	
Variable	Coefficient	P-value	Coefficient	P-value	Coefficient	P-value	Coefficient	P-value
P_NEWS	0.302	[.000]	0.404	[.000]	0.260	[.000]	0.295	[.000]
P_NEWS (−1)	−0.084	[.000]	−0.363	[.000]	−0.050	[.000]	−0.274	[.000]
P_NEWS (−2)	−0.039	[.000]	−0.033	[.000]	−0.023	[.000]	−0.019	[.015]
P_NEWS (−3)	−0.025	[.000]	−0.011	[.165]	−0.015	[.001]	−0.011	[.129]
M_NEWS	0.007	[.250]	0.050	[.000]	0.047	[.000]	0.045	[.000]
M_NEWS (−1)	−0.009	[.174]	−0.052	[.000]	−0.017	[.001]	−0.042	[.000]
M_NEWS (−2)	−0.011	[.091]	0.001	[.889]	0.004	[.405]	0.004	[.622]
M_NEWS (−3)	−0.020	[.002]	−0.001	[.918]	0.000	[.978]	−0.003	[.684]
SLEEP	0.000	[.999]	0.020	[.311]	0.036	[.001]	0.001	[.959]
SLEEP(−1)	−0.033	[.013]	−0.008	[.704]	0.011	[.351]	0.015	[.420]
SLEEP(−2)	0.011	[.418]	0.013	[.525]	−0.014	[.210]	−0.038	[.041]
SLEEP(−3)	0.005	[.680]	−0.027	[.162]	0.006	[.601]	0.024	[.182]
HEALTH	0.179	[.000]	0.206	[.000]	0.172	[.000]	0.174	[.000]
HEALTH (−1)	−0.047	[.011]	−0.165	[.000]	−0.048	[.006]	−0.176	[.000]
HEALTH (−2)	−0.035	[.061]	0.006	[.827]	−0.014	[.404]	0.008	[.773]
HEALTH (−3)	−0.038	[.037]	−0.053	[.046]	−0.012	[.466]	−0.003	[.923]
NOANXIETY	0.293	[.000]	0.187	[.000]	0.228	[.000]	0.288	[.000]
NOANXIETY (−1)	−0.087	[.000]	−0.166	[.000]	−0.059	[.000]	−0.301	[.000]
NOANXIETY (−2)	−0.020	[.284]	0.026	[.348]	−0.021	[.191]	0.043	[.106]
NOANXIETY (−3)	−0.064	[.000]	−0.039	[.142]	−0.052	[.001]	−0.036	[.163]
NOCLASS	0.078	[.004]	0.034	[.394]	0.055	[.016]	0.008	[.838]
NOCLASS (−1)	−0.035	[.227]	−0.093	[.034]	−0.038	[.119]	−0.076	[.061]
NOCLASS (−2)	−0.039	[.173]	−0.010	[.823]	−0.001	[.969]	0.059	[.145]
NOCLASS (−3)	−0.016	[.541]	0.030	[.459]	0.016	[.489]	−0.015	[.689]
constant			0.036	[.637]	−0.564	[.000]	0.018	[.812]
adjusted R^2	0.535		0.392		0.445		0.311	
Number of observations	7,249		7,249		7,211		7,211	
Hausman test		[.027]		[1.000]		[.532]		[1.000]

Third, focusing on the significant estimates, the estimates of the current variables and those of the lagged variables take the opposite signs for *P_NEWS*, *M_NEWS*, *HEALTH*, and *NOANXIETY*. These results imply that the long-run effect of these variables on happiness (*CHANGE* and *DIFFERENCE*) is smaller than their short-run effects, suggesting that the respondents adapt to the level of happiness brought about with these variables.

Fourth, the absolute values of the estimates of the significant lagged variables of *DIFFERENCE* are larger than those of *CHANGE* in all cases, suggesting that adaptation is larger for *DIFFERENCE* than for *CHANGE*.

The fourth fact, which is the most important fact for this chapter to determine, is the cause of the difference between *CHANGE* and *DIFFERENCE* (and thus between *LEVEL* and *INTEG*). In order to confirm the difference in the degree of adaptation between *CHANGE* and *DIFFERENCE*, we calculate the short-run effect, long-run effect, and adaptation ratio, which are defined as follows: the short-run effect is the coefficients of the current variables, the long-run effect is the sum of the significant coefficients of the current and lagged variables, and the adaptation ratio is defined as $\left(1 - \frac{\text{long-run effect}}{\text{short-run effect}}\right) \times 100\ (\%)$. We do not calculate them if the coefficient of the current variable is insignificant (i.e., if the short-run effect is zero).

Table 17.4 presents the results. The adaptation ratios are close to 100 % for all the variables for the case of *DIFFERENCE* for both waves, implying that none of the variables has any effect on happiness (*DIFFERENCE*, and therefore *LEVEL*) in the

Table 17.4 Adaptation ratio of *CHANGE* and *DIFFERENCE*

		2008		2009	
		CHANGE	*DIFFERENCE*	*CHANGE*	*DIFFERENCE*
P_NEWS	Short-run effect	0.302	0.404	0.260	0.295
	Long-run effect	0.153	−0.003	0.172	0.003
	Adaptation ratio (%)	49.3	100.8	34.1	99.1
M_NEWS	Short-run effect	0	0.050	0.047	0.045
	Long-run effect	NA	−0.003	0.030	0.003
	Adaptation ratio (%)	NA	105.2	36.0	93.2
SLEEP	Short-run effect	0	0	0.036	0
	Long-run effect	NA	NA	0.036	NA
	Adaptation ratio (%)	NA	NA	0.0	NA
HEALTH	Short-run effect	0.179	0.206	0.172	0.174
	Long-run effect	0.094	−0.012	0.125	−0.002
	Adaptation ratio (%)	47.6	105.7	27.6	101.1
ANXIETY	Short-run effect	0.293	0.187	0.228	0.288
	Long-run effect	0.143	0.021	0.117	−0.012
	Adaptation ratio (%)	51.4	88.8	48.6	104.2
NOCLASS	Short-run effect	0.078	0	0	0
	Long-run effect	0.078	NA	NA	NA
	Adaptation ratio (%)	0.0	NA	NA	NA

long-run. On the other hand, the adaptation ratios for *CHANGE* are approximately 50 % for the 2008-survey and approximately 30 % for 2009-survey, suggesting that adaptation is not perfect for *CHANGE*.

The results suggest that the reason that the mean of *DIFFERENCE* is not statistically different from zero and *LEVEL* fluctuates around a constant level is that the subjects fully adapt to the situation: although *DIFFERENCE* is significantly and largely affected by the current variables, the effect is cancelled in 3 days. In contrast, *CHANGE* also adapts to the situation; however, the adaptation is much weaker than that for *DIFFERENCE*. The difference in the magnitude of adaptation is the cause of the divergence between *LEVEL* and *INTEG*.

5 Discussion and Conclusions

In this chapter, we investigated whether the level of happiness and the integrated process of changes in happiness are the same process. We found that they follow different processes: although the level is stationary, the integration of changes is non-stationary with an apparent rising trend.

Despite the fact that mathematically, the integration of changes is the same as the level, why do these two variables diverge? We examined two possible reasons and found that *DIFFERENCE* is fully affected by adaptation, whereas *CHANGE* is partially affected by adaptation. Thus, in the long-run, the effects of various impacts on *DIFFERENCE* are completely cancelled in the following 3 days, whereas those on *CHANGE* are only partially cancelled. This is the reason why *INTEG*, which is the integration of *CHANGE*, and *LEVEL*, which is the integration of *DIFFERENCE*, diverge. Overall, the empirical outcomes are robust across the waves.

Our results have an important implication for the Easterlin paradox, which is the phenomenon that subjective happiness, which corresponds to *LEVEL* in this chapter, is stable irrespective of whether the standard of living (GDP) improves or deteriorates. The relative income hypothesis and adaptation hypothesis are known to offer effective explanations of the paradox (Clark et al. 2008; Knight and Song 2009), and they imply that if adaptation does not occur, the Easterlin paradox should, if not completely, partially disappear. Thus, our results suggest that if we ask about the change in happiness, *CHANGE*, and construct its integrated process, *INTEG*, then *INTEG* may not exhibit the Easterlin paradox. This inference is based on our results that adaptation affects *CHANGE* only partially, whereas it completely affects *DIFFERENCE*.

The relationship between subjective happiness and utility is not understood fully.[21] We believe, however, that an important distinction between the two is that decision utility is constructed from comparisons of two ex-ante states, whereas

[21] Kimball and Willis (2006) theoretically examined the relationship between them. Many economists think that comparison of subjective happiness among individuals lacks a solid basis,

subjective happiness is based on the introspection of the current feelings of an individual. Since utility is based on a comparison of ex-ante states, it should be free from adaptation. Thus, utility is expected to increase when the standard of living (GDP) improves.

In fact, in a survey conducted in Japan in 2008, we asked respondents whether they would have preferred to have been born in 1910, 1950, or 1980, and many selected the later period, suggesting that they preferred a higher standard of living when they compared the periods. We also asked Japanese respondents whether they would have preferred to have been born in Italy or Indonesia, and Singapore or Mexico. These two pairs of countries differ significantly with respect to GDP, but according to the World Value Survey, the average subjective happiness of the nations is almost the same. Most respondents chose Italy (84 %) and Singapore (68 %); both these countries enjoy higher GDPs.

The Easterlin paradox means that economic growth does not lead to an improvement in subjective happiness, which raises a question regarding the role of economic growth. However, our results suggest that *INTEG* (*CHANGE*) may be a closer concept to utility than *LEVEL* (*DIFFERENCE*) in that the former is freer from adaptation. This implies the possibility that the paradox will disappear if we measure subjective happiness by the sum of changes in happiness.

Let us examine the above speculation on the basis of our survey conducted in Japan from fiscal years 2003 to 2009. In the survey, we investigated the level of happiness (Q1) and the change in happiness compared with the level that existed a few years ago. From the former question, we defined *LEVEL* as the average of the answer. In the latter question, respondents were requested to select from the following options: 1. Happier than a few years ago, 2. Same as a few years ago, 3. Unhappier than a few years ago.[22] We defined *CHANGE* as two minus the answer to this question, which takes the value of 1, 0, or -1. We used the average of *CHANGE* over all respondents and calculate *INTEG* as before. Figure 17.6 presents the values of *LEVEL* and *INTEG* obtained subsequently. Although *LEVEL* is almost constant around 6.4, *INTEG* increases from 6.4 to 7.1, reflecting that *CHANGE* is positive for all the years. Thus, the result is essentially similar to those using the daily data in this chapter. In the figure, we also show "consumption of household," as a proxy for the standard of living, which seems to correspond more with *INTEG* than with *LEVEL*.[23] Indeed, its correlation coefficient is -0.22 with *LEVEL* and 0.74 with *INTEG*. These results suggest that the Easterlin paradox is seen between *LEVEL*

whereas researchers in the field of economics of happiness estimate the happiness function using data on subjective happiness.

[22]To be precise, "4. Do not know" is included in the options. In 2008 and 2009, the comparison is made with "a year ago" instead of "a few years ago."

[23]Here, "consumption of household" is normalized so that the value of the first year equals 6.38, that is, the value of *LEVEL* in that year.

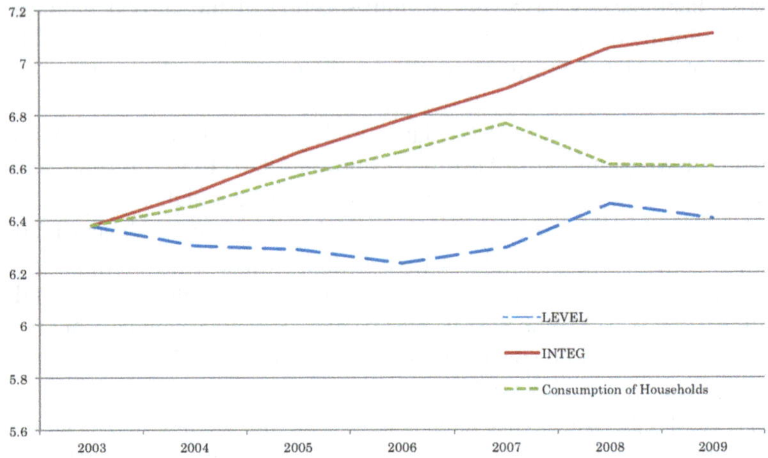

Fig. 17.6 The Easterlin paradox

and "consumption of household," but not between *INTEG* and "consumption of household."[24]

A problem of this analysis is that the data spans only 7 years. In order to obtain more reliable results, it is necessary to conduct a longitudinal survey that investigates the changes in happiness and examines if the integrated process of the change in happiness corresponds to the standard of living (GDP). This is an important subject for future research.

Acknowledgments We would like to extend our heartfelt gratitude to Masahiko Shibamoto and Frans van Winden for their comments and acknowledge financial support from the Global Center of Excellence (GCOE) program at Osaka University. This chapter was presented at Monetary Economics Workshop (MEW) and the 2011 Spring Meeting of the Japanese Economic Association.

Addendum: "Ladder of Life Question" from Gallop World Poll, and Easterlin Paradox[25]

The Easterlin Paradox implies that the average happiness level of a country remains constant over a long period. However, the paradox is sometimes demonstrated using scatterplots of various countries' GDP and average happiness. Figure 17.7 is an example. Among poor countries, higher income generally correlates with higher

[24]When we use GDP instead of consumption of household, its coefficient is −0.49 with *LEVEL* and 0.40 with *INTEG*.

[25]This addendum has been newly written for this book chapter.

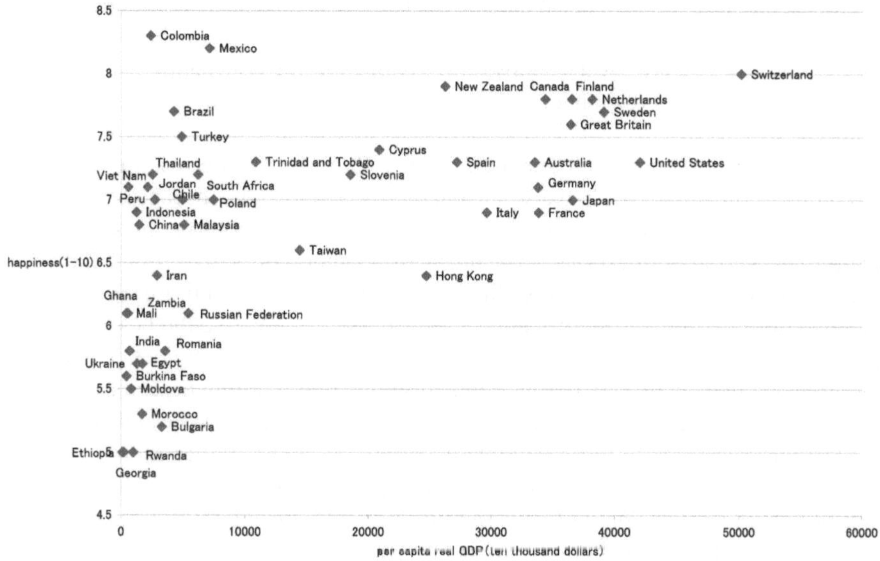

Fig. 17.7 Scatterplots of various countries' GDP and average happiness

happiness, while among wealthier countries, no clear relation between per capita income and happiness is recognized. In a word, the figure reveals that happiness becomes independent of income where income exceeds a certain level; this is the Easterlin Paradox.

However, in recent years, challenges to this paradox have appeared. For example, Deaton (2008) and Stevenson and Wolfers (2008), using the Gallop World Poll conducted in 2006 which investigated 132 countries, establish a clear positive link between average levels of subjective well-being and GDP per capita across countries, and find no evidence of a satiation point beyond which wealthier countries have no further increases in subjective well-being as income rises.[26]

Graham (2011) sums up the reasons why this result is obtained from the Gallop World Poll as follows: First, it is reasonable that wealthier people are happier, and in addition, freedom, stable employment and good health are easier to come by in wealthier countries. Second, later surveys, including the Gallop World Poll, include many more observations from small poor countries than do earlier surveys. Third, the Gallop World Poll uses Cantril's "ladder of life question," (or "Self-Anchoring Striving Scale"), which asks: "Here is a picture of a ladder. Suppose that we say the top of the ladder represents the best possible life for you and the bottom represents

---

[26]Stevenson and Wolfers (2008) derived the same conclusion based on several other surveys. However, Di Tella and MacCulloch (2010) still support the view that once basic needs have been satisfied, there is full adaptation to further economic growth, although that process may take a long period of time. Thus, the controversy is not settled yet.

the worst possible life for you. Where on the ladder do you feel you personally stand at the present time?" Comparing with usual question such as "In general, how happy would you say you are—very happy, fairly happy, or not very happy?" the "ladder of life question" asks respondents to make a relative comparison when they assess their lives.

What is important in this appendix is that Cantril's "ladder of life question" strengthens the relationship between happiness and income because it requires respondents to make a comparison. On this point, Deaton (2008) argues that when people answer such questions, they must assess their life satisfaction relative to some benchmark, such as their own life in the past, or the lives of those around them. He also offers a simpler interpretation: "When asked to imagine the best and worst possible lives for themselves, people use a global standard." Using data from Latin America, Graham et al. (2010) report that differences in framing these questions can have important effects on the measured relationship between income and happiness. "Questions that provide more tangible economic or status frames seem to have a closer relationship with income than do more open-ended questions." This result, as was argued in the text, suggests that the Easterlin Paradox emerges when questions are based on subjective happiness elicited by "overall questions"; once we introduce the element of "comparison" to the questions that measure happiness, happiness begins to correlate with income (standard of living).

References

Bruni L, Porta PL (2005) Economics and happiness: framing the analysis. Oxford University Press, New York

Choi I (2001) Unit root tests for panel data. J Int Money Financ 20(2):249–272

Clark AE, Oswald AJ (1996) Satisfaction and comparison income. J Public Econ 61(3):359–381

Clark AE, Frijters P, Shields MA (2008) Relative income, happiness, and utility: an explanation for the Easterlin paradox and other puzzles. J Econ Lit 46(1):95–144

Csikszentmihalyi M, Hunter J (2003) Happiness in everyday life: the uses of experience sampling. J Happiness Stud 4:185–199

Deaton A (2008) Income, health, and well-being around the world: evidence from the Gallup World Poll. J Econ Perspect 22(2):53–72

Di Tella R, MacCulloch R (2010) Happiness adaptation to income beyond "basic needs". In: Diener E, Helliwell J, Kahnemann D (eds) International differences in well-being. Oxford University Press, Oxford, pp 217–246, Chapter 8

Di Tella R, Haisken-DeNew J, MacCulloch RJ (2007) Happiness adaptation to income and to status in an individual panel, NBER working paper, no. 13159

Dickey DA, Fuller WA (1979) Distribution of the estimators for autoregressive time series with a unit root. J Am Stat Assoc 74(366):427–431

Dolan P, Peasgood T, White M (2008) Do we really know what makes us happy? A review of the economic literature on the factors associated with subjective well-being. J Econ Psychol 29(1):94–122

Duesenberry JS (1949) Income, savings, and the theory of consumer behaviour. Harvard University Press, Cambridge

Easterlin RA (1974) Does economic growth improve the human lot? Some empirical evidence. In: David PA, Reder MW (eds) Nations and households in economic growth: essays in Honor of Moses Abramowitz. Academic, New York, pp 89–125
Easterlin RA (2005) Building a better theory of well-being. In: Bruni L, Porta PL (eds) Economics and happiness. Oxford University Press, Oxford, pp 29–64
Frank RH (2005) Does absolute income matter? In: Bruni L, Porta PL (eds) Economics and happiness. Oxford University Press, Oxford, pp 65–90
Frey BS, Stutzer A (2002a) Happiness and economics. Princeton University Press, Princeton
Frey BS, Stutzer A (2002b) What can economists learn from happiness research? J Econ Lit 40(2):402–435
Graham C (2011) The pursuit of happiness. Brookings Institution Press, Washington, DC
Graham C, Chattopadhyay S, Picon M (2010) The Easterlin and other paradoxes: why both sides of the debate may be correct. In: Diener E, Helliwell J, Kahnemann D (eds) International differences in well-being. Oxford University Press, Oxford, pp 247–288, Chapter 9
Kahneman D, Krueger AB (2006) Developments in the measurement of subjective well-being. J Econ Perspect 20(1):3–24
Kahneman D, Krueger AB, Schkade D, Schwartz N, Stone AA (2004a) A survey method for characterizing daily life experience: the day reconstruction method. Science 306:1776–1780
Kahneman D, Krueger AB, Schkade D, Schwartz N, Stone AA (2004b) Toward National Well-Being Accounts. The American Economic Review 94(2): Papers and Proceedings: 429–439
Kimball M, Willis R (2006) Utility and happiness. mimeo
Knight J, Song L (2006) Subjective well-being and its determinants in rural China. China Econ Rev 20(4):635–649
Kwiatkowski D, Phillips PCB, Schmidt P, Shin Y (1992) Testing the null hypothesis of stationarity against the alternative of a unit root: how sure are we that economic time series have a unit root? J Econ 54(1–3):159–178
Scollon CN, Kim-Prieto C, Diener E (2003) Experience sampling: promises and pitfalls, strengths and weaknesses. J Happiness Stud 4:5–34
Stevenson B, Wolfers J (2008) Economic growth and subjective well-being: reassessing the Easterlin Paradox. Brookings Papers on Economic Activity, Spring 2008:1–102
Tsutsui Y, Ohtake F (2012) Asking about changes in happiness in a daily web survey and its implication for the Easterlin paradox. Jpn Econ Rev 63(1):38–56

Chapter 18
Welfare States and the Redistribution of Happiness

Hiroshi Ono and Kristen Schultz Lee

Abstract We use data from the 2002 International Social Survey Programme, with roughly 42,000 individuals nested within 29 countries, to examine the determinants of happiness in a comparative perspective. We hypothesize that social democratic welfare states redistribute happiness among policy-targeted demographic groups in these countries. The redistributive properties of the social democratic welfare states generate an alternate form of "happiness inequality" in which winners and losers are defined by marital status, presence of children and income. We apply multilevel modeling and focus on public social expenditures (as percentage of GDP) as proxy measures of state intervention at the macro-level, and happiness as the specific measure of welfare outcome at the micro-level. We find that aggregate happiness is not greater in the social democratic welfare states, but happiness closely reflects the redistribution of resources in these countries. Happiness is redistributed from low-risk to high-risk individuals. For example, women with small children are significantly happier, but single persons are significantly less happy in the welfare states. This suggests that pro-family ideology of the social democratic welfare states protects families from social risk and improves their well-being at the cost of single persons. Further, we find that the happiness gap between high versus low-income earners is considerably smaller in the social democratic welfare states, suggesting that happiness is redistributed from the privileged to the less privileged.

The original article first appeared in Social Forces 92(2):789–814, 2013. A newly written addendum has been added to this book chapter.

Hiroshi Ono co-authored this chapter while he was a faculty member at Texas A&M University, Department of Sociology.

H. Ono (✉)
Graduate School of International Corporate Strategy, Hitotsubashi University, Tokyo, Japan
e-mail: hono@ics.hit-u.ac.jp

K.S. Lee
Department of Sociology, The University at Buffalo, SUNY, Buffalo, NY, USA
e-mail: kslee4@buffalo.edu

S. Ikeda et al. (eds.), *Behavioral Economics of Preferences, Choices, and Happiness*, DOI 10.1007/978-4-431-55402-8_18

Keywords Happiness • Welfare states • Redistribution • Taxes • Family

1 Introduction

The extent to which the state and the market provide for the welfare of citizens has been the subject of great debate in political economy and in public policy. Esping-Andersen (1999) work on the "varieties of welfare capitalism" is a notable example of how modern capitalist societies can be categorized according to their contrasting positions regarding the roles of the state and the market. As happiness becomes vital in defining the nation's health and well-being, there is renewed interest in studying the association between happiness and the role of the state. While the goal of any society is to improve the welfare of its citizens, there is greater disagreement regarding how this can be achieved. Would individuals be happier if the state played an active role? Or should the pursuit of happiness be left to individual choice and market forces?

Against this backdrop, the concept of happiness becomes a pawn in the debates between competing ideologies, with political and economic systems pitted against each other. Indeed there is now a growing body of research that examines the "political economy of happiness" (see for example, Bjørnskov et al. 2007; Radcliff 2001; Rothstein 2010 and Veenhoven 2000). However, aside from the politics, international comparisons using rigorous analytical methods remain few.

In this chapter, we examine the determinants of happiness in an international context. We treat happiness as a measure of subjective well-being.[1] Following Veenhoven (1991), happiness is conceived here as one's overall appreciation of life, including both an affective and cognitive component. We argue that happiness is best understood as an individual-level outcome that is simultaneously shaped by larger social forces. At the macro-level, we are primarily interested in studying how the countries' welfare expenditures and taxes affect the happiness of their citizens. Is happiness greater in the social democratic welfare states? The pursuit for the "optimal level" of state or market intervention may be quantitatively and qualitatively difficult to assess. State intervention and welfare are both empirically vague notions that require more precise specifications. We focus on particular measures, mainly public social expenditures and tax revenue as share of GDP, as proxy measures of state intervention, and happiness as the specific measure of welfare outcome. The "happiness equation" would then have aggregate happiness on the left-hand side, and macro-level predictors on the right-hand side. Note, however, that this question by itself has a strictly macro-level orientation. Indeed, methodologically, one of the shortcomings of earlier studies that examine welfare capitalism and its outcomes is that they have been limited to the macro-level

[1]The other commonly used measure of subjective well-being is life satisfaction. Blanchflower and Oswald (2004) have shown that the form of the well-being equation is nearly identical whether one uses happiness or life satisfaction as the outcome variable.

(Esping-Andersen 1999). Underlying this macro formulation is the assumption that *all* persons, regardless of socioeconomic status or demographics, are made better off (or worse off) in the social democratic welfare states. This line of inquiry may be empirically interesting to the study of political economy, but sociologists are more keen on probing the macro-micro link (Coleman 1990), i.e. how do macro-level forces affect micro-level outcomes?

Our second question explores this interaction effect, specifically by asking: Who gains and who loses *within* the social democratic welfare states? The operations of the social democratic welfare states must be considered in conjunction with *both* distinguishable features – universalism and redistribution. The social democratic welfare states provide a universal safety net with comprehensive coverage of social risks. These countries achieve egalitarianism through the massive redistribution of income, and the transfer of resources from low risk to high risk groups. If happiness follows this path, then we may in fact observe a similar pattern whereby happiness is redistributed from the privileged to the less privileged. The beneficiaries of the social democratic welfare states gain at the cost of the benefactor.

At the micro-level, we focus especially on the institutions of family and marriage. According to Esping-Andersen (1999), social policy is the "public management of social risk" (p. 36). Under this framework, the family is a social institution that is exposed to higher risk, at least in comparison to non-family units such as single persons. Accordingly, the social democratic welfare states maintain a strong pro-family ideology, where considerable resources are allocated to improve the welfare and well-being of families. These countries also allow for flexible family forms whereby cohabiting persons receive similar (if not identical) benefits as do married persons. Our primary focus on the institutions of family and marriage thus allows us to better isolate the association between state intervention and happiness. We take advantage of hierarchically structured data with individuals nested within countries. We apply a multilevel modeling approach to reveal how macro-level forces affect the micro-level foundations of society.

2 Background

2.1 Happiness in Social Context: The Market Versus the State

The state can take a direct role in improving social welfare, through greater involvement and direct subsidies in the everyday lives of their citizens. Our analytical framework begins with the idea that countries can be mapped along a continuum of state's involvement in providing social welfare. The measure of our central interest is the public social expenditure (PSE), here defined as welfare expenditures as a percentage share of GDP, excluding education. We use PSE as a proxy measure which captures the extent of government's role in providing for the welfare of its citizens.[2] Our framework is a modification of Esping-Andersen (1990, 1999)'s welfare regime typology. While Esping-Andersen outlines welfare systems according to the role of market, state and family, we are primarily concerned with the distinction between market versus the state.

On one end of the continuum lies the market-based economies characterized by low PSE and low involvement by the state. These countries maintain "a political commitment to minimize the state, to individualize risks, and to promote market solutions" (Esping-Andersen 1999: 75). On the other end of this spectrum lies welfare capitalism characterized by high PSE and extensive involvement of the state. The extreme manifestation of this welfare state model is the social democratic welfare state. Denmark, Norway and Sweden are the notable countries that fall in this category. This Scandinavian Welfare Model is first and foremost identified by "unusually heavy social spending, benefits and services of high standards, and a high degree of government intervention" (Esping-Andersen and Korpi 1987: 42). It is also distinguished by its universalism and comprehensive provision of welfare services and transfers (Kangas and Palme 1993).

Welfare provision by the state is a form of social insurance, because it lays out a safety net that ensures a basic standard of living for their citizens, and protects their citizens from unforeseen events or social risk in general. The specifics of this involve such measures as government subsidized healthcare, generous and far-reaching family policies, and extensive care for the elderly. The social welfare programs help to reduce poverty, and the overall level of economic and social inequality (Kenworthy 1999; Korpi and Palme 1998; Lindbeck 1997), thereby creating the potential for greater social solidarity (Esping-Andersen 1990; Kenworthy 2004). For example, OECD (2008) data shows that the tax and transfer systems reduced income inequality by 45 % in Denmark, Sweden and Belgium, compared to 17 % in the U.S., and less than 8 % in South Korea.

The arrangement in the social democratic welfare states therefore contrasts greatly to that observed in other countries where the market plays a greater role in providing for benefits and services. Social insurance is replaced by private insurance, and many of the publicly provided services such as healthcare and childcare are replaced by market mechanisms (Esping-Andersen and Korpi 1987). The market-based system generates a more stratified society consisting of those who can afford such services versus those who cannot.

The other feature of the social democratic welfare states is its massive resource redistribution scheme. The state collects revenue through a combination of progressive income taxes, where the rich are taxed at higher rates compared to the poor,

[2] A common critique of using PSE as a proxy for the welfare state is that social expenditures may not adequately capture the state's commitment to welfare (Esping-Andersen and Korpi 1987; Pacek and Radcliff 2008). Indeed, Esping-Andersen (1999) and others have proposed alternative measures to approximate the quality of the welfare state. However, these alternative measures are usually limited in scope and coverage of countries. The utility of the PSE measure, in spite of its shortcomings, is that the data are available for all countries included in the ISSP dataset.

flat consumption taxes, flat social security taxes, and heavy taxation on addiction goods such as alcohol and tobacco (Lindert 2004; Steinmo 1989). Tax revenue is then returned in the form of social programs that are intended to benefit those that paid into the system. Ultimately, however, "there is a definitive redistributive element to all social spending" (Lindert 2004, p. 6). Income redistribution, and consequently income compression, is most extreme in the Scandinavian welfare states.

It should thus be emphasized that even within the social democratic welfare state, *some persons benefit more than do others.* As Esping-Andersen (1990) has noted, the distribution policy of the welfare states alters social relations, but the process itself can create an alternative system of stratification. Some types of social insurance benefit all citizens, but others are targeted specifically for families with small children. This pro-family policy is based on the view that families are exposed to greater social risk than are single persons. For example, in the case of healthcare, a single person may only be concerned with her own health. But a parent in a family of four must ensure that she is protected against the risk of illness not only for herself, but also for her spouse and two children.

In many of the European countries, non-marital cohabitation is now institutionalized; it is considered to be a socially acceptable alternative family form (Märtinson 2007; Soons and Kalmijn 2009). The state does not discriminate between married persons and cohabiting persons in determining the eligibility of social benefits, and in the level of their benefits. The inclusion of cohabiters in social benefits is both the consequence and the driving force for greater social acceptance of cohabitation as a legally-recognized alternative to marriage.

Universal welfare can only be sustained through high taxes. Indeed the citizens of the Scandinavian welfare states benefit from the most generous level of social insurance, but they also pay the highest taxes in the world in terms of both average and marginal taxes (OECD 2009b). The rich are taxed heavily to subsidize the poor. Hence, while the benefits of the welfare states are many, so are the costs associated with this system. The effect of the welfare provision on happiness must be evaluated in light of its costs and benefits.

Social democratic welfare states encourage family formation through non-discriminatory treatment of cohabitation, and their strong support for families with small children. Consequently, it can be argued that the pro-family bias leads to a less generous treatment of those without children, particularly of single persons. In terms of costs, single people on average pay *higher* personal income tax and contributions to social security (as percentage of gross wage earnings) than do married persons (OECD 2009b).[3] While single persons do benefit from some forms of social insurance such as sick leave, unemployment, healthcare, and old age assistance, they obviously do not qualify for the benefits that are targeted for families with children. Hence, in this regard, the social democratic welfare state is partial

[3]This is based on OECD's comparison between single persons with no children, and married one earner couples with two children.

to families, and single persons bear the costs of the pro-family policy. From the perspective of costs, benefits and incentives, the social democratic welfare states' pro-family policy is one that encourages their citizens to have children.

2.2 Happiness at the Individual Level

Much of the previous research on happiness has focused on the demographic and socioeconomic characteristics associated with greater happiness. Scholars have argued that general well-being reflects a composite of satisfaction in different life domains such as work, family, and housing (Campbell et al. 1976). There is an overall positive association between income and happiness within countries (Blanchflower and Oswald 2004; Clark and Oswald 1996; Easterlin 2001; Schyns 2002). Past research has explored variations in happiness over the life span (Rodgers 1982). Recent work in this area finds that there is an overall increase in happiness with age (Yang 2008) and that family, income, and health, become increasingly important in explaining happiness with age (Margolis and Myrskylä 2013). Overall, women report greater life happiness than do men (e.g. Aldous and Ganey 1999).

An extensive literature documents the relationship between marriage and general happiness (see for example, Nock 1995; Waite and Gallagher 2000), and confirms first and foremost the positive effects of marriage relative to being single. Married individuals are also found to be happier than cohabiters (Stack and Eshleman 1998; Waite and Gallagher 2000), although the happiness gap between married and cohabiting individuals varies depending on the social context, such as the religious and gender climate (Lee and Ono 2012). Several different explanations for the happiness gap between married and cohabiting individuals have been proposed: the relatively weaker bond between cohabiters (Waite and Gallagher 2000), the protective effects of being married which include social and financial support as well as greater health (Skinner et al. 2002; Stack and Eshleman 1998), the incomplete institutionalization of cohabitation, the relatively weaker social support received by cohabiters (Nock 1995; Skinner et al. 2002), as well as to the selection effects into marriage (Stack and Eshleman 1998). Overall, most research has attributed the relationship between marriage and happiness to the protective effects of marriage (Skinner et al. 2002; Stack and Eshleman 1998) or to a combination of protection and selection effects (Nock 1995), rather than to selection effects alone.

Although the relationship between children and well-being varies depending on the timing of childbirth, the age of the child, social class, parent gender, and marital status among other factors (Umberson et al. 2010), the overall consensus is that parents of minor co-resident children report poorer life satisfaction than childless persons (McLanahan and Adams 1987; Simon 2008). Working mothers in particular experience lower levels of well-being associated with parenting because of their greater involvement in child care, compared to fathers (Nomaguchi et al. 2005).

What has been given less attention in the literature, however, is the role played by the social-institutional context in shaping the happiness of individuals and families.[4] Such an approach is particularly important when we examine happiness across a wide spectrum of countries.

2.3 *Macro-micro Interaction*

While some scholars contend that happiness is greater in the social democratic welfare states (Pacek and Radcliff 2008; Radcliff 2001), others argue that there is no clear link (Bjørnskov et al. 2007; Veenhoven 2000). These contrasting views stem in part from differences in methodologies employed. We argue that aggregate measures of happiness at the country-level in and by themselves are not informative from the perspective of welfare and distribution policies. Aggregate rankings of happiness assume that all demographic groups report the same level of happiness and thus fail to capture the social mechanisms that relate macro-level forces to happiness at the micro-level.[5] To take one example, suppose we observe that families with small children are happier compared to their counterparts in the (benchmark) market-based economies. This positive association may not be the same across countries, but greater in the social democratic welfare states because they offer extensive benefits for family support. The institutional support provided by the social democratic welfare states may compensate for the burden of parenting, which may lead to greater happiness for families in the social democratic welfare states in comparison to the market-based economies. In fact, recent research has found cross-national differences in the association between parenthood and happiness (Margolis and Myrskylä 2011).

The effects of public social expenditures on happiness may not be symmetrical between men and women. Cross-national research has in fact shown how macro-level forces can affect the happiness of men and women in different ways. For example, Bjørnskov et al. (2007)'s more nuanced empirical analysis of government size on life satisfaction shows that women benefit more in countries with greater government consumption compared to men in these countries. Societal factors such as traditional gender beliefs can also lead to a happiness gap between men and women (Lee and Ono 2012).

To the extent that women of all countries take on a disproportionate share of raising children, women may benefit more from the pro-family policies of the social democratic welfare states than do men. As Esping-Andersen (1999) explains, "the

[4]Exceptions include Diener et al. (2000a), Soons and Kalmijn (2009), and Stack and Eshleman (1998) who examine happiness among cohabiters and married couples cross-nationally, and Margolis and Myrskylä (2011) who study how happiness varies across countries depending on the family support system.

[5]We acknowledge that there are cross-cultural variations in subjective well-being. The positivity score as described by Diener et al. (2000b) may be one method to address these variations.

Nordic welfare state remains the only ones where social policy is explicitly designed to maximize women's economic independence" (p. 45). The institutionalization of cohabitation in the European countries can also be viewed as a movement towards greater female autonomy in these countries (Märtinson 2007).

In sum, we expect to find a pattern of "happiness redistribution" in the social democratic welfare states which mirrors the pattern of resource redistribution in these countries. Happiness is redistributed from low risk to high risk persons, and from privileged to less privileged persons. We examine these redistributive effects in the areas of family, marriage, and income.

3 Hypotheses

We use public social expenditures (PSE) as a proxy measure that captures the degree of state intervention in social welfare. PSE distinguishes the market-based economies (our benchmark) from the social democratic welfare states. We employ multilevel models and specify macro-micro interactions with PSE and individual-level covariates in order to capture the extent to which state intervention affects individual happiness.

In addressing our first research question about differences in happiness across countries, we do not expect aggregate happiness to vary by level of public social expenditures. Instead, in response to our second research question, we expect that public social expenditures will be associated with the redistribution of happiness *within* countries. This redistribution will create an alternate form of "happiness inequality" with different winners and losers within the high PSE countries.

First, in line with the social democratic welfare states' pro-family ideology, we expect redistribution to be most evidently observed among the institutions of family and marriage. We expect cohabiters and parents to be relatively happier in high PSE countries. And second, income redistribution in the social democratic welfare states is achieved through taxation, and by transferring money from high-income earners to low-income earners. We expect happiness redistribution in the social democratic welfare states to occur in the same direction as income redistribution. Mirroring the largely compressed distribution of income in these countries, we expect the happiness gap between the rich and the poor to be smaller in the social democratic welfare states.

4 Data and Methods

We analyze data from the 2002 International Social Survey Program's (ISSP) "Family and Changing Gender Roles" module.[6] These data allow us to examine the family characteristics related to happiness in nationally representative samples

[6]The data used here were made available by the Zentralarchiv fuer Empirische Sozialforschung. Data were collected by independent institutions in each country as documented in ISSP (2004).

Table 18.1 Descriptive statistics by country

	Public social expenditures (PSE) as % of GDP[a]	Tax revenue as % of GDP[b]	Happiness[c]	
			Mean	S.D.
Australia	17.3	30.5	5.38	(0.92)
Austria	26.0	43.4	5.55	(0.93)
Belgium	24.7	46.8	5.20	(0.90)
Brazil	16.2	38.8	5.42	(0.89)
Chile	11.2	17.1	5.54	(1.02)
Cyprus	21.8	36.6	5.29	(1.08)
Czech Republic	19.5	36.3	5.03	(0.99)
Denmark	29.2	50.0	5.34	(0.96)
Finland	24.2	43.6	5.24	(0.96)
France	28.5	46.1	5.25	(0.95)
Germany East	27.4	40.6	5.03	(0.91)
Germany West	27.4	40.6	5.16	(0.85)
Hungary	20.1	37.3	5.04	(1.11)
Israel	20.0	36.8	5.34	(1.10)
Latvia	8.6	30.4	4.85	(0.97)
Mexico	4.3	9.7	5.58	(1.06)
New Zealand	18.1	36.5	5.48	(0.96)
Norway	21.3	43.6	5.30	(0.92)
Philippines	4.7	14.4	5.41	(1.25)
Poland	20.5	33.8	4.97	(1.03)
Portugal	18.9	37.0	5.19	(1.06)
Russia	10.0	36.9	4.87	(1.14)
Slovak Republic	15.7	29.5	4.88	(1.05)
Spain	19.6	37.3	5.26	(0.89)
Sweden	29.8	49.7	5.24	(0.97)
Switzerland	17.5	30.1	5.52	(0.77)
Taiwan	5.7	12.4	5.19	(1.10)
U.K.	21.8	39.0	5.42	(1.00)
USA	14.5	28.2	5.52	(0.96)

[a]Source: OECD (2009a and various years)
[b]Source: Index of Economic Freedom, Heritage Foundation, 2002
[c]The data are country averages aggregated from the 2002 ISSP data

of the adult population in 29 countries in different geographic regions and stages of economic development. These countries are listed in Table 18.1.

In all of our analyses, we exclude respondents over the age of 75 in order to minimize the heterogeneity resulting from old age, attributable to mortality, declines in physical health, and retirement and also to create consistent age ranges across

Neither the original data collectors nor the Zentralarchiv bear any responsibility for the analyses or conclusions presented here.

countries. We chose 75 as the maximum age in order to achieve consistency across countries (Finland did not include respondents over the age of 74 and Latvia over the age of 75 in their samples) and on the basis of a sensitivity analysis in which we tested our models with different age cutoffs (at age 55, 65, and 75). Results of these additional tests confirmed that our analysis is robust to different specification of age limits and only 4.5 % of the total sample is lost through this age restriction. We also removed respondents under the age of 18 from the analysis (an additional 0.6 % of the original sample) because the legal age of marriage is 18 and above in all of the countries that we consider here. In addition, only three countries in our sample included respondents under the age of 18. The final sample size for our analysis is 42,187 respondents.

The ISSP has broader geographic coverage than do other datasets, e.g. the European Social Survey. In comparison to some cross-national studies that may focus exclusively on advanced economies of the world, the ISSP includes a wide range of countries with regard to GDP, PSE, and other macro-level indicators, which allows us to capture variations in these measures across countries. However, there is an overall underrepresentation of developing countries in the ISSP, and this may be a shortcoming of the dataset.

4.1 Individual-Level Variables

The dependent variable in all equations is the respondent's report of their general life happiness. Respondents were asked: "If you were to consider your life in general, how happy or unhappy would you say you are, on the whole?" Responses range from *1 = completely unhappy* to *7 = completely happy.* Country-level means of self-reported happiness are presented in Table 18.1. Individual-level covariates include the respondent's gender (*1 = female*), presence of children under 18 in the home (*1 = present*), and marital status (mutually exclusive dummy variables for married, single, cohabiting, divorced/separated, and widowed). Depending on the model, one marital status dummy variable is excluded from the analysis to serve as the reference category. Standard control variables for the respondent's age, age-squared, employment status (*1 = full-time employment*), and educational attainment (*1 = has completed a college degree or more*) are also included in the analysis.

We control for individual income. Because income varies considerably across countries in both absolute and relative terms, income is generally not comparable between countries. We follow the convention used by Ruiter and van Tubergen (2009) among others, and estimated Z-scores of individual incomes per country. We imputed missing income cases on the basis of other attributes included in the equations. These income measures should thus be interpreted as relative (and not absolute) income. They capture income differences within countries, but not across countries.

4.2 Country-Level Variables

Table 18.1 shows descriptive statistics of key indicators by country. Public social expenditures (PSE) is the percentage share of GDP spent on welfare excluding education (source: OECD various years).[7] "Tax" is tax revenue as percentage of GDP (source: Index of Economic Freedom, Heritage Foundation 2002). And "happiness" is the mean value of happiness assigned to the country aggregated from the individual-level variables.

We include PSE as a proxy for the extent of welfare spending by country. Depending on the analysis involved, we also examine how taxes (at the country-level) affect people's happiness. Because the two are highly correlated, we include one or the other in our models, and not both.

We designate East Europe as the control variable that will be used consistently across all models. Eastern Europe is coded one if the country belongs to the former Soviet bloc and zero otherwise. There are several reasons for using East Europe as our country-level covariate. First, preliminary tests revealed that East Europe has the strongest (negative) correlation with happiness among other country-level variables tested, e.g. log GDP, and Gini index of inequality.[8] This negative correlation is consistent with previous empirical findings (e.g. Bjørnskov et al. (2007), Deaton (2008) and Guriev and Zhuravskaya (2009)). Including Eastern Europe significantly improves the fit of our model estimations. Second, East Europe is uncorrelated with PSE which allows us to avoid problems of collinearity between the country-level variables. And third, we take advantage of the fact that East Europe is negatively associated with GDP per capita, and use this as one measure to control for macroeconomic performance.

4.3 Multilevel Models

Multilevel models (estimated using HLM software) are used to address the non-independence of observations from the same country (Raudenbush and Bryk 2002). When such clustering is ignored, the standard errors of the parameters tend to be underestimated (Guo and Zhao 2000). We estimate 2-level ordered logistic regression models, predicting general happiness. The Level-1(individual-level) ordinal logistic regression model is as follows:

[7]We used data from the OECD Factbook 2002 to match the year of the ISSP data (which was conducted in 2002). We referred to other years (2000–2006) of the OECD Factbook and OECD Social Expenditure Database for countries that were not included in the 2002 edition.

[8]Lower happiness in Eastern Europe and transition economies is a consistent finding in empirical research. See for example, Deaton (2008) and Guriev and Zhuravskaya (2009).

$$\log\left(\frac{\varphi_{mij}}{1-\varphi_{mij}}\right) = \beta_{0j} + \sum_{q=1}^{Q}\beta_{qj}X_{q1j} + \sum_{m=2}^{M}\delta_m \tag{18.1}$$

where ϕ_{mij} is the probability that respondent i in country j is at or above response option m in their response to the question of how happy they are with their life in general. β_{0j} is the intercept for country j and β_{qj} is the coefficient for independent variable q in country j. δ_m is a threshold that separates categories m – 1 and m.

The Level-2 (country-level) equations model the intercept (Eq. 18.2a) and the slopes of female (Eq. 18.2b), cohabiting (Eq. 18.2c), married (or single in the case of Table 18.2, Model 2; Eq. 18.2d), and children under 18 in the home (Eq. 18.2e) as randomly varying across countries. Although cross-level interaction terms are included with some of the other individual-level variables, the error terms of all other independent variables are modeled as fixed across countries unless otherwise noted. We followed a "step-up" strategy as described by Raudenbush and Bryk (2002) in building our models. We started by treating the level-1 variables of greatest theoretical importance as random. When we added additional random coefficients beyond these key variables, data sparseness led to problems with model convergence. In this way, we made modeling decisions by considering both theory and data constraints. For example, in the case of Model 1 in Table 18.2, we have the following set of Level-2 equations with random error terms:

$$\beta_{0j} = \gamma_{00} + \gamma_{01}(E.\ Europe)_j + \gamma_{02}(PSE)_j + u_{0j} \tag{18.2a}$$

$$Female:\quad \beta_{1j} = \gamma_{10} + \gamma_{11}(PSE)_j + u_{1j} \tag{18.2b}$$

$$Cohabiting:\quad \beta_{2j} = \gamma_{20} + \gamma_{21}(PSE)_j + u_{2j} \tag{18.2c}$$

$$Married:\quad \beta_{3j} = \gamma_{30} + \gamma_{31}(PSE)_j + u_{3j} \tag{18.2d}$$

$$Children\ under\ 18:\quad \beta_{4j} = \gamma_{40} + \gamma_{41}(PSE)_j + u_{4j} \tag{18.2e}$$

The coefficient for country-level PSE in Eq. 18.2b (γ_{11}) indicates the interaction of PSE and gender (female). Similarly in Eqs. 18.2c, 18.2d and 18.2e the coefficient for PSE indicates the interaction of PSE with cohabiting (γ_{21}), being married (γ_{31}), and having children under 18 (γ_{41}), respectively. All variables in the equations are grand mean centered unless noted otherwise.

The performance of the multilevel models may be sensitive to outliers if the level-2 random effects do not share a multivariate normal distribution. We conducted diagnostic tests to check the normality assumption of level-2 random effects following the procedures outlined in Raudenbush and Bryk (2002). These robustness checks revealed that our hypothesis tests and confidence intervals for the fixed effects coefficients are not sensitive to outliers and influential observations.

Table 18.2 Ordered logit regression models predicting general happiness

	(1)	(2)
Country-level variables		
Intercept	−2.428*** (0.109)	−2.423*** (0.057)
East Europe	−0.805*** (0.108)	−0.786*** (0.124)
Public social expenditures (PSE) as % of GDP	−0.013 (0.009)	−0.013 (0.008)
Individual-level variables		
Female	0.009 (0.039)	0.026 (0.041)
Female X Country-level PSE	0.102 (0.005)	0.009 (0.006)
Cohabiting	0.627*** (0.057)	−0.340*** (0.048)
Cohabit X Country-level PSE	0.042*** (0.008)	0.027** (0.008)
Married	0.991*** (0.051)	
Married X Country-level PSE	0.020*** (0.004)	
Divorced/Separated		−1.139*** (0.081)
Widowed		−0.989*** (0.094)
Single		−0.874*** (0.063)
Single X Country-level PSE		−0.010* (0.005)
Child under 18 in the home	−0.022 (0.024)	0.0001 (0.024)
Child X Country-level PSE	0.007 (0.003)	0.010* (0.004)
Age	−0.108*** (0.010)	−0.100*** (0.010)
Age square	0.001*** (0.0001)	0.001*** (0.0001)
College education	0.154** (0.052)	0.151** (0.051)
Full-time employment	0.055 (0.032)	0.060 (0.032)
Income Z score	0.109*** (0.013)	0.112*** (0.012)

(continued)

Table 18.2 (continued)

	(1)	(2)
Threshold levels (δ)		
δ_2	1.991*** (0.131)	1.991*** (0.131)
δ_3	4.066*** (0.132)	4.065*** (0.132)
δ_4	5.646*** (0.141)	5.646*** (0.142)
δ_5	7.038*** (0.190)	7.039*** (0.190)
δ_6	8.541*** (0.263)	8.542*** (0.263)
Variance components		
Intercept	0.086***	0.086***
Female	0.036***	0.035***
Child under 18	0.014**	0.020***
Cohabit	0.039**	0.023*
Married	0.018***	
Single		0.020**

*$p < .05$; **$p < .01$; ***$p < .001$ (two-tailed tests). Robust standard errors in parentheses

4.4 Modeling Income and Happiness

We hypothesize that the happiness gap between the rich and the poor will be smaller in the social democratic welfare states. We model the relationship between income and happiness, and the intervening role of PSE and taxes. Most countries employ progressive taxation, with high-income earners facing higher marginal tax rates than do low-income earners. Marginal tax rates are generally higher in the Scandinavian welfare states (OECD 2009b), as previously discussed. The mechanism of redistribution, where money income is transferred from the rich to the poor, has an equalizing effect where the after-tax income of the rich and the poor is compressed. If money and happiness are closely linked, then the happiness gained from money income may be smaller in high-PSE/ high-taxed countries, because the income distribution will be more compressed in these countries. This can be shown as follows.

Let happiness (U) be a function of income (I) and taxes (T) such that:

$$U = f\,(I, T) \tag{18.3}$$

The change in happiness from a change in income (dU/dI) is the marginal utility of income. With taxes in the equation, the marginal utility of income can be expressed as the total derivative:

$$\frac{dU}{dI} = \underset{(-)}{\frac{\partial U}{\partial T}} \cdot \underset{(+)}{\frac{dT}{dI}} + \underset{(+)}{\frac{\partial U}{\partial I}} \tag{18.4}$$

Here, dT/dI is the marginal tax rate which is always positive. $\partial U/\partial T$, the pure effect of taxes on happiness, is negative because people prefer lower (rather than higher) taxes. Finally, $\partial U/\partial I$, the pure effect of income on happiness, is positive since higher income is associated with higher happiness.

Equation (18.4) thus leads to several predictions. First, dU/dI is *always lower* in countries with high (versus low) marginal tax rates. Since Scandinavian countries have the highest marginal tax rates in the world, Eq. (18.4) would predict that dU/dI in Scandinavia is smaller compared to other countries. Note that this condition holds true even if $\partial U/\partial I = 0$. Second, if the indirect effect $\left(\frac{\partial U}{\partial T} \cdot \frac{dT}{dI}\right)$ was sufficiently negative, then this may offset the positive effect of $\partial U/\partial I$, in which case the total effect of income on happiness (dU/dI) may be zero or even negative. And third, under an unlikely scenario, there may be no taxes, or all citizens face the same lump sum tax regardless of income level. In this case, $dT/dI = 0$ and Eq. (18.4) would collapse, such that $dU/dI = \partial U/\partial I$. The effect of taxes on happiness can be disregarded, and dU/dI would be the same in all countries.

Empirically, happiness as a function of income (I) is:

$$Y_{ij} = \beta_{0j} + \beta_{1j} I_{ij} + r_{ij} \tag{18.5}$$

where r_{ij} is the observation- and group-specific residual. If we allow the intercept (β_0) and coefficient (β_1) to vary by country-level TAX, we get:

$$\beta_{0j} = \gamma_{00} + \gamma_{01} TAX_j + u_{0j} \tag{18.6a}$$

$$\beta_{1j} = \gamma_{10} + \gamma_{11} TAX_j + u_{1j} \tag{18.6b}$$

where the u's are the residual terms. Combining Eqs. (18.5) and (18.6), we get:

$$Y_{ij} = \left(\gamma_{00} + \gamma_{10} I_{ij} + \gamma_{01} TAX_j + \gamma_{11} I_{ij} TAX_j\right) + \left(u_{0j} + u_{1j} I_{ij} + r_{ij}\right) \tag{18.7}$$

The expected value of happiness (U) is then:

$$U_{ij} = \left(\gamma_{00} + \gamma_{01} TAX_j\right) + \left(\gamma_{10} + \gamma_{11} TAX_j\right) I_{ij} \tag{18.8}$$

The marginal utility of income is the change in happiness from a change in income:

$$dU/dI = \gamma_{10} + \gamma_{11} TAX_j \tag{18.9}$$

where γ_{10} is the main effect of income on happiness. γ_{11} is the indirect effect manifested through taxes which is expected to be negative. Note that the same predictions hold true if we were to substitute TAX with PSE, since these two measures are highly correlated, and they move in the same direction.

5 Findings

We present our findings from the multilevel models (Tables 18.2 and 18.3). We begin by investigating our first research question: is happiness greater in the social democratic welfare states? Consistently, the results show that happiness in Eastern European countries is significantly lower than in other countries. In all models, PSE at the country-level is slightly negative but not significant. Hence the answer to our first research question is that aggregate happiness does *not* vary by the size of the welfare state.[9] The relationship between PSE and happiness is *not* manifested universally across all citizens, but indirectly with some socioeconomic and demographic groups benefiting more than others.

This leads us to our second research question: Who gains and who loses in the social democratic welfare state? The task is to examine the cross-level interaction effects of PSE with the demographic groups that are specifically targeted by social insurance. We first examine the hypothesis that cohabiters and parents will be happier in countries with high PSE. We present our findings in the order of marriage and family, followed by a separate analysis by gender. In our discussions, a low PSE country refers to a country with the minimum level of PSE, and a high PSE country refers to a country with the maximum level of PSE. In all models, college education and income are positive and significant. Age and age-squared are negative and positive respectively, suggesting that happiness is U-shaped as a function of age. We do not know, however, if these age differences reflect changes in happiness associated with aging or cohort differences in happiness. Where relevant, we report the regions of significance, following the algorithm described by Preacher et al. (2006).

In Model 1, the intercept, and the coefficients for female, the presence of a child under age 18, cohabiting and married are modeled as randomly varying. The random coefficients are specified to be the same in Model 2, with the one exception that the variable married is replaced with the variable single.

First, women and men are equally happy. On the whole, their happiness does not vary by the size of the welfare state. This finding, however, requires further elaboration because the happiness of women and men depends largely on the presence of family. We will explore the interactions between gender, family and PSE in separate analysis below.

Second, married persons report greater happiness than do unmarried persons. This gap in happiness by marital status is greater in the high PSE countries, as evidenced by the positive coefficients for being married (0.991) and its interaction with PSE (0.020). In these countries, the predicted odds of higher happiness for married people are more than three times compared to non-married, non-cohabiting individuals. But in low PSE countries, the same odds ratio drops to about two. Note

[9]In results not shown here, we estimated a model that includes all level-2 and level-1 covariates shown in Table 18.2, but without the interaction effects. Results of this model confirmed that public social expenditures (PSE) has no direct effect on happiness at the country-level.

Table 18.3 Ordered logit regression models predicting general happiness by gender

	Women	Men
Country-level variables		
Intercept	−2.405*** (0.103)	−2.477*** (0.123)
East Europe	−0.789*** (0.120)	−0.905*** (0.104)
Public social expenditures (PSE) as % of GDP	−0.008 (0.008)	−0.020 (0.010)
Individual-level variables		
Cohabiting	0.495*** (0.074)	0.798*** (0.072)
Cohabit X Country-level PSE	0.050*** (0.011)	0.033*** (0.009)
Married	0.863*** (0.056)	1.156*** (0.065)
Married X Country-level PSE	0.022*** (0.004)	0.018** (0.005)
Child under 18 in the home	−0.085* (0.035)	0.006 (0.034)
Child X Country-level PSE	0.011* (0.005)	0.0001 (0.004)
Age	−0.092*** (0.010)	−0.130*** (0.013)
Age square	0.001*** (0.0001)	0.001*** (0.0001)
College education	0.160** (0.060)	0.156** (0.060)
Full-time employment	−0.015 (0.034)	0.148** (0.058)
Income Z score	0.083*** (0.017)	0.116*** (0.017)
Threshold levels (δ)		
δ_2	1.961*** (0.118)	2.032*** (0.152)
δ_3	4.009*** (0.118)	4.151*** (0.155)
δ_4	5.540*** (0.126)	5.808*** (0.177)
δ_5	6.952*** (0.180)	7.172*** (0.227)
δ_6	8.483*** (0.256)	8.633*** (0.314)
Variance components		
Intercept	0.101***	0.082***
Child under 18	0.020**	0.017*
Cohabit	0.085**	0.033
Married	0.027**	0.028*

*$p < .05$; **$p < .01$; ***$p < .001$ (two-tailed tests). Robust standard errors in parentheses

Table 18.4 Predicted odds of selecting one of the three highest categories of happiness for key demographic groups

	Min PSE	Max PSE
Married	8.301	6.764
Un-married	4.074	2.034
Cohabit	4.222	5.950
Single	3.467	2.052
Women – Married with kids	6.330	6.810
Women – Cohabiting with kids	2.931	6.373

All covariates are centered except for the covariate for the key demographic group which is left uncentered

here that married persons are not necessarily happier in the high PSE countries than are their counterparts in the low PSE countries. In fact, when we account for the intercepts and interactions with PSE, married persons actually report lower happiness in the social democratic welfare states (see Table 18.4). The interaction effect between married and PSE is positive, but it is offset by the negative main effect of PSE at the country level.

Third, cohabiting persons are more likely to report greater happiness than are other unmarried persons, and this difference is greater in the high PSE countries. Both the coefficients for cohabiting (0.627) and its interaction with PSE (0.042) are positive. Cohabiters' odds of reporting a higher level of happiness are not statistically different than those for non-married, non-cohabiting individuals in low PSE countries, but this gap widens as we move towards high PSE countries and achieves statistical significance for countries where PSE is greater than 9.2. At the highest end of the PSE scale (at PSE = 29.8), cohabiters have nearly three times greater odds of reporting a higher level of happiness than non-married, non-cohabiting individuals. Cohabiters in the social democratic welfare states enjoy comparable benefits to those of married couples. This inclusive, non-discriminatory policy is associated with greater happiness.

And fourth, having children under 18 in the home (hereafter children) is not associated with happiness overall in this model. The relationship between children and happiness will be examined in greater detail in our subsequent analysis, which separates the sample into men and women.

In Model 2, we include the dummy variables for single, widowed, and divorced/separated (combined category) in place of married. For clarification, the dummy variables for marital status are mutually exclusive, so married becomes the default reference category here. The coding scheme in Model 2 thus allows us to better isolate the difference between being single compared to being married. Here we find that on average, single persons are more likely to report lower happiness than are married persons, as evidenced by the negative coefficient for single (−0.874). More interestingly, this negative coefficient is even stronger among single persons in high-PSE countries (the coefficient for the interaction of single and PSE is −0.010). This is essentially the opposite of what we observe for married and cohabiting persons in Model 1. The policies of the social democratic welfare states are explicit family-support policies put in place to protect and to improve the welfare of married and cohabiting persons. Consequently, single persons report relatively lower levels of happiness in the social democratic welfare states.

We find that the coefficient for cohabitation is now negative (−0.340), indicating that cohabiting persons are less happy than are married persons. However, we also find that this gap between married and cohabiting persons becomes statistically insignificant at the high end of the PSE scale (the interaction term for cohabiting and PSE is 0.027), specifically in countries where PSE is greater than 26.2. This finding suggests that the happiness of cohabiting persons reaches parity with that of married persons in the high PSE countries. Overall in Models 1 and 2 of Table 18.2, we find support for the hypothesis that the happiness gap between cohabiters and married people is smaller in countries with high levels of public spending (with no statistical difference in happiness between these groups in the high PSE countries). On the other hand, the gap between singles and married people is greater in high PSE countries (with singles reporting less happiness than married people in high PSE countries). In these first two models, we did not find support for the prediction that parents of small children are happier in high PSE countries; this will be further tested in the separate gender models that follow.

5.1 The Happiness Gap Between Men and Women

If women are more likely to take on a disproportionate share of family responsibilities, then women, and particularly those with children, may benefit more than do men under the pro-family policies of the social democratic welfare states. We examine this more closely by analyzing the sample of men and women separately. Table 18.3 shows the results. Our analysis reveals a number of similarities as well as dissimilarities between the sexes.[10]

Marriage and cohabitation are associated with higher odds of greater happiness for both genders, especially among the higher PSE countries. For women, the coefficients for married (0.863) and its interaction with PSE (0.022) are both positive as well as the coefficients for cohabiting (0.495) and its interaction with PSE (0.050). This means that in high PSE countries, the predicted odds of reporting higher happiness are about three times greater for married women, and 2.8 times greater for cohabiting women, than for non-married, non-cohabiting women. The coefficients for college education and income on happiness are roughly the same for men and women, with regard to both magnitude and direction of the coefficients. There is a somewhat stronger negative association between age and happiness for men than for women. Full-time employment is associated with higher happiness for men, but it does nothing to improve happiness for women.

The relationship between having children and happiness exposes the gender asymmetries of parenthood commonly discussed in the literature, mainly that the

[10]When differences are noted in the coefficients for men and women, the statistical significance of these differences were tested using the Wald test.

burden of raising children falls disproportionately on women (e.g. Lee and Ono 2008). The direct effect of children is negative for women (−0.085), but this coefficient is not statistically significant for men. More interestingly, the interaction with PSE is positive for women (0.011), but there is no association for men. A Wald test of the gender difference in coefficients for the interaction of children and PSE indicates that these coefficients are marginally different for men and women, at the .10 level. This means that while children are more strongly associated with lower happiness for women than for men overall, there is only marginal statistical evidence that the association between children and happiness varies by PSE in different ways for men and women.

To elaborate on the relationship between happiness and children for women, the default is that the presence of small children in the home is associated with *lower* happiness for women. However, women in the social democratic welfare states receive extensive institutional support to alleviate the constraints imposed on families with children. The positive gain in happiness is large enough to offset the disutility of having small children in high PSE countries. Empirically, we find that the happiness gap for women is statistically significant for countries in the lower end of the PSE scale, but becomes *insignificant* for countries with PSE greater than 21. In other words, the happiness gap between women with and without children disappears in the high PSE countries.

Table 18.4 shows the predicted odds of selecting one of the three highest categories of happiness for the key demographic groups that we examined here. These predictions take into consideration the intercepts and interaction effects of PSE on happiness, and were generated from the coefficients estimated from our models. We also include predicted odds for groups who stand to benefit most from the policies of the social democratic welfare state, namely married and cohabiting women with children.

The predictions show that happiness changes in the expected direction as we move from low- to high-PSE countries. The only exception is for married people and this, we argue, is because the benefits of marriage in the social democratic welfare state accrue primarily to women with children. The pro-family ideology encourages union formation and childbearing and discourages people from remaining single or childfree. Women, who take on the disproportionate share of child-care, stand to benefit from the institutional support provided by the social democratic welfare states. This targeted strategy results in greater happiness for women with small children. Overall, the findings from Tables 18.3 and 18.4 support the hypothesis that cohabiters and parents of small children, more specifically mothers, report greater happiness in countries with higher levels of public spending.

5.2 Income and Happiness

Our results thus far show that higher income is associated with greater happiness. But does this positive association vary across countries with respect to tax revenues and welfare spending at the country level? We next examine our hypothesis that the happiness gap between rich and poor will be smaller in countries with high PSE.

Table 18.5 shows the results of our analysis on income and happiness. In both models, we confirm that income is positively associated with happiness ($\gamma_{10} = 0.111$). More interestingly, we find that the interaction between income and PSE (−0.005), and the interaction between income and taxes ($\gamma_{11} = -0.003$) are both negative. These findings suggest that the marginal utility of income is significantly smaller in the high-PSE/ tax countries than in the low-PSE/tax countries.

Using the coefficients from Table 18.5, we can illustrate how happiness changes with income as we move from low- to high-PSE countries (see Fig. 18.1). In

Table 18.5 Ordered logit regression models predicting general happiness

	(1) Income Z-score X Country-level PSE	(2) Income Z-score X Country-level tax
Country-level variables		
Intercept	−2.426*** (0.110)	−2.431*** (0.106)
East Europe	−0.814*** (0.107)	−0.781*** (0.098)
Public social expenditures (PSE) as % of GDP	−0.010 (0.009)	
Tax revenue as % of GDP		−0.011 (0.006)
Individual-level variables		
Income Z score	0.111*** (0.015)	0.111*** (0.014)
X Country-level interaction	−0.005*** (0.001)	−0.003*** (0.001)
Threshold levels (δ)		
δ_2	1.992*** (0.131)	1.992*** (0.131)
δ_3	4.067*** (0.133)	4.068*** (0.133)
δ_4	5.648*** (0.142)	5.648*** (0.142)
δ_5	7.041*** (0.190)	7.041*** (0.190)
δ_6	8.543*** (0.263)	8.543*** (0.263)
Variance components		
Intercept	0.085***	0.079***
Income Z score	0.004**	0.003**

Models also control for the same variables shown in Model 1 of Table 18.3 minus the interaction effects. These control variables are suppressed from the output

*$p < .05$; **$p < .01$; ***$p < .001$ (two-tailed tests). Robust standard errors in parentheses

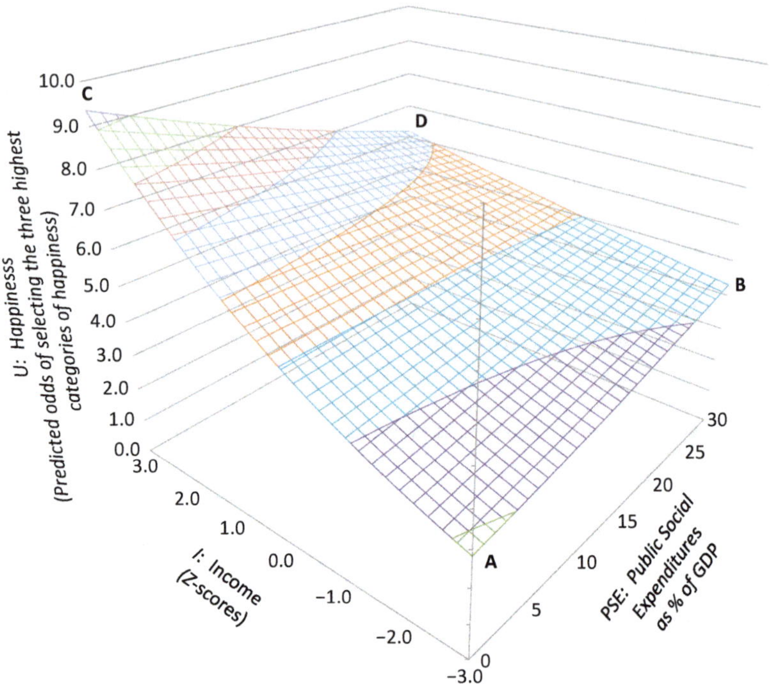

Fig. 18.1 Happiness as a function of income and public social expenditures (PSE)

this three-dimensional illustration, the vertical axis is the predicted log odds of belonging to one of the three highest categories of happiness (U). One horizontal axis is income (I) expressed in Z-scores, and the other is PSE. For reference, we indicate the four corners of the graph. Point A is the lowest income group in the lowest PSE country; at the other extreme is point D which is the highest income group in the highest PSE country. The slope of AC and BD is the marginal utility of income (dU/dI), i.e. it measures how happiness changes as income grows. The slope of AB and CD captures the change in happiness as a function of PSE ($dU/dPSE$). From Eq. (18.5), $dU/dPSE = \gamma_{01} + \gamma_{11}\, I$: the slope is determined by the sum of the pure effect of PSE on happiness (γ_{01}) plus the interaction effect (γ_{11}) of PSE on I. We highlight our findings below.

First, dU/dI is greater in the low-PSE countries than in the high-PSE countries. From Fig. 18.1, we can see that the slope of AC is steeper than the slope of BD. Higher income is associated with higher happiness in all countries, but this association is much stronger in the low-PSE countries. Second, $dU/dPSE$ is positive for the low-income group, but negative for the high-income group. Low-income earners are happier if they live in high-PSE countries than in low-PSE countries. In contrast, high-income earners are happier if they live in low-PSE countries than in high-PSE countries. According to our simulations, happiness for the highest income group in the highest-PSE country (at point D) is approximately equal to the happiness in the income group $Z = 0.9$ in the lowest-PSE country.[11]

Does money buy happiness? Our answer is yes, but with qualifications. The gain in happiness derived from money incomes is not uniform across countries. Specifically, people in the low-tax/low-PSE countries stand to benefit most from higher incomes when it comes to happiness. In contrast, people in the high-tax/high-PSE countries derive little happiness from money income.

Our findings are largely consistent with our hypothesis: Happiness redistribution in the social democratic welfare states mirrors income redistribution in these countries. The redistributive mechanism of "spreading the wealth around" among the social democratic welfare states diminishes the marginal utility of income, which equalizes people's happiness regardless of their income levels. Clearly, we see that the distribution of happiness is compressed much like income in these countries. There is a smaller happiness gap between the rich and the poor, suggesting a more egalitarian society with less economic and social inequality.

The fact that poor persons are happier in high PSE countries (than in low PSE countries) suggests that the social welfare programs not only improve the economic well-being of the poor and protect them from poverty, but they also improve their subjective well-being. Further, the fact that rich persons are less happy in the high PSE countries may indicate that the poor achieve greater happiness *at the cost of rich persons* in these countries.

We note here that since PSE and GDP per capita are correlated, it may be difficult to distinguish the association between PSE and income from that between GDP and income. It is possible that PSE and GDP per capita are both proxies for the standard of living, thus leading to the same predictions of marginal utility. Our results should be interpreted with this alternative explanation in mind.[12]

6 Summary and Discussion

What makes people happy? We offer a classic sociological explanation: *It depends on whom you ask, and it depends on the institutional context.* The social democratic welfare state does not produce greater happiness for the whole, but makes some

[11]This can be calculated for any range of PSE and/or income by manipulating equation (18.5). For example, in order to estimate income (I) in the lowest PSE country (PSE_{min}) that matches happiness in the highest income category (I_{max}) in the highest PSE country (PSE_{max}), we solve for:

$$I = \frac{\gamma_{01}\,(PSE_{\max} - PSE_{\min}) + \gamma_{11} PSE_{\max} I_{\max} + \gamma_{10} I_{\max}}{\gamma_{10} + \gamma_{11} PSE_{\min}}$$

[12]We also reran all models in Table 18.2 by replacing PSE with logged GDP per capita. Most interaction effects become insignificant, specifically: (GDP per capita and) * married, * having children, and * single. These interaction effects are key to understanding the relationship between welfare states and happiness. The results suggest that PSE is a reliable measure of welfare expenditures and that it is not just serving as a proxy for GDP per capita.

people happier and others less so. Studying happiness in the social democratic welfare states requires unpacking the various interactions between the macro and the micro. Aggregate happiness does not vary by the size of the welfare state. Public social expenditures do not raise happiness for all citizens. Rather, our multilevel analysis clearly shows that social insurance improves the life conditions in the demographics groups it targets specifically, but worsens them in others.

Our key contribution is in the discovery that the redistribution of happiness in the social democratic welfare states mirrors the redistribution of resources and income in these countries. The transfer of resources from low-risk to high-risk individuals in the social democratic welfare states is associated with a leveling effect in happiness in these countries. It is a pro-family policy that is associated with greater happiness for women with small children and cohabiting persons. The redistribution of income reduces the happiness gap between the rich and the poor: The happiness of the poor is lifted, and the happiness of the rich is lowered. Our findings are thus consistent with the ideological foundations of the social democratic welfare states. By providing a generous safety net against social risk, the welfare states have made the "pursuit of happiness" more accessible for high-risk groups.

Aside from the obvious disutility associated with high taxes, our analysis has also uncovered some areas where the social democratic welfare state may be associated with *lower* happiness. High taxes and high expenditures on social welfare do not make everyone happy across the board. The beneficiaries of the social democratic welfare states achieve happiness at the cost of the benefactor. By attempting to rectify inequality through distribution mechanisms, the social democratic welfare state generates an alternate form of "happiness inequality" in which winners and losers are defined by marital status, presence of children and income. While the system looks after the welfare of families, it is less generous in its treatment of unmarried and single persons. On average, single people face a higher tax burden than do married persons, but they gain the least in return. Indeed, the tax system implicitly encourages union formation, be it marriage or cohabitation, and even more, to have children. This incentive structure is attributed to one of the leading causes for the recovery of fertility in Sweden during the 1990s.[13]

Methodologically, we have demonstrated the strengths of multilevel modeling as an effective strategy for examining happiness across countries by uncovering the mechanisms that shape macro- and micro-level variations in happiness. We first showed that aggregate happiness is lower in the East European countries. But aside from this there are few country-level factors that are associated with happiness. At the individual-level, we find that characteristics such as income

[13]The taxation scheme resembles lex Julia et Papia which was legislated in ancient Rome to encourage family formation. The law offered incentives for marriage and procreation, and penalized single persons by imposing heavier taxes. It should be noted that single persons in the U.S. may also feel that taxes favor married persons with children. See for example, "Lifestyle and Taxes: Writers discuss incentives to marry, procreate and buy a home" (*New York Times*, April 13, 2013). The article centers around the discussion of "lifestyle discrimination," or the idea that taxes implicitly discriminate against single persons.

(Blanchflower and Oswald 2004), the presence of children (Umberson et al. 2010), and marital status (Nock 1995; Waite and Gallagher 2000) are important correlates of happiness. Cross-national variation in happiness is best explained not by looking at country- or individual-level factors alone, but by looking at their interactions. This conclusion would have been overlooked had we employed methods that do not account for cross-level interactions. The significant associations found in the macro-micro interactions underscore the importance of considering the social and institutional context in which respondents live.

By considering public social expenditures, we gain insight into how the policies of the social democratic welfare state differentially impact individuals and families. Most importantly, our work has shown that happiness is socially embedded in a larger cultural and institutional framework. Understanding what makes people happy requires a deeper analysis of the social mechanisms that link individual actors to their social-institutional environments.

Acknowledgements Ono acknowledges financial support from Texas A&M University, Office of the Vice President for Research and Japan Society for Promotion of Science Grant-in-Aid for Scientific Research (Grant Number C- 23530261). We thank Christopher Browning for helpful suggestions and support.

Addendum: Towards the Sociology of Happiness[14]

The pursuit of happiness is one of the most basic assumptions underlying the analysis of human behavior. And yet, it is only in recent years that scholars have become seriously engaged in "happiness science." The study of what makes people happy is far from complete. Despite the accumulation of wealth and higher standards of living in richer societies, people claim to be no happier today than they did 50 years ago. The disconnect between economic well-being and subjective well-being has led to a renewed interest in the study of happiness. Happiness research is now mainstream in the public discourse, discussed widely in policy circles, academia, and the popular media. Across the social sciences, it is flourishing, with each discipline making their own contributions to the discovery of why some people are happier than others.

Our approach to the happiness question, grounded instead in sociology, offers the complexity that a realistic answer demands. We account for social context, including critical perspectives of the question from which other disciplines have had to abstract. Admitting social context into the analysis allows us to observe that what makes people happy in one social setting may not do so in another. And, just as important, that happiness found usually owes to the right mix of social context and individual factors. While economists search for a universal model of happiness,

[14]This addendum has been newly written by Hiroshi Ono for this book chapter.

sociologists seek answers that are specific to the institutional context, as we illustrate empirically in the three studies that we have published to date.

Our first study examined happiness in marriage in the U.S. and in Japan (Lee and Ono 2008). We selected these two countries because of salient difference in gender roles, with Japan representing a society with a more traditional division of labor between the sexes. The two-country comparison revealed that there is a big difference between what makes a marriage happy in the U.S. and what makes it so in Japan. We also found significant differences between men and women *within* countries. For example, in the realm of money, we discovered that women in the U.S. find happiness in marriage through their financial independence. In contrast, women in Japan are more likely to achieve happiness in marriage through dependence; they are happier if they are married to husbands with high income. These findings reminded us of the importance of accounting for social institutions, as well as the perils of generalizing findings across varying institutional contexts.

Our second study was more ambitious. Encouraged by the importance of accounting for social context, we took on the greater task of comparing a larger number of countries, to see if we could find correlates of happiness both at the societal level, and at the individual level. We chose the International Social Survey Programme (ISSP) data for our study because of its design and breadth of coverage – 30 plus countries, with individuals nested within countries – which was ideal for applying hierarchical linear modeling (or multi-level modeling). We quickly learned that there was a lot to discover. Our research, which was originally titled, "the social-institutional bases of happiness," became too large for a single paper, and we decided to split our study into two separate works.

The second paper focused on the happiness gap between married and cohabitating persons across countries (Lee and Ono 2012). We hypothesized that this gap is not universal across countries, but instead depended on the social-institutional context of the countries involved. We first confirmed the so-called marriage premium, with married persons overall reporting greater happiness than cohabiting persons. But more importantly, we found that the marriage premium varied across different social contexts in the case of women (but not men). Specifically, the premium was greatest in societies that upheld traditional gender beliefs (with respect to the division of labor between the sexes, views on marriage and family, etc.), but nonexistent in societies that upheld egalitarian gender views. The marriage premium also varied across the spectrum of religious context, with larger premiums found in deeply religious societies, and no premium found in secular societies.

And this brings us to our third paper, featured here in this chapter, which focused on the redistributive mechanisms of social democratic welfare states and their effects on happiness. We were originally inspired to study this topic circa 2009 when the results of an OECD study on happiness were released. The study reported that the happiest country in the world was Denmark, followed closely by Finland, Netherlands and Sweden (OECD 2009a). The media's reaction to this announcement was decidedly predictable. Since the high-taxed countries of Scandinavia occupied the top of the happiness rankings, a number of media outlets jumped to the conclusion that "the happiest people on earth are heavily taxed," thereby alluding to the positive correlation (and perhaps even causation) between taxes and happiness.[15]

We argue that aggregate measures of happiness at the country level are not informative from the perspective of welfare and distribution policies. Aggregate rankings of happiness assume that *all* demographic groups are equally happy within countries. For example, what does it mean that Sweden ranks high on the happiness scale? Are we to assume that everyone in Sweden is happy across the board, and increasing social welfare spending (or taxes for that matter) is the path to greater happiness for all demographic groups? The aggregated view overlooks the redistribution mechanisms that relate macro level forces to happiness and well-being at the individual level.

The welfare states have constructed generous safety nets for high-risk individuals by transferring resources from low-risk to high-risk groups. We hypothesize that *redistribution in itself creates new inequalities*, by lowering the happiness of low-risk persons, and improving the happiness of high-risk groups. We test these redistribution effects in the areas of family, marriage, and earned income.

Suppose we take the example of parenting. In Sweden, families with small children benefit greatly from the welfare state's pro-family policies. Considerable resources are allocated in favor of families, so Sweden is a happy place indeed to raise small children. But overlooked is the fact that Sweden is less generous to single persons, who stand to gain little from the pro-family policy. Sweden is a less happy place to be single.

By unpacking the redistributive policies of the welfare states, we show that the social democratic welfare state does not produce greater happiness overall, but rather makes some people happier and others less so. Redistribution involves tradeoffs. If a government is to improve the welfare of particular demographic groups, it does so at the expense of others.

Our research offers a classic sociological explanation to the question: What makes people happy? It depends on whom you ask, and where.

Hiroshi Ono
Hitotsubashi University

References

Aldous J, Ganey R (1999) Family life and the pursuit of happiness – the influence of gender and race. J Fam Issues 20:155–180

Bjørnskov C, Dreher A, Fischer JAV (2007) The bigger the better? Evidence of the effect of government size on life satisfaction around the world. Public Choice 130:267–292

---

[15]See for example, Kostigen, Thomas. 2009. "The happiest taxes on earth: More people are satisfied in heavily tariffed nations." *Market Watch*, as well as a number of blog entries, for example, "Study shows 'socialist' highly taxed countries have happiest people." (*Oprah.com*, May 18, 2009), and "High taxes lead to happiness" (*TaxProf Blog*, July 7, 2010).

Blanchflower D, Oswald A (2004) Well-being over time in Britain and the USA. J Public Econ 88:1359–1386
Campbell A, Converse P, Rodgers WL (1976) The quality of American life: perceptions, evaluations, and satisfactions. Russell Sage, New York
Clark A, Oswald AJ (1996) Satisfaction and comparison income. J Public Econ 61:359–381
Coleman JS (1990) Foundations of social theory. Belknap Press of Harvard University Press, Cambridge
Deaton A (2008) Income, health, and well-being around the world: evidence from the Gallup World Poll. J Econ Perspect 22:53–72
Diener E, Gohm CL, Suh E, Oishi S (2000a) Similarity of the relations between marital status and subjective well-being across cultures. J Cross-Cult Psychol 31:419–436
Diener E, Scollon CKN, Oishi S, Dzokoto V, Suh EM (2000b) Positivity and the construction of life satisfaction judgments: global happiness is not the sum of its parts. J Happiness Stud 1:159–176
Easterlin RA (2001) Income and happiness: towards a unified theory. Econ J 111:465–484
Esping-Andersen G (1990) The three worlds of welfare capitalism. Princeton University Press, Princeton
Esping-Andersen G (1999) Social foundations of postindustrial economies. Oxford University Press, Oxford
Esping-Andersen G, Korpi W (1987) From poor relief to institutional welfare states: the development of Scandinavian social policy. In: Erikson R, Hansen EJ, Ringen S, Uusitalo H (eds) The Scandinavian model: welfare states and welfare research. M.E. Sharpe, Armonk, pp 39–74
Guo G, Zhao H (2000) Multilevel modeling for binary data. Annu Rev Sociol 26:441–462
Guriev S, Zhuravskaya E (2009) (Un)Happiness in transition. J Econ Perspect 23:143–168
Heritage Foundation (2002) Index of economic freedom. Available from www.heritage.org/index/
International Social Survey Programme (ISSP) (2004) ISSP 2002 codebook: family and changing gender roles III. Zentralarchiv fuer Empirische Sozialforschung, Koeln
Kangas O, Palme J (1993) Statism eroded? Labor-market benefits and challenges to the Scandinavian welfare states. In: Hansen EJ, Ringen S, Uusitalo H, Erikson R (eds) Welfare trends in the Scandinavian countries. M.E. Sharpe, Armonk, pp 3–24
Kenworthy L (1999) Do social-welfare policies reduce poverty? A cross-national assessment. Soc Forces 77:1119–1139
Kenworthy L (2004) Egalitarian capitalism: jobs, incomes, and growth in affluent countries. Russell Sage, New York
Korpi W, Palme J (1998) The paradox of redistribution and strategies of equality: welfare state institutions, inequality, and poverty in the Western countries. Am Sociol Rev 63:661–687
Lee KS, Ono H (2008) Specialization and happiness in marriage: a U.S.-Japan comparison. Soc Sci Res 37:1216–1234
Lee KS, Ono H (2012) Marriage, cohabitation, and happiness: a cross-national analysis of 27 countries. J Marriage Fam 74:953–972
Lindbeck A (1997) The Swedish experiment. J Econ Lit 35:1273–1319
Lindert P (2004) Growing public: social spending and economic growth since the eighteenth century, vol 1. Cambridge University Press, Cambridge
Margolis R, Myrskylä M (2011) A global perspective on happiness and fertility. Popul Dev Rev 37:29–56
Margolis R, Myrskylä M (2013) Family, money, and health: regional differences in the determinants of life satisfaction over the life course. Adv Life Course Res 18:115–126
Märtinson VK (2007) Families in different contexts: a comparison of European, British, and U.S. union formation and family patterns. In: Lovell SA, Holman TB (eds) The family in the new millennium, vol 1. Praeger, Westport, pp 124–152
McLanahan S, Adams J (1987) Parenthood and psychological well-being. Annu Rev Sociol 13:237–257
Nock SL (1995) A comparison of marriages and cohabiting relationships. J Fam Issues 16:53–76

Nomaguchi KM, Milkie M, Bianchi SM (2005) Time strains and psychological well-being: do dual-earner mothers and fathers differ? J Fam Issues 26:756–792
Ono H, Lee KS (2013) Welfare states and the redistribution of happiness. Soc Forces 92:789–814
Organisation for Economic Co-operation and Development (OECD) (2008) Growing unequal? Income distribution and poverty in OECD countries. OECD, Paris
Organisation for Economic Co-operation and Development (OECD) (2009a and various years) OECD factbook. OECD, Paris
Organisation for Economic Co-operation and Development (OECD) (2009b) Taxing wages 2009. OECD, Paris
Pacek A, Radcliff B (2008) Assessing the welfare state: the politics of happiness. Perspect Polit 6:267–277
Preacher KJ, Curran PJ, Bauer DJ (2006) Computational tools for probing interaction effects in multiple linear regression, multilevel modeling, and latent curve analysis. J Educ Behav Stat 31:437–448
Radcliff B (2001) Politics, markets, and life satisfaction: the political economy of human happiness. Am Polit Sci Rev 95:939–952
Raudenbush SW, Bryk AS (2002) Hierarchical linear models: applications and data analysis methods. Sage, Thousand Oaks
Rodgers W (1982) Trends in reported happiness within demographically defined subgroups, 1957–78. Soc Forces 60:826–842
Rothstein B (2010) Happiness and the welfare state. Soc Res 77:441–468
Ruiter S, van Tubergen F (2009) Religious attendance in cross-national perspective: a multilevel analysis of 60 countries. Am J Sociol 115:863–895
Schyns P (2002) Wealth of nations, individual income and life satisfaction in 42 countries: a multilevel approach. Soc Indic Res 60:5–40
Simon RW (2008) The joys of parenthood, reconsidered. Contexts 7:40–45
Skinner KB, Bahr SJ, Crane DR, Call VRA (2002) Cohabitation, marriage, and remarriage: a comparison of relationship quality over time. J Fam Issues 23:74–90
Soons JPM, Kalmijn M (2009) Is marriage more than cohabitation? Well-being differences in 30 European countries. J Marriage Fam 71:1141–1157
Stack S, Eshleman JR (1998) Marital status and happiness: a 17-nation study. J Marriage Fam 60:527–536
Steinmo S (1989) Political institutions and tax policy in the United States, Sweden, and Britain. World Polit 41:500–535
Umberson D, Pudrovska T, Reczek C (2010) Parenthood, childlessness, and well-being: a life course perspective. J Marriage Fam 72:612–629
Veenhoven R (1991) Is happiness relative? Soc Indic Res 28:195–223
Veenhoven R (2000) Well-being in the welfare state: level not higher, distribution not more equitable. J Comp Policy Anal 2:91–125
Waite LJ, Gallagher M (2000) The case for marriage: why married people are happier, healthier, and better off financially. Doubleday, New York
Yang Y (2008) Social inequalities in happiness in the United States, 1972 to 2004: an age-period-cohort analysis. Am Sociol Rev 73:204–226

Part VI
Decisions

Chapter 19
Revealed Attention

Yusufcan Masatlioglu, Daisuke Nakajima, and Erkut Y. Ozbay

Abstract The standard revealed preference argument relies on an implicit assumption that a decision maker considers all feasible alternatives. However, the marketing and psychology literatures provide well-established evidence that consumers do not consider all brands in a given market before making a purchase (Limited Attention). In this chapter, we illustrate how one can deduce both the decision maker's preference and the alternatives to which she pays attention and inattention from the observed behavior. We illustrate how seemingly compelling welfare judgements without specifying the underlying choice procedure are misleading. Further, we provide a choice theoretical foundation for maximizing a single preference relation under limited attention.

Keywords Revealed preferences • Awareness • Attention • Consideration set

JEL Classification D11; D81

The original article first appeared in the American Economic Review 102(5):2183–2205, 2012. A newly written addendum has been added to this book chapter.

Y. Masatlioglu
Department of Economics, University of Michigan, Ann Arbor, MI, USA
e-mail: yusufcan@umich.edu

D. Nakajima (✉)
Department of Economics, Otaru University of Commerce, Otaru, Japan
e-mail: nakajima@res.otaru-uc.ac.jp

E.Y. Ozbay
Department of Economics, University of Maryland, College Park, MD, USA
e-mail: ozbay@umd.edu

S. Ikeda et al. (eds.), *Behavioral Economics of Preferences, Choices, and Happiness*, DOI 10.1007/978-4-431-55402-8_19

1 Introduction

Revealed preference is one of the most influential ideas in economics and has been applied to a number of areas of economics, including consumer theory.[1] According to standard revealed preference theory, x is revealed to be preferred to y if and only if x is chosen when y is also available (Samuelson 1938). Any choice reversal, therefore, observed both empirically and experimentally, is attributed to irrationality since it cannot be expressed as a preference maximization.

The revealed preference argument relies on the implicit assumption that a decision maker (DM) considers all feasible alternatives. Without the full consideration assumption, the standard revealed preference method can be misleading. It is possible that the DM prefers x to y but she chooses y when x is present simply because she does not realize that x is also available (Hausman 2008). For example, while using a search engine, a DM might only pay attention to alternatives appearing on the first page of the results since it takes too much time to consider all the search results. She then picks the best alternative of those on the first page, say y. It is possible that her most preferred item, x, does not appear on the first page. Therefore we, as outside observers, cannot conclude that y is better than x even though y is chosen when x is available. Nevertheless, as in the above example, the DM may have a well-defined preference and is maximizing her preference within her bounded understanding of what is available.[2]

This example immediately raises a question: How can we elicit her (stable) preference without the full attention assumption? We consider a DM who picks her most preferred item from the alternatives she pays attention to, not from the entire feasible set. Then we shall illustrate when and how one can deduce both the DM's preferences and the alternatives to which she does or does not pay attention from her observed choices. Furthermore, we illustrate the problem of the welfare judgement without specifying the underlying choice procedure by showing an example where our method and the conservative criterion of Bernheim and Rangel (2007, 2009) result in the completely opposite implication.

The marketing literature calls the set of alternatives to which a DM pays attention in her choice process as the *consideration set* (Wright and Barbour 1977). The formation of the consideration set has been extensively studied in the marketing and finance literatures (e.g. Hauser and Wernerfelt 1990; Roberts and Lattin 1991). It has been argued that due to cognitive limitations, DMs cannot pay attention to all the available alternatives. As Simon (1957) pointed out, being able to consider all possible alternatives is as hard as comparing them for decision makers. Therefore, a DM with limited cognitive capacity (possibly stemming from unawareness as

[1] Varian (2006) provides a nice survey of revealed preference analysis.

[2] As argued in Aumann (2005), this behavior is still considered rational (at least boundedly rational) since she is choosing the best alternative under her limited information about what is available.

demonstrated in Goeree (2008)[3]), restricts her attention only to a small fraction of the objects present in the associated market (Stigler 1961; Pessemier 1978; Chiang et al. 1998).[4] In sum, a DM intentionally or unintentionally filters out some alternatives to prevent her cognitive capacity from being overloaded (Broadbent 1958).

The common property in the formation of consideration sets is that it is unaffected when an alternative she does not pay attention to becomes unavailable. This basic property of the attention filter, which is also documented in the psychology literature (Broadbent 1958), can be interpreted as the minimal condition. This property is trivially satisfied in classical choice theory where it is assumed that the DM is able to pay attention to all the available alternatives. Additionally, it is normatively appealing especially when a DM pays attention to all of items she is aware of and is unaware that she is unaware of other items. For example, if a PC buyer is not only unaware of a particular PC, but she is also unaware that she overlooks that PC, then, even when that PC becomes unavailable, she will not recognize such a change. Therefore, her consideration set will stay the same.

Interestingly, this property is also satisfied when the DM actually chooses the consideration sets by taking the cost of investigation and the expected benefit into account. Suppose the DM excludes x from her consideration. If x becomes unavailable, she has no reason to add or remove any alternative to her consideration set because she could have done so when x was available. Therefore, her consideration set is not affected when x becomes unavailable. Furthermore, this property is also satisfied when the formation is based on many decision heuristics, such as paying attention only to the N-most advertised alternatives or the products appearing in the first page of search results. As a result, our property is appealing from both normative and descriptive point of views.

In this chapter, we refer to the consideration sets satisfying this property as *attention filters*. Under this structure, it is possible to elicit the DM's preference whenever a choice reversal is observed.[5] For example, assume that she chooses x, but removing y changes her choice. This can happen only when her consideration set has changed. This would be impossible if she did not pay attention to y. Hence, y must have been considered (*Revealed Attention*). Given the fact that x is chosen while y draws her attention, we conclude that she prefers x over y (*Revealed*

[3]Lavidge and Steiner (1961) presented awareness of an item as a necessary condition to be in the consideration set. How unawareness alters the behavior of the DM has been studied in various contexts such as game theory (Heifetz et al., 2010, Dynamic unawareness and rationalizable behavior, unpublished; Ozbay, 2008, Unawareness and strategic announcements in games with uncertainty, unpublished), and contract theory (Filiz-Ozbay, 2010, Incorporating awareness into contract theory, unpublished).

[4]In addition, in financial economics it is shown that investors reach a decision within their limited attention (Huberman and Regev 2001). Similar examples can be found in job search (Richards et al. 1975), university choice (Dawes and Brown 2005), and airport choice (Basar and Bhat 2004).

[5]Without any structure on the formation of the consideration sets, any choice behavior can be rationalized by any preference (Hausman 2008).

Preference). In sum, whenever her choice changes as a consequence of removing an unchosen alternative, the initially chosen alternative is preferred to the removed one.

Given that our identification strategy relies on the particular choice procedure, where she maximizes her preference within her attention filter, it is natural to ask the falsifiability of our model. We show that our model is fully characterized by weakening the Weak Axiom of the Revealed Preference (WARP). This result renders our model behaviorally testable.

Our method to distinguish between a preference and attention/inattention generates several policy implications. For instance, if a product of a firm is unpopular in the market place, there could be two different explanations: (i) the product has a low evaluation by consumers or (ii) it does not attract attention of consumers. Identifying the right reason will lead to different strategies for the firm to improve the sales.

Our paper also contributes to the recent discussion about welfare analysis under non-standard individual behavior.[6] We elicit the DM's preference in a positive approach, which is based on a particular choice procedure. Bernheim and Rangel (2009) criticize such an approach by arguing that it is not necessary to explain the behavior to make a welfare analysis. Instead, they make welfare arguments directly from the choice data without assuming any choice procedure (model-free). Particularly, they claim that y is strictly welfare improving over x if y is sometimes chosen when x is available but x is never chosen when y is present. However, this intuitive criterion of welfare analysis is meaningful only if the DM considers all the presented alternatives.[7] In Sect. 3, we discuss this issue in detail to illustrate the problem of the naive use of the model-free approach. Indeed, we provide an example where their welfare implication contradicts our revealed preference (hence the actual preference); that is, y is revealed to be preferred to x even when x is strictly welfare improving over y in Bernheim and Rangel's (2009) sense.

So far we have discussed how one can elicit DM's preference and consideration sets in our model. In doing so, we impose a relatively weak condition on the formation of consideration sets so that our approach is applicable to a wide range of choice data. As a result, although our model is refutable, it provides an alternative explanation for several frequently observed behaviors that cannot be captured by the standard choice theory: Attraction Effect, Cyclical Choice, and Choosing Pairwisely Unchosen (see Anomalies section). Our explanations for these choice patterns solely depend on limited attention, hence seemingly irrational behaviors can be explained

[6]See Ambrus and Rozen (2010, Rationalizing choice with multi-self models, unpublished), Apesteguia and Ballester (2010, A measure of rationality and welfare, unpublished), Cherepanov et al. (2010, Rationalization, unpublished), Chambers and Hayashi (2008), Green and Hojman (2008), Manzini and Mariotti (2012), Masatlioglu and Nakajima (2009, Choice by iterative search, unpublished), Noor (2011), and Rubinstein and Salant (2009).

[7]Indeed, Bernheim and Rangel (2007) mention that if we know the DM believes that she is choosing from a set that is other than the objective feasible set, we should take it into account for the welfare analysis (Section III B).

without introducing changing preference. Nevertheless, depending on the intended application, it is possible to analyze this framework under different restrictions on consideration sets.

There are several related models where the final choice is made after eliminating several items, which can be interpreted as a choice with limited consideration such as applying a rationale to eliminate alternatives (Manzini and Mariotti 2007; Apesteguia and Ballester, 2009, Choice by sequential procedures, unpublished; Houy 2007; Houy and Tadenuma 2009), considering only the N-most eye-catching alternatives (Salant and Rubinstein 2008), focusing only on alternatives a decision maker can rationalizes to choose by some other criterion (Cherepanov et al., 2010, Rationalization, unpublished) and considering only alternatives belonging to undominated categories (Manzini and Mariotti 2012). Our model is both descriptively and behaviorally distinct from these models. In addition, unlike our model, these models implicitly assume that a DM considers all feasible alternatives at the first stage and *intentionally* eliminates several alternatives. Therefore, their stories are not applicable to cases where the source of limited consideration is unawareness of some alternatives.

Finally, we would like to compare our model to several other models involving consideration sets in decision theory. Lleras et al. (2010, When more is less: choice by limited consideration, unpublished) study a different model of choice under limited consideration where a product attracting attention in a crowded supermarket shelf will be noticed when there are fewer products.[8] Masatlioglu and Nakajima (2009, Choice by iterative search, unpublished) propose a model of an iterative search where a decision maker cannot consider all alternatives, which can be because of unawareness like our model. The difference is that they emphasize that a consideration set depends on the initial starting point and evolves dynamically during the course of search. In the models of Caplin and Dean (2011) and Caplin et al. (2009), a decision maker goes through alternative sequentially and, at any given time, chooses the best one among those she has searched. Unlike our model, their "choice process" data includes not only the DM's choice without time limit, but also what she would choose if she were suddenly forced to quit the search at any given time.

Eliaz and Spiegler (2011) analyze a market where firms would like to manipulate consumers' consideration sets by using costly marketing devices. Eliaz et al. (2011) study a very concrete and reasonable way to construct a consideration set. Indeed, some of the consideration sets we shall present as examples are within their models. However, contrary to our model, in their paper, the decision maker's consideration set (called *finalists*) is observed and is directly investigated. In our model the consideration set is an object that must be inferred from the DM's final choice.

The outline of this chapter is as follows: Sect. 2 introduces the basic notations and definitions. In Sect. 3, we provide two characterizations for the revealed preference

[8] While this paper is complementary to our paper, their implications are completely different We discuss it in the Conclusion section.

and the revealed (in)attention from observed choice data. Section 4 provides a simple behavioral test for our model and discusses the related literature. Then, in Sect. 5, we illustrate that our limited attention model is capable of accommodating several frequently observed behaviors. Finally, the Further Comments on Revealed Preference and the Conclusion sections conclude the paper.

2 The Model

Throughout this chapter, let X be a finite set of alternatives that may be available for a decision maker to choose. $\mathscr{X}$ denotes the set of all non-empty subsets of X, which is interpreted as the collection of all the (objective) feasible sets observed by a third party.

2.1 Attention Filters

In our model, a decision maker picks the best element from those she pays attention to (her consideration set). Our goal is to elicit her preference along with her attention and inattention from her actual choice data. However, this is impossible without any knowledge about her attention and inattention. One can always claim that she picks an alternative because she ignores everything else so one cannot infer her preference at all.

We now propose a property how consideration sets change as feasible sets change, instead of explicitly modeling how the feasible set determines the consideration set. This approach makes it possible to apply our method to elicit the preference without relying on a particular formation of the consideration set. We shall explain that this property is normatively compelling in several situations and is indeed true in many heuristics people actually use in real life.

Let S be a feasible set the decision maker is facing. She does not pay attention to all alternatives in S. Let $\Gamma(S)$ be the (non-empty) set of elements to which she pays attention. Formally, Γ is a mapping from $\mathscr{X}$ to $\mathscr{X}$ with $\emptyset \neq \Gamma(S) \subset S$. We call Γ a consideration set mapping. Of all consideration set mappings, we focus on those having the following property:

Definition 1 A consideration set mapping Γ is an **attention filter** if for any S, $\Gamma(S) = \Gamma(S \setminus x)$ whenever $x \notin \Gamma(S)$.[9]

[9]Throughout the paper, unless it leads to confusion, we abuse the notation by suppressing set delimiters, e.g. writing $c(xy)$ instead of $c(\{x, y\})$ or $\Gamma(xy)$ instead of $\Gamma(\{x, y\})$ or $S\backslash x$ instead of $S\backslash\{x\}$.

This definition says that if an alternative does not attract an attention of the decision maker, her consideration set does not change when such an item becomes unavailable.

To illustrate that this is a normatively appealing property, we shall provide two examples where the decision maker's consideration set mapping should be an attention filter. The first example is based on unawareness. Imagine a decision maker (wrongly) believes $\Gamma(S)$ is her feasible set (S is the actual one). That is, she is not only unaware of alternatives in $S \setminus \Gamma(S)$ and but unaware that she is unaware of these alternatives. If so, she will not recognize the change of the feasible set when such an item becomes unavailable so her consideration set should not change. This is exactly what the property dictates.

The second one is choosing rationally what to consider (or not to consider). Because of scarcity of time and/or complexity of decision problems, a decision maker selectively focuses on a smaller set of alternatives and ignores the rest. Suppose she knows S is her entire feasible set. Then, she picks her consideration set $\Gamma(S)$ optimally based on her prior beliefs about the value of alternatives and the cost of inspecting them. Then, her consideration set mapping must satisfy our property. To see this, imagine that she considers only a and b when her feasible set is $\{a, b, c, d\}$ ($\Gamma(abcd) = \{a, b\}$). Assume that d becomes unavailable now. She has no reason to add c to her consideration set because she could have done so when d was available. For the same reason, it is not rational to remove b (or a) from her consideration set. Therefore, it must be $\Gamma(abc) = \{a, b\}$. That is, her consideration set mapping is an attention filter. Notice that this must be true whatever beliefs and cost function she has.[10]

Furthermore, in addition to being normatively appealing, our condition is also descriptively appealing. Many heuristics that are actually used to narrow down the set of choosable options generate attention filters. We list some of them.

▷ **Top N:** A decision maker considers only top N alternatives according to some criterion that is different from her preference. For instance:

- Consider only the three cheapest suppliers in the market (Dulleck et al. 2008).
- Consider the N most advertised products in the market.
- Consider the products that appear in the first page of the websearch and/or sponsored links (Hotchkiss et al., 2004, The role of search in business to business buying decisions a summary of research conducted, unpublished).
- Consider the first N available alternatives according to an exogenously given order (Salant and Rubinstein 2008).[11]

[10]The only exception is that the feasible set itself conveys some information that affects her belief or cost function.

[11]Salant and Rubinstein (2008) characterizes this class of choice functions by assuming N is observable.

▷ **Top on each criterion:** A decision maker has several criteria and considers only the best alternative(s) on each criterion (modeled as a complete and transitive binary relation). For instance:

- Consider only a job candidate if she is the best in a program. Or consider the top-two job candidates from all first-tier schools and the top candidate from second-tier schools.
- Consider only the cheapest car, the safest car, and the most fuel efficient car in the market.[12]

▷ **Most popular category:** A decision maker considers alternatives that belong to the most popular "category" in the market. For instance:

- There are several bike shops in the DM's town. The DM first checks online to find the store offering the largest variety of bikes and goes to that store. Therefore, the DM only considers bikes sold in the selected store.[13] Zyman (1999) provides real-world evidence for such behavior. The sale of Sprite is increased dramatically when they are simply repositioned from the category of lemon-limes (less popular category) to soda (more popular category).

2.2 *Choice with Limited Attention*

In the previous subsection, we defined the concept of the attention filter and discussed features that make it both normatively and descriptively appealing. Now we define the choice behavior of a decision maker who picks the best element from her consideration set according to the complete and transitive preference. Formally, a choice function assigns a unique element to each feasible set. That is, $c : \mathscr{X} \to X$ with $c(S) \in S$ for all $S \in \mathscr{X}$.

Definition 2 A choice function c is a **choice with limited attention (CLA)** if there exists a complete and transitive preference $\succ$ over X and an attention filter Γ such that $c(S)$ is the $\succ$-best element in $\Gamma(S)$.[14]

In the following sections, we answer the following questions under the assumption that decision maker follows a choice with limited attention but her preference and attention filter is not observable: (1) How can we identify her preference and

[12]This heuristic is very close to "Rationalization" of Cherepanov et al. (2010, Rationalization, unpublished). Indeed, it is a special version of Rationalization. In their model, unlike "the top on each criterion", depending on the feasible set, different sets of criteria might be utilized to eliminate alternatives in the first stage. See Sect. 4 for further discussion.

[13]For instance, suppose store A deals with Makers 1 and 2's bikes while store B sells bikes from Makers 2 and 3. Then, the DM compares the number of Makers 1 and 2's bikes with that of Makers 2 and 3's to choose which store to visit.

[14]That is, $c(S) \in \Gamma(S)$ and $c(S) \succ x$ for all $x \in \Gamma(S) \setminus c(S)$.

attention filter through her choice data? (2) Which choice functions are compatible with the model of a choice with limited attention?

3 Revealed Preference and (In)Attention

In this section, we illustrate how to infer (1) the DM's preference and (2) what the DM pays (and does not pay) attention to from her observed choice that is a CLA. The standard theory concludes that x is preferred to y when x is chosen while y is available. To justify such an inference, one must implicitly assume that she has paid attention to y. Without this hidden assumption, we cannot make any inference because she may prefer y but overlooks it. Therefore, eliciting the DM's preference is no longer trivial because her choice can be attributed to her preference or to her inattention.[15]

This observation suggests that multiple pairs of a preference and an attention filter can generate the same choice behavior. To illustrate this, consider the choice function with three elements exhibiting a cycle:

$$c(xyz) = x, \quad c(xy) = x, \quad c(yz) = y, \quad c(xz) = z.$$

One possibility is that the DM's preference is $z \succ_1 x \succ_1 y$ and she overlooks z both at $\{x, y, z\}$ and $\{y, z\}$. Another possibility is that her preference is $x \succ_2 y \succ_2 z$ and she does not pay attention to x only at $\{x, z\}$ (see Table 19.1 for the corresponding attention filters).

We cannot identify which of them is her true preference. Nevertheless, if only these two pairs represent c, we can unambiguously conclude that she prefers x to y because both of them rank x above y. For the same reason, we can infer that she pays attention to both x and y at $\{x, y, z\}$ (Table 19.1). This example makes it clear that we need to define revealed preference when multiple representations are possible.

Table 19.1 Two possible representations for the cyclical choice

		Attention filter			
Preference		$\{x, y, z\}$	$\{x, y\}$	$\{y, z\}$	$\{x, z\}$
$z \succ_1 x \succ_1 y$	Γ_1	xy	xy	y	xz
$x \succ_2 y \succ_2 z$	Γ_2	xyz	xy	yz	z

[15] In the extreme case where the choice data satisfy the weak axiom of revealed preference, we have no way of knowing whether the decision maker is aware of all alternatives and maximizing a particular preference, or whether she only pays attention to the one she chooses. In the latter, her preference has no significant importance. In Sect. 6, we discuss the situations where one can pin down the preference even in this extreme case.

Definition 3 Assume c is a choice by limited attention and there are k different pairs of preference and attention filter representing c, $(\Gamma_1, \succ_1), (\Gamma_2, \succ_2), \ldots, (\Gamma_k, \succ_k)$. In this case,

- x is *revealed to be preferred* to y if $x \succ_i y$ for all i,
- x is *revealed to attract attention* at S if $\Gamma_i(S)$ includes x for all i,
- x is *revealed **not** to attract attention* at S if $\Gamma_i(S)$ excludes x for all i.

This definition is very conservative: we say x is revealed to be preferred to y only when all possible representations agree on it. We do not want make any false claims or claims that we are not sure. This conservative approach makes it possible that a social planner is always safe to follow our welfare recommendations.

If one wants to know whether x is revealed to be preferred to y, it would appear necessary to check for every $(\Gamma_i, \succ_i)$ whether it represents her choice or not. However, this is not practical especially when there are many alternatives. Instead we shall now provide a handy method to obtain the revealed preference, attention and inattention completely.

In the example above, when Γ is an attention filter, it is possible to determine the relative ranking between x and y. To see this, note that if the DM pays attention to x and z at both $\{x, z\}$ and $\{x, y, z\}$, then we should not observe choice reversal. If there is a choice reversal, then this means that her attention set changes when y is removed from $\{x, y, z\}$. This is possible only when she pays attention to y at $\{x, y, z\}$ (*Revealed Attention*). Given the fact that x is chosen from $\{x, y, z\}$ we conclude that the DM prefers x over y (*Revealed Preference*). This observation can be easily generalized. Whenever the choices change as a consequence of removing an alternative, the initially chosen alternative is preferred to the removed one. Formally, for any distinct x and y, define:

$$xPy \text{ if there exists T such that } \mathrm{c(T)} = \mathrm{x} \neq \mathrm{c(T \setminus y)}. \tag{19.1}$$

By the argument analogous to the one above, if xPy then x is revealed to be preferred to y. In addition, since the underlying preferences are transitive, we also conclude that she prefers x to z if xPy and yPz for some y, even when xPz is not directly revealed from the choice. Therefore, the transitive closure of P, denoted by P_R, must also be part of her revealed preference. One may wonder whether some revealed preference is overlooked by P_R. The next theorem states that the answer is no: P_R is the revealed preference in our model.

Theorem 1 (Revealed Preference) *Suppose c is a CLA. Then, x is revealed to be preferred to y if and only if* xP_Ry.

Theorem 1 illustrates that welfare analysis is possible even with non-standard choices. In addition, it provides a guideline for a policy maker.

The revealed preference characterized by Theorem 1 is independent of *how* her consideration set is formed, as long as her consideration set mapping is an attention filter. Therefore, it is applicable to many situations. However, depending on how her consideration set is formed, it may appear to be inappropriate to base the welfare analysis solely on our revealed preference. For instance, one can interpret her attention/inattention as some reflection of her preference and argue that it should be incorporated to the welfare analysis. We do not disagree with such attempts, but to do so the policy maker must have more concrete views about the DM's actual consideration set formation. In those cases, our revealed preference is what the policy maker can say without knowledge of the DM's underlying consideration set formation process.

Notice that our analysis is a model-based approach as the welfare criterion is obtained assuming a particular underlying choice procedure: a choice with limited attention. On the other hand, Bernheim and Rangel (2009) propose that one should make a welfare judgement only when the choices are unambiguous. Their intuition is that if x is never chosen while y is present and y is chosen at least once when x is available, then y should be strictly welfare improving over x. Since this intuitive criterion is independent of the underlying model, their approach is called model-free. Using Theorem 1, we are able to illustrate in a reasonable example that the above intuition might deceive us. In the next example, while x is never chosen when y is present, y is chosen at least once over x. Nevertheless, Theorem 1 dictates that x is revealed to be preferred to y.

Example 1 There are four products x, y, z, and t. Each of them is packed in a box. Consider a supermarket which displays these products in its two aisles according to the following rules: (i) Each aisle can carry at most two products, (ii) x and y cannot be placed into the same aisle because they are packed in big boxes, (iii) the supermarket fills the first aisle first and uses the second aisle only if it is necessary, (iv) y and z are put into the first aisle whenever they are available, (v) t is placed in the first aisle only after all other available items are put in an aisle and still the first aisle has a space. Consider a costumer with preference $t \succ x \succ z \succ y$ (not observable) and she only visits the first aisle and picks her most preferred item displayed in that aisle.

It is easy to see that her consideration set mapping is an attention filter as the supermarket does not changes its lineups in its first aisle when something in the second aisle become unavailable. Hence Theorem 1 is applicable.

Since x never appears in the first aisle when y is available, she never chooses x whenever y is feasible (and y is chosen when only x and y are available). Thus, the criterion by Bernheim and Rangel (2009), although it is very conservative to make a welfare statement, conclude that y is welfare improving over x, which is opposite to her true preference.

In contrast to Bernheim and Rangel (2009), our model correctly identifies her true preference between y and x by Theorem 1. To see this, suppose all of four products are available. Then, y and z are placed in the first aisle so z is chosen. When y becomes unavailable, then x is moved to the first aisle and is chosen. Furthermore, when z is also sold out, then x and t are placed in the first aisle so she picks t. In sum, her choices will be $c(xyzt) = z$, $c(xzt) = x$ and $c(xt) = t$. Then, when only choice is observable, our model concludes that the DM prefers z over y and x over z. Therefore, we can identify her preference between x and y correctly.

This example highlights the importance of knowledge about the underlying choice procedure when we conduct welfare analysis.[16] In other words, welfare analysis is more delicate task than it looks.

Next, we investigate when we can unambiguously conclude that the DM pays (or does not pay) attention to an alternative. Consider the choice reversal above, from which we have concluded that she prefers x to y. Therefore, whenever y is chosen, she must not have paid attention to x (*Revealed Inattention*).

As we illustrate, we infer that x is revealed to attract attention at S whenever x is chosen from S or removing x from S causes a choice reversal. Furthermore, it is possible to reach the same conclusion even when removing x from S does not cause a choice reversal. Imagine that the DM chooses the same item, say $\alpha \neq x$, from S and T and removing x from T causes a choice reversal, so we know $x \in \Gamma(T)$ for sure. Now collect all items that belong to either S or T but not to both. Suppose all of those items are revealed to be preferred to α. Then, those items cannot be in $\Gamma(S)$ or $\Gamma(T)$. Therefore, removing those items from S or T cannot change her consideration set. Hence, we have

$$\Gamma(S) = \Gamma(S \cap T) = \Gamma(T)$$

and can conclude that x is considered at S.

The following theorem summarizes this observation and also provides the full characterization of revealed attention and inattention.

Theorem 2 (Revealed (In)Attention) *Suppose c is a CLA. Then,*

(1) x is revealed not to attract attention at S if and only if $xP_Rc(S)$,
(2) x is revealed to attract attention at S if and only if there exists T (possibly equal to S) such that:

(i) $c(T) \neq c(T \setminus x)$,
(ii) $yP_Rc(S)$ for all $y \in S \setminus T$,
$zP_Rc(T)$ for all $z \in T \setminus S$.

Theorem 2 identifies both revealed attention and inattention. This information is as important as the revealed preference. For example, if a product is not popular in a market, it is very important for a firm to know the reason, which can either be that it is not liked by consumers or that it does not attract the attentions of consumers.

4 Characterization

The two preceding theorems characterize revealed preference and revealed (in)attention. However, they are not applicable unless the observed choice behavior is a CLA. Therefore, a question to ponder is: how can we test whether a choice

[16] For a detailed discussion of this subject, see Manzini and Mariotti (2009, Choice based welfare economics for boundedly rational agents, unpublished).

data is consistent with CLA? Surprisingly, it turns out that CLA can be simply characterized by only one behavioral postulate of choice.

Before we state the postulate, recall the sufficient and necessary condition for observed behavior to be consistent with the preference maximization under the full attention assumption: the Weak Axiom of Revealed Preference (WARP). WARP is equivalent to stating that every set S has the "best" alternative x^* in the sense that it must be chosen from any set T whenever x^* is available and the choice from T lies in S. Formally,

WARP: For any nonempty S, there exists $x^* \in S$ such that for any T including x^*,

$$\text{if } c(T) \in S, \text{ then } c(T) = x^*.$$

Because of the full attention assumption, being feasible is equal to attracting attention. However, this is no longer true when we allow for the possibility of limited attention. To conclude that x^* is chosen from T, we not only need to make sure that the chosen element from T is in S and x^* is available but also that x^* attracts attention. As we have discussed, we can infer this when removing x^* from T changes the DM's choice, which is the additional requirement for x^* to be chosen from T. This discussion suggests the following postulate, which is a weakening of WARP:

WARP with Limited Attention - WARP(LA): For any nonempty S, there exists $x^* \in S$ such that, for any T including x^*,

$$\text{if } c(T) \in S \text{ and } c(T) \neq c(T \setminus x^*), \text{ then } c(T) = x^*.$$

WARP with Limited Attention indeed guarantees that the binary relation P defined in (19.1) is acyclic and it fully characterizes the class of choice functions generated by an attention filter. The next lemma makes it clear that WARP(LA) is equivalent to the fact that P has no cycle.

Lemma 1 *P is acyclic if and only if c satisfies WARP with Limited Attention.*

Proof (The if-part) Suppose P has a cycle: $x_1 P x_2 P \cdots P x_k P x_1$. Then for each $i = 1, \dots, k-1$ there exists T_i such that $x_i = c(T_i) \neq c(T_i \setminus x_{i+1})$ and $x_k = c(T_k) \neq c(T_k \setminus x_1)$. Consider the set $\{x_1, \dots, x_k\} \equiv S$. Then, for every $x \in S$, there exists T such that $c(T) \in S$ and $c(T \setminus x) \neq c(T)$ but $x \neq c(T)$, so WARP with Limited Attention is violated.

(The only-if part) Suppose P is acyclic. Then every S has at least one element x such that there is no $y \in S$ with yPx, which means that there is no $y \in S$ with $y = c(T) \neq c(T \setminus x)$. Equivalently, whenever $c(T) \in S$ and $c(T) \neq c(T \setminus x)$, it must be $x = c(T)$, which is WARP with Limited Attention.

Theorem 3 (Characterization) *c satisfies WARP with Limited Attention if and only if c is a CLA.*

Theorem 3 shows that a CLA is captured by a single behavioral postulate. This makes it possible to test our model non-parametrically by using the standard revealed-preference technique *à la* Samuelson and to derive the decision maker's preferences and attention filter based on Theorems 1 and 2 from the observed choice data.

As we mentioned in the introduction, there are several related decision theoretic models where the final choice is made after eliminating several items, which are similar to a CLA such as Manzini and Mariotti (2007, 2012), Cherepanov et al. (2010, Rationalization, unpublished) and Lleras et al. (2010, When more is less: choice by limited consideration, unpublished). We shall illustrate that our model is different from these models both in a descriptive sense and in a behavior sense.

To show the difference more starkly, we compare our model with the "Rationalization" concept in Cherepanov et al. (2008). At first glance, Rationalization would appear to be a special case of our model. In fact this is not the case. In the Rationalization model, the decision-maker chooses the best alternative among those she can rationalize. The set of rationalizable alternatives is defined by her set of rationales. Each rationale is a transitive binary relation which may or may not be complete. The set of rationalizable alternatives in S consists of all the alternatives that dominate all other alternatives according to at least one of her rationales. Formally,

$$\Gamma_{CFS}(S) = \{y \in S \mid \exists R_i \text{such that } yR_ix \text{ for all } x \in S\},$$

where each R_i is a rationale (a transitive binary relation).

In general, Γ_{CFS} is not an attention filter. To see this, consider three alternatives x, y, z and two rationales: xR_1yR_1z and yR_2x. First, observe that when all options are present, then x is rationalizable but z is not. On the other hand, y is rationalizable only when z is removed because R_2 does not compare y and z. That is, $z \notin \Gamma_{CFS}(xyz)$ but $\Gamma_{CFS}(xyz) \neq \Gamma_{CFS}(xy)$ – whereas our framework requires $\Gamma_{CFS}(xyz) = \Gamma_{CFS}(xy)$. This example shows that there are rationales which do not satisfy the conditions of our model. At the same time, it is easy to show that for any rationalization,

$$x \in \Gamma_{CFS}(S) \Rightarrow x \in \Gamma_{CFS}(T) \text{ for all } x \in T \subset S.$$

This property does not necessarily hold in our framework (e.g., Most Popular Category). Hence, there are attention filters which do not satisfy the conditions of their model. In short, neither model is a special case of the other.

One can modify Rationalization to make it a proper special case of our model. The necessary modification requires that the admissible rationales are not only transitive but are also complete.[17] If Rationalization were restricted in this way, each rationalizable alternative is an attention filter (though the converse is still not true).

[17] "The top on each criterion" introduced in Sect. 2.1 coincides with the rationalization model when all rationales are complete.

We now demonstrate how these models differ from the CLA model behaviorally by means of examples. First, we shall present an example of a CLA that cannot be explained by any of these models. Although these models have different characterizations, all of them satisfy the axiom called Weak-WARP (Manzini and Mariotti 2007) so we only need to show that it violates that axiom. The Weak-WARP states that if x is chosen over y both from the pair and from a larger set, y cannot be chosen from anywhere between. Formally,

Weak-WARP. Suppose $\{x, y\} \subset T \subset S$. If $x = c(xy) = c(S)$, then $y \neq c(T)$.

Consider the following example of a CLA:

Example 2 There are four alternatives x, y, a, b. The alternatives a and b are never chosen (unless there is no other alternative) but they alter the attention of the decision maker. Her preference is $y \succ x \succ a \succ b$ and picks the best alternative from those she considers. She considers y only when either a or b is feasible but not both and always considers all other alternatives. It is easy to see that her consideration set mapping is an attention filter so her choice function satisfies WARP(LA). However, it does not satisfy Weak-WARP because $c(xy) = c(xyab) = x$ (y is not considered) but $c(xya) = y$.

Conversely, none of the above alternative models is a special case of the CLA model. In Example 3, we present a model of Rational Shortlist Method of Manzini and Mariotti (2007) that cannot be a CLA. One can easily verify that the exactly same choice function can be generated by other models mentioned above. The rational shortlist model consists of two rationales P_1 and P_2 where P_1 has no cycle (not necessarily transitive) and P_2 is a complete and transitive order.[18] The decision is made applying these rationales sequentially to eliminate alternatives. Consider the following example of the rational shortlist model:

Example 3 The first rationale (not transitive[19]) and the second rationale (transitive) are:

$$tP_1y, \ yP_1x, \ zP_1x, \ zP_1s,$$

$$sP_2xP_2yP_2zP_2t.$$

For instance, if the feasible set is $\{s, y, z\}$, s is eliminated in the first stage by z and she picks y in the second stage by comparing y and z according to P_2. However,

[18]Actually, Manzini and Mariotti (2007) do not require the second rationale (P_2) to be complete and transitive (it only requires P_2 to be asymmetric). We put the stronger requirement on P_2 in order to highlight that the difference between these models is generated by the first stage, not by the incompleteness or intransitivity of the second rationale, which corresponds to the DM's preference in our model.

[19]One can show that if P_1 is transitive, the first stage elimination generates an attention filter so the resulting choice will be a CLA as long as P_2 is complete and transitive.

this choice function would generate contradictory revealed preferences if it were a CLA:

- zPt since $z = c(yzt)$ and $y = c(yz)$,
- tPy since $t = c(xyt)$ and $x = c(xt)$,
- yPz since $y = c(syz)$ and $s = c(sy)$.

Thus, it cannot be explained by a CLA by Lemma 1. Hence, this choice cannot be a part of our model.

5 Anomalies

Our limited attention model is capable of accommodating several frequently observed behaviors: Attraction Effect, Cyclical Choice, and Choosing Pairwisely Unchosen. Our explanations for these choice patterns solely depend on limited attention, hence seemingly irrational behaviors can be explained without introducing changing preference. We will overview them and illustrate how our model accommodates them. In addition to that, we elicit the DM's preference, attention and inattention from such choice data.

5.1 Attraction Effect

The attraction effect refers to a phenomenon where adding an irrelevant alternative to a choice set affects the choice.[20] A typical attraction effect choice patterns is

$$c(xyd) = y, \;\; c(xy) = x, \;\; c(yd) = y, \;\; c(xd) = x.$$

Here d is the irrelevant alternative that shifts the choice from x to y.[21] Thus, d is the decoy of y. Lehmann and Pan (1994) experimentally show that introducing new products causes an attraction effect particularly by affecting the composition

[20]This phenomenon is well-documented and robust in behavioral research on marketing (Huber et al. 1982; Tversky and Simonson 1993), including choices among monetary gambles, political candidates, job candidates, environmental issues, and medical decision making. Advertising irrelevant alternatives is commonly used as a marketing strategy to invoke the attraction effect on the customers.

[21]The standard continuity is inconsistent with the attraction effect: $x = c(x, d_n, y)$ for all n but y is chosen at the limit ($y = c(x, y)$) where $\{d_n\}$ is a sequence of x's decoys converging to x. Nevertheless, the model can still enjoy a weaker continuity along with the attraction effect. For example, assume $y_n \to y$ and $y, y_n \notin S$, then

$$\text{If} y_n \notin c(S \cup y_n) \text{then} \{y\} \neq c(S \cup y_n).$$

of consideration sets. How the CLA model accommodates the attraction effect is in line with their findings. One possible representation is that the DM's preference is $y \succ x \succ d$ and she considers y only when d is present (otherwise, she considers everything). It is clear that her consideration set mapping is an attention filter.

Now we elicit the preference of a decision maker whose choice behavior follows the same pattern above without knowing her preference and consideration sets. By Theorem 1, $y = c(xyd) \neq c(xy)$ imply that y is revealed to be preferred to d. That is, our model judges that she prefers y over its own decoy.

Although most of the research on attraction effect is centered around with one decoy option, a natural extension of the attraction effect is to include additional decoys. In particular, what happens if a decoy of x is additionally introduced to the aforementioned example? Teppan and Felfernig (2009) demonstrated that displaying both a decoy of x and a decoy of y along with x and y will lead the DM to choose as if there were no decoys.[22]

Formally, suppose that there are two decoys d_x and d_y of x and y, respectively. That is,

$$c(xyd_xd_y) = x, \quad c(xyd_y) = y, \quad c(xy) = x.$$

The most of the theoretical literature, including the ones that can accommodate the attraction effect with one decoy option, cannot accommodate this choice behavior.[23] Nevertheless, the CLA model can accommodate this behavior: she considers y only when d_y is present but d_x is not. She ignores x when d_y is available but not d_x. Then she will exhibit the above choice as long as she prefers x over d_x and y over d_y.

Again, assume we have no prior information about the DM's preference and consideration sets. The first two choices reveal that she pays attention to d_x at $\{x, y, d_x, d_y\}$ so prefers x over d_x. Similarly, the second and third tell us she prefers y over d_y. Therefore, our approach again elicits her preference between an alternative and its decoy.

Here, we rely on the paper by Lehmann and Pan (1994) which experimentally suggest that attraction effect is due to the composition of consideration sets. However, there are other explanations for attraction effect (Huber et al. 1982). For

---

Indeed, one can show that the CLA is continuous in this sense if $\succ$ is continuous and the attention filter satisfies: (a) $y_n \notin \Gamma(S \cup y_n)$ implies $y \notin \Gamma(S \cup y)$ and (b) $z \in \Gamma(S \cup y_n)$ implies $z \in \Gamma(S \cup y)$ when $y_n \to y$.

[22]Eliaz and Spiegler (2011) studied a game theoretical model where firms would like to influence consumers' consideration sets by introducing costly decoys.

[23]This generalized attraction effect is another example that lies outside of recent models provided in Cherepanov et al. 2008, Manzini and Mariotti (2012) and Lleras et al. (2010, When more is less: choice by limited consideration, unpublished) since it does not satisfy Weak-WARP. There are two exceptions: Ok et al. (2010, Revealed (p)reference theory, unpublished) and de Clippel and Eliaz (2012). However, these two models can accommodate neither Cyclical nor Choosing Pairwisely choice patterns.

example, one explanation concerns the decision-maker being able to "give a reason" for the choice of x over y or vice versa. An asymmetrically dominated alternative gives such a reason. It seems that each explanation could be more appropriate than the others depending on the environment.

5.2 Cyclical Choice

May (1954) provides the first experiment where cyclical choice patterns are observed and these results have been replicated in many different choice environments (e.g. Tversky 1969; Loomes et al. (1991); Manzini and Mariotti 2009; Mandler et al., 2010, A million answers to twenty questions: choosing by checklist, unpublished). Consider a cyclical choice pattern:

$$c(xyz) = x, \quad c(xy) = x, \quad c(yz) = y, \quad c(xz) = z.$$

We have already illustrated that this choice pattern can be captured by our model at the beginning of Sect. 3. Now let us elicit the preference. Since the DM exhibits a choice reversal when y is removed from $\{x, y, z\}$, we can identify that y attracts her attention when these three elements are present. So, we can conclude that she prefers x over y. However, as illustrated before, we cannot determine the ranking of z.

5.3 Choosing Pairwisely Unchosen

In this choice pattern, the DM chooses an alternative that is never chosen from pairwise comparisons:

$$c(xyz) = z, \quad c(xy) = x, \quad c(yz) = y, \quad c(xz) = x.$$

Since removing x or y from $\{x, y, z\}$ changes her choice, it is revealed that z is better than x and y but we cannot determine her preference between x and y. Since her revealed preference has no cycle, her behavior is captured by our model through Lemma 1 and Theorem 3.

Note that the best element, z, is not chosen in any binary choice so we can conclude that she pays attention to z only when x and y are present. Applying Theorem 2, we can pin down her consideration set uniquely except when her feasible set is $\{x, y\}$ (Table 19.2).

One possible story that generates such an attention pattern is "searching more when the decision is tough." Several items are hard to find even if they are feasible. The decision maker first considers alternatives that are feasible and easy to find and if there is an item that dominates all others, she chooses it immediately. Otherwise, she makes an extensive search to find all feasible items. In the former case, the

Table 19.2 Choosing pairwisely unchosen

	zP_Rx and zP_Ry			
Revealed preference	$\{x, y, z\}$	$\{x, y\}$	$\{y, z\}$	$\{x, z\}$
Revealed attention	xyz	x	y	x
Revealed inattention	–	–	z	z

consideration set consists only of easily found (and feasible) alternatives and in the latter case it coincides with the feasible set. Given this story, suppose her true preference is $z \succ x \succ y$ where the decision between x and y is very tough and z is hard to find. She makes an extensive search to find z only if she sees both x and y. If either x or y is missing, she does not bother to search, and therefore overlooks z.

6 Further Comments on Revealed Preference

In this section, we discuss the boundaries of our revealed preference approach. First of all, our revealed preference could be very incomplete; in other words, it only provides coarse welfare judgements. In the extreme case where the choice data satisfies WARP, Theorems 1 and 2 do not provide any identification of the preference and attention/inattention. This is because the DM's behavior can be attributed fully to her preference or to her inattention (never considering anything other than her actual choice). Thus, we cannot make any statement without imposing any additional assumption. This extreme example illustrates the limitation of choice data, which alone is not enough to identify her preferences. Notice that the classical revealed preference is not an exception since it implicitly assumes the full attention.

Nevertheless, a policy maker may be *forced* to make a welfare judgement even when our revealed preference is silent. There are three directions to deal with incompleteness of our revealed preference: (1) looking for additional data other than choice data, (2) imposing additional structures on attention filter, and/or (3) utilizing other methods as long as the resulting revealed preference includes ours. We will discuss each of them in detail.

◇ Additional Data: The idea of our (direct) revealed preference is that we can conclude x is preferred to y if x is chosen while y receives attention, which is inferred because removing y changes her choice. However, if we know y is considered for some other reason, we will naturally make the same conclusion even without observing such a choice change. One can obtain such information from many sources, such as eye-tracking, fMRI and the tracking system in the internet commerce.[24] If the policy maker believes that these sources are trustworthy, he can utilize them to obtain additional information about preferences.

[24]In this regard, our theory highlights the importance of other tools (besides observed choice) which can shed light on the choice process rather than outcome.

Furthermore, additional information about preferences can also have a cascading effect. For instance, the choice data may not reveal the ranking between x and y but some laboratory experiment or survey study may have already found that x is better than y. In such a case, the policy maker can add $x \succ y$ to the revealed preference generated by our method (Theorem 1), say $P' = P_R \cup \{(x, y)\}$. By using the transitive closure of P', denoted by P'_R, the policy maker can obtain more attention/inattention information as in Theorem 2. Indeed, Theorems 1 and 2 are exactly applicable by replacing P_R with the transitive closure of P'_R.

Similarly, a policy maker may know the consumer pays attention to x under certain decision problem. This information immediately generates more information about her preference, (the chosen element here is better than x), which tells more about her attention/inattention like in the previous case.

◇ Further Restrictions on Consideration Sets: The other direction is to impose additional restrictions on Γ. For example, if the source of limited attention is simply the abundance of alternatives, one reasonable restriction is that the decision maker considers at least two alternatives for each decision problem. That is $|\Gamma(S)| \geqslant 2$. Under this restriction, the choice data reveals the consumer's preference completely. This result is trivial but still it is important in order to identify whether an unchosen alternative attracts attention. Our approach will provide an answer for the revealed attention. The revealed attention and inattention will be characterized by Theorem 2 by replacing P_R with the completely identified preference.

Notice that the classical revealed preference can be seen as one of such an attempt with the strongest assumption on the consideration set $\Gamma(S) = S$. Our model highlights that we need to assume *how* choices are made in order to make a meaningful revealed preference exercise. The assumption about *what* are chosen (like WARP) is not enough.

◇ Other Methods: One can combine our methodology with others which try to make the welfare analysis without relying on a particular choice procedure, such as Apesteguia and Ballester (2010, A measure of rationality and welfare, unpublished) and Bernheim and Rangel (2009). What is common between our model and theirs is that all try to respect consumer's choice for the welfare judgment as much as possible. The difference is that our model does so only when the consumer actually considers other unchosen alternatives.

Now imagine that a policy maker knows/believes a consumer behaves according to our model. Then, he should first elicit her preference based on our method. Admittedly, it only provides an incomplete ranking (and empty if the choice data satisfies WARP). If the policy maker is *forced* to make a complete welfare judgement with a risk of making mistakes, he can apply the other methods with the constraint of respecting the revealed preference generated by our model. In other words, these methods should be used to break the incompleteness of our revealed preference.

For instance, consider Apesteguia and Ballester's approach. They first axiomatically construct an index to measure the consistency between choice data and a certain preference, and of all complete and transitive preferences pick the one that minimizes the inconsistency for the welfare analysis. However, if the policy maker knows the decision maker follows a choice with limited attention, he should first elicit her preference based on our method and then pick the inconsistency-minimizing preference *only from those that are consistent with our revealed preference*. The resulting welfare judgment can be wrong (can be different from her actual preference). Nevertheless, this sequential process eliminates certain mistakes the policy maker would make if he simply applied the other model-free methods. For instance, applying Apesteguia and Ballester's approach directly to Example 1 will lead the wrong conclusion: y is welfare improving over x but this sequential advocacy certainly kills such a mistake.

7 Conclusion

Limited attention has been widely studied in economics: neglecting the nontransparent taxes (Chetty et al. 2009), inattention to released information (DellaVigna and Pollet 2007), costly information acquisition (Gabaix et al. 2006), and rational inattention in macroeconomics (Sims 2003). For example, Goeree (2008) shows that relaxing the full attention assumption by allowing customers to be unaware of some computers in the market is enough to explain the high markups in the PC industry.

In this chapter, we study the implications of limited attention on revealed preference. We illustrate when and how one can deduce both the preference and consideration sets of a DM who follows a CLA. The distinction between a preference and an (in)attention is crucial. For instance, if a product is not popular in a market, it is very important for a firm to know the reason, which can either be that it is not liked by consumers or that it does not attract the attentions of consumers. Our model provides a theoretical framework to distinguish these two possibilities. Similarly, a social planner can find a proper strategy to make sure that people choose the right option in 401(K) plans and health insurance. Hence, in a welfare analysis it is important to understand the underlying model of the DM.

Since revealed preference and (in)attention are the main focus of the paper, we impose a rather weak restriction on consideration sets. Such a weak condition allows us to apply our revealed preference and (in)attention theorems to seemingly irrational choice patterns (i.e. Attraction Effect, Cyclical Choice, and Choosing Pairwisely Unchosen). Nevertheless, depending on the intended application, our framework can be used to analyze choices under different restrictions on consideration sets.

◇ In many real-world markets, products compete with each other for the space in the consideration set of the DM, who has cognitive limitations. In these situations, if an alternative attracts attention when there exist many others, then it is easier to be considered when some of other alternatives become unavailable. If a product is able to attract attention in a crowded supermarket shelf, the same product will be noticed when there are fewer alternatives, i.e., $x \in \Gamma(T)$ implies $x \in \Gamma(S)$ whenever

$x \in S \subset T$. Lleras et al. (2010, When more is less: choice by limited consideration, unpublished) extensively study consideration sets which satisfy this property. They also consider the cases where both conditions are satisfied.

◇ Lleras et al. (2010, When more is less: choice by limited consideration, unpublished) also consider another special case whereby the decision maker overlooks or disregards an alternative because it is dominated by another item in some aspect. Imagine Maryland's economics department is hiring one tenure-track theorist. Since there are too many candidates in the job market to consider all of them, the department asks other departments to recommend their best theory student. Therefore, a candidate from Michigan is ignored if and only if there is another Michigan candidate who is rated better by Michigan. In this case, Maryland's filter is represented by a irreflexive and transitive order as long as each department's ranking over its students is rational. Formally, given an irreflexive and transitive order $\rhd$,[25] the attention filter consists of alternatives which are undominated with respect to this order, $\Gamma_{\rhd}(S) = \{x \in S | \nexists y \in S \text{ s.t.} y \rhd x\}$.

Appendix

Proofs

Notice that the if-parts of Theorems 1 and 2 have been already shown in the main text. The following proofs use these results.

Proof of Theorem 3

Suppose c is a CLA represented by $(\succ, \Gamma)$. Then Theorem 1(if part) implies that $\succ$ must include P so P must be acyclic. Therefore, by Lemma 1, c must satisfy WARP(LA).

Now suppose that c satisfies WARP(LA). By Lemma 1, P is acyclic so there is a preference $\succ$ that includes P. Pick any such preference arbitrarily and define

$$\Gamma(S) = \{x \in S \,:\, c(S) \succ x\} \cup \{c(S)\}. \tag{19.2}$$

Then, it is clear that $c(S)$ is the unique $\succ$-best element in $\Gamma(S)$ so all we need to show is that Γ is an attention filter. Suppose $x \in S$ but $x \notin \Gamma(S)$ (so $x \neq c(S)$). By construction, $x \succ c(S)$ so it cannot be $c(S)Px$. Hence, it must be $c(S) = c(S \setminus x)$ so we have $\Gamma(S) = \Gamma(S \setminus x)$. □

[25] This order is not necessarily complete, as in this example; Michigan does not compare its students with candidates from other schools.

Proof of Theorem 1 (The Only-If Part)

Suppose $xP_{R}y$ does not hold. Then there exists a preference that includes P_R and ranks y better than x. The proof of Theorem 3 shows that c can be represented by such a preference so x is not revealed to be preferred to y. □

Proof of Theorem 2 (The Only-If Parts)

(Revealed Inattention) Suppose x is not revealed to be preferred to $c(S)$. Then pick a preference that includes P_R and puts $c(S)$ above x. The proof of Theorem 3 shows that c can be represented by such a preference and an attention filter Γ with $x \in \Gamma(S)$.

(Revealed Attention) Suppose there exists no T which satisfies the condition. We shall prove that if c is a CLA then it can be represented by some attention filter Γ with $x \notin \Gamma(S)$. If $c(S)P_Rx$ does not hold, we have already shown that c can be represented with $x \succ c(S)$ and $x \notin \Gamma(S)$ so x is not revealed to attract attention at S, so we focus on the case when $c(S)P_Rx$.

Now construct a binary relation, $\tilde{P}$, where $a\tilde{P}b$ if and only if "aP_Rb" or "$a = c(S)$ and not $bP_Rc(S)$." That is, $\tilde{P}$ puts $c(S)$ as high as possible as long as it does not contradict P_R. Since P_R is acyclic and c is represented by an attention filter, one can show that $\tilde{P}$ is also acyclic. Given this, take any preference relation $\succ$ that includes $\tilde{P}$, which includes P_R as well. We have already shown that $\tilde{\Gamma}(S) \equiv \{z \in S : c(S) \succ z\} \cup \{c(S)\}$ is an attention filter and $(\tilde{\Gamma}, \succ)$ represents c. Now define Γ as follows:

$$\Gamma\left(S'\right) = \begin{cases} \tilde{\Gamma}\left(S'\right) & \text{for } S' \notin \mathcal{D}, \\ \tilde{\Gamma}\left(S'\right) \setminus x & \text{for } S' \in \mathcal{D}, \end{cases}$$

where $\mathcal{D}$ is a collections of sets such that

$$\mathcal{D} = \left\{ S' \subset X : \begin{array}{c} c\left(S'\right) = c\left(S\right) \quad \text{and} \\ zP_Rc\left(S\right) \ \text{for all } z \in \left(S \setminus S'\right) \cup \left(S' \setminus S\right). \end{array} \right\}$$

That is, Γ is obtained from $\tilde{\Gamma}$ by removing from x any budget set S' where $c(S) = c(S')$ and any item that belongs to S or S' but not to both is revealed to be better than $c(S)$. Notice that x cannot be $c(S)$ because if this true, the condition of the statement is satisfied for $T = S$. Hence, $\Gamma(S') \subset \tilde{\Gamma}(S')$ always includes $c(S')$. Furthermore the proof of Theorem 3 shows that $(\tilde{\Gamma}, \succ)$ represents c. Therefore, $(\Gamma, \succ)$ also represents c so we only need to show that Γ is an attention filter.

To do that, it is useful to notice that $\tilde{\Gamma}$ is an attention filter and $c(T') = c(T'')$ whenever $\tilde{\Gamma}(T') = \tilde{\Gamma}(T'')$ because $(\tilde{\Gamma}, \succ)$ represents c.

Suppose $y \notin \Gamma(T)$. We shall prove $\Gamma(T) = \Gamma(T \setminus y)$.

Case I: $y = x$
If $T \notin \mathscr{D}$, then we have $\Gamma(T) = \tilde{\Gamma}(T) = \tilde{\Gamma}(T \setminus x) = \Gamma(T \setminus x)$. If $T \in \mathscr{D}$, then it must be $c(T) = c(T \setminus x)$ (otherwise, the condition of the statement is satisfied) so by construction of $\tilde{\Gamma}$ and Γ, we have $\Gamma(T) = \tilde{\Gamma}(T) \setminus x = \tilde{\Gamma}(T \setminus x) = \Gamma(T \setminus x)$.

Case II: $T \in \mathscr{D}$ and $y \neq x$
Since $y \notin \Gamma(T)$ is equivalent to $y \notin \tilde{\Gamma}(T)$, we have $\tilde{\Gamma}(T) = \tilde{\Gamma}(T \setminus y)$. Therefore, $c(T \setminus y) = c(T) = c(S)$. By construction of Γ and $\tilde{\Gamma}$, it must be $y \succ c(S)$, which implies $yP_{Rc}(S)$ by construction of $\succ$. Therefore, $T \setminus y \in \mathscr{D}$. Therefore, $\Gamma(T) = \tilde{\Gamma}(T) \setminus x = \tilde{\Gamma}(T \setminus y) \setminus x = \Gamma(T \setminus y)$.

Case III: $T \notin \mathscr{D}$ and $y \neq x$
If $T \setminus y \in \mathscr{D}$, analogously to the previous case, we have $c(T) = c(T \setminus y) = c(S)$ and $yP_R c(S)$ so it must be $T \in \mathscr{D}$, which is a contradiction. Hence, $T \setminus y \notin \mathscr{D}$ so we have $\Gamma(T) = \tilde{\Gamma}(T) = \tilde{\Gamma}(T \setminus y) = \Gamma(T \setminus y)$. □

Addendum[26]

The article in this chapter, since first presented in 2008, have triggered many interesting studies.[27] It is not possible to address all of them so I am presenting two most closely related ones in this addendum.

Incorporating Auxiliary Data

As we discuss in Sect. 6, it is not always possible to *completely* elicit DM's preference from her choice data, which contains only pairs of a feasible set and her choice. In many environments, we can access data beyond feasible sets. For instance, marketing analysts knows the amount of time and money spent on advertisements for each product.

Consider the following situation. The DM chooses x from a certain set of alternatives. Now her choice suddenly shifts to y when a third product z is more advertised. I argue that she prefers y to z. To see this, suppose she does not pay attention to z in the latter environment. Then, it is hard to imagine she does so in the former case where z is less advertised. Thus, z is never considered in neither environment. Extending the idea of attention filters, I conclude that the advertising such an ignored product will not affect her attention span, so should not cause the choice shift. This is a contradiction so she must have considered z when it is more advertised. Thus, we can conclude she prefers y to z.

[26]This addendum has been newly written by Daisuke Nakajima for this book chapter.

[27]Nakajima appreciates the financial support provided by Japan Society for the Promotion of Science (JSPS KAKENHI Grant Number 26780113).

Iwata (2013) generalizes this idea, which illustrates how to utilize observable salience factors possessed by each alternative in each decision problem. Iwata's model, called generalized CLA, consists of a stable preference and a consideration set mapping like our original CLA model. The difference is that Iwata's consideration set mapping now depends not only on a feasible set but also on salience factors of all alternatives. Adapting the idea of our attention filter, Iwata requires DM's attention filter unaffected when an unconsidered alternative is removed or when an unconsidered alternative's salience decreases. Iwata defines revealed preference, attention and inattention as we do, and characterizes them like our Theorems 1 and 2.

Limited Data

We assume all choice data are available. That is, DM's choices from all subsets of X are all observed. Although this requirement is not uncommon among the theoretical literatures, it sounds too much in many of empirical and experimental settings.

The lack of complete choice data does not undermine the effectiveness of our identification. We can conclude that the DM prefers x to y based only on as few as two decision problems. Nevertheless, de Clippel and Rozen (2014) illustrates Theorems 1 and 3 cannot be literally extended when choice data is limited. Example 2 in their study demonstrates this issue as follows. Suppose there are five potentially available alternatives a, b, d, e, f, but we observe only five choice data:

$$c(ae) = e, \ \ c(ef) = f, \ \ c(abd) = d, \ \ c(ade) = a.c(bde) = b.$$

Suppose c is a CLA. This data contains only one choice reversals (between *ade* and *ad*) so $a \succ d$ seems the only revealed preference.

We can, however, also conclude that the DM prefers b to e. Imagine that the DM faced another binary decision problem between b and d. He would choose d. To see this, note that $a \notin \Gamma(ade)$ because $a \succ c(ade) = d$. Thus, removing a would not affect her consideration span nor her choice so it would be $c(bd) = d$. Notice that we observe $c(bde) = b$ so removing e from *bde*, although it is not actually observed, would cause a choice reversal. Considering these hypothetical choices, we must conclude she prefers b over e. This example shows that, when the choice data is limited, Theorem 1 overlooks some identifiable parts of the DM's preference.

Now imagine that we have one more extra choice data $c(bef) = e$, which is the original version of Example 2 in Clippel and Rozen's paper. This extra information, together with $c(ef) = d$, makes it possible to identify $e \succ b$. This does not sound a contradiction if we do not imagine that the DM could face the choice between b and d. Thus one may wonder these six data are compatible with the CLA model but we have already shown that the first five data reveals $b \succ e$ by considering the hypothetical binary choice. In sum, this example illustrates that data seemingly satisfying the WALP(LA) may not be explained by the CLA model.

de Clippel and Rozen (2014) emphasize the second issue, and propose the remedy of the behavioral characterization of the CLA model (Proposition 2). Nevertheless, they remark that their results illustrates a weakness of our theory as follows:

> Being subject to this pitfall is not a weakness of a theory. Rather, the moral is that one cannot limit the test of consistency to finding a story that explains the observed data, without thinking whether that story extends. This extensibility problem is precisely avoided (for any theory) by employing Definition 1.

In line with their remark, I would like to emphasize the following point: the first issue (the overlooked revealed preference) shows that our model can generate more preference information by the careful investigations rather than mindlessly applying Theorem 1. It does not show a pitfall of but a power of our model, which is more than it appears to have.

References

Aumann RJ (2005) Musings on information and knowledge. Econ J Watch 2(1):88–96

Basar G, Bhat C (2004) A parameterized consideration set model for airport choice: an application to the San Francisco bay area. Trans Res Part B Methodol 38(10):889–904

Bernheim BD, Rangel A (2007) Toward choice-theoretic foundations for behavioral welfare economics. Am Econ Rev 97(2):464–470

Bernheim BD, Rangel A (2009) Beyond revealed preference: choice-theoretic foundations for behavioral welfare economics. Q J Econ 124(1):51–104

Broadbent DE (1958) Perception and communication. Pergamon, New York

Caplin A, Dean M (2011) Search, choice, and revealed preference. Theor Econ 6:19–48

Caplin A, Dean M, Martin D (2009) Search and satisficing. Am Econ Rev 101:2899–2922. doi: 10.1257/aer.101.7.2899

Chambers CP, Hayashi T (2008) Choice and individual welfare. HSS California Institute of Technology Working Paper 1286

Cherepanov V, Feddersen T, Sandroni A (2013) Rationalization. Theor Econ 8:775–800

Chetty R, Looney A, Kroft K (2009) Salience and taxation: theory and evidence. Am Econ Rev 99(4):1145–1177

Chiang J, Chib S, Narasimhan C (1998) Markov chain Monte Carlo and models of consideration set and parameter heterogeneity. J Econ 89(1–2):223–248

Dawes PL, Brown J (2005) The composition of consideration and choice sets in undergraduate university choice: an exploratory study. J Market High Educ 14(2):37–59

de Clippel G, Eliaz K (2012) Reason-based choice: a bargaining rationale for the attraction and compromise effects. Theor Econ 7:125–162

de Clippel G, Rozen K (2014) Bounded rationality and limited datasets. Mimeo. http://www.econ.brown.edu/fac/Geoffroy_declippel/GK_BRLimitedData.pdf

DellaVigna S, Pollet J (2007) Demographics and industry returns. Am Econ Rev 97:1167–1702

Dulleck U, Hackl F, Weiss B, Winter-Ebmer R (2008) Buying online: sequential decision making by shopbot visitors. Wien economics series, vol 225. Institut für Höhere Studien

Eliaz K, Spiegler R (2011) Consideration sets and competitive marketing. Rev Econ Stud 78(1):235–262

Eliaz K, Richter M, Rubinstein A (2011) An etude in choice theory: choosing the two finalists. Econ Theory 46(2):211–219

Gabaix X, Laibson D, Moloche G, Weinberg S (2006) Costly information acquisition: experimental analysis of a boundedly rational model. Am Econ Rev 96(4):1043–1068

Goeree MS (2008) Limited information and advertising in the US personal computer industry. Econometrica 76:1017–1074
Green JR, Hojman D (2008) Choice, rationality and welfare measurement. Harvard Institute of Economic Research Discussion Paper No. 2144
Hauser JR, Wernerfelt B (1990) An evaluation cost model of evoked sets. J Consum Res 16:383–408
Hausman D (2008) Mindless or mindfull economics: a methodological evaluation. In: Caplin A, Schotter A (eds) The foundations of positive and normative economics: a handbook. Oxford University Press, New York, pp 125–155
Houy N (2007) Rationality and order-dependent sequential rationality. Theory Decis 62(2):119–134
Houy N, Tadenuma K (2009) Lexicographic compositions of multiple criteria for decision making. J Econ Theory 144(4):1770–1782
Huber J, Payne JW, Puto C (1982) Adding asymmetrically dominated alternatives: violations of regularity and the similarity hypothesis. J Consum Res 9(1):90–98
Huberman G, Regev T (2001) Contagious speculation and a cure for cancer: a nonevent that made stock prices soar. J Financ 56(1):387–396
Iwata Y (2013) Generalized revealed attention. Mimeo, Nishogakusha University, Tokyo
Lavidge RJ, Steiner GA (1961) A model for predictive measurements of advertising effectiveness. J Market 25:59–62
Lehmann DR, Pan Y (1994) Context effects, new brand entry, and consideration sets. J Market Res 31(3):364–374
Loomes G, Starmer C, Sugden R (1991) Observing violations of transitivity by experimental methods. Econometrica 59(2):425–439
Manzini P, Mariotti M (2007) Sequentially rationalizable choice. Am Econ Rev 97(5):1824–1839
Manzini P, Mariotti M (2009) Choice over time. In: Anand P, Pattanaik P, Puppe C (eds) Oxford handbook of rational and social choice, chapter 10. Oxford University Press, New York
Manzini P, Mariotti M (2012) Categorize then choose: boundedly rational choice and welfare. J Eur Econ Assoc 10(5). doi: 10.2307/23251215.
Masatlioglu Y, Nakajima D, Ozbay EY (2012) Revealed attention. Am Econ Rev 102(5):2183–2205
May KO (1954) Intransitivity, utility, and the aggregation of preference patterns. Econometrica 22:1–13
Noor J (2011) Temptation and revealed preference. Econometrica 79(2):601–644
Pessemier EA (1978) Stochastic properties of changing preferences. Am Econ Rev 68(2):380–385
Richards MD, Sheridan JE, Slocum JW (1975) Comparative analysis of expectancy and heuristic models of decision behavior. J Appl Psychol 60(3):361–368
Roberts JH, Lattin JM (1991) Development and testing of a model of consideration set composition. J Market Res 28(4):429–440
Rubinstein A, Salant Y (2009) Eliciting welfare preferences from behavioral datasets. Rev Econ Stud 79(1). doi: 10.2307/41407054.
Salant Y, Rubinstein A (2008) Choice with frames. Rev Econ Stud 75:1287–1296
Samuelson PA (1938) A note on the pure theory of consumers' behavior. Econometrica (February) 61–71
Simon HA (1957) Models of man: social and rational: mathematical essays on rational human behavior in a social setting. Wiley, New York
Sims CA (2003) Implications of rational inattention. J Monet Econ 50(3):665–690
Stigler GJ (1961) The economics of information. J Politi Econ 69(3):213–225
Teppan EC, Felfernig A (2009) Minimization of product utility estimation errors in recommender result set evaluations. In: WI-IAT 2009 proceedings of the 2009 IEEE/ WIC/ACM international joint conference on web intelligence and intelligent agent technology, vol 1. University of Milano-Bicocca, Milan, pp 20–27
Tversky A (1969) Intransitivity of preferences. Psychol Rev 76:31–48
Tversky A, Simonson I (1993) Context-dependent preferences. Manag Sci 39(10):1179–1189

Varian HR (2006) Revealed preference. In: Szenberg M, Ramrattan L, Gottesman AA (eds) Samuelsonian economics and the twenty-first century. Oxford University Press, New York, pp 99–115

Wright P, Barbour F (1977) Phased decision strategies: sequels to an initial screening. In: Starr MK, Zeleny M (eds) Studies in management sciences, multiple criteria decision making. North-Holland, Amsterdam, pp 91–109

Zyman S (1999) The end of marketing as we know it. Harper Collins, New York

Chapter 20
Subjective Random Discounting and Intertemporal Choice

Youichiro Higashi, Kazuya Hyogo, and Norio Takeoka

Abstract This chapter provides an axiomatic foundation for a particular type of preference shock model called the *random discounting representation* where a decision maker believes that her discount factors change randomly over time. For this purpose, we formulate an infinite horizon extension of Dekel, Lipman, and Rustichini (Econometrica 69:891–934, 2001), and identify the behavior that reduces all subjective uncertainties to those about future discount factors. We also show uniqueness of subjective belief about discount factors. Moreover, a behavioral comparison about preference for flexibility characterizes the condition that one's subjective belief second-order stochastically dominates the other. Finally, the resulting model is applied to a consumption-savings problem.

Keywords Random discounting • Preference for flexibility • Subjective states

1 Introduction

1.1 Objective and Outline

In intertemporal decision making, a decision maker (DM) faces two kinds of trade-offs among alternatives. The first is a trade-off from the difference of alternatives within a time period and the second is an intertemporal trade-off between different

The original article first appeared in the Journal of Economic Theory 144:1015–1053, 2009. A newly written addendum has been added to this book chapter.

Y. Higashi
Faculty of Economics, Okayama University, Okayama, Japan
e-mail: higashi@e.okayama-u.ac.jp

K. Hyogo
Faculty of Economics, Ryukoku University, Kyoto, Japan
e-mail: hyogo@econ.ryukoku.ac.jp

N. Takeoka (✉)
Faculty of Economics, Yokohama National University, Yokohama, Japan
e-mail: takeoka@ynu.ac.jp

S. Ikeda et al. (eds.), *Behavioral Economics of Preferences, Choices, and Happiness*, DOI 10.1007/978-4-431-55402-8_20

time periods. Anticipating intertemporal trade-offs seems more difficult than anticipating trade-offs within a period. Thus, we consider a DM who is certain about ranking of alternatives within a period, and at the same time is uncertain about future intertemporal discount rates.

In addition, several authors have mentioned psychological reasons for uncertainty about discount factors. As Yaari (1965) and Blanchard (1985) point out, a discount factor admits an interpretation as a probability of death. Depending on the future prospects of diseases, armed conflicts, and discoveries in medical treatments, the probabilities of death will change over time. An alternative interpretation is to think not of an agent but of a dynasty, in which case a discount factor is regarded as a degree of altruism. The bequest motives of the current generations may fluctuate over time because they may die without descendants. Becker and Mulligan (1997) suggest a model in which a discount factor depends on the quantity of resources the DM invests into making future pleasures less remote. For example, schooling may focus students' attention on the future, and parents would spend resources on teaching their children to make better future plan. The choice of investment or effort level in these activities is affected by economic variables, for instance, interest rates or the DM's wealth, which are uncertain by their own nature. Thus, these uncertainties may lead to random discounting.[1]

Moreover, random discounting has been used in several macroeconomic models with infinite horizon since it is a useful device for generating heterogeneity among agents, in particular, for realistic wealth heterogeneity in quantitative models. For example, see Krusell and Smith (1998) and Chatterjee et al. (2007). However, preference shock to discounting is often postulated in an ad hoc way since shock cannot be observed directly by analysts. The reliance on these unobservable entities seems problematic.

In this chapter, we provide an axiomatic foundation for the random discounting model, in which the DM believes that her discount factors change randomly over time. Therefore, we demonstrate that there exists a behavior which can, in principle, pin down expected shocks to discount factors. For this purpose, we extend the two-period framework of Kreps (1979, 1992) and Dekel et al. (2001) (hereafter DLR) to an infinite horizon setting. They axiomatize a preference shock model by considering preference over menus (opportunity sets) of alternatives. If a DM is aware of uncertainties regarding her future preference over alternatives, then ranking of menus reflects how she perceives those uncertainties. Kreps and DLR derive the set of future preferences from the ranking of menus.

Behavioral characterization of random discounting shows that uncertainty about future preferences, whether it is about future discount factors or other aspects of preference, leads to a demand for flexibility—larger menus are preferred. This observation is made on the basis of Kreps and DLR. However, if uncertainty is only about discount factors, then flexibility has value only in limited cases. The

[1]See Mehra and Sah (2002, Section 1.1, pp. 871–873) for more examples about fluctuations in subjective parameters.

behavioral characterization of random discounting takes the form of identifying primarily the instances where flexibility has no value (see the example that follows shortly for elaboration).

To analyze sequential decision making, we adopt the same domain of choice used by Gul and Pesendorfer (2004). Let C be the outcome space (consumption set), which is a compact metric space. There exists a compact metric space $\mathscr{Z}$ such that $\mathscr{Z}$ is homeomorphic to $\mathscr{K}(\Delta(C\times\mathscr{Z}))$, where $\Delta(C\times\mathscr{Z})$ is the set of lotteries, that is, all Borel probability measures over $C\times\mathscr{Z}$ and $\mathscr{K}(\cdot)$ denotes the set of all non-empty compact subsets of "·". An element of $\mathscr{Z}$, called a menu, is an opportunity set of lotteries over pairs of current consumption and future menus. Preference $\succsim$ is defined on $\mathscr{Z}\simeq\mathscr{K}(\Delta(C\times\mathscr{Z}))$.

We consider the following timing of decisions: In period 0, the DM chooses a menu x. In period 1^-, current discount factor α becomes known to the DM, and she chooses a lottery l out of the menu x in period 1. In period 1^+, the DM receives a pair (c,x') according to realization of the lottery l, and consumption c takes place. The DM expects another discount factor α' to be realized in the following period. Subsequently, she chooses another lottery l' out of the menu x', and so on.

Notice that our primitive $\succsim$ is preference in period 0. Thus, beyond period 0, the time line in Fig. 20.1 is not part of the formal model. However, if the DM has in mind this time line and anticipates uncertain discount factors to be resolved over time, then $\succsim$ should reflect the DM's perception of those uncertainties. Hence, our domain can capture the expectation of random discounting.

We provide an axiomatic foundation for the following functional form, called the *random discounting representation*: there exists a non-constant, continuous, mixture linear function $u:\Delta(C)\to\mathbb{R}$, and a probability measure μ over [0, 1] with $\mathbb{E}_\mu[\alpha]<1$, such that $\succsim$ is represented numerically by the functional form,

$$U(x)=\int_{[0,1]}\max_{l\in x}\left((1-\alpha)u(l_c)+\alpha\int_{\mathscr{Z}}U(z)\,\mathrm{d}l_z\right)\mathrm{d}\mu(\alpha),$$

where l_c and l_z are the marginal distributions of l on C and $\mathscr{Z}$, respectively.

The above functional form can be interpreted as follows: the DM behaves as if she has in mind the time line described above, and anticipates a discount factor α to be realized with probability μ in every time period. After the realization of α, the DM evaluates a lottery by the weighted sum of its instantaneous expected utility $u(l_c)$ and its expected continuation value $\int U(z)\,\mathrm{d}l_z$. The same representation

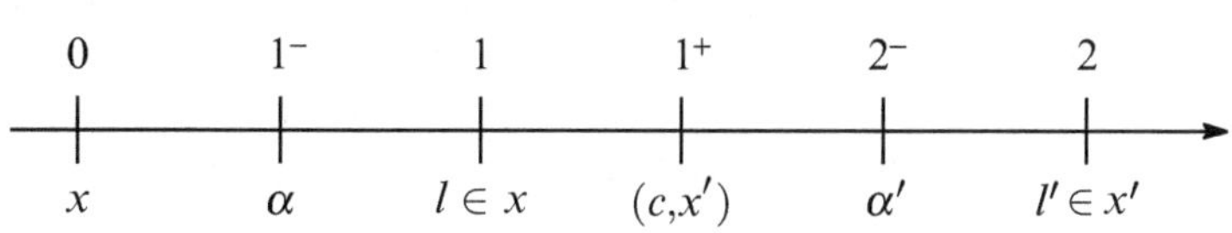

Fig. 20.1 Timing of decisions

U is used to evaluate menus at all times. Hence, the representation has a stationary recursive structure and the DM's belief about future discount factors is constant over time.

We show uniqueness of the DM's belief μ. That is, the components (u, μ) of the representation are uniquely derived from preference. This result is in stark contrast to that of Kreps (1979, 1992) and DLR. Since future preference is state-dependent in their model, arbitrary manipulations on subjective probabilities are possible. In our model, a future utility function over $\Delta(C \times \mathscr{Z})$ is state-dependent as in DLR (α corresponds to a subjective state). However, notice that both the instantaneous expected utility u and the utility U over menus are independent of subjective states, and state-dependent components, $1 - \alpha$ and α, add up to one. Hence, the representation cannot be maintained under arbitrary manipulations. A combination of the additive recursive structure and the normalization of discount factors ensures uniqueness.

Owing to uniqueness result, it is meaningful to compare subjective beliefs among agents. We provide a behavioral condition capturing a situation where one agent is more uncertain about discount factors than the other. For objective uncertainty, second-order stochastic dominance is widely used to describe such a comparison (Rothschild and Stiglitz 1970). If agent 2 perceives greater uncertainty about discount factors than agent 1, the former is more reluctant to make a commitment to a specific plan than the latter. This greater demand for flexibility is the behavioral manifestation of greater uncertainty about future discount factors. An implication of the behavioral comparison similar to DLR is also investigated and it shows contrasting results.

The resulting model is applied to a consumption-savings problem and it analyzes how uncertainty about discount factors affects savings behavior. By assuming an instantaneous utility function to be CRRA with the parameter $\sigma < 1$ (or $\sigma > 1$), savings rates increase (or decrease) when the DM becomes more uncertain about future discount factors in the sense of second-order stochastic dominance. This result can be interpreted based on the DM's attitude toward flexibility. It is noted that uncertainty about discount factors has an opposite effect on savings when compared to uncertainty about interest rates.

1.2 Motivating Example

To understand the behavior that characterizes the random discounting model, we consider a simple example as follows: Let C stand for a set of monetary payoffs.

Suppose that DM faces uncertainty about future discount factors. As pointed out by Kreps (1979) and DLR, she may keep her options open until the uncertainty is resolved, that is, she may exhibit preference for flexibility. On considering two alternatives, $(\$60, \{(\$100, z)\})$ and $(\$100, \{(\$50, z)\})$ in $\Delta(C \times \mathscr{Z})$, chosen in period 1, there might be a difference in consumption levels between periods 1 and 2. However, from period 3 onward, both alternatives guarantee the same opportunity set z. We assume that $\{(\$60, \{(\$100, z)\})\} \succsim \{(\$100, \{(\$50, z)\})\}$. This ranking under commitment reflects the DM's ex ante perspective on random discount factors. The DM, on average, believes that she will be patient in period 1 and prefer $(\$60, \{(\$100, z)\})$ to $(\$100, \{(\$50, z)\})$. However, the DM may still prefer keeping $(\$100, \{(\$50, z)\})$ as an option if there is a possibility of becoming impatient in period 1, in which case $(\$100, \{(\$50, z)\})$ would be more attractive than $(\$60, \{(\$100, z)\})$. Hence, the DM may exhibit preference for flexibility as

$$\left\{(\$60, \{(\$100, z)\}), (\$100, \{(\$50, z)\})\right\} \succ \left\{(\$60, \{(\$100, z)\})\right\}$$
$$\succsim \{(\$100, \{(\$50, z)\})\}.$$

However, if the DM is uncertain *only* about future discount factors, then other forms of flexibility may not be valued. In that case, the DM would be sure of her preference over consumption in the next period (in this example, consumption is scalar, and hence, greater consumption is preferred to less), and also other preference over menus for the rest of the horizon. Therefore, uncertainty is relevant for rankings only when an intertemporal trade-off must be made, as in comparing $(\$60, \{(\$100, z)\})$ and $(\$100, \{(\$50, z)\})$, between consumption for period 1 and the menu for period 2 onward. Hence, some forms of flexibility are *not* valuable on uncertainty related to future discount factors.

To illustrate further, consider a lottery l, yielding

$$(\$0, \{(\$0, z)\}) \text{ or } (\$120, \{(\$200, z)\})$$

with an equal probability of one-half. For current consumption, l induces the lottery yielding \$0 or \$120 with a probability of one-half, while it induces the lottery over menus with an equal chance of $\{(\$0, z)\}$ or $\{(\$200, z)\}$. If \$60 and $\{(\$100, z)\}$ are both preferred to these induced lotteries respectively, then the DM does not face an intertemporal trade-off between $(\$60, \{(\$100, z)\})$ and l. Irrespective of how patient she will be in the next period, l will not be chosen over $(\$60, \{(\$100, z)\})$. Since there is no benefit in keeping l as an option with $(\$60, \{(\$100, z)\})$, the DM will exhibit

$$\{(\$60, \{(\$100, z)\}), l\} \sim \{(\$60, \{(\$100, z)\})\} \succsim \{l\}.$$

In a later section, we formally provide axioms consistent with these behavior.

1.3 *Related Literature*

1.3.1 Macroeconomics

Random discounting in a number of infinite-horizon macroeconomic models, where its role broadly appears, generates suitable heterogeneity across agents. Models of wealth inequality based on standard and identical preferences and on uninsurable shocks to income can explain only a small part of the observed wealth inequality. Krusell and Smith (1998) consider shocks to discount factors and succeed in relating wealth heterogeneity predicted by the model to the observed data in the United States. Dutta and Michel (1998) use random discounting to model imperfect altruism to future generations, and derive a stationary wealth distribution where fewer agents hold higher levels of wealth. Karni and Zilcha (2000) prove that if the agents have random discount factors, in a steady-state competitive equilibrium, agents other than the most patient agents hold capital. This contrasts with the result in deterministic economies where only the most patient agents hold capital (see Becker 1980). Chatterjee et al. (2007) construct a general equilibrium model where agents with random discounting are allowed to default. They are able to match a default rate consistent with data partly because agents with low discount factors tend to consume more and default more frequently.

In models of monetary economics, random discounting also plays an important role. In a two-period model with random discounting, Goldman (1974) shows the possibility that an agent holds money that yields a lower interest than other interest-bearing assets. If the discount factor is random, after finding the discount factor, the agent may be willing to change her portfolio consisting of money and other assets. Since the transaction cost of money is lower than that of other assets, money allows the agent to change the portfolio more easily, and hence, can be valuable for the agent with random discounting.

Atkeson and Lucas (1992) and Farhi and Werning (2007) consider an intergenerational model, where each generation is composed of a continuum of agents who live for one-period and are altruistic to a descendant. Agents are ex ante identical but they experience taste-shocks to the degree of altruism (or discount factor), which are private information. The authors investigate the property of the second-best allocations of consumption. In these papers, agent's private information about taste-shocks is elicited through an incentive-compatible mechanism, while in the present chapter, the information is elicited indirectly from the observable behavior of the agent.

1.3.2 Axiomatic Models

To provide a foundation for random discounting, we follow studies of preference on the opportunity set approach. Koopmans (1964) first introduces an opportunity set as a choice object to model sequential decision making and emphasizes that intertemporal choice may be essentially different from a once-and-for-all decision making. He points out that if a DM perceives uncertainty about future preferences, she may strictly prefer to leave some options open rather than to choose a completely specified future plan.

Kreps (1979, 1992) interprets uncertain future preferences as subjective uncertainties of the DM, and provides an axiomatic foundation for the subjective state space. Dekel et al. (2001) refine Kreps's idea and show uniqueness of the subjective state space. Furthermore, Dekel et al. (2007) modify the argument of DLR surrounding the additive representation with subjective states. In this line of research, our result can be viewed as an infinite-horizon extension of DLR, where the DM's subjective state space is specified to the set of sequences of discount factors.

Several authors provide sequential choice models consistent with preference for flexibility. Rustichini (2002) follows the same idea as DLR and considers closed subsets of C^{∞} as choice objects. In this framework, all subjective uncertainties are resolved one period ahead. Kraus and Sagi (2006) follow the dynamic model of Kreps and Porteus (1978) and consider a sequence of preferences without the completeness axiom. Each incomplete preference is represented by the decision rule of the form, where one choice object is preferred to another if the former is unanimously preferred to the latter with respect to a set of uncertain future preferences. This uncertainty leads to preference for flexibility. Takeoka (2007) introduces objective states into DLR's model and considers preference over menus of menus of Anscombe-Aumann acts, which is viewed as a three-period extension of DLR. He derives a subjective decision tree and a subjective probability measure on it as components of representation.

2 Model

2.1 Domain

Let C be the outcome space (consumption set), which is assumed to be compact and metric. Let $\Delta(C)$ be the set of lotteries, that is, all Borel probability measures over C. Under the weak convergence topology, $\Delta(C)$ is also compact and metric. Gul and Pesendorfer (2004) show that there exists a compact metric space $\mathscr{X}$ such that $\mathscr{X}$ is homeomorphic to $\mathscr{K}(\Delta(C \times \mathscr{X}))$, where $\mathscr{K}(\cdot)$ denotes the set of non-empty compact subsets of "$\cdot$".[2] Generic elements of $\mathscr{X}$ are denoted by $x, y, z, \cdots$. Each such object is called a menu (or an opportunity set) of lotteries over pairs of current consumption and menu for the rest of the horizon.

Preference $\succsim$ is defined on $\mathscr{X} \simeq \mathscr{K}(\Delta(C \times \mathscr{X}))$. We have in mind the timing of decisions as mentioned in Fig. 20.1.

An important subdomain of $\mathscr{X}$ is the set $\mathscr{L}$ of perfect commitment menus where DM is committed in every period. We identify a singleton menu with its only element. Then a perfect commitment menu can be viewed as a multistage lottery, considered by Epstein and Zin (1989), that is, $\mathscr{L}$ is a subdomain of $\mathscr{X}$ satisfying $\mathscr{L} \simeq \Delta(C \times \mathscr{L})$. A formal treatment is found in Appendix section "Perfect Commitment Menus".

[2] The set $\mathscr{K}(\Delta(C \times \mathscr{X}))$ is endowed with the Hausdorff metric. Details are relegated to Appendix section "Hausdorff Metric".

The following examples illustrate that the recursive domain $\mathscr{X}$ can accommodate sequential decision problems.

Example 1 (Consumption-Savings Problem) Given a constant interest rate $r > 0$ and an initial savings $s > 0$, DM decides a current consumption c and savings s' carried over to the next period within the wealth of $(1 + r)s$. That is, the DM faces the budget constraint,

$$B(s) = \{(c, s') \in \mathbb{R}^2_+ \,|\, c + s' = (1 + r)s\},$$

which is translated into the menu $x(s) = \{(c, x(s'))| (c, s') \in B(s)\}$. If r is random, $x(s)$ can be modified to a set of lotteries.

Example 2 (Durable Goods) A durable good provides flow of services, $c = \{c_t\}_{t=1}^{\infty}$ over certain time periods. The durability of goods depends both on the physical property and intensive use of goods. Let $\{c = \{c_t\}_{t=1}^{\infty} \,|\, f(c) \le 0\}$ be the feasible set of flow of services associated with a durable good, where f is a technology frontier. Given the history of consumptions up to period $t-1$, denoted by $c^{t-1} = (c_1, \cdots, c_{t-1})$, c_t is a feasible consumption in period t if and only if $f(c^{t-1}, c_t, c) \le 0$ for some c. In other words, the DM faces the menu as

$$x_f(c^{t-1}) = \{(c_t, x_f(c^{t-1}, c_t)) \,|\, f(c^{t-1}, c_t, c) \le 0 \text{ for some sequence c}\}.$$

The DM prefers one durable good f to another g if and only if $x_f(c^0) \succsim x_g(c^0)$.

Example 3 (Sampling Problem) Given a wage offer w, which is a random sample from a distribution F, a DM has to decide whether to accept or reject the offer. If the DM accepts w, she receives current payoff from w and nothing for the rest of the horizon. Otherwise, the DM continues sampling, and receives a new random sample w' in the next period. Sampling is repeated until the DM accepts an offer. This decision problem can be described formally as follows: given a current offer w, define the menu $x(w) \equiv \{\text{accept}w, \text{continue}\}$. The object "accept w" is the consumption stream $(w, \{(0, \{(0, \cdots)\})\})$, and "continue" is the lottery over menus of the form $x(w') = \{\text{acceptw}', \text{continue}\}$, where w' is given according to the distribution F.

2.2 Random Discounting Representations

By taking any non-constant, continuous, mixture linear function $u : \Delta(C) \to \mathbb{R}$ and any Borel probability measure μ over $[0, 1]$ with the mean $\bar{\alpha} \equiv \mathbb{E}_{\mu}[\alpha] < 1$ we consider the functional form $U : \mathscr{X} \to \mathbb{R}$ defined as

$$U(x) = \int_{[0,1]} \max_{l \in x} \left((1 - \alpha)u(l_c) + \alpha \int_{\mathscr{X}} U(z)\, \mathrm{d}l_z \right) \mathrm{d}\mu(\alpha), \qquad (20.1)$$

where l_c and l_z denote the marginal distributions of l on C and $\mathscr{X}$, respectively.

The functional form (20.1) can be interpreted as follows: the DM behaves as if she has in mind the time line described in Fig. 20.1 and anticipates uncertainty about discount factors, which is captured by μ over $[0, 1]$. On the other hand, she is certain about future risk preference, u over $\Delta(C)$. Moreover, she is also certain about future ranking of menus, which is identical with the current ranking U. That is, the representation has a stationary and recursive structure. After considering the realization of discount factor α, the DM chooses a lottery out of the menu to maximize the "ex post" utility function,

$$(1-\alpha)u(l_c) + \alpha \int_{\mathscr{Z}} U(z)\, \mathrm{d}l_z, \tag{20.2}$$

which is the weighted sum of expected utilities from current consumption and the opportunity set for the rest of the horizon. The functional form (20.1) states that the DM evaluates a menu x by taking the expected value of these maximum values with respect to her subjective belief μ over discount factors.

Definition 1 Preference $\succsim$ on $\mathscr{Z}$ admits a random discounting representation if $\succsim$ can be represented numerically by the functional form U as given by (20.1) with components (u, μ).

A random discounting representation coincides with a stationary cardinal utility function on the subdomain $\mathscr{L}$ of perfect commitment menus. Since the DM has no opportunity for choice, random discounting does not matter on this subdomain. The functional form (20.1) reduces to

$$U(l) = (1-\bar{\alpha})u(l_c) + \bar{\alpha} \int_{\mathscr{L}} U(l')\, \mathrm{d}l_L(l'),$$

where l_c and l_L denote the marginal distributions of $l \in \Delta(C \times \mathscr{L})$ on C and $\mathscr{L}$, respectively. This is a standard stationary recursive utility with a deterministic discount factor $\bar{\alpha} < 1$.

Apart from the difference of choice objects,[3] a random discounting representation is a special case of DLR's additive representation of the form that

$$U(x) = \int_S \max_{l \in x} V(l, s)\, \mathrm{d}\mu(s), \tag{20.3}$$

where S is a state space, μ is a non-negative measure on S, and $V(\cdot, s)$ is a state-dependent expected utility function. Indeed, the ex post utility function (20.2) can be written as

$$V(l, s) = (1-\alpha(s))u(l_c) + \alpha(s) \int_{\mathscr{Z}} U(z)\, \mathrm{d}l_z \tag{20.4}$$

with an index $s \in S$.

[3]DLR consider preference over $\mathscr{K}(\Delta(C))$ with finite set C.

DLR have a model of the form (20.3) with a signed measure μ, where choice based on some subjective states may be negatively evaluated from the ex ante perspective. The DM having such a representation does not necessarily desire flexibility. Similarly, it is possible to consider functional form (20.1) by assuming μ as a signed measure. For example, Gul and Pesendorfer (2004) correspond to the case where μ has one "regular" discount factor $\alpha > 0$ with a positive weight and a completely myopic discount factor $\alpha = 0$ with a negative weight.[4] In this chapter, however, we do not focus on this general model. First, unless some further restriction is imposed such as in Gul and Pesendorfer (2004), a model with a signed measure does not necessarily have a clear implication of how choice behavior evolves over time. Such a model is not appropriate as a dynamic model, while the random discounting representation can generate a stochastic choice according to the probability measure. Second, as Koopmans (1964) and Kreps (1979) point out, a dynamic model consistent with preference for flexibility is of its own interest.

3 Foundations

3.1 Axioms

The axioms which we consider on $\succsim$ are the following. The first two axioms are standard and need no explanation.

Axiom 1 (Order) $\succsim$ is complete and transitive.

Axiom 2 (Continuity) For all $x \in \mathscr{Z}$, $\{z \in \mathscr{Z} | x \succsim z\}$ and $\{z \in \mathscr{Z} | z \succsim x\}$ are closed.

For any $l \in \Delta(C \times \mathscr{Z})$, l_c and l_z denote the marginal distributions of l on C and on $\mathscr{Z}$, respectively.

Axiom 3 (Nondegeneracy) There exist $l, l' \in \Delta(C \times \mathscr{Z})$ such that $l_c \neq l'_c$, $l_z = l'_z$, and $\{l\} \succ \{l'\}$.

The lotteries l and l' differ only in the distribution of current consumption. Thus, strict preference for l over l' presumably reveals that the DM's risk preference over C is not constant.

The next three axioms are the same as those in Gul and Pesendorfer (2004).

Axiom 4 (Commitment Independence) For all $l, l', l'' \in \Delta(C \times \mathscr{Z})$ and for all $\lambda \in (0, 1)$,

$$\{l\} \succ \{l'\} \Rightarrow \{\lambda l + (1-\lambda)l''\} \succ \{\lambda l' + (1-\lambda)l''\}.$$

[4] A sophisticated DM, who is fully aware of time-inconsistency caused by hyperbolic discounting, may be viewed as a limiting case of their model, where the DM never exercises self-control at the moment of choice.

For all $l, l' \in \Delta(C \times \mathscr{X})$, $\{l\} \succsim \{l'\}$ means commitment preference, which reflects the DM's ex ante perspective on future preference over lotteries. Axiom 4 states that commitment preference over lotteries satisfies the vNM independence.

Axiom 5 (Stationarity) For all $x, y \in \mathscr{X}$ and $c \in C$, $\{(c, x)\} \succsim \{(c, y)\} \Leftrightarrow x \succsim y$.

Since current consumption is the same, the ranking between $\{(c, x)\}$ and $\{(c, y)\}$ reflects how the DM evaluates x and y in the next period. Thus, Stationarity means that the ranking over menus is identical across time.

In general, belief about future discount factors may depend on the history of consumptions and realizations of discount factors up to that period. Stationarity, however, excludes such history-dependent beliefs: the DM is sure that her belief about discount factors will not change over time. We adopt Stationarity because it seems sensible as a first step and because the general model seems much more difficult to characterize and is beyond our grasp at this time.

For any $(c, x), (c', x') \in C \times \mathscr{X}$ and $\lambda \in [0, 1]$, the notation

$$\lambda \circ (c, x) + (1 - \lambda) \circ (c', x')$$

denotes the lottery over $C \times \mathscr{X}$ yielding (c, x) with probability λ and yielding (c', x') with probability $1 - \lambda$.

For any $x, x' \in \mathscr{X}$ and $\lambda \in [0, 1]$, define the mixture of two menus by considering the mixtures element by element between x and x', that is,

$$\lambda x + (1 - \lambda)x' \equiv \{\lambda l + (1 - \lambda)l' | l \in x,\ l' \in x'\} \in \mathscr{X}.$$

If the DM identifies a two-stage lottery $\lambda \circ l + (1 - \lambda) \circ l'$ with its reduced lottery $\lambda l + (1 - \lambda)l'$, $\lambda x + (1 - \lambda)x'$ can also be viewed as a set of two-stage lotteries.

Axiom 6 (Timing Indifference) For all $x, x' \in \mathscr{X}$, $c \in C$, and $\lambda \in (0, 1)$,

$$\{\lambda \circ (c, x) + (1 - \lambda) \circ (c, x')\} \sim \{(c, \lambda x + (1 - \lambda)x')\}.$$

Notice that $\lambda \circ (c, x) + (1 - \lambda) \circ (c, x')$ is the lottery yielding (c, x) with probability λ and yielding (c, x') with probability $1 - \lambda$, while $(c, \lambda x + (1 - \lambda)x')$ is the degenerate lottery that assigns the pair of consumption c and menu $\lambda x + (1 - \lambda)x'$ of two-stage lotteries. Hence, these two lotteries differ in timing of resolution of randomization λ. For the former, the DM makes choice out of a menu (either x or x') after the resolution of λ, while for the latter, this order is reversed, that is, the choice out of the menu $\lambda x + (1 - \lambda)x'$ is made before the resolution of λ. Timing Indifference suggests that the DM does not care about this difference in timing. Timing Indifference can be justified by the same argument as in DLR. Suppose that a DM is uncertain about future preference over $\Delta(C \times \mathscr{X})$, yet she surely anticipates that it will satisfy the expected utility axioms. Let l and l' be a rational choice from x and x', respectively, with respect to a future preference. Therefore, $(c, \lambda l + (1 - \lambda)l')$

is the expected choice from $\lambda \circ (c, x) + (1 - \lambda) \circ (c, x')$. On the other hand, if the future preference satisfies the expected utility axioms, $(c, \lambda l + (1 - \lambda)l')$ is a rational choice from $(c, \lambda x + (1 - \lambda)x')$ as well. Therefore, irrespective of the future preference, the two menus will ensure indifferent consequences.[5]

Axioms 1, 2, and 4–6 appear in Gul and Pesendorfer (2004).[6] They consider a DM facing self-control problems. Such a DM may be better off by restricting available options and, hence, exhibits preference for commitment rather than for flexibility. A key axiom of their model is called *Set Betweenness*: for any $x, y \in \mathscr{X}$,

$$x \succsim y \Rightarrow x \succsim x \cup y \succsim y.$$

Even if $x \succsim y$, the DM may rank x over $x \cup y$ because y may contain a tempting option and choosing from $x \cup y$ may require costly self-control to the DM.

We adopt the following two axioms, which distinguish our model from theirs. As mentioned in Sect. 1.2, the DM facing uncertainty about her future preferences may want to keep options open as much as possible. This is because flexibility allows the DM to make a decision contingent upon realization of her future preference. This informational advantage leads to preference for flexibility. Such a DM would rank $x \cup y$ over x even though $x \succsim y$. To accommodate such behavior, we follow Kreps and DLR, and assume (instead of Set Betweenness):

Axiom 7 (Monotonicity) For all $x, y \in \mathscr{X}$, $y \subset x \Rightarrow x \succsim y$.

This axiom states that a bigger menu is always weakly preferred. That is, Monotonicity is consistent with preference for flexibility.[7]

Monotonicity is consistent with any kind of uncertainty about future preferences. To identify behavior that reduces uncertainty about future preferences to that about future discount factors, we need to impose a qualification on the attitude toward flexibility. The DM facing random discount factors is sure how she evaluates consumption in the next period and a menu from that time period onward. Thus, uncertainty is relevant only when an intertemporal trade-off must be made. As mentioned in Sect. 1.2, such a DM should not value flexibility provided by "dominated lotteries", which are now described formally.

Let $l_c \otimes l_z$ denote the product measure on $C \times \mathscr{X}$ that consists of marginal distributions $l_c \in \Delta(C)$ and $l_z \in \Delta(\mathscr{X})$. We define dimension-wise dominance as follows:

[5]The DM may care about timing of resolution of risk and prefer earlier or later resolution of multistage lotteries. Such distinction is examined in Kreps and Porteus (1978). Epstein et al. (2007) argue against Timing Indifference and provide a model with nonlinear future preferences.

[6]Their Nondegeneracy axiom requires the existence of menus x, y with $x \succ y$ and $x \subset y$. That is, this axiom captures preference for commitment—a DM may prefer a smaller menu.

[7]A sophisticated DM with hyperbolic discounting exhibits preference for commitment rather than for flexibility. Thus, such a DM is excluded by this axiom.

Definition 2 For all $l, l' \in \Delta(C \times \mathscr{X})$, l dominates l' if $\{l_c \otimes l'_z\} \succsim \{l'_c \otimes l'_z\}$ and $\{l'_c \otimes l_z\} \succsim \{l'_c \otimes l'_z\}$, where l_c (resp. l_z) denotes the marginal distribution of l on C (resp. $\mathscr{X}$).

If the DM is certain about her risk preferences over $\Delta(C)$ and over $\Delta(\mathscr{X})$ in future, the commitment rankings appearing in the above definition should reflect those preferences. Since $l_c \otimes l'_z$ and $l'_c \otimes l'_z$ differ only in marginal distributions on C, the ranking $\{l_c \otimes l'_z\} \succsim \{l'_c \otimes l'_z\}$ reflects that l_c is preferred to l'_c in terms of the future risk preference over $\Delta(C)$. Similarly, the ranking $\{l'_c \otimes l_z\} \succsim \{l'_c \otimes l'_z\}$ should reveal the DM's future preference for l_z over l'_z. If l dominates l', the marginal distributions of l on C and $\mathscr{X}$ are both preferred to those of l'. Hence, l will definitely be chosen over l' by the DM who is certain about her future risk preferences over C and $\mathscr{X}$.

For any $l \in \Delta(C \times \mathscr{X})$, let $O(l)$ be the set of all lotteries dominated by l, that is,

$$O(l) \equiv \{l' \in \Delta(C \times \mathscr{X}) \mid \text{l dominates l}'\}. \tag{20.5}$$

If $\succsim$ satisfies Order, $l \in O(l)$. Thus, a DM having preference for flexibility weakly prefers $O(l)$ to $\{l\}$. However, there is no reason to choose a dominated lottery $l' \in O(l)$ over l. Hence, $O(l)$ should be indifferent to $\{l\}$.

The same intuition should hold between a general menu x and the set

$$O(x) \equiv \bigcup_{l \in x} O(l), \tag{20.6}$$

that is, $O(x)$ is the set of all lotteries dominated by some lottery in x. Lemma 3 (i) in Appendix section "Proof of Theorem 1" shows that $O(x)$ is a well-defined choice object, that is, $O(x) \in \mathscr{X}$ for all x.

Axiom 8 (Marginal Dominance) For all $x \in \mathscr{X}$, $x \sim O(x)$.

Marginal Dominance states that the DM should not care about dominated lotteries. Since $x \subset O(x)$ when $\succsim$ satisfies Order, the DM having preference for flexibility weakly prefers $O(x)$ to x. Thus, this axiom is a counterpoint to Monotonicity, and shows that it is not useful to keep dominated lotteries within the menu, that is, $x \succsim O(x)$. Such behavior can be justified if the DM believes that her future risk preference over $\Delta(C)$ is separated from her future ranking of menus, and these two preferences are known to the DM without uncertainty. Then, dominated lotteries are definitely useless because they give less utilities in the future, both immediate and remote, and hence the DM exhibits $x \sim O(x)$.

Marginal Dominance involves a form of separability of preferences between immediate and remote future. Two remarks are in order: First, under this axiom, the DM cares only about the marginal distributions on C and $\mathscr{X}$—the correlation between immediate consumption and the future opportunity set does not matter. Second, Marginal Dominance is stronger than the Separability axiom stated by Gul and Pesendorfer (2004), which requires a form of separability only in the singleton sets. That is, for any $c, c' \in C$ and $x, x' \in \mathscr{X}$,

$$\left\{\frac{1}{2}\circ(c,x)+\frac{1}{2}\circ(c',x')\right\}\sim\left\{\frac{1}{2}\circ(c',x)+\frac{1}{2}\circ(c,x')\right\}.$$

If $\succsim$ satisfies Marginal Dominance, for all $l\in\Delta(C\times\mathscr{X})$, we have $\{l\}\sim O(l)=O(l_c\otimes l_z)\sim\{l_c\otimes l_z\}$. Thus, both the above singleton menus are indifferent to

$$\left\{\left(\frac{1}{2}\circ c+\frac{1}{2}\circ c'\right)\otimes\left(\frac{1}{2}\circ x+\frac{1}{2}\circ x'\right)\right\},$$

which results in Separability.

3.2 Representation Results

It is now appropriate to state the main theorem.

Theorem 1 *If preference $\succsim$ satisfies Order, Continuity, Nondegeneracy, Commitment Independence, Stationarity, Timing Indifference, Monotonicity, and Marginal Dominance, then there exists a random discounting representation (u,μ).*

Conversely, for any pair (u,μ) with $\bar{\alpha}<1$, there exists a unique functional form U that satisfies functional equation (20.1) and the preference it represents satisfies all the axioms.

The above theorem is closely related to DLR's study, and the role of the axioms may be well understood when compared with their axioms. DLR show that preference over menus of lotteries admits the additive representation (20.3) with a non-negative measure if and only if it satisfies Order, Continuity, Monotonicity, and the following axiom[8]:

Axiom 9 (Independence) For all x,y,z and $\lambda\in(0,1]$,

$$x\succ y\Rightarrow\lambda x+(1-\lambda)z\succ\lambda y+(1-\lambda)z.$$

Indeed, Commitment Independence, Stationarity, and Timing Indifference imply Independence.[9] Marginal Dominance plays a key role in restricting subjective states (future preferences) to differ only in intertemporal trade-offs between the immediate and remote future. The recursive form of the representation is due to Stationarity. For an outline of the proof of sufficiency, see Sect. 3.4. A formal proof is relegated to Appendix section "Proof of Theorem 1".

According to the above argument, a natural strategy to obtain a random discounting representation would be to establish the additive representation (20.3) on

---

[8]Dekel et al. (2007) fill a gap in DLR surrounding this representation result.

[9]See Gul and Pesendorfer (2004, p. 125, footnote 7) for more details.

$\mathcal{K}(\Delta(C \times \mathcal{X}))$, and to manipulate the representation to convert the subjective state space S to the set of discount factors $[0, 1]$ using the additional axioms (especially Marginal Dominance). However, we do not follow this strategy mainly because the first step is not immediate: DLR consider menus of lotteries over finite alternatives as choice objects and, hence, can regard the compact set of expected utility functions over lotteries as the subjective state space, while in this chapter, choice objects are menus of lotteries over a compact set. Thus, instead of dealing with the set of all mixture linear functions over the compact set, we start off with the subjective state space $[0, 1]$ of discount factors and establish our functional form by adapting DLR's argument. For an outline of the proof of sufficiency, see Sect. 3.4.

The next result considers uniqueness of the representation. If preference admits two distinct random discounting representations, say (u, μ) and (u', μ'), we cannot know which belief actually captures the DM's subjective uncertainty about discount factors. Therefore, we have the following uniqueness result. A proof can be found in Appendix section "Proof of Theorem 2".

Theorem 2 *If two random discounting representations, U and U', with components (u, μ) and (u', μ') respectively, represent the same preference, then:*

(i) u and u' are cardinally equivalent; and
(ii) $\mu = \mu'$.

Theorem 2 pins down a subjective probability measure μ over the set of future discount factors, which is interpreted as the set of subjective states of the DM. Our result is in contrast to Kreps (1979, 1992) and DLR, where probability measures over subjective states are not identified; since the ex post utility functions are state-dependent as shown in (20.3), probabilities assigned to those states can be manipulated arbitrarily. Formally, let ν be a probability measure which is absolute continuous with respect to μ. Then there is a function f such that $V'(l, s) = V(l, s)f(s)$ and

$$U(x) = \int_S \max_{l \in x} V'(l, s)\, \mathrm{d}\nu(s),$$

which means that μ cannot be identified. On the other hand, our representation has an additive recursive structure, that is, the ex post utility functions are specified as shown in (20.4). Notice that both the instantaneous expected utility u and the utility U over menus are independent of subjective states, and state-dependent components, $1-\alpha(s)$ and $\alpha(s)$, add up to one for all s. Under the above manipulation, the representation is maintained only when $f(s) = 1$ almost surely, and thus $\nu = \mu$. Therefore, it is a combination of the additive recursive structure and the normalization of discount factors that ensures uniqueness of subjective beliefs.[10]

[10]To prevent arbitrary manipulations, DLR (p. 912) suggest that probability measures can be identified if some aspect of the ex post utility functions is state-independent. Such a condition is satisfied in our model.

3.3 Special Case: Deterministic Discounting

We imagine a "standard" DM with deterministic discounting, who is not anticipating any uncertainty about future discount factors. Such a DM should not care about flexibility, and should evaluate a menu by its best element according to a fixed weak order over singleton sets. That is,

$$x \succsim y \Leftrightarrow \{l^x\} \succsim \{l^y\}, \tag{20.7}$$

where $\{l^x\} \succsim \{l\}$ and $\{l^y\} \succsim \{l'\}$ for all $l \in x$ and $l' \in y$. Kreps (1979) characterizes such a standard DM based on the next axiom:

Axiom 10 (Strategic Rationality) For all $x, y \in \mathscr{X}$, $x \succsim y \Rightarrow x \sim x \cup y$.

Strategic Rationality states that as long as x is preferred to y, the DM does not care whether options in y are added into x or not. This axiom is more restrictive than Monotonicity, and excludes preference for flexibility.[11]

Strategic Rationality is not enough to characterize deterministic discounting because it does not impose any restriction on the commitment ranking. The next axiom requires the dimension-wise dominance on singleton sets.

Axiom 11 (Commitment Marginal Dominance) For all $l \in \Delta(C \times \mathscr{X})$, $\{l\} \sim O(l)$.

This axiom is weaker than Marginal Dominance, but the intuition is the same as before.

The next corollary of Theorem 3.1 characterizes deterministic discounting. Appendix section "Proofs of Corollary 1 and Proposition 1" can be referred for a proof.

Corollary 1 *Preference $\succsim$ satisfies Order, Continuity, Nondegeneracy, Commitment Independence, Stationarity, Timing Indifference, Strategic Rationality, and Commitment Marginal Dominance if and only if $\succsim$ admits a random discounting representation (u, μ) such that μ is degenerate.*

As mentioned above, Strategic Rationality implies Monotonicity. To verify that the set of axioms in Corollary 1 implies Marginal Dominance, we provide a further perspective on Strategic Rationality. A standard DM, who surely anticipates her preference in the next period, will rank menus according to the decision rule (20.7). Consequently, she should be indifferent between committing to a lottery $l \in \Delta(C \times \mathscr{X})$ and having its "lower contour set"

$$O^*(l) \equiv \{l' \in \Delta(C \times \mathscr{X}) \mid \{l\} \succsim \{l'\}\},$$

---

[11]Strategic Rationality implies Monotonicity. Indeed, assume $y \subset x$. Arguing by contradiction, suppose $y \succ x$. Strategic Rationality implies $x = x \cup y \sim y \succ x$, which is a contradiction.

which is the set of all lotteries that are no more desired than l with respect to commitment ranking. Accordingly, arranging $O^*(x) \equiv \cup_{l \in x} O^*(l)$ for all $x \in \mathscr{X}$, the standard DM will satisfy the next axiom:

Axiom 12 (Dominance) For all $x \in \mathscr{X}$, $x \sim O^*(x)$.

This axiom states that DM does not care about keeping a lottery which is no more desired than some lottery in the menu in terms of commitment ranking. Even if $\{l\} \succsim \{l'\}$, the support of l may be different from that of l', that is, these lotteries may differ in intertemporal trade-offs, and hence, the DM facing uncertainty about discount factors may be better off by keeping l' as an option. However, Dominance implies that if $\{l\} \succsim \{l'\}$, the DM surely anticipates not to choose l' in the next period, and does not care about flexibility regarding intertemporal trade-offs in the future. Hence, this axiom is a necessary condition for deterministic discounting.

As one might imagine, Dominance has close relations to Strategic Rationality and Marginal Dominance.

Proposition 1 *Assume that $\succsim$ satisfies Order and Continuity.*

(i) Strategic Rationality is equivalent to Dominance.
(ii) Dominance and Commitment Marginal Dominance imply Marginal Dominance.

See Appendix section "Proofs of Corollary 1 and Proposition 1" for a proof. From this proposition, Strategic Rationality and Commitment Marginal Dominance together with the other axioms imply the set of axioms in Theorem 1.

3.4 *Proof Sketch for Sufficiency of Theorem 1*

As mentioned in Sect. 3.2, Commitment Independence, Stationarity, and Timing Indifference imply Independence. Focusing on the subdomain $\mathscr{X}_1 \subset \mathscr{X}$ consisting of convex menus, the mixture space theorem delivers a mixture linear representation $U : \mathscr{X}_1 \to \mathbb{R}$. We have to show that U can be rewritten as the desired form.

Marginal Dominance implies that the DM is certain about her future risk preferences over C and $\mathscr{X}$. Let $u : \Delta(C) \to \mathbb{R}$ and $W : \Delta(\mathscr{X}) \to \mathbb{R}$ be

$$u(l_c) \equiv U(\{l_c \otimes \underline{l}_z\}) \text{ and } W(l_z) \equiv U(\{\underline{l}_c \otimes l_z\}),$$

where $\underline{l} \in \Delta(C \times \mathscr{X})$ is a minimal lottery in terms of commitment ranking. These two functions should represent those future preferences.

Monotonicity captures preference for flexibility, which presumably reflects uncertainty about future preferences. Since u and W are sure for the DM, all the uncertainties about future preferences are effectively reduced to those about future discount factors. The DM should expect her future preference over $\Delta(C \times \mathscr{X})$ to have the form of

$$(1-\alpha)u(l_c) + \alpha W(l_z),$$

where $\alpha \in [0, 1]$ is a subjective weight between u and W.

We identify a menu x with its "support function" $\sigma_x : [0, 1] \to \mathbb{R}$, defined by

$$\sigma_x(\alpha) \equiv \max_{l \in x} (1-\alpha)u(l_c) + \alpha W(l_z), \text{ for all } \alpha \in [0, 1].$$

That is, $\sigma_x = \sigma_y \Leftrightarrow x = y$. This identification ensures that the mapping σ embeds the set of menus into the space of real-valued continuous functions on [0, 1], and hence, the functional $V(f) = U(\sigma^{-1}(f))$ is well-defined on the image of σ. Following the similar argument by DLR (and Dekel et al. 2007), we show that there exists a unique probability measure μ over [0, 1] such that $V(f)$ can be written as $\int f(\alpha)\,\mathrm{d}\mu(\alpha)$, and hence,

$$U(x) = V(\sigma_x) = \int_{[0,1]} \left(\max_{l \in x} (1-\alpha)u(l_c) + \alpha W(l_z) \right) \mathrm{d}\mu(\alpha).$$

The remaining step is to show that U has a stationary and recursive form as desired. Since $W(l_z)$ is a mixture linear function, it has the expected utility form $\int_{\mathscr{Z}} W(z)\,\mathrm{d}ł_z$. By Stationarity, W and U must represent the same preference. Moreover, Timing Indifference implies that W is mixture linear with respect to the mixture operation over menus. Hence, $W(z)$ can be written as an affine transformation of $U(z)$. Manipulating the functional form appropriately, we obtain the desired representation. Finally, Continuity and Nondegeneracy imply $\bar{\alpha} < 1$.

4 Greater Demand for Flexibility and Greater Uncertainty

We would like to analyze the situation where one agent is more uncertain about discount factors than another. We provide behavioral comparisons about preference for flexibility and characterize intuitive properties of subjective beliefs.

Consider two agents: Agent i has preference $\succsim^i$ on $\mathscr{Z}$, $i = 1, 2$. Since we are interested in comparing preference for flexibility, we focus on agents having identical commitment rankings. Recall that $\mathscr{L}$ is the set of multistage lotteries. If an element of $\mathscr{L}$ is chosen, there remains no opportunity for choice over the rest of the horizon. We say that $\succsim^1$ and $\succsim^2$ are equivalent on $\mathscr{L}$ if, for all $l, l' \in \mathscr{L}$,

$$\{l\} \succ^1 \{l'\} \Leftrightarrow \{l\} \succ^2 \{l'\}.$$

A DM's preference for flexibility is captured by the Monotonicity axiom, that is, the DM prefers bigger menus. Hence, one can say that agent 2 has greater demand for flexibility than agent 1 if agent 2 strictly prefers a bigger menu whenever agent 1 does so. Such a behavioral comparison is provided by DLR. Formally:

Definition 3 Agent 2 *desires more flexibility than* agent 1 if, for all $x, y \in \mathscr{X}$ with $y \subset x$, $x \succ^1 y \Rightarrow x \succ^2 y$.

In a two-period model, DLR show that, under Definition 3, the subjective state space of agent 2 is bigger than that of agent 1. That is, greater demand for flexibility reflects greater uncertainty about future contingencies. In particular, in the case of their additive representation, the subjective state space corresponds to a support of non-negative measure. By analogy of DLR, one might expect that greater demand for flexibility reflects a bigger support of the subjective belief about discount factors.

Since a menu in $\mathscr{X}$ is an infinite horizon decision problem, preference for flexibility on $\mathscr{X}$ reflects the agent's belief about sequence of discount factors over the rest of the horizon, while μ is her belief about discount factors only in the immediate future. To obtain a characterization result, it is relevant to specify preference for flexibility attributable solely to belief about the immediate future. To formalize the idea, define "the two-period domain" as

$$\mathscr{X}^1 \equiv \mathscr{K}(\mathscr{L}) \subset \mathscr{X}.$$

Holding a menu $x \in \mathscr{X}^1$, the agent can postpone a decision only until period 1, from which point on she has to make a commitment. A comparison of preference for flexibility on $\mathscr{X}^1$ corresponds to DLR's two-period case.

Definition 4 Agent 2 *desires more flexibility in the two-period model than* agent 1 if, for all $x, y \in \mathscr{X}^1$ with $y \subset x$, $x \succ^1 y \Rightarrow x \succ^2 y$.

The next theorem is a counterpart of DLR. A proof is found in Appendix section "Proof of Theorem 3".

Theorem 3 *Assume that* $\succsim^i$, $i = 1, 2$, *satisfy all the axioms of Theorem 1 and are equivalent on* $\mathscr{L}$. *The following conditions are equivalent:*

(a) *Agent 2 desires more flexibility in the two-period model than agent 1.*
(b) *There exist random discounting representations* U^i *with* (u^i, μ^i), $i = 1, 2$, *such that (i)* $u^1 = u^2$, *and (ii) the support of* μ^2 *set-theoretically includes that of* μ^1.

Two remarks are in order: First, although μ^i is constant over time, condition (b) does not imply that agent 2 desires more flexibility than agent 1. Indeed, under condition (b), we may find two menus z and z' such that $U^1(z) > U^1(z')$ and $U^2(z) \leq U^2(z')$. Considering $x \equiv \{(c, z), (c, z')\}$ and $y \equiv \{(c, z')\}$ for some $c \in C$, we have $y \subset x$ and $U^1(x) > U^1(y)$, yet $U^2(x) = U^2(y)$. Second, although our functional form is a special case of DLR's, Theorem 3 does not follow directly from Theorem 2 (p. 910) of DLR regarding the characterization of Definition 4. DLR consider menus of lotteries over finite outcomes, while in our study, choice objects are menus of lotteries on a compact outcome space.

We next consider another behavioral comparison about preference for flexibility. If agent 2 faces more uncertainty about discount factors than agent 1, agent 2 is presumably more averse to making a commitment to a specific plan than agent 1 is. That is,

Definition 5 Agent 2 is *more averse to commitment than* agent 1 if, for all $x \in \mathscr{X}$ and $l \in \mathscr{L}$, $x \succ^1 \{l\} \Rightarrow x \succ^2 \{l\}$.

This condition states that if agent 1 strictly prefers a menu x to a completely spelled-out future plan $\{l\}$, so does agent 2. Since l does not necessarily belong to x, Definition 5 is independent of Definition 3.

In a similar way to Definition 4, the above condition can be restricted to the two-period domain.

Definition 6 Agent 2 is *more averse to commitment in the two-period model than* agent 1 if, for all $x \in \mathscr{X}^1$ and $l \in \mathscr{L}$, $x \succ^1 \{l\} \Rightarrow x \succ^2 \{l\}$.

Several authors adopt conditions identical to Definitions 5 and 6 in different contexts. Ahn (2008) considers preference over subsets of lotteries and interprets those subsets as ambiguous objects. Since singleton sets are then regarded as options without ambiguity, a similar comparison with Definition 5 shows that agent 1 is more ambiguity averse than agent 2. By taking preference over menus of lotteries, Sarver (2008) models a DM who anticipates regret from choice in the future and, hence, may prefer smaller menus. In his model, the identical comparison is interpreted as agent 1 being more regret prone than agent 2.[12]

Now the implication of the above behavioral comparison is considered. We show that Definition 5 characterizes second-order stochastic dominance in terms of subjective beliefs. In case of objective uncertainty, second-order stochastic dominance has been widely used to describe increasing uncertainty since Rothschild and Stiglitz (1970).

Definition 7 Consider probability measures μ^1 and μ^2 over $[0,1]$. Say that μ^1 exhibits second-order stochastic dominance over μ^2 if, for all continuous and concave functions $v : [0,1] \to \mathbb{R}$,[13]

$$\int_{[0,1]} v(\alpha)\,\mathrm{d}\mu^1(\alpha) \geq \int_{[0,1]} v(\alpha)\,\mathrm{d}\mu^2(\alpha).$$

Rothschild and Stiglitz (1970) show that the above condition holds if and only if μ^2 is obtained as μ^1 plus some "noise".[14] Thus, second-order stochastic dominance is a natural ordering on probability measures to describe increasing uncertainty. One immediate observation is that $\mathbb{E}_{\mu^1}[\alpha] = \mathbb{E}_{\mu^2}[\alpha]$ if μ^1 exhibits second-order stochastic dominance over μ^2 because $v(\alpha) = \alpha$ is a convex and concave function.

We may now state a characterization result.

[12]In literature on ambiguity in the Savage-type model, Epstein (1999) and Ghirardato and Marinacci (2002) adopt closely related conditions to capture comparative attitudes toward ambiguity aversion. They compare an arbitrary act with an unambiguous act instead of comparing an arbitrary menu with a commitment menu.

[13]Notice that continuity is not redundant because a concave function is continuous in the interior of the domain. In the original definition by Rothschild and Stiglitz (1970), continuity is not imposed.

[14]Their argument for this equivalence works even when continuity is imposed on v.

Theorem 4 *Assume that $\succsim^i$, $i = 1, 2$, satisfy all the axioms of Theorem 1. Then the following conditions are equivalent:*

(a) Agent 2 is more averse to commitment than agent 1.
(b) Agent 2 is more averse to commitment in the two-period model than agent 1.
(c) There exist random discounting representations U^i with (u^i, μ^i), $i = 1, 2$, such that (i) $u^1 = u^2$, and (ii) μ^1 exhibits second-order stochastic dominance over μ^2.

A formal proof is relegated to Appendix section "Proof of Theorem 4". By definition, condition (a) implies condition (b). The intuition behind (b)⇒(c) is as follows: Definition 6 implies that $\succsim^1$ and $\succsim^2$ are equivalent on $\mathscr{L}$, and hence part (i) is obtained. Furthermore, together with this observation, Definition 6 implies that $U^2(x) \geq U^1(x)$ for all $x \in \mathscr{X}^1$. Since, for all x, the function

$$\max_{l \in x} \left((1-\alpha)u(l_c) + \alpha \int_{\mathscr{X}} U^i(z)\, \mathrm{d}l_z \right) \tag{20.8}$$

is convex in α, the ranking $U^2(x) \geq U^1(x)$ means that the integral of a convex function of the form (20.8) with respect to μ^2 is always bigger than that corresponding to μ^1. As the last step, we show that any continuous convex function v on $[0, 1]$ can be arbitrarily approximated by a function of the form (20.8) if an affine transformation of u is chosen appropriately.

Unlike Theorem 3, condition (c) implies condition (a). That is, condition (c) is sufficient to show relative aversion to commitment with respect to not only "two-period menus" $x \in \mathscr{X}^1$ but also all infinite horizon decision problems $x \in \mathscr{X}$. In the proof, by exploiting the property of second-order stochastic dominance, we show that condition (c) ensures $U^2(x) \geq U^1(x)$ for all $x \in \mathscr{X}$, which implies $U^2(x) \geq U^1(x) > U^1(\{l\}) = U^2(\{l\})$ as desired.

5 Consumption-Savings Decisions Under Random Discounting

In this section, we apply the resulting model to a consumption-savings problem and analyze how random discounting affects consumption-savings decisions. We focus on the situation where the DM becomes more uncertain about discount factors in the sense of second-order stochastic dominance. We will characterize savings behavior when the DM has a CRRA utility function on consumption.

Recall Example 1 in Sect. 2.1. Assume that an interest rate r is constant as in the example. Given the savings s from the previous period, the DM evaluates $x(s)$ according to the random discounting representation,

$$U(x(s)) = \int \max_{(c,x(s'))\in x(s)} \Big((1-\alpha)u(c) + \alpha U(x(s')) \Big)\, \mathrm{d}\mu(\alpha). \tag{20.9}$$

Throughout this section, the DM is assumed to have a CRRA utility function over instantaneous consumption, that is, $u(c) = c^{1-\sigma}/(1-\sigma)$ for $\sigma > 0$, $\sigma \neq 1$. As is well-known, the inverse of σ is the elasticity of intertemporal substitution.

We examine the effect of the DM being more uncertain about future discount factors. Suppose that the DM changes her belief μ^1 to μ^2, where μ^1 second-order stochastically dominates μ^2. Let U^i denote the random discounting representation with components (u, μ^i), $i = 1, 2$.

After realization of $\alpha \in (0, 1)$, the DM faces the following problem:

$$\begin{aligned} V_{\mu^i}(s,\alpha) &\equiv \max_{(c,x(s'))\in x(s)} (1-\alpha)u(c) + \alpha U^i(x(s')) \\ &= \max_{(c,s')\in B(s)} (1-\alpha)u(c) + \alpha U^i(x(s')). \end{aligned} \tag{20.10}$$

Here, the current discount factor is known as α and the DM believes discount factors to follow distribution μ^i over the rest of the horizon. From (20.9) and (20.10), the Bellman equation is obtained as

$$V_{\mu^i}(s,\alpha) = \max_{(c,s')\in B(s)} \left((1-\alpha)u(c) + \alpha \int V_{\mu^i}(s',\alpha')\, \mathrm{d}\mu^i(\alpha') \right). \tag{20.11}$$

Let $g_{\mu^i}(s,\alpha)$ denote the savings function which solves problem (20.11).

We state the main result in this section. A proof is relegated to Appendix section "Proof of Theorem 5".

Theorem 5 *Assume that μ^1 second-order stochastically dominates μ^2 and $\bar{\alpha} \equiv \mathbb{E}_{\mu^1}[\alpha] = \mathbb{E}_{\mu^2}[\alpha] < 1/(1+r)^{1-\sigma}$. Then:*

(i) the DM saves a constant fraction of wealth, that is,

$$g_{\mu^i}(s,\alpha) = SR_{\mu^i}(\alpha)(1+r)s,$$

where the savings rate $SR_{\mu^i}(\alpha) \in (0,1)$ is uniquely determined, and;

(ii) for all $\alpha \in (0,1)$, $SR_{\mu^1}(\alpha) \lesseqgtr SR_{\mu^2}(\alpha)$ if $\sigma \lesseqgtr 1$.

Part (i) is a characterization of the savings function, and is based on the assumption that u is a CRRA utility function. Owing to part (i), we can focus on the savings rate rather than the savings function to analyze the savings behavior of the DM. Part (ii) concerns a comparative analysis. Depending on the relative size of σ compared to one, the savings rate increases or decreases as the DM becomes more uncertain about discount factors.

To obtain the intuition behind part (ii), for each s, define the number $\theta^i(s)$ by

$$V_{\bar{\alpha}}(\theta^i(s)) = \int V_{\mu^i}(s, \alpha')\,\mathrm{d}\mu^i(\alpha'), \tag{20.12}$$

where $V_{\bar{\alpha}}$ is the value function of the savings problem when a discount factor is constant over time and equal to the average $\bar{\alpha}$, that is, for all s, $V_{\bar{\alpha}}(s)$ is defined as

$$V_{\bar{\alpha}}(s) = \max_{(c,s')\in B(s)} (1-\bar{\alpha})u(c) + \bar{\alpha}V_{\bar{\alpha}}(s'). \tag{20.13}$$

Let $\mathbf{c}^i = (c_1^i, c_2^i, \cdots)$ be a solution to (20.13) that attains the maximum value $V_{\bar{\alpha}}(\theta^i(s))$. Then, the discounted sum of $\mathbf{c}^i$ is equal to $\theta^i(s)$, that is, $\theta^i(s) = \sum_{t=1}^{\infty} c_t^i/(1+r)^t$, and (20.12) is equivalent to saying that $\{\mathbf{c}^i\} \sim^i x(s)$. Since the DM desires flexibility, $\theta^i(s)$ must be greater than s so as to compensate the DM for being committed to $\mathbf{c}^i$. Hence, the ratio $\phi^i \equiv \theta^i(s)/s$ is interpreted as *the commitment premium*.[15] As uncertainty increases, the DM becomes more averse to commitment, and hence, ϕ^i increases. From (20.12), maximization problem (20.10) is rewritten as

$$\max_{(c,s')\in B(s)} (1-\alpha)u(c) + \alpha V_{\bar{\alpha}}(\phi^i s').$$

That is, increasing uncertainty has the same effect as if the rate of return from savings increases in the consumption-savings model with no uncertainty. Therefore, the substitution and income effects lead to the desired result.

Part (ii) of Theorem 5 includes, as a special case, a comparison between random and deterministic discounting with the same mean. According to the theorem, the savings increase or decrease depending on parameter σ when the DM becomes uncertain about discount factors, which implies that observed over-savings or under-savings behavior may be explained by subjective uncertainty about discount factors. Salanié and Treich (2006) provide the same observation in a three-period model.

Instead of uncertainty about discount factors, uncertainty about interest rates has been discussed in studies on consumption-savings, for example, Levhari and Srinivasan (1969), Sandmo (1970) and Rothschild and Stiglitz (1971). They report that increasing uncertainty will decrease (increase) savings in case of $\sigma < (>) 1$, which is the opposite to Theorem 5 (ii). Under risk aversion, the certainty equivalent of an uncertain interest rate always decreases as uncertainty increases. Hence, increasing uncertainty has the same effect as if the interest rate decreases in the consumption-savings problem with no uncertainty, while the commitment premium increases as discount factors become more uncertain. Thus, substitution and income effects lead to opposite implications.

Acknowledgements We would like to thank Larry Epstein for his illuminating guidance and constant support. We also thank Árpád Ábrahám, Larry Blume, Atsushi Kajii, Tomoyuki Nakajima,

[15] Since u is CRRA, ϕ^i is independent of s.

Jean-Marc Tallon, Katsutoshi Wakai, and the audiences of the 2005 JEA Spring Meeting, CETC 2006, and RUD 2006, Hosei, Keio, Kobe, Kyoto, Osaka, and Shiga Universities for useful comments. Detailed suggestions by an anonymous associate editor and two referees led to substantial improvements. Takeoka gratefully acknowledges the financial support by Grant-in-Aid for Scientific Research and MEXT.OPENRESEARCH(2004-2008). All remaining errors are the author's responsibility.

Appendices

Hausdorff Metric

Let X be a compact metric space with a metric d. Let $\mathscr{K}(X)$ be the set of all non-empty compact subsets of X. For $x \in X$ and $A, B \in \mathscr{K}(X)$, let

$$d(x, B) \equiv \min_{x' \in B} d(x, x'),\ d(A, B) \equiv \max_{x \in A} d(x, B).$$

For all $A, B \in \mathscr{K}(X)$, define *the Hausdorff metric* d_H by

$$d_H(A, B) \equiv \max[d(A, B), d(B, A)].$$

Then, d_H satisfies (i) $d_H(A, B) \geq 0$, (ii) $A = B \Leftrightarrow d_H(A, B) = 0$, (iii) $d_H(A, B) = d_H(B, A)$, and (iv) $d_H(A, B) \leq d_H(A, C) + d_H(C, B)$. Moreover, $\mathscr{K}(X)$ is compact under the Hausdorff metric.

Perfect Commitment Menus

We follow the construction of menus by Gul and Pesendorfer (2004, Appendix A) (hereafter GP) and define the set $\mathscr{L}$ of perfect commitment menus. Then we show that $\mathscr{L}$ is homeomorphic to $\Delta(C \times \mathscr{L})$. That is, a perfect commitment menu can be viewed as a multistage lottery.

Let C denote the outcome space (consumption set), which is a compact metric space. We define the set of one-period consumption problems as $\mathscr{Z}_1 \equiv \mathscr{K}(\Delta(C))$. For $t > 1$, define the set of t-period consumption problems inductively as $\mathscr{Z}_t \equiv \mathscr{K}(\Delta(C \times \mathscr{Z}_{t-1}))$. Let $\mathscr{Z}^* \equiv \Pi_{t=1}^{\infty} \mathscr{Z}_t$. A menu is a *consistent* element of $\mathscr{Z}^*$.

Formally, define $G_1 : C \times \mathscr{Z}_1 \to C$, $F_1 : \Delta(C \times \mathscr{Z}_1) \to \Delta(C)$, and $\overline{F}_1 : \mathscr{K}(\Delta(C \times \mathscr{Z}_1)) \to \mathscr{K}(\Delta(C))$ as follows:

$$G_1(c, z_1) \equiv c,\ F_1(\mu_2)(E) \equiv \mu_2(G_1^{-1}(E)) \text{ and } \overline{F}_1(z_2) \equiv \{F_1(\mu_2) \mid \mu_2 \in z_2\},$$

for E in the Borel σ−algebra of C. For $t > 1$, we define inductively $G_t : C \times \mathscr{Z}_t \to C \times \mathscr{Z}_{t-1}$, $F_t : \Delta(C \times \mathscr{Z}_t) \to \Delta(C \times \mathscr{Z}_{t-1})$, and $\overline{F}_t : \mathscr{K}(\Delta(C \times \mathscr{Z}_t)) \to$

$\mathscr{K}(\Delta(C \times \mathscr{Z}_{t-1}))$ by

$$G_t(c, z_t) \equiv (c, G_{t-1}(z_t)), \ F_t(\mu_{t+1})(E) \equiv \mu_{t+1}(G_t^{-1}(E)), \text{ and}$$

$$\overline{F}_t(z_{t+1}) \equiv \{F_t(\mu_{t+1}) \mid \mu_{t+1} \in z_{t+1}\},$$

for E in the Borel σ−algebra of $C \times \mathscr{Z}_{t-1}$. Finally, we define $\{z_t\}_{t=1}^{\infty} \in \mathscr{Z}^*$ is *consistent* if $z_{t-1} = \overline{F}_{t-1}(z_t)$ for every $t > 1$.

We identify a singleton menu with its only element by slightly abusing notation. Let $\mathscr{L}_1 \equiv \Delta(C) \subset \mathscr{Z}_1$. An element of $\mathscr{L}_1$ is a one-period "commitment" consumption problem. For $t > 1$, we define $\mathscr{L}_t$ inductively as $\mathscr{L}_t \equiv \Delta(C \times \mathscr{L}_{t-1}) \subset \mathscr{Z}_t$. An element of $\mathscr{L}_t$ is a t-period "commitment" consumption problem. Let $\mathscr{L}^* \equiv \Pi_{t=1}^{\infty}\mathscr{L}_t$. We define the set of perfect commitment menus as $\mathscr{L} \equiv \mathscr{Z} \cap \mathscr{L}^*$. Thus, an element in $\mathscr{L}$ is a menu in which the DM is committed in every period.

Proposition 2 *$\mathscr{L}$ is homeomorphic to $\Delta(C \times \mathscr{L})$.*

Proof GP construct a homeomorphism $f : \mathscr{Z} \to \mathscr{K}(\Delta(C \times \mathscr{Z}))$. Note that $\mathscr{L}$ is compact since $\mathscr{L}_t$ is compact for every t. It is sufficient to check that $f(\mathscr{L}) = \Delta(C \times \mathscr{L})$.

Definition 8 Let $Y_1 \equiv \hat{L}_1 \equiv \Delta(C)$ and for $t > 1$ let $Y_t \equiv \Delta(C \times \Pi_{n=1}^{t-1}\mathscr{Z}_n)$ and $\hat{L}_t \equiv \Delta(C \times \Pi_{n=1}^{t-1}\mathscr{L}_n)$. Define $Y^{kc} \equiv \{\{\hat{\mu}_t\} \in \Pi_{t=1}^{\infty}Y_t \mid \text{marg}_{C\times\Pi_{n=1}^{t-1}\mathscr{Z}_n}\hat{\mu}_{t+1} = \hat{\mu}_t\}$. Let $\hat{L}^{kc} = Y^{kc} \cap \Pi_{t=1}^{\infty}\hat{L}_t$.

GP show that for every $\{\hat{\mu}_t\} \in Y^{kc}$ there exists a unique $\mu \in \Delta(C\times\mathscr{Z}^*)$ such that $\text{marg}_C\mu = \hat{\mu}_1$ and $\text{marg}_{C\times\Pi_{n=1}^{t}\mathscr{Z}_n}\mu = \hat{\mu}_t$. Then they define $\psi : Y^{kc} \to \Delta(C \times \mathscr{Z}^*)$ as the mapping that associates this μ with the corresponding $\{\hat{\mu}_t\}$.

Step 1: $\psi(\hat{L}^{kc}) = \Delta(C \times \mathscr{L}^*)$.

Note that, for a sequence $\{\hat{l}_t\} \in \hat{L}^{kc}$, it holds that

$$\text{marg}_{C\times\Pi_{n=1}^{t-1}\mathscr{L}_n}\hat{l}_{t+1} = \text{marg}_{C\times\Pi_{n=1}^{t-1}\mathscr{Z}_n}\hat{l}_{t+1} = \hat{l}_t.$$

The same argument of Lemma 3 in GP shows that there exists a homeomorphism $\psi' : \hat{L}^{kc} \to \Delta(C\times\mathscr{L}^*)$ such that $\text{marg}_C\psi'(\{\hat{l}_t\}) = \hat{l}_1$ and $\text{marg}_{C\times\Pi_{n=1}^{t-1}\mathscr{L}_n}\psi'(\{\hat{l}_t\}) = \hat{l}_t$. The uniqueness part of the Kolmogorov's Existence Theorem implies that $\psi' = \psi|_{\hat{L}^{kc}}$. Step 1 thus follows.

Definition 9 Let $D_t \equiv \{(z_1, \ldots, z_t) \in \Pi_{n=1}^{t}\mathscr{Z}_n \mid z_k = \overline{F}_k(z_{k+1}), \ \forall k = 1, \ldots, t-1\}$ and $D_t^L \equiv D_t \cap \Pi_{n=1}^{t}\mathscr{L}_n$. Define $M^c \equiv \{\{\mu_t\} \in \Delta(C)\times\Pi_{t=1}^{\infty}\Delta(C\times\mathscr{Z}_t) \mid F_t(\mu_{t+1}) = \mu_t, \ \forall t \geq 1\}$. Let $Y^c \equiv \{\{\hat{\mu}_t\} \in Y^{kc} \mid \hat{\mu}_{t+1}(C \times D_t) = 1, \forall t \geq 1\}$ and $\hat{L}^c \equiv Y^c \cap \hat{L}^{kc}$.

Note that $\mathscr{L} = M^c \cap \mathscr{L}^*$. GP show that for every $\{\mu_t\} \in M^c$ there exists a unique $\{\hat{\mu}_t\} \in Y^c$ such that $\hat{\mu}_1 = \mu_1$ and $\text{marg}_{C\times\mathscr{Z}_{t-1}}\hat{\mu}_t = \mu_t$ for every $t \geq 2$.

Then they define $\phi : M^c \to Y^c$ as the mapping that associates this $\{\mu_t\}$ with the corresponding $\{\hat{\mu}_t\}$.

Step 2: $\phi(\mathscr{L}) = \hat{L}^c$.

It is straightforward from the definition of ϕ that $\phi(\mathscr{L}) \supset \hat{L}^c$. We show $\phi(\mathscr{L}) \subset \hat{L}^c$ or $\phi(\mathscr{L}) \subset \Pi_{t=1}^{\infty}\hat{L}_t$ by mathematical induction. Take $\{l_t\} \in \mathscr{L}$ and let $\{\hat{\mu}_t\} \equiv \phi(\{l_t\}) \in Y^c$. By definition, $\hat{\mu}_1 = l_1 \in \Delta(C) = \hat{L}_1$ and $\hat{\mu}_2 = \mathrm{marg}_{C\times \mathscr{Z}_1}\hat{\mu}_2 = l_2 \in \Delta(C \times \mathscr{L}_1) = \hat{L}_2$.

Suppose that $\hat{\mu}_k \in \hat{L}_k$ for every $k = 1, 2, \ldots, t$. Since $\{\hat{\mu}_t\}$ is a Kolmogorov consistent sequence, $\mathrm{marg}_{C\times\Pi_{n=1}^{t-1}\mathscr{Z}_n}\hat{\mu}_{t+1} = \hat{\mu}_t \in \hat{L}_t$. Thus, $\hat{\mu}_{t+1} \in \Delta(C\times\Pi_{n=1}^{t-1}\mathscr{L}_n\times \mathscr{Z}_t)$. The definition of ϕ implies that $\mathrm{marg}_{C,\mathscr{Z}_t}\hat{\mu}_{t+1} = l_{t+1} \in \Delta(C\times \mathscr{L}_t)$. Therefore, $\hat{\mu}_{t+1} \in \hat{L}_{t+1} = \Delta(C \times \Pi_{n=1}^{t}\mathscr{L}_n)$.

Step 3: $\psi(\hat{L}^c) = \{l \in \Delta(C \times \mathscr{L}^*) \mid l(C \times \mathscr{L}) = 1\}$.

Since $\hat{L}^c = \{\{\hat{l}_t\} \in \hat{L}^{kc} \mid \hat{l}_{t+1}(C \times D_t^L) = 1, \forall t \geqq 1\}$, Step 3 follows from the same argument of Lemma 5 in GP.

GP define $\xi : \mathscr{Z} \to \mathscr{K}(M^c)$ as $\xi(z) \equiv \{\{\mu_t\} \in M^c \mid \mu_t \in z_t,\ \forall t \geq 1\}$. Note that ξ is identity on $\mathscr{L}$. Finally, the homeomorphism $f : \mathscr{Z} \to \mathscr{K}(\Delta(C \times \mathscr{Z}))$ is given by $f(z) = \psi \circ \phi(\xi(z))$. Then the above steps imply that $f(\mathscr{L}) = \psi \circ \phi(\xi(\mathscr{L})) = \psi \circ \phi(\mathscr{L}) = \Delta(C \times \mathscr{L})$.

Proof of Theorem 1

Necessity

Necessity of the axioms is routine. We show that for any (u, μ) there exists U satisfying the functional equation.

Let $\mathscr{U}$ be the Banach space of all real-valued continuous functions on $\mathscr{Z}$ with the sup-norm metric. Define the operator $T : \mathscr{U} \to \mathscr{U}$ by

$$T(U)(x) \equiv \int_{[0,1]} \max_{l\in x}\left((1-\alpha)u(l_c) + \alpha\int_{\mathscr{Z}} U(z)\,\mathrm{d}l_z\right)\mathrm{d}\mu(\alpha).$$

Since $T(U)$ is continuous, the operator T is well-defined. To show T is a contraction mapping, it suffices to verify that (i) T is monotonic, that is, $T(U) \geq T(V)$ whenever $U \geq V$, and (ii) T satisfies the discounting property, that is, there exists $\delta \in [0, 1)$ such that for any U and $c \in \mathbb{R}$, $T(U + c) = T(U) + \delta c$.

Step 1: T is monotonic.

Take any $U, V \in \mathscr{U}$ with $U \geq V$. Since $\int U(z)\,\mathrm{d}l_z \geq \int V(z)\,\mathrm{d}l_z$ for all $l \in \Delta(C \times \mathscr{Z})$, we have

$$\max_{l\in x}\left((1-\alpha)u(l_c)+\alpha\int_{\mathscr{Z}}U(z)\,\mathrm{d}l_z\right)\geq\max_{l\in x}\left((1-\alpha)u(l_c)+\alpha\int_{\mathscr{Z}}V(z)\,\mathrm{d}l_z\right)$$

for all x and α, and hence $T(U)(x)\geq T(V)(x)$ as desired.

Step 2: T satisfies the discounting property.

Let $\delta\equiv\bar{\alpha}$. By assumption, $\delta\in[0,1)$. For any $U\in\mathscr{U}$ and $c\in\mathbb{R}$,

$$\begin{aligned}T(U+c)&=\int_{[0,1]}\max_{l\in x}\left((1-\alpha)u(l_c)+\alpha\int_{\mathscr{Z}}(U(z)+c)\,\mathrm{d}l_z\right)\mathrm{d}\mu(\alpha)\\&=T(U)+\bar{\alpha}c=T(U)+\delta c.\end{aligned}$$

By Steps 1 and 2, T is a contraction mapping. Thus, the fixed point theorem (See Bertsekas and Shreve 1978, p. 55) ensures that there exists a unique $U^*\in\mathscr{U}$ satisfying $U^*=T(U^*)$. This U^* satisfies Eq. (20.1).

Sufficiency

Lemma 1 *Commitment Independence, Stationarity, and Timing Indifference imply Independence, that is,*

$$x\succ y\;\Rightarrow\;\lambda x+(1-\lambda)z\succ\lambda y+(1-\lambda)z,$$

for all $x,y,z\in\mathscr{Z}$ *and* $\lambda\in(0,1)$.

Proof Let $x\succ y$. From Stationarity, $\{(c,x)\}\succ\{(c,y)\}$. For any $\lambda\in(0,1)$, Commitment Independence implies $\{\lambda\circ(c,x)+(1-\lambda)\circ(c,z)\}\succ\{\lambda\circ(c,y)+(1-\lambda)\circ(c,z)\}$. From Timing Indifference, $\{(c,\lambda x+(1-\lambda)z)\}\succ\{(c,\lambda y+(1-\lambda)z)\}$. Again, from Stationarity, $\lambda x+(1-\lambda)z\succ\lambda y+(1-\lambda)z$. □

Let $\overline{\text{co}}(x)$ denote the closed convex hull of x. As in DLR, Order, Continuity, and Independence imply $x\sim\overline{\text{co}}(x)$. Hence we can pay attention to the sub-domain

$$\mathscr{Z}_1\equiv\{x\in\mathscr{Z}\,|\,x=\overline{\text{co}}(x)\}.$$

Since $\mathscr{Z}_1$ is a mixture space, Order, Continuity, and Independence ensure that $\succsim$ can be represented by a mixture linear function $U:\mathscr{Z}_1\to\mathbb{R}$. Nondegeneracy implies U is not constant. Since $C\times\mathscr{Z}$ is compact, there exist a maximal and a minimal lottery $\bar{l},\underline{l}\in\Delta(C\times\mathscr{Z})$ with respect to $U(\{\cdot\})$. Without loss of generality, assume $U(\{\bar{l}\})=1$ and $U(\{\underline{l}\})=0$.

Define $u:\Delta(C)\to\mathbb{R}$ and $W:\Delta(\mathscr{Z})\to\mathbb{R}$ by

$$u(l_c)\equiv U(\{l_c\otimes\underline{l}_z\}),\;\;W(l_z)\equiv U(\{\underline{l}_c\otimes l_z\}),$$

where $\underline{l}_c$ and $\underline{l}_z$ be the marginal distributions of $\underline{l}$ on C and $\mathscr{Z}$.

Lemma 2 *(i) For any $l_c, l'_c \in \Delta(C)$ and $l_z, l'_z \in \Delta(\mathscr{Z})$,*

$$u(l_c) \geq u(l'_c) \;\Leftrightarrow\; U(\{l_c \otimes l_z\}) \geq U(l'_c \otimes l_z),$$
$$W(l_z) \geq W(l'_z) \;\Leftrightarrow\; U(\{l_c \otimes l_z\}) \geq U(l_c \otimes l'_z).$$

(ii) u and W are mixture linear.

Proof (i) Consider the restriction of U on $\Delta(C \times \mathscr{Z})$. Let $U(c, z) \equiv U(\{(c, z)\})$. First we will claim that there exist $\bar{u} : C \to \mathbb{R}$ and $\bar{W} : \mathscr{Z} \to \mathbb{R}$ such that $U(c, z) = \bar{u}(c) + \bar{W}(z)$. Since

$$O\left(\frac{1}{2} \circ (c, z) + \frac{1}{2} \circ (c', z')\right) = O\left(\frac{1}{2} \circ (c', z) + \frac{1}{2} \circ (c, z')\right),$$

Marginal Dominance implies

$$U\left(\left\{\frac{1}{2} \circ (c, z) + \frac{1}{2} \circ (c', z')\right\}\right) = U\left(\left\{\frac{1}{2} \circ (c', z) + \frac{1}{2} \circ (c, z')\right\}\right).$$

Mixture linearity of U implies

$$U(c, z) + U(c', z') = U(c', z) + U(c, z').$$

Define $\bar{u}(c) \equiv U(c, z')$ and $\bar{W}(z) \equiv U(c', z) - U(c', z')$ for an arbitrarily fixed (c', z'). Then, $U(c, z) = \bar{u}(c) + \bar{W}(z)$.
By the above claim, for any $l \in \Delta(C \times Z)$,

$$U(\{l\}) = \int U(c, z)\, \mathrm{d}l(c, z) = \int (\bar{u}(c) + \bar{W}(z))\, \mathrm{d}l(c, z) = \int \bar{u}(c)\, \mathrm{d}l_c(c) + \int \bar{W}(z)\, \mathrm{d}l_z(z).$$

Thus,

$$\begin{aligned}
u(l_c) \geq u(l'_c) &\Leftrightarrow U(\{l_c \otimes \underline{l}_z\}) \geq U(\{l'_c \otimes \underline{l}_z\}) \\
&\Leftrightarrow \int \bar{u}(c)\, \mathrm{d}l_c(c) + \int \bar{W}(z)\, \mathrm{d}\underline{l}_z(z) \geq \int \bar{u}(c)\, \mathrm{d}l'_c(c) + \int \bar{W}(z)\, \mathrm{d}\underline{l}_z(z) \\
&\Leftrightarrow \int \bar{u}(c)\, \mathrm{d}l_c(c) \geq \int \bar{u}(c)\, \mathrm{d}l'_c(c) \\
&\Leftrightarrow \int \bar{u}(c)\, \mathrm{d}l_c(c) + \int \bar{W}(z)\, \mathrm{d}l_z(z) \geq \int \bar{u}(c)\, \mathrm{d}l'_c(c) + \int \bar{W}(z)\, \mathrm{d}l_z(z)
\end{aligned}$$

$$\Leftrightarrow U(\{l_c \otimes l_z\}) \geq U(\{l'_c \otimes l_z\}).$$

The symmetric argument can be applied to W.

(ii) We want to show $u(\lambda l_c + (1-\lambda)l'_c) = \lambda u(l_c) + (1-\lambda)u(l'_c)$ for any l_c, l'_c and $\lambda \in [0,1]$. Since

$$O((\lambda l_c + (1-\lambda)l'_c) \otimes l_z) = O(\lambda l_c \otimes l_z + (1-\lambda)l'_c \otimes l_z),$$

Marginal Dominance implies

$$U(\{(\lambda l_c + (1-\lambda)l'_c) \otimes l_z\}) = U(\{\lambda l_c \otimes l_z + (1-\lambda)l'_c \otimes l_z\}).$$

Since $U(\{\cdot\})$ is mixture linear,

$$\begin{aligned} u(\lambda l_c + (1-\lambda)l'_c) &= U(\{(\lambda l_c + (1-\lambda)l'_c) \otimes \underline{l}_z\}) \\ &= U(\{\lambda l_c \otimes \underline{l}_z + (1-\lambda)l'_c \otimes \underline{l}_z\}) \\ &= \lambda U(\{l_c \otimes \underline{l}_z\}) + (1-\lambda)U(\{l'_c \otimes \underline{l}_z\}) \\ &= \lambda u(l_c) + (1-\lambda)u(l'_c). \end{aligned}$$

By the symmetric argument, we can show that W is mixture linear. □

Next we show several properties of the Marginal Dominance operator.

Lemma 3 *(i) For any $x \in \mathscr{X}$, $O(x) \in \mathscr{X}$.*
(ii) If x is convex, so is $O(x)$.
(iii) $O : \mathscr{X} \to \mathscr{X}$ is Hausdorff continuous.

Proof (i) Since $\Delta(C \times \mathscr{Z})$ is compact, it suffices to show that $O(x)$ is a closed subset of $\Delta(C \times \mathscr{Z})$. Let $l^n \to l$ with $l^n \in O(x)$. By definition, there exists a sequence $\{\bar{l}^n\}$ with $\bar{l}^n \in x$ such that $\{\bar{l}^n_c \otimes l^n_z\} \succsim \{l^n_c \otimes l^n_z\}$ and $\{l^n_c \otimes \bar{l}^n_z\} \succsim \{l^n_c \otimes l^n_z\}$. Since x is compact, without loss of generality, we can assume that $\{\bar{l}^n\}$ converges to a limit $\bar{l} \in x$. Since $l^n_c \to l_c$ and $l^n_z \to l_z$, $\bar{l}^n_c \to \bar{l}_c$ and $\bar{l}^n_z \to \bar{l}_z$, Continuity implies $\{\bar{l}_c \otimes l_z\} \succsim \{l_c \otimes l_z\}$ and $\{l_c \otimes \bar{l}_z\} \succsim \{l_c \otimes l_z\}$. Hence, $l \in O(x)$.

(ii) Take $l, l' \in O(x)$ and $\lambda \in [0,1]$. Let $l^\lambda \equiv \lambda l + (1-\lambda)l'$. We want to show $l^\lambda \in O(x)$. By definition, there exist $\bar{l}, \bar{l}' \in x$ such that $\{\bar{l}_c \otimes l_z\} \succsim \{l_c \otimes l_z\}$, $\{l_c \otimes \bar{l}_z\} \succsim \{l_c \otimes l_z\}$, $\{\bar{l}'_c \otimes l'_z\} \succsim \{l'_c \otimes l'_z\}$, and $\{l'_c \otimes \bar{l}'_z\} \succsim \{l'_c \otimes l'_z\}$. Let $\bar{l}^\lambda \equiv \lambda \bar{l} + (1-\lambda)\bar{l}' \in x$. From Commitment Independence,

$$\{\lambda \bar{l}_c \otimes l_z + (1-\lambda)\bar{l}'_c \otimes l'_z\} \succsim \{\lambda l_c \otimes l_z + (1-\lambda)l'_c \otimes l'_z\}.$$

Since $O(l_c \otimes l_z) = O(l)$, Marginal Dominance implies $\{l_c \otimes l_z\} \sim \{l\}$. By the same reason, $\{l'_c \otimes l'_z\} \sim \{l'\}$, $\{l^\lambda_c \otimes l^\lambda_z\} \sim \{l^\lambda\}$, and

$$\{(\lambda\bar{l}_c + (1-\lambda)\bar{l}'_c) \otimes (\lambda l_z + (1-\lambda)l'_z)\} \sim \{\lambda\bar{l}_c \otimes l_z + (1-\lambda)\bar{l}'_c \otimes l'_z\}.$$

Thus,

$$\begin{aligned}\{\bar{l}^\lambda_c \otimes l^\lambda_z\} &= \{(\lambda\bar{l} + (1-\lambda)\bar{l}')_c \otimes (\lambda\bar{l} + (1-\lambda)\bar{l}')_z\} \\ &= \{(\lambda\bar{l}_c + (1-\lambda)\bar{l}'_c) \otimes (\lambda l_z + (1-\lambda)l'_z)\} \\ &\sim \{\lambda\bar{l}_c \otimes l_z + (1-\lambda)\bar{l}'_c \otimes l'_z\} \succsim \{\lambda l_c \otimes l_z + (1-\lambda)l'_c \otimes l'_z\} \\ &\sim \{\lambda l + (1-\lambda)l'\} \sim \{l^\lambda_c \otimes l^\lambda_z\}.\end{aligned}$$

Similarly, $\{l^\lambda_c \otimes \bar{l}^\lambda_z\} \succsim \{l^\lambda_c \otimes l^\lambda_z\}$. Hence, $l^\lambda \in O(x)$.

(iii) Let $x^n \to x$. We want to show $O(x^n) \to O(x)$. By contradiction, suppose otherwise. Then, there exists a neighborhood $\mathscr{U}$ of $O(x)$ such that $O(x^\ell) \notin \mathscr{U}$ for infinitely many ℓ. Let $\{x^\ell\}_{\ell=1}^\infty$ be the corresponding subsequence of $\{x^n\}_{n=1}^\infty$. Since $x^n \to x$, $\{x^\ell\}_{\ell=1}^\infty$ also converges to x. Since $\{O(x^\ell)\}_{\ell=1}^\infty$ is a sequence in a compact metric space $\mathscr{X}$, there exists a convergent subsequence $\{O(x^m)\}_{m=1}^\infty$ with a limit $y \neq O(x)$. As a result, now we have $x^m \to x$ and $O(x^m) \to y$. In the following argument, we will show that $y = O(x)$, which is a contradiction.

Step 1: $O(x) \subset y$.

Take any $l \in O(x)$. Then, there exists $\bar{l} \in x$ such that $\{\bar{l}_c \otimes l_z\} \succsim \{l_c \otimes l_z\}$ and $\{l_c \otimes \bar{l}_z\} \succsim \{l_c \otimes l_z\}$. Since $x^m \to x$, we can find a sequence $\{\bar{l}^m\}_{m=1}^\infty$ such that $\bar{l}^m \in x^m$ and $\bar{l}^m \to \bar{l}$.

Now we will construct a sequence $\{l^m\}_{m=1}^\infty$ with $l^m \in O(x^m)$ satisfying $l^m \to l$. Let $l^-_c \in \Delta(C)$ be a worst element with respect to u and $l^-_z \in \Delta(\mathscr{X})$ be a worst element with respect to W. For all sufficiently large k, let $B_k(l)$ be the $1/k$-neighborhood of l with respect to the weak convergence topology. There exists $0 < \lambda^k < 1$ such that $l^k \equiv \lambda^k l + (1-\lambda^k)(l^-_c \otimes l^-_z) \in B_k(l)$. By construction, $l^k \to l$. Since u is mixture linear from Lemma 2 (ii), $u(l_c) > u(l^k_c)$ if $u(l_c) > u(l^-_c)$, and $u(l_c) = u(l^k_c)$ if $u(l_c) = u(l^-_c)$. In the case of former, since $\bar{l}^m \to \bar{l}$, by Continuity, there exists m^k_1 such that for all $m \geq m^k_1$, $u(\bar{l}^m_c) > u(l^k_c)$. In the case of latter, for all m, $u(\bar{l}^m_c) \geq u(l^-_c) = u(l^k_c)$. In both cases, we have $u(\bar{l}^m_c) \geq u(l^k_c)$ for all $m \geq m^k_1$. Since W is mixture linear from Lemma 2 (ii), by the same argument, there exists m^k_2 such that for all $m \geq m^k_2$, $W(\bar{l}^m_z) \geq W(l^k_z)$. Therefore, for all $m \geq m^k \equiv \max[m^k_1, m^k_2]$, $u(\bar{l}^m_c) \geq u(l^k_c)$ and $W(\bar{l}^m_z) \geq W(l^k_z)$, that is, $\{\bar{l}^m_c \otimes l^k_z\} \succsim \{l^k_c \otimes l^k_z\}$ and $\{l^k_c \otimes \bar{l}^m_z\} \succsim \{l^k_c \otimes l^k_z\}$. Hence, we have $l^k \in O(\bar{l}^m) \subset O(x^m)$ for all $m \geq m^k$. Since $m^{k+1} \geq m^k$ for all k, define $l^m \equiv l^k$ for all m satisfying $m^k \leq m < m^{k+1}$. Then, $\{l^m\}_{m=1}^\infty$ is a required sequence.

Since $l^m \to l$ and $O(x^m) \to y$ with $l^m \in O(x^m)$, we have $l \in y$. Thus, $O(x) \subset y$.

Step 2: $y \subset O(x)$.

Take any $l \in y$. Since $O(x^m) \to y$, we can find a sequence $l^m \in O(x^m)$ with $l^m \to l$. By definition, there is $\bar{l}^m \in x^m$ such that $\{\bar{l}^m_c \otimes l^m_z\} \succsim \{l^m_c \otimes l^m_z\}$ and $\{l^m_c \otimes \bar{l}^m_z\} \succsim \{l^m_c \otimes l^m_z\}$. Since $\Delta(C \times \mathscr{Z})$ is compact, we can assume $\{\bar{l}^m\}$ converges to a limit $\bar{l} \in \Delta(C \times \mathscr{Z})$. Since $\bar{l}^m \to \bar{l}$ and $x^m \to x$ with $\bar{l}^m \in x^m$, we have $\bar{l} \in x$. From Continuity, $\{\bar{l}_c \otimes l_z\} \succsim \{l_c \otimes l_z\}$ and $\{l_c \otimes \bar{l}_z\} \succsim \{l_c \otimes l_z\}$. Thus, $l \in O(x)$. □

From Marginal Dominance, $x \sim O(x)$. Hence we can pay attention to the subdomain,

$$\mathscr{Z}_2 \equiv \{x \in \mathscr{Z}_1 | x = O(x)\}.$$

From Lemma 3 (iii), $\mathscr{Z}_2$ is compact. Moreover, Lemma 3 (i) and (ii) imply that any $x \in \mathscr{Z}_2$ is compact and convex.

For each $x \in \mathscr{Z}_2$ and $\alpha \in [0, 1]$, define

$$\sigma_x(\alpha) \equiv \max_{l \in x}\Big((1-\alpha)u(l_c) + \alpha W(l_z)\Big). \tag{20.14}$$

Let $\mathscr{C}([0, 1])$ be the set of real-valued continuous functions on $[0, 1]$ with the supnorm. The above formulation (20.14) defines the mapping $\sigma : \mathscr{Z}_2 \to \mathscr{C}([0, 1])$.

Lemma 4 *(i) σ is continuous.*
(ii) For all $x, y \in \mathscr{Z}_2$ and $\lambda \in [0, 1]$, $\lambda\sigma_x + (1-\lambda)\sigma_y = \sigma_{O(\lambda x+(1-\lambda)y)}$.
(iii) σ is injective.

Proof (i) Let

$$V(x) \equiv \{(u, w) | u = u(l_c), w = W(l_z), l \in x\} \subset \mathbb{R}^2.$$

Since u and W are continuous and $C \times \mathscr{Z}$ is compact, there exists a compact set $L \subset \mathbb{R}^2$ such that $V(x) \subset L$ for all x. Hence, $V(x)$ is also compact and, moreover, convex because u and W are mixture linear. Let $\mathscr{K}(L)$ be the set of non-empty compact subsets of L with the Hausdorff metric.

Step 1: The map $V : \mathscr{Z}_2 \ni x \mapsto V(x) \in \mathscr{K}(L)$ is Hausdorff continuous.

Take a sequence $x^n \to x$ with $x^n, x \in \mathscr{Z}_2$. We want to show that $V(x^n) \to V(x)$. By contradiction, suppose otherwise. Then, there exists a neighborhood $\mathscr{U}$ of $V(x)$ such that $V(x^m) \notin \mathscr{U}$ for infinitely many m. Let $\{x^m\}_{m=1}^{\infty}$ be the corresponding subsequence of $\{x^n\}_{n=1}^{\infty}$. Since $x^n \to x$, $\{x^m\}_{m=1}^{\infty}$ also converges to x. Since $\{V(x^m)\}_{m=1}^{\infty}$ is a sequence in a compact metric space $\mathscr{K}(L)$, there exists a convergent subsequence $\{V(x^\ell)\}_{\ell=1}^{\infty}$ with a limit $z \neq V(x)$. As a result, now we have $x^\ell \to x$ and $V(x^\ell) \to z$.

In the following argument, we will show that $z = V(x)$, which is a contradiction. Take any $(\bar{u}, \bar{w}) \in V(x)$. There exists $\bar{l} \in x$ such that $\bar{u} = u(\bar{l}_c)$ and $\bar{w} = W(\bar{l}_z)$. Since $x^\ell \to x$, we can find $\{l^\ell\}_{\ell=1}^{\infty}$ such that $l^\ell \to \bar{l}$ with $l^\ell \in x^\ell$. Let $(u^\ell, w^\ell) \equiv$

$(u(l_c^\ell), W(l_z^\ell)) \in V(x^\ell)$. The conditions $(u^\ell, w^\ell) \to (\bar{u}, \bar{w})$ and $V(x^\ell) \to z$ with $(u^\ell, w^\ell) \in V(x^\ell)$ imply $(\bar{u}, \bar{w}) \in z$. Thus, $V(x) \subset z$.

For the other direction, take any $(\bar{u}, \bar{w}) \in z$. Since $V(x^\ell) \to z$, we can find $\{(u^\ell, w^\ell)\}_{\ell=1}^\infty$ such that $(u^\ell, w^\ell) \to (\bar{u}, \bar{w})$ with $(u^\ell, w^\ell) \in V(x^\ell)$. There exists $l^\ell \in x^\ell$ satisfying $(u^\ell, w^\ell) = (u(l_c^\ell), W(l_z^\ell))$. Since $\Delta(C \times \mathscr{Z})$ is compact, there exists a convergent subsequence $\{l^k\}_{k=1}^\infty$ with a limit $\bar{l}$. By continuity of u and W, $(u(\bar{l}_c), W(\bar{l}_z)) = (\bar{u}, \bar{w})$. Moreover, since $l^k \to \bar{l}$, $x^k \to x$ with $l^k \in x^k$, we have $\bar{l} \in x$. Thus $(\bar{u}, \bar{w}) \in V(x)$, which implies $z \subset V(x)$.

Step 2: $d_{\text{supnorm}}(\sigma_x, \sigma_y) \leq d_{\text{Hausdorff}}(V(x), V(y))$.

For any $\alpha \in [0, 1]$, by definition,

$$\left|\sigma_x(\alpha) - \sigma_y(\alpha)\right| = \left|\max_{l \in x}\Big((1-\alpha)u(l_c) + \alpha W(l_z)\Big) - \max_{h \in y}\Big((1-\alpha)u(l_c) + \alpha W(l_z)\Big)\right|$$
$$= \left|\max_{(u,w) \in V(x)} ((1-\alpha)u + \alpha w) - \max_{(u,w) \in V(y)} ((1-\alpha)u + \alpha w)\right|.$$

Let $(u^{\alpha x}, w^{\alpha x}) \in V(x)$ and $(u^{\alpha y}, w^{\alpha y}) \in V(y)$ be maximizers for the maximization problems, respectively. Without loss of generality, assume

$$(1-\alpha)u^{\alpha x} + \alpha w^{\alpha x} \geq (1-\alpha)u^{\alpha y} + \alpha w^{\alpha y}.$$

Let

$$H^{\alpha y} \equiv \{(u, w) | (1-\alpha)u + \alpha w = (1-\alpha)u^{\alpha y} + \alpha w^{\alpha y}\}$$

and $(u^*, w^*) \in H^{\alpha y}$ be a point solving

$$\min_{(u,w) \in H^{\alpha y}} \|(u, w) - (u^{\alpha x}, w^{\alpha x})\|.$$

Then, by the Schwarz inequality,

$$\begin{aligned}
&\left|\max_{(u,w) \in V(x)} ((1-\alpha)u + \alpha w) - \max_{(u,w) \in V(y)} ((1-\alpha)u + \alpha w)\right| \\
&= |((1-\alpha)u^{\alpha x} + \alpha w^{\alpha x}) - ((1-\alpha)u^{\alpha y} + \alpha w^{\alpha y})| \\
&= |((1-\alpha)u^{\alpha x} + \alpha w^{\alpha x}) - ((1-\alpha)u^* + \alpha w^*)| \\
&= |(1-\alpha)(u^{\alpha x} - u^*) + \alpha(w^{\alpha x} - w^*)| \\
&\leq \|(u^{\alpha x} - u^*, w^{\alpha x} - w^*)\| \|(1-\alpha, \alpha)\| \leq \|(u^{\alpha x} - u^*, w^{\alpha x} - w^*)\| \\
&\leq \min_{(u,w) \in V(y)} \|(u^{\alpha x}, w^{\alpha x}) - (u, w)\| \leq d_{\text{Hausdorff}}(V(x), V(y)).
\end{aligned}$$

Since this inequality holds for all α,

$$d_{\text{supnorm}}(\sigma_x, \sigma_y) = \sup_{\alpha \in [0,1]} \left| \sigma_x(\alpha) - \sigma_y(\alpha) \right| \leq d_{\text{Hausdorff}}(V(x), V(y)).$$

From Steps 1 and 2, σ is continuous.

(ii) Fix $\alpha \in [0, 1]$. Let $l^x \in x$ and $l^y \in y$ satisfy

$$(1-\alpha)u(l^x_c) + \alpha W(l^x_z) = \max_{l \in x}((1-\alpha)u(l_c) + \alpha W(l_z)),$$
$$(1-\alpha)u(l^y_c) + \alpha W(l^y_z) = \max_{l \in y}((1-\alpha)u(l_c) + \alpha W(l_z)).$$

Since $\lambda l^x + (1-\lambda)l^y \in \lambda x + (1-\lambda)y$, mixture linearity of u and W implies

$$\begin{aligned}
&\lambda\sigma_x(\alpha) + (1-\lambda)\sigma_y(\alpha) \\
&= \lambda((1-\alpha)u(l^x_c) + \alpha W(l^x_z)) + (1-\lambda)((1-\alpha)u(l^y_c) + \alpha W(l^y_z)) \\
&= (1-\alpha)u(\lambda l^x_c + (1-\lambda)l^y_c) + \alpha W(\lambda l^x_z + (1-\lambda)l^y_z) \\
&- \max_{l \in \lambda x + (1-\lambda)y}((1-\alpha)u(l_c) + \alpha W(l_z)) \\
&= \max_{l \in O(\lambda x + (1-\lambda)y)}((1-\alpha)u(l_c) + \alpha W(l_z)) = \sigma_{O(\lambda x + (1-\lambda)y)}(\alpha).
\end{aligned}$$

(iii) Take $x, x' \in \mathscr{X}_2$ with $x \neq x'$. Without loss of generality, assume $x \not\subset x'$. Take $\tilde{l} \in x \setminus x'$. Let $\tilde{u} = u(\tilde{l}_c)$ and $\tilde{w} = W(\tilde{l}_z)$. Let

$$V' \equiv \{(u, w) | u = u(l_c), w = W(l_z), l \in x'\} \subset \mathbb{R}^2.$$

We will claim that $(\{(\tilde{u}, \tilde{w})\} + \mathbb{R}^2_+) \cap V' = \emptyset$. Suppose otherwise. Then, there exists $l' \in x'$ such that $u(l'_c) \geq \tilde{u}$ and $W(l'_z) \geq \tilde{w}$. That is, $U(\{l'_c \otimes \underline{l}_z\}) \geq U(\{\tilde{l}_c \otimes \underline{l}_z\})$ and $U(\{\underline{l}_c \otimes l'_z\}) \geq U(\{\underline{l}_c \otimes \tilde{l}_z\})$. From Lemma C.2 (i), $U(\{l'_c \otimes \tilde{l}_z\}) \geq U(\{\tilde{l}_c \otimes \tilde{l}_z\})$ and $U(\{\tilde{l}_c \otimes l'_z\}) \geq U(\{\tilde{l}_c \otimes \tilde{l}_z\})$. Thus, $\tilde{l} \in O(l') \subset O(x')$. Since $O(x') = x'$, this is a contradiction.

Since the above claim holds, by the separating hyperplane theorem, there exists $\alpha \in [0, 1]$ and $\gamma \in \mathbb{R}$ such that $(1-\alpha)\tilde{u} + \alpha\tilde{w} > \gamma > (1-\alpha)u' + \alpha w'$ for all $(u', w') \in V'$. Equivalently,

$$(1-\alpha)u(\tilde{l}_c) + \alpha W(\tilde{l}_z) > \gamma > (1-\alpha)u(l'_c) + \alpha W(l'_z),$$

for all $l' \in x'$. Hence,

$$\begin{aligned}
\sigma_x(\alpha) &= \max_{l \in x}((1-\alpha)u(l_c) + \alpha W(l_z)) \geq (1-\alpha)u(\tilde{l}_c) + \alpha W(\tilde{l}_z) \\
&> \max_{l' \in x'}((1-\alpha)u(l'_c) + \alpha W(l'_z)) = \sigma_{x'}(\alpha).
\end{aligned}$$

Therefore, $\sigma_x \neq \sigma_{x'}$. □

Let $C \subset \mathscr{C}([0,1])$ be the range of σ.

Lemma 5 *(i) C is convex.*
(ii) The zero function belongs to C.
(iii) The constant function equal to a positive number $c > 0$ belongs to C.
(iv) The supremum of any two points $f, f' \in C$ belongs to C. That is, $\max[f(\alpha), f'(\alpha)]$ belongs to C.
(v) For all $f \in C$, $f \geq 0$.

Proof (i) Take any $f, f' \in C$ and $\lambda \in [0,1]$. There are $x, x' \in \mathscr{X}_2$ satisfying $f = \sigma_x$ and $f' = \sigma_{x'}$. From Lemma 4 (ii),

$$\lambda f + (1-\lambda) f' = \lambda \sigma_x + (1-\lambda)\sigma_{x'} = \sigma_{O(\lambda x + (1-\lambda)x')} \in \mathscr{X}_2.$$

Hence, C is convex.
(ii) Let $x \equiv O(\underline{l}) \in \mathscr{X}_2$. Then, for all α,

$$\begin{aligned}\sigma_x(\alpha) &= \max_{l \in O(\underline{l})} (1-\alpha)u(l_c) + \alpha W(l_z) = (1-\alpha)u(\underline{l}_c) + \alpha W(\underline{l}_z) \\ &= (1-\alpha)U(\{\underline{l}_c \otimes \underline{l}_z\}) + \alpha U(\{\underline{l}_c \otimes \underline{l}_z\}) = 0.\end{aligned}$$

(iii) Recall that $\bar{l}$ is a maximal element of $U(\{\cdot\})$. Without loss of generality, assume $u(\bar{l}_c) \geq W(\bar{l}_z)$. From Nondegeneracy, there exists l_z^* such that $W(l_z^*) > W(\underline{l}_z) = 0$. Since $u(\bar{l}_c) \geq W(l_z^*) > 0 = u(\underline{l}_c)$, continuity of u implies that there exists l_c^* such that $u(l_c^*) = W(l_z^*)$. Let $c \equiv W(l_z^*) > 0$ and $x \equiv O(l_c^* \otimes l_z^*) \in \mathscr{X}_2$. Then, for all α,

$$\sigma_x(\alpha) = \max_{l \in O(l_c^* \otimes l_z^*)} (1-\alpha)u(l_c) + \alpha W(l_z) = (1-\alpha)u(l_c^*) + \alpha W(l_z^*) = c.$$

(iv) There exist $x', x \in \mathscr{X}_2$ such that $f = \sigma_x$ and $f' = \sigma_{x'}$. Let $f'' \equiv \sigma_{O(\text{co}(x \cup x'))} \in C$. Then, $f''(\alpha) = \max[\sigma_x(\alpha), \sigma_{x'}(\alpha)]$.
(v) There exists $x \in \mathscr{X}_2$ such that $f = \sigma_x$. Since $O(\underline{l}) \subset x$, Lemma 5 (ii) implies $f(\alpha) = \sigma_x(\alpha) \geq \sigma_{O(\underline{l})}(\alpha) = 0$, for any α. □

Define $T : C \to \mathbb{R}$ by $T(f) \equiv U(\sigma^{-1}(f))$. Notice that $T(0) = 0$ and $T(c) = c$, where 0 and c are identified with the zero function and the constant function equal to $c > 0$, respectively. Since U and σ are continuous and mixture linear, so is T.

Lemma 6 *$T(\beta f + \gamma f') = \beta T(f) + \gamma T(f')$ as long as $f, f', \beta f + \gamma f' \in C$, where $\beta, \gamma \in \mathbb{R}_+$.*

Proof For any $\beta \in [0,1]$, $T(\beta f) = T(\beta f + (1-\beta)0) = \beta T(f) + (1-\beta)T(0) = \beta T(f)$, where 0 is the zero function. For any $\beta > 1$, let $f'' \equiv \beta f$. Since

$T\left(\frac{1}{\beta}f''\right) = \frac{1}{\beta}T(f'')$, $\beta T(f) = T(\beta f)$. Additivity follows from $T(f+f') = 2T\left(\frac{1}{2}f + \frac{1}{2}f'\right) = T(f) + T(f')$. □

By the same argument as in DLR, we will extend T to $\mathscr{C}([0,1])$ step by step. For any $r \geq 0$, let $rC \equiv \{rf | f \in C\}$ and $H \equiv \cup_{r \geq 0} rC$. For any $f \in H \setminus 0$, there is $r > 0$ satisfying $(1/r)f \in C$. Define $T(f) \equiv rT((1/r)f)$. From linearity of T on C, $T(f)$ is well-defined. That is, even if there is another $r' > 0$ satisfying $(1/r')f \in C$, $rT((1/r)f) = r'T((1/r')f)$. It is easy to see that T on H is mixture linear. By the same argument in Lemma 6, T is also linear.

Let

$$H^* \equiv H - H = \{f_1 - f_2 \in \mathscr{C}([0,1]) | f_1, f_2 \in H\}.$$

For any $f \in H^*$, there are $f_1, f_2 \in H$ satisfying $f = f_1 - f_2$. Define $T(f) \equiv T(f_1) - T(f_2)$. We can verify that $T : H^* \to \mathbb{R}$ is well-defined. Indeed, suppose that f_1, f_2, f_3 and f_4 in H satisfy $f = f_1 - f_2 = f_3 - f_4$. Since $f_1 + f_4 = f_2 + f_3$, $T(f_1) + T(f_4) = T(f_2) + T(f_3)$ by linearity of T on H.

Lemma 7 *H^* is dense in $\mathscr{C}([0,1])$.*

Proof From the Stone-Weierstrass theorem, it is enough to show that (i) H^* is a vector sublattice, (ii) H^* separates the points of $[0,1]$; that is, for any two distinct points $\alpha, \alpha' \in [0,1]$, there exists $f \in H^*$ with $f(\alpha) \neq f(\alpha')$, and (iii) H^* contains the constant functions equal to one. By the exactly same argument as Lemma 11 (p. 928) in DLR, (i) holds. To verify condition (ii), take $\alpha, \alpha' \in [0,1]$ with $\alpha \neq \alpha'$. Without loss of generality, $\alpha' > \alpha$. Let $x \equiv O(\bar{l}_c \otimes \underline{l}_z)$. Then, $\sigma_x \in C \subset H^*$. Since $u(\bar{l}_c) > 0$ and $W(\underline{l}_z) = 0$,

$$\sigma_x(\alpha) = (1-\alpha)u(\bar{l}_c) + \alpha W(\underline{l}_z) > (1-\alpha')u(\bar{l}_c) + \alpha' W(\underline{l}_z) = \sigma_x(\alpha').$$

Finally, condition (iii) directly follows from Lemma 5 (iii) and the definition of H. □

Lemma 8 *There exists a constant $K > 0$ such that $T(f) \leq K\|f\|$ for any $f \in H^*$.*

Proof We use the same argument as in Theorem 2 of Dekel et al. (2007).[16] First, we claim that T is increasing in the pointwise order. Indeed, take any $g', g \in H^*$ with $g' \geq g$. Since H^* is a vector space, $g' - g \in H^*$. Hence there exist $f, f' \in C$ and $r > 0$ such that $r(f' - f) = g' - g \geq 0$. Thus $f' \geq f$ pointwise. Since $T(f') \geq T(f)$ by Monotonicity, $T(r(f' - f)) \geq T(0) = 0$ implies $T(g' - g) \geq 0$. That is, we have $T(g') \geq T(g)$.

[16]They fix the argument (Lemma 12, p. 929) of DLR.

For all $f \in H^*$, we have $f \leq \|f\|\mathbf{1}$, where $\mathbf{1} \in H$ is the function identically equal to 1. Since T is increasing, $T(f) \leq \|f\|T(\mathbf{1})$. Thus $K \equiv T(\mathbf{1})$ is the desired object. □

By Lemma 8 and the Hahn-Banach theorem, we can extend $T : H^* \to \mathbb{R}$ to $\overline{T} : \mathscr{C}([0, 1]) \to \mathbb{R}$ in a linear, continuous and increasing way. Since H^* is dense in $\mathscr{C}([0, 1])$ by Lemma 7, this extension is unique.

Now we have the following commutative diagram:

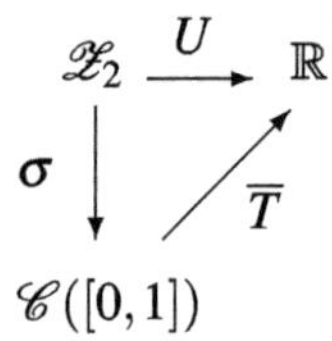

Since $\overline{T}$ is a positive linear functional on $\mathscr{C}([0, 1])$, the Riesz representation theorem ensures that there exists a unique countably additive probability measure μ on [0, 1] satisfying

$$\overline{T}(f) = \int_{[0,1]} f(\alpha)\mathrm{d}\mu(\alpha),$$

for all $f \in \mathscr{C}([0, 1])$. Thus we have

$$U(x) = \overline{T}(\sigma(x)) = \int_{[0,1]} \max_{l \in x} ((1-\alpha)u(l_c) + \alpha W(l_z))\, \mathrm{d}\mu(\alpha).$$

For any $x \in \mathscr{X}$, let δ_x be the degenerate measure at x. Denote $W(\delta_x)$ by $W(x)$.

Lemma 9 $U(x) \geq U(y) \Leftrightarrow W(x) \geq W(y)$.

Proof First of all,

$$W(l_z) = \int_{\Delta(\mathscr{X})} W(x)\mathrm{d}l_z(x).$$

Since

$$U(\{(c, x)\}) = \int ((1-\alpha)u(c) + \alpha W(x))\, \mathrm{d}\mu(\alpha) = (1-\bar{\alpha})u(c) + \bar{\alpha}W(x),$$

Stationarity implies that $U(x) \geq U(y) \Leftrightarrow U(\{(c, x)\}) \geq U(\{(c, y)\}) \Leftrightarrow W(x) \geq W(y)$. □

Lemma 10 *There exist* $\beta > 0$ *and* $\zeta \in \mathbb{R}$ *such that* $W(x) = \beta U(x) + \zeta$.

Proof Since U is mixture linear, there exists $(\underline{c}, \underline{z}) \in C \times \mathscr{Z}$ such that $\{\underline{l}\} \sim \{(\underline{c}, \underline{z})\}$. Thus $W(l_z) = U(\{\underline{c} \otimes l_z\})$. We have

$$\begin{aligned} U(\{\lambda \circ (\underline{c}, x) + (1-\lambda) \circ (\underline{c}, y)\}) &= U(\{\underline{c} \otimes (\lambda \circ x + (1-\lambda) \circ y)\}) \\ &= W(\lambda \circ x + (1-\lambda) \circ y), \end{aligned}$$

and $U(\{(\underline{c}, \lambda x + (1-\lambda)y)\}) = W(\lambda x + (1-\lambda)y)$. Since W is mixture linear over $\Delta(\mathscr{Z})$, Timing Indifference implies

$$\lambda W(x) + (1-\lambda)W(y) = W(\lambda \circ x + (1-\lambda) \circ y) = W(\lambda x + (1-\lambda)y).$$

Hence, W is mixture linear over $\mathscr{Z}_1$. From Lemma 9, we know $U(x)$ and $W(x)$ represent the same preference. Since both functions are mixture linear, there exist $\beta > 0$ and $\zeta \in \mathbb{R}$ such that $W(x) = \beta U(x) + \zeta$. □

We will claim that β can be normalized to one. Define $W^* : \Delta(\mathscr{Z}) \to \mathbb{R}$ by $W^*(l_z) = W(l_z)/\beta$. For any $x \in \mathscr{D}$, define $\sigma_x^* : [0,1] \to \mathbb{R}$ by

$$\sigma_x^*(\alpha) \equiv \max_{l \in x}\Big((1-\alpha)u(l_c) + \alpha W^*(l_z)\Big).$$

Since W^* is continuous and mixture linear, the same arguments up to Lemma 9 work even for σ^*. Thus, there exists a probability measure μ^* on $[0,1]$ such that

$$U(x) = \int_{[0,1]} \max_{l \in x}\big((1-\alpha)u(l_c) + \alpha W^*(l_z)\big)\, \mathrm{d}\mu^*(\alpha).$$

By definition, $W^*(z) = U(z) + \zeta/\beta$.

Lemma 11 *$\bar{\alpha} < 1$, where $\bar{\alpha}$ is the mean of μ^*.*

Proof Since U is not constant, there exist x and x' such that $U(x) > U(x')$. For any fixed c, let

$$x^t \equiv \{(c, \{(c, \{\cdots\{(c, x)\}\cdots\})\})\},\ x'^t \equiv \{(c, \{(c, \{\cdots\{(c, x')\}\cdots\})\})\}.$$

Then,

$$U(x^t) - U(x'^t) = (1-\bar{\alpha})\bar{\alpha}^t U(x) - (1-\bar{\alpha})\bar{\alpha}^t U(x') = (1-\bar{\alpha})(U(x) - U(x'))\bar{\alpha}^t.$$

Since Continuity requires $U(x^t) - U(x'^t) \to 0$ as $t \to \infty$, we must have $\bar{\alpha} < 1$. □

Define $\zeta^* \equiv \zeta/\beta$ and

$$u^*(l_c) \equiv u(l_c) + \frac{\bar{\alpha}}{1-\bar{\alpha}}\zeta^*.$$

Then

$$\begin{aligned}
U(x) &= \int_{[0,1]} \max_{l \in x} \left((1-\alpha)u(l_c) + \alpha \int_{\mathscr{X}} W^*(z)\, \mathrm{d}l_z(z) \right) \mathrm{d}\mu^*(\alpha) \\
&= \int_{[0,1]} \max_{l \in x} \left((1-\alpha)u(l_c) + \alpha \int_{\mathscr{X}} (U(z) + \zeta^*)\, \mathrm{d}l_z(z) \right) \mathrm{d}\mu^*(\alpha) \\
&= \int_{[0,1]} \max_{l \in x} \left((1-\alpha) \left(u(l_c) + \frac{\bar{\alpha}}{1-\bar{\alpha}} \zeta^* \right) + \alpha \int_{\mathscr{X}} U(z)\, \mathrm{d}l_z(z) \right) \mathrm{d}\mu^*(\alpha) \\
&= \int_{[0,1]} \max_{l \in x} \left((1-\alpha)u^*(l_c) + \alpha \int_{\mathscr{X}} U(z)\, \mathrm{d}l_z(z) \right) \mathrm{d}\mu^*(\alpha).
\end{aligned}$$

Therefore the functional form U with components (u^*, μ^*) is the required representation.

Proof of Theorem 2

(i) Since mixture linear functions u and u' represent the same conditional preference over $\Delta(C)$, by the standard argument, u' is rewritten as an affine transformation of u. That is, u and u' are cardinally equivalent.

(ii) From (i), there exist $\gamma > 0$ and $\zeta \in \mathbb{R}$ such that $u' = \gamma u + \zeta$. Since U and U' are mixture linear functions representing the same preference, there exist $\gamma^* > 0$ and $\zeta^* \in \mathbb{R}$ such that $U' = \gamma^* U + \zeta^*$. Let x_c be the perfect commitment menu to c, that is, $x_c \equiv \{(c, \{(c, \{\cdots\})\})\}$. Since $U(x_c) = u(c)$ and $U'(x_c) = u'(c)$, we have $U'(x_c) = \gamma U(x_c) + \zeta$, which implies $\gamma^* = \gamma$ and $\zeta^* = \zeta$. Now we have

$$\begin{aligned}
U'(x) &= \int_{[0,1]} \max_{l \in x} \left((1-\alpha)u'(l_c) + \alpha \int_{\mathscr{X}} U'(z)\mathrm{d}l_z \right) \mathrm{d}\mu'(\alpha) \\
&= \int_{[0,1]} \max_{l \in x} \left((1-\alpha)(\gamma u(l_c) + \zeta) + \alpha \int_{\mathscr{X}} (\gamma U(z) + \zeta)\mathrm{d}l_z \right) \mathrm{d}\mu'(\alpha) \\
&= \gamma \int_{[0,1]} \max_{l \in x} \left((1-\alpha)u(l_c) + \alpha \int_{\mathscr{X}} U(z)\, \mathrm{d}l_z \right) \mathrm{d}\mu'(\alpha) + \zeta.
\end{aligned}$$

Hence,

$$U''(x) \equiv \int_{[0,1]} \max_{l \in x} \left((1-\alpha)u(l_c) + \alpha \int_{\mathscr{X}} U(z)\, \mathrm{d}l_z \right) \mathrm{d}\mu'(\alpha)$$

also represents the same preference. Since $U' = \gamma U + \zeta$ and $U' = \gamma U'' + \zeta$, we must have $U(x) = U''(x)$ for all x. For all $x \in \mathscr{X}$ and $\alpha \in [0, 1]$, let

$$\sigma_x(\alpha) \equiv \max_{l \in x} \left((1-\alpha)u(l_c) + \alpha \int U(z)\, dl_z(x) \right).$$

Then,

$$U(x) = \int \sigma_x(\alpha)\, d\mu(\alpha) = \int \sigma_x(\alpha)\, d\mu'(\alpha) = U''(x). \tag{20.15}$$

If x is convex, σ_x is its support function. Equation (20.15) holds also when σ_x is replaced with $a\sigma_x - b\sigma_y$ for any convex menus x, y and $a, b \geq 0$. From Lemma C.6, the set of all such functions is a dense subset of the set of real-valued continuous functions over [0, 1]. Hence, Eq. (20.15) holds when σ_x is replaced with any real-valued continuous function. Hence, the Riesz representation theorem implies $\mu = \mu'$.

Proofs of Corollary 1 and Proposition 1

First we show Proposition 1. For all x, let l^x denote a best element in x with respect to commitment ranking.

Lemma 12 *$\succsim$ satisfies Dominance if and only if, for all x, $x \sim \{l^x\}$.*

Proof If $\succsim$ satisfies Dominance, $\{l^x\} \sim O^*(l^x) = O^*(x) \sim x$. Conversely, by definition of $O^*(x)$, l^x is a best element in $O^*(x)$. Thus $x \sim \{l^x\} \sim O^*(x)$. □

(i) By Lemma 12, it suffices to show that Strategic Rationality is equivalent to the condition that $x \sim \{l^x\}$ for all x. First suppose that $\succsim$ satisfies $x \sim \{l^x\}$. Since $x \succsim y$ implies $\{l^x\} \succsim \{l^y\}$, l^x is a best element of $x \cup y$ with respect to commitment ranking. Hence $x \sim \{l^x\} \sim x \cup y$.

Next suppose $\succsim$ satisfies Strategic Rationality. Take any finite menu x, denoted by $\{l_1, l_2, \cdots, l_N\}$. Without loss of generality, let $l^x = l_1$. Since $\{l_1\} \succsim \{l_2\}$, Strategic Rationality implies $\{l_1, l_2\} \sim \{l_1\}$. Since $\{l_1, l_2\} \sim \{l_1\} \succsim \{l_3\}$, again by Strategic Rationality, $\{l_1, l_2, l_3\} \sim \{l_1, l_2\} \sim \{l_1\}$. Repeating the same argument finite times, $x \sim \{l^x\}$. For any menu x, Lemma 0 of Gul and Pesendorfer (2001, p. 1421) shows that there exists a sequence of finite subsets x^n of x converging to x in the sense of the Hausdorff metric. Since l^x is a best element of x and $x^n \subset x$, applying the above claim, $x^n \cup \{l^x\} \sim \{l^x\}$. Thus, by Continuity, $x = x \cup \{l^x\} \sim \{l^x\}$ as $n \to \infty$.

(ii) For all x, choose any $l \in O(x)$. By definition, there exists $l' \in x$ such that $l \in O(l')$. From part (i), preference satisfies Monotonicity. Applying Commitment Marginal Dominance and Monotonicity, we have $\{l^x\} \succsim \{l'\} \sim O(l') \succsim \{l\}$. Hence, l^x is a best element in $O(x)$. Therefore, by Lemma 12, $x \sim \{l^x\} \sim O(x)$.

Turn to the proof of Corollary 1. If part: The representation has the form of

$$U(x) = \max_{l \in x} \left\{ (1-\alpha)u(l_c) + \alpha \int_{\mathscr{X}} U(z)\, \mathrm{d}l_z \right\},$$

for some $\alpha \in [0, 1)$. Thus it is easy to verify that $U(x) \geq U(y)$ implies $U(x) = U(x \cup y)$.

Only-if part: From Proposition 1, $\succsim$ satisfies all the axioms of Theorem 1. Hence $\succsim$ admits a random discounting representation U with components (u, μ). By contradiction, suppose $\#\mathrm{supp}(\mu) \neq 1$. Then, there exist $\alpha', \alpha'' \in \mathrm{supp}(\mu)$ with $\alpha'' > \alpha'$. Let $u(\Delta(C))$ denote the image of $\Delta(C)$ under u. Let $U(\mathscr{L})$ denote the image of $\mathscr{L} \subset \mathscr{X}$ under U. Since $U(\mathscr{L})$ and $u(\Delta(C))$ are non-degenerate intervals of $\mathbb{R}_+$, take $p_1 \in u(\Delta(C))$ and $p_2 \in U(\mathscr{L})$ from the relative interiors. Take two points $(p_1', p_2'), (p_1'', p_2'') \in \mathbb{R}^2_+$ such that $p_1'' > p_1 > p_1', p_2' > p_2 > p_2''$, and

$$(1-\alpha')p_1' + \alpha' p_2' = (1-\alpha')p_1 + \alpha' p_2, \text{ and } (1-\alpha'')p_1'' + \alpha'' p_2'' = (1-\alpha'')p_1 + \alpha'' p_2. \tag{20.16}$$

Since p_1 belongs to the relative interior of $u(\Delta(C))$, p_1', p_1'' can be taken to be in $u(\Delta(C))$. Similarly, we can assume p_2', p_2'' belong to $U(\mathscr{L})$. Then we have

$$(1-\alpha')p_1' + \alpha' p_2' > (1-\alpha')p_1'' + \alpha' p_2'', \text{ and } (1-\alpha'')p_1'' + \alpha'' p_2'' > (1-\alpha'')p_1' + \alpha'' p_2'. \tag{20.17}$$

Indeed, by contradiction, suppose $(1-\alpha')p_1'' + \alpha' p_2'' \geq (1-\alpha')p_1' + \alpha' p_2'$. By (20.16), $(1-\alpha')p_1'' + \alpha' p_2'' \geq (1-\alpha')p_1 + \alpha' p_2$. Since $p_1'' > p_1$, $p_2'' < p_2$, and $\alpha'' > \alpha'$, we have $(1-\alpha'')p_1'' + \alpha'' p_2'' > (1-\alpha'')p_1 + \alpha'' p_2$, which contradicts (20.16). The same argument can be applied to the other case. Now take lotteries $l_c', l_c'' \in \Delta(C)$ and $l', l'' \in \mathscr{L}$ such that $u(l_c') = p_1'$, $u(l_c'') = p_1''$, $U(\{l'\}) = p_2'$, and $U(\{l''\}) = p_2''$. Taking (20.17) and continuity of the inner product together, there exist open neighborhoods $B(\alpha')$ and $B(\alpha'')$ satisfying

$$\begin{aligned}
&(1-\alpha)u(l_c') + \alpha U(\{l'\}) > (1-\alpha)u(l_c'') + \alpha U(\{l''\}), \text{ and} \\
&(1-\tilde{\alpha})u(l_c'') + \tilde{\alpha} U(\{l''\}) > (1-\tilde{\alpha})u(l_c') + \tilde{\alpha} U(\{l'\}),
\end{aligned} \tag{20.18}$$

for all $\alpha \in B(\alpha')$ and $\tilde{\alpha} \in B(\alpha'')$. Since α', α'' belong to the support of μ, $\mu(B(\alpha')) > 0$ and $\mu(B(\alpha'')) > 0$. Thus, by (20.18) and the representation,

$$U(\{l_c' \otimes \{l'\}, l_c'' \otimes \{l''\}\}) > \max[U(\{l_c' \otimes \{l'\}\}), U(\{l_c'' \otimes \{l''\}\})],$$

which contradicts Strategic Rationality.

Proof of Theorem 3

((a)⇒(b)) Since $\succsim^1$ and $\succsim^2$ are equivalent on $\mathscr{L}$, we have condition (i). Let $u^i(\Delta(C))$ denote the image of $\Delta(C)$ under u^i. Let $U^i(\mathscr{L})$ denote the image of $\mathscr{L} \subset \mathscr{X}$ under U^i. Let l_c^+ and l_c^- be a maximal and a minimal lottery with respect to u^i. Since $u^i(l_c^+) \geq U^i(\{l\}) \geq u^i(l_c^-)$ for all $l \in \mathscr{L}$, we have $U^1(\mathscr{L}) = u^1(\Delta(C)) = u^2(\Delta(C)) = U^2(\mathscr{L})$. Let $\text{supp}(\mu^i)$ denote the support of μ^i. By contradiction, suppose that there exists $\alpha^* \in \text{supp}(\mu^1)$ with $\alpha^* \notin \text{supp}(\mu^2)$. Since $\text{supp}(\mu^2)$ is a relative closed set of [0, 1], there exists a relative open interval (α^a, α^b) of α^* such that $(\alpha^a, \alpha^b) \cap \text{supp}(\mu^2) = \emptyset$. Since $u^1(\Delta(C))$ is a non-degenerate interval of $\mathbb{R}_+$, take $p_1 \in u^1(\Delta(C))$ and $p_2 \in U^1(\mathscr{L})$ from the relative interior. Take (p_1^a, p_2^a) and (p_1^b, p_2^b) such that $p_1^a > p_1 > p_1^b$, $p_2^b > p_2 > p_2^a$,

$$(1-\alpha^a)p_1^a + \alpha^a p_2^a = (1-\alpha^a)p_1 + \alpha^a p_2, \text{ and}$$
$$(1-\alpha^b)p_1^b + \alpha^b p_2^b = (1-\alpha^b)p_1 + \alpha^b p_2.$$

Then we have

$$(1-\alpha)p_1^b + \alpha p_2^b > \max[(1-\alpha)p_1 + \alpha p_2,\ (1-\alpha)p_1^a + \alpha p_2^a] \text{ for all } \alpha > \alpha^b,$$
$$(1-\alpha)p_1 + \alpha p_2 > \max[(1-\alpha)p_1^a + \alpha p_2^a,\ (1-\alpha)p_1^b + \alpha p_2^b] \text{ for all } \alpha \in (\alpha^a, \alpha^b),$$
$$(1-\alpha)p_1^a + \alpha p_2^a > \max[(1-\alpha)p_1 + \alpha p_2,\ (1-\alpha)p_1^b + \alpha p_2^b] \text{ for all } \alpha < \alpha^a.$$

Since (p_1^a, p_2^a) and (p_1^b, p_2^b) can be chosen sufficiently close to (p_1, p_2), assume without loss of generality that $p_1^a, p_1^b \in u^1(\Delta(C))$ and $p_2^a, p_2^b \in U^1(\mathscr{L})$. Thus there exist $l_c, l_c^a, l_c^b \in \Delta(C)$ and $l, l^a, l^b \in \mathscr{L}$ such that $u^i(l_c) = p_1, u^i(l_c^a) = p_1^a, u^i(l_c^b) = p_1^b$, $U^i(\{l\}) = p_2, U^i(\{l^a\}) = p_2^a$, and $U^i(\{l^b\}) = p_2^b$. Define $x \equiv \{l_c \otimes \{l\}, l_c^a \otimes \{l^a\}, l_c^b \otimes \{l^b\}\} \in \mathscr{X}^1$ and $y \equiv \{l_c^a \otimes \{l^a\}, l_c^b \otimes \{l^b\}\} \in \mathscr{X}^1$. Since $(\alpha^a, \alpha^b) \cap \text{supp}(\mu^2) = \emptyset$, $U^2(x) = U^2(y)$. On the other hand, since $\mu^1((\alpha^a, \alpha^b)) > 0$, $U^1(x) > U^1(y)$. This contradicts the assumption that $\succsim^2$ desires more flexibility in the two-period model than $\succsim^1$.

((b)⇒(a)) Assume that $u^1 = u^2$ and $\text{supp}(\mu^1) \subset \text{supp}(\mu^2)$. Since $\succsim^i, i = 1, 2$ are equivalent on $\mathscr{L}$, we have $\overline{\alpha}^1 = \overline{\alpha}^2$. Consequently, $U^1(\{l\}) = U^2(\{l\})$ for all $l \in \mathscr{L}$. Now take all $x, y \in \mathscr{X}^1$ with $y \subset x$ and assume $x \succ^1 y$. There exists $\alpha^* \in \text{supp}(\mu^1)$ such that

$$\max_{l \in x}(1-\alpha^*)u^1(l_c) + \alpha^* U^1(\{l_L\}) > \max_{l \in y}(1-\alpha^*)u^1(l_c) + \alpha^* U^1(\{l_L\}). \quad (20.19)$$

By continuity of the representation, there exists an open neighborhood $O \subset [0, 1]$ of α^* such that strict inequality (20.19) holds for all $\alpha \in O$. Since $\alpha^* \in \text{supp}(\mu^1) \subset \text{supp}(\mu^2)$, $\mu^2(O) > 0$. Moreover, since $u^1 = u^2$ and $U^1(\{l\}) = U^2(\{l\})$ for all $l \in \mathscr{L}$,

$$\max_{l\in x}(1-\alpha)u^2(l_c)+\alpha U^2(\{l_L\}) > \max_{l\in y}(1-\alpha)u^2(l_c)+\alpha U^2(\{l_L\})$$

for all $\alpha \in O$, which implies $U^2(x) > U^2(y)$.

Proof of Theorem 4

By definition, (a) implies (b). We show that (b)⇒(c) and (c)⇒(a). To show (b)⇒(c), we prepare two lemmas.

Lemma 13 *Suppose that $\succsim^i$ satisfies all the axioms of Theorem 1. If agent 2 is more averse to commitment in the two-period model than agent 1, then $x \succsim^1 \{l\} \Rightarrow x \succsim^2 \{l\}$ for all $x \in \mathscr{X}^1$ and $l \in \mathscr{L}$.*

Proof It suffices to show that $x \sim^1 \{l\} \Rightarrow x \succsim^2 \{l\}$. If agent 1 strictly prefers l to the worst lottery $\underline{l}$, then $x \succ^1 \{\lambda l + (1-\lambda)\underline{l}\}$ for all $\lambda \in (0,1)$. By assumption, $x \succ^2 \{\lambda l + (1-\lambda)\underline{l}\}$. Thus Continuity implies $x \succsim^2 \{l\}$ as $\lambda \to 1$. If l is indifferent to $\underline{l}$, consider the best lottery $\bar{l}$. Since $\{\bar{l}\} \succsim x$ for all $x \in \mathscr{X}^1$, mixture linearity of the representation implies $U^1(\lambda x + (1-\lambda)\{\bar{l}\}) > U^1(\{l\})$ for all $\lambda \in (0,1)$. By assumption, $\lambda x + (1-\lambda)\{\bar{l}\} \succ^2 \{l\}$. Thus Continuity implies $x \succsim^2 \{l\}$ as $\lambda \to 1$. □

Lemma 14 *Agent 2 is more averse to commitment in the two-period model than agent 1 if and only if there exist random discounting representations U^i with (u^i, μ^i), $i = 1, 2$ such that (i) $u^1 = u^2$ and $\bar{\alpha}^1 = \bar{\alpha}^2$, and (ii) $U^1(x) \le U^2(x)$ for all $x \in \mathscr{X}^1$.*

Proof Necessity follows because $U^2(x) \ge U^1(x) > U^1(\{l\}) = U^2(\{l\})$ for all $x \in \mathscr{X}^1$. We prove sufficiency. By Lemma 13, $\succsim^1$ and $\succsim^2$ are equivalent on $\mathscr{L}$. Thus there exist random discounting representations satisfying (i), and hence $U^1(\{l\}) = U^2(\{l\})$ for all $l \in \mathscr{L}$. Note that for all $x \in \mathscr{X}^1$ there exists $l \in \mathscr{L}$ such that $x \sim^1 \{l\}$ or $U^1(x) = U^1(\{l\})$. By Lemma 13, $x \sim^1 \{l\}$ implies that $x \succsim^2 \{l\}$ or $U^2(x) \ge U^2(\{l\}) = U^1(\{l\}) = U^1(x)$. □

We show that, for all continuous and convex functions v of α, there is a sequence $\{v_n\}$ of functions of the form (20.8) such that $v \ge v_n$,

$$\sup_{\alpha} |v(\alpha) - v_n(\alpha)| < \frac{1}{n}, \text{and} \int v_n(\alpha)\, d\mu^1(\alpha) \le \int v_n(\alpha)\, d\mu^2(\alpha)$$

for all $n = 1, 2, \cdots$. Then the result follows from the dominated convergence theorem.

Let $v : [0,1] \to \mathbb{R}$ be a continuous convex function. Then, for every $\hat{\alpha} \in [0,1]$, there exists a vector $p_{\hat{\alpha}} \in \mathbb{R}^2$ such that for all $\alpha \in [0,1]$,

$$v(\alpha) \ge (1-\alpha)p_{\hat{\alpha},1} + \alpha p_{\hat{\alpha},2}$$

with equality for $\hat{\alpha}$. Fix n. Since $v(\alpha) - \{(1-\alpha)p_{\hat{\alpha},1} + \alpha p_{\hat{\alpha},2}\}$ is continuous with respect to α, there exists an open neighborhood $B(\hat{\alpha})$ of $\hat{\alpha}$ such that for every $\alpha \in B(\hat{\alpha})$

$$0 \leq v(\alpha) - \{(1-\alpha)p_{\hat{\alpha},1} + \alpha p_{\hat{\alpha},2}\} < \frac{1}{n}.$$

It follows from the compactness of [0, 1] that there exists a finite set $\{\hat{\alpha}_i\}_{i=1}^M \subset [0,1]$ such that $\{B(\hat{\alpha}_i)\}_{i=1}^M$ is a covering of [0, 1].

We define $v_n : [0,1] \to \mathbb{R}$ by

$$v_n(\alpha) = \max_i [(1-\alpha)p_{\hat{\alpha}_i,1} + \alpha p_{\hat{\alpha}_i,2}].$$

Then it is straightforward that $v(\alpha) \geq v_n(\alpha)$ for every $\alpha \in [0,1]$. Moreover, we see that

$$\sup_\alpha |v(\alpha) - v_n(\alpha)| < \frac{1}{n}.$$

In fact, pick an arbitrary $\alpha \in [0,1]$. Then there is $j \in M$ such that $\alpha \in B(\hat{\alpha}_j)$. This implies

$$0 \leq v(\alpha) - v_n(\alpha) \leq v(\alpha) - \{(1-\alpha)p_{\hat{\alpha}_j,1} + \alpha p_{\hat{\alpha}_j,2}\} < \frac{1}{n}.$$

Finally we see that

$$\int v_n(\alpha)\, \mathrm{d}\mu^1(\alpha) \leq \int v_n(\alpha)\, \mathrm{d}\mu^2(\alpha).$$

Since $u(\Delta(C))$ and $U^1(\mathscr{L}) = U^2(\mathscr{L})$ are closed intervals, we can assume, without loss of generality, that there exist $\{l_{c,i}\}_{i=1}^M \subset \Delta(C)$ and $\{l_i\}_{i=1}^M \subset \mathscr{L}$ satisfying

$$u^1(l_{c,i}) = u^2(l_{c,i}) = p_{\hat{\alpha}_i,1}, \text{and} U^1(\{l_i\}) = U^2(\{l_i\}) = p_{\hat{\alpha}_i,2}.$$

Thus we can rewrite v_n by

$$v_n(\alpha) = \max_i (1-\alpha)u^1(l_{c,i}) + \alpha U^1(\{l_i\}) = \max_i (1-\alpha)u^2(l_{c,i}) + \alpha U^2(\{l_i\}).$$

Consider the menu $x^n = \{l_{c,i} \otimes \{l_i\} | i = 1, \cdots, M\} \in \mathscr{X}^1$. Then it follows from Lemma 14 that

$$\int v_n(\alpha)\, \mathrm{d}\mu^1(\alpha) = U^1(x^n) \leq U^2(x^n) = \int v_n(\alpha)\, \mathrm{d}\mu^2(\alpha),$$

which completes the proof.

((c)⇒(a)) Let $\mathscr{U}$ be the Banach space of all real-valued continuous functions on $\mathscr{X}$. Define the operator $T^i : \mathscr{U} \to \mathscr{U}$ by

$$T^i(U)(x) \equiv \int \max_{l \in x} \left((1-\alpha)u(l_c) + \alpha \int_{\mathscr{X}} U(z)\,\mathrm{d}l_z \right) \mathrm{d}\mu^i(\alpha).$$

Pick $x \in \mathscr{X}$ arbitrarily. Note that, for all $U \in \mathscr{U}$, $\max_{l \in x}\big((1-\alpha)u(l_c) + \alpha \int_{\mathscr{X}} U(z)\,\mathrm{d}l_z\big)$ is continuous and convex with respect to α. Hence it holds that $T^1(U)(x) \leq T^2(U)(x)$ for all $x \in \mathscr{X}$.

For $i = 1, 2$, let $T^{i,n}$ denote the operation defined as n-times iterations of T^i. We show, by mathematical induction, that $T^{1,n}(U)(x) \leq T^{2,n}(U)(x)$ for all $x \in \mathscr{X}$ and $n = 1, 2, \cdots$. Assume that $T^{1,k}(U)(x') \leq T^{2,k}(U)(x')$ for all $x' \in \mathscr{X}$. Pick $x \in \mathscr{X}$ arbitrarily. Then it holds that $T^2(T^{1,k}(U))(x) \leq T^2(T^{2,k}(U))(x)$. Moreover, since $T^{1,k}(U)$ is in $\mathscr{U}$, we have $T^1(T^{1,k}(U))(x) \leq T^2(T^{1,k}(U))(x)$. These together imply $T^{1,k+1}(U)(x) \leq T^{2,k+1}(U)(x)$ for all $x \in \mathscr{X}$. Therefore, it holds that $U^1(x) \leq U^2(x)$ since $T^{i,n}(U)$ converges to U^i. The desired result follows because $U^2(x) \geq U^1(x) > U^1(\{l\}) = U^2(\{l\})$ for all $x \in \mathscr{X}$ and $l \in \mathscr{L}$.

Proof of Theorem 5

(i) We can solve (20.11) by the guess-and-verify method. Let

$$V_\mu(s,\alpha) \equiv A_\mu(\alpha)\frac{s^{1-\sigma}}{1-\sigma}. \tag{20.20}$$

Considering the F.O.C. of

$$\max_{s'} \left((1-\alpha)\frac{((1+r)s - s')^{1-\sigma}}{1-\sigma} + \alpha \int \left(A_\mu(\alpha')\frac{s'^{1-\sigma}}{1-\sigma} \right) \mathrm{d}\mu(\alpha') \right), \tag{20.21}$$

we have

$$(1-\alpha)((1+r)s - s')^{-\sigma} = \alpha \overline{A}_\mu s'^{-\sigma},$$

where $\overline{A}_\mu \equiv \int A_\mu(\alpha')\,\mathrm{d}\mu(\alpha')$. By rearrangement, we can obtain the savings function

$$s' = SR(\alpha, \overline{A}_\mu)(1+r)s, \text{ where } SR(\alpha, \overline{A}_\mu) \equiv \frac{(\alpha\overline{A}_\mu)^{\frac{1}{\sigma}}}{(1-\alpha)^{\frac{1}{\sigma}} + (\alpha\overline{A}_\mu)^{\frac{1}{\sigma}}}. \tag{20.22}$$

Substituting (20.22) into (20.21) and comparing the coefficients with (20.20),

$$A_\mu(\alpha) = \left((1-\alpha)^{\frac{1}{\sigma}} + (\alpha\overline{A}_\mu)^{\frac{1}{\sigma}} \right)^\sigma (1+r)^{1-\sigma}. \tag{20.23}$$

For all $\alpha \in [0, 1]$ and $A \geq 0$, define $f(\alpha, A)$ and $F(A)$ as

$$f(\alpha, A) \equiv \left((1-\alpha)^{\frac{1}{\sigma}} + (\alpha A)^{\frac{1}{\sigma}}\right)^{\sigma} (1+r)^{1-\sigma}, \; F(A) \equiv \int f(\alpha, A)\, \mathrm{d}\mu(\alpha). \quad (20.24)$$

From (20.23), $\overline{A}_{\mu}$ is characterized as a solution of $\overline{A}_{\mu} = F(\overline{A}_{\mu})$. We want to show that there exists a unique $\overline{A} > 0$ satisfying this equation. Note first that $F(0) = (1-\bar{\alpha})(1+r)^{1-\sigma} > 0$. Since $\lim_{A\to\infty} F(A) \to \infty$, the L'Hopital's rule implies

$$\lim_{A\to\infty} \frac{F(A)}{A} = \lim_{A\to\infty} F'(A).$$

Since

$$F'(A) = \int \frac{\partial f}{\partial A}\, \mathrm{d}\mu(\alpha) = \int (1+r)^{1-\sigma} \alpha^{\frac{1}{\sigma}} \left((1-\alpha)^{\frac{1}{\sigma}} + (\alpha A)^{\frac{1}{\sigma}}\right)^{\sigma-1} A^{\frac{1}{\sigma}-1} \mathrm{d}\mu(\alpha)$$
$$= \int (1+r)^{1-\sigma} \alpha^{\frac{1}{\sigma}} \left(\left(\frac{1-\alpha}{A}\right)^{\frac{1}{\sigma}} + \alpha^{\frac{1}{\sigma}}\right)^{\sigma-1} \mathrm{d}\mu(\alpha),$$

we have $\lim_{A\to\infty} F'(A) = \bar{\alpha}(1+r)^{1-\sigma} < 1$. Hence, there exists a sufficiently large number $\tilde{A}$ such that $F(\tilde{A}) < \tilde{A}$. By continuity of F, there exists $\overline{A} > 0$ such that $\overline{A} = F(\overline{A})$. Finally, since

$$F'' = \int \frac{\partial^2 f}{\partial A^2}\, \mathrm{d}\mu(\alpha)$$
$$= \frac{1-\sigma}{\sigma}(1+r)^{1-\sigma} \int \alpha^{\frac{2}{\sigma}} (1-\alpha)^{\frac{1}{\sigma}} \left((1-\alpha)^{\frac{1}{\sigma}} + (\alpha A)^{\frac{1}{\sigma}}\right)^{\sigma-2} A^{\frac{1}{\sigma}-2}\, \mathrm{d}\mu(\alpha),$$

F is either strictly convex or concave depending on $\sigma \lesseqgtr 1$. Since $\lim_{A\to\infty} F'(A) < 1$, $\overline{A}$ must be unique.

(ii) From (20.22), it is easy to verify that $\frac{\partial SR(\alpha,A)}{\partial A} > 0$. Thus it suffices to show that $\overline{A}_{\mu^1} \lesseqgtr \overline{A}_{\mu^2}$ if $\sigma \lesseqgtr 1$. Note first that f defined as (20.24) is strictly convex or strictly concave in α according as $\sigma < 1$ or $\sigma > 1$. Indeed, for any $\alpha \in (0, 1)$ and $A > 0$,

$$\frac{\partial^2 f}{\partial \alpha^2} = (1+r)^{1-\sigma} \frac{1-\sigma}{\sigma} \left((1-\alpha)^{\frac{1}{\sigma}} + (\alpha A)^{\frac{1}{\sigma}}\right)^{\sigma-2}$$
$$\times \left(2(\alpha(1-\alpha))^{\frac{1}{\sigma}-1} A^{\frac{1}{\sigma}} + (1-\alpha)^{\frac{1}{\sigma}-2} (\alpha A)^{\frac{1}{\sigma}} + \alpha^{\frac{1}{\sigma}-2}((1-\alpha)A)^{\frac{1}{\sigma}}\right) \gtreqless 0$$

whenever $\sigma \lesseqgtr 1$. Since μ^1 second-order stochastically dominates μ^2,

$$\overline{A}_{\mu^2} = \int f(\alpha, \overline{A}_{\mu^2})\, \mathrm{d}\mu^2(\alpha) \gtreqless \int f(\alpha, \overline{A}_{\mu^2})\, \mathrm{d}\mu^1(\alpha) \quad (20.25)$$

depending on $\sigma \lesseqgtr 1$. Let $F^1(A) \equiv \int f(\alpha, A)\, d\mu^1(\alpha)$. We know from the proof of part (i) that $F^1(0) > 0$ and $\overline{A}_{\mu^1}$ is a unique positive solution of $F^1(A) = A$. Hence, $F^1(A) \gtreqless A$ if$A \lesseqgtr \overline{A}_{\mu^1}$. Taking this observation and (20.25) together, $\overline{A}_{\mu^2} \gtreqless \overline{A}_{\mu^1}$ if $\sigma \lesseqgtr 1$.

Addendum: Recent Developments[17]

If a DM is uncertain about her future preference, she may prefer to leave some options open rather than choose a completely spelled-out future plan. This behavior is called *preference for flexibility* and is admitted as an important aspect of sequential decision making. Kreps (1979, 1992) and Dekel et al. (2001) provide a behavioral foundation for preference for flexibility and derive the set of future preferences, called *the subjective state space*, from observable choice behavior. Although the preference for flexibility arises inherently in a dynamic setup, the derivation of the subjective state space has been considered within a two-period model. Higashi et al. (2009) extend their model to an infinite-horizon setting and specify the subjective state space to be the set of sequences of discount factors.

In Higashi et al. (2009), the belief of future discount factors is assumed to be constant, and hence, the DM's attitude toward flexibility is the same over time. Some recent works consider more general models for preference for flexibility in a dynamic setup. Krishna and Sadowski (2014) provide a complementary result to ours. To introduce their model, let S be a finite set of objective states. A *state-contingent infinite-horizon consumption problem (S-IHCP)* is a function specifying for each $s \in S$ an opportunity set of lotteries over pairs of current consumption and an S-IHCP in the next period. They show that there exists a compact metric space $\mathscr{F}$, which is linearly homeomorphic to $\mathscr{H}(\mathscr{K}(\Delta(C \times \mathscr{F})))$, where $\mathscr{H}(X)$ means the set of functions from S to a compact metric space X.[18] A generic element of $\mathscr{F}$ is denoted by f and for lottery $l \in \Delta(C \times \mathscr{F})$ its marginals on C and $\mathscr{F}$ are denoted by l_c and l_f, respectively. A preference $\succsim$ is defined on $\mathscr{F} \simeq \mathscr{H}(\mathscr{K}(\Delta(C \times \mathscr{F})))$.

Krishna and Sadowski (2014) consider the following representation. The DM has a subjective belief about objective states S captured by a Markov process, that is, a pair of a transition probability $\Pi : S \times S \to [0, 1]$ and a stationary distribution (or initial prior) π over S. The subjective state space of this model is the set of all vN-M functions over C denoted by $\mathscr{U} := \left\{u \in \mathbb{R}^C : \sum u_i = 0\right\}$. A belief about subjective states depends on objective states, that is, for each $s \in S$, μ_s is a probability measure on $\mathscr{U}$. Finally, let $\delta \in (0, 1)$ be a discount factor. A preference $\succsim$ on $\mathscr{F}$ admits a representation of Dynamic Preference for Flexibility (a DPF representation) with components $((\Pi, \pi), (\mu_s)_{s \in S}, \delta)$ if $V_0(f) \equiv \sum_s V(f, s)\pi(s)$ represents $\succsim$, where

[17] This addendum has been newly written for this book chapter.

[18] In their model, C is assumed to be finite.

$V(\cdot, s) : \mathscr{F} \to \mathbb{R}$ is defined as

$$V(f, s) = \sum_{s' \in S} \Pi(s, s') \left[\int_{\mathscr{U}} \max_{l \in f(s')} [u(l_c) + \delta V(l_f, s')] \, \mathrm{d}\mu_{s'}(u) \right],$$

and $V(l_f, s') \equiv \int V(g, s') \, \mathrm{d}l_f(g)$. Since π is a stationary distribution, which satisfies $\pi(s') = \sum_s \pi(s)\Pi(s, s')$, the representation is rewritten as

$$V_0(f) = \sum_s \pi(s) \left[\int_{\mathscr{U}} \max_{l \in f(s)} [u(l_c) + \delta V(l_f, s)] \, \mathrm{d}\mu_s(u) \right].$$

In this representation, the Markov process represented by Π captures persistent shocks on objective states, and the probability measures $(\mu_s)_{s \in S}$ correspond to unobservable transitory shocks on future utilities. Therefore, an attitude toward flexibility may change according to realization of objective states. Krishna and Sadowski prove that a preference $\succsim$ satisfies suitable axioms if and only if it has a DPF representation. Moreover, they prove that $(\mu_s)_{s \in S}$ are unique up to a common scaling, and (Π, π) and δ are unique.[19]

There are two remarks related to our study (Higashi et al. 2009). First, their DPF representation allows persistent shocks on subjective states, while preference shocks are i.i.d. in our model. Second, a DPF representation can capture a random discounting by specifying $\mu_s(\{\lambda \bar{u} : \lambda \geq 0\}) = 1$ for some fixed $\bar{u} \in \mathscr{U}$. As a special case, a random discount factor representation is behaviorally characterized.

Another attempt to accommodate a changing preference for flexibility is made by Higashi et al. (2014). In this paper, we extend the previous model in order to allow the situation where a prior action affects future attitude toward flexibility. For example, imagine a DM who invested in self-improvement such as health investment or education is more likely to expect new information about her future preference, and hence may want to have greater demand for flexibility. More formally, we incorporate the histories of past consumption, $h = (c_{-T}, \cdots, c_{-1})$, into Higashi et al. (2009) and consider a set of preferences $\{\succsim_h\}_{h \in H}$. The following recursive representation is axiomatized: there exist a non-constant continuous function $u : C \to \mathbb{R}$ and a history-dependent probability measure μ_h on the set $[0, 1]$ of discount factors such that for all h, $\succsim_h$ on $\mathscr{X}$ is represented by

$$V(x, h) = \int_{[0,1]} \max_{l \in x} \int_{C \times \mathscr{X}} \Big((1 - \alpha)u(c) + \alpha V(z, hc) \Big) \mathrm{d}l(c, z) \, \mathrm{d}\mu_h(\alpha),$$

[19] In the supplement to Krishna and Sadowski (2014), Krishna and Sadowski (2013) show a similar result for a preference $\succsim$ on $\mathscr{X} \simeq \mathscr{K}(\Delta(C \times \mathscr{X}))$.

where $hc = (c_{-T+1}, \cdots, c_{-1}, c)$ denotes an updated history of $h = (c_{-T}, \cdots, c_{-1})$. This representation can capture a changing future attitude toward flexibility from past consumption.

As an application of the random discounting, Higashi et al. (2014) investigate impatience comparisons within the random discounting model. Time preference has been measured as the magnitude of the discount factor, which is elicited from choices among consumption streams with a time trade-off. This elicitation implicitly assumes that choices are made under commitment. In sequential decision making, however, the degree of impatience may be affected by two potentially conflicting effects: one is pure time preference, which is a preference for early consumption, and the other is preference for flexibility, which is an attitude of leaving one's options open until the future.

In this paper, we consider preference over menus of consumption streams in two periods and provide behavioral definitions for impatience comparisons among menus having a time trade-off. If one menu includes more options allowing earlier consumption than another menu (such as $x = \{(100, 0), (70, 35)\}$ vs $y = \{(50, 60), (0, 120)\}$), an agent expecting to be more impatient in the future will tend to choose the former. Thus, if agent 2 is more impatient than agent 1, we require that

$$x \succsim^1 y \Rightarrow x \succsim^2 y.$$

This is a natural extension of impatience comparisons made under commitment. We show that in the random discounting model, the relative degree of impatience is measured as a probability shift in the *monotone likelihood ratio order (MLR)*, which is characterized via behavioral comparisons among menus defined as above.

References

Ahn DS (2008) Ambiguity without a state space. Rev Econ Stud 75:3–28

Atkeson A, Lucas RE Jr (1992) On efficient distribution with private information. Rev Econ Stud 59:427–453

Becker R (1980) On the long run steady state in a simple equilibrium with heterogeneous households. Quart J Econ 90:375–382

Becker GS, Mulligan CB (1997) The endogenous determination of time preference. Quart J Econ 112:729–758

Bertsekas DP, Shreve SE (1978) Stochastic optimal control: the discrete time case. Academic, New York

Blanchard, OJ (1985) Debt, deficits, and finite horizons. J Polit Econ 93:223–247

Chatterjee S, Corbae D, Nakajima M, Rios-Rull, JV (2007) A quantitative theory of unsecured consumer credit with risk of default. Econometrica 75:1525–1589

Dekel E, Lipman B, Rustichini A (2001) Representing preferences with a unique subjective state space. Econometrica 69:891–934

Dekel E, Lipman B, Rustichini A, Sarver T (2007) Representing preferences with a unique subjective state space: a corrigendum. Econometrica 75:591–600

Dutta J, Michel P (1998) The distribution of wealth with imperfect altruism. J Econ Theory 82:379–404
Epstein, LG (1999) A definition of uncertainty aversion. Rev Econ Stud 66:579–608
Epstein LG, Zin S (1989) Substitution, risk aversion, and the temporal behavior of consumption and asset returns: a theoretical framework. Econometrica 57:937–969
Epstein LG, Marinacci M, Seo K (2007) Coarse contingencies and ambiguity. Theor Econ 2:355–394
Farhi E, Werning I (2007) Inequality and social discounting. J Polit Econ 115:365–402
Ghirardato P, Marinacci M (2002) Ambiguity made precise: a comparative foundation. J Econ Theory 102:251–289
Goldman SM (1974) Flexibility and the demand for money. J Econ Theory 9:203–222
Gul F, Pesendorfer W (2001) Temptation and self-control. Econometrica 69:1403–1435
Gul F, Pesendorfer W (2004) Self-control and the theory of consumption. Econometrica 72:119–158
Higashi Y, Hyogo K, Takeoka N (2009) Subjective random discounting and intertemporal choice. J Econ Theory 144:1015–1053
Higashi Y, Hyogo K, Takeoka N (2014) Stochastic endogenous time preference. J Math Econ 51:77–92
Higashi Y, Hyogo K, Takeoka N, Tanaka H (2014) Comparative impatience under random discounting. Working paper
Karni E, Zilcha I (2000) Saving behavior in stationary equilibrium with random discounting. Econ Theory 15:551–564
Koopmans TC (1964) On flexibility of future preference. In: Shelley MW, Bryan GL (ed) Human judgments and optimality, chap 13. Academic, New York
Kraus A, Sagi JS (2006) Inter-temporal preference for flexibility and risky choice. J Math Econ 42:698–709
Kreps DM (1979) A representation theorem for preference for flexibility. Econometrica 47:565–578
Kreps DM (1992) Static choice and unforeseen contingencies. In: Dasgupta P, Gale D, Hart O, Maskin E (ed) Economic analysis of markets and games: essays in honor of Frank Hahn. MIT, Cambridge, pp 259–281
Kreps DM, Porteus EL (1978) Temporal resolution of uncertainty and dynamic choice theory. Econometrica 46:185–200
Krishna RV, Sadowski P (2013) Supplement to dynamic preference for flexibility: unobservable persistent taste shocks. Working paper
Krishna RV, Sadowski P (2014) Dynamic preference for flexibility. Econometrica 82:655–703
Krusell P, Smith A (1998) Income and wealth heterogeneity in the macroeconomy. J Polit Econ 106:867–896
Levhari D, Srinivasan TN (1969) Optimal savings under uncertainty. Rev Econ Stud 36:153–163
Mehra R, Sah R (2002) Mood fluctuations, projection bias, and volatility of equity prices. J Econ Dyn Control 26:869–887
Rothschild M, Stiglitz JE (1970) Increasing risk I: a definition. J Econ Theory 2:225–243
Rothschild M, Stiglitz JE (1971) Increasing risk II: its economic consequences. J Econ Theory 3:66–84
Rustichini A (2002) Preference for flexibility in infinite horizon problems. Econ Theory 20:677–702
Salanié F, Treich N (2006) Over-savings and hyperbolic discounting. Eur Econ Rev 50:1557–1570
Sandmo A (1970) The effect of uncertainty on saving decisions. Rev Econ Stud 37:353–360
Sarver T (2008) Anticipating regret: why fewer options may be better. Econometrica 76:263–305
Takeoka N (2007) Subjective probability over a subjective decision tree. J Econ Theory 136:536–571
Yaari ME (1965) Uncertain lifetime, life insurance, and the theory of the consumer. Rev Econ Stud 32:137–150

Chapter 21
A Geometric Approach to Temptation

Koji Abe

Abstract We provide a simple geometric proof of the Gul and Pesendorfer's (Econometrica 69(6):1403–1435, 2001) utility representation theorem about choice under temptation without self-control. We extract two incomplete orders from preferences: temptation relation and resistance relation. We characterize those relations geometrically and obtain temptation utility using a separation method à la Aumann (Econometrica 30(3):445–462, 1962).

Keywords Temptation • No self-control • Temptation utility

1 Introduction

Over the last decade, a great deal of progress has been made in our understanding of the theory of temptation. Gul and Pesendorfer (2001) reinterpret Strotz's (1955) time inconsistency model as a temptation model, and they provide a preference foundation for the model.

We provide a simple geometric proof of the Strotz representation theorem. In the menu choice setting of Gul and Pesendorfer (2001), we extract two kinds of dynamic considerations, temptation and resistance, from preferences and explore those geometry. We view temptation as an anticipation to choose an undesired alternative. Resistance prevails when an individual is free from worries of temptation. Applying a geometric approach, we derive an expected utility that represents those considerations.

The geometric approach is able to trace the idea back to Aumann (1962). He considers a one-way expected utility representation for incomplete (but reflexive and

The original article first appeared in the Journal of Mathematical Economics 48:92–97, 2012. A newly written addendum has been added to this book chapter.

K. Abe (✉)
Faculty of International Social Sciences, Yokohama National University, 79-4 Tokiwadai, Hodogaya, Yokohama, Kanagawa 240-8501, Japan
e-mail: abe@ynu.ac.jp

S. Ikeda et al. (eds.), *Behavioral Economics of Preferences, Choices, and Happiness*, DOI 10.1007/978-4-431-55402-8_21

transitive) preferences that satisfy Independence and some continuity. Here, the term "one-way" means that the representation preserves the ranking of the underlying preferences but we cannot recover the preferences from the representation because of its incompleteness. To obtain such a one-way representation, he considers the convex cone defined by directions of (strict) preferences and shows that the cone is open in the space generated by the cone. As a result, he obtains a hyperplane through zero that does not intersect the cone. The normal to this hyperplane in the direction of the half-space occupied by the cone then provides a desired one-way expected utility.

Incompleteness of preferences naturally comes up in the study of temptation. Observed choice affected by temptation does not define a complete order because we can identify temptation only when the tempting alternative is undesired for the individual. We construct a temptation utility using Aumann's approach. The point is that, although there are many utility functions that represent temptation considerations in the one-way representation's sense, requiring to simultaneously represent resistance considerations narrows the candidates of expected utilities down to a single candidate.

Our geometric approach has two contributions in the theory of temptation. First, providing a proof of the Strotz representation theorem is itself important because the proof of Gul and Pesendorfer (2001) has a gap. The gap arises when they measure temptation. Suppose that an individual is indifferent between $\{x\}$ and $\{x, y\}$. Then, the individual finds no value from flexibility of $\{x, y\}$ in spite of adding y. They interpret this as meaning that the individual anticipates that x is chosen from $\{x, y\}$ later, and hence they consider that such indifferences reveal anticipated temptation. By verifying that the elicited temptation relation satisfies standard expected utility axioms, they then try to obtain its expected utility representation, which was supposed to be a numerical measure of temptation. However, as we show in Sect. 6, the relation does not satisfy continuity in general.

Eliciting temptation by anticipated ex-post choices is legitimate when $\{y\} \succ \{x, y\} \sim \{x\}$ because in this case we can naturally interpret that the *undesired* x is chosen from $\{x, y\}$. However, if $\{x\} \sim \{x, y\} \succ \{y\}$, then we cannot distinguish a possibility that x is more tempting than y from another possibility that x and y have the same temptation ranking because both would lead to an anticipation of x from $\{x, y\}$ in the ex-post choice. Hence, anticipated ex-post choices do not properly capture the ranking of temptation of alternatives.

We can identify a temptation ranking only when the tempting alternative is undesired for the individual. This implies that observed temptation considerations define an incomplete order. This is exactly the reason why this chapter adopts a separation method à la (Aumann 1962). Separating the incomplete order from its dual (resistance relation), we successfully obtain a linear temptation utility that is consistent with the above-mentioned identification problem.

The second contribution is that our geometric approach provides refined testable implications of the Strotz model. We extract two incomplete orders, temptation relation and resistance relation, from preferences. This enable us to conduct a test of implications of the two incomplete orders directly in addition to a test of menu preferences itself. To characterize those relations geometrically, we explore some properties of them and show that they are transitive and satisfy independence. Since a numerical measure of temptation is derived as a linear utility that is characterized by temptation and resistance relations, the properties of those relations are testable predictions of a model with linear temptation utility. This means that if an individual's choices do not obey the prediction of a Strotz model, then the properties of those relations will be useful in exploring the nature of observed violations and in considering a minimally extended model that accommodates the violations.[1]

This chapter is organized as follows. Section 2 summarizes the Strotz representation theorem. Section 3 is the heart of our geometric approach. In this section, we explore our notions of temptation and resistance, and derive those cone representations. Section 4 shows that the Strotz representation theorem directly follows from the result of Sect. 3. Section 5 complements a technical issue on an infinite dimensional setting. Section 6 discusses the relation between our approach and the Gul and Pesendorfer's approach. We demonstrate the gap of their proof with a concrete example.

2 The Strotz Representation Theorem

Let Z be a finite set of prizes. (Although our approach works likewise in an infinite Z case, we assume Z is finite in main sections in this chapter, which is enough to develop our geometric approach and allows us to avoid awkward expressions relevant to an infinite dimensional setting. Instead, Sect. 5 explains how the proofs are adjusted in case of infinite Z.) Let Δ be the set of all probability vectors over Z, that is, the probability simplex of $\mathbb{R}^{|Z|}$. Let $\mathscr{A}$ be the set of all compact subsets of Δ and be endowed with the Hausdorff metric. For any $\alpha \in [0, 1]$ and $A, B \in \mathscr{A}$, we let $\alpha A + (1 - \alpha)B := \{z \in \Delta \mid z = \alpha x + (1 - \alpha)y, x \in A, y \in B\}$. A typical element A of $\mathscr{A}$ is called a menu (of lotteries).

Let $\mathscr{C}$ be the set of continuous affine mappings from Δ to reals; that is, $f \in \mathscr{C}$ if and only if f is continuous on Δ and satisfies $f(\alpha x + (1 - \alpha)y) = \alpha f(x) + (1 - \alpha)f(y)$ for all $x, y \in \Delta$ and for all $\alpha \in [0, 1]$. For any $f \in \mathscr{C}$, we let $M_f(A) = \arg\max_{y \in A} f(y)$.

[1]As in the literature of non-expected utility theories, identifying the nature of violations of a particular model (expected utility model in the literature) is an important issue in order to develop a new model that accommodates the violations. See for example MacCrimmon and Larsson (1979) and Machina (1983). In the literature of temptation, Noor and Takeoka (2010) extend the Gul–Pesendorfer's self-control model to admit an individual's ability to exert self-control to depend on the faced menu. Providing a minimal generalization to the Gul–Pesendorfer model, they retain linearity of temptation utility. To this end, they characterize linear temptation utility in a way similar to ours.

We consider a Strotz model defined as follows.[2]

Definition 1 A utility function U on menus is said to be a Strotz model if it is a function of the form:

$$U(A) = \max_{x \in M_v(A)} u(x)$$

for some $u, v \in \mathscr{C}$. We call u a commitment utility, and v a temptation utility.

Gul and Pesendorfer (2001) provided a preference foundation for the model of utility function. Let $\succsim$ be a binary relation over $\mathscr{A}$. We say that $\succsim$ is:

- Upper semi-continuous if the sets $\{B \in \mathscr{A} | B \succsim A\}$ are closed,
- Lower mixture continuous if $A \succ B$ and $B \succ C$ imply $\alpha A + (1-\alpha)C \succ B$ for some $\alpha \in (0, 1)$,
- Lower semi-continuous on singletons if the sets $\{\{x\} \in \mathscr{A} | \{y\} \succsim \{x\}\}$ are closed.

The following axioms are considered.

Axiom 1 (Preference) $\succsim$ is a complete and transitive binary relation.

Axiom 2 (Semi-Continuity) $\succsim$ is upper semi-continuous, lower mixture continuous, and lower semi-continuous on singletons.

Axiom 3 (Independence) $A \succ B$ and $\alpha \in (0, 1)$ imply $\alpha A + (1-\alpha)C \succ \alpha B + (1-\alpha)C$.

Axiom 4 (No Self-Control) For any $A, B \in \mathscr{A}$, $A \sim A \cup B$ or $B \sim A \cup B$.

Axiom 1 is a standard revealed preference axiom. Axioms 2 and 3 are a variant of the von Neumann and Morgenstern axioms adapted to the preferences-over-menus setting. Axiom 4 is viewed as intuitive notions of behavior under temptation without self-control as we explain below.

Imagine a situation in which an individual first chooses a menu and then selects an alternative from that menu. Suppose that the individual evaluates a menu by its best element. Such an individual's behavior is represented by a utility function U of the form $U(A) = \max_{x \in A} u(x)$ for some $u \in \mathscr{C}$. Observe that an individual with this type of utility function follows a regularity called Strategic Rationality: $A \succsim B$ implies $A \sim A \cup B$.[3] Clearly, any strategically rational decision maker does not exhibit a desire for commitment, where by 'desire for commitment' we mean that an individual strictly prefers a subset of a menu to the menu itself.

Desire for commitment is an implication of temptation. An individual may strictly prefer menu A to menu $A \cup B$ to avoid succumbing to temptation that is anticipated as follows: The individual anticipates that he/she will be tempted to

---

[2]We borrow the term "Strotz model" from Gul and Pesendorfer (2005).

[3]See Kreps (1988).

select an alternative when facing menu $A \cup B$, and this alternative is undesired for him/her.

Axiom 4 relaxes Strategic Rationality and allows a possibility that $A \succ A \cup B \sim B$. This possibility is viewed as meaning that a tempting alternative is in B and the individual succumbs to the temptation when facing menu $A \cup B$. In other wards, whenever temptation presents itself, the individual cannot resist it.[4] Thus, Axiom 4 is called No Self-Control.

Gul and Pesendorfer (2001) showed the following representation theorem.

The Strotz Representation Theorem: $\succsim$ *satisfies Preference, Semi-Continuity, Independence, and No Self-Control if and only if it has a Strotz representation, that is, there exists a Strotz model* U *such that* $A \succsim B$ *if and only if* $U(A) \geq U(B)$.

3 Geometry of Temptation

This section explores some geometric properties of $\succsim$ that satisfies No Self-Control (and von Neumann and Morgenstern type axioms). Specifically, we extract behavior that displays temptation and geometrically characterize the behavior. We use the geometric characterization to prove the representation theorem in the next section.

Before proceeding, we note a basic result that will prove useful in what follows.

Lemma 1 (Lemma 1, Gul and Pesendorfer (2001)) $\succsim$ *satisfies Preference, Semi-Continuity, and Independence if and only if there exists an upper semi-continuous affine function* $U : \mathscr{A} \to \mathbb{R}$ *that represents* $\succsim$ *and that is continuous when restricted over singletons.*

We define u by $u(x) := U(\{x\})$ for all $x \in \Delta$ as in Gul and Pesendorfer (2001). Since u represents preferences that the individual would like to commit to, it is called a commitment utility. Any commitment utility defined in this manner is continuous and affine from Lemma 1.

Let us now consider a nontrivial preference relation $\succsim$, that is, there are $x, y \in \Delta$ such that $\{x\} \succ \{y\}$. Then, No Self-Control induces the following two strict partial orders.[5]

- A temptation relation T^* is defined by yT^*x if $\{x\} \succ \{x, y\} \sim \{y\}$.
- A resistance relation R^* is defined by xR^*y if $\{x\} \sim \{x, y\} \succ \{y\}$.

The temptation relation displays a desire for commitment in a binary menu. Suppose $\{x\} \succ \{y\}$. We view $\{x\} \succ \{x, y\}$ as meaning that the individual desires to commit to $\{x\}$ because y is more tempting than x. The resistance relation is a dual

[4]See Kreps (1979) and Gul and Pesendorfer (2005) for another interpretation of Axiom 4. Those authors provide a behavioral foundation for Strotz's model of changing tastes (Strotz 1955) in the environment with menus of deterministic options.

[5]The fact that these orders are strict partial orders is proved in Lemma 2 below.

of temptation. We view $\{x, y\} \succ \{y\}$ as meaning that the individual selects x when facing $\{x, y\}$. This means that the individual is free from worries of temptation.

The next fact is worth pointing out, and we may use this fact repeatedly without warning below: When $\succsim$ satisfies No Self-Control, $\{x\} \succ \{y\}$ implies exactly one of either yT^*x or xR^*y holds.

The following properties of two relations are the fundamentals for our geometric approach, where we say that a binary relation B satisfies:

- Asymmetry when xBy implies $\neg(yBx)$,
- Transitivity when xBy and yBz imply xBz,
- Strong Independence when for any $\alpha \neq 0$, xBy if and only if $[\alpha x+(1-\alpha)z]B[\alpha y+(1-\alpha)z]$,
- Strong Archimedeanity if xBy and $x'By'$ imply that there is an $\alpha \in (0, 1)$ such that $[\alpha x + (1-\alpha)y']B[\alpha y + (1-\alpha)x']$.

Lemma 2 *Suppose that $\succsim$ satisfies Preference, Semi-Continuity, Independence, and No Self-Control. Then, the following hold.*

- *Two relations T^* and R^* are Asymmetric and Transitive (that is, strict partial orders), and they satisfy Strong Independence.*
- *The temptation relation T^* is Strong Archimedean.*

Proof We will prove the assertions only about T^* and omit the similar proof of R^*.

First, Asymmetry is obvious by definition.

Second, we show that T^* is Transitive. Suppose that zT^*y and yT^*x. Then, $\{x\} \succ \{z\}$. Let us show zT^*x, that is, $\{x\} \succ \{x, z\} \sim \{z\}$. Suppose to the contrary that xR^*z; $\{x\} \sim \{x, z\} \succ \{z\}$. Observe that we have $\{x\} \sim \{x, z\} \succ \{x, y\} \sim \{y\} \succ \{y, z\} \sim \{z\}$. Since U is affine, we have $.5\{x, z\} + .5\{y\} \succ .5\{x, y\} + .5\{y, z\}$. This is equivalent to $\{.5x + .5y, .5y + .5z\} \succ \{.5x + .5y, .5y + .5z, .5z + .5x, y\}$. We similarly have $.5\{x\} + .5\{y, z\} \succ .5\{x, y\} + .5\{y, z\}$, and this is equivalent to $\{.5x + .5y, .5z + .5x\} \succ \{.5x + .5y, .5y + .5z, .5z + .5x, y\}$. Then, No Self-Control implies $\{.5x + .5y, .5y + .5z, .5z + .5x\} \succ \{.5x + .5y, .5y + .5z, .5z + .5x, y\}$, because $\{.5x+.5y, .5y+.5z\} \cup \{.5x+.5y, .5z+.5x\} = \{.5x+.5y, .5y+.5z, .5z+.5x\}$. On the other hand, $.5\{x, y\}+.5\{y\} \succ .5\{x, y\}+.5\{y, z\}$. This is equivalent to $\{.5x+.5y, y\} \succ \{.5x + .5y, .5y + .5z, .5z + .5x, y\}$. Then, No Self-Control implies $\{.5x + .5y, .5y + .5z, .5z + .5x, y\} \succ \{.5x + .5y, .5y + .5z, .5z + .5x, y\}$, because $\{5x + .5y, .y\} \cup \{.5x + .5y, .5y + .5z, .5z + .5x\} = \{.5x + .5y, .5y + .5z, .5z + .5x, y\}$. This is a contradiction.

Third, Strong Independence of T^* immediately follows from the affine property of U.

Lastly, we show that T^* is Strong Archimedean. Suppose that yT^*x and $y'T^*x'$. We can then take an $\alpha^* \in (0, 1)$ such that $\{\alpha^*x + (1-\alpha^*)y'\} \sim \{\alpha^*y + (1-\alpha^*)x'\}$, and $\alpha > \alpha^*$ implies $\{\alpha x + (1-\alpha)y'\} \succ \{\alpha y + (1-\alpha)x'\}$. Since $\succsim$ is upper semi-continuous, it is impossible that $\{\alpha x + (1-\alpha)y'\} \sim \{\alpha x + (1-\alpha)y', \alpha y + (1-\alpha)x'\} \succ \{\alpha y + (1-\alpha)x'\}$ for any $\alpha \in (\alpha^*, 1)$. Hence, there must be an $\alpha \in (\alpha^*, 1)$ such that $\{\alpha x + (1-\alpha)y'\} \succ \{\alpha x + (1-\alpha)y', \alpha y + (1-\alpha)x'\}$, that is, $[\alpha y + (1-\alpha)x']T^*[\alpha x + (1-\alpha)y']$.

We now consider geometric representations of the two strict partial orders. Let us define two cones corresponding to the two relations as follows. (We denote the zero vector of $\mathbb{R}^{|Z|}$ by θ.)

- A temptation cone is defined by $\mathscr{T}^* = \{\lambda(y-x) \mid \lambda > 0,\ yT^*x\}$.
- A resistance cone is defined by $\mathscr{R}^* = \{\lambda(y-x) \mid \lambda > 0,\ xR^*y\}$.

Temptation cone is defined as the set of 'tempting directions', and resistance cone is defined as the set of 'resisting directions'. We now show that those cones possess some properties similar to the properties of the corresponding binary relation shown in Lemma 2. Before doing so, two definitions are introduced. The first is on a cone representation of a binary relation: For a binary relation B on a domain, we say that the cone $\{\lambda(y-x) \mid \lambda > 0,\ xBy\}$ represents B when $\lambda'(y'-x') \in \{\lambda(y-x) \mid \lambda > 0,\ xBy\}$ for some $\lambda' > 0$ and x', y' in the domain of B implies $x'By'$. The second is on an algebraic continuity of a cone: A face of a convex cone C is a nonempty convex subset F of C such that $s, t \in C$ and $\alpha s + (1-\alpha)t \in F$ for some $\alpha \in (0, 1)$ imply $s, t \in F$. A convex cone C is said to be faceless if C is the only face of C. It is known, for example from the equivalence between (a) and (e) of Proposition 10.7 in Glöckner (2003), that C is a faceless convex cone of a finite dimensional linear space like $\mathbb{R}^{|Z|}$ if and only if C is (topologically) open in the subspace generated by C. We will make full use of this property of faceless convex cone later.

Lemma 3 *Suppose that $\succsim$ satisfies Preference, Semi-Continuity, Independence, and No Self-Control. Then, the following hold.*

- *Two cones $\mathscr{T}^*$, $\mathscr{R}^*$ are convex cones that represent their corresponding relations, respectively.*
- $\mathscr{T}^* \cap \mathscr{R}^* = \emptyset$.
- *The temptation cone $\mathscr{T}^*$ is faceless.*

Proof For the first assertion of this lemma, the reader may consult with Shapley and Baucells (1998, Lamma 1.3) or Dubra et al. (2004, Lemma 2) for a proof of the fact that the desired properties follow if the relations are strict partial orders and satisfy Strong Independence. The second assertion of this lemma then follows from the fact that $\{x\} \succ \{y\}$ implies exactly one of either yT^*x or xR^*y holds.

We prove the third assertion. We say that a cone C is Archimedean (in the sense of Fishburn 1972) if $s, t \in C$ implies $\lambda s - t \in C$ for some $\lambda > 0$ and $s - \mu t \in C$ for some $\mu > 0$. We first claim:

Claim 1 The cone $\mathscr{T}^*$ is Archimedean.

To see it, take $s, t \in \mathscr{T}^*$ arbitrarily. We can write $s = \beta(x-y)$ and $t = \gamma(x'-y')$ with some $\beta > 0$, xT^*y, $\gamma > 0$, and $x'T^*y'$. By Strong Archimedeanity of T^*, $[\alpha x + (1-\alpha)y']T^*[\alpha y + (1-\alpha)x']$ for some $\alpha \in (0, 1)$. Hence, $\alpha(x-y) - (1-\alpha)(x'-y') = [\alpha x + (1-\alpha)y'] - [\alpha y + (1-\alpha)x'] \in \mathscr{T}^*$. Let $\mu = \gamma/(1-\alpha) > 0$. Since $\mathscr{T}^*$ is a cone, $\alpha\mu(x-y) - \gamma(x'-y') \in \mathscr{T}^*$. Let $\lambda = (\alpha\mu)/\beta > 0$. Then, by construction, $\lambda s - t = \lambda\beta(x-y) - \gamma(x'-y') = \alpha\mu(x-y) - \gamma(x'-y') \in \mathscr{T}^*$. We can similarly prove $s - \mu t \in C$ for some $\mu > 0$.

We now prove that the cone $\mathscr{T}^*$ is faceless. Suppose to the contrary that $\mathscr{T}^*$ has a face $F \neq \mathscr{T}^*$. Take $s \in F$ and $t \in \mathscr{T}^* \setminus F$ arbitrarily. Since $\mathscr{T}^*$ is Archimedean, there is a $\lambda > 0$ such that $s - \lambda t \in \mathscr{T}^*$. Observe that

$$\frac{1}{1+\lambda}[s - \lambda t] + \frac{\lambda}{1+\lambda}t = \frac{1}{1+\lambda}s + \theta = \frac{1}{1+\lambda}s \in F,$$

because any face of a cone is a subcone in the cone (Lemma 10.2 in Glöckner 2003). This means that $t \in F$ from the definition of face. This is a contradiction.

Remark 1 Our characterization of T^* and R^*, especially transitivity and strong independence, will be used to test the Strotz model. First, it is helpful to design an experiment or a questionnaire. Since Independence and/or No Self-Control are written in terms of choices over *all* menus, testing literally them entails a comprehensive examination of choices that uses not only small menus but large menus. The properties of T^* and R^* provide simple testable implications of the model that are written by menus that include at most two elements.

Second, as we show in the next section, temptation utility v is characterized by T^* and R^*. This means that the properties of those relations are testable predictions of a model with linear temptation utility. That is, if an individual's choices do not obey the prediction of a Strotz model, then the properties of T^* and R^* will be useful in exploring the nature of observed violations and in considering a minimally extended model that accommodates the violations.

Remark 2 Our geometric approach is useful in the theory of menu preferences beyond the Strotz model. Gul and Pesendorfer (2001) propose and axiomatize another model of utility function of the form

$$U(A) = \max_{x \in A} \{u(x) + v(x)\} - \max_{y \in A} \{v(y)\}$$

for some $u, v \in \mathscr{C}$. This is a continuous model that describes an individual's costly self-control behavior. The key axiom for this model is Set Betweenness. This relaxes No Self-Control and allows a possibility that $A \succ A \cup B \succ B$. This possibility displays the notion of temptation and costly self-control. Suppose that B contains a tempting alternative. We can view $A \cup B \succ B$ as meaning that when facing menu $A \cup B$, the individual uses self-control and can resist the temptation. We then interpret $A \succ A \cup B$ as meaning that exercising self-control is costly.

We can explore similar geometric properties for this model by considering weaker version of temptation and resistance relations in addition to T^* and R^*. Define T by yTx if $\{x\} \succ \{x, y\}$, and R by xRy if $\{x, y\} \succ \{y\}$.[6] Then, Gul and Pesendorfer's self-control axioms imply that all of T, T^*, R, R^* are transitive and satisfy strong independence. Hence, these properties become refined testable

[6]No Self-Control implies $T = T^*$ and $R = R^*$. But, these equalities do not necessarily hold under Set Betweenness.

predictions for Gul and Pesendorfer's self-control model as in the above remark. We follow this approach in Abe (2011) to prove the representation theorem for this model, and show that $u+v$ in the representation is characterized by T^* and R while v is characterized by T and R^*.[7]

4 The Geometric Proof of the Strotz Representation Theorem

In this section, we prove the Strotz representation theorem by applying a separation argument based on the fact established in Lemma 3. Specifically, we prove that any regular no self-control preference relation admits a Strotz representation.

If $\succsim$ satisfies Axioms 1–4, then we say that $\succsim$ is a no self-control preference relation. A no self-control preference relation $\succsim$ is regular if there are $x', y', x'', y'' \in \Delta$ such that $\{x'\} \succ \{x', y'\} \sim \{y'\}$ and $\{x''\} \sim \{x'', y''\} \succ \{y''\}$.[8]

Consider the linear subspace spanned by $\mathscr{T}^*$ and denote it by $\text{span}(\mathscr{T}^*)$. It can be written as $\text{span}(\mathscr{T}^*) = \mathscr{T}^* - \mathscr{T}^*$ since $\mathscr{T}^*$ is a cone. As the following lemma shows, this space is rich enough for our separation argument in Lemma 5.

Lemma 4 $\Delta - \Delta \subsetneq \text{span}(\mathscr{T}^*)$.

Proof See Appendix.

Note that this lemma immediately implies that $\mathscr{R}^* \subsetneq \text{span}(\mathscr{T}^*)$. Our separation argument is as follows.

Lemma 5 *There exists a linear functional* $L : \text{span}(\mathscr{T}^*) \to \mathbb{R}$ *such that* $L(t) > 0 \geq L(r)$ *for all* $t \in \mathscr{T}^*$ *and all* $r \in \mathscr{R}^*$.

Proof From Lemma 3, $\mathscr{T}^*$ is faceless. Hence, it is open in $\text{span}(\mathscr{T}^*)$ equipped with the Euclidian topology (Proposition 10.7 in Glöckner 2003). Since $\mathscr{T}^*$ and $\mathscr{R}^*$ are disjoint, nonempty, convex sets in linear space $\text{span}(\mathscr{T}^*)$ from Lemma 3 and 4, we can apply a separating hyperplane theorem (See for example Theorem 3.4 in Rudin 1991) to conclude that there is a continuous linear functional L on $\text{span}(\mathscr{T}^*)$ such that L openly separates $\mathscr{T}^*$ from $\mathscr{R}^*$. Since $\mathscr{T}^*$ and $\mathscr{R}^*$ are cones by definition, the linear functional must satisfy the desired property.

[7]Recently, Kopylov (2009a) proved the self-control representation theorem for a more general choice object than the one considered here and applied it to characterize various models associated with temptation. His proof is not geometric but rather constructive and shorter than existing proofs.

[8]It is straightforward to verify that the regularity defined here is equivalent to that of Gul and Pesendorfer (2001). It is also straightforward to prove the Strotz representation theorem in the non-regular case. Set $v := u$ for the case that $\{x\} \succ \{y\}$ implies $\{x\} \sim \{x, y\}$ and $v := -u$ for the case that $\{x\} \succ \{y\}$ implies $\{x, y\} \sim \{y\}$. We can then easily prove that U is the Strotz model with u and v.

Fix $x_0 \in \Delta$ arbitrarily. Define $v : \Delta \to \mathbb{R}$ by $v(x) := L(x - x_0)$. Then, v is affine (and hence continuos), and xT^*y (resp., xR^*y) implies $v(x) > v(y)$ (resp., $v(x) \geq v(y)$) by construction. Moreover, if $\{x\} \succ \{y\}$, then it must hold under No Self-Control that $v(x) \geq v(y)$ implies xR^*y and that $v(x) < v(y)$ implies yT^*x.[9,10]

Using these properties of v, we can prove the Strotz representation theorem.

Lemma 6 *The representation U is the Strotz model with u and v.*

Proof We first prove the Strotz representation theorem for finite menus. Consider a finite menu $A \in \mathscr{A}$. Pick a $x^* \in \text{argmax}_{x \in M_v(A)} u(x)$. Since $A = \cup_{y \in A}\{x^*, y\}$, we have $U(\{x^*, y\}) = U(A)$ for some $y \in A$ from No Self-Control. If $\{x^*\} \sim \{y\}$, then No Self-Control ensures that $U(A) = \text{argmax}_{x \in M_v(A)} u(x) = u(x^*)$. If $\{x^*\} \succ \{y\}$, then $v(x^*) \geq v(y)$ implies x^*R^*y. Hence, $U(A) = u(x^*)$. Finally, consider the case of $\{y\} \succ \{x^*\}$. Then, yR^*x^* or x^*T^*y. Suppose yR^*x^*. This implies $v(y) \geq v(x^*)$. This contradicts $x^* \in \text{argmax}_{x \in M_v(A)} u(x)$ in the case of $\{y\} \succ \{x^*\}$. Hence, x^*T^*y. This implies $U(A) = u(x^*)$.

We can extend the Strotz representation from finite menus to the entire $\mathscr{A}$ by applying Lemma 8 in Gul and Pesendorfer (2001).

5 Infinite Z Case

Our geometric approach works for infinite Z case as well as for finite Z case. Let Z be a compact metric space of prizes. Following Gul and Pesendorfer (2001), we consider Δ as the set of all Borel probability measures over Z and endow it with the topology of weak convergence. The set of menus is defined as before and denoted by $\mathscr{A}$. Then, each of Δ and $\mathscr{A}$ becomes a compact metric space (See for example Theorem 15.11 and Theorem 3.85, respectively, in Aliprantis and Border 2006).

In this general setup, we need to adjust some proofs provided in earlier sections. It is sufficient to care two things. First, we need another linear space that contains Δ. Instead of $\mathbb{R}^{|Z|}$, take the linear space (over $\mathbb{R}$) as the set of all finite Borel signed measures over Z.

Second, we have to care the relation between facelessness and topological continuity in an infinite dimensional space. From the equivalence between (a) and (d) of Proposition 10.7 in Glöckner (2003), we have the following fact: A convex cone C is faceless if and only if it is open in span(C) equipped with the finest locally convex topology, where the topology is defined as follows. A set C of a real linear space V is radial at x if C contains a line segment through x in each direction.

[9] Recently, an independent work, Noor and Takeoka (2010), adopts a similar method to ours for characterizing of temptation utility and prove the menu-dependent self-control representation theorem.

[10] This means that $\{-u, v\}$ is an expected multi-utility representation of T^* in the sense of Shapley and Baucells (1998) and Dubra et al. (2004).

(Formally, C is radial at x if for any $y \neq x$, there is a $z \neq x$ such that $[x, z] \subseteq [x, y] \cap C$, where $[x, z] := \{\alpha x + (1 - \alpha)z \in V | \alpha \in [0, 1]\}$.) A set C is absorbing if it is radial at θ. A set C is circled if $|\lambda| \leq 1$ implies $\lambda x \in C$ for all $x \in C$. The set of all absorbing convex circled subsets of V forms a local base for a locally convex topology, which is the finest (strongest) locally convex topology on V (Kelly and Namioka 1976, Problem I on p.53).

Then, we adjust proofs of Lemma 5 and 6. We can obtain a desired linear functional L as in the proof of Lemma 5 except that the continuity of the functional must be adjusted. The functional is just continuous on span($\mathscr{T}^*$) in the finest locally convex topology. As a result, we cannot automatically conclude that function v defined from L is continuous in the weak convergence topology. Since this continuity is needed not only in the representation itself, but also in Lemma 6 where we use this continuity to apply Lemma 8 of Gul and Pesendorfer (2001), we have to prove it additionally as below.

Proof (Supplement to the proof of Lemma 6) We show that v is continuous with respect to the topology of weak convergence. Let us first show that if z_n weakly converges to z, then $\lim_{n\to\infty} v(z_n)$ exists. Take $x, y \subset \Delta$ with yT^*x arbitrarily. Then, $u(x) > u(y)$ and $v(y) > v(x)$. Suppose that $v(z_n)$ diverges to positive infinity. Then, $v(z_n) > v(z) + 1$ holds for all sufficiently large n. Take an $\alpha \in (0, 1)$ such that $\alpha v(x) + (1 - \alpha)v(z_n) > \alpha v(y) + (1 - \alpha)v(z)$ for all such large n. Since U is a Strotz representation for binary menus as shown in the first half of Lemma 6, this implies $U(\{\alpha x + (1 - \alpha)z_n, \alpha y + (1 - \alpha)z\}) = U(\{\alpha x + (1 - \alpha)z_n\})$. However, then

$$\begin{aligned}&\limsup_{n\to\infty} U(\{\alpha x + (1 - \alpha)z_n, \alpha y + (1 - \alpha)z\})\\&= U(\{\alpha x + (1 - \alpha)z\})\\&> U(\{\alpha x + (1 - \alpha)z, \alpha y + (1 - \alpha)z\}),\end{aligned}$$

where the inequality follows from yT^*x with independence. This contradicts upper semi-continuity of U. Hence, $v(z_n)$ is bounded from above. Similarly, $v(z_n)$ is bounded from below. Thus, we can take a convergent subsequence in $v(z_n)$. Moreover, any convergent subsequence in $v(z_n)$ has the same limit. To see this, suppose to the contrary that there are $z_{n_1(m)}$ and $z_{n_2(m)}$ such that $\lim_{m\to\infty} v(z_{n_1(m)}) = v_1$, $\lim_{m\to\infty} v(z_{n_2(m)}) = v_2$, and $v_1 > v_2$. Then, $v(z_{n_1(m)}) > (2v_1 + v_2)/3$ and $(v_1 + 2v_2)/3 > v(z_{n_2(m)})$ hold for sufficiently large m. Take an $\alpha \in (0, 1)$ such that $\alpha v(x) + (1 - \alpha)v(z_{n_1(m)}) > \alpha v(y) + (1 - \alpha)v(z_{n_2(m)})$ for all such large m. Since U is a Strotz representation for binary menus, this implies $U(\{\alpha x + (1 - \alpha)z_{n_1(m)}, \alpha y + (1 - \alpha)z_{n_2(m)}\}) = U(\{\alpha x + (1 - \alpha)z_{n_1(m)}\})$. However, then

$$\begin{aligned}&\limsup_{m\to\infty} U(\{\alpha x + (1 - \alpha)z_{n_1(m)}, \alpha y + (1 - \alpha)z_{n_2(m)}\})\\&= U(\{\alpha x + (1 - \alpha)z\})\\&> U(\{\alpha x + (1 - \alpha)z, \alpha y + (1 - \alpha)z\}),\end{aligned}$$

where the inequality follows from yT^*x with independence. This contradicts upper semi-continuity of U. Hence, any convergent subsequence in $v(z_n)$ converges to the same limit point. Therefore, the original bounded sequence $v(z_n)$ converges to the same limit point; that is, $\lim v(z_n)$ exists.

Given the existence of $\lim v(z_n)$, the proof of $v(z) = \lim v(z_n)$ is accomplished by a similar procedure. Since such a proof appears on pages 1429–1430 in Gul and Pesendorfer (2001), we omit the proof.

6 Discussion

We compare our geometric approach with Gul and Pesendorfer's approach to prove the theorem. They first pay attention to a particular binary relation in the underlying preferences that are thought to display temptation. Specifically, they attempted to elicit temptation considerations by taking particular note of $\{x\} \sim \{x, y\}$ in the case of $\{x\} \not\succsim \{y\}$ and said that x is more tempting than y.[11] Write it xPy. They then tried to obtain its expected utility representation, unlike our geometric approach, by verifying that it satisfies standard expected utility axioms. This expected utility was supposed to be a temptation utility.

Unfortunately, their proof has a gap. We show it by counterexample. Let $Z = \{c_1, c_2, c_3\}$ and $x = (x_1, x_2, x_3) \in \Delta$, where c_i occurs with probability x_i. Consider (continuous) affine functions $u(x) = x_1$ and $v(x) = x_3$. Let us define a binary relation $\succsim$ over $\mathscr{A}$ by the Strotz model with the functions (u, v). By the Strotz representation theorem, the binary relation $\succsim$ satisfies Axioms 1–4. Examine temptation relation P for the binary relation $\succsim$. Let $x = (1, 0, 0)$, $y = (0, 1, 0)$, and $w = (0, 0, 1)$. Then $\{x\} \succ \{x, w\} \sim \{w\}$ and $\{x\} \sim \{x, y\} \succ \{y\}$; that is, $wPxPy$. However, $\{x\} \succ \{x, \beta w + (1-\beta)y\} \sim \{\beta w + (1-\beta)y\}$ for any $\beta \in (0, 1)$. This means that there is no $\beta \in (0, 1)$ such that $xP[\beta w + (1-\beta)y]$, so P does not satisfy continuity although it is needed in their proof of the theorem.

Reconsider temptation relation P, which is saying that x is more tempting than y if $\{x\} \sim \{x, y\}$ in the case of $\{x\} \not\succsim \{y\}$. This is legitimate when $\{y\} \succ \{x, y\} \sim \{x\}$ because the fact that the individual finds no value from flexible menu $\{x, y\}$ is naturally interpreted as anticipating that the undesired x is chosen from $\{x, y\}$. However, if $\{x\} \sim \{x, y\} \succ \{y\}$, then we cannot distinguish a possibility that x is more tempting than y from another possibility that x and y have the same temptation ranking because both would lead to an anticipation of x from $\{x, y\}$ in the ex-post choice. Hence, we cannot identify a temptation ranking with the anticipated ex-post choices. This is the gap in Gul and Pesendorfer (2001).[12]

[11] To be precise, they say that x is more tempting than y when $\{x\} \sim \{x, y\}$ in the case of $\{x\} \not\succsim \{y\}$ and when $\{y\} \sim \{y, z\}$ implies $\{x\} \sim \{x, z\}$ in the case of $\{x\} \sim \{y\}$.

[12] To be more exact, the identification problem causes discontinuity of P as in the counterexample. Hence, its expected utility representation does not exist in general. Note that the finite alternatives

We can identify a temptation ranking only when the tempting alternative is undesired for the individual. This implies that observed temptation considerations are a part of the temptation order considered by Gul and Pesendorfer (2001) and define an incomplete order. This chapter directly treats this incomplete order and obtains a temptation utility using a separation method à la Aumann (1962). Separating the incomplete order from its dual (resistance relation), we obtain a linear temptation utility that is consistent with the above-mentioned identification problem. In this sense, our approach completes the idea in the approach taken by Gul and Pesendorfer (2001).

Acknowledgements I would like to express my appreciation to Hideo Suehiro for invaluable discussions and encouragement. I would also like to thank Kazuya Hyogo, Hajime Kobayashi, Noriaki Matsushima, Eiichi Miyagawa, Wolfgang Pesendorfer, and Norio Takeoka for their valuable comments and suggestions. Very useful remarks of two anonymous reviewers and the editor have lead to an improved presentation of the results. Responsibility for any remaining errors rests with the author. The addendum part was supported by JSPS KAKENHI Grant Number 24730166.

Appendix: Omitted Proof

Proof (Proof of Lemma 4) Take $x, y \in \Delta$ with xT^*y arbitrarily. Let us first show that $z - y \in \text{span}(\mathscr{T}^*)$ for any $z \in \Delta$. Consider the linear subspace spanned by $S := \{x - y, z - y\}$ and denote it by span(S). If these underlying vectors are linearly dependent, then $z - y = \lambda(x - y) \in \text{span}(\mathscr{T}^*)$ for some $\lambda \neq 0$. Assume that these vectors are linearly independent, that is, span(S) has dimension 2. Define the set $\mathscr{T}^*(y) := \{z' - y | z'T^*y\}$ and let $\mathscr{T}^*{}_s(y)$ denote the intersection of $\mathscr{T}^*(y)$ and span(S). It is straightforward to verify that $\mathscr{T}^*{}_s(y)$ is a convex set. Moreover, this has dimension 2. Suppose to the contrary that $\mathscr{T}^*{}_s(y)$ has dimension 1. Then, for any $\alpha \in (0, 1)$,

$$[\alpha x + (1 - \alpha)z] - y = \alpha(x - y) + (1 - \alpha)(z - y) \notin \mathscr{T}^*{}_s(y).$$

This means that $yR^*[\alpha x + (1 - \alpha)z]$ for all $\alpha \in (\alpha^*, 1)$, where $\alpha^* \in (0, 1)$ is a number such that $\{y\} \succ \{\alpha^* x + (1 - \alpha^*)z\}$. As we stated in the proof of Lemma 2, this contradicts Upper Semi-Continuity of $\succsim$. Thus, $\mathscr{T}^*{}_s(y)$ has dimension 2. We can then take an algebraically relative interior point $z' - y \in \mathscr{T}^*{}_s(y)$ (see p.9 in Holmes 1975). From its algebraic properties, there is a $\lambda > 0$ such that

$$[z' - \lambda(z - y)] - y = z' - y - \lambda(z - y) \in \mathscr{T}^*{}_s(y).$$

setting as in Kreps (1979) and Gul and Pesendorfer (2005) is free from this gap. It is because only important thing in the finite setting is that the relation has a utility representation, not expected utility representation.

This means that $[z' - \lambda(z - y)]T^*y$ for some $\lambda > 0$. Hence,

$$-\lambda(z - y) = [z' - \lambda(z - y)] - y - (z' - y) \in \text{span}(\mathscr{T}^*).$$

As a result, $z - y \in \text{span}(\mathscr{T}^*)$.

We now show that $\Delta - \Delta \subsetneq \text{span}(\mathscr{T}^*)$. Take $z, z' \in \Delta$ arbitrarily. Then, as shown above, both $z - y$ and $z' - y$ are in $\text{span}(\mathscr{T}^*)$. Therefore, $z - z' = (z - y) - (z' - y) \in \text{span}(\mathscr{T}^*)$. This completes the proof.

Addendum: On the Geometry of Temptation and Self-Control[13]

As stated in Remark 2, Abe (2011) demonstrates the usefulness of our geometric approach to menu preferences beyond the Strotz model. By taking the geometric approach, Abe (2011) provides an alternative proof of the costly self-control representation theorem in Gul and Pesendorfer (2001).[14,15] Here, we briefly supplement Remark 2 by providing an outline of the proof provided in Abe (2011).

We begin by summarizing Gul and Pesendorfer's costly self-control representation theorem.

Definition 2 A utility function U on menus is said to be a Gul and Pesendorfer's costly self-control model, hereafter referred to as a costly self-control model, if it is a function of the form:

$$U(A) = \max_{x \in A} \{u(x) + v(x)\} - \max_{y \in A} \{v(y)\}$$

for some $u, v \in \mathscr{C}$.

The costly self-control models are characterized by a behavioral regularity on menu preferences named Set Betweenness.

Axiom 4′ (Set Betweenness) $A \succsim B$ implies $A \succsim A \cup B \succsim B$.

[13] This addendum has been newly written for this book chapter.

[14] Gul and Pesendorfer (2001) proves the theorem by directly constructing a temptation utility. This constructive approach and the geometric approach taken here bring us additional but different benefits beyond just establishing the representation theorem. The former directly tells us how to calibrate temptation, whereas the latter directly defines temptation and self-control in terms of preferences, so that it directly relates temptation and self-control utilities to the particular intuitive properties of the underlying preferences.

[15] As Gul and Pesendorfer (2001, footnote 6) conjecture, there is another approach to prove the theorem that is based on a representation theorem characterizing a general model called a finite additive expected utility representation. See Dekel et al. (2009) for the case of finite Z and Kopylov (2009b) for a more general choice object.

Set Betweenness relaxes No Self-Control and allows for the possibility that $A \succ A \cup B \succ B$. This possibility displays the notion of temptation and costly self-control. Suppose that B contains a tempting alternative. We can view $A \cup B \succ B$ as meaning that when facing menu $A \cup B$, the individual uses self-control and can resist the temptation. We then interpret $A \succ A \cup B$ as meaning that exercising self-control is costly. The main theorem in Gul and Pesendorfer (2001) is summarized as follows.[16]

The Costly Self-Control Representation Theorem. *$\succsim$ satisfies Preference, Continuity, Independence, and Set Betweenness if and only if it has a costly self-control representation, that is, there exists a costly self-control model U such that $A \succsim B$ if and only if $U(A) \geq U(B)$.*

We provide the proof outline on the sufficiency of the axioms in Abe (2011). In what follows, let U be a utility representation of $\succsim$ derived as in Lemma 1 and u be a commitment utility derived by restricting U on singleton menus. Consider a nontrivial preference relation $\succsim$, that is, there are $x, y \in \Delta$ such that $\{x\} \succ \{y\}$. The proof outline is as follows. First, in a similar way as in Sect. 3, we can characterize the geometry of temptation under Set Betweenness. Specifically, Set Betweenness induces the following four strict partial orders satisfying Strong Independence.

- A weak temptation relation T is defined by yTx if $\{x\} \succ \{x, y\}$.
- A strong temptation relation T^* is defined by yT^*x if $\{x\} \succ \{x, y\} \sim \{y\}$.
- A weak resistance relation R is defined by xRy if $\{x, y\} \succ \{y\}$.
- A strong resistance relation R^* is defined by xR^*y if $\{x\} \sim \{x, y\} \succ \{y\}$.

Furthermore, the weak temptation relation T and the weak resistance relation R are both Strong Archimedean. Define four cones corresponding to the four relations as follows.

- A weak temptation cone is defined by $\mathscr{T} = \{\lambda(y - x) \mid \lambda > 0,\ yTx\}$.
- A strong temptation cone is defined by $\mathscr{T}^* = \{\lambda(y - x) \mid \lambda > 0,\ yT^*x\}$.
- A weak resistance cone is defined by $\mathscr{R} = \{\lambda(y - x) \mid \lambda > 0,\ xRy\}$.
- A strong resistance cone is defined by $\mathscr{R}^* = \{\lambda(y - x) \mid \lambda > 0,\ xR^*y\}$.

Then, the four cones $\mathscr{T}$, $\mathscr{T}^*$, $\mathscr{R}$, and $\mathscr{R}^*$ are convex cones that represent their corresponding relations, respectively. Furthermore, the weak temptation cone $\mathscr{T}$ and the weak resistance cone $\mathscr{R}$ are both faceless.

Second, we derive affine numerical representations of temptation and resistance (self-control) by the separation argument, and obtain $v, w \in \mathscr{C}$ such that for any $x, y \in \Delta$ with $\{x\} \succ \{y\}$, (i) $\{x\} \succ \{x, y\}$ if and only if $v(y) > v(x)$ and (ii)

[16]Let $\succsim$ be a binary relation over $\mathscr{A}$. Say that $\succsim$ is continuous if the sets $\{B \in \mathscr{A} | B \succsim A\}$ and $\{B \in \mathscr{A} | A \succsim B\}$ are closed.

Axiom 2′ (Continuity) $\succsim$ is continuous.

Unlike the Strotz models, the costly self-control models are continuous in menu. Hence, compared with the Strorz representation theorem, Axiom 2 is strengthened to Axiom 2′ in the costly self-control representation theorem.

$\{x,y\} \succ \{y\}$ if and only if $w(x) > w(y)$. We determine temptation utility v by openly separating $\mathscr{T}$ from $\mathscr{R}^*$ and self-control utility w by openly separating $\mathscr{R}$ from $\mathscr{T}^*$. Note that if $u(x) > u(y)$, then, by construction, $v(x) \geq v(y)$ implies $w(x) > w(y)$. With this fact, we can show that self-control utility w must be written by $w = au + bv + c$ for some constant $a, b > 0$ and $c \in \mathbb{R}$. This means that the indifference curve of w lies between those of u and v when they pass a common point, and this also implies $w(x) > w(y)$ and $v(y) > v(x)$ if and only if $\{x\} \succ \{x,y\} \succ \{y\}$.

Third, we can characterize U with w and v. The next lemma establishes this.

Lemma 7 *$U(\{x,\cdot\})$ is cardinally equivalent to $-v$ over set $\{y \in \Delta \mid w(x) \geq w(y)$ and $v(y) \geq v(x)\}$.*[17]

This lemma states that the ranking of $\{x,y\}$ and $\{x,z\}$ is determined by the temptation ranking of y and z when both y and z are more tempting than x but when the individual can resist the temptations.[18] This observation leads us to the desired form of representation. Suppose $\{x\} \succ \{x,y\} \succ \{y\}$. Take a z such that $w(x) = w(z)$ and $v(y) = v(z)$. The facts derived in the second step imply $\{x\} \succ \{x,z\} \sim \{z\}$. Combining this with the above lemma, we then find $\{x,y\} \sim \{x,z\} \sim \{z\}$. Recall from the second step that an appropriate scale-normalized commitment utility is the difference between the self-control utility and the scale-normalized temptation utility: $au + c = w - bv$. Therefore, we can calibrate the utility value of $\{x,y\}$ by the difference between the self-control utility of z and the normalized temptation utility of z. By way of choosing z, we can calibrate the utility value of $\{x,y\}$ by the difference between the self-control utility of x and the normalized temptation utility of y, that is, $w(x) - bv(y)$. This means that the utility value of $\{x,y\}$ is measured by Gul and Pesendorfer's costly self-control representation form $\hat{u}(x) + \hat{v}(x) - \hat{v}(y)$ if we define $\hat{u} = au + c$ and $\hat{v} = bv$. More formally, we can prove the next lemma in this line and hence complete the proof.

Lemma 8 *Define $\hat{U}$ and $\hat{v}$ by $\hat{U} := aU + c$ and $\hat{v} := bv$ with a, b, c derived in the second step. Let $\hat{u}$ be the restriction of $\hat{U}$ on singleton menus. Then, $\hat{U}$ is a representation of $\succsim$ and a costly self-control model.*

References

Abe K (2011) A geometric approach to temptation and self-control. Mimeograph, Osaka University

Abe K (2012) A geometric approach to temptation. J Math Econ 48(2):92–97

---

[17] Similarly, we can show that $U(\{\cdot,x\})$ is cardinally equivalent to w over set $\{y \in \Delta \mid w(y) \geq w(x)$ and $v(x) \geq v(y)\}$.

[18] Similarly, the ranking of $\{x,y\}$ and $\{x,z\}$ is determined by the self-control ranking of y and z when x is more tempting than both y and z but when the individual can resist the temptation.

Aliprantis CD, Border KC (2006) Infinite dimensional analysis, 3rd edn. Springer, Berlin
Aumann RJ (1962) Utility theory without the completeness axiom. Econometrica 30(3):445–462
Dekel E, Lipman BL, Rustichini A (2009) Temptation-driven preferences. Rev Econ Stud 76(3):937–971
Dubra J, Maccheroni F, Ok EA (2004) Expected utility theory without the completeness axiom. J Econ Theory 115(1):118–133
Fishburn PC (1972) Alternative axiomatizations of one-way expected utility. Ann Math Stat 43(5):1648–1651
Glöckner H (2003) Positive definite functions on infinite-dimensional convex cones. Memoirs Am Math Soc 166(789):1–128
Gul F, Pesendorfer W (2001) Temptation and self-control. Econometrica 69(6):1403–1435
Gul F, Pesendorfer W (2005) The revealed preference theory of changing tastes. Rev Econ Stud 72(2):429–448
Holmes RB (1975) Geometric functional analysis and its applications. Springer, New York
Kelly JL, Namioka I (1976) Linear topological spaces. Springer, New York (Reprint of the 1963 edition published by Van Nostrand, Princeton)
Kopylov I (2009a) Temptations in general settings. B.E. J Theor Econ (Advances) 9(1):Article 31
Kopylov I (2009b) Finite additive utility representations for preferences over menus. J Econ Theory 144(1):354–374
Kreps DM (1979) On sophisticated choice of opportunity sets. Stanford GSB Research Papers No. 494, Stanford University
Kreps DM (1988) Notes on the theory of choice. Westview Press, Boulder
MacCrimmon KR, Larsson S (1979) Utility theory: axioms versus 'Paradoxes'. In: Allais M, Hagen Ole (eds) Expected utility hypotheses and the Allais paradox. D. Reidel, Dordrecht, pp 333–409
Machina MJ (1983) Generalized expected utility analysis and the nature of observed violations of the independence axiom," In: Stigum BP, Wenstøp F (ed) Foundations of utility and risk theory with applications. D. Reidel, Dordrecht, pp 263–293
Noor J, Takeoka N (2010) Menu-dependent self-control. Mimeograph, Boston University and Yokohama National University
Rudin W (1991) Functional analysis, 2nd edn. McGraw-Hill, Boston
Shapley LS, Baucells M (1998) A theory of multiperson utility. Working Paper No. 779, Department of Economics, UCLA
Strotz RH (1955) Myopia and inconsistency in dynamic utility maximization. Rev Econ Stud 23(3):165–180

Part VII
Biological Foundation

Chapter 22
Prediction of Immediate and Future Rewards Differentially Recruits Cortico-Basal Ganglia Loops

Saori C. Tanaka, Kenji Doya, Go Okada, Kazutaka Ueda, Yasumasa Okamoto, and Shigeto Yamawaki

Abstract Evaluation of both immediate and future outcomes of an action is a critical requirement for intelligent behavior. We investigated brain mechanisms for reward prediction at different time scales in an fMRI experiment using a Markov decision task. When subjects learned actions from immediate rewards, significant activity was found in the lateral orbitofrontal cortex and the striatum. When subjects learned to acquire large future rewards despite small immediate losses, the dorsolateral prefrontal cortex, inferior parietal cortex, dorsal raphe nucleus, and cerebellum were also activated. Computational model-based regression analysis using the predicted future rewards and prediction errors estimated from subjects' performance data revealed graded maps of time scale within the insula and the striatum, where ventroanterior parts were responsible for predicting immediate rewards and dorsoposterior parts for future rewards. These results suggest differential involvement of the cortico-basal ganglia loops in reward prediction at different time scales.

Keywords Decision making • Delay discounting • fMRI • Striatum • Neuroeconomics

---

The original article first appeared in Nature Neuroscience 7(8):887–893, 2004. A newly written addendum has been added to this book chapter.

S.C. Tanaka (✉)
ATR Brain Information Communication Research Lab. Group, 2-2-2 Hikaridai, Seika-cho, Soraku-gun, Kyoto 619-0288, Japan
e-mail: xsaori@atr.jp

K. Doya
Neural Computation Unit, Okinawa Institute of Science and Technology, 1919-1 Tancha, Onna, Okinawa 904-0495, Japan

G. Okada • K. Ueda • Y. Okamoto • S. Yamawaki
Department of Psychiatry and Neurosciences, Hiroshima University, 1-2-3 Kasumi, Minamiku, Hiroshima 734-8551, Japan

S. Ikeda et al. (eds.), *Behavioral Economics of Preferences, Choices, and Happiness*, DOI 10.1007/978-4-431-55402-8_22

1 Introduction

In our daily life, we make decisions based on the prediction of rewards at different time scales; for example, a decision to undertake hard daily exercises to achieve a major future goal, or to resist a sweet temptation if it may lead to a future disaster. Patients with damage in the prefrontal cortex often have trouble in daily decision making, which requires assessment of future outcomes (Bechara et al. 2000; Mobini et al. 2002). Lesions in the core of the nucleus accumbens in rats result in the choice of a small immediate reward rather than a larger future reward (Cardinal et al. 2001). Low activity of the central serotonergic system is associated with impulsive behaviors in humans (Rogers et al. 1999a), and animal experiments have shown that lesions in the ascending serotonergic pathway cause the choice of small immediate rewards as opposed to larger future rewards (Evenden and Ryan 1996; Mobini et al. 2000). A possible mechanism underlying these observations is that different sub-loops of the topographically organized cortico-basal ganglia network are specialized for reward prediction at different time scales and that they are differentially activated by the ascending serotonergic system (Doya 2002). To test whether there are distinct neural pathways for reward prediction at different time scales, we developed a Markov decision task, in which an action does not only affect the immediate reward but also the future states and rewards, and we analyzed subjects' brain activities using functional MRI. Recent functional brain imaging studies have shown the involvement of specific brain areas, such as the orbitofrontal cortex (OFC) and the ventral striatum, in prediction and perception of rewards (Berns et al. 2001; Breiter et al. 2001; O'Doherty et al. 2002, 2003b). However, in previous studies, rewards were given either independent of subject's actions or as a function of the current action. Our Markov decision task probes decision making under a dynamic context with small losses followed by a large positive reward. The results of the block-design analysis suggest differential involvement of brain areas in decision making by prediction of rewards at different time scales. By analyzing subjects' performance data according to a theoretical model of reinforcement learning, we revealed a gradient of activation within the insula and the striatum for prediction of rewards at different time scales.

2 Methods

2.1 Subjects

Twenty healthy, right-handed volunteers (18 males and 2 females), aged 22–34 years gave informed consent to participate in the experiment, which was conducted with the approval of the ethics and safety committees of Advanced Telecommunications Research Institute International and Hiroshima University.

2.2 Behavioral Task

In the Markov decision task (Fig. 22.1), one of three states is visually presented to the subject using three different figures, and the subject selects one of two actions by pressing one of two buttons using their right hand (Fig. 22.1a). In the SHORT condition (Fig. 22.1b), action a_1 results in a small positive reward $+ r_1$ (10, 20, or 30 yen, with equal probabilities), while action a_2 results in a small loss $-r_1$, at any of the three states. Thus, the optimal behavior is to collect small positive rewards at each state by taking action a_1. In the LONG condition (Fig. 22.1c), however, the reward setting is changed so that action a_2 gives a large positive reward $+ r_2$ (90, 100, or 110 yen) at state s_3, and action a_1 gives a large loss $-r_2$ at state s_1. Thus, the optimal behavior is to receive small losses at states s_1 and s_2 to obtain a large positive reward

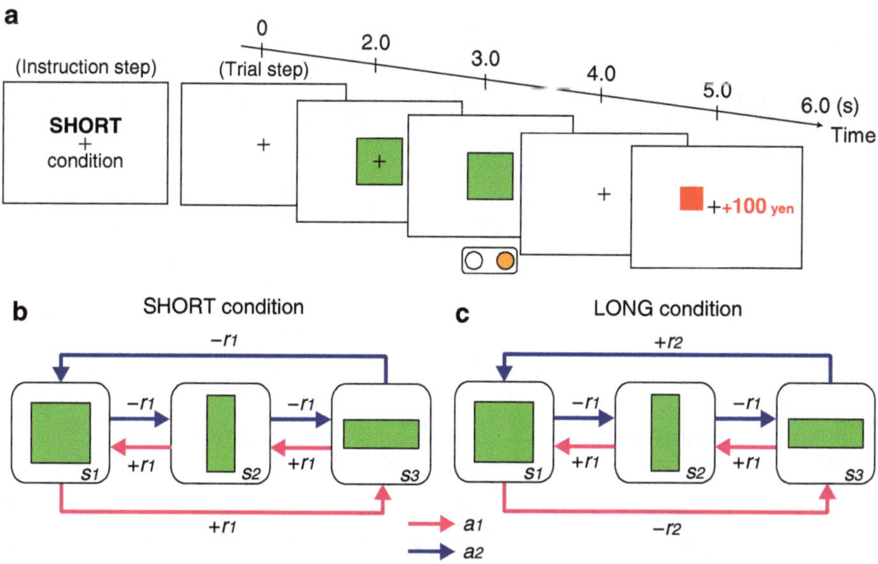

Fig. 22.1 Experimental design. (**a**) Sequences of stimulus and response events in the task. At the beginning of each condition block, the condition is informed by displaying character (6 s), such as the "SHORT condition" (instruction step). In each trial step, a fixation point is presented on the screen, and after 2 s, one of three figures (*square, vertical rectangle, and horizontal rectangle*) is presented. As the fixation point vanishes after 1 s, the subject presses either the right or left button within 1 s. After a short delay (1 s), a reward for the current action is presented by a number and the past cumulative reward is shown by a bar graph. Thus, one trial takes 6 s. (**b and c**) The rules of the reward and state transition for action a_1 (*red arrow*) and action a_2 (*magenta arrow*) in the SHORT (**b**) and LONG (**c**) conditions. The small reward r_1 is either 10, 20, or 30 yen, with equal probability, and the large reward r_2 is either 90, 100, or 110 yen. The rule of state transition is the same for all conditions; $s_3 \rightarrow s_2 \rightarrow s_1 \rightarrow s_3 \ldots$ for action a_1, and $s_1 \rightarrow s_2 \rightarrow s_3 \rightarrow s_1 \ldots$ for action a_2. Although the optimal behaviors are opposite (SHORT: a_1, LONG: a_2), the expected cumulative reward during one cycle of the optimal behavior is 60 yen in both the SHORT ($+20 \times 3$) and LONG ($-20 - 20 + 100$) conditions

at state s_3 by taking action a_2 at each state. There were two control conditions: NO condition, where the reward was always zero, and RANDOM condition, where the reward was positive ($+r_1$) or negative ($-r_1$) with equal probability regardless of state and action.

Subjects performed four trials in a NO condition block, 15 trials in a SHORT condition block, four trials in a RANDOM condition block, and 15 trials in a LONG condition block. A set of four condition blocks (NO, SHORT, RANDOM, LONG) was repeated four times (see Fig. 22.2a). Subjects are informed of the current condition at the beginning of each condition block by a text on the screen, for example, "SHORT condition" ("instruction step", first slide in Fig. 22.1a); thus, the entire experiment consisted of 168 steps (152 trial steps and 16 instruction steps), taking about 17 min. The mappings of the three states to the three figures and the two buttons to the two actions are randomly set at the beginning of each experiment,

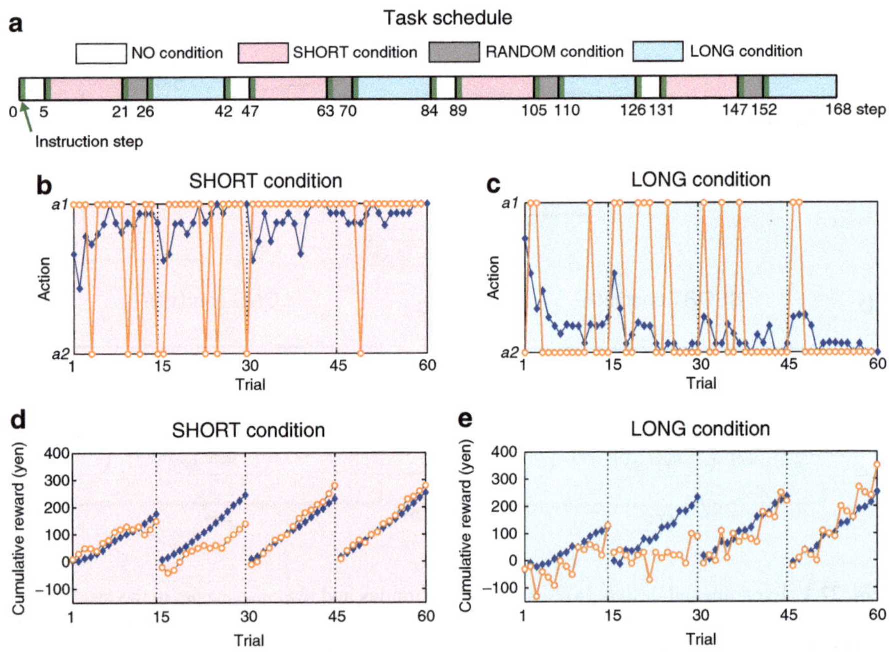

Fig. 22.2 Task schedule and behavioral results. (**a**) A set of four condition blocks, NO (four trials), SHORT (15 trials), RANDOM (four trials), and LONG (15 trials), is repeated four times. At the beginning of each condition block, the task condition is presented to the subject (instruction step); thus, the entire experiment consisted of 168 steps (152 trial steps and 16 instruction steps). (**b** and **c**) The selected action of a representative single subject (*orange*) and the group average ratio of selecting a_1 (*blue*) in the (**b**) SHORT and (**c**) LONG conditions. (**d** and **e**) The accumulated reward in each block of a representative single subject (*orange*) and the group average (*blue*) in the (**d**) SHORT and (**e**) LONG conditions. To clearly show the learning effects, data from four trial blocks in the SHORT and LONG conditions are concatenated, with the dotted lines indicating the end of each condition block

so that subjects must learn the amount of rewards associated with each figure-button pair in both SHORT and LONG conditions. Furthermore, in the LONG condition, subjects have to learn the subsequent figure for each figure-action pair and take into account the amount of reward expected from the subsequent figure in selecting a button.

2.3 *fMRI Imaging*

A 1.5-Tesla scanner (Shimadzu-Marconi, MAGNEX ECLIPSE, Japan) was used to acquire both structural T1-weighted images (TR = 12 ms, TE = 4.5 ms, flip angle = 20 deg, matrix = 256 × 256, FoV = 256 mm, thickness = 1 mm, slice gap = 0 mm) and T2*-weighted echo planar images (TR = 6 s, TE = 55 ms, flip angle = 90 deg, 50 transverse slices, matrix = 64 × 64, FoV = 192 mm, thickness = 3 mm, slice gap = 0 mm) with blood oxygen level-dependent (BOLD) contrast.

Because the aim of the present study was to specify brain activities for reward prediction over multiple trial steps, we acquired functional images every 6 s (TR = 6 s) in synchronization with single trial. Although shorter TR and event-related paradigm are often used in experiments that aim to distinguish brain activities for events within a trial, such as conditioned stimuli, action and reward (Breiter et al. 2001; Knutson et al. 2001, 2003; O'Doherty et al. 2003b), analysis of those finer events in time were not the focus of the current study. With this longer TR, the BOLD signal in a single scan contained a mixture of responses for a reward predictive stimulus and reward feedback. However, because of the progress of learning and the stochasticity of the amount of reward, the time courses of reward prediction $V(t)$ and prediction error $\delta(t)$ over the 168 trial steps were significantly different with each other. Thus, we could separate activities for reward prediction and outcomes by using both reward prediction $V(t)$ and reward outcome $r(t)$ in multiple regression analysis as described below.

2.4 *Data Analysis*

The data were pre-processed and analyzed with SPM99 (Friston et al. 1995; Wellcome Department of Cognitive Neurology, London, UK). The first two volumes of images were discarded to avoid T1 equilibrium effects. The images were realigned to the first image as a reference, spatially normalized with respect to the Montreal Neurological Institute EPI template, and spatially smoothed with a Gaussian kernel (8 mm, full-width at half-maximum).

We conducted two types of analysis. One was block-design analysis using four boxcar regressors covering the whole experiment convolved with a hemodynamic response function as the reference waveform for each condition (NO, SHORT, RANDOM, and LONG). We did not find substantial differences between SHORT vs. NO and SHORT vs. RANDOM contrasts, or between LONG vs. NO and LONG vs. RANDOM contrasts. Thus, we report here only the results with the NO condition as the control condition. The other method was multivariate regression analysis using explanatory variables, representing the time course of the reward prediction $V(t)$ or reward prediction error $\delta(t)$ at six different timescales γ, estimated from subjects' performance data (described below).

In both analyses, images of parameter estimates for the contrast of interest were created for each subject. These were then entered into a second-level group analysis using a one-sample t-test at a threshold of $P < 0.001$, uncorrected for multiple comparisons (random effects analysis) and extent threshold of 4 voxels. Small-volume correction (SVC) was done at a threshold of $P < 0.05$, using an ROI within the striatum (including the caudate and putamen), which was defined anatomically based on a normalized T1 image.

2.5 *Procedures of Performance-Based Regression Analysis*

The time course of reward prediction $V(t)$ and reward prediction error $\delta(t)$ were estimated from each subject's performance data, i.e. state $s(t)$, action $a(t)$, and reward $r(t)$, as follows.

(1) **Reward prediction:** To estimate how much of a forthcoming reward a subject would have expected at each step during the Markov decision task, we took the definition of the value function (1) and reformulated it based on the recursive structure of the task. Namely, if the subject starts from a state s(t) and comes back to the same state after k steps, the expected cumulative reward V(t) should satisfy the consistency condition

$$V(t) = r(t+1) + \gamma r(t+2) + \cdots + \gamma^{k-1} r(t+k) + \gamma^k V(t).$$

Thus, for each time t of the data file, we calculated the weighted sum of the rewards acquired until the subject returned to the same state and estimated the value function for that episode as

$$\widehat{V}(t) = \frac{\left[r(t+1) + \gamma r(t+2) + \cdots + \gamma^{k-1} r(t+k)\right]}{1-\gamma^k}.$$

The estimate of the value function $V(t)$ at time t was given by the average of all previous episodes from the same state as at time t

$$V(t) = \frac{1}{L}\sum_{l=1}^{L} \widehat{V}(t_l),$$

where $\{t_1, \ldots, t_L\}$ are the indices of time visiting the same state as $s(t)$, i.e. $s(t_1) = \ldots = s(t_L) = s(t)$.

(2) **Reward prediction error:** the TD error (2) was calculated from the difference between the actual reward $r(t)$ and the temporal difference of the estimated value function $V(t)$.

We separately calculated the time courses of $V(t)$ and $\delta(t)$ during SHORT and LONG conditions; we concatenated data of four blocks in the SHORT condition, and calculated $V(t)$ and $\delta(t)$ as described above. We used the same process for the LONG condition data. During the NO and RANDOM conditions, the values of $V(t)$ and $\delta(t)$ were fixed to zero. Finally, we reconstructed the data corresponding to the real time course of experiment. We used one of these, $V(t)$ and $\delta(t)$, as the explanatory variable in a regression analysis by SPM. To remove any effects of factors other than reward prediction, concurrently we used possibly relevant explanatory variables, namely the four box-car functions representing each condition (NO, SHORT, RANDOM, and LONG). Because the immediate reward prediction $V(t)$ with $\gamma = 0$ and reward outcome $r(t)$ can coincide if learning is perfect, we included the reward outcome $r(t)$ in regression analysis with $V(t)$. Thus, the significant correlation with $V(t)$ (Fig. 22.6a, b) should represent a predictive component rather than a reward outcome.

The amplitude of explanatory variables $\delta(t)$ with all γ were large in early trials and decreased as subjects learned the task. This decreasing trend causes a risk that areas that are activated early in trials, e. g. those responsible for general attentiveness or novelty, have correlations with $\delta(t)$. Because our aim in regression analysis was to clarify the brain structures for reward prediction at specific time scales, we removed the areas that had similar correlation to $\delta(t)$ at all settings of γ from considerations in Fig. 22.6 and Table 22.3.

To compare the results of regression analysis with six different values of γ, we used display software that can overlay multiple activation maps in different colors on a single brain structure image. When a voxel is significantly activated in multiple values of γ, it is shown by a mosaic of multiple colors, with apparent subdivision of the voxel (Fig. 22.6).

3 Results

3.1 Behavioral Results

In the Markov decision task (Fig. 22.1; see Methods for details), one of three states is visually presented to the subject using three different figures, and the subject selects one of two actions by pressing the right or left button (Fig. 22.1a). For each state, the subject's action affects not only the reward given immediately but also the state subsequently presented (Fig. 22.1b, c).

While the rule of state transition is fixed during the entire experiment, the rules of reward delivery are changed according to task conditions. In the SHORT condition, action a_1 gives a small positive reward $+r_1$ (20 yen average) and action a_2 gives a small loss $-r_1$ at all three states (Fig. 22.1b). The optimal behavior for maximizing the total outcomes is to collect small positive rewards by taking action a_1 at each state. In the LONG condition, while action a_2 at state s_3 gives a big bonus $+r_2$ (100 yen average), action a_1 at state s_1 results in a big loss $-r_2$ (Fig. 22.1c). The optimal behavior is to receive small losses at state s_1 and s_2 to obtain a large positive reward at state s_3 by taking action a_2 at each state, opposite to the optimal behavior in the SHORT condition; this behavior produces a net positive outcome during one cycle. Thus in the LONG condition, the subject has to select an action by taking into account both the immediate reward and the future reward expected from the subsequent state, while the subjects need to consider only the immediate outcome in the SHORT condition. Subjects performed 15 trials in a SHORT condition block and 15 trials in a LONG condition block; four condition blocks were performed (see Methods for Behavioral task and Fig. 22.2a for Task schedule).

All subjects successfully learned the optimal behaviors: taking action a_1 in the SHORT condition (Fig. 22.2b) and action a_2 in the LONG condition (Fig. 22.2c). Cumulative rewards within each 15 trials in the SHORT (Fig. 22.2d) and LONG (Fig. 22.2e) conditions also indicate successful learning. It can be seen from the single subject data in the LONG condition (Fig. 22.2e, orange) that the subject learned to lose small amounts ($-r_1$) twice to get a big bonus ($+r_2$). The average cumulative reward in the last block was 254 yen in the SHORT condition and 257 yen in the LONG condition, which was 84.7 % and 85.7 %, respectively, of the theoretical optimum of 300 yen.

3.2 Block-Design Analysis

First, in order to find the brain areas that are involved in immediate reward prediction, we compared brain activity during the SHORT condition and the NO condition, in which reward was always zero. In the SHORT vs. NO contrast, a significant increase in activity was observed in the lateral OFC (Fig. 22.3a), the insula and the occipitotemporal area (OTA) (Fig. 22.3b), as well as in the striatum, the globus pallidus (GP) (Fig. 22.3c) and the medial cerebellum (Fig. 22.3d) (threshold of $P < 0.001$, uncorrected for multiple comparisons). These areas may be involved in reward prediction that only takes into account an immediate outcome. In the LONG condition, subjects need to predict both immediate and future rewards for optimal actions. Thus, in order to reveal the areas that are specific to future reward prediction, we compared the brain activity during LONG and SHORT conditions. In the LONG vs. SHORT contrast, a robust increase in activity was observed in the ventrolateral prefrontal cortex (VLPFC), the insula, the dorsolateral prefrontal

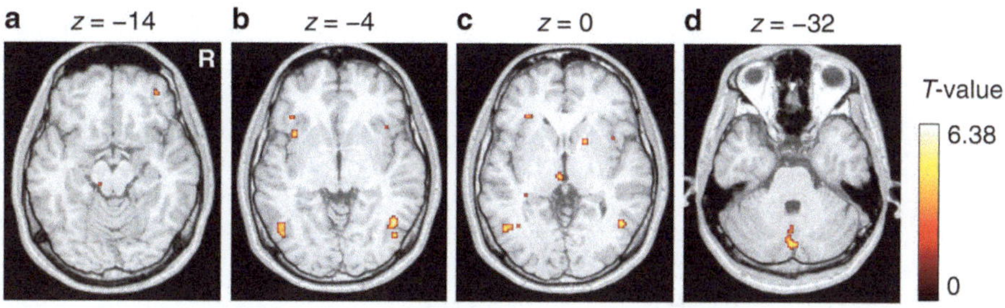

Fig. 22.3 Brain areas activated in the SHORT vs. NO contrast ($p < 0.001$, uncorrected; extent threshold of 4 voxels). (**a**) Lateral OFC. (**b**) Insula. (**c**) Striatum. (**d**) Medial cerebellum

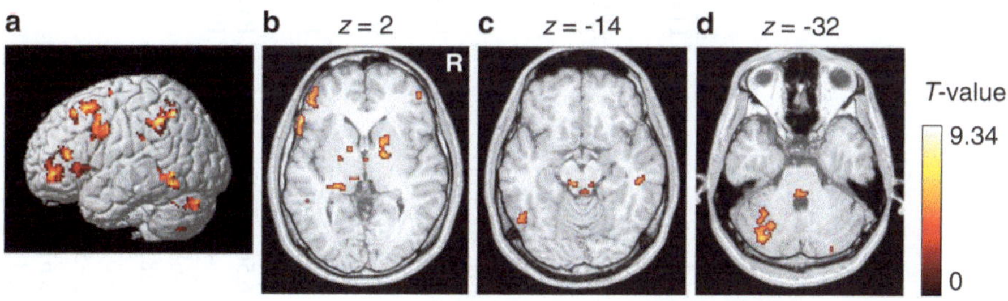

Fig. 22.4 Brain areas activated in the LONG vs. SHORT contrast ($p < 0.0001$, uncorrected; extent threshold of 4 voxels for illustration purposes). (**a**) DLPFC, IPC, PMd. (**b**) GP, striatum. (**c**) Dorsal raphe nucleus. (**d**) Left lateral cerebellum

cortex (DLPFC), the dorsal premotor cortex (PMd), the inferior parietal cortex (IPC) (Fig. 22.4a), the striatum, GP (Fig. 22.4b), the dorsal raphe nucleus (Fig. 22.4c), the lateral cerebellum (Fig. 22.4d), the posterior cingulate cortex, and the subthalamic nucleus ($P < 0.001$, uncorrected). Especially, activations in the striatum were highly significant (threshold at $P < 0.05$, corrected for a small volume when using the region of interest of the striatum anatomically defined). These areas are specifically involved in decision making based on the prediction of reward in multiple steps in the future. In the LONG vs. NO contrast, the activated areas were approximately the union of the areas activated in the SHORT vs. NO and LONG vs. SHORT contrasts. These results were consistent with our expectation that both immediate and future reward prediction were required in the LONG condition. The results of block-design analysis, including the LONG vs. NO contrast, are summarized in the Table 22.1. Activities in both SHORT and LONG conditions were stronger in the first two blocks, when subjects were involved in active trial and error, than in the last two blocks when the subjects' behaviors became repetitive.

We compared the activities in the SHORT vs. NO contrast and the LONG vs. SHORT contrast in three regions (Fig. 22.5); namely the lateral prefrontal cortex (lateral OFC and VLPFC), the insula, and the anterior striatum, where significant activities were found in both contrasts. In the lateral PFC (Fig. 22.5a), although the

Table 22.1 Areas significantly activated in the block-design analysis

	SHORT vs. NO		LONG vs. NO		LONG vs. SHORT	
	Area (BA)	T-value (Tal x, y, z)	Area (BA)	T-value (Tal x, y, z)	Area (BA)	T-value (Tal x, y, z)
Cerebral cortex	lOFC (11)	3.98 (38, 46, −14)	lOFC (11)	5.86 (−46, 50, −8)	VLPFC (10)	6.71 (−48, 43, −2)
	Insula (13)	4.43 (−36, 13, −4)		5.69 (42, 46, −11)		6.06 (46, 47, 3)
	OTA (37)	5.15 (−48, −62, 1)	DLPFC (46)	5.92 (−42, 35, 9)	DLPFC (46)	5.77 (−40, 35, 9)
		6.32 (46, −68, −3)	Insula (13)	4.99 (−34, 19, −8)	Insula (13)	4.93 (−30, 18, 1)
			mPFC (9)	7.54* (4, 40, 26)	PCC (23)	6.36 (−10, −26, 29)
			PMd (6)	6.56 (−40, 5, 27)	PMd (6) IPC (40)	6.75 (−42, 2, 31)
				6.68 (38, 3, 24)		6.79 (−49, −43, 41)
			IPC (40)	6.07 (−55, −21, 40)		6.06 (48, −41, 35)
				6.61 (51, −31, 40)		

Basal ganglia	Putamen	4.54 (18, 10, 0)	Putamen	7.72* (14, 10, 0)	Putamen	5.87† (18, 12, 3)
	Medial GP	3.96 (−16, −10, −8)	Caudate head	7.89* (−4, 4, −2)		5.99† (−12, 0, 4)
			Lateral GP	7.69* (−20, −8, 0)	Lateral GP	6.38† (−20, −8, 0)
					STN	5.13 (−8, −12, −4)
Brainstem					Dorsal raphe	5.27 (4, −35, −10)
Cerebellum	Vermis	4.98 (0, −75, −23)	Vermis	6.3 (0, −60, −26)		
			Hemisphere	6.94 (−34, −69, −20)	Hemisphere	8.05* (14, −52, −39)
						7.49* (−28, −62, −31)

All other regions are $p < 0.001$, uncorrected for the whole brain
Extent threshold of 4 voxels
The numbers in parentheses show the Brodmann area (BA)
Abbreviations: *Tal* Talairach coordinates, *lOFC* lateral orbitofrontal cortex, *OTA* occipitotemporal area, *PCC* posterior cingulate cortex, *STN* subthalamic nucleus, *VLPFC* ventrolateral prefrontal cortex
*$p < 0.05$, corrected for the whole brain
†$p < 0.05$, corrected for a small volume restricted to the striatum

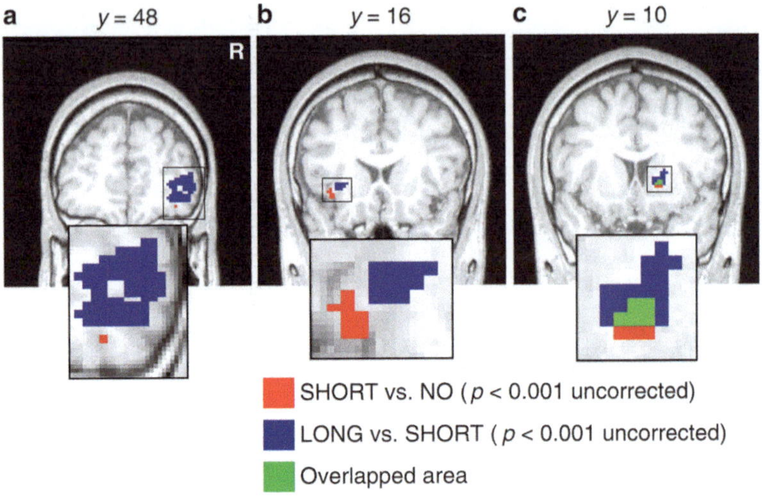

Fig. 22.5 Comparison of brain areas activated in the SHORT vs. NO contrast (*red*) and the LONG vs. SHORT contrast (*blue*). These figures show activation maps focused on (**a**) the lateral OFC (*red*: (x, y, z) = (38, 46, −14), *blue*: (46, 47, 3)), (**b**) the insula (*red*: (−36, 13, −4), *blue*: (−30, 18, 1)), and (**c**) the striatum (*red*: (18, 10, 0), *blue*: (18, 12, 3)) where we observed significant activation in both contrast. The overlapped area is indicated in *green*

activities in lateral OFC for the SHORT vs. NO contrast (red) and in the VLPFC for the LONG vs. SHORT contrast (blue) were close in location, they were clearly apart on the cortical surface. Activities in the insula were also separated (Fig. 22.5b). In the anterior striatum (Fig. 22.5c), we found limited overlaps between the two contrasts (green). In all three areas, activities in the SHORT vs. NO contrast were found in the ventral parts, while activities in the LONG vs. SHORT contrast were found in the dorsal parts.

These results of block-design analysis suggest differential involvement of brain areas in predicting immediate and future rewards.

3.3 Performance-Based Multiple Regression Analysis

In order to further clarify the brain structures specific to reward prediction at different time scales, we estimated how much reward the subjects should have predicted on the basis of their performance data and used their time courses as the explanatory variables of regression analysis. We took the theoretical framework of temporal difference (TD) learning (Sutton and Barto 1998), which has been successfully used for explaining reward-predictive activities of the midbrain dopaminergic system as well as those of the cortex and the striatum (Berns et al. 2001; Doya 2000; Houk et al. 1995; McClure et al. 2003; O'Doherty et al. 2003b; Schultz et al. 1997). In TD learning theory, the predicted amount of future reward starting from a state *s(t)* is formulated as the "value function"

$$V(t) = E\left[r(t+1) + \gamma r(t+2) + \gamma^2 r(t+3) + \cdots\right]. \tag{22.1}$$

Any deviation from the prediction is given by the TD error

$$\delta(t) = r(t) + \gamma V(t) - V(t-1), \tag{22.2}$$

which is a crucial learning signal for reward prediction and action selection. The "discount factor" γ ($0 \leq \gamma < 1$) controls the time scale of prediction; while only the immediate reward $r(t+1)$ is considered with $\gamma = 0$, rewards in the longer future are taken into account with γ closer to 1.

We estimated the time courses of reward prediction $V(t)$ and prediction error $\delta(t)$ from each subject's performance data and used them as the explanatory variables in multiple regression analysis with fMRI data (see Methods). In our Markov decision task, the minimum value of γ needed to find the optimal action in the LONG condition is 0.36, while any small value of γ is sufficient in the SHORT condition. From the results of block-design analysis, we assumed that different cortico-basal ganglia network are specialized for reward prediction at different time scales and that they work in parallel, depending on the requirement of the task. Thus, we varied the discount factor γ as 0, 0.3, 0.6, 0.8, 0.9, and 0.99: small γ for immediate reward prediction and large γ for long future reward prediction.

We observed a significant correlation with reward prediction $V(t)$ in the medial prefrontal cortex (mPFC: including the anterior cingulate cortex (ACC) and the medial OFC) (Fig. 22.6a) and bilateral insula (Fig. 22.6b), left hippocampus, and left temporal pole ($P < 0.001$, uncorrected; see Table 22.2). These figures show the correlated voxels within these areas using a gradient of colors for different discount factor γ (red for $\gamma = 0$, blue for $\gamma = 0.99$). The activities of the mPFC, temporal pole, and hippocampus correlated with reward prediction with a longer time scale ($\gamma \geq 0.6$). Furthermore, in the insula, we found a graded map of activities for reward prediction at different time scales (Fig. 22.6b). While the activity in the ventroanterior part correlated with reward prediction at a shorter time scale, the activity in the dorsoposterior part correlated with reward prediction at a longer time scale.

The red and blue lines in Fig. 22.6b, c show the vertical positions of activity peaks in the SHORT vs. NO and LONG vs. SHORT contrasts, respectively, in the insula and the striatum (Fig. 22.5b, c). The coincidence of the ventroanterior-dorsoposterior maps and the ventroanterior-dorsoposterior shifts in activities indi-

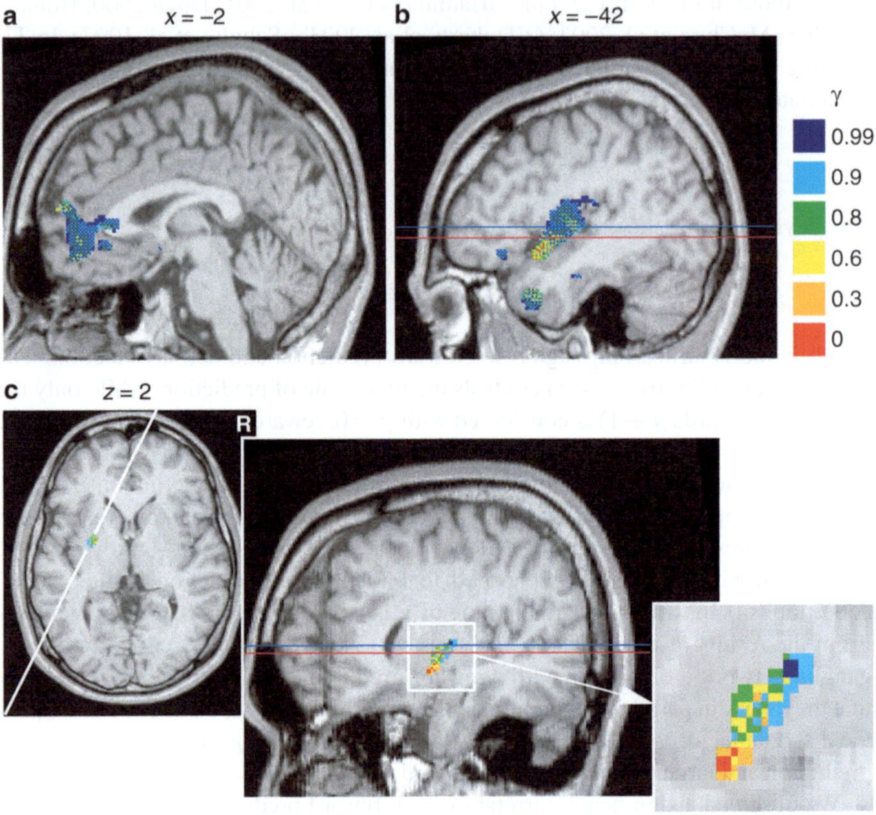

Fig. 22.6 Voxels with a significant correlation (height threshold of $p < 0.001$, uncorrected; extent threshold of 4 voxels) with reward prediction $V(t)$ and prediction error $\delta(t)$ are shown in different colors for different settings of the discount factor. Voxels correlated with two or more regressors are shown by a mosaic of colors. (**a** and **b**) Significant correlation with reward prediction $V(t)$. (**a**) mPFC. (**b**) Insula. (**c**) Significant correlation with reward prediction error $\delta(t)$ restricted to region of interest of the striatum (slice at *white line* in horizontal slice at $z = 2$ mm). Note the ventroanterior to dorsoposterior gradient with the increase in γ both in the insula and the striatum. Red and blue lines correspond to the z-coordinate levels of activation peaks in the insula and striatum shown in Fig. 22.5b, c (*red* for the SHORT vs. NO and *blue* for the LONG vs. SHORT contrasts)

cate that, while the ventroanterior parts with smaller γ were predominantly active in the SHORT condition, the dorsoposterior parts with larger γ became more active in the LONG condition.

We also found significant correlation with reward prediction error $\delta(t)$ with a wide range of time scale in the basal ganglia (Fig. 22.6c) ($P < 0.001$, uncorrected; see Table 22.3 and Methods). Again, we found a graded map, which had a short time scale in the ventroanterior part and a long time scale in the dorsoposterior part.

Table 22.2 Areas with significant correlation with reward prediction $V(t)$ estimated with different discount factors γ

	$\gamma = 0$	$\gamma = 0.3$	$\gamma = 0.6$	$\gamma = 0.8$	$\gamma = 0.9$	$\gamma = 0.99$
Area (BA)	T-value (Tal x, y, z)	T-value (Tal x, y, z)	T-value (Tal x, y, z)	T-value (Tal x, y, z)	T-value (Tal x, y, z)	T-value Tal (x, y, z)
Insula cortex (13)	4.02 (−42,7,–9)	4.84 (−42,7,–10)	6.06 (−42,4,–7)	7.04 (−42,–10,4)	7.84* (−42,–10,4)	7.82* (−42,–10,4)
		4.24 (44,–4,–5)	5.5 (42,–4,–3)	6.53 (42,–2,–3)	6.74 (42,–2,–3)	6.73 (40,–4,–1)
mPFC/ACC (11/9/32/24)			4.45 (−2,46,–16)	6.3 (−6,44,–6)	7.41 (−4,44,–6)	7.79* (−4,44,–6)
Hippocampus			3.66 (−30,–18,–14)	4.57 (−30,–20,–16)	4.79 (−30,–20,–16)	4.84 (−30,–20,–16)
Temporal pole (38)			5.01 (−44,10,–31)	5.42 (−44,10,–31)	5.26 (−44,10,–32)	5.01 (−44,10,–32)

All other regions are $p < 0.001$, uncorrected for the whole brain
Extent threshold of 4 voxels
$*p < 0.05$, corrected for the whole brain

Table 22.3 Voxels with significant correlation with reward prediction error $\delta(t)$ estimated with different discount factors γ

	$\gamma = 0$	$\gamma = 0.3$	$\gamma = 0.6$	$\gamma = 0.8$	$\gamma = 0.9$	$\gamma = 0.99$
	T-value (Tal x, y, z)	T-value (Tal x, y, z)	T-value (Tal x, y, z)	T-value (Tal x, y, z)	T-value (Tal x, y, z)	T-value (Tal x, y, z)
Putamen	4.55 (−24, 4, −7)	4.58 (−26, 5, −9)	4.44 (−26, 2, −2)	4.66 (−26, 2, −2)	5.23 (−28, −6, 6)	4.15 (−28, −6, 6)

All areas are $p < 0.001$, uncorrected for the whole brain
Extent threshold of 4 voxels

4 Discussion

The results of the block-design and performance-based regression analyses suggest differential involvement of brain areas in action learning by prediction of rewards at different time scales. Both block-design and performance-based regression analyses found activities in the insula and the anterior striatum. Activations of the ventral part in the SHORT vs. NO contrast and the dorsal part in the LONG vs. SHORT contrast in each area (Fig. 22.5) are consistent with the ventroanterior-dorsoposterior maps of the discount factor γ found in performance-based regression analysis (Fig. 22.6).

The insula takes a pivotal position in reward processing by receiving primary taste and visceral sensory input (Mesulam and Mufson 1982) and sending output to the OFC (Cavada et al. 2000) and the striatum (Chikama et al. 1997). Previous studies showed that the insula is activated with anticipation of primary reward (O'Doherty et al. 2002) and that insular lesion causes deficits in incentive learning for primary reward (Balleine and Dickinson 2000). Our results confirm the role of the insula in prediction of non-primary, monetary reward (Knutson et al. 2003), and further suggest heterogeneous organization within the insula. Previous imaging studies also showed involvement of the insula, especially ventroanterior part, in processing of aversive outcomes (O'Doherty et al. 2003a; Ullsperger and von Cramon 2003). Thus a possible interpretation of the activation of the insula in LONG condition is that it was due to the losses that subjects acquired before getting a large reward. However, we also ran a regression analysis using losses and found significant correlation in ventroanterior part of insula. Anatomical and physiological studies of insula also showed involvement of its ventroanterior part in perception of aversive stimuli (Mesulam and Mufson 1982). Thus we argue that the activation of dorsoposterior insula is not simply due to losses in LONG condition.

Previous brain imaging and neural recording studies suggest a role for the striatum in prediction and processing of reward (Breiter et al. 2001; Elliott et al. 2000, 2003; Haruno et al. 2004; Knutson et al. 2001, 2003; Koepp et al. 1998; O'Doherty et al. 2002; Pagnoni et al. 2002; Schultz et al. 1997). Consistent with previous fMRI studies (Berns et al. 2001; McClure et al. 2003; O'Doherty et al. 2003b), our results showed striatal activities correlated with the error of reward prediction. The reinforcement learning models of the basal ganglia (Doya 2000; Houk et al. 1995; Schultz et al. 1997) posit that the striatum learns reward prediction and action selection based on the reward prediction error $\delta(t)$ represented by the dopaminergic input. Correlation of the striatal activity with reward prediction error $\delta(t)$ could be due to dopamine-dependent plasticity of cortico-striatal synapses (Reynolds and Wickens 2002).

In lateral OFC, DLPFC, PMd, IPC, and dorsal raphe, we found significant activities in the block-design analyses, but there was not strong correlation in regression analyses. This may be because these areas perform functions that are helpful for reward prediction and action selection, but their activities do not directly represent the amount of predicted reward or prediction error at a specific time scale.

In reinforcement learning theory, an optimal action selection is realized by taking the action a that maximizes the 'action value' $Q(s, a)$ at a given state s. The action value is defined as

$$Q(s,a) = E\left[r(s,a) + \gamma V\left(s'(s,a)\right)\right] \tag{22.3}$$

and represents the expected sum of the immediate reward $r(s, a)$ and the weighted future rewards $V(s'(s, a))$, where $s'(s, a)$ means the next state reached by taking an action a at a state s (Doya 2000; Sutton and Barto 1998). According to this framework, we can see that prediction of immediate reward $r(s, a)$ is helpful for action selection based on rewards at either short or long time scales, i.e. with any value of discount factor γ. On the other hand, prediction of state transition $s'(s, a)$ is helpful only in long-term reward prediction with positive γ.

In the lateral OFC, we observed significant activity in both the SHORT vs. NO and the LONG vs. NO contrasts (Table 22.1), but no significant correlation with reward prediction $V(t)$ or reward prediction error $\delta(t)$ in regression analysis. This suggests that the lateral OFC takes the role of predicting immediate reward $r(s, a)$, which is used for action selection in both SHORT and LONG conditions, but not in the NO condition. This interpretation is consistent with previous studies demonstrating the OFC's role in prediction of rewards, immediately following sensorimotor events (Critchley et al. 2001; Tremblay and Schultz 2000), and action selection based on reward prediction (Critchley et al. 2001; O'Doherty et al. 2003a; Rolls 2000).

In the DLPFC, PMd, and IPC, there were significant activities in both the LONG vs. NO and the LONG vs. SHORT contrasts (Table 22.1) but no significant correlation with either $V(t)$ or $\delta(t)$. A possible interpretation is that this area is involved in prediction of future state $s'(s, a)$ in the LONG condition but not in the SHORT or NO conditions. This interpretation is consistent with previous studies showing the role of these cortical areas in imagery (Hanakawa et al. 2002), working memory and planning (Baker et al. 1996; Owen et al. 1996).

The dorsal raphe nucleus was activated in the LONG vs. SHORT contrast, but not correlated with $V(t)$ or $\delta(t)$. In consideration of its serotonergic projection to the cortex and the striatum and serotonin's implication with behavioral impulsivity (Evenden and Ryan 1996; Mobini et al. 2000; Rogers et al. 1999a), a possible role for the dorsal raphe nucleus is to control the effective time scale of reward prediction (Doya 2002). Its higher activity in the LONG condition, where a large setting of γ is necessary, is consistent with this hypothesis.

Let us consider the present experimental results in light of the anatomy of cortico-basal ganglia loops, as illustrated in Fig. 22.7. The cortex and the basal ganglia both have parallel loop organization, with four major loops (limbic, cognitive, motor, and oculomotor) and finer, topographic sub-loops within each major loop (Middleton and Strick 2000). Our results suggest that the areas within the limbic loop (Haber et al. 1995), namely the lateral OFC and ventral striatum, shown on the left side of Fig. 22.7, are involved in immediate reward prediction. On the other hand, areas within the cognitive and motor loops (Middleton and Strick 2000), including the DLPFC, IPC, PMd, and dorsal striatum, shown on the right side of Fig. 22.7, are involved in activated in future reward prediction. The connections from the insula to the striatum are topographically organized, with the ventral/anterior, agranular cortex projecting to the ventral striatum and the dorsal/posterior, granular cortex projecting to the dorsal striatum (Chikama et al. 1997) (rainbow-colored arrow shown in Fig. 22.7). The graded maps shown in Fig. 22.6b, c are consistent with this topographic cortico-striatal organization and suggest that areas that project to the more dorsoposterior part of the striatum are involved in reward prediction at a longer time scale. These results are consistent with the observations that localized damages within the limbic and cognitive loops manifest as deficits in evaluation of future rewards (Bechara et al. 2000; Cardinal et al. 2001; Eagle et al. 1999; Pears et al. 2003; Rolls 2000) and learning of multi-step behaviours (Hikosaka et al. 1999). The parallel learning mechanisms in the cortico-basal ganglia loops used for reward prediction at a variety of time scales may have the merit of enabling flexible selection of a relevant time scale appropriate for the task and the environment at the time of decision making.

A possible mechanism for selection or weighting of different cortico-basal ganglia loops with an appropriate time scale is serotonergic projection from the dorsal raphe nucleus (Doya 2002) (green arrows shown on the Fig. 22.7), which was activated in the LONG vs. SHORT contrast. Although serotonergic projection is supposed to be diffuse and global, differential expression of serotonergic receptors in the cortical areas and in the ventral and dorsal striatum (Compan et al. 1998; Mijnster et al. 1997) would result in differential modulation. The mPFC, which had significant correlation with reward prediction $V(t)$ at long time scales ($\gamma \geq 0.6$), may regulate the activity of the raphe nucleus through reciprocal connection (Celada et al. 2001; Martin-Ruiz et al. 2001). This interpretation is consistent with previous studies using experimental tasks that require long-range prospects for problem solving, such as the gambling problem (Bechara et al. 2000) or delayed reward task (Mobini et al. 2002), that showed involvement of the medial OFC. Future studies using the Markov decision task under pharmacological manipulation of the serotonergic system should clarify the role of serotonin in regulating the time scale of reward prediction.

Recent brain imaging and neural recording studies reported involvement of a variety of cortical areas and the striatum in reward processing

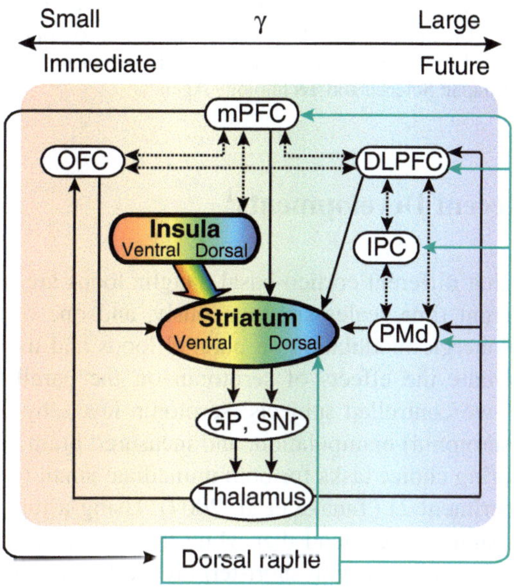

Fig. 22.7 A schematic diagram of the brain areas involved in reward prediction at different time scales. The *doted lines* indicate a cortico-cortico connection, and the *green arrows* indicate the serotonergic pathways from the dorsal raphe. The 'limbic loop' (including lateral OFC and ventral striatum) is involved in short-term reward prediction. The 'cognitive and motor loops' (including DLPFC, PMd, and dorsal striatum) are involved in long-term reward prediction. Ventroanterior-to-dorsoposterior topographical projections from the insula to the striatum are involved in short-to-long term reward prediction (*rainbow-colored arrow*). The mPFC and dorsal raphe, which are reciprocally connected, may regulate these loops by cortico-cortical and cortico-striatal projections from mPFC and serotonergic projections from dorsal raphe. *SNr* substantia nigra pars reticulate

(Berns et al. 2001; Breiter et al. 2001; Critchley et al. 2001; Elliott et al. 2000, 2003; Haruno et al. 2004; Hikosaka and Watanabe 2000; Knutson et al. 2001, 2003; Koepp et al. 1998; Matsumoto et al. 2003; McClure et al. 2003; O'Doherty et al. 2002, 2003a, b; Pagnoni et al. 2002; Rogers et al. 1999b; Shidara and Richmond 2002). Although some neural recording studies have used experimental tasks that require multiple trial steps for getting rewards (Hikosaka and Watanabe 2000; Shidara and Richmond 2002), none of the previous functional brain imaging studies addressed the issue of reward prediction at different time scales, and considered only rewards immediately following stimuli or actions. We could extract specific functions of OFC, DLPFC, mPFC, insula and cortico-basal ganglia loops by developing a novel Markov decision task and a reinforcement learning model-based regression analysis method. Our regression analysis not only extracted brain activities specific to reward prediction, but also revealed a novel topographic organization in reward prediction (Fig. 22.6). The combination of our Markov decision task with event-related fMRI and magnetoencephalography (MEG) should further clarify the functions used for reward prediction and perception at different time scales, and at finer spatial and temporal resolutions.

Acknowledgments We thank K. Samejima, N. Schweighofer, M. Haruno, H. Imamizu, S. Higuchi, T. Yoshioka, T. Chaminade, and M. Kawato for helpful discussions and technical advice. This research was funded by "Creating the Brain", Core Research for Evolutional Science and Technology (CREST), Japan Science and Technology Agency.

Addendum: Recent Developments[1]

We hypothesized that different cortico-basal ganglia loops are involved in reward prediction at different time scales simultaneously, and one of these time scales is chosen by serotonergic modulation on parallel loops and used in actual action selection. To elucidate the effects of serotonin on the parallel cortico-striatum loop mechanisms, we controlled subjects' serotonin levels by dietary tryptophan (the precursor of serotonin) manipulation, and measured brain activity at different serotonin levels during choice tasks for both immediate-small reward and delayed-large reward (Experiment 2) (Tanaka et al. 2007). Using a regression analysis of reward prediction signals, we found that while the activity in the ventral part of the striatum correlated strongly with short-term reward prediction at low serotonin levels, those of the dorsal part strongly correlated with long-term reward prediction at high serotonin levels. This result supports the possibility that serotonin controls the time scale of reward prediction by differentially regulating the activity within the striatum.

We found similar graded time-scale maps for reward prediction in the striatum in our previous experiment (Experiment 1) (Tanaka et al. 2004) and later experiment (Experiment 2) (Tanaka et al. 2007). In both maps, the ventral parts are correlated with reward prediction at shorter time scales, indicated by smaller γ values, whereas dorsal parts are correlated with reward prediction at longer time scales (larger γ values). Are both maps graded on the same time scale? That is, is a particular part of the graded map involved in reward prediction at a particular time scale? If so, a question arises as to whether this map is graded in theoretical time or real time. To answer these questions, we verify the graded maps in the striatum that we found in Experiments 1 and 2.

To verify the ventral-dorsal-directed gradient of both maps, we compared the spatial distribution of the maps along the z-axis. The theoretical time scale, discount factor γ, and the real time scale, decay time constant $\tau = \Delta t/(1-\gamma)$, depended on the duration of a single trial of behavioral task Δt. Figure 22.8 shows the number of voxels at each z-level that were significantly correlated with reward prediction at each time scale in γ (Fig. 22.8a) and τ (Fig. 22.8b) grading. The colored lines in Fig. 22.8 indicate the z-level of the median of each colored voxels. Figure 22.9 plots the z-level of the median against γ (Fig. 22.9a) and τ (Fig. 22.9b). For γ grading,

[1] This addendum has been newly written by Saori C. Tanaka for this book chapter (partly taken from the doctoral dissertation "Functional model of serotonin in human reward system based on reinforcement learning theory" by Saori C. Tanaka, 2006).

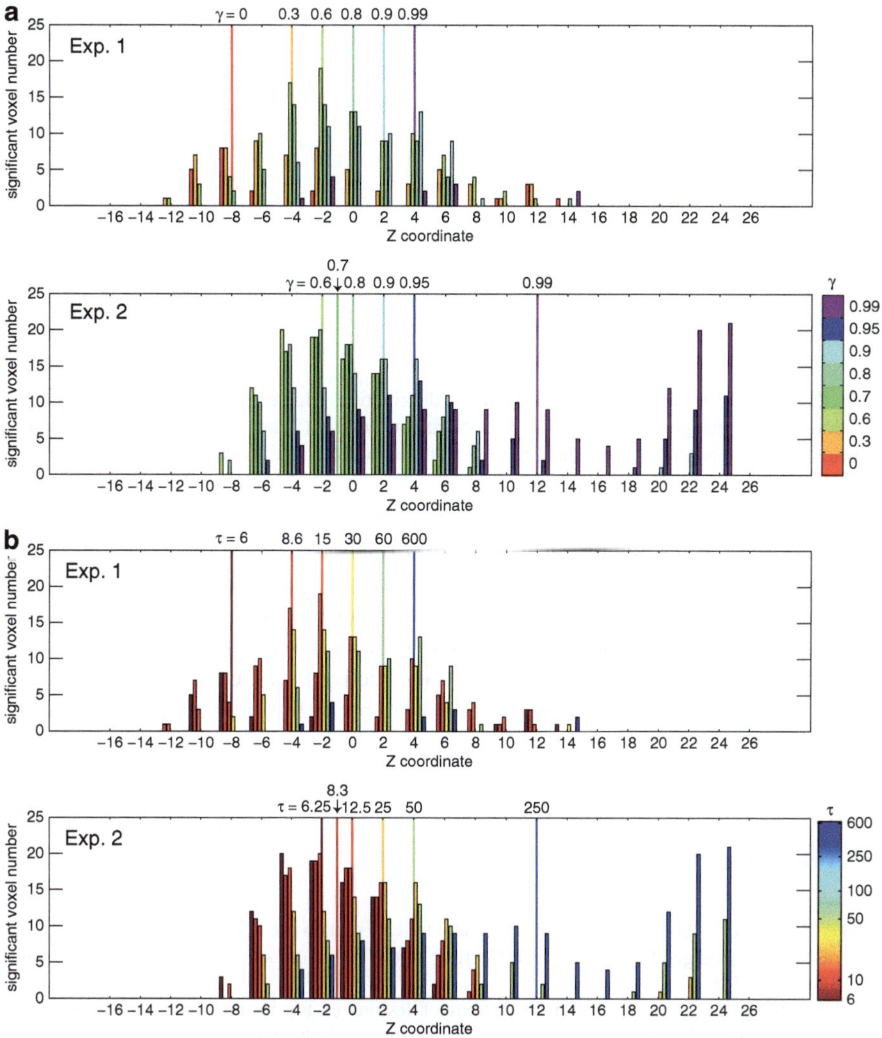

Fig. 22.8 The number of voxels at each z-level that were significantly correlated with reward prediction at each time scale in Experiment 1 and 2 in (**a**) γ-grading and (**b**) τ-grading. *Colored lines* show the median z-coordinate of voxel distribution with each time scale. Although there are gradients of time scales from ventral (low z-level) to dorsal (high z-level) both in Experiments1 and 2, we can see good consistency of time scales between Experiments 1 and 2 only in γ-grading (Note that different color scales are used in γ-grading and τ-grading)

we can see that voxels correlated at the same γ are distributed at about the same z-level, except for $\gamma = 0.99$ in Experiment 2. In contrast, for τ grading, there is no consistency in the distribution along the z-axis. This result suggests that the graded maps found in Experiments 1 and 2 are involved in reward prediction at a common "theoretical" time scale.

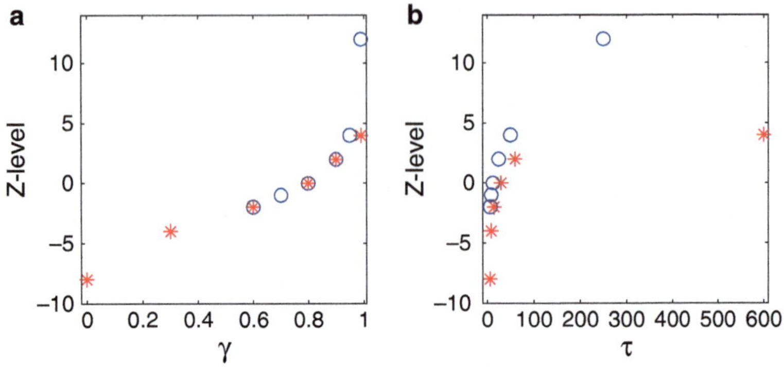

Fig. 22.9 The median z-coordinate of voxel distribution with each time scale. (**a**) In the γ-grading, we can see good fitting of data in both Experiments 1 (*) and 2 (∘) by the same function. (**b**) In the τ-grading, in contrast, this seems difficult to be explained by the same function

These results indicate that particular parts of the striatum are involved in reward prediction not at absolute time scales but at relative time scales depending on the task. In the real world, we need to solve problems with variable time scales. At some times we choose an action producing a reward after several seconds or minutes, and at other times, we make decisions that reap rewards several years later. In this case, the relative grading of a time scale may be effective because the broader region of the striatum can be engaged to compute reward prediction with a limited number of striatal neurons.

References

Baker SC, Rogers RD, Owen AM, Frith CD, Dolan RJ, Frackowiak RS, Robbins TW (1996) Neural systems engaged by planning: a PET study of the Tower of London task. Neuropsychologia 34(6):515–526

Balleine BW, Dickinson A (2000) The effect of lesions of the insular cortex on instrumental conditioning: evidence for a role in incentive memory. J Neurosci 20(23):8954–8964

Bechara A, Damasio H, Damasio AR (2000) Emotion, decision making and the orbitofrontal cortex. Cereb Cortex 10(3):295–307

Berns GS, McClure SM, Pagnoni G, Montague PR (2001) Predictability modulates human brain response to reward. J Neurosci 21(8):2793–2798

Breiter HC, Aharon I, Kahneman D, Dale A, Shizgal P (2001) Functional imaging of neural responses to expectancy and experience of monetary gains and losses. Neuron 30(2):619–639

Cardinal RN, Pennicott DR, Sugathapala CL, Robbins TW, Everitt BJ (2001) Impulsive choice induced in rats by lesions of the nucleus accumbens core. Science 292(5526):2499–2501

Cavada C, Company T, Tejedor J, Cruz-Rizzolo RJ, Reinoso-Suarez F (2000) The anatomical connections of the macaque monkey orbitofrontal cortex. A review. Cereb Cortex 10(3):220–242

Celada P, Puig MV, Casanovas JM, Guillazo G, Artigas F (2001) Control of dorsal raphe serotonergic neurons by the medial prefrontal cortex: involvement of serotonin-1A, GABA(A), and glutamate receptors. J Neurosci 21(24):9917–9929

Chikama M, McFarland NR, Amaral DG, Haber SN (1997) Insular cortical projections to functional regions of the striatum correlate with cortical cytoarchitectonic organization in the primate. J Neurosci 17(24):9686–9705

Compan V, Segu L, Buhot MC, Daszuta A (1998) Selective increases in serotonin 5-HT1B/1D and 5-HT2A/2C binding sites in adult rat basal ganglia following lesions of serotonergic neurons. Brain Res 793(1–2):103–111

Critchley HD, Mathias CJ, Dolan RJ (2001) Neural activity in the human brain relating to uncertainty and arousal during anticipation. Neuron 29(2):537–545

Doya K (2000) Complementary roles of basal ganglia and cerebellum in learning and motor control. Curr Opin Neurobiol 10(6):732–739

Doya K (2002) Metalearning and neuromodulation. Neural Netw 15(4–6):495–506

Eagle DM, Humby T, Dunnett SB, Robbins TW (1999) Effects of regional striatal lesions on motor, motivational, and executive aspects of progressive-ratio performance in rats. Behav Neurosci 113(4):718–731

Elliott R, Friston KJ, Dolan RJ (2000) Dissociable neural responses in human reward systems. J Neurosci 20(16):6159–6165

Elliott R, Newman JL, Longe OA, Deakin JF (2003) Differential response patterns in the striatum and orbitofrontal cortex to financial reward in humans: a parametric functional magnetic resonance imaging study. J Neurosci 23(1):303–307

Evenden JL, Ryan CN (1996) The pharmacology of impulsive behaviour in rats: the effects of drugs on response choice with varying delays of reinforcement. Psychopharmacology (Berl) 128(2):161–170

Friston KJ, Holmes AP, Worsley KJ, Poline JP, Frith CD, Frackowiak RSJ (1994) Statistical parametric maps in functional imaging: a general linear approach. Hum Brain Mapp 2:189–210

Haber SN, Kunishio K, Mizobuchi M, Lynd-Balta E (1995) The orbital and medial prefrontal circuit through the primate basal ganglia. J Neurosci 15(7 Pt 1):4851–4867

Hanakawa T, Honda M, Sawamoto N, Okada T, Yonekura Y, Fukuyama H, Shibasaki H (2002) The role of rostral Brodmann area 6 in mental-operation tasks: an integrative neuroimaging approach. Cereb Cortex 12(11):1157–1170

Haruno M, Kuroda T, Doya K, Toyama K, Kimura M, Samejima K, Imamizu H, Kawato M (2004) A neural correlate of reward-based behavioral learning in caudate nucleus: a functional magnetic resonance imaging study of a stochastic decision task. J Neurosci 24(7):1660–1665

Hikosaka K, Watanabe M (2000) Delay activity of orbital and lateral prefrontal neurons of the monkey varying with different rewards. Cereb Cortex 10(3):263–271

Hikosaka O, Nakahara H, Rand MK, Sakai K, Lu X, Nakamura K, Miyachi S, Doya K (1999) Parallel neural networks for learning sequential procedures. Trends Neurosci 22(10):464–471

Houk JC, Adams JL, Barto AG (1995) A model of how the basal ganglia generate and use neural signals that predict reinforcement. In: Houk JC, Davis JL, Beiser DG (eds) Models of information processing in the basal ganglia, Computational neuroscience. MIT Press, Cambridge, MA, pp 249–270

Knutson B, Adams CM, Fong GW, Hommer D (2001) Anticipation of increasing monetary reward selectively recruits nucleus accumbens. J Neurosci 21(16):RC159

Knutson B, Fong GW, Bennett SM, Adams CM, Hommer D (2003) A region of mesial prefrontal cortex tracks monetarily rewarding outcomes: characterization with rapid event-related fMRI. Neuroimage 18(2):263–272

Koepp MJ, Gunn RN, Lawrence AD, Cunningham VJ, Dagher A, Jones T, Brooks DJ, Bench CJ, Grasby PM (1998) Evidence for striatal dopamine release during a video game. Nature 393(6682):266–268

Martin-Ruiz R, Puig MV, Celada P, Shapiro DA, Roth BL, Mengod G, Artigas F (2001) Control of serotonergic function in medial prefrontal cortex by serotonin-2A receptors through a glutamate-dependent mechanism. J Neurosci 21(24):9856–9866

Matsumoto K, Suzuki W, Tanaka K (2003) Neuronal correlates of goal-based motor selection in the prefrontal cortex. Science 301(5630):229–232

McClure SM, Berns GS, Montague PR (2003) Temporal prediction errors in a passive learning task activate human striatum. Neuron 38(2):339–346

Mesulam MM, Mufson EJ (1982) Insula of the old world monkey. III: efferent cortical output and comments on function. J Comp Neurol 212(1):38–52

Middleton FA, Strick PL (2000) Basal ganglia and cerebellar loops: motor and cognitive circuits. Brain Res Brain Res Rev 31(2–3):236–250

Mijnster MJ, Raimundo AG, Koskuba K, Klop H, Docter GJ, Groenewegen HJ, Voorn P (1997) Regional and cellular distribution of serotonin 5-hydroxytryptamine2a receptor mRNA in the nucleus accumbens, olfactory tubercle, and caudate putamen of the rat. J Comp Neurol 389(1):1–11

Mobini S, Chiang TJ, Ho MY, Bradshaw CM, Szabadi E (2000) Effects of central 5-hydroxytryptamine depletion on sensitivity to delayed and probabilistic reinforcement. Psychopharmacology (Berl) 152(4):390–397

Mobini S, Body S, Ho MY, Bradshaw CM, Szabadi E, Deakin JF, Anderson IM (2002) Effects of lesions of the orbitofrontal cortex on sensitivity to delayed and probabilistic reinforcement. Psychopharmacology (Berl) 160(3):290–298

O'Doherty JP, Deichmann R, Critchley HD, Dolan RJ (2002) Neural responses during anticipation of a primary taste reward. Neuron 33(5):815–826

O'Doherty J, Critchley H, Deichmann R, Dolan RJ (2003a) Dissociating valence of outcome from behavioral control in human orbital and ventral prefrontal cortices. J Neurosci 23(21):7931–7939

O'Doherty JP, Dayan P, Friston K, Critchley H, Dolan RJ (2003b) Temporal difference models and reward-related learning in the human brain. Neuron 38(2):329–337

Owen AM, Doyon J, Petrides M, Evans AC (1996) Planning and spatial working memory: a positron emission tomography study in humans. Eur J Neurosci 8(2):353–364

Pagnoni G, Zink CF, Montague PR, Berns GS (2002) Activity in human ventral striatum locked to errors of reward prediction. Nat Neurosci 5(2):97–98

Pears A, Parkinson JA, Hopewell L, Everitt BJ, Roberts AC (2003) Lesions of the orbitofrontal but not medial prefrontal cortex disrupt conditioned reinforcement in primates. J Neurosci 23(35):11189–11201

Reynolds JN, Wickens JR (2002) Dopamine-dependent plasticity of corticostriatal synapses. Neural Netw 15(4–6):507–521

Rogers RD, Everitt BJ, Baldacchino A, Blackshaw AJ, Swainson R, Wynne K, Baker NB, Hunter J, Carthy T, Booker E, London M, Deakin JF, Sahakian BJ, Robbins TW (1999a) Dissociable deficits in the decision-making cognition of chronic amphetamine abusers, opiate abusers, patients with focal damage to prefrontal cortex, and tryptophan-depleted normal volunteers: evidence for monoaminergic mechanisms. Neuropsychopharmacology 20(4):322–339

Rogers RD, Owen AM, Middleton HC, Williams EJ, Pickard JD, Sahakian BJ, Robbins TW (1999b) Choosing between small, likely rewards and large, unlikely rewards activates inferior and orbital prefrontal cortex. J Neurosci 19(20):9029–9038

Rolls ET (2000) The orbitofrontal cortex and reward. Cereb Cortex 10(3):284–294

Schultz W, Dayan P, Montague PR (1997) A neural substrate of prediction and reward. Science 275(5306):1593–1599

Shidara M, Richmond BJ (2002) Anterior cingulate: single neuronal signals related to degree of reward expectancy. Science 296(5573):1709–1711

Sutton RS, Barto AG (1998) Reinforcement learning. MIT Press, Cambridge, MA

Tanaka SC, Doya K, Okada G, Ueda K, Okamoto Y, Yamawaki S (2004) Prediction of immediate and future rewards differentially recruits cortico-basal ganglia loops. Nat Neurosci 7(8):887–893

Tanaka SC, Schweighofer N, Asahi S, Shishida K, Okamoto Y, Yamawaki S, Doya K (2007) Serotonin differentially regulates short- and long-term prediction of rewards in the ventral and dorsal striatum. PLoS One 2(12):e1333

Tremblay L, Schultz W (2000) Reward-related neuronal activity during go-nogo task performance in primate orbitofrontal cortex. J Neurophysiol 83(4):1864–1876

Ullsperger M, von Cramon DY (2003) Error monitoring using external feedback: specific roles of the habenular complex, the reward system, and the cingulate motor area revealed by functional magnetic resonance imaging. J Neurosci 23(10):4308–4314

Chapter 23
Second-to-Fourth Digit Ratio and the Sporting Success of Sumo Wrestlers

Rie Tamiya, Sun Youn Lee, and Fumio Ohtake

Abstract The second (index finger) to fourth (ring finger) digit length ratio (2D:4D) is known to be a putative marker of prenatal exposure to testosterone. It has been reported that fetal and adult testosterone may be critical for development of physical and mental traits such as cardiovascular system, reaction time, aggressiveness, and masculinity. Testosterone-driven attributes are associated with success in male-to-male physical competition, which may be proxied by ability in sports. Many researchers have found that 2D:4D is sexually dimorphic and a negative correlate of athletic performance. This study aims to investigate the associations of 2D:4D with measures of power as another possible testosterone-associated trait, using ability in sumo wrestling as a proxy for male physical competiveness. The measures of sumo performance comprised the sumo ranks and winning percentages of 142 Japanese professional sumo wrestlers. We found that sumo wrestlers with low 2D:4D had higher sumo ranks and better winning records. The significant negative associations between 2D:4D and the athletic prowess of sumo wrestlers provide further evidence of the possible link between high testosterone levels and muscle strength. The relatively small effect sizes found in this study, however, imply that 2D:4D may be a weaker predictor for sports requiring explosive power than for those requiring endurance.

The original article first appeared in the Evolution and Human Behavior 33:130–136, 2012. A newly written addendum has been added to this book chapter.

R. Tamiya
Yamaguchi Branch, NHK (Japan Broadcasting Corporation), Tokyo 753-0075, Japan
e-mail: lapoire_cestmoi@yahoo.co.jp

S.Y. Lee
Faculty of International Studies, Meiji Gakuin University, Yokohama 244-8539, Japan
e-mail: sylee@k.meijigakuin.ac.jp

F. Ohtake (✉)
Institute of Social and Economic Research, Osaka University, 6-1 Mihogaoka, Ibaraki, Osaka 567-0047, Japan
e-mail: ohtake@iser.osaka-u.ac.jp

S. Ikeda et al. (eds.), *Behavioral Economics of Preferences, Choices, and Happiness*, DOI 10.1007/978-4-431-55402-8_23

Keywords 2nd:4th digit ratio • Sumo • Sports ability • Testosterone • Promotion

1 Introduction

The second (index finger) to fourth (ring finger) digit length ratio (2D:4D) has been known to be fixed *in utero* and sexually dimorphic such that 2D:4D is negatively correlated to the level of prenatal testosterone exposure, and males have lower mean 2D:4D than females (van Honka et al. 2011). Evidence suggests high testosterone levels have been shown to enhance confidence (Boissy and Bouissou 1994), improve spatial ability (Puts et al. 2008), reduce reaction times (Salminen et al. 2004), stimulate development of the cardiovascular system (Manning and Bundred 2000), and increase perceived dominance, masculinity, and aggression (Neave et al. 2003).

These testosterone-associated, sex-dependent abilities are associated with success in male-to-male physical competition, which may be proxied by sports and athletic disciplines (Manning and Taylor 2001) to investigate the relationship of these abilities with 2D:4D. Many studies have found a significant negative association between 2D:4D and performance in sports and activities, such as rugby (Bennett et al. 2010), fencing (Voracek et al. 2006), skiing (Manning 2002), football (Manning and Taylor 2001), and gym-based exercises (Honekopp et al. 2006). Performance in these sports and activities is dependent on both a well-developed cardiovascular system and muscle strength. A more direct relationship between 2D:4D and muscle strength was found in studies on hand-grip strength (Fink et al. 2006a, b), isometric strength of elite players (Hansen et al. 1999), and sprinting speed (Manning and Hill 2009). It has yet to be established whether a combination of cardiovascular efficiency, muscle power, and other testosterone-driven attributes or only one particular characteristic correlates to success in sports. Some evidence, however, has suggested that 2D:4D may be a strong predictor for performance in sports requiring endurance but a weak predictor for performance in sports requiring power (Manning and Hill 2009).

The aim of the present study was to investigate the relative strength of the association between 2D:4D and performance in sumo wrestling, a sport requiring explosive power. The winner of a sumo bout is determined if the opponent is forced out of the sumo ring (18 ft^2 and 2 ft high) or if the opponent touches the ground with any part of his body other than the bottom of his feet (Nihon Sumo Kyokai n.d.). Matches often end in less than a minute (average, 6–10 s) and occasionally last for several minutes. Thus, the decisive attributes of success in sumo bouts are thought to be as follows: rapid reaction time, which is involved in the initial charge in a sumo bout (*Tachiai*), and explosive power and visual-spatial awareness, which are required to force the opponent out of the ring, judging the distance between oneself and the opponent as well as that between oneself and the edge of the ring (Benjamin 2010). We hypothesized that if the link between sumo performance and prenatal testosterone exposure as measured by 2D:4D is found to be strong, the explosive power may be a significant attribute that is influenced by testosterone exposure.

2 Methods and Materials

2.1 Sumo Ranking System

Professional sumo wrestling consists of six divisions (Table 23.1). Wrestlers start their careers in *Jonokuchi*, and they can be promoted up to *Makuuchi*. Wrestlers in the top two divisions, *Makuuchi* and *Jyuryo*, are the only full-fledged professionals who are rewarded with high social status and monetary incentives (Nema 2008). This study investigates wrestlers in these top two divisions.

The official tournament is held in the odd months every year and lasts for 15 consecutive days. Wrestlers must win majority of their matches (*kachi-koshi*) to be promoted within or between the divisions, e.g., a record of 8–7 or better for *Makuuchi* and *Jyuryo*. In contrast, from the *Komusubi* rank upward, achieving *kachi-koshi* is not sufficient for promotion to a higher rank. Promotion to these top four ranks is discretionary and sometimes contentious, as the rules are not set in stone. However, there are some consensual criteria. For promotion to *Komusubi* and *Sekiwake*, a convincing record in the previous tournament (e.g., 10–5 or better), and for promotion to *Ozeki*, at least 30 wins over the last three consecutive tournaments are often considered the minimum standard. For *Yokozuna*, there are additional criteria such as the quality of the wins, dignity and skill (*hinkaku*) along with two consecutive championships. There is no demotion from *Yokozuna*, but a *Yokozuna* wrestler has to retire if he can no longer perform as expected (Nihon Sumo Kyokai n.d.).

2.2 Handprints

As top professional sumo wrestlers in Japan are expected to provide a handprint of their right or left hands, the Tokyo Sumo Museum possesses an entire collection of handprints collected from 1790 to present. We took photos of 341 handprints of top professional sumo wrestlers ranked in the *Makuuchi* and *Jyuryo* divisions (Fig. 23.1). For the top *Yokozuna* rank, we collected all existing handprints because they have no prospects of future promotion. From *Ozeki* (second highest rank) to *Maegashira* (fifth highest rank), we collected handprints for all wrestlers who entered the *Makuuchi* division after World War II and were retired at the time of sample collection. For *Jyuryo* (second highest division), only a limited number of samples was obtained, namely those of wrestlers who were active in the *Heisei* era (from 1998 to present) and were retired when the sample was collected.

Analyzing professional athletes who are deceased or retired at the time of sample collection is advantageous because the samples are not truncated. Current athletes may have future chances of promotion, and thus, including those who might perform better in the future could underestimate the results of the analysis. Furthermore, the winning records of our study sample were obtained from actual sports competitions, where a judge can police the contest and intense rivalries exist. This is in contrast to

Table 23.1 Divisions and ranks in professional sumo wrestling

	Position	Division (Number of wrestlers)	Rank (Number of wrestlers)		Sub-rank
↑	Professional wrestlers	***Makuuchi*** (40 or less)	**1**	***Yokozuna*** (0 or more)	
			2	***Ozeki*** (1 or more)	
			3	***Sekiwake*** (1 or more)	
			4	***Komusubi*** (1 or more)	
			5	***Maegashira*** (approximately 32)	Maegashira 1 ⋮ Maegashira 16
		Jyuryo (26 or less)	**6**	***Jyuryo*** (26 or less)	Jyuryo 1 ⋮ Jyuryo 13
	Training wrestlers	*Makushita* (fixed at 120)			Makushita 1 ⋮ Makuhsita 60
		Sandanme (fixed at 200)			Sandanme 1 ⋮ Sandanme 100
		Jonidan (350 or more)			Jonidan 1 ⋮ Jonidan 10 ⋮
		Jonokuchi (100 or more)			Jonokuchi 1 ⋮ Jonokuchi 10 ⋮

Sumo wrestling is divided into six divisions, with five ranks within the top division *Makuuchi* and sub-ranks in divisions from *Maegashira* downward. Each sub-rank can have two wrestlers. The total number of wrestlers in *Maegashira* can vary from 32 to 36 in 16 to 18 sub-ranks because the number of wrestlers in the top 4 ranks in the same division is not fixed, but the number of wrestlers in *Jyuryo* is typically fixed at 26 wrestlers in 13 sub-ranks

previous studies that assessed the measures of muscle strength through experimental tests (Fink et al. 2006a, b; Hansen et al. 1999; Manning and Hill 2009).

2.3 2D:4D Measurement

A total of 341 photos were first classified by two observers into three grades from A to C according to the clarity of the crease of each index and ring finger, and only

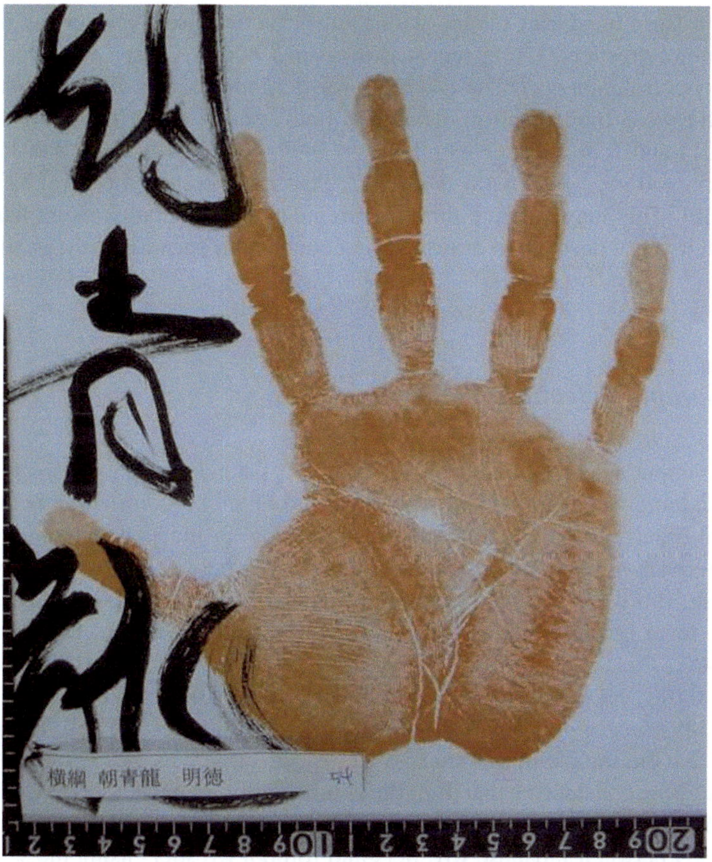

Fig. 23.1 An example of a sumo wrestler's handprint. Sumo wrestlers in higher divisions are asked by the Tokyo Sumo Museum to leave their handprints with their autographs

handprints with A grades (153 photos) for both fingers from both observers were selected. The lengths of the index and ring fingers were then measured to the nearest 0.1 mm from the mid-point of the finger crease proximal to the palm to the tip of the finger using a digital vernier caliper. The measurements were made twice separately by each of the three independent measurers, and the measurers were blind to the expected results regarding the correlation between 2D:4D and sports performance as well as the names and rankings of wrestlers.

Digit ratios may be estimated differently depending on the methods used to measure finger lengths; the mean 2D:4D calculated from photocopies has been found to be lower than that calculated from the direct measurement of fingers (Manning et al. 2005) or from self-measurement 2D:4D Caswell and Manning (2009). For studies concerning the link between 2D:4D and traits with small effect sizes, direct measurements have been used (Manning et al. 2010). In this context, we examined the differences in the measurement protocols by comparing 2D:4D measured from handprint photos with that measured directly from the fingers of living sumo wrestlers. Using repeated-measures ANOVA tests, we calculated the intraclass correlation (r_1). The r_1 values for the indirect and direct measurements of 2D:4D were high and significant for both second ($r_1 = 0.99$, $F_{1,8} = 29.142$, $P < 0.001$) and fourth finger lengths ($r_1 = 0.99$, $F_{1,8} = 31.36$, $P < 0.001$) and for 2D:4D ($r_1 = 0.96$, $F_{1,8} = 5.48$, $P < 0.047$; Pearson correlation (r) = 0.823, $N = 9$, $p = 0.006$). This may validate the measurements of digit ratios using handprints, although it is not possible to draw a strong conclusion because of the small sample size.

2.4 Sample Selection

As the sample selection based on the quality of handprint photos may not have been random, we examined the potential problem of correlation between the selection criterion and athletic performance using an independent samples t-test. The difference in mean winning percentage (DWP) between the selected wrestlers and those who were excluded because of unclear handprints was not significant at the 5 % level for any rank in the *Makuuchi* division (*Yokozuna*: DWP = −0.036, $t_{53} = 1.457$, $P = 0.151$; *Ozeki*: DWP = 0.004, $t_{23} = -0.252$, $P = 0.803$; *Sekiwake*: DWP = 0.011, $t_{56} = -1.864$, $P = 0.068$; *Komusubi*: DWP = 0.006, $t_{43} = -1.146$, $P = 0.258$; *Maegashira*: DWP = −0.002, $t_{132} = 0.281$, $P = 0.779$). These results suggest that the sample of this study is free of selection bias.

In addition, considering that digit ratios and confounding factors may vary across ethnicities (Manning et al. 2007a), we examined differences in mean height, weight, and 2D:4D between Japanese wrestlers and foreign wrestlers using the same t-test. A statistically significant difference was observed between the two groups (height: $t_{151} = -3.528$, $P < 0.001$; weight: $t_{151} = -4.736$, $P < 0.001$; 2D:4D: $t_{151} = -2.495$, $P = 0.013$). Therefore, we eliminated foreign wrestlers ($N = 11$) in the subsequent analyses, leaving a total of 142 samples.

2.5 Measurement of Performance in Sumo Wrestlers and Potential Confounders

In this study, three measures of athletic ability in sumo wrestling were used as dependent variables. The first dependent variable was the highest sumo rank that each wrestler reached before his retirement (Editorial of Sumo 2001), which was converted into a binary variable equal to 1 when sumo wrestlers were ranked higher than *Maegashira* and equal to 0 otherwise (hereafter denoted as "rank above *Maegashira*"). The second dependent variable was sumo ranks ordered from the following list on a scale of 1–6 (hereafter "rank"): *Jyuryo* (the lowest rank),

Maegashira, *Komusubi*, *Sekiwake*, *Ozeki*, and *Yokozuna* (the highest rank). The last dependent variable was the lifetime winning percentage in the *Makuuchi* division, which is a continuous variable calculated as a ratio of the number of sumo bouts that each wrestler had in *Makuuchi* division to the number of his wins in the same division (hereafter "winning percentage") (Nihon Sumo Kyokai n.d.). For *Jyuryo* wrestlers who had no matches in *Makuuchi* and thus no records, their winning percentages were censored at zero.

As potential confounding variables, we considered the height and weight of sumo wrestlers, which were measured at their highest levels. In addition, as it is reported that the negative relationship between 2D:4D and prenatal testosterone levels is particularly strong for the right hand (Manning 2008), we considered the effect of the difference due to right and left handprints (hereafter "R/L hand").

Means and SDs for dependent and independent variables drawn from 142 Japanese wrestlers were as follows: rank above *Maegashira* (=1), 0.598 ± 0.491; rank (range: 1–6), 3.345 ± 1.580; winning percentage, 0.456 ± 0.181 %; 2D:4D, 0.952 ± 0.035; height, 182.525 ± 6.027 cm; weight, 143.559 ± 25.644 kg; R/L hand (right hand = 1), 0.507 ± 0.501.

3 Results

The r_1 values for the six measurements of 2D:4D made by three independent measurers (two measurements each) were large and significant (first measurer: $r_1 = 0.99$, $F_{1,141} = 241.26$, $P < 0.001$; second measurer: $r_1 = 0.99$, $F_{1,141} = 191.60$, $P < 0.001$; third measurer: $r_1 = 0.99$, $F_{1,141} = 1.68.98$, $P < 0.001$; six measurements: $r_1 = 0.98$, $F_{5,705} = 7.15$, $P < 0.001$). The digit ratio was calculated each time, and the average of the six digit ratios was used as the 2D:4D for each sumo wrestler. Table 23.2 reports the mean values of rank and winning percentage divided into three groups based on the tertiles of 2D:4D. A wrestler with a lower digit ratio tended to have a higher career rank and a larger winning percentage and was likely to be promoted to a rank above *Maegashira*. As expected, 2D:4D was a significant negative correlate of winning percentage (Fig. 23.2) and rank (Fig. 23.3). To test for differences in means of 2D:4D between two groups (wrestlers ranked above and up to *Maegashira*), one-way ANOVA was conducted with 2D:4D as the dependent variable and the two groups as the fixed factor. This analysis revealed significant differences between the two groups regarding 2D:4D ($F_{1,141} = 5.04$, $P = 0.022$, $\eta^2 = 0.036$).

Considering the characteristics of the three dependent variables and the possible effects of confounding factors, we conducted a regression analysis using the following models. First, we examined the relationship of 2D:4D with sumo rank. Because the first (rank) and second (rank above *Maegashira*) dependent variables are constrained to range between 1 and 6 and between 0 and 1, respectively, we used a rank-ordered probit model and a binary probit model, respectively, adjusting for confounders (Table 23.3). The results, after controlling for confounding factors,

Table 23.2 Average rank and winning percentage based on 2D:4D classification

2D:4D (mean ± SD)	Average rank	Ratio above *Maegashira*	Average winning percentage
Low (0.914 ± 0.018)	3.562 ± 1.583	0.666 ± 0.476	0.477 ± 0.176
Medium (0.952 ± 0.007)	3.425 ± 1.556	0.683 ± 0.485	0.462 ± 0.180
High (0.984 ± 0.016)	3.042 ± 1.587	0.489 ± 0.505	0.428 ± 0.189
Whole (0.95 ± 0.032)	3.345 ± 1.580	0.598 ± 0.491	0.456 ± 0.181
r (Pearson correlation)	−0.178	−0.192	−0.174
P	0.034	0.022	0.038
Observations	142	142	142

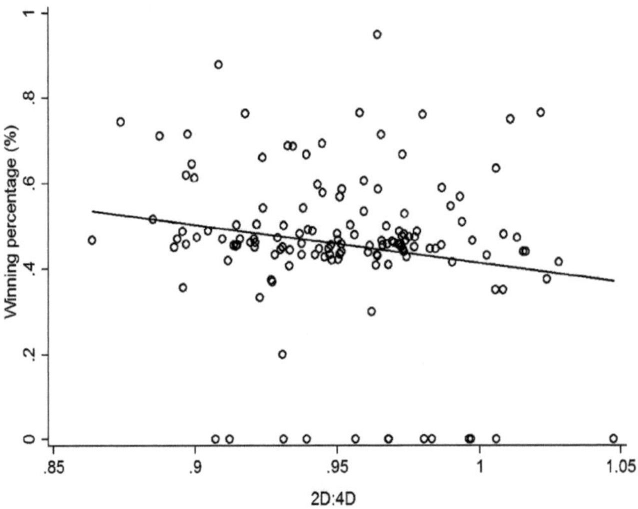

Fig. 23.2 The relationship between the left and right hand 2D:4D of 142 sumo wrestlers and their winning percentages in *Makuuchi*. Subjects with low 2D:4D had higher winning percentages than those with high 2D:4D ($r = -0.186$, $P = 0.026$)

revealed that the estimated coefficient for 2D:4D was negative and statistically significant (Model I: $P = 0.010$, Model II: $P = 0.018$, Model III: $P = 0.013$, Model IV: $P = 0.021$). However, when the analysis was performed on a limited number of samples that included only wrestlers ranked above *Maegashira*, the effect of 2D:4D on the rankings of the sumo wrestlers disappeared (Model V: $P = 0.837$).

Next, we investigated the association between 2D:4D and the third dependent variable, i.e., winning percentage. Here we used a Tobit model on the whole sample because the winning percentage was censored at zero for *Jyuryo* wrestlers. For the sub-sample ranked above *Maegashira*, which was not censored, we used OLS models (Table 23.4). We obtained results similar to those obtained in the probit models in Table 23.3. In both Models I (Tobit) and II (OLS), after the effects of confounding factors were removed, 2D:4D had a significant negative association

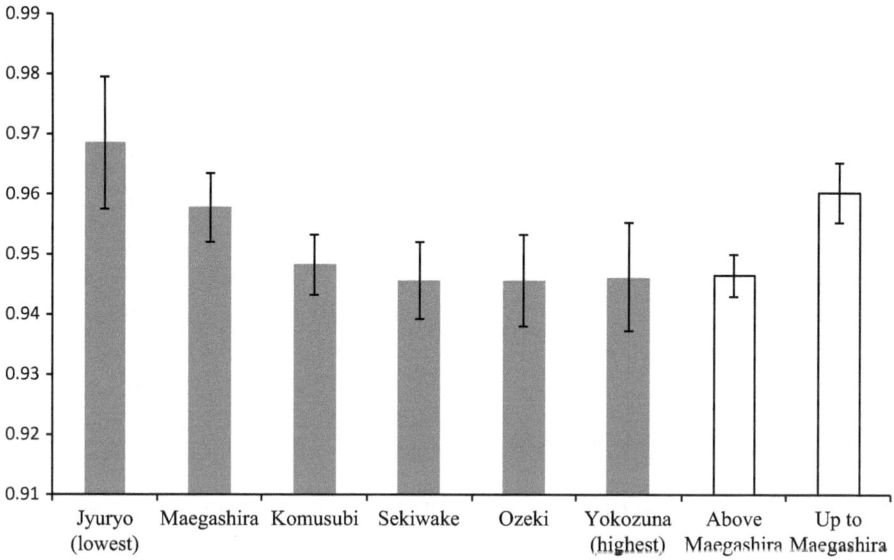

Fig. 23.3 Mean 2D:4D by rank. The *first six bars* show the mean 2D:4D by rank, and the *last two bars* show the mean 2D:4D of wrestlers ranked up to *Maegashira* (0.960, $N=57$) and that of wrestlers ranked above *Maegashira* (0.946. $N=85$), respectively. The *error bars* represent standard errors. The difference in 2D:4D between these two groups (above and up to *Maegashira*) was 0.013 (independent samples *t*-test: $P=0.022$)

Table 23.3 2D:4D and rank

	Probit (Rank above *Maegashira* = 1)		Ordered Probit (Rank: 1–6)		
	Whole		Whole		Above *Maegashira*
	I	II	III	IV	V
2D:4D	−2.830***	−2.627**	−6.344**	−5.995**	−0.759
	(1.093)	(1.108)	(2.565)	(2.591)	(3.695)
Height	0.010*	0.014**	0.026**	0.034**	0.011
	(0.006)	(0.007)	(0.014)	(0.016)	(0.019)
Weight		−0.002		−0.004	0.003
		(0.001)		(0.003)	(0.005)
2D:4D × R/L hand		0.002		0.009	0.097
		(0.084)		(0.186)	(0.252)
Observations	142	142	142	142	85
(Pseudo) R-squared	0.039	0.05	0.017	0.02	0.005

The coefficients reported in Models I and II are the average marginal effects based on the probability that the wrestler reaches a rank above *Maegashira* from an infinitesimal change in 2D:4D. Models III and IV show maximum likelihood estimates of an ordered probit model. Standard errors are reported in brackets

*Means significantly different from zero at the 10 % level (two-tailed t-test); **at the 5 % level; and ***at the 1 % level

Table 23.4 2D:4D and winning percentage

	Whole		Above *Maegashira*
	I	II	III
Estimation Method	Tobit	Tobit	OLS
2D:4D	−1.065** (0.465)	−1.005** (0.469)	−0.136 (0.397)
Height	0.004** (0.002)	0.002** (0.002)	0.001 (0.002)
Weight		−0.000 (0.000)	0.000 (0.000)
2D:4D × R/L hand		−0.006 (0.034)	−0.001 (0.027)
Observations	142	142	85
Log likelihood	10.049	10.429	–
R-squared	–	–	0.01

This table shows Tobit and OLS regressions of 2D:4D and confounding factors on the winning percentage. Standard errors are reported in brackets
*Means significantly different from zero at the 10 % level (two-tailed t test); **at the 5 % level; and ***at the 1 % level

with winning percentage (Model I: $P = 0.024$, Model II: $P = 0.034$); however, when subjects were limited to sumo wrestlers ranked above *Maegashira*, 2D:4D had no significant effect on winning percentage (Model III: $P = 0.733$).

4 Discussion

In our findings, 2D:4D was significantly correlated with the performance of sumo wrestlers. As predicted by the hypothesis, sumo wrestlers with lower 2D:4D had higher career ranks and better winning percentages, which suggests that a high level of testosterone may positively correlate with athletic prowess and thus with career promotion in sumo wrestling. The significant association between 2D:4D and ability in sumo wrestling remained after controlling for height, weight, and R/L hand. Both height and weight are considered as the most important criteria to win a sumo bout; however, weight did not have a significant effect on sumo performance. A possible reason is that to be most competitive, a sumo wrestler is expected to gain weight until reaching the ideal weight for his height (Benjamin 2010). Hence, the marginal effect of a change in weight near the optimal level on the expected value of sumo performance is reduced to nearly zero when height is kept constant.

If we limited the subjects to sumo wrestlers ranked above *Maegashira*, no significant correlation was observed before or after controlling for confounding factors (Tables 23.3 and 23.4). This nonlinearity might be associated with the different promotion systems used for divisions above and up to *Maegashira*. Promotion above *Maegashira* depends not only on the majority of wins but also on the quality of the performance, the rank of the opponents, and the attitude of the wrestler toward sumo practice. Because these endogenous factors, in addition to individual sports performance, affect promotion to upper ranks and winning percentage, the effect of 2D:4D did not appear to be significant among wrestlers in the top four ranks. However, between wrestlers in these four ranks and those in the other ranks (binary probit model; Table 23.3) and among wrestlers in the lower ranks, the relationships of 2D:4D with rank and winning percentage were significant.

Many studies have investigated the effect of prenatal testosterone exposure on success in athletic competitions by examining the association between 2D:4D and sports performance. Manning et al. (2007b) suggested that 2D:4D predicts more variance in performance in sports requiring endurance than in those requiring muscle strength. The authors provided the most compelling evidence on 2D:4D and its strong relationship with performance in sports requiring endurance such that 2D:4D explained approximately 25 % of the variance in middle- and long-distance running performance for both males and females. Comparatively, rowing ergometer performance, which requires a high level power output in addition to a well-developed cardiovascular system, exhibited a strong correlation with 2D:4D ($r = 0.50$ and 0.37 for right and left-hand 2D:4D, respectively) (Longman et al. 2011); this correlation was similar in magnitude to that for endurance running. This provides some support for a link between 2D:4D and measures of power.

In contrast, the effect sizes of 2D:4D on success in sports that are more directly linked to muscle strength have been found to be relatively small. Sprinting speed, which more strongly reflects strength and speed than endurance, was weakly related to 2D:4D ($r = -0.12$ to -0.15) (Manning and Hill 2009). In addition, Fink et al. (2006a, b) found a rather weak but significant relationship between hand-grip strength and right hand 2D:4D in both Indian and German samples (India, $\eta^2 = 0.046$; Germany, $\eta^2 = 0.073$). After adjustment for age, weight, and height in this same study, significant differences in 2D:4D were observed between hand-grip strength groups (India, $\eta_p^2 = 0.073$; Germany, $\eta_p^2 = 0.077$). The strengths of the association found in our study ($r = -0.174$ to -0.192; $\eta^2 = 0.036$) are similar to those found for sprinting speed and hand-grip strength. This result may provide further evidence for the significant link between 2D:4D and measures of power and imply that the association between 2D:4D and sports performance is related more to endurance than power and acceleration (Manning et al. 2007b).

Abilities in sumo wrestling can be explained by the theoretical framework of intrasexual selection in that men are often selected to compete against each other to attract women. Such intrasexual selection favors the evolution of mechanisms that promote sex-dependent characters involved in success in male-to-male combat (Darwin 1871) that in turn enhance the evolution of physical abilities such as strength and speed (Thornhill 1980). Male-to-male combat can be represented by male sports, and monetary and status rewards of success in sports can often serve as resources that make the winners more desirable to females (Manning and Taylor 2001). Sumo wrestling is one sport representing male-to-male combat that is associated with the evolution of male strength and size because of intrasexual selection.

In conclusion, the results of the present study indicate that early-life testosterone exposure may be a precursor of muscle strength associated with intrasexual selection. This suggests that 2D:4D, a marker of prenatal testosterone exposure, may be a significant predictor for performance in sports requiring power, although the effect sizes are smaller than those found in sports requiring endurance.

Acknowledgements We thank Mr. Fumihiko Nakamura of the Sumo Museum for his helpful advice and research assistance, particularly for taking photos of the handprints. We are also grateful to living sumo wrestlers for their research assistance for direct measurements of the finger lengths. This work was supported by the Global COE Program of Osaka University and a Grant-in-Aid for Scientific Research (22653030) from the Japan Society for the Promotion of Science. A part of this study is the result of "Development of biomarker candidates for social behavior" performed under the Strategic Research Program for Brain Sciences by the Ministry of Education, Culture, Sports, Science and Technology in Japan.

Addendum: Related Literature and Further Analysis[1]

In this chapter, we investigated the correlation between the relative length of the second and fourth digits (subsequently referred to as the 2D:4D ratio, or simply 2D:4D) and physical competition which is proxied by sports ability. The 2D:4D ratio has been suggested as a marker of prenatal exposure to testosterone and these testosterone-driven attributes are known to be associated with physical performance in a wide range of sports. In our study, the athletic performance in sports is measured by the career ranks and winning percentages of 142 Japanese professional sumo wrestlers and the 2D:4D is measured from their handprints collected from 1970 to present. The results indicate that sumo wrestlers with lower 2D:4D ratios tend to have a higher winning percentage and higher rank performance. This provides further evidence of the positive correlation between high testosterone levels and ability in sports that are mainly dependent on muscle strength.

The contribution of our work to the extant literature is manifold, due to (i) the consideration given to the ethnicity differences and sexual dimorphism of the 2D:4D ratio, (ii) the analysis of the explosive power as a significant testosterone-driven attribute, and (iii) the comparison of the effect size of the 2D:4D ratio between sports requiring endurance and those requiring power. These three points have been explored and discussed in recent studies, using different measurement and analysis methods. Our findings are consistent with the results yielded by these studies, and thus further contribute to clarifying the possible link between the 2D:4D ratio and athletic performance. A purpose of this addendum to review some recent studies that elucidate the three points noted above, as well as a few recent studies that yielded results conflicting with those reported in the previous studies (see Sects. A1 and A2).

[1] This addendum has been newly written for this book chapter.

Another purpose of this addendum is to introduce some recent literature in relation to the phenomenon of interest, focusing on how 2D:4D is related to individual characteristics, such as personality, behavioral and psychological traits, as well as educational and career success (see Sects. A3 and A4).

A1. Ethnicity Differences and Sexual Dimorphism of the 2D:4D Ratio

In this work, we postulate that the 2D:4D digit ratios and confounding factors may vary across ethnicities (Manning et al. 2003a, b, 2007a). Thus, the analyses performed are based on the handprints of Japanese sumo wrestlers. The importance of considering ethnicity when attempting to ascertain the significance of the 2D:4D ratio was emphasized in the recent study conducted by Zhao et al. (2012). In their work, the authors collected the 2D:4D data of adult participants, all of whom were of Han ethnic origin and resided in a remote village in the Qinling Mountains in China. Their results indicate that the mean 2D:4D ratio among the individuals of Han ethnicity is lower than that of Caucasians and Blacks, and even that of Chinese individuals included in a multi-national sample investigated by Manning et al. (2007a). This finding suggests that ethnical combinations should be considered for the analysis of the significance of the 2D:4D digit ratio.

While our results only provide additional evidence of a significant relationship between the 2D:4D ratio and "male" sports ability, using male-to-male athletic performance in professional sumo wrestling as a proxy for testosterone exposure, authors of several previous studies reported difference between the sexes. Their findings indicate that, compared to females, males tend to have longer fourth digits relative to second digits. Moreover, these studies suggest that the 2D:4D ratio and physical performance are significantly correlated in men, but not in women (Gallup et al. 2007; van Anders 2007). Honekopp and Watson (2010), however, claim that the sex difference is mitigated by the hand and measurement type, which can possibly distort the finger's soft tissue. The presence of a moderate difference between the male and female 2D:4D ratios, as well as a significant relationship between the 2D:4D value and sport ability in females, is supported by Honekopp et al. (2006) and Voracek et al. (2010).

In contrast, some recent studies yielded findings in accordance with the view that 2D:4D is sexually dimorphic and insignificantly related to female physical performance. Zhao et al. (2012) found that the 2D:4D ratio in the right hand is negatively correlated with handgrip strength in males but not in females, using the sample comprising 54 males and 55 females of the same ethnicity. The authors interpreted this finding as an indicator of sexual selection operating on fetal programming. In their recent study, Peeters et al. (2013) found no relation between 2D:4D and physical fitness component in adolescent girls, and Longman et al. (2011) found insignificant relationship between the 2D:4D ratio and rowing ergometer performance in females. These contradictory results suggest that the relationship between female athletic performance and prenatal testosterone levels has not yet been established.

A2. The Effect of the 2D:4D Ratio on Endurance and Muscle Strength

The relationship between 2D:4D and physical competition is analyzed using ability in various sports, such as rugby, fencing, skiing, and football (see literature sources cited in Introduction). Achieving success in these sports requires a well-developed cardiovascular system and muscle strength. In this chapter, we aimed to clarify the role of prenatal testosterone as a determinant of strength or power utilized in sumo wrestling, which was previously measured by assessing the hand-grip strength, isometric strength or sprinting speed (Fink et al. 2006a, b; Manning and Hill 2009). Our results indicate that, while there is a statistically significant correlation between the 2D:4D ratio and these measures of power, the predictive power of 2D:4D is relatively small. This finding is consistent with those reported in previous studies, where the 2D:4D ratio was found to be more strongly related to sports requiring endurance than sports requiring power and acceleration (Manning et al. 2007b; Manning and Hill 2009).

Honekopp and Schuster (2010) report that, in their study, the 2D:4D ratio was strongly correlated with endurance running performance. In contrast, the correlation between 2D:4D and sprinting speed was very weak and insignificant when the 2D:4D ratio for the left hand was used as a proxy for prenatal testosterone stimulation. In a recent study, Hill et al. (2012) investigated the potential role of maximal oxygen uptake ($\dot{V}O_{2\,max}$, $\upsilon - \dot{V}O_{2\,max}$, or LA_{max}) in explaining the mechanism behind the strong predictive power of the 2D:4D ratio for middle- and long-distance running performance, as $\dot{V}O_{2\,max}$ is known as an important determinant of success in sports requiring endurance (Foster 1983; Manning et al. 2007b). However, their findings failed to reveal a significant relationship between maximum oxygen uptake and the 2D:4D ratio (measured in both right and left hand). This is in contrast to the view of Manning and colleagues (2007b), who suggested presence of a possible link between maximum oxygen uptake and 2D:4D that predicts 25 % of variance in endurance running performance. This disparity suggests that the mechanism behind the 2D:4D ratio and sports requiring endurance should be further analyzed. However, it should be also noted that the obtained results cannot be directly comparable because of the inherent differences in the background characteristics of the samples used for analysis and methodologies.

In addition to cardiovascular system, the 2D:4D ratio is also indicative of one's muscle strength, as it is known to be sensitive to testosterone. In line with our findings, Zhao et al. (2012) reported a significant correlation between the 2D:4D ratio and male muscle strength measured by handgrip strength. However, following their recent study, Folland et al. (2012) reported a contradictory result, indicating that 2D:4D is not significantly correlated with muscle strength. The authors used knee extensor strength as a physiological parameter that served as a proxy for muscle strength, and their results were based on the data pertaining to Caucasian men aged around 20. According to the authors, absence of significant correlation in their data can potentially be due to the systemic difference between locomotor muscle strength in the knee and the hand musculo-skeletal system contributing to the handgrip strength. These mixed results suggest that further analysis is needed to clarify whether there is a direct link between the 2D:4D digit ratio and sports requiring muscle strength and the magnitude of the effect of 2D:4D on muscle strength in comparison with cardiovascular system.

A3. The Link Among the 2D:4D Ratio, Masculinity, and Psychological Traits

In addition to the overall physical performance in competitive sports, a few recent studies have investigated a possible link between the 2D:4D ratio and psychology, behavioral characteristics in particular. Corrado and Perciavalle (2013) used tests designed to measure specific psychological features and mood states in elite female water polo players and found that anger was significantly correlated with the 2D:4D ratio. Honekopp and Watson (2011) meta-analyzed the existing literature on physical aggression predicted by the difference in the 2D:4D digit ratio, and found evidence of a significant association between 2D:4D and physical aggression in males, although the correlation coefficient was very low. Honekopp (2013) investigated the relationship between the 2D:4D ratio and male facial attractiveness, which is thought to be mediated by facial masculinity. The results yielded by the random-effects meta-analyses indicate that the relationships are weak and statistically insignificant, which suggests that facial masculinity influenced by the 2D:4D ratio may not contribute to male facial attractiveness, as was previously suggested by Scott et al. (2013).

In a recent study on facial aggressiveness, Třebický et al. (2013) focused on the perception of aggressiveness and fighting ability, which may be linked to male-to-male physical competition.[2] The authors found that facial perception is associated with perceived aggressiveness, which is further positively correlated with winning ratios of MMA fighters when other confounding variables, such as weight, are adequately controlled for. Another recent study that focused on the effect of masculinity (Mayew et al. 2013) revealed its association with labor market success, as the earnings of CEOs with more masculine voices were higher than those of their less masculine counterparts.[3]

[2,3]The authors of these two recent studies cited Tamiya et al. (2012) in order to support their hypotheses in relation to male-to-male competition, masculinity and their effect sizes.

A4. A Possible Link Between the 2D:4D Ratio and Educational and Labor Market Outcomes

A few recent studies have investigated whether testosterone has both organizational and activational effects on academic performance and labor market outcomes, such career choices and earnings. Coco et al. (2011) examined the effect of the 2D:4D ratio on the performance of a group of 48 male students on the admission test to the medical school. Their findings indicate that prenatal traits affected their participants' performance in relation to the decision-making process and the degree of risk taking. Sapienza et al. (2009) analyzed the difference in the risk aversion in financial decision-making between sexes, using the data pertaining to approximately 500 MBA students. According to their findings, higher levels of circulating testosterone are related with lower risk aversion in females, and students with high testosterone and low risk aversion levels tend to choose risky careers in finance after graduation. Coates et al. (2009) also predicted that risk-sensitive trading in the financial world is affected by prenatal testosterone levels. More specifically, the authors found that the long-term profitability and longevity of male trades in risk-taking trading is predicted by the difference in the 2D:4D digit ratios.

Personality traits have also been analyzed in association with the 2D:4D ratio. Hampson et al. (2008) found that the 2D:4D ratio was significantly, albeit weakly, correlated with both aggression and sensation seeking in both males and females. This suggests that prenatal exposure to testosterone may predict selective sex-dependent characteristics expressed by later personality traits. Fink et al. (2006a, b) provided additional evidence that supports an organizing effect of testosterone on sensation seeking personality characteristics. This is in line with the work of Fink et al. (2004), which examined the effect of the 2D:4D ratio on Big Five personality domains, which are a broadly accepted model of personality and are based on five personality facets—extraversion, agreeableness, conscientiousness, emotional stability, and openness to experiences. They found week but significant but correlations between neuroticism and agreeableness and the right hand 2D:4D digit ratio. Several studies have recently focused on personality traits as an important predictor of educational attainment (Borghans et al. 2006; Heckman et al. 2006) and earnings (Heineck and Anger 2010). These findings indicate that the educational and career success may be determined through personality and behavioral characteristics that are found to be affected by prenatal biological traits.

In sum, several recent studies have investigated the relationships among the 2D:4D ratio, physical competition and behavioral traits. Their findings contribute to the extant knowledge on the differences in the 2D:4D ratios among ethnical groups, as well as between sexes. Moreover, they help elucidate the mechanism behind the correlations between the 2D:4D ratio and athletic performance in sports requiring cardiovascular system and muscular strength. Finally, they highlight the possible link between 2D:4D and behavioral traits, as well as educational and labor market outcomes. Overall, the results presented here suggest that the difference in later development is partly caused by the difference in the *in utero* testosterone levels. Further analysis will be necessary to establish how biological traits affect the later success in life.

References

Benjamin D (2010) Sumo: a thinking fan's guide to Japan's national sport. Tuttle Publishing, North Clarendon

Bennett M, Manning JT, Cook CJ et al (2010) Digit ratio (2D:4D) and performance in elite rugby players. J Sports Sci 28:1415–1421

Boissy A, Bouissou MF (1994) Effects of androgen treatment on behavioral and physiological responses of heifers to fear-eliciting situations. Horm Behav 28:66–83

Borghans L, Meijers F, ter Weel B (2006) The role of noncognitive skills in explaining cognitive test scores. Econ Inq 46(1):2–12

Casewell N, Manning JT (2009) A comparison of finger 2D:4D by self-report direct measurement and experimenter measurement from photocopy: methodological issues. Arch Sex Behav 38:143–148

Coates JM, Gurnell M, Rustichini A (2009) Second-to-fourth digit ratio predicts success among high-frequency financial traders. Proc Natl Acad Sci U S A 106:623–628

Coco M, Perciavalle V, Maci T et al (2011) The second-to-fourth digit ratio correlates with the rate of academic performance in medical school students. Mol Med Rep 4:471–476

Corrado DD, Perciavalle V (2013) Digit ratio (2D:4D) and mood states in elite female water polo players. Sport Sci Health 9:19–23

Darwin C (1871) The descent of man and selection in relation to sex, vol 1. John Murray, London

Editorial of Sumo (2001) Ozumo Jinbutsu Daijiten [Grand Sumo Encyclopedia], vol 1. Baseball Magazine Company, Tokyo (in Japanese)

Fink B, Manning JT, Neave N (2004) Second to fourth digit ratio and the 'Big Five' personality factors. Pers Individ Differ 37(3):495–503

Fink B, Neave N, Laughton K et al (2006a) Second to fourth digit ratio and sensation seeking. Pers Individ Differ 41(7):1253–1262

Fink B, Thanzami V, Seydel H et al (2006b) Digit ratio and hand-grip strength in German and Mizos men: cross-cultural evidence for an organizing effect of prenatal testosterone on strength. Am J Hum Biol 18:776–782

Folland JP, McCauley TM, Phypers C et al (2012) Relationship of 2D:4D finger ratio with muscle strength, testosterone, and androgen receptor CAG repeat genotype. Am J Phys Anthropol 148:81–87

Foster C (1983) VO2max and training indices as determinants of competitive running performance. J Sports Sci 1:13–22

Gallup AC, White DD, Gallup GG (2007) Handgrip strength predicts sexual behavior, body morphology, and aggression in male college students. Evol Hum Behav 28:423–429

Hampson E, Ellis CL, Tenk CM (2008) On the relation between 2D:4D and sex-dimorphic personality traits. Arch Sex Behav 37(1):133–144

Hansen L, Bangsbo J, Twisk J et al (1999) Development of muscle strength in relation to training level and testosterone in young male soccer players. J Appl Physiol 87:1141–1147

Heckman JJ, Stixrud N, Urzua S (2006) The effects of cognitive and noncognitive abilities on labor market outcomes and social behavior. J Labor Econ 24(3):411–482

Heineck G, Anger S (2010) The returns to cognitive abilities and personality traits in Germany. Labour Econ 17(3):535–546

Hill R, Simpson B, Manning J et al (2012) Right-left digit ratio (2D:4D) and maximal oxygen uptake. J Sports Sci 30(2):129–134

Honekopp J (2013) Digit ratio (2D:4D) and male facial attractiveness: new data and a meta-analysis. Evol Psychol 11(5):944–952

Honekopp J, Schuster M (2010) A meta-analysis on 2D:4D and athletic prowess: substantial relationships but neither hand out-predicts the other. Pers Individ Differ 48:4–10

Honekopp J, Watson S (2010) Meta-analysis of digit ratio 2D:4D shows greater sex difference in the right hand. Am J Hum Biol 22:619–630

Honekopp J, Watson S (2011) Meta-analysis of the relationship between digit-ratio (2D:4D) and aggression. Pers Individ Differ 51:381–386

Honekopp J, Manning T, Muller C (2006) Digit ratio (2D:4D) and physical fitness in males and females: evidence for effects of prenatal androgens on sexually selected traits. Horm Behav 49:545–549

Longman D, Stock JT, Wells JC (2011) Digit ratio (2D:4D) and rowing ergometer performance in males and females. Am J Phys Anthropol 144:337–341

Manning JT (2002) The ratio of 2nd to 4th digit length and performance in skiing. J Sports Med Phys Fitness 42:446–450

Manning JT (2008) The finger book: sex, behaviour and disease revealed in the fingers, vol 2. Faber and Faber, London

Manning JT, Bundred PE (2000) The ratio of 2nd to 4th digit length: a new predictor of disease predisposition? Med Hypotheses 54:855–857

Manning JT, Hill MR (2009) Digit ratio (2D:4D) and sprinting speed in boys. Am J Hum Biol 21:210–213

Manning JT, Taylor RP (2001) 2nd to 4th digit ratio and male ability in sport: implications for sexual selection in humans. Evol Hum Behav 22:61–69

Manning JT, Bundred PE, Newton DJ et al (2003a) The second to fourth digit ratio and variation in the androgen receptor gene. Evol Hum Behav 24:399–405

Manning JT, Henzi P, Venkatramana P et al (2003b) Second to fourth digit ratio: ethnic differences and family size in English, Indian and South African populations. Ann Hum Biol 30:579–588

Manning JT, Fink B, Neave N et al (2005) Photocopies yield lower digit ratios (2D:4D) than direct finger measurements. Arch Sex Behav 34:329–333

Manning JT, Churchill AJG, Peters M (2007a) The effects of sex, ethnicity, and sexual orientation on self-measured digit ratio (2D:4D). Arch Sex Behav 36:223–233

Manning JT, Morris L, Caswell N (2007b) Endurance and digit ratio (2D:4D): implications for fetal testosterone effects on running speed and vascular health. Am J Hum Biol 19:416–421

Manning JT, Baron-Cohen S, Wheelwright S et al (2010) Is digit ratio (2D:4D) related to systemizing and empathizing? Evidence from direct finger measurements reported in the BBC internet survey. Pers Individ Differ 48:767–771

Mayew WJ, Parsons CA, Venkatachalam M (2013) Voice pitch and the labor market success of male chief executive officers. Evol Hum Biol 34:243–248

Neave N, Laing S, Fink B et al (2003) Second to fourth digit ratio, testosterone and perceived male dominance. Proc R Soc Lond Ser B Biol Sci 270:2167–2172

Nema H (2008) Sumo no Ban Zu Ke [Sumo Ranking System] (in Japanese). Available via http://ozumou.com/banduke.html. Accessed 15 Jan 2011

Nihon Sumo Kyokai (n.d.) Grand Sumo Home Page. Available via http://sumo.goo.ne.jp/eng/. Accessed 5 Nov 2010

Peeters MW, Aken KV, Claessens AL (2013) The left hand second to fourth digit ratio (2D:4D) is not related to any physical fitness component in adolescent girls. PLoS One 8(4):e59766

Puts DA, McDaniel MA, Jordan CL et al (2008) Spatial ability and prenatal androgens: meta-analyses of congenital adrenal hyperplasia and digit ratio (2D: 4D) studies. Arch Sex Behav 37:100–111

Salminen EK, Portin RI, Koskinen A et al (2004) Associations between serum testosterone fall and cognitive function in prostate cancer patients. Clin Cancer Res 10:7575–7582

Sapienza P, Zingales L, Maestripieri D (2009) Gender differences in financial risk aversion and career choices are affected by testosterone. Proc Natl Acad Sci U S A 106(36):15268–15273

Scott IML, Clark AP, Boothroyd LG et al (2013) Do men's faces really signal heritable immunocompetence? Behav Ecol 24:579–589

Tamiya R, Lee SY, Ohtake F (2012) Second-to-fourth digit ratio and the sporting success of sumo wrestlers. Evol Hum Behav 33(2):130–136

Thornhill R (1980) Sexual selection within mating swarms of the lovebug, *Plecia Nearctica* (Diptera: Bibionidae). Anim Behav 28:405–412

Třebický V, Havlíček J, Roberts SC et al (2013) Perceived aggressiveness predicts fighting performance in mixed-martial-arts fighters. Psychol Sci 24(9):1664–1672

van Anders SM (2007) Grip strength and digit ratios are not correlated in women. Am J Hum Biol 19:437–439

van Honka J, Schutter DJ, Bos PA et al (2011) Testosterone administration impairs cognitive empathy in women depending on second-to-fourth digit ratio. Proc Natl Acad Sci U S A 108:3448–3452

Voracek M, Reimer B, Ertl C et al (2006) Digit ratio (2D:4D), lateral preferences, and performance in fencing. Percept Mot Skills 103:427–446

Voracek M, Reimer B, Dressler SG (2010) Digit ratio (2D:4D) predicts sporting success among female fencers independent from physical, experience, and personality factors. Scand J Med Sci Sports 20:853–860

Zhao D, Kamarul Li B, Yu K et al (2012) Digit ratio (2D:4D) and handgrip strength in subjects of Han ethnicity: impact of sex and age. Am J Phys Anthropol 149:266–271

Part VIII
Investor Behavior

Chapter 24
Investors' Herding on the Tokyo Stock Exchange

Yoshio Iihara, Hideaki Kato, and Toshifumi Tokunaga

Abstract Herding occurs when a group of investors intensively buy or sell the same stock at the same time. This study examines the tendency of individual, institutional and foreign investors to herd in Japan, where the yearly change in ownership is used as a proxy for investor herding. Using 20 years of aggregate data, we examine how investor herding is related to stock return performance around the herding interval. Both institutional and foreign investor herding impact stock prices. Further, Japanese institutional investors seem to follow positive-feedback trading strategies, and subsequent return reversals imply that these investors' trades destabilize stock prices. On the other hand, foreign investors' trades are related to information. Our results are robust to the effect of firm size, to portfolio formation methods, to initial ownership levels, and to the chosen time period.

Keywords Ownership • Positive-feedback trading • Return reversal

1 Introduction

A number of recent studies have documented investor-herding behaviour in stock markets. Herding occurs when a group of investors intensively buy or sell the same stock at the same time. Several studies in the USA document individual investor trading behaviour and conclude that they are irrational and trade on noise. For example, Lakonishok et al. (1994) posit that individual investors may make

The original article first appeared in the International Review of Finance 2:71–98, 2001. A newly written addendum has been added to this book chapter.

Y. Iihara

H. Kato
Nagoya University, Nagoya, Japan
e-mail: kato@soec.nagoya-u.ac.jp

T. Tokunaga (✉)
Musashi University, Tokyo, Japan
e-mail: t-tkng@cc.musashi.ac.jp

S. Ikeda et al. (eds.), *Behavioral Economics of Preferences, Choices, and Happiness*, DOI 10.1007/978-4-431-55402-8_24

judgment errors by extrapolating past growth rates of stocks and believe that such growth rates will persist into the future. De Long et al. (1990) also argue that individual investors place more weight on recent news and overreact.

Scharfstein and Stein (1990) suggest that institutional investors will rationally herd because of concerns about their own reputations when they are evaluated relative to each other. Each money manager prefers to mimic the actions of other managers rather than taking the risk of appearing to have low ability. In addition, institutional investors may pursue short-term trading strategies based not on fundamentals, but on technical analysis (a feedback trading strategy).[1]

On the other hand, institutional investor trading may be based on information, and thus would counter changes in the sentiment of other investors. Because institutional investors tend to be well informed from a variety of news sources, they are in a better position to evaluate the fundamental value of a stock. They purchase undervalued stocks and sell overvalued stocks. Several US studies (for example, Nofsinger and Sias 1999) support this view.

Although a number of studies have been carried out on herding and positive-feedback trading using US data, no studies have been conducted on Japanese markets. Since Japanese stock markets are the second largest in the world, an analysis of Japanese markets is important. In addition, because of a different institutional environment and a different corporate culture, both Japanese institutional and individual investors may not behave in the same way as their American counterparts.

In addition to individual and institutional investors, we add foreign investors to our analysis. The analysis of foreign investor behaviour in Japan is particularly interesting because foreign investors may not follow the same trading strategy as Japanese investors, as they are not likely to be motivated by the same career or culture concerns. Shiller et al. (1996) provide striking evidence that expectations about market returns differ very significantly between the USA and Japan. Using survey data, they report that the Japanese were uniformly more optimistic in their short-run expectations for the stock market than were the Americans. This suggests that geographic location or country of origin may have some bearing on information acquisition and beliefs about different country returns.

Foreign investor transactions on the Tokyo Stock Exchange (TSE) have increased dramatically in the past several years, and their annual trading volume has exceeded individual investor annual trading volume since 1994. Foreign investor annual trading volume jumped from 13 % of total trading volume in 1990 to 41 % in 1998, which is close to that of Japanese institutional investors. Thus, foreign investors play a significant role in pricing securities and their trades may impact stock prices.

Our analysis of foreign investors is similar to the analysis of Choe et al. (1999), who examine the impact of foreign investors on stock returns in Korea and find

[1]This may not be the case if other investors underreact to news. Brennan and Cao (1997) argue that foreign investors may appear to be positive-feedback traders but their trade may be related to information if they trade a large volume almost simultaneously, and the market underreacts to news.

strong evidence of positive-feedback trading and herding before Korea's economic crisis period but no evidence during the crisis period. In addition, they find no evidence that foreign investor trades destabilize stock prices.

We follow the approach used by Nofsinger and Sias (1999). The herding interval is 1 year and the change in ownership is used as a proxy of investor herding. Using aggregate data, we analyze how investor herding is related to stock returns. Accordingly, we analyze the cross-sectional relation between changes in ownership and stock returns for three different types of investors: individual, institutional and foreign.[2] We also examine how ownership change is related to post-herding returns and pre-herding returns.

Our analysis exhibits a strong positive relationship between annual changes in ownership and herding period returns for both institutional and foreign investors. On the other hand, a negative relationship is observed for individual investors. These results suggest that both institutional and foreign investors engage in intra-year positive feedback trading, or their trade impacts stock prices more than individual investors.[3] Analysis of post-herding returns reveals evidence that foreign investor herding is related to information but institutional investor herding is not. Furthermore, institutional investors seem to follow positive feedback trading because the relationship between the pre-herding period returns and ownership change is significantly positive. No such relations are observed for foreign investors.

The organization of the paper is as follows: Section 2 presents data and sample statistics. Section 3 discusses methodology and ownership structure of Japanese firms. Section 4 investigates the relationship between change in ownership and excess returns surrounding the herding period. Section 5 examines the sensitivity of our results when we adjust for relevant factors, and Sect. 6 concludes with a brief summary and discussion.

2 Data

We divide investors into three groups: individual, institutional and foreign. Following Nofsinger and Sias (1999), we examine change in ownership over 1-year periods.[4] The more shares a certain type of investor purchases, the greater the herding. For example, if change in ownership is primarily initiated by institutional investors' buy herding, then order flow imbalance is likely to drive the stock

[2]Nofsinger and Sias (1999) did not include foreign investors in their analysis.

[3]The positive relationship between ownership change and returns may be observed when these investors successfully forecast short-term returns.

[4]One limitation of these data is that we do not know when the change in ownership takes place during a particular year. Unfortunately, we are unable to obtain shorter holding period data. Monthly and weekly ownership information is not available.

Table 24.1 Summary statistics of the firms listed on the Tokyo Stock Exchange

	First section firms	Second section firms
Number of firms	901 (1975)	497 (1975)
	1,327 (1997)	478 (1997)
Daily trading value (billion)	53 (1975)	1.3 (1975)
	434 (1997)	8.4 (1997)
Daily trading volume (million shares)	178 (1975)	4 (1976)
	430 (1997)	8 (1997)
Total market value (billion)	41,468 (1975)	1,776 (1975)
	273,907 (1997)	7,022 (1997)

price higher. In this case, we predict that institutional buying should result in a simultaneous increase in institutional ownership and positive excess returns.

The data consist of monthly stock returns, annual market capitalization and annual fractions of shares held by a variety of investors for all non-financial firms listed on the TSE during the period from 1975 to 1996.[5] The TSE, which accounts for more than 90 % of the total market capitalization of Japanese equity, consists of two sections, the First Section and the Second Section.[6] The difference between the two sections is similar to the difference between the NYSE and the AMEX in the USA.[7] Table 24.1 presents summary statistics for both sections. The First Section dominates the Second Section in terms of the number of listed firms, trading volume, trading value and market capitalization.

3 Methodology

In order to examine the relationship between change in ownership and returns, March is used as a base month. Since the ownership structure information is available at the company's fiscal year end, only firms whose fiscal years end in March are selected for our analysis.[8] As shown in Fig. 24.1, a substantial majority of Japanese firms have their fiscal years end in March. Approximately 84 % of Japanese firms had their fiscal years end in March in 1996. In addition, March fiscal

[5]We use the PACAP database for our analysis. We subscribe to this database from the Pacific Basin Financial Center at the University of Rhode Island. This database is com parable to CRSP and COMPUSTAT in the USA.

[6]In addition to these two sections, the TSE also includes a Foreign Section and the Mothers Section, which specializes in new and small firm stocks. The former includes 29 foreign firms. The latter contains 40 young growing firms started in 2000.

[7]The AMEX has recently merged with the NASDAQ.

[8]The ownership structure for March firms is not significantly different from that for non-March firms during our sample period.

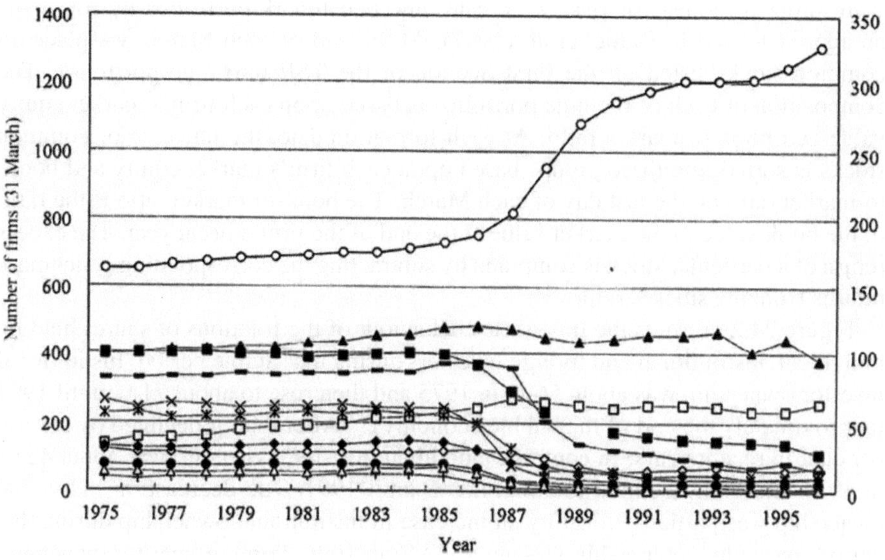

Fig. 24.1 The number of firms based on fiscal year, 1975 to 1996

year end firms are scattered across all industries.[9] Therefore, March fiscal year end firms can be considered to be good representatives of the firms listed on the TSE.[10]

At the end of each March, all firms listed on the TSE whose fiscal year ends in March are sorted into five portfolios based upon ownership change over the following year. Since we have three different types of investors – individual, institutional and foreign – five portfolios are created for each of these three types of investors. Ownership is measured as the fraction of shares held by these investors on 31 March; thus, for the first year, the change in ownership is measured as the fraction of shares held by these three types of investors on 31 March 1976 less the fraction held on 31 March 1975. As a result, the number of firms for this study ranges from 642 to 1,244.[11]

[9]No concentration of fiscal year end in the other months is observed. One exception is retail industry. In addition to March, February is also a popular fiscal year end month for this industry.

[10]Although March fiscal year end firms dominate on the TSE, the selection bias may drive our results. In order to investigate if including only firms with a fiscal year ending in March biases our results, we added firms with a fiscal year end from the previous October to the current March to our sample and conducted the same analysis. Though we obtain slightly weaker results because of measurement error, the results do not qualitatively change. Therefore, we report results using firms with a fiscal year ending in March in this chapter. We thank the referee for suggesting this procedure.

[11]All the sample firms must have their fiscal year ends in March in at least two consecutive years to compute ownership change.

In order to adjust for risk, we create nine benchmark portfolios by following an approach used in Daniel et al. (1997). At the end of each March, we place all common stocks listed on the First Section of the TSE into nine portfolios. The composition of each of the nine portfolios is based upon each firm's market equity value and book-to-market ratio. At each formation date, the universe of common stocks is sorted into three groups based upon each firm's market equity and book-to-market ratio on the last day of each March. The book-to-market ratio is the ratio of the book value to the market value at the end of the firm's fiscal year. The excess return of a particular stock is computed by subtracting the corresponding benchmark returns from the stock's return.[12]

Figure 24.2 presents the time series behaviour of the fractions of shares held by individual, institutional and foreign investors during the sample period. Institutional investor ownership was about 56 % in 1975 and then rose to about 71 % until 1991 (approximately the end of the bubble economy).[13] After that, it declined by several per cent in recent years. In contrast, individual investor ownership was about 42 % in 1975 and then declined to about 25 % until 1991. The decrease in individual ownership was partially offset by an increase in institutional ownership during this period. Individual ownership was about 27 % in 1996. Foreign investor ownership was relatively small until the early 1980s and the gradually increased to about 6.7 % in 1996. Though foreign investors' ownership was relatively small, their transactions are not negligible. Their trading volume increased dramatically from 13 % of total volume in 1990 to 41 % of total volume in 1999. Their trading volume is currently close to that of institutional investors.

The market capitalization (size of the firm) may be an important factor for certain types of investors in the selection of portfolios. For example, Kang and Stulz (1997) document that foreign investors tend to hold shares of large firms in the Japanese market. Institutional investors may hold the stock of large, we known firms for window dressing purposes. Figure 24.3 presents the time series behaviour of ownership of three different investors based upon firm size. Consistent with the findings of Kang and Stulz, foreign investors tend to hold large-firm stocks. Individual investors, on the other hand, hold more small-firm stocks than large-firm stocks. Institutional investors held slightly more large-firm stocks during the late 1970s and late 1980s.

[12]Though Daniel et al. adjust for industry effects, we did not make such adjustment. In addition, we did not take momentum into account because there is no evidence of such an effect in Japan (see Iihara et al. 2004). Chan et al. (1991) document that both firm size and book-to-market are important for pricing stock in Japan. Daniel et al. (2000) examine the Japanese data to see if the characteristic model provides a better description of the cross-sectional variation of stock returns than the three factor model.

[13]The institutional investors consist of financial and non-financial firms. This increase is mainly caused by the increase in ownership by financial firms. The share held by financial firms was about 25 % in 1975 and then rose to about 33 %. On the other hand, the share held by not financial firms has been about 30 % during our sample period.

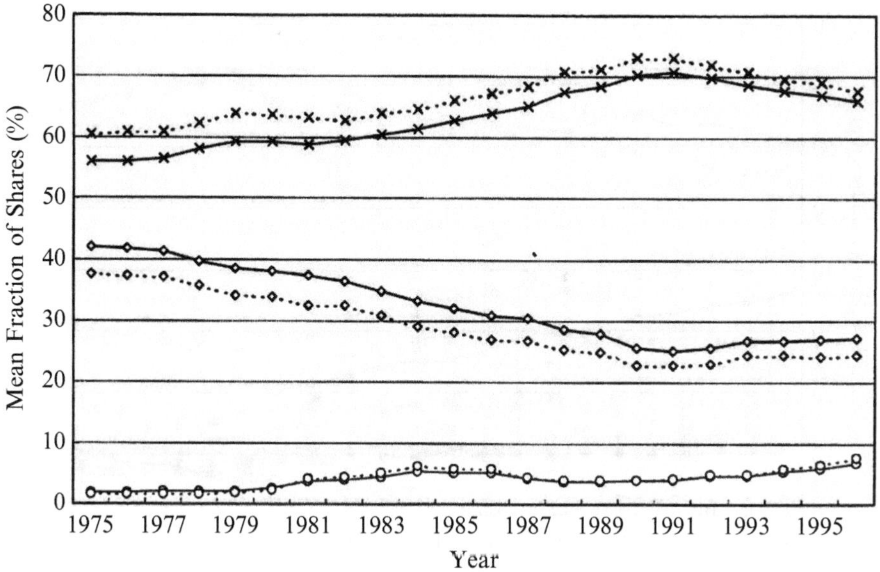

Fig. 24.2 The mean fractions of shares held by individual, institutional and foreign investors based of sections of Tokyo Stock Exchange and fiscal year, 1975 to 1996The mean fractions of shares are defined as annual cross-sectional averages of the ratio of the number of shares held by each of the three types of investors to the number of shares outstanding. The *continuous line* marked with '◇' corresponds to individual investors for all firms listed on either the First or Second Section of the Tokyo Stock Exchange (TSE). The *dashed line* marked with '◇' corresponds to individual investor for all firms listed on the First Section of the TSE whose fiscal year ends in March. The *continuous line* marked with '×' corresponds to institutional investors for all firms listed on either First or Second Section of the TSE. The *dashed line* marked with '×' corresponds to institutional investors for all firms listed on the First Section of the TSE whose fiscal year ends in March. The *continuous line* marked 'o' corresponds to foreign investors for all firms listed on either First or Second Section of the TSE. The *dashed line* marked with 'o' corresponds to foreign investors for all firms listed on the First Section of the TSE whose fiscal year ends in March

The ownership structure may be different for the *keiretsu* group firms that dominate Japanese markets. There are six major city-bank-centred *keiretsu* groups.[14] In addition, Toyota, Panasonic and other firms have their own *keiretsu* groups for efficiency in their distribution systems. A majority of Japanese firm belong to at least one of these *keiretsu* groups. Though we predict significantly higher institutional holdings for *keiretsu* firms than for non-*keiretsu* firms because of mutual shareholdings among the group firms, we do not observe any significant

[14]Six city-bank-centred *keiretsu* groups ma y no longer exist in their traditional form in Japan because of mergers among city banks. For example, Fuji merged with Daiichi-Kangyo and Sumitomo merged with Sakura (Mitsui and Taiyo–Kobe). Furthermore, Sanwa plans to merge with Tokai. However, *keiretsu* analysis may be important because city-bank-centred *keiretsu* still existed during our sample period.

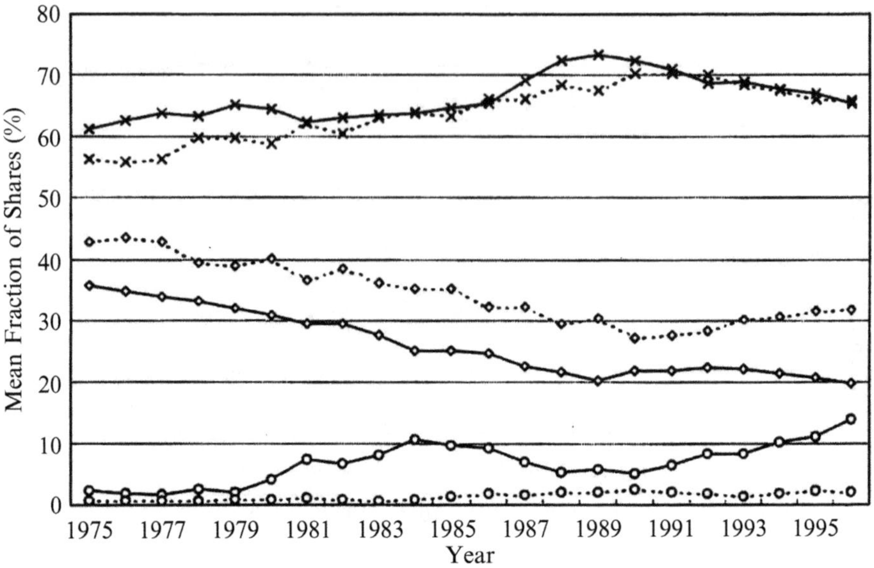

Fig. 24.3 The mean fractions of shares held by individual, institutional, and foreign investors based on firm size, 1975 to 1996All firms listed on the First Section of the Tokyo Stock Exchange whose fiscal year ends in March are sorted into five groups based on the market capitalization at the beginning of each April. The firms in each initial capitalization quintile are then further sorted into three groups based on investor type. The mean fractions of shares based upon firm size are defined as annual cross-sectional averages of the ratio of the number of shares held by each of the three types of investors to the number of shares outstanding. The *continuous line* marked '◇' corresponds to individual investors for the largest capitalization group. The *dashed line* marked with '◇' corresponds to individual investors for the smallest capitalization group. The *continuous line* marked with '×' corresponds to institutional investors for the largest capitalization group. The *dashed line* marked with '×' corresponds to institutional investors for the smallest capitalization group. The *continuous line* marked with '∘' corresponds to foreign investors for the largest capitalization group. The *dashed line* marked with '∘' corresponds to foreign investors for the smallest capitalization group

differences between these two groups. We also examine the industry effect to see if any specific ownership structures are observed among the nine industries: agriculture and fishery, construction, manufacturing, wholesale and retail, financial institutions, real estate, transportation and communication utilities, and services. No significant differences are observed among these industries with respect to ownership structure.

4 Change in Ownership and Excess Returns

We examine the relation between change in ownership and excess returns for three different types of investors: individual, institutional and foreign. A mentioned in the previous section, we form five ownership change-base portfolios for each of these three investor types, following the procedure adopted by Nofsinger and Sias (1999). We compute the time series average of portfolio excess returns over all event years surrounding the portfolio formation.[15] We focus on the excess returns of three time periods to examine the following issue. The pre-herding period excess returns are used to test for evidence of feedback trading. The herding period excess returns are examined to test for price pressure and information effects. The post-herding period excess returns are examined to test for information effects. The portfolios are formed at month 0 and the change in ownership is measured in the herding period. The timeline of the period is as follows:

```
      |------------------------|------------------------|------------------------|
month –12                      0                        12                       24
      pre-herding period      herding period      post-herding period
```

We also calculate the average excess ownership, average excess capitalization an average excess book-to-market ratio for each portfolio to examine the characteristics of that portfolio.[16]

4.1 *Individual Investor Herding*

Table 24.2 presents the cross-sectional average characteristics for each of the five portfolios that are formed from a ranking on the change in ownership of firm during a given year. Panel A presents time-series averages of these portfolio measures (over all event years), and the difference between the raw value and the cross-sectional average of each variable for the particular year. Initial ownership increases as the ownership change decreases. Individual investors tend to sell stocks that they own in greater amounts than the average stock and buy those that they own in lesser amounts. This indicates that ownership is mean reverting. If an individual tends to be overweighted in a particular stock in a particular year, he will tend to reduce his holdings in the following year. Neither firm size nor the book-to-market ratio exhibits any significant pattern across portfolios.

[15]The annual ownership change may be significantly influenced by equity offerings or stock repurchases. Though stock repurchase has not been allowed until recently in Japan, equity offerings are one of the major financing methods used by Japanese firms over the past 15 years. In unreported results, we tested the effect of seasoned equity offerings on our analysis by discarding firms whose change in number of shares outstanding is greater than 10 % from our sample. We repeated this procedure with 20 % as well. In both cases, the results remain qualitatively unchanged. We did not adjust for the effect of delisted firms because the number of delisted firms is very small (about four firms a year in our sample period).

[16]Excess values are computed as the difference between the raw value and the cross-sectional average of each variable for the particular year. We calculate size and book-to-market at the beginning of the herding period.

Table 24.2 Characteristics of individual ownership-change portfolios

	Quintile 1 (decrease)	Quintile 2	Quintile 3	Quintile 4	Quintile 5 (increase)	*F*
A: Individual ownership statistics						
ΔIndividual (%)	−5.9727 (−12.17)	−1.7484 (−7.78)	−0.3858 (−3.31)	0.7169 (6.77)	3.7885 (21.19)	183.61
Initial ownership (excess % values)	5.2640 (3.94)	0.2930 (0.20)	−1.2997 (−0.99)	−1.9320 (−1.93)	−2.3253 (−2.79)	6.6191
Book/market (excess % values)	−0.0008 (−0.04)	0.0110 (0.39)	0.0268 (0.94)	0.0024 (0.08)	−0.0393 (−1.62)	0.8574
Size (excess % values)	−3924.28 (−2.81)	1466.46 (0.66)	986.15 (0.51)	311.77 (0.12)	1159.90 (0.30)	0.7846
ΔInstitutional (%)	4.1399 (6.68)	1.2238 (2.65)	0.3564 (−0.96)	−0.4597 (−8.00)	−2.7245 (−14.18)	68.2125
ΔForeign (%)	1.8445 (5.41)	0.5402 (2.39)	0.0345 (−2.45)	−0.2569 (−5.22)	−1.0125 (−5.65)	33.4027
B: Herding year excess returns (t = 0–11)						
Equal weighted	25.2876 (8.91)	5.3968 (5.17)	−5.3833 (−4.79)	−10.2108 (−7.73)	−13.2342 (−7.39)	79.44
Value weighted	22.7843 (7.21)	7.3718 (3.73)	−2.2566 (−1.75)	−10.2560 (−5.66)	−16.7670 (−6.56)	47.51
C: Post-herding year excess returns (t = 12–23)						
Equal weighted	0.1534 (0.13)	0.5065 (0.89)	1.1328 (1.06)	1.7945 (2.11)	−0.7131 (−0.54)	0.86
Value weighted	−1.0586 (−0.76)	0.5526 (0.19)	−0.9519 (−0.45)	0.3088 (0.25)	−2.0752 (−1.13)	0.30
D: Pre-herding year excess returns (t = −12 to −1)						
Equal weighted	3.6050 (2.76)	0.9489 (0.91)	−4.3485 (−3.57)	−3.2057 (−3.21)	4.8998 (2.12)	7.84
Value weighted	−0.4660 (−0.27)	0.3161 (0.14)	−3.1785 (−1.80)	−1.9631 (−1.02)	−2.2989 (−0.78)	0.43

Each March (1976–1996), all firms listed on the First and Second Sections of the Tokyo Stock Exchange whose fiscal year ends in March are sorted into five portfolios based on the fractions of shares held by individual investors. Panel A reports the time-series mean of the annual cross-sectional average characteristics for each portfolio. All the excess values are computed as the difference between the raw value and the cross-sectional average of each variable for the particular year. ΔIndividual is the raw change in individual ownership less the annual cross-sectional average change. Initial ownership, Size and Book/market are initial characteristics ($t = 0$) for each ΔInstitutional quintile ($t = 0$ to 11). ΔInstitutional and ΔForeign are fractions of shares held by institutional and foreign investors for each ΔIndividual quintile ($t = 0$ to 11), respectively. Panel B, C and D present annual size and book-to-market adjusted returns. The period $t = 0$ to 11 indicates the 12 months during the herding year, the period $t = 12$ to 23 indicates the first year following the herding year and the periods $t = -12$ to -1 indicates 1 year prior to the herding year. The *F* value is based on the null hypothesis that the time-series means of cross-sectional averages do not differ across the five portfolios

Panel B reports the average annual excess returns (both equal and value weighted returns) over the same period. The results demonstrate a strong negative relation between changes in individual ownership and excess returns. The firms in the largest ownership increase quintile (Q5 portfolio) suffer average excess returns of −13.23 % (equal weighted returns), which is statistically significant at the 1 % level. Alternatively, the firms in the large ownership decrease quintile (Q1 portfolio) gain excess returns of 25.28 % (equal weighted returns), which is statistically significant at the 1 % level. The results do not differ significantly when value weighted returns are used. The results here are consistent with US findings presented by Nofsinger and Sias (1999), who report that individual investor herding impacts stock price less than other investor herding. Our results also imply that herding does not impact stock price and individual investors follow intra-year negative feedback trading.

Panel C documents post-herding period excess returns. Q1 to Q5 portfolio (except the equal weighted Q4 portfolio return) post-herding period returns are not significantly different from zero. These results are not consistent with US findings, which show that the firms in the largest ownership decrease quintile continue to exhibit significantly positive excess returns.

The results in Panel D are mixed. The equal weighted pre-herding excess returns for the firms in the Q1 portfolio are significantly positive. The firms in the Q5 portfolio also exhibit significantly positive excess returns in the year prior to the herding period. However, the value weighted pre-herding excess returns are insignificant for both the Q1 and the Q5 portfolios. Our results in Panel C and D are somewhat different from the US results documented by Nofsinger and Sias (1999).

4.2 Institutional Investor Herding

Table 24.3 presents the time series average of the annual cross-sectional mean characteristics for the institutional ownership-change portfolios. The institutional investors tend to sell the stocks that they own more than the cross-sectional average ownership share, as shown in Panel A. On the other hand, they purchase the stocks that they own less than the cross-sectional average. The pattern is similar to that of the individual investors. As regards firm size and the book-to-market ratio, no significant patterns are observed. When institutional investors increase their ownership, individual investors decrease their ownership more than foreign investors.

In contrast to the case of individual investors, herding period excess returns increase as the ownership change increases, as shown in Panel B. The firms in the largest ownership increase portfolio exhibits positive equal weighted excess returns of 17.07 %, which is statistically significant at the 1 % level. On the other hand, the largest ownership decrease portfolio exhibits significantly negative returns of −4.92 %. The results do not substantially change when the value weighted returns are used. The results show that institutional investors' herding impacts stock prices more than other investors' herding, which is consistent with the US findings. The results also suggest that institutional investors strongly follow intra-year positive feedback trading.

Table 24.3 Characteristics of institutional ownership-change portfolios

	Quintile 1 (decrease)	Quintile 2	Quintile 3	Quintile 4	Quintile 5 (increase)	*F*
A: Institutional ownership statistics						
ΔIndividual (%)	−3.9062	−0.8789	0.2197	1.5110	5.5596	159.79
	(−23.02)	(−6.34)	(1.42)	(6.09)	(11.30)	
Initial ownership (excess % values)	3.1128	2.2146	0.8134	−0.9704	−5.1704	11.0917
	(4.19)	(2.72)	(0.75)	(−0.89)	(−4.61)	
Book/market (excess % values)	−0.0286	0.0069	0.0271	0.0130	−0.0185	0.7560
	(−1.14)	(0.24)	(0.92)	(0.47)	(−0.91)	
Size (excess % values)	−72.04	2792.19	−211.02	−1252.79	−1256.35	0.5093
	(−0.03)	(0.94)	(−0.11)	(−0.81)	(−0.51)	
ΔInstitutional (%)	2.3958	0.4966	−0.3850	−1.3697	−4.7777	90.3321
	(11.24)	(11.25)	(2.50)	(−2.83)	(−8.43)	
ΔForeign (%)	1.5014	0.3860	0.1672	−0.1457	−0.7610	25.0616
	(4.72)	(1.37)	(−0.95)	(−3.59)	(−5.15)	
B: Herding year excess returns (*t* = *0–11*)						
Equal weighted	−4.9183	−7.3768	−4.4636	1.5984	17.0706	36.92
	(−3.16)	(−5.54)	(−4.04)	(2.17)	(6.32)	
Value weighted	−6.4974	−6.4475	−3.1434	2.5251	8.6150	10.00
	(−3.18)	(−3.24)	(−2.12)	(1.50)	(3.01)	
C: Post-herding year excess returns (*t* = *12–23*)						
Equal weighted	0.7383	2.0486	2.3508	−0.0243	−2.3012	4.18
	(0.89)	(2.29)	(2.31)	(−0.03)	(−2.51)	
Value weighted	0.0582	1.2459	2.9170	−3.0074	−4.4235	2.30
	(0.04)	(0.69)	(1.25)	(−1.45)	(−1.98)	
D: Pre-herding year excess returns (*t* = *−12 to −1*)						
Equal weighted	2.9278	−2.7108	−4.0956	−0.3319	6.1211	8.47
	(1.58)	(−1.91)	(−3.46)	(−0.43)	(3.65)	
Value weighted	−1.9618	−3.3743	−3.6841	−0.1127	4.7517	2.59
	(−0.91)	(−1.23)	(−2.61)	(−0.07)	(1.98)	

Each March (1976–1996), all firms listed on the First and Second Sections of the Tokyo Stock Exchange whose fiscal year ends in March are sorted in to five portfolios based on the fractions of shares held by institutional investors. Panel A reports the time-series mean of the annual cross-sectional average characteristics for each portfolio. All the excess values are computed as the difference between the raw value and the cross-sectional average of each variable for the particular year. ΔInstitutional is the raw change in individual ownership less the annual cross-sectional average change. Initial ownership, Size and Book/market are initial characteristics ($t = 0$) for each ΔInstitutional quintile ($t = 0$ to 11). ΔIndividual and ΔForeign are fractions of shares held by individual and foreign investors for each ΔInstitutional quintile ($t = 0$ to 11), respectively. All other details are as for Table 24.2

The results in Panel B show that institutional herding is associated with a large price change over the herding year. If institutional herding is related to information, then institutional herding over the herding year should not drive stock prices away from their fundamental values. This conjecture is tested by computing post-herding returns, as shown in Panel C. Because post-herding excess returns for the firms in the Q5 portfolio are significantly negative, subsequent return reversals are observed.

No such reversals are observed for Q1 portfolio. Similarly, stocks heavily sold experience insignificantly negative future returns but stocks heavily bought show significantly negative future return when the value weighted returns are used. The results here differ from the US findings, which document no subsequent return reversals for the largest ownership-increase portfolio.

Significant return reversals may imply that herding year positive returns are due to stock market overreaction. For example, Japanese institutional investor may be so overconfident that they are reluctant to revise their estimate in a timely manner. Alternatively, return reversals may imply that herding year positive returns are due to trend chasing strategies. Japanese institutional investors may be acting out of concern for their own reputation. Therefore, they may mimic each other and follow a trend chasing strategy, which is unrelated to information. In either case, our results suggest that Japanese institutional investors' trades destabilize stock prices.

Panel D documents pre-herding excess returns for five portfolios. The equal weighted Q5 portfolio exhibits significantly positive excess returns for the pre-herding year, which is consistent with positive-feedback trading. The Q1 portfolio, on the other hand, is not significant. The results do not change when value weighted returns are used. Institutional investors purchase past winners but do not necessarily sell past losers, which is consistent with the results documented by Grinblatt et al. (1995). In sum, the results suggest that institutional investors may overreact or follow trend-chasing investment strategies that destabilize stock prices.[17] Our results show that their herding impacts stock prices more than that of other investors or/and they may simply follow intra-year positive feedback trading.

4.3 Foreign Investors' Herding

Table 24.4 presents the characteristics of foreign ownership-change portfolios. The initial ownership level does not exhibit a significant pattern. No significant patterns are observed for firm size and the book-to-market ratio. When foreign investors increase their ownership, individual investors decrease their ownership more than institutional investors.

A positive relation between changes in foreign ownership and the equal weighted excess returns during the herding year is observed, as presented in Panel B. The same relation exists for value weighted returns. This suggests that foreign investor s follow intra-year positive feedback trading or/and foreign investors' herding impacts stock prices more than other investors' herding. In the previous section, we document that institutional investors' trading impacts stock price more than that

[17]As mentioned in footnote 12, institutional investors consist of financial and non-financial firms. We conduct the same analysis using March fiscal year end firms to see if there are any differences between financial and non-financial firms in terms of herding, pre-herding and post-herding returns. Financial firms exhibit stronger patterns than non-financial firms.

Table 24.4 Characteristics of foreign ownership-change portfolios

	Quintile 1 (decrease)	Quintile 2	Quintile 3	Quintile 4	Quintile 5 (increase)	*F*
A: Institutional ownership statistics						
ΔIndividual (%)	−2.3829 (−7.20)	−0.3406 (−3.83)	0.0126 (0.44)	0.4585 (4.77)	3.3943 (9.44)	84.07
Initial ownership (excess % values)	3.3693 (4.52)	−1.1153 (−3.88)	−2.1109 (−15.73)	−0.9047 (−2.89)	0.7617 (1.44)	22.2633
Book/market (excess % values)	−0.0290 (−1.26)	0.0013 (0.05)	0.0122 (0.38)	0.0071 (0.26)	0.0084 (0.35)	0.3921
Size (excess % values)	1213.74 (0.54)	−3007.63 (−1.65)	−3480.74 (−1.55)	2275.59 (0.83)	2999.00 (1.14)	1.6483
ΔInstitutional (%)	0.6092 (6.48)	−0.2555 (2.28)	−0.4147 (1.67)	−0.6864 (0.20)	−2.8924 (−6.22)	29.9461
ΔForeign (%)	1.7875 (4.48)	0.6072 (0.45)	0.4141 (−0.46)	0.2305 (−1.29)	−0.5036 (−2.92)	10.2145
B: Herding year excess returns (t = 0–11)						
Equal weighted	−6.3843 (−4.58)	−6.7475 (−4.83)	−4.1468 (−4.19)	0.3651 (0.25)	18.7678 (7.31)	42.05
Value weighted	−6.4071 (−4.13)	−7.8361 (−3.11)	−5.4911 (−2.26)	−2.2591 (−1.13)	12.4685 (5.42)	14.35
C: Post-herding year excess returns (t = 12–23)						
Equal weighted	−2.3860 (−1.40)	−0.7539 (−0.66)	1.0784 (0.91)	2.4673 (2.12)	2.4378 (1.23)	2.04
Value weighted	−2.9086 (−1.62)	−2.1530 (−1.22)	1.0831 (0.55)	0.5634 (0.18)	−0.3067 (−0.15)	0.60
D: Pre-herding year excess returns (t = −12 to −1)						
Equal weighted	7.6946 (2.96)	−3.0225 (−2.58)	−4.9004 (−2.83)	−1.5179 (−1.63)	3.4898 (2.00)	8.83
Value weighted	2.8569 (1.94)	−1.0835 (−0.44)	−5.9116 (−2.55)	−3.3209 (−1.55)	−1.6892 (−0.85)	2.32

Each March (1976–1996), all firms listed on the First and Second Sections of the Tokyo Stock Exchange whose fiscal year ends in March are sorted into five portfolios based on the fractions of shares held by foreign investors. Panel A reports the time-series mean of the annual cross-sectional average characteristics for each portfolio. All the excess values are computed as the difference between the raw value and the cross-sectional average of each variable for the particular year. ΔForeign is the raw change in foreign ownership less the annual cross-sectional average change. Initial ownership, Size and Book/market are initial characteristics ($t = 0$) for each ΔForeign quintile ($t = 0$ to 11). ΔIndividual and ΔInstitutional are fractions of shares held by individual and institutional investors for each ΔForeign quintile ($t = 0$ to 11), respectively. All other details are as for Table 24.2

of other investors. The results here raise the following interesting question. Does the foreign investors' herding impact stock prices more than institutional investors' herding? We examine this issue below.

The post-herding excess returns are insignificant for the firms in all quintile portfolios. In contrast to the case of Japanese institutional investors, return reversals are not observed in the following year for both equal and value weighted excess returns. Lack of subsequent return reversals is consistent with the hypothesis that the herding year returns are due to information and changes in foreign ownership are correlated with information. Both intra-year positive feedback trading and lack of subsequent return reversals are consistent with Brennan and Cao (1997), who argue that foreign investor trade is related to information and does not destabilize stock prices.

The results of pre-herding period returns are mixed, as presented in Panel D. The pre-herding period returns for the firms in equal weighted Q1 and Q5 portfolios are significantly positive. The results change when value weighted returns are used. The pre-herding excess returns become insignificant. The result that foreign investors simultaneously buy and sell past winners may be driven by small firm stocks.

Lack of return reversals in the subsequent period is consistent with the view that foreign investors are well informed and that their trades are related to information. The evidence here is very similar to the US evidence regarding institutional investors.

4.4 *Pairwise Relationship*

In the previous two sections, we document that both institutional and foreign investors' herding impacts stock prices more than other investors' herding. The interesting question to be asked is whether foreign investors' herding impacts stock prices more than institutional investors' herding. In order to examine this issue, the effect of individual investor s should be limited. We exclude firms that belong to the Q1 and Q5 portfolios in Table 24.2 (individual investors) from our sample. In this way, individual investors' ownership change is relatively small for the rest of the sample, so we can directly compare the relationship between institutional and foreign investors in terms of owner ship change and excess returns.

Using this subsample, we form five portfolios based upon the institutional ownership change. We also form five portfolios based upon the foreign ownership change using the same sample. Then, the firms that belong to the largest decrease portfolio among the institutional owner ship change-based portfolios, as well as the largest increase portfolio among the foreign ownership change-based portfolios, are put into the G1 portfolio. The firms that belong to the second largest decrease portfolio among institutional ownership change-based portfolios, as well as to the second largest increase portfolio among the foreign ownership change-based portfolios, are put into the G2 portfolio. In a similar way, the rest of the firms are put into the G3, G4 and G5 portfolios, respectively.

The G1 to G5 portfolios represent the ranking portfolios based upon ownership change between institutional and foreign investors. The G1 portfolio correspond s to the largest foreign ownership increase with the largest institutional ownership decrease. On the other hand, the G5 corresponds to the largest foreign ownership decrease with the largest institutional ownership increase. We also form

Table 24.5 Herding year pairwise excess returns

G1	G2	G3	G4	G5
Large decrease/ large increase	Quintile 2/ quintile 4	Quintile 3/ quintile 3	Quintile 4/ quintile 2	Large increase/ large decrease
A: Individual/institutional				
14.4135	−0.2268	−6.7546	−11.1078	−13.8028
(5.77)	(−0.15)	(−3.83)	(−6.88)	(−7.61)
B: Institutional/foreign				
4.3173	−7.2460	−5.6153	−7.2019	−0.6512
(2.87)	(−3.23)	(−2.62)	(−4.20)	(−0.34)
C: Foreign/individual				
−15.9772	−13.3020	−5.2098	0.5486	21.4676
(−8.53)	(−6.88)	(−2.39)	(0.27)	(8.00)

In Panel A, each March (1976–1996), all firms listed on the First Section of the Tokyo Stock Exchange whose fiscal year ends in March are sorted into five portfolios based on the fractions of shares held by foreign investors. We exclude firms that belong to the Q1 and the Q5 portfolios in Table 24.4 (foreign investors) from our sample. Using this subsample, we form five portfolios based upon the institutional ownership change. We also form five portfolios based upon the individual ownership change using the same sample. Then, the firms that belong to the largest decrease portfolio among the institutional ownership change-based portfolios and the largest increase portfolio among the individual ownership change-based portfolios are put into the G1 portfolio. The firms that belong to the second largest decrease portfolio among institutional ownership change-based portfolios and the second largest increase portfolio among the individual ownership change-based portfolios are put into the G2 portfolio. In a similar way, the rest of the firms are put into the G3, G4 and G5 portfolios. Panel A presents the time-series mean of annual cross-sectional average excess returns for the relationship between individual and institutional investors. We follow the same procedure by excluding firms that belong to the Q1 and the Q5 portfolios in Table 24.2 (individual investors) to examine the relationship between institutional and foreign investors. Panel B presents the time-series mean of annual cross-sectional average excess returns for the relationship between institutional and foreign investors. Similarly, Panel C presents the time-series mean of annual cross-sectional average excess returns for the relationship between individual and foreign investors

five portfolios in a similar way to analyze the relationship between individual and institutional investors and the relationship between individual and foreign investors.

Panel B of Table 24.5 presents the herding period pairwise excess returns for five portfolios ranked by ownership change of foreign and institutional investors.[18] The excess returns of portfolio G1 are significantly positive but the excess return of portfolios G2 to G4 are significantly negative. Portfolio G5 is insignificant. This result indicates that foreign investors' herding impacts stock prices more than institutional investors' herding after controlling for the effect of individual investors. Panels A and C show the relationships between individual and institutional (or

[18]The results using the equal weighted excess returns are presented. The results do not substantially change when the value weighted excess return are used.

foreign) investors. Consistent with previous findings, both institutional and foreign investors' herding impacts stock prices more than individual investors' herding.

5 Sensitive Analysis[19]

Individual investors' herding does not impact stock price, and intra-year negative feedback trading is observed. On the other hand, we find that both institutional and foreign investors' herding impacts stock prices. While positive feedback trading is observed for both institutional and foreign investors, subsequent return reversals are observed only for institutional investors. In this section, we investigate the robustness of our results by examining the way the five portfolios are formed, time stability, initial ownership level and the effect of firm size.

5.1 Time Stability and Portfolio Formation

In the previous section, we followed Nofsinger and Sias's procedure to form the ownership-change portfolios every year. This approach may not be appropriate when we examine the time stability of the results by splitting the sample period into several subperiods because of the small number of time series observations. Since Japan experienced a bubble economy in the late 1980s, it is interesting to see how investors' behaviour is different before, during and after the bubble period. In addition, foreign investors' presence on the Tokyo markets may have become more significant after the bubble period. Furthermore, if the variance of the change in ownership is not stable through time, Nofsinger and Sias's procedure may not provide convincing results. In order to test the robustness of our results, we directly form portfolios based upon change in ownership for each subperiod as well as for the entire sample period, instead of forming portfolios every year.

Table 24.6 presents both the Q5 portfolio (largest ownership increase) and the Q1 portfolio (largest ownership decrease) returns for the herding period, the pre-herding period and the post-herding period. The sample period is divided into three subsample periods: pre-bubble economy (1976–1984), bubble economy (1985–1989) and post-bubble economy (1990–1996). The herding period excess returns of both portfolios are stable through time for all three types of investors (individual, institutional and foreign). The results are similar to those in Panel B of Tables 24.2, 24.3, and 24.4.

[19]Our results may be driven by several extreme outliers. In order to examine this possibility, we exclude the observations from the sample if either the change in ownership or excess return exceeds 10 %. The results remain qualitatively unchanged. Results using equal weighted excess returns are presented in this section.

Table 24.6 Portfolio formation and time stability

	$t = 0$ to 11			$t = -12$ to -1			$t = 12$ to 23		
	Quintile 1 Large decrease	Quintile 5 Large increase	Q5–Q1	Quintile 1 Large decrease	Quintile 5 Large increase	Q5–Q1	Quintile 1 Large decrease	Quintile 5 Large increase	Q5–Q1
A: Individual investor									
Subperiod 1: 1976–1984	29.7348 (17.19)	−10.9311 (−11.68)	−40.6659 (−20.67)	4.3388 (3.72)	9.6022 (6.32)	5.2634 (2.75)	0.0091 (0.01)	1.0787 (0.96)	1.0697 (0.64)
Subperiod 2: 1985–1989	34.5191 (14.09)	−25.1873 (−23.64)	−59.7064 (−22.35)	0.8035 (0.37)	4.0574 (1.84)	3.2539 (1.05)	0.9740 (0.57)	−6.5615 (−4.13)	−7.5355 (−3.24)
Subperiod 3: 1990–1996	12.001 (13.18)	−6.6457 (−11.05)	−18.7458 (−17.08)	2.9552 (3.54)	−1.3509 (−1.74)	−4.3061 (−3.78)	−2.5189 (−4.73)	2.0667 (2.60)	4.5857 (4.79)
Full period	23.3517 (25.42)	−12.2422 (−24.97)	−35.5939 (−34.18)	2.3623 (3.09)	2.9789 (3.88)	0.6165 (0.57)	−0.4007 (−0.60)	−0.4054 (−0.64)	−0.0047 (−0.01)
B: Institutional investor									
Subperiod 1: 1976–1984	−2.9563 (−2.57)	21.9431 (12.45)	24.8994 (11.83)	9.6032 (6.81)	3.4003 (2.96)	−6.2030 (−3.41)	1.1833 (1.05)	−0.7725 (−0.64)	−1.9558 (−1.18)
Subperiod 2: 1985–1989	−12.6069 (−8.56)	22.7937 (9.23)	35.4005 (12.31)	−0.9351 (−0.48)	8.9789 (3.73)	9.9141 (3.19)	−2.5476 (−1.62)	−2.5192 (−1.53)	0.0284 (0.01)
Subperiod 3: 1990–1996	−0.1770 (−0.26)	6.6041 (7.52)	6.7811 (6.14)	−1.8455 (−2.67)	4.3951 (5.10)	6.2406 (5.65)	2.4971 (3.11)	−3.3641 (−6.68)	−5.8613 (−6.18)
Full period	−3.1457 (−5.72)	15.4720 (17.03)	18.6177 (17.54)	2.2007 (3.25)	4.8002 (5.78)	2.5995 (2.43)	1.2950 (2.15)	−2.4021 (−3.67)	−3.6971 (−4.16)

C: Foreign investor									
Subperiod 1: 1976–1984	−4.1892 (−3.48)	23.9817 (15.25)	28.1709 (14.22)	7.8770 (5.74)	9.0396 (7.55)	1.1626 (0.64)	0.0427 (0.04)	4.6742 (3.50)	4.6315 (2.61)
Subperiod 2: 1985–1989	−13.5571 (−9.29)	20.1538 (11.26)	33.7108 (14.59)	11.1625 (5.14)	−2.4548 (−1.42)	−13.6173 (−4.90)	−8.0886 (−4.95)	1.2516 (0.78)	9.3402 (4.08)
Subperiod 3: 1990–1996	−4.0725 (−6.97)	8.9254 (13.10)	12.9979 (14.49)	4.3378 (5.59)	0.5964 (0.97)	−3.7414 (−3.77)	−1.6162 (−2.88)	1.4726 (2.67)	3.0888 (3.93)
Full period	−6.5773 (−10.74)	15.4755 (22.44)	22.0528 (23.91)	7.2015 (8.97)	2.1545 (3.83)	−5.0369 (−5.13)	−3.3504 (−5.59)	1.9298 (3.15)	5.2802 (6.16)

All firms listed on the First Section of the TSE whose fiscal year ends in March are sorted into five portfolios based on the fractions of shares held by each of three investors. Instead of forming five portfolios each year, we form five portfolios each period by aggregating the data. Three subperiods are chosen to examine time stability, pre-bubble economy, bubble economy and post-bubble economy periods. Panel A presents the results based upon individual investors' ownership change. Q1 represents the portfolio with the largest decrease in individual ownership and Q5 the portfolio with the largest increase in individual ownership. Similarly, Panel B corresponds to institutional investors and Panel C corresponds to foreign investors. Excess returns are computed for the previous 6 months of the herding year, the herding year and the year following the herding year

As regards individual investors, the pre-herding excess returns of the Q1 portfolio are positive over time. The pre-herding excess returns of the Q5 portfolio are positive or insignificantly different from zero. The differences between the Q1 and the Q5 portfolio in terms of pre-herding excess returns are positive for earlier periods but insignificant for later sample periods. The results are similar to Panel C of Table 24.2. As regards institutional investors, Q5 portfolio pre-herding excess returns are significantly positive for all the periods. This suggests trend-chasing behaviour by institutional investors. The results are similar to Panel C of Table 24.3. As regards foreign investors, Q1 portfolio pre-herding excess returns are significantly positive over time. On the other hand, Q5 portfolio excess returns are positive (in the earlier period) or insignificant (in the later periods). Significantly positive returns for the entire period seem to be caused by significantly positive returns in the earlier period. In the early days when the presence of foreign investors was not significant, foreign investors may have followed a trend chasing strategy. Overall, foreign investors sell winners, which is similar to the results shown in Panel C of Table 24.4.

As regards post-herding period returns for the entire sample period, both Q1 and Q5 portfolio returns of individual investors are insignificant. This is consistent with the results in Panel B of Table 24.2. The patterns are not stable through time. As for institutional investors, the results of the entire sample period are similar to those shown in Panel B of Table 24.3. Portfolio Q5 exhibits negative returns through time and the difference between portfolios Q5 and Q1 is negative or insignificant. Return reversals are observed for most time periods. As for foreign investors, portfolio Q5 post-herding excess returns are significantly greater than portfolio Q1 post-herding excess returns for all periods. No return reversals are observed in the subsequent period for portfolio Q5. Instead, the stocks they purchase outperform the stocks they sell. Our results are robust under different portfolio formation approaches and different time periods.

5.2 *Initial Ownership Level*

Individual investors tend to increase their holdings of a particular stock if their holdings are less than the cross-sectional average. The same patterns are observed for institutional investors. In other words, both types of investors sell the highest ownership firms and buy the lowest ownership firms. However, the foreign investors do not necessarily increase their holdings when their initial ownership level is less than the average, though they tend to decrease their holdings when their initial ownership level is greater than the average. The patterns are weak compared to those of individual and institutional investors.

In order to examine how this affects our results, all firms are sorted into five groups based on the initial individual ownership level for each year. The stocks in the largest and the smallest initial ownership groups are then further sorted into five portfolios based on change in ownership. We compute the time series average of the excess returns for these five portfolios of two extreme groups to see if they have different patterns. We conduct the same analysis for both institutional and foreign investors. The results are presented in Table 24.7.

Panel A presents the results for individual investors. No significant differences in patterns with respect to both herding period and post-herding period excess returns are observed for the two groups. For the pre-herding period, the lowest ownership group shows higher returns than the highest ownership group.

Panel B shows the results for institutional investors. The basic patterns of herding period excess returns are similar for both groups. Positive (negative) excess returns are observed when institutional investors increase (decrease) their holdings. Both

Table 24.7 Highest and lowest initial ownership groups sorted by subsequent ownership changes

	Quintile 1 (decrease in ownership)	Quintile 2	Quintile 3	Quintile 4	Quintile 5 (increase in ownership)	*F* value
A: Individual investor						
Highest initial ownership						
Excess returns ($t = 0$ to 11)	27.5008 (6.77)	7.6755 (3.28)	−2.9952 (−1.77)	−8.6404 (−4.80)	−15.5212 (−5.96)	42.46
Excess returns ($t = 12$ to 23)	−0.4956 (−0.18)	1.5841 (1.18)	3.1277 (2.56)	1.6265 (0.77)	3.8857 (2.31)	0.77
Excess returns ($t = -12$ to -1)	4.1673 (1.57)	−3.4196 (−1.52)	−4.3675 (−2.38)	−11.4402 (−5.41)	−2.6184 (−1.21)	6.26
Lowest initial ownership						
Excess returns ($t = 0$ to 11)	21.8774 (7.27)	−0.8378 (−0.45)	−7.5916 (−4.09)	−9.5833 (−6.03)	−11.6504 (−4.28)	38.19
Excess returns ($t = 12$ to 23)	−1.3795 (−0.81)	0.1644 (0.10)	−0.3167 (−0.22)	−1.1656 (−0.75)	−1.1830 (−0.54)	0.15
Excess returns ($t = -12$ to -1)	9.0043 (3.17)	4.0051 (2.10)	1.0110 (0.47)	2.6913 (1.41)	12.5428 (3.47)	3.46
B: Institutional investor						
Highest initial ownership						
Excess returns ($t = 0$ to 11)	−3.9606 (−1.85)	−6.3154 (−3.64)	−6.4814 (−3.83)	−3.4025 (−1.78)	11.8769 (3.48)	12.04
Excess returns ($t = 12$ to 23)	−4.9478 (−3.52)	1.3954 (1.51)	4.1105 (2.02)	−0.7777 (−0.42)	−3.8887 (−1.57)	4.18
Excess returns ($t = -12$ to -1)	7.7540 (2.32)	0.7587 (0.36)	−2.5246 (−1.10)	−1.9107 (−1.07)	4.1863 (1.96)	3.24
Lowest initial ownership						
Excess returns ($t = 0$ to 11)	−8.4087 (−2.62)	−4.5934 (−2.95)	−3.1291 (−1.87)	4.2319 (2.46)	18.9115 (5.41)	19.95
Excess returns ($t = 12$ to 23)	2.6515 (1.23)	4.6221 (2.33)	2.2187 (2.39)	−0.8837 (−0.62)	−2.7641 (−1.23)	2.64
Excess returns ($t = -12$ to -1)	−3.1699 (−1.52)	−5.9054 (−4.20)	−4.5289 (−2.90)	1.4454 (0.80)	8.3400 (2.54)	7.36

(continued)

Table 24.7 (continued)

	Quintile 1 (decrease in ownership)	Quintile 2	Quintile 3	Quintile 4	Quintile 5 (increase in ownership)	*F* value
C: Foreign investor						
Highest initial ownership						
Excess returns ($t=0$ to 11)	−4.5999 (−1.37)	−6.6778 (−3.24)	−2.4895 (−1.40)	3.5552 (1.07)	18.3029 (4.94)	12.30
Excess returns ($t=12$ to 23)	−2.8030 (−0.94)	−0.8879 (−0.46)	−3.8911 (−2.02)	4.1807 (1.14)	3.3642 (1.03)	1.63
Excess returns ($t=-12$ to -1)	18.0551 (3.70)	12.8483 (4.24)	4.7760 (2.28)	5.4838 (2.37)	10.8541 (2.79)	2.60
Lowest initial ownership						
Excess returns ($t=0$ to 11)	−1.9344 (−0.94)	−4.8769 (−2.34)	−1.0532 (−0.43)	−1.1378 (−0.50)	10.8623 (4.25)	7.39
Excess returns ($t=12$ to 23)	−0.9475 (−0.58)	4.6597 (1.80)	3.1665 (1.49)	−0.5087 (−0.33)	1.4578 (0.85)	1.48
Excess returns ($t=-12$ to -1)	−5.8542 (−2.90)	−3.7573 (−1.41)	−2.2031 (−1.09)	−3.2428 (−2.58)	−0.4954 (−0.28)	0.98

At the beginning of each April (1975–1995), all firms listed on the First and Second Sections of the Tokyo Stock Exchange whose fiscal year ends in March are sorted into five portfolios based on the fractions of shares held by each of the three types of investors. Panel A reports the time-series mean of the annual size and book-to-market adjusted excess returns over the herding year ($t=0$ to 11), the post-herding year ($t=12$ to 23) and the pre-herding year ($t=-12$ to -1) for stocks in the highest/lowest initial ownership quintile sorted into subsequent ($t=0$ to 11) changes in individual ownership quintiles. Panel B reports the same data for institutional ownership quintiles and Panel C for foreign ownership quintiles. t-values (in parentheses) are calculated from time-series standard errors of annual cross-sectional averages

groups show significantly negative post-herding returns and significantly positive pre herding returns for portfolio Q5. The results indicate the presence of return reversals and trend chasing behaviour by institutional investors, which is consistent with our previous finding.

Panel C reports the results for foreign investors. With respect to both herding period and post-herding period excess returns, the basic patterns are the same. For the pre-herding period, the highest initial ownership group shows higher positive returns than the lowest group. This suggests that when the stock outperforms (underperforms) the market, foreign investors' ownership of the stock is far above (below) the average. However, previous period returns do not explain foreign investor ownership change in the following period. This is consistent with our previous finding. In sum, we observe a similar pattern of excess returns surrounding the herding period for both the highest and the lowest initial ownership groups. Our results do not change after the initial ownership level is taken in to account.

5.3 Firm Size and Feedback Trading

Nofsinger and Sias (1999) document that institutional feedback trading is largely restricted to smaller capitalization stocks.[20] In this section, we examine the relationship between firm size, feedback trading and change in ownership. In order to examine the size effect on our results, all firms are sorted into five group by firm size for each year. Both the largest and the smallest size group firms are then further sorted into five portfolios based upon change in ownership of individual investors. We compute the time series average of the cross-sectional mean excess returns for these five portfolios to see if there are any different patterns between the two extreme size groups. In addition to herding period excess returns, we also calculate pre-herding period and post-herding period excess returns. We conduct the same analysis for both institutional and foreign investors. The results are presented in Table 24.8.

Panel A of Table 24.8 shows the relation between change in ownership and excess returns of herding, pre-herding and post-herding periods for individual investor. The basic patterns are the same for both herding and post-herding period return between the two size groups. However, significantly positive pre-herding period returns are observed for the large size group, while significantly negative pre-herding period returns are observed for the small size group. This is also true for both institutional

Table 24.8 Largest and smallest size groups sorted by subsequent ownership changes

	Quintile 1 (decrease in ownership)	Quintile 2	Quintile 3	Quintile 4	Quintile 5 (increase in ownership)	*F* value
A: Individual investor						
Largest size						
Excess returns ($t = 0$ to 11)	22.5245 (6.18)	6.6377 (3.36)	−1.0315 (−0.68)	−8.9923 (−4.94)	−16.1890 (−7.54)	40.71
Excess returns ($t = 12$ to 23)	−0.9448 (−0.57)	0.9306 (0.51)	2.1299 (0.91)	−1.4608 (−0.89)	0.4646 (0.23)	0.58
Excess returns ($t = -12$ to -1)	8.9331 (4.47)	6.8561 (3.42)	7.7495 (2.36)	5.6172 (3.28)	13.1703 (3.20)	1.09
Smallest size						
Excess returns ($t = 0$ to 11)	26.1382 (4.97)	5.2170 (2.33)	−4.1524 (−1.85)	−8.6965 (−4.31)	−6.9227 (−3.13)	22.07
Excess returns ($t = 12$ to 23)	0.6301 (0.38)	3.9765 (1.64)	4.1752 (2.14)	2.6641 (1.99)	2.4755 (1.41)	0.59
Excess returns ($t = -12$ to -1)	−5.1656 (−3.75)	−9.1033 (−4.12)	−14.0210 (−5.89)	−15.2589 (−7.06)	−8.0607 (−3.62)	4.03

(continued)

[20] Lakonishok et al. (1992) present evidence that pension fund feedback trading is limited to smaller firm stocks.

Table 24.8 (continued)

	Quintile 1 (decrease in ownership)	Quintile 2	Quintile 3	Quintile 4	Quintile 5 (increase in ownership)	*F* value
B: Institutional investor						
Largest size						
Excess returns ($t = 0$ to 11)	−3.6810 (−1.54)	−3.8820 (−2.09)	−2.1164 (−1.17)	3.0615 (1.59)	9.8443 (4.34)	8.09
Excess returns ($t = 12$ to 23)	0.3378 (0.20)	2.2416 (0.90)	3.0884 (1.81)	−1.1205 (−0.64)	−3.4693 (−2.80)	2.08
Excess returns ($t = -12$ to -1)	6.6972 (2.47)	8.6940 (3.39)	4.3520 (2.00)	6.2721 (31.0)	16.5008 (4.61)	3.14
Smallest size						
Excess returns ($t = 0$ to 11)	−3.9412 (−1.65)	−6.0939 (−3.62)	−3.1815 (−1.78)	3.0537 (1.57)	21.5928 (4.21)	15.29
Excess returns ($t = 12$ to 23)	0.7814 (0.63)	4.7615 (3.36)	6.1113 (2.44)	2.8984 (1.49)	−0.6618 (−0.37)	2.30
Excess returns ($t = -12$ to -1)	−6.6445 (−3.05)	−12.9487 (−6.06)	−15.0303 (−6.35)	−10.9622 (−4.92)	−5.8273 (−4.27)	3.63
C: Foreign investor						
Largest size						
Excess returns ($t = 0$ to 11)	−7.7583 (−3.69)	−4.7551 (−2.37)	−3.3965 (−2.86)	3.2949 (1.37)	15.7376 (4.93)	17.00
Excess returns ($t = 12$ to 23)	−1.7231 (−0.85)	−1.2280 (−0.68)	−1.1435 (−0.58)	2.9142 (1.10)	2.3505 (0.90)	0.98
Excess returns ($t = -12$ to -1)	17.1327 (4.40)	7.1364 (3.13)	4.4175 (1.81)	7.3621 (3.31)	6.9139 (2.99)	3.31
Smallest size						
Excess returns ($t = 0$ to 11)	−1.7273 (−0.93)	−2.1310 (−0.75)	−1.0798 (−0.43)	−1.2195 (−0.50)	17.3160 (5.11)	10.07
Excess returns ($t = 12$ to 23)	0.9619 (0.52)	2.7271 (0.84)	5.1912 (1.65)	2.2570 (0.94)	2.7726 (0.69)	0.26
Excess returns ($t = -12$ to -1)	−12.4771 (−5.17)	−14.8989 (−5.21)	−11.3748 (−6.42)	−8.0967 (−4.40)	−5.1339 (−3.69)	3.26

At the beginning of each April (1975–1995), all firms listed on the First and Second Sections of the Tokyo Stock Exchange whose fiscal year ends in March are sorted into five portfolios based on the firm size. Panel A reports the time-series mean of the annual size and book-to-market adjusted excess returns over the herding year ($t = 0$ to 11), the post-herding year ($t = 12$ to 23) and the pre-herding year ($t = -12$ to -1) for stocks in the largest/smallest size sorted into subsequent ($t = 0$ to 11) changes in individual ownership quintiles. Panel B reports the same data for institutional ownership quintiles and Panel C for foreign ownership quintiles. *t*-values (in parentheses) are calculated from time-series standard errors of annual cross-section al averages

investors and foreign investors. This may make sense since the large size group tends to contain more winners, while the small size group tends to include more losers. Nofsinger and Sias (1999) present similar results but the conclude that institutional feedback trading is largely restricted to small firm stocks by showing higher lag performance in portfolio Q1 for the large size group. Our results, however, are opposite for institutional investors because the portfolio Q5 return is higher than the portfolio Q1 return for the large size group. Institutional feedback trading is largely restricted to large firm stocks in Japan.

Panel B presents results for institutional investors. The basic patterns do not change for herding period excess returns. With regard to post-herding period returns, return reversals are observed only for large firm stocks. In other words, small firm stocks exhibit higher post-herding returns than large firm stocks. This finding may be similar to US results, which show stronger subsequent performance in small firm stocks. Panel C presents results for foreign investor. The results do not differ between the two groups for both herding and post-herding period returns. In sum, we confirm our previous results when the firm size effect is considered.[21]

6 Conclusions

This study examines the herding behaviour of investors in Japanese markets by examining the cross-sectional relationship between the change in ownership an stock returns using 20 years of aggregate data. Previous studies examined the herding behaviour of both individual and institutional investors in the USA. In addition to analyzing both individual and institutional investors, we examine foreign investors to determine whether their behaviour is different from that of institutional/individual investors. We find both institutional and foreign investors' herding impacts stock prices more than individual investors' herding. When we minimize the effect of individual investors, foreign investors' herding is greater than that of institutional investors in terms of impacting stock prices. Our finding is also consistent with intra-year positive feedback trading by both institutional and foreign investors. Our results also suggest that both institutional and foreign investors are able to forecast short-term stock returns.

[21]We conducted a similar analysis considering the book-to-market effect. We obtained similar results to the firm size effect analysis. The results for high book-to-market stocks are similar to those of small firm stocks and the results for low book-to-market stocks are similar to those of large firm stocks.

Positive feedback trading, which is largely restricted to large firm stocks, is observed for Japanese institutional investors. The presence of subsequent return reversals is consistent with the view that institutional investors' trades destabilize stock prices. This is different from the US finding of no return reversals. Foreign investors do not seem to follow trend-chasing investment strategies. Their trades may be related to information because subsequent return reversals are not observed. In fact, the stocks foreign investors purchase subsequently outperform those they sell. Foreign investors' herding behaviour seems to be similar to the herding behaviour of the US institutional investors, as documented by Nofsinger and Sias (1999). Our results are robust regardless of portfolio formation method, initial ownership level, time periods chosen and firm size.

Acknowledgements We are grateful to Marc Bremer, Takao Kobayashi, Sheridan Titman and Toshiki Yotsuzuka for their helpful comments. We also thank Ed Skrzypczak for editing the paper.

Addendum: Worldwide Empirical Studies of Investor Herding in Global Stock Markets[22]

One of the motivations for our paper was a presentation given by Professor John Nofsinger at the Financial Management Association (FMA) annual meeting held in Hawaii, October 1997. His paper, written with Professor Richard Sias, was elected "Best of the Best Paper" at the meeting. Even now, we distinctly remember that the standees came out to the hall of the Hilton Hawaiian Village Waikiki Beach Resort to listen to his presentation. The paper was titled, "Herding and Feedback Trading by Institutional and Individual Investors," published in the *Journal of Finance* in 1999 and now an indispensable prior research and empirical study on herding.

Around 1997, the term "herding" was hardly heard in Japan. Nofsinger and Sias (1999) made a significant contribution to the global development of empirical studies on herding. Several reasons why their paper became important and indispensable for subsequent empirical studies on herding are its simple herding measurement, the explicit interaction among investors, and the easy data collection method. In our paper, which focuses on the foreign investor who played a role that gradually became important in stock price formation in Japan, we analyzed the relationship between stock price movements and herding based on the empirical method of Nofsinger and Sias (1999), and found new evidence of foreign investor behavior.

Table 24.9 summarizes several studies that analyzed herding behavior in the global stock markets. For Asian stock markets, researchers tended to concentrate on foreign investor herding behavior. In addition, some papers report on the asymmetry of herding on the basis of an upward and a downward state of the stock market and a high and low state of market volatility besides others.

[22]This addendum has been newly written by Toshifumi Tokunaga for this book chapter.

Table 24.9 Worldwide herding behavior

Paper	Stock exchange	Factor
Kim and Nofsinger (2005)	Japan	Keiretsu
Choe et al. (1999)	Korea	Foreign investor's herding
Jeon and Moffett (2010)	Korea	Foreign investor's herding
Lao and Singh (2011)	China, India	Up and/or down
Hsieh (2013)	Taiwan	Ins. vs. Ind.
Bowe and Domuta (2004)	Jakarta	Foreign investor's herding
Phansatan et al. (2012)	Thai	Foreign investor's herding
Balcilar et al. (2013)	Gulf Arab (5 SEs)	Volatility
Wylie (2005)	U.K.	Fund manager behavior
Economou et al. (2011)	South Europe (4 SEs)	Volatility, up and/or down
Goodfellow et al. (2009)	Poland	Ins. vs. Ind.
Lin and Swanson (2008)	U.S.	Up and/or down
Kim and Nofsinger (2005)	Japan	Keiretsu

"Ins." and "ind." denote institutional investor and individual investor, respectively. "Up" and "down" denote the upward state and the downward state of the stock market, respectively

The greatest difficulty of empirical analyses on herding behavior is how we measure the magnitude of herding using published trading data. As we mentioned in footnote 3, our data based on financial statements are not precise because herding is then measurable only in 1-year intervals. More detailed data are required to analyze short-term herding behavior. Empirical studies on herding behavior are expected to increase if investor trading data that are measurable at shorter intervals become easily available in Japan.

References

Balcilar M, Demirer R, Hammoudeh S (2013) Investor herds and regime-switching: evidence from Gulf Arab stock markets. J Int Financ Mark Inst Money 23:295–321

Bowe M, Domuta D (2004) Investor herding during financial crisis: a clinical study of the Jakarta Stock Exchange. Pac Basin Financ J 12:387–418

Brennan M, Cao H (1997) International portfolio investment flows. J Financ 52:1851–1880

Chan L, Hamao Y, Lakonishok J (1991) Fundamentals and stock returns in Japan. J Financ 46:1739–1789

Choe H, Kho BC, Stulz R (1999) Do foreign investors destabilize stock markets? The Korean experience in 1997. J Financ Econ 56:743–766

Daniel K, Grinblatt M, Titman S, Wermers R (1997) Measuring mutual fund performance with characteristic based benchmarks. J Financ 52:1035–1058

Daniel K, Titman S, Wei J (2000) Explaining the cross-section of stock returns in Japan: factors or characteristics? J Financ 54:227–264

De Long B, Shleifer A, Summers L, Waldmann R (1990) Noise trader risk in financial markets. J Polit Econ 98:703–738

Economou F, Kostakis A, Philippas N (2011) Cross-country effects in herding behaviour: evidence from four south European markets. J Int Financ Mark Inst Money 21:443–460

Goodfellow C, Bohl MT, Gebka B (2009) Together we invest? Individual and institutional investors' trading behaviour in Poland. Int Rev Financ Anal 18:212–221

Grinblatt M, Titman S, Wermers R (1995) Momentum investment strategies, portfolio performance and hedging: a study of mutual fund behavior. Am Econ Rev 85:1088–1105

Hsieh SF (2013) Individual and institutional herding and the impact on stock returns: evidence from Taiwan stock market. Int Rev Financ Anal 29:175–188

Iihara Y, Kato H, Tokunaga T (2004) The winner-loser effect in Japanese stock returns. Japan World Econ 16:471–485

Jeon JQ, Moffett CM (2010) Herding by foreign investors and emerging market equity returns: evidence from Korea. Int Rev Econ Financ 19:698–710

Kang J, Stulz R (1997) Why is there a home bias? An analysis of foreign portfolio equity ownership in Japan. J Financ Econ 46:3–28

Kim KM, Nofsinger JR (2005) Institutional herding, business groups, and economic regimes: evidence from Japan. J Bus 78(1):213–242

Lakonishok J, Shleifer A, Vishny R (1992) The impact of institutional trading on stock prices. J Financ Econ 32:23–43

Lakonishok J, Shleifer A, Vishny R (1994) Contrarian investment, extrapolation, and risk. J Financ 49:1541–1578

Lao P, Singh H (2011) Herding behaviour in the Chinese and Indian stock markets. J Asian Econ 22:495–506

Lin AY, Swanson PE (2008) Foreigners' perceptions of U.S. markets: do foreigners exhibit herding tendencies? J Econ Bus 60:179–203

Nofsinger J, Sias R (1999) Herding and feedback trading by institutional an individual investors. J Financ 54:2263–2295

Phansatan S, Powell JG, Tanthanongsakkun S, Treepongkaruna S (2012) Investor type trading behavior and trade performance: evidence from the Thai stock market. Pac Basin Financ J 20:1–23

Scharfstein D, Stein J (1990) Herd behavior and investment. Am Econ Rev 80:465–479

Shiller R, Konya M, Tsutsui Y (1996) Why did the Nikkei crash? Expanding the scope of expectation data collections. Rev Econ Stat 78:156–164

Wylie S (2005) Fund manager herding: a test of the accuracy of empirical results using U.K. data. J Bus 78(1):381–403

Chapter 25
The Characteristics of Online Investors

Konari Uchida

Abstract Using survey data, we explore the characteristics of Japanese online investors. Our main findings are as follows. First, young men are more likely to engage in online trading. Second, employed investors trade online more frequently, implying that proximity to the information network of the workplace affects investor decisions to trade online. Third, we do not find that investors who are more satisfied with their past returns tend to invest online more often. Thus, the self-attribution bias is not supported for Japanese online traders. Finally, Japanese online investors prefer capital gains, do not prefer low-volatility stocks, refer to chart data, make investment decisions more frequently, and tend to choose stocks to buy and sell on their own. These characteristics of Japanese online investors are consistent with those of overconfident investors.

Keywords Online investor • Overconfidence • Investor survey

1 Introduction

The advent of online trading is one of the most notable recent changes in the stock markets. In the U.S., there were reportedly more than 20 million online brokerage accounts in 2001, up from just 1.5 million in 1996.[1] In Japan, which lagged the U.S. in its use, the increase in online trading has also been dramatic. The increase began in 1999, along with the liberalization of commissions for security trading.[2] For the

The original article first appeared in the Journal of Behavioral Finance 7:168–177, 2006. A newly written addendum has been added to this book chapter.

[1]See the web site of the *Wall Street Journal* (http://investing.wsj.com/stocks.html).

[2]Prior to the liberalization, the commission rate was fixed at 1.15 % for trades with a value of less than 1 million yen (about U.S. $9,000).

K. Uchida (✉)
Faculty of Economics, Kyushu University, Fukuoka, Japan
e-mail: kuchida@econ.kyushu-u.ac.jp

S. Ikeda et al. (eds.), *Behavioral Economics of Preferences, Choices, and Happiness*, DOI 10.1007/978-4-431-55402-8_25

6 months ending in September 2002, it is estimated that online trading accounted for 52 % of all retail stock trading value.[3]

This chapter explores the characteristics of Japanese online investors. The recent increase in online investors has led to an increased interest in examining their attitudes and motives as a way to further understand market movements.

To be able to investigate individual investor tendencies, however, we need detailed data on their trading patterns and preferences. And although there is a paucity of such data, we do have access to survey data from Dr. Mizuno, a Japanese finance researcher, who conducted a study in 2001 with the Financial Media Company. His survey includes information about individual investor preferences and attitudes, as well as frequency of Internet usage for investments.

Several earlier studies have investigated who engages in online trading and what characteristics such traders have using U.S. data (Barber and Odean 2002; Choi et al. 2002). These studies found that young men are more likely to use the Internet for investing, and that online investors tend to increase turnover and decrease their performance after switching to online trading. Using Japanese data, we can test the universality of these characteristics. Because Japanese are generally thought of as more conservative or modest than Americans, a comparison of U.S. and Japanese online investor characteristics would be meaningful.

Research concerning online investors frequently focuses on the phenomenon of overconfidence. Overconfidence occurs when people believe their predictions about random events like stock returns are more precise than they really are. Earlier U.S. studies have found that online investors experience increased turnover and decreased performance after switching to online trading, two common traits of overconfident investors. Using the survey data, we examine whether the characteristics of Japanese online investors are consistent with those of overconfident investors.

Our main findings are as follows. First, young men are more likely to invest online, which is consistent with U.S. studies. Second, investors trade more frequently online when they are at work. This means that investors away from the information network of the workplace may be less likely to engage in online trading.

Third, we do not find that investors who are more satisfied with their past returns are more likely to invest online. This evidence does not support the self-attribution bias for Japanese online traders, which is inconsistent with U.S. results (Barber and Odean 2002), but is consistent with Daniel et al. (1998) and Kitayama et al. (1995).

Finally, the characteristics of Japanese online investors are different from those of traditional investors. Specifically, Japanese online investors prefer higher capital gains, choose low-volatility stocks less often, use chart data more frequently, and are more likely to choose stocks to buy and sell themselves. In other words, they are more active, more speculative, and more confident. These characteristics of Japanese online investors are also consistent with those of overconfident investors.

[3]See the *Nihon Keizai Shimbun*, February 12, 2002.

2 Data Description

In 2001, Dr. Mizuno conducted a survey on the behavioral principles of Japanese individual investors in cooperation with the Financial Media Company, the publisher of *Japanese Investor,* one of the most important Japanese quarterly journals for individual investors. *Japanese Investor* has a circulation of approximately 10,000. The Financial Media Company mailed the questionnaire at the end of April 2001 to 2,800 individual investors randomly selected from *Japanese Investor* subscribers. The subscribers who received the questionnaire were asked to mail it back to the Financial Media Company from April 30–May 14, 2001. During this period, 1,068 responses were received (a 38 % response rate).

This survey is extremely valuable, since it is so difficult to obtain large sample data about the preferences and attitudes of Japanese individual investors. We will refer to the survey as MF survey hereafter.

Table 25.1 gives the survey results for the entire sample in the third column. Panel A gives demographic data on the respondents. Approximately 88 % were male. This figure is higher than that in Barber and Odean (2001) (77.2 %), and is attributable to the subscriber structure of *Japanese Investor*.

Panel A of Table 25.1 also describes the occupation status of the respondents. We define a respondent who answered "no occupation" or "housewife" as an investor with no occupation. About 40 % are classified this way.

The mean age of all respondents was about 55, which is relatively close to Barber and Odean (2001) (51.6), and the Omega company investigated in Choi et al. (2002) (52.8). The average investment career is 18 years, and its percentiles of 25th and 50th are 7 and 15 years, respectively (not reported). This figure suggests that our sample consists mainly of investors with relatively long investment careers, which may be attributable to the fact that our sample selection method is based on subscribers of an investment journal.

Panel B summarizes the respondents' answers to each question. The survey asked: "Do you use the Internet for investing?" The response choices were (1) *frequently use*, (2) *sometimes use*, and (3) *never*. About half the respondents frequently or sometimes use online trading.

The next question asked which form of return, capital gains or dividends, is preferred. This was designed to reveal the level of speculativeness among Japanese investors. The response choices were (1) *dividend*, (2) *capital gains*, and (3) *indifferent*. Table 25.1 shows that, again, roughly half the respondents prefer capital gains over dividends.

The MF survey then asked "Which stock would you prefer, a high- or a low-volatility stock, provided their expected returns were the same?" This question is intended to reveal risk tolerance. The responses were (1) *high-volatility stock*, (2) *low-volatility stock*, and (3) *indifferent*. Approximately 33 % chose (1) *high-volatility stock,* and approximately 50 % chose (3) *indifferent.* This result may be surprising, since Japanese investors are generally considered more conservative and highly risk-averse.

Table 25.1 Survey results

Panel A: Demographic characteristics of respondents

		Entire sample		Group A		Group B		Group C		
		Number	%	Number	%	Number	%	Number	%	Chi-square
Gender	Male	905	87.78 %	293	90.71 %	161	86.10 %	439	86.42 %	4.27
	Female	126	12.22 %	30	9.29 %	26	13.90 %	69	13.58 %	
	Total	1,031	100.00 %	323	100.00 %	187	100.00 %	508	100.00 %	
Occupation	Employed	567	60.45 %	235	78.07 %	125	71.84 %	207	44.71 %	96.53***
	No occupation	371	39.55 %	66	21.93 %	49	28.16 %	256	55.29 %	
	Total	938	100.00 %	301	78.07 %	174	100.00 %	463	100.00 %	
		Mean	Standard deviation	Mean	Standard deviation	Mean	Standard deviation	Mean	Standard deviation	
Age		54.33	14.84	46.04	13.28	50.83	14.24	60.91	12.83	
	Number of respondents	988		310		181		485		
Length of investment experience		18.07	13.40	12.78	10.90	16.10	11.88	22.38	14.03	
	Number of respondents	999		317		184		486		

Panel B: Answer to main questionnaires

Questions	Answer	Number	%	Number	%	Number	%	Number	%	Chi-square
Do you use the Internet for investments?	(1) frequently use	327	31.66 %							
	(2) sometimes use	193	18.68 %							
	(3) never	513	49.66 %							
	Total	1,033	100.00%							
Which form of return do you prefer, dividends or capital gains?	(1) dividends	397	38.36%	103	31.79%	71	37.17%	218	42.91%	10.86**
	(2) capital gains	515	49.76%	178	54.94%	95	49.74%	237	46.65%	
	(3) indifferent	123	11.88%	43	13.27%	25	13.09%	53	10.43%	
	Total	1,035	100.00 %	324	100.00 %	191	100.00 %	508	100.00 %	
Would you prefer a high- or low-volatility stock, provided their expected returns were the same?	(1) high-volatility stocks	355	34.27 %	102	31.29 %	61	32.11 %	186	36.61 %	27.82***
	(2) low-volatility stocks	235	22.68 %	49	15.03 %	47	24.74 %	136	26.77 %	
	(3) indifferent	446	43.05 %	175	53.68 %	82	43.16 %	186	36.61 %	
	Total	1,036	100.00 %	326	100.00 %	190	100.00 %	508	100.00 %	
Do you refer to past stock price movements (charts) in picking stocks to buy and sell?	(1) refer very much	448	43.37%	199	61.42%	63	32.98%	179	35.38%	77.92***
	(2) refer very little	544	52.66 %	121	37.35 %	125	65.45 %	293	57.91 %	
	(3) not at all	41	3.97 %	4	1.23 %	3	1.57 %	34	6.72 %	
	Total	1,033	100.00 %	324	100.00 %	191	100.00 %	506	100.00 %	

(continued)

Table 25.1 (continued)

Panel B: Answer to main questionnaires

Questions	Answer	Number	%	Number	%	Number	%	Number	%	Chi-square
How do you pick stocks to buy and sell?	(1) by myself	769	76.21%	278	87.97%	147	81.22%	338	72.22%	32.04***
	(2) by consulting with specialists	204	20.22 %	28	8.86%	27	14.92 %	113	24.15 %	
	(3) mainly take buy-and-hold strategy	36	3.57 %	10	3.16 %	7	3.87 %	17	3.63 %	
	Total	1,009	100.00 %	316	100.00 %	181	100.00 %	468	100.00 %	
Are you satisfied with your past returns from stocks?	(1) satisfied	77	7.47 %	25	7.81 %	16	8.38 %	34	6.71 %	2.25
	(2) somewhat satisfied	284	27.55 %	94	29.38 %	53	27.75 %	135	26.63 %	
	(3) somewhat unsatisfied	320	31.04 %	98	30.63 %	61	31.94 %	158	31.16 %	
	(4) unsatisfied	350	33.95 %	103	32.19 %	61	31.94 %	180	35.50 %	
	Total	1,031	100.00 %	320	100.00 %	191	100.00 %	507	100.00 %	
Are you satisfied with your past returns from mutual funds?	(1) satisfied	14	1.55%	4	1.45%	5	2.89%	5	1.12%	6.98
	(2) somewhat satisfied	86	9.49 %	28	10.14 %	17	9.83 %	41	9.17%	
	(3) somewhat unsatisfied	240	26.49 %	79	28.62 %	52	30.06 %	107	23.94 %	
	(4) unsatisfied	566	62.47 %	165	59.78 %	99	57.23 %	294	65.77 %	
	Total	906	100.00 %	276	100.00 %	173	100.00 %	447	100.00 %	

Group A: respondents who frequently use online trading.
Group B: respondents who sometimes use online trading.
Group C: respondents who have never used online trading.

To explore whether Japanese investors rely on chart analysis, which usually produces no excess returns in the semi-strong form of efficient markets, the MF survey asked: "Do you refer to past stock price movements (charts) in choosing stocks to buy and sell?" Table 25.1 indicates that almost all the respondents use chart analysis.

The next question is "How do you pick stocks to buy and sell?" This was designed to analyze how heavily Japanese investors rely on their own abilities to gather and analyze securities information. The responses were (1) *by myself*, (2) *by consulting with specialists like financial institution staff and financial planners*, and (3) *mainly use a buy-and-hold strategy*. Surprisingly, about 75 % answered (1) *by myself*. This may be because our sample consists of more experienced and eager individual investors.

The MF survey next asked: "Are you satisfied with your past returns from stocks?" and "Are you satisfied with your past returns from mutual funds?" It is striking that only 33 % answered (1) *satisfied* or (2) *somewhat satisfied* about stocks, and only 11 % answered (1) or (2) about mutual funds. We interpret this surprisingly low figure as reflecting the recent serious downturn in Japanese stock prices.

As described earlier, the mean (median) of an investment career is 18 (15) years. During the 15 years prior to 2001, the Japanese stock market experienced both tremendous gains and tremendous losses. The Tokyo Stock Exchange Price Index (TOPIX) climbed from 1,324.26 in 1986, to 2,177.96 in 1989, and then dropped to 1,195.10 by 2001. Therefore, Japanese investors with less than 10 years of investment experience, roughly 30 % of our sample, are likely to have lost money during their entire investment careers. Investors with 15 years' experience are likely to feel unsatisfied because they lost money during the latter half of their whole investment careers.

3 Who Tends to Invest Online in Japan?

Using the self-reported data, this section explores who is likely to engage in online investing in Japan. Investigating U.S. individual investors, Barber and Odean (2002) and Choi et al. (2002) found that young men are more likely to use online trading. Choi et al. (2002) also argued that the information network of the workplace affects the decision to go online, which implies that retired and terminated participants of 401(k) plans may be less likely to use the web.

3.1 Univariate Analysis

We divided the respondents into three groups, A, B, and C. Respondents who frequently use online trading were placed into Group A. Those who sometimes use online trading were placed into Group B, and those who never use it in Group C.

The three right-hand columns in Panel A of Table 25.1 describe the demographic characteristics and answers to each of the questions for Groups A, B, and C, respectively. They also give the results of chi-square statistics that test whether the answer distribution is uniform across the three groups for each of the questions.

Panel A shows there are more men in Group A (90.7 %) than in Groups B and C (86.1 % and 86.4 %). However, the significance level of the chi-square is marginal.

The percentage of respondents with no occupation seems clearly different among the three groups. Approximately 80 % in Group A are employed; only 45 % in Group C are employed. The chi-square statistic is statistically significant here at the 1 % level.

It is clear that younger respondents have a higher frequency of online trading. The average age for Groups A and B is 46.0 and 50.8, respectively; for Group C it is 60.9. Likewise, the longer a respondent's investment experience, the lower the frequency of online trading. The mean length of investment experience is 12.8 and 16.1 years for Groups A and B, respectively; the respondents in Group C have over 20 years of investment experience on average.

The right-hand three columns of Panel B show answer distributions about each questionnaire for Groups A, B, and C, respectively. We are primarily interested in the degree of satisfaction with past investments. Barber and Odean (2002) found that those who switch to online trading perform well prior to going online. Because return data for each respondent is not available, however, we cannot conduct the same test as Barber and Odean (2002). Instead, we use self-reported data on the degree of respondent satisfaction.

Panel B does not appear to present a clear relationship between degree of satisfaction with past returns and frequency of online trading. The percentage of respondents who answered "satisfied" or "somewhat satisfied" with their past returns from stocks is about 37 % for Group A, 36 % for Group B, and 33 % for Group C. The chi-square statistic is insignificant. Likewise, the percentage of respondents who answered "satisfied" or "somewhat satisfied" with their past mutual fund returns is about 12 % for Group A, slightly higher than for Group C (10 %), but lower than for Group B (13 %). The chi-square statistic is insignificant again.

Overall, the univariate analysis finds that young and less experienced investors who are employed trade online more frequently. We do not find that investors who are more satisfied with their past returns tend to be more frequent online traders.

3.2 Logistic Regression Result

We next conduct logistic regressions whose dependent variable is an online trader dummy. The online trader dummy has a value of 1 if a respondent frequently or sometimes engages in online trading (respondents from Groups A or B), and 0 for never having used it (respondents from Group C).

The independent variables are as follows. The dummy for gender has a value of 1 for male respondents, and 0 for female respondents. Age and length of investment

Table 25.2 Logistic regression results of the determinants of going online

Constant	3.25*** (8.15)
Gender dummy (male = 1, female = 0)	0.51** (2.07)
Age	−6.33E-02*** (−8.82)
Length of investment experience	−7.88E-03 (−1.05)
No occupation dummy	−0.36* (−1.91)
Satisfied with past returns from stocks	1.19E-02 (0.04)
Somewhat satisfied with past returns from stocks	0.28 (1.45)
Somewhat unsatisfied with past returns from stocks	−1.26E-02 (−0.07)
Chi-square	216.27***
Log likelihood	−517.62
Pseudo R-squared	0.17
Number of observations	903

The dependent variable is the online trader dummy which takes on a value of one if a responder frequently or sometimes uses online trading and zero if he/she has never used it
T-statistics are shown in *parentheses*
***, **, *: significant at the 1 %, 5 %, and 10 % level, respectively

career are also included as independent variables. The no occupation dummy is a binary variable with a value of 1 if a respondent answered "no occupation" or "housewife," and 0 otherwise. Finally, three dummy variables, "satisfied," "somewhat satisfied," and "somewhat unsatisfied" with past returns are added. If a respondent answered "satisfied with past returns," the dummy takes a value of 1 and the other two dummies have a value of 0.

The logistic regression results are given in Table 25.2. The three dummy variables indicate the degree of respondent satisfaction with past returns from stocks. Table 25.2 shows the gender dummy has a positive and significant coefficient. This suggests that men have a higher probability of trading online when controlling for the effects of age, occupation status, and degree of satisfaction with past returns. This evidence is consistent with previous U.S. findings.

Age has a negative and significant coefficient. Together with the univariate analysis findings, this suggests that younger generations trade online more frequently, consistent with Barber and Odean's (2002) and Choi et al. (2002) results for U.S. investors.

The coefficient of the investment career is negative. However, the significance level is marginal. Therefore, we do not find evidence of a positive relationship between length of investment career and frequency of online investing when controlling for the effects of age, occupation status, and degree of satisfaction with past returns.

The no occupation dummy has a negative and significant coefficient, consistent with the univariate analysis findings. This implies that investors away from the information network of the workplace are less likely to engage in online trading in Japan. Together with Choi, Laibson, and Metrick's (2002) evidence, we conclude that the workplace affects investor decisions to trade online, both in the U.S. and in Japan. Given that online trading in 401(k) plans by participants of the same company is expected to be affected more highly by the information network of the workplace, we believe our research shows broad evidence of its effect on online trading.

Finally, no dummy variables indicating degree of respondent satisfaction with past returns have significant coefficients. Along with the univariate analysis, we fail to find evidence that the degree of investor satisfaction with past returns affects frequency of online trading.

Barber and Odean (2002) investigated returns data for U.S. online investors, and found that past returns are positively associated with investor frequency of online trading. They also found that investors who have had positive investment experiences are more likely to invest online. This evidence suggests that successful investors may become overconfident through the self-attribution bias, which refers to the psychological phenomenon of attributing success to one's own abilities, even when it is clearly caused by external factors. Thus these types of investors may be more motivated to trade online.

However, our evidence suggests that the self-attribution bias is not evident for Japanese online investors. Kitayama, Takagi, and Matsumoto (1995) found that the self-attribution bias is less evident in Japan. Daniel et al. (1998) pointed out that, due to the lack of the self-attribution bias, short-term momentum and long-term return reversals are not observed in Japan. Thus, our finding can be attributed to the fact that Japanese investors tend to be less susceptible to this bias.[4]

4 Characteristics of Japanese Online Traders

We now focus on Japanese online investor preferences for (1) capital gains versus dividends, (2) volatility, (3) chart analysis for investment information, and (4) method of stock selection.

4.1 Preference for Capital Gains Over Dividends

Table 25.1 shows that the proportion of respondents who preferred dividends over capital gains is higher for Group C (42.9 %) than for Groups A (31.8 %) and B (37.2 %). The fraction of respondents who prefer capital gains is higher for Group A (54.9 %) than for Groups B (49.7 %) and C (46.7 %). The chi-square statistic

[4]The long-term slump of recent Japanese stock prices can be another cause for this finding. During the 1990s, the Japanese stock market declined, losing about one-half its value from its peak. We consider it difficult for investors who beat the market but still bore losses to be overconfident.

is significant at the 5 % level. These figures show that online traders prefer capital gains over dividends, suggesting they are more active and more speculative.

We also conduct a logistic regression of a dummy variable that takes a value of 1 if a respondent prefers capital gains, and 0 otherwise. The online trader dummy and some demographic variables are adopted as independent variables. Model 1 in Table 25.3 finds that the online trader dummy has a positive and significant coefficient, suggesting that online traders tend to be more active and more speculative after controlling for respondent gender, age, and length of investment experience.

4.2 Risk Tolerance

Investor risk tolerance is represented by preference for volatility. Table 25.1 shows that the percentage of Group A respondents with a preference for low-volatility stocks is about 15 %, much lower than for Groups B and C (24.7 % and 26.8 %, respectively). Also, the percentage of respondents who are indifferent between low- and high-volatility stocks is much higher for Group A (63.7 %) than for Groups B (43.2 %) and C (36.6 %). These figures imply that online investors are less risk-averse than non-online investors. The chi-square statistic is statistically significant at the 1 % level.

Model 2 in Table 25.3 presents the result of a logistic regression for the dummy variable with a value of 1 if a respondent prefers low-volatility stocks, and 0 otherwise. The online trader dummy has a negative and significant coefficient, suggesting that online traders are more risk-tolerant.

4.3 Referring to Charts

The degree of using past stock price movements (charts) to choose stocks represents an important investor characteristic. Table 25.1 clearly shows that Group A has a much higher proportion of respondents who use charts frequently (61.4 %) than Groups B and C (33.0 % and 35.4 %, respectively). The proportion of respondents who do not refer to charts at all is much higher for Group C (6.7 %) than for Groups A and B (1.2 % and 1.6 %, respectively). The chi-square statistic is statistically significant at the 1 % level.

Likewise, the logistic regression, using a dummy variable with a value of 1 if a respondent refers to charts very much and 0 otherwise, finds the online trader dummy has a positive and significant coefficient (Model 3 in Table 25.3). These results indicate that online traders tend to use charts more often, implying that online traders desire access to vast quantities of real-time information on security price movements. This investment style is also consistent with the tendency of online traders to be less risk-averse and prefer capital gains.

Table 25.3 Logistic regression results of the respondents' characteristics

	Model 1	Model 2	Model 3
Dependent variable (all dependent variables are binary ones)	1 if a respondent prefers capital gains and 0 otherwise	1 if a respondent prefers low-volatility stocks and 0 otherwise	1 if a respondent refers to charts very much and 0 otherwise
Constant	−0.65* (−1.83)	−1.07** (−2.55)	−1.09*** (−2.94)
Online trader dummy	0.31** (2.12)	−0.44** (−2.51)	0.67*** (4.45)
Gender	0.15 (0.75)	−0.15 (−0.62)	0.47** (2.19)
Age	0.01 (1.22)	0.01 (1.11)	0.00 (0.64)
Length of investment experience	−1.86E-03 (−0.29)	−0.01* (−1.91)	−0.01 (−1.27)
Chi-squared	5.73	11.99	33.13
Log likelihood	−654.92	−501.80	−631.84
Pseud R-squared	0.04	0.01	0.03
Number of observations	949	949	947

T-statistics are shown in *parentheses*
***, **, *: significant at the 1 %, 5 %, and 10 % level, respectively

4.4 *Method of Choosing Stocks*

Finally, we compare the method of choosing stocks among the three groups. Table 25.1 shows that the fraction of respondents who chose stocks on their own increases as the frequency of online trading increases. The percentages are about 88.0 % for Group A, 81.2 % for Group B, and 72.2 % for Group C. On the other hand, the fraction of respondents who choose stocks by consulting with specialists is much higher for Group C (24.2 %) than for Groups A and B (8.9 % and 14.9 %, respectively). The chi-square statistic is statistically significant.

We also conduct a logistic regression for the dummy variable with a value of 1 if respondents primarily choose stocks on their own, and 0 otherwise. The regression result shows that the online trader dummy has a positive and statistically significant coefficient (untabulated). This suggests that online investors are more likely to rely on their own judgments when valuing stocks.

Overall, Japanese online investors have different characteristics than traditional investors. They are more likely to prefer capital gains, less likely to prefer low-volatility stocks, more likely to use past price (chart) data, and tend to choose stocks themselves. In other words, they are more active, speculative, and confident.

5 Discussion

Previous research has argued that online investors exhibit overconfidence. It is critical to consider whether the characteristics of Japanese online investors are consistent with those of overconfident investors. Such an analysis would contribute to the universality of results found in earlier U.S. works.

5.1 *Investor Overconfidence*

Overconfidence means that people believe their predictions about random events like stock returns are more precise than they actually are. Odean (1998) showed that online investors trade more actively and speculatively than rational investors, and, as a result, they may lower their expected utilities.

Since online trading decreases transaction costs per trade and increases ease of trading, it may be highly appealing to overconfident investors. Moreover, once investors trade online, they may become more overconfident. A series of psychological studies have found that people tend to become overconfident when they are given more information (illusion of knowledge). Since online trading gives investors access to less costly and vast quantities of information, it may make them more overconfident.

Moreover, online trading is likely to delude investors via the illusion of control, the phenomenon whereby people believe their personal involvement improves the probability of a favorable outcome. Larger (1975) found that choice, task familiarity, competition, and active involvement lead to the illusion of control. Of these key factors, active involvement is offered by online trading, because investors can place their orders themselves.

Barber and Odean (2002) reported that investors trade more actively, more speculatively, and less profitably after first engaging in online trading than before. Choi et al. (2002) showed that turnover in 401(k) accounts increased by 50 % after starting to trade online.

5.2 *Japanese Online Investors and Overconfidence*

Note that we cannot analyze whether Japanese online investors are overconfident in the same way as U.S. studies. The lack of data in Japan does not allow us to test whether online investor performance is inferior to traditional investor performance, or whether online investors increased turnover or performed worse after starting to trade online. Nevertheless, we believe our self-reported data suggest that the characteristics of Japanese online investors are consistent with those of overconfident investors for the following reasons.

First, our data show that Japanese online investors tend to choose stocks on their own. The illusion of control often means that people expect their personal involvement to increase the probability of a favorable outcome. The illusion of control may be consistent with the behavioral pattern of overconfident investors.

Second, the evidence that Japanese online traders prefer capital gains over dividends suggests they are more active and more speculative. This implies that Japanese online traders have higher turnovers than traditional investors. The fact that the turnover of the Japanese stock market has increased since 1999, when online trading began to expand, reinforces this inference.[5]

Third, Japanese online investors are less risk-averse, and prefer low-volatility stocks less than non-online investors. Previous studies showed that overconfident investors reduce their perception of risk and may become overly risk-tolerant because they believe the probability of success is higher than it really is. Thus, our finding is consistent with the finding of risk tolerance for overconfident investors.

Finally, Japanese online investors are found to frequently use chart analysis to obtain past price data. This evidence leads us to conjecture that online investors tend to have access to vast quantities of real-time information on their desktops. This may lead to the illusion of knowledge, a characteristic typical of overconfident investors.

Moreover, it is well-known that analyzing past price movements cannot produce excess returns in a semi-strong efficient market. Thus, the finding of a heavy reliance on chart data implies that Japanese online investors are more likely to perform below

[5] A similar view was described in the *Nihon Keizai Shimbun* on February 2, 2002.

the market, although we cannot directly compare their performance with market returns. This inference is reinforced by the result of a survey conducted by *Nikkei Money* in 2002, another major Japanese investment journal. The survey found that just 31 % of Japanese online investors profit from their investments. If their raw returns are not higher than the market's, they must ultimate lose money, because trading more frequently means paying more commissions.

In sum, the characteristics of Japanese online investors are consistent with those of overconfident investors, except that the self-attribution bias is not evident.

6 Concluding Remarks

Using the survey data, we study the characteristics of Japanese online investors. We summarize our main findings as follows. First, young men are more likely to engage in online trading, which is consistent with previous U.S. studies.

Second, employed investors are more like to engage in online trading. Investors away from the information network of a workplace are less likely to join online trading. This evidence, consistent with Choi et al. (2002), presents more broad evidence of how the information network of a workplace affects online trading.

Third, we do not find that investors who are more satisfied with their past returns are more likely to trade online. This evidence, which does not support the self-attribution bias for Japanese online investors, is inconsistent with the result for U.S. online investors (Barber and Odean 2002), but is consistent with Kitayama, Takagi, and Matsumoto (1995) and Daniel et al. (1998).

Finally, Japanese online investors have different characteristics than investors who have never invested online. They prefer capital gains, higher-volatility stocks, use chart analysis more frequently, and tend to choose stocks to buy and sell on their own. In other words, they are more active, more speculative, and more confident.

We believe this research takes an important step forward in exploring the characteristics of Japanese online investors.

Acknowledgments I thank Professor Hiroshi Mizuno for providing the survey data and for useful comments and advice.

Addendum: The Internet and the Stock Market[6]

Literature of behavioral finance points out overconfidence (tendency of individuals to consider themselves better than the average) as a cognitive bias that significantly impacts economic activities. Examples are CEOs' overconfidence influencing

[6]This addendum has been newly written for this book chapter.

corporate investment decisions (Malmendier and Tate 2005a, b, 2008), financing (Malmendier et al. 2011), optimal compensation contracts (Gervais et al. 2011), and innovation (Galasso and Simcoe 2011; Hirshleifer et al. 2012); overconfident investors showing different trading patterns and performance (Grinblatt and Keloharju 2009; Wang 2001); the existence of overconfident investors affecting stock prices, volatility, and trading volume (Daniel et al. 1998; Hirshleifer and Luo 2001; Scheinkman and Xiong 2003; Statman et al. 2006); peoples' overconfidence affecting their productivity (Kinari et al. 2011); and so on. In such, it is important to uncover how people become overconfident.

Camerer and Lovallo (1999) show that overconfidence is especially evident among highly skilled people. Previous studies also premise that men are more overconfident than women (Camerer and Lovallo 1999). Additionally, online trading potentially facilitates overconfidence in people. Since the Internet enables users to gather vast amounts of information with a trivial cost, online traders are likely to have the illusion of control, which is an important source of overconfidence. Furthermore, Internet users are likely to be caught up in self-attribution bias, which is another source of overconfidence. Therefore, researchers should pay particular attention to online trading as a source of overconfidence, since online investing is a growing and non-reversible phenomenon. For example, in December 2013, SBI securities, the largest online brokerage firm in Japan, intermediated for securities transactions for approximately 11.1 trillion JPY, which is almost 10 times the amount shown in December 2003 (about 1.36 trillion JPY). This fact implies that overconfident investors, who may generate volatile markets with high trading volume, have significantly increased during the past 10 years.

As introduced in the main chapter, Barber and Odean (2002) and Choi et al. (2002) provided the seminal works on characteristics and performance of online investors. Their findings support the idea that online investors are overconfident. In addition, this chapter argues that Japanese online investors show characteristics of overconfident investors by investigating results from the Japanese investor survey conducted in 2001. This supplemental chapter reviews previous studies, including recent ones, on online investors to enrich our understanding of the issue.

Another important topic in this line of research is who goes online for stock trading. Literature on information systems has suggested that peoples' decisions to use the Internet are affected by their perception of ease of use, benefits, security risk, and so on (e.g., Davis 1989). As for online trading, Lee (2009) conducted an investor survey in Taiwan and constructed proxy variables for investors' trust in the Internet, its perceived benefits, and its perceived risk.[7] Lee (2009) finds that trust and perceived benefits are positively associated with online trading adoption

[7] Specifically, trust is ascertained from the respondent's answers to the following questions: "I know it is trustworthy"; "I know it is not opportunistic"; and "I believe it is predictable." Perceived benefit is ascertained from answers to the following: "Online trading transaction costs are very low"; "Online trading transaction speed is very fast"; and "all the information from the transaction can be viewed through a website and is transparent." Finally, perceived risk is ascertained from: "I would not feel secure sending private personal information on the Internet"; "If online trading

while the perceived risk is negatively related.[8] In general, younger generations are more focusing on the benefits of the Internet. This fact will generate continuous increases in online trading. In addition, daily communication with colleagues will allow employed people to gain access to information on benefits and ease of Internet usage, as well as solutions to technical problems that may be encountered. Taken together, Lee's (2009) finding is consistent with Choi et al.'s (2002) and this chapter's finding that young and employed investors tend to trade online.

Interestingly, wide variations exist in online trading usage across countries. For instance, Lee (2009) notes that 54 % of the total market turnover was driven by online trading in Korea for the year of 2005, while only 13.2 % of the total turnover was online in Taiwan. In addition to the tax treatment and nation-level Internet environments, some cultural and psychological factors may generate the difference. It would be an interesting study to consider whether peoples' country-level characteristics affect usage of online trading, since the proportion of online traders (i.e., overconfident investors) over all investors will affect the market characteristics.

We need online investors' trading records and performance data to examine accurately whether online investors are overconfident; they should trade very frequently and experience negative excess returns after transaction costs. However, research that addresses the issue in a convincing manner is limited due to the severe difficulty in obtaining such data, with the exception of Barber and Odean (2002) and Choi et al. (2002). Oh et al. (2008) offer recent and exceptional research that traces online investors' performance; in such, they obtain data of daily online trading activities from the Korea Stock Exchange. Oh et al. (2008) find that Korean online investors underperform non-online investors, and argue that individual investors' poor performance is attributable to online trading. This result is consistent with the idea that online investors are overconfident. However, we should note that their online trading data are collected at the aggregate-level (not at the individual investor-level) and do not allow them to distinguish the effects of online trading from those of other investor characteristics (gender, age, income, and so on). Accordingly, their analysis cannot rule out the effect of the young men, which means young men invest online more likely and they are overconfident.

Since we do not have investors' realized return data, this chapter examines preferences of Japanese online investors to investigate whether they are overconfident. Vople et al. (2002) conducted an Internet survey for 530 investors regarding investment literacy. They point out that online investors should improve their knowledge, since the average respondent answered only half of the questions

---

errors were to occur, I worry that I would be unable to get compensation"; and "I worry about the occurrence of fraud and hacker intrusion while trading online."

[8]Huang et al. (2005) identify factors that significantly affect Taiwanese brokerages' adoption of an Internet trading system: organization size (number of employees); IT maturity (Number of MIS department staff, Local network, Website); and Marketing supply.

correctly. However, they find that investors who have traded online have more superior knowledge than non-online traders. This result does not support the notion that online investors are overconfident.

We have mainly discussed whether online investors are overconfident. Meanwhile, we should keep in mind that the Internet has various positive aspects. Online trading decreases transaction costs considerably and Internet usage allows investors to access vast amounts of information, which helps their decisions. Rubin and Rubin (2010) find that the frequency with which firms' entries on Wikipedia are edited is negatively related to analysts' forecast errors and analysts' forecast dispersion, while being positively associated with the change in bid-ask spreads during analysts' recommendation days. They argue that Internet information processing increases informed investors. The Internet also provides firms with a new medium of investor relation (IR) activities. Many researchers investigate characteristics of corporate online information reporting (Deller et al. 1999; Geerings et al. 2003; Hedlin 1999; Xiao et al. 2002). For instance, Bollen et al. (2006) show evidence that firm size, internationalization (foreign listing and foreign revenue), proportion of shares available to individual investors and disclosure environment are significantly related to the extent of online IR activities. Therefore, it is important to accumulate research on the Internet and the capital market from various perspectives.

References

Barber BM, Odean T (2001) Boys will be boys: gender, overconfidence, and common stock investment. Q J Econ 116:261–292

Barber BM, Odean T (2002) Online investors: do the slow die first? Rev Financ Stud 15:455–487

Bollen L, Hassink H, Bozic G (2006) Measuring and explaining the quality of internet investor relations activities: a multinational empirical analysis. Int J Account Inf Syst 7:273–298

Camerer C, Lovallo D (1999) Overconfidence and excess entry: an experimental approach. Am Econ Rev 89:306–318

Choi JJ, Laibson D, Metrick A (2002) How does the internet affect trading? evidence from investor behavior in 401(k) plans. J Financ Econ 64:397–421

Daniel K, Hirshleifer D, Subrahmanyam A (1998) Investor psychology and security market under- and over-reactions. J Financ 53:1839–1885

Davis FD (1989) Perceived usefulness, perceived ease of use, and use acceptance of information technology. MIS Q 13(3):318–339

Deller D, Stubenrath M, Weber C (1999) A survey on the use of the internet for investor relations in the USA, the UK and Germany. Eur Acc Rev 8:351–364

Galasso A, Simcoe TS (2011) CEO overconfidence and innovation. Manag Sci 57:1469–1484

Geerings J, Bollen LHH, Hassink HED (2003) Investor relations on the internet: a survey of the Euronext zone. Eur Acc Rev 12:567–579

Gervais S, Heaton JB, Odean T (2011) Overconfidence, compensation contracts, and capital budgeting. J Financ 66:1735–1777

Grinblatt M, Keloharju M (2009) Sensation seeking, overconfidence, and trading activity. J Financ 64:549–578

Hedlin P (1999) The internet as a vehicle for investor relations: the Swedish case. Eur Acc Rev 8:373–381

Hirshleifer D, Luo GY (2001) On the survival of overconfident traders in a competitive securities market. J Financ Mark 4:73–84
Hirshleifer D, Low A, Teho SH (2012) Are overconfident CEOs better innovators? J Financ 67:1457–1498
Huang S-M, Hung Y-C, Yen D (2005) A study on decision factors in adopting an online stock trading system by brokers in Taiwan. Decis Support Syst 40:315–328
Kinari Y, Mizutani N, Ohtake F, Okudaira H (2011) Overconfidence and productivity. SSRN working paper. http://ssrn.com/abstract=1904692
Kitayama S, Takagi H, Matsumoto H (1995) Causal attribution of success and failure: cultural psychology of the Japanese self. Jpn Psychol Rev 38:247–280
Larger EJ (1975) The illusion of control. J Pers Soc Psychol 32:311–328
Lee M-C (2009) Predicting and explaining the adoption of online trading: an empirical study in Taiwan. Decis Support Syst 47:133–142
Malmendier U, Tate G (2005a) CEO overconfidence and corporate investment. J Financ 60:2661–2700
Malmendier U, Tate G (2005b) Does overconfidence affect corporate investment? CEO overconfidence measures revisited. Eur Financ Manage 11:649–659
Malmendier U, Tate G (2008) Who makes acquisitions? CEO overconfidence and the market's reaction. J Financ Econ 89:20–43
Malmendier U, Tate G, Yan J (2011) Overconfidence and early life experiences: the impact of managerial traits on corporate financial policies. J Financ 66:1687–1733
Odean T (1998) Volume, volatility, price and profit when all traders are above average. J Financ 53:1887–1934
Oh NY, Parwada JT, Walter TS (2008) Investors' trading behavior and performance: online versus non-online equity trading in Korea. Pac Basin Financ J 16:26–43
Rubin A, Rubin E (2010) Informed investors and the internet. J Bus Financ Acc 37:841–865
Scheinkman JA, Xiong W (2003) Overconfidence and speculative bubbles. J Polit Econ 111:1183–1220
Statman M, Thorley S, Vorkink K (2006) Investor overconfidence and trading volume. Rev Financ Stud 19:1531–1565
Uchida K (2006) The characteristics of online investors. J Behav Financ 7:168–177
Vople PP, Kotel JE, Chen H (2002) A survey of investment literacy among online investors. J Financ Couns Plan 13(1):1–13
Wang AF (2001) Overconfidence, investor sentiment, and evolution. J Financ Intermed 10:138–170
Xiao Z, Jones M, Lymer A (2002) Immediate trends in internet reporting. Eur Acc Rev 11:245–275

Chapter 26
Can Margin Traders Predict Future Stock Returns in Japan?

Takehide Hirose, Hideaki Kiyoshi Kato, and Marc Bremer

> *Why do the mechanisms of borrowing securities and selling them short appear so underdeveloped? Why are some crucial securities that arbitrageurs need missing altogether? (From Ch. 7, Open Problems) Andrei Shleifer, Inefficient Markets (2000).*

Abstract A growing body of literature suggests that investor sentiment affects stock prices both at the firm level and at the market level. This study examines the relationship between investor behavior and stock returns focusing on Japanese margin transactions using weekly data from 1994 to 2003. Margin trading is dominated by individual investors in Japan. In analysis at the firm level, we find a significant cross-sectional relationship between margin buying and stock returns. Both market-level and firm-level analyses show that margin buying traders follow herding behavior. They seem to follow positive feedback trading behavior for small-firm stocks and negative feedback trading behavior for large firm stocks. Our results show that information about margin buying helps predict future stock returns, especially for small-firm stocks at short horizons. The predictive power does not diminish even after controlling for firm size and liquidity.

Keywords Behavioral finance • Investor sentiment • Margin trading • Japan • Herding behavior

---

The original article first appeared in the Pacific-Basin Financial Journal 17:41–57, 2009. A newly written addendum has been added to this chapter.

T. Hirose (✉)
Sumitomo Mitsui Trust Bank, Tokyo, Japan
e-mail: Hirose_Takehide@smtb.jp

H.K. Kato
Graduate School of Economics, Nagoya University, Nagoya, Japan
e-mail: kato@soec.nagoya-u.ac.jp

M. Bremer
School of Business Administration, Nanzan University, Nagoya, Japan
e-mail: bremerm@ic.nanzan-u.ac.jp

S. Ikeda et al. (eds.), *Behavioral Economics of Preferences, Choices, and Happiness*, DOI 10.1007/978-4-431-55402-8_26

1 Introduction

A growing section of the finance literature suggests that investor sentiment affects stock prices both at the firm level and at the market level. This chapter extends this literature by linking investor sentiment to margin trades and examines how these quantities predict future stock returns in Japan. De Long et al. (1990) demonstrate that if risk-averse arbitrageurs know that prices may diverge further away from their fundamental values before they converge, they will take smaller positions when betting against mispricing. Therefore, if the sentiments of noise traders are systematically correlated and there are constraints on arbitrage, their investment behavior may predict future market prices. Yet, the direction of causality is not entirely clear because the behavior of noise traders may be influenced by the market.

Fisher and Statman (2000) examine the usefulness of a variety of sentiment variables in predicting short-horizon market returns. Baker and Wurgler (2006) examine how investor sentiment affects the cross-section of stock returns. When sentiment is pessimistic, subsequent returns are relatively high for smaller stocks, high-volatility stocks, unprofitable stocks, non-dividend-paying stocks, extreme-growth stocks, and distressed stocks. When sentiment is optimistic, these patterns attenuate or, in several cases, fully reverse. Brown and Cliff (2004) document that returns cause sentiment rather than vice versa. In his analysis of volatility, Brown (1999) finds deviations from the mean level of investor sentiment are positively related to volatility during the same period. Wang et al. (2006) examine the relationship between sentiment, returns, and volatility and find that investor sentiment is caused by returns and volatility rather than vice versa. In addition, lagged returns cause volatility.

Odean's (1998) model shows that investor overconfidence will increase trading volume. Gervais and Odean (2001) argue that high past market returns may cause overconfidence in individual investors if they happened to invest in stocks in the same period. Using monthly market data, Statman et al. (2006) show that investor overconfidence is positively related to trading volume. Baker and Stein (2004) propose a model that explains why increases in liquidity are associated with lower subsequent returns at both the firm level and the aggregate level. When short sales are constrained, unusually high liquidity is a symptom of market domination by irrational investors who underreact to the information contained in order flow.

Individual investors have long been considered to be noise traders. They are less informed or trade for non-informational reasons. Nevertheless, if their trades are correlated and arbitrage is limited in someway, their investments will change asset prices. Lee et al. (1991) argue that the discount on closed-end funds can be explained by the irrational behavior of individual investors. Because of leverage, margin transactions are sometimes considered speculative and major players in these transactions tend to be individual investors. Therefore, we argue that margin transactions tend to reflect individual investor sentiment.

This study examines the relationship between investor behavior and stock returns by focusing on margin transactions in Japan. Margin trades are widely thought to be dominated by individual investors in Japan. First, we confirm that margin transactions are indeed dominated by individual investors. Second, we examine how margin transactions are related to stock returns. We look for specific patterns that are consistent with apparently irrational behavior. Our market-level analysis shows that margin buying is dominated by individual investors, but that margin selling is not. In analysis at the firm level, we find a significant cross-sectional relationship between margin buying and stock returns. We do not find significant patterns for margin selling. Both the market-level and firm-level analyses show that margin buying traders follow herding behavior. They seem to follow positive feedback trading behavior for small-firm stocks and negative feedback trading behavior for large firm stocks. As predicted, margin traders heavily impact the stock prices of small firms over a certain period of time. The deviation from previous value exists longer and is more pronounced for small-firm stocks that are mainly owned by individual investors. Our results show that information about margin buying shares outstanding helps predict future stock returns, especially for small-firm stocks. The predictive power does not diminish even after controlling for liquidity. This is consistent with De Long et al. (1990), who show that stock prices deviate from their fundamental values for a certain period of time due to excess demand by noise traders.

This is the first comprehensive study of Japanese margin trading using weekly data over a long period of time. These weekly data cover most stocks eligible for margin trades. Standardized margin trades have been practiced in Japan for more than 50 years. In contrast to the United States, the Japanese margin trading system is advanced and highly centralized. The Japanese system allows stockbrokers to borrow securities and funds from specialized securities finance companies when there is a shortage of securities and funds. Because of this highly evolved system, margin traders almost always use the standardized margin trading system when they can satisfy its requirements. Japanese margin data are complete and market-wide compared to U.S. data, which include margin transactions for only the largest brokerage firms. Furthermore, individual firm data are not available in the U.S.

The structure of the chapter is as follows. The next section describes and compares margin transactions in Japan and the U.S. The third section discusses Japanese margin data. The fourth section discusses results for the aggregate market. The fifth section examines margin transactions and stock returns at the firm level. A brief conclusion follows.

2 Margin Transactions in Japan

There are two types of margin transactions that are currently practiced in Japan; the first is negotiation based margin trading and the second is standardized margin trading. Negotiation margin transactions are usually between large financial institutions. The terms and fees are freely negotiated. On the other hand, standardized margin trades must follow specific rules determined by the stock exchange. The stock exchange determines which stocks are eligible for margin trading on the basis of liquidity. Standardized margin trading in Japan is similar to margin trading in the U.S., but certain features are importantly different.

Japan started its standardized margin transactions system in 1951. Loans and borrowed stock certificates for these margin transactions are provided by specialized securities finance companies, the largest of these being the Japan Securities Finance Company. The goal of the system was to stabilize and expand Japan's securities market amid the confusion of the early postwar period. The system allows stockbrokers to easily borrow securities and funds from securities finance companies. This process is called a security loan transaction (*taishaku torihiki*). The system's intent is to attract more individual investors. Standardized margin transactions work in the following way: brokers accepting orders from investors for standardized margin transactions will check their inventory of stocks, and match the order with other orders for the same stock by other investors. When the margin order by an investor cannot be met with the inventory that is on hand or that is available through the matching process, brokers will then go to securities finance companies to fill the gap. It is likely that standardized margin transactions are mainly used by individual investors because they are less creditworthy. The transactions are quite convenient for individuals because various conditions, especially interest rates, are fixed by the system with little regard to their creditworthiness, unlike other transaction modes.[1]

Accelerated financial deregulation, due to the Japanese version of the financial Big Bang, triggered the full-scale start of ordinary security loan transactions in December 1998. In this system, ordinary loan transactions were liberalized so that the borrowing rate and repayment period can be freely negotiated by investors and brokers. This was the start of negotiation based margin trading. Although this type of margin transaction is available for almost all Tokyo Stock Exchange (TSE) stocks and is more flexible, the major investors in ordinary loan transactions are institutions, not individuals. Individual investors are usually less creditworthy than institutional investors, hence this type of transaction is usually not available to them. Since this margin system is relatively new, its volume is still much smaller than that of standardized margin transactions.

It is highly likely that the buying entities and the selling entities in margin transactions are different investors. The buying entities, who effectively borrow

[1]Standardized margin transaction positions are required to be closed out within 6 months. Before the Japanese Big Bang, brokerage commissions, margin interest, *shinagashi-ryo* (premium charges), administration fees, and *haito-chosei-gaku* (ex-dividend adjustment) were determined by the stock exchange. After the Big Bang, only *shinagashi-ryo* and *haito-chosei-gaku* have been regulated. When stock loans outstanding exceed outstanding loans between the brokers and the securities finance companies, the cost of providing securities is charged to all the investors who sell the particular stock on margin; this is *shinagashi-ryo*. Though stockbrokers can now set their own conditions on margin transactions, they generally set the same conditions as security loans transactions. Both for standardized margin trades and for negotiation based margin trades, investors deposit 300,000 yen plus an additional 30 % or more of the contract's value with their broker. These deposit levels are determined by cabinet office regulations and stock exchange rules. Investors are obligated to contribute additional funds to their margin account when a paper loss is incurred.

money from their brokers, are likely to be individual investors. Institutional investors do not have to borrow money from their brokers to invest. On the other hand, margin selling entities are not necessarily individual investors. Institutional investors will sell short just like individual investors. In summary, we argue that margin buying is mainly the activity of individual investors, but margin selling will be conducted by both institutions and individuals. Therefore, the analysis of margin buying is particularly interesting because these transactions are likely to be a result of individual investor sentiment.

3 Data

Our sample consists of all stocks eligible for margin transactions listed on the 1st and 2nd sections of the TSE during the period from December 17, 1994 through May 17, 2003.[2] The number of margin shares outstanding is collected from weekly TSE reports.[3] The final sample has 431 observations and 494,460 firm-weeks from a possible 440 observations and 834,491 firm-weeks.

This study examines the relationship between short-term stock returns and margin trading using both aggregate market-level data and firm-level transaction data. In the market-level analysis, we aggregate the number of shares outstanding of all margin transactions for all eligible stocks. Figure 26.1 shows aggregate margin transaction shares outstanding (on the left-hand axis) and a TSE index (on the right-hand axis).[4]

While it is premature to draw conclusions, the figure shows a high degree of co-movement between margin buying and stock prices. The co-movement is especially striking from the late 1990s. The number of shares outstanding for margin buying rose substantially from 1999, whereas the number of selling shares outstanding stayed relatively lower until late 2001. On average, the number of shares outstanding for margin buying was almost double that of selling for much of the sample period. Table 26.1 shows basic summary statistics for our margin transactions data. We also show summarized trading volume for all stocks in this table. Average margin buying outstanding is much higher than that of margin selling.

[2]In some of the subsequent analysis we divide this sample into two sub-periods: December 17, 1994 to March 6, 1999 and March 13, 1999 to May 17, 2003. We explore these sub-periods because of a substantial increase in margin buying that started in late 1998/early 1999. This increase could indicate a change in the trading behavior of investors and may correspond to a telecommunications/internet bubble and/or financial deregulation in the late 1990s.

[3]The TSE publishes the previous Friday's closing number of margin shares outstanding on Tuesday. We use outstanding margin shares measured in terms of trading units that adjust for stock splits. We exclude data for weeks in the very few cases where the TSE did not make a margin announcement.

[4]This TSE index is the TOPIX that is described below. The Nikkei 225, another well-known index, also suggests that stock prices and margin purchases move together.

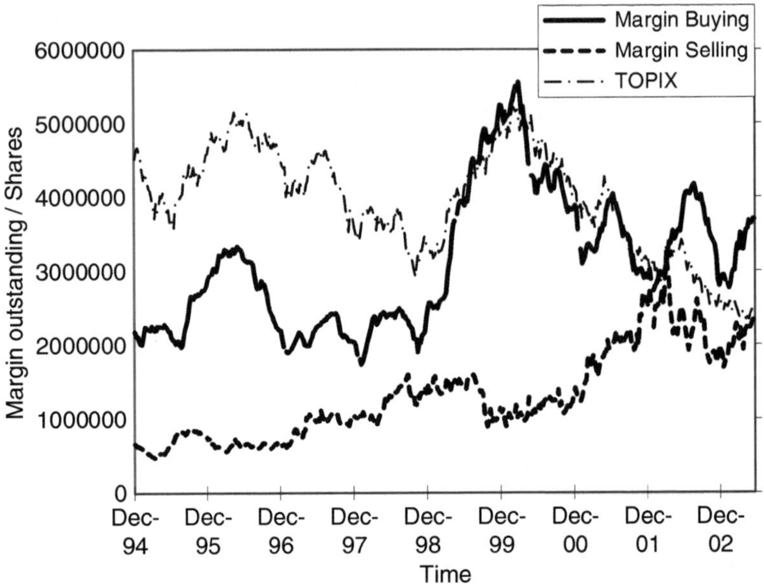

Fig. 26.1 Aggregate outstanding margin transactions. This figure shows aggregate shares outstanding of margin transactions for all eligible stocks listed on the Tokyo Stock Exchange (TSE) 1st and 2nd sections. The TOPIX is a value-weighted index of 1st section of the TSE stock prices. The sample period is from December 17, 1994 to May 17, 2003 on a weekly basis. Shares outstanding of margin transactions are made public by the TSE. The shares are adjusted for stock splits and scaled by trading units. There are 431 observations

This indicates that the market for margin buying is much larger and more liquid. The average change in margin buying outstanding is almost equal to the average change in margin selling outstanding. The standard deviation of the shares outstanding for buying is somewhat larger than that of selling. We also compute the serial correlation of all of the variables. The change in margin buying is serially correlated at lag one. This means that an increase in MBO this week is followed by an increase in MBO in the subsequent week. As expected, the levels of both margin buying and margin selling are highly serially correlated.

In the market-level analysis, we examine the relationship between the weekly change in margin transactions outstanding and both market returns and market volatility. We are concerned with how margin traders' investment behavior is related to market returns and volatility. De Long et al. (1990) demonstrate that if risk averse, well-informed investors know prices may diverge further away from fundamental values before eventually converging, they may take smaller positions when they attempt to arbitrage mispricing. Hence, the sentiment of herding noise traders may predict future prices and volatility. We argue that MBO is a plausible proxy of the sentiment of Japanese noise traders. In addition, we investigate the relationship between margin transactions outstanding and trading volume because Baker and Stein (2004) predict that high liquidity is a symptom of market domination by

Table 26.1 Summary statistics for aggregate margin transactions

	Level				Change			
	MBO	MSO	Net	Trading volume	MBO	MSO	Net	Trading volume
Mean	3,121,125	1,318,303	1,802,822	1,318,303	5,151	5,515	−364	3,461
Median	2,988,254	1,171,622	1,541,737	1,171,622	2,807	1,040	−5,561	8,365
Max	5,554,973	3,248,912	4,492,425	3,423,105	262,299	445,466	390,196	1,223,126
Min	1,738,647	473,832	−243,315	291,574	−298,561	−416,613	−550,634	−915,943
Standard deviation	905,610	601,211	932,311	601,211	82,063	87,504	116,685	252,935
Skewness	0.632	0.707	0.911	0.707	−0.143	0.245	−0.245	0.147
Kurtosis	2.558	2.600	3.395	2.600	4.416	7.522	5.216	5.237
Ac(1)	0.994	0.984	0.992	0.810	0.427	−0.015	0.200	−0.249
Ac(2)	0.984	0.969	0.980	0.710	0.227	−0.031	0.104	−0.176
Ac(3)	0.973	0.955	0.967	0.678	0.191	−0.016	0.055	−0.096

This table shows summary statistics of the aggregate shares outstanding of margin transactions. MBO and MSO refer to shares outstanding of margin buying and margin selling, respectively. The "Net" column shows statistics for margin buying less margin selling. Shares outstanding of margin transactions and trading volume are in trading units. Trading volume is defined as average daily trading volume for the week. The sample period is from December 17, 1994 to May 17, 2003. Ac(x) in the leftmost column is the xth order's serial correlation

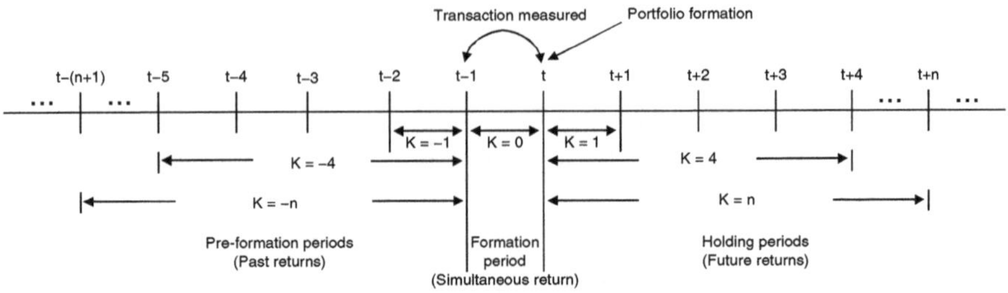

Fig. 26.2 Return periods. The values denoted by $K=0$ describe returns in the week which measure the change in shares outstanding of margin transactions. The $K=-n$ returns are average weekly returns over the pre-formation n weeks. The $K=n$ returns are average weekly returns over the holding period n weeks

irrational investors.[5] The important question to be asked is who the major margin traders are. In order to identify major margin traders, we use investor data from the Tokyo Stock Exchange to focus on four types of investors: individuals, financial institutions, securities firms, and foreign investors. Financial institutions include insurance companies, long-term credit banks, regional banks, and trust banks.

We use the Tokyo Stock Exchange Price Index (TOPIX) to calculate market returns. The TOPIX is a value weighted market index of all firms listed on the 1st section of the TSE. Figure 26.2 shows the return period construction; t is the weekend measurement point. The returns in the portfolio formation period, from weekend $t-1$ to weekend t, are described as $K=0$. The returns in the next n weeks measured as holding periods are described as $K=n$, and in the pre-formation periods, from weekend $t-n$ to weekend $t-1$, are described as $K=-n$. Average weekly rates of return in these periods are calculated and used in the analysis. The same return definitions are used in the firm-level analysis.

In the firm-level analysis, we examine the behavior of individual stock returns when margin traders change their aggregate position. We rank individual stocks and create five portfolios on the basis of the change in their buying position from the previous week. Five portfolios are also created on the basis of the change in their selling position from the previous week. We examine the excess returns of these portfolios before and after the formation period to investigate the characteristics of margin traders. We use the Fama and French (1993, 1995) three-factor model to compute these excess returns. The intercept of these Fama–French regressions is used as a proxy of excess returns. In addition, the relationship between margin transactions and liquidity, which is often used as a proxy for investor sentiment, is analyzed.

[5]Trading volume is defined as the total number of shares traded during a given week on the TSE in terms of trading units after adjustment for stock splits.

4 Market-Level Analysis

In this section, aggregate market data for margin transactions are used to investigate: (1) the relationship between margin shares outstanding (change in margin shares outstanding) and market returns; (2) the relationship between margin shares outstanding (change in margin shares outstanding) and market volatility; (3) major margin traders; and, (4) the relationship between the change in margin shares outstanding and trading volume.

4.1 Relationship with Market Returns and Volatility

In order to examine the relationship between market returns and margin shares outstanding, we estimate a simple regression. This analysis illustrates how margin traders' transactions are related to past and future weekly market returns. If margin traders follow positive feedback trading behavior, market returns in the previous several weeks should be positively correlated with the change/level of margin shares outstanding. If their trades impact on stock prices, the market returns in the same week will also be positively related.

Examining the relationship between future market returns and margin shares outstanding is also interesting. If margin traders do not rely on information, we should observe return reversals in the following week. We estimate the regression using margin information as a dependent variable for the past and contemporaneous returns and as an explanatory variable for the future returns. Table 26.2 shows the relationship between market returns and margin shares outstanding. In the case of margin buying, the level of margin buying outstanding (MBO) is weakly positively related to previous market returns. MBO becomes higher when market returns are high in the previous 52 weeks; this is consistent with positive feedback trading.[6] Stronger patterns are observed when the change in margin buying outstanding (ΔMBO) is used instead of MBO.[7] On the other hand, neither MBO nor ΔMBO is significantly related to market returns in the same week. Margin buyer transactions

[6] An interesting point could be made here that it is not really margin buying that is linked to market returns, but rather total trading volume. The idea is that total buying in the stock market volume displays positive feedback trading behavior. We argue that MBO uniquely captures the sentiment of individual Japanese investors, but perhaps MBO just tracks all buying on the Tokyo Stock Exchange. To test this, we also examine the relation between total buying (VOL) and the TOPIX return in Table 26.2. The table shows that there is no meaningful relation between total buying and past market returns.

[7] The change in MBO (MSO) is calculated as the difference between MBO (MSO) this week and last week. We also use the deviation from the previous 52-week mean of MBO (MSO) instead of previous week of MBO (MSO) when we compute ΔMBO (ΔMSO). The results remain qualitatively unchanged. We only report results that use the former definition of ΔMBO (ΔMSO).

Table 26.2 The relationship between aggregate margin transactions and market returns

	Past market returns						Future market returns				
	K=−52	−13	−4	−2	−1	K=0	K=1	2	4	13	52
MBO	0.488 (2.07)	2.107 (1.71)	3.642 (0.85)	5.148 (0.61)	7.238 (0.44)	−4.364 (−0.27)	−0.088 (−0.62)	−0.035 (−0.25)	−0.027 (−0.19)	−0.088 (−0.61)	−0.176 (−1.18)
MSO	−0.235 (−1.34)	−0.587 (−0.69)	−0.561 (−0.20)	−0.922 (−0.16)	−3.000 (−0.28)	−3.470 (−0.32)	−0.174 (−0.81)	−0.140 (−0.67)	−0.117 (−0.56)	−0.084 (−0.40)	−0.124 (−0.47)
ΔMBO	0.003 (0.13)	0.258 (2.38)	1.901 (5.54)	5.023 (7.24)	10.365 (7.45)	−0.067 (−0.05)	−1.760 (−1.12)	−0.386 (−0.25)	0.605 (0.39)	1.146 (0.71)	0.610 (0.31)
ΔMSO	−0.006 (−0.21)	−0.044 (−0.35)	−0.046 (−0.11)	0.029 (0.95)	−0.501 (−0.32)	4.850 (3.09)	0.739 (0.50)	−0.353 (−0.25)	−0.438 (−0.30)	0.099 (0.06)	−0.131 (−0.07)
VOL	−0.048 (−0.28)	−0.120 (−0.16)	1.762 (0.70)	3.999 (0.79)	9.647 (1.00)	14.795 (1.54)	0.064 (0.27)	0.233 (0.15)	−0.029 (−0.13)	−0.117 (−0.49)	−0.337 (−1.24)
ΔVOL	−0.007 (−0.09)	−0.165 (−0.47)	−0.716 (−0.61)	−2.580 (−1.10)	−5.422 (−1.21)	12.583 (2.83)	0.438 (0.86)	0.545 (1.12)	0.188 (0.38)	0.138 (0.27)	0.024 (0.04)

This table shows OLS regression results for aggregate margin transactions. Market returns are calculated from the TOPIX index. MBO and MSO refer to shares outstanding of margin buying and margin selling respectively. VOL is stock market trading volume, or "total buying". The *K* columns show return periods used in the regressions. For $K=-52$ to K = 0, the estimated equation is $X=\alpha+\beta$ (return or volatilities). In this case, the variable *X* in the leftmost column is the explained variable. For $K=1$ to $K=52$, the estimated equation is (return or volatilities) $=\alpha+\beta X$. In this case, the variable *X* in the leftmost column is the explanatory variable. Stocks are adjusted for splits. The numeraire of margin transactions is 1000s of trading units for prior regressions and millions of trading units for later regressions. T-statistics are shown in parentheses

do not seem to impact stock prices. In general, margin buyers (we argue individual Japanese investors) seem to have positive feedback trading behavior consistent with Odean (1998).

In the case of margin selling, neither the level of margin selling shares outstanding (MSO) nor the change in margin selling shares outstanding (ΔMSO) is significantly related to market returns in previous weeks. However, the contemporaneous relationship between ΔMSO and market returns is positive, significant. This suggests that margin selling does not impact stock prices. Instead, these trades are passive and provide liquidity to the market.

Table 26.2 also shows that the change in margin shares outstanding is not related to future market returns. Information about aggregate margin transactions does not help predict future market returns. Assuming that margin traders' activities represent investor sentiment, our results are consistent with Brown and Cliff's (2004) argument that stock returns determine sentiment rather than vice versa. We discuss this issue in more detail in the following section.

4.2 Characteristics of Margin Transactions

Time-series models are used to investigate how liquidity and purchases by investors are related to margin transactions. First, we identify which type of investor dominates in this market. Secondly, the relationship between margin transactions and liquidity is examined. Table 26.3 shows results for MBO (Panel A) and MSO (Panel B). The following regression equation is estimated in this analysis:

$$X_t = \alpha + \gamma \Delta Volume_t + \sum \theta_j Investors(j)_t + \sum \beta_j \ Control\ Variables + \varepsilon_t \quad (26.1)$$

where X represents ΔMBO or ΔMSO. The TOPIX is used as a proxy for the market rate of return, a control variable. The number of shares traded in the week is defined to be trading volume. The number of shares purchased by each investor type in a particular week is the proxy for investor activity. In separate unreported work, we find current volatility and past market returns are related to ΔMBO; hence we include these variables in the regression as control variables.[8] ΔMBO, ΔMSO, trading volume, and the number of shares purchased by each investor are measured during the $K = 0$ period.

Table 26.3 shows that the coefficient for individual investors is significantly positive for ΔMBO. This means that margin purchases are mainly conducted by individual investors. Generally, institutional investors such as trust banks, life insurance companies, and investment trust companies are well capitalized, so they have less need to borrow money through margin transactions. The result that margin

[8] As was shown in Table 26.1, past ΔMBO is serially correlated at lag one. And as was shown in Table 26.2, past and contemporaneous returns are related to the change in margin transactions.

Table 26.3 Time-series regression analysis of changes in aggregate margin transactions

	Investor classification				
ΔVOL	Indi.	Foreign	Fin.	Broker	Adjusted R^2
Panel A: ΔMBO					
0.004 (1.39)					0.25
	0.599 (5.66)	0.108 (1.64)	−0.043 (−0.62)	−0.059 (−0.89)	0.42
0.005 (2.35)	0.606 (5.77)	0.092 (1.41)	−0.041 (−0.60)	−0.074 (−0.12)	0.43
Panel B: ΔMSO					
0.018 (5.43)					0.12
	−0.125 (−0.83)	−0.004 (−0.05)	−0.030 (−0.30)	−0.066 (−0.61)	0.01
0.019 (5.60)	−0.075 (−0.53)	−0.049 (−0.58)	−0.019 (−0.20)	−0.112 (−1.10)	0.12

$X_t = \alpha + \gamma \Delta Volume_t + \sum \theta_j Investors(j)_t + \sum \beta_j \; Control\ Variables + \varepsilon_t$
X represents ΔMBO or ΔMSO. ΔX_t is defined as $X_t - X_{t-1}$. This table shows time-series regression results for margin transactions. Market returns (R_t and R_{t-1}) and lagged X (X_{t-1}) are used as control variables. Margin buying (ΔMBO) or selling (ΔMSO) are defined as the change in shares outstanding of margin buys or sales for the week. ΔVolume_t is defined as $\text{Volume}_t - \text{Volume}_{t-1}$. Volume is share volume in trading units. Returns are rates of return in percent form. The market returns are from the TOPIX. Investor classification means net purchase amounts (in millions of yen) for each investor class. Indi., Foreign, Fin. and Brok stand for individuals, foreigners, financial institutions, and stockbrokers, respectively. T-statistics are shown in parentheses. These regressions are adjusted for heteroskedasticity

buying is dominated by individual investors is consistent with conventional wisdom. Therefore, it is likely that margin buying information reflects individual investor sentiment. On the other hand, margin selling is not significantly related to any particular investor type.

Our results are consistent with Gervais and Odean's (2001) overconfidence hypothesis; they argued that past high market returns make investors overconfident. In their model, investors learn about their own investment abilities through their investment experience. In particular, investors tend to overestimate their own abilities in the early stages of their trading careers. The fact that the main participants in Japanese standardized margin buying are unsophisticated individual investors, whose access to information is inferior to that of institutional investors, together with the fact that margin transactions are relatively speculative investments, may have made positive feedback trading in margin buying appear more conspicuous. However, the apparent link between overconfidence and positive feedback trading cannot be formally tested with the available data. Our data do not allow us to identify individual agents' trades, so we cannot determine whether the individual investors who traded successfully at $K = -1$ are the same investors who traded at $K = 1$ with excessive confidence. Still, our results for margin buying do suggest that investor sentiment is affected by past market returns.

Both margin buying and selling significantly increase as market volume increases. The increase in margin buying is consistent with Baker and Stein's (2004) argument that high liquidity is a symptom of market domination by irrational, individual investors. Margin traders provide liquidity to the market and their activities are not negligible. Our results imply that the change in margin buying reflects individual investor sentiment.

5 Firm-Level Analysis

The previous section showed that: (1) Japanese margin buying is mainly by individual investors; (2) it has a positive feedback bias; and, (3) margin transactions do not have a large impact on stock prices at the market level. These results suggest that the change in margin buying reflects individual investor sentiment.

In this section, we investigate whether there is a cross-sectional relationship between margin transactions and stock returns at the individual firm level. We conduct quintile analysis in order to determine how margin transactions influence individual stock returns. All eligible stocks are first sorted by the margin transaction measures at the end of each week as shown in Fig. 26.2. We construct five equal weighted portfolios on the basis of these margin transaction measures, each containing an equal number of stocks. The smallest margin transaction stocks are in the Q1 portfolio and the largest in the Q5 portfolio. We rebalance these portfolios at each weekend and compute these portfolios' returns. We use the Fama and French (1993, 1995) three-factor model to adjust for risk.

If there is a cross-sectional relationship between margin transactions and stock returns, we should observe significant differences between the returns of sorted portfolios after adjusting for risk. The next part in this section analyzes the relationship between margin transactions and liquidity, a proxy of investor sentiment.

5.1 Cross-Sectional Characteristics of Margin Transactions

In the previous section, we showed that for Japanese margin transactions, especially for margin buying, investors seem to follow positive feedback trading behavior. Initially, we confirm that this tendency is also observed in the cross-sectional analysis. The change in margin transactions may be related to trading volume or the total number of shares issued by each firm. In order to standardize the change in margin transactions, we divide margin shares outstanding by total number of shares issued and trading volume. In subsequent analysis, we use these standardized ΔMBO (ΔMSO).[9]

[9]Since the results are qualitatively similar, we do not report results for standardized ΔMBO (ΔMSO) using trading volume.

Table 26.4 The persistence of margin transactions in the following weeks

	Period	Q1 (decrease)	Q2	Q3	Q4	Q5 (increase)	Q1–Q5 (difference)
ΔMBO/OUTS	$K=-1$	−0.043	−0.009	−0.003	0.003	0.058	−0.101
		(−15.36)	(−12.90)	(−7.02)	(5.47)	(19.76)	(−34.46)
	$K=0$	−0.122	−0.019	−0.002	0.011	0.137	−0.259
		(−46.78)	(−30.58)	(−8.33)	(18.91)	(32.67)	(−56.54)
	$K=1$	−0.049	−0.007	−0.000	0.006	0.055	−0.104
		(−17.85)	(−8.80)	(−0.15)	(9.19)	(18.37)	(−33.64)
ΔMSO/OUTS	$K=-1$	−0.004	−0.004	−0.005	−0.005	0.023	−0.027
		(−2.06)	(−10.28)	(−14.26)	(−12.27)	(18.29)	(−13.31)
	$K=0$	−0.100	−0.012	−0.001	0.008	0.111	−0.211
		(−60.00)	(−30.28)	(−4.65)	(21.91)	(57.11)	(−80.44)
	$K=1$	−0.021	0.005	0.006	0.005	0.011	−0.032
		(−16.70)	(11.42)	(13.22)	(10.23)	(6.62)	(−16.76)

This table shows margin transaction characteristics for portfolios shown in the leftmost column. Stocks are sorted into portfolios by the margin transaction indicator shown in the leftmost column. Margin buying (ΔMBO) or selling (ΔMSO) are defined as the change in shares outstanding of margin buys or sales for the week. OUTS is the total shares issued. The rows labeled $K=0$ show characteristics for the week in which the portfolio is formed. The rows labeled $K=1$ and $K=-1$ show the characteristics in the next week and in the previous week, respectively. The Q1 portfolio has the smallest sorted indicators, and Q5 has the largest. T-statistics are shown in parentheses

Initially, we examine the persistence of margin transactions. From the market-level analysis, we found serial correlation in the change in margin buying; it is interesting to investigate whether similar patterns are observed at the portfolio level. The results are shown in Table 26.4. Stocks with high margin purchases tend to be also bought on margin in the following week.[10] The general pattern observed for margin buying also exists for margin selling. The main result from Table 26.4 is consistent with that of our market-level analysis. Margin buying traders, who are mainly individual investors, seem to herd on particular stocks for several weeks.

In the market-level analysis, we observed positive feedback trading behavior for margin buying. We investigate if similar patterns are present for individual stocks. We examine how the cross-sectional difference in margin transactions affects the cross-sectional difference in returns. If there are significant impacts on stock prices caused by these transactions, information on margin trades will help make subsequent stock returns predictable.

Table 26.5 shows excess returns using the three-factor model for margin buying sorted portfolios. The leftmost column shows the period of the excess return; each value in the body of the table shows the weekly average excess return during each

[10]This is true for both of the sub-periods as well. Apparently the substantial increase in aggregate margin buying from the late 1990s is not associated with a change in margin-trading behavior. We also examine the persistence of margin transactions from $t=-4$ to $t=4$ in work not reported here. The results are essentially the same, hence we report only $t=-1$ and $t=1$ in Table 26.4.

Table 26.5 Fama–French three-factor model alphas for portfolios sorted by margin buying

	Excess returns					
K=	Q1 (decrease)	Q2	Q3	Q4	Q5 (increase)	Q1–Q5 (difference)
−20	−0.03 (−1.74)	−0.03 (−2.32)	0.02 (2.01)	−0.00 (−0.19)	0.04 (2.63)	−0.06 (−5.92)
−4	0.12 (3.54)	0.06 (2.28)	0.02 (1.09)	−0.12 (−5.13)	−0.00 (−0.14)	0.13 (4.91)
−1	0.37 (5.02)	0.27 (5.11)	−0.00 (−0.02)	−0.31 (−6.33)	−0.18 (−2.57)	0.55 (10.19)
0	0.92 (12.14)	0.53 (9.84)	0.01 (0.10)	−0.76 (−14.76)	−0.59 (−6.47)	1.50 (18.54)
1	−0.16 (−2.25)	−0.19 (−3.54)	−0.09 (−1.85)	0.08 (1.60)	0.32 (4.63)	−0.48 (−8.55)
4	−0.07 (−2.07)	−0.08 (−3.08)	−0.05 (−2.16)	0.02 (0.61)	0.09 (3.11)	−0.16 (−7.16)
20	−0.03 (−1.95)	−0.01 (−0.90)	−0.01 (−1.10)	0.00 (0.33)	0.00 (0.17)	−0.03 (−3.57)

At the end of each week, five groups of stocks are formed. The stocks are sorted by margin buying indicators in ascending order. These portfolios are equal-weighted. Q1 is the portfolio that has the smallest margin buying values (ΔMBO/OUTS), Q5 has largest values. ΔMBO is the change in margin buying shares outstanding. OUTS is total shares issued. This variable is defined as net margin buying (New contracts − Settled contracts). The numbers in the $K=0$ rows are Fama–French three-factor model alphas when margin transactions are measured. Those in the $K=n/-n$ rows show average alphas over n post-/pre-formation weeks. T-statistics are shown in parentheses. The null hypothesis is that the alpha = 0

measurement period. Since the Q5 portfolio returns before and during the formation period are significantly negative, margin buyers seem to follow negative feedback trading behavior. The rightmost column (Q1–Q5) shows the difference in quintile portfolio excess returns. The returns for the rows labeled $K=-4$, and -1 show that portfolio Q1 realizes higher returns than Q5 a few weeks before the formation period. Investors who reduce their buying position may have realized a higher return in the past. On the other hand, portfolio Q5 has high excess return in the following week. The excess returns decrease as the change in MBO gets smaller in the following few weeks ($K=1$, $K=4$). These results imply that information about margin trading may help predict future stock returns. High levels of margin buying tend to precede positive excess returns.[11] This result is consistent with the model developed by Chordia and Subrahmanyam (2004) that describes the relationship between microstructure and returns. They argue that positively autocorrelated order imbalances[12] (plausibly related to our MBO variable) predict future returns because

[11]In sub-period analysis not reported here, the association between margin buying and future excess returns is somewhat stronger in the 1999 to 2003 period.

[12]Order imbalance is a measure of buying/selling pressure. Chordia and Subrahamyan calculate order imbalance using an algorithm developed by Lee and Ready (1991) that classifies a trade as

Table 26.6 Fama–French three-factor model alphas for portfolios sorted by margin selling

K=	Excess returns Q1 (decrease)	Q2	Q3	Q4	Q5 (increase)	Q1–Q5 (difference)
−20	0.16	−0.02	−0.08	−0.08	0.03	0.13
	(11.50)	(−1.18)	(−6.29)	(−6.39)	(2.11)	(14.63)
−4	0.29	−0.03	−0.19	−0.15	0.16	0.12
	(9.15)	(−1.30)	(−7.47)	(−6.21)	(5.15)	(5.34)
−1	0.21	−0.12	−0.29	−0.13	0.45	−0.25
	(3.33)	(−2.41)	(−5.79)	(−2.59)	(6.55)	(−5.21)
0	−1.34	−0.85	−0.33	0.42	2.07	−3.42
	(−21.90)	(−15.81)	(−6.61)	(8.05)	(24.45)	(−45.08)
1	−0.12	0.07	0.09	−0.07	0.02	−0.14
	(−2.05)	(1.25)	(1.71)	(−1.35)	(0.35)	(−3.33)
4	−0.11	0.03	0.04	−0.01	−0.03	−0.08
	(−3.94)	(1.25)	(1.39)	(−0.29)	(−1.26)	(−4.39)
20	−0.07	0.01	0.03	0.02	−0.04	−0.03
	(−4.96)	(0.79)	(2.23)	(1.32)	(−3.11)	(−3.80)

At the end of each week, five groups of stocks are formed. The stocks are sorted by margin selling indicators in ascending order. These portfolios are equal-weighted. Q1 is the portfolio that has the smallest margin selling values (ΔMSO/OUTS), Q5 has the largest values. ΔMSO is the change in margin selling shares outstanding. OUTS is total shares issued. This variable is defined as net margin selling (New contracts − Settled contracts). The numbers in the $K=0$ rows are Fama–French three-factor model alphas when margin transactions are measured. Those in the $K=n/-n$ rows show the average alphas over n post-/pre-formation weeks. T-statistics are shown in parentheses. The null hypothesis is that the alpha = 0

of the way risk-averse market-makers resolve inventory and adverse selection issues. Their empirical analysis of NYSE order imbalances support their model. Our result is also similar to Barber et al. (2006) and Hvidkjaer (2008) who study the trading behavior of individual American investors. They find that stock heavily purchased by individuals (assuming that small trades are by individuals) in 1 week earn high returns in the subsequent week. Stocks heavily sold in 1 week earn poor returns in the following week.

Here our focus moves to the change in margin selling outstanding. This analysis is shown in Table 26.6. The table shows that the Q1 and Q5 portfolios have significantly positive excess returns in the weeks before portfolio formation. At $K=0$, the excess returns have opposite signs. The Q1 excess return is significantly negative and the Q5 excess return is significantly positive. The patterns of Q1 and Q5 portfolios indicate that margin sellers sell (buy back) shares when stock prices rise (fall). Margin sellers' transactions seem to push stock prices back to their fundamental values quickly since we observe insignificant excess returns after

buyer (seller) originated if the price is closer to the ask (bid) price of the prevailing quote. We do not have bid/ask data, so we are unable to make an exact comparison of Japanese margin buying to Chordia and Subrahamyan's order imbalance result for the NYSE.

the $K = 0$ formation period. These results are consistent with the view that margin sellers are information-based traders. This is consistent with the findings in the previous section.

Using cross-sectional return data, we do not find positive feedback trading behavior for margin buying traders, though their position changes imply herding on particular stocks. Margin buying traders seem to follow negative feedback trading behavior instead. Margin buying traders increase or decrease their positions in a timely fashion. When their position increases (decreases), the following period's stock returns become significantly positive (negative). We argue that margin buying trades, which we view as herding by individual Japanese investors, perhaps in conjunction with the trades of risk-averse market makers and constrained arbitragers, impact on stock prices in the following period. When investor sentiment is optimistic, the following period's excess returns are significantly positive. Our results show that information about margin buying shares outstanding helps predict future stock returns in Japan.

In order to understand the relationship between investor behavior and stock returns around the formation week, we plot in Fig. 26.3 excess returns, ΔMBO, and ΔMSO for both the Q1 and Q5 portfolios during the period from 10 weeks before to 10 weeks after the formation week.[13] Margin traders' activities are concentrated in the few weeks before and after the formation week. Japanese margin traders' sentiments seem to be short-term. The behavioral finance literature generally assumes investor sentiments are longer lasting, on the order of months and years. However, we argue that Japanese margin traders will tend to have much shorter-lived sentiments. There are good reasons to believe this is true. By regulation, standardized margin positions must be closed out within 6 months. While it is possible to circumvent this regulation, doing so can be inconvenient and costly.[14]

Figure 26.3 shows that the margin trading patterns of the Q1 and Q5 portfolios are symmetric. Margin buying traders gradually increase (decrease) their positions in the 10 weeks before and after the $K = 0$ formation week though stock prices do not change very much until the $K = -1$ previous week. Margin traders significantly increase (decrease) their positions as stock prices fall (rise) over the 3 weeks before the $K = 0$ formation week. Trades by margin buyers seem to impact stock prices in the following week. Margin sellers seem to change their positions at the same time as margin buyers. It is at least possible that the small excess returns after the portfolio formation week are partially due to margin sellers' trades.

[13]We examined periods up to 20 weeks before and after the formation period, but no significant patterns are observed beyond 10 weeks.

[14]One further reason for short-term sentiment is that the managements of Japanese firms are obligated to make public announcements when they anticipate that earnings in the current accounting period will be substantially different from what were originally forecast. Accounting periods were general six months in the period for our data, though Japanese firms now generally report quarterly results. These earnings revision announcements, or lack of announcements, provide important short-term information that traders might rationally use in their decision to roll over or close out their margin positions.

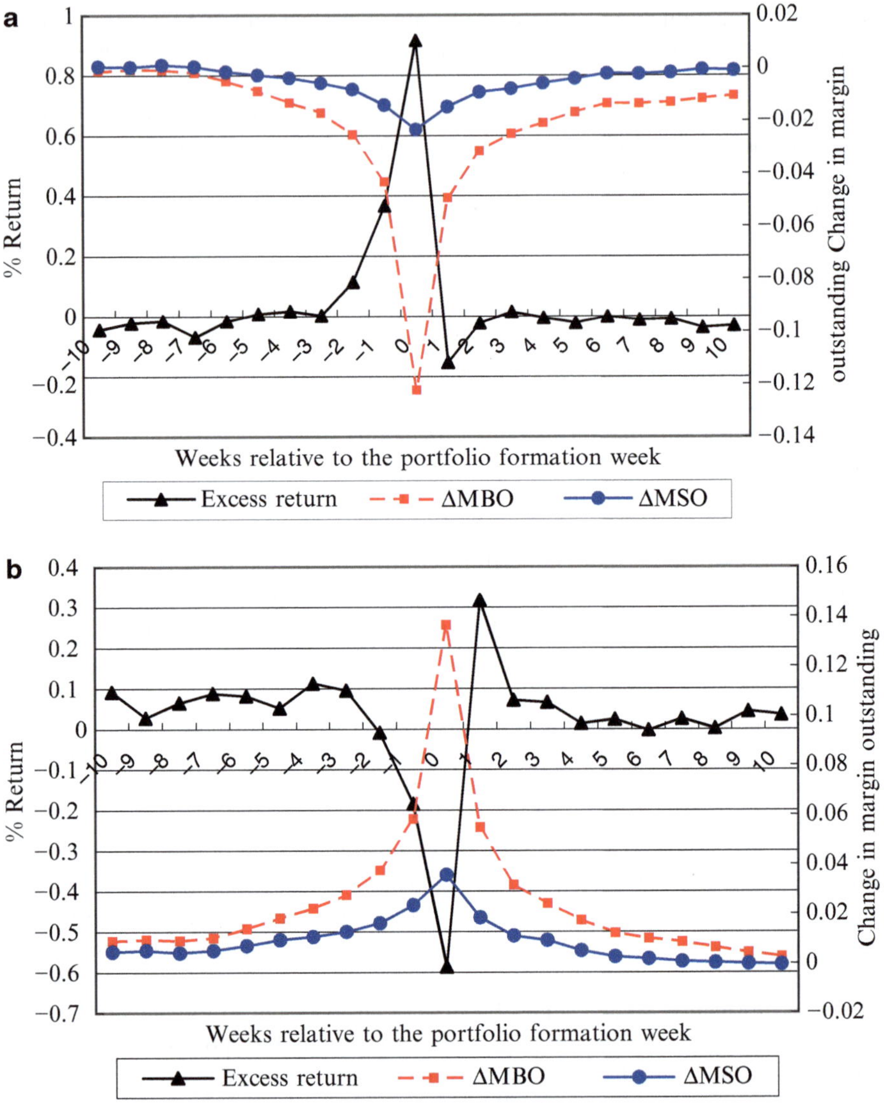

Fig. 26.3 (**a**) Excess returns and margin transaction characteristics for the ΔMBO/OUTS Q1 portfolio (smallest margin transaction stocks). (**b**) Excess returns and margin transaction characteristics for the ΔMBO/OUTS Q5 portfolio (largest margin transaction stocks)

Though we find evidence of significant excess returns for the Q5 portfolio in the following week, this does not necessarily prove the existence of economically meaningful profits. Because information about margin trading is released on Tuesday in the following week, it may not be possible to construct a Q5 portfolio to capture the following week's excess returns. In the following two sections, we examine how these margin buying results are related to firm size and liquidity.

5.2 *Firm Size*

Firm size may be an important factor in the analysis of investor sentiment since small-firm stocks are less liquid and more volatile. Small firm, less liquid stocks also potentially cause significant inventory, adverse selection and portfolio problems for market-makers and arbitragers. We expect to observe stronger, clearer results for the stocks of small firms. In order to examine this issue, we construct double sorted portfolios. Stocks are first sorted into three portfolios on the basis of firm size; these portfolios are then each sorted into five sub-portfolios using the change in margin buying outstanding indicator. The results are presented in Table 26.7. Both large- and small-firm excess returns are significantly positive in the $K = 1$ period (Panel C) for the Q5 portfolio. Surprisingly, our findings in the previous section are mainly observed for large firm stocks. Individual investors buy more (a significant 0.065)

Table 26.7 Fama–French three-factor model alphas for firm-size sorted portfolios

	Q1		Q5		Q1–Q5	
	Return	ΔMBO/ OUTS	Return	ΔMBO/ OUTS	Return	ΔMBO/ OUTS
Panel A: K=−1						
Small	−0.05 (−0.58)	−0.065 (−12.61)	0.29 (2.86)	0.087 (16.23)	−0.34 (−4.31)	−0.152 (−26.73)
Large	0.87 (15.16)	−0.016 (−15.83)	−0.65 (−11.84)	0.023 (17.01)	1.53 (23.01)	−0.040 (−29.53)
Small-large	−0.92 (−11.32)	−0.048 (−9.75)	0.94 (9.71)	0.064 (11.91)		
Panel B: K=0						
Small	−0.02 (−0.19)	−0.179 (−37.38)	0.42 (3.32)	0.204 (27.60)	−0.44 (−3.78)	−0.384 (−47.41)
Large	2.36 (32.48)	−0.061 (−35.84)	−1.92 (−27.20)	0.065 (29.86)	4.28 (39.80)	−0.126 (−39.11)
Small-Large	−2.38 (−24.44)	−0.119 (−23.20)	2.34 (19.84)	0.139 (18.87)		
Panel C: K=1						
Small	−0.10 (−1.08)	−0.075 (−15.01)	0.46 (5.01)	0.086 (15.99)	−0.56 (−6.98)	−0.161 (−27.43)
Large	−0.25 (−4.92)	−0.019 (−17.72)	0.21 (3.84)	0.021 (14.86)	−0.46 (−7.68)	−0.039 (−28.57)
Small-Large	0.15 (1.79)	−0.056 (−11.44)	0.25 (2.89)	0.066 (12.23)		

Stocks are classified into three groups by market capitalization. For each size, sorted portfolios are formed on ΔMBO/OUTS. ΔMBO is the change in margin buying shares outstanding. OUTS is total shares issued. The left-hand values in each cell are portfolio returns. The right-hand values are the average of ΔMBO/OUTS. Five equal-weighted portfolios are formed at $K = 0$. Panels A, B and C show mean returns and ΔMBO/OUTS at $K = -1$, 0 and 1, respectively. The rightmost column shows the Q1 portfolio minus the Q5 portfolio characteristic. Fama–French three-factor model alphas are reported. T-statistics are in parentheses

on margin at period $K = 0$ of large firm stocks that were down (a significant -0.65) at period $K = -1$. However, individual investors buy more (a significant 0.204) on margin at period $K = 0$ of small firms that were up (a significant 0.29) at period $K = -1$. Margin traders seem to follow negative feedback trading behavior for large firm stocks and positive feedback trading for small-firm stocks. The excess returns of the Q1 portfolio for both large and small firms during the 3-week period are consistent with this conjecture. The change in margin buying for the Q5 portfolio is positive, significant for all three periods regardless of firm size. We find evidence of price continuation for small-firm stocks. Small-firm stocks that were bought heavily at $K = 0$ (a significant 0.204) had significant positive returns (0.46) at $K = 1$. Market-maker inventory concerns as suggested by Chordia and Subrahmanyam (2004) and the difficulty in arbitraging small-firm stock mispricings seem plausible explanations for this result.

It is highly unlikely that individual investors use the three-factor model to examine past stock performance when they trade stocks. We therefore conduct the same analysis again using raw returns. The results remain essentially unchanged. These results indicate that the predictive power of margin buying is significant regardless of the firm size. Our results are not consistent with the view that margin buying traders are noise traders. Instead, they seem to time the market very well when they trade, or perhaps microstructure issues limit the ability of the market to quickly correct mispricings.

In order to fully understand the relationship between investor behavior and stock returns around the formation week, we plot in Fig. 26.4 excess returns, ΔMBO, and ΔMSO for the smallest and largest firm groups of the Q1 and Q5 portfolios over the period from 10 weeks before to 10 weeks after the formation week.[15] The patterns for small-firm stocks are interesting. Contrary to our previous findings, we observe significant positive excess returns a few weeks before and after the formation period for the Q5 portfolio. This is consistent with our finding in the market-level analysis that margin buyers follow positive feedback trading. Since margin buyers' sentiments are optimistic for some reason, their trades perhaps in conjunction with risk-averse market-makers push up these stock prices after the formation period for a few weeks. However, we do not observe an opposite pattern for the Q1 portfolio. Since we observe positive excess returns for the Q5 portfolio a few weeks after the formation week, a trading strategy on the basis of margin trading information may be profitable. The results are consistent with De Long et al. (1990).

In the case of large firm stocks, margin traders seem to follow negative feedback trading behavior. We observe positive excess returns for the Q5 portfolio and negative excess returns for the Q1 portfolio in the following week. The patterns of excess returns and the change in MBO are symmetric between the Q1 and Q5 portfolios surrounding the formation period. The significantly positive (negative) excess returns over the following week indicate that margin traders' transactions

[15]We also expand our estimation period up to 20 weeks before and after the formation period; however, no significant patterns are observed beyond 10 weeks.

a

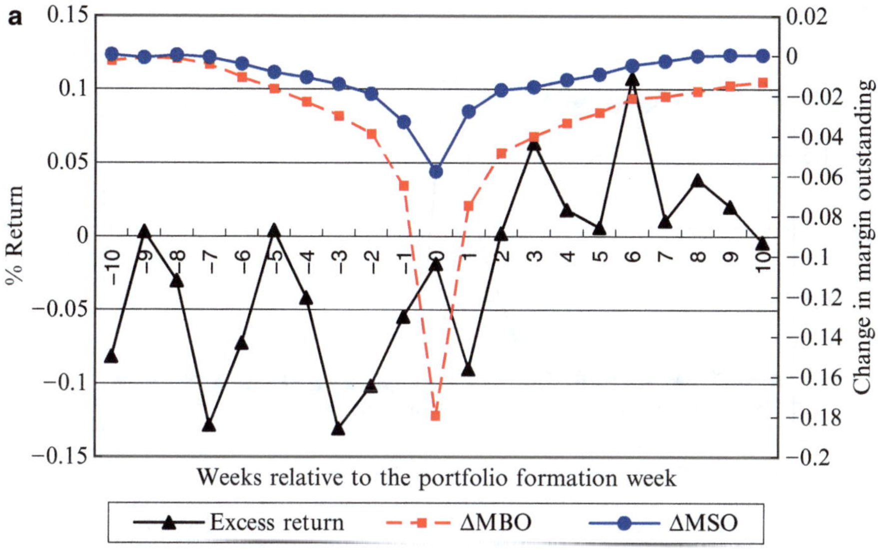

b

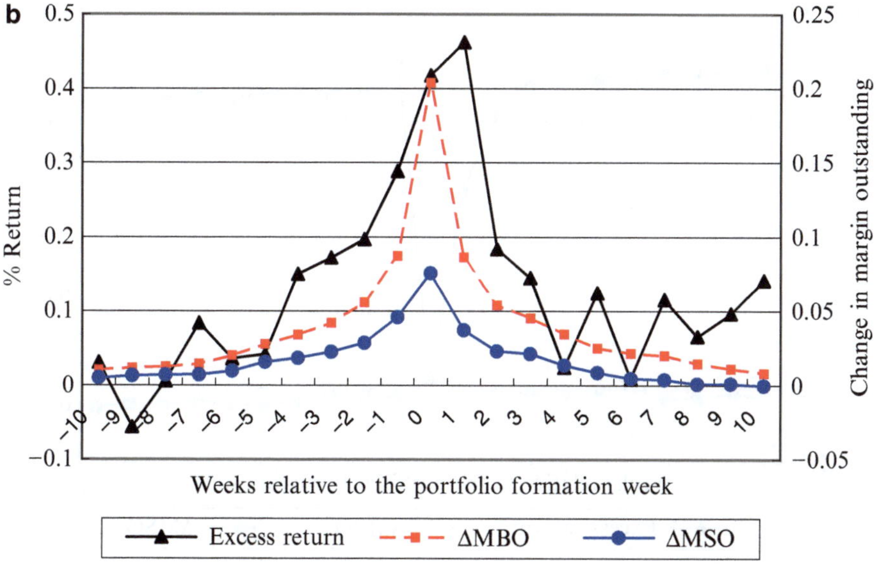

Fig. 26.4 (**a**) Excess returns and margin transaction characteristics for the ΔMBO/OUTS, small firms Q1 portfolio (smallest margin transaction stocks). (**b**) Excess returns and margin transaction characteristics for the ΔMBO/OUTS, small firms Q5 portfolio (largest margin transaction stocks). (**c**) Excess returns and margin transaction characteristics for the ΔMBO/OUTS, large firms Q1 portfolio (smallest margin transaction stocks). (**d**) Excess returns and margin transaction characteristics for the ΔMBO/OUTS, large firms Q5 portfolio (largest margin transaction stocks)

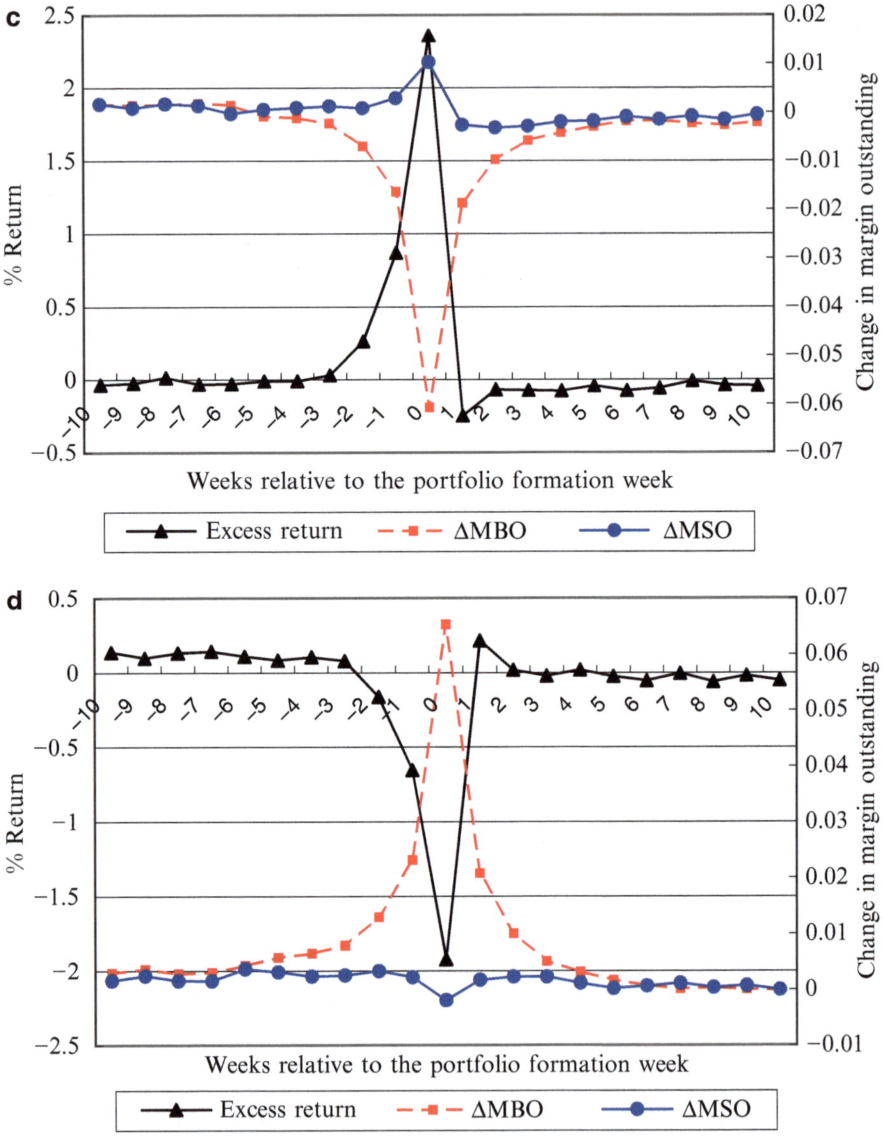

Fig. 26.4 (continued)

impact large firm stock prices though the effect is not as striking as that for small-firm stocks. In addition, significant excess returns are not observed after the second week. The market quickly absorbs the excess demand/supply of margin traders for large firm stocks that are mainly traded by institutional investors. Since information about margin transactions is released on Tuesday in the following week, it is very unlikely that a margin information-based trading strategy can earn economic profits.

5.3 Liquidity

The results so far suggest that the predictive power of margin buying information is different from firm size anomalies. Our market-level analysis shows that margin transactions are significantly positively related to liquidity. A growing body of empirical literature suggests that liquidity predicts stock returns. Brennan and Subrahmanyam (1996) and Brennan et al. (1998) find that measures of increased liquidity are associated with lower future returns. Both Odean (1998) and Baker and Stein (2004) argue that overconfident investors generate high liquidity, which may result from optimistic investor sentiment. If investor sentiment dominates the market, stocks with high trading volume may experience subsequent poor performance. Since Japanese margin buying is mainly the activity of individual investors, the margin buying effect documented in this chapter should be a good proxy for short-term investor sentiment. Our question here is how the margin buying effect is related to liquidity.

To examine this issue, we again apply a double-sorted portfolio approach similar to that employed in the previous section. The analysis asks whether the margin buying effect disappears after controlling for liquidity or if the difference in returns caused by liquidity disappears after controlling for the margin buying effect.[16] Twenty-five portfolios are created by sorting all stocks on the basis of the weekly turnover ratio (ΔTOR) before being sorted into quintile portfolios on the basis of changes in margin transactions outstanding.[17] The first round of sorting adjusts for the effects of liquidity and the second round of sorting for the effect of margin buying.[18] The results are presented in Table 26.8, which shows portfolio excess returns in the following week ($K = 1$) for 25 portfolios.

The bottom row of Table 26.8 shows average excess returns in the following week for margin buying ranked portfolios. The rightmost column of Table 26.8 shows the difference in average excess returns in the following week for liquidity ranked portfolios. Both margin buying and liquidity are significantly positively related to future returns. The difference in excess returns between the first and the fifth portfolios sorted on turnover ratios is significant only for the largest and the second largest change in margin buying portfolios. On the other hand, the difference in excess returns between the first and the fifth portfolios sorted on change in margin buying is significant for all liquidity ranked portfolios. Our results indicate that the margin buying effect is independent of liquidity while the liquidity effect is present only for the stocks in which margin traders increase their positions.

---

[16]We also conduct the same analysis for margin selling. We do not find any meaningful patterns for margin selling.

[17]TOR is defined as average shares traded each day/number of shares outstanding. We proxy liquidity with volume in the form of TOR.

[18]We also examine the difference in portfolio returns ($K = 1$) between the first and fifth portfolios sorted on the change in margin transactions outstanding after being sorted by the change in the weekly turnover. The results remain qualitatively unchanged.

Table 26.8 Double-sorted portfolio market model alphas: ΔTOR (First) and margin transactions (Second)

	Q1 (decrease)	Q2	Q3	Q4	Q5 (increase)	Q1–Q5 (difference)	Average
Q1 (TOR decrease)	−0.22 (−2.55)	−0.20 (−2.74)	−0.13 (−2.16)	−0.02 (−0.33)	0.11 (1.24)	−0.34 (−3.99)	−0.09 (−1.50)
Q2	−0.20 (−2.61)	−0.22 (−3.52)	−0.09 (−1.59)	0.04 (0.70)	0.27 (3.84)	−0.47 (−7.62)	−0.04 (−0.75)
Q3	−0.14 (−2.04)	−0.18 (−2.95)	−0.07 (−1.14)	0.06 (0.98)	0.29 (4.39)	−0.43 (−7.84)	−0.01 (−0.13)
Q4	−0.16 (−2.16)	−0.19 (−3.19)	−0.11 (−2.04)	0.16 (2.65)	0.38 (5.43)	−0.54 (−8.71)	0.02 (0.29)
Q5 (TOR increase)	−0.12 (−1.34)	−0.14 (−1.98)	−0.01 (−0.13)	0.26 (3.52)	0.40 (3.70)	−0.52 (−4.94)	0.08 (1.24)
Q1–Q5 (difference)	−0.11 (−1.21)	−0.06 (−0.83)	−0.12 (−1.67)	−0.28 (−3.97)	−0.29 (−2.86)		−0.17 (−3.05)
Average	−0.17 (−2.51)	−0.18 (−3.46)	−0.08 (−1.79)	0.10 (2.07)	0.29 (4.56)	−0.46 (−9.40)	−0.01

This table shows two-dimensional classifications by ΔTOR and margin buying (ΔMBO/OUTS). TOR is the weekly trading volume turnover ratio, a liquidity proxy. ΔMBO is the change in margin buying shares outstanding. OUTS is total shares issued. Stocks are first sorted by ΔTOR at $K = 0$ into five groups. Stocks are then sorted on the change in margin buying shares outstanding for each portfolio. Twenty-five portfolios are formed with approximately the same number of stocks in each week. The table reports Fama–French three-factor model alphas for each equal-weighted portfolio. T-statistics are shown in parentheses

6 Conclusion

This study examines the relationship between investor behavior and stock returns focusing on Japanese margin transactions. We use weekly margin transactions data from 1994 to 2003 for our analysis. Our market-level analysis shows that Japanese margin buying is dominated by individual investors. Individual investors appear to follow positive feedback trading behavior because the change in margin buying shares outstanding is positively autocorrelated, and is positively related to stock market performance in the recent past. Aggregate margin selling transactions, however, are practiced by all investors and may be strongly influenced by institutions. This is consistent with the conventional wisdom that institutional investors do not need to borrow money to purchase stocks. We do not find evidence of positive feedback behavior for margin selling.

Our individual firm-level analysis shows that margin buying investors do not follow positive feedback trading behavior. Instead, they seem to follow negative feedback trading. Margin buying investors increase their positions in particular stocks when the recent performance of the market was high but the recent performance of these stocks was poor. Interestingly, excess returns of these stocks in the following week are significantly positive. On the other hand, the subsequent excess returns of stocks in which margin traders reduce their positions are significantly negative. Margin traders' herding behavior seems to impact stock prices in the following week. One possible explanation is that the trading decisions of risk-averse market-makers and constrained arbitragers contribute to the relation between margin buying and subsequent returns. Analysis of firm size suggests that margin traders follow positive feedback trading behavior for small-firm stocks and negative feedback trading for large firm stocks. Yet, predictability persists regardless of firm size. In addition, the predictive power of margin trades does not diminish after adjusting for liquidity.

It is extremely puzzling that individual Japanese margin traders follow positive feedback trading behavior for small-firm stocks while also following negative feedback trading behavior for large firm stocks. How individual Japanese margin traders can so effectively time the market and the related microstructure issues for market-makers is an intriguing topic for future research.

Addendum: Further Analysis[19]

Hirose (2007) extended this research in much greater detail. His findings are consistent with the notion that the short-term change in margin buying shares outstanding is a proxy for transactions by noise traders and that margin selling shares outstanding is a proxy for fundamental investors' positions from a long term perspective. He examines the relationship between margin shares outstanding and long-term stock returns. Because such security loan transactions have monthly periodicity, they are suitable to examine the long term performance of margin transaction-driven trading strategies.

The results are shown in Table 26.9. From a long-term perspective, margin selling shares outstanding predicts the cross-sectional variation of future long-term returns. High margin selling shares outstanding are associated with long-term negative excess returns in the future. This means that margin sellers can earn excess returns in the long-run.

This finding is consistent with the following explanation. Margin buyers follow biased trading in the short term, and margin sellers tend to take opposite positions to margin buyers. Consistent results can be seen in Fig. 26.3 and for small firms in Fig. 26.4. Hirose (2007) also examines the daily transitions of margin shares outstanding and prices around the days when stocks were designated as margin restricted issues. Herding and positive feedback trading biases of margin buyers can push margin buying shares outstanding to high levels. Some margin sellers seem to be fundamental investors, such as institutional investors. They tend to sell short based upon the level of overpricing, and margin selling shares outstanding becomes higher simultaneously. Because margin selling is not large enough to arbitrage away the mispricing, noise trading by margin buyers can push prices away from

[19]This addendum has been newly written for this book chapter.

Table 26.9 Long term Fama-French model alphas for portfolios sorted by security loan transactions

	D1 (low)	D2	D3	D4	D5	D6	D7	D8	D9	D10 (high)	D1–D10 (difference)
Panel A: CLO											
1M	−0.32 (−2.02)	−0.04 (−0.35)	0.15 (1.10)	0.08 (0.51)	0.01 (0.06)	0.02 (0.12)	0.21 (1.06)	0.14 (0.67)	0.16 (0.68)	−0.50 (−1.80)	0.17 (0.53)
2M	−0.25 (−2.34)	−0.02 (−0.27)	0.13 (1.32)	0.12 (1.05)	0.01 (0.06)	0.01 (0.06)	0.11 (0.83)	0.13 (0.92)	0.15 (1.13)	−0.52 (−2.95)	0.27 (1.27)
3M	−0.21 (−2.34)	−0.02 (−0.31)	0.12 (1.54)	0.03 (0.36)	0.04 (0.40)	−0.04 (−0.38)	0.10 (0.93)	0.12 (0.98)	0.14 (1.13)	−0.48 (−3.55)	0.28 (1.68)
6M	−0.14 (−2.33)	0.01 (0.19)	0.02 (0.39)	−0.00 (−0.02)	0.02 (0.35)	−0.03 (−0.43)	0.02 (0.28)	0.09 (0.96)	0.14 (1.55)	−0.44 (−4.36)	0.30 (2.49)
9M	−0.13 (−2.81)	0.00 (0.01)	−0.01 (−0.16)	−0.01 (−0.31)	−0.01 (−0.14)	−0.04 (−0.66)	0.01 (0.10)	0.07 (0.98)	0.12 (1.47)	−0.39 (−4.53)	0.27 (2.80)
12M	−0.12 (−3.57)	−0.01 (−0.27)	−0.03 (−0.74)	−0.02 (−0.42)	−0.01 (−0.30)	−0.04 (−0.83)	0.00 (0.01)	0.06 (1.01)	0.11 (1.58)	−0.35 (−4.79)	0.23 (2.99)
Panel B: SLO											
1M	0.27 (1.90)	0.24 (1.68)	0.15 (1.01)	0.30 (1.94)	0.00 (0.02)	0.09 (0.52)	−0.03 (−0.19)	−0.16 (−0.91)	−0.30 (−1.72)	−0.64 (−2.97)	0.91 (3.88)
2M	0.19 (1.83)	0.22 (2.09)	0.19 (1.84)	0.20 (1.87)	0.09 (0.75)	0.05 (0.45)	−0.06 (−0.54)	−0.12 (−1.01)	−0.26 (−2.20)	−0.63 (−4.22)	0.82 (4.80)
3M	0.19 (2.21)	0.21 (2.44)	0.18 (2.18)	0.16 (1.81)	0.08 (0.78)	0.04 (0.38)	−0.07 (−0.75)	−0.12 (−1.24)	−0.25 (−2.58)	−0.61 (−5.12)	0.80 (5.84)
6M	0.14 (2.30)	0.14 (2.42)	0.15 (2.43)	0.14 (2.24)	0.04 (0.57)	0.03 (0.40)	−0.05 (−0.64)	−0.12 (−1.64)	−0.19 (−2.58)	−0.60 (−7.19)	0.74 (7.96)
9M	0.10 (2.14)	0.12 (2.56)	0.13 (2.69)	0.12 (2.47)	0.02 (0.36)	0.01 (0.21)	−0.03 (−0.59)	−0.10 (−1.77)	−0.20 (−3.31)	−0.56 (−8.17)	0.66 (9.16)
12M	0.09 (2.24)	0.13 (3.39)	0.13 (3.31)	0.11 (2.58)	0.02 (0.38)	−0.01 (−0.14)	−0.04 (−0.91)	−0.10 (−2.00)	−0.20 (−3.81)	−0.53 (−8.59)	0.62 (9.53)

CLO and SLO mean cash loans outstanding and security loans outstanding of security loan companies, respectively. OUTS means shares outstanding of the stocks. The leftmost column shows the return measuring period in months after portfolio formation. Figures are average alphas over the measuring periods. t-statistics are shown in parentheses. The null hypothesis is that the alpha is zero (Source: Hirose 2007)

their fundamental values in the short term. But, in the long term, the mispricing is resolved and margin sellers can earn excess returns in the long-run.

The change in margin buying shares outstanding helps predict the cross-sectional variation of short-term returns and margin selling shares outstanding helps predict the cross-sectional variation of long-term returns. Margin buying transactions in the short-term are a proxy for noise trades and the level of margin selling shares outstanding is a proxy of fundamental investors' positions from a long-term perspective. Margin transactions contain useful information about the trading behavior of both noise traders and fundamental investors.

References

Baker M, Stein JC (2004) Market liquidity as a sentiment indicator. J Financ Mark 7:271–299

Baker M, Wurgler J (2006) Investor sentiment and the cross-section of stock returns. J Financ 61:1645–1680

Barber B, Odean T, Zhu N (2006) Do noise traders move markets? Working paper, University of California, Davis, Graduate School of Management

Brennan M, Subrahmanyam A (1996) Market microstructure and asset pricing: on the compensation for illiquidity in stock returns. J Financ Econ 41:441–464

Brennan M, Chordia T, Subrahmanyam A (1998) Alternative factor specifications, security characteristics, and the cross-section of expected stock returns. J Financ Econ 49:345–373

Brown GW (1999) Volatility, sentiment and noise traders. Financ Anal J 55:82–90

Brown GW, Cliff MT (2004) Investor sentiment and the near-term stock market. J Empir Financ 11:1–27

Chordia T, Subrahmanyam A (2004) Order imbalance and individual stock returns: theory and evidence. J Financ Econ 72:485–518

De Long BJ, Shliefer A, Summers LH, Waldmann R (1990) Noise trader risk in financial markets. J Polit Econ 98:703–738

Fama EF, French KR (1993) Common risk factors in the returns on stocks and bonds. J Financ Econ 33:3–56

Fama EF, French KR (1995) Size and book-to-market factors in earnings and returns. J Financ 50:131–155

Fisher KL, Statman M (2000) Investor sentiment and stock returns. Financ Anal J 56:16–23

Gervais S, Odean T (2001) Learning to be overconfident. Rev Financ Stud 14:1–27

Hirose T (2007) Investor sentiment through margin trading and stock price movements Kobe University, Dissertation (in Japanese)

Hirose T, Kato HK, Bremer M (2009) Can margin traders predict future stock returns in Japan? Pac Basin Financ J 17:41–57

Hvidkjaer S (2008) Small trades and the cross-section of stock returns. Rev Financ Stud 21: 1123–1151

Lee CMC, Ready MJ (1991) Inferring trade direction from intraday data. J Financ 46:733–746

Lee CMC, Shleifer A, Thaler RH (1991) Investor sentiment and the closed-end fund puzzle. J Financ 46:75–109

Odean T (1998) Volume, volatility, price and profit when all traders are above average. J Financ 53:1887–1934

Shleifer A (2000) Inefficient markets: an introduction to behavioral finance. Oxford University Press, London

Statman M, Thorley S, Vorkink K (2006) Investor overconfidence and trading volume. Rev Financ Stud 19:1531–1565

Wang Y-H, Keswani A, Taylor SJ (2006) The relationships between sentiment, returns and volatility. Int J Forecast 22:109–123

Index

S. Ikeda et al. (eds.), *Behavioral Economics of Preferences, Choices, and Happiness*, DOI 10.1007/978-4-431-55402-8

MIX
Papier aus verantwortungsvollen Quellen
Paper from responsible sources
FSC® C105338

If you have any concerns about our products,
you can contact us on
ProductSafety@springernature.com

In case Publisher is established outside the EU,
the EU authorized representative is:
Springer Nature Customer Service Center GmbH
Europaplatz 3, 69115 Heidelberg, Germany

Printed by Libri Plureos GmbH
in Hamburg, Germany